ESSENTIALS OF ENTREPRENEURSHIP AND SMALL BUSINESS MANAGEMENT

Fourth Edition

THOMAS W. ZIMMERER
St. Leo University

NORMAN M. SCARBOROUGH
Presbyterian College

PEARSON
Prentice
Hall

Pearson Education International

KT-377-855

Acquisitions Editor: David Parker
VP/Editorial Director: Jeff Shelstad
Editorial Assistant: Melissa Yu
Media Project Manager: Jessica Sabloff
Executive Marketing Manager: Shannon Moore
Marketing Assistant: Patrick Danzuso
Senior Managing Editor (Production): Judy Leale
Production Editor: Theresa Festa
Production Assistant: Joe DeProspero
Permissions Supervisor: Suzanne Grappi
Manufacturing Buyer: Michelle Klein
Design Director: Maria Lange
Designer: Michael J. Fruhbeis
Interior Design: Michael J. Fruhbeis
Cover Design: Michael J. Fruhbeis
Photo Researcher: Sheila Norman
Manager, Print Production: Christy Mahon
Composition/Full-Service Project Management: Preparé, Inc.
Printer/Binder: Courier-Westford

Pearson Education LTD.
Pearson Education Australia PTY, Limited
Pearson Education Singapore, Pte. Ltd
Pearson Education North Asia Ltd
Pearson Education Canada, Ltd.
Pearson Educación de Mexico, S.A. de C.V.
Pearson Education -- Japan
Pearson Education Malaysia, Pte. Ltd
Pearson Education, Upper Saddle River, New Jersey

10 9 8 7 6 5 4 3
ISBN 0-13-191856-7

BRIEF CONTENTS

CONTENTS

The twenty-first century has dawned with entrepreneurship as a major force shaping the global economy. The future growth of this economy lies in the hands of men and women committed to achieving success through innovative customer-focused new products and services. At the heart of this global movement are entrepreneurs who demonstrate their willingness to assume the risks associated with creating new business ventures. Those who possess the spirit of entrepreneurial leadership have led, and will continue to lead, the economic revolution that has proved repeatedly to raise the standard of living for people everywhere. We hope that you will join this economic revolution to bring about lasting, positive changes in your own community and around the world.

This fourth edition of *Essentials of Entrepreneurship and Small Business Management* introduces you to the processes of new venture creation and the critical knowledge you need to manage your business once it is formed. We hope that you will follow your dream of becoming a successful entrepreneur with the help of this textbook and your instructor.

Text Features

- Sections 2, 3, and 4 focus on "Building a Business Plan," and Section 5 covers "Putting the Business Plan to Work."
- Chapter 2, "Inside the Entrepreneurial Mind: From Ideas to Reality," explains the creative process entrepreneurs use to generate business ideas and to recognize entrepreneurial opportunities. Students learn to *think like entrepreneurs*.
- Chapter 7, "E-Commerce and the Entrepreneur," serves as a practical guide to using the Web to conduct business in the twenty-first century.
- The **You Be the Consultant** feature challenges students to *apply* what they've learned. Each chapter contains at least two of these boxed illustrations based on actual companies that pose a problem situation and include questions to focus attention on key issues and to launch lively class discussions. Featured companies include Tommy Bahama, JetBlue Airlines, NFL Films, and many others.
- Sample business plan for *Sluggers*, an indoor pitching/batting cage, included both in the text *and* on the Web site.
- New, attractive layout includes in-margin glossary and learning objectives.
- **Business Plan Pro**, the best-selling business planning software package from Palo Alto Software, is a valuable tool that helps students build winning business plans for their entrepreneurial ideas. The end-of-chapter Business Plan Pro exercises enable students to apply the knowledge they've gained from reading the chapter to using Business Plan Pro. A brief user guide is available in the instructor's manual.
- **The Business Disc** is a sophisticated experiential learning simulation, which leads students through the steps of planning and managing a small business. Using video vignettes, students interact with scores of real people as they build and operate any kind of business: service, retail or manufacturing. The end-of-chapter Business Disc exercises enable students to link the chapter content to The Business Disc experience.

Supplements

- A dedicated student Web site at www.prenhall.com/zimmerer, which includes section level learning modules for each chapter. Learning modules include a pre-test, content summary, learning application and post-test. Each chapter includes between three and five learning modules for depth of coverage. In addition the Web site includes more than 1,000 links to relevant small business sites, and other valuable teaching and learning resources including a handy "Before You Start Checklist" designed to help entrepreneurs make sure they have everything they need to launch a successful business and a "Business Plan Evaluation Scale" that allows entrepreneurs to measure the quality of their business plans.

- The following videos are provided to adopters and the video guide is available in the instructor's manual and on the text Web site.

  - *Joan Rivers Worldwide Enterprises*—Entrepreneurship, small business management
  - *The WaggingTail.com*—Entrepreneurship, technology, differentiation, and customer service
  - *Build-A-Bear Workshop*—Strategic management, focus strategy, competitive advantage
  - *Zoots*—Marketing, customer service, convenience, competitive advantage, social responsibility
  - *Strike Holdings LLC*—Marketing, target market, advertising, innovation, competitive advantage
  - *The Golf Network*—E-commerce, marketing, target market, pricing, advertising, innovation
  - *Bay Partners*—Sources of financing, venture capital
  - *MyTeam.com*—Sources of financing, venture capital
  - *Crunch Fitness*—Location, international business, differentiation
  - *Neema Clothing*—Purchasing, quality management, electronic data interchange, managing inventory
  - *CESSI (Cherry Engineering Support Services Inc)*—Leadership, managing people, motivation, disabilities, staffing, social responsibility
  - *Second Gear Bicycles*—Ethics and social responsibility
- Instructor's Manual and Test Item File
- Instructor's Resource Center on CD contains the Instructor's Manual, Test Item File, computerized test bank, PowerPoints, and Transparency Masters.
- Blackboard, WebCT and Prentice Hall's own OneKey are available for course management solutions.

Beyond the Textbook   As you can see, the authors have used their combined 60 years of teaching experience (and their 54 years of experience writing textbooks) to produce a book that contains a multitude of both student- and professor-friendly features. We trust that this edition of *Essentials of Entrepreneurship and Small Business Management*, 4/E will help the next generation of entrepreneurs reach their full potential and achieve their dreams of success as independent business owners. It is their dedication, perseverance, and creativity that keep the world's economy moving forward.

ACKNOWLEDGMENTS

Working with every author team is a staff of professionals who work extremely hard to bring a book to life. They handle the thousands of details involved in transforming a rough manuscript into the finished product you see before you. Their contributions are immeasurable, and we appreciate all they do to make this book successful. We have been blessed to work with the following outstanding publishing professionals:

David Parker, acquisitions editor, whose wisdom and guidance throughout this project was invaluable.

Melissa Yu, editorial assistant, who was always just an e-mail away when we needed her help with a seemingly endless number of details.

Theresa Festa, production editor, who skillfully guided the book through the long and sometimes difficult production process.

Sheila Norman, photo researcher, who took our ideas for photos and transformed them into meaningful images.

Donna Mulder, copy editor, whose linguistic polishing made the content of this edition flow smoothly.

Shannon Moore, marketing manager, whose input helped focus this edition on an evolving market.

Special thanks to the following academic reviewers whose thought provoking inputs helped shape this and past editions of our two books, *Essentials of Entrepreneurship and Small Business Management* and *Effective Small Business Management*:

Nancy Bowman, Baylor University

John deYoung, Cumberland Community College

Art Elkins, University of Massachusetts

W. Bruce Erickson, University of Minnesota

Gregory Worosz, Schoolcraft College

Annamary Allen, Broome Community College

Tom Bergman, Northeastern State University

Charles Hubbard, University of Arkansas

E.L. (Betty) Kinarski, Seattle University

Michael S. Broida, Miami University

Richard Cuba, University of Baltimore

Kathy J. Daruty, L.A. Pierce College

Stuart Devlin, New Mexico State University

George J. Foegen, Metropolitan State College of Denver

Martin K. Marsh, California State University–Bakersfield

Charles H. Matthews, University of Cincinnati

Louis D. Ponthieu, University of North Texas

Nick Sarantakes, Austin Community College

Barry L. Van Hook, Arizona State University

Bernard W. Weinrich, St. Louis Community College

Dick LaBarre, Ferris State University

Deborah Streeter, Cornell University

James Walker, Morhead State University

Bill Snider, Cuesta College

Fred Hughes, Faulkner University

William Meyer, TRICOMP, Cary, NC

Michael Dickson, Columbus State Community College

Kevin Banning, University of Florida

Paul Lamberson, Riverton, WY

R.D. Butler, Trenton State College

David O'Dell, McPherson State College

Donald Wilkinson, East Tennessee State University

Joseph Salamone, State University of New York at Buffalo

Milton Miller, Carteret Community College

Professor M. Ala, California State University–Los Angeles

Sol Ahiarah, Buffalo State College

John E. Butler, University of Washington

Mary Lou Lockerby, College of DuPage

Jan Feldbauer, Austin Community College

Gita DeSouza, Pennsylvania State University

Pamela Clark, Angelo State University

John Todd, University of Arkansas

Peter Mark Shaw, Tidewater Community College

John Phillips, University of San Francisco

Ralph Jagodka, Mt. San Antonio College

Marcella Norwood, University of Houston

Khaled Sartawi, Fort Valley State University

Lon Addams, Weber State University

John Moonen, Daytona Beach Community College

Jack Sheeks, Broward Community College

Linda Newell, Saddleback College

James Browne, University of Southern Colorado

John McMahon, Mississippi County Community College

Charles Toftoy, George Washington University

Ben Powell, University of Alabama

Kyoung-Nan Kwon, Michigan State University

Judy Dietert, Southwest Texas State University

Many thanks to Linzie Steele Batchelor who was gracious enough to allow us to use her superb business plan as a model from which others can learn.

We also are grateful to our colleagues who support us in the sometimes grueling process of writing a book: Foard Tarbert, Sam Howell, Jerry Slice, Meredith Holder, Suzanne Smith, Jody Lipford, George Dupuy, and Debby Young of Presbyterian College and Dr. Douglas Astolfi of Saint Leo University.

A very special acknowledgement to Pat Guinn, whose talent in manuscript typing is legendary. Finally, we thank Cindy Scarborough and Linda Zimmerer, for their love, support, and understanding while we worked many long hours to complete *Essentials of Entrepreneurship and Small Business Management*, Fourth Edition. For them, this project represents a labor of love.

Norman M. Scarborough
William H. Scott III Associate Professor of Information Science
Presbyterian College
Clinton, South Carolina
e-mail:nmscarb@presby.edu

Thomas W. Zimmerer
Dean, School of Business
Professor of Management
Saint Leo University
St. Leo, Florida
e-mail:tom.zimmerer@saintleo.edu

Chapter

1

The Foundations of Entrepreneurship

Great things are done by people who think great thoughts and then go out into the world to make their dreams come true.

—Anonymous

Follow the grain in your own wood.

—Howard Thurman

LEARNING OBJECTIVES

Upon completion of this chapter, you will be able to:

1. **DEFINE** the role of the entrepreneur in business—in the United States and across the world.

2. **DESCRIBE** the entrepreneurial profile and evaluate your potential as an entrepreneur.

3. **DESCRIBE** the benefits and drawbacks of entrepreneurship.

4. **EXPLAIN** the forces that are driving the growth of entrepreneurship.

5. **EXPLAIN** the cultural diversity of entrepreneurship.

6. **DESCRIBE** the important role small businesses play in our nation's economy.

7. **DESCRIBE** the 10 deadly mistakes of entrepreneurship and explain how to avoid them.

8. **PUT** failure into proper perspective.

9. **EXPLAIN** how entrepreneurs can avoid becoming another failure statistic.

Learning Objective

1. Define the role of the entrepreneur in business—in the United States and across the world.

THE WORLD OF THE ENTREPRENEUR

Welcome to the world of the entrepreneur! Across the globe, growing numbers of people are realizing their dreams of owning and operating their own businesses. Although the level of entrepreneurial activity in the United States is down from record levels a few years ago, entrepreneurship continues to thrive in our nation. Every year, American entrepreneurs start between 3 million and 4.5 million businesses, and the level of interest in pursuing entrepreneurship as a career remains high among people in all age groups.[1] Eighty-four percent of those who launch businesses are doing so for the first time.[2] This entrepreneurial spirit is the most significant economic development in recent business history. Around the globe, these heroes of the new economy are reshaping the business environment, creating a world in which their companies play an important role in the vitality of the global economy. With amazing vigor, their businesses have introduced innovative products and services, pushed back technological frontiers, created new jobs, opened foreign markets, and, in the process, provided their founders with the opportunity to do what they enjoy most.

Interest in entrepreneurship has never been higher than it is at the beginning of the twenty-first century. A recent study by Ernst & Young found that 78 percent of influential Americans believe that entrepreneurship will be *the* defining trend of this century. Which entrepreneurial opportunity topped their list? No surprise here: the Internet.[3] The future of entrepreneurial activity looks incredibly bright, given that the past two decades have seen record numbers of entrepreneurs launching businesses. Many of the world's largest companies continue to engage in massive downsizing campaigns, dramatically cutting the number of managers and workers on their payrolls. This flurry of "pink slips" has spawned a new population of entrepreneurs: "castoffs" from large corporations (in which many of these individuals thought they would be lifetime ladder-climbers) with solid management experience and many productive years left before retirement.

This downsizing has all but destroyed the long-standing notion of job security in large corporations. As a result, members of Generation X (those born between 1965 and 1976) and Generation Y (those born between 1977 and 1994) no longer see launching a business as being a risky career path. Having watched large companies lay off their parents after many years of service, these young people see entrepreneurship as the ideal way to create their own job security and success! They are eager to control their own destinies.

The downsizing trend among large companies has created a more significant philosophical change. It has ushered in an age in which "small is beautiful." Twenty-five years ago, competitive conditions favored large companies with their hierarchies and layers of management; today, with the pace of change constantly accelerating, fleetfooted, agile, small companies have the competitive advantage. These nimble competitors can dart into and out of niche markets as they emerge and recede; they can move faster to exploit market opportunities; and they can use modern technology to create within a matter of weeks or months products and services that once took years and all of the resources a giant corporation could muster. The balance has tipped in favor of small, entrepreneurial companies. Howard Stevenson, Harvard's chaired professor of entrepreneurship, says, "Why is it so easy [for small companies] to compete against giant corporations? Because while they [the giants] are studying the consequences, [entrepreneurs] are changing the world."[4]

One of the most comprehensive studies of global entrepreneurship shows a significant gap in the rate of new business formation among the nations of the world when measured by total entrepreneurial activity or TEA (see Figure 1.1). The study found that 10.5 percent of the adult population in the United States is working to start a business. Thailand and India led the world in entrepreneurial activity with 18.9 percent and 17.9 percent respectively, whereas only 1.8 percent of adults in Japan were trying to launch companies. The study also concluded that these different rates of entrepreneurial activity may account for as much as one-third of the variation in the rates of economic growth among these nations.[5]

The United States and many other nations are benefiting from this surge in global entrepreneurial activity. Eastern European countries, China, Vietnam, and many others whose economies were state controlled and centrally planned are now fertile ground for growing small businesses. Even in stately Great Britain, where the total entrepreneurial activity index is a meager 5.4, entrepreneurship is becoming more popular.

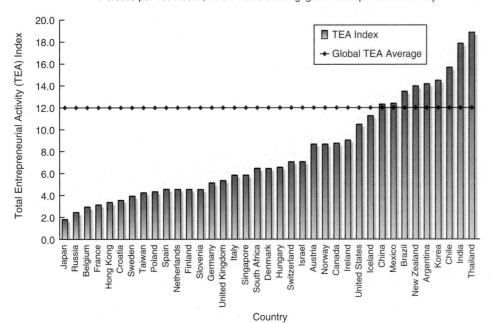

Persons per 100 Adults, 18-64 Years Old Engaged in Entrepreneurial Activity

A Company Example

When attorney Chantelle Ludski went to London to practice international corporate law, she decided to transform her love of the food business into reality by launching a restaurant with a partner. Soon she decided to pursue an M.B.A. at the London Business School and noticed a tremendous business opportunity: The campus she attended had no coffee shop, and students were clamoring for one! As she developed her business plan, Ludski decided to make her shop unique by offering only organically grown coffee and foods. Ludski used part of her student loan to fund her start-up. Since fresh! opened for business, the company has added other retail locations and a wholesale warehouse that supplies one of the largest supermarkets in the United Kingdom. Ludski is now exploring franchise plans for the United Kingdom. "There are more people in the UK who are thinking of starting their own businesses than there were 10 years ago," she says.[6]

Wherever they may choose to launch their companies, these business builders continue to embark on one of the most exhilarating—and one of the most frightening—adventures ever known: launching a business. It's never easy, but it can be incredibly rewarding, both financially and emotionally. One writer calls it "life without a safety net—thrilling and dangerous."[7] Still, true entrepreneurs see owning a business as the real measure of success. Indeed, entrepreneurship often provides the only avenue for success to those who otherwise might have been denied the opportunity.

Who are these entrepreneurs, and what drives them to work so hard with no guarantee of success? What forces lead them to risk so much and to make so many sacrifices in an attempt to achieve an ideal? Why are they willing to give up the security of a steady paycheck working for someone else to become the last person to be paid in their own companies? This chapter will examine the entrepreneur, the driving force behind the American economy.

WHAT IS AN ENTREPRENEUR?

Learning Objective

2. Describe the
entrepreneurial profile.

An **entrepreneur** is one who creates a new business in the face of risk and uncertainty for the purpose of achieving profit and growth by identifying significant opportunities and assembling the necessary resources to capitalize on them. Although many people come up with great business ideas, most of them never act on their ideas. Entrepreneurs do. Researchers have invested a great deal of time and effort over the last few decades trying to paint a clear picture of "the entrepreneurial personality." Although these studies have identified several characteristics entrepreneurs tend to exhibit, none of them has isolated a set of traits required for success. We now turn to a brief summary of the entrepreneurial profile.[8]

entrepreneur—one who creates a new business in the face of risk and uncertainty for the purpose of achieving profit and growth by identifying significant opportunities and assembling the necessary resources to capitalize on them.

1. *Desire for responsibility.* Entrepreneurs feel a deep sense of personal responsibility for the outcome of ventures they start. They prefer to be in control of their resources and use those resources to achieve self-determined goals.

2. *Preference for moderate risk.* Entrepreneurs are not wild risk takers but are instead calculating risk takers. Unlike "high-rolling, riverboat" gamblers, they rarely gamble. Their goals may appear to be high—even impossible—in others' eyes, but entrepreneurs see the situation from a different perspective and believe that their goals are realistic and attainable. They usually spot opportunities in areas that reflect their knowledge, backgrounds, and experiences, which increases their probability of success. One writer observes:

   Entrepreneurship is not the same thing as throwing darts and hoping for the best. It is about planning and taking calculated risks based upon knowledge of the market, the available resources or products, and a predetermined measure of the potential for success.[9]

   In other words, successful entrepreneurs are not as much risk takers as they are risk eliminators, removing as many obstacles to the successful launch of their ventures as possible. One of the most successful ways of eliminating risks is to build a solid business plan for a venture.

3. *Confidence in their ability to succeed.* Entrepreneurs typically have an abundance of confidence in their ability to succeed. They tend to be optimistic about their chances for success. In its recent *National Small Business Poll*, the National Federation of Independent Businesses (NFIB) found that business owners rated the success of their companies quite high—an average of 7.3 on a scale of 1 (a total failure) to 10 (an extreme success).[10] This high level of optimism may explain why some of the most successful entrepreneurs have failed in business—often more than once—before finally succeeding.

4. *Desire for immediate feedback.* Entrepreneurs enjoy the challenge of running a business, and they like to know how they are doing and are constantly looking for feedback. "I love being an entrepreneur," says Nick Gleason, cofounder of CitySoft Inc., a Web-page design firm based in Cambridge, Massachusetts. "There's something about the sheer creativity and challenge of it that I like."[11]

5. *High level of energy.* Entrepreneurs are more energetic than the average person. That energy may be a critical factor given the incredible effort required to launch a start-up company. Long hours and hard work are the rule rather than the exception, and the pace can be grueling.

   A Company Example

   *For example, when Colin Angle and Helen Greiner, MIT graduates whose joint interest in robotics brought them together to form a business venture, **iRobot**, they and their six employees routinely spent 18 hours a day creating software and assembling prototype robots. Their hard work has paid off, however; their company has become the leader in the field of robotics. iRobot has developed a multitude of robots for a wide variety of market segments, ranging from My Real Baby ("an interactive, robotic, artificially-intelligent, emotionally-responsive baby doll") for kids and Roomba (an automatic vacuum cleaner) for busy homeowners to the MicroRig (a device that takes sensors to the bottom of oil wells) for industry and Ariel (a robot capable of removing obstacles on land and underwater) for the military.[12]*

6. *Future orientation.* Entrepreneurs have a well-defined sense of searching for opportunities. They look ahead and are less concerned with what they did yesterday than with what they might do tomorrow. Not satisfied to sit back and revel in their success, real entrepreneurs stay focused on the future. "As you grow a company, your goals become more ambitious and expansive," says Beth Cross, cofounder of Ariat International Inc., a maker of quality footware for equestrians.[13]

Entrepreneurs see potential where most people see only problems or nothing at all, a characteristic that often makes them the objects of ridicule (at least until their ideas become huge successes). Whereas traditional managers are concerned with managing available *resources*, entrepreneurs are more interested in spotting and capitalizing on *opportunities*. The United States leads the world in the percentage of opportunity entrepreneurs, those who start businesses because they spot an opportunity in the marketplace, compared to necessity entrepreneurs, those who start businesses because they cannot find work any other way.[14]

serial entrepreneurs—entrepreneurs who repeatedly start businesses and grow them to a sustainable size before striking out again.

Serial entrepreneurs, those who repeatedly start businesses and grow them to a sustainable size before striking out again, push this characteristic to the maximum.

*Patrick Brandt has been an entrepreneur his entire life, owning a lemonade stand as a kid and a lawn care service in college. In 1996, Brandt launched Cyberpix, an e-commerce service that allowed photographers to catalog and distribute their work online. Even though Cyberpix ended in failure, Brandt's entrepreneurial spirit kept him going. In 1999, he launched **Skywire Technology**, a company that invests in promising new technology businesses, and Skywire Software, a software development company.[15]*

7. *Skill at organizing*. Building a company "from scratch" is much like piecing together a giant jigsaw puzzle. Entrepreneurs know how to put the right people together to accomplish a task. Effectively combining people and jobs enables entrepreneurs to transform their visions into reality.

8. *Value of achievement over money*. One of the most common misconceptions about entrepreneurs is that they are driven wholly by the desire to make money. To the contrary, *achievement* seems to be entrepreneurs' primary motivating force; money is simply a way of "keeping score" of accomplishments—a symbol of achievement. One business researcher says, "What keeps the entrepreneur moving forward is more complex—and more profound—than mere cash. It's about running your own show. It's about doing what is virtually impossible."[16]

Other characteristics frequently exhibited by entrepreneurs include:

High degree of commitment. Entrepreneurship is hard work, and launching a company successfully requires total commitment from an entrepreneur. Business founders often immerse themselves completely in their companies. Most entrepreneurs have to overcome seemingly insurmountable barriers to launch a company and to keep it growing. That requires commitment.

Tolerance for ambiguity. Entrepreneurs tend to have a high tolerance for ambiguous, ever-changing situations, the environment in which they most often operate. This ability to handle uncertainty is critical because these business builders constantly make decisions using new, sometimes conflicting information gleaned from a variety of unfamiliar sources. Based on his research, entrepreneurial expert Amar Bhidé says that entrepreneurs exhibit "a willingness to jump into things when it's hard to even imagine what the possible set of outcomes will be."[17]

Flexibility. One hallmark of true entrepreneurs is their ability to adapt to the changing demands of their customers and their businesses. In this rapidly changing global economy, rigidity often leads to failure. As our society, its people, and their tastes change, entrepreneurs must be willing to adapt their businesses to meet those changes. When their ideas fail to live up to their expectations, successful entrepreneurs change them!

*In 1917, Ed Cox invented a presoaped steel-wool scouring pad that was ideal for cleaning pots and used it as a "calling card" in his sales calls. Although his efforts at selling pots proved futile, Cox noticed how often his prospects asked for the soap pads. He quickly forgot about selling pots and shifted his focus to selling the scouring pads, which his wife had named **S.O.S.** ("Save Our Saucepans"), and went on to start a business that still thrives today.[18]*

Tenacity. Obstacles, obstructions, and defeat typically do not dissuade entrepreneurs from doggedly pursuing their visions. They simply keep trying. "The economy gets good and bad," says Nancy Koehn, a Harvard professor who studies entrepreneurs, "but entrepreneurs will always be with us."[19]

What conclusion can we draw from the volumes of research conducted on the entrepreneurial personality? Entrepreneurs are not of one mold; no one set of characteristics can predict who will become entrepreneurs and whether or not they will succeed. Indeed, *diversity* seems to be a central characteristic of entrepreneurs. One researcher of the entrepreneurial personality explains, "Entrepreneurs don't fit any statistical norm . . . Most are aberrant or a bit odd by nature."[20]

As you can see from the examples in this chapter, *anyone*—regardless of age, race, gender, color, national origin, or any other characteristic can become an entrepreneur (although not everyone should). There are no limitations on this form of economic expression. Entrepreneurship is not a mystery; it is a practical discipline. Entrepreneurship is not a genetic trait; it is a skill that most people can learn. The editors of *Inc.* magazine claim, "Entrepreneurship is more mundane than it's sometimes portrayed. . . . You don't need to be a person of mythical proportions to be very, very successful in building a company."[21]

THE BENEFITS OF ENTREPRENEURSHIP

Surveys show that owners of small businesses believe they work harder, earn more money, and are happier than if they worked for a large company. Before launching any business venture, every potential entrepreneur should consider the benefits of small business ownership.

Opportunity to Create Your Own Destiny

Owning a business provides entrepreneurs the independence and the opportunity to achieve what is important to them. Entrepreneurs want to "call the shots" in their lives, and they use their businesses to make that desire a reality.

A Company Example

*After spending years in the construction business, **Doug Danforth** decided to pursue his dream of opening a flower shop in his hometown of Green Bay, Wisconsin. "I had managed two floral shops years before I went into the construction business, and I liked it a lot," he says. Danforth scraped together $900 of his own money, convinced family members to put up a small amount of cash, and launched his shop, which he has built into a thriving business. "I wanted to control my own destiny," he says. "I knew I wanted to be my own boss."* [22]

Like Doug Danforth, entrepreneurs reap the intrinsic rewards of knowing they are the driving forces behind their businesses.

Opportunity to Make a Difference

Increasingly, entrepreneurs are starting businesses because they see an opportunity to make a difference in a cause that is important to them. Whether it is providing low-cost, sturdy housing for families in developing countries or establishing a recycling program to preserve the Earth's limited resources, entrepreneurs are finding ways to combine their concerns for social issues and their desire to earn a good living.

A Company Example

*Tony Golobic, CEO of **GreatAmerica Leasing Corporation**, a company that leases everything from computers to X-ray machines, is using the resources of his company to give back to his hometown of Cedar Rapids, Iowa. Golobic, an immigrant from Slovenia whose first job in the United States was as a janitor, established a computer center that provides both computer access and instruction for local kids. The company also provides a bus to transport kids to the center from nearby schools.* [23]

Opportunity to Reach Your Full Potential

Too many people find their work is boring, unchallenging, and unexciting. But not entrepreneurs! To them, there is little difference between work and play; the two are synonymous. Entrepreneurs' businesses become their instruments for self-expression and self-actualization. They know that the only boundaries on their success are those imposed by their own creativity, enthusiasm, and vision. Owning a business gives them a sense of empowerment. Barbie Dallman, who left the security (and the hassles) of corporate life at age 30 to start a résumé service, says, "Starting my own business was a spiritual awakening. I found out what was important to me—being able to follow my own interests." [24]

Opportunity to Reap Impressive Profits

Although money is not the primary force driving most entrepreneurs, the profits their businesses can earn are an important motivating factor in their decisions to launch companies. Most entrepreneurs never become super-rich, but many of them do become quite wealthy. In fact, nearly 75 percent of those on the *Forbes* list of the 400 richest Americans are first-generation entrepreneurs! [25] According to research by Thomas Stanley and William Danko, self-employed business owners make up two-thirds of American millionaires. "Self-employed people are four times more likely to be millionaires than people who work for others," says Danko. [26] The typical millionaire's business is not a glamorous, high-tech enterprise; more often, it is something much less glamorous—scrap metal, welding, auctioneering, garbage collection, and the like.

When Michael Dell started a business selling custom-made PCs and components in his dorm room at the University of Texas, reaching the list of the most wealthy people in the United States was only a dream. Yet, Dell has realized that dream. **Dell Computer** *sells more than $50 million worth of computer products on the Internet each day, and the financial wealth he reaps from the success of his company keeps Dell near the top of* Forbes *list with a net worth of $16.5 billion!*[27]

Table 1.1 offers a brief profile of some of the wealthiest Americans in history.

Opportunity to Contribute to Society and Be Recognized for Your Efforts

Often small business owners are among the most respected and most trusted members of their communities. Business deals based on trust and mutual respect are the hallmark of many established small companies. These owners enjoy the trust and recognition they receive from the customers whom they have served faithfully over the years. Playing a vital role in their local business systems and knowing that their work has a significant impact on how smoothly our nation's economy functions is yet another reward for small business managers.

Opportunity to Do What You Enjoy and Have Fun at It

A common sentiment among small business owners is that their work really isn't work. Most successful entrepreneurs choose to enter their particular business fields because they have an interest in them and enjoy those lines of work. They have made their avocations (hobbies) their vocations (work) and are glad they did! These entrepreneurs are living Harvey McKay's advice: "Find a job doing what you love, and you'll never have to work a day in your life." The journey rather than the destination is the entrepreneur's greatest reward.

Mike Becker transformed his passion for nostalgia-based toys into a successful business venture, **Funko Inc.** *Becker invested $35,000 of his own money to resurrect the bobblehead, a toy that was popular in the 1950s and 1960s. His first product was a bobblehead of the restaurant icon Big Boy, but the company's sales took off when Becker landed the rights to distribute Austin Powers bobbleheads after the first hit movie. Since its founding in 1998, Funko has sold more than 1.5 million bobbleheads to small gift, novelty, and collectible stores across the country. "As long as I'm doing what I want to do and we're making a profit" says Becker, "I can't imagine anything better."* [28]

Not only has Becker found a way to make a living, but more importantly, he is doing something he loves!

THE POTENTIAL DRAWBACKS OF ENTREPRENEURSHIP

Although owning a business has many benefits and provides many opportunities, anyone planning to enter the world of entrepreneurship should be aware of its potential drawbacks. Individuals who prefer the security of a steady paycheck, a comprehensive benefit package, a two-week paid vacation, and the support of a corporate staff probably should not go into business for themselves. Some of the disadvantages of entrepreneurship include the following:

TABLE 1.1

Wealthiest Americans in History

Source: Adapted from "The World's Richest People," *Forbes*, February 26, 2003, www.forbes.com/lists/2003/02/26/billionaireland.html; "Richest Americans in History," *Forbes ASAP*, August 24, 1998, p. 32; Rachel Emma Silverman, "Rich & Richer: Fifty of the Wealthiest People of the Past 1,000 Years," *Wall Street Journal Reports: The Millenium*, January 11, 1999, pp. R6–R10.

Who	Comment	Business	Wealth as a % of the U.S. Economy*
John D. Rockefeller (1839–1937)	America's first billionaire. Created America's most powerful monopoly, the Standard Oil Company.	Oil	1.53%
Cornelius Vanderbilt (1794–1877)	Known as the "Commodore." Borrowed $100 from his mother at age 12 to start what became the Staten Island Ferry.	Railroad and shipping	1.15%
John Jacob Astor (1763–1848)	A German-born immigrant who began as a fur trader.	New York real estate	0.93%
Stephen Girard (1750–1831)	Largest investor in the First Bank of the United States. Once loaned the U.S. Treasury $8 million to finance the War of 1812.	Shipping and banking	0.67%
Andrew Carnegie (1835–1919)	A "rags to riches" story. Started as a bobbin boy and went on to found U.S. Steel.	Steel	0.60%
Bill Gates (1955–)	Dropped out of Harvard and launched Microsoft Corporation with Paul Allen. Wealthiest man in the world today.	Computer software	0.43%
Alexander Turney Stewart (1803–1876)	Founded the first department store in the United States.	Retail	0.56%
Frederick Weyerhauser (1834–1914)	Made his fortune as America's demand for lumber exploded.	Timber	0.55%
Larry Ellison (1944-)	Started Oracle Corporation with $2,000 of his own money. (Now second largest maker of computer software behind Microsoft.)	Computer software	0.15%
Michael Dell (1965-)	Started Dell Computer from his dormitory room at the University of Texas. Sales now exceed $35 billion a year.	Computers	0.11%

*Calculated by dividing person's total wealth by the U.S. GDP at the time of death, or if person is still living, by 2001 GDP.

Uncertainty of Income

Opening and running a business provides no guarantees that an entrepreneur will earn enough money to survive. Some small businesses barely earn enough to provide the owner-manager with an adequate income. In a business's early days the owner often has trouble meeting financial obligations and may have to live on savings. The steady income that comes with working for someone else is absent. The owner is always the last one to be paid.

Risk of Losing Your Entire Investment

The small business failure rate is relatively high. According to recent research, 35 percent of new businesses fail within two years, and 54 percent shut down within four years. Within six years, 64 percent of new businesses will have folded. Studies also show that when a company creates at least one job in its early years, the probability of failure after six years plummets to 35 percent![29]

YOU Be the Consultant . . .

A Pigskin Revolution

In 1962, Ed Sabol was selling coats in his father-in-law's Philadelphia clothing business, and he was miserable. "It was like going to the dentist every morning," he recalls. Ed's passion was using the Bell & Howell movie camera (a precursor to today's digital video camera) that his mother-in-law gave him as a wedding present to film his son Steve at practically everything he did, especially his high school football games. When local high schools saw the quality of Ed's films, they asked Sabol to film their games too. Then Sabol read a newspaper article about a local company, Tlra, that had paid $1,500 for the rights to film the 1961 National Football League (NFL) championship game. (The Super Bowl had not been invented yet!) Sabol resolved to win the rights to the 1962 game, even though his football-filming experience was limited to his son's high school games. He called NFL commissioner Pete Rozelle and submitted what proved to be the winning bid of $3,000.

It was a good move for both Rozelle and Sabol. More than 40 years later, Rozelle still considers the 1962 championship game between the Green Bay Packers and the New York Giants to be the best football film ever made. Filming the game made it clear to Sabol that producing films of football games was what he was meant to do. Using the skills he had learned as a coat salesman, Sabol pitched to Rozelle the idea that the NFL needed its own film company to produce highlight films for the 14 teams that made up the league at that time. "We'd call it NFL Films," says Sabol. "He loved the idea." Sabol agreed to produce the highlight films in exchange for $12,000 from each team that would provide the capital to fund NFL Films. His assignment was to preserve the history of the game and to promote NFL football to the nation's sports fans. "In the early 1960s, baseball was the number one sport, college football number two, and boxing number three," recalls Ernie Accorsi, a 30-year NFL veteran. Then "pro football took over the country, and NFL Films had a lot to do with it."

What set NFL Films apart from its rivals was applying cinematography to capturing the power, the finesse, and the spirit of the game rather than merely documenting the action. Sabol dramatized the game by using theatrical music, slow motion, multiple angles, and intense close-ups. Ground-level shots from strategically positioned cameramen, the sounds of players smashing into one another, and artful editing gave viewers the feeling of being in the middle of the action. John Facenda, known as "The Voice of Doom," provided the poetic voiceovers that elevated every film to the level of majestic drama. Sabol's approach to NFL games was more like that of legendary Hollywood film director Billy Wilder than a newsman capturing shots for the evening sports segment. NFL

Steve Sabol and the camera his Dad used to launch NFL Films.

Sources: Adapted from Ilan Mochari, "Archive," *Inc.*, November 2002, p. 124; David Lidsky, "This Is NFL Films," *FSB*, September 2002, pp. 45–50; NFL Films, www.nflfilms.com.

Films' creative approach to the game has garnered the company 82 Emmy Awards to date, making it the most honored filmmaker in sports. "Imagine what would happen if Cezanne, Picasso, or Monet took a look at the NFL," says one newspaper columnist. "The result would be NFL Films."

When Ed Sabol retired from NFL Films in 1987 at the age of 71, his son, Steve, took over as company president and has carefully guided the company to new heights. For years, Steve was the creative and artistic genius behind the company, carefully building a culture of innovation and creativity among employees. Explaining his management philosophy, Steve says, "Leadership is the liberation of talent. We put people in positions to be as creative as they possibly can." At one time, Steve awarded a member of the NFL Films team $1,000 for the most spectacular failure of the year. "We weren't celebrating failure, but ingenuity, the willingness to take risks," he says.

Experienced cinematographers who document a game's action and drama are a key part of the company's success. NFL Films sends at least two cinematographers to every game, and the entire crew shoots more than 1,000 miles of 16-mm film each season! (Nearly 30 crew members cover the Super Bowl, using more than 25 miles of film for that one game.) "Trees" are those in charge of stationary cameras positioned high above the action and are responsible for capturing every play in the game. "Moles" are crew members who move around the field with hand-held cameras, shooting from the players' perspective. They must have the ability to understand the flow of the game and to anticipate where the best shots will be.

"Weasels" cover everything except the on-field action. They find the drama on the sidelines with players and coaches and sometimes film the fans in the stands or in the parking lots. NFL Films now produces more than 400 hours of original programming each year for broadcast over a variety of channels.

Innovation remains an important part of NFL Films' continued success. The company recently moved into a 200,000-square-foot facility containing the latest in video technology that will enable it to stay at the forefront of filmmaking. NFL Films has come a long way since its humble beginnings, but in many ways it remains a family business—one that revolutionized the way America watches football.

1. Identify the entrepreneurial traits that Ed Sabol and his son Steve exhibit.

2. How would you characterize the Sabols' philosophy, beliefs, and values? How important are a business founder's philosophy, beliefs, and values to a small business as it grows?

3. What factors have led to NFL Films' success?

Before "reaching for the golden ring," entrepreneurs should ask themselves if they can cope psychologically with the consequences of failure:

What is the worst that could happen if I open my business and it fails?

How likely is the worst to happen? (Am I truly prepared to launch my business?)

What can I do to lower the risk of my business failing?

If my business were to fail, what is my contingency plan for coping?

Long Hours and Hard Work

Business start-ups often demand that owners keep nightmarish schedules. According to a recent Dun & Bradstreet survey, 65 percent of entrepreneurs devote 40 or more hours per week to their companies (see Figure 1.2). In many start-ups, six- or seven-day workweeks with no paid vacations are the norm. In fact, one study by American Express found that 29 percent of small business owners had no plans to take a summer vacation. The primary reason? "Too busy."[30] These owners feel the pressure because they know that when the business closes, the revenue stops coming in, and customers go elsewhere. "You must have stamina to see it through," says Chantelle Ludski, founder of London-based fresh!, an organic food company. "I put in many 16-hour workdays. Holidays and time off are things that go out the window!"[31]

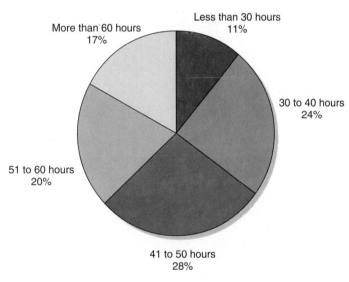

FIGURE 1.2 Number of Hours per Week Entrepreneurs Devote to Their Businesses

Sources: Adapted from *Dun & Bradstreet 21st Annual Small Survey Summary Report,* 2002, p. 35.

Lower Quality of Life Until the Business Gets Established

The long hours and hard work needed to launch a company can take their toll on the remainder of the entrepreneur's life. Business owners often find that their roles as husbands or wives and fathers or mothers take a back seat to their roles as company founders. Part of the problem is that half of all entrepreneurs launch their businesses between the ages of 25 and 39, just when they start their families (see Figure 1.3). As a result, marriages, families, and friendships are too often casualties of small business ownership. "The traits that make you a successful entrepreneur are not the things you can turn off when you walk in the door at home," says one entrepreneurial researcher, describing how owning a business often conflicts with one's family and social life.[32]

High Levels of Stress

Starting and managing a business can be an incredibly rewarding experience, but it also can be a highly stressful one. Entrepreneurs often have made significant investments in their companies, have left behind the safety and security of a steady paycheck, and have mortgaged

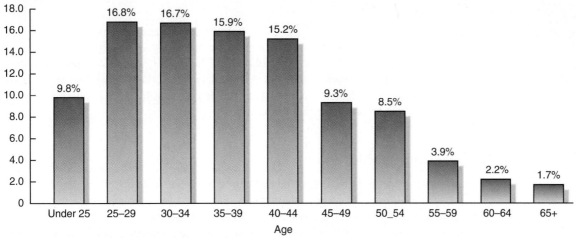

FIGURE 1.3 Owner Age When Business Formed

Source: National Federation of Independent Business and Wells Fargo Bank, 1999.

everything they own to get into business. Failure may mean total financial ruin, and that creates intense levels of stress and anxiety! Sometimes entrepreneurs unnecessarily bear the burden of managing alone because they cannot bring themselves to delegate authority and responsibility to others in the company, even though their employees are capable.

*Jo DeMars, founder of **DeMars and Associates**, a company that manages warranty disputes and arbitration for automakers, guided her company's growth for 13 years by micromanaging every aspect of it. Both DeMars and the company paid a price, however. "I was burned out and exhausted," she says. Because she was so focused on day-to-day issues, DeMars was neglecting the company's strategic management. Her solution was to take a four-month sabbatical and to allow her management team (and a trusted consultant) to run the company, which thrived in her absence. Now back at the helm, DeMars encourages employees to make daily decisions while she focuses on broader issues, such as writing the company's first comprehensive business plan and creating a new division.*[33]

Complete Responsibility

It's great to be the boss, but many entrepreneurs find that they must make decisions on issues about which they are not really knowledgeable. Many business owners have difficulty finding advisors. A recent national small business poll conducted by the National Federation of Independent Businesses found that 34 percent of business owners have no one person to turn to for help when making a critical business decision.[34] When there is no one to ask, the pressure can build quickly. The realization that the decisions they make are the cause of success or failure has a devastating effect on some people. Small business owners discover quickly that *they* are the business.

Discouragement

Launching a business is a substantial undertaking that requires a great deal of dedication, discipline, and tenacity. Along the way to building a successful business, entrepreneurs will run headlong into many different obstacles, some of which appear to be insurmountable. In the face of such difficulties, discouragement and disillusionment are common emotions. Successful entrepreneurs know that every business encounters rough spots along the way, and they wade through difficult times with lots of hard work and an abundant reserve of optimism.

BEHIND THE BOOM: WHAT'S FEEDING THE ENTREPRENEURIAL FIRE?

What forces are driving this entrepreneurial trend in our economy? Which factors have led to this age of entrepreneurship? Some of the most significant ones include the following:

Learning Objective

4. Explain the forces that are driving the growth of entrepreneurship.

Entrepreneurs as Heroes

An intangible but very important factor is the attitude that Americans have toward entrepreneurs. As a nation we have raised them to hero status and have held out their accomplishments as models to follow. Business founders such as Bill Gates (Microsoft Corporation), Mary Kay Ash (Mary Kay Cosmetics), Jeff Bezos (Amazon. com), Michael Dell (Dell Computer Corporation), and Ben Cohen and Jerry Greenfield (Ben & Jerry's Homemade Inc.) are to entrepreneurship what Tiger Woods and Kurt Warner are to sports.

Entrepreneurial Education

Colleges and universities have discovered that entrepreneurship is an extremely popular course of study. Disillusioned with corporate America's downsized job offerings and less promising career paths, a rapidly growing number of students see owning a business as an attractive career option. Today more than 1,500 colleges and universities offer courses in entrepreneurship and small business to some 15,000 students. Many colleges and universities have difficulty meeting the demand for courses in entrepreneurship and small business.

Demographic and Economic Factors

Nearly two-thirds of entrepreneurs start their businesses between the ages of 25 and 44, and much of our nation's population falls into that age range. Plus, the economic growth that spanned most of the 1980s and 1990s created a significant amount of wealth among people of this age group and many business opportunities on which they can capitalize.

Shift to a Service Economy

The service sector produces 92 percent of the jobs and 85 percent of the gross domestic product (GDP) in the United States, which represents a sharp rise from just a decade ago. Because of their relatively low start-up costs, service businesses have become very popular among entrepreneurs. The booming service sector continues to provide many business opportunities, and not all of them are in high-tech fields.

A Company Example

*For example, Christopher Kelly and Michele Fitzgerald, two part-time actors, launched **L.A. Bike Tours** in 1999 to appease their passion for film-related trivia and Hollywood legends. The entrepreneurs offer tours of Hollywood, Beverly Hills, and Venice Beach—all on bicycles! More than just the average "see-the-stars'-homes" tours, L.A. Bike Tours offers customers interesting, fact-filled, leisurely paced tours of the region's most alluring sites. "There's something about being out in the open that's so different from being in an enclosed vehicle," says Fitzgerald. "It makes you feel more a part of the experience." Some tours have special themes, such as the Marilyn Monroe tour, which focuses on the life of the famous actress, and the Death and Despair tour at Halloween that features some of Hollywood's ghastliest stories. Although sales started slowly, Kelly and Fitzgerald's specialty travel business has tapped into one of the fastest-growing segments of tourism, and sales are climbing.[35]*

Technological Advancements

With the help of modern business machines such as personal computers, laptop computers, fax machines, copiers, color printers, answering machines, and voice mail, even one person working at home can look like a big business. At one time, the high cost of such technological wizardry made it impossible for small businesses to compete with larger companies that could afford the hardware. Today, however, powerful computers and communication equipment are priced within the budgets of even the smallest businesses. Although entrepreneurs may not be able to manufacture heavy equipment in their spare bedrooms, they can run a service- or information-based company from their homes very effectively and look like any *Fortune* 500 company to customers and clients.

Independent Lifestyle

Entrepreneurship fits the way Americans want to live—independent and self-sustaining. People want the freedom to choose where they live, the hours they work, and what they do. Although financial security remains an important goal for most entrepreneurs, many place top priority on lifestyle issues such as more time with family and friends, more leisure time, and more control over work-related stress.

E-Commerce and the World Wide Web

The proliferation of the **World Wide Web**, the vast network that links computers around the globe via the Internet and opens up oceans of information to its users, has spawned thousands of entrepreneurial ventures since its beginning in 1993. Online commerce is growing rapidly (see Figure 1.4), creating many opportunities for Web-savvy entrepreneurs. Travel services, computer hardware and software, books, music, videos, and consumer electronics are among the best-selling items on the Web, but entrepreneurs are learning that they can use this powerful tool to sell just about anything! Approximately 57 percent of small businesses use the Internet for business-related purposes, but only 33 percent have Web sites. Those that do have Web sites reap benefits quickly. The most commonly cited benefit of launching a Web site is additional customers; in fact, after launching a site, 41 percent of small companies reported an increase in sales. Fifty-five percent of small companies with Web sites report that their sites are either breaking even or are earning a profit.[36] These "netpreneurs" are using their Web sites to connect with their existing customers and, ultimately, to attract new ones. "Small businesses that use the Web to market their products and services outperform those that don't," says an executive at Verizon, which sponsors an annual small business Internet survey. "The promise of the Internet is starting to pay off."[37]

> **World Wide Web**—*the vast network that links computers around the globe via the Internet and opens up oceans of information to its users. A major business opportunity for entrepreneurs.*

A Company Example

*The Web has stimulated growth at **Timbuk2 Designs**, a small San Francisco company that makes customized carrying cases for bicycle messengers. The company's original business plan called for customers to design their own bags at bicycle shops across the country. Because Timbuk2 could charge extra for custom-designed bags that included unique features, accessories, and colors, profit margins were attractive. Most stores that sold Timbuk2 bags, however, wanted only to stock its basic bags in standard colors. In 1999 founder Rob Honeycutt and president Brennan Mulligan decided to abandon the idea of offering customized bags through retail outlets. They concluded that the best way to reach the company's target customers who wanted customized bags was through the Web. When the company introduced a "Build Your Own" feature on its Web site, sales exploded. More than 30 percent of Timbuk2's total sales and 50 percent of its gross profit come from its Web site. "For us, (e-commerce) is the best thing that's ever happened," says Mulligan.[38]*

International Opportunities

No longer are small businesses limited to pursuing customers within their own borders. The shift to a global economy has opened the door to tremendous business opportunities for entrepreneurs willing to reach across the globe. Although the United States is an attractive market

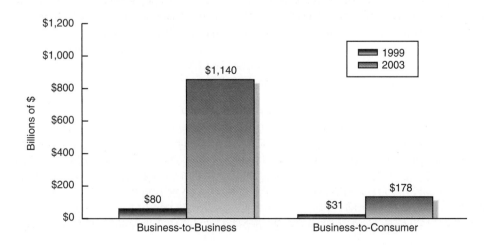

FIGURE 1.4 Online Commerce

Source: International Data Corporation.

for entrepreneurs, approximately 95 percent of the world's population lives outside its borders. World-altering changes such as the crumbling of the Berlin Wall, the collapse of Communism, and breaking down trade barriers through trade agreements have changed the world order and have opened more of the world market to entrepreneurs. Today, small businesses can have a global scope from their inception. Small companies comprise 97 percent of all businesses engaged in exporting, yet they account for only 30 percent of the nation's export sales.[39] Most small companies do not take advantage of export opportunities, often because their owners don't know how or where to start an export initiative. Although terrorism and global recessions have slowed the growth of international trade somewhat, global opportunities for small businesses have a long-term positive outlook.

Although going global can be fraught with dangers and problems, many entrepreneurs are discovering that selling their products and services in foreign markets is really not that difficult. Small companies that have expanded successfully into foreign markets tend to rely on the following strategies:

- Researching foreign markets thoroughly.
- Focusing on a single country initially.
- Utilizing government resources designed to help small companies establish an international presence.
- Forging alliances with local partners.

*From its founding in 1966, **Kelley Manufacturing Company**, a Tifton, Georgia–based maker of peanut harvesting equipment, focused almost exclusively on the domestic market. Then, in 1999, the managers at the employee-owned business decided that the time was right to explore global markets. The company's export strategy has succeeded, and Kelley now sells its products on four continents, making it the world's largest manufacturer of peanut harvesting equipment.[40]*

THE CULTURAL DIVERSITY OF ENTREPRENEURSHIP

As we have seen, virtually anyone has the potential to become an entrepreneur. Indeed, diversity is a hallmark of entrepreneurship. We now explore the diverse mix of people who make up the rich fabric of entrepreneurship.

Young Entrepreneurs

Young people are setting the pace in starting businesses. Disenchanted with their prospects in corporate America and willing to take a chance at controlling their own destinies, scores of young people are choosing entrepreneurship as their primary career path. A study by Babson College found that members of Generation X (those born between 1965 and 1976) are three times more likely than those in other age groups to launch businesses. Members of this generation are responsible for about 80 percent of all business start-ups, making Generation X the most entrepreneurial generation in history![41] There is no slowdown in sight as this generation flexes its entrepreneurial muscle. Generation X might be more appropriately called "Generation E."

Even teenagers and those in their early twenties (the Millenium Generation, born after 1982), show high levels of interest in entrepreneurship. Young entrepreneur camps are popping up all around the country to teach youthful business-building wannabes how to launch and run a business, and many of them are fulfilling their dreams.

*Tyler Dikman was just 15 years old when he started **CoolTronics**, a Tampa, Florida–based computer supply company, after he learned how to fix computers in an internship at Merrill Lynch. When he launched his company, Tyler "didn't even have a car. My clients would pick me up," he recalls. As his business grew, Tyler took over his father's study and turned it into the company headquarters. "The living room became shipping dock A," he says. Now in college, Tyler continues to run the business, which has sales of more than $1 million.[42]*

Because of young people such as Tyler, the future of entrepreneurship looks very bright.

YOU Be the Consultant . . .

Never Too Young

When Erica Gluck was just seven years old, she wanted to earn her own money so badly that she threatened to sell her teddy bears on the sidewalk. Instead, she approached the owners of a pasta shop where she and her family often shopped and asked if she could sell their pasta at weekend farmers' markets near San Diego. "I really loved [their pasta]," Erica says, "and I wanted everyone else to try it." She bought 120 packages at $1.25 with the intent of selling them for twice their cost. "We figured the worst that could happen is that we'd be eating pasta every night for a month," recalls Erica's mother, Mary. Their supply sold out quickly, and a new business, Erica's Pasta, was born. The company has expanded over the years and now sells pesto, olive oils, and hearth-baked breads in addition to pasta. Erica's parents now work for the business full-time, and Erica helped her father, Chris, write a pasta cookbook that includes kid-friendly recipes that the company sells through a separate division called Pasta Press. Erica's little sister Katie has created her own business as well: Katie's Koop, which sells fresh eggs at the farmers' markets. Both girls give 10 percent of their earnings to their church, save 50 percent, and spend the rest. "We would never have done this if it weren't for Erica," admits Mary.

While a junior in college, Adam Witty got the inspiration for his business after repeatedly watching his busy father's Orlando Magic tickets go unused when his schedule changed unexpectedly at the last minute. "I remember seeing Dad throw away Magic tickets because he couldn't attend the game, and he couldn't find anyone else on such short notice to use them," says Witty. He launched TicketAdvantage, a Web-based company that provides an online matching service for ticket holders and ticket buyers. Using TicketAdvantage's secure transaction system, single-game ticket buyers can purchase from season ticket holders seats that would normally not be available. In addition to the National Basketball Association, Witty's company has partnered with almost every major sports organization, including the Women's National Basketball Association, the National Football League, Major League Baseball, Major League Soccer, the National Hockey League, the National Collegiate Athletic Association, the Arena Football League, and National Association of Stock Car Automobile Racing. Witty developed the concept for TicketAdvantage in his Clemson University dorm room and used the resources of the university's Spiro Center for Entrepreneurial Leadership to polish his idea.

Budding entrepreneurs at the University of Maryland can take advantage of a special program the school designed to "create a culture for entrepreneurship." The university's Hinman Campus Entrepreneurship Opportunities program provides space in a specially outfitted dormitory for 100 students who want to build their own companies. Students not only share living space with other like-minded entrepreneurial types, an ideal setting for encouraging start-ups, but they also have access to amenities such as a professionally appointed conference room, wireless Internet access, smart whiteboards, ample computer facilities, videoconferencing equipment, copiers, and a phone system that rings simultaneously home and cellular phones so that no one misses an important business call. Weekly presentations from entrepreneurs, venture capitalists, attorneys, and others help students define their business ideas and develop their business plans. Two hundred students applied for the 100 available spots in the dorm with its incubator-like business environment. The program, which won the Price Institute Innovative Entrepreneurship Educators Award, is working. Twenty of the students already have launched companies, including a medical software company and a textbook sales business. "It's often over those late-night pizzas where the best ideas are born," says one official. One student entrepreneur in the program agrees, "A lot of it is the community. Being around people in the program inspires one to think about other opportunities out there. What I've learned here is how to plan, how to make a business actually work."

Think you're too young to be an entrepreneur? No way! Tyler Dikman, who started a computer supply company at age 15, says, "I wish I would have started the business earlier. You can what-if yourself forever, but I do wish I had started when I was 13."

1. In addition to the normal obstacles of starting a business, what other barriers do young entrepreneurs face?

2. What advantages do young entrepreneurs have when launching a business?

3. What advice would you offer a fellow college student about to start a business?

4. Work with a team of your classmates to develop ideas about what your college or university could do to create a culture of entrepreneurship on your campus or in your community.

Sources: Julie Sloane, "Most Likely to Succeed," *FSB*, November 2002, p. 22; Ellen McCarthy, "A Dorm for Dreamers," *Washington Post*, October 30, 2002, p. E1; "Hinman CEOs Living-Learning Entrepreneurship Program," www.hinmanceos.umd.edu; Teresa Hopkins, "The Winning Ticket," *Clemson World*, Summer 2002, pp. 12–13; Glenn D. Bridges, "Clemson Program Incubates Future Business Leaders," *GSA Business*, February 25, 2002, p. 6; Janet Bodnar, "No Kidding," *Kiplinger's Personal Finance Magazine*, September 2001, pp. 110–113.

Women Entrepreneurs

Despite years of legislative effort, women still face discrimination in the workforce. However, small business has been a leader in offering women opportunities for economic expression through employment and entrepreneurship. Increasing numbers of women are discovering that the best way to break the "glass ceiling" that prevents them from rising to the top of many organizations is to start their own companies. Nearly 6 percent of adult women now own their own businesses.[43] In fact, women are opening businesses at a rate about twice that of the national average.[44] Women entrepreneurs have even broken through the comic strip barrier. Blondie Bumstead, long a typical suburban housewife married to Dagwood, now owns her own catering business with her best friend and neighbor Tootsie Woodly! Although about 69 percent of women-owned businesses are concentrated in retailing and services (as are most businesses), female entrepreneurs are branching out rapidly into previously male-dominated industries. According to the Center for Women's Business Research, the fastest growing-industries for women-owned companies are construction, agribusiness, transportation, communications, and utilities.[45]

Although the businesses women start tend to be smaller than those men start, their impact is anything but small. Women-owned companies employ more than 9.2 million workers and generate sales of more than $1.15 trillion a year! Women own about 28 percent of all privately held businesses in the United States, a number that grew by 37 percent between 1997 and 2002.[46] Although their businesses tend to grow more slowly than those owned by men, women-owned businesses have a higher survival rate than U.S. businesses overall. Female entrepreneurs today are more likely than ever to be highly educated and to have managerial experience in the industries in which they start their companies.[47]

A Company Example

*Darlene Ryan, president of **PharmaFab Inc.**, a pharmaceutical manufacturer, is typical of this new generation of women entrepreneurs. Ryan holds bachelor's degrees in mathematics and German as well as an M.B.A. in accounting and finance; she is also a certified public accountant. Ryan, who was recently honored as a finalist for Entrepreneur of the Year, has taken her company from $395,000 in annual sales to more than $20 million in just six years![48]*

Minority Enterprises

Another rapidly growing segment of the small business population is minority-owned businesses. Hispanics, Asians, and African Americans, respectively, are the minority groups most likely to become entrepreneurs. Like women, minorities cite discrimination as a principal reason for their limited access to the world of entrepreneurship. Minority-owned businesses have come a long way in the past decade, however, and their success rate is climbing.

A Company Example

*While working for IBM, Erika Amoako-Agyei accepted an assignment in West Africa, where she was introduced to contemporary African art. "The work was uniquely African but very sophisticated," she says. She and her husband Nathaniel met many of the artists and began building their own collection. Three years later, the couple returned to the United States and decided to launch **Gold Coast Imports**, a company that would bring this unique art to the U.S. market. Financed by personal savings and a small bank loan, the business struggled early on but became profitable in just its second year. Today the company imports art from 26 countries and counts basketball star Penny Hardaway among its customers. The company recently was featured on MTV Cribs, which led to a boost in sales.[49]*

A recent study by the Small Business Administration (SBA) reported that minorities now own 15 percent of all businesses.[50] Minority-owned businesses generate $591 billion in annual revenues and employ more than 4.5 million workers.[51] The future is promising for this new generation of minority entrepreneurs, who are better educated, have more business experience, and are better prepared for business ownership than their predecessors.

Immigrant Entrepreneurs

The United States has always been a "melting pot" of diverse cultures, and many immigrants have been drawn to this nation by its promise of economic freedom. Unlike the unskilled "huddled masses" of the past, today's immigrants arrive with more education and experience. Although many of them come to the United States with few assets, their dedication and desire to succeed enable them to achieve their entrepreneurial dreams.

Don Chang came to the United States from South Korea when he was 24 and took on a variety of low-level jobs, including some in the garment industry, to support himself. After learning to speak English, Chang decided to get into the garment business himself and used his $11,000 savings to purchase a troubled clothing store in Los Angeles. He worked long hours each day as the store's chief salesperson, buyer, manager, and janitor. Chang's company, **Forever 21***, now has 135 stores in 23 states and Canada that sell inexpensive, chic fashions for girls and young women.*[52]

A Company Example

Part-Time Entrepreneurs

Starting a part-time business is a popular gateway to entrepreneurship. Part-time entrepreneurs have the best of both worlds: They can ease into business for themselves without sacrificing the security of a steady paycheck and benefits. Approximately 15 million Americans are self-employed part-time. A major advantage of going into business part-time is the lower risk in case the venture flops. Many part-timers are "testing the entrepreneurial waters" to see whether their business ideas will work, whether there is sufficient demand for their products and services, and whether they enjoy being self-employed. As they grow, many part-time enterprises absorb more of the entrepreneur's time until they become full-time businesses.

Joe Carmen decided to keep his job at a technology firm when he started his online guitar string company, **StringThis! Inc.** *Carmen created a Web site and filled customer orders in the evenings and on weekends. Two years after start-up, however, Carmen transformed his business into a full-time venture when his company downsized and he was laid off. Carmen rewrote his business plan and made a few adjustments in the way he ran the business. Within a year, he received a lucrative offer to sell the business and accepted it. He is now planning the launch of his next business, which will be a full-time venture.*[53]

A Company Example

Home-Based Businesses

Home-based businesses are booming! Fifty-three percent of all businesses are home based, but about 80 percent of them are very small with no employees.[54] Several factors make the home many entrepreneurs' first-choice location:

- Operating a business from home keeps start-up and operating costs to a minimum.
- Home-based companies allow owners to maintain a flexible lifestyle and workstyle. Many home-based entrepreneurs relish being part of the "open-collar workforce."
- Technology, which is transforming many ordinary homes into "electronic cottages," allows entrepreneurs to run a huge variety of businesses from their homes.

In the past, home-based businesses tended to be rather unexciting cottage industries such as crafts or sewing. Today's home-based businesses are more diverse; modern home-based entrepreneurs are more likely to be running high-tech or service companies with millions of dollars in sales. The average home-based entrepreneur works 61 hours a week and earns an income of just over $50,000. Studies by Link Resources Corporation, a research and consulting firm, suggest that the success rate for home-based businesses is high: 85 percent of such businesses are still in operation after three years.[55]

Over the years, Andy Wiese noticed that his beloved dogs made a mess of his cars whenever he took them for rides, so the German-born entrepreneur began designing and building car beds and barriers in his home. He soon realized that he could sell his products to dog lovers and that home was the ideal location from which to launch the business. Although the business has grown significantly since its launch in 1986, Wiese, his wife Melissa, and their twin daughters continue to run **Meblo, Inc.** *from their five-acre home in northern California. The Weises outsource all of the manufacturing operations to companies in California, England, and China, but company headquarters, warehouses, and shipping facilities are all home based.*[56]

A Company Example

Table 1.2 offers 18 "rules" home-based entrepreneurs should follow to be successful.

TABLE 1.2

Follow These Rules for a
Successful Home-Based Business

Sources: Lynn Beresford, Janean Chun,
Cynthia E. Griffin, Heather Page, and
Debra Phillips, "Homeward Bound,"
Entrepreneur, September 1995,
pp. 116–118; Jenean Huber, "House
Rules," *Entrepreneur*, March 1993,
pp. 89–95; Hal Morris, "Home-Based
Businesses Need Extra Insurance," *AARP
Bulletin*, November 1994, p. 16;
Stephanie N. Mehta, "What You Need,"
Wall Street Journal, October 14, 1994,
p. R10; Jeffery Zbar, "Home Free,"
Business Start-Ups, June 1999, pp. 31–37.

Rule 1. Do your homework. Much of a home-based business's potential for success depends on how much preparation an entrepreneur makes *before* ever opening for business. The library is an excellent source for research on customers, industries, competitors, and the like.

Rule 2. Find out what your zoning restrictions are. In some areas local zoning laws make running a business from home illegal. Avoid headaches by checking these laws first. You can always request a variance.

Rule 3. Choose the most efficient location for your office. About half of all home-based entrepreneurs operate out of spare bedrooms. The best way to determine the ideal office location is to examine the nature of your business and your clients. Avoid locating your business in your bedroom or your family room.

Rule 4. Focus your home-based business idea. Avoid the tendency to be "all things to all people." Most successful home-based businesses focus on a particular customer group or on some specialty.

Rule 5. Discuss your business rules with your family. Running a business from your home means you can spend more time with your family . . . and that your family can spend more time with you. Establish the rules for interruptions up front.

Rule 6. Select an appropriate business name. Your first marketing decision is your company's name, so make it a good one! Using your own name is convenient, but it's not likely to help you sell your product or service.

Rule 7. Buy the right equipment. Modern technology allows a home-based entrepreneur to give the appearance of any *Fortune* 500 company—but only if you buy the right equipment. A well-equipped home office should have a separate telephone line, a computer, a laser or inkjet printer, a fax machine (or board), a copier, a scanner, and an answering machine (or voice mail), but realize that you don't have to have everything from Day One.

Rule 8. Dress appropriately. Being an "open-collar worker" is one of the joys of working at home. But, when you need to dress up (to meet a client, make a sale, meet your banker, close a deal), do it! Avoid the tendency to lounge around in your bathrobe all day.

Rule 9. Learn to deal with distractions. The best way to fend off the distractions of working at home is to create a business that truly interests you. Budget your time wisely. Your productivity determines your company's success.

Rule 10. Realize that your phone can be your best friend . . . or your worst enemy. As a home-based entrepreneur, you'll spend lots of time on the phone. Be sure you use it productively.

Rule 11. Be firm with friends and neighbors. Sometimes friends and neighbors get the mistaken impression that because you're at home, you're not working. If someone drops by to chat while you're working, tactfully ask that person to come back "after work."

Rule 12. Take advantage of tax breaks. Although a 1993 Supreme Court decision tightened considerably the standards for business deductions for an office at home, many home-based entrepreneurs still qualify for special tax deductions on everything from computers to cars. Check with your accountant.

Rule 13. Make sure you have adequate insurance coverage. Some homeowner's policies provide adequate coverage for business-related equipment, but many home-based entrepreneurs have inadequate coverage on their business assets. Ask your agent about a business owner's policy (BOP), which may cost as little as $300 to $500 per year.

Rule 14. Understand the special circumstances under which you can hire outside employees. Sometimes zoning laws allow in-home businesses, but they prohibit hiring employees. Check zoning laws carefully.

Rule 15. Be prepared if your business requires clients to come to your home. Dress appropriately. (No pajamas!) Make sure your office presents a professional image.

Rule 16. Get a post office box. With burglaries and robberies on the rise, you're better off using a "P.O. Box" address rather than your specific home address. Otherwise you may be inviting crime.

Rule 17. Network, network, network. Isolation can be a problem for home-based entrepreneurs, and one of the best ways to combat it is to network. It's also a great way to market your business.

Rule 18. Be proud of your home-based business. Merely a decade ago there was a stigma attached to working from home. Today, home-based entrepreneurs and their businesses command respect. Be proud of your company!

cathy® by Cathy Guisewite

Family Businesses

A **family-owned business** is one that includes two or more members of a family with financial control of the company. Family businesses are an integral part of our economy. Of the 25 million businesses in the United States, 90 percent are family owned and managed. These companies account for 60 percent of total U.S. employment, pay 65 percent of all wages, and generate 50 percent of the nation's GDP. Not all of them are small; 37 percent of the *Fortune* 500 companies are family businesses.[57]

"When it works right," says one writer, "nothing succeeds like a family firm. The roots run deep, embedded in family values. The flash of the fast buck is replaced with long-term plans. Tradition counts."[58] Despite their magnitude, family businesses face a major threat, a threat from within: management succession. Only 30 percent of family businesses survive to the second generation, just 12 percent make it to the third generation, and only 3 percent survive into the fourth generation and beyond. Business periodicals are full of stories describing bitter disputes among family members that have crippled or destroyed once thriving businesses.

To avoid such senseless destruction of valuable assets, founders of family businesses should develop plans for management succession long before they plan to retire.

*For example, after he underwent quadruple heart bypass surgery at age 42, George Davenport, second-generation owner of **D&D Motors**, a successful auto dealership established by Davenport's father in 1937, decided it was time to develop a management succession plan for the family business. "I've spent my whole life building this business," he says. "I'd roll over in my grave if they shut it down after I die." With the help of a family business consultant, the family created a comprehensive succession plan that addressed management as well as estate planning issues. Today, all three of Davenport's children hold offices in the company, each in charge of the area that best suits his or her skills.[59]*

Copreneurs

Copreneurs are entrepreneurial couples who work together as co-owners of their businesses. Unlike the traditional "Mom and Pop" (Pop as "boss" and Mom as "subordinate"), copreneurs "are creating a division of labor that is based on expertise as opposed to gender," says one expert.[60] Studies show that companies co-owned by spouses represent one of the fastest-growing business sectors.

Managing a small business with a spouse may appear to be a recipe for divorce, but most copreneurs say this isn't so. "There is nothing more exciting than nurturing a business and watching it grow with someone you love," says Marcia Sherrill, who, with her husband, William Kleinberg, runs Kleinberg Sherrill, a leather goods and accessories business.[61] Successful copreneurs learn to build the foundation for a successful working relationship before they ever launch their companies. Some of the characteristics they rely on include:

- an assessment of whether their personalities will mesh—or conflict—in a business setting.
- mutual respect for each other and one another's talents.
- compatible business and life goals—a common vision.
- a view that they are full and equal partners, not a superior and a subordinate.
- complementary business skills that each acknowledges and appreciates and that lead to a unique business identity for each spouse.
- the ability to keep lines of communication open, talking and listening to each other.

family-owned business—
one that includes two or more members of a family with financial control of the company.

A Company Example

copreneurs—*entrepreneurial couples who work together as co-owners of their businesses.*

- a clear division of roles and authority, ideally based on each partner's skills and abilities, to minimize conflict and power struggles.
- the ability to encourage each other and to lift up a disillusioned partner.
- separate work spaces that allow them to escape when the need arises.
- boundaries between their business life and their personal life.
- a sense of humor.
- the realization that not every couple can work together.

Although copreneuring isn't for everyone, it works extremely well for many couples and often leads to successful businesses. "Both spouses are working for a common purpose but also focusing on their unique talents," says a family business counselor. "With all these skills put together, one plus one equals more than two."[62]

A Company Example

*In 1995, Dennis and Susie Thompson left the security of their well-paying corporate jobs to operate a **Great Harvest** bakery franchise. Their corporate jobs kept them so busy that they "never saw each other," says Susie, so they decided to run the bakery together. Early on, while the Thompsons were defining their roles and settling in to them, disagreements were common. Their business succeeded partly because the copreneurs established a clear division of responsibilities and stuck to it. Dennis handles production and operations; Susie is responsible for marketing and management. The couple has since opened a second franchise and credit their joint efforts for their success. "A lot of husbands and wives can't work together," says Dennis, "but for us it worked out great."[63]*

Corporate Castoffs

Concentrating on shedding the excess bulk that took away their flexibility and speed, many large American corporations have been downsizing in an attempt to regain their competitive edge. For more than a decade, one major corporation after another has announced layoffs—and not just among blue-collar workers. Companies are cutting back their executive ranks as well. Millions of people have lost their jobs.

These corporate castoffs have become an important source of entrepreneurial activity. Some 20 percent of these discharged corporate managers have become entrepreneurs, and many of those left behind in corporate America would like to join them. One study by Accountemps found that nearly half of the executives surveyed believed their peers would take the entrepreneurial plunge if they only had the money to do so. Four years before, just one-third of corporate executives were inclined to start their own companies.[64]

Many corporate castoffs are deciding that the best defense against future job insecurity is an entrepreneurial offense.

A Company Example

*Between them, Tom Rogers and Gene Neill had 45 years of experience at a factory owned by one of the largest paper machinery companies in the world. Both assumed that they one day they would retire from the company; unfortunately, the corporation declared bankruptcy, and the factory closed, throwing hundreds of people out of work. Within days, Rogers and Neill became entrepreneurs, launching **GT Flow Technology**, a company that occupies a small but profitable niche manufacturing a product called a headbox sheet that is an essential component in the paper-making process. "We had two choices," explains Neill. "We could go out and find other jobs with big companies, or we could try this." After banks refused their start-up loan requests, the corporate castoffs mortgaged their houses to raise the $80,000 they needed to launch GT Flow Technology. They repaid their mortgages within the first nine months of operation and earned a small profit in their first year in business. Both men agree that they are far better off owning their own company than they were working for the giant corporation.[65]*

Corporate Dropouts

The dramatic downsizing of corporate America has created another effect among the employees left after restructuring: a trust gap. The result of this trust gap is a growing number of dropouts from the corporate structure who then become entrepreneurs. Although their workdays may grow longer and their incomes may shrink, those who strike out on their own often find their work more rewarding and more satisfying because they are doing what they enjoy. Other entrepreneurs are inspired to launch their companies after being treated unfairly by large impersonal corporate entities.

In the 1950s, Marion Kauffman was so successful as a salesperson for a pharmaceutical company that his pay exceeded that of the company president, who promptly cut Kauffman's sales territory. Kauffman managed to rebuild sales so that he once again earned more than the boss, who then cut Kauffman's commission rate. Outraged, Kauffman left to start his own business, **Marion Laboratories***, which he sold to Dow Chemical Company in 1989 for $5.2 billion! Before his death in 1993, Kauffman established the Ewing Marion Kauffman Foundation in Kansas City, Missouri, to promote entrepreneurship.*[66]

Because they have college degrees, a working knowledge of business, and years of management experience, both corporate dropouts and castoffs may ultimately increase the small business survival rate. A recent survey by Richard O'Sullivan found that 64 percent of people starting businesses have at least some college education, and 14 percent have advanced degrees.[67] Better-trained, more experienced entrepreneurs are less likely to fail.

THE POWER OF "SMALL" BUSINESS

Of the 25 million businesses in the United States today, approximately 24.75 million, or 99 percent, can be considered "small." Although there is no universal definition of a small business (the U.S. Small Business Administration has more than 800 definitions of a small business based on industry categories), a common delineation of a **small business** is one that employs fewer than 100 people. They thrive in virtually every industry, although the majority of small companies are concentrated in the retail and service industries (see Figure 1.5). Although they may be small businesses, their contributions to the economy are anything but small. For example, small companies employ 51 percent of the nation's private sector workforce, even though they possess less than one-fourth of total business assets. Almost 90 percent of small businesses employ fewer than 20 workers. Because they are primarily labor intensive, small businesses actually create more jobs than do big businesses. In fact, small companies have created two-thirds to three-fourths of the net new jobs in the U.S. economy.[68]

small business—*one that employs fewer than 100 people.*

gazelles—*small companies that are growing at 20 percent or more per year with at least $100,000 in annual sales; they create 70 percent of net new jobs in the economy.*

David Birch, president of the research firm Cognetics, says that the ability to create jobs is not distributed evenly across the small business sector. His research shows that just 3 percent of these small companies created 70 percent of the net new jobs in the economy, and they did so across all industry sectors, not just in "hot" industries. Birch calls these job-creating small companies "**gazelles**," those growing at 20 percent or more per year with at least $100,000 in annual sales. His research also identified "mice," small companies that never grow much and don't create many jobs. The majority of small companies are "mice." Birch tabbed the country's largest businesses "elephants," which have continued to shed jobs for several years.[69]

Not only do small companies lead the way in creating jobs, but they also bear the brunt of training workers for them. One study by the Small Business Administration concluded that small businesses are the leaders in offering training and advancement opportunities to workers. Small companies offer more general skills instruction and training than large ones, and their employees receive more benefits from the training than do those in larger firms. Although their training programs tend to be informal, in-house, and on-the-job, small companies teach employees valuable skills, from written communication to computer literacy.[70]

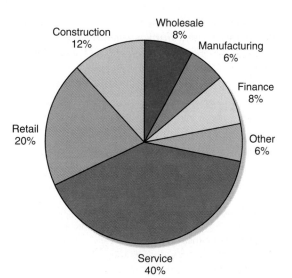

Wholesale 8%
Construction 12%
Manufacturing 6%
Finance 8%
Other 6%
Service 40%
Retail 20%

FIGURE 1.5 A Profile of Small Businesses by Industry

Source: U.S. Small Business Administration, 2002.

Small businesses also produce 51 percent of the country's private GDP and account for 47 percent of business sales.[71] In fact, the U.S. small business sector is the world's third largest economy, trailing only the entire U.S. economy and Japan![72] Small companies are incubators of new ideas, products, and services. Research conducted for the National Science Foundation concluded that small firms create four times more innovations per research and development (R&D) dollar than medium-sized firms and 24 times as many as large companies. In another study of the most important technological innovations introduced into the U.S. market, researchers found that, on average, smaller companies contributed 20 percent more of these innovations per employee than did large companies.[73] Traditionally, small businesses have played a vital role in innovation, and they continue to do so today. Many important inventions trace their roots to an entrepreneur, including the zipper, FM radio, the laser, air conditioning, the escalator, the lightbulb, the personal computer, and the automatic transmission.

Learning Objective

7. Describe the 10 deadly mistakes of entrepreneurship and explain how to avoid them.

THE 10 DEADLY MISTAKES OF ENTREPRENEURSHIP

Because of their limited resources, inexperienced management, and lack of financial stability, small businesses suffer a mortality rate significantly higher than that of larger, more established businesses. Figure 1.6 illustrates the small business survival rate over a 10-year period. Exploring the circumstances surrounding business failure may help to avoid it.

YOU Be the Consultant . . .

A Chilly Idea

When 25-year-old Willis Carrier invented the air conditioner in 1902, he originally did not intend it to make humans more comfortable. Instead, he saw practical application for his device in manufacturing operations that needed to control heat and humidity. Carrier's first customer was a frustrated printer whose presses turned out blurry color images because the heat and humidity in the plant caused the paper's dimensions to change, which misaligned the colored inks. Other early adopters included a textile mill in Belmont, North Carolina, that had problems with the heat generated by the weaving process that made its cotton yarns fuzzy and hard to weave and a candy maker whose chocolate melted in the summer.

In 1922, the Carrier Engineering Company, which Carrier and six friends formed in 1915 with $32,600 they scraped together, developed the centrifugal chiller, the first practical method of air conditioning large spaces. It wasn't until 1924 that Carrier began to market the centrifugal chiller for applications other than manufacturing. The company's first customer of air conditioning for human comfort was the J.L. Hudson Department Store in Detroit, Michigan. The store was famous for its bargain sales in the basement of its building and for the many shoppers who fainted as the heat from the throng of customers overwhelmed the crude ventilation system. The store's basement sales became even more popular after Carrier's air-conditioning system cooled the basement—and soon the rest of the store as well. Air conditioning caught on among the general public after the owner of three Houston movie theaters installed units, enabling patrons to enjoy a respite from the sweltering summer heat. Soon theaters nationwide adopted the idea, often advertising "Air Conditioning" in bigger letters on their marquees than the name of the movie! Government buildings began to install air

conditioning, including the House of Representatives in 1928, the Senate in 1929, the White House in 1930, and the U.S. Supreme Court in 1931. It wasn't until after World War II that sales of small units designed for homes took off.

Throughout the 1950s, Carrier air conditioners became smaller and more powerful, opening new markets for cooling train cars, buses, ocean liners, and even cars. Carrier units were used to cool a special traveling display for Gargantua, a large gorilla that attracted huge audiences throughout Europe and the United States. Today, Carrier systems control the climate in the Sistine Chapel, the Library of Congress, and George Washington's historic Mount Vernon home as well as in millions of homes, factories, and businesses.

The company's first foreign sale was to a Japanese silk factory in 1907. Today the company sells its air-conditioning products in more than 171 countries around the globe and generates sales of $9 billion a year. Like many entrepreneurs throughout history, Willis Carrier could not have predicted the impact that his small company would have on the world when the idea for air conditioning hit him as he stood on a chilly, fog-shrouded platform waiting for a train. Yet, like many entrepreneurs, the world was never the same because of his ideas and his business. Geraud Davis, current president of Carrier Corporation, says, "A humble but determined man, he truly changed the way we work and live."

1. Was launching a business any easier in Willis Carrier's day than it is today? Explain.

2. Explain how Willis Carrier exhibited the entrepreneurial spirit.

3. Develop a list of other entrepreneurs whose products, services, or businesses changed the world. Select one that interests you and prepare a short report on him or her.

Sources: Adapted from Aaron Steetman, "Air Conditioning's 100th Anniversary," *Region Focus*, Fall 2002, p. 40; Mike Hofman, "Archive," *Inc.*, July 2002, p. 116; "Carrier History," Carrier Corporation, www.global.carrier.com/details/0,1240,CLI1_DIV28_ETI23,00.html.

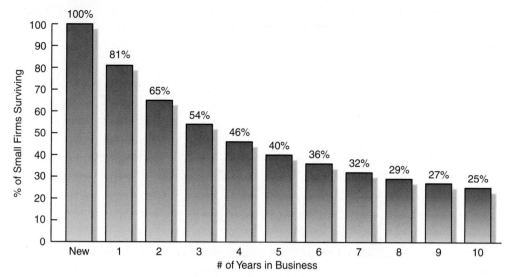

Management Mistakes

In most small businesses, poor management is the primary cause of business failure. Sometimes the manager of a small business does not have the capacity to operate it successfully. The owner lacks the leadership ability, sound judgment, and knowledge necessary to make the business work. Many managers simply do not have what it takes to run a small enterprise. "What kills companies usually has less to do with insufficient money, talent, or information than with something more basic: a shortage of good judgment and understanding at the very top," says one business researcher.[74]

Lack of Experience

Small business managers need to have experience in the field they want to enter. For example, if an entrepreneur wants to open a retail clothing business, she should first work in a retail clothing store. This will provide practical experience as well as knowledge about the nature of the business, which can spell the difference between failure and success. One aspiring entrepreneur who wanted to launch a restaurant went to work for a national chain known for its high-quality management training program after he graduated from college. After completing the training program, he took on a variety of tasks—from cook to manager—in one of the chain's restaurants. He took advantage of every subsequent training opportunity the company offered and asked lots of questions. He began developing a business plan based on his idea for a restaurant, and after nearly five years, he left to start his own restaurant. He credits the knowledge and experience he gained during that time for much of his success in the business.

Ideally, a prospective entrepreneur should have adequate technical ability (a working knowledge of the physical operations of the business and sufficient conceptual ability); the power to visualize, coordinate, and integrate the various operations of the business into a synergistic whole; and the skill to manage the people in the organization and motivate them to higher levels of performance.

Poor Financial Control

Sound management is the key to a small company's success, and effective managers realize that any successful business venture requires proper financial control. Business success also requires having a sufficient amount of capital on hand at start-up. Undercapitalization is a common cause of business failure because companies run out of capital before they are able to generate positive cash flow. Many small business owners make the mistake of beginning their businesses on a "shoestring," which can be a fatal error. Entrepreneurs tend to be overly optimistic and often misjudge the financial requirements of going into business. As a result, they start off undercapitalized and can never seem to catch up financially as their companies consume increasing amounts of cash to fuel their growth.

**"I introduced the world's first
nose-top computer 18 months ago.
Sales are slower than originally anticipated."**

Another aspect of adequate financial control is implementing proper cash management techniques. Many entrepreneurs believe that profit is what matters most in a new venture, but cash is the most important financial resource a company owns. Maintaining adequate cash flow to pay bills on time is a constant challenge for entrepreneurs, especially those in the turbulent start-up phase, or for established companies experiencing rapid growth. Fast-growing companies devour cash fast! Poor credit screening, sloppy debt collection practices, and undisciplined spending habits are common factors in many business bankruptcies. One Internet company that ultimately went bust spent valuable cash on frivolous items such as a $40,000 conference table and a huge office aquarium that cost $4,000 a month to maintain![75]

Weak Marketing Efforts

Sometimes entrepreneurs make the classic *Field of Dreams* mistake. Like Kevin Costner's character in the movie, they believe that if they "build it," customers automatically "will come." Although the idea makes for a great movie plot, in business, it almost never happens. Building a growing base of customers requires a sustained, creative marketing effort. Keeping them coming back requires providing them with value, quality, convenience, service, and fun—and doing it all quickly! As you will see in Chapter 6, "Building a Powerful Marketing Plan," small companies do not have to spend enormous sums of money to sustain a successful marketing effort. Creative entrepreneurs find innovative ways to market their businesses effectively to their target customers without breaking the bank.

Failure to Develop a Strategic Plan

Too many small business managers neglect the process of strategic planning because they think that it is something that only benefits large companies. "I don't have the time" or " We're too small to develop a strategic plan," they rationalize. Failure to plan, however, usually results in failure to survive. Without a clearly defined strategy, a business has no sustainable basis for creating and maintaining a competitive edge in the marketplace. Building a strategic plan forces an entrepreneur to assess *realistically* a proposed business's potential. Is it something customers are willing and able to purchase? Who are the target customers? How will the business attract and keep those customers? What is the company's basis for serving customers' needs better than existing companies? How will the business gain a sustainable edge over its rivals? We will explore these and other vital issues in Chapter 3, "Strategic Management and the Entrepreneur."

Uncontrolled Growth

Growth is a natural, healthy, and desirable part of any business enterprise, but it must be planned and controlled. Management expert Peter Drucker says that start-up companies can expect to outgrow their capital bases each time sales increase 40 to 50 percent.[76] Ideally, expansion should be financed by the profits they generate ("retained earnings") or by capital contributions from the owners, but most businesses wind up borrowing at least a portion of the capital investment.

Expansion usually requires major changes in organizational structure, business practices such as inventory and financial control procedures, personnel assignments, and other areas. But the most important change occurs in managerial expertise. As the business increases in size and complexity, problems increase in magnitude, and the entrepreneur must learn to deal with them. Sometimes entrepreneurs encourage rapid growth, only to have the business outstrip their ability to manage it.

Jill and Doug Smith, co-owners of **Buckeye Beans & Herbs***, "got a hangover" when their specialty food company began growing rapidly. Sales were climbing by 50 percent a year, but profit margins were shrinking. To save their business, the Smiths curbed sales growth, eliminated customers that were cutting into profit margins (many of whom were large chain stores), and hired a chief financial officer. Their efforts at refocusing put their company back on track.[77]*

A Company Example

Poor Location

For any business, choosing the right location is partly an art—and partly a science. Too often, business locations are selected without proper study, investigation, and planning. Some beginning owners choose a particular location just because they noticed a vacant building. But the location question is much too critical to leave to chance. Especially for retailers, the lifeblood of the business—sales—is influenced heavily by choice of location.

Before Dylan and Elise Fager bought their **Mailboxes, Etc.** *(MBE) franchise, they invested a great deal of time researching the ideal site. Their final choice was a site across the street from a major shopping mall, which generated lots of customer traffic every day. The Fagers' research also showed them that the site was within five miles of 2 to 3 million square feet of office space, providing prime access to large numbers of potential customers. The Fagers' franchise was so successful that they quickly opened a second MBE franchise in the downtown district. A major advantage of that site was a complete lack of nearby competition.[78]*

A Company Example

Improper Inventory Control

Normally, the largest investment a small business owner makes is in inventory, yet inventory control is one of the most neglected managerial responsibilities. Insufficient inventory levels result in shortages and stockouts, causing customers to become disillusioned and leave. A more common situation is that the manager has not only too much inventory but also too much of the *wrong type* of inventory. Many small firms have an excessive amount of cash tied up in an accumulation of useless inventory. Computerized point-of-sale systems are now priced low enough to be affordable for small businesses, and they can track items as they come in and go out, allowing business owners to avoid inventory problems.

Incorrect Pricing

Establishing prices that will generate the necessary profits means that business owners must understand how much it costs to make, market, and deliver their products and services. Too often, entrepreneurs simply charge what competitors charge or base their prices on some vague idea of "selling the best product at the lowest price," both of which are dangerous. Small business owners usually underprice their products and services. The first step in establishing accurate prices is to know what a product or service costs to make or to provide. Then business owners can establish prices that reflect the image they want to create for their companies, always, of course, with an eye on the competition.

Inability to Make the "Entrepreneurial Transition"

Making it over the "entrepreneurial start-up hump" is no guarantee of business success. After the start-up, growth usually requires a radically different style of management, one that entrepreneurs are not necessarily good at. The very abilities that make an entrepreneur successful often lead to managerial ineffectiveness. Growth requires entrepreneurs to delegate authority and to relinquish hands-on control of daily operations—something many entrepreneurs simply cannot do. Growth pushes them into areas where they are not capable, yet they continue to make decisions rather than involve others.

Table 1.3 explains some of the most common symptoms of these 10 deadly mistakes.

TABLE 1.3

Symptoms of the 10 Deadly Mistakes of Entrepreneurship

Sources: Adapted from Ram Charan and Jerry Useem, "Why Companies Fail," *Fortune,* May 27, 2002, pp. 50–62; Frederick J. Beste III, "Avoiding the Traps Set for Small Firms," *Nation's Business,* January 1999, p. 10; Mel Mandell, "Fifteen Start-Up Mistakes," *Business Start-Ups,* December 1995, p. 22; Kenneth Labich, "Why Companies Fail," *Fortune,* November 14, 1994, pp. 52–68; Sharon Nelton, "Ten Key Threats to Success," *Nation's Business,* June 1992, pp. 22–30; Robert J. Cook, "Famous Last Words," *Entrepreneur,* June 1994, pp. 122–128; David M. Anderson, "Deadly Sins," *Entrepreneur B.Y.O.B.,* August 2001, pp. 107–109; Geoff Williams, "100 Million Dollars Baked in a Pie," *Entrepreneur, B.Y.O.B.,* September 2001, pp. 107–109.

Entrepreneurs whose businesses fail usually can look back on their experiences and see what they did wrong, vowing never to make the same mistake again. If you find yourself making any of the following statements as you launch your business, look out! You may become a victim of one of the 10 deadly mistakes of entrepreneurship.

"We've got a great product (or service)! It will sell itself." Don't get so caught up in your product or service that you forget to evaluate whether real, live customers are willing and able to pay for it. Oh . . . and no product or service has ever "sold itself."

"With a market this big, we only need a tiny share of it to become rich." Entrepreneurs tend to be overly optimistic in their sales, profits, and cash flow estimates, especially in the beginning. Most don't realize until they get into business how tough it really is to capture even a tiny share of the market.

"Strategic plan?! We don't need a strategic plan, that's only for big corporations." One of the quickest and surest paths to failure is neglecting to build a strategic plan. That defines some point of distinction for your company. A plan helps you focus on what you can do for your customers that your competitors cannot.

"What a great business idea! It's cheap, easy to start, and it's the current rage." Because a business idea is cheap and easy to start does not necessarily make it attractive. Too many entrepreneurs get clobbered in such businesses once the market matures and the competition gets stiff or the fad passes.

"We may not know what we're doing yet, but we've got enough capital to last us until we do. We'll figure it out as we go." Everything—especially launching a business—takes longer and costs more than you think. Experienced entrepreneurs call it "the rule of two and three": Start-ups take either twice as long or need three times as much money (or both) to get off the ground as the founders forecast. Plan accordingly.

"Our forecast shows that we'll be making profits within three months, and that's very conservative . . . really." Everyone expects entrepreneurs to be optimistic about their ventures' future, but you have to temper your optimism with reality. Launching a business on the basis of one set of forecasts is asking for trouble. Make sure you develop at least three sets of forecasts—pessimistic, most likely, and optimistic—and have contingency plans for all three.

"It's a good thing that we've got enough capital to last us the few months until we hit our breakeven point." Attracting adequate start-up financing is essential to launching your business, but you also have to have access to *continuing* sources of funding. Growing businesses consume cash, and fast-growing businesses consume cash even faster. Don't become a victim of your own success; make sure you establish reliable sources of capital once your business is up and running.

"We'll make it easy for customers to buy from us. We'll extend credit to almost anyone to make a sale." One of the shortest routes to cash flow problems is failing to manage customer credit. It's easy to make a sale, but remember: Sales don't count unless you actually collect the payments from them. Watch for slow-paying customers.

"We're in the big time now. Our largest customer is [insert name of large customer here]." Landing a big customer is great, but it's dangerous to become overly dependent on a single customer for most of your sales. What happens if that customer decides to squeeze you for price concessions or to go to a competitor?

"Let's have our annual meeting in the Cayman Islands. We're the only 'stockholders,' and, besides, we deserve it. We've worked hard." Avoid the tendency to drain cash out of your business unnecessarily. A good rule of thumb: Don't start your business unless you have enough savings to support yourself (without taking cash from it) until the business breaks even.

TABLE 1.3 (continued)

"Let's go with this location. I know it's 'off the beaten path,' but it's so much cheaper!" For some businesses, choice of location is not a crucial issue. However, if your company relies on customers coming into your place of business to make sales, do not settle for the cheapest location. There's a reason such places are cheap! It's better to pay a higher price for a location that produces adequate sales volume.

"Computer?! I don't know anything about computers. A legal pad and an adding machine are all I need to manage my business!" These days almost any business—no matter how small—can benefit from a computer. First, find the software that will help you maintain control over your business; then buy the computer that will run it. Don't forget to budget both time and money for training and support.

"We're so small here. Everybody knows what our goals and objectives are." Just because a business is small doesn't necessarily mean that everyone who works there understands where you are trying to take the company. Do not assume that people will read your mind concerning your company's mission, goals, and objectives. You must communicate your vision for the business to everyone involved in it.

"This business is so easy it can run itself." Don't fool yourself. The only place a business will run itself is downhill! You must manage your company, and one of the most important jobs you have as leader is to prioritize your business's objectives.

"Of course our customers are satisfied! I never hear them complain." Most customers never complain about poor service or bad quality. They simply refuse to do business with you again. More often than not, the service and level of "personal treatment" that customers receive is what allows many small businesses to gain an edge over their larger rivals. Unfortunately, it's also one of the most overlooked aspects of a business. Set up a system to get regular feedback from your customers.

"What do you mean we're out of cash? We've been making a profit for months now, and sales are growing." Don't confuse cash and profits. You cannot spend profits—just cash. Many businesses fail because their founders mistakenly assume that if profits are rising, so is the company's cash balance. To be successful, you must manage both profits and cash!

PUTTING FAILURE INTO PERSPECTIVE

Learning Objective
8. Put failure into the proper perspective.

Because they are building businesses in an environment filled with uncertainty and shaped by rapid change, entrepreneurs recognize that failure is likely to be part of their lives, but they are not paralyzed by that fear. "The excitement of building a new business from scratch is greater than the fear of failure," says one entrepreneur who failed in business several times before finally succeeding.[79] Entrepreneurs use their failures as a rallying point and as a means of refocusing their business ventures for success. They see failure for what it really is: an opportunity to learn what does not work! Successful entrepreneurs have the attitude that failures are simply stepping-stones along the path to success.

Failure is a natural part of the creative process. The only people who never fail are those who never do anything or never attempt anything new. Baseball fans know that Babe Ruth held the record for career home runs (714) for many years, but how many know that he also held the record for strikeouts (1,330)? Successful entrepreneurs know that hitting an entrepreneurial home run requires a few strikeouts along the way, and they are willing to accept them. Failure is an inevitable part of being an entrepreneur, and true entrepreneurs don't quit when they fail. One entrepreneur whose business burned through $800 million of investors' money before folding says, "If you're an entrepreneur, you don't give up when times get tough."[80]

One hallmark of successful entrepreneurs is the ability to fail *intelligently*, learning why they failed so that they can avoid making the same mistake again. They know that business success does not depend on their ability to avoid making mistakes but to be open to the lessons each mistake teaches. They learn from their failures and use them as fuel to push closer to their ultimate target. Entrepreneurs are less worried about what they might lose if they try something and fail than about what they might lose if they fail to try.

Entrepreneurial success requires both persistence and resilience, the ability to bounce back from failure. Thomas Edison discovered about 1,800 ways not to build a lightbulb before hitting on a design that worked. Walt Disney was fired from a newspaper job because, according to his boss, he "lacked ideas." Disney also went bankrupt several times before he created Disneyland.

YOU Be the Consultant . . .

If at First You Don't Succeed, So What!?

"Would you like for me to give you a formula for success? It's quite simple, really: Double your rate of failure. You are thinking of failure as the enemy of success. But it isn't at all. You can be discouraged by failure, or you can learn from it. So go ahead and make mistakes. Make all you can. Because remember, that's where you will find success."

—Thomas J. Watson
Founder, IBM

Thomas Watson understood what true entrepreneurs know: Failure is a necessary and important part of the entrepreneurial process and it does not have to be permanent. Some of the world's greatest entrepreneurs failed (some of them many times) before they finally succeeded. Henry Ford's first business, The Detroit Automobile Company, failed less than two years after Ford and his partners started it. Ford's second auto company also failed, but his third attempt in the then-new auto manufacturing business was, of course, a huge success. The Ford Motor Company, which is still controlled by the Ford family, is a major player in the automotive industry and is one of the largest companies in the world. Milton Hershey launched his first candy shop at age 18 in Philadelphia; it failed after six years. Four more attempts at building a candy business also failed before Hershey finally hit on success with the Lancaster Caramel Company, the business that was the parent of the famous Hershey Foods Corporation. Today, Hershey is the leading manufacturer of chocolate products in the United States and exports to more than 90 countries.

In post–World War II Japan, Masaru Ibuka and Akio Morita formed a partnership to produce an automatic rice cooker. Unfortunately, their machine burned the rice and was a flop. Their company sold just 100 cookers. Ibuka and Morita refused to give up, however, and created another company to build an inexpensive tape recorder that they sold to schools. Their tape recorder proved to be successful, and the company eventually became the consumer electronics giant Sony Corporation.

Rick Rosenfield and Larry Flax wrote a screenplay that never sold, started an Italian restaurant that went bankrupt, and developed a mobile skateboard park that quickly flopped. Then, in 1984, they tried the restaurant business again, launched the California Pizza Kitchen, and struck pay dirt! The California Pizza Kitchen is now a successful and well-recognized chain.

Gail Borden (1801–1874) also knew about failure because he had a geat deal of experience with it. One of his first inventions, the Terraqueous Wagon, a combination of wagon and sailboat that was designed to travel on both land and water, sank on its first trial run. Several years later, returning to the United States from London where he had been promoting another invention, the condensed meat biscuit (a concoction of dehydrated meat and flour), Borden saw four babies die from tainted milk. Afterward, he dropped the meat biscuit to focus on making milk safer for human consumption. He knew that the key was to remove the water from the milk, but the challenge was to do so without affecting its taste. For two years, he worked without success, always ending up with scorched milk. Ultimately, Borden developed a vacuum condensation process that successfully removed the water from milk without adversely affecting its flavor. After three unsuccessful attempts, Borden finally won a patent for his process in 1856 and set up a manufacturing plant. It failed. A second attempt to produce condensed milk also failed. Undaunted, Borden convinced New York financier Jeremiah Milbank to invest in a new milk-processing venture, and this one succeeded! The New York Condensed Milk Company supplied much-needed nourishment to troops during the Civil War before becoming a staple in American households. Today, Borden Inc. is a multibillion-dollar conglomerate that still manufactures condensed milk using the same process that Borden developed 150 years ago. When he died in 1874, Gail Borden was buried beneath a tombstone that read, "I tried and failed; I tried again and succeeded."

1. Do the entrepreneurs described here exhibit the true entrepreneurial spirit? If so, how?

2. How do these entrepreneurs view failure? Is their view typical of most entrepreneurs?

3. James Joyce said, "Mistakes are the portals of discovery." What did he mean? Do you agree? Why is Joyce's idea important to entrepreneurs?

Sources: Adapted from "Gail Borden," www.famoustexans.com/ GailBorden.htm; Jeffrey Shuman and David Rottenberg, "Famous Failures," *Business Start-Ups*, February 1999, pp. 32–33; Francis Huffman, "A Dairy Tail," *Entrepreneur*, August 1993, p. 182; Bob Gatty, "Building on Failure," *Nation's Business*, April 1987, pp. 50–51.

HOW TO AVOID THE PITFALLS

Learning Objective

9. Explain how entrepreneurs can avoid becoming another failure statistic.

We have seen the most common reasons behind many small business failures. Now we must examine the ways to avoid becoming another failure statistic and gain insight into what makes a successful business. The suggestions for success follow naturally from the causes of business failure.

Know Your Business in Depth

We have already emphasized the need for the right type of experience in the business you plan to start. Get the best education in your business area that you possibly can *before* you set out on your own. Become a serious student of your industry. Read everything you can—trade journals, business periodicals, books, research reports—relating to your industry and learn what it takes to succeed in it. Personal contact with suppliers, customers, trade associations, and others in the same industry is another excellent way to get that knowledge.

A Company Example

*Before she launched **Executive Temporaries**, Suzanne Clifton contacted other entrepreneurs in the temporary personnel services business (far enough away from her home base to avoid competitors) to find out "what it takes to operate this kind of business." She picked up many valuable tips and identified the key factors required for success. Today her company is a highly respected leader in the industry.[81]*

Successful entrepreneurs are like sponges, soaking up as much knowledge as they can from a variety of sources.

Develop a Solid Business Plan

For any entrepreneur, a well-written business plan is a crucial ingredient in preparing for business success. Without a sound business plan, a firm merely drifts along without any real direction. Unfortunately, most entrepreneurs never take the time to develop a solid business plan. Not only does a plan provide a pathway to success, but it also creates a benchmark against which an entrepreneur can measure actual company performance.

A business plan allows entrepreneurs to replace sometimes faulty assumptions with facts before making the decision to go into business. The planning process forces entrepreneurs to ask and then answer some difficult, challenging, and crucial questions.

A Company Example

*In his freshman year at Princeton, Tom Szaky created a business plan that helped him launch **TerraCycle International**, a company that uses red worms to compost food waste into nutrient-rich soil. Szaky's ingenious plan is to sell waste disposal services to restaurants, schools, penitentiaries, and other institutions and allow the worms to transform the waste into organic soil, which the company will sell at premium prices to garden centers, nurseries, supermarkets, and other retail outlets. Because many of its key "employees" are worms and because the company can sell the organic soil it produces at premium prices, TerraCycle offers waste-disposal fees that are 25 percent below those of traditional waste-disposal companies. Szaky's research told him that the organic segment of the potting soil industry is a multibillion-dollar business and has been growing at double-digit rates for the past several years. TerraCycle recently signed a contract with clients across northern New Jersey to process 130 tons of food waste a day! Szaky's plans include expansion into the global market, and the company already has inquiries from potential partners in four countries.[82]*

We will discuss the process of developing a business plan in Chapter 11, "Crafting a Winning Business Plan."

Manage Financial Resources

The best defense against financial problems is developing a practical information system and then using this information to make business decisions. No entrepreneur can maintain control over a business unless she is able to judge its financial health.

The first step in managing financial resources effectively is to have adequate start-up capital. Too many entrepreneurs begin their businesses with too little capital. One experienced business owner advises, "Estimate how much capital you need to get the business going and then double that figure." His point is well taken; it almost always costs more to launch a business than any entrepreneur expects.

The most valuable financial resource to any small business is *cash*. Although earning a profit is essential to its long-term survival, a business must have an adequate supply of cash to pay its bills and meets its obligations. Some entrepreneurs count on growing sales to supply their company's cash needs, but it almost never happens. Growing companies usually consume more cash than they generate; and the faster they grow, the more cash they gobble up! We will discuss cash management techniques in Chapter 9, "Managing Cash Flow."

Understand Financial Statements

Every business owner must depend on records and financial statements to know the condition of her business. All too often entrepreneurs use these only for tax purposes and not as vital management control devices. To truly understand what is going on in the business, an owner must have at least a basic understanding of accounting and finance.

When analyzed and interpreted properly, these financial statements are reliable indicators of a small firm's health. They can be quite helpful in signaling potential problems. For example, declining sales, slipping profits, rising debt, and deteriorating working capital are all symptoms of potentially lethal problems that require immediate attention. We will discuss financial statement analysis in Chapter 10, "Creating a Successful Financial Plan."

Learn to Manage People Effectively

No matter what kind of business you launch, you must learn to manage people. Every business depends on a foundation of well-trained, motivated employees. No business owner can do everything alone. The people an entrepreneur hires ultimately determine the heights to which the company can climb–or the depths to which it can plunge. Attracting and retaining a corps of quality employees is no easy task, however. It remains a challenge for every small business owner. "In the end, your most dominant sustainable resource is the quality of the people you have," says one small business expert.[83] We will discuss the techniques of managing and motivating people effectively in Chapter 15, "Leading the Growing Company and Planning for Management Succession."

Keep in Tune with Yourself

"Starting a business is like running a marathon. If you're not physically and mentally in shape, you'd better do something else," says one business consultant.[84] Your business's success will depend on your constant presence and attention, so it is critical to monitor your health closely. Stress is a primary problem, especially if it is not kept in check.

Successful entrepreneurs recognize that their most valuable asset is their time, and they learn to manage it effectively to make themselves and their companies more productive. None of this, of course, is possible without passion—passion for their businesses, their products or services, their customers, their communities. Passion is what enables a failed entrepreneur to get back up, try again, and make it to the top.

CHAPTER SUMMARY

1. Define the role of the entrepreneur in business—in the United States and across the world.

Entrepreneurship is thriving in the United States, but this wave of entrepreneurship is not limited to the United States; many nations across the globe are seeing similar growth in their small business sectors. A variety of competitive, economic, and demographic shifts have created a world in which "small is beautiful."

Capitalist societies depend on entrepreneurs to provide the drive and risk taking necessary for the system to supply people with the goods and services they need.

2. Describe the entrepreneurial profile and evaluate your potential as an entrepreneur.

Entrepreneurs have some common characteristics, including a desire for responsibility, a preference for moderate risk, confidence in their ability to succeed, desire for immediate feedback, a high energy level, a future orientation, skill at organizing, and a value of achievement over money. In a phrase, they are tenacious high achievers.

3-A. Describe the benefits of entrepreneurship.

Driven by these personal characteristics, entrepreneurs establish and manage small businesses to gain control over their lives, make a difference in the world, become self-fulfilled, reap unlimited profits, contribute to society, and do what they enjoy doing.

3-B. Describe the drawbacks of entrepreneurship.

Entrepreneurs also face certain disadvantages, including uncertainty of income, the risk of losing their investments (and more), long hours and hard work, a lower quality of life until the business gets established, high stress levels, and complete decision-making responsibility.

4. Explain the forces that are driving the growth of entrepreneurship.

Several factors are driving the boom in entrepreneurship, including entrepreneurs portrayed as heroes, better entrepreneurial education, economic and demographic factors, a shift to a service economy, technological advancements, more independent lifestyles, and increased international opportunities.

5. Explain the cultural diversity of entrepreneurship.

Several groups are leading the nation's drive toward entrepreneurship: women, minorities, immigrants, part-timers, home-based business owners, family business owners, copreneurs, corporate castoffs, and corporate dropouts.

6. Describe the important role small businesses play in our nation's economy.

The small business sector's contributions are many. Small business make up 99 percent of all businesses, employ 51 percent of the private sector workforce, create two-thirds to three-fourths of the net new jobs in the economy, produce 51 percent of the country's private gross domestic product (GDP), and account for 47 percent of all business sales.

7. Describe the 10 deadly mistakes of entrepreneurship and explain how to avoid them.

There are no guarantees that the business will make a profit or even survive. SBA statistics show that 64 percent of new businesses will fail within six years. The 10 deadly mistakes of entrepreneurship include management mistakes, lack of experience, poor financial control, weak marketing efforts, failure to develop a strategic plan, uncontrolled growth, poor location, lack of inventory control, incorrect pricing, and inability to make the "entrepreneurial transition."

8. Put failure into the proper perspective.

Entrepreneurs recognize that failure is a natural part of the creative process. Successful entrepreneurs have the attitude that failures are simply stepping stones along the path to success, and they refuse to be paralyzed by a fear of failure.

9. Explain how entrepreneurs can avoid becoming another failure statistic.

Entrepreneurs can employ several general tactics to avoid pitfalls. Entrepreneurs should know their businesses in depth, prepare a solid business plan, manage financial resources effectively, understand financial statements, learn to manage people, and try to stay healthy.

DISCUSSION QUESTIONS

1. What forces have led to the boom in entrepreneurship in the United States and across the globe?
2. What is an entrepreneur? Give a brief description of the entrepreneurial profile.
3. *Inc.* magazine claims, "Entrepreneurship is more mundane than it's sometimes portrayed . . . you don't need to be a person of mythical proportions to be very, very successful in building a company." Do you agree? Explain.
4. What are the major benefits of business ownership?
5. Which of the potential drawbacks to business ownership are most critical?
6. Briefly describe the role of the following groups in entrepreneurship: women, minorities, immigrants, part-timers, home-based business owners, family business owners, copreneurs, corporate castoffs, and corporate dropouts.
7. What is a small business? What contributions do small businesses make to our economy?
8. Describe the small business failure rate.
9. Outline the causes of business failure. Which problems cause most business failures?
10. How does the typical entrepreneur view the possibility of business failure?
11. How can the small business owner avoid the common pitfalls that often lead to business failures?
12. Why is it important to study the small business failure rate and the causes of business failures?
13. Explain the typical entrepreneur's attitude toward risk.
14. Are you interested in one day launching a small business? If so, when? What kind of business? Describe it. What can you do to ensure its success?

THE BUSINESS DISC

Launch *The Business Disc* and take the Entrepreneurial Attitude Survey. Your answers to the questions and scenarios will produce a score on the following six dimensions to assess your entrepreneurial characteristics:

1. creativity
2. self-reliance
3. drive, discipline, and determination
4 energy
5. risk-taking
6. communications

How did you score on the survey's six dimensions? Is your score much higher (or lower) in one particular area? Did the results surprise you? Is a high score on surveys such as this one a prerequisite for success as an entrepreneur? Explain. Do you think you would make a good entrepreneur? Explain. How well does your entrepreneurial score fit with the perceptions of those who know you best—family, friends, teachers, and others?

BUSINESS PLAN PRO

Business PlanPro

Most students using this textbook are committed to becoming entrepreneurs or they have been assigned the development of a business plan as an important part of the class. In either case you will discover that the Business Plan Pro is a software tool that will assist you in the process. At the end of each chapter there will be suggestions as to materials relevant in the chapter that should be added to the business plan being created with the help of your Business Plan Pro software. If you add material to the plan as you proceed through the textbook, you will find that the final business plan seems to come together more easily.

For this chapter please go to the section that asks if you are building a business plan for a "Start-Up" business or an "Ongoing" Business. Chose the one you plan to do.

The second step is to select if you are planning a "For-Profit" or "Not-For-Profit" business.

Third, will you be selling products, services, or both?

Fourth, do you manage inventories in the business you are developing this plan for?

Fifth, will the business sell or credit?

Sixth, does the business have a Web site?

Seventh, what Standard Industrial Classification System (SIC) does your business fit in? If you do not know, use the SIC code search to find the best fit for your business.

Eighth, choose a start date for the business. You might want to assume that for the class project business plan the start date is at the end of the term.

Ninth, choose the length of the term for the business plan. If your instructor wants you to build a business plan longer than three years, you will need to select the long-term business plan. If you are creating, this plan for a business you plan to actually start or acquire, our advice is to select the long-term business plan option.

Tenth, choose the name of your business and then, if the business is hypothetical, select a location, phone, fax and e-mail for the business. If it is an actual business, provide the correct information.

Eleventh, select a title for your business plan. Normally this will be the name of the business, (i.e. Betty Lou's Auto Parts)

That was not difficult at all and now you have established a document that you will continue to build throughout the term. If you change your mind about the type of business, it does not take but a few minutes to start again. This is a software tool that is included to assist you in converting what you are reading, discussing, and learning into the basics of a business.

1. Choose an entrepreneur in your community and interview him or her. What's the "story" behind the business? How well does the entrepreneur fit the entrepreneurial profile described in this chapter? What advantages and disadvantages does the owner see in owning a business? What advice would he or she offer to someone considering launching a business?

2. Select one of the categories under the section "The Cultural Diversity of Entrepreneurship" in this chapter and research it in more detail. Find examples of business owners in that category. Prepare a brief report for your class.

3. Search through recent business publications (especially those focusing on small companies) and find an example of an entrepreneur, past or present, who exhibits the entrepreneurial spirit of striving for success in the face of failure. Prepare a brief report for your class.

2

Inside the Entrepreneurial Mind: From Ideas to Reality

Imagination is more important than knowledge. Knowledge is limited. Imagination encircles the world.

—Albert Einstein

Creativity is the power to connect the seemingly unconnected.

—William Plomer

LEARNING OBJECTIVES

Upon completion of this chapter, you will be able to:

1. **EXPLAIN** the differences among creativity, innovation, and entrepreneurship.

2. **DESCRIBE** why creativity and innovation are such an integral part of entrepreneurship.

3. **UNDERSTAND** how the two hemispheres of the human brain function and what role they play in creativity.

4. **EXPLAIN** the 10 "mental locks" that limit individual creativity.

5. **UNDERSTAND** how entrepreneurs can enhance their own creativity and that of their employees as well.

6. **DESCRIBE** the steps in the creative process.

7. **DISCUSS** techniques for improving the creative process.

8. **DESCRIBE** the protection of intellectual property involving patents, trademarks, and copyrights.

One of the tenets of entrepreneurship is the ability to create new and useful ideas that solve the problems and challenges people face every day. Entrepreneurs achieve success by creating value in the marketplace when they combine resources in new and different ways to gain a competitive edge over rivals. From Alexander Fleming's pioneering work that resulted in a cure for infections (penicillin) and the founders of the Rocket Chemical Company's fortieth try to create an industrial lubricant (WD-40) to Jeff Bezos's innovative use of the World Wide Web in retailing (Amazon. com) and Ted Turner's unique approach to the availability of television news (CNN), entrepreneurs' ideas have transformed the world.

As you learned in Chapter 1, entrepreneurs can create value in a number of ways—inventing new products and services, developing new technology, discovering new knowledge, improving existing products or services, finding different ways of providing more goods and services with fewer resources, and many others. Indeed, finding new ways of satisfying customers' needs, inventing new products and services, putting together existing ideas in new and different ways, and creating new twists on existing products and services are hallmarks of the entrepreneur!

*For instance, while in an exercise class, Linda Turner came up with an idea for practical lingerie for pregnant women. "I was watching a woman who was hugely pregnant holding up her belly and thought, 'There must be something out there to help her.'" Hours of research, interviews with hundreds of pregnant women, and a patent search turned up nothing, and Turner knew she had a business in the making. She needed a prototype, so she bought a jog bra and a heavy girdle and sewed them together to make the first Bellybra. "It was one of the most ridiculous things I'd ever seen," she recalls, "but it worked." A pregnant friend tested Turner's crude prototype and gave it a rave review. Turner applied for a patent and in 1991 licensed her new product idea to Basic Comfort, a small baby products business looking for new ideas. In 2000, Turner and Basic Comfort terminated their licensing agreement, and Turner formed **T&J Designs**, LLC with partner Cindy Koch to market the doctor-recommended Bellybra.[1]*

Like many innovators, Turner created a successful business by taking two everyday items that have existed for many years and combining them in a different way.

CREATIVITY, INNOVATION, AND ENTREPRENEURSHIP

A recent study by the Small Business Administration found that small firms produce more economically and technically important innovations than larger firms.[2] What is the entrepreneurial "secret" for creating value in the marketplace? In reality, the "secret" is no secret at all: It is applying creativity and innovation to solve problems and to exploit opportunities that people face every day. **Creativity** is the ability to develop new ideas and to discover new ways of looking at problems and opportunities. **Innovation** is the ability to *apply* creative solutions to those problems and opportunities to enhance or to enrich people's lives. Harvard's Theodore Levitt says that creativity is *thinking* new things, and innovation is *doing* new things. In short, entrepreneurs succeed by *thinking and doing* new things or old things in new ways. Simply having a great new idea is not enough; transforming the idea into a tangible product, service, or business venture is the essential next step. Management legend Peter Drucker says "Innovation is the specific instrument of entrepreneurs, the means by which they exploit change as an opportunity for a different business or a different service."[3]

creativity—*the ability to develop new ideas and to discover new ways of looking at problems and opportunities.*

innovation—*the ability to apply creative solutions to problems and opportunities to enhance or to enrich people's lives.*

Successful entrepreneurs come up with ideas and then find ways to make them work to solve a problem or to fill a need. In a world that is changing faster than most of us ever could have imagined, creativity and innovation are vital to a company's success—and survival. That's true for businesses in every industry—from automakers to tea growers—and for companies of all sizes. However, creativity and innovation are the signature of small, entrepreneurial businesses. Creative thinking has become a core business skill, and entrepreneurs lead the way in developing and applying that skill. In fact, creativity and innovation often lie at the heart of small companies' ability to compete successfully with their larger rivals. Even though they cannot outspend their larger rivals, small companies can create powerful, effective competitive advantages over big companies by "out-creating" and "out-innovating" them! If they fail to do so, entrepreneurs don't stay in business very long. Leadership expert Warren Bennis says, "Today's successful companies live and die according to the quality of their ideas."[4]

Sometimes creativity involves generating something from nothing. However, creativity is more likely to result in elaborating on the present, of putting old things together in new ways, or of taking something away to create something simpler or better. In some cases, a creative idea springs up from the most unexpected places. Edwin Land, one of America's most prolific inventors, credits his three-year-old daughter with the idea of the Polaroid instant camera. On a vacation trip in 1943, she asked why she couldn't see the photograph Land had just taken of her. During the next hour, as he walked around with his family, Land's mind was at work on his daughter's question. Before long, he had worked out the concept of building the camera that launched the era of instant photography. "The camera and the film became clear to me," Land recalls. "In my mind they were so real that I spent several hours describing them." Land's invention—instant photography—was so outlandish that only a child could conceive of it![5]

More often, creative ideas arise when entrepreneurs look at something old and think something new or different. Legendary Notre Dame football coach Knute Rockne, whose teams dominated college football in the 1920s, got the idea for his constantly shifting backfields while watching a burlesque chorus routine! Rockne's innovations in the backfield (which included the legendary "Four Horsemen") and his emphasis on the forward pass (a legal but largely unused tactic in his era) so befuddled opposing defenses that his teams compiled an impressive 105-12-5 record. Similarly, military tacticians, needing better camouflage designs to protect troops and equipment in World War I, borrowed ideas from the "cubist" art of Picasso and Braque. Their improved camouflage patterns helped the Allies win the war.[6] More recently, one entrepreneur helped solve a problem that plagued U.S. troops in the deserts of Saudi Arabia and Kuwait during Desert Storm. U.S. military experts discovered that enemy aircraft were able to detect the location of troops and equipment by looking for the repeating patterns in the camouflage used to hide them. The entrepreneur began selling the military a special camouflage whose pattern never repeated. He developed it using technology he was already employing to produce multicolored, multipatterned area rugs (each one unique) for the home market.

Entrepreneurs also create innovations to solve problems they observe, often problems they face themselves.

A Company Example

*When Carl Goldberg was involved in an auto accident, he almost lost his beloved 100 pound chocolate Labrador retriever, Maxie, who flew into the windshield on impact. Goldberg decided that he would never put his dog at risk again, and he thought that other pet lovers would want to protect their dogs while on the road. With the help of Maxie's vet, Goldberg spent six years and $500,000 developing the Ruff Rider canine vehicle restraint system, which is orthopedically and ergonomically correct for dogs. The canine seat belt has three movement settings and comes in nine sizes to accommodate dogs weighing from just six pounds to 200 pounds. Goldberg has patented the device, and **Ruff Rider LLC** generates sales of more than $1 million a year![7]*

Entrepreneurship is the result of a disciplined, systematic process of applying creativity and innovation to needs and opportunities in the marketplace. It involves applying focused strategies to new ideas and new insights to create a product or a service that satisfies customers' needs or solves their problems. It is much more than random, disjointed tinkering with a new gadget. Millions of people come up with creative ideas for new or different products and services; most of them, however, never do anything with them. Entrepreneurs are those who connect their creative ideas with the purposeful action and structure of a business. Thus, successful entrepreneurship is a constant process that relies on creativity, innovation, and application in the marketplace.

Innovation must be a constant process because most ideas don't work and most innovations fail. One writer explains, "Trial—and lots of error—is embedded in entrepreneurship."[8] Karen Anne Zien, cofounder of Polaroid Corporation's Creativity and Innovation Lab, estimates that for every 3,000 new product ideas, four make it to the development stage, two are actually launched, and only one becomes a success in the market. These new products are crucial to companies' success, however. Robert Cooper, a researcher who has analyzed thousands of new product launches, says that, on average, new products account for a whopping 40 percent of companies' sales.[9] Still, successful entrepreneurs recognize that failure often accompanies innovation, and they are willing to accept their share of failures because they know that failure is merely part of the creative process. Entrepreneurship requires business owners to be bold enough to try their new ideas, flexible enough to throw aside those that do not work, and wise enough to learn about what will work based on their observations of what did not. We now turn our attention to creativity, the creative process, and methods of enhancing creativity.

CREATIVITY—A NECESSITY FOR SURVIVAL

In this fiercely competitive, fast-faced, global economy, creativity is not only an important source for building a competitive advantage, but it also is a necessity for survival. When developing creative solutions to modern problems, entrepreneurs must go beyond merely using whatever has worked in the past. History is not always a reliable predictor of the future in business. Making the inferential leap from what has worked in the past to what will work today (or in the future) requires entrepreneurs to cast off the limiting assumptions, beliefs, and behaviors and to develop new insights into the relationship between resources, needs, and value. In other words, they must change their perspectives, looking at the world in new and different ways.

Entrepreneurs must always be on guard against traditional assumptions and perspectives about how things ought to be because they are certain killers of creativity. Such self-imposed mental constraints and other paradigms that people tend to build over time push creativity right out the door. A **paradigm** is a preconceived idea of what the world is, what it should be like, and how it should operate. These ideas become so deeply rooted in our minds that they become immovable blocks to creative thinking—even though they may be outdated, obsolete, and no longer relevant. In short, they act as logjams to creativity. Look, for example, at the following illustrations and read the text aloud:

paradigm—*a preconceived idea of what the world is, what it should be like, and how it should operate.*

Paris	Once	A Bird
in the	in a	in the
the Spring time	a Lifetime	the Hand

If you're like most people, you didn't notice the extra word in each phrase ("Paris in the the spring time"). Why? Part of the reason is that we see what we expect to see! Past experiences shape the ways in which we perceive the world around us ("We've always done it this way"). That's why children are so creative and curious about new possibilities; society has not yet brainwashed them into an attitude of conformity, nor have they learned to accept *traditional* solutions as the *only* solutions. Retaining their creative "inner child," entrepreneurs are able to throw off the shackles on creativity and see opportunities for creating viable businesses where most people see what they've always seen (or, worse yet, see nothing).

Many years ago, during an international chess competition, Frank Marshall made what has become known as one of the most beautiful—and one of the most creative—moves ever made on a chessboard. In a crucial game in which he was evenly matched with a Russian master player, Marshall found his queen under serious attack. Marshall had several avenues of escape available for his queen. Knowing that the queen is one of the most important offensive players on the chessboard, spectators assumed that Marshall would make a conventional move and push his queen to safety.

Using all the time available to him to consider his options, Marshall picked up his queen—and paused—and put it down on the most *illogical* square of all—a square from which the queen could easily be captured by any one of three hostile pieces. Marshall had done the unthinkable! He had sacrificed his queen, a move typically made only under the most desperate of circumstances. All the spectators—even Marshall's opponent—groaned in dismay. Then the Russian, and finally the crowd, realized that Marshall's move was, in reality, a brilliant one. No matter how the Russian opponent took the queen, he would eventually be in a losing position. Seeing the inevitable outcome, the Russian conceded the game. Marshall had won the match in a rare and daring fashion: He had won by sacrificing his queen![10]

What lesson does this story hold for entrepreneurs? By suspending conventional thinking long enough to even consider the possibility of such a move, Marshall was able to throw off the usual paradigms constraining most chess players. He had looked beyond the traditional and orthodox strategies of the game and was willing to take the risk of trying an unusual tactic to win. The result: He won. Although not every creative business opportunity that entrepreneurs take will be successful, many who, like Frank Marshall, are willing to go beyond conventional wisdom will be rewarded for their efforts. Successful entrepreneurs, those who are constantly pushing technological and economic boundaries forward, must ask: "Is it time to sacrifice the queen?"

Merely generating one successful creative solution to address a problem or a need usually is not good enough to keep an entrepreneurial enterprise successful in the long run, however. Success—even survival—in this fiercely competitive, global environment requires entrepreneurs to tap their creativity (and that of their employees) constantly. Entrepreneurs can be sure that if they have developed a unique, creative solution to solve a problem or to fill a need, a competitor (perhaps one or six times zones away) is hard at work developing an even more creative solution to render theirs obsolete. This extremely rapid and accelerating rate of change has created an environment in which staying in a leadership position requires constant creativity, innovation, and entrepreneurship. A company that has achieved a leadership position in an industry but then stands still creatively is soon toppled from its number-one perch.

Can Creativity Be Taught?

For many years, conventional wisdom held that a person was either creative (i.e., imaginative, free-spirited, entrepreneurial) or not (i.e., logical, narrow-minded, rigid). Today we know better. Research shows that *anyone* can learn to be creative. "Every person can be taught techniques and behaviors that help them generate more ideas," says Joyce Wycoff, author of several books on creativity.[11] The problem is that in most organizations, employees have never been expected to be creative. Also, many businesses fail to foster an environment that encourages creativity among employees. Restricted by their traditional thinking patterns, most people never tap into their pools of innate creativity, and the company becomes stagnant. Creative exercises such as the one illustrated in Figure 2.1 can help adults reconnect with the natural creativity they exhibited so willingly as children.

FIGURE 2.1 How Creative Are You? Can you recognize the well-known phrases these symbols represent?

Sources: Tery Stickels, "Frame Games," *USA Weekend*, January 3–5, 2003, p. 14; January 14–16, 2000; January 21–23, 2000; June 22–24, 2001; June 29–July 1, 2001; July 6–8, 2001; April 29, 2001; May 18–20, 2001; January 17–19, 2003; July 28–30, 2000; September 9, 2001; November 29–December 1, 2002; Gavin DeBecker, "Thinking Caps," *USA Weekend*, July 30–August 1, 1999; April 9–11, 1999; February 5–7, 1999; June 4–6, 1999; June 11–13, 1999; July 2–4, 1999; January 22–24, 1999; January 15–17, 1999; August 6–8, 1999.

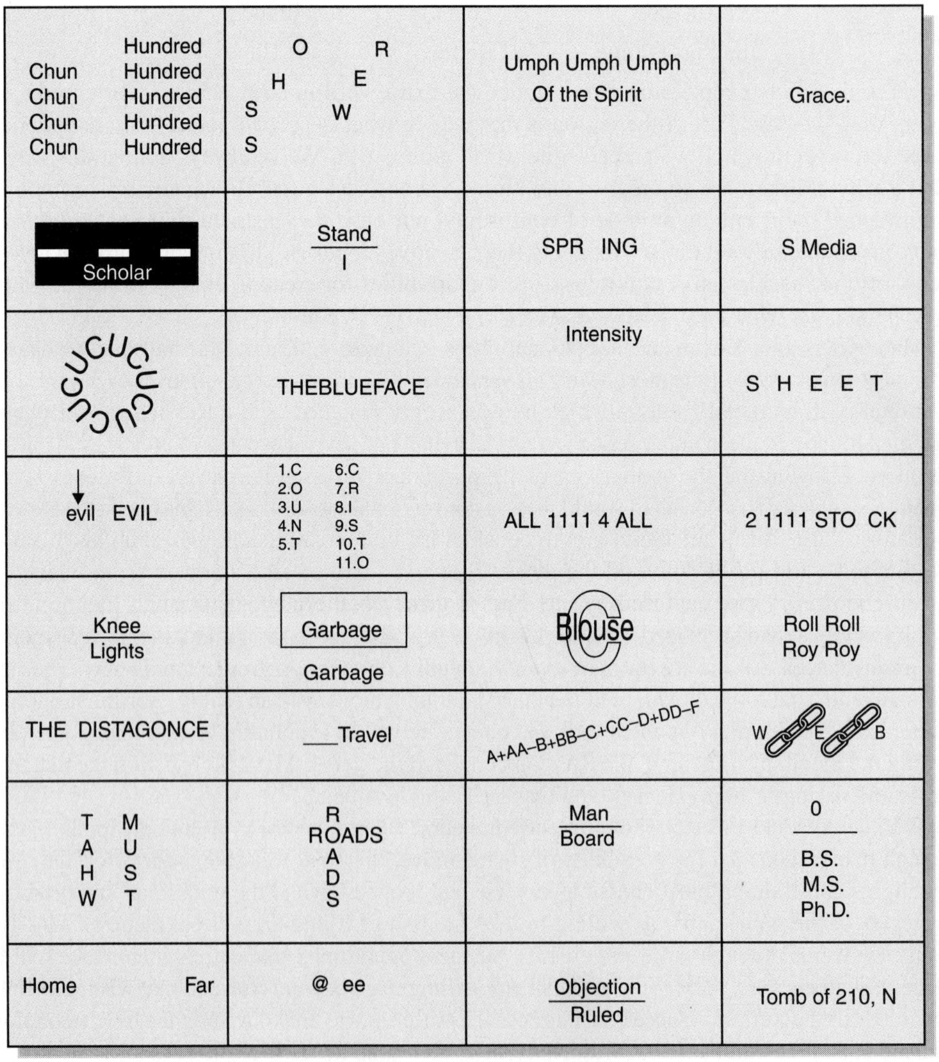

Entrepreneurs and the people who work for them can learn to think creatively, and they must for their companies' sake! "Innovation and creativity are not just for artists," says Wycoff. "These are skills with a direct, bottom-line payoff."[12]

A Company Example

For instance, Mary Naylor, owner of Capitol Concierge, a company that provides concierge services in office building lobbies, looks to an unusual source for new ideas about how to promote her business: junk mail. "I collect junk mail and keep it in a box I call 'Mary's Ideas,'" says Naylor. "I get inspiration from things most people throw away. When I want to kick start my creative processes, I go to my box and see what's new."[13]

Before entrepreneurs can draw on their own creative capacity or stimulate creativity in their own organizations, they need to understand creative thinking.

CREATIVE THINKING

Learning Objective

3. Understand how the two hemispheres of the human brain function and what role they play in creativity.

Research into the operation of the human brain shows that each hemisphere of the brain processes information differently and that one side of the brain tends to be dominant over the other. The human brain develops asymmetrically, and each hemisphere tends to specialize in certain functions. The left-brain is guided by linear, vertical thinking (from one logical conclusion to the next) whereas the right-brain relies on kaleidoscopic, lateral thanking (considering a problem from all sides and jumping into it at different points). The left-brain handles language, logic, and symbols; the right-brain takes care of the body's emotional, intuitive, and spatial functions. The left-brain processes information in a step-by-step fashion, but the right-brain processes it intuitively—all at once, relying heavily on images.

Left-brain vertical thinking is narrowly focused and systematic, proceeding in a highly logical fashion from one point to the next. Right-brain lateral thinking, on the other hand, is somewhat unconventional, unsystematic, and unstructured, much like the image of a kaleidoscope, whirling around to form one pattern after another. It is this right-brain–driven, lateral thinking that lies at the heart of the creative process. Those who have learned to develop their right-brain thinking skills tend to:

- always ask the question, "Is there a better way?"
- challenge custom, routine, and tradition.
- be reflective, often staring out windows, deep in thought. (How many traditional managers would stifle creativity by snapping these people out of their "daydreams," chastising them for "loafing," and admonishing them to "get back to work"?)
- be prolific thinkers. They know that generating lots of ideas increases the likelihood of coming up with a few highly creative ideas.
- play mental games, trying to see an issue from different perspectives.
- realize that there may be more than one "right answer."
- see mistakes and failures as mere "pit stops" on the way to success.
- see problems as springboards for new ideas.
- relate seemingly unrelated ideas to a problem to generate innovative solutions.
- have "helicopter skills," the ability to rise above the daily routine to see an issue from a broader perspective and then swooping back down to focus on an area in need of change.

A Company Example

Stanford Ovshinsky, now 80, has used right-brain thinking to generate the ideas that have led him to earn an amazing 274 patents. Ovshinsky, who skipped college to become a toolmaker and machinist, used his firsthand knowledge of machinery to earn his first patent in the 1940s for a high-speed, automated machine tool he designed. His curiosity led him to study neurophysiology, from which he branched into a field known as disordered materials physics. In 1960, he founded a company, Energy Conversion Devices, that has produced low-cost solar-powered batteries, a rechargeable battery that powers hybrid electric cars, rewritable CDs and DVDs, and many other important inventions. Most of his patents and his company's products derive from Ovshinsky's ability to translate his knowledge of unstructured elements and superconductivity into useful products that produce clean energy. "Most people think in two dimensions," says a long-time colleague. "Stan thinks not only in three dimensions but also in different colors."[14]

Although each hemisphere of the brain tends to dominate in its particular functions, the two halves normally cooperate, with each part contributing its special abilities to accomplish those tasks better suited to its mode of information processing. Sometimes, however, the two hemispheres may even compete with each other, or one half may choose not to participate. Some researchers have suggested that each half of the brain has the capacity to keep information from the other! The result, literally, is that "the left hand doesn't know what the right hand is doing." Perhaps the most important characteristic of this split-brain phenomenon is that an individual can learn to control which side of the brain is dominant in a given situation. In other words, a person can learn to "turn down" the dominant left hemisphere (focusing on logic and linear thinking) and "turn up" the right hemisphere (focusing on intuition and unstructured thinking) when a situation requiring creativity arises.[15] To get a little practice at this "shift," try the visual exercises presented in Figure 2.2. When viewed from one perspective, the picture in the middle portrays an attractive young lady with a feather in her hair and a boa around her shoulders. Once you shift your perspective, however, you will see an old woman with a large nose wearing a scarf on her head! This change in the image seen is the result of a shift from one hemisphere in the viewer's brain to the other. With practice, a person can learn to control this mental shift, tapping the pool of creativity that lies hidden within the right side of the brain. This ability has tremendous power to unleash the creative capacity of entrepreneurs. The need to develop this creative ability means that exploring inner space (the space within our brains)—not outer space—becomes the challenge of the century.

Entrepreneurship requires both left- and right-brain thinking. Right-brain thinking draws on the power of divergent reasoning, which is the ability to create a multitude of original, diverse ideas. Left-brain thinking counts on convergent reasoning, the ability to evaluate multiple ideas and choose the best solution to a given problem. Entrepreneurs need to rely on right-brain thinking to generate innovative product, service, or business ideas. Then they must use left-brain thinking to judge the market potential of the ideas they generate. Successful entrepreneurs have learned to coordinate the complementary functions of each hemisphere of the brain, using their brains' full creative power. Otherwise, entrepreneurs, who rarely can be accused of being "halfhearted" about their business ideas, run the risk of becoming "half-headed."

How can entrepreneurs learn to tap their innate creativity more readily? The first step is to break down the barriers to creativity that most of us have erected over the years. We now turn our attention to these barriers and some suggested techniques for tearing them down.

YOU Be the Consultant . . .

The Spirit of Entrepreneurship in the Olympics

Entrepreneurs aren't the only ones who use creativity to create competitive advantages for themselves. Throughout history, Olympic athletes have pushed back the frontiers of their sports by developing new techniques, improved training methods, and innovative solutions to existing problems. Two of the best examples of applying creativity to their sports were figure skater Sonja Henie and high jumper Dick Fosbury. Although their sports are at different extremes of the Olympic spectrum, both of these athletes relied on the creative process to throw off the paradigms that bound the other athletes competing in these sports.

Before Sonja Henie came along, figure skating routines were exactly that—routine. In competitions, skaters performed a series of precise moves that emphasized accuracy and control. But when the young Norwegian glided onto the ice, skating changed forever. Bringing the beauty and movement of ballet to the skating rink, Henie transformed the sport into the graceful combination of motion, music, and muscle that it remains today. From 1927 to 1936, Henie dominated ice skating by creatively blending her graceful ballet skills with her strength on the ice. She won 10 straight world championships, eight European titles, and a record three Olympic gold medals. Trained in both dance and ballet as a child, Henie cast aside the existing paradigms of what ice skating was as she recognized the possibilities of transferring dance movements onto the ice.

After winning her last world championship in 1936, Henie used her dance and skating skills to get into show business. She became an international star in movies and in traveling ice shows that gave her the freedom to use her creative genius on the ice. Even her glamorous and daring costumes proved to be an exciting innovation in ice skating as they emphasized the grace and flow of her movements. Later generations of ice skaters would push the sport even farther. Tenely Albright (1956 Olympics) and Peggy Fleming (1968

(continued on page 42)

FIGURE 2.2   What do you see?

Source: *Entrepreneurship and New Venture Formation* by Zimmerer and Scarborough, © 1995. Reprinted by permission of Prentice Hall, Inc., Upper Saddle River, NJ.

A. Which do you see? The goblet or the famous twins?

B. Describe the lady you see in this drawing. How old is she, how attractive, what kind of covering on her head etc.?

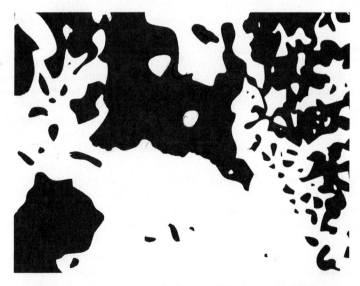

C. In these patches of black and white, do you see the face of Christ?

Olympics) introduced spins, twirls, and leaps. More recently, Tara Lipinsky, Kristi Yamaguchi, Nancy Kerrigan, Katarina Witt, and others have injected an element of gymnastics to ice skating, performing triple jumps and double and triple Axels. Yet every one of these champions owes a debt of gratitude to Sonja Henie, the daring young skater who had the creativity and the courage to make innovations on the ice.

Until 1968, much like ice skating, the sport of high jumping had changed little since its origins in ancient Greece. Athletes sprinted toward the bar and then leaped forward and upward, rolling over the bar face down. In the 1968 Olympics in Mexico City, Dick Fosbury revolutionized the sport with his innovative style of high jumping. He approached the bar at a different angle and then curved his body over the bar face up, kicking his legs over the end of the jump. Based on the principles of biomechanics, the "Fosbury Flop," as the style became known, transfers the weight of the jumper over the bar in stages. It also requires less energy and is more efficient. The result of Fosbury's innovation? An Olympic gold medal, a new world high jump record (Fosbury broke the old record by 6 cm), and the satisfaction of creating a new style of high jumping used by athletes across the world even today.

Sonja Henie and Dick Fosbury became champions by applying creativity and innovation to the sports they loved so much. Similarly, entrepreneurs can become "champions" in their industries by using their creative spirits to come up with new ideas, better products and services, and innovative techniques. Successful entrepreneurs rely on their ability to see the same things everyone else sees and to dream what no one else dreams.

1. What is a paradigm? How does a paradigm stifle creativity?

2. Work with a small group of your classmates to identify a local business that is bound by a paradigm. What impact is this paradigm having on the business? Identify the paradigm and then generate as many creative suggestions as you can in 20 minutes that would change this paradigm.

3. What can entrepreneurs do to throw off existing paradigms?

Sonja Heine was an early innovator in figure skating, which enabled her to dominate the sport for many years.

Source: "Innovations of the Olympic Games," *Fortune*, January 27, 1992, pp. 28–29. Photo courtesy of Corbis Bettmann, © Bettmann/Corbis.

BARRIERS TO CREATIVITY

Learning Objective

4. Understand the 10 "mental locks" that limit individual creativity.

The number of potential barriers to creativity is virtually limitless—time pressures, unsupportive management, pessimistic co-workers, overly rigid company policies, and countless others. Perhaps the most difficult hurdles to overcome, however, are those that individuals impose on themselves. In his book *A Whack on the Side of the Head*, Roger von Oech identifies 10 "mental locks" that limit individual creativity:[16]

1. *Searching for the one "right" answer.* Deeply ingrained in most educational systems is the assumption that there is one "right" answer to a problem. The average student who has completed four years of college has taken more than 2,600 tests, so it is not unusual for this one-correct-answer syndrome to become an inherent part of our thinking. In reality, however, most problems are ambiguous. Depending on the questions one asks, there may be (and usually are) several "right" answers.

A Company Example

When representatives from Jacksonville, Florida, made a proposal to the National Football League (NFL) to host the Super Bowl in 2005, they knew that they had to overcome one major disadvantage: a lack of high-end hotel space, always a key factor in the NFL's bid requirements. The team's approach was based on the assumption that there was more than one right answer to providing upscale hotel space, and they came up with an innovative solution: They would dock cruise ships along the St. Johns River that would serve as floating hotels, putting guests within easy walking distance of the football stadium! Shortly after the meeting, NFL officials named Jacksonville the host city for the 2005 Super Bowl, making it the smallest city ever to host the big game.[17]

2. *Focusing on "being logical."* Logic is a valuable part of the creative process, especially when evaluating ideas and implementing them. However, in the early imaginative phases of the process, logical thinking can restrict creativity. Focusing too much effort on being logical also discourages the use of one of the mind's most powerful creations: intuition. Von Oech advises us to "think something different" and to use nonlogical thinking freely, especially in the imaginative phase of the creative process. Intuition, which is based on the accumulated knowledge and experiences a person encounters over the course of a lifetime and resides in the subconscious, can be unlocked. It is a crucial part of the creative process because using it often requires one to tear down long-standing assumptions that limit creativity and innovation.

Dan Murphy is an entrepreneur who challenges traditional assumptions, and his efforts may revolutionize agriculture across the world. Murphy is using seawater rather than fresh water to irrigate commercial crops in arid areas where fresh water is scarce! For instance, in Mexico's Baja Peninsula, Murphy's company, Saline Seed, is raising salicornia (a succulent sprout that sells for as much as $1 an ounce in some areas!), the world's first commercial crop to be grown in soil irrigated by seawater. Murphy, who spent years involved in sea agriculture, reasoned that because all life derived from seawater, plants retain some genetic memory of salt water. Murphy's idea was to "train" plants over several generations to drink seawater. Starting with salicornia, Murphy's company has branched out into other types of plants and is now developing seawater-tolerant ornamental shrubs and grasses that would be ideal for golf courses, farmers, and residential developments.[18]

3. *Blindly following the rules.* We learn at a very early age not to "color outside the lines," and we spend the rest of our lives blindly obeying such rules. Sometimes creativity depends on our ability to break the existing rules so that we can see new ways of doing things. Consider, for example, the top row of letters on a standard typewriter or computer keyboard:

QWERTYUIOP

In the 1870s, Sholes & Company, a leading manufacturer of typewriters, began receiving numerous customer complaints about its typewriter keys sticking together when typists' fingers were practiced enough to go really fast. Company engineers came up with an incredibly creative solution to eliminate the problem of sticking keys. They designed a less efficient keyboard configuration, placing the letters *O* and *I* (the third and sixth most commonly used letters of the alphabet) so that the weakest fingers (the ring and little fingers) would strike them. By slowing down typists with this inefficient keyboard, the engineers solved the sticking keys problem. Today, despite the fact that computer technology has eliminated all danger of sticking keys, this same inefficient keyboard configuration remains the industry standard!

4. *Constantly being practical.* Imagining impractical answers to "what if" questions can be powerful stepping-stones to creative ideas. Suspending practicality for a while frees the mind to consider creative solutions that otherwise might never arise. Whenever Thomas Edison hired an assistant to work in his creative laboratory, he would tell the new employee, "Walk through town and list 20 things that interest you." When the worker returned, Edison would ask him to split the list into two columns. Then he would say, "Randomly combine objects from column A and column B and come up with as many inventions as you can." Edison's methods for stimulating creativity in his lab proved to be successful; he holds the distinction of being the only person to have earned a patent every year for 65 consecutive years![19]

5. *Viewing play as frivolous.* A playful attitude is fundamental to creative thinking. There is a close relationship between the "haha" of humor and the "aha" of discovery. Play gives us the opportunity to reinvent reality and to reformulate established ways of doing things. Children learn when they play, and so can entrepreneurs. Watch children playing and you will see them invent new games, create new ways of looking at old things, and learn what works (and what doesn't) in their games.

Entrepreneurs can benefit from playing in the same way that children do. They, too, can learn to try new approaches and discover what works and what doesn't. Creativity results when entrepreneurs take what they have learned at play, evaluate it, corroborate it with other knowledge, and put it into practice. For instance, a group of fund-raisers was discussing the arrangements for an upcoming annual fund-raising banquet (which had been the organization's primary source of income for many years). Lamenting the declining turnout over the past several years and the multitude of other organizations that were using banquets as a source of revenue, one officer jokingly said, "Maybe we should have a 'nonbanquet,' where people pay not to tie up several hours, eat rubber chicken, and listen to some dull speaker talk about a topic they'd rather not hear about." The other officers laughed at the idea initially and then began throwing in humorous ideas of their own. The group mustered the courage to try out this creative solution, and their "nonbanquet" was a tremendous success. It raised more money than the organization had ever raised before, and no one had to attend!

6. *Becoming overly specialized.* Defining a problem as one of "marketing" or "production," or some other area of specialty limits the ability to see how it might be related to other issues. Creative thinkers tend to be "explorers," searching for ideas outside their areas of specialty. The idea for the roll-on deodorant stick came from the ballpoint pen. The famous Mr. Potato Head toy was invented by a father sitting with his family at the dinner table and noting how much fun his children had playing with their food. Velcro was invented by a man who, while hiking one day to take a break from work, had to stop to peel sticky cockleburrs from his clothing. As he picked them off, he noticed how their hooked spines caught on and held tightly to the cloth. As he resumed his hike, he began to think about the possibilities of using a similar design to fasten objects together. Thus was born Velcro!

7. *Avoiding ambiguity.* Ambiguity can be a powerful creative stimulus; it encourages us to "think something different." Being excessively detailed in an imaginative situation tends to stifle creativity. Ambiguity, however, requires us to consider at least two different, often contradictory notions at the same time, which is a direct channel to creativity. Ambiguous situations force us to stretch our minds beyond their normal boundaries and to consider creative options we might otherwise ignore. Although ambiguity is not a desired element when entrepreneurs are evaluating and implementing ideas, it is a valuable tool when they are searching for creative ideas and solutions. Entrepreneurs are famous for asking a question and then going beyond the first answer to explore other possible answers. The result is that they often find business opportunities by creating ambiguous situations.

A Company Example

*Copreneurs Tom and Sally Fegley, owners of **Tom and Sally's Handmade Chocolates**, considered the possibility of other answers to the question "What uses exist for chocolate sauce?" Although most people see chocolate sauce merely as a topping for ice cream or other desserts, their friend Larry (whom they have nicknamed 'Dirty Larry') came up with a different idea. The Fegleys were trying to come up with an innovative recipe that would keep their string of awards at a local, fund-raising event devoted to celebrating chocolate, the Brown-Out. Their fun-loving friend suggested they shoot for the Most Decadent Award. "I'll go naked," he said. "You paint melted chocolate all over my body, and you'll win!" Although the Fegleys declined Larry's offer, his suggestion got them thinking. Before long, Tom had whipped up a batch of chocolate dessert topping, labeled it "Chocolate Body Paint," and included the following directions on the bottle: "Heat to 98.6 degrees, apply liberally, and let your imagination run wild." Today Chocolate Body Paint is the Fegley's best-selling product, and it has won awards and has been featured in publications ranging from the* Wall Street Journal *to* Playboy *magazine. "Never judge an idea by its source," advises Sally.[20]*

8. *Fearing looking foolish.* Creative thinking is no place for conformity! New ideas rarely are born in a conforming environment. People tend toward conformity because they don't want to look foolish. The fool's job is to whack at the habits and rules that keep us thinking in the same old ways. In that sense, entrepreneurs are top-notch "fools." They are constantly questioning and challenging accepted ways of doing things and the assumptions that go with them. Noted entrepreneurship theorist Joseph Schumpeter wrote that entrepreneurs perform a vital function—"creative destruction"—in which they rethink conventional assumptions and discard those that are no longer useful. According to Schumpeter, "The function of entrepreneurs is to reform or revolutionize the pattern of production by exploiting an invention or, more generally, an untried technological possibility for producing a new commodity or producing an old one in a new way, by opening up a new source of supply of materials or a new outlet for products, by reorganizing an industry or so on."[21] In short, entrepreneurs look at old ways of doing things and ask, "Is there a better way?" By destroying the old, they create the new.

One way entrepreneurs often engage in creative destruction is by reversing their thinking. For example, one agricultural entrepreneur had been trying to solve a common problem that automatic picking machines have when picking the fruit from apple trees. The machines, which are quite efficient at picking apples growing on the outer limbs of the trees, often miss or damage the fruit growing on the inner limbs. For years, he worked to develop a machine with the dexterity to pick apples in both locations but to no avail. Finally, this entrepreneur reversed his thinking and began to focus his efforts, not on the picking machine but *on the apple tree!* Working with horticulturists, he was able to develop a new breed of tree whose fruit grew only on the outer limbs, where standard picking machines could easily get to it! By reversing his thinking, he solved the problem and created a new business opportunity.

9. *Fearing mistakes and failure.* Creative people realize that trying something new often leads to failure; however, they do not see failure as an end. It represents a learning experience on the way to success. As you learned in Chapter 1, failure is an important part of the creative process; it signals entrepreneurs when to change their course of action. Entrepreneurship is all about the opportunity to fail! Many entrepreneurs failed numerous times before they succeeded. Despite their initial setbacks, they were able to set aside the fear of failure and kept trying.

   The key, of course, is to see failure for what it really is: a chance to learn how to succeed. Entrepreneurs who willingly risk failure and learn from it when it occurs have the best chance of succeeding at whatever they try. Charles F. Kettering, a famous inventor of lighting and ignition systems in automobiles, among other things, explains, "You fail because your ideas aren't right, but you should learn to fail intelligently. When you fail, find out *why* you failed and each time it will bring you nearer to the goal."[22] Successful entrepreneurs equate failure with innovation rather than with defeat.

10. *Believing that "I'm not creative."* Some people limit themselves because they believe creativity belongs only to the Einsteins, Beethovens, and da Vincis of the world. Unfortunately, this belief often becomes a self-fulfilling prophecy. A person who believes he is not creative will, in all likelihood, behave that way and will make that belief come true. Successful entrepreneurs recognize that thinking "I'm not creative" is merely an excuse for inaction. *Everyone* has within him or her the potential to be creative; not everyone will tap that potential, however. Successful entrepreneurs find a way to unleash their creative powers on problems and opportunities.

By avoiding these 10 mental locks, entrepreneurs can unleash their own creativity and the creativity of those around them as well. Successful entrepreneurs are willing to take some risks, explore new ideas, play a little, ask "what if?" and learn to appreciate ambiguity. By doing so, they develop the skills, attitudes, and motivation that make them much more creative—one of the keys to entrepreneurial success. Table 2.1 lists some questions designed to spur imagination.

HOW TO ENHANCE CREATIVITY

Enhancing Organizational Creativity

Creativity doesn't just happen in organizations; entrepreneurs must establish an environment in which creativity can flourish—for themselves and for their workers. New ideas are fragile creations, but the right company culture can encourage people to develop and cultivate them. Ensuring that workers have the freedom and the incentive to be creative is one of the best ways to achieve innovation. "Developing a corporate culture that both fosters and rewards creativity . . . is critical because companies must be able to churn out innovations at a fast pace since technology has shortened product life cycles," says Geoff Yang, successful entrepreneur and venture capitalist.[23] Entrepreneurs can stimulate their own creativity and encourage it among workers by:

Embracing diversity. One of the best ways to cultivate a culture of creativity is to hire a diverse workforce. When people solve problems or come up with ideas, they do so within the framework of their own experience. Hiring people from different backgrounds, cultural experiences, hobbies, and interests provides a company with a crucial raw material needed for creativity.

Expecting creativity. Employees tend to rise—or fall—to the level of expectations entrepreneurs have of them. One of the best ways to communicate the expectation of creativity is to give employees permission to be creative. At one small company that manufactures industrial equipment, the owner put a "brainstorming board" in a break area. Anyone facing a sticky problem simply posts it on a brightly colored piece of paper on the board. Other workers are invited to share ideas and suggestions by writing them on white pieces of paper and posting

TABLE 2.1

Questions to Spur the Imagination

Sources: Adapted from Leigh Buchanan, Thea Singer, Christopher Caggiano, Ilan Mochari, and Tahl Raz, "If You Come, They Will Build It," *Inc.*, August 2002, p. 70; Creativity Web, "Question Summary.0" www.ozemail.com/au/~caveman/Creative/Techniques/osb_quest.html; *Bits & Pieces*, February 1990, p. 20; *Bits & Pieces*, April 29, 1993, "Creativity Quiz," *In Business*, November/December 1991, p. 18; Doug Hall, *Jump Start Your Brain* (New York: Warner Books, 1995), pp. 86–87; Christine Canabou, "Imagine That," *Fast Company*, January 2001, p. 56.

People learn at an early age to pursue answers to questions. Creative people, however, understand that good *questions* are extremely valuable in the quest for creativity. Some of the greatest breakthroughs in history came as a result of creative people asking thought-provoking questions. Bill Bowerman, contemplating a design for the soles of running shoes over a breakfast of waffles, asked, "What would happen if I poured rubber into my waffle iron?" He did, and that's how Nike shoes came to be. (Bowerman's rubber-coated waffle iron is on display in the Nike Town superstore and museum in Chicago.) Albert Einstein, creator of the theory of relativity, asked, "What would a light wave look like to someone keeping pace with it?" Masura Ibuka, who created the Sony Walkman, asked, "Why can't we remove the recording function and speaker and put headphones on the recorder?" William Riblich, CEO of Foster-Miller Inc., a company that develops production equipment for businesses, says his company routinely asks, "In what other ways can we use this particular technology?" Answering that question enabled Foster-Miller to adapt a metallurgical heat-treating technology for use in a candy manufacturing process.

The following questions can help spur your imagination:

1. Is there a new way to do it?
2. Can you borrow or adapt it?
3. Can you give it a new twist?
4. Do you merely need more of the same?
5. Less of the same?
6. Is there a substitute?
7. Can you rearrange the parts?
8. What if you do just the opposite?
9. Can you combine ideas?
10. Can you put it to other uses?
11. What else could we make from this?
12. Are there other markets for it?
13. Can you reverse it?
14. What idea seems impossible but, if executed, would revolutionize your business?

them around the problem. The board has generated many creative solutions that otherwise would not have come up.

Expecting and tolerating failure. Creative ideas will produce failures as well as successes. People who never fail are not being creative. Creativity requires taking chances, and managers must remove employees' fear of failure. The surest way to quash creativity throughout an organization is to punish employees who try something new and fail.

Encouraging curiosity. Entrepreneurs and their employees constantly should ask "what if" questions and take a "maybe we could . . ." attitude. Doing so allows them to break out of assumptions that limit creativity.

Viewing problems as challenges. Every problem offers the opportunity for innovation. Entrepreneurs who allow employees to dump all of their problems on their desks to be "fixed" do nothing to develop creativity within those employees.

Providing creativity training. Almost everyone has the capacity to be creative, but developing that capacity requires training. One writer claims, "What separates the average person from Edison, Picasso, or even Shakespeare isn't creative capacity—it's the ability to tap that capacity by encouraging creative impulses and then acting upon them."[24] Training accomplished through books, seminars, workshops, and professional meetings can help everyone learn to tap their creative capacity.

Providing support. Entrepreneurs must give employees the tools and the resources they need to be creative. One of the most valuable resources is time. Advanced Tissue Sciences, a company that makes products to replace or repair damaged tissue and organs and has appeared on *Inc.* magazine's list of the 500 fastest-growing firms, allows employees to spend up to 20 percent of their time working on "pet projects" that they find exciting and believe have potential. "That keeps their energy and their enthusiasm alive," says founder Gail Naughton.[25] Entrepreneurs should remember that creativity often requires nonwork phases, and allowing employees time to "daydream" is an important part of the process.

Developing a procedure for capturing ideas. Workers in every organization come up with creative ideas; however, not every organization is prepared to capture those ideas. The unfortunate result is that ideas that may have vaulted a company ahead or made people's lives better simply evaporate. George Calhoun, chairperson of Isco International, a company that makes wireless communications products, routinely sends employees to work with customers all over the globe, knowing that they will come back with insights and ideas they might never have had. The company captures those ideas in "trip reports" that employees make upon their return.[26]

Rewarding creativity. Entrepreneurs can encourage creativity by rewarding it when it occurs. Financial rewards can be effective motivators of creative behavior, but nonmonetary rewards such as praise, recognition, and celebration can be more powerful incentives.

A Company Example

Digital Communications Corporation, a small company that develops advanced wireless technologies, recognizes employees who develop patentable inventions with stock options, cash awards, and honors at an Inventors' Dinner. The reward system works; within two years after implementing it, the number of patent applications Digital Communications filed increased by a factor of five![27]

Modeling creative behavior. Creativity is "caught" as much as it is "taught." Companies that excel at innovation find that the passion for creativity starts at the top. Entrepreneurs who set examples of creative behavior, take chances, and challenge the status quo will soon find their employees doing the same. Table 2.2 describes 10 "secrets" for leading innovation in an organization.

Building a creative environment takes time, but the payoffs can be phenomenal. 3M, a company that is famous for cultivating a creative environment, estimates that 70 percent of its annual sales come from creative ideas that originated from its workforce. As one creativity consultant explains, "For your employees to be more creative, you have to create an environment that values their creativity."[28]

TABLE 2.2

10 "Secrets" for Leading Creativity

Source: Katherine Catlin, "10 Secrets to Leading Innovation," *Entrepreneur,* September 2002, p. 72. Reprinted with permission of Entrepreneur Media, Inc., www.entrepreneur.com

Leaders at innovative companies know that their roles in stimulating creativity and establishing a culture that embraces and encourages creativity are vital. Katherine Catlin, founder of a consulting firm specializing in leadership and innovation, has identified the following characteristics exhibited by leaders of innovation.

1. *They think.* These leaders invest time in thinking because they recognize the power of their own creativity and the ideas it generates.

2. *They are visionaries.* These people are totally focused on the values, vision, and mission of their companies and express them through their companies' products and services as well as through its culture. They are able to communicate to others exactly what they want to accomplish.

3. *They listen to customers.* They recognize that customers or potential customers can be a valuable source of new ideas for product or service development and improvement, sales techniques, and market positioning.

4. *They understand how to manage ideas.* As they search for new ideas and creative solutions, these managers look to a variety of sources—customers, employees, the board of directors, and even their own dreams.

5. *They are people centered.* These leaders hire people for their creative abilities and then place them in a setting that enables that creativity to blossom. They see their employees and their employees' ideas as an important part of their companies' competitive edge.

6. *They maintain a culture of "change."* These leaders do not simply manage change; they embrace it. They seek out change, recognizing that there is a constant need to improve.

7. *They maximize team synergy, balance, and focus.* Realizing that teamwork fosters creativity and innovation, these leaders bring together people from diverse backgrounds into teams to maximize their companies' creative output.

8. *They hold themselves and others accountable for extremely high standards of performance.* These leaders demand results of the highest quality from themselves and their employees and are unwilling to settle for anything less.

9. *They refuse to take "no" for an answer.* These leaders persist in the face of adversity even when others say it cannot be done.

10. *They love what they do and have fun doing it.* These leaders' passion for their work is contagious, empowering everyone in the organization to accomplish everything they possibly can.

Enhancing Individual Creativity

Just as entrepreneurs can cultivate an environment of creativity in their organizations by using the techniques described previously, they also can enhance their own creativity by using the following techniques:

Allow yourself to be creative. As we have seen, one of the biggest obstacles to creativity occurs when a person believes that he or she is not creative. Giving yourself the permission to be creative is the first step toward establishing a pattern of creative thinking.

Give your mind fresh input every day. To be creative, your mind needs stimulation. Do something different each day—listen to a new radio station, take a walk through a park or a shopping center, or pick up a magazine you never read.

*When Janet Harris Lange, founder of **Agenda Dynamics Inc.**, a meeting and event management company, needs a fresh idea for an upcoming event, she makes an effort to expose her mind to new stimuli. In the past, she has walked through a second-hand thrift shop, shopped in a dime store, talked with children, and put on funny hats to generate creative ideas for her clients' events, something that is vital to her company's success. "To be better than the competition, I have to employ creative thinking," she says.[29]*

Recognize the creative power of mistakes. Innovations sometimes are the result of serendipity, finding something while looking for something else, and sometimes they arise as a result of mistakes. Creative people recognize that even their errors may lead to new ideas, products, and services. Charles Goodyear worked for five years trying to combine rubber with a variety of chemicals to prevent it from being too soft in hot weather and too brittle in cold weather. One cold night in 1839, Goodyear was combining rubber, sulfur, and white lead when he accidentally spilled some of the mixture on a work stove. The substances melted together to form a new compound that had just the properties Goodyear was looking for! Goodyear named the process he discovered accidentally "vulcanization," and today practically every product made from rubber depends on it.[30]

Keep a journal handy to record your thoughts and ideas. Creative ideas are too valuable to waste so always keep a journal nearby to record them as soon as you get them. Patrick McNaughton invented the neon blackboards that restaurants use to advertise their specials. In addition to the neon blackboard, McNaughton has invented more than 30 new products, many of which are sold through the company that he and his sister, Jamie, own. McNaughton credits much of his creative success to the fact that he writes down every idea he gets and keeps it in a special folder. "There's no such thing as a crazy idea," he insists.[31]

Listen to other people. No rule of creativity says that an idea has to be your own! Sometimes the best business ideas come from someone else, but entrepreneurs are the ones to act on them.

*J. S. Fletcher and Kathy Newburn decided to launch their business, **YourNovel.com**, a business that writes customized romance novels, after a friend mentioned the idea as a passing comment. Since launching their business more than a decade ago, the couple (who decided to marry after they started their business together) has written 10 novels under the pseudonym Fletcher Newbern. Customers go to the company's Web site, fill out a questionnaire that gathers all of the necessary information, pick the setting (which ranges from a dude ranch on the open plains to the mountains of North Carolina), and select the type of novel they want ("mild" or "wild").[32]*

Kathy Newburn and J.S. Fletcher got the idea for YourNovel.com from a friend's passing comment at a party.

Courtesy of YourNovel.com, Inc.

YOU Be the Consultant . . .

The Creative Side of Entrepreneurship

When St. Petersburg, one of the most splendid, harmonious cities in Europe, was being laid out early in the eighteenth century, many large boulders brought by a glacier from Finland had to be removed. One particularly large rock was in the path of one of the principal avenues that had been planned, and bids were solicited for its removal. The bids submitted were very high. This was understandable, because at that time modern equipment did not exist and there were no high-powered explosives. As officials pondered what to do, a peasant presented himself and offered to get rid of the boulder for a much lower price than those submitted by other bidders. Since they had nothing to lose, officials gave the job to the peasant.

The next morning he showed up with a crowd of other peasants carrying shovels. They began digging a huge hole next to the rock. They propped up the rock with timbers to prevent it from rolling into the hole. When the hole was deep enough, the timber props were removed and the rock dropped into the hole below the street level. Then they covered it with dirt and carted the excess dirt away.

It's an early example of what creative thinking can do to solve a problem. The unsuccessful bidders only thought about moving the rock from one place to another on the city's surface. The peasant looked at the problem from another angle. He considered another dimension—up and down. He couldn't lift it up, so he put it underground!

Managers at the Cleveland Museum used a similar kind of creative thinking to ensure the success of a dazzling exhibit of ancient Egyptian treasures. Taking a different marketing approach, museum managers held a free private showing for the city's taxi drivers. Some of the museum's snooty, blue-blooded patrons scoffed at the idea and dismissed it as an exercise in foolishness. After all, they said, taxi drivers aren't known for their polish or their culture. But the museum managers persisted. Impress the cab drivers, they reasoned, and the "cabbies" would be more likely to recommend the new exhibit to their customers, who would, in turn, flock to the museum. That's exactly what happened. During the exhibit's run in Cleveland, the museum enjoyed shoulder-to-shoulder attendance, thanks to talkative cab drivers and creative museum managers!

The principal at one Oregon middle school used creativity to solve a maintenance problem. Girls would put on lipstick in the bathrooms and then press their lips to the mirror, leaving dozens of sticky lip prints that the maintenance crew had to scrub off. The principal invited all of the girls to the bathroom, where she explained the problem and the time and cost associated with cleaning the mirrors every day. She then asked the maintenance man to demonstrate how difficult it was to scrub off the lipstick. He took out a long-handled squeegee, dipped it in a toilet, and proceeded to clean the mirror with it. Since then, no lip prints have appeared on the mirrors in the girls' bathrooms!

1. Contact a local small business owner and ask about a problem that his or her company is facing. Work with a small team of your classmates and use the type of creative thinking described here to generate potential solutions to the problem. Remember to think creatively!

Sources: Bernard Percy and Marina Leight, "Side by Sick" *Converge*, April–May 2002, p. 11; Charles R. Davey, "Oddball Ideas Aren't So Odd," *Industry Week*, August 3, 1992, p. 7; *Bits & Pieces*, October 15, 1992, pp. 8–10.

Talk to a child. As we grow older, we learn to conform to society's expectations about many things, including creative solutions to problems. Children place very few limitations on their thinking; as a result, their creativity is practically boundless. (Remember all of the games you and your fiends invented when you were young?)

Keep a toy box in your office. Your box might include silly objects such as wax lips, a yoyo, a Slinky, fortune cookie sayings, feathers, a top, a compass, or a host of other items. When you are stumped, pick an item at random from the toy box and think about how it relates to your problem.

Read books on stimulating creativity or take a class on creativity. Creative thinking is a technique that anyone can learn. Understanding and applying the principles of creativity can improve dramatically anyone's ability to develop new and innovative ideas.

Take some time off. Relaxation is vital to the creative process. Getting away from a problem gives the mind time to reflect on it. It is often during this time, while the subconscious works on a problem, that the mind generates many creative solutions, One creativity expert claims that fishing is the ideal activity for stimulating creativity. "Your brain is on high alert in case a fish is around," he says, "but your brain is completely relaxed. This combination is the time when you have the 'Aha!' moment."[33]

THE CREATIVE PROCESS

Although creative ideas may appear to strike as suddenly as a bolt of lightning, they are actually the result of the creative process, which involves seven steps:

1. preparation
2. investigation
3. transformation
4. incubation
5. illumination
6. verification
7. implementation

Step 1. Preparation. This step involves getting the mind ready for creative thinking. Preparation might include a formal education, on-the-job training, work experience, and taking advantage of other learning opportunities. This training provides a foundation on which to build creativity and innovation. As one writer explains, "Creativity favors the prepared mind."[34] For example, Dr. Hamel Navia, a scientist at tiny Vertex Pharmaceuticals, recently developed a promising new drug to fight the AIDS virus. His preparation included earning an advanced degree in the field of medicine and learning to use computers to create 3-D images of the protein molecules he was studying.[35] How can you prepare your mind for creative thinking?

■ Adopt the attitude of a lifelong student. Realize that educating yourself is a neverending process. Look at every situation you encounter as an opportunity to learn.

A Company Example

Ravi Vaidyanathan, a research scientist at **Orbital Research Inc.**, *a small high-tech firm based in Cleveland, began studying the reflexes of the cockroach after observing its uncanny ability to escape an approaching shoe. Vaidyanathan used what he learned from the insect to create a neural network called BioAVERT based on a mathematical algorithm for the company that promises to improve the navigation systems in cars, ships, airplanes, and other methods of transportation. "By mimicking a cockroach," he says, "we're able to come up with a neural network for very fast responses."*[36]

■ Read . . . a lot . . . and not just in your field of expertise. Many innovations come from blending ideas and concepts from different fields in science, engineering, business, and the arts. Reading books, magazines, and papers covering a wide variety of subject matter is a great way to stimulate your creativity.

■ Clip articles of interest to you and create a file for them. Over time, you will build a customized encyclopedia of information from which to draw ideas and inspiration.

■ Take time to discuss your ideas with other people, including those who know little about the topic as well as experts in the field. Sometimes the apparently simple questions an "unknowledgeable" person asks lead to new discoveries and to new approaches to an old problem.

A Company Example

Dave Wiggins, president of **American Wilderness Experience, Inc.**, *an adventure travel company, gets valuable ideas from his wife, Carol, a network of business advisors, and his employees. The idea for the company's most popular trip, snowmobiling in Yellowstone National Park, came from one of the company's guides. "I find it extremely helpful to get different perspectives from people I respect and trust," says Wiggins.*[37]

■ Join professional or trade associations and attend the meetings. There you have the chance to brainstorm with others who have similar interests. Learning how other people have solved a particular problem may give you fresh insight into solving it.

■ Invest time in studying other countries and their cultures; then travel there. Our global economy offers incredible business opportunities for entrepreneurs with the necessary knowledge and experience to recognize them. One entrepreneur began a lucrative business exporting a variety of consumer products to Latvia after he accompanied his daughter there on a missionary trip. He claims that he never would have seen the opportunity had he not traveled to Latvia with his daughter.

■ Develop listening skills. It's amazing what you can learn if you take the time to listen to other people—especially those who are older and have more experience. Try to learn something from everyone you meet.

Step 2. Investigation. This step requires developing a solid understanding of the problem, situation, or decision at hand. To create new ideas and concepts in a particular field, an individual first must study the problem and understand its basic components. Creative thinking comes about when people make careful observations of the world around them and then investigate the way things work (or fail to work). For example, Dr. Navia and another scientist at Vertex had spent several years conducting research on viruses and on a protein that blocks a virus enzyme called protease. His exploration of the various ways to block this enzyme paved the way for his discovery.

A Company Example

*For Joe Moya and Joe Raia, cofounders of **Joe Designer Inc.**, the creative process is the key to their company's success. Joe Designer has created and developed a myriad of award-winning designs for companies ranging from Betty Crocker to Kodak. Raia explains the importance of the investigation phase as he and Moya prepare their creative team for an assignment. "We familiarize ourselves with market trends, the past history of the product," he says. "We research by flipping through magazines. We pin articles, photos, everything upon the walls and familiarize the whole team with what the history is and what we want to achieve."* [38]

Step 3. Transformation. Transformation involves viewing the similarities and the differences in the information collected. This phase requires two types of thinking: convergent and divergent. **Convergent thinking** is the ability to see the *similarities* and the connections among various data and events.

convergent thinking—*the ability to see similarities and the connections among various data and events.*

A Company Example

*While working for Dow Chemical Company, Mike Biddle was disturbed by the difficulties of recycling and reusing the high-tech plastics he and his team developed for the aerospace industry. When he left Dow in 1992, Biddle decided to start **MBA Polymers Inc.**, a research and development company that focuses on recycling the plastic from consumer durables such as computers, monitors, televisions, and other common products. Traditional plastics recycling equipment was not durable enough to handle the job. The first barrier Biddle and former Dow co-worker Trip Allen had to overcome was finding a way to separate the plastic components from other materials such as glass, metal, and paper. Using convergent thinking, Biddle and Allen searched for similarities in the equipment used by other industries such as mining, agriculture, and food processing, where sorting and separating materials is an important part of the process. Creative thinking led them to adapt a machine that was used to shred nail-filled wooden pallets to separate metals from the plastic; they used a piece of farm equipment that separated wheat from chaff to remove paper labels from the plastic mix. They modified a mining machine that extracted minerals from rocks to separate different grades of plastic. The founders' ability to use convergent thinking allows MBA Polymers to produce recycled plastic that is 20 to 25 percent cheaper than virgin plastic. The company now churns out more than 500,000 pounds of recycled plastic each month.* [39]

Divergent thinking is the ability to see the differences among various data and events. While developing his AIDS-fighting drug, Dr. Navia studied the work of other scientists whose attempts at developing an enzyme-blocking drug had failed. He was able to see the similarities and differences between his research and others' research and to build on their successes while avoiding their failures.

divergent thinking—*the ability to see differences among various data and events.*

How can you increase your ability to transform the information collected into a purposeful idea?

■ Evaluate the parts of the situation several times, trying to grasp the "big picture." Getting bogged down in the details of a situation too early in the creative process can diminish creativity. Look for patterns that emerge.

■ Rearrange the elements of the situation. By looking at the components of an issue in a different order or from a different perspective, you may be able to see the similarities and the differences among them more readily. Rearranging them also may help uncover a familiar pattern that had been masked by an unfamiliar structure.

- Before locking into one particular approach to a situation, remember that several approaches might be successful. If one approach produces a dead end, don't hesitate to jump quickly to another. Considering several approaches to a problem or opportunity simultaneously would be like rolling a bowling ball down each of several lanes in quick succession. The more balls you roll down the lanes, the greater is the probability of hitting at least one strike. Resist the temptation to make snap judgments on how to tackle a problem or opportunity. The first approach may not be the best one.

Step 4. Incubation. The subconscious needs time to reflect on the information collected. To an observer, this phase of the creative process would be quite boring; it looks as though nothing is happening! In fact, during this phase, it may appear that the creative person is *loafing.* Incubation occurs while the individual is away from the problem, often engaging in some totally unrelated activity. Dr. Navia's creative powers were working at a subconscious level even when he was away from his work and not even thinking about his research on AIDS-fighting drugs.

How can you enhance the incubation phase of the creative process, letting ideas marinate in your mind?

- Walk away from the situation. Often doing something totally unrelated to it will give your subconscious mind the chance to work on the problem or opportunity. One expert suggests that the "three b's"—bath, bed, and bus—are conducive to creativity. "I do some of my best thinking in my hot tub at home," says American Wilderness Experience's Dave Wiggins. "I sit there, look at the stars, and come up with some pretty good ideas."[40]

- Take the time to daydream. Although it may *look* as if you're doing nothing, daydreaming is an important part of the creative process. That's when your mind is most free from paradigms and other self-imposed restrictions on creativity. Feel free to let your mind wander, and it may just stumble onto a creative solution.

- Relax—and play—regularly. Perhaps the worst thing you can do for creativity is to work on a problem or opportunity constantly. Soon enough, fatigue walks in and creativity walks out! Great ideas often are incubated on the golf course, on the basketball court, in the garden, or in the hammock.

- Dream about the problem or opportunity. Although you may not be able to dream on command, thinking about an issue just before you drift off to sleep can be an effective way to encourage your mind to work on it while you sleep, a process called lucid dreaming. When he gets in bed, prolific inventor, serial entrepreneur, and author Ray Kurzweil focuses on a particular problem, sometimes imagining that he is giving a speech about his success at solving it. "This has the purpose of seeding your subconscious to influence your dreams," he explains. Often, while he is asleep, ideas and potential solutions to the problem drift into his dreams. When he begins to awaken but is still in that netherland of semi-sleep, Kurzweil merges the logic of conscious thought with the content of his dreams. The process often produces astonishing insights that Kurzweil says he otherwise might have missed.[41]

- Work on the problem or opportunity in a different environment—somewhere other than the office. Take your work outside on a beautiful fall day or sit on a bench in a mall. The change of scenery will likely stimulate your creativity.

Step 5. Ilumination. This phase of the creative process occurs at some point during the incubation stage when a spontaneous breakthrough causes "the lightbulb to go on." It may take place after five minutes—or five years. In the illumination stage, all of the previous stages come together to produce the "Eureka factor"—the creation of the innovative idea. In one study of 200 scientists, 80 percent said that at least once a solution to a problem had "just popped into their heads"—usually when they were away from the problem.[42] For Dr. Navia, the illumination stage occurred one day while he was reading a scientific journal. As he read, Dr. Navia says he was struck with a "hallucination" of a novel way to block protease.

Although the creative process itself may last for months or even years, the suddenness with which the illumination step occurs can be deceiving. For example:

One night, Kent Murphy, an electrical engineer, began dreaming about what it would be like to be a photon of light. "I was riding a ray of light moving through the fiber," he recalls about his dream. Murphy, who holds 30 patents, used the insight from his dream to invent a fiber-optic gauge that monitors on a real-time basis the structural wear in airplanes.[43] Barry

Kemp says that the idea for the TV series *Coach* popped into his head—characters, plot line, and all—at 3 o'clock in the morning. He got up and scribbled seven pages of notes that became the foundation for the successful sit-com. A professor of mathematical sciences came up with an important new theory to explain how gravity works in the rotation of spiral galaxies, a problem that has perplexed physicists and astronomers for decades, while gazing at a ceiling fan in a restaurant. Like a point on the blade of a ceiling fan, he thought (he was daydreaming at the time), the speed of a star in a spinning galaxy is slower if it lies closer to the axis. He developed an equation to test his theory and then compared its results to various measurements of galactic rotation. The results were consistent with reality, and the theory worked![44]

Step 6. Verification. Validating the idea as accurate and useful, for entrepreneurs, may include conducting experiments, running simulations, test marketing a product or service, establishing small-scale pilot programs, building prototypes, and many other activities designed to verify that the new idea will work and is practical to implement. The goal is to subject the innovative idea to the test of cold, hard reality. At this phase, appropriate questions to ask include:

■ Is it *really* a better solution to a particular problem or opportunity? Sometimes an idea that appears to have a bright future in the lab or on paper dims considerably when put to the test of reality.

■ Will it work?

■ Is there a need for it?

■ If so, what is the best application of this idea in the marketplace?

■ Does this product or service idea fit into our core competencies?

■ How much will it cost to produce or to provide?

■ Can we sell it at a reasonable price that will produce adequate sales, profit, and return on investment for our business?

Ramtron International Corporation, a maker of memory chips, uses a "product justification form" to collect information from the idea generator as well as from other departments in the company so it can verify the potential of each idea.[45] To test the value of his new drug formulation, Dr. Navia used powerful computers at Vertex Pharmaceuticals to build 3-D Tinkertoy-like models of the HIV virus and then simulated his new drug's ability to block the protease enzyme. Subsequent testing of the drug verified its safety. "I was convinced that I had an insight that no one else had," he recalls.[46]

Step 7. Implementation. The focus of this step is to transform the idea into reality. Plenty of people come up with creative ideas for promising new products or services, but most never take them beyond the idea stage. What sets entrepreneurs apart is that they *act* on their ideas. An entrepreneur's philosophy is "ready, aim, fire," not "ready, aim, aim, aim, aim . . ."

NCT Group, a small company, had developed a system that sent mirror images of sound waves through ceramic tiles to cancel out noise. One day, an engineer wondered what would happen if he sent music instead of "anti-noise" through the tiles. He connected a radio to the unit, and from the flat tiles came the sound of the Beatles! The company took the engineer's discovery and developed 2-inch-thick, wall-mounted speakers that produce high-quality audio for the consumer market! Another small business, Cygnus Inc., had created a patch that was designed to deliver drugs through the wearer's skin. While taking apart a patch one day, a researcher realized that not only did it deliver drugs, but it also absorbed material from the body. Cygnus transformed the discovery into a line of watchlike devices that monitor the glucose levels of diabetic patients.[47]

A Company Example

The key to both companies' success was their ability to take a creative idea for a useful new product and turn it into a reality. As one creativity expert explains, "Becoming more creative is really just a matter of paying attention to that endless flow of ideas you generate, and learning to capture and act upon the new that's within you."[48]

For Dr. Navia and Vertex Pharmaceuticals, the implementation phase required testing the drug's ability to fight the deadly virus in humans. If it proved to be effective, Vertex would complete the process by bringing the drug to market. In this final phase of testing, Navia was so certain that he was on the verge of a major breakthrough in fighting AIDS that he couldn't sleep at night. Unfortunately, the final critical series of tests proved that Dr. Navia's flash of

YOU Be the Consultant . . .

Reinventing the Wheel

Brian Le Gette and Ron Wilson have built a highly successful company, Big Bang Products, by focusing their creativity on everyday products that most people never think about: sunglasses, gloves, beach chairs, stadium seats, and others. It all started, however, when Le Gette and Wilson, both trained as engineers, became friends while studying at Wharton Business School. They decided that they could come up with a better design for earmuffs, one that would enable them to keep their ears warm without looking like dorks. In their first year of business school, Le Gette and Wilson designed an expandable, collapsible, fleece-covered ear warmer that wrapped around the back of the wearer's head rather than over the top. Their design was lighter, less bulky, and looked much better than traditional earmuffs. "We thought the engineering would be relatively simple," says Wilson. But to make it so it stayed on people's heads was complex. On a shopping spree at Wal-Mart, the duo bought a variety of plastic items they could cut apart and reglue or rivet together to make a crude prototype.

Le Gette and Wilson decided that their design had market potential, so in 1993 they charged $7,500 of start-up expenses on their credit cards and launched Big Bang Products. By the fall of 1994, they were selling their distinctive earmuffs to fellow students on the University of Pennsylvania's main thoroughfare. Then came a big break. Two of their classmates had landed internships at shopping network QVC and convinced Le Gette and Wilson to pitch their earmuffs on television. The first 5,000 earmuffs sold out in just eight-and-a-half minutes. By 1997, they had sold more than 600,000 earmuffs on QVC!

Later that year, they raised $2 million in capital, hired five employees, and turned their attention to innovating other mundane products including a radio-controlled toy hang glider, a stadium seat filled with self-inflating foam, and a pop-open beach mat, all of which they sold on QVC. The duo gained a reputation for getting products from the idea stage to market with incredible speed. The beach mat, for instance, went from prototype to market in just eight weeks! "Innovation is the easy part," says Le Gette. "The difficult part is choosing the right innovation."

Big Bang Products now has annual sales of more than $35 million and is growing rapidly. In addition to QVC, the company's products are sold through retailers such as Nordstrom, REI, Target, Eddie Bauer, and others. Le Gette and Wilson now focus their attention on a narrower line of products, those with the greatest market potential, but they remain true to their original business concept: innovating everyday products. One of their latest innovations is a pair of gloves equipped with "exhale heating technology," a small port the wearer blows into to warm his or her hands. The company is working with the Department of Defense about the gloves' potential military applications. The company's sunglasses have pivoting temples that fold in from of the lenses, making them less likely to get scratched and easier to put into a pocket. "We have an inexhaustible desire to question the things that most people think have already been answered," says Le Gette. "And that's how we succeed at reinventing the wheel."

1. What is Big Bang Products' competitive edge in the marketplace?

2. Try the company's approach yourself. Work with a team of your classmates to select an everyday product and brainstorm ways it could be improved.

3. How would you determine the market potential of your new and improved design?

Sources: Adapted from Donna Fenn, "The B-School Boys," *Inc.*, September 2002, p. 78; Big Bang Products, www.bigbangproducts.com/aboutus/history/history.asp#.

---

creativity was, as he now says, "completely, totally, and absolutely incorrect." Although his intuition proved to be wrong this time, Dr. Navia's research into fighting AIDS continues. Much of the current work at Vertex is based on Dr. Navia's original idea. Although it proved to be incorrect, his idea has served a valuable purpose: generating new ideas. "We are now applying a powerful technology in HIV research that wasn't used before, one inspired by a hunch," he says.[49]

TECHNIQUES FOR IMPROVING THE CREATIVE PROCESS

Teams of people working together usually can generate more and more creative ideas. Three techniques that are especially useful for improving the quality of creative ideas from teams are brainstorming, mind-mapping, and rapid prototyping.

Brainstorming

Brainstorming is a process in which a small group of people interact with very little structure with the goal of producing a large *quantity* of novel and imaginative ideas. The goal is to create an open, uninhibited atmosphere that allows members of the group to "freewheel" ideas. Participants should suggest any ideas that come to mind *without evaluating or criticizing them.* As group members interact, each idea sparks the thinking of others, and the spawning of ideas becomes contagious. For a brainstorming session to be successful, entrepreneurs should follow these guidelines:

Brainstorming—*a process in which a small group of people interact with very little structure with the goal of producing a large quantity of novel and imaginative ideas.*

- Keep the group small—five to eight members. If possible, include people with different backgrounds and perspectives. At Joe Design Inc., every employee in the small firm takes part in brainstorming sessions. "We bring in everybody from the bookkeeper to the office manager because they see things completely differently than we do," says Raia.[50]
- Company rank and department affiliation are irrelevant. Every member of the brainstorming team is on equal ground.
- Have a well-defined problem for the group to address, but don't reveal it ahead of time. Otherwise, participants will discuss their ideas, criticize them, and engage in other creativity-limiting activities. Stating the problem in the form of a "why," "how," or "what" question often helps.
- Limit the session to 40 to 60 minutes. Beyond that, participants grow weary and creativity flags.
- Appoint someone (preferably not a brainstorming participant) to the job of recorder. The recorder should write all ideas on a flip chart or board so that everyone can see them.
- Use a seating pattern that encourages communication and interaction (e.g., circular or U-shaped arrangements).
- Throw logic out the window. The best brainstorming sessions are playful and anything but logical.
- Encourage *all* ideas from the team, even wild and extreme ones. Not only can ideas that initially seem crazy get the group's creative juices flowing, but they also can spread creativity like wildfire. In addition, the group often can polish some of these wild ideas into practical, creative solutions.
- Establish a goal of *quantity* of ideas over *quality* of ideas. There will be plenty of time later to evaluate the ideas generated. At Ideo Inc., a Silicon Valley design firm, brainstorming teams shoot for at least 150 ideas in a 30- to 45-minute session.[51] When chemist Linus Pauling received his second Nobel Prize, someone asked him how he came up with so many great ideas. Pauling replied simply, "I come up with lots of ideas."[52]
- *Forbid* evaluation or criticism of any idea during the brainstorming session. No idea is a bad idea. Criticism slams the brakes on the creative process instantly!

© 1998 RANDY GLASBERGEN.
E-MAIL: RANDY@GLASBERGEN.COM
REPRINTED BY PERMISSION OF RANDY GLASBERGEN.

"Sometimes you get a brainstorm, sometimes you just get the clouds."

■ Encourage participants to use "idea hitch-hiking," building new ideas on those already suggested. Often some of the best solutions are those that are piggybacked on others.

Brainstorming is a powerful tool; teams of workers using brainstorming will produce a greater quantity of ideas and higher-quality ideas than individuals working alone on the same problem. Several software packages, including IdeaFisher Pro, ThoughtPath, and Inspiration, are designed to guide both individuals and teams of people through the brainstorming process.

Mind-Mapping

Another useful tool for jump-starting creativity is mind-mapping, an extension of brainstorming. One strength of mind-mapping is that it reflects the way the brain actually works. Rather than throwing out ideas in a linear fashion, the brain jumps from one idea to another. In many creative sessions ideas are rushing out so fast that many are lost if a person attempts to shove them into a linear outline. Creativity suffers. **Mind-mapping** is a graphical technique that encourages thinking on both sides of the brain, visually displays the various relationships among ideas, and improves the ability to view a problem from many sides.

The mind-mapping process works this way:

■ Start by writing down or sketching a picture symbolizing the problem or area of focus in the center of a large blank page. Tony Buzan, originator of the mind-mapping technique, suggests using ledger paper or covering an entire wall with butcher paper to establish a wide open attitude toward creativity.

■ Write down *every* idea that comes into your mind, connecting each idea to the central picture or words with a line. Use key words and symbols to record ideas in shorthand. Work as quickly as possible for no more than 20 minutes, doing your best to capture the tide of ideas that flows from your brain. Just as in brainstorming, do not judge the quality of your ideas; just get them onto the paper. Build new ideas on the backs of existing ones. If you see a connection between a new idea and one already on the paper, connect them with a line. If not, simply connect the idea to the center symbol. You will organize your ideas later in the process.

■ When the flow of ideas slows to a trickle, stop! Don't try to force creativity.

■ Allow your mind to rest for a few minutes and then begin to integrate the ideas on the page into a mind map. Use colored pens and markers to connect ideas with similar themes or to group ideas into related clusters. As you organize your thoughts, look for new connections among your ideas. Sometimes the brain needs time to process the ideas in a mind map. (Recall the incubation stage of the creative process.) Walking away from the mind map and the problem for a few minutes or a few hours may lead to several new ideas or to new relationships among ideas. One entrepreneur created the format for his company's business plan with a mind map rather than with a traditional linear outline. When he finished, he not only knew what he should include in his plan but he also had a clear picture of the order in which to sequence the elements.

Rapid Prototyping

Generating creative ideas is a critical step in the process of taking an idea for a product or a service successfully to the market. However, entrepreneurs find that most of their ideas won't work, and that's where rapid prototyping plays an important part in the creative process. The premise behind **rapid prototyping** is that transforming an idea into an actual model will point out flaws in the original idea and will lead to improvements in its design. "If a picture is worth a thousand words, a prototype is worth ten thousand," says Steve Vassallo of Ideo Inc.[53]

The three principles of rapid prototyping are the three R's: rough, rapid, and right. Models do not have to be perfect; in fact, in the early phases of developing an idea, perfecting a model usually is a waste of time. The key is to make the model good enough to determine what works and what does not. Doing so allows an entrepreneur to develop prototypes rapidly, moving closer to a successful design with each iteration. The final R, *right*, means building lots of small models that focus on solving particular problems with an idea. "You're not trying to build a complete model," says Vassallo. "You're just focusing on a small section of it."[54]

mind-mapping—*a graphical technique that encourages thinking on both sides of the brain, visually displays the various relationships among ideas, and improves the ability to view a problem from many sides.*

rapid prototyping—*the process of creating a model of an idea, enabling an entrepreneur to discover flaws in the idea to make improvements in the design.*

YOU Be the Consultant . . .

Evaluating Ideas for Their Market Potential

Legend has it that in 1899, Charles H. Duell, U.S. Commissioner of Patents, advised President McKinley to close the U.S. Patent Office because "everything that can be invented has been invented." Duell was way off the mark, of course; the U.S. Patent and Trademark Offce has issued more than 7 million patents since 1899. However, does a great idea that earns a patent mean that the inventor has the foundation for a successful business?

Not necessarily. Alden McMurtrys, a Connecticut tinkerer, in 1911 rushed to the U.S. Patent Office with his immortal design for the bubble-hat. It used a hidden gas canister to send soap bubbles out of a hat—perfect, Mr. McMurtrys thought, for showstopping chorus numbers. It never became a commercial success. Other patents that demonstrate Americans' creative if not always marketable ideas include the underwater airplane, protective glasses for chickens, a 12-foot-long TV remote control, bird diapers, and a dog-shaped vacuum cleaner.

How can an entrepreneur evaluate the market potential of a new product or service idea? The following questions can help any entrepreneur or inventor assess the profit potential of a creative idea:

- What benefits does the product or service offer customers? Is there a real need for it?
- Have you pinpointed the exact problems or difficulties your idea aims to solve? Have you considered the problems or difficulties it might create?
- On a scale of 1 to 10, how difficult will it be to execute the idea and sell it commercially?
- Does the product or service have natural sales appeal? Can customers afford it? Will they buy it? Why?
- What existing products or services would compete with your idea? Is your product or service superior to these competing products or services? If so, in what way?
- On a scale of 1 to 10, how easily can potential customers understand the benefits of your new product or service idea? Are they obvious?
- On a scale of 1 to 10, how complex is the product or service? If it is a product, can you make a prototype of it yourself?
- On a scale of 1 to 10, how complex is the distribution or delivery system necessary to get the product or service into customers' hands?
- How unique is your product or service? How easily can other companies imitate your idea?
- How much will it cost to produce or provide the product or service? To distribute it?

To evaluate creative ideas for their commercial potential, Mail Boxes Etc. relies on a set of 20 criteria, each weighted to reflect its importance, and a scoring scale of minus 2 to plus 2. By multiplying an idea's score on each criteria by the criteria's weight, managers calculate a total score that gives them a sense of an idea's market potential. Michael Michalko, author of *Cracking Creativity: The Secrets of Creative Geniuses*, suggests using the PMI (plus, minus, interesting) technique. "First, list all of the positive (plus) aspects of the idea," he says. "Then list all of the negative (minus) aspects of the idea. Last, list everything that's interesting [about it], but you're not sure if it's a plus or a minus." Evaluating an idea in this way will lead to one of three results. "You'll decide it's a bad idea, you'll decide it's a good idea, or you'll recycle it into something else," says Michalko.

Try your hand at this process. Assume the role of consultant and help Randi Altschul evaluate the market potential of her business idea. One day, Randi was trying to use her malfunctioning cellular phone in her car when she became so frustrated that she was tempted to throw the expensive phone out the window. That's when the idea of a disposable cellular phone came to her. Using her background in inventing board games, Randi worked with engineers to design an ultrathin (the equivalent of three credit cards), inexpensive phone whose circuitry is printed in conductive ink. The 2-inch by 3-inch phone gives users 60 minutes of calling time (outgoing calls only) and a hands-free attachment, all for an estimated average price of $20 (and a $2 to $3 rebate for returning the phone instead of tossing it). Randi and partner Lee Volte are working through their company, Dieceland Technologies, to apply the same technology used in the cell phone to create a paper laptop computer that they expect to serve as an Internet access device that will sell for $20.

1. Use the resources on the World Wide Web and your library to explore the prospects for Randi Altschul's cell phone.

2. Use the information you collect to answer as many of the questions listed here as possible. Conduct a PMI (plus, minus, interesting) analysis for Randi's idea.

Sources: Adapted from Mary Bellis, "Disposable Cell Phone—Phone Card Phone," *Inventors*, inventors.about.com/librag/weekly/aa2280lb.htm; Joshua Hyatt, "Inside an Inventive Mind," *FSB*, March 2002, p. 26; Jane Bahls, "Got a Winner?" *Business Start-Ups*, March 1999, pp. 6–7; Patricia L. Fry, "Inventor's Workshop," *Business Start-Ups*, August 1997, pp. 34–37; Peter Carbonara, "What Do You Do with a Great Idea?" *Business Start-Ups*, August/September, pp. 28–58; Michael W. Miller, "It Seemed Like a Good Idea," *Wall Street Journal*, May 24, 1993, p. R24; Don Debelak, "Ready or Not?" *Business StartUps*, January 1998, pp. 62–65; Karen Axelton, "Imagine That!" *Business Start-Ups*, April 1998, p. 96; Susan Greco, "Where Great Ideas Come From," *Inc.*, April 1998, pp. 76–86; Ross McDonald, "Patent Office Gold," *Kiplinger's Personal Finance Magazine*, June 2002, p. 124; Michael S. Malone, "The Smother of Invention," *Forbes ASAP*, June 24, 2002, pp. 32–40.

Learning Objective

8. Describe the protection of intellectual property rights involving patents, trademarks, and copyrights.

patent—*a grant from the federal government's Patent and Trademark Office to the inventor of a product, giving the exclusive right to make, use, or sell the invention in this country for 20 years from the date of filing the patent application.*

PROTECTING YOUR IDEAS

Once entrepreneurs come up with an innovative idea for a product or service that has market potential, their immediate concern should be to protect it from unauthorized use. Entrepreneurs must understand how to put patents, trademarks, and copyrights to work for them.

Patents

A **patent** is a grant from the federal government's Patent and Trademark Office (PTO) to the inventor of a product, giving the exclusive right to make, use, or sell the invention in this country for 20 years from the date of filing the patent application. The purpose of giving an inventor a 20-year monopoly over a product is to stimulate creativity and innovation. After 20 years, the patent expires and cannot be renewed. Most patents are granted for new product inventions, but *design patents*, extending for 14 years beyond the date the patent is issued, are given to inventors who make new, original, and ornamental changes in the design of existing products that enhance their sales. Inventors who develop a new plant can obtain a *plant patent*, provided they can reproduce the plant asexually (e.g., by grafting or cross-breeding rather than planting seeds). To be patented, a device must be new (but not necessarily better!), not obvious to a person of ordinary skill or knowledge in the related field, and useful. A device *cannot* be patented if it has been publicized in print anywhere in the world or if it has been used or offered for sale in this country prior to the date of the patent application. A U.S. patent is granted only to the true inventor, not to a person who discovers another's invention. No one can copy or sell a patented invention without getting a license from its creator. A patent does not give one the right to make, use, or sell an invention but the right to exclude others from making, using, or selling it.

Although inventors are never assured of getting a patent, they can enhance their chances considerably by following the basic steps suggested by the PTO. Before beginning the often lengthy and involved procedure, inventors should obtain professional assistance from a patent practitioner—a patent attorney or a patent agent—who is registered with the PTO. Only those attorneys and agents who are officially registered may represent an inventor seeking a patent. A list of registered attorneys and agents is available at the PTO's Web site. Approximately 98 percent of all inventors rely on these patent experts to steer them through the convoluted process. Legal fees for filing a patent application range from $3,000 to $10,000, depending on the complexity of the product.[55] One study reports that for the typical small business, obtaining a patent and maintaining it for 20 years costs about $10,000.[56]

THE PATENT PROCESS. Since George Washington signed the first patent law in 1790, the U.S. Patent and Trademark Office (www.uspto.gov) has issued patents on everything imaginable (and some unimaginable items, too), including mousetraps (of course!), Robert Fulton's steamboat, animals (genetically engineered mice), Thomas Edison's lightbulb, games, and various fishing devices. The PTO also has issued patents on business processes—methods of doing business—including Amazon. com's controversial patent on its "1-Click" technology, which allows users to store their customer information in a file and then recall it with one mouse click at checkout. To date the PTO has issued more than 7 million patents, and it receives more than 340,000 new applications each year (see Figure 2.3).[57] To receive a patent, an inventor must follow these steps:

Establish the invention's novelty. An invention is not patentable if it is known or has been used in the United States or has been described in a printed publication in this or a foreign country.

Document the device. To protect their patent claims, inventors should be able to verify the date on which they first conceived the idea for their inventions. Inventors can document a device by keeping dated records (including drawings) of their progress on the invention and by having knowledgeable friends witness these records. Inventors also can file a disclosure document with the PTO—a process that includes writing a letter describing the invention and sending a check for $10 to the PTO. A disclosure document is *not* a patent application, but it does provide evidence of the date an inventor conceived an invention.

Search existing patents. To verify that the invention truly is new, not obvious, and useful, an inventor must conduct a search of existing patents on similar products. The purpose of the

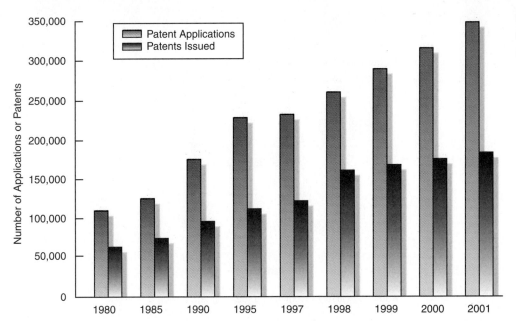

FIGURE 2.3 Number of Patent Applications and Patents Issued

search is to determine whether or not the inventor has a chance of getting a patent. Most inventors hire professionals trained in conducting patent searches to perform the research. Inventors themselves can conduct an online search of all patents granted by the PTO since 1976 from the office's Web site. An online search of these patents does not include sketches; however, subscribers to Delphion's Research Intellectual Property Network can access patents, including sketches, as far back as 1971 at www.delphion.com.

Study search results. Once the patent search is finished, inventors must study the results to determine their chances of getting a patent. To be patentable, a device must be sufficiently different from what has been used or described before and must not be obvious to a person having ordinary skill in the area of technology related to the invention.

Submit the patent application. If an inventor decides to seek a patent, he or she must file an application describing the invention with the PTO. The typical patent application runs 20 to 40 pages, although some, especially those for biotech or high-tech products, are tens of thousands of pages long. The longest patent application to date is one for a gene patent that was 6 million pages long![58] Most inventors hire patent attorneys or agents to help them complete their patent applications. Figure 2.4 shows a portion of the application for a rather unusual patent, number 3,771,192.

Prosecute the patent application. Before the PTO will issue a patent, one of its examiners studies the application to determine whether or not the invention warrants a patent. Approval of a patent normally takes about two years from the date of filing. If the PTO rejects the application, the inventor can amend the application and resubmit it to the PTO.

Defending a patent against "copycat producers" can be expensive and time-consuming but often is necessary to protect an entrepreneur's interest. The average cost of a patent infringement lawsuit is about $1 million if the case goes to trial (about half that if the parties settle before going to trial), but the odds of winning are in the patent holder's favor. More than 60 percent of those holding patents win their infringement suits.[59]

A Company Example

Knockoffs of its famous "Big Bertha" golf club have kept **Callaway Golf Company** *busy defending its patents against counterfeiters. The company recently discovered a company making a look-a-like driver called the "Big Bursa." Experts estimate that in some cases, the knockoffs, with their steeply discounted prices, actually outsell the original clubs![60]*

The World Wide Web has only compounded the problem of counterfeit sales, especially among luxury items such as Luis Vuitton and Coach bags, Cartier jewelry, and Chanel perfumes. The World Wide Web accounts for 10 percent of the total counterfeit market, which is double the amount of legitimate retail sales through e-commerce.[61]

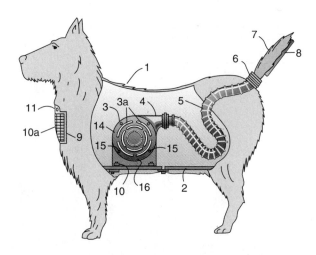

FIGURE 2.4 Dog-Shaped Vacuum Cleaner, Patent Number 3,771,192

[57]   **ABSTRACT**

A toy dog closely resembling a real dog and having a hollow interior in which is mounted a vacuum cleaner having a suction hose which is retractable from the tail end of the dog. This enables vacuuming a dog after a hair cut and grooming without causing fear to the dog, inasmuch as the vacuum cleaner noise is greatly muffed by such enclosure. The vacuum cleaner is convertible to a blower and air issuing from the tail end can be heated so as to serve as a dryer.

5 Claims, 5 Drawing Figures

Trademarks

trademark—*any distinctive word, phrase, symbol, design, name, logo, slogan, or trade dress that a company uses to identify the origin of a product or to distinguish it from other goods on the market.*

A **trademark** is any distinctive word, phrase, symbol, design, name, logo, slogan, or trade dress that a company uses to identify the origin of a product or to distinguish it from other goods on the market. (A *service mark* is the same as a trademark except that it identifies and distinguishes the source of a service rather than a product.) A trademark serves as a company's "signature" in the marketplace. A trademark can be more than just a company's logo, slogan, or brand name; it can also include symbols, shapes, colors, smells, or sounds. For instance, Coca-Cola holds a trademark on the shape of its bottle, and NBC owns a trademark on its three-toned chime. Motorcycle maker Harley-Davidson has applied for trademark protection for the shape of its oil tanks and the throaty rumbling sound its engines make![62]

trade dress—*the unique combination of elements that a company uses to create a product's image and to promote it.*

Components of a product's identity such as these are part of its **trade dress**, the unique combination of elements that a company uses to create a product's image and to promote it. For instance, a Mexican restaurant chain's particular decor, color schemes, design, and overall "look and feel" would be its trade dress. To be eligible for trademark protection, trade dress must be inherently unique and distinctive to a company, and another company's use of that trade dress must be likely to confuse customers.

A Company Example

*The **Zippo Manufacturing Company**, which has been making its distinctive metal cigarette lighter since 1932, has trademarked the shape of its classic lighter with the PTO to protect it from an onslaught of cheap imitations. Every year, the company sells more than 12 million lighters with their gently curved metal case, beveled edges, and distinctive flip-top. Zippo estimates that look-a-like knockoffs, many of which are made in China, have been skimming off as much as 30 percent of the company's sales by infringing on its trade dress.[63]*

There are 1.5 million trademarks registered in the United States, 900,000 of which are in actual use. Federal law permits a manufacturer to register a trademark, which prevents other companies from employing a similar mark to identify their goods. Before 1989, a business could not reserve a trademark in advance of use. Today, the first party who either uses a trademark in commerce or files an application with the PTO has the ultimate right to register that trademark. Unlike patents and copyrights, which are issued for limited amounts of time, trade-

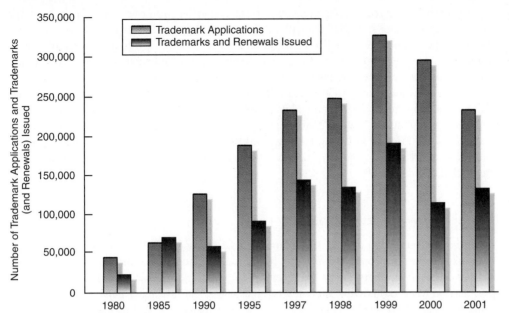

FIGURE 2.5 Trademark Application and Trademarks Issued

Source: U.S. Patent and Trademark Office.

marks last indefinitely as long as the holder continues to use it. However, a trademark cannot keep competitors from producing the same product and selling it under a different name. It merely prevents others from using the same or confusingly similar trademark for the same or similar products. Figure 2.5 shows the number of trademark applications filed and the number of trademarks issued in recent years.

Many business owners are confused by the use of the symbols ™ and ®. Anyone who claims the right to a particular trademark (or service mark) can use the ™ (or ^SM) symbols without having to register the mark with the PTO. The claim to that trademark or service mark may or may not be valid, however. Only those businesses that have registered their marks with the PTO can use the ® symbol. Entrepreneurs do not have to register trademarks or service marks to establish their rights to those marks; however, registering a mark with the PTO does give entrepreneurs greater power in protecting their marks. Filing an application to register a trademark or service mark is relatively easy, but it does require a search of existing names.

A Company Example

*Nancy Ganz, founder of **Bodyslimmers**® **by Nancy Ganz**, registered the name she gave her hipshaping undergarment, Hipslip®, with the PTO as soon as she coined the name. With her company's sales now exceeding $10 million, Ganz has successfully defended her trademark against several competitors who unlawfully sold similar products using the Hipslip® name. "Shielding your trademarks isn't hard," she says. "If you let things slide long enough, you could learn the hard way how much it costs to have your name taken in vain."* [64]

An entrepreneur may lose the exclusive right to a trademark if it loses its unique character and becomes a generic name. *Aspirin, escalator, thermos, brassiere, super glue, yo-yo*, and *cellophane* all were once enforceable trademarks that have become common words in the English language. These generic terms can no longer be licensed as trademarks.

Copyrights

A **copyright** is an exclusive right that protects the creators of original works of authorship such as literary, dramatic, musical, and artistic works (e.g., art, sculptures, literature, software, music, videos, video games, choreography, motion pictures, recordings, and others). The internationally recognized symbol © denotes a copyrighted work. A copyright protects only the form in which an idea is expressed, not the idea itself. A copyright on a creative work comes into existence the moment its creator puts that work into a tangible form. Just as with a trademark, obtaining basic copyright protection does not require registering the creative work with the U.S. Copyright Office (http://lcweb.loc.gov/copyright).

copyright—*an exclusive right that protects the creators of original works of authorship such as literary, dramatic, musical, and artistic works.*

Registering a copyright does give creators greater protection over their work, however. Copyright applications must be filed with the Copyright Office in the Library of Congress for a fee of $30 per application. A valid copyright on a work lasts for the life of the creator plus 70 years after his or her death. When a copyright expires, the work becomes public property and can be used by anyone free of charge.

Because they are so easy to duplicate, computer software programs, videotapes, CDs, and DVDs are among the most often pirated items by copyright infringers. Experts estimate that the global software industry loses $12 billion each year to pirates who illegally copy programs and that Hollywood loses $2 billion to those who forge counterfeit movies and sell them. Because they are so adept at plying their trade, video pirates often manage to beat genuine distributors to the market with movies![65]

Protecting Intellectual Property

Acquiring the protection of patents, trademarks, and copyrights is useless unless an entrepreneur takes action to protect those rights in the marketplace. Unfortunately, not every businessperson respects others' rights of ownership to products, processes, names, and works and infringes on those rights with impunity. In other cases, the infringing behavior simply is the result of a lack of knowledge about other's rights of ownership. The primary weapon an entrepreneur has to protect patents, trademarks, and copyrights is the legal system. The major problem with relying on the legal system to enforce ownership rights is the cost of infringement lawsuits, which can quickly exceed the budget of most small businesses.

If an entrepreneur has a valid patent, trademark, or copyright, stopping an infringer often requires nothing more than a stern letter from an attorney threatening a lawsuit. Often offenders don't want to get into expensive legal battles and agree to stop their illegal behavior. If that tactic fails, the entrepreneur may have no choice but to bring an infringement lawsuit.

Legal battles always involve costs. Before bringing a lawsuit, an entrepreneur must consider the following issues:

- Can the opponent afford to pay if you win?

- Do you expect to get enough from the suit to cover the costs of hiring an attorney and preparing a case?

- Can you afford the loss of time, money, and privacy from the ensuing lawsuit?

CHAPTER SUMMARY

1. Explain the differences among creativity, innovation, and entrepreneurship.

- The entrepreneur's "secret" for creating value in the marketplace is applying creativity and innovation to solve problems and to exploit opportunities that people face every day. Creativity is the ability to develop new ideas and to discover new ways of looking at problems and opportunities. Innovation is the ability to apply creative solutions to those problems and opportunities to enhance or to enrich people's lives. Entrepreneurship is the result of a disciplined, systematic process of applying creativity and innovation to needs and opportunities in the marketplace.

2. Describe why creativity and innovation are such an integral part of entrepreneurship.

- Entrepreneurs must always be on guard against existing paradigms—preconceived ideas of what the world is, what it should be like, and how it should operate—because they are logjams to creativity. Successful entrepreneurs often go beyond conventional wisdom as they ask "why not . . . ?"

- Success—even survival—in this fiercely competitive, global environment requires entrepreneurs to tap their creativity (and that of their employees) constantly.

3. Understand how the two hemispheres of the human brain function and what role they play in creativity.

■ For years, people assumed that creativity was an inherent trait. Today, however, we know better. Research shows that almost anyone can learn to be creative. The left hemisphere of the brain controls language, logic, and symbols, processing information in a step-by-step fashion. The right hemisphere handles emotional, intuitive, and spatial functions, processing information intuitively. The right side of the brain is the source of creativity and innovation. People can learn to control which side of the brain is dominant in a given situation.

4. Explain the 10 "mental locks" that limit individual creativity.

The number of potential barriers to creativity is limitless, but entrepreneurs commonly face 10 "mental locks" on creativity: searching for the one "right" answer; focusing on "being logical"; blindly following the rules; constantly being practical; viewing play as frivolous; becoming overly specialized; avoiding ambiguity; fearing looking foolish; fearing mistakes and failure; and believing that "I'm not creative."

5. Understand how entrepreneurs can enhance the creativity of their employees as well as their own creativity.

■ Entrepreneurs can stimulate creativity in their companies by expecting creativity; expecting and tolerating failure; encouraging curiosity; viewing problems as challenges; providing creativity training; providing support; rewarding creativity; and modeling creativity.

■ Entrepreneurs can enhance their own creativity by using the following techniques: allowing themselves to be creative; giving their minds fresh input every day; keeping a journal handy to record their thoughts and ideas; reading books on stimulating creativity or taking a class on creativity; taking some time off to relax.

6. Describe the steps in the creative process.

■ The creative process consists of seven steps: Step 1. Preparation—involves getting the mind ready for creative thinking; Step 2. Investigation—requires the individual to develop a solid understanding of the problem or decision; Step 3. Transformation—involves viewing the similarities and the differences in the information collected; Step 4. Incubation—allows the subconscious mind to reflect on the information collected; Step 5. Illumination—occurs at some point during the incubation stage when a spontaneous breakthrough causes "the lightbulb to go on"; Step 6. Verification—involves validating the idea as accurate and useful; and Step 7. Implementation—involves transforming the idea into a business reality.

7. Discuss techniques for improving the creative process.

Three techniques that are especially useful for improving the creative process:

■ Brainstorming is a process in which a small group of people interact with very little structure with the goal of producing a large *quantity* of novel and imaginative ideas.

■ Mind-mapping is a graphical technique that encourages thinking on both sides of the brain, visually displays the various relationships among ideas, and improves the ability to view a problem from many sides.

■ Rapid prototyping is based on the premise that transforming an idea into an actual model will point out flaws in the original idea and will lead to improvements in its design.

8. Describe the protection of intellectual property involving patents, trademarks, and copyrights.

■ A patent is a grant from the federal government that gives an inventor exclusive rights to an invention for 20 years.

■ A trademark is any distinctive word, symbol, or trade dress that a company uses to identify its product and to distinguish it from other goods. It serves as a company's "signature" in the marketplace.

■ A copyright protects original works of authorship. It covers only the form in which an idea is expressed, not the idea itself, and lasts for 70 years beyond the creator's death.

DISCUSSION QUESTIONS

1. Explain the differences among creativity, innovation, and entrepreneurship.
2. How are creativity, innovation, and entrepreneurship related?
3. Why are creativity and innovation so important to the survival and success of a business?
4. One entrepreneur claims, "Creativity unrelated to a business plan has no value." What does this mean? Do you agree?
5. What is a paradigm? What impact do paradigms have on creativity?
6. Can creativity be taught or is it an inherent trait? Explain.
7. How does the human brain function? What operations does each hemisphere specialize in? Which hemisphere is the "seat" of creativity?

8. Briefly outline the 10 "mental locks" that can limit individual creativity. Give an example of a situation in which you subjected yourself to one of these mental locks.

9. What can entrepreneurs do to stimulate their own creativity and to encourage it among workers?

10. Explain the steps of the creative process. What can an entrepreneur do to enhance each step?

11. Explain the differences among a patent, a trademark, and a copyright. What form of intellectual property does each protect?

THE BUSINESS DISC

Launch *The Business Disc*. Before you begin working through the exercises on the disc, you may want to see the brief overview of the process by using the disc's preview feature. Once you feel comfortable with the process, start the business disc program and work with Harry, your host, accountant, and consultant, to determine the type of business you will launch. Be sure to use the techniques discussed in Chapter 2 to stimulate creative thinking and to avoid the barriers to creativity. Complete the business profile form.

As you work your way through *The Business Disc* you can, at any time, use the "Go To" menu to return to earlier parts of the program for review. However, you should never use the "Go To" menu to skip ahead because you will miss data entry and decision points, and will ultimately have to start over. Be sure to exit the program by clicking "File" and "Exit" or by pressing the F4 function key. This will save your data.

BUSINESS PLAN PRO

Business PlanPro

Did you develop some innovative ideas about different kind of businesses? If so, you may want to include these in the sections in *Business Plan Pro* called "Your Company" and "What You Are Selling".

At this point it is too premature to complete these sections accurately, but do not let your ideas elude you; put them down in the plan so you can rework them later.

1. Your dinner guests are to arrive in five minutes, and you've just discovered that you forgot to chill the wine!! Wanting to maintain your reputation as the perfect host or hostess, you must tackle this problem with maximum creativity. What could you do? Generate as many solutions as you can in five minutes working alone. Then work with two or three students in a small group to brainstorm the problem.

2. Work with a group of your classmates to think of as many alternative uses for the commercial lubricant WD-40 as you can. Remember to think *fluidly* (generating a quantity of ideas) and *flexibly* (generating unconventional ideas).

3. Review the following list of household appliances. Working with a small group of your classmates, select one and use the brainstorming technique to develop as many alternative uses for the appliance as you can in 15 minutes. Remember to abide by the rules of brainstorming! The appliances are the dishwasher, clothes dryer, curling iron, toaster oven, iron, microwave oven, coffeemaker, and any others you want to use.

4. A major maker of breakfast cereals was about to introduce a new multigrain cereal. Its principal selling point is that it features "three great tastes" in every bowl: corn, rice, and wheat. Because a cereal's name is an integral part of its marketing campaign, the company hired a costly consulting firm to come up with the right name for the new product. The consulting firm tackled the job using "a combination of structural linguistics and personal creativity." One year and many dollars later, the consulting firm gave its recommendation.

   Take 20 minutes to list names that you think would be appropriate for this cereal. Make brief notes about why you think each name is appropriate.

   Your professor may choose to prepare a list of names from all of the members of your class and may take a vote to determine the "winner."

5. Each hemisphere of the brain processes information differently, and one hemisphere tends to dominate the other. Consider the following lists of words and decide which one best describes the way you make decisions and solve problems:

Metaphor	Logic
Dream	Reason
Humor	Precision
Ambiguity	Consistency
Play	Work
Approximate	Exact
Fantasy	Reality
Paradox	Direct
Diffuse	Focused
Hunch	Analysis
Generalization	Specific
Child	Adult

   If you chose the list on the left, you tend to engage in "soft" thinking, which suggests a rightbrain orientation. If you chose the list on the right, you tend to engage in "hard" thinking, which suggests a left-brain orientation.

   Creativity relies on both "soft" and "hard" thinking. Each plays an important role in the creative process but at different phases.

   A. Identify which type of thinking—"soft" or "hard"—would be more useful in each of the seven stages of the creative process.
   B. List five things you can do to develop your thinking skills in the area ("soft" or "hard") that least describes your decision-making style.

6. Interview at least two entrepreneurs about their experiences as business owners. Where did their business ideas originate? How important are creativity and innovation to their success? How do they encourage an environment of creativity in their businesses?

Chapter

3

Strategic Management and the Entrepreneur

Vision without action is a daydream. Action without vision is a nightmare.

—Japanese Proverb

One ship drives east and another drives west
with the self-same winds that blow;
'Tis the set of the sails
And not the gales
That tells them the way to go.

—Ella Wheeler Wilcox

LEARNING OBJECTIVES

Upon completion of this chapter, you will be able to:

1. **UNDERSTAND** the importance of strategic management to a small business.

2. **EXPLAIN** why and how a small business must create a competitive advantage in the market.

3. **DEVELOP** a strategic plan for a business using the nine steps in the strategic planning process.

4. **DISCUSS** the characteristics of low-cost, differentiation, and focus strategies and know when to employ them.

5. **UNDERSTAND** the importance of controls such as the balanced scorecard in the planning process.

Few activities in the life of a business are as vital—or as overlooked—as that of developing a strategy for success. Too often, entrepreneurs brimming with optimism and enthusiasm launch businesses destined for failure because their founders never stop to define a workable strategy that sets them apart from their competition. Because they tend to be people of action, entrepreneurs often find the process of developing a strategy dull and unnecessary. Their tendency is to start a business, try several approaches, and see what works. Without a cohesive plan of action, however, these entrepreneurs have as much chance of building a successful business as a defense contractor attempting to build a jet fighter without blueprints. Companies lacking clear strategies may achieve some success in the short run, but as soon as competitive conditions stiffen or an unanticipated threat arises, they usually "hit the wall" and fold. Without a basis for differentiating itself from a pack of similar competitors, the best a company can hope for is mediocrity in the marketplace.

In today's global competitive environment, any business, large or small, that is not thinking and acting strategically is extremely vulnerable. Every business is exposed to the forces of a rapidly changing competitive environment, and in the future small business executives can expect even greater change and uncertainty. From sweeping political changes around the planet and rapid technological advances to more intense competition and newly emerging global markets, the business environment has become more turbulent and challenging to business owners. Although this market turbulence creates many challenges for small businesses, it also creates opportunities for those companies that have in place strategies to capitalize on them. Historically important, entrepreneurs' willingness to create change, to experiment with new business models, and to break traditional rules has become more important than ever.

Perhaps the biggest change business owners face is unfolding now: the shift in the world's economy from a base of *financial* to *intellectual* capital. "Knowledge is no longer just a factor of production," says futurist Alvin Toffler. "It is the *critical* factor of production."[1] Today, a company's intellectual capital is likely to be the source of its competitive advantage in the marketplace. **Intellectual capital** is comprised of three components:[2]

intellectual capital—*a key source of a company's competitive advantage that is comprised of (1) human capital, (2) structural capital, and (3) customer capital.*

1. *human capital*, the talents, skills, and abilities of a company's workforce.
2. *structural capital*, the accumulated knowledge and experience that a company possesses. It can take many forms including processes, software, patents, copyrights, and, perhaps most important, the knowledge and experience of the people in a company.
3. *customer capital*, the established customer base, positive reputation, ongoing relationships, and goodwill a company builds up over time with its customers.

Increasingly, entrepreneurs are recognizing that the capital stored in these three areas forms the foundation of their ability to compete effectively and that they must manage this intangible capital base carefully. Every business uses all three components in its strategy, but the emphasis they place on each component varies.

A Company Example

*For example, **The Container Store**, a Dallas-based chain that sells a complete line of storage and organization products, relies heavily on human capital as the basis for its competitive advantage in the marketplace. The company subjects all job applicants to a thorough screening process, carefully selecting only those who demonstrate a passion for what lies at the heart of its competitive edge: customer service. Most of the Container Store employees have college degrees, something that its competitors cannot claim. The company also invests significant capital in its employees, spending 10 times the industry average on employee training and development! Because of its employee-friendly policies, The Container Store is consistently listed on Fortune's "100 Best Companies to Work For" list. The company is growing rapidly and with just 28 locations is generating more than $300 million in sales!*[3]

This knowledge shift will create as much change in the world's business systems as the Industrial Revolution did in the agricultural-based economies of the 1800s. The knowledge revolution will spell disaster for those companies who are not prepared for it, but it will spawn tremendous opportunities for those entrepreneurs equipped with the strategies to exploit these opportunities. Management legend Jack Welch, who masterfully guided General Electric for many years, says, "Intellectual capital is what it's all about. Releasing the ideas of people is what we've got to do if we are going to win."[4] However, in practice, releasing people's ideas is much more difficult than it appears. The key is to encourage employees to generate a large volume of ideas, recognizing that only a few (the best) will survive. According to Gary Hamel, author of *Inside the Revolution*, "If you want to find a few ideas with the power to enthrall customers, foil competitors, and thrill investors, you must first generate hundreds and potentially thousands of unconventional strategic ideas. Put simply, you have to crush a lot of rock to find a diamond."[5] In other words, small companies must use the creative techniques discussed in Chapter 2 as one source of competitive advantage.

The rules of the competitive game of business have changed dramatically. To be successful, entrepreneurs can no longer do things in the way they've always done them. Fortunately, successful entrepreneurs have at their disposal a powerful weapon to cope with a hostile, ever-changing environment: the process of strategic management. **Strategic management** involves developing a game plan to guide a company as it strives to accomplish its vision, mission, goals, and objectives and to keep it from straying off its desired course. The idea is to give the owner a blueprint for matching the company's strengths and weaknesses to the opportunities and threats in the environment.

BUILDING A COMPETITIVE ADVANTAGE

The goal of developing a strategic plan is to create for the small company a **competitive advantage**—the aggregation of factors that sets a small business apart from its competitors and gives it a unique position in the market superior to its competition. From a strategic perspective, the key to business success is to develop a unique competitive advantage, one that creates value for customers and is difficult for competitors to duplicate.

*Early in its existence, the **Blockbuster Video** chain gained a significant advantage over rival video rental stores when it negotiated a deal with the major movie studios to purchase videos for just $6 each, plus 40 percent of the rental fees. The agreement meant that Blockbuster could lower the cost of its inventory to less than one-tenth of that of its competitors, who were still paying an average of $65 per video! Blockbuster's significantly lower costs meant that it could stock thousands more video titles than any of its rivals, enabling the company to offer customers a tangible benefit (greater selection and in-stock guarantees) while creating a sizable competitive advantage in the market.[6]*

Building a competitive advantage alone is not enough; the key to success is building a *sustainable* competitive advantage. In the long run, a company gains a sustainable competitive advantage through its ability to develop a set of core competencies that enables it to serve its selected target customers better than its rivals. **Core competencies** are a unique set of capabilities that a company develops in key areas, such as superior quality, customer service, innovation, team building, flexibility, responsiveness, and others that allow it to vault past competitors. Typically, a company is likely to build core competences in no more than five or six (sometimes fewer) areas. These core competencies become the nucleus of a company's competitive advantage and are usually quite enduring over time. Markets, customers, and competitors may change, but a company's core competencies are more durable, forming the building blocks for everything a company does. To be effective, these competencies should be difficult for competitors to duplicate, and they must provide customers with an important perceived benefit. Small companies' core competencies often have to do with the advantages of their size—for example, agility, speed, closeness to their customers, superior service, and ability to innovate. In short, their smallness is an advantage, allowing them to do things that their larger rivals cannot. The key to success is building these core competencies (or identifying the ones a company already has) and then concentrating them on providing superior service and value for its target customers.

*Blockbuster Video's early market dominance in the video rental business has not gone unchallenged. One of the most serious challenges comes from **Netflix**, a small company that has created a unique online DVD rental service. Software entrepreneur Reed Hastings saw the World Wide Web as a way to revolutionize the delivery of videos to consumers and launched the company in 1997 by investing his own money and raising $120 million in equity capital. For a monthly subscription fee, customers can log onto the Netflix Web site and pick the movies they*

strategic management—*the process of developing a game plan to guide a company as it strives to accomplish its vision, mission, goals, and objectives and to keep it from straying off course.*

Learning Objective

2. Explain why and how a small business must create a competitive advantage in the market.

A Company Example

competitive advantage—*the aggregation of factors that sets a small business apart from its competitors and gives it a unique position in the market superior to its competition.*

core competencies—*a unique set of lasting capabilities that a company develops in key operational areas that allow it to vault past competitors.*

A Company Example

want to rent and the order in which they want to receive them. The order goes to the Netflix regional distribution center (there are 12 centers with plans to expand to 25) that is closest to the customer, where employees fill the order. Customers can keep a DVD as long as they want without incurring any late fees, and shipping (both ways) is free. When a customer returns a DVD, a computer scans it, looks up the next video on the customer's order, and sends it out. About 95 percent of DVDs come in and go out on the same day. Netflix is building its competitive advantage on several core competencies. Hastings created the business system that drives Netflix using his extensive knowledge of computer software. One venture capitalist says, "[Netflix's] film recommendation software, its merchandising, and the inventory control systems are so sophisticated. It isn't that they couldn't be replicated, but they're hard to do, and it'll take a lot of money, time, and commitment to get it right as Netflix has." CineMatch, the company's proprietary film suggestion software, uses customers' ratings from past films they have rented to suggest new ones. Netflix also has entered into revenue-sharing deals with 50 film distributors, including most of the major studios, giving it an inventory of more than 13,500 titles, including lesser-known, niche films as well as box office hits. The largest Blockbuster Video stores have 7,000 to 8,000 titles. One of the most important issues Netflix faces is market size. Can the company increase its customer base from 742,000 to its target of 8 million within eight years?[7]

No business can be everything to everyone. In fact, one of the biggest pitfalls many entrepreneurs stumble into is failing to differentiate their companies from the crowd of competitors. Entrepreneurs often face the challenge of setting their companies apart from their larger, more powerful competitors (who can easily outspend them) by using their creativity and the special abilities their businesses offer customers. Developing core competencies does *not* necessarily require a company to spend a great deal of money. It does, however, require an entrepreneur to use creativity, imagination, and vision to identify those things that it does best and that are most important to its target customers. Businesses have an infinite number of ways to create a competitive edge, but building strategy around a company's core competencies allows it to gain a sustainable competitive advantage based on what it does best.

A Company Example

*For example, **Tom's of Maine** has built its reputation over the past 35 years as a back-to-nature company that sells all-natural personal care products with environmentally friendly packaging and donates 10 percent of its pretax profits to charity. Founder Tom Chappell's company competes in the same industry as giants such as Unilever, Colgate-Palmolive, and Procter & Gamble by focusing on its base of environmentally conscious customers and by promoting itself as a company "working with nature to make a difference." Gearing up for growth, Tom's of Maine recently introduced a line of herbal remedy products as well as a line of toothpastes for adults and children. Like all of its other products, the new toothpastes contain no artificial flavors, dyes, sweeteners, or preservatives, nor are they tested on animals. Tom's of Maine is the only company to have a complete line of all-natural fluoride toothpastes that are approved by the American Dental Association. The toothpastes and all of the company's product extensions are based on its core competency of developing and manufacturing all-natural, environmentally friendly products that meet the highest standards of quality and safety. Another core competency is the company's stellar reputation among a loyal customer base as a business with a deep sense of ethics and social responsibility.*[8]

When it comes to developing a strategy for establishing a competitive advantage, small companies such as Tom's of Maine have a variety of natural advantages over their larger competitors. Small businesses often have narrower product lines, more clearly defined customer bases, and more specific geographic market areas than big businesses. Entrepreneurs usually are in close contact with their markets, giving them valuable knowledge on how to best serve their customers' needs and wants. Because of the simplicity of their organizational structures, small business owners are in touch with employees daily, often working side by side with them, allowing them to communicate strategic moves firsthand. Consequently, small businesses find that strategic management comes more naturally to them than to larger companies with their layers of bureaucracy and far-flung operations.

Strategic management can increase a small company's effectiveness, but entrepreneurs first must have a process designed to meet their needs and their business's special characteristics. It is a mistake to attempt to apply a big business's strategic development techniques to a small business because a small business is not a little big business. Because of their size and their particular characteristics—

small resource base, flexible managerial style, informal organizational structure, and adaptability to change—small businesses need a different approach to the strategic management process. In developing a strategic management procedure for a small business, an entrepreneur should:

- Use a relatively short planning horizon—two years or less for most small companies.
- Be informal and not overly structured; a shirt-sleeve approach is ideal.
- Encourage the participation of employees and outside parties to improve the reliability and creativity of the resulting plan.
- Not begin with setting objectives, as extensive objective setting early on may interfere with the creative process of strategic management.
- Maintain flexibility; competitive conditions change too rapidly for any plan to be considered permanent.
- Focus on strategic *thinking*, not just planning, by linking long-range goals to day-to-day operations.

THE STRATEGIC MANAGEMENT PROCESS

Learning Objective

3. Develop a strategic plan for a business using the nine steps in the strategic planning process.

Strategic planning is a continuous process that consists of nine steps:

Step 1. Develop a clear vision and translate it into a meaningful mission statement.

Step 2. Assess the company's strengths and weaknesses.

Step 3. Scan the environment for significant opportunities and threats facing the business.

Step 4. Identify the key factors for success in the business.

Step 5. Analyze the competition.

Step 6. Create company goals and objectives.

Step 7. Formulate strategic options and select the appropriate strategies.

Step 8. Translate strategic plans into action plans.

Step 9. Establish accurate controls.

Step 1. Develop a Clear Vision and Translate It into a Meaningful Mission Statement

VISION.   Throughout history, the greatest political and business leaders have been visionaries. Whether the vision is as grand as Martin Luther King, Jr.'s "I have a dream" speech or as simple as Ray Kroc's devotion to quality, service, cleanliness, and value at McDonald's, the purpose is the same: to focus everyone's attention on the same target and to inspire them to reach it. The vision touches everyone associated with the company—employees, investors, lenders, customers, and the community. It is an expression of what the owner stands for and believes in. Highly successful entrepreneurs are able to communicate their vision and their enthusiasm about that vision to those around them.

A vision is the result of an entrepreneur's dream of something that does not exist yet and the ability to paint a compelling picture of that dream for everyone to see. A clearly defined vision helps a company in three ways:

1. *Vision provides direction.* Entrepreneurs who spell out the vision for their company focus everyone's attention on the future and determine the path the business will take to get there.
2. *Vision determines decisions.* The vision influences the decisions, no matter how big or how small, that owners, managers, and employees make every day in a business. This influence can be positive or negative, depending on how well defined the vision is.
3. *Vision motivates people.* A clear vision excites and ignites people to action. People want to work for a company that sets its sights high.

Vision is based on an entrepreneur's values. Explaining how an entrepreneur's values are the nucleus around which a company grows, author and consultant Ken Blanchard says, "Winning companies first emphasize values—the beliefs that you, as the business owner, have about your employees, customers, quality, ethics, integrity, social responsibility, growth, stability, innovation, and flexibility. Managing by values—not by profits—is a powerful process."[9] Successful entrepreneurs build their businesses around a set of three to six core values, which might range from respect for the individual and innovation to creating satisfied customers and making the world a better place.

*In 1957, eighteen years after they had launched the company bearing their names, Bill Hewlett and Dave Packard were pleased with their company's rapid growth but were concerned that the business might lose its "small company atmosphere." The **Hewlett-Packard** cofounders took 20 of their best employees to an upscale resort in California's wine country (on one of the first recorded corporate retreats) to define the type of culture HP would foster. By the end of the retreat, the team had drafted a set of values that ultimately became the basis of "the HP Way," the highly admired culture the company is known for even today.*[10]

Indeed, truly visionary entrepreneurs see their companies' primary purpose as more than just "making money." One writer explains, "Almost all workers are making decisions, not just filling out weekly sales reports or tightening screws. They will do what they think best. If you want them to do as the company thinks best too, then you must [see to it that] that they have an inner gyroscope aligned with the corporate compass."[11] That gyroscope's alignment depends on the entrepreneur's values and how well he or she transmits them throughout the company.

The best way to put values into action is to create a written mission statement that communicates those values to everyone the company touches.

mission statement—*an enduring declaration of a company's purpose that addresses the first question of any business venture: What business are we in?*

MISSION.   The **mission statement** addresses the first question of any business venture: What business are we in? Establishing the purpose of the business in writing must come first in order to give the company a sense of direction. "If you don't reduce [your company's purpose] to paper, it just doesn't stick," says the owner of an architectural firm. "Reducing it to paper really forces you to think about what you are doing."[12] As an enduring declaration of a company's purpose, a mission statement is the mechanism for making it clear to everyone the company touches "why we are here" and "where we are going."

*Truett Cathy, founder of the highly successful restaurant chain **Chick-fil-A**, recalls a time when his business was struggling because of intensifying competition from big hamburger chains. With 200 outlets at the time, the company was struggling to keep operating costs under control as inflation threatened to push them ever higher. Cathy scheduled an executive retreat at a lake outside of Atlanta, where managers could relax and talk about their concerns and ideas for the company. His oldest son Dan, director of operations, asked, "Why are we in business? Why are we here?" Cathy was about to tell his son that this retreat was no time to dwell on philosophical issues because there were bigger problems to solve. "Then," recalls Cathy, "I realized he was serious. His question both challenged and inspired us." In the ensuing brainstorming session, the group defined values that became Chick-fil-A's mission statement: "To glorify God by being faithful stewards of all that is entrusted to us. To have a positive influence on all who come in contact with Chick-fil-A." With their purpose clearly defined, the management team went on to lead the company in a growth spurt, where sales climbed 30 percent a year. Today the company has more than 1,000 restaurants across the country (none of which are open on Sundays).*[13]

Without a concise, meaningful mission statement, a small business risks wandering aimlessly in the marketplace, with no idea of where to go or how to get there. The mission statement sets the tone for the entire company and focuses its attention on the right direction.

ELEMENTS OF A MISSION STATEMENT. A sound mission statement need not be lengthy to be effective. Some of the key issues an entrepreneur and employees should address as they develop a mission statement for the company include:

- What are the basic beliefs and values of the organization? What do we stand for?
- Who are the company's target customers?
- What are our basic products and services? What customer needs and wants do they satisfy?
- Why should customers do business with us rather than the competitor down the street (or across town, on the other coast, on the other side of the globe)?
- What constitutes value to our customers? How can we offer them better value?
- What is our competitive advantage? What is its source?
- In which markets (or market segments) will we choose to compete?
- Who are the key stakeholders in our company and what effect do they have on it?

Pepper . . . and Salt

THE WALL STREET JOURNAL

**"Please pardon our appearance while
we re-think our original theme."**

A company's mission statement may be the most essential and basic communication that it puts forward. If the people on the plant, shop, retail, or warehouse floor don't know what a company's mission is, then, for all practical purposes, it does not have one! The mission statement expresses the firm's character, identity, and scope of operations, but writing it is only half the battle, at best. The most difficult part is living that mission every day. *That's* how employees decide what really matters. To be effective, a mission statement must become a natural part of the organization, embodied in the minds, habits, attitudes, and decisions of everyone in the company every day. According to the *Workplace 2000 Employee Insight Survey*, 89 percent of employees say their companies have mission statements. Unfortunately, only 23 percent of workers believe their company's mission statement has become a way of doing business![14] One business writer claims, "If what you say about your firm's values and mission isn't true, you're in worse trouble than if you'd never articulated it in the first place."[15] Five years after founding Field Trip Factory Inc., a business that organizes life skill educational field trips for students, Susan Singer saw the need to update the company's mission statement. At a company retreat, she and her employees decided that their existing mission statement no longer reflected what the company actually stood for and did. A brainstorming session yielded a new mission statement that Singer says is helping her company improve its bottom line. "It became so clear what we do versus what we want to be," she says.[16]

A well-used mission statement serves as a strategic compass for a small company.

A Company Example

Ben & Jerry's Homemade Inc. *relies on a three-part mission statement that its managers and employees live out every day; consider the message its sends to company stakeholders:*[17]

Product Mission: To make, distribute & sell the finest quality all natural ice cream & euphoric concoctions with a continued commitment to incorporating wholesome, natural ingredients and promoting business practices that respect the Earth and the Environment.

Economic Mission: To operate the Company on a sustainable financial basis of profitable growth, increasing value for our stakeholders & expanding opportunities for development and career growth for our employees.

Social Mission: To operate the company in a way that actively recognizes the central role that business plays in society by initiating innovative ways to improve the quality of life locally, nationally & internationally.

Underlying the mission of Ben & Jerry's is the determination to seek new and creative ways of addressing all three parts, while holding a deep respect for individuals inside and outside the Company and for the communities of which they are a part.

A company may have a powerful competitive advantage, but it is wasted unless (1) the owner has communicated that advantage to workers, who, in turn, are working hard to communicate it to customers and potential customers and (2) customers are recommending the company to their friends because they understand the benefits they are getting from it that they cannot get elsewhere. *That's* the real power of a mission statement. Table 3.1 offers some useful tips on writing a mission statement.

Step 2: Assess the Company's Strengths and Weaknesses

Having defined the vision for her company and translated that vision into a meaningful mission statement, an entrepreneur can turn her attention to assessing company strengths and weaknesses. Building a successful competitive strategy requires a business to magnify its strengths and overcome or compensate for its weaknesses. **Strengths** are positive internal factors that a company can use to accomplish its mission, goals, and objectives. They might include special skills or knowledge, a positive public image, an experienced sales force, and many other factors.

strengths—*positive internal factors that a company can use to accomplish its mission, goals, and objectives.*

TABLE 3.1

Tips for Writing a Powerful Mission Statement

Sources: Adapted from Ken Blanchard, "The New Bottom Line," *Entrepreneur*, February 1998, pp. 127–131; Alan Farnham, "Brushing Up Your Vision Thing," *Fortune*, May 1, 1995, p. 129; Sharon Neiton, "Put Your Purpose in Writing," *Nation's Business*, February 1994, pp. 61–64; Jacquelyn Lynn, "Single-Minded," *Entrepreneur*, January 1996, p. 97.

A mission statement is a useful tool for getting everyone fired up and heading in the same direction, but writing one is not as easy as it may first appear. Here are some tips for writing a powerful mission statement:

- *Keep it short.* The best mission statements are just a few sentences long. If they are short, people will tend to remember them better.
- *Keep it simple.* Avoid using fancy jargon just to impress outsiders such as customers or suppliers. The first and most important use of a mission statement is inside a company.
- *Get everyone involved.* If the boss writes the company mission statement, who is going to criticize it? Although the entrepreneur has to be the driving force behind the mission statement, everyone in the company needs the opportunity to have a voice in creating it. Expect to write several drafts before you arrive at a finished product.
- *Keep it current.* Mission statements can get stale over time. As business and competitive conditions change, so should your mission statement. Make a habit of evaluating your mission statement periodically so that it stays fresh.
- *Make sure your mission statement reflects the values and beliefs you hold dear.* They are the foundation on which your company is built.
- *Make sure your mission statement includes values that are worthy of your employees' best efforts.* One entrepreneur says that a mission statement should "send a message to employees, suppliers, and customers as to what the purpose of the company is aside from just making profits."
- *Make sure your mission statement reflects a concern for the future.* Business owners can get so focused on the present that they forget about the future. A mission statement should be the first link to the company's future.
- *Keep the tone of the mission statement positive and upbeat.* No one wants to work for a business with a pessimistic outlook on the world.
- *Consider using your mission statement to lay an ethical foundation for your company.* This is the ideal time to let employees know what your company stands for—and what it won't stand for.
- *Look at other companies' mission statements to generate ideas for your own.* Two books, *Say It and Live It: The 50 Corporate Mission Statements That Hit the Mark* (Currency/Doubleday) and *Mission Statements: A Guide to the Corporate and Nonprofit Sectors* (Garland Publishing), are useful resources.
- *Make sure that your mission statement is appropriate for your company's culture.* Although you should look at other companies' mission statements, do not make the mistake of trying to copy them. Your company's mission statement is unique to you and your company.
- *Use it.* Don't go to all of the trouble of writing a mission statement just to let it collect dust. Post it on bulletin boards, print it on buttons and business cards, stuff it into employees' pay envelopes. Talk about your mission statement often, and use it to develop your company's strategic plan. That's what it's for!

Weaknesses are negative internal factors that inhibit a company's ability to accomplish its mission, goals, and objectives. Lack of capital, a shortage of skilled workers, and an inferior location are examples of weaknesses.

Identifying strengths and weaknesses helps owners understand their business as it exists (or, for a start-up, will exist). An organization's strengths should originate in the core competencies that are essential to gaining an edge in each of the market segments in which the firm competes. The key to building a successful strategy is using the company's underlying strengths as its foundation and matching those strengths against competitors' weaknesses.

One effective technique for taking this strategic inventory is to prepare a "balance sheet" of the company's strengths and weaknesses (see Table 3.2). The positive side should reflect important skills, knowledge, or resources that contribute to the firm's success. The negative side should record honestly any limitations that detract from the company's ability to compete. This balance sheet should analyze all key performance areas of the business—human resources, finance, production, marketing, product development, organization, and others. This analysis should give owners a more realistic perspective of their businesses, pointing out foundations on which they can build future strengths and obstacles that they must remove for business progress. This exercise can help entrepreneurs move from their current position to future actions.

Step 3: Scan the Environment for Significant Opportunities and Threats Facing the Business

OPPORTUNITIES. Once entrepreneurs have taken an internal inventory of company strengths and weaknesses, they must turn to the external environment to identify any opportunities and threats that might have a significant impact on the business. **Opportunities** are positive external options that a firm can exploit to accomplish its mission, goals, and objectives. The number of potential opportunities is limitless, so entrepreneurs need to analyze only those factors that are most significant to the business (probably two or three at most).

When identifying opportunities, an entrepreneur must pay close attention to new potential markets. Are competitors overlooking a niche in the market? Is there a better way to reach customers? Can we develop new products that offer customers better value? What opportunities are trends in the industry creating? For instance, analysts predict that the restaurant industry as a whole in the United States will grow by just 2 percent a year until 2010. This uninspired growth is causing problems for many segments of the industry; the profits of fast-food chains such as McDonald's and Burger King are under pressure as firms emphasize low-cost (and low-profit) value meals. Full-service restaurants offer the freshly prepared foods diners are demanding now, but for them speed and efficiency remain a serious challenge as busy customers demand ever-faster service. The *real* opportunity for growth in the restaurant industry is occurring in the middle ground, the "fast casual" segment. The restaurants experiencing the greatest success are those that focus on dinner, the most popular meal for customers outside the home, outpacing both breakfast and lunch combined. Diners also spend 40 percent more on dinner than on lunch. Café Express, a chain of fast-casual restaurants in which Wendy's

Strengths (Positive Internal Factors)	Weaknesses (Negative Internal Factors)

TABLE 3.2

Identifying Company Strengths and Weaknesses

International is an investor, uses "oasis tables," where customers can customize their dishes with a variety of toppings, ranging from parmesan cheese to capers. The chain benefits not only from satisfied customers getting exactly what they want quickly but also from lower labor costs because a smaller waitstaff is required. Many fast-casual chains are experiencing profit margins that are two to three times higher than those in other segments of the industry.[18]

Opportunities almost always arise as a result of factors that are beyond entrepreneurs' control. Constantly scanning for those opportunities that best match their companies' core competencies and strengths and then pouncing on them ahead of competitors is the key to success. As horrific as they were, the terrorist attacks on the United States, which posed serious threats to thousands of small businesses, also created unusual opportunities for others.

A Company Example

*After the attacks, **Tempest Publishing**, a small publisher of books and reports on bio-terrorism, saw demand for its daily terrorism reports and books such as* First Responder Chem-Bio Handbook *skyrocket. Founder Ben Venzke was able to boost significantly both sales and profits as the company's books began to outsell the popular Harry Potter books on Amazon.com. Another company, **Big Toys Coach Works**, experienced a huge increase in the demand for its customized, specially outfitted sports utility vehicles that come complete with bulletproof, bomb-resistant bodies and features such as wireless Internet access, televisions, refrigerators, and bars.[19] The majority of the company's customers are corporate executives, movie stars, and other VIPs in search of security and who are capable of buying customized vehicles whose prices can run upwards of $175,000![20]*

THREATS. **Threats** are negative external forces that inhibit a company's ability to achieve its mission, goals, and objectives. Threats to the business can take a variety of forms, such as competitors entering the local market, a government mandate regulating a business activity, an economic recession, rising interest rates, technological advances making a company's product obsolete, and many others. Many small retailers face a threat from "big box" retailers such as Wal-Mart, Home Depot, Circuit City, and others offering lower prices because of their high-volume purchasing power, huge advertising budgets, and megastores that attract customers from miles around. Kenneth Stone, a professor at Iowa State University and a leading researcher on Wal-Mart's impact on small companies, says that after Wal-Mart entered Iowa in 1983, 23 percent of drugstores and 45 percent of hardware stores disappeared.[21] However, small businesses with the proper strategies in place do *not* have to fold in the face of intense competition.

A Company Example

After Wal-Mart, Home Depot, and Lowe's opened next to their second-generation small hardware store in Greenville, South Carolina, Terry and Debbie Dobson changed their competitive strategy and refocused their business more on gifts and less on the standard hardware items their larger rivals sold. The Dobsons now rely on a focus strategy that emphasizes unique gifts and home décor items with a distinctively local flavor and specialty hardware items overlooked by their big box competitors. The Dobsons continue to set their business apart by offering a high level of personal service, including knowledgeable, long-time employees and a home delivery service that customers love![22]

Although they cannot control the threats themselves, entrepreneurs such as the Dobsons must prepare a plan for shielding their businesses from these threats.

Figure 3.1 illustrates that opportunities and threats are products of the interactions of forces, trends, and events outside the direct control of the business. These external forces will have a direct impact on the behavior of the markets in which the business operates, the behavior of competitors, and the behavior of customers. Table 3.3 provides a form that allows business owners to take a strategic inventory of the opportunities and threats facing their companies.

A Company Example

*As part of updating the business plan for his small metal-plating business, **AlumiPlate Inc.**, David Dayton prepared an analysis of the company's strengths, weaknesses, opportunities, and threats (a SWOT analysis) and found it to be an extremely useful part of the planning process. Dayton and his 14 employees identified high barriers to new competitors as one of AlumiPlate's major strengths and its proprietary aluminum coating technology as its greatest opportunity. The team saw the inability to produce a high-volume production demonstration as the company's greatest weakness, and its greatest threat was the heavy demands being placed on key personnel. Dayton and his employees went on to explore the ways AlumiPlate could use its strengths to exploit the best opportunities facing it; they also considered the ways in which its weaknesses make it vulnerable to threats.[23]*

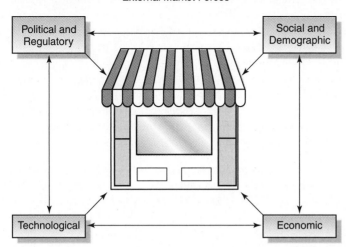

External Market Forces

Political and Regulatory

Social and Demographic

Technological

Economic

FIGURE 3.1 The Power of External Forces

These interactions of strengths and weaknesses and opportunities and threats can be the most revealing aspects of using a SWOT analysis as part of a strategic plan. This analysis also requires entrepreneurs to take an objective look at their businesses and the environment in which they operate as they address many issues fundamental to their companies' success in the future.

Step 4: Identify the Key Factors for Success in the Business

Every business is characterized by controllable variables that determine the relative success of market participants. Identifying and manipulating these variables is how a small business gains a competitive advantage. By focusing efforts to maximize their companies' performance on these key success factors, entrepreneurs can achieve dramatic market advantages over their competitors. Companies that understand these key success factors tend to be leaders of the pack, whereas those that fail to recognize them become also-rans.

Key success factors come in a variety of different patterns depending on the industry. Simply stated, they are the factors that determine a company's ability to compete successfully in an industry. Many of these sources of competitive advantages are based on cost factors such as manufacturing cost per unit, distribution cost per unit, or development cost per unit. Some are less tangible and less obvious but are just as important, such as superior product quality, solid relationships with dependable suppliers, number of services offered, prime store locations, available customer credit, and many others. For example, one restaurant owner identified the following key success factors:

key success factors—*the factors that determine a company's ability to compete successfully in an industry.*

- tight cost control (labor costs, 15–18 percent of sales, and food costs, 35–40 percent of sales)
- trained, dependable, honest in-store managers
- close monitoring of waste
- careful site selection (the right location)
- maintenance of food quality

Opportunities (Positive External Factors)	Threats (Negative External Factors)

TABLE 3.3

Identifying Opportunities and Threats

YOU Be the Consultant . . .

Something New, Something Blue

The past few years have been brutal to the airline industry as terrorism, economic recession, and war have taken their toll. Companies with long histories have experienced turbulence in their operating and financial performances, forcing some to declare bankruptcy. Yet there are bright spots among the black clouds of this troubled industry, and one of those is JetBlue Airlines. Launched in February 2000 by David Neeleman, JetBlue has quickly become one of the biggest success stories in the industry, generating a load factor (average percentage of seats filled) of more than 80 percent, the highest in the industry. Neeleman modeled his company after another success story in the airline industry and a company with which he has experience—Southwest Airlines. In 1993, Southwest founder Herb Kelleher bought Morris Air, a discount carrier that Neeleman had founded, for $128 million and hired Neeleman. The restless entrepreneur was not happy in a structured environment he did not control, and he was fired from Southwest.

Because he had signed a five-year noncomplete agreement when he sold Morris Air to Southwest Airlines, Neeleman was legally prevented from doing what he really wanted to do: launch another airline. While he waited for the five-year restriction to expire, Neeleman started Open Skies, a ticketless airline reservation system, which he later sold to Hewlett-Packard for $22 million. In 1997, he began planning the airline that would become JetBlue, incorporating what he had learned at Morris Air and from the many airline executives he had peppered with questions over the years. Neeleman had proved one thing at Morris Air—that innovative, high-quality airline service coupled with low fares will attract a strong and loyal base of customers—and he decided to follow that strategy again.

JetBlue's success stems from several strategic moves. First, like Southwest Airlines, the company flies only point-to-point routes rather than the traditional hub-and-spoke routes its larger rivals fly. The hub-and-spoke system feeds planes from smaller cities into a few central points, allowing carriers to serve small markets such as Altoona, Pennsylvania, and Asheville, North Carolina. The problem with the system is that it creates logistical nightmares because a delay anywhere in the system ripples throughout. The result is that JetBlue planes spend an average of 12 hours a day in the air, compared to just 9 to 11 hours a day for its competitors—an important difference because planes are generating revenue only when they are in the air. Plus, its on-time performance record of 83 percent tops the industry.

Unlike Southwest, however, JetBlue focuses on longer flights and uses larger planes. JetBlue's average flight is 1,055 miles versus Southwest's 528 miles. Southwest jets seat 135 passengers, and JetBlue's planes accommodate 162 passengers. Both companies use only one type of jet (Boeing 737s for Southwest and Airbus A320s for JetBlue), which enables them to keep maintenance costs low. "That way we don't have to spend money and time training our pilots, flight attendants, and technicians on different models," says Neeleman. Rather than purchase used planes, the new planes in JetBlue's fleet mean that its maintenance costs, for now, are lower than any other carrier in the industry. Neeleman also decided to upholster every seat in leather; this luxury costs $15,000 more per plane, but it sends an important signal to passengers, and the leather surfaces are easier to maintain and last much longer. JetBlue provides no in-flight meals, but every seatback contains a television that offers 24-channel satellite reception.

Another advantage JetBlue has over its rivals is that its workforce is nonunion, which means its labor cost is below that of other airlines and it has more flexibility in job assignments. Pilots even pitch in to help flight attendants clean cabins, which keeps flight turnaround times short. Reservation takers work from their homes, creating significant cost savings for them and for the company. Because the company offers stock options to its workers, employees often are willing to work for lower salaries.

Wanting to avoid the mistake of making passengers feel like cattle, Neeleman is fanatical about his company's customer service. He hitches a ride on at least one flight a week, always chatting with customers and asking for feedback from them. It is not uncommon for him to pitch in to help baggage handlers load and unload planes. Neeleman insists on being paged whenever a JetBlue flight is more than one minute late. (He even takes his pager to bed!) "Employees at other airlines get so caught up in procedure—rules, rules, rules—that they often forget there is a paying customer there," he says. Even the company's Web site focuses on simplicity and ease of use, and customers have responded; half of its fares are booked online (compared to the industry average of 10 percent), which saves the company $5 per transaction. The essence of JetBlue's strategy is to excel at offering low-cost features that its competitors overlook, that make a positive impression on customers, and that distinguish its brand.

The future poses challenges for JetBlue. How much longer can the company keep labor unions at bay? Unionization would boost labor costs by 25 percent, erasing a major cost advantage. In a related issue, as employees mature, they are more likely to demand traditional benefits and pension plans rather than rely on stock options for their retirement. As the company's fleet grows older, its maintenance costs will rise; one expert estimates that by the time its planes are seven years old, maintenance costs will increase 25 percent over current levels to $1.6 million each per year. Finally, can JetBlue beat the odds and growing pains to survive? Since 1980, entrepreneurs have launched 27 airline companies that went public, but only eight have survived.

1. Go online to the JetBlue Web site or to business magazine Web sites to learn more about JetBlue. Prepare an analysis of the company's strengths, weaknesses, opportunities, and threats.

2. Identify the sources of JetBlue's competitive advantages. Are these sources sustainable?

3. What strategic advice can you offer David Neeleman to ensure JetBlue's future success?

Sources: Melanie Wells, "Lord of the Skies," *Forbes*, October 14, 2002, pp. 130–138; "How to Shake Up a Calcified Industry," *Business 2.0*, December 2002/January 2003, p. 92; Amy Goldwasser, "Something Stylish, Something Blue," *Business 2.0*, February 2002, pp. 94–95; JetBlue Airways, www.jetblue.com.

TABLE 3.4

Identifying Key Success Factors

List the specific skills, characteristics, and core competencies that your business must possess if it is to be successful in its market segment.

Key Success Factor	How your company rates . . .
1	Low 1 2 3 4 5 6 7 8 9 10 High
2	Low 1 2 3 4 5 6 7 8 9 10 High
3	Low 1 2 3 4 5 6 7 8 9 10 High
4	Low 1 2 3 4 5 6 7 8 9 10 High
5	Low 1 2 3 4 5 6 7 8 9 10 High
Conclusions:	

- consistency
- cleanliness
- friendly and attentive service from a well-trained waitstaff

These controllable variables determine the ability of any restaurant in the market segment to compete. Restaurants lacking these key success factors are not likely to survive, but those that build their strategies with these factors in mind will prosper. However, before any entrepreneurs can build a strategy on the foundation of the industry's key success factors, they must identify them. Table 3.4 presents a form to help owners identify the most important success factors in the industry and the implications for their companies.

Entrepreneurs must use the information gathered to analyze their businesses, their competitors, and their industries to isolate sources of competitive advantage. They must then determine how well their businesses meet these criteria for successfully competing in the market. Highly successful companies know and understand these relationships, but marginal competitors are mystified by the factors that determine success in that particular business. For example, a small manufacturer of cosmetics may discover that shelf space, broad exposure, efficient distribution, and long production runs are crucial to business success. On the other hand, a small retail chain owner may find that broad product lines, customer credit, personalized service, capable store management, and reliable sources of supply determine success in that industry.

Step 5: Analyze the Competition

When a recent survey asked small business owners to identify the greatest challenge they faced in the coming year, the overwhelming response was *competition*.[24] In another survey, CEOs across the globe said the World Wide Web and e-commerce will increase the ferocity of the competition they face in the future. Twenty percent said that e-commerce will *completely* reshape the ways in which they do business.[25] As these studies suggest, keeping tabs on rivals' movements through competitive intelligence programs is a vital strategic activity. "Business is like any battlefield. If you want to win the war, you have to know who you're up against," says one small business consultant.[26] Unfortunately, most businesses are not very good at competitive intelligence; 97 percent of U.S. businesses do not systematically track the progress of their key competitors.[27] The primary goals of a competitive intelligence program include the following:

- Avoiding surprises from existing competitors' new strategies and tactics.
- Identifying potential new competitors.
- Improving reaction time to competitors' actions.
- Anticipating rivals' next strategic moves.

COMPETITOR ANALYSIS. Sizing up the competition gives business owners a more realistic view of the market and their company's position in it. Yet not every competitor warrants the same level of attention in the strategic plan. *Direct competitors* offer the same products and services, and customers often compare prices, features, and deals from these competitors as they shop. *Significant competitors* offer some of the same products and services. Although their product or service lines may be somewhat different, there is competition with them in several key areas. *Indirect competitors* offer the same or similar products or services only in a few areas, but their target customers seldom overlap yours. Entrepreneurs should monitor closely the actions of their direct competitors, maintain a solid grasp of where their significant competitors are heading, and spend only minimal resources tracking their indirect competitors.

A competitive intelligence exercise enables entrepreneurs to update their knowledge of competitors by answering the following questions:

- Who are our competitors? Where are they located? (The Yellow Pages is a great place to start.)
- What distinctive competencies have they developed?
- How do their cost structures compare to ours? Their financial resources?
- How do they market their products and services?
- What do customers say about them? How do customers describe their products or services, their way of doing business, and the additional services they might supply?
- What are their key strategies?
- What are their strengths? How can our company surpass them?
- What are their primary weaknesses? How can our company capitalize on them?
- Are new competitors entering the business?

A small business owner can collect a great deal of information about rivals through low-cost competitive intelligence (CI) methods including the following:

- Read industry trade publications for announcements and news stories about competitors.
- Ask questions of customers and suppliers on what they hear competitors may be doing. In many cases, this information is easy to gather because some people love to gossip.
- Regularly debrief employees, especially sales representatives and purchasing agents. Experts estimate that 70 to 90 percent of the competitive information a company needs already resides with employees who collect it in their routine dealings with suppliers, customers, and other industry contacts.[28]
- Attend trade shows and collect competitors' sales literature.
- Watch for employment ads from competitors; knowing what types of workers competitors are hiring can tell you a great deal about their future plans.
- Conduct patent searches (see Chapter 2) for patents that competitors have filed. This gives important clues about new products they are developing.
- Environmental Protection Agency reports can provide important information about the factories of manufacturing companies, including the amounts and the kinds of emissions released. A private group, Environmental Protection, also reports emissions for specific plants.[29]
- Learn about the kinds and amounts of equipment and raw materials competitors are importing by studying the *Journal of Commerce Port Import Export Reporting Service (PIERS)* database. These clues can alert an entrepreneur to new products a competitor is about to launch.
- If appropriate, buy competitors' products and assess their quality and features. Benchmark their products against yours. The owner of a mail-order gourmet brownie business periodically places orders from her primary rivals and compares their packaging, pricing, service, and quality to her own.[30]
- Obtain credit reports on each of your major competitors to evaluate their financial condition. Dun & Bradstreet and other research firms also enable entrepreneurs to look up profiles of competitors that can be helpful in a strategic analysis.
- Publicly held companies must file periodic reports with the Securities and Exchange Commission (SEC), including quarterly 10-Q and annual 10-K reports. These are available at the SEC's Web site.
- Check out the resources of your local library, including articles, computerized databases, and online searches. Press releases, which often announce important company news, can be an important source of competitive intelligence. Many companies supply press releases through the PR Newswire. For local competitors, review back issues of the area newspaper for articles on and advertisements by competitors.
- Use the vast resources of the World Wide Web to learn more about your competitors. The Web enables small companies to uncover valuable competitive information at little or no cost. (Refer to our Web site at www.prenhall.com/zimmerer for an extensive listing of more than 1,200 useful small business Web sites.)

■ Visit competing businesses periodically to observe their operations. Tom Stemberg, CEO of Staples, a chain of office supply superstores, says, "I've never visited a store where I didn't learn something."[31]

Using the information gathered, a business owner can set up teams of managers and employees to evaluate each competitor and make recommendations on specific strategic actions that will improve the firm's competitive position against each.

Entrepreneurs can use the results of their competitive intelligence efforts to construct a competitive profile matrix for their most important competitors. A **competitive profile matrix** allows owners to evaluate their firms against major competitors on the key success factors for that market segment. The first step is to list the key success factors identified in Step 5 of the strategic planning process (refer to Table 3.4) and to attach weights to them reflecting their relative importance. (For simplicity, the weights in this matrix add up to 1.00). In this example, notice that product quality is weighted twice as heavily (twice as important) as is price competitiveness.

The next step is to identify the company's major competitors and to rate each one (and your company) on each of the key success factors:

If factor is a:	Rating is:
Major weakness	1
Minor weakness	2
Minor strength	3
Major strength	4

Once the rating is completed, the owner simply multiplies the weight by the rating for each factor to get a weighted score and then adds up each competitor's weighted scores to get a total weighted score. Table 3.5 shows a sample competitive profile matrix for a small company. The results should show which company is strongest, which is weakest, and which of the key success factors each one is best and worst at meeting. By carefully studying and interpreting the results, entrepreneurs can begin to envision the ideal strategy for building a competitive edge in their market segments.

KNOWLEDGE MANAGEMENT.   Unfortunately, many small companies fail to gather competitive intelligence because their owners mistakenly assume that it is too costly or simply unnecessary. In reality, the cost of collecting information about competitors and the competitive environment typically is minimal, but it does require discipline. Thanks in large part to the Internet, "All companies, large and small, have virtually the same access to information," says competitive intelligence consultant Leonard Fuld.[32] Identifying and organizing the information a company possesses and then getting it efficiently to those who need it when they need it is the real challenge. In an age where knowledge is the primary source of a company's competitive edge, the key is learning how to *manage* the knowledge and information a company accumulates. A study by software firm Business Objects found that 90 percent of managers admit they make most of their decisions using instinct because they lack the right information when they need it![33]

Knowledge management is the practice of gathering, organizing, and disseminating the collective wisdom and experience of a company's employees for the purpose of strengthening its competitive position. "Knowledge management allows you to determine the explicit knowledge that is somewhere in your organization and that you can leverage rather than having to reinvent the wheel," says Dorothy Leonard-Barton, author of *Wellsprings of Knowledge*.[34] Business owners

> **competitive profile matrix**—*a tool that allows business owners to evaluate their company against major competitors on the key success factors for that market.*

> **knowledge management**—*the practice of gathering, organizing, and disseminating the collective wisdom and experience of a company's employees for the purpose of strengthening its competitive position.*

TABLE 3.5

Sample Competitive Profile Matrix

Key Success Factors	Your Business			Competitor I		Competitor 2	
			Weighted		Weighted		Weighted
(from Step 5)	Weight	Rating	Score	Rating	Score	Rating	Score
Market Share	0.10	3	0.30	2	0.20	3	0.30
Price Competitiveness	0.20	I	0.20	3	0.60	4	0.80
Financial Strength	0.10	2	0.20	3	0.30	2	0.20
Product Quality	0.40	4	1.60	2	0.80	I	0.40
Customer Loyalty	0.20	3	0.60	3	0.60	2	0.40
Total	**1.00**		**2.90**		**2.50**		**2.10**

who practice knowledge management realize that knowledge is power and that managing it can produce huge benefits. Because of their size and simplicity, small businesses have an advantage over large companies when it comes to managing employees' collective knowledge.

The first step in creating a knowledge management program is to take an inventory of the special knowledge a company possesses that gives it a competitive advantage. This involves assessing the knowledge bank that employees at all levels of the organization have compiled over time. The second step is to organize the essential knowledge and disseminate it throughout the company to those who need it. High-tech solutions such as e-mail, computerized databases, document sharing, and special knowledge management software that allows many different employees to work on a project simultaneously are important tools, but low-tech methods such as whiteboards, Post-it Notes, and face-to-face meetings can be just as effective in small companies. "To understand and respond to the kaleidoscopic patterns of new opportunities and potential dangers to its mission, an organization must mobilize the distributed intelligence of its members and listen to the collective knowledge of the whole," says one expert.[35]

A Company Example

*For Ben Farrell, owner of **Phase Two Strategies**, a San Francisco public relations firm, keeping up with news stories about clients and their industries is essential. Farrell and his staff used to spend many hours poring over stacks of magazines and newspapers to sift out the information they needed. Recently, however, Phase Two Strategies switched to Lexis-Nexis Tracker, an online news retrieval service that allows staffers to set up search criteria and then create a Web page with hyperlinks to relevant stories. The new system not only saves time and increases productivity, but it also allows Phase Two Strategies to serve its customers more effectively.[36]*

A Company Example

*Shari Franey, CEO of **Performance Personnel**, a staffing company with offices in six locations across Pennsylvania, also uses e-mail and voice-mail systems as part of her company's knowledge management program. These tools worked well, but Franey quickly saw their limitations and instituted a series of meetings designed exclusively to allow employees to share useful information with one another. The meetings disseminate vital information throughout the company and build a sense of camaraderie among employees.[37]*

Step 6. Create Company Goals and Objectives

Before entrepreneurs can build a comprehensive set of strategies, they must first establish business goals and objectives, which give them targets to aim for and provide a basis for evaluating their companies' performance. Without them, it is impossible to know where a business is going or how well it is performing. The following conversation between Alice and the Cheshire Cat, taken from Lewis Carroll's *Alice in Wonderland*, illustrates the importance of creating meaningful goals and objectives as part of the strategic management process:[38]

"Would you tell me please, which way I ought to go from here?" asked Alice.

"That depends a good deal on where you want to get to," said the Cat.

"I don't much care where . . . ," said Alice.

"Then it doesn't matter which way you go," said the Cat.

A small business that "doesn't much care where" it wants to go (i.e., one that has no goals and objectives) will find that "it really doesn't matter which way" it chooses to go (i.e., its strategy is irrelevant).

goals—*the broad, long-range attributes a business seeks to accomplish; they tend to be general and sometimes even abstract.*

GOALS. Goals are the broad, long-range attributes that a business seeks to accomplish; they tend to be general and sometimes even abstract. Goals are not intended to be specific enough for a manager to act on but simply state the general level of accomplishment sought. Do you want to boost your market share? Does your cash balance need strengthening? Would you like to enter a new market or increase sales in a current one? Do you want to develop new products or services? Researchers Jim Collins and Jerry Porras studied a large group of businesses and determined that one of the factors that set apart successful companies from unsuccessful ones was the formulation of very ambitious, clear, and inspiring long-term goals. Collins and Porras called them BHAGs ("Big Hairy Audacious Goals," pronounced "bee-hags") and say that their main benefit is to inspire and focus a company on important actions that are consistent with its overall mission.[39]

Addressing these broad issues will help you focus on the next phase—developing specific, realistic objectives.

OBJECTIVES. **Objectives** are more specific targets of performance than goals. Common objectives concern profitability, productivity, growth, efficiency, markets, financial resources, physical facilities, organizational structure, employee welfare, and social responsibility. Because some of these objectives might conflict with one another, it is important to establish priorities. Which objectives are most important? Which are least important? Arranging objectives in a hierarchy according to their priority can help an entrepreneur resolve conflicts when they arise. Well-written objectives have the following characteristics:

objectives—*more specific targets of performance, commonly addressing areas such as profitability, productivity, growth, and other key aspects of a business.*

They are specific. Objectives should be quantifiable and precise. For example, "to achieve a healthy growth in sales" is not a meaningful objective; however, "to increase retail sales by 12 percent and wholesale sales by 10 percent in the next fiscal year" is precise and spells out exactly what management wants to accomplish.

They are measurable. Managers should be able to plot the organization's progress toward its objectives; this requires a well-defined reference point from which to start and a scale for measuring progress.

They are assignable. Unless an entrepreneur assigns responsibility for an objective to an individual, it is unlikely that the company will ever achieve it. Creating objectives without giving someone responsibility for accomplishing it is futile.

They are realistic, yet challenging. Objectives must be within the reach of the organization or motivation will disappear. In any case, managerial expectations must remain high. In other words, the more challenging an objective is (within realistic limits), the higher the performance will be. Set objectives that will challenge you and your employees.

They are timely. Objectives must specify not only what is to be accomplished but also when it is to be accomplished. A time frame for achievement is important.

They are written down. This writing process does not have to be complex; in fact, the manager should make the number of objectives relatively small, from five to fifteen.

The strategic planning process works best when managers and employees are actively and jointly involved in setting objectives. Developing a plan is top management's responsibility, but executing it falls to managers and employees; therefore, encouraging them to participate broadens the plan's perspective and increases the motivation to make the plan work. In addition, managers and employees know a great deal about the organization and usually are willing to share this knowledge.

Step 7. Formulate Strategic Options and Select the Appropriate Strategies

By this point in the strategic management process, entrepreneurs should have a clear picture of what their businesses do best and what their competitive advantages are. They also should understand their firms' weaknesses and limitations as well as those of its competitors. The next step is to evaluate strategic options and then prepare a game plan designed to achieve the stated mission, goals, and objectives.

STRATEGY. A **strategy** is a road map of the actions an entrepreneur draws up to fulfill a company's mission, goals, and objectives. In other words, the mission, goals, and objectives spell out the ends, and the strategy defines the means for reaching them. A strategy is the master plan that covers all of the major parts of the organization and ties them together into a unified whole. The plan must be action oriented; it should breathe life into the entire planning process. An entrepreneur must build a sound strategy based on the preceding steps that uses the company's core competencies and strengths as the springboard to success. Joseph Picken and Gregory Dess, authors of *Mission Critical: The 7 Strategic Traps That Derail Even the Smartest Companies*, write, "A flawed strategy—no matter how brilliant the leadership, no matter how effective the implementation—is doomed to fail. A sound strategy, implemented without error, wins every time."[40]

Learning Objective

4. Discuss the characteristics of low-cost, differentiation, and focus strategies and know when to employ them.

strategy—*a road map of the actions an entrepreneur draws up to fulfill a company's mission, goals, and objectives.*

YOU Be the Consultant . . .

Snow and Soda: A Profitable Mix

The Crowleys truly are a family of entrepreneurs. Chris and Ralph Crowley manage the bottling plant their great-grandfather, Denis, purchased in 1916. Today a fourth-generation family business with $200 million in annual sales, Polar Beverages is the second-largest independent soft-drink bottler in the nation and the largest in the Northeast. Their younger siblings, David, Jeff, and Carolyn, operate a nearby ski resort, Wachusett Mountain, which they rescued from near bankruptcy in 1982. Since then, the younger Crowleys have transformed Wachusett Mountain into one of the most popular winter resorts in New England. What's surprising is how this generation of Crowleys learn from each other as they run what seem to be totally disparate and unrelated businesses and then apply their knowledge to their respective companies. It's a talent they learned from their late father. "A lot of what we do at the ski area is directly linked to our experience watching Dad run Polar," says David.

Although many ski resorts have struggled to survive in recent years (the number of resorts across the United States has dropped from 735 in 1982 to just 483 in 2003), Wachusett has earned a profit every year since the Crowleys bought it. The Crowleys generate an operating profit margin of about 35 percent, compared to the national average of 12 percent. This family of entrepreneurs has developed a strategy that works well for both businesses, and, surprisingly, many of the elements are common to both businesses. For instance, both the bottling plant and the ski resort share a common threat: unused capacity. In the bottling plant, one hour of downtime means that 72,000 bottles of soft drinks or water do not get bottled, a fact that is not lost on Chris and Ralph. However, the younger Crowleys recognize that unused capacity at their ski resort means lost revenue as well. To keep unused capacity to a minimum, they market the resort to specific target groups at different times of the day. In other words, the Crowleys do not see their target market as simply "skiers." David explains, "It's seniors, housewives, and third-shift factory workers from 9 A.M. to 2:30 P.M., teenage groups [from] 3 P.M. to 7 , and race clubs and families who like lower ticket prices [from] 7 P.M. to 10 P.M." On weekends, families and "night owls" are the primary customers. The result is that the resort is filled with customers almost every minute of its 14 hours of operation a day.

One of their most successful strategies has proved to be working with local schools to provide afternoon activities for children. They came up with the idea when they first took over Wachusett Mountain 20 years ago, and the program has been expanding ever since. On a typical afternoon when school is over, 65 yellow school buses pull up and deposit 2,500 teenagers ready to ski and have fun! Sales of burgers and fries skyrocket. Around 7 P.M., long after most ski resorts have closed, the teens have gone home, and a new crowd emerges: ski racers and singles. More than 800 adult racers belong to the Wachusett Racing League, and most of them are devoted skiers. The Crowleys recently began targeting corporate customers with the addition of Mountain Suite, luxury boxes with beautiful views and easy access to everything. A suite rents for $350 a day or $50,000 for the season. In their second year of operation, the suites generated enough revenue to cover the mortgage on the lodge expansion.

Another highly successful tactic stems from the Crowleys' clear understanding of their customers and also is aimed at minimizing unused capacity. The Century Pass allows skiers to use the slopes in off-peak hours at greatly reduced prices ($189 for a Century Pass versus $595 for an unlimited annual pass). Wachusett sells 15,000 Century Passes a year, and the steady stream of customers generates a handsome profit in food and beverage sales as well.

A few years ago in the Polar plant, Chris and Ralph noticed that the 20-liter jugs of bottled water they were producing left a lot of wasted space on their delivery trucks. So they redesigned the bottles—they are shaped like squat rectangles—and found immediate benefits. "They pack more efficiently, don't break as much, and cost $1.50 less each to make." Seeing a parallel in their ski operation, the younger Crowleys focused their attention on the "truck" they have to fill and empty as efficiently as possible: the rental shop, where 3,000 skiers and snowboarders arrive at 7:30 on weekend mornings. Skiers spend an average of 50 minutes in the typical rental shop, but Carolyn and Jeff have managed to cut that time to 10 minutes! "It's like the [bottling] plant," explains Carolyn. "You're watching bottles go through the manufacturing process and making sure none of them sit still too long." One technique that works for Wachusett is not allowing customers to try on ski boots; servers simply ask what size a customer wears and give them the appropriate pair. The resort stocks step-in snowboard bindings only to speed up that process as well.

On the surface, Polar Beverages and Wachusett Mountain do not appear to have much in common, but the family members who run both businesses see enough overlapping aspects to use the lessons learned in one operation to make the other more effective and efficient as well. While watching 1,200 cans a minute whir past as one of his machines fills cans of Polar Orange Dry Soda, Chris Crowley exclaims, "Look at all those skiers getting on chairlifts."

1. Explain the core competencies that Wachusett Mountain has built. What is the source of its core competencies?

2. Identify Wachusett Mountain's strengths, weaknesses, opportunities, and threats.

3. Explain how Wachusett Mountain uses knowledge management to build a competitive advantage. What other steps would you suggest the company take in this area?

Sources: Paul Hochman, "Crossing Over," *FSB*, December 2002/January 2003, pp. 71–73; Polar Beverages, www.polarbev.com; Wachusett Mountain, www.wachusett.com.

*Don Todrin and Fred Seibert, cofounders of **True Confections**, compete quite successfully in the $20 billion-a-year candy industry dominated by three giants, Nestlé, Hershey, and Mars. The small company succeeds by concentrating on a niche, selling entertainment-licensed candies mainly through novelty, gift, and fashion stores as well as on the Web. Their candy wrappers feature stars such as Scooby Doo, SpongeBob Squarepants, and characters from Austin Powers and The Lord of the Rings. "We're not really selling chocolate bars," says Todrin. "We're selling entertainment impulse items." True Confections is built on Todrin's background in the confectionery business and Seibert's experience at entertainment companies Hanna-Barbera, Nickelodeon, and MTV. The two entrepreneurs use their company's size to their advantage, quickly shifting their product line to include on their wrappers the latest "hot" characters.[41]*

A successful strategy is comprehensive and well integrated, focusing on establishing the key success factors that the manager identified in Step 4. For instance, if maximum shelf space is a key success factor for a small manufacturer's product, the strategy must identify techniques for gaining more in-store shelf space (e.g., offering higher margins to distributors and brokers than competitors do, assisting retailers with in-store displays, or redesigning a wider, more attractive package).

THREE STRATEGIC OPTIONS. Obviously, the number of strategies from which the small business owner can choose is infinite. When all the glitter is stripped away, however, three basic strategies remain. In his classic book, *Competitive Strategy*, Michael Porter defines these strategies: (1) cost leadership, (2) differentiation, and (3) focus (see Figure 3.2).[42]

COST LEADERSHIP. A company pursuing a **cost leadership strategy** strives to be the lowest-cost producer relative to its competitors in the industry. Low-cost leaders have a competitive advantage in reaching buyers whose primary purchase criterion is price, and they have the power to set the industry's price floor. This strategy works well when buyers are sensitive to price changes, when competing firms sell the same commodity products, and when companies can benefit from economies of scale. Not only is a low-cost leader in the best position to defend itself in a price war, but it also can use its power to attack competitors with the lowest price in the industry.

There are many ways to build a low-cost strategy, but the most successful cost leaders know where they have cost advantages over their competitors, and they use these as the foundation for their strategies. For instance, because it is not unionized, JetBlue Airlines has a significant advantage over its rivals in labor cost. Its labor cost is just 25 percent of revenues compared to 33 to 44 percent of revenues for its competitors, and the company uses this to deploy its fleet of planes more efficiently and more profitably than its competition.[43]

cost leadership strategy—*a strategy in which a company strives to be the low-cost producer relative to its competitors in the industry.*

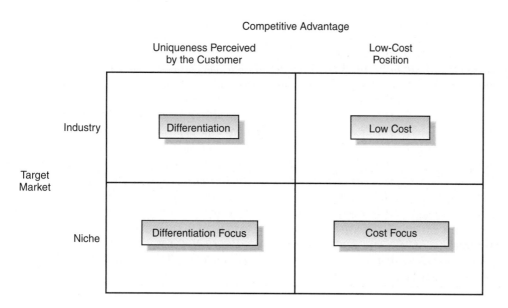

FIGURE 3.2 Three Strategic Options

American Champion Aircraft, a maker of small, lightweight, single-propeller airplanes that once was in bankruptcy, also has a significant cost advantage over its rivals, enabling it to sell its planes for as much as $100,000 less than comparable planes from competitors. In 1988, Jerry and Charlene Mehlhaff bought the company for its salvage value of just $400,000 and began rebuilding the company. They invested $1.7 million to modernize the production process, hired a crew of nonunion workers, and began making airplanes in 1991, earning a profit that first year. Because American Champion's nonunion workforce molds and manufactures 90 percent of its aircrafts' parts, the Mehlhaffs estimate that they save in costs at least $30,000 per plane! The primary components the company purchases from suppliers are the Textron Lycoming four-cylinder engine and propeller. Each aircraft is custom-made, and options such as sophisticated navigation electronics and vacuum-pump fuel systems can add as much as 50 percent to the base prices of $71,000 to $111,000, depending on the model. Still, an American Champion top-of-the-line airplane goes for about $150,000, which is $100,000 less than many comparable single-propeller aircraft sell for.[44]

Of course, there are dangers in following a cost leadership strategy. Sometimes a company focuses exclusively on lowering manufacturing costs, without considering the impact of purchasing, distribution, or overhead costs. Another danger is misunderstanding the firm's true cost drivers. For instance, one food processing plant drastically underestimated its overhead costs and, as a result, was selling its products at a loss. Finally, a firm may pursue a low-cost leadership strategy so zealously that it essentially locks itself out of other strategic choices.

Under the right conditions, a cost-leadership strategy executed properly can be an incredibly powerful strategic weapon. Small discount retailers that live in the shadows of Wal-Mart and thrive even when the economy slows succeed by relentlessly pursuing low-cost strategies. Small chains such as Fred's, Dollar General, Family Dollar, and 99 Cents Only cater to low- and middle-income customers who live in inner cities or rural areas. They offer inexpensive products such as food, health and beauty products, cleaning supplies, clothing, and seasonal merchandise, and many of the items they stock are closeout buys (purchases made as low as 10 cents on the dollar) on brand-name merchandise. These companies also strive to keep their overhead costs as low as possible. For instance, 99 Cents Only, whose name describes its merchandising strategy, is housed in a no-frills warehouse in an older section of City of Commerce, California.[45] The success of these stores proves that companies pursuing a cost leadership strategy must emphasize cost containment in *every* decision, from where to locate the company headquarters to which items to stock.

differentiation strategy—*a strategy in which a company seeks to build customer loyalty by positioning its goods or services in a unique or different fashion.*

DIFFERENTIATION. A company following a **differentiation strategy** seeks to build customer loyalty by positioning its goods or services in a unique or different fashion. That, in turn, enables the business to command a higher price for its products or services than competitors. There are many ways to create a differentiation strategy, but the key is to be special at something that is important to the customer. In other words, a business strives to be better than its competitors at something customers value.

*Although it sells a wide variety of clothing, **It's A Wrap! Production Wardrobe Sales** is not the typical clothing store. The Burbank, California–based company sells wardrobe in volume from the sets of film, television shows, commercials, and the fashion runway. Jan Hallman Dion, a former movie studio employee, came up with her business idea in 1981 after she coordinated an auction to sell wardrobe, props, and equipment from several of the studio's recent movies. She opened a small store in Studio City that sold movie clothes to eager customers who wanted to wear what the stars had worn! It's A Wrap! has experienced significant growth over the years and has expanded into larger quarters twice, now occupying a location with 10,000 square feet of showroom space. The company's location is perfect for implementing Dion's differentiation strategy because Burbank is home to dozens of movie and television studios. It's A Wrap! is literally in the backyards of its suppliers! Dion's company makes the studios' job of disposing of thousands of items much easier, providing valuable services such as instant pickup, computerized inventory control, and private sales. The store's inventory changes daily, depending on which items television or movie studios are selling. Garments come from every kind of show or movie imaginable—from sitcoms and soap operas to war movies and westerns—and every one comes with a certificate of authenticity verifying its origin. It's A Wrap! has been featured in several magazines and on many television shows, including* The Oprah Winfrey Show *and* CNN's Financial Report.[46]

If a small company can improve a product's (or service's) performance, reduce the customer's cost and risk of purchasing it, or both, it has the potential to differentiate. To be successful, a business must make its product or service truly different, at least in the eyes of its customers.

Entrepreneur Yngve Bergqvist has no trouble setting his hotel in Jukkasjärvi, Sweden, apart from others. Located 125 miles above the Arctic Circle, the aptly named **Ice Hotel** *offers travelers a unique experience.* Everything *in the hotel—walls, beds, night tables, chairs, cinema, bars—is made from 30,000 tons of snow and 10,000 tons of crystal-clear ice harvested from the Torne River! Each of the 60 rooms is unique, designed by a different artist from around the world. Guests sleep in insulated sleeping bags on ice beds covered with thin mattresses and plenty of reindeer blankets. Because temperatures inside the hotel typically hover at 5 degrees below zero (centigrade), guests cannot take their luggage to their ice rooms; it will freeze! Amenities include an ice bar, an ice chapel, an ice cinema, and an ice art exhibition. The 30,000-square-foot Ice Hotel is open from December through April (it melts in the spring), but during its brief existence, it will accommodate some 5,000 guests at rates ranging from $200 to $500 per night. Countless rock groups, including Van Halen, have shot music videos at the Ice Hotel. It's not about comfort," says co-owner Arne Bergh. "It's a journey, an adventure."* [47]

Although few businesses are innately as unique as the Ice Hotel, the goal for a company pursuing a differentiation strategy is to create that kind of uniqueness in the minds of its customers. The key to a successful differentiation strategy is to build it on core competencies, those a small company is uniquely good at doing in comparison to its competitors. Common bases for differentiation include superior customer service, special product features, complete product lines, instantaneous parts availability, absolute product reliability, supreme product quality, and extensive product knowledge. To be successful, a differentiation strategy must create the perception of value in the customer's eyes. No customer will purchase a good or service that fails to produce its perceived value, no matter how real that value may be. One business consultant advises, "Make sure you tell your customers and prospects what it is about your business that makes you different. Make sure that difference is in the form of a true benefit to the customer." [48]

There are risks in pursuing a differentiation strategy. One danger is trying to differentiate a product or service on the basis of something that does not boost its performance or lower its cost to customers. Business owners also must consider how long they can sustain a product's or service's differentiation; changing customer tastes make the basis for differentiation temporary at best. Imitations and "knockoffs" from competitors also pose a threat to a successful differentiation

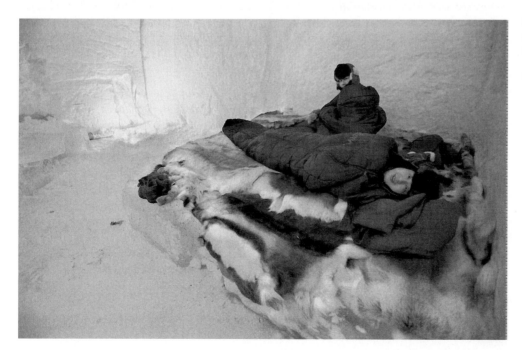

Guests at the Ice Hotel pay up to $500 a night to bundle up and sleep in an ice bed covered with reindeer blankets.

Courtesy of AP/Wide World Photos.

strategy. For instance, entrepreneurs have built an ice hotel in Finland to compete with the original ice hotel in Sweden. Designers of high-priced original clothing see much cheaper knockoff products on the market shortly after their designs hit the market. Another pitfall is overdifferentiating and charging so much that the company prices its products out of the market. The final risk is focusing only on the physical characteristics of a product or service and ignoring important psychological factors such as status, prestige, and image, which can be powerful sources of differentiation.

focus strategy—*a strategy in which a company selects one or more market segments, identifies customers' special needs, wants, and interests, and approaches them with a good or service designed to excel in meeting those needs, wants, and interests.*

FOCUS. A **focus strategy** recognizes that not all markets are homogeneous. In fact, in any given market, there are many different customer segments, each having different needs, wants, and characteristics. The principal idea of this strategy is to select one (or more) segment(s), identify customers' special needs, wants, and interests, and approach them with a good or service designed to excel in meeting these needs, wants, and interests. Focus strategies build on *differences* among market segments.

A successful focus strategy depends on a small company's ability to identify the changing needs of its targeted customer group and to develop the skills required to serve them. That means an entrepreneur and everyone in the organization must have a clear understanding of how to add value to the product or service for the customer. How does the product or service meet the customer's needs at each stage—from raw material to final sale?

Rather than attempting to serve the total market, the focusing firm specializes in serving a specific target segment or niche. A focus strategy is ideally suited to many small businesses, which often lack the resources to reach the overall market. Their goal is to serve their narrow target markets more effectively and efficiently than do competitors that pound away at the broad market. Common bases for building a focus strategy include zeroing in on a small geographic area, targeting a group of customers with similar needs or interests (e.g., left-handed people), specializing in a specific product or service (e.g., Batteries Plus, a store that sells and services every kind of battery imaginable), or selling specialized knowledge (e.g., restoring valuable and priceless works of art).

A Company Example

*After taking over the painting business his father had started in 1947, Paul Thomarios had transformed the company into the dominant force in the Akron, Ohio, market. Thomarios discovered the foundation of a profitable niche strategy in 1996 when he landed a contract to restore and paint a Saturn V rocket from the Apollo Space Program for the National Aeronautic Space Agency's (NASA) John F. Kennedy Space Center. Today, the **Apostolos Group** generates 25 percent of its $15 million in sales by restoring and repainting "the tons of old rockets out there," says Thomarios. In addition to NASA, the company's customers include the Detroit Science Center and the U.S. Space and Rocket Center in Huntsville, Alabama.*[47]

The most successful focusers build a competitive edge by concentrating on specific market niches and serving them better than any other competitor can. Essentially, this strategy depends on creating value for the customer either by being the lowest-cost producer or by differentiating the product or service in a unique fashion but doing it in a narrow target segment. To be worth targeting, a niche must be large enough to be profitable, reasonably reachable through advertising media, and capable of sustaining a business over time (i.e., not a passing fad).

A Company Example

*Dan Panoz, founder of **Panoz Auto Development**, is implementing a focus strategy in an industry dominated by global giants where many entrepreneurs before him have flamed out: the auto industry. Like Preston Tucker (whose company lasted from 1946 to 1948), Henry Kaizer (1946–1958), and John DeLorean (1981–1983), Panoz is building his business in a niche: hand-built sports cars. The challenges are formidable, and the capital requirements are high, even for a niche player. At the world's least automated auto assembly line, each Panoz Esperante requires 200 hours to assemble, about 10 times longer than it takes Toyota to build a Camry. Panoz has done a masterful job of taking stock components (mostly from the Ford SVT Mustang Cobra) and transforming them into a high-performance car that one auto magazine called "the world's best engineered, best-built, low-volume car." Priced at $80,000, Panoz is aiming the Esperante directly at men in their forties and fifties who earn annual incomes of more than $150,000 and are auto enthusiasts. The typical*

Dan Panoz, whose company relies on a focus strategy, inspect a high-performance Panoz Esperante.

Courtesy of AP/Wide World Photos.

customer owns two or three other cars, and many travel to the factory near Atlanta to pick out special leather and wood trim and to watch their cars being built. Panoz is shooting for a target of producing 30 cars a month, and his calculations show that once he sells 200 cars, he can begin to earn a profit. Once he works the kinks out of the assembly process, Panoz plans to introduce model variations, such as a hardtop Esperante, to reach his ultimate goal of selling 1,000 cars a year.[50]

As Panoz's venture suggests, pursuing a focus strategy is not without risks. Companies sometimes must struggle to capture a large enough share of a small market to be profitable. If a small company is successful in a niche, there is also the danger of larger competitors entering the market and eroding it. Panoz's constant struggle to keep costs down is typical; the small volume of business that some niches support can raise production costs, making a company vulnerable to lower-cost competitors as their prices spiral upward. Sometimes a company with a successful niche strategy gets distracted by its success and tries to branch out into other areas. As it drifts farther away from its core strategy, it loses its competitive edge and runs the risk of confusing or alienating its customers.

Victoria's Secret, the mail-order company once known for its niche in lingerie, runs the risk of losing its appeal to its traditional customers as the business has strayed from its roots. In addition to its wide selection of lingerie, Victoria's Secret sells wedding gowns, jeans and casual wear, shoes, and career clothing. Muddying its image with customers puts a company in danger of losing its identity.

An effective strategic plan identifies a complete set of success factors—financial, operating, and marketing—that, taken together, produce a competitive advantage for a small company. The resulting action plan distinguishes a business from its competitors by exploiting its competitive advantage. The focal point of this entire strategic plan is the customer. The customer is the nucleus of the business, and a competitive strategy will succeed only if it is aimed at serving target customers better than the competition does. An effective strategy draws out the competitive advantage in a small company by building on its strengths and by making the customer its focus. It also designates methods for overcoming a firm's weaknesses, and it identifies opportunities and threats that demand action.

STRATEGY IN ACTION.   The strategies a small business selects depend on its competitive advantages in the market segments in which it competes. In some cases, the business will implement multiple strategies across several segments. When a business has a well-defined strategic advantage, it may pursue highly aggressive growth strategies in an attempt to increase its market share. This is especially true when a business achieves a "first-mover" advantage in a market with little direct competition. By being the first in the market, it establishes name recognition and a loyal customer base. Starbucks Coffee continues to reap the benefits of being the first company to establish a chain of upscale retail coffeehouses in major markets after Howard Shultz traveled to Milan, Italy, and noticed the tremendous popularity of espresso bars. A year later, in 1984, Schultz launched his coffee bar concept as a test in Seattle, Washington. Today, the chain has nearly 6,000 locations around the globe! Aggressive strategies sometimes can backfire if larger competitors decide to fight back. In many cases, the old adage of being the "big frog in a small pond" allows a small business to earn a handsome profit in a market niche without attracting the attention of larger competitors.

Small companies must develop strategies that exploit all of the competitive advantages of their size by:

■ Responding quickly to customers' needs.

■ Remaining flexible and willing to change.

■ Constantly searching for new, emerging market segments.

■ Building and defending market niches.

■ Erecting "switching costs," the costs a customer incurs by switching to a competitor's product or service, through personal service and loyalty.

■ Remaining entrepreneurial and willing to take risks and act with lightning speed.

■ Constantly innovating.

Step 8. Translate Strategic Plans into Action Plans

No strategic plan is complete until it is put into action. Entrepreneurs must convert strategic plans into operating plans that guide their companies on a daily basis and become a visible, active part of the business. No small business can benefit from a strategic plan sitting on a shelf collecting dust.

YOU Be the Consultant . . .

One-of-a-Kind Chip Maker

Mark and Stacy Andrus, cofounders of Stacy's Pita Chip Company, have become experts at keeping costs low in their small Randolph, Massachusetts–based company that makes crispy, low-fat chips from pita bread. Housed in an old brick warehouse, the only exterior "sign" identifying the company is a sheet of paper taped to the door. The interior is spotless but contains no frills; the approach is strictly utilitarian. The Andruses' office is decorated in the style of late college or perhaps early yard sale. Stacy's office chair is a castoff from her aunt's old dining room set. The company's location speaks volumes about its founders' philosophy: Make every penny count. Even their salaries are "scavenger-level," says Stacy. "*Everything* goes into the business."

Leaving behind their careers as a psychologist (Mark) and a social worker (Stacy), the couple decided to get into the pita chip–making business. Both self-confessed "foodies," the Andruses worked in restaurants during their college years in California. There they learned that they loved the food business but that they did not want to work for someone else. When they returned to New England, they developed a plan to open a bistro offering the fresh California-style food they knew and enjoyed. Debt from college, however, altered their plans. They started with a pushcart from which they sold hot dogs, sausages, and chili at local festivals and events. Soon they took their cart to Boston's financial district and changed their menu to "Stacy's D'Lites," handmade pita-wrapped sandwiches. Their cart-based menu was perfect for their target customers; during the two-hour lunch rush, the Andruses typically sold 200 wraps, and the line of waiting customers would stretch to 30 or 40 people! "Invariably," says Mark, "the last people in line would trickle away, so we wanted to do something to get them to wait."

What they did was recycle each day's leftover pita bread. Every night, Mark would take the leftover bread, coat it with cinnamon, sugar, or garlic and Parmesan, cut it into wedges, and bake it. Customers loved the chips! In 1996, the Andruses made a decision to stop making sandwiches and focus instead on making pita chips. Their goal was to mass-produce them and sell them nationwide. In keeping with their low-cost philosophy, the Andruses took a low-budget approach, renting space at the Boston Pretzel Bakery and using the bakery's equipment in the off-hours. They cut, bagged, and labeled their chips by hand! The one thing they refused to scrimp on, however, were the ingredients. Because their maximum production rate was just seven cases of chips per 10-hour day, the Andrus's first-year sales were just $25,000. As sales grew steadily, they began investing in automated equipment and moved into the space the company occupies today. They cleaned, stripped, repaired, and painted the entire 10,000-square-foot facility themselves. (David built his "cubicle" from plywood salvaged from a shipping crate from a packaging machine!) The second year of operation produced sales of $450,000.

The Andruses needed capital to expand, but without an extensive track record, they knew they had to prepare a stellar business plan. With Stacy as the majority owner, Stacy's Pita Chip Company qualified for a special Small Business Administration guaranteed loan to assist women entrepreneurs through BankBoston, where many of their former sandwich-cart customers worked. They qualified for $360,000 in loans. "I had a good, solid business plan," says Stacy, "and we had the demand." Her plan included a letter from an airline executive stating that his company would purchase 1 million bags of Stacy's pita chips if the company could turn them out.

As sales continued to climb, the Andruses began looking for more automated equipment to help them increase their production levels. They could not find the automated slicer they needed, and having one custom-built would cost them at least $100,000, which they could not afford. After searching for a year, they finally found a used carrot-cutting machine that the Campbell Soup Company had used for 40 years! The price was a much more affordable $18,000. Mark modified the antique, and it is still in use today. When the Andruses needed an oven with a conveyor belt and adjustable temperature, velocity, and airflow controls, they could not find a used one, nor could they afford the $160,000 a new one would cost. Their solution: They struck a deal with an oven company to build two ovens for $80,000; they purchased one, and the oven maker kept the other to use as a prototype to boost its sales. As sales climbed, they bought a second oven from a bankrupt baker for just $13,000, charging the purchase to a credit card because no bank would lend them the money! "Now we can do 700 cases a day," says Mark.

The Andruses spend very little on advertising, instead relying on the methods they used when they sold food from a pushcart. They make personal appearances at trade shows, cooking demonstrations, public appearances, and grocery stores across the nation, giving out free samples to passersby.

Despite the intense workload they face and the constant challenges of running a business, the Andruses know they made the right choice when they started Stacy's Pita Chip Company. "When we talked about starting our own business, we thought, if we don't do it now, we're going to someday look back and think, "we wish we had," says Mark. "The only regrets you have are for the things you don't try," adds Stacy.

1. Which of the three basic strategies described in this chapter are Mark and Stacy Andrus using? Explain. How effective is it?

2. When it comes to implementing their strategy, how do the Andruses use their size to their advantage? How would you rate the level of creativity they exhibit in managing their business?

3. What suggestions would you offer the Andruses to improve the company's future?

Sources: Anne Stuart, "The Pita Principle," *Inc.*, August 2001, pp. 58–64; Stacy's Pita Chip Company, www.pitachips.com.

IMPLEMENT THE STRATEGY. To make the plan workable, the business owner should divide the plan into projects, carefully defining each one by the following:

Purpose. What is the project designed to accomplish?

Scope. Which areas of the company will be involved in the project?

Contribution. How does the project relate to other projects and to the overall strategic plan?

Resource requirements. What human and financial resources are needed to complete the project successfully?

Timing. Which schedules and deadlines will ensure project completion?

Once entrepreneurs assign priorities to projects, they can begin to implement the strategic plan.

Involving employees and delegating adequate authority to them is essential since these projects affect them most directly. If an organization's people have been involved in the strategic management process to this point, they will have a better grasp of the steps they must take to achieve the organization's goals as well as their own professional goals. Early involvement of the workforce in the strategic management process is a luxury that larger businesses cannot achieve. Commitment to reaching the company's objectives is a powerful force, but involvement is a prerequisite for achieving total employee commitment. Without a team of committed, dedicated employees, a company's strategy usually fails.

Step 9. Establish Accurate Controls.

So far, the planning process has created company objectives and has developed a strategy for reaching them, but rarely, if ever, will the company's actual performance match stated objectives. Entrepreneurs quickly realize the need to control actual results that deviate from plans.

Learning Objective

5. Understand the importance of controls such as the balanced scorecard in the planning process.

CONTROLLING THE STRATEGY. Planning without control has little operational value; therefore, a sound planning program requires a practical control process. The plans created in the strategic planning process become the standards against which actual performance is measured. It is important for everyone in the organization to understand—and to be involved in—the planning and controlling process.

Controlling projects and keeping them on schedule means that an entrepreneur must identify and track key performance indicators. The source of these indicators is the operating data from the company's normal business activity; they are the guideposts for detecting deviations from established standards. Accounting, production, sales, inventory, quality, customer service and satisfaction, and other operating records are primary sources of data that managers can use to control activities. For example, on a customer service project, performance indicators might include the number of customer complaints, the number of orders returned, the percentage of on-time shipments, and a measure of order accuracy.

To judge the effectiveness of their strategies, many companies are developing **balanced scorecards**, a set of measurements unique to a company that includes both financial and operational measures and gives managers a quick yet comprehensive picture of the company's overall performance. One writer says that a balanced scorecard:

balanced scorecard—*a set of measurements unique to a company that includes both financial and operational measures and gives a quick yet comprehensive picture of the company's overall performance.*

> is a sophisticated business model that helps a company understand what's really driving its success. It acts a bit like the control panel on a spaceship—the business equivalent of a flight speedometer, odometer, and temperature gauge all rolled into one. It keeps track of many things, including financial progress and softer measurements—everything from customer satisfaction to return on investment—that need to be managed to reach the final destination: profitable growth.[51]

Rather than sticking solely to the traditional financial measures of a company's performance, the balanced scorecard gives managers a comprehensive view from *both* a financial and an operational perspective. The premise behind such a scorecard is that relying on any single measure of company performance is dangerous. Just as a pilot in command of a jet cannot fly safely by focusing on a single instrument, an entrepreneur cannot manage a company by concentrating on a single measurement. The complexity of managing a business demands that an entrepreneur be able to see performance measures in several areas simultaneously. "Knowing whether an enterprise is viable or not doesn't mean looking at just the bottom line," says one manager.[52] Scorecards that combine relevant results from all aspects of the operation allow everyone in the organization to see how their job performance connects to a company's mission, goals, and objectives.

When creating a balanced scorecard for their companies, entrepreneurs should establish goals for each critical indicator of company performance and then create meaningful measures for each one.

*For example, Court Coursey, founder of **Certifiedmail.com**, a company that delivers certified mail electronically, has developed a scorecard that encompasses measures on everything from financial performance to employee satisfaction. Every quarter, Coursey presents Certifiedmail.com's one-page scorecard to his 10 employees for review. "It's a good way to get a grasp of the company and how it's performing," he says. The scorecard gives Coursey important feedback that allows him to adjust his management style and the company's direction when necessary. The scorecard already has improved Certifiedmail.com's performance. One of Coursey's top priorities is cost control, and the scorecard recently pointed out a wasteful practice that he halted. "[The scorecard] showed me a way to save money," he says. "And it was something I may not have seen without this feedback."*[53]

Ideally, a balanced scorecard looks at a business from four important perspectives (see Figure 3.3):[54]

Customer Perspective: How do customers see us? Customers judge companies by at least four standards: time (how long it takes the company to deliver a good or service), quality (how well a company's product or service performs in terms of reliability, durability, and accuracy), performance (the extent to which a good or service performs as expected), and service (how well a company meets or exceeds customers' expectations of value). Because customer-related goals are external, managers must translate them into measures of what the company must do to meet customers' expectations.

Internal Business Perspective: At what must we excel? The internal factors that managers should focus on are those that have the greatest impact on customer satisfaction and retention and on company effectiveness and efficiency. Developing goals and measures for factors such as quality, cycle time, productivity, costs, and others that employees directly influence is essential.

FIGURE 3.3 The Balanced Scorecard Links Performance Measures

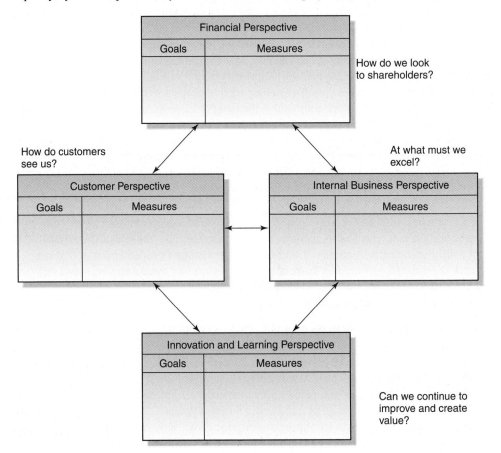

Innovation and Learning Perspective: Can we continue to improve and create value? This view of a company recognizes that the targets required for success are never static; they are constantly changing. If a company wants to continue its pattern of success, it cannot stand still; it must continuously improve. A company's ability to innovate, learn, and improve determines its future. These goals and measures emphasize the importance of continuous improvement in customer satisfaction and internal business operations.

Financial Perspective: How do we look to shareholders? As the most traditional performance measures, financial standards tell how much the company's overall strategy and its execution are contributing to its bottom line. These measures focus on such factors as profitability, growth, and shareholder value. On balanced scorecards, companies often break their financial goals into three categories: survival, success, and growth.

Although the balanced scorecard is a vital tool that helps managers keep their companies on track, it is also an important tool for changing behavior in an organization and for keeping everyone focused on what really matters. As conditions change, managers must make corrections in performances, policies, strategies, and objectives to get performance back on track. A practical control system is also economical to operate. Most small businesses have no need for a sophisticated, expensive control system. The system should be so practical that it becomes a natural part of the management process.

CONCLUSION

The strategic planning process does *not* end with the nine steps outlined here; it is an ongoing procedure that entrepreneurs must repeat. With each round, managers and employees gain experience, and the steps become much easier. The planning process outlined here is designed to be as simple as possible. No small business should be burdened with an elaborate, detailed formal planning process that it cannot easily use. Such processes require excessive amounts of time to operate, and they generate a sea of paperwork. Entrepreneurs need neither.

What does this strategic planning process lead to? It teaches business owners a degree of discipline that is important to business survival. It helps them learn about their businesses, their core competencies, their competitors, and, most important, their customers. Although strategic planning cannot guarantee success, it does dramatically increase a small firm's chances of survival in a hostile business environment.

CHAPTER SUMMARY

1. Understand the importance of strategic management to a small business.

Because they are affected by the forces of a rapidly changing competitive environment, small businesses need the guidance that strategic management can provide. Strategic management enables a company to set itself apart from the competition.

2. Explain why and how a small business must create a competitive advantage in the market.

The goal of developing a strategic plan is to create for the small company a unique image in the minds of its potential customers. A company builds a competitive edge on its core competencies, which are a unique set of capabilities that a company develops in key operational areas, such as quality, service, innovation, team building, flexibility, responsiveness, and others that allow it to vault past competitors. They are what the company does best and are the focal point of the

strategy. This step must identify target market segments and determine how to position the firm in those markets. Entrepreneurs must identify some way to differentiate their companies from competitors.

3. Develop a strategic plan for a business using the nine steps in the strategic planning process.

Small businesses need a strategic planning process designed to suit their particular needs.

Step 1. Develop a clear vision and translate it into a meaningful mission statement.

Step 2. Assess the company's strengths and weaknesses. Strengths are positive internal factors; weaknesses are negative internal factors.

Step 3. Scan the environment for significant opportunities and threats facing the business. Opportunities are positive external options; threats are negative external forces.

Step 4. Identify the key factors for success in the business. In every business, key factors determine the success of the firms in it, and so they must be an integral part of a company's strategy. Key success factors are relationships between a controllable variable and a critical factor influencing the firm's ability to compete in the market.

Step 5. Analyze the competition. Business owners should know their competitors almost as well as they know their own business. A competitive profile matrix is a helpful tool for analyzing competitors' strengths and weaknesses.

Step 6. Create company goals and objectives. Goals are the broad, long-range attributes that the firm seeks to accomplish. Objectives are quantifiable and more precise; they should be specific, measurable, assignable, realistic, timely, and written down. The process works best when managers and employees are actively involved.

Step 7. Formulate strategic options and select the appropriate strategies. A strategy is the game plan the firm plans to use to achieve its objectives and mission. It must center on establishing for the firm the key success factors identified earlier.

Step 8. Translate strategic plans into action plans. No strategic plan is complete until the owner puts it into action.

Step 9. Establish accurate controls. Actual performance rarely, if ever, matches plans exactly. Operating data from the business assembled into a comprehensive scorecard serve as an important guidepost for determining how effective a company's strategy is. This information is especially helpful when plotting future strategies.

The strategic planning process does not end with these nine steps; rather, it is an ongoing process that an entrepreneur will repeat.

4. Discuss the characteristics of low-cost, differentiation, and focus strategies and know when to employ them.

Three basic strategic options are cost leadership, differentiation, and focus. A company pursuing a cost leadership strategy strives to be the lowest-cost producer relative to its competitors in the industry. A company following a differentiation strategy seeks to build customer loyalty by positioning its goods or services in a unique or different fashion. In other words, the firm strives to be better than its competitors at something that customers value. A focus strategy recognizes that not all markets are homogeneous. The principal idea of this strategy is to select one (or more) segment(s), identify customers' special needs, wants, and interests, and approach them with a good or service designed to excel in meeting these needs, wants, and interests. Focus strategies build on *differences* among market segments.

5. Understand the importance of controls such as the balanced scorecard in the planning process.

Just as a pilot in command of a jet cannot fly safely by focusing on a single instrument, an entrepreneur cannot manage a company by concentrating on a single measurement. A balanced scorecard is a set of measures unique to a company that includes both financial and operational measures and gives managers a quick yet comprehensive picture of the company's total performance.

DISCUSSION QUESTIONS

1. Why is strategic planning important to a small company?

2. What is a competitive advantage? Why is it important for a small business to establish one?

3. What are the steps in the strategic management process?

4. "Our customers don't just like our ice cream," write Ben Cohen and Jerry Greenfield, cofounders of Ben and Jerry's Homemade, Inc. "They like what our company stands for. They like how doing business with us makes them feel." What do they mean?

5. What are strengths, weaknesses, opportunities, and threats? Give an example of each.

6. Explain the characteristics of effective objectives. Why is setting objectives important?

7. What are business strategies?

8. Describe the three basic strategies available to small companies. Under what conditions is each most successful?

9. Explain how a company can gain a competitive advantage using each of the three strategies described in this chapter: cost leadership, differentiation, and focus. Give an example of a company that is using each strategy.

10. How is the controlling process related to the planning process?

11. What is a balanced scorecard? What value does it offer entrepreneurs who are evaluating the success of their current strategies?

THE BUSINESS DISC

Launch *The Business Disc*. From the menu across the top of your screen, select the "Reference" option and then click on "General Information." Here you will find several reference guides that offer useful information to entrepreneurs. Click on "Strategic Planning for the Growing Business" and review the concepts in this reference guide and in Chapter 2. Write down your company's mission statement. Next, identify the primary strengths and weaknesses your business can rely on. Develop a list of the top two or three opportunities and threats your start-up business faces. Now, establish meaningful goals and objectives for your business start-up. (Be sure to select a reasonable time frame; six months to one year is probably best.) Finally, describe the strategy you plan to use to develop a competitive edge for your business. How will you set your company apart while attracting and retaining customers?

BUSINESS PLAN PRO

Business PlanPro

As you study the concepts of organizational objectives, mission, and the key success factor for a business, go to the "Concept Kick-Off" section of *Business Plan Pro* and begin work on each sub-section.

Objectives Drawing upon the criteria in Chapter 3 which defines objectives, list the three or four most critical objectives your business must achieve to be viable.

Mission In this section enter the mission statement for your business. In most cases it will take a half-dozen re-writes of the mission statement before it states exactly what you want it to say. Our suggestion is to then ask four or five acquaintances to read the mission statement and tell you what they think you have said.

Keys to Success In step four of the strategic planning process you were asked to identify the key success factor(s) for a business. Applying that material to your proposed venture, enter your key success factor(s).

Other key aspects about your business that relate to this chapter can be inserted in sub-sections such as "Company Summary" and "What You Are Selling." This material will not complete the sections but will allow you to capture your thoughts while they are fresh in your mind.

1. Contact the owner of a small business that competes directly with an industry giant (such as Home Depot, Wal-Mart, Barnes & Noble, or others). What does the owner see as his or her competitive advantage? How does the business communicate this advantage to its customers? What competitive strategy is the owner using? How successful is it? What changes would you suggest the owner make?

2. In his book, *The HP Way*, Dave Packard, cofounder of Hewlett-Packard, describes the seven commitments of the HP Way:

    ■ Profit—the ultimate source of corporate strength.

    ■ Customers—constant improvement in the value of the products and services the company offers them.

    ■ Field of interest—seeking new opportunities but limiting them to complementary products and services based on company core competences.

    ■ Growth—a measure of strength and a requirement for survival.

    ■ Employees—provide opportunities for advancement, share in their success, and offer job security based on performance.

    ■ Organization—foster individual motivation, initiative, and creativity by giving employees the freedom to work toward established goals and objectives.

    ■ Citizenship—contribute in a positive way toward the community and society at large.

    In what ways do these values help HP define its vision? Its competitive edge? How important is it for entrepreneurs to define a system of values to guide their companies?

3. Contact a local entrepreneur and help him or her devise a balanced scorecard for his or her company. What goals did you and the owner establish in each of the four perspectives? What measures did you use to judge progress toward those goals?

4. Use the strategic tools provided in this chapter to help a local small business owner discover his or her firm's strengths, weaknesses, opportunities, and threats; identify the relevant key success factors; and analyze its competitors. Help the owner devise a strategy for success for his or her business.

5. Choose an entrepreneur in your community and interview him or her. Does the company have a strategic plan? A mission statement? Why or why not? What does the owner consider the company's strengths and weaknesses to be? What opportunities and threats does the owner perceive? What image is the owner trying to create for the business? Has the effort been successful? (Do you agree?) Which of the generic competitive strategies is the company following? Who are the company's primary competitors? How does the owner rate his or her chances for success in the future (use a low (1) to high (10) scale). When you have completed the interview, use the following evaluation questionnaire to rate the company's strategic orientation. Compare your evaluation with other classmates. What, if any, generalizations can you draw from the interview?

Is the Owner Managing the Business Strategically?

Rate your present managerial actions on each of the following questions:

1. In the past two years have you written or reviewed your firm's mission statement?

    Yes (10 pts.)

    No (0 pts.)   Q.1. _____

2. Are you confident that your employees are aware of the key underlying values that drive the business?

   Absolutely (10 pts.)

   Generally (7 pts.)

   Not sure (3 pts.)

   I have never shared with them my values (0 pts.)   Q.2. _____

3. Does each manager have a clear set of performance objectives for his area of responsibility?

   Yes (10 pts.)

   Some do (5 pts.)

   No (0 pts.)   Q.3. _____

4. Do you regularly meet with your key managers and employees to discuss the behaviors of your competitors?

   Regularly and often (10 pts.)

   Informally, but not a scheduled event (5 pts.)

   Never have done so (0 pts.)   Q.4. _____

5. Would your employees be able to accurately describe the strategies your firm is attempting to employ?

   Definitely (10 pts.)

   Most of them (5 pts.)

   The firm's strategies have never been explained to them (0 pts.)   Q.5. _____

6. Do all employees understand that through the achievement of success for the organization they enhance the opportunity for achieving their own personal goals?

   Definitely (10 pts.)

   Most do (7 pts.)

   A few do (4 pts.)

   It has never been explained to them (0 pts.)   Q.6. _____

7. Do you annually conduct an environmental scanning exercise with your managers in an attempt to identify future opportunities for the firm?

   Yes (10 pts.)

   Informally (5 pts.)

   No (0 pts.)   Q.7. _____

8. Can all of your managers explain the impact of their performance, and that of their staff, on the performance of the total organization?

   Absolutely (10 pts.)

   Generally (7 pts.)

   Not sure (3 pts.)

   No (0 pts.)   Q.8. _____

9. Has your business been moving in a clear and positive direction over the past three years?

Definitely (10 pts.)

Generally (7 pts.)

Not sure (3 pts.)

No (0 pts.)   Q.9. _____

10. Do you and your key managers think and behave strategically?

Always (10 pts.)

Generally (7 pts.)

Not sure (3 pts.)

Seldom (0 pts.)   Q.10. _____

Total points _____

Maximum Score 100

Minimum Score 0

Grading Your Firm:

A+ 95–100 pts.

A 90–94 pts.

B+ 85–89 pts.

B 80–84 pts.

C+ 75–79 pts.

C 70–74 pts.

D+ 65–69 pts.

D 60–64 pts.

F below 60 pts.

Your recommendations:

Chapter 4

Forms of Business Ownership and Franchising

First Law of Bridge: It's always the partner's fault.

—Anonymous

Humans must breathe, but corporations must make money.

—Alice Embree

LEARNING OBJECTIVES

Upon completion of this chapter, you will be able to:

1. **EXPLAIN** the advantages and the disadvantages of the three major forms of business ownership: the sole proprietorship, the partnership, and the corporation.

2. **DISCUSS** the advantages and the disadvantages of the S corporation, the limited liability company, the professional corporation, and the joint venture.

3. **DESCRIBE** the three types of franchising: trade name, product distribution, and pure.

4. **EXPLAIN** the benefits and the drawbacks of buying a franchise.

5. **UNDERSTAND** the laws covering franchise purchases.

6. **DISCUSS** the *right* way to buy a franchise.

7. **OUTLINE** the major trends shaping franchising.

Every business operates as some form of legally recognized entity. It may be as simple as sole proprietorship or as complex as a C corporation. The form of business ownership that an entrepreneur selects may have some very significant implications as the business goes forward. What form of ownership is "best" depends on the characteristics of the business and its owner(s). This chapter is designed to allow you to review the advantages and disadvantages of the most common forms of business ownership and then to apply your analytical skills in evaluating these choices in light of the specific circumstances surrounding the new business and its owner(s). Matching the personal circumstances of the owner(s) and the size and nature of the business with the ownership options can result in the avoidance of problems later. Although the decision regarding the selected form of ownership is not irreversible, changing from one ownership form to another can be difficult, time consuming, complicated, and expensive. Consequently, attention to the detailed components of each form of ownership can be very beneficial.

The following are seven critical considerations, which normally comprise the basis of your review and evaluation prior to the final selection of the form of ownership. Clearly, some criteria are more important than others at difficult times in the life of the business.

Tax considerations. The graduated tax rates under each form of ownership, the government's constant tinkering with the tax code, and the year-to-year fluctuations in a company's income mean that entrepreneurs must calculate the firm's tax bill under each ownership option every year.

Liability exposure. Certain forms of ownership offer business owners greater protection from personal liability that might result from financial problems, faulty products, and a host of other difficulties. Entrepreneurs must decide the extent to which they are willing to assume personal responsibility for their companies' obligations.

Start-up capital requirements. Forms of ownership differ in their ability to raise start-up capital. How much capital entrepreneurs need and where they plan to get it make some forms of ownership superior to others.

Control. By choosing certain forms of ownership, entrepreneurs automatically give up some control over the company. Entrepreneurs must decide early on how much control they are willing to sacrifice in exchange for help from other people in building a successful business.

Business goals. How big and how profitable entrepreneurs plan for the business to become will influence the form of ownership chosen. Businesses often switch forms of ownership as they grow, but moving from some formats to others can be extremely complex and expensive.

Management succession plans. When choosing a form of ownership, business owners must look ahead to the day when they will pass their companies on to the next generation or to a buyer. Some forms of ownership make this transition much smoother than others.

Cost of formation. Certain forms of ownership are much more costly and involved to create than others. Entrepreneurs must weigh carefully the benefits and the costs of the particular form they choose.

Entrepreneurs have a wide choice of forms of business ownership. In recent years, various hybrid forms of ownership have emerged. This chapter will attempt to outline the key features of the most common forms of ownership, beginning with the sole proprietorship, the partnership, and the corporation. Franchising will be addressed later in the chapter.

Learning Objective

1-A. Explain the advantages and disadvantages of the sole proprietorship.

sole proprietorship—
a business owned and managed by one individual.

THE SOLE PROPRIETORSHIP

Without question the simplest and most popular form of ownership remains the **sole proprietorship**. The sole proprietorship, as its name implies, is a business owned and managed by one individual. The normal perception of sole proprietorships is that they are a small and insignificant part of the national as well as global economy. This could not be further from the truth. The latest government figures place the number of domestic sole proprietorships at approximately 18 million with sales in excess of $1 trillion.[1] Estimates place sole proprietorships at 73 percent of all U.S. businesses. The reasons for their popularity can be found in the advantages of this form of ownership providing, however, its disadvantages are never overlooked.

The Advantages of a Proprietorship

SIMPLE TO CREATE. One of the most attractive features of a proprietorship is how fast and simple it is to begin. If an entrepreneur wants to operate a business under his own name (e.g., Strossner's Bakery), he simply obtains the necessary licenses from state, county, and/or local governments and begins operation. For most entrepreneurs, it would not be impossible to start a proprietorship in a single day.

LEAST COSTLY FORM OF OWNERSHIP TO BEGIN. In addition to being easy to begin, the proprietorship is generally the least expensive form of ownership to establish. There is no need to create and file the legal documents that are recommended for partnerships and required for corporations. An entrepreneur simply goes to the city or county government, states the nature of the business he will start, and pays the appropriate fees and license costs. Paying these fees and license costs gives the entrepreneur the right to conduct business in that particular jurisdiction.

Someone planning to conduct business under a trade name should acquire a certificate of doing business under an assumed name from the secretary of state. The fee for filing this certificate usually is nominal. Acquiring this certificate involves conducting a legal search to ensure that the name chosen is not already registered as a trademark or a service mark with the secretary of state. Filing this certificate also notifies the state who the owner of the business is. In a proprietorship, the owner *is* the business.

PROFIT INCENTIVE. One major advantage of the proprietorship is that once the owner pays all of the company's expenses, she can keep the remaining profits (less taxes, of course). The profit incentive is a powerful one, and profits represent an excellent way of "keeping score" in the game of the business.

TOTAL DECISION-MAKING AUTHORITY. Because the sole proprietor is in total control of operations, she can respond quickly to changes, which is an asset in a rapidly shifting market. The freedom to set the company's course of action is a major motivational force. For those who thrive on the enjoyment of seeking new opportunities in business, the freedom of fast, flexible decision making is vital. Many sole proprietors simply thrive on the feeling of control they have over their personal financial future and the recognition they earn as the "owner" of the business.

NO SPECIAL LEGAL RESTRICTIONS. The proprietorship is the least regulated form of business ownership. In a time when government requests for information seem never ending, this feature has much merit.

EASY TO DISCONTINUE. If the entrepreneur decides to discontinue operations, he can terminate the business quickly, even though he will still be personally liable for any outstanding debts and obligations that the business cannot pay.

The Disadvantages of a Proprietorship

UNLIMITED PERSONAL LIABILITY. Probably the greatest disadvantage of a sole proprietorship is the **unlimited personal liability** of the owner, which means that the sole proprietor is personally liable for all of the business's debts. Remember: In a sole proprietorship, the owner *is* the business. He owns all of the business's assets, and if the business fails, creditors can force the sale of these assets to cover its debts. If unpaid business debts remain, creditors can also force the sale of the proprietor's *personal* assets to recover payment. In short, the company's debts are the owner's debts. Laws vary from one state to another, but most states require creditors to leave the failed business owner a minimum amount of equity in a home, a car, and some personal items. The reality: *Failure of a business can ruin a sole proprietor financially.*

unlimited personal liability—*a situation in which the sole proprietor is personally liable for all of the business's debts.*

LIMITED SKILLS AND CAPABILITIES. A sole proprietor may not have the wide range of skills that running a successful business requires. Each of us has areas in which our education, training, and work experiences have taught us a great deal; yet there are other areas where our decision-making ability is weak. Many business failures occur because owners lack the skills, knowledge, and experience in areas that are vital to business success. Owners tend to push aside problems they don't understand or don't feel comfortable with in favor of those they can solve more easily. Unfortunately, the problems they set aside seldom solve themselves. By the time an owner decides to ask for help in addressing these problems, it may be too late to save the company.

FEELINGS OF ISOLATION. Running a business alone allows an entrepreneur maximum flexibility, but it also creates feelings of isolation—that there is no one else to turn to for help in solving problems or getting feedback on a new idea. Most sole proprietors will honestly admit that there are times when they feel the pressure of being alone and being fully and completely responsible for every major business decision. It's a challenge to learn what you need to know about aspects of the business with which you may have had little, or no, previous experience.

LIMITED ACCESS TO CAPITAL. If the business is to grow and expand, a sole proprietor generally needs additional financial resources. However, many proprietors have already put all they have into their businesses and have used their personal resources as collateral on existing loans, making it difficult to borrow additional funds. A sole proprietorship is limited to whatever capital the owner can contribute and whatever money he can borrow. In short, proprietors, unless they have great personal wealth, find it difficult to raise additional money while maintaining sole ownership. Most banks and other lending institutions have well-defined formulas for determining borrowers' eligibility. Unfortunately, many sole proprietorships cannot meet those borrowing requirements, especially in the early days of operation.

LACK OF CONTINUITY FOR THE BUSINESS. Lack of continuity is inherent in a sole proprietorship. If the proprietor dies, retires, or becomes incapacitated, the business automatically terminates. Unless a family member or employee can take over (which means that person is now a sole proprietor), the business could be in jeopardy. Because people look for secure employment and an opportunity for advancement, proprietorships, being small, often have trouble recruiting and retaining good employees. If no one is trained to run the business, creditors can petition the courts to liquidate the assets of the dissolved business to pay outstanding debts.

Some entrepreneurs find that forming partnerships is one way to overcome the disadvantages of the sole proprietorship. For instance, when one person lacks specific managerial skills or has insufficient access to needed capital, he can compensate for these weaknesses by forming a partnership with someone with complementary management skills or money to invest.

YOU Be the Consultant . . .

Where Do Small Business Owners Turn for Advice? It's All in the Family

A recent survey conducted by the National Federation of Independent Business and Wells Fargo reveals that when it comes to advice, blood is thicker than water. Of the businesses responding to the survey, 56 percent consulted family members for advice on critical decisions. This was greater than their partners or co-owners (16%) or professionals (accountants, attorneys, consultants) (14%). Family members whom owners turn to are as follows:

Spouse	62% of the time
Son	11% of the time
Father	9.5% of the time
Brother	8.8% of the time

1. Who else could provide a business owner with objective advice?

2. Is the person to whom you turn to for advice a source of potential problems? Explain.

Source: Richard Breeden, "The Big Decision" *Wall Street Journal*, September 24, 2002, p. B6.

THE PARTNERSHIP

A **partnership** is an association of two or more people who co-own a business for the purpose of making a profit. In a partnership the co-owners (partners) share the business's assets, liabilities, and profits according to the terms of a previously established partnership agreement.

The law does not require a partnership agreement (also known as the articles of partnership), but it is wise to work with an attorney to develop one that spells out the exact status and responsibility of each partner. All too often the parties think they know what they are agreeing to, only to find later that no real meeting of the minds took place. The **partnership agreement** is a document that states in writing all of the terms of operating the partnership and protects each partner involved. Every partnership should be based on a written agreement. "When two entrepreneurial personalities are combined, there is a tremendous amount of strength and energy, but it must be focused in the same direction, or it will tear the relationship apart," explains one business writer. "A good partnership agreement will guide you through the good times, provide you with a method for handling problems, and serve as the infrastructure for a successful operation."[2]

When no partnership agreement exists, the Uniform Partnership Act (UPA) governs a partnership, but its provisions may not be as favorable as a specific agreement hammered out among the partners. Creating a partnership agreement is not costly. In most cases the partners can discuss each of the provisions in advance. Once they have reached an agreement, an attorney can draft the formal document. Banks will often want to see a copy of the partnership agreement before lending the business money. Probably the most important feature of the partnership agreement is that it resolves potential sources of conflict that, if not addressed in advance, could later result in partnership battles and the dissolution of an otherwise successful business. Spelling out details—especially sticky ones such as profit splits, contributions, workloads, decision-making authority, dispute resolution, dissolution, and others—in a written agreement at the outset will help avoid damaging tension in a partnership that could lead to a business "divorce." Business divorces, like marital ones, are almost always costly and unpleasant for everyone involved.

It may be impossible to overstate the need to approach the formation of a business partnership in an objective, impersonal, logical, and rational manner. In reality, there is a tendency for partnerships to be created by individuals who don't believe that it is necessary to draw up a partnership agreement. As a result, if and when a disagreement arises between or among the partners, there is no written record of what was agreed to and how a disagreement is to be resolved. Thousands of businesses close each year because the founders saw no need for a partnership agreement with, like in some marriages, "irreconcilable differences" being the stated reason for dissolution of the business.[3]

Generally, a partnership agreement can include any terms the partners want (unless they are illegal). The standard partnership agreement will likely include the following:

1. *Name of the partnership.*
2. *Purpose of the business.* What is the reason the business was brought into being?
3. *Domicile of the business.* Where will the principal business be located?
4. *Duration of the partnership.* How long will the partnership last?
5. *Names of the partners and their legal addresses.*
6. *Contributions of each partner to the business*, at the creation of the partnership and later. This would include each partner's investment in the business. In some situations a partner may contribute assets that are not likely to appear on a balance sheet. Experience, sales contacts, or a good reputation in the community may be reasons for asking a person to join the partnership.
7. Agreement on *how the profits or losses will be distributed.*
8. An agreement on *salaries or drawing rights* against profits for each partner.
9. Procedure for *expansion through the addition of new partners.*
10. If the partners *voluntarily dissolve the partnership, how will the partnership's assets be distributed?*
11. *Sale of partnership interest.* The articles of partnership should include terms defining how a partner can sell his or her interest in the business.

Learning Objective

1-B. Explain the advantages and disadvantages of the partnership.

partnership—*an association of two or more people who co-own a business for the purpose of making a profit.*

partnership agreement—*a document that states in writing all of the terms of operating the partnership and protects the interest of each partner.*

12. *Salaries, draws, and expense accounts for the partners*. How much money will each partner draw from the business? Under what circumstances? How often?

13. *Absence or disability of one of the partners*. If a partner is absent or disabled for an extended period of time, should the partnership continue? Will the absent or disabled partner receive the same share of profits as she did prior to her absence or disability? Should the absent or disabled partner be held responsible for debts incurred while unable to participate?

14. *Dissolution of the partnership*. Under what circumstances will the partnership dissolve? How will the assets of the business be valued for dissolution?

15. *Alterations or modifications of the partnership agreement*. No document is written to last forever. Partnership agreements should contain provisions for alterations or modifications.

The Uniform Partnership Act

The Uniform Partnership Act (UPA) codifies the body of law dealing with partnerships in the United States (except in Louisiana, which has not adopted the UPA and where state law governs in the absence of a partnership agreement). Under the UPA, the three key elements of any partnership are common ownership interest in a business, sharing the business's profits and losses, and the right to participate in managing the operation of the partnership. Under the act each partner has the *right* to:

1. share in the management and operations of the business.
2. share in any profits the business might earn from operations.
3. receive interest on additional advances made to the business.
4. be compensated for expenses incurred in the name of the partnership.
5. have access to the business's books and records.
6. receive a formal accounting of the partnership's business affairs.

The UPA also sets forth the partners' general obligations. Each partner is *obligated* to:

1. share in any losses sustained by the business.
2. work for the partnership without salary.
3. submit differences that may arise in the conduct of the business to majority vote or arbitration.
4. give the other partner complete information about all business affairs.
5. give a formal accounting of the partnership's business affairs.

Beyond what the law prescribes, a partnership is based above all else on mutual trust and respect. Any partnership missing these elements is destined to fail.

YOU Be the Consultant . . .

How Will the Assets of the Business Be Valued for Dissolution?

PARTNERSHIPS, DEATH, AND FEUDS

At the age of 81, a New York City real estate mogul, Seymour Milstein, died leaving his billion-dollar real estate empire in turmoil. Some two dozen real estate partnerships held with his brother, Paul, must now, by partnership law, be dissolved. The family must either form a new partnership, split the property, or liquidate the assets. Family feuding may result in the total liquidation of all the real estate partnerships and an end to the business.

1. What provisions of a partnership agreement could have eliminated this problem?

Source: Joanne Gordon, "Kickin' Cousins," *Forbes*, November 26, 2001, pp. 52–53.

The Advantages of the Partnership

EASY TO ESTABLISH   Like the proprietorship, the partnership is easy and inexpensive to establish. The owners must obtain the necessary business licenses and submit a minimal number of forms. In most states, partners must file a certificate for conducting business as partners if the business is run under a trade name.

COMPLEMENTARY SKILLS.   In a sole proprietorship, the owner must wear lots of different hats, and not all of them will fit well. In successful partnerships, the parties' skills and abilities usually complement one another, strengthening the company's managerial foundation.

DIVISION OF PROFITS.   There are no restrictions on how partners distribute the company's profits as long as they are consistent with the partnership agreement and do not violate the rights of any partner. The partnership agreement should articulate the nature of each partner's contribution and proportional share of the profits. If the partners fail to create an agreement, the UPA says that the partners share equally in the partnership's profits, even if their original capital contributions are unequal.

LARGER POOL OF CAPITAL.   The partnership form of ownership can significantly broaden the pool of capital available to a business. Each partner's asset base improves the business's ability to borrow needed funds; together the partners' personal assets will support a larger borrowing capacity.

ABILITY TO ATTRACT LIMITED PARTNERS.   When partners share in owning, operating, and managing a business, they are **general partners**. General partners have unlimited liability for the partnership's debts and usually take an active role in managing the business. Every partnership must have at least one general partner although there is no limit on the number of general partners a business can have.

> **general partners**—*partners who share in owning, operating, and managing a business and who have unlimited personal liability for the partnership's debts.*

Limited partners cannot participate in the day-to-day management of a company, and they have limited liability for the partnership's debts. If the business fails, they lose only what they have invested in it and no more. Limited partners usually are just financial investors in a business. A limited partnership can attract investors by offering them limited liability and the potential to realize a substantial return on their investments if the business is successful. Many individuals find it very profitable to invest in high-potential small businesses, but only if they avoid the disadvantages of unlimited liability while doing so.

> **limited partners**—*partners who do not take an active role in managing a business and whose liability for the partnership's debts is limited to the amount they have invested.*

LITTLE GOVERNMENTAL REGULATION.   Like the proprietorship, the partnership form of operation is not burdened with red tape.

FLEXIBILITY.   Although not as flexible as sole ownership, the partnership can generally react quickly to changing market conditions because no giant organization stifles quick and creative responses to new opportunities.

TAXATION.   The partnership itself is not subject to federal taxation. It serves as a conduit for the profit or losses it earns or incurs; its net income or losses are passed along to the partners as personal income, and the partners pay income tax on their distributive shares. The partnership, like the proprietorship, avoids the "double taxation" disadvantage associated with the corporate form of ownership.

The Disadvantages of the Partnership

UNLIMITED LIABILITY OF AT LEAST ONE PARTNER.   At least one member of every partnership must be a general partner. The general partner has unlimited personal liability, even though he is often the partner with the least personal resources.

CAPITAL ACCUMULATION.   Although the partnership form of ownership is superior to the proprietorship in its ability to attract capital, it is generally not as effective as the corporate form of ownership, which can raise capital by selling shares of ownership to outside investors.

DIFFICULTY IN DISPOSING OF PARTNERSHIP INTEREST WITHOUT DISSOLVING THE PARTNERSHIP.   Most partnership agreements restrict how a partner can dispose of his share of the business. Often a partner is required to sell his interest to the remaining partner(s). Even if the original agreement contains such a requirement and clearly delineates how the value of each partner's ownership will be determined, there is no guarantee that the other partner(s) will have the financial resources to buy the seller's interest. When the money is not available to purchase a partner's interest, the other partner(s) may be forced either to accept a new partner or to dissolve the partnership, distribute the remaining assets, and begin again. When a partner withdraws from the partnership, the partnership ceases to exist unless there are specific provisions in the partnership agreement for a smooth transition. When a general partner dies, becomes incompetent, or withdraws from the business, the partnership automatically dissolves, although it may not terminate. Even when there are numerous partners, if one chooses to disassociate her name from the business, the remaining partners will probably form a new partnership.

LACK OF CONTINUITY. If one partner dies, complications arise. Partnership interest is often nontransferable through inheritance because the remaining partner(s) may not want to be in a partnership with the person who inherits the deceased partner's interest. Partners can make provisions in the partnership agreement to avoid dissolution due to death if all parties agree to accept as partners those who inherit the deceased's interest.

POTENTIAL FOR PERSONALITY AND AUTHORITY CONFLICTS. Being in a partnership is much like being in a marriage. Making sure partners' work habits, goals, ethics, and general business philosophy are compatible is an important step in avoiding a nasty business divorce. It may often sound foolish, but it is valuable to engage in serious and lengthy discussions between or among potential partners on each of these topics. Never blindly assume that you know how a potential partner might act in a difficult situation. It is important to remember that an unethical action by a partner will always reflect on you.

No matter how compatible partners are, friction among them is inevitable. The key is having a mechanism such as a partnership agreement and open lines of communication for controlling it. The demise of many partnerships can often be traced to interpersonal conflicts and the lack of a procedure to resolve those conflicts.

In many instances, the unlimited personal liability of each partner in a general partnership is a major barrier to attracting needed capital. As a result, limited partnerships have become more popular.

YOU Be the Consultant . . .

Rosabeth Moss Kanter on Partnerships

Avoiding ugly and costly business divorces that too often put an end to businesses requires an ongoing and active effort. Howard Professor Rosabeth Moss Kanter suggests from her experience that partners follow the following six rules:

1. Take a close look at what you're getting. Do your research and test your assumptions before you construct the partnership agreement.

2. Invest in the relationship, not just the deal making. Relationships between or among partners must continuously be strengthened. If this role is delegated or ignored, the partnership will fail.

3. Get connected through many people. Have those whom you do business with meet the staff as well as your partners. Through these connections, relationships can be built at many levels in the organization.

4. Respect differences and expect to work out conflicts. When potential sources of conflict exist, address them immediately. Festering wounds seldom heal without medication.

5. Be prepared to change. Be open to new opportunities and share what you see with your partners. Partnerships need to evolve to survive.

6. Help everyone succeed. Work hard to see that every partner plays a role in the business that allows him or her the opportunity to be successful and become viewed by others as a significant player in the business.

1. If you were asked to add a "seventh rule," what would it be?

Source: Rosabeth Moss Kanter, "Six Rules for a Happy Marriage . . .Uh, Partnership," *Business 2.0*, April 2002, p. 114.

Limited Partnerships

A **limited partnership**, which is a modification of a general partnership, is composed of at least one general partner and at least one limited partner. In a limited partnership the general partner is treated, under the law, exactly as in a general partnership. The limited partner is treated more as an investor in the business venture; limited partners have limited liability. They can lose only the amount invested in the business.

limited partnership—*a partnership composed of at least one general partner and at least one limited partner.*

Most states have ratified the Revised Uniform Limited Partnership Act. The formation of a limited partnership requires its founder to file a certificate of limited partnership in the state in which the limited partnership plans to conduct business. The certificate of limited partnership should include the following information:

1. the name of the limited partnership.
2. the general character of its business.
3. the address of the office of the firm's agent authorized to receive summonses or other legal notices.
4. the name and business address of each partner, specifying which ones are general partners and which are limited partners.
5. the amount of cash contributions actually made, and agreed to be made in the future, by each partner.
6. a description of the value of noncash contributions made or to be made by each partner.
7. the times at which additional contributions are to be made by any of the partners.
8. whether and under what conditions a limited partner has the right to grant limited partner status to an assignee of his or her interest in the partnership.
9. if agreed upon, the time or the circumstances when a partner may withdraw from the firm (unlike the withdrawal of a general partner, the withdrawal of a limited partner does *not* automatically dissolve a limited partnership).
10. if agreed upon, the amount of, or the method of determining, the funds to be received by a withdrawing partner.
11. any right of a partner to receive distributions of cash or other property from the firm, and the times and circumstances for such distributions.
12. the time or circumstances when the limited partnership is to be dissolved.
13. the rights of the remaining general partners to continue the business after withdrawal of a general partner.
14. any other matters the partners want to include.

The general partner has the same rights and duties as under a general partnership: the right to make decisions for the business, to act as an agent for the partnership, to use the property of the partnership for normal business, and to share in the business's profits. The limited partner does not have the right to take an active role in managing the business. In fact, if he or she takes part in managing the business, a limited partner may actually forfeit limited liability, taking on the liability status of a general partner. Limited partners can, however, make management suggestions to the general partners, inspect the business, and make copies of business records. A limited partner is, of course, entitled to a share of the business's profits as agreed on and specified in the certificate of limited partnership. The primary disadvantage of limited partnerships is the complexity and the cost of establishing them.

A Company Example

*"Cot" Campbell of **Dogwood Stable** brought the "sport of kings" to a larger audience of thrill-seeking investors when he created the first limited partnership in thoroughbred racing. Dogwood Stable has had 58 stable winners including the Preakness. Currently Dogwood Stable has 60 horses in competition, all owned by members of limited partnerships. Dogwood Stable retains five percent ownership as the general partner and sells four 23.75 percent shares to limited partners.*[4]

limited liability partnership—*a special type of limited partnership in which all partners, who in many states must be professionals, are limited partners.*

Limited Liability Partnerships

Many states now recognize **limited liability partnerships (LLPs)** in which *all* partners in a business are limited partners, having only limited liability for the debts of the partnership. Most states restrict LLPs to certain types of professionals such as attorneys, physicians, dentists, accountants, and others. Just as with any limited partnership, the partners must file a certificate of limited partnership in the state in which the partnership will conduct business, and the partnership must identify itself as an LLP to those with whom it does business. Also, like every partnership, an LLP does not pay taxes; its income is passed through to the limited partners, who pay taxes on their shares of the company's income.

Master Limited Partnership

master limited partnership—*a partnership whose shares are traded on stock exchanges, just like a corporation's.*

A relatively new form of business structure, **master limited partnerships (MLPs)**, are just like regular limited partnerships, except their shares are traded just like shares of common stock. They provide most of the same advantages to investors as a corporation—including limited liability. Operationally, a master limited partnership behaves like a corporation, and some even trade on major stock exchanges. In 1987, congressional legislation provided that any MLPs not involved in natural resources or real estate would be taxed as corporations and, consequently, eliminated their ability to avoid double taxation.

CORPORATIONS

Learning Objective

1-C. Explain the advantages and disadvantages of the corporation.

corporation—*a separate legal entity apart from its owners that receives the right to exist from the state in which it is incorporated.*

domestic corporation—*a corporation doing business in the state in which it is incorporated.*

foreign corporation—*a corporation doing business in a state other than the one in which it is incorporated.*

alien corporation—*a corporation formed in another country but doing business in the United States.*

The corporation is the most complex of the three major forms of business ownership. It is a separate entity apart from its owners and may engage in business, make contracts, sue and be sued, own property, and pay taxes. The Supreme Court has defined the **corporation** as "an artificial being, invisible, intangible, and existing only in contemplation of the law."[5] Because the life of the corporation is independent of its owners, the shareholders can sell their interests in the business without affecting its continuation.

Corporations (also known as C corporations) are creations of the state. When a corporation is founded, it accepts the regulations and restrictions of the state in which it is incorporated and any other state in which it chooses to do business. A corporation doing business in the state in which it is incorporated is a **domestic corporation**. When a corporation conducts business in another state, that state considers it to be a **foreign corporation**. Corporations formed in other countries but doing business in the United States are **alien corporations**.

Generally, the corporation must report annually its financial operations to its home state's secretary of state. These financial reports become public record. If a corporation's stock is sold in more than one state, the corporation must comply with federal regulations governing the sale of corporate securities. There are substantially more reporting requirements for a corporation than for the other forms of ownership.

How to Incorporate

Most states allow entrepreneurs to incorporate without the assistance of an attorney. Some states even provide incorporation kits to help in the incorporation process. Although it is cheaper for entrepreneurs to complete the process themselves, it is not always the best idea. In some states, the application process is complex, and the required forms are confusing. The price for filing incorrectly can be high. If an entrepreneur completes the incorporation process improperly, it is generally invalid.

Once the owners decide to form a corporation, they must choose a state in which to incorporate. If the business will operate within a single state, it is probably most logical to incorporate in that state. States differ—sometimes rather dramatically—in the requirements they place on the corporations they charter and how they treat corporations chartered in other states. They also differ in the tax rate they impose on corporations, the restrictions placed on their activities, the capital required to incorporate, and the fees or organization tax charged to incorporate. Delaware, for instance, offers low incorporation fees and minimal legal requirements.

Every state requires a certificate of incorporation or charter to be filed with the secretary of state. The following information is generally required to be included in the certificate of incorporation:

The corporation's name. The corporation must choose a name that is not so similar to that of another firm in the state that it causes confusion or lends itself to deception. It must also include a term such as *corporation, incorporated, company,* or *limited* to notify the public that they are dealing with a corporation.

The corporation's statement of purpose. The incorporators must state in general terms the intended nature of the business. The purpose must, of course, be lawful. An illustration might be "to engage in the sale of office furniture and fixtures." The purpose should be broad enough to allow for some expansion in the activities of the business as it develops.

The corporation's time horizon. In most cases corporations are formed with no specific termination date; they are formed "for perpetuity." However, it is possible to incorporate for a specific duration (e.g., 50 years).

Names and addresses of the incorporators. The incorporators must be identified in the articles of incorporation and are liable under the law to attest that all information in the articles of incorporation is correct. In some states one or more of the incorporators must reside in the state in which the corporation is being created.

Place of business. The street and mailing address of the corporation's principal office must be listed. For a domestic corporation, this address must be in the state in which incorporation takes place.

Capital stock authorization. The articles of incorporation must include the amount and class (or type) of capital stock the corporation wants to be authorized to issue. This is not the number of shares it must issue; a corporation can issue any number of shares up to the amount authorized. This section must also define the different classifications of stock and any special rights, preferences, or limits each class has.

Capital required at the time of incorporation. Some states require a newly formed corporation to deposit in a bank a specific percentage of the stock's par value prior to incorporating.

Provisions for preemptive rights, if any, that are granted to stockholders.

Restrictions on transferring shares. Many closely held corporations—those owned by a few shareholders, often family members—require shareholders interested in selling their stock to offer it first to the corporation. (Shares the corporation itself owns are called **treasury stock**.) To maintain control over their ownership, many closely held corporations exercise this right, known as the **right of first refusal**.

Names and addresses of the officers and directors of the corporation.

Rules under which the corporation will operate. **Bylaws** are the rules and regulations the officers and directors establish for the corporation's internal management and operation.

Once the secretary of state of the incorporating state has approved a request for incorporation and the corporation pays its fees, the approved articles of incorporation become its charter. With the charter in hand, the next order of business is to hold an organizational meeting for the stockholders to formally elect directors who, in turn, will appoint the corporate officers.

The Advantages of the Corporation

LIMITED LIABILITY OF STOCKHOLDERS. Because it is a separate legal entity, a corporation allows investors to limit their liability to the total amount of their investment in the business. This legal protection of personal assets beyond the business is of critical concern to many potential investors.

This shield of limited liability may not be impenetrable, however. Because start-up companies are so risky, lenders and other creditors require the owners to personally guarantee loans made to the corporation. Robert Morris Associates, a national organization of bank loan officers, estimates that 95 percent of small business owners have to sign personal guarantees to get the financing they need. By making these guarantees, owners are putting their personal assets at risk (just as in a proprietorship) despite choosing the corporate form of ownership.

The corporate form of ownership does not protect its owners from being held personally liable for fraudulent or illegal acts under what is known as the "alter ego doctrine." The act of disregarding the corporate entity and pursuing the stockholders is referred to as "piercing the corporate veil" and can occur under the following circumstances:

1. When corporate assets are used for personal reasons or commingled with personal assets.
2. Failure to act in a responsible manner and creating an unwarranted level of financial risk for the stockholders.

treasury stock—*the shares of its own stock that a corporation owns.*

right of first refusal—*a provision requiring shareholders who want to sell their stock to offer it first to the corporation.*

bylaws—*the rules and regulations the officers and directors establish for a corporation's internal management and operation.*

3. Financial misrepresentations, such as operating with more than one set of books.

4. Taking actions in the name of the corporation that were not authorized by the board of directors.

Problems almost always revolve around actions and decisions that fail to maintain the integrity of the corporation.

ABILITY TO ATTRACT CAPITAL. Based on the protection of limited liability, corporations have proved to be the most effective form of ownership for accumulating large amounts of capital. Limited only by the number of shares authorized in its charter (which can be amended), the corporation can raise money to begin business and expand as opportunity dictates by selling shares of its stock to investors. A corporation can sell its stock to a limited number of private investors (a private placement) or to the public (a public offering).

ABILITY TO CONTINUE INDEFINITELY. Unless a corporation fails to pay its taxes or is limited to a specific length of life by its charter, it can continue indefinitely. The corporation's existence does not depend on the fate of any single individual. Unlike a proprietorship or partnership in which the death of a founder ends the business, a corporation lives beyond the lives of those who gave it life. This perpetual life gives rise to the next major advantage—transferable ownership.

TRANSFERABLE OWNERSHIP. If stockholders in a corporation are displeased with the business's progress, they can sell their shares to someone else. Millions of shares of stock representing ownership in companies are traded daily on the world's stock exchanges. Shareholders can also transfer their stock through inheritance to a new generation of owners. During all of these transfers of ownership, the corporation continues to conduct business as usual.

Unlike that of large corporations whose shares are traded on organized stock exchanges, the stock of many small corporations is held by a small number of people ("closely held"), often company founders, family members, or employees. The small number of people holding the stock means that the resale market for shares is limited, which could make the transfer of ownership more difficult.

The Disadvantages of Corporations

COST AND TIME INVOLVED IN THE INCORPORATION PROCESS. Corporations can be costly and time-consuming to establish. The owners are giving birth to an artificial legal entity, and the gestation period can be prolonged for the novice. In some states an attorney must handle the incorporation process, but in most states entrepreneurs can complete all of the required forms alone. However, an owner must exercise great caution when incorporating without the help of an attorney. Also, incorporating a business requires a variety of fees that are not applicable to proprietorships or partnerships. Creating a corporation can cost between $500 and $2,500, typically averaging around $1,000.

DOUBLE TAXATION. Because a corporation is a separate legal entity, it must pay taxes on its net income at the federal level, in most states, and to some local governments as well. Before stockholders receive a penny of its net income as dividends, a corporation must pay these taxes at the *corporate* tax rate. Then stockholders must pay taxes on the dividends they receive from these same profits at the *individual* tax rate. Thus, a corporation's profits are taxed twice. This **double taxation** is a distinct disadvantage of the corporate form of ownership.

double taxation—
disadvantage of the corporate form of ownership in which a corporation's profits are taxed twice: at the corporate rate and at the individual rate (on the portion of profits distributed as dividends).

POTENTIAL FOR DIMINISHED MANAGERIAL INCENTIVES. As corporations grow, they often require additional managerial expertise beyond that which the founder can provide. Because she created the company and often has most of her personal wealth tied up in it, the entrepreneur has an intense interest in making it a success and is willing to make sacrifices for it. Professional managers the entrepreneur brings in to help run the business as it grows do not always have the same degree of interest in or loyalty to the company. As a result, the business may suffer without the founder's energy, care, and devotion. One way to minimize this potential problem is to link managers' (and even employees') compensation to the company's financial performance through a profit-sharing or bonus plan. Corporations can also stimulate managers' and employees' incentives on the job by creating an employee stock ownership plan (ESOP) in which managers and employees become part or whole owners in the company.

LEGAL REQUIREMENTS AND REGULATORY RED TAPE. Corporations are subject to more legal, reporting, and financial requirements than other forms of ownership. Corporate officers must meet more stringent requirements for recording and reporting management decisions and actions. They must also hold annual meetings and consult the board of directors about major decisions that are beyond day-to-day operations. Managers may be required to submit some major decisions to the stockholders for approval. Corporations that are publicly held must file quarterly and annual reports with the Securities and Exchange Commission (SEC).

POTENTIAL LOSS OF CONTROL BY THE FOUNDER(S). When entrepreneurs sell shares of ownership in their companies, they relinquish some control. Especially when they need large capital infusions for start-up or growth, entrepreneurs may have to give up *significant* amounts of control, so much, in fact, that the founders become minority shareholders. Losing majority ownership—and, therefore, control—in their company leaves the founders in a precarious position. They no longer have the power to determine the company's direction; "outsiders" do. In some cases, founders' shares have been so diluted that majority shareholders actually vote them out of their jobs!

Microsoft Inc. was founded as a partnership between Bill Gates and Paul Allen in 1975. At that time, Bill Gates owned 50 percent of the business. As the company grew, it needed additional capital and Gates and Allen decided to take Microsoft public, selling shares of common stock to investors. The effect has been to reduce Bill Gates's percentage of ownership to 18.5 percent. But not to worry, the Forbes *list of the world's wealthiest people places Mr. Gates's net worth at $40 billion!*

This example illustrates the nature of the dilemma: Often growth requires the sale of ownership (stock) to acquire the needed cash to reach the firm's market potential. Most people believe that Bill Gates made the correct decision, even if his percentage of ownership in Microsoft has been reduced.

OTHER FORMS OF OWNERSHIP

In addition to the sole proprietorship, the partnership, and the corporation, entrepreneurs can choose from other forms of ownership, including the S corporation, the limited liability company, the professional corporation, and the joint venture.

Learning Objective
2. Discuss the advantages and disadvantages of the S corporation, the limited liability company, the professional corporation, and the joint venture.

The S Corporation

In 1954 the Internal Revenue Service (IRS) Code created the subchapter S corporation. In recent years the IRS has changed the title to S corporation and has made a few modifications in its qualifications. An **S corporation** is a distinction that is made only for federal income tax purposes and is, in terms of legal characteristics, no different from any other corporation. Although Congress recently simplified some of the rules and requirements for S corporations, a business seeking S status still must meet the following criteria:

S corporation—*a corporation that retains the legal characteristics of a regular (C) corporation but has the advantage of being taxed as a partnership if it meets certain criteria.*

1. It must be a domestic (U.S.) corporation.
2. It cannot have a nonresident alien as a shareholder.
3. It can issue only one class of common stock, which means that all shares must carry the same rights (e.g., the right to dividends or liquidation rights). The exception is voting rights, which may differ. In other words, an S corporation can issue voting and nonvoting common stock.
4. It must limit its shareholders to individuals, estates, and certain trusts, although tax-exempt creations such as employee stock ownership plans (ESOPs) and pension plans can now be shareholders.
5. It cannot have more than 75 shareholders (increased from 35), which is an important benefit for family businesses making the transition from one generation of owners to another.
6. Less than 25 percent of the corporation's gross revenues during three successive tax years must be from passive sources.

You must elect S status with the Internal Revenue Service (IRS) by filing with it within the first two and a half months of the corporation's first taxable year. Failure to meet this deadline results in the firm being treated as a C corporation until timely filing of an S corporation election.

An S corporation election may be filed at any time during the 12 months that precede the taxable year for which the election is to be effective. If you make the election within the first two and a half months of the taxable year, it is effective for the current year, providing that the corporation was eligible to make an S election for the entire year. If a corporation satisfies the definition for an S corporation, the owners must actually elect to be treated as one. The election is made by filing IRS Form 2553 at any time during the year, and *all* shareholders must consent to have the corporation treated as an S corporation.

THE ADVANTAGES OF AN S CORPORATION. The S corporation retains all of the advantages of a regular corporation, such as continuity of existence, transferability of ownership, and limited personal liability for its owners. The most notable provision of the S corporation is that it passes all of its profits or losses through to the individual shareholders, and its income is taxed only once at the individual tax rate. Thus, electing S corporation status avoids a primary disadvantage of the regular (or C) corporation—double taxation. In essence, the tax treatment of an S corporation is exactly like that of a partnership; its owners report their proportional shares of the company's profits on their individual income tax returns and pay taxes on those profits at the individual rate (even if they never take the money out of the business).

Another advantage the S corporation offers is avoiding the tax C corporations pay on assets that have appreciated in value and are sold. Also, owners of S corporations enjoy the ability to make year-end payouts to themselves if earnings are high. In a C corporation, owners have no such luxury because the IRS watches for excessive compensation to owners and managers.

One significant change to the laws governing S corporations that benefits entrepreneurs involves subsidiary companies. Before 1998, if entrepreneurs owned separate but affiliated companies, they had to maintain each one as a distinct S corporation with its own accounting records and tax return. Under current law, business owners can set up all of these affiliated companies as qualified S corporation subsidiaries ("Q Subs") under the umbrella of a single company, each with its own separate legal identity, and still file a single tax return for the parent company. For entrepreneurs with several lines of businesses, this change means greatly simplified tax filing. Owners also can use losses from one subsidiary company to offset profits from another to minimize their tax bills. "The advent of the Q Sub has made [S corporations] more useful and popular than ever," says one tax expert.[6]

DISADVANTAGES OF AN S CORPORATION. Tax implications always factor into an entrepreneur's choice of a form of ownership. Periodically, Congress changes the tax rates for both individuals (hence S corporations) and C corporations, which can reverse instantly any tax advantage one form of ownership has over another. For example, from 1993 to 2002, the maximum individual tax rate was 4.6 percent *higher* than the maximum corporate tax rate, which made S corporations *less* attractive to entrepreneurs. In 2003, however, Congress realigned the tax code, making the maximum corporate tax rate 4 percent higher than the maximum individual rate. This change made the S corporation once again the preferred form of ownership from a tax perspective. In addition to the tax implications of choosing a form of ownership, owners should consider the size of the company's net income, the tax rates of its shareholders, plans to sell the company, and the impact of the C corporation's double taxation penalty on income distributed as dividends.

Another disadvantage of the S corporation is that the costs of many fringe benefits—insurance, meals, lodging, and so on—paid to shareholders with 2 percent or more of stock cannot be deducted as business expenses for tax purposes; these benefits are considered to be taxable income. In addition, S corporations offer shareholders only a limited range of retirement benefits, whereas regular corporations make a wide range of retirement plans available.

WHEN IS AN S CORPORATION A WISE CHOICE? Choosing S corporation status is usually beneficial to start-up companies anticipating net losses and to highly profitable firms with substantial dividends to pay out to shareholders. In these cases the owner can use the loss to offset other income or is in a lower tax bracket than the corporation, thus saving money in the long run. Companies that plan to reinvest most of their earnings to finance growth also find S corporation status favorable. Small business owners who intend to sell their companies in the near future will prefer S over C status because the taxable gains on the sale of an S corporation are generally lower than those of a C corporation.

On the other hand, small companies with the following characteristics are *not* likely to benefit from S corporation status:

- highly profitable personal service companies with large numbers of shareholders, in which most of the profits are passed on to shareholders as compensation or retirement benefits.
- fast-growing companies that must retain most of their earnings to finance growth and capital spending.
- corporations in which the loss of fringe benefits to shareholders exceeds tax savings.
- corporations in which the income before any compensation to shareholders is less than $100,000 per year.
- corporations with sizable net operating losses that cannot be used against S corporation earnings.

LIQUIDATION OF AN S CORPORATION   Although, just like a C corporation, the S corporation has perpetual life, the time may come when the stockholders wish to dissolve the company. To liquidate an S corporation its owners must complete the following:

- Pay all taxes, debts, and creditors.
- Obtain the written approval of shareholders to dissolve the company.
- File a statement of intent to dissolve with the secretary of state's office in the state in which the S corporation resides.
- Distribute all assets of the corporation to shareholders.

The Limited Liability Company (LLC)

A relatively new creation, the **limited liability company (LLC)** is, like an S corporation, a cross between a partnership and a corporation. LLCs, however, are not subject to many of the restrictions currently imposed on S corporations and offer more flexibility than S corporations. For example, S corporations cannot have more than 75 shareholders, none of whom can be foreigners or corporations. S corporations are also limited to only one class of stock. LLCs eliminate those restrictions. An LLC must have at least two owners (called "members"), but it offers its owners limited liability without imposing any requirements on their characteristics or any ceiling on their numbers. Unlike a limited partnership, which prohibits limited partners from participating in the day-to-day management of the business, an LLC does not restrict its members' ability to become involved in managing the company.

> **limited liability company (LLC)**—*a relatively new form of ownership that, like an S corporation, is a cross between a partnership and a corporation; it is not subject to many of the restrictions imposed on S corporations.*

In addition to offering its members the advantage of limited liability, LLCs also avoid the double taxation imposed on C corporations. Like an S corporation, an LLC does not pay income taxes; its income flows through to the members, who are responsible for paying income taxes on their shares of the LLC's net income. Because they are not subject to the many restrictions imposed on other forms of ownership, LLCs offer entrepreneurs another significant advantage: flexibility. Like a partnership, an LLC permits its members to divide income (and, thus, tax liability) as they see fit.

These advantages make the LLC an ideal form of ownership for small companies in virtually any industry—retail, wholesale, manufacturing, real estate, or service. Because they offer the tax advantage of a partnership, the legal protection of a corporation, and maximum flexibility, LLCs have become an extremely popular form of ownership among entrepreneurs.

*For example, Marian Fletcher launched a profitable party planning and catering service in 1995 as a sole proprietorship. Her company, **Let's Go Party**, grew quickly, and Fletcher wanted to bring her daughter into the business as an owner. Reviewing the advantages and disadvantages of each form of ownership led Fletcher to create an LLC. "We decided this was the best way to go for us," she says. "In case anything happens, my daughter and I won't be liable for anything more than what we have invested in the company already." Fletcher, who set up her LLC without the help of an attorney for just $50, also found the LLC's tax treatment to be a major advantage for her and her daughter.*[7]

A Company Example

Creating an LLC is much like creating a corporation. Forming an LLC requires an entrepreneur to file two documents with the secretary of state: the articles of organization and the operating agreement. The LLC's **articles of organization**, similar to the corporation's articles of incorporation, actually creates the LLC by establishing its name and address, its method of

> **articles of organization**—*the document that creates an LLC by its name, its method of management, its duration, and other details.*

management (board managed or member managed), its duration, and the names and addresses of each organizer. In most states the company's name must contain the words "limited liability company," "limited company," or the letters "L.L.C." or "L.C." Unlike a corporation, an LLC does not have perpetual life; in most states an LLC's charter may not exceed 30 years. However, the same factors that would cause a partnership to dissolve would also cause the dissolution of an LLC before its charter expires.

operating agreement—*the document that establishes for an LLC the provisions governing the way it will conduct business.*

The **operating agreement**, similar to a corporation's bylaws, outlines the provisions governing the way the LLC will conduct business, such as members' capital contributions to the LLC, the admission or withdrawal of members, distributions from the business, and how the LLC will be managed. To ensure that their LLCs are classified as a partnership for tax purposes, entrepreneurs must draft the operating agreement carefully. The operating agreement must create an LLC that has more characteristics of a partnership than of a corporation to maintain this favorable tax treatment. Specifically, an LLC cannot have any more than *two* of the following four corporate characteristics:

1. *Limited liability.* Limited liability exists if no member of the LLC is personally liable for the debts or claims against the company. Because entrepreneurs choosing this form of ownership usually do so to get limited liability protection, the operating agreement almost always contains this characteristic.

2. *Continuity of life.* Continuity of life exists if the company continues to exist in spite of changes in stock ownership. To avoid continuity of life, any LLC member must have the power to dissolve the company. Most entrepreneurs choose to omit this characteristic from their LLC's operating agreements.

3. *Free transferability of interest.* Free transferability of interest exists if each LLC member has the power to transfer his or her ownership to another person freely and without the consent of other members. To avoid this characteristic, the operating agreement must state that a recipient of a member's LLC stock cannot become a substitute member without the consent of the remaining members.

4. *Centralized management.* Centralized management exists if a group that does not include all LLC members has the authority to make management decisions and to conduct company business. To avoid this characteristic, the operating agreement must state that the company elects to be "member managed."

Despite their universal appeal to entrepreneurs, LLCs suffer some disadvantages. They can be expensive to create, often costing between $1,500 and $5,000. Although an LLC may be ideally suited for an entrepreneur launching a new company, it may pose problems for business owners considering converting an existing business to an LLC. Switching to an LLC from a general partnership, a limited partnership, or a sole proprietorship by reorganizing to bring in new owners is usually not a problem. However, owners of corporations and S corporations would incur large tax obligations if they converted their companies to LLCs.

To date, the biggest disadvantage of the LLC stems from its newness. However, every state now recognizes the LLC as a legal form of ownership, and the Uniform Limited Liability Act exists at the federal level.

The Professional Corporation

Professional corporations are designed to offer professionals—lawyers, doctors, dentists, accountants, and others—the advantages of the corporate form of ownership. They are ideally suited for professionals, who must always be concerned about malpractice lawsuits, because they offer limited liability. For example, if three doctors formed a professional corporation, none of them would be liable for the others' malpractice. (Of course, each would be liable for his or her own actions.) Owners create a professional corporation in the same way as a regular corporation. Such corporations are often identified by the abbreviations P.C. (professional corporation), P.A. (professional association), or S.C. (service corporation). A professional corporation has the following additional limitations beyond the standard corporation:

- All shares of stock of the corporation must be owned and held by individuals licensed in the profession of the corporation.

- At least one of the incorporators must be licensed in the profession.

- At least one director and one officer must be licensed in the profession.

- The articles of incorporation, in addition to all other requirements, must designate the personal services to be provided by the corporation.

- The professional corporation must obtain from the appropriate licensing board a certification that declares the shares of stock are owned by individuals who are duly licensed in the profession.

The Joint Venture

A joint venture is very much like a partnership, except that it is formed for a specific, limited purpose. For instance, suppose that you have a 500-acre tract of land 60 miles from Chicago that has been cleared and is normally used in agricultural production. You have a friend who has solid contacts among major musical groups and would like to put on a concert. You expect prices for your agricultural products to be low this summer, so you and your friend form a joint venture for the specific purpose of staging a three-day concert. Your contribution will be the exclusive use of the land for one month, and your friend will provide all the performers as well as technicians, facilities, and equipment. All costs will be paid out of receipts and the net profits will be split, with you receiving 20 percent for the use of your land. When the concert is over, the facilities removed, and the accounting for all costs completed, you and your friend split the profits 20-80, and the joint venture terminates.

In any endeavor in which neither party can effectively achieve the purpose alone, a joint venture becomes a common form of ownership. The "partners" form a new joint venture for each new project they undertake. The income derived from a joint venture is taxed as if it arose from a partnership.

Table 4.1 provides a summary of the key features of the major forms of ownership discussed in this chapter.

TABLE 4.1

Characteristics of the Major Forms of Ownership

Feature	Sole Proprietorship	Partnership	C Corporation	S Corporation	Limited Liability Company
Owner's personal liability	Unlimited	Unlimited for general partners Limited for limited partners	Limited	Limited	Limited
Number of owners	1	2 or more (at least 1 general partner required)	Any number	Maximum of 75 (with restriction on who they are)	2 or more
Tax liability	Single tax: proprietor pays at individual rate	Single tax: partners pay on their proportional shares at individual rate	Double tax: corporation pays tax and shareholders pay tax on dividends distributed	Single tax: owners pay on their proportional shares at individual rate	Single tax: members pay on their proportional shares at individual rate
Maximum tax rate	35%	35%	39%	35%	35%
Transferability of ownership	Fully transferable through sale or transfer of company assets	May require consent of all partners	Fully transferable	Transferable (but transfer may affect S status)	Usually requires consent of all members
Continuity of business	Ends on death or insanity of proprietor or upon termination by proprietor	Dissolves upon death, insanity, or retirement of a general partner (business may continue)	Perpetual life	Perpetual life	Perpetual life
Cost of formation	Low	Moderate	High	High	High
Liquidity of owner's investment in business	Poor to average	Poor to average	High	High	High
Complexity of formation	Extremely low	Moderate	High	High	High
Ability to raise capital	Low	Moderate	Very high	Moderate to high	High
Formation procedure	No special steps required other than buying necessary licenses	No written partnership agreements required (but highly advisable)	Must meet formal requirements specified by state law	Must follow same procedures as C corporation, then elect S status with IRS	Must meet formal requirements specified by state law

FRANCHISING

It is almost impossible to find a town or village that does not have a franchised business of some type. The variety among these businesses is staggering. Most of us would immediately identify the fast-food restaurants that exist in every community, but we may not so easily recognize franchises such as Service Master and Clean Net USA (commercial/residential contract cleaning businesses) or Curves for Women, a women's fitness and weight loss center.

Today, approximately 4,500 franchisers operate more than 600,000 franchise outlets throughout the world, and more are opening at an incredible pace. A new franchise opens somewhere in the world every 6.5 minutes![8] Franchises account for 44 percent of all retail sales, totaling more than *$1 trillion*, and they employ some 8 million people in more than 100 major industries.[9] Much of the popularity of franchising stems from its ability to offer those who lack business experience the chance to own and operate a business with a high probability of success. This booming industry has moved far beyond the traditional boundaries of fast food into fields as diverse as maid services and bakeries to computer sales and pet-sitting.

In **franchising**, semi-independent business owners (franchisees) pay fees and royalties to a parent company (franchiser) in return for the right to become identified with its trademark, to sell

franchising—*a system of distribution in which semi-independent business owners (franchisees) pay fees and royalties to a parent company (franchiser) in return for the right to become identified with its trademark, to sell its products or services, and often to use its business format and system.*

its products or services, and often to use its business format and system. Franchisees do not establish their own autonomous businesses; instead, they buy a "success package" from the franchiser, who shows them how to use it. Franchisees, unlike independent business owners, don't have the freedom to change the way they run their businesses—for example, shifting advertising strategies or adjusting product lines—but they do have a formula for success that the franchiser has worked out. Most franchisers are selling a successful business model. Many successful franchisers claim that neglecting to follow the formula is one of the chief reasons that franchisees fail.

For example, Anita Schlachter, co-owner of a highly successful Maaco (automotive services) franchise with her husband and her son, is convinced that the system the franchiser taught them is the key to their company's progress and growth to date. The Schlachters follow the franchiser's plan, using it as a road map to success. "If you listen to what your franchiser says and follow its policies and procedures, you'll be successful," she says. "Those who think they know more should not go into franchising." [10]

A Company Example

In 1992, Gary Heavin launched Curves, a women-only fitness center. The company began franchising in 1995 and now has more than 6,000 franchised outlets around the globe, making it one of the fastest growing franchises in the United States.

Courtesy of Curves International

trade-name franchising—*a system of franchising in which a franchisee purchases the right to use the franchiser's trade name without distributing particular products under the franchiser's name.*

Franchising is based on a continuing relationship between a franchiser and a franchisee. The franchiser provides valuable services such as market research, a proven business system, name recognition, and many other forms of assistance; in return, the franchisee pays an initial franchise fee as well as an ongoing percentage of sales to the franchiser as royalties and agrees to operate the outlet according to the franchiser's system. Because franchisers develop the business systems their franchisees use and direct their distribution methods, they maintain substantial control over their franchisees. This standardization lies at the core of franchising's success as a method of distribution.

TYPES OF FRANCHISING

Learning Objective

3. Describe the three types of franchising: tradename, product distribution, and pure.

There are three basic types of franchising: trade-name franchising, product distribution franchising, and pure franchising. **Trade-name franchising** involves a brand name such as True Value Hardware or Western Auto. Here the franchisee purchases the right to use the franchiser's trade name without distributing particular products exclusively under the franchiser's name. **Product distribution franchising** involves a franchiser licensing a franchisee to sell specific products under the franchiser's brand name and trademark through a selective, limited distribution network. This system is commonly used to market automobiles (Chevrolet, Oldsmobile, Chrysler), gasoline products (Exxon, Sunoco, Texaco), soft drinks (Pepsi-Cola, Coca-Cola), bicycles (Schwinn), appliances, cosmetics, and other products. These two methods of franchising allow franchisees to acquire some of the parent company's identity.

product distribution franchising—*a system of franchising in which a franchiser licenses a franchisee to sell its products under the franchiser's brand name and trademark through a selective, limited distribution network.*

pure franchising—*a system of franchising in which a franchiser sells a franchisee a complete business format and system.*

Pure (or comprehensive or business format) **franchising** involves providing the franchisee with a complete business format, including a license for a trade name, the products or services to be sold, the physical plant, the methods of operation, a marketing strategy plan, a quality control process, a two-way communications system, and the necessary business services. The franchisee purchases the right to use all of the elements of a fully integrated business operation. Pure franchising is the most rapidly growing of all types of franchising and is common among fast-food restaurants, hotels, business service firms, car rental agencies, educational institutions, beauty aid retailers, and many others. Although product and trade-name franchises annually ring up more than sales than pure franchisees, pure franchising outlets' sales are growing much faster.

THE BENEFITS OF BUYING A FRANCHISE

Learning Objective

4-A. Explain the benefits of buying a franchise.

A franchisee gets the opportunity to own a small business relatively quickly and, because of the identification with an established product and brand name, a franchise often reaches the breakeven point faster than an independent business would. Still, most new franchise outlets don't break even for at least six to eighteen months.

Franchisees also benefit from the franchiser's business experience. In fact, experience is the essence of what a franchisee is buying from a franchiser. Many entrepreneurs go into business by themselves and make many costly mistakes. Given the thin margin for error in the typical start-up, a new business owner cannot afford to make many mistakes. In a franchising arrangement, the franchiser already has worked out the kinks in the system by trial and error, and franchisees benefit from that experience. Franchisers have climbed up the learning curve and can share with franchisees the secrets of success they have discovered in the industry. For many "first-time" entrepreneurs, access to business models with a proven track record is the safest way to own a business. One critical question every potential entrepreneur must ask is, "What can a franchise do for me that I cannot do for myself?" The answer to this question will depend on the entrepreneur's situation and is not as important as the systematic evaluation of the franchise opportunity. After careful deliberation, one person may conclude that the franchise offers nothing that she could not do independently, and another may decide that a franchise is the key to success as a business owner. Franchisees often cite the following advantages:

Management Training and Support

Recall from Chapter 1 that one of the leading causes of business failure is incompetent management. Franchisers are well aware of this and, in an attempt to reduce the number of franchise casualties, offer managerial training programs to franchisees prior to opening a new outlet.

Many franchisers, especially the well-established ones, also provide follow-up training and counseling services. This service is vital because most franchisers do not require a franchisee to have experience in the business. These programs teach franchisees the details they need to know for day-to-day operations as well as the nuances of running their businesses successfully.

Training programs often involve both classroom and on-site instruction to teach franchisees the basic operations of the business. Before beginning operations, McDonald's franchisees spend 14 days in Illinois at Hamburger University where they learn everything from how to scrape the grill correctly to the essential elements of managing a business with high community visibility and great profit potential. Maaco franchisees spend four weeks at the company's headquarters delving into a five-volume set of operations manuals and learning to run an auto services shop. H & R Block trains its franchisees to unravel the mysteries of tax preparation, whereas Dunkin' Donuts trains a franchisee for as long as five weeks in everything from accounting to dough making. To ensure franchisees' continued success, many franchisers supplement their start-up training programs with ongoing instruction and support. Franchisers offer these training programs because they realize that their ultimate success depends on the franchisee's success.

Despite the positive features of training, inherent dangers exist in the trainer–trainee relationship. Every would-be franchisee should be aware that, in some cases, "assistance" from the franchiser tends to drift into "control" over the franchisee's business. Also, some franchisers charge fees for their training services, so franchisees should know exactly what they are agreeing to, and what it costs.

Brand-Name Appeal

Licensed franchisees purchase the right to use a nationally known and advertised brand name for a product or service. Thus, franchisees have the advantage of identifying their businesses with a widely recognized trademark, which usually provides a great deal of drawing power. Customers recognize the identifying trademark, the standard symbols, the store design, and the products of an established franchise. Indeed, one of the basic tenets of franchising is cloning the franchiser's success. For example, nearly everyone is familiar with the golden arches of McDonald's or the red roof of the Red Roof Inn and the standard products and quality offered at each. A customer is confident that the quality and content of a meal at McDonald's in Fort Lauderdale will be consistent with a meal at a San Francisco McDonald's. There is undoubtedly value in operating a franchise that has a positive brand reputation. Be equally aware, however, that the actions by the franchiser or the actions of other franchisees can harm the value of the brand name and, consequently, have a negative impact on your business. For example, approximately 10 years ago, one of the worst cases of *E. coli* food poisoning ever recorded in the United States hit western Washington. More than 800 people received treatment at local hospitals. Four children died and many others were left with lifelong medical challenges. The source of the food poisoning was undercooked, contaminated beef served at local fast-food restaurants. This tragic event led to a drop in sales throughout the entire chain of restaurants.

Standardized Quality of Goods and Services

Because franchisees purchase a license to sell the franchiser's product or service and the privilege of using the associated brand name, the quality of the goods or service sold determines the franchiser's reputation. Building a sound reputation in business is not achieved quickly, although destroying a good reputation takes no time at all. If some franchisees were allowed to operate at substandard levels, the image of the entire chain would suffer irreparable damage; therefore, franchisers normally demand compliance with uniform standards of quality and service throughout the entire chain. In many cases, the franchiser conducts periodic inspections of local facilities to assist in maintaining acceptable levels of performance.

A Company Example

For instance, John Schnatter, founder of **Papa John's**, *a fast-growing pizza franchise, makes personal visits to some of his franchisees' stores four to five times each week to make sure they are performing up to the company's high quality standards. Franchisees say that Schnatter, known for his attention to detail, often checks pizzas for air bubbles in the crust or tomato sauce for freshness. "Pizza is Schnatter's life, and he takes it very seriously," says one industry analyst.*[11]

Maintaining quality is so important that most franchisers retain the right to terminate the franchise contract and to repurchase the outlet if the franchisee fails to comply with established standards.

National Advertising Programs

An effective advertising program is essential to the success of virtually all franchise operations. Marketing a brand-name product or service over a wide geographic area requires a far-reaching advertising campaign. A regional or national advertising program benefits all franchisees. Normally, such an advertising campaign is organized and controlled by the franchiser. It is financed by each franchisee's contribution of a percentage of monthly sales, usually 1 to 5 percent, or a flat monthly fee. For example, Subway franchisees must pay 3.5 percent of gross revenues to the Subway national advertising program. These funds are pooled and used for a cooperative advertising program, which has more impact than if the franchisees spent the same amount of money separately.

Many franchisers also require franchisees to spend a minimum amount on local advertising. To supplement their national advertising efforts, both Wendy's and Burger King require franchisees to spend at least 3 percent of gross sales on local advertising. Some franchisers assist each franchisee in designing and producing its local ads. Many companies help franchisees create promotional plans and provide press releases and advertisements for grand openings.

Financial Assistance

Because they rely on their franchisees' money to grow their businesses, franchisers typically do not provide any extensive financial help for franchisees. Franchisers rarely make loans to enable franchisees to pay the initial franchise fee. However, once a franchiser locates a suitable prospective franchisee, it may offer the qualified candidate direct financial assistance in specific areas, such as purchasing equipment, inventory, or even the franchise fee. Because the start-up costs of some franchises are already at breathtaking levels, some franchisers find that they must offer direct financial assistance.

A Company Example

*For example, **US Franchise Systems**, franchiser of Microtel Inn and Hawthorn Suites hotels, has set up a subsidiary, US Funding Corporation, that makes available to its franchisees $200 million in construction and mortgage financing. Not only has the in-house financing program cut the time required to open a new hotel franchise, but it also has accelerated the franchise's growth rate.*[12]

Nearly half of the International Franchise Association's members indicate that they offer some type of financial assistance to their franchises; however, only one-fourth offer direct financial assistance. In most instances, financial assistance from franchisers takes a form other than direct loans, leases, or short-term credit. Franchisers usually are willing to assist qualified franchisees in establishing relationships with banks, private investors, and other sources of funds. Such support and connections from the franchiser enhance a franchisee's credit standing because lenders recognize the lower failure rate among established franchises.

Preferred relationships between lenders and franchisers can be critical because finding financing for a franchise can be challenging, just like attracting capital for any business start-up.

A Company Example

*For instance, when Jana Sappenfield began searching for $1.6 million of the $1.9 million needed to purchase a **Primrose School** franchise, the franchiser helped her connect with Newcourt/AT&T, a Small Business Administration–certified lender that has established preferred relationships with about 25 different franchised companies. "They were familiar with Primrose," says Sappenfield, "so no time was wasted researching or approving the franchiser." Because Primrose School had already accepted Sappenfield's application for a franchise, her loan request sailed easily through Newcourt/AT&T's approval process. "We know the leadership and have an understanding of the selection criteria at the franchises we work with regularly," says a top executive at Newcourt/AT&T. "Consequently, when an approved loan application comes in from a [preferred franchise], we are certain the candidate is qualified." Sappenfield's first Primrose School franchise was so successful that she has since purchased a second one.*[13]

Proven Products and Business Formats

What a franchisee essentially purchases is a franchiser's experience, expertise, and products. A franchise owner does not have to build the business from scratch. Instead of being forced to rely solely on personal ability to establish a business and attract a clientele, a franchisee can depend on the methods and techniques of an established business. These standardized procedures and operations greatly enhance the franchisee's chances of success and avoid the most inefficient type of learning—trial and error. In addition, a franchisee does not have to struggle for recognition in the local marketplace as much as an independent owner might.

Centralized Buying Power

A significant advantage a franchisee has over an independent small business owner is participation in the franchiser's centralized and large-volume buying power. If franchisers sell goods and supplies to franchisees (not all do), they may pass on to franchisees any cost savings from quantity discounts they earn by buying in volume. For example, it is unlikely that a small, independent ice cream parlor could match the buying power of Baskin-Robbins with its 4,500-plus retail ice cream stores. In many instances, economies of scale simply preclude the independent owner from competing head-to-head with a franchise operation.

Site Selection and Territorial Protection

A proper location is critical to the success of any small business, and franchises are no exception. In fact, franchise experts consider the three most important factors in franchising to be *location, location,* and *location*. Becoming affiliated with a franchiser may be the best way to get into prime locations. Many franchisers will make an extensive location analysis for each new outlet, including researching traffic patterns, zoning ordinances, accessibility, and population density. McDonald's, for example, is well known for its ability to obtain prime locations in high-traffic areas. Although choosing a location is the franchisee's responsibility, the franchiser usually reserves the right to approve the final site. Choosing a suitable location requires a location analysis, including studies of traffic patterns, zoning ordinances, accessibility, population density, and demographics.

Some franchisers offer franchisees territorial protection, which gives existing franchisees the right to exclusive distribution of brand name goods or services within a particular geographic area. A clause establishing such a protective zone that bars other outlets from the same franchise area gives franchisees significant protection and security. The size of a franchisee's territory varies from industry to industry. For example, one national fast-food restaurant agrees not to license another franchisee within a mile and one-half of existing locations. But one soft-serve ice cream franchiser defines its franchisees' territories on the basis of zip code designations. The purpose of such protection is to prevent an invasion of the existing franchisee's territory and the accompanying dilution of sales. As existing markets have become increasingly saturated with franchise outlets, the placement of new outlets has become a source of friction between franchisers and franchisees. Existing franchisees charge that franchisers are encroaching on their territories by granting new franchises so close to them that their sales are diluted. Although most franchises offer their franchisees some type of territorial protection, be absolutely sure that the territorial protection clause is specific and enforceable.

Greater Chance for Success

Investing in a franchise is not risk free. Between 200 and 300 new franchise companies enter the market each year, and not all of them survive. But available statistics suggest that franchising is less risky than building a business from the ground up. General statistics are useful, but the most valuable numbers are the percentages of successful franchises for any specific business opportunity. Historically, the success rates among franchises are higher than nonfranchise start-ups. This success rate for franchises is attributed to the broad range of services, assistance, and support the franchiser provides. Any statistics regarding the success of a given franchise must be interpreted, however. For example, sometimes when a franchise is in danger of failing, the franchiser often repurchases or relocates the outlet and does not report it as a failure. As a result, some franchisers boast of never experiencing a failure.

The risk involved in purchasing a franchise in the final analysis is largely dependent on the entrepreneur's managerial skills and motivation, and on the franchiser's business experience and system. In light of this risk, many franchise owners prefer the feeling of "not being in this alone" and are convinced that franchising has been a crucial part of their success.

THE DRAWBACKS OF BUYING A FRANCHISE

Learning Objective

4-B. Explain the drawbacks of buying a franchise.

Obviously, the benefits of franchising can mean the difference between success and failure for a small business. However, the franchisee must sacrifice some freedom to the franchiser. The prospective franchisee must explore other limitations of franchising before undertaking this form of ownership.

Franchise Fees and Profit Sharing

Virtually all franchisers impose some type of fees and demand a share of the franchisee's sales revenues in return for the use of the franchiser's name, products or services, and business system. The fees and the initial capital requirements vary among different franchisers, even among those in similar industries. For example, Subway reports start-up cost of $52,000–$191,000, Quizno's $208,400–$243,800, Sonic Drive-In Restaurant $288,100–1,200,000, Hardee's $770,800–$1,100,000, McDonald's $489,900–$1,500,000, and Taco Bell $3,000,000. These start-up cost are influenced by the cost of land and construction.

Start-up costs for franchises often include numerous additional fees. Most franchises impose a franchise fee up front for the right to use the company name. Other start-up costs might include site purchase and preparation, construction, signs, fixtures, equipment, management assistance, and training. Some franchise fees include these costs whereas others do not. For example, Closets by Design, a company that designs and installs closet and garage organizers, entertainment centers, and home office systems, charges a franchise fee ranging from $19,500 to $34,900, which includes both a license for an exclusive territory and management training and support. Before signing any contract, a prospective franchisee should determine the total cost of a franchise, something every franchiser is required to disclose in item 10 of its Uniform Franchising Offering Circular (see "Franchising and the Law" later in this chapter).

Franchisers also impose continuing royalty fees as profit-sharing devices. The royalty usually involves a percentage of gross sales with a required minimum or a flat fee levied on the franchise. Royalty fees range from 1 percent to 11 percent although most franchises assess a rate between 3 percent and 7 percent. The Atlanta Bread Company, for example, charges franchisees a royalty of 5 percent of gross sales, which is payable weekly. These ongoing royalties can increase a franchisee's overhead expenses significantly. Because the franchiser's royalties and fees are calculated as a percentage of a franchisee's sales, the franchiser gets paid—even if the franchisee fails to earn a profit. Sometimes unprepared franchisees discover (too late) that a franchiser's royalties and fees are the equivalent of the normal profit margin for a franchise. To avoid such problems, a prospective franchisee should find out which fees are required (some are merely recommended) and then determine which services and benefits the fees cover. One of the best ways to do this is to itemize what you are getting for your money and then determine whether the cost corresponds to the benefits provided. Be sure to get the details on all expenses—amount, time of payment, and financing arrangements; find out which items, if any, are included in the initial franchise fee and which ones are "extra." Even owning a high-profile franchise such as McDonald's does not guarantee success. In fact, 8 percent of McDonald's franchisees sell their rights back to the company under financial stress.[14]

Strict Adherence to Standardized Operations

Although the franchisee owns the business, she does not have the autonomy of an independent owner. To protect its public image, the franchiser requires that the franchisee maintain certain operating standards. If a franchise constantly fails to meet the minimum standards established for the business, the franchiser may terminate its license. Determining compliance with standards is usually accomplished by periodic inspections. At times, strict adherence to franchise standards may become a burden to the franchisee. The owner may believe that the written reports the franchiser demands require an excessive amount of time. In other instances, the owner may be required to enforce specific rules she believes are inappropriate or unfair.

Restrictions on Purchasing

In the interest of maintaining quality standards, franchisees may be required to purchase products, special equipment, or other items from the franchiser or from an "approved" supplier. For example, Kentucky Fried Chicken requires that franchisees use only seasonings blended by a particular company because a poor image could result from franchisees using inferior products to cut costs. Under some conditions, such purchase arrangements may be challenged in court as a violation of antitrust laws, but generally franchisers have a legal right to see that franchisees maintain acceptable quality standards. A franchiser may legally set the prices paid for the products it sells but may not establish the retail prices to be charged on products sold by the franchisee. A franchiser can suggest retail prices for the franchisee's products and services but cannot force the franchisee to abide by them.

Limited Product Line

In most cases, the franchise agreement stipulates that the franchise can sell only those products approved by the franchiser. Unless willing to risk license cancellation, a franchisee must avoid selling any unapproved products through the franchise.

A franchise may be required to carry an unpopular product or be prevented from introducing a desirable one by the franchise agreement. A franchisee's freedom to adapt a product line to local market conditions is restricted. But some franchisers solicit product suggestions from their franchisees.

*In fact, a **McDonald's** franchisee, Herb Peterson, created the highly successful Egg McMuffin while experimenting with a Teflon-coated egg ring that gave fried eggs rounded corners and a poached appearance. Peterson put his round eggs on English muffins, adorned them with Canadian bacon and melted cheese, and showed his creation to McDonald's chief Ray Kroc. Kroc devoured two of them and was sold on the idea when Peterson's wife suggested the catchy name. In 1975, McDonald's became the first fast-food franchise to open its doors for breakfast, and the Egg McMuffin became a staple on the breakfast menu.*[15]

Unsatisfactory Training Programs

Every would-be franchisee must be wary of the unscrupulous franchiser who promises extensive services, advice, and assistance but delivers nothing. For example, one owner relied on the franchiser to provide what had been described as an "extensive, rigorous training program" after paying a handsome technical assistance fee. The program was nothing but a set of pamphlets and do-it-yourself study guides. Other examples include those impatient entrepreneurs who paid initial franchise fees without investigating the business and never heard from the franchiser again. Although disclosure rules have reduced the severity of the problem, dishonest characters still thrive on unprepared prospective franchisees.

Market Saturation

As the owners of many fast-food and yogurt and ice cream franchises have discovered, market saturation is a very real danger. Although some franchisers offer franchisees territorial protection, others do not. Territorial encroachment has become a hotly contested issue in franchising as growth-seeking franchisers have exhausted most of the prime locations and are now setting up new franchises in close proximity to existing ones. In some areas of the country, franchisees are upset, claiming that their markets are oversaturated and their sales are suffering.

Less Freedom

When franchisees sign a contract, they agree to sell the franchiser's product or service by following its prescribed formula. This feature of franchising is the source of the system's success, but it also gives many franchisees the feeling that they are reporting to a "boss." Franchisers want to ensure success, and most monitor their franchisees' performances closely to make sure franchisees follow the system's specifications. Strict uniformity is the rule rather than the exception. Entrepreneurs who want to be their own bosses often are disappointed with a franchise because highly independent, "go-my-own-way" individuals may find a conflict in basic philosophy with a "go-by-the-rules" franchise contract. Table 4.2 describes 10 myths of franchising.

FRANCHISING AND THE LAW

Learning Objective

5. Understand the laws covering franchise purchases.

The franchising boom spearheaded by McDonald's and others in the late 1950s brought with it many prime investment opportunities. However, the explosion of legitimate franchises also ushered in with it numerous fly-by-night franchisers who defrauded their franchisees. In response to these specific incidents and to the potential for deception inherent in a franchise

TABLE 4.2

10 Myths of Franchising

Sources: Adapted from Andrew A. Caffey, "There's More to a franchise Than Meets the Eye," *Entrepreneur,* www.entrepreneurmag.com; Andrew A. Caffey, "Myth vs. Reality, *Entrepreneur,* www.entrepreneurmag.com/page.hts?N =7118&Ad=S; Chieh Chieng, "Do You Want to Know a Secret?" *Entrepreneur,* January 1999, pp. 174–178; Ten Most Common Mistakes Made by Franchise Buyers," *Franchise Doctor,* www.franchisedoc.com/mistakes.html.

Myth #1. Franchising is the safest way to go into business because franchises never fail. Although the failure rate for franchises is lower than that of independent businesses, there are no guarantees of success. Franchises can—and do—fail. Potential franchisees must exercise the same degree of caution in judging the risk of a franchise as they would any other business.

Myth #2. I'll be able to open my franchise for less money than the franchiser estimates. Launching a business, including a franchise, normally takes more money and more time than entrepreneurs estimate. Be prepared. One franchisee of a retail computer store advises, "If a franchiser tells you you'll need $100,000 to get started, you better have $150,000."

Myth #3. The bigger the franchise organization, the more successful I'll be. Bigger is not always better in the franchise industry. Some of the largest franchise operations are struggling to maintain their growth rates because the best locations are already taken. Market saturation is a significant problem for many large franchises, and smaller franchises are accounting for much of the growth in the industry.

Myth #4. I'll use 80 percent of the franchiser's business system, but I'll improve on it by substituting my experience and know-how. When franchisees buy a franchise, they are buying, in essence, the franchiser's experience and know-how. Why pay all of that money to a franchiser if you aren't willing to use its system?

Myth #5. All franchises are the same. Each franchise has its own unique requirements, procedures, and culture. Naturally, some will suit you better than others. Avoid the tendency to select the franchise offering the lowest cost; ask the franchiser and existing franchisees lots of questions to determine whether you'll be comfortable in that system.

Myth #6. I don't have to be a "hands-on" manager. I can be an absentee owner and still be very successful. Most franchisers shy away from absentee owners. They know that franchise success requires lots of hands-on attention, and the owner is the best person to provide that.

Myth #7. Anyone can be a satisfied, successful franchise owner. With more than 4,500 franchises available, the odds of finding a franchise that appeals to your tastes is high. However, not everyone is cut out to be a franchisee. Those "free spirits" who insist on doing things their way will most likely be miserable in a franchise.

Myth #8. Franchising is the cheapest way to get into business for yourself. Although bargains do exist in franchising, the price tag for buying into some systems is breathtaking, sometimes running into several hundreds of thousands of dollars. Franchisers look for candidates who are on solid financial footing.

Myth #9. The franchiser will solve my business problems for me; after all, that's why I pay an ongoing royalty. Although franchisers offer franchisees start-up and ongoing training programs, they will not run their franchisees' businesses for them. Your job is to take the formula that the franchiser has developed and make it work in your location. Expect to solve many of your own problems.

Myth #10. Once I open my franchise, I'll be able to run things the way *I* want to. Franchisees are not free to run their businesses any way they see fit. Every franchisee signs a contract that requires him or her to run the business according to the franchiser's requirements. Franchisees who violate the terms of that agreement run the risk of having their franchise relationship canceled.

relationship, California in 1971 enacted the first Franchise Investment Law. The law (and those of 16 other states that have since passed similar laws) requires franchisers to register a **Uniform Franchise Offering Circular (UFOC)** and deliver a copy to prospective franchisees before any offer or sale of a franchise. The UFOC establishes full disclosure guidelines for any company selling franchises.

In October 1979, the Federal Trade Commission (FTC) enacted the Trade Regulation Rule, requiring all franchisers to disclose detailed information on their operations at the first personal meeting, or at least 10 days before a franchise contract is signed, or before any money is paid. The FTC rule covers *all* franchisers, even those in the 33 states lacking franchise disclosure laws. The purpose of the regulation is to assist the potential franchisee's investigation of the franchise deal and to introduce consistency into the franchiser's disclosure statements. In 1994, the FTC modified the requirements for the UFOC, making more information available to prospective franchisees and making the document shorter and easier to read and understand. The FTC's philosophy is not so much to prosecute abusers as to provide information to prospective franchisees and help them make intelligent decisions. Although the FTC requires each franchiser to provide a potential franchisee with this information, it does not verify its accuracy. Prospective franchisees should use these data only as a starting point for the investigation. The Trade Regulation Rule requires a franchiser to include 23 major topics in its disclosure statement:

1. Information identifying the franchiser and its affiliates and describing their business experience and the franchises being sold.

2. Information identifying and describing the business experience of each of the franchiser's officers, directors, and management personnel responsible for the franchise program.

3. A description of the lawsuits in which the franchiser and its officers, directors, and managers have been involved. Although most franchisers will have been involved in some type of litigation, an excessive number of lawsuits, particularly if they relate to the same problem, is alarming.

4. Information about any bankruptcies in which the franchiser and its officers, directors, and managers have been involved.

5. Information about the initial franchise fee and other payments required to obtain the franchise, including the intended use of the fees. Initial fees typically range from $10,000 to $50,000.

6. A description of any continuing payments franchisees are required to make after start-up, including royalties, service fees, training fees, lease payments, advertising or marketing charges, and others.

7. A detailed description of the payments a franchisee must make to fulfill the initial investment requirement and how and to whom they are made. The categories covered are the initial franchise fee, equipment, opening inventory, initial advertising fee, signs, training, real estate, working capital, legal, accounting, and utilities. These estimates, usually stated in the form of a range of numbers, give prospective franchisees an idea of how much their total start-up costs will be.

8. Information about quality restrictions on goods, services, equipment, supplies, inventory, and other items used in the franchise and where franchisees may purchase them, including restricted purchases from the franchiser.

9. A statement (in tabular form) of the franchisee's obligations under the franchise contract, including items such as selecting a site, paying fees, maintaining quality standards, keeping records, transferring or renewing the franchise relationship, and others.

10. A description of any financial assistance available from the franchiser in the purchase of the franchise.

11. A description of all obligations the franchiser must fulfill in helping a franchisee prepare to open, open, and operate a unit plus information covering location selection methods and the training program provided to franchisees. In addition to the training they provide new franchisees, many franchisers offer help with a grand opening for each outlet and on-site management assistance for a short time to get franchisees started.

12. A description of any territorial protection that will be granted to the franchise and a statement as to whether the franchiser may locate a company-owned store or other outlet in that territory.

13. All relevant information about the franchiser's trademarks, service marks, trade names, logos, and commercial symbols, including where they are registered. Look for a strong trade or service mark that is registered with the U.S. Patent and Trademark Office.

Uniform Franchise Offering Circular (UFOC)—*a document that every franchiser is required by law to give prospective franchisees before any offer or sale of a franchise; it outlines 23 important pieces of information.*

14. Similar information on any patents and copyrights the franchiser owns and the rights to these transferred to franchisees.

15. A description of the extent to which franchisees must participate personally in the operation of the franchise. Many franchisers look for "hands-on" franchisees and discourage "absentee owners."

16. A description of any restrictions on the goods or services franchises are permitted to sell and with whom franchisees may deal. The agreement usually restricts franchisees to selling only those items approved by the franchiser.

17. A description of the conditions under which the franchise may be repurchased or refused renewal by the franchiser, transferred to a third party by the franchisee, and terminated or modified by either party. This section also addresses the method established for resolving disputes.

18. A description of the involvement of celebrities and public figures in the franchise.

19. A complete statement of the basis for any earnings claims made to the franchisee, including the percentage of existing franchises that have actually achieved the results that are claimed. New rules put two requirements on franchisers making earnings claims: (a) Any earnings claim must be included in the UFOC, and (b) the claim must "have a reasonable basis at the time it is made." However, franchisers are *not* required to make any earnings claims at all; in fact, only about 25 percent of franchisers make earnings claims in their circulars, primarily because of liability concerns about committing such numbers to paper.

20. Statistical information about the present number of franchises, the number of franchises projected for the future, the number of franchises terminated, the number the franchiser has not renewed, the number repurchased in the past, and a list of the names and addresses (organized by state) of other franchisees in the system.

21. The franchiser's financial statements.

22. A copy of all franchise and other contracts (leases, purchase agreements, etc.) the franchisee will be required to sign.

23. A standardized, detachable "receipt" to prove that the prospective franchisee received a copy of the UFOC.

The information contained in the UFOC does not fully protect a potential franchise from deception, nor does it guarantee success. It does, however, provide enough information to begin a thorough investigation of the franchiser and the franchise deal.

THE *RIGHT* WAY TO BUY A FRANCHISE

Learning Objective

6. Discuss the *right* way to buy a franchise.

The UFOC is a powerful tool designed to help would-be franchisees select the franchise that is right for them and to avoid being duped by dishonest franchisers. The best defenses a prospective entrepreneur has against unscrupulous franchisers are preparation, common sense, and patience. By investigating thoroughly before investing in a franchise, a potential franchisee minimizes the risk of being hoodwinked into a nonexistent business. Asking the right questions and resisting the urge to rush into an investment decision helps a potential franchisee avoid being taken by unscrupulous operators.

Potential franchisees must beware because franchise fraud still exists in this rapidly growing field. A recent conference of state securities regulators named "illegal franchise offers" as one of the top 10 financial frauds in the United States.[16] The president of one franchise consulting firm estimates that 5 to 10 percent of franchisers are dishonest—"the rogue elephants of franchising." Dishonest franchisers tend to follow certain patterns, and well-prepared franchisees who know what to look for can avoid trouble. The following clues should arouse the suspicion of an entrepreneur about to invest in a franchise:

■ Claims that the franchise contract is a standard one and that "you don't need to read it."

■ A franchiser who fails to give you a copy of the required disclosure document at your first face-to-face meeting.

■ A marginally successful prototype store or no prototype at all.

■ A poorly prepared operations manual outlining the franchise system or no manual (or no system) at all.

■ Oral promises of future earnings without written documentation.

■ A high franchisee turnover rate or a high termination rate.

■ An unusual amount of litigation brought against the franchiser.

- Attempts to discourage you from allowing an attorney to evaluate the franchise contract before you sign it.
- No written documentation to support claims and promises.
- A high-pressure sale—sign the contract now or lose the opportunity.
- Claiming to be exempt from federal laws requiring complete disclosure of franchise details.
- "Get-rich-quick schemes," promises of huge profits with only minimum effort.
- Reluctance to provide a list of present franchisees for you to interview.
- Evasive, vague answers to your questions about the franchise and its operation.

Not every franchise "horror story" is the result of dishonest franchisers. More often than not, the problems that arise in franchising have more to do with franchisees who buy legitimate franchises without proper research and analysis. They end up in businesses they don't enjoy and that they are not well suited to operate. How can you avoid this mistake? The following steps will help you make the right choice:

Evaluate Yourself

Before looking at any franchise, entrepreneurs should study their own traits, goals, experience, likes, dislikes, risk orientation, income requirements, time and family commitments, and other characteristics. Will you be comfortable working in a structured environment? What kinds of franchises fit your desired lifestyle? In what region of the country or world do you want to live and work? What is your ideal job description? Knowing what you enjoy doing (and what you don't want to do) will help you narrow your search. The goal is to find the franchise that is right—*for you*! One characteristic successful franchisees have in common is that they genuinely enjoy their work. Table 4.3 provides a test for prospective franchisees that helps them evaluate their franchise potential.

Research Your Market

Before shopping for a franchise, research the market in the area you plan to serve. How fast is the overall area growing? In which areas is that growth occurring fastest? Investing some time at the library developing a profile of the customers in your target area is essential; otherwise, you will be flying blind. Who are your potential customers? What are their characteristics? Their income and education levels? What kinds of products and services do they buy? What gaps exist in the market? These gaps represent potential franchise opportunities for you. Market research also should confirm that a franchise is not merely part of a fad that will quickly fade. Steering clear of fads and into long-term trends is one way to sustain the success of a franchise.

A Company Example

*Before **Papa John's Pizza** allows franchisees to open any store, it requires them to spend six months to a year evaluating the market potential of the local area. "We don't just move into an area and open up 200 stores," says one manager. "We do it one store at a time."*[17]

Consider Your Franchise Options

The International Franchise Association publishes the *Franchise Opportunities Guide*, which lists its members and some basic information about them. Many cities host franchise trade shows throughout the year, where hundreds of franchisers gather to sell their franchises. Attending one of these franchise showcases is a convenient, efficient way to collect information about a variety of available opportunities. Many small business magazines such as *Entrepreneur, Inc., FSB,* and others devote at least one issue to franchising, where they often lists hundreds of franchises. These guides can help you find a suitable franchise within your price range.

Get a Copy of the Franchiser's UFOC

Once you narrow down your franchise choices, you should contact each franchise and get a copy of its UFOC. Then read it! This document is an important tool in your search for the right franchise, and you should make the most of it. When evaluating a franchise opportunity, what should a potential franchisee look for? Although there's never a guarantee of success, the following characteristics make a franchise stand out:

- *A unique concept or marketing approach.* "Me-too" franchises are no more successful than "me-too" independent businesses. Pizza franchiser Papa John's has achieved an impressive growth rate by emphasizing the quality of its ingredients, whereas Domino's is known for its fast delivery.

- *Profitability.* A franchiser should have a track record of profitability and so should its franchisees. If a franchiser is not profitable, its franchisees are not likely to be either. Franchisees who follow the business format should expect to earn a reasonable rate of return.

- *A registered trademark.* Name recognition is difficult to achieve without a well-known and protected trademark.

- *A business system that works.* A franchiser should have in place a system that is efficient and is well documented in its manuals.

- *A solid training program.* One of the most valuable components of a franchise system is the training it offers franchisees. The system should be relatively easy to teach.

- *Affordability.* A franchisee should not have to take on an excessive amount of debt to purchase a franchise. Being forced to borrow too much money to open a franchise outlet can doom a business from the outset. Respectable franchisers verify prospective franchisees' financial qualifications as part of the screening process.

- *A positive relationship with franchisees.* The most successful franchises are those that see their franchisees as partners . . . and treat them accordingly.

The UFOC covers the 23 items discussed in the previous section and includes a copy of the company's franchise agreement and any contracts accompanying it. Although the law requires a UFOC to be written in plain English rather than "legalese," it is best to have an attorney experienced in franchising to review the UFOC and discuss its provisions with you. Watch for clauses that give the franchiser absolute control and discretion. The franchise contract summarizes the details that will govern the franchiser–franchisee relationship over its life. It outlines *exactly* the rights and the obligations of each party and sets the guidelines that govern the franchise relationship. Because franchise contracts typically are long term (50 percent run for 15 years or more), it is extremely important for prospective franchisees to understand the terms *before* they sign the contract.

franchisee turnover rate—
the rate at which franchisees leave a franchise system.

One of the most revealing items in the UFOC is the **franchisee turnover rate**, the rate at which franchisees leave the system. If the turnover rate is less than 5 percent, the franchise is probably sound. However, a franchise turnover rate approaching 20 percent is a sign of serious, underlying problems in a franchise. Satisfied franchisees are not inclined to leave a successful system.

Talk to Existing Franchisees

One of the best ways to evaluate the reputation of a franchiser is to interview (in person) several franchise owners who have been in business at least one year about the positive and the negative features of the agreement and whether the franchiser delivered what was promised. Did the franchise estimate their start-up costs accurately? Do they get the support the franchiser promised them? Has the franchise met their expectations concerning profitability and return on investment? Knowing what they know now, would they buy the franchise again?

A Company Example

*Bob Phillips, a CPA looking to make a career change, wanted to make sure that he purchased the right franchise, so he invested time poring over the UFOCs he had collected from the dozen franchises that interested him. Rather than rely on the documents alone to judge the franchises, Phillips made calls to franchisees that he randomly selected from the lists included in the UFOCs (item 20). His conversations with franchisees convinced him that **Ranch 1**, a chain of fast-food grilled chicken stores, was the best choice for him. "Almost every one wanted a second location," he says. "That's indicative of a healthy franchise system." Phillips is convinced that his thorough research led him to the right franchise. Today he owns two Ranch 1 franchises that generate more than $2 million in sales, and he plans to open eight more outlets within three years.*[18]

TABLE 4.3

A Test for Prospective Franchisees

Sources: Adapted from Erika Kotite, "Is Franchising for You?" *Franchise & Business Opportunities 1995,* pp. 14–18; Heather Page, "True Confessions," *Entrepreneur,* January 1996, pp. 184–186: *Franchise Solutions.* www.franchisesolutions.com.

Of those people who set out to buy a franchise, only 15 percent actually buy one. Some of that 15 percent make the wrong decision. They discover too late that they are not cut out to be franchisees. Do you have what it takes to be a successful franchisee? The following quiz will help you determine your "franchise quotient."

1. You own a company. How much operational detail are you comfortable with?
    a. I want direct control over all operations.
    b. I delegate less than half.
    c. I delegate more than half.

2. You have three job offers with comparable salary and benefits. Choose one.
    a. Small company but high management responsibility and exposure.
    b. Midsized company with less personal exposure but more prestigious name.
    c. Large company with least personal exposure but very well-known name.

3. You reach a major stumbling block on a project. You:
    a. Seek help from others immediately.
    b. Think it through and then present possible solutions to your superior.
    c. Keep working until you resolve it on your own.

4. Which investment sounds most appealing?
    a. Five percent fixed return over a period of time.
    b. From –20 percent to +50 percent loss or return over a period of time, depending on changing economic situations.

5. Which business arrangement is most appealing?
    a. You're the sole owner.
    b. You're in a partnership and own a majority of the stock.
    c. You're in an equal partnership.

6. Your company's sales technique increases sales 10 percent per year. You used a technique elsewhere you feel will result in 15 percent to 20 percent annual increases, but it requires extra time and capital. You:
    a. Avoid the risk and stay with the present plan.
    b. Suggest your new method, showing previous results.
    c. Privately use your system, and show the results later.

7. You suggest your system to your boss, and he says, "Don't rock the boat." You:
    a. Drop your different approach.
    b. Approach your boss at a later time.
    c. Go to your boss's boss with your suggestion.
    d. Use your own system anyway.

8. Which would mean the most to you?
    a. Becoming the president of a company.
    b. Becoming the highest-paid employee of a company.
    c. Winning the highest award for achievement in your profession.

9. What three activities do you find most appealing?
    a. Sales and marketing.
    b. Administration.
    c. Payroll.
    d. Training.
    e. Customer service.
    f. Credit and collections.
    g. Management.

10. What work pace do you generally prefer?
    a. Working on one project until it is completed.
    b. Working on several projects at one time.

Scoring: 1. A=5, B=3, C=1. 2. A=3, B=2, C=1. 3. A=1, B=5, C=7. 4. A=2, B=6. 5. A=7, B=5 C=2.
6. A=1, B=6, C=10. 7. A=1, B=5, C=8, D=10. 8. A=8, B=2, C=5. 9. A=10, B=1, C=3, D=3,
E=8, F=2, G=5. 10. A=3, B=6.

Total Score:

20–33   You're a corporate player and are happiest in a structured environment. Franchising suits you.
34–71   You're a potentially good franchisee.
72–85   You're an entrepreneur who prefers total independence.

Interviewing past franchisees to get their perspectives on the franchiser–franchisee relationship is also helpful. Why did they leave? Franchisees of some companies have formed associations, which might provide prospective franchisees with valuable information. Other sources of information include the American Association of Franchisees and Dealers, the American Franchise Association, and the International Franchise Association.

Ask the Franchiser Some Tough Questions

Take the time to ask the franchiser questions about the company and its relationship with its franchisees. You will be in this relationship a long time, and you need to know as much about it as you possibly can beforehand. What is its philosophy concerning the relationship? What is the company culture like? How much input do franchisees have into the system? What are the franchise's future expansion plans? How will they affect your franchise? Are you entitled to an exclusive territory? Under what circumstances can either party terminate the franchise agreement? What happens if you decide to sell your franchise in the future? Under what circumstances would you not be entitled to renew the agreement? What kind of profits can you expect? (If the franchiser made no earnings claims in item 19 of the UFOC, why not?) Does the franchiser have a well-formulated strategic plan?

Make Your Choice

The first lesson in franchising is "Do your homework *before* you get out your checkbook." Once you have done your research, you can make an informed choice about which franchise is right for you. Then it is time to put together a solid business plan that will serve as your road map to success in the franchise you have selected. The plan is also a valuable tool to use as you arrange the financing for your franchise. We will discuss the components of a business plan in Chapter 11.

TRENDS SHAPING FRANCHISING

Learning Objective

7. Outline the major trends shaping franchising.

Franchising has experienced three major growth waves since its beginning. The first wave occurred in the early 1970s when fast-food restaurants used the concept to grow rapidly. The fast-food industry was one of the first to discover the power of franchising, but other businesses soon took notice and adapted the franchising concept to their industries. The second wave took place in the mid-1980s as our nation's economy shifted heavily toward the service sector. Franchises followed suit, springing up in every service business imaginable—from maid services and copy centers to mailing services and real estate. The third wave began in the early 1990s and continues today. It is characterized by new, low-cost franchises that focus on specific market niches. In the wake of major corporate downsizing and the burgeoning costs of traditional franchises, these new franchises allow would-be entrepreneurs to get into proven businesses faster and at lower costs. These companies feature start-up costs in the $2,000 to $250,000 range and span a variety of industries—from leak detection in homes and auto detailing to day care and tile glazing. Other significant trends affecting franchising are discussed next.

Changing Face of Franchisees

Franchisees today are better educated, are more sophisticated, have more business acumen, and are more financially secure than those of just 20 years ago. Franchising is attracting skilled, experienced businesspeople whose goal is to own multiple outlets that cover entire states or regions.

A Company Example

*For instance, when **Krispy Kreme Doughnuts** began to move its popular product north from its southern stronghold, the Lev family—father Howard, sons Russel and Mel, and nephew John Faber—bought the franchise for the entire state of New York. While on a trip to the South, Mel discovered the tasty orbs and brought some back to his family, who quickly devoured them. Once they returned to their home in New York, the Levs decided to become franchisees. All experienced in business (Howard and Mel once owned a shirt-making company), the Levs and Faber have opened 10 stores and have plans for dozens more.[19] James A. Cosentino's Krispy Kreme in West Palm Beach, Florida, has customers waiting at the front door at 5:30 A.M. The franchise agreement requires the franchisee to pay Krispy Kreme 4.5 percent of total sales as a royalty fee, plus an additional 2.0 percent to help pay for brand development and public relations.*

YOU Be the Consultant . . .

The Opportunity of a Lifetime

"Honey, I think I've found it!" said Joe Willingham to his wife Allie. "This is just what I've been looking for, and just in time, too. My severance package from the company runs out next month. The man said that if we invested in this franchise now, we could be bringing in good money by then. It's that easy!"

Allie knew Joe had been working hard at finding another job since he had been a victim of his company's latest downsizing, but jobs were scarce even for someone with his managerial experience and background in manufacturing. "Nobody wants to hire a 51-year-old man with experience when they can hire 23-year-old college graduates at less than half the salary and teach them what they need to know," Joe told her after months of fruitless job hunting. That's when Joe got the idea of setting up his own business. Rather than start an independent business from scratch, Joe felt more comfortable, given his 26-year corporate career, opening a franchise. "A franchiser can give me the support I need," he told Allie.

"Tell me about this franchise," Allie said.

"It's a phenomenal opportunity for us," Joe said, barely able to contain his excitement. "I saw this booth for American Speedy Print at the Business Expo this morning. There were all kinds of franchises there, but this one really caught my eye," Joe said as he pulled a rather plain-looking photocopy of a brochure from his briefcase.

"Is that their brochure?" asked Allie.

"Well, the company is growing so fast that they have temporarily run out of their normal literature. This is just temporary."

"Oh . . .You would think that a printing franchise could print flashier brochures even on short notice, but I guess . . . ," said Allie.

"The main thing is the profit potential this business has," said Joe. "I met one of their franchisees. I tell you the guy was wearing a $2,000 suit if ever there was one, and he had expensive jewelry dripping from his fingers. He's making a mint with this franchise, and he said we could, too!"

Joe continued, "With the severance package I have from the company, we could pay the $10,000 franchise fee and lease most of the equipment we need to get started. It'll take every penny of my package, but, hey, it's an investment in our future. The representative said the company would help us with our grand opening and would also help us compile a list of potential customers."

"What would you print?" asked Allie.

"Anything!" said Joe. "The franchisee I talked to does flyers, posters, booklets, newsletters, advertising pieces . . .you name it!"

"Wow! It seems like you'd need lots of specialized equipment to do all of that. How much does the total franchise package cost?" said Allie.

"Well, I'm not exactly sure. He never gave me an exact figure, but we can lease all the equipment we need from the franchiser!"

"Is this all of the material they gave you? I thought franchisers were supposed to have some kind of information packet to give to people," said Allie.

"Yeah, I asked him about that," said Joe. "He said that American Speedy Print is just a small franchise. They'd rather put their money into building a business and helping their franchisees succeed than into useless paperwork that nobody reads anyway. It makes sense to me."

"I guess so . . . ," Allie said reluctantly.

"I think we need to take this opportunity, hon," Joe said, with a look that spoke of determination and enthusiasm. "Besides, he said that there was another couple in this county that is already looking at this franchise, and that the company will license only one franchisee in this area. They don't want to saturate the market. He thinks they may take it. I think we have to move on this now, or we'll lose the opportunity of a lifetime."

Allie had not seen Joe exhibit this much enthusiasm and excitement for anything since he had lost his job at the plant. Piles of rejection letters from his job search had sapped Joe's zest for living. Allie was glad to see "the old Joe" return, but she still had her doubts about the franchise opportunity Joe was describing.

"It might just be the opportunity of a lifetime, Joe," she said. "But don't you think we need to find out a little more about this franchise before we invest that much money? I mean . . ."

"Hon, I'd love to do that, but like the man said, we may miss out on the opportunity of a lifetime if we don't sign today. I think we've got to move on this thing now!"

1. What advice would you offer Joe about investing in this franchise?

2. Map out a plan for Joe to use in finding the right franchise for him. What can Joe do to protect himself from making a bad franchise investment?

3. Summarize the advantages and disadvantages Joe can expect if he buys a franchise.

International Opportunities

One of the major trends in franchising is the internationalization of American franchise systems. Increasingly, franchising is becoming a major export industry for the United States. Growing numbers of U.S. franchises are moving into international markets to boost sales and profits as the domestic market becomes saturated. According to a report by Arthur Andersen, 44 percent of U.S. franchisers have international locations, up from 34 percent in 1989. International expansion is a relatively new phenomenon in franchising, however; approximately

McDonald's has achieved much success around the world by adapting its menu to satisfy local tastes. The company has more than 30,000 restaurants in 119 countries.

Courtesy of CORBIS BETTMANN, © Morton Beebe/CORBIS

75 percent of franchisers established their first foreign outlet within the past 10 years.[20] Canada is the primary market for U.S. franchisers, with Mexico, Japan, and Europe following. These markets are most attractive to franchisers because they are similar to the U.S. market—rising personal incomes, strong demand for consumer goods, growing service economies, and spreading urbanization.

As they venture into foreign markets, franchisers have learned that adaptation is one key to success. Although a franchise's overall business format may not change in foreign markets, some of the details of operating its local outlets must. For instance, fast-food chains in other countries often must make adjustments to their menus to please locals' palates. In Japan, McDonald's (known as "Makudonarudo") outlets sell teriyaki burgers, rice burgers, and katsu burgers (cheese wrapped in a roast pork cutlet topped with katsu sauce and shredded cabbage) in addition to their traditional American fare. In the Philippines, the McDonald's menu includes a spicy Filipino-style burger, spaghetti, and chicken with rice.

Countries that recently welcomed the free market system are turning to franchising to help them move toward a market economy. Some countries of Eastern Europe, including Hungary, Poland, and Yugoslavia, already have attracted franchises. Even Russia is fertile ground for franchising. McDonald's scored a hit with its 700-seat restaurant in Moscow. Despite being one of the largest McDonald's outlets in the world, "The waiting line winds along busy Pushkin Square for well over 500 yards," reports one Soviet magazine.[21] Franchisers in these countries must have patience, however. Lack of capital, archaic infrastructure, and a shortage of hard currencies mean that profits will be slow in coming. Most franchisers recognize the difficulties of developing franchises in foreign markets and start slowly.

It is valuable to have owners of American franchises be natives of the country in which the franchise is located. For example, Brambang Rachmadi owns 85 McDonald's restaurants in his native Indonesia. Following the September 11, 2001, terrorist attacks in the United States, it was feared that the natives of Indonesia, a Muslim country, might have within its population anti-American radicals who would attack American targets in Indonesia. Mr. Rachmadi immediately took the offensive to defend his McDonald's by erecting a 6-foot-high banner stating that "In the name of Allah, the merciful and the gracious, McDonald's Indonesia is owned by an indigenous Muslim."[22]

Smaller, Nontraditional Locations

intercept marketing—*the principle of putting a franchise's products or services directly in the paths of potential customers, wherever they may be.*

As the high cost of building full-scale locations continues to climb, more franchisers are searching out nontraditional locations in which to build smaller, less expensive outlets. Based on the principle of **intercept marketing**, the idea is to put a franchise's products or services directly in the paths of potential customers, wherever that may be. Locations within locations have become popular. Franchises are putting scaled-down outlets on college campuses, in high school cafeterias, in sports arenas, in hospitals, on airline flights, and in zoos. St. Louis–based Pizzas of Eight already has outlets inside convenience stores, supermarkets, and bowling alleys and plans to open others in video stores.[23] Many franchisees have discovered that smaller outlets in these nontraditional locations generate nearly the same sales volume as full-sized outlets at just a fraction of the cost!

A Company Example

Steve Siegel, owner of 35 **Dunkin' Donut** *shops in the Boston area, recently began branching out into small, nontraditional locations where pedestrian traffic counts are high. One of his most profitable spots measures just 64 square feet, but because it is in a business district filled with office workers, it generates a high volume of sales.*[24] *Such locations will be a key to continued franchise growth in the domestic market.*

Conversion Franchising

conversion franchising—*a franchising trend in which owners of independent businesses become franchisees to gain the advantage of name recognition.*

The recent trend toward **conversion franchising**, in which owners of independent businesses become franchisees to gain the advantage of name recognition, will continue. In a franchise conversion, the franchiser gets immediate entry into new markets and experienced operators; franchisees get increased visibility and often a big sales boost. It is not unusual to experience an increase of 20 percent or better in gross sales. The biggest force in conversion franchising has been Century 21, the real estate sales company.

Multiple-Unit Franchising

Multiple-unit franchising became extremely popular in the early 1990s. In multiple unit franchising, a franchisee opens more than one unit in a broad territory within a specific time period. Multiple ownership of franchise units has expanded in recent years. It is now becoming more common for one franchisee to own 60, 70, or even 200 units. Franchisers are finding it's far more efficient in the long run to have one well-trained franchisee operate a number of units than to train many franchisees. The popularity of multiple-unit franchising has paralleled the trend toward increasingly experienced, sophisticated franchisees, who set high performance goals that a single outlet cannot meet. The typical multiple-unit franchisee owns between three and six units, but some franchisees own many more.

multiple-unit franchising— *a method of franchising in which a franchisee opens more than one unit on a broad territory within a specific time period.*

Master Franchising

A **master franchise** (or subfranchise) gives a franchisee the right to create a semi-independent organization in a particular territory to recruit, sell, and support other franchisees. A master franchisee buys the right to develop subfranchises within a broad geographic area or, sometimes, an entire country. Subfranchising "turbocharges" a franchiser's growth. Many franchisers use it to open outlets in international markets more quickly and efficiently because the master franchisees understand local laws and the nuances of selling in local markets. For instance, a master franchisee with TCBY International, a yogurt franchise, has opened 21 stores in China and Hong Kong. Based on his success in these markets, the company has sold him the master franchise in India.[25]

master franchise—*a method of franchising that gives a franchisee the right to create a semi-independent organization in a particular territory to recruit, sell, and support other franchisees.*

Piggybacking (or Combination Franchising)

Some franchisers also are discovering new ways to reach customers by teaming up with other franchisers selling complementary products or services. A growing number of companies are **piggybacking** outlets—combining two or more distinct franchises under one roof. This "buddy system" approach works best when the two franchise ideas are compatible and appeal to similar customers. For example, franchisers Dunkin' Donuts, Togos' Eatery sandwich shops, and ice cream retailer Baskin-Robbins are working together to build hundreds of combination outlets, a concept that has proved to be highly successful.[26] Properly planned, piggybacked franchises can magnify many times over the sales and profits of individual, self-standing outlets. One Baskin Robbins franchisee saw his sales climb 25 percent when he added a Blimpie Subs and Salads franchise to his existing ice cream shop. Another enterprising franchisee who combined Shell Oil (gas station), Charley's Steakery (sandwich shop), and TCBY (frozen yogurt) franchises under one roof in Columbus, Ohio, says that sales are running 10 percent higher than the three outlets would generate in separate locations.[27]

Serving Aging Baby Boomers

Now that dual-career couples have become the norm, especially among baby boomers, the market for franchises offering convenience and timesaving devices is booming. Customers are willing to pay for products and services that will save them time or trouble, and franchises are ready to provide them. Franchisees of Around Your Neck go into the homes and offices of busy male executives to sell men's apparel and accessories ranging from shirts and ties to custom-made suits. Other areas in which franchising is experiencing rapid growth include home delivery of meals, house-cleaning services, continuing education and training (especially computer and business training), leisure activities (such as hobbies, health spas, and travel-related activities), products and services aimed at home-based businesses, and health care.

CONCLUSION

Franchising has proved its viability in the U.S. economy and has become a key part of the small business sector because it offers many would-be entrepreneurs the opportunity to own and operate a business with a greater chance for success. Despite its impressive growth rate to date, the franchising industry still has a great deal of room to grow. Global companies, as well as U.S. firms, are finding that they can achieve growth through franchising, and we can anticipate that the franchising phenomenon will continue in the future.

CHAPTER SUMMARY

1-A. Explain the advantages and the disadvantages of the sole proprietorship.

A sole proprietorship is a business owned and managed by one individual and is the most popular form of ownership.

Sole proprietorships offer these *advantages*: They are simple to create; they are the least costly form to begin; the owner has total decision-making authority; there are no special legal restrictions; and they are easy to discontinue.

They also suffer from these *disadvantages*: unlimited personal liability of owner; limited managerial skills and capabilities; limited access to capital; and lack of continuity.

1-B. Explain the advantages and the disadvantages of the partnership.

A partnership is an association of two or more people who co-own a business for the purpose of making a profit. Partnerships offer these *advantages*: ease of establishing; complementary skills of partners; division of profits; larger pool of capital available; ability to attract limited partners; little government regulation flexibility; and tax advantages.

Partnerships suffer from these *disadvantages*: unlimited liability of at least one partner; difficulty in disposing of partnership interest; lack of continuity; potential for personality and authority conflicts; and partners bound by the law of agency.

1-C. Explain the advantages and the disadvantages of the corporation.

A corporation, the most complex of the three basic forms of ownership, is a separate legal entity. To form a corporation, an entrepreneur must file the articles of incorporation with the state in which the company will incorporate. Corporations offer these *advantages*: limited liability of stockholders; ability to attract capital; ability to continue indefinitely; and transferable ownership.

Corporations suffer from these *disadvantages*: cost and time involved in incorporating; double taxation; potential for diminished managerial incentives; legal requirements and regulatory red tape; and potential loss of control by the founder(s).

2. Discuss the advantages and the disadvantages of the S corporation, the limited liability company, the professional corporation, and the joint venture.

Entrepreneurs can also choose from several other forms of ownership, including S corporations, and limited liability companies. An S corporation offers its owners limited liability protection but avoids the double taxation of C corporations.

A limited liability company, like an S corporation, is a cross between a partnership and a corporation, yet it operates without the restrictions imposed on an S corporation. To create an LLC, an entrepreneur must file the articles of organization and the operating agreement with the secretary of state.

A professional corporation offers professionals the benefits of the corporate form of ownership.

A joint venture is like a partnership, except that it is formed for a specific purpose.

3. Describe the three types of franchising: trade name, product distribution, and pure.

Trade-name franchising involves a franchisee purchasing the right to become affiliated with a franchiser's trade-name without distributing its products exclusively.

Product distribution franchising involves licensing a franchisee to sell products or services under the franchiser's brand name through a selective, limited distribution network.

Pure franchising involves selling a franchisee a complete business format.

4. Explain the benefits and the drawbacks of buying a franchise.

Franchises offer many *benefits*: management training and support; brand-name appeal; standardized quality of goods and services; national advertising programs; financial assistance; proven products and business formats; centralized buying power; territorial protection; and a greater chance of success.

Franchising also suffers from certain *drawbacks*: franchise fees and profit sharing; strict adherence to standardized operations; restrictions on purchasing; limited product lines; unsatisfactory training programs; market saturation; and less freedom.

5. Understand the laws covering franchise purchases.

The Federal Trade Commission (FTC) enacted the Trade Regulation Rule in 1979, which requires all franchisers to disclose detailed information on their operations at the first personal meeting or at least 10 days before a franchise contract is signed, or before any money is paid. The FTC rule covers *all* franchisers. The Trade Regulation Rule requires franchisers to provide information on 23 topics in their disclosure statements.

Seventeen states have passed their own franchise laws requiring franchisers to provide prospective franchisees a Uniform Franchise Offering Circular (UFOC).

6. Discuss the *right* way to buy a franchise.

The following steps will help you make the right franchise choice: Evaluate yourself; research your market; consider your franchise options; get a copy of the franchiser's UFOC; talk to existing franchisees; ask the franchiser some tough questions; and make your choice.

7. Outline the major trends shaping franchising.

Key trends shaping franchising today include the changing face of franchisees; international franchise opportunities; smaller, nontraditional locations; conversion franchising; multiple-unit franchising; master franchising; and piggybacking (or combination franchising).

DISCUSSION QUESTIONS

1. What factors should an entrepreneur consider before choosing a form of business ownership?
2. Why are sole proprietorships so popular as a form of ownership?
3. How does personal conflict affect partnerships?
4. What issues should the articles of partnership address? Why are the articles important to a successful partnership?
5. Can one partner commit another to a business deal without the other's consent? Why?
6. What issues should the certificate of incorporation cover?
7. How does an S corporation differ from a regular corporation?
8. What role do limited partners play in a partnership? What happens if a limited partner takes an active role in managing the business?
9. What advantages does a limited liability company offer over an S corporation? A partnership?
10. How is an LLC created? What criteria must an LLC meet to avoid double taxation?
11. Briefly outline the advantages and disadvantages of the major forms of ownership.
12. What is franchising?

13. Describe the three types of franchising and give an example of each.
14. Discuss the advantages and the limitations of franchising for the franchisee.
15. Why might an independent entrepreneur be dissatisfied with a franchising arrangement?
16. What kinds of clues should tip off prospective franchisees that they are dealing with a disreputable franchiser?
17. What steps should potential franchisees take before investing in a franchise?
18. What is the function of the FTC's Trade Regulation Rule? Outline the protection the Trade Regulation Rule gives all prospective franchisees.
19. Describe the current trends in franchising.
20. One franchisee says, "Franchising is helpful because it gives you somebody [the franchiser] to get you going, nurture you, and shove you along a little. But the franchiser won't make you successful. That depends on what you bring to the business, how hard you are prepared to work, and how committed you are to finding the right franchise for you." Do you agree? Explain.

THE BUSINESS DISC

Launch *The Business Disc* and proceed to the section where Harry describes the basic forms of ownership. Although you may actually plan to create a corporation (either an S corporation or a C corporation) the Disc gives you two choices: a sole proprietorship or a partnership. For purposes of using the Disc, pick one of these as your form of ownership. What factors did you consider when making your choice? What are the advantages and the disadvantages of the form of ownership you chose?

If you are planning to buy a franchise, you should review the reference material on franchising on *The Business Disc*. From the menu across the top of your screen, select the "Reference" option and then click on "General Information." Click on "Complete Workshop on Franchising." Review the concepts in this reference guide and in Chapter 4. Then click on "Evaluating Franchises" and review the information in this reference guide. Develop a list of questions to ask the franchisers you are considering. Which franchise did you choose? Why?

Business PlanPro

Go to the section of the Business PlanPro called "Your Company" and complete the section concerning the form of ownership for your business. Use the comparison matrix of the major forms of ownership in Table 4.1 on page 116 to help you select the form of ownership that is best for you. Which factors are most relevant to your choice? Are you considering a franchise? If so, what are the advantages and disadvantages of buying a franchise? Use the process described on pages 127 to 130 to choose the ideal franchise for you. Which factors are most relevant to your choice?.

BEYOND THE CLASSROOM . . .

1. Interview five local small business owners. What form of ownership did each choose? Why? Prepare a brief report summarizing your findings, and explain advantages and disadvantages those owners face because of their choices.

2. Invite entrepreneurs who operate as partners to your classroom. Do they have a written partnership agreement? Are their skills complementary? How do they divide responsibility for running their company? How do they handle decision making? What do they do when disputes and disagreements arise?

3. Visit a local franchise operation. Is it a trade-name, product distribution, or pure franchise? To what extent did the franchisee investigate before investing? What assistance does the franchiser provide? How does the franchisee feel about the franchise contract he or she signed? What would he or she do differently now?

4. a. Consult a copy of the International Franchise Association publication *Franchise Opportunities Handbook* (the library should have a copy). Write several franchisers in a particular business category and ask for their franchise packages. Write a report comparing their treatment of the topics covered by the Trade Regulation Rule.

   b. Analyze the terms of their franchise contracts. What are the major differences? Are some terms more favorable than others? If you were about to invest in the franchise, which terms would you want to change?

5. Ask a local franchisee to approach his or her regional franchise representative about leading a class discussion on franchising.

6. Contact the International Franchise Association (1350 New York Avenue, N.W., Suite 900, Washington, DC, 20005-4709, (202-628-8000) for a copy of *Investigate Before Investing*. Prepare a report outlining what a prospective franchisee should do before buying a franchise.

A Franchiser Evaluation Checklist
THE FRANCHISER AND THE FRANCHISE

1. Is the potential market for the product or service adequate to support your franchise? Will the prices you charge be in line with the market?

2. Is the market's population growing, remaining static, or shrinking? Is the demand for your product or service growing, remaining static, or shrinking?

3. Is the product or service safe and reputable?

4. Is the product or service a fad, or is it a durable business idea?

5. What will the direct and indirect competition be in your sales territory? Do any other franchisees operate in this general area?

6. Is the franchise international, national, regional, or local in scope? Does it require full- or part-time involvement?

7. How many years has the franchiser been in operation? Does it have a sound reputation for honest dealings with franchisees?

8. How many franchise outlets now exist? How many will there be a year from now? How many outlets are company owned?

9. How many franchises have failed? Why?

10. What service and assistance will the franchiser provide? What training programs are offered? Are they continuous in nature?

11. Will the franchise perform a location analysis to help you find a suitable site?

12. Will the franchiser offer you exclusive distribution rights for the length of the agreement, or may it sell to other franchises in this area?

13. What facilities and equipment are required for the franchise? Who pays for construction? Is there a lease agreement?

14. What is the total cost of the franchise? What are the initial capital requirements? Will the franchiser provide financial assistance? Of what nature? What is the interest rate? Is the franchiser financially sound enough to fulfill all its promises?

15. How much is the franchise fee? Exactly what does it cover? Are there any confining fees? What additional fees are there?

16. Does the franchiser provide an estimate of expenses and income? Are they reasonable for your particular area? Are they sufficiently documented?

17. How risky is the franchise opportunity? Is the return on the investment consistent with the risks?

18. Does the franchiser offer a written contract that covers all the details of the agreement? Have your attorney and your accountant studied its terms and approved it? Do you understand the implications of the contract?

19. What is the length of the franchise agreement? Under what circumstances can it be terminated? If you terminate the contract, what are the costs to you? What are the terms and costs of renewal?

20. Are you allowed to sell the franchise to a third party? If so, will you receive the proceeds?

21. Is there a national advertising program? How is it financed? What media are used? What help is provided for local advertising?

22. Once you open for business, *exactly* what support will the franchiser offer you?

23. How does the franchise handle complaints from and disputes with franchisees? How well has the system worked?

THE FRANCHISEES

1. Are you pleased with your investment in this franchise?
2. Has the franchiser lived up to its promises?
3. What was your greatest disappointment after getting into this business?
4. How effective was the training you received in helping you run the franchise?
5. What are your biggest challenges and problems?
6. What is your franchise's cash flow like?
7. How much money are you making on your investment?
8. What do you like most about being a franchisee? Least?
9. Is there a franchisee advisory council that represents franchisees?
10. Knowing what you know now, would you buy this franchise again?

YOURSELF

1. Are you qualified to operate a franchise successfully? Do you have adequate drive, skills, experience, education, patience, and financial capacity? Are you prepared to work hard?
2. Are you willing to sacrifice some autonomy in operating a business to own a franchise?
3. Can you tolerate the financial risk? Would business failure wipe you out financially?
4. Can you juggle multiple tasks simultaneously and prioritize various projects so that you can accomplish those that are most important?
5. Are you genuinely interested in the product or service you will be selling? Do you enjoy this kind of business? Do you like to sell?
6. Do you enjoy working with and managing people? Are you a "team player"?
7. Will the business generate enough profit to suit you?
8. Has the franchiser investigated your background thoroughly enough to decide if you are qualified to operate the franchise?
9. What can this franchiser do for you that you cannot do for yourself?

Chapter 5

Buying an Existing Business

Goodwill, like a good name, is gotten by many actions, and lost by one.

—Lord Jeffrey

Experience is what you get looking for something else.

—Mary Pettibone Poole

LEARNING OBJECTIVES

Upon completion of this chapter, you will be able to:

1. **UNDERSTAND** the advantages and disadvantages of buying an existing business.

2. **DEFINE** the steps involved in the *right* way to buy a business.

3. **EXPLAIN** the process of evaluating an existing business.

4. **DESCRIBE** the various techniques for determining the value of a business.

5. **UNDERSTAND** the seller's side of the buyout decision and how to structure the deal.

6. **UNDERSTAND** how the negotiation process works and identify the factors that affect the negotiation process.

Each year, more than 500,000 businesses are bought and sold. Many entrepreneurs don't start new businesses but instead focus their attention on finding an existing business that has potential but is poorly managed and can be bought at "the right price." Each circumstance is unique, but the process of evaluating a potential acquisition is not. The importance of the analysis and evaluation process cannot be underestimated. A business that looks good on the surface may have flaws at its core. The "due diligence" process in analyzing and evaluating an existing business is just as time consuming as the development of a comprehensive business plan for a start-up. The due diligence process will uncover the negative as well as the positive components of any business. This process takes time and a lot of homework to verify all the facts and figures. Be patient and, as the process implies, be diligent. Be sure that you know the answers to the following fundamental questions:

- Is the right type of business for sale in a market in which you want to operate?
- What experience do you have in this particular business and the industry in which it operates?
- How critical is experience in the business to your ultimate success? Where should such a business be located?
- What price and payment method are reasonable for you and acceptable to the seller?
- Should you start the business and build it from the ground up or should you shop around to buy an existing company?
- What is this company's potential for success?
- What changes will you have to make—and how extensive will they be—to realize the business's full potential?
- Will the company generate sufficient cash to pay for itself and leave you with a suitable rate of return on your investment?

Learning Objective

1-A. Understand the advantages of buying an existing business.

BUYING AN EXISTING BUSINESS

Advantages of Buying an Existing Business

A SUCCESSFUL EXISTING BUSINESS MAY CONTINUE TO BE SUCCESSFUL. Purchasing a thriving business at an acceptable price increases the likelihood of success. The previous management already has established a customer base, built supplier relationships, and set up a business system. The new owner's objective should be to make those modifications that will attract new customers while retaining the firm's existing customers. Maintaining the proper balance of old and new is not an easy task, however. The customer base inherited in a business purchase can carry an entrepreneur while he studies how the business has become successful and how he can build on that success. Time spent learning about the business and its customers before introducing changes will increase the probability that any changes made will be successful.

AN EXISTING BUSINESS MAY ALREADY HAVE THE BEST LOCATION. When the location of the business is critical to its success (as is often the case in retailing), it may be wise to purchase a business that is already in the right place. Opening in a second-choice location and hoping to draw customers may prove fruitless. In fact, an existing business's biggest asset may be its location. If this advantage cannot be matched by other locations, an entrepreneur may have little choice but to buy instead of build. As part of its expansion plans, one fast-food chain recently purchased a smaller chain, not so much for its customer base or other assets but for its prime store locations.

EMPLOYEES AND SUPPLIERS ARE ESTABLISHED. An existing business already has experienced employees, so there are fewer problems associated with the transition phase. Experienced employees can help the company earn money while a new owner learns the business. Many new owners find it valuable to ask the employees what ideas they might have that would increase sales or reduce cost. In many cases, the previous owner may not have involved the employees in this fashion and never gained the advantages found in the wisdom of employees. Few people know a job better than those who are performing it.

In addition, an existing business has an established set of suppliers with a history of business dealings. Those vendors can continue to supply the business while the new owner investigates the products and services of other suppliers. Often the new owner is not pressured to choose a supplier quickly without thorough investigation. However, a supplier may want to ensure that the new owners are competent to run the business.

Reid Chase and Scott Semel purchased **Cole-Kramer Imports**, *a high-end candy company, that distributed Swiss candies. The Swiss supplier worked with the new owners who aggressively expanded the product offerings and grew the sales from $600,000 in 1994 to $40 million in 2001.*[1]

A Company Example

EQUIPMENT IS INSTALLED AND PRODUCTIVE CAPACITY IS KNOWN.   Acquiring and installing new equipment exerts a tremendous strain on a fledgling company's financial resources. In an existing business, a potential buyer can determine the condition of the plant and equipment and its capacity before buying. The previous owner may have established an efficient production operation through trial and error, although the new owner may need to make modifications to improve it. In many cases, entrepreneurs can purchase physical facilities and equipment at prices significantly below their replacement costs.

INVENTORY IS IN PLACE AND TRADE CREDIT IS ESTABLISHED.   The proper amount of inventory is essential to both cost control and sales volume. If a business has too little inventory, it will not have the quantity and variety of products to satisfy customer demand. But if a business has too much inventory, it is tying up excessive capital, thereby increasing costs and reducing profitability. Owners of successful, established businesses have learned the proper balance between these extremes. Previous owners have established trade credit relationships that can benefit the new owner. No supplier wants to lose a good customer.

THE NEW BUSINESS OWNER HITS THE GROUND RUNNING.   The entrepreneur who purchases an existing business saves the time, costs, and energy required to launch a new business. The day she takes over the ongoing business is the day her revenues begin. Entrepreneurs who buy an existing *successful* business do not have to invest a lifetime in building a company to enjoy success.

THE NEW OWNER CAN USE THE EXPERIENCE OF THE PREVIOUS OWNER. Even if the previous owner is not around after the sale, new owners will have access to all of the business's records that they reviewed during the due diligence process, which can guide them until they become acclimated to the business and the local market. They can trace the impact on costs and revenues of the major decisions that the previous owner made and can learn from his mistakes and profit from his achievements. In many cases, the previous owner spends time in an orientation period with the new owner, giving the new manager the opportunity to learn about the policies and procedures in place and the reasons for them. Previous owners also can be extremely helpful in unmasking the unwritten rules of business in the area, critically important intangibles, and whom you can and cannot trust. After all, owners who sell out want to see the buyer succeed in carrying on their businesses.

EASIER FINANCING.   Attracting financing to purchase an existing business often is easier than finding the money to launch a company from scratch. Many existing businesses already have established relationships with lenders, which may open the door to financing through traditional sources such as banks. As we will see later in this chapter, many business buyers also have access to another important source of financing: the seller.

IT'S A BARGAIN.   Some existing businesses may be real bargains. The current owners may need to sell on short notice, which may lead to them selling the business at a low price. Many small companies operate in profitable but tiny niches, making it easy for potential buyers to overlook them. The more specialized the business is, the greater the likelihood is that a bargain might be found. If special skills or training is required to operate the business, the number of potential buyers will be significantly smaller. If the owner wants a substantial down payment or the entire selling price in cash, few buyers may qualify; however, those who do may be able to negotiate a good deal.

Learning Objective

I-B. Understand the disadvantages of buying an existing business.

Disadvantages of Buying an Existing Business

"IT'S A LOSER."   A business may be for sale because it has never been profitable. Such a situation may be disguised; owners can employ various creative accounting techniques that make a firm's financial picture appear much brighter than it really is. The reason that a business is for sale will seldom be stated honestly as "It's losing money." If there is an area of business where the maxim "let the buyer beware" still prevails, it is in the sale of a business. Any buyer unprepared to do a complete and thorough analysis of the business may be stuck with a real loser.

Although buying a money-losing business is risky, it is not necessarily taboo. If your analysis of a company shows that it is poorly managed or suffering from neglect, you may be able to turn it around. However, if you do not have a well-defined plan for improving a struggling business, do *not* consider buying it!

A Company Example

After deciding to become entrepreneurs by buying a business, Jim Sally and Tom Marenyi established the criteria their acquisition must meet: a quality product, a good name, market potential, and a solid formula they could improve upon. They soon discovered **Woodplay**, *a small company that manufactured wooden playsets for the residential market. Although the company was known for its outstanding line of well-made redwood products and had good name recognition in an attractive niche, Woodplay had fallen on hard times and was in bankruptcy. Looking beyond the company's immediate financial problems, Sally and Marenyi recognized that Woodplay had great potential. They purchased the company's assets and invested several hundred thousand dollars of their own money in working capital. "The first thing we had to do was stabilize the business," says Marenyi. They quickly eliminated Woodplay's two weakest product lines, added two new ones, and began building a network of national dealers. Within two years, Sally and Marenyi found themselves turning down orders because they could not keep up with the demand for their products! Today, Woodplay is thriving, and in addition to expanding their dealer network, Sally and Marenyi are working to build retail locations to sell their state-of-the-art product line.*[2]

THE PREVIOUS OWNER MAY HAVE CREATED ILL WILL.   Just as ethical, socially responsible business dealings create goodwill for a company, improper business behavior creates ill will. The due diligence process may reveal that customers, suppliers, creditors, or employees have extremely negative feelings about the behavior of the previous owner. Business relations may have begun to deteriorate, but their long-term effects may not yet appear in the business's financial statements. Ill will can permeate a business for years.

EMPLOYEES INHERITED WITH THE BUSINESS MAY NOT BE SUITABLE.   Previous managers may have kept marginal employees because they were close friends or because they started off with the company. The new owner, therefore, may have to make some very unpopular

Courtesy of WoodPlay.

termination decisions. For this reason, employees often do not welcome a new owner because they feel threatened. If the new owner plans to make changes in the business, its current employees may not suit her needs. Others may not be able to adapt to the new owner's management style, and a culture clash results. A successful new operating strategy can seldom be effectively implemented by incompetent employees. If your due diligence efforts uncovered that the current employees are a significant cause of the problems the business faces, you must have a preemptive plan to correct this weakness or your new strategic efforts may fail miserably.

THE BUSINESS LOCATION MAY HAVE BECOME UNSATISFACTORY. What was once an ideal location may have become obsolete as market and demographic trends changed. Large shopping malls, new competitors, or highway reroutings can spell disaster for small retail shops. Prospective buyers should always evaluate the existing market in the area surrounding an established business as well as its potential for expansion. Remember, you are buying the future, not the past. A location in decline may never recover. If business success is tied to location, do not acquire a business where the demographic trends are turning negative. The value of the business will erode faster than the neighborhood.

EQUIPMENT AND FACILITIES MAY BE OBSOLETE OR INEFFICIENT. Potential buyers sometimes neglect to have an expert evaluate a firm's facilities and equipment before they purchase it. Only later do they discover that the equipment is obsolete and inefficient, and consequently the business may suffer losses from excessively high operating costs. The equipment may have been well suited to the business they purchased but not to the business they want to build. Modernizing equipment and facilities is seldom inexpensive.

CHANGE AND INNOVATION ARE DIFFICULT TO IMPLEMENT. It is easier to plan for change than it is to implement it. Methods previously used in a business may have established precedents that are hard to modify. For example, if the previous owner allowed a 10 percent discount to customers purchasing a hundred or more units in a single order, it may be almost impossible to eliminate the discount practice without losing some of those customers. The previous owner's policies, even if proven unwise, still affect the changes a new owner can make. Reversing a downward slide in sales can be just as difficult. Implementing changes to bring in new business and convince former clients to return can be an expensive and laborious process. Never underestimate the effort, time, and expense it takes to change the negative momentum of a business in trouble. Before a business can go forward, it must stop going backward.

INVENTORY MAY BE OUTDATED OR OBSOLETE. Inventory is valuable only if it is salable. Smart buyers know better than to trust the inventory valuation on a firm's balance sheet. Some of it may actually appreciate in value in periods of rapid inflation, but more likely it has depreciated. A prospective buyer must judge inventory on the basis of its market value, not its book value.

TABLE 5.1

Valuing Accounts Receivable

A prospective buyer asked the current owner of a business about the value of her accounts receivable. The owner's business records showed $101,000 in receivables. But when the prospective buyer aged the accounts and multiplied them by his estimated collection probabilities, he discovered their *real* value.

Age of Accounts	Amount	Collection Probability	Value
0–30 days	$ 40,000	95%	$ 38,000
31–60 days	25,000	88%	22,000
61–90 days	14,000	70%	9,800
91–120 days	10,000	40%	4,000
121–150 days	7,000	25%	1,750
151-plus days	5,000	10%	500
Total	**$101,000**		**$76,050**

Had he blindly accepted the seller's book value of these accounts receivable, this prospective buyer would have overpaid nearly $25,000 for them!

*For example, generations of customers have enjoyed shopping at a Clemson, South Carolina, landmark, **Judge Kellers General Store**. Inventory can be traced back to the founder, three generations ago. Excellent service and friendly and honest owners made shopping a delight, but if you were to evaluate its inventory you might discover some items that were outdated.*

ACCOUNTS RECEIVABLE MAY BE WORTH LESS THAN FACE VALUE. Like inventory, accounts receivables rarely are worth their face value. The prospective buyer should age the accounts receivable (a breakdown of accounts 30, 60, 90, and 120 days old and beyond) to determine their collectibility. The older the receivables are, the less likely they are to be collected and, consequently, the lower their value is. Table 5.1 shows a simple but effective method of evaluating accounts receivable once they have been aged.

When one buyer was considering purchasing an existing business, his research showed that a substantial volume of accounts receivable was well past due. Further investigation revealed that the company and its largest customer were locked in a nasty fight over these outstanding accounts. The buyer decided to withdraw his preliminary offer.[3]

THE BUSINESS MAY BE OVERPRICED. Each year, many people purchase businesses at prices far in excess of their value, which can impair the companies' ability to earn a profit and generate a positive cash flow. If a buyer accurately values a business's accounts receivable, inventories, and other assets, she will be in a better position to negotiate a price that will allow the business to be profitable. Making payments on a business that was overpriced is a millstone around the new owner's neck, making it difficult to carry this excess weight and keep the business afloat.

Although most buyers do not realize it, the price they pay for a company typically is not as crucial to its continued success as the terms on which they make the purchase. Of course, wise business buyers will try to negotiate a fair and reasonable price, but they are often equally interested in the more specific terms of the deal—for instance, how much cash they must pay out and when, how much of the price the seller is willing to finance and for how long, the interest rate at which the deal is financed, and other such terms. Their primary concern is making sure that the deal does not endanger the company's future financial health and that it preserves the company's cash flow.

THE STEPS IN ACQUIRING A BUSINESS

Learning Objective

2. Define the steps involved in the *right* way to buy a business.

Buying an existing business can be risky if approached haphazardly. Studies show that more than 50 percent of all business acquisitions fail to meet the buyer's expectations. To avoid costly mistakes, an entrepreneur-to-be should follow a logical, methodical approach:[4]

- Analyze your skills, abilities, and interests to determine what kind(s) of businesses you should consider.
- Prepare a list of potential candidates.
- Investigate those candidates and evaluate the best one(s).
- Explore financing options.
- Ensure a smooth transition.

Analyze Your Skills, Abilities, and Interests

The first step in buying a business is *not* searching out potential acquisition candidates. Every entrepreneur considering buying a business should begin by conducting a self-audit to determine the ideal business for him or her. The primary focus is to identify the type of business *you* will be happiest and most successful owning. Consider, for example, the following questions:

- What business activities do you enjoy most? Least? Why?
- Which industries or markets offer the greatest potential for growth?
- Which industries interest you most? Least? Why?
- What kind of business do you want to buy?
- What kinds of businesses do you want to *avoid*?
- What do you expect to get out of the business?
- How much time, energy, and money can you put into the business?

- What business skills and experience do you have? Which ones do you lack?
- How easily can you transfer your skills and experience to other types of businesses? In what kinds of businesses would that transfer be easiest?
- How much risk are you willing to take?
- Are you willing and able to turn around a struggling business?
- What size company do you want to buy?
- Is there a particular geographic location you desire?

Answering these and other questions beforehand will allow you to develop a list of precise criteria a company must meet before it becomes a purchase candidate. Addressing these issues early in the process will also save a great deal of time, trouble, and confusion as you wade through a multitude of business opportunities. The better you know yourself—your skills, competencies, and interests—the more likely you will be to find and manage a successful business.

Prepare a List of Potential Candidates

Once you know what your goals are for acquiring a business, you can begin your search. Do *not* limit yourself to only those businesses that are advertised as being "for sale." In fact, the **hidden market** of companies that might be for sale but are not advertised as such is one of the richest sources of top-quality businesses. Many businesses that can be purchased are not publicly advertised but are available through business brokers and other professionals. Although they maintain a low profile, these hidden businesses represent some of the most attractive purchase targets a prospective buyer may find. How can you tap into this hidden market of potential acquisitions? Typical sources include the following:

hidden market—*low-profile companies that might be for sale but are not advertised as such.*

- Business brokers
- Bankers
- Accountants
- Investment bankers
- Industry contacts—suppliers, distributors, customers, insurance brokers, and others
- Networking—social and business contacts with friends and relatives
- Knocking on the doors of businesses you'd like to buy (even if they're not advertised as being for sale)
- Trade associations
- Newspapers and trade journals listing businesses for sale

In recent years, the World Wide Web also has become an important tool for entrepreneurs looking to buy businesses. In the past, the market for businesses was highly fragmented and unstructured, making it difficult for entrepreneurs to conduct an organized, thorough search for companies that might meet their purchase criteria. Today, hundreds of business brokers have established Web sites that list thousands of companies for sale in practically every industry imaginable, enabling entrepreneurs to search the entire country for that perfect business from the comfort of their own homes. Using the Web, potential buyers can eliminate the companies that do not suit them and can conduct preliminary research on those that look most promising. The more opportunities entrepreneurs have to find and evaluate potential acquisitions, the greater the likelihood of finding a match that meets their criteria.

INVESTIGATE AND EVALUATE CANDIDATE BUSINESSES AND EVALUATE THE BEST ONE. Finding the right company requires patience. Although some buyers find a company after only a few months of looking, the typical search takes much longer, as much as two or three years. Once you have a list of prospective candidates, it is time to do your homework. The next step is to investigate the candidates in more detail:

- What are the company's strengths? Weaknesses?
- Is the company profitable? What is its overall financial condition?
- What is its cash flow cycle? How much cash will the company generate?
- Who are its major competitors?
- How large is the customer base? Is it growing or shrinking?
- Are the current employees suitable? Will they stay?
- What is the physical condition of the business, its equipment, and its inventory?
- What new skills must you learn to be able to manage this business successfully?

Determining the answers to these (and other questions addressed in this chapter) will allow a prospective buyer to develop a list of the most attractive prospects and to prioritize them in descending order of attractiveness. This process also will make the task of valuing the business much easier.

Explore Financing Options

Placing a value on an existing business (a topic we will discuss later in this chapter) represents a major hurdle for many would-be entrepreneurs. The next challenging task in closing a successful deal is financing the purchase. Although financing the purchase of an existing business usually is easier than financing a new one, some traditional lenders shy away from deals involving the purchase of an existing business. Those who are willing to finance business purchases normally lend only a portion of the value of the assets, so buyers often find themselves searching for alternative sources of funds. Fortunately, most business buyers have access to a ready source of financing: the seller. Once a seller finds a suitable buyer, she typically will agree to finance anywhere from 30 percent to 80 percent of the purchase price. Usually, a deal is structured so that the buyer makes a down payment to the seller, who then finances a note for the balance. The buyer makes regular principal and interest payments over time—perhaps with a larger balloon payment at the end—until the note is paid off. The terms and conditions of such a loan are a vital concern to both buyer and seller. They cannot be so burdensome that they threaten the company's continued existence; that is, the buyer must be able to make the payments to the seller out of the company's cash flow. At the same time, the deal must give the seller the financial security she is seeking from the sale. Defining reasonable terms is the result of the negotiation process between the buyer and the seller.

Ensure a Smooth Transition

Once the parties strike a deal, the challenge of making a smooth transition immediately arises. No matter how well planned the sale is, there are *always* surprises. For instance, the new owner may have ideas for changing the business—sometimes radically—that cause a great deal of stress and anxiety among employees and the previous owner. Charged with such emotion and uncertainty, the transition phase is always difficult and frustrating—and sometimes painful. To avoid a bumpy transition, a business buyer should do the following:

- Concentrate on communicating with employees. Business sales are fraught with uncertainty and anxiety, and employees need reassurance.

- Be honest with employees. Avoid telling them only what they want to hear. Share with the employees your vision for the business with the intent of generating a heightened level of motivation and support.

- Listen to employees. They have intimate knowledge of the business and its strengths and weaknesses and usually can offer valuable suggestions.

- Consider asking the seller to serve as a consultant until the transition is complete. The previous owner can be a valuable resource, especially to an inexperienced buyer.

Table 5.2 describes 15 steps potential buyers should take to increase the probability that the businesses they buy are the right ones for them.

EVALUATING AN EXISTING BUSINESS—THE DUE DILIGENCE PROCESS

Learning Objective
3. Explain the process of evaluating an existing business.

When evaluating an existing business, a lone buyer quickly feels overwhelmed by the tremendous number and complexity of the issues involved. Therefore, a smart buyer will assemble a team of specialists to help in investigating the potential business opportunity. This team is usually composed of a banker, an accountant familiar with the particular industry, an attorney, and perhaps a small business consultant or a business broker. The cost of such a team can range from $3,000 to $20,000, but most buyers agree that using a team significantly lowers the likelihood of making a bad buy. Because making a bad purchase will cost many times the expense of a team of experts, most buyers see it as a wise investment. It is important for a buyer to trust the members of the business evaluation team. With this team assembled, the potential buyer is ready to explore the business opportunity by examining five critical areas.

TABLE 5.2

15 Steps to Buying the Company That's Right for You

Source: The Magazine for Growing Companies by Jay Finegan. © 1991 by Bus Innovator Group Resources/*Inc.* Reproduced by permission of Bus Innovator Group Resources/*Inc.* in the format Textbook via Copyright Clearance Center.

1. *Make sure you shouldn't be starting a company instead.* You should have solid reasons for buying a company rather than starting one—and you should know what they are.

2. *Determine the kind of business you want—and whether you're capable of running it.* This requires an unflinching assessment of your own strengths, weaknesses, personality, and goals.

3. *Consider the lifestyle you want.* What are you expecting from the business? Money? Freedom? Flexibility?

4. *Consider the location you want.* What part of the country (or world) do you want to live in?

5. *Reconsider lifestyle.* You may own this business for a long, long time; it had better be one you enjoy.

6. *Cozy up to lenders in advance.* Visit potential lenders long before you need to borrow any money. Develop a rapport with them.

7. *Prepare to sell yourself to the sellers.* You're buying their "baby," and they'll want to make sure you're the right person for the job!

8. *Once you've defined the kind of business you're after, find the right company.* Three major sources of potential candidates are: (1) the network of businesspeople and advisers in the area, (2) business brokers specializing in companies of the size or type you want to buy, and (3) businesses that technically are not for sale (but are very attractive).

9. *Choose the right seller.* Is she honest? What's the *real* reason she's selling the business?

10. *Do your research before agreeing to a price.* Ask lots of questions and get the facts to help you estimate the company's value.

11. *Make sure your letter of intent is specific.* It should establish deadlines, escape clauses, payment terms, confidentiality, and many other key issues.

12. *Don't skimp on due diligence.* Don't believe everything you see and hear; a relentless investigation will show whether the seller is telling the truth. Not all of them will.

13. *Be skeptical.* Don't fall in love with the deal; look for reasons *not* to buy the company.

14. *Don't forget to assess the employees.* You're not just buying a company; you're also buying the people who go with it.

15. *Make sure the final price reflects the company's real value.* Don't lower your chances of success by paying too much for the business.

1. Why does the owner want to sell?
2. What is the physical condition of the business?
3. What is the potential for the company's products or services?
4. What legal aspects should you consider?
5. Is the business financially sound?

Why Is the Business for Sale?

WHY DOES THE OWNER WANT TO SELL?   Every prospective business buyer should investigate the *real* reason the business owner wants to sell. A study by the Geneva Corporation found that the most common reasons that owners of small and medium-sized businesses gave for selling were boredom and burnout.[5] Others decided to cash in their business investments and diversify into other types of assets.

Smart business buyers know that the biggest and most unpleasant surprises can crop up outside the company's financial records and may never appear on the spreadsheets designed to analyze a company's financial position. For instance, a business owner might be looking to sell his business because a powerful new competitor is about to move into the market, a major highway rerouting will cause customer traffic to evaporate, the lease agreement on the ideal location is about to expire, or the primary customer base is declining. Every prospective buyer should investigate thoroughly any reason a seller gives for wanting to sell a business.

Businesses do not last forever, and smart entrepreneurs know when the time has come to sell. Some owners consider their behavior ethical only if they do not make false or misleading statements. Never expect to get a full disclose of the whole story. In most business sales, the buyer bears the responsibility of determining whether the business is a good value. The best way to do that is to get out into the local community, talk to people, and ask a lot of questions. Visiting local business owners may reveal general patterns about the area and its overall vitality. The local Chamber of Commerce also may have useful information. Suppliers, customers, and even competitors may be able to shed light on why a business is up for sale. By combining this information with an analysis of the company's financial records, the potential buyer should be able to develop a clearer picture of the business and its real value.

The Condition of the Business

WHAT IS THE PHYSICAL CONDITION OF THE BUSINESS?   A prospective buyer should evaluate the business's assets to determine their value. Are they reasonably priced? Are they obsolete? Will they need to be replaced soon? Do they operate efficiently? The potential buyer should check the condition of both the equipment and the building. It may be necessary to hire a professional to evaluate the major components of the building—its structure and its plumbing, electrical, and heating and cooling systems. Unexpected renovations are rarely inexpensive or simple and can punch a gaping hole in a buyer's financial plans.

How fresh is the firm's inventory? Is it consistent with the image the new owner wants to project? How much of it would the buyer have to sell at a loss? A potential buyer may need to get an independent appraisal to determine the value of the firm's inventory and other assets because the current owner may have priced them far above their actual value. These items typically comprise the largest portion of a business's value, and a potential buyer should not accept the seller's asking price blindly. Remember: *Book value is not the same as market value.* Usually, a buyer can purchase equipment and fixtures at substantially lower prices than book value. Value is determined in the market, not on a balance sheet.

Other important factors that the potential buyer should investigate include the following:

ACCOUNTS RECEIVABLE.   If the sale includes accounts receivable, the buyer should check their quality before purchasing them. How creditworthy are the accounts? What portion of them is past due? How likely are you to be able to collect them? By aging the accounts receivable, a buyer can judge their quality and determine their value. (Refer to Table 5.1.)

LEASE ARRANGEMENTS.   Is the lease included in the sale? When does it expire? What restrictions does it have on renovation or expansion? The buyer should determine *beforehand* what restrictions the landlord has placed on the lease and negotiate any changes prior to purchasing the business.

BUSINESS RECORDS.   Well-kept business records can be a valuable source of information and can tell a prospective buyer a lot about the company's pattern of success (or lack of it). Unfortunately, many business owners are sloppy recordkeepers. Consequently, the potential buyer and his team may have to reconstruct some critical records. It is important to verify as much information about the business as possible. For instance, does the owner have customer or mailing lists? These lists can be a valuable marketing tool for a new business owner.

INTANGIBLE ASSETS.   Does the sale include any intangible assets such as trademarks, patents, copyrights, or goodwill? How long do patents have left to run? Is the trademark threatened by lawsuits for infringement? Does the company have logos or slogans that are unique or widely recognized? Determining the value of such intangibles is much more difficult than computing the value of the tangible assets.

LOCATION AND APPEARANCE.   The location and the overall appearance of the building are important factors for a prospective buyer to consider. What had been an outstanding location in the past may be totally unacceptable today. Even if the building and equipment are in good condition and are fairly priced, the business may be located in a declining area. What kinds of businesses are in the area? Every buyer should consider the location's suitability several years into the future.

The potential buyer should also check local zoning laws to ensure that any changes he wants to make are legal. In some areas, zoning laws are very difficult to change and, as a result, can restrict the business's growth.

Table 5.3 offers a checklist of items every business buyer should investigate before closing a deal.

TABLE 5.3

A Business Buyer's Checklist

Sources: Adapted from "Look Before You Buy," Business Resale Network. www.br.network.com/features/bybl.html; "Making an in-Depth Evaluation," Business Resale Network, www.br.network.com/features/bybl.html; Norm Brodsky, "Caveat Emptor," *Inc.*, August 1998, pp. 31–32; "Basics of Buying a Business," American Express Small Business Exchange. home3.americanexpress.com/smallbusiness/resources/starting/buybiz.shtml.

Buildings, furnishings, and fixtures. Every buyer should get a list of all of the fixed assets included in the purchase and then determine their condition, age, usefulness, and value.

Inventory. Inventory may be the biggest part of a business sale, and it can be one of the trickiest parts of the deal. What inventory is on hand? What is its condition? How salable is it? What is its value? (Remember not to confuse *book value* with *market value*.) What is the company's merchandise return policy? How high is its return rate?

Financial statements. Although small business owners are notoriously poor recordkeepers, a business buyer must have access to a company's financial statements for the past five years. This is the only way a buyer can judge the earning power of a company. The most reliable financial statements are those that have been audited by a certified public accountant. Comparing financial ratios against industry standards found in reports from Robert Morris & Associates and Dun & Bradstreet can reveal important patterns.

Tax returns. A good accountant should be able to reconcile the owner's or company's tax returns with its financial statements.

Sales records. A prospective buyer should determine sales patterns by getting a monthly breakdown by product categories, sales representatives, cash versus credit, and any other significant factor for the company for three years. It is also a good idea to identify the company's top 10 customers and review their purchases over the past three years. For what percentage of total sales did these 10 customers account?

Accounts receivable. Age the company's accounts receivable to see how many are current and how many are past due. Identify the top 10 accounts and check their credit ratings.

Accounts payable. Conduct an analysis similar to the one for accounts receivable for the company's accounts payable. Past-due accounts are an indication that a business is experiencing cash flow difficulties.

Legal documents. A prospective buyer should investigate all significant contracts (especially long-term ones) a company has with vendors, suppliers, distributors, lenders, employees, unions, customers, landlords, and others. Can the current owner assign the rights and obligations of these existing contracts to the buyer? If the company is incorporated, it is wise to check the articles of incorporation (or its articles of organization and operating agreement if it is a limited liability company).

Patents, trademarks, and copyrights. Reviewing the documentation for any patents, trademarks, and copyrights the company holds is vital.

Lawsuits. Is the company facing any lawsuits, either current or pending?

Liabilities. It is essential that the seller provide the buyer with a complete list of liabilities that are outstanding against the company, including accounts and notes payable, loans, liens by creditors against business assets, lawsuits, and others.

Advertising and sales literature. A business buyer should study the company's advertising and sales literature to get an idea of the image it is projecting to its customers and the community. Talking to customers, suppliers, bankers, attorneys, and other local business owners will provide clues about the company's reputation.

Organization chart. Current employees can be a vital asset to a business buyer (if they are willing to stay after the sale). Ask the seller to develop an organization chart, showing the company's chain of command, and get copies of employees' job descriptions so you can understand who is responsible for which duties.

Insurance coverage. Evaluate the types and amounts of insurance coverage the company currently has, including workers' compensation. Is it sufficient? If not, will you be able to obtain the necessary coverage at a reasonable price?

Products and Services

WHAT IS THE POTENTIAL FOR THE COMPANY'S PRODUCTS OR SERVICES? No one wants to buy a business with a shrinking customer base. A thorough market analysis can lead to an accurate and realistic sales forecast for an existing business. This research will tell a buyer whether or not he should consider buying a particular business and will help spot trends in the business's sales and customer base.

CUSTOMER CHARACTERISTICS AND COMPOSITION. Before purchasing an existing business, a buyer should analyze both existing and potential customers. Discovering why customers buy from the business and developing a profile of the entire customer base can help the buyer identify a company's strengths and weaknesses. The entrepreneur should determine the answers to the following questions:

■ Who are my customers in terms of race, age, gender, and income level? What is their demographic profile?

■ Why do they buy?

■ What do the customers want the business to do for them? What needs are they satisfying?

- How often do customers buy? Do they buy in seasonal patterns?
- How loyal are my present customers?
- Is it practical or even possible to attract new customers? If so, are the new customers significantly different from existing customers?
- Does the business have a well-defined customer base? Is it growing? Do these customers come from a large geographical area or do they all live near the business?

Analyzing the answers to these questions can help a potential buyer create and implement a more powerful marketing plan. Most likely he will try to keep the business attractive to existing customers, while changing some features of its marketing plan to attract new customers.

COMPETITOR ANALYSIS. A potential buyer must identify the company's direct competition—those businesses in the immediate area that sell similar products or services. The potential profitability and survival of the business may well depend on the behavior of these competitors. An important factor to consider is the trend in the competition. How many competitors have opened in recent years? How many have closed in the past five years? What caused these failures? Has the market already reached the saturation point? Being a latecomer in an already saturated market is not the path to long-term success.

When evaluating the competitive environment, a prospective buyer should address other questions:

- Which competitors have survived, and what characteristics have led to their success?
- How do competitors' sales volumes compare with those of the business under consideration?
- What unique services do competitors offer?
- How well organized and coordinated are the marketing efforts of competitors?
- What are the competitors' reputations?
- What are the strengths and weaknesses of the competition? Which competitor is strongest?
- What competitive edge does each competitor have?
- How can you gain market share in this competitive environment?

Legal Aspects

WHAT LEGAL ASPECTS SHOULD YOU CONSIDER? Business buyers must be careful to avoid several legal pitfalls as they negotiate the final deal. The biggest potential traps include liens, bulk transfers, contract assignments, covenants not to compete, and ongoing legal liabilities.

LIENS. The key legal issue in the sale of any asset is typically the proper transfer of good title from seller to buyer. However, because most business sales involve a collection of assorted assets, the transfer of a good title is more complex. Some business assets may have **liens** (creditors' claims) against them and, unless they are satisfied before the sale, the buyer must assume them and is financially responsible for them. One way to reduce this potential problem is to include a clause in the sales contract stating that any liability not shown on the balance sheet at the time of sale remains the responsibility of the seller. A prospective buyer should have an attorney thoroughly investigate all of the assets for sale and their lien status before buying any business.

lien—*a creditor's claim against an asset.*

BULK TRANSFERS. To protect against surprise claims from the seller's creditors after purchasing a business, the buyer should meet the requirements of a **bulk transfer** under Section 6 of the Uniform Commercial Code. Suppose that an owner owing many creditors sells his business to a buyer. The seller, however, does not use the proceeds of the sale to pay his debts to business creditors. Instead, he pockets them to use for his own benefit. Without the protection of a bulk transfer, those creditors could make claim to the assets that the buyer purchased in order to satisfy the previous owner's debts (within six months). To be effective, a bulk transfer must meet the following criteria:

bulk transfer—*protects the buyer of a business's assets from the claims unpaid creditors might have against those assets.*

- The seller must give the buyer a signed, sworn list of existing creditors.
- The buyer and the seller must prepare a list of the property included in the sale.
- The buyer must keep the list of creditors and the list of property for six months.
- The buyer must give written notice of the sale to each creditor at least 10 days before he takes possession of the goods or pays for them (whichever is first).

By meeting these criteria, a buyer acquires free and clear title to the assets purchased, which are not subject to prior claims from the seller's creditors. Because Section 6 can create quite a burden on a business buyer, 16 states have repealed it, and more may follow. About a half-dozen states have revised Section 6 to make it easier for buyers to notify creditors. Under the revised rule, if a business has more than 200 creditors, the buyer may notify them by public notice rather than by contacting them individually.

CONTRACT ASSIGNMENTS. A buyer must investigate the rights and the obligations he would assume under existing contracts with suppliers, customers, employees, lessors, and others. To continue the smooth operation of the business, the buyer must assume the rights of the seller under many existing contracts. Assuming these rights and obligations means having the seller assign existing contracts to the new owner. For example, the current owner may have four years left on a 10-year lease and will need to assign this contract to the buyer. To protect her interest, the buyer (who is the assignee) should notify the other party involved in the contract of the assignment. In the previous example, the business buyer should notify the landlord promptly of the lease assignment from the previous owner.

Generally, the seller can assign any contractual right to the buyer, unless the contract specifically prohibits the assignment or the contract is personal in nature. For instance, loan contracts sometimes prohibit assignments with **due-on-sale clauses**. These clauses require the buyer to pay the full amount of the remaining loan balance or to finance the balance at prevailing interest rates. Thus, the buyer cannot assume the seller's loan (at a lower interest rate). Also, a seller usually cannot assign his credit arrangements with suppliers to the buyer because they are based on the seller's business reputation and are personal in nature. If such contracts are crucial to the business operation and cannot be assigned, the buyer must renegotiate new contracts. A prospective buyer also should evaluate the terms of any other unique contracts the seller has, including patent, trademark, or copyright registrations, exclusive agent or distributor contracts, real estate leases, financing and loan arrangements, and union contracts.

COVENANTS NOT TO COMPETE. One of the most important and most often overlooked legal considerations for a prospective buyer is negotiating a **covenant not to compete** (or a **restrictive covenant**) with the seller. Under a restrictive covenant, the seller agrees not to open a new competing business within a specific time period and geographic area. (The covenant should be negotiated with the *owner*, not with the corporation, because if the corporation signs the agreement, the owner may not be bound.) However, the covenant must be a part of a business sale and must be reasonable in scope in order to be enforceable. Although some states place limitations on the enforceability of restrictive covenants, business buyers should insist on the seller signing one. Without this protection, a buyer may find his new business eroding beneath his feet. For example, Bob purchases a tire business from Alexandra, whose reputation in town for selling tires is unequaled. If Bob fails to negotiate a restrictive covenant, nothing can stop Alexandra from opening a new shop next to her old one and keeping all of her customers, thereby driving Bob out of business. A reasonable covenant in this case might restrict Alexandra from opening a tire store within a three-mile radius for three years. Every business buyer should negotiate a covenant not to compete with the seller.

ONGOING LEGAL LIABILITIES. Finally, a buyer must look for any potential legal liabilities the purchase might expose. These typically arise from three sources: (1) physical premises, (2) product liability claims, and (3) labor relations. First, the buyer must examine the physical premises for safety. Are employees at risk because of asbestos or some other hazardous material? If a manufacturing environment is involved, does it meet Occupational Safety and Health Administration (OSHA) and other regulatory agency requirements?

One entrepreneur who purchased a retail business located in a building that once housed a gasoline service station was quite surprised when the Environmental Protection Agency informed him that he would have to pay for cleaning up the results of an old, leaking gas tank that still sat beneath the property. Even though he had no part in running the old gas station and did not know the leaking tank was there, he was responsible for the cost of the cleanup! Removing the tank and cleaning up the site cost him several thousand dollars that he had not budgeted.

Second, the buyer must consider whether existing products contain defects that could result in **product liability lawsuits**, which claim that a company is liable for damages and injuries caused by the products or services it makes or sells. Existing lawsuits might be an omen of more to follow. In addition, the buyer must explore products that the company has discontinued because he

due-on-sale clause—*loan contract provision that prohibits a seller from assigning a loan arrangement to the buyer. Instead, the buyer is required to finance the remaining loan balance at prevailing interest rates.*

covenant not to compete (or restrictive covenant)—*an agreement between a buyer and a seller in which the seller agrees not to compete with the buyer within a specific time period and geographic area.*

A Company Example

might be liable for them if they prove to be defective. The final bargain between the parties should require the seller to guarantee that the company is not involved in any product liability lawsuits.

Third, what is the relationship between management and employees? Does a union contract exist? The time to discover sour management–labor relations is before the purchase, not after.

If the buyer's investigation reveals such potential liabilities, it does not necessarily eliminate the business from consideration. Insurance coverage can shift such risks from the potential buyer, but the buyer should check to see whether the insurance will cover lawsuits resulting from actions predating the purchase.

Financial Soundness of the Business

IS THE BUSINESS FINANCIALLY SOUND? A prospective buyer must analyze the financial records of a target business to determine its condition. He shouldn't be afraid to ask an accountant for help. Accounting systems and methods can vary tremendously from one type of business to another and can be quite confusing to a novice. Current profits can be inflated by changes in the accounting procedure or in the method for recording sales. For the buyer, the most dependable financial records are audited statements, those prepared by a CPA firm in accordance with generally accepted accounting principles (GAAP). Unfortunately, audited records do not exist in many small companies that are for sale. In some cases, a potential buyer has to hire an accountant to construct reliable financial statements because the owner's accounting and recordkeeping is so sloppy.

When evaluating the financial status of any business prospect, a buyer must remember that any investment in a company should produce a reasonable salary for her, an attractive return on the money she invests, and enough to cover the amount she must borrow to make the purchase. Otherwise, it makes no sense to purchase the business. Because most investors know that they can earn at least 8 to 10 percent a year by investing wisely in the stock market, they expect any business they buy to earn at least that amount plus an extra return that reflects the additional risk of buying a business. Many owners expect to earn a return of at least 15 percent to 30 percent on the amount invested in their businesses.

A buyer also must remember that she is purchasing the future profit potential of an existing business. To evaluate the firm's profit potential, she should review past sales, operating expenses, and profits as well as the assets used to generate those profits. She must compare current balance sheets and income statements with previous ones and then develop pro forma statements for the next two or three years. Sales tax records, income tax returns, and financial statements are valuable sources of information.

Are profits consistent over the years, or are they erratic? Is this pattern typical in the industry, or is it a result of unique circumstances or poor management? Can the business survive with such a serious fluctuation in revenues, costs, and profits? If these fluctuations are caused by poor management, can a new manager turn the business around?

Some of the financial records that a potential buyer should examine include the following:

INCOME STATEMENTS AND BALANCE SHEETS FOR THE PAST THREE TO FIVE YEARS. It is important to review data from several years because creative accounting techniques can distort financial data in any single year. Even though buyers are purchasing the future profits of a business, they must remember that many businesses intentionally show low profits in order to minimize the owners' tax bills. Low profits should prompt a buyer to investigate their causes.

INCOME TAX RETURNS FOR THE PAST THREE TO FIVE YEARS. Comparing basic financial statements with tax returns can reveal discrepancies of which the buyer should be aware. Some small business owners **skim** from their businesses—take money from sales without reporting it as income. Owners who skim will claim their businesses are more profitable than their tax returns show. Although such underreporting is illegal and unethical, it is surprisingly common. Do *not* pay for undocumented, "phantom" profits the seller claims exist. In fact, you should consider whether you want to buy a business from someone who admits to doing business unethically.

OWNER'S COMPENSATION (AND THAT OF RELATIVES). The owner's compensation is especially important in small companies; and the smaller the company is, the more important it will be. Although many companies do not pay their owners what they are worth, others compensate their owners lavishly. The buyer must consider the impact of fringe benefits—company cars, insurance contracts, country club memberships, and the like. It is important to adjust the company's income statements for the salary and fringe benefits that the seller has paid himself and others.

product liability lawsuits—*lawsuits that claim a company is liable for damages and injuries caused by the products it makes or sells.*

skimming—*taking money from sales without reporting it as income.*

CASH FLOW. Most buyers understand the importance of evaluating a company's profitability, but fewer recognize the necessity of analyzing its cash flow. They assume that if profits are adequate, there will be sufficient cash to pay all of the bills and to fund an attractive salary for themselves. *That is not necessarily the case*! Before you agree to a deal, you should sit down with an accountant and convert the target company's financial statements into a cash flow forecast. Not only must this forecast take into account existing debts and obligations but also any modifications the buyer would make in the business. It must also reflect the repayment of any financing the buyer arranges to purchase the company. Will the company generate enough cash to be self-supporting? How much cash will it generate for you?

A potential buyer must look for suspicious deviations from normal (in either direction) for sales, expenses, profits, cash flow, assets, and liabilities. Have sales been increasing or decreasing? Is the equipment really as valuable as it is listed on the balance sheet? Are advertising expenses unusually high or low? How is depreciation reflected in the financial statements?

This financial information gives a buyer the opportunity to verify the seller's claims about the business's performance. Sometimes, however, an owner will take short-term actions that produce a healthy financial statement but weaken the firm's long-term health and profit potential. For example, a seller might lower costs by gradually eliminating equipment maintenance or boost sales by selling to marginal businesses that will never pay their bills. Such techniques can artificially inflate assets and profits, but a well-prepared buyer should be able to see through them.

YOU Be the Consultant . . .

Escaping a High-Tech World for a Low-Tech One

Mike and Nancy Lusby knew that it was time for a change in their lives. Mike, the director of operations for a high-tech company in Silicon Valley, had just learned that his $70,000-a-year job was being eliminated. Nancy was the manager of the finance department at a high-tech lab in Silicon Valley, and, although she enjoyed her work, she had grown weary of office politics and the three-hour round-trip commutes to work and back. The Lusbys decided that it was time to realize their dream of becoming entrepreneurs.

Rather than start their own company from scratch, however, the Lusbys wanted to buy a business. They knew that they did not want to own a high-tech company and that they did want a business that included living quarters. The couple spent a considerable amount of time scouring advertisements for businesses in magazines and newspapers, ultimately narrowing their choices to three: hardware stores, bed-and-breakfast inns, and general stores. "I've always loved hardware stores," says Mike, but they don't usually come with a place to live. B&Bs provide you housing, but you're on call 24 hours a day." The couple decided to focus on general stores.

Mike contacted a dozen general stores and visited them but ultimately rejected them all because they were either "boring" or they were too far from good schools for the couple's young daughters. The prospects of finding a suitable general store were fading. "We were down to our last $1,000 in my severance pay, and I spent it on a plane tickets to fly to New Hampshire," Mike says. There he visited the Brick Store, which is listed on the Interior Department's National Register of Historic Places as the oldest continuously operated general store in the United States. Mike immediately recognized the Brick Store's drawing

power and marketing potential; he also fell in love with the business, which was started in 1790. The brick building that houses the store today was built in 1804 after a fire destroyed the original location. The two-story, Federal-style building came complete with large white columns and an inviting porch. Its old-world charm was hard for the Lusbys—and for customers—to resist. Plus, there was plenty of room upstairs for the family to live. The Ammonoosuc River flowed by just beyond the Brick Store, and the town of Bath was filled with picturesque, calendar-like scenes of New England. Nearby was the longest covered bridge in New Hampshire.

The Lusbys were ready to buy the Brick Store. The asking price was $390,000 but the owner accepted the Lusbys' offer of $300,000. The Lusbys took much of their savings and a gift from Nancy's parents to make a down payment of $140,000 and borrowed the balance from a local bank. Although their previous business experience came in handy when they set up a mail-order business to keep revenue coming in during the off-season (January through April), the Lusbys knew they had a lot to learn about retailing. Product lines run into the hundreds—from pocketknives and jellies to weathervanes and worms—all with profit margins as varied as the products themselves. They discovered that the store's tourist traffic arrives in May, swells throughout the summer, and blossoms in September and October. In fact, the Brick House brings in 40 percent of its annual sales in just six weeks during September and October. After that, business slows to a trickle. Fortunately for the Lusbys, three long-time employees agreed to stay on to teach the New England newcomers the daily details of running the store.

After the Lusbys took over the Brick Store, they discovered several problems that caused them so much concern that they actually returned to California for a brief time. They learned that in the future a new highway will divert approximately 20 percent of the store's traffic. In addition, the Lusbys' early experience in the store did not measure up to the expectations that the previous owner's rather spotty financial records had created. Fortunately, the business broker, whom the Lusbys did not know before buying the store, became a friend and was able to show them that the store could generate enough profits to support itself and them. The Lusbys also discovered how much they enjoyed their new lifestyle and location. "One winter day, [we] sat down and figured out how much we'd have to earn at other jobs to support this kind of life," says Mike. "It came to $75,000 a year." The Lusbys not only are making a comfortable living running the Brick Store, but their commute to work is now much shorter. A short stroll down the steps from the living quarters puts them at work in a beautiful, 200-year-old general store with a tremendous sense of history.

1. Suppose that the Lusbys came to you for advice on buying the Brick Store. What would you have told them?

2. Should the Lusbys have done anything differently in their quest to buy a business? Explain.

Source: Adapted from Lee Smith, "From High Tech . . . to Low Tech," *Fortune,* November 9, 1998, pp. 228[A]–228[D].

Source: Courtesy of The Brick Store.

1. Identify and approach candidate	2. Sign nondisclosure statement	3. Sign letter of intent	4. Buyer's due diligence investigation	5. Draft the purchase agreement	6. Close the final deal	7. Begin the transition

→ Negotiations →

FIGURE 5.1

The Acquisition Process

Sources: Adapted from *Buying and Selling: A Company Handbook.* Price Waterhouse (New York: 1993) pp. 38–42. Charles F. Claeys, "The Intent to Buy," *Small Business Reports.* May 1994, pp. 44–47.

1. *Approach the candidate.* If a business is advertised for sale, the proper approach is through the channel defined in the ad. Sometimes buyers will contact business brokers to help them locate potential target companies. If you have targeted a company in the "hidden market," an introduction from a banker, accountant, or lawyer often is the best approach. During this phase, the seller checks out the buyer's qualifications, and the buyer begins to judge the quality of the company.
2. *Sign a nondisclosure document.* If the buyer and the seller are satisfied with the results of their preliminary research, they are ready to begin serious negotiations. Throughout the negotiation process, the seller expects the buyer to maintain strict confidentiality of all the records, documents, and information

he or she receives during the investigation and negotiation process. The nondisclosure document is a legally binding contract that ensures the secrecy of the parties' negotiations.
3. *Sign a letter of intent.* Before a buyer makes a legal offer to buy the company, he or she typically will ask the seller to sign a letter of intent. The letter of intent is a nonbinding document that says that the buyer and the seller have reached a sufficient "meeting of the minds" to justify the time and expense of negotiating a final agreement. The letter should state clearly that it is nonbinding, giving either party the right to walk away from the deal. It should also contain a clause calling for "good faith negotiations" between the parties. A typical letter of intent addresses terms such as price, payment, categories of assets to be sold, and a deadline for closing the final deal.
4. *Buyer's due diligence.* While

negotiations are continuing, the buyer is busy studying the business and evaluating its strengths and weaknesses. In short, the buyer must "do his or her homework" to make sure that the business is a good value.
5. *Draft the purchase agreement.* The purchase agreement spells out the parties' final deal. It sets forth all of the details of the agreement and is the final product of the negotiation process.
6. *Close the final deal.* Once the parties have drafted the purchase agreement, all that remains to making the deal official is the closing. Both buyer and seller sign the necessary documents to make the sale final. The buyer delivers the required money, and the seller turns the company over to the buyer.
7. *Begin the transition.* For the buyer, the *real* challenge now begins: making the transition to a successful business owner!

Finally, a potential buyer should walk away from a deal—no matter how good it may appear on the surface—if the present owner refuses to disclose his company's financial records.

Buying an existing business is a process filled with potential missteps along the way. The expression "Let the buyer beware" should govern your thoughts and actions throughout the entire process. However, by following the due diligence procedure just discussed, a buyer can dramatically lower the probability of getting "burned" with a business that does not suit her personality or one that is in on the verge of failure. Figure 5.1 illustrates the sequence of events leading up to a successful negotiation with a seller.

Learning Objective

4. Describe the various techniques for determining the value of a business.

METHODS FOR DETERMINING THE VALUE OF A BUSINESS

Business valuation is partly an art and partly a science. Part of what makes establishing a reasonable price for a privately held business so difficult is the wide variety of factors that influence its value: the nature of the business itself, its position in the market or industry, the outlook for the market or industry, the company's financial status, its earning capacity, any intangible assets it may own (e.g., patents, trademarks, or copyrights), the value of other similar publicly held companies, and many other factors.

Computing the value of the company's tangible assets normally poses no major problem, but assigning a price to the intangibles, such as goodwill, almost always creates controversy. The seller expects goodwill to reflect the hard work and long hours invested in building the business. The buyer, however, is willing to pay extra only for those intangible assets that produce exceptional income. So, how can the buyer and the seller arrive at a fair price? There are few hard-and-fast rules in establishing the value of a business, but the following guidelines are helpful:

■ The wisest approach is to compute a company's value using several techniques and then to choose the one that makes the most sense.

■ The deal must be financially feasible for both parties. The seller must be satisfied with the price received for the business, but the buyer cannot pay an excessively high price.

■ The potential buyer must have access to the business records.

■ Valuations should be based on facts, not fiction.

■ No surprise is the best surprise. Both parties should commit to dealing with one another honestly and in good faith.

The main reason that buyers purchase existing businesses is to get their future earning potential. The second most common reason is to obtain an established asset base; it is much easier to buy assets than to build them. Although evaluation methods should take these characteristics into consideration, too many business sellers and buyers depend on rules of thumb that ignore the unique features of small companies. Often these rules of thumb are based on multiples of a company's net earnings or sales and vary by industry.

The next section describes three basic techniques and several variations on them for determining the value of a hypothetical business, Lewis Electronics.

Basic Balance Sheet Methods: Net Worth = Assets – Liabilities

balance sheet technique—
a method of valuing a business based on the value of the company's net worth (net worth = total assets – total liabilities).

BALANCE SHEET TECHNIQUE.   The **balance sheet technique** is one of the most commonly used methods of evaluating a business although it is not highly recommended because it oversimplifies the valuation process. This method computes the company's net worth or owner's equity (net worth = total assets – total liabilities) and uses this figure as the value. The problem with this technique is that it fails to recognize reality: Most small businesses have market values that exceed their reported book values.

The first step is to determine which assets are included in the sale. In most cases, the owner has some personal assets that he does not want to sell. Professional business brokers can help the buyer and the seller arrive at a reasonable value for the collection of assets included in the deal. Remember that net worth on a financial statement will likely differ significantly from actual net worth in the market. Figure 5.2 shows the balance sheet for Lewis Electronics. Based on this balance sheet, the company's net worth is $266,091 – $114,325 = $151,766.

FIGURE 5.2   Balance Sheet for Lewis Electronics

Lewis Electronics
Balance Sheet
June 30, 200x

Assets

Current Assets:

Cash	$11,655	
Accounts Receivable	15,876	
Inventory	56,523	
Supplies	8,574	
Prepaid Insurance	5,587	
Total Current Assets		$ 98,215

Fixed Assets:

Land		$24,000	
Buildings	$141,000		
less accumulated depreciation	51,500	89,500	
Office Equipment	$ 12,760		
less accumulated depreciation	7,159	5,601	
Factory Equipment	$ 59,085		
less accumulated depreciation	27,850	31,235	
Trucks and Autos	$ 28,730		
less accumulated depreciation	11,190	17,540	
Total Fixed Assets			$167,876
Total Assets			$266,091

Liabilities

Current Liabilities:

Accounts Payable	$19,497	
Mortgage Payable (current portion)	5,215	
Salaries Payable	3,671	
Note Payable	10,000	
Total Current Liabilities		$ 38,383

Long-Term Liabilities:

Mortgage Payable	$54,542	
Note Payable	21,400	
Total Long-Term Liabilities		$ 75,942
Total Liabilities		$114,325

Owners' Equity

Owners' Equity	$151,766
Total Liabilities and Owners' Equity	$266,091

VARIATION: ADJUSTED BALANCE SHEET TECHNIQUE.   A more realistic method for determining a company's value is to adjust the book value of net worth to reflect *actual* market value. The values reported on a company's books may either overstate or understate the true value of assets and liabilities. Typical assets in a business sale include notes and accounts receivable, inventories, supplies, and fixtures. If a buyer purchases notes and accounts receivable, he should estimate the likelihood of their collection and adjust their value accordingly.

In manufacturing, wholesale, and retail businesses, inventory is usually the largest single asset in the sale. Taking a physical inventory count is the best way to determine accurately the quantity of goods to be transferred. The sale may include three types of inventory, each having its own method of valuation: raw materials, work-in-process, and finished goods. The buyer and the seller must arrive at a method for evaluating the inventory. First-in, first-out (FIFO), last-in, first-out (LIFO), and average costing are three frequently used techniques, but the most common methods use the cost of last purchase and the replacement value of the inventory. Before accepting any inventory value, the buyer should evaluate the condition of the goods.

adjusted balance sheet technique—*a method of valuing a business based on the market value of the company's net worth (net worth = total assets − total liabilities).*

One young couple purchased a lumber yard without sufficiently examining the inventory. After completing the sale, they discovered that most of the lumber in a warehouse they had neglected to inspect was warped and was of little value as building material. The bargain price they paid for the business turned out not to be the good deal they had expected.

To avoid such problems, some buyers insist on having a knowledgeable representative on an inventory team to count the inventory and check its condition. Nearly every sale involves merchandise that cannot be sold, but by taking this precaution, a buyer minimizes the chance of being stuck with worthless inventory. Fixed assets transferred in a sale might include land, buildings, equipment, and fixtures. Business owners frequently carry real estate and buildings at prices well below their actual market value. Equipment and fixtures, depending on their condition and usefulness, may increase or decrease the true value of the business. Appraisals of these assets on insurance policies are helpful guidelines for establishing market value. Also, business brokers can be useful in determining the current market value of fixed assets. Some

FIGURE 5.3 Balance Sheet for Lewis Electronics Adjusted to Reflect Market Value

Lewis Electronics
Adjusted Balance Sheet
June 30, 200x

Assets

Current Assets:

Cash	$ 11,655	
Accounts Receivable	10,051	
Inventory	39,261	
Supplies	7,492	
Prepaid Insurance	5,587	
Total Current Assets		$ 74,046

Fixed Assets:

Land		$ 39,900	
Buildings	$177,000		
less accumulated depreciation	51,500	125,500	
Office Equipment	$ 11,645		
less accumulated depreciation	7,159	4,486	
Factory Equipment	$ 50,196		
less accumulated depreciation	27,850	22,346	
Trucks and Autos	$ 22,550		
less accumulated depreciation	11,190	11,360	
Total Fixed Assets			$200,592
Total Assets			$274,638

Liabilities

Current Liabilities:

Accounts Payable	$ 19,497	
Mortgage Payable (current portion)	5,215	
Salaries Payable	3,671	
Note Payable	10,000	
Total Current Liabilities		$ 38,383

Long-Term Liabilities:

Mortgage Payable	$ 54,542	
Note Payable	21,400	
Total Long-Term Liabilities		$ 75,942
Total Liabilities		$114,325

Owners' Equity

Owners' Equity	$160,313
Total Liabilities and Owners' Equity	$274,638

brokers use an estimate of what it would cost to replace a company's physical assets (less a reasonable allowance for depreciation) to determine value. For Lewis Electronics, the adjusted net worth is $274,638 − $114,325 = $160,313 (see the adjusted balance sheet in Figure 5.3), indicating that some of the entries in its books did not accurately reflect true market value.

Business evaluations based on balance sheet methods suffer one major drawback: They do not consider the future earning potential of the business. These techniques value assets at current prices and do not consider them as tools for creating future profits. The next method for computing the value of a business is based on its expected future earnings.

EARNINGS APPROACH.   The buyer of an existing business is essentially purchasing its future income. The **earnings approach** focuses on the future income potential of a business and assumes that a company's value depends on its ability to generate consistent profits over time. There are three variations of the earnings approach.

earnings approach—*a method of valuing a business that recognizes that a buyer is purchasing the future income (earnings) potential of a business.*

VARIATION 1: EXCESS EARNINGS METHOD.   This method combines both the value of a business's existing assets (minus its liabilities) and an estimate of its future earnings potential to determine its selling price. One advantage of this technique is that it offers an estimate of goodwill. **Goodwill** is an intangible asset that often creates problems in a business sale. In fact, the most common method of valuing a business is to compute its tangible net worth and then to add an often arbitrary adjustment for goodwill. In essence, goodwill is the difference between an established, successful business and one that has yet to prove itself. It is based on the company's reputation and its ability to attract customers. A buyer should not accept blindly the seller's arbitrary adjustment for goodwill because it is likely to be inflated. The *real* value of a company's goodwill lies in its financial value to the buyer, not in its emotional value to the seller.

goodwill—*an intangible asset that reflects the value of a company's reputation, its established customer and supplier contacts, name recognition, and other factors.*

The excess earnings method provides a consistent and realistic approach for determining the value of goodwill. It measures goodwill by the amount of profit the business earns above that of the average firm in the same industry. It also assumes that the owner is entitled to a reasonable return on the firm's adjusted tangible net worth.

Step 1. *Compute adjusted tangible net worth.* Using the adjusted balance sheet method of valuation, the buyer should compute the firm's adjusted tangible net worth. Total tangible assets (adjusted for market value) minus total liabilities yields adjusted tangible net worth. In the Lewis Electronics example, adjusted tangible net worth is $274,638 − $114,325 = $160,313 (refer to Figure 5.3).

Step 2. *Calculate the opportunity costs of investing in the business.* **Opportunity cost** represents the cost of forgoing a choice. If a buyer chooses to purchase the assets of a business, he cannot invest his money elsewhere. Therefore, the opportunity cost of the purchase would be the amount that the buyer could earn by investing the same amount *in a similar-risk investment.*

opportunity cost—*the cost of the next best alternative choice; the cost of giving up one alternative to get another.*

There are three components in the rate of return used to value a business: (1) the basic, risk-free return, (2) an inflation premium, and (3) the risk allowance for investing in the particular business. The basic, risk-free return and the inflation premium are reflected in investments such as U.S. treasury bonds. To determine the appropriate rate of return for investing in a business, the buyer must add to this base rate a factor reflecting the risk of purchasing the company. The greater the risk is, the higher the rate of return will be. A normal-risk business typically indicates a 25 percent rate of return. In the Lewis Electronics example, the opportunity cost of the investment is $160,313 × 25% = $40,078.

The second part of the buyer's opportunity cost is the salary that she could earn working for someone else. For the Lewis Electronics example, if the buyer purchases the business, she must forgo the $25,000 salary that she could earn working elsewhere. Adding these amounts together yields a total opportunity cost of $65,078.

Step 3. *Project net earnings.* The buyer must estimate the company's net earnings for the upcoming year before subtracting the owner's salary. Averages can be misleading, so the buyer must be sure to investigate the trend of net earnings. Have they risen steadily over the past five years, dropped significantly, remained relatively constant, or fluctuated wildly? Past income statements provide useful guidelines for estimating earnings. In the Lewis Electronics example, the buyer and his accountant project net earnings for the upcoming year to be $74,000.

Step 4. *Compute extra earning power.* A company's extra earning power is the difference between forecasted earnings (step 3) and total opportunity costs (step 2). Many small businesses that are for sale do not have extra earning power (i.e., excess earnings), and they show marginal or no profits. The extra earning power of Lewis Electronics is $74,000 − $65,000 = $8,922.

Step 5. *Estimate the value of intangibles.* The owner can use the extra earning power of the business to estimate the value of its intangible assets—that is, its goodwill. Multiplying the extra earning power by a years-of-profit figure yields an estimate of the intangible assets' value. The years-of-profit figure for a normal-risk business ranges from 3 to 4. A very high-risk business may have a years-of-profit figure of 1, whereas a well-established firm might use a figure of 7. For Lewis Electronics, the value of intangibles (assuming normal risk) would be $8,922 \times 3 = $26,766.

Step 6. *Determine the value of the business.* To determine the value of the business, the buyer simply adds together the adjusted tangible net worth (step 1) and the value of the intangibles (step 5). Using this method, the value of Lewis Electronics is $160,313 + $26,766 = $187,079.

The buyer and the seller should consider the tax implications of including in the purchase the value of goodwill and the value of a covenant not to compete. Because the *buyer* can amortize both the cost of goodwill and a covenant over 15 years, the tax treatment of either would be the same for him or her. However, the *seller* would prefer to have the amount of the purchase price in excess of the value of the assets allocated to goodwill, which is a capital asset. The gain on the capital asset would be taxed at the lower capital gains rates. If that same amount were allocated to a restrictive covenant (which is negotiated with the seller personally, not the business), the seller must treat it as ordinary income, which would be taxed at regular rates that are higher than the capital gains rates.

VARIATION 2: CAPITALIZED EARNINGS APPROACH. Another earnings approach capitalizes expected net earnings to determine the value of a business. The buyer should prepare his own pro forma income statement and should ask the seller to prepare one also. Many appraisers use a five-year weighted average of past sales (with the greatest weights assigned to the most recent years) to estimate sales for the upcoming year.

Once again, the buyer must evaluate the risk of purchasing the business to determine the appropriate rate of return on the investment. The greater the perceived risk, the higher the return that the buyer requires. Risk determination is always somewhat subjective, but it is necessary for proper evaluation.

capitalized earnings approach—*a method of valuing a business that divides estimated earnings by the rate of return the buyer could earn on a similar-risk investment.*

The **capitalized earnings approach** divides estimated net earnings (*after* subtracting the owner's reasonable salary) by the rate of return that reflects the risk level. For Lewis Electronics, the capitalized value (assuming a reasonable salary of $25,000) is:

$$\frac{\text{Net earnings (after deducting owner's salary)}}{\text{Rate of return}} = \frac{\$74,000 - \$25,000}{25\%} = \$196,000$$

Clearly, firms with lower risk factors are more valuable (a 10 percent rate of return would yield a value of $499,000 for Lewis Electronics) than are those with higher risk factors (a 50 percent rate of return would yield a value of $99,800). Most normal-risk businesses use a rate-of-return factor ranging from 25 to 30 percent. The lowest risk factor that most buyers would accept for any business ranges from 15 to 20 percent.

discounted future earnings approach—*a method of valuing a business that forecasts a company's earnings several years into the future and then discounts them back to their present value.*

VARIATION 3: DISCOUNTED FUTURE EARNINGS APPROACH. This variation of the earnings approach assumes that a dollar earned in the future is worth less than that same dollar today. Therefore, using this approach, the buyer estimates the company's net income for several years into the future and then discounts these future earnings back to their present value. The resulting present value is an estimate of the company's worth.

The reduced value of future dollars represents the cost of the buyer's giving up the opportunity to earn a reasonable rate of return by receiving income in the future instead of today, a concept known as the time value of money. To illustrate the importance of the time value of money, consider two $1 million sweepstake winners. Rob wins $1 million in a sweepstakes, but he receives it in $50,000 installments over 20 years. If Rob invested every installment at 15 percent interest, he would have accumulated $5,890,505.98 at the end of 20 years. Lisa wins $1 million in another sweepstakes, but she collects her winnings in one lump sum. If Lisa invested her $1 million today at 15 percent, she would have accumulated $16,366,537.39 at the end of 20 years. The difference in their wealth is the result of the time value of money.

DISCOUNTED FUTURE EARNINGS APPROACH. The **discounted future earnings approach** has five steps:

Step 1. *Project future earnings for five years into the future.* One way is to assume that earnings will grow by a constant amount over the next five years. Perhaps a better method is to develop three forecasts—an optimistic, a pessimistic, and a most likely—for each year and then find a weighted average using the following formula:

$$\text{Forecasted earnings for year } i = \frac{\text{(Optimistic earnings for year } i) + \text{(Most likely forecast for year } i \times 4) + \text{(Pessimistic forecast for year } i)}{6}$$

For Lewis Electronics, the buyer's forecasts are:

Year	Pessimistic	Most Likely	Optimistic	Weighted Average
XXX1	65,000	74,000	92,000	75,500
XXX2	74,000	90,000	101,000	89,167
XXX3	82,000	100,000	112,000	99,000
XXX4	88,000	109,000	120,000	107,333
XXX5	88,000	115,000	122,000	111,667

Buyers must remember that the farther into the future they forecast, the less reliable their estimates will be.

Step 2. *Discount these future earnings at the appropriate present value rate.* The rate that the buyer selects should reflect the rate he could earn on a similar-risk investment. Because Lewis Electronics is a normal-risk business, the buyer chooses a present value rate of 25 percent.

Year	Income Forecast (Weighted Average)	Present Value Factor (at 25%)*	Net Present Value
XXX1	75,500	.8000	60,400
XXX2	89,167	.6400	57,067
XXX3	99,000	.5120	50,688
XXX4	107,333	.4096	43,964
XXX5	111,667	.3277	36,593
		Total	248,712

*The appropriate present value factor can be found by looking in published present value tables, by using modern calculators or computers, or by solving this formula:

$$\text{Present value factor} = \frac{1}{(1 + k)^t}$$
$$\text{where } k = \text{rate of retur}$$
$$t = \text{year}(t = 1, 2, 3 \ldots, n).$$

Step 3. *Estimate the income stream beyond five years.* One technique suggests multiplying the fifth-year income by 1/rate of return. For Lewis Electronics, the estimate is:

$$\text{Income beyond year 5} = \$111,667 \times \frac{1}{25\%} = \$446,668$$

Step 4. *Discount the income estimate beyond five years using the present value factor for the sixth year.* For Lewis Electronics:

$$\text{Present value of income beyond year 5} = \$446,668 \times 0.2622 = \$117,116$$

Step 5. *Compute the total value of the business.* Add the present value of the company's estimated earnings for years 1 through 5 (step 2) and the present value of its earnings from years 6 on (step 4):

$$\text{Total value} = \$248,712 + \$117,116 = \$365,828$$

The primary advantage of this technique is that it evaluates a business solely on the basis of its future earning potential, but its reliability depends on making forecasts of future earnings and on choosing a realistic present value rate. In other words, a company's present value is tied to its future performance, which is not always easy to project. The discounted cash flow technique is especially well suited for valuing service businesses (whose asset bases are often very thin) and for companies experiencing high growth rates.

market approach—*a method of valuing a business that uses the price/earnings (P/E) ratio of similar, publicly held companies to determine value.*

MARKET APPROACH. The **market** (or price/earnings) **approach** uses the price/earnings ratios of similar businesses to establish the value of a company. According to one valuation expert, among professional appraisers, the most widely recognized and applied standard of value is 'fair market value,' as defined by the Internal Revenue Service: the price at which property would change hands between a willing buyer and a willing seller, neither under any compulsion to buy or sell and both having reasonable knowledge of the relevant facts.[6] The buyer must use businesses whose stocks are publicly traded in order to get a meaningful comparison. A company's price/earnings ratio (or P/E ratio) is the price of one share of its common stock in the market divided by its earnings per share (after deducting preferred stock dividends). To get a representative P/E ratio, the buyer should average the P/E ratios of as many similar businesses as possible.

To compute the company's value, the buyer multiplies the average price/earnings ratio by the private company's estimated earnings. For example, suppose that the buyer found four companies comparable to Lewis Electronics whose stocks are publicly traded. Their price/earnings ratios are:

Company 1	3.3
Company 2	3.8
Company 3	4.7
<u>Company 4</u>	<u>4.1</u>
Average P/E ratio	3.975

Using this average P/E ratio produces a value of $294,150:

$$\text{Value} = \text{Average P/E ratio} \times \text{Estimated net earnings} = 3.975 \times \$74,000 = \$294,150$$

The biggest advantage of the market approach is its simplicity. But this method does have several disadvantages, including the following:

Necessary comparisons between publicly traded and privately owned companies. Because the stock of privately owned companies is illiquid, the P/E ratio used is often subjective and lower than that of publicly held companies.

Unrepresentative earnings estimates. The private company's net earnings may not realistically reflect its true earning potential. To minimize taxes, owners usually attempt to keep profits low and rely on fringe benefits to make up the difference.

Finding similar companies for comparison. Often it is extremely difficult for a buyer to find comparable publicly held companies when estimating the appropriate P/E ratio.

Applying the after-tax earnings of a private company to determine its value. If a prospective buyer is using an after-tax P/E ratio from a public company, he also must use the after-tax earnings from the private company.

Despite its drawbacks, the market approach is useful as a general guideline to establishing a company's value.

Which of these methods is best for determining the value of a small business? Simply stated, there is no single best method. Valuing a business is partly an art and partly a science. Using these techniques, a range of values will emerge. Buyers should look for values that might cluster together and then use their best judgment to determine their offering price. Table 5.4 summarizes the valuation techniques covered in this chapter.

BALANCE SHEET TECHNIQUE

Book value of net worth = Total assets − Total liabilities

$$= \$266{,}091 - \$114{,}325 = \$151{,}766$$

Variation: Adjusted Balance Sheet Technique

Net worth adjusted to reflect market value = $274,638 − $114,325 = $160,313

EARNINGS APPROACH

Variation 1: Excess Earnings Method

Step 1: Adjusted tangible net worth = $274,638 − $114,325 = $160,313

Step 2: Opportunity costs = Opportunity cost of investing + Salary forgone

$$= \$160{,}313 \times 25\% + \$25{,}000 = \$65{,}078$$

Step 3: Estimated net earnings = $74,000

Step 4: Extra earning power = Estimated net earning − Total opportunity costs

$$= \$74{,}000 - \$65{,}078$$
$$= \$8{,}922$$

Step 5: Value of intangibles (goodwill) = Extra earning power × Years-of-profit figure

$$= \$8{,}922 \times 3$$
$$= \$26{,}766$$

Step 6: Value of business = Tangible net worth + Value of intangibles

$$= \$160{,}313 + 26{,}766$$
$$= \$187{,}079$$

Variation 2: Capitalized Earnings Approach

$$\text{Value} = \frac{\text{Net earnings (after deducting owner's salary)}}{\text{Rate of return on a similar risk investment}}$$

$$= \frac{\$74{,}000 - \$25{,}000}{25\%} = \$196{,}000$$

Variation 3: Discounted Future Earnings Approach

Step 1: Project future earnings.

Year	Pessimistic	Most Likely	Optimistic	Weighted Average*
XXX1	$65,000	$ 74,000	$ 94,000	$ 75,500
XXX2	74,000	90,000	101,000	89,167
XXX3	82,000	100,000	112,000	99,000
XXX4	88,000	109,000	120,000	107,333
XXX5	88,000	115,000	122,000	111,667

$$^{*}\ \text{Weighted average} = \frac{P + 4 \times ML + O}{6}$$

Step 2: Discount future earnings using the appropriate present value factor.

Year	Forecasted Earnings	Present Value Factor	Net Present Value
XXX1	$ 75,500	.8000	$ 60,400
XXX2	89,167	.6400	57,067
XXX3	99,000	.5120	50,688
XXX4	107,333	.4096	43,964
XXX5	111,667	.3277	36,593
Total			$248,712

Step 3: Estimate income stream beyond five years.

$$\text{Income stream} = \text{Fifth-year forecasted income} \times \frac{1}{\text{Rate of return}}$$

$$= \$111{,}667 \times \frac{1}{25\%}$$

$$= \$446{,}668$$

(continued on the next page)

TABLE 5.4

What's It Worth? A Summary of Business Valuation Techniques

Source: "Cashing Out and Maintaining Control" by Peter Collins, Small Business reports, Dec. 1989, p. 28. Reprinted by permission of JBS and Emerald, www.emeraldinsight.com.

TABLE 5.4 (continued)

Step 4: Discount income stream beyond five years (using sixth-year present value factor).

Present value of income stream = $446,668 × .2622 = $117,116

Compute total value.

Total value = $248,712 + $117,116 = $365,828

MARKET APPROACH

Value = Estimated earnings × Average price/earnings ratio of representative companies
= $74,000 × 3.975 = $294,150

Which value is correct? Remember: There is no best method of valuing a business. These techniques provide only estimates of a company's worth. The particular method used depends on the unique qualities of the business and the special circumstances surrounding the sale.

UNDERSTANDING THE SELLER'S SIDE

Learning Objective

5. Understand the seller's side of the buyout decision and how to structure the deal.

Few events are more anticipated—and more emotional—for entrepreneurs than selling a business. It often produces vast personal wealth and a completely new lifestyle, and this newly gained wealth offers freedom and the opportunity to catch up on all the things the owners missed out on while building the business. Yet, many entrepreneurs who sell out experience a tremendous void in their lives. We might call this difficulty "separation anxiety" because for many owners their entire lives have been linked to their businesses. The businesses they owned were the focal point in their lives in the communities in which they lived and a part of their identities. In many cases the values that an owner exhibited through the business are an overwhelming concern at the time of sale. Will the new owner display the same values in managing the business I built?

Gary Hirshberg, who was the founder and CEO of Stonyfield Farms, a Londonderry, New Hampshire, yogurt producer, ran the business in compliance with his values regarding social responsibility. When negotiations with the French firm, Groupe Danone, began, Hirshberg made a condition of the sale that the acquirer must retain all of the company's employees. This condition was similar to the terms in the Ben & Jerry's Homemade sale to Cenilever.[7]

Selling a business involves developing a plan that maximizes the value of the business. Before selling her business, an entrepreneur must ask herself some important questions: Do you want to walk away from the business completely, or do you plan to stay on after the sale? If you decide to stay on, how involved do you want to be in running the company? How much can you realistically expect to get for the business? Is this amount of money sufficient to maintain your desired lifestyle? Rather than sell the business to an outsider, should you be transferring ownership to your kids or to your employees? Who are the professionals—business brokers, accountants, attorneys, tax advisors—you will need to help you close the sale successfully? How do you expect the buyer to pay for the company? Are you willing to finance at least some of the purchase price?

A seller who has answered these fundamental questions is prepared to move forward in an organized and professional fashion.

Structuring the Deal

Next to picking the right buyer, planning the structure of the deal is one of the most important decisions a seller can make. Entrepreneurs who sell their companies without considering the tax implications of the deal can wind up paying the IRS as much as 70 percent of the proceeds in the form of capital gains and other taxes![8] A skilled tax advisor or financial planner can help business sellers legally minimize the bite various taxes take out of the proceeds of the sale.

Exit Strategy Options

STRAIGHT BUSINESS SALE.   A straight business sale may be best for those entrepreneurs who want to step down and turn over the reins of the company to someone else.

*For instance, Richie Stachowski recently sold his toy company, **Short Stack Inc.**, to Wild Planet Toys of San Francisco because the business had grown so rapidly that Richie wanted more time to focus on other activities. The success of his three-year-old company, which sold worldwide more than 1 million water toys such as the Water Talkie (a device that allows swimmers to communicate underwater) and the Bin-Aqua-Lar (underwater binoculars), had won Richie several national awards and an appearance on* The David Letterman Show. *But he wanted time to pursue more normal activities—those suited for a 13-year-old boy! (Richie started Short Stack when he was just 10.) The sale of the company to Wild Planet Toys will net Richie an estimated $1 million per year for the next several years.[9]*

An initial question that owners need to answer is whether they want to sell the stock in the business or the assets of the business. Which choice is best for the seller and the buyer depends on the form of ownership. In an S corporation, the seller does not care if stock or assets are sold because the tax considerations are the same. Owners of C corporations are far better off selling stock rather than selling assets. Buyers will generally prefer to acquire the "hard" assets of the business, thus avoiding any potential hidden liabilities.[10] Despite these concerns, more than 90 percent of sales involve stock.

In every case, an intelligent entrepreneur always consults an attorney or tax advisor to obtain advice as to what form of sales will best suit their unique situation and personal desires. Know in advance what options you would prefer and which purchase options you would not accept. For example, although selling the business outright is the cleanest exit path for an entrepreneur, it may have negative tax consequences, and it often excludes the option of "staying on" and exiting gradually.

FORM A FAMILY LIMITED PARTNERSHIP. An entrepreneur could transfer her business to her children but still maintain control over it by forming a family limited partnership. The entrepreneur would take the role of the general partner with the children becoming limited partners in the business. The general partner keeps just 1 percent of the company, but the partnership agreement gives her total control over the business. The children own 99 percent of the company but have little or no say over how to run the business. Until the founder decides to step down and turn over the reins of the company to the next generation, she continues to run the business and sets up significant tax savings for the ultimate transfer of power.

SELL A CONTROLLING INTEREST. Sometimes business owners sell the majority interest in their companies to investors, competitors, suppliers, or large companies with an agreement that they will stay on after the sale as managers or consultants.

*For instance, Leon and Pam Seidman sold 55 percent of **Cosmic Pet Products**, a catnip business Leon started while in college, to Four Paws Pet Products, a much larger company. Four Paws gives the Seidmans the autonomy to run the business as they did before the sale, although the Seidmans do work with Four Paws on strategic planning and pricing issues. For both the Seidmans and Four Paws, the sale has produced positive outcomes. The Seidmans still get to run the day-to-day operations of the business they love without having to worry about the financial struggles of keeping a small company going. With the Seidmans' help, Four Paws has improved Cosmic Pet Products' distribution and pricing and built it into the largest catnip company in the country, commanding 60 percent of the market![11]*

RESTRUCTURE THE COMPANY. Another way for business owners to cash out gradually is to replace the existing corporation with a new one, formed with other investors. The owner essentially is performing a leveraged buyout of his own company. For example, assume that you own

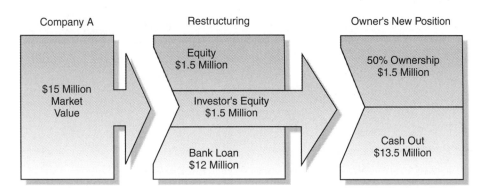

FIGURE 5.4 Restructuring a Business for Sale

Source: Peter Collins, "Cashing Out and Maintaining Control," *Small Business Reports,* December 1989, p. 28.

a company worth $15 million. You form a new corporation with $12 million borrowed from a bank and $3 million in equity: $1.5 million of your own equity and $1.5 million in equity from an investor who wants you to stay on with the business. The new company buys your company for $15 million. You net $13.5 in cash ($15 million – your $1.5 million equity investment) and still own 50 percent of the new leveraged business (see Figure 5.4).[12]

SELL TO AN INTERNATIONAL BUYER. In an increasingly global marketplace, small U.S. businesses have become attractive buyout targets for foreign companies. Foreign buyers—mostly European—buy more than 1,000 U.S. businesses each year. Despite the publicity that Japanese buyouts get, England leads the list of nations acquiring U.S. companies. Small business owners are receptive to international offers.

A Company Example

*Consider the opportunity presented to Jim Dolce, founder of **Redstone Communications**, by the German firm, Siemens, that paid Dolce $500 million for his 18-month-old telecommunications business and then hired him to stay on and run the company.*[13]

In today's global economic environment, it is not unprecedented to find buyers for a business, viewed as having great financial potential, from around the world. In many instances, foreign companies buy U.S. businesses to gain access to a lucrative, growing market. They look for a team of capable managers, whom they typically retain for a given time period. They also want companies that are profitable, stable, and growing.

Selling to foreign buyers can have disadvantages, however. They typically purchase 100 percent of a company, thereby making the previous owner merely an employee. Relationships with foreign owners also can be difficult to manage.

USE A TWO-STEP SALE. For owners wanting the security of a sales contract now but not wanting to step down from the company's helm for several years, a two-step sale may be ideal. The buyer purchases the business in two phases—getting 20 to 70 percent today and agreeing to buy the remainder within a specific time period. Until the final transaction takes place, the entrepreneur retains at least partial control of the company.

employee stock ownership plan (ESOP)—*an employee benefit plan in which a trust created for employees purchases stock in their employer's company.*

ESTABLISH AN EMPLOYEE STOCK OWNERSHIP PLAN (ESOP). Some owners cash out by selling to their employees through an **employee stock ownership plan (ESOP)**. An ESOP is a form of employee benefit plan in which a trust created for employees purchases their employer's stock. Here's how an ESOP works: The company transfers shares of its stock to the ESOP trust, and the trust uses the stock as collateral to borrow enough money to purchase the shares from the company. The company guarantees payment of the loan principal and interest and makes tax-deductible contributions to the trust to repay the loan (see Figure 5.5). The company then distributes the stock to employees' accounts based on a predetermined formula. In addition to the tax benefits an ESOP offers, the plan permits the owner to transfer all or part of the company to employees as gradually or as suddenly as preferred.

To use an ESOP successfully, a small business should be profitable (with pretax profits exceeding $100,000) and should have a payroll of more than $500,000 a year. Generally, companies with fewer than 15 to 20 employees do not find ESOPs beneficial. For companies that prepare properly, however, ESOPs offer significant financial and managerial benefits. An owner has great flexibility to set her retirement pace. An ESOP allows all parties to benefit and the transfer of ownership can be timed to meet the goals of the entrepreneur.

FIGURE 5.5

A Typical Employee Stock Ownership Plan (ESOP)

Source: From Sharing Ownership with Employees by Corey Rosen, Small Business Reports, Dec. 1990, p. 63. Reprinted by permission of JBS and Emerald, www.emeraldinsight.com.

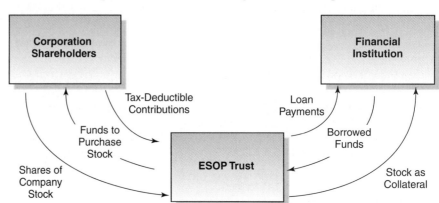

YOU Be the Consultant . . .

A Seller's Tale

Joseph Grassadonia loves the ocean so much that he planned his life around it, including starting businesses that would allow him to have both the time and the money to enjoy the sun and surf of California's beaches. Over the years, Grassadonia launched six magazines, including his most recent, *Dive Travel*. He compares the thrill and challenge of starting and managing a magazine to surfing and catching the ultimate wave. "When you're surfing and you're totally in control of the wave, and the equipment is right and everything is working, it's exhilarating," he says. After five years of running *Dive Travel*, however, Grassadonia says he got to the point where it wasn't fun anymore. "That's when I knew I had to sell," he recalls.

Actually, Grassadonia knew he would eventually sell *Dive Travel* from the day he started it. Managing and growing a magazine is "not my forte," he says. He began shopping for a business broker and settled on a local company to help him sell the company. The first order of business was to put a price tag on *Dive Travel*, something that proved to be a more emotional experience for Grassadonia than he had imagined. Although he knew that a company's value depends on the cash it can generate, he couldn't help but recall all of the energy, time, and talent he had invested in building the magazine from nothing to its current level. "This business is a chunk of my life. How do you put a value on that?" he asks philosophically.

Grassadonia had built *Dive Travel* into a successful publication. "We do business with just about every major advertiser in the marketplace," he says. "It would be very expensive to try and [re]create that." Using *Dive Travel's* sales of $324,000 and earnings of $50,000, the broker suggested an asking price of $500,000. For the next year, the business attracted very few leads—not an unusual pattern in selling a business. Ads in industry trade journals produced only a few nibbles but no serious buyers. Waiting to sell was wearing on Grassadonia, so he and the broker reduced the price to $450,000. Several more months slipped by with no interest from buyers, and Grassadonia was beginning to wonder if *anyone* wanted to buy *Dive Travel*.

Finally, Susan Wilmink and Thomas Schneck contacted Grassadonia's broker about *Dive Travel*. The couple was living in Germany, where Wilmink worked for a large international magazine publisher and Schneck owned a software company. The only problem was that Wilmink and Schneck couldn't afford to buy *Dive Travel* outright. They proposed that Grassadonia sell them a controlling interest in the company and stay on as a consultant for three years. Grassadonia hesitated at first but then agreed to stay on as long as Wilmink and Schneck took over the day-to-day operations of running the business. A major factor in his decision was Wilmink's presentation on how she and Schneck planned to run the company—from adding a World Wide Web site to repositioning the magazine. "Susan came in with a vision," says Grassadonia.

Negotiating the final deal took another six months, and at times the discussions became heated. At one such emotional moment, Barkley, Grassadonia's 13-year-old golden retriever, walked over to Wilmink's chair, jumped up, and licked her face. That broke the tension, everyone started laughing, and Wilmink decided to name the new business Barkley Publishing. The final price the parties agreed on was $215,000 for the 51 percent controlling interest Wilmink and Schneck got. Wilmink became the new president and publisher, and Grassadonia agreed to stay on as a paid consultant for three years. At the end of that time, he would sell his stock, with Wilmink and Schneck getting the right of first refusal. In addition, Grassadonia got a percentage of the company's revenues over the three years.

The deal has worked to everyone's satisfaction. Grassadonia has the freedom to surf whenever he pleases, and Wilmink and Schneck have the company they wanted. *Dive Travel's* circulation has more than doubled, revenues have nearly doubled, and profits are up.

1. Why is the process of valuing a business so difficult for the entrepreneur who founded it?

2. Which method(s) of valuing a business do you think would be most appropriate in placing a realistic value on *Dive Travel*? Explain.

3. Evaluate the final deal the parties struck from both the buyers' and the seller's perspectives. Do you think the deal was fair?

Source: Inc., Adapted from Christopher Caggiano, "The Seller," June 1996, pp. 54–56.

NEGOTIATING THE DEAL

Learning Objective

6. Understand how the negotiation process works and identify the factors that affect the negotiation process.

Although determining the value of a business for sale is an important step in the buying process, it is not the final one. The buyer must sit down with the seller to negotiate the actual selling price for the business and, more importantly, the terms of the deal. The final deal the buyer strikes depends, in large part, on her negotiating skills. The first rule of negotiating a deal is to avoid confusing price with value. Value is what the business is actually worth; price is what the buyer agrees to pay. In a business sale, the party who is the better bargainer usually comes out on top. The seller is looking to:

- get the highest price possible for the business.
- sever all responsibility for the company's liabilities.

- avoid unreasonable contract terms that might limit his future opportunities.
- maximize the cash he gets from the deal.
- minimize the tax burden from the sale.
- make sure the buyer will be able to make all future payments.

The buyer seeks to:

- get the business at the lowest possible price.
- negotiate favorable payment terms, preferably over time.
- get assurances that he is buying the business he thinks he is getting.
- avoid putting the seller in a position to open a competing business.
- minimize the amount of cash paid up front.

FACTORS AFFECTING THE NEGOTIATION PROCESS. Before beginning negotiations, a buyer should take stock of some basic issues. How strong is the seller's desire to sell? Is the seller willing to finance part of the purchase price? What terms does the buyer suggest? Which ones are most important to him? Is it urgent that the seller close the deal quickly? What deal structure best suits your needs? What are the tax consequences for both parties? Will the seller sign a restrictive covenant? Is the seller willing to stay on with the company for a time as a consultant? What general economic conditions exist in the industry at the time of the sale? Sellers tend to have the upper hand in good economic times, and buyers will have an advantage during recessionary periods in an industry.

The Negotiation Process

On the surface, the negotiation process appears to be strictly adversarial. Although each party may be trying to accomplish objectives that are at odds with those of the opposing party, the negotiation process does not have to turn into a nasty battle of wits with overtones of "If you win, then I lose." The negotiation process will go much more smoothly and much faster if both parties work to establish a cooperative relationship based on honesty and trust from the outset. A successful deal requires both parties to examine and articulate their respective positions while trying to understand the other party's position. Recognizing that neither of them will benefit without a deal, both parties must work to achieve their objectives while making certain concessions to keep the negotiations alive.

To avoid a stalled deal, a buyer should go into the negotiation with a list of objectives ranked in order of priority. Once she has developed her own list of priorities, it is useful to develop what she perceives to be the seller's list. That requires learning as much as possible about the seller. Knowing which terms are most important (and which are least important) to her and to the seller enables a buyer to make concessions without "giving away the farm" and without getting bogged down in "nit-picking," which often leads to a stalemate. If, for instance, the seller insists on a term that the buyer cannot agree to, she can explain why and then offer to give up something in exchange. The buyer also should identify the one concrete objective that sits at the top of that list, the one thing she absolutely must come away from the negotiations with. The final stage of preparing for the actual negotiation is to study her list and the one she has developed based on her perceptions of the seller to determine where the two mesh and where they conflict. The key to a successful negotiation is to use this analysis to look for areas of mutual benefit and to use them as the foundation for the negotiation.

Figure 5.6 offers five tips on making the negotiation process a successful one.

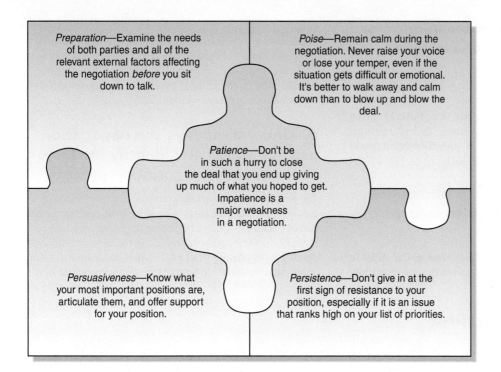

Preparation—Examine the needs of both parties and all of the relevant external factors affecting the negotiation *before* you sit down to talk.

Poise—Remain calm during the negotiation. Never raise your voice or lose your temper, even if the situation gets difficult or emotional. It's better to walk away and calm down than to blow up and blow the deal.

Patience—Don't be in such a hurry to close the deal that you end up giving up much of what you hoped to get. Impatience is a major weakness in a negotiation.

Persuasiveness—Know what your most important positions are, articulate them, and offer support for your position.

Persistence—Don't give in at the first sign of resistance to your position, especially if it is an issue that ranks high on your list of priorities.

CHAPTER SUMMARY

1. Understand the advantages and disadvantages of buying an existing business.

The *advantages* of buying an existing business: A successful business may continue to be successful; the business may already have the best location; employees and suppliers are already established; equipment is installed and its productive capacity known; inventory is in place and trade credit established; the owner hits the ground running; the buyer can use the expertise of the previous owner; and the business may be a bargain.

The *disadvantages* of buying an existing business: An existing business may be for sale because it is deteriorating; the previous owner may have created ill will; employees inherited with the business may not be suitable; its location may have become unsuitable; equipment and facilities may be obsolete; change and innovation are hard to implement; inventory may be outdated; accounts receivable may be worth less than face value; and the business may be overpriced.

2. Define the steps involved in the *right* way to buy a business.

Buying a business can be a treacherous experience unless the buyer is well prepared. The right way to buy a business is to analyze your skills, abilities, and interests to determine the ideal business for you; prepare a list of potential candidates, including those that might be in the hidden market; investigate and evaluate candidate businesses and evaluate the best one; explore financing options before you actually need the money; and, finally, ensure a smooth transition.

3. Explain the process of evaluating an existing business.

Rushing into a deal can be the biggest mistake a business buyer can make. Before closing a deal, every business buyer should investigate five critical areas: (1) Why does the owner wish to sell? Look for the *real* reason. (2) Determine the physical condition of the business. Consider both the building and its location. (3) Conduct a thorough analysis of the market for your products or services. Who are the present and potential customers? Conduct an equally thorough analysis of competitors, both direct and indirect. How do they operate and why do customers prefer them? (4) Consider all of the legal aspects that might constrain the expansion and growth of the business. Did you comply with the provisions of a bulk transfer? Negotiate a restrictive covenant? Consider ongoing legal liabilities? (5) Analyze the financial condition of the business, looking at financial statements, income tax returns, and especially cash flow.

4. Describe the various techniques for determining the value of a business.

Placing a value on a business is partly an art and partly a science. There is no single best method for determining the value of a business. The following techniques (with several variations) are useful: the balance sheet technique (adjusted balance sheet technique); the earnings approach (excess earnings method, capitalized earnings approach, and discounted future savings approach); and the market approach.

5. Understand the seller's side of the buyout decision and how to structure the deal.

Selling a business takes time, patience, and preparation to locate a suitable buyer, strike a deal, and make the transition.

Sellers must always structure the deal with tax consequences in mind. Common exit strategies include a straight business sale, forming a family limited partnership, selling a controlling interest in the business, restructuring the company, selling to an international buyer, using a two-step sale, and establishing an employee stock ownership plan (ESOP).

6. Understand how the negotiation process works and identify the factors that affect the negotiation process.

The first rule of negotiating is never to confuse price with value. In a business sale, the party who is the better negotiator usually comes out on top. Before beginning negotiations, a buyer should identify the factors that are affecting the negotiations and then develop a negotiating strategy. The best deals are the result of a cooperative relationship between the parties based on trust.

DISCUSSION QUESTIONS

1. What advantages can an entrepreneur who buys a business gain over one who starts a business "from scratch"?
2. How would you go about determining the value of the assets of a business if you were unfamiliar with them?
3. Why do so many entrepreneurs run into trouble when they buy an existing business? Outline the steps involved in the *right* way to buy a business.
4. When evaluating an existing business that is for sale, what areas should an entrepreneur consider? Briefly summarize the key elements of each area.
5. How should a buyer evaluate a business's goodwill?
6. What is a restrictive covenant? Is it fair to ask the seller of a travel agency located in a small town to sign a restrictive covenant for one year covering a 20-square-mile area? Explain.
7. How much negative information can you expect the seller to give you about the business? How can a prospective buyer find out such information?

8. Why is it so difficult for buyers and sellers to agree on a price for a business?
9. Which method of valuing a business is best? Why?
10. Outline the different exit strategy options available to a seller.
11. Explain the five Ps of a successful negotiation process. What tips would you offer someone about to enter into negotiations to buy a business?
12. One entrepreneur who recently purchased a business advises buyers to expect some surprises in the deal no matter how well prepared they may be. He says that potential buyers must build some "wiggle room" into their plans to buy a company. What steps can buyers take to ensure that they have sufficient "wiggle room"?

THE BUSINESS DISC

Launch *The Business Disc* and continue from where you left off until you have completed the Cash Flow projections for the full year. To understand how the program calculates and automatically fills numbers into some parts of the form see the Owner's Manual. From the Main Menu click Owner's Manual. Then scroll down to "Cash Flow Statement" at the bottom of page 5.

BUSINESS PLAN PRO

Business PlanPro

This chapter has dealt with the acquisition of an existing business. If you are developing a business plan for a company you plan to buy, go to the "Company Summary" section of the Business PlanPro and include the results of the due diligence process there. Be sure to include in the financial section income statements, balance sheets, and cash flow statements for the business for the past three years as well as forecasts for the next three years.

1.   Ask several new owners who purchased existing businesses the following questions:

   a. How did you determine the value of the business?

   b. How close was the price paid for the business to the value assessed prior to purchase?

   c. What percentage of the accounts receivable was collectible?

   d. How accurate have the projections been concerning customers (sales volume and number of customers, especially)?

2.   Visit a business broker and ask him how he brings a buyer and seller together. What does he do to facilitate the sale? What methods does he use to determine the value of a business?

3.   Invite an attorney to speak to your class about the legal aspects of buying a business. How does the attorney recommend business buyers protect themselves legally in a business purchase?

Chapter

6

Building a Powerful Marketing Plan

*If one takes care of the means,
the end will take care of itself.*

—Mohandas Gandhi

*This fishing lure manufacturer
I know had all these flashy
green and purple lures. I asked,
"Do fish take these?" "Charlie,"
he said, "I don't sell these
lures to fish."*

—Charles Munger

LEARNING OBJECTIVES

Upon completion of this chapter, you will be able to:

1. **DESCRIBE** the principles of building a guerrilla marketing plan and explain the benefits of preparing one.

2. **EXPLAIN** how small businesses can pinpoint their target markets.

3. **DISCUSS** the role of market research in building a guerrilla marketing plan and outline the market research process.

4. **DESCRIBE** how a small business can build a competitive edge in the marketplace using guerrilla marketing strategies: customer focus, quality, convenience, innovation, service, and speed.

5. **DISCUSS** the marketing opportunities the World Wide Web (WWW) offers entrepreneurs and how to best take advantage of them.

6. **DISCUSS** the "four Ps" of marketing—product, place, price, and promotion—and their role in building a successful marketing strategy.

The culmination of the next five chapters is the creation of an important business tool: the *business plan*, a valuable document that defines *what* an entrepreneur plans to accomplish in both quantitative and qualitative terms and *how* she plans to accomplish it. A business plan consolidates many of the topics we have discussed in preceding chapters with those of the next four chapters to produce a concise statement of how an entrepreneur plans to achieve success in the marketplace.

Too often, business plans describe in great detail what the entrepreneur intends to accomplish (e.g., "the financials") and pay little, if any, attention to the strategies to achieve those targets. Too many entrepreneurs squander enormous effort pulling together capital, people, and other resources to sell their products and services because they fail to determine what it will take to attract and keep a profitable customer base. Sometimes they fail to determine if a profitable customer base even exists! To be effective, a solid business plan must contain both a financial plan *and* a marketing plan. Like the financial plan, an effective marketing plan projects numbers and analyzes them but from a different perspective. Rather than focus on cash flow, net income, and owner's equity, the marketing plan concentrates on the *customer*.

This chapter is devoted to creating an effective marketing plan, which is a subset of a total business plan. Before producing reams of computer-generated spreadsheets of financial projections, an entrepreneur must determine what to sell, to whom and how, on what terms and at what price, and how to get the product or service to the customer. In short, a marketing plan identifies a company's target customers and describes how that business will attract and keep them. Its primary focus is capturing and maintaining a competitive edge for a small business.

BUILDING A GUERRILLA MARKETING PLAN

Learning Objective

1. Describe the principles of building a guerrilla marketing plan and explain the benefits of preparing one.

Marketing—*the process of creating and delivering desired goods and services to customers, involves all of the activities associated with winning and retaining loyal customers.*

guerrilla marketing strategies—*unconventional, low-cost, creative marketing strategies designed to give small companies an edge over their larger, richer, more powerful rivals.*

Marketing is the process of creating and delivering desired goods and services to customers and involves all of the activities associated with winning and retaining loyal customers. The secret to successful marketing is to understand what your target customers' needs, demands, and wants are before your competitors can; offer them the products and services that will satisfy those needs, demands, and wants; and provide customers service, convenience, and value so that they will keep coming back. Unfortunately, there appears to be a sizable gap between sound marketing principles and actual marketing practices among small businesses. One study of small company marketing practices by Dun & Bradstreet revealed many serious weaknesses. For instance, the study found that just one in five small business owners creates a strategic marketing plan and that the most common sales approach is to react to customer orders rather than to proactively seek them out. (Efforts are so passive that walk-in traffic was cited as the most popular sales method.) The study also revealed that word-of-mouth promotion and referrals comprise the typical small company's marketing efforts.[1]

In a small business, the marketing function cuts across the entire company, affecting every aspect of its operation—from finance and production to hiring and purchasing—as well as the company's ultimate success. As the global business environment becomes more turbulent and competition becomes more intense, small business owners must understand the importance of developing creative marketing strategies; their success and survival depend on it. A marketing plan is *not* just for megacorporations competing in international markets. Although they may be small in size and cannot match their larger rivals' marketing budgets, entrepreneurial companies are not powerless when it comes to developing effective marketing strategies. By using **guerrilla marketing strategies**—unconventional, low-cost, creative techniques—small companies can wring as much or more "bang" from their marketing bucks. For instance, facing the power of discount giants such as Wal-Mart, Target, and "category killer" superstores such as Best Buy and Circuit City determined to increase their market shares, small retail shops are turning to guerrilla marketing tactics to lure new customers and to keep existing ones. One small retailer explains, "If the chains are the steamships plowing through the ocean, then we have to be the cigarette [racing] boats zipping around and through them, changing direction on a dime. That must be our advantage when going up against the tremendous cash and resources of the biggies."[2]

An effective marketing campaign does *not* require an entrepreneur to spend large amounts of money, but it does demand creativity and ingenuity.

*Tory Johnson used the network of connections she had developed at her jobs with ABC and NBC News to launch **Women for Hire**, a New York City–based executive search firm that specializes in matching high-profile female employees with large companies in major cities across the United States. In her first year of operation, Johnson convinced a friend who worked in the marketing department at* Cosmopolitan *magazine to introduce her to top marketing managers. In the meeting, she pitched the idea of collaborating with* Cosmopolitan *to sponsor career fairs aimed at upscale professional women, a market that both the magazine and Johnson's company were targeting.* Cosmopolitan *managers agreed and gave Johnson free space in their magazine to promote the career fairs and the right to use the* Cosmopolitan *name and logo in her own promotional materials. Johnson even convinced them to sponsor free "goodie bags" for participants. The career fairs were a huge hit, and their success earned Johnson an interview on NBC's* The Today Show, *giving her company even more national exposure. Johnson's guerrilla marketing techniques have helped her company generate more than $1 million in annual sales.*[3]

A sound guerrilla marketing plan reflects a company's understanding of its *customer* and recognizes that satisfying the customer is the foundation of every business. Its purpose is to build a strategy of success for a business—but *from the customer's point of view*. Indeed, the customer is the central player in the cast of every business venture. According to marketing expert Ted Levitt, the primary purpose of a business is not to earn a profit; instead, it is "to create and keep a customer. The rest, given reasonable good sense, will take care of itself."[4] Every area of the business must practice putting the customer first in planning and actions.

A guerrilla marketing plan should accomplish four objectives:

1. It should pinpoint the specific target markets the small company will serve.
2. It should determine customer needs and wants through market research.
3. It should analyze the firm's competitive advantages and build a guerrilla marketing strategy around them.
4. It should help create a marketing mix that meets customer needs and wants.

The rest of this chapter focuses on building a customer orientation into these four objectives of the small company's marketing plan.

PINPOINTING THE TARGET MARKET

Learning Objective

2. Explain how small businesses can pinpoint their target markets.

One of the first steps in building a guerrilla marketing plan is to identify a small company's **target market**—the specific group of customers at whom the company aims its goods or services. The more a business learns about its local markets, its customers and their buying habits and preferences, the more precisely it can focus its marketing efforts on the group(s) of prospective and existing customers who are most likely to buy its products or services. Most marketing experts contend that the greatest marketing mistake small businesses make is failing to define clearly the target market to be served. In other words, most small businesses follow a "shotgun approach" to marketing, firing marketing blasts at every customer that they see, hoping to capture just some of them. Although this approach can work to get a small business established, it can lead to serious problems for a company using it to try to grow. Most entrepreneurs simply cannot use shotgun marketing techniques and compete successfully with larger rivals and their deep pockets. These entrepreneurs develop new products that do not sell because they are not targeted at a specific audience's needs; they broadcast ads that attempt to reach everyone and end up reaching no one; they spend precious time and money trying to reach customers who are not the most profitable; and many of the customers they attract leave because they do not know what the company stands for. Why, then, is the shotgun approach so popular? Because it is easy and does not require market research or a marketing plan! The problem is that the shotgun approach is a sales-driven rather than a customer-driven strategy. Smart entrepreneurs know that they do not have the luxury of wasting resources; they must follow a more targeted, "rifle" approach to marketing.

To be customer driven, an effective marketing program must be based on a clear, concise definition of a company's target customers. Failing to pinpoint their target markets is especially ironic because small firms are ideally suited to reaching small, often more concentrated market

target market—*the specific group of customers at whom a company aims its goods or services.*

segments that their larger rivals overlook or consider too small to be profitable. A target-focused marketing strategy can be a powerful strategic weapon for any company that lacks the financial and physical resources of its competitors. Customers respond when companies take the time to learn about their unique needs and offer products and services designed to satisfy them.

A Company Example

*For instance, when Marvin and Helene Gralnick launched **Chico's FAS** in 1983, they targeted women of the baby-boomer generation who had plenty of purchasing power and wanted fashionable but comfortable clothing. The Gralnicks focused on clothing designed for real women with all of their curves and imperfections, rather than styles that only supermodels and pop stars could wear. That meant pants that drape rather than cling and tops that covered the derriere. Chico's marketing strategy is the same today. "Our customer wants to be current," says chief financial officer Charles Kleman, "but she also wants a more comfortable fit." Understanding its customers' preferences, Chico's clothing is exclusive to its stores and Web site; customers will not see the same items sold elsewhere. The company's unique sizing also flatters its target customers as well. Its size 0 fits 4–6, size 1 fits 8–10, size 2 fits 10–12, and its largest size, 3, fits 14–16. Chico's trains its sales clerks extensively in identifying the four basic body types and in selecting the right styles that best fit each type. The company very cleverly has no mirrors in the dressing room so that customers must come outside to see themselves—and to be "accessorized" by a sales clerk. Chico's marketing approach has worked so well that even during economic recessions its sales have continued to grow.[5]*

Like Chico's, the most successful businesses have well-defined portraits of the customers they are seeking to attract. From market research, they know their customers' income levels, lifestyles, buying patterns, likes and dislikes, and even their psychological profiles. These companies establish prices appropriate to their target customers' buying power, product lines that appeal to their tastes, and service they expect. In essence, the target customer permeates the entire business—from the merchandise sold to the location, layout, and decor of the store. They have an advantage over their larger rivals because the images they have created for their companies appeal to their target customers, and that's why they prosper. Without a clear picture of its target market and the image it must create to attract those customers, a small company will try to reach almost everyone and usually ends up appealing to almost no one.

The nation's increasingly diverse population offers businesses of all sizes tremendous marketing opportunities if they target specific customers, learn how to reach them, and offer goods and services designed specifically for them. Because of this diversity, a "one-size-fits-all" approach to marketing no longer works. The 2000 U.S. census shows that Hispanic Americans are now the nation's largest minority, followed by African Americans and Asian Americans. More than 13 percent of the U.S. population is of Hispanic origin, but because they hail from more than 20 countries, this diverse market also requires a targeted marketing approach.[6]

A Company Example

*Entrepreneur Wilfredo Leon is aiming squarely at this fast-growing market by publishing **Latino**, the first Hispanic newspaper in South Carolina. Leon is publishing the paper in Spanish, but many other publishers of newspapers and magazines aimed at the Hispanic market use English or a combination of English and Spanish.[7] Strategy Research Corporation, a marketing research firm, says that 45.4 percent of Hispanics prefer to read magazines and newspapers in English, and 43 percent prefer Spanish.[8]*

Sometimes new target markets emerge on their own, much to the surprise of a small business owner.

A Company Example

*When Steve Pateman took over the shoe manufacturing company his grandfather had founded, the family business was struggling as a result of intense global competition and rising costs in its core market—high-quality, traditional men's shoes. Pateman was forced to cut the company's workforce from 77 to just 22 employees. Then Pateman received a phone call from a customer with an unusual request: Could he manufacture women's shoes for cross-dressing men? Pateman's company began manufacturing women's shoes in men's sizes and soon developed a complete product line under the **Divine** label that includes faux leopard thigh boots with seven-and-a-half-inch heels! The business has rehired many workers, takes orders from all across the globe, and generates 50 percent of its sales from the transvestite market.[9]*

DETERMINING CUSTOMER NEEDS AND WANTS THROUGH MARKET RESEARCH

Learning Objective

3. Discuss the role of market research in building a guerrilla marketing plan and outline the market research process.

The changing nature of the U.S. population is a potent force altering the landscape of business. Shifting patterns in age, income, education, race, and other population characteristics (which are the subject of **demographics**) will have a major impact on companies, their customers, and the way they do business with those customers. Businesses that ignore demographic trends and fail to adjust their strategies accordingly run the risk of becoming competitively obsolete.

A demographic trend is like a train; a business owner must find out early on where it's going and decide whether or not to get on board. Waiting until the train is roaring down the tracks and gaining speed means it's too late to get on board. However, by checking the schedule early and planning ahead, an entrepreneur may find himself at the train's controls wearing the engineer's hat! Similarly, small companies that spot demographic trends early and act on them can gain a distinctive edge in the market. An entrepreneur's goal is to make sure her company's marketing plan is on track with the most significant trends that are shaping the industry.

Trends are powerful forces and can be a business owner's greatest friend or greatest enemy. In the restaurant industry, traditional fast-food chains are struggling to sustain mediocre growth rates, whereas restaurants based on the "fast casual" concept make up the hottest sector (refer to Chapter 3). In fact, fast-food giants McDonald's and Wendy's have purchased promising companies in the fast casual sector such as Boston Market, Panera Bread, Chipotle, and Baja Fresh. Several factors are driving this trend: consumers who are "burned out" on burgers and concerned about the health considerations of fast-food diets, the growing population of empty-nest baby boomers who are tired of cooking, and the increasing purchasing power of members of Generation X, who never enjoyed cooking at home.[10] For entrepreneurs who are observant and position their companies to intercept them, trends can be to their companies what the perfect wave is to a surfer. For entrepreneurs who ignore them or discount their importance, trends can leave their companies stranded like a boat stuck in the mud at low tide.

The increasing cultural diversity in the United States is providing tremendous business opportunities for entrepreneurs who are fast enough and savvy enough to capitalize on them. Demographic patterns indicate that by 2050, the population of Caucasians will shrink to 53 percent of the nation's population from 72 percent in 2000, but the populations of other groups such as Hispanic Americans and Asian Americans will climb rapidly. The population of Asian Americans, for instance, now boasts the highest rate of education of any segment and has an average household income that exceeds that of Caucasian households by $10,000. Recognizing the potential of this demographic trend, Lubna Khalid, a former model of Pakistani descent, launched Real Cosmetics, a company that produces a line of cosmetics aimed specifically at Asian women.[11]

demographics—*the study of important population characteristics such as age, income, education, race, and others.*

The Value of Market Research

By performing some basic market research, small business owners can detect key demographic and market trends. Indeed, *every* business can benefit from a better understanding of its market, customers, and competitors. "Market information is just as much a business asset and just as important as your inventory or the machine you have in the back room," says one marketing consultant.[12] **Market research** is the vehicle for gathering the information that serves as the foundation for the marketing plan. It involves systematically collecting, analyzing, and interpreting data pertaining to a company's market, customers, and competitors. The objective of market research is to learn how to improve the level of satisfaction for existing customers and to find ways to attract new customers. Market research answers questions such as: Who are my customers and potential customers? What are they looking for? What kind of people are they? Where do they live? How often do they buy these products or services? What models, styles, colors, or flavors do they prefer? Why do or don't they buy from my business? How do the strengths of my product or service serve their needs and wants? What hours do they prefer to shop? How do they perceive my business? Which advertising media are likely to reach them? How do customers perceive my business versus my competitors? This information is an integral part of developing a marketing plan that produces sales.

When marketing their goods and services, small companies must avoid mistakes because there is no margin for error when funds are scarce and budgets are tight. Small businesses simply cannot afford to miss their target markets, and market research can help them zero in on the bull's-eye.

market research—*the vehicle for gathering the information that serves as the foundation for the marketing plan; it involves systematically collecting, analyzing, and interpreting data pertaining to a company's market, customers, and competitors.*

*Jim Ammeen, CEO of **Neema Clothing Ltd.**, a small manufacturer of men's tailored clothing, says that the marketing strategy behind his company's impressive growth rate (700 percent since its inception) is the result of deliberate market research. Studying statistics on the U.S. men's clothing industry he had gathered from various sources, Ammeen noticed that "80 percent of the suits retailed for less than $300, yet the majority of manufacturers were pricing their suits in the $500-to-$700 range. I was able to direct Neema's efforts toward capturing business that the competition was overlooking," he says. Neema Clothing continues to thrive by focusing its niche strategy on marketing quality tailored suits and sport coats that fit within this most popular price range.[13]*

One of the worst—and most common—mistakes entrepreneurs make is assuming that a market exists for their product or service. The time to find out if customers will buy your product or service is *before* you invest thousands of dollars to launch it! Market research can tell entrepreneurs whether or not a sufficient customer base exists and how likely those customers are to purchase their products or services. In addition to collecting and analyzing demographic data about the people in a particular geographic area and comparing the results to the profile of a typical customer, entrepreneurs can learn much by actually observing, mingling with, and interviewing customers as they shop. The founder of one snack-food company says that he learns a great deal about packaging and design and product placement by hanging around the aisles of grocery stores and watching shoppers' buying behavior. Other companies videotape customers while they are shopping to get a clear picture of their buying habits. Hands-on market research techniques such as these allow entrepreneurs to get past the barriers that consumers often put up and to uncover their true preferences and hidden thoughts.

Market research does *not* have to be time consuming, complex, or expensive to be useful. By applying the same type of creativity to market research that they display when creating their businesses, entrepreneurs can perform effective market research "on the cheap."

*Inexpensive market research is one key to success for the Southern California retail chain **Hot Topic**. No one could confuse one of the chain's 346 stores with Gap or American Eagle, which sells jeans, crop-tops, and khaki pants to athletic-looking young people. Since Orv Madden founded the first Hot Topic store in Montclair, California, in 1989, market research has led the company to target "alternative" teens, who make up 17 percent of all high school students. At Hot Topic, angst-filled teens browse among displays of fishnet stockings, blue hair dye, glow-in-the-dark tongue rings, black Gothic patent leather platform boots with 4-inch heels, red feather "blood angel" wings, and pink fur pants. To stay on the cutting edge of the ever-changing fashion tastes of its customers, Hot Topics sends its buyers to rock concerts and raves its "alternative" customers frequent to see and to photograph what performers and fashion-forward fans are wearing. The company also surveys teens who come into its stores about their favorite bands, clothing preferences, and ideas.[14]*

As Hot Topic proves, meaningful market research for a small business can be informal; it does not have to be highly sophisticated or expensive to be valuable.

Many entrepreneurs are discovering the power, the speed, the convenience, and the low cost of conducting market research over the World Wide Web. Online surveys, customer opinion polls, and other research projects are easy to conduct, cost virtually nothing, and help companies connect with their customers. With Web-based surveys, businesses can get real-time feedback from customers, often using surveys they have designed themselves.

Faith Popcorn, a marketing consultant, encourages small business owners to be their own "trend-tracking sleuths." Merely by observing their customers' attitudes and actions, small business owners can shift their product lines and services to meet changing tastes in the market. To spot significant trends, Popcorn suggests the following:[15]

■ Read as many current publications as possible, especially ones you normally would not read.

■ Watch the top 10 TV shows because they are indicators of consumers' attitudes and values and what they're going to be buying.

■ See the top 10 movies. They also influence consumer behavior, from language to fashions. In the 1930s, Hollywood star Clark Gable took off his shirt in *It Happened One Night* and revealed a bare chest; undershirt sales soon took a dive. After Will Smith and Tommy Lee Jones donned Ray-Ban sunglasses in *Men in Black*, sales of the sunglasses tripled![16]

- Talk to at least 150 customers a year about what they're buying and why. Make a conscious effort to spend time with some of your target customers, preferably in an informal setting, to find out what they are thinking.

- Talk with the 10 smartest people you know. They can offer valuable insights and fresh perspectives that you may not have considered.

- Listen to your children. ("They can be tremendous guides for you," says Popcorn.)

Next, entrepreneurs should make a list of the major trends spotted and should briefly describe how well their products or services match these trends. Companies whose products or services are diverging from major social, demographic, and economic trends rather than converging with them, must change their course or run the risk of failing because their markets can evaporate before their eyes. How can entrepreneurs find the right match among trends, their products or services, and the appropriate target markets? Market research!

How to Conduct Market Research

The goal of market research is to reduce the risks associated with making business decisions. It can replace misinformation and assumptions with facts. Opinion and hearsay are not viable foundations on which to build a solid marketing strategy. Successful market research consists of four steps: define the objective, collect the data, analyze and interpret the data, and draw conclusions and act.

STEP 1: DEFINE THE OBJECTIVE. The first and most crucial step in market research is defining the research objective clearly and concisely. A common error at this stage is to confuse a symptom with the true problem. For example, dwindling sales is not a problem; it is a symptom. To get to the heart of the matter, entrepreneurs must list all the possible factors that could have caused it. Do we face new competition? Are our sales representatives impolite or unknowledgeable? Have customer tastes changed? Is our product line too narrow? Do customers have trouble finding what they want? Is our Web site giving customers what they want? Is it easy to navigate? One entrepreneur wanting to discover the possible causes of his company's poorly performing Web site videotaped customers as they used it and then interviewed them. After studying the videos and listening to their comments, he redesigned the site to make it easier for users to maneuver through its pages, and he refocused its content.

In some cases, business owners may be interested in researching a specific type of question. What are the characteristics of my customers? What are their income levels? What radio stations do they listen to? Why do they shop here? What factors are most important in their buying decisions?

STEP 2: COLLECT THE DATA. The marketing approach that dominates today is **individualized (one-to-one) marketing**, gathering data on individual customers and then developing a marketing program designed specifically to appeal to their needs, tastes, and preferences. In a society where people feel so isolated and interactions are so impersonal, one-to-one marketing gives a business a competitive edge. Companies following this approach know their customers, understand how to give them the value they want, and perhaps most important, know how to make them feel special and important. The goal is to treat each customer as an individual.

Individualized marketing requires business owners to gather and assimilate detailed information about their customers, however. Fortunately, owners of even the smallest companies now have access to affordable technology that creates and manages computerized databases, allowing them to develop close, one-to-one relationships with their customers. Much like gold nuggets waiting to be discovered, significant amounts of valuable information about customers and their buying habits is hidden *inside* many small businesses, tucked away in computerized databases. For most business owners, collecting useful information about their customers and potential new products and markets is simply a matter of sorting and organizing data that are already floating around somewhere in their companies. One marketing research expert explains the situation this way:[17]

> You know a lot about your customers. You know who they are, where they live, what their buying habits are. And if you're like most companies, you've done absolutely nothing with that pile of market intelligence. It just sits there, earning you no money and creating zero shareholder value.

individualized (one-to-one marketing)—*a system based on gathering data on individual customers and developing a marketing program designed to appeal specifically to their needs, tastes, and preferences.*

The key is to mine the data that most companies have at their disposal and turn it into useful information that allows the company to "court" its customers with special products, services, ads, and offers that appeal most to them.

A Company Example

*For example, at **Silverman's**, a men's clothing chain in the Dakotas, owner Stephen Silverman and a salesperson recently were reviewing a customer's purchasing history on a computer that doubles as a cash register. The flowchart revealed that he has spent more than $2,000 to date and had shopped four times in the previous six months. Looking at the average time between his visits, they noted that he should be coming in soon. Examining the profile more closely, they saw that this customer prefers double-breasted suits, likes Perry Ellis and Christian Dior suits in gray or blue and has one shoulder slightly lower than the other. He also was among the customers who received a direct-mail ad featuring the upcoming season's new suits. Then, as if on cue, the customer walked in the door! The salesperson greeted him enthusiastically, personally, and knowledgeably. Within 15 minutes, he completed the sale, and the customer raved about how much he enjoys shopping at Silverman's because they know just what he likes and make it so easy to buy! Silverman's chalks up another sale to a satisfied, loyal customer thanks to its "segment of one" marketing strategy.[18]*

Figure 6.1 shows how to develop a successful one-to-one marketing strategy.

How can entrepreneurs collect such valuable market and customer information? Two basic methods are available: conducting *primary research*, data you collect and analyze yourself, and gathering *secondary research*, data that have already been compiled and are available, often at a very reasonable cost (even free).

A Company Example

*To help its distributors sell its software that allows businesses to enhance the features of their existing telephone systems more easily, **Sylantro Systems** conducted extensive market research on how customers would use the company's software, how much they would be willing to pay for it, and which features were most important to them. Managers first searched for secondary research that would help them answer the questions they had posed but found nothing of great value. Turning to primary research, Sylantro set up focus groups, bringing in people from a variety of business situations, and discovered some surprising results. As participants talked, they revealed that many of the components of Sylantro's existing marketing strategy were not important to them and that other parts the company had not emphasized really mattered! Using the focus groups' responses, Sylantro revamped its marketing strategy, which then produced much better results.[19]*

FIGURE 6.1 How to Become an Effective One-to-One Marketer

Source: Adapted from Susan Greco, "The Road to One-to-One Marketing," *Inc.*, October 1995, pp. 56–66.

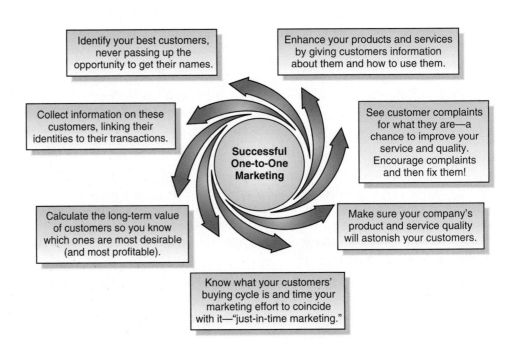

Identify your best customers, never passing up the opportunity to get their names.

Enhance your products and services by giving customers information about them and how to use them.

Collect information on these customers, linking their identities to their transactions.

See customer complaints for what they are—a chance to improve your service and quality. Encourage complaints and then fix them!

Successful One-to-One Marketing

Calculate the long-term value of customers so you know which ones are most desirable (and most profitable).

Make sure your company's product and service quality will astonish your customers.

Know what your customers' buying cycle is and time your marketing effort to coincide with it—"just-in-time marketing."

Primary research techniques include:

- *Customer surveys and questionnaires.* Keep them short. Word your questions carefully so that you do not bias the results and use a simple ranking system (e.g., a 1-to-5 scale, with 1 representing "unacceptable" and 5 representing "excellent"). Test your survey for problems on a small number of people before putting it to use. Web surveys are inexpensive, easy to conduct, and provide feedback fast. Femail Creations, a mail-order company that sells clothing, accessories, and gifts to women, uses Web surveys to gather basic demographic data about its customers and to solicit new product ideas as well. Customer responses have led to profitable new product lines for the small company.[20]

- *Focus groups.* Enlist a small number of customers to give you feedback on specific issues in your business—quality, convenience, hours of operation, service, and so on. Listen carefully for new marketing opportunities as customers or potential customers tell you what is on their minds. Once again, consider using the Web; one small bicycle company conducts 10 online focus groups each year at virtually no cost and gains valuable marketing information from them.

- *Daily transactions.* Sift as much data as possible from existing company records and daily transactions—customer warranty cards, personal checks, frequent-buyer clubs, credit applications, and others.

- *Other ideas.* Set up a suggestion system (for customers and employees) and use it. Establish a customer advisory panel to determine how well your company is meeting various needs. Talk with suppliers about trends they have spotted in the industry. Contact customers who have not bought anything in a long time and find out why. Contact people who are not customers and find out why. Teach employees to be good listeners and then ask them what they hear.

Secondary research, which is usually less expensive to collect than primary data, includes the following sources:

- *Business directories.* To locate a trade association, use *Business Information Sources* (University of California Press) or the *Encyclopedia of Associations* (Gale Research). To find suppliers, use *The Thomas Register of American Manufacturers* (Thomas Publishing Company) or *Standard and Poor's Register of Corporations, Executives, and Industries* (Standard and Poor Corporation). *The American Wholesalers and Distributors Directory* includes details on more than 18,000 wholesalers and distributors.

- *Direct-mail lists.* You can buy mailing lists for practically any type of business. *The Standard Rates and Data Service (SRDS) Directory of Mailing Lists* (Standard Rates and Data) is a good place to start looking.

- *Demographic data.* To learn more about the demographic characteristics of customers in general, use *The Statistical Abstract of the United States* (Government Printing Office). Profiles of more specific regions are available in *The State and Metropolitan Data Book* (Government Printing Office). *The Sourcebook of Zip Code Demographics* (CACI, Inc.) provides detailed breakdowns of the population in every zip code in the country. *Sales and Marketing Management's Survey of Buying Power* (Bill Communications) has statistics on consumer, retail, and industrial buying.

- *Census data.* The Bureau of the Census publishes a wide variety of reports that summarize the wealth of data found in its census database, which is available at most libraries and at the Census Bureau's Web site (www.census.gov).

- *Forecasts.* The *U.S. Global Outlook* traces the growth of 200 industries and gives a five-year forecast for each one. Many government agencies, including the Department of Commerce, offer forecasts on everything from interest rates to the number of housing starts. Again, a government librarian can help you find what you need.

- *Market research.* Someone may already have compiled the market research you need. *The FINDex Worldwide Directory of Market Research Reports, Studies, and Surveys* (Cambridge Information Group) lists more than 10,600 studies available for purchase. Other directories of business research include *Simmons Study of Media and Markets* (Simmons Market Research Bureau Inc.) and the *A.C. Neilsen Retail Index* (A.C. Neilsen Company).

- *Articles.* Magazine and journal articles pertinent to your business are a great source of information. Use the *Reader's Guide to Periodical Literature*, the *Business Periodicals Index* (similar to the *Reader's Guide* but focuses on business periodicals), and *Ulrich's Guide to International Periodicals* to locate the ones you need.

- *Local data.* Your state Department of Commerce and your local chamber of commerce will very likely have useful data on the local market of interest to you. Call to find out what is available.

- *World Wide Web.* Most entrepreneurs are astounded at the marketing information that is available on the World Wide Web (WWW). Using one of the search engines, you can gain access to a world of information—literally!

data mining—*a process in which computer software that uses statistical analysis, database technology, and artificial intelligence finds hidden patterns, trends, and connections in data so that business owners can make better marketing decisions and predictions about customers' behavior.*

Thanks to advances in computer hardware and software, data mining, once available only to large companies with vast computer power, is now possible for even very small businesses. **Data mining** is a process in which computer software that uses statistical analysis, database technology, and artificial intelligence finds hidden patterns, trends, and connections in data so that business owners can make better marketing decisions and predictions about customers' behavior. By finding relationships among the many components of a data set, identifying clusters of customers with similar buying habits, and predicting customers' buying patterns, data mining gives entrepreneurs incredible marketing power. Popular data mining software packages include Clementine, DataScope Pro, MineSet, Nuggets, and many others.

For an effective individualized marketing campaign to be successful, business owners must collect three types of information:

1. *Geographic.* Where are my customers located? Do they tend to be concentrated in one geographic region?
2. *Demographic.* What are the characteristics of my customers (age, education levels, income, gender, marital status, and many other features)?
3. *Psychographic.* What drives my customers' buying behavior? Are they receptive to new products or are they among the last to accept them? What values are most important to them?

STEP 3: ANALYZE AND INTERPRET THE DATA. The results of market research alone do not provide a solution to the problem; business owners must attach some meaning to them. What do the facts mean? Is there a common thread running through the responses? Do the results suggest any changes needed in the way the business operates? Are there new opportunities the owner can take advantage of? There are no hard-and-fast rules for interpreting market research results; entrepreneurs must use judgment and common sense to determine what the results of their research mean.

STEP 4: DRAW CONCLUSIONS AND ACT. The market research process is not complete until the business owner acts on the information collected. In many cases, the conclusion is obvious once a small business owner interprets the results of the market research. Based on her understanding of what the facts really mean, the owner must then decide how to use the information in the business. For example, the owner of a retail shop discovered from a survey that her customers preferred evening shopping hours over early morning hours. She made the schedule adjustment, and sales began to climb.

Learning Objective
4. Describe how a small business can build a competitive edge in the marketplace using guerrilla marketing strategies.

PLOTTING A GUERRILLA MARKETING STRATEGY: HOW TO BUILD A COMPETITIVE EDGE

A competitive edge is crucial for business success. A small company has a competitive edge when customers perceive that its products or services are superior to those of its competitors. A business owner can create this perception in a variety of ways. Small companies sometimes try to create a competitive edge by offering the lowest prices. This approach may work for many products and services—especially those that customers see as being commodities—but price can be a dangerous criterion on which to build a competitive edge. Independent hardware stores have discovered that large chains can use their buying power to get volume discounts and undercut the independents' prices. Individual store owners are finding new ways, such as personal service and advice, individual attention, charge accounts, and convenience, to differentiate themselves and to retain customer loyalty. "Instead of being forced out of business by the 'category killers,'" says a retail expert, "small retailers are thriving by providing the services and products that larger stores are not able to."[21]

Successful entrepreneurs often use the special advantages that flow from their companies' small size to build a competitive edge over their larger rivals. Their close contact with the customer, personal attention, focus on service, and organizational and managerial flexibility provide a solid foundation from which to build a towering competitive edge in the market. Small companies can exploit their size to become more effective than their larger rivals at **relationship marketing** or **customer relationship management (CRM)**—developing, maintaining, and managing long-term relationships with customers so that they will want to keep

relationship marketing (or customer relationship management)—*the process of developing, maintaining, and managing long-term relationships with customers so they will keep coming back to make repeat purchases.*

YOU Be the Consultant . . .

Data Mining: A Sure Bet for Harrah's

More than 25 million customers of Harrah's Entertainment, the parent company of 26 gambling casinos in 13 states, use personalized frequent gambler cards (just like the ones shoppers use in grocery stores) called Total Rewards to earn free trips, meals, hotel rooms, and other perks from Harrah's. As good a deal as that is for the company's loyal customers, it's an even better deal for Harrah's. Harrah's uses the data it collects to refine its customer base, which is now divided into 90 distinct demographic and psychographic segments, and to customize its marketing efforts to individual customers' preferences. When customers swipe their cards, the company knows which games they played, how many machines they played, how many wagers they made, the amount of their average wager, the total amount wagered, as well as the history of their gambling behavior at every Harrah's casino across the country. Harrah's collects all these data about its customers' gambling tendencies in its information technology center in Memphis, Tennessee, and then uses data mining software to extract meaningful information about how best to market to them.

Unlike most of its casino competitors, Harrah's does not target the "high roller," wealthy patrons who are capable of gambling hundreds of thousands of dollars at a time. Known to insiders as "whales," these big-stakes gamblers wager (and often lose) huge sums of money, but casinos must court them with expensive, palatial suites, free shopping trips, free chartered flights, and other pricey "comps." Competition for this small, jet-set group is intense. Instead, Harrah's targets its best and most profitable customers, "avid experienced players," who are low rollers with modest incomes and who spend between $100 and $499 per trip. Harrah's still offers "comps"—free trips, dinners, tickets to a show, or hotel rooms—to its best customers, but they are much less expensive than those the high rollers expect. As a result, Harrah's casinos emphasize the games that will attract its target customers, slot machines and video poker machines, rather than baccarat that the billionaire players prefer. Analysis shows that 30 percent of Harrah's avid experienced players account for 80 percent of its revenues and nearly 100 percent of its profits. Why? Most of them are locals who visit Harrah's casinos regularly. Harrah's, of course, knows this, and markets to them accordingly.

Harrah's CEO, Gary Loveman, was once a Harvard University professor who had done consulting work with Harrah's after it had invested in a $17 million computer system to harvest data from its customers across all of its casinos, which at the time was a revolutionary idea in the industry. The company hired Loveman in 1998 to orchestrate a plan for analyzing and using the data it collected as a potent marketing force. Loveman says that the entire data mining system is all about getting to know Harrah's customers so well through data profiling that the company can offer them the perfect reason to wager at Harrah's rather than at a competing casino. "All we used to know was how much money we made on each machine, but we couldn't connect what kind of customer used them," he says. "This is the replacement of intuition and hunch with science." The model uses neural networks and other sophisticated techniques of analysis to compare how much customers are capable of spending on gaming, how much they are actually spending, and how best to close that gap.

The payoff has been exceptional; Harrah's sales, profits, market share, and customer response rate to promotions have climbed dramatically. When Loveman started work, Harrah's was getting 36 cents of the total gaming dollars its customers spent. "We realized that if we could just get to 40 cents, that would be monstrous," he says. As a result of its more targeted marketing efforts, Harrah's "wallet share" currently stands at 42 cents! For the past three years, Harrah's return on investment has been the highest in the industry. The casino, once considered an "also-ran" in the industry, is now the second largest casino operator in the United States. One analyst praises the company, saying, "Especially in Las Vegas, where their property is not the top draw, they clearly are outperforming other [casinos]."

Loveman enjoys his work, but his professorial side still shines through. "I love the business," he says. "I like the fact that customers enjoy what we sell. I like the mathematics—and the fact that at its base, gambling is a statistical activity."

1. Work with a group of your classmates in a brainstorming session to identify other industries that could benefit from a data collection and mining system like the one Harrah's uses so effectively. In what ways could these businesses use data to become more effective marketers?

2. Discuss the ethical issues that Harrah's faces as a result of its data collection and data mining efforts.

3. What benefits does Harrah's gain from these efforts? What benefits do Harrah's customers gain?

Sources: Carol Pogash, "From Harvard Yard to Vegas Strip," *Forbes ASAP*, October 7, 2001, pp. 48–52; Joe Ashbrook Nickell, "Welcome to Harrah's," *Business 2.0*, pp. 49–54; "About Us," Harrah's Entertainment, www.harrahs.com/about_us/index.html.

coming back to make repeat purchases (see Figure 6.2). This concept recognizes that customers have a lifetime value to a business and that keeping the best customers over time may be a company's greatest sustainable advantage. CRM puts the customer at the center of a company's thinking, planning, and action and shifts the focus away from a product or service to customers and their needs and wants. CRM requires business owners to take the following steps:

FIGURE 6.2

The Relationship Marketing
Process

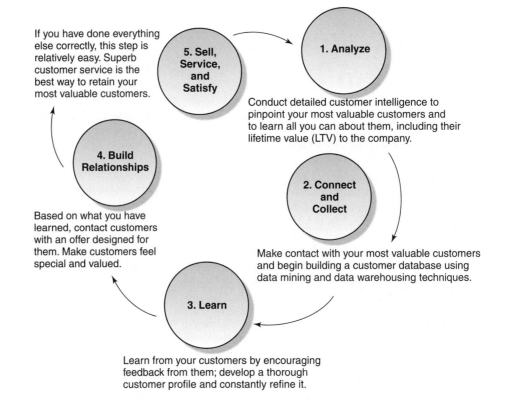

Collect meaningful information about existing customers and compile it in a database.

Mine the database to identify the company's best and most profitable customers, their needs, and their buying habits. In most companies, a small percentage of customers accounts for the majority of sales and profits. These are the customers on whom a business should focus its attention and efforts.

Use the mined information to develop lasting relationships with these "best" customers, the ones that offer the most attractive lifetime values to the company, and to serve them better. This often requires entrepreneurs to "fire" some customers that require more attention, time, and expense than they generate in revenue for the business. Failure to do so, reduces a company's return on its CRM effort.

Attract more customers who fit the profile of the company's best customers.

Business owners are discovering that even though they may be providing their customers with satisfactory service and value, many of their customers do not remain loyal, choosing instead to buy from other companies. Businesses that provide poor customer service are in grave danger. Hepworth, a consulting firm that specializes in customer retention, measures its clients' **revenue at risk**, which calculates the sales revenue a company would lose by measuring the percentage of customers that would leave because of poor service. According to Hepworth's research, for companies that score in the top 25 percent on customer loyalty, revenue at risk averages just 3 percent. However, for companies that rate loyalty scores in the bottom 25 percent, poor customer service puts at risk an average of more than 12 percent of company revenue.[22] Today, earning customers' loyalty requires businesses to take customer focus and service to unprecedented levels, and that requires building long-term relationships with customers. To make customer relationship management work, a small business must achieve the highest of the four levels of customer involvement illustrated in Figure 6.3.

Table 6.1 describes the differences between relationship marketing and its polar opposite, transaction selling.

revenue at risk—*a measure that calculates the sales revenue a company would lose by measuring the percentage of customers that would leave because of poor service.*

Guerrilla Marketing Principles

To be successful guerrilla marketers, entrepreneurs must be as innovative in creating their marketing strategies as they are in developing new product and service ideas. Table 6.2 describes several low-cost, highly effective guerrilla marketing tactics small businesses have used to outperform their larger rivals.

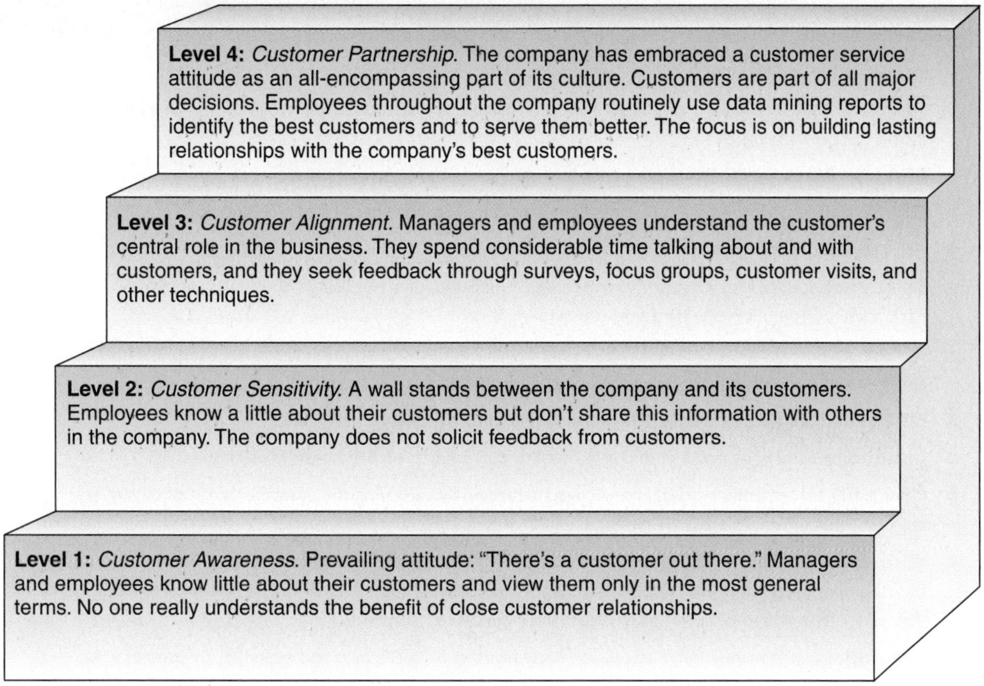

FIGURE 6.3 Four Levels of Customer Sensitivity

Level 4: *Customer Partnership.* The company has embraced a customer service attitude as an all-encompassing part of its culture. Customers are part of all major decisions. Employees throughout the company routinely use data mining reports to identify the best customers and to serve them better. The focus is on building lasting relationships with the company's best customers.

Level 3: *Customer Alignment.* Managers and employees understand the customer's central role in the business. They spend considerable time talking about and with customers, and they seek feedback through surveys, focus groups, customer visits, and other techniques.

Level 2: *Customer Sensitivity.* A wall stands between the company and its customers. Employees know a little about their customers but don't share this information with others in the company. The company does not solicit feedback from customers.

Level 1: *Customer Awareness.* Prevailing attitude: "There's a customer out there." Managers and employees know little about their customers and view them only in the most general terms. No one really understands the benefit of close customer relationships.

From a broader perspective, the following principles can help business owners create powerful, effective guerrilla marketing strategies.

FIND A NICHE AND FILL IT. As we saw in Chapter 3, Strategic Management and the Entrepreneur, many successful small companies choose their niches carefully and defend them fiercely rather than compete head-to-head with larger rivals. A niche strategy allows a small company to maximize the advantages of its size and to compete effectively even in industries

TABLE 6.1

The Differences Between Relationship Marketing and Transaction Selling

Sources: Adapted from Timothy M. Baye, "Relationship Marketing: A Six-Step Guide for the Business Start-Up," *Small Business Forum,* Spring 1995, pp. 26–41.

Feature	Relationship Marketing	Transaction Selling
Duration	Ongoing	Distinct beginning and end; one-transaction attitude
Key Concepts	Collaboration and cooperation	Negotiation
Driven by	Commitment and trust	Making profitable short-term transactions
Style	Mutual dependence	Independence
Business Plan Implications	Build a network of relationships with dependable suppliers and customers that will lead to long-term profitability	Maximize short-term profits; make the bottom line look good, whatever the long-term costs
Primary Advantage	Intimate knowledge of customers' needs, wants, and preferences developed over time	Cash in hand
Primary Disadvantage	Dependence on other partners in the web of relationships	Losing the sale if a competitor makes the customer a better offer
Foundation	Knowledge based	Bottom line oriented
Outlook	Increasing in popularity	On the decline

TABLE 6.2

Guerrilla Marketing Tactics

Sources: Adapted from Jay Conrad Levinson, "Attention Getters," *Entrepreneur*, March 1998, p. 88; Lynn Beresford, Janean Chun, Cynthia E. Griffin, Heather Page, and Debra Phillips, "Marketing 101," *Entrepreneur*, May 1996, pp. 104–114; Guen Sublette, "Marketing 101," *Entrepreneur*, May 1995, pp. 86–98; Denise Osburn, "Bringing Them Back for More," *Nation's Business*, August 1995, p. 31R; Jay Conrad Levinson, "Survival Tactics," *Entrepreneur*, March 1996, p. 84; Tom Stein, "Outselling the Giants," *Success*, May 1996, pp. 38–41.

- Help organize and sponsor a service- or community-oriented project.
- Sponsor offbeat, memorable events. Build a giant banana split or rent a theater for a morning and invite kids for a free viewing.
- Always be on the lookout for new niches to enter. Try to develop multiple niches.
- Offer to speak about your business, industry, product, or service to local organizations.
- Ask present customers for referrals.
- Sell at every opportunity. One brewery includes a mini-catalog advertising T-shirts and mugs in every six-pack it sells. Orders for catalog items are climbing fast.
- Develop a sales "script" that asks customers a series of questions to hone in on what they are looking for and that will lead them to the conclusion that your product or service is IT!!
- Offer customers gift certificates. They really boost your cash flow.
- Create samples of your product and give them to customers. You'll increase sales later.
- Offer a 100 percent, money-back, no-hassles guarantee. By removing the customer's risk of buying, you increase your product's attractiveness.
- Create a "frequent buyer" program. Remember how valuable existing customers are. Work hard to keep the customers you have! One coffee shop kept its customers coming back with a punch-card promotion that gave a free pound of coffee after a customer purchased 9 pounds.
- Clip articles that feature your business and send reprints to customers and potential customers. Keep reminding them of who you are and why you're valuable to them.
- Test how well your ads "pull" with coded coupons that customers bring in. Focus your ad expenditures on those media that produce the best results for you.
- Create "tip sheets" to pass out to customers and potential customers (e.g., landscape tips on lawn maintenance).
- Find ways to make your product or service irresistible to your customers. One furniture company mails a Polaroid photo of big-ticket items customers are considering, and sales closing rates have climbed 25 percent.
- Create an award for your community (e.g., a landscape company presented a "best yard" award each season).
- Conduct a contest in the community (e.g., a photographer sponsored a juried photo contest for different age groups).
- Collect testimonials from satisfied customers and use them in ads, brochures, and so on. Testimonials are one of the most effective forms of advertising!
- Get a former journalist to help you write a story "pitch" for local media.
- Show an interest in your customers' needs. If you spot a seminar that would be of interest to them, tell them! Become a valuable resource for them.
- Find unique ways to thank customers (especially first-time buyers) for their business—a note, a lunch, a gift basket, and so on.
- Give loyal customers a "freebie" occasionally. You might be surprised at how long they will remember it.
- Create a newsletter that features your customers or clients and their businesses (e.g., a photo of a client using your product in his business).
- Cooperate with other businesses selling complementary products and services in marketing efforts and campaigns, a process called fusion marketing. Share mailing lists and advertising time or space, or work together on a special promotion.
- Use major competitors' coupons against them. The owner of an independent sandwich shop routinely pulled business from a nearby national chain by advertising that he would accept its coupons.
- Market your company's uniqueness. Many customers enjoy buying from small companies that are different and unique. The owners of the only tea plantation in the United States used that fact to their advantage in establishing a customer base.

dominated by giants. Focusing on niches that are too small to be attractive to large companies is a common recipe for success among thriving small companies. "Finding such unserved niches is an excellent way to begin 'whupping' the big guys, if not in their own back yard, at least on the same street," says one marketing expert.[23]

Pepper . . . and Salt

FROM THE WALL STREET JOURNAL-PERMISSION CARTOON FEATURE SYNDICATE.

THE WALL STREET JOURNAL

LITZLER

"Exhaustive research efforts have narrowed your niche market down to Henry Finkleton of Newburg Heights here."

A Company Example

A fourth-generation family business founded in 1920, **G. Lieberman and Sons** *was for many years a wholesale distributor of hosiery, underwear, and nightwear. A few years ago, however, owners Steven Katz and Constance Barsky saw sales of pantyhose slip as women increasingly rebelled against the discomfort pantyhose caused. They also noticed another unusual trend emerging: men buying pantyhose—not for their wives or girlfriends, but for themselves! Typically, these were not cross-dressers but men who stood all day and needed the support for better blood circulation in their legs, men who worked outside in extremely cold weather looking for warmth, and even athletes whose sports kept them outside in inclement conditions. ("Great catch, Joe, and by the way, what shade are your pantyhose?") "There's a whole underground culture of normal, mainstream guys who wear hose," says Katz. Katz and Barsky saw an opportunity to capture a significant share of this niche and developed Activskin Performance Wear, pantyhose with male-friendly features such as a fly in the front that they sell exclusively on the company's Web site.*[24]

Niche markets such as this one are ideally suited for small businesses. "If a small business follows the principles of targeting, segmenting, and differentiating, it doesn't have to collapse to larger companies," says marketing expert Phil Kotler.[25]

DON'T JUST SELL—ENTERTAIN. Numerous surveys have shown that consumers are bored with shopping and that they are less inclined to spend their scarce leisure time shopping than ever before. Winning customers today requires more than low prices and wide merchandise selection; increasingly, businesses are adopting strategies based on **entertailing**, the notion of drawing customers into a store by creating a kaleidoscope of sights, sounds, smells, and activities, all designed to entertain—and, of course, sell (think Disney). The primary goal of entertailing is to catch customers' attention and engage them in some kind of entertaining experience so that they shop longer and buy more goods or services. Entertailing involves "making [shopping] more fun, more educational, more interactive," says one retail consultant.[26]

Research supports the benefits of entertailing's hands-on, interactive, educational, approach to selling; one study found that, when making a purchase, 34 percent of consumers are driven more by emotional factors such as fun and excitement than by logical factors such as price and convenience.[27] Entertailing's goal, of course, is not only to entertain but also to boost sales.

entertailing—*a marketing concept designed to draw customers into a store by creating a kaleidoscope of sights, sounds, smells, and activities, all designed to entertain—and, of course, sell.*

A Company Example

*Few retailers practice entertailing as well as **Cabela's**, an innovative company that sells a wide selection of outdoor gear, mostly to hunters and fishermen. The company generates impressive sales through its catalog operations, its Web site, and its eight stores, all of which are located in small towns in rural America. (Sydney, Nebraska, is host to one store and company headquarters.) What is even more amazing is that Cabela's has achieved its position as one of the hottest retailers in the industry by targeting unusual customers: men who typically hate to shop! Men (and often their families) routinely drive hundreds of miles to visit a Cabela's store, where they spend hours shopping for everything from guns and decoys to fishing rods and tents. The stores' immense drawing power is due in part to the breadth and depth of the company's product lines. (Cabela's product lines run six to ten times deeper than a typical discounter selling outdoor equipment.) Yet, brothers Jim and Dick Cabela know that entertaining customers encourages them to shop longer and spend more. They spend lavishly on each store they build, including glass ceilings that let in natural light and aquariums containing 8,000 gallons of freshwater and game fish in natural settings. A major component of their entertailing strategy is the 45 percent of the floor space taken up by nature scenes situated throughout the stores. One features a waterfall spilling into a stream stocked with trout. Others show off museum-quality taxidermy work. Shoppers stop to marvel at a mountain populated by a grizzly bear, caribou, and big-horn sheep or a display of an African savannah with two lions attacking a zebra. Each store contains about 400 displays, some of which cost more than $10,000. Cabela's may be the only company in the world to have an executive whose title is taxidermy purchasing specialist! Obviously a hit with its prime target audience—men who enjoy the outdoors—Cabela's also is popular with their wives and children because of the expanded line of gifts and clothing it offers.[28]*

STRIVE TO BE UNIQUE. One of the most effective guerrilla marketing tactics is to create an image of uniqueness for your business. Entrepreneurs can achieve a unique place in the market in a variety of ways, including through the products and services they offer, the marketing and promotional campaigns they use, the store layouts they design, and the business strategies they employ. A few years ago, Fritz Kropf saw sales at his Kansas City restaurant dwindling and realized that his was "just another burger joint." To distinguish his business from its many competitors, Fritz came up with a unique (and patented) invention his customers love. Guests place their orders using telephones located on their tables. A few minutes later, a whistle blows, and a small train travels across a suspended track and drops a box of hamburgers and fries onto a platform, which is then lowered to the table.[29] Like Fritz's Restaurant, the goal is to stand out from the crowd; few things are as uninspiring to customers as a "me-too" business that offers nothing unique.

A Company Example

*One company that holds a unique place in the travel market is **Space Adventures**, primarily because of the services it sells. The company's goal is to sell space travel to civilians. Through its Steps to Space programs, the company already has sold about 350 tickets at $95,000 each for suborbital space flights scheduled to begin in the near future. Until the technology needed to get people into space on a routine basis emerges, the start-up company will generate sales by selling space-related adventure tours such as high-altitude flights at supersonic speed in Russian MiG fighter jets, zero-gravity flights in specially designed jets, video birthday cards from astronauts aboard orbiting space stations, and more mundane Earth-bound trips to view solar eclipses and space observatories.[30]*

CREATE AN IDENTITY FOR YOUR BUSINESS. Some of the most powerful marketers are those companies that have a clear sense of who they are, what they stand for, and why they exist. Defining their vision for their companies in a meaningful way is one of the most challenging tasks facing entrepreneurs. As we learned in Chapter 3, that vision stems from the beliefs and values of the entrepreneur and is reflected in a company's culture, ethics, and business strategy. Although it is intangible, this vision is a crucial ingredient in a successful guerrilla marketing campaign. Once this vision is firmly planted, guerrilla marketers can use it to market their companies and their products and services. Entrepreneurs often have unique and interesting stories about how they started their companies, and their stories, when told in the right way, can be an important part of an effective emotional marketing strategy.

A Company Example

*Ivan Juzang, founder of **MEE Productions**, a communications research and media company located in Philadelphia, discovered early on the marketing power his entrepreneurial story had with customers and investors. For an M.B.A. class he was taking at Wharton, Juzang wrote a business plan for a company that would make videos that would blend hip-hop music with inspirational self-help messages aimed at young people. During the business plan competition, the*

Focus on the Customer

Too many businesses have lost sight of the important component of every business: the customer. Wooing disillusioned customers back will require businesses to focus on them as never before. Businesses must realize that everything in the business—even the business itself—depends on creating a satisfied customer. One entrepreneur says, "If you're not taking care of your customers and nurturing that relationship, you can bet there's someone else out there who will."[34]

Businesses are just beginning to discover the true costs of poor customer relations. For instance:

- Sixty-seven percent of customers who stop patronizing a particular store do so because an indifferent employee treated them poorly.[35]
- Ninety-six percent of dissatisfied customers never complain about rude or discourteous service, but …
- Ninety-one percent will not buy from the business again.
- One hundred percent of those unhappy customers will tell their "horror stories" to at least nine other people.
- Thirteen percent of those unhappy customers will tell their stories to at least twenty other people.[36]

According to the authors of *Keeping Customers for Life*, "The nasty result of this customer indifference costs the average company from 15 to 30 percent of gross sales."[37] Because 70 percent of the average company's sales come from present customers, few can afford to alienate any shoppers. In fact, the typical business loses 20 percent of its customers each year. But a recent study by the consulting firm Bain & Co. shows that companies that retain just 5 percent more customers experience profit increases of at least 25 percent and, in some cases, as much as 95 percent![38] Studies by the Boston Consulting Group also show that customer retention results in above-average profits and superior growth in market share.[39] Powell's Books, a Portland, Oregon, landmark known as the "City of Books" for its huge inventory, has built a solid base of loyal customers in its 30-plus year history, enabling the company to compete successfully against industry giants Barnes and Noble and Books-a-Million. Powell's Books has hosted several weddings for customers who met there, and one customer's ashes are interred (at his request) in one of the columns made to look like a stack of books at the northwest entrance to the store. Now *that's* customer loyalty![40]

Because about 20 percent of a typical company's customers account for about 80 percent of its sales, it makes more sense to focus resources on keeping the best (and most profitable) customers than to spend them chasing "fair weather" customers who will defect to any better deal that comes along. Suppose that a company increases its customer base by 20 percent each year, but it retains only 85 percent of its existing customers. Its effective growth rate is just 5 percent per year [20% − (100% − 85%) = 5%] . If this same company can raise its customer retention rate to 95 percent, its net growth rate *triples* to 15 percent [20% − (100% − 95%) = 15%] .[41]

Although winning new customers keeps a company growing, keeping existing ones is essential to success. Attracting a new customer actually costs *five times* as much as keeping an existing one. Therefore, small business owners would be better off asking, "How can we improve customer value and service to encourage our existing customers to do more business with us?" rather than "How can we increase our market share by 10 percent?" The *real* key to marketing success lies in a company's existing customer base!

A Company Example

*At **Chico's**, the clothing store targeting women of the baby-boomer generation, customers who purchase $500 in merchandise become members of Chico's Passport Club, which gives them a variety of perks, including a 5 percent discount on all purchases. The club already has 435,000 members, and another 2 million are working toward the $500 goal. Chico's management is well aware of the benefits of retaining these loyal customers. "[Club members] spend 40 percent more than the usual customer and come in six times as often," says chief financial officer Charles Klemen.*[42]

The most successful small businesses have developed a customer focus and have instilled a customer satisfaction attitude *throughout* the company. Companies with world-class customer attitudes set themselves apart by paying attention to "little things" such as remembering a customer's unique preferences or sending a customer a copy of an article of interest to her. Taking care of the small interactions a company has with its customers adds up to a positive service experience. For example, a small flower shop offers a special service for customers who forget that special event. The shop will insert a card reading, "Please forgive us! Being short-handed this week, we were unable to deliver this gift on time. We hope the sender's thoughtfulness will not be less appreciated because of our error. Again, we apologize."[43] At the New Orleans Superdome, managers installed a Fanlink system so that hungry fans can use their cell phones or PDAs to place a credit card order for snacks and drinks. It takes about two minutes to place an order, which concession workers read from a computer terminal and then fill and deliver to the designated seat.[44] Avis, the care rental company that "tries harder," breaks down the entire car rental process into more than 100 incremental steps and analyzes each one in meticulous detail from the customer's perspective to improve its customers' experiences. The company frequently surveys customers to determine the factors that are most important to them (convenience, speed, safety, customer service, and price often top the list) and then sets out to find ways to incorporate those into every transaction. The Avis Preferred service program that makes rental car pickup a snap and shaves 10 minutes off the average pickup time is just one example of Avis's customer-focused efforts.[45]

How do these companies stay focused so intently on their customers? They constantly ask customers four basic questions and then act on what they hear:

1. What are we doing right?
2. How can we do that even better?
3. What have we done wrong?
4. What can we do in the future?

A Company Example

*Leslie Blodgett, owner of **Bare Escentuals**, generates nearly one-fourth of her company's sales from her appearances on shopping network QVC and finds that staying close to her QVC customers improves her business. Before launching any new product, Blodgett contacts 1,000 customers by phone and e-mail and sends samples for them to try. "If they don't like it, we won't launch it," she says. Some customer ideas turn out to be huge sellers. After one woman called into QVC and asked for a travel-size brush kit, Blodgett developed one and sent it to her "testers," who overwhelmingly approved it. Six months later, when Blodgett debuted the kit on QVC, she sold $67,000 of the kits per minute on the show!*[46]

Table 6.3 offers some basic strategies for developing and retaining loyal customers.

Devotion to Quality

In this intensely competitive global business environment, quality goods and services are a prerequisite for success—and even survival. According to one marketing axiom, the worst of all marketing catastrophes is to have great advertising and a poor-quality product. Customers have come to expect and demand quality goods and services, and those businesses that provide them consistently have a distinct competitive advantage. Research by Josh Gordon, author of *Selling*

TABLE 6.3

Strategies for Developing and Retaining Loyal Customers

Sources: Adapted from Jerry Fisher, "The Secret's Out," *Entrepreneur*, May 1998, pp. 112–119; Laura M. Litvan, "Increasing Revenue with Repeat Sales," *Nation's Business*, January 1996, pp. 36–37; "Encourage Customers to Complain," *Small Business Reports*, June 1990, p. 7; Dave Zielinski, "Improving Service Doesn't Require a Big Investment," *Small Business Reports*, February 1991, p. 20; John H. Sheridan, "Out of the Isolation Booth," *Industry Week*, June 19, 1989, pp. 18–19; Lin Grensing-Pophal, "At Your Service," *Business Start-Ups*, May 1995, pp. 72–74.

- Identify your best customers and give them incentives to return. Focus resources on the 20 percent of customers that account for 80 percent of sales.

- When you create a dissatisfied customer, fix the problem fast. One study found that, given the chance to complain, 95 percent of customers will buy again *if* a business handles their complaints promptly and effectively. The worst way to handle a complaint is to ignore it, to pass it off to a subordinate, or to let a lot of time slip by before dealing with it.

- Make sure your business system makes it easy for customers to buy from you. Eliminate unnecessary procedures that challenge customers' patience.

- *Encourage* customer complaints. You can't fix something if you don't know it's broken. Find out what solution the customer wants and try to come as close to that as possible.

- Contact lost customers to find out why they left. You may uncover a problem you never knew existed.

- Ask employees for feedback on improving customer service. A study by Technical Assistance Research Programs (TARP), a customer service research firm, found that front-line service workers can predict nearly 90 percent of the cases that produce customer complaints. Emphasize that *everyone* is part of the customer satisfaction team.

- Get total commitment to superior customer service from top managers—and allocate resources appropriately.

- Allow managers to wait on customers occasionally. It's a great dose of reality. The founder of a small robot manufacturer credits such a strategy with saving his company. "We now require every officer of this company—including myself—to meet with customers at least four times a month," he says.

- Carefully select and train *everyone* who will deal with customers. Never let rude employees work with customers.

- Develop a service theme that communicates your attitude toward customers. Customers want to feel they are getting something special.

- Reward employees "caught" providing exceptional service to the customer.

- Get in the habit of calling customers by name. It's one of the most meaningful ways of connecting with your customers.

- Remember: The customer pays the bills. Special treatment wins customers and keeps them coming back.

2.0, shows that almost 60 percent of customers who change suppliers say they switched because of problems with a company's products or services.[47]

Today, quality is more than just a slogan posted on the company bulletin board; world-class companies treat quality as a strategic objective—an integral part of a company's strategy and culture. This philosophy is called **total quality management (TQM)**—quality not just in the product or service itself but in *every* aspect of the business and its relationship with the customer and *continuous improvement* in the quality delivered to customers.

Companies on the cutting edge of the quality movement are developing new ways to measure quality. Manufacturers were the first to apply TQM techniques, but retail, wholesale, and service organizations have seen the benefits of becoming champions of quality. They are tracking customer complaints, contacting "lost" customers, and finding new ways to track the cost of quality (COQ) and their return on quality (ROQ). ROQ recognizes that although any improvement in quality may improve a company's competitive ability, only those improvements that produce a reasonable rate of return are worthwhile. In essence, ROQ requires managers to ensure that the quality improvements they implement will more than pay for themselves.

The key to developing a successful TQM philosophy is seeing the world from the customer's point of view. In other words, quality must reflect the needs and wants of the customer. How do customers define quality? According to one survey, Americans rank quality components in this order: reliability (average time between failures), durability (how long it lasts), ease of use, a known or trusted brand name, and, last, a low price.[48] When buying services, customers look for similar characteristics: tangibles (equipment, facilities, and people), reliability (doing what you

total quality management (TQM)—*the philosophy of producing a high-quality product or service and achieving quality in every aspect of the business and its relationship with the customer; the focus is on continuous improvement in the quality delivered to customers.*

say you will do), responsiveness (promptness in helping customers and in solving problems), and assurance and empathy (conveying a caring attitude). For example, the owner of a very successful pest-control company offers his customers a unique, unconditional guarantee: If the company fails to eliminate all roach and rodent breeding and nesting areas on a client's premises, it will refund the customer's last 12 monthly payments and will pay for one year's service by another exterminator. The company has had to honor its guarantee only once in 17 years.

The benefits of a successful TQM philosophy can be substantial, sometimes making the difference between success and failure.

A Company Example

*At **Rockwell Collins**, a company that makes a multitude of avionics devices—from weather radar systems to complex GPS systems that prevent midair collisions—employees have become devotees of TQM. In the five years after implementing radical process improvement, or RPI, company sales climbed 88 percent and profits more than doubled. Rockwell Collins's shift to lean manufacturing methods has generated cost savings in excess of $100 million a year! Recently, a team of employees was using Post-it Notes to diagram an assembly line for one of its products in an attempt to reduce its cycle time. Although the existing line took more than 60 hours to build the device, the team's analysis showed the actual working time to be less than 2 hours! Their goal: redesign the process using the principles of TQM and lean manufacturing. "There's a shorter list of what we didn't change than what we did change around here," says CEO Clayton Jones.[49]*

Companies successful in capturing a reputation for top quality products and services rely on the following guidelines to "get it right the first time":

- Build quality into the process; don't rely on inspection to obtain quality.
- Foster teamwork and dismantle the barriers that divide disparate departments.
- Establish long-term ties with select suppliers; don't award contracts on low price alone.
- Provide managers and employees the training needed to participate fully in the quality improvement program.
- Empower workers at all levels of the organization; give them authority and responsibility for making decisions that determine quality.
- Get managers' commitment to the quality philosophy. Otherwise, the program is doomed. Describing his leadership role in his company's TQM philosophy, one CEO says, "People look to see if you just talk about it or actually do it."[50]
- Rethink the processes the company uses now to get its products or services to its customers. Employees at Analog Devices redesigned its production process, significantly lowered the defect rate on its silicon chips, and saved $1.2 million a year.[51]
- Be willing to make changes in processes wherever they may be necessary.
- Reward employees for quality work. Ideally, workers' compensation is linked clearly and directly to key measures of quality and customer satisfaction.
- Develop a company-wide strategy for constant improvement of product and service quality.

Attention to Convenience

Ask customers what they want from the businesses they deal with and one of the most common responses is "convenience." In this busy, fast-paced world of dual-career couples and lengthy commutes to and from work, customers increasingly are looking for convenience. Convenience is the driving force behind the boom in home cleaning services. The U.S. Department of Commerce reports that 80 percent of two-income families now use home-cleaning services.[52] Several studies also have found that customers rank easy access to goods and services at the top of their purchase criteria. Unfortunately, too few businesses deliver adequate levels of convenience, and they fail to attract and retain customers. One print and framing shop, for instance, alienated many potential customers with its abbreviated business hours—9 to 5 daily, except for Wednesday afternoons, Saturdays, and Sundays when the shop was closed! Other companies make it a chore to do business with them. In an effort to defend themselves against unscrupulous customers, these businesses have created elaborate procedures for exchanges, refunds, writing checks, and other basic transactions. One researcher claims, "What they're doing is treating the 98 percent of honest customers like crooks to catch the 2 percent who are crooks."[53]

Successful companies go out of their way to make sure that it is easy for customers to do business with them. The HomeBased Warehouse in San Bernadino, California, has borrowed an idea from fast-food restaurants to make buying lumber more convenient for its customers: drive-in windows. More than 200 cars a day pull in and load up with lumber before driving to the cashier's booth to pay. The drive-thru "has increased [sales] volume and enhanced contractor business. They like the time-saving [convenience] of being able to drive in, load up, and cash out at the outside register," says one manager.[54] In Las Vegas, a couple can pull up into the Tunnel of Vows at the famous Little White Chapel, and an ordained minister at the drive-thru window will marry them! Business has been so brisk that the owner of the chapel recently expanded the tunnel to include "a romantic ceiling with cherubs and starlights."[55]

How can a business owner boost the convenience level of her business? By conducting a "convenience audit" from the customer's point of view to get an idea of its ETDBW ("Easy To Do Business With") index:

- Is your business located near your customers? Does it provide easy access?

- Are your business hours suitable to your customers? Should you be open evenings and weekends to serve them better?

- Would customers appreciate pickup and delivery service? The owner of a restaurant located near a major office complex installed a Web site and a fax machine to receive orders from busy office workers; a crew of employees would deliver lunches to the workers at their desks!

- Does your company make it easy for customers to make purchases on credit or with credit cards?

- Are your employees trained to handle business transactions quickly, efficiently, and politely? Waiting while rude, poorly trained employees fumble through routine transactions destroys customer goodwill.

- Does your company offer "extras" that make customers' lives easier? With a phone call to one small gift store, a customer in need of a special gift simply tells how much she wants to spend, and the owner takes care of the rest—selecting the gift, wrapping it, and shipping it. All the customer has to do is pay the invoice when it arrives in the mail.

- Can you adapt existing products to make them more convenient for customers? When J.M. Smucker Company began test-marketing a premade, frozen peanut butter and jelly sandwich, CEO Tim Smucker was amazed at the results. The sandwiches, called Uncrustables, generated $20 million in sales, and Smucker now sells them nationwide.[56]

- Does your company handle telephone calls quickly and efficiently? Long waits "on hold," transfers from one office to another, and too many rings before answering signal customers that they are not important. Jerre Stead, CEO of Ingram Micro Inc., a distributor of computer products, expects every telephone call to the company to be answered within three seconds![57]

John and Amy Malik operate a small restaurant, a catering business, and a cooking instruction center under the umbrella of **Culinary Capers**. *But their latest venture, an in-home cooking service, is the fastest growing of their businesses. With their "elite hired spatula service," the Maliks target busy upscale customers for whom entertaining is important but who lack the time to host elaborate events. Lavish meals prepared in the homes of foreign dignitaries, business executives, and public officials can cost $125 per person or more! The Maliks charged $5,000 for one recent event. A typical menu might include handmade lobster ravioli, foie gras terrine, a lobster sausage salad, and braised quail over risotto. The Maliks begin some of the food preparation in the kitchen of Culinary Capers, but the actual cooking and final assembly take place in customers' homes. Although their menus and their prices are the antithesis of any fast-food restaurant, the Mahliks' "slow-food" business does have one thing in common with their fast-food counterparts: the convenience it offers their customers!*[58]

Concentration on Innovation

Innovation is the key to future success. Markets change too quickly and competitors move too fast for a small company to stand still and remain competitive. Because they cannot outspend their larger rivals, small companies often turn to superior innovation as the way to gain a competitive edge. "Never stop innovating or taking risks," says Michael Dell, founder of Dell Computer. "Keep raising the bar, not just for the industry but for yourself."[59]

Thanks to their organizational and managerial flexibility, small businesses often can detect and act on new opportunities faster than large companies. Innovation is one of the hallmarks of entrepreneurs, and it shows up in the new products, unique techniques, and unusual marketing approaches they introduce. Despite their limited resources, small businesses frequently are leaders in innovation. For instance, in the hotly competitive pharmaceutical industry, the dominant drugs in many markets were discovered by small companies rather than the industry giants such as GlaxoSmithKline or Upjohn with their multimillion dollar R&D budgets.

Obviously, there is more to innovation than spending megadollars on research and development. "It takes money to fund a business," says one small business advisor, "but it's continuous creativity that keeps the venture running smoothly and profitably."[60] How do small businesses manage to maintain their leadership role in innovating new products and services? They use their size to their advantage, maintaining their speed and flexibility much like a martial arts expert does against a larger opponent. Their closeness to their customers enables them to read subtle shifts in the market and to anticipate trends as they unfold. Their ability to concentrate their efforts and attention in one area also gives small businesses an edge in innovation. One venture capitalist explains, "Small companies have an advantage: a dedicated management team totally focused on a new product or market."[61]

Entrepreneur Francisco Guerra created **Drink Safe Technology Inc.** *with a partner in 2000 to market a new product they invented: a drink coaster and test strips that signal when a drink has been spiked with a foreign substance such as GHB, the "date rape drug." Place a few drops onto one of the company's coasters and it turns blue if a foreign substance is present. The Drink Safe products are not Guerra's first entrepreneurial innovations. He also is the founder of Snow Masters, a maker of machines that manufacture fake snow, and Foammasters, a company that makes foam cannons. Guerra's innovative new product struck a vein with consumers; first-year revenues for Drink Safe Technology topped $20 million!*[62]

Dedication to Service and Customer Satisfaction

Customer service has become a lost art in our society. A recent survey by the Pew Charitable Trusts found that 46 percent of customers had walked out of a store within the past year because of poor service.[63] Smart companies are rediscovering that unexpected, innovative, customized service can be a powerful strategic weapon. Providing incomparable service—not necessarily a low price—is one of the most effective ways to attract and maintain a growing customer base. In fact, a recent study of consumer behavior reported that 73 percent of customers buy for reasons other than price![64] "If you want to be a great marketer," says Pat Croce, entrepreneur and former owner of the Philadelphia 76ers professional basketball team, "you have to fulfill what you are selling with customer service, with exceeding expectations, with giving a little extra, with surprising the customer."[65]

Although more companies than ever before are preaching customer service to employees, the reality is that most Americans still rate U.S. companies low on customer service. In one survey of 200 companies, 57 percent of the managers said that "customer service" is their top priority. However, 73 percent said that the only way to survive is with "price competition."[66] This short-run philosophy short-circuits real progress toward superior customer service. "Sales starts a customer relationship," says one customer service expert. "Service turns it into a profitable or unprofitable relationship."[67]

Successful businesses recognize that superior customer service is only an intermediate step toward the goal of *customer satisfaction*. These companies seek to go beyond customer satisfaction, striving for *customer astonishment*! They concentrate on providing customers with quality, convenience, and service *as their customers define those terms*.

*After 26 years in the retail boat business, William McGill, owner of **MarineMax**, an association of luxury boat retailers, recognized that his industry was characterized by extremely poor service. McGill saw an opportunity to differentiate MarineMax by offering customers unparalleled service and "no-haggle" prices. For inexperienced customers or those who are just plain nervous about taking a new boat out by themselves for the first time, MarineMax will provide a captain at no extra charge. The captain will keep coming back until the customer learns to handle the boat alone. The company also has a staff of repair technicians who are on call 24 hours a day. Every MarineMax boat over 20 feet in length carries a full two-year warranty from bow to stern, twice as long as the typical warranty in the industry. Because McGill has learned that his customers' families influence how often they upgrade to bigger (and more expensive) boats, he sponsors regular seminars and fun events to teach spouses and kids how to get the most out of their boats—and to look at new, larger models. MarineMax also perpetuates customer loyalty through its "getaways," trips that range from one-day outings on a Minnesota lake to two-week trips to the Bahamas. The company services all boats before a trip and sends along a crew of technicians to fix any problems that crop up. All of this superior service costs MarineMax money, and McGill's prices reflect the extra costs. The company figures that 2.5 percent to 6 percent of a boat's price goes to cover the extra service it provides. Customers do not seem to mind slightly higher prices, however; MarineMax's profit margin is more than twice the industry average, and sales are climbing!*[68]

Certainly the least expensive—and the most effective—way to achieve customer satisfaction is through friendly, personal service. Numerous surveys of customers in a wide diversity of industries—from manufacturing and services to banking and high tech—conclude that the most important element of service is "the personal touch." Calling customers by name, making attentive, friendly contact, and truly caring about their needs and wants are much more essential than any other factor—even convenience, quality, and speed! In our society, business transactions have become so automated that the typical customer is starved for personal attention. Genuine customer service requires a business to bridge that service gap, to treat each customer as an individual, and to transform "high-tech" applications into a "high-touch" attitude.

How can a company achieve stellar customer service and satisfaction?

LISTEN TO CUSTOMERS. The best companies constantly listen to their customers and respond to what they hear! This allows them to keep up with customers' changing needs and expectations. The best way to find out what customers really want and value is to ask them. Businesses rely on a number of techniques including surveys, focus groups, telephone interviews, comment cards, suggestion boxes, toll-free "hot lines," and regular one-on-one conversations (perhaps the best technique). The Internet is another useful tool for getting feedback from customers; many companies solicit complaints, suggestions, and ideas through their Web sites.

It is important for entrepreneurs to keep customer feedback in its proper perspective, however. Although listening to customers does produce valuable feedback for business owners in many areas, it is *not* a substitute for an innovative company culture, solid market research, and a well-devised marketing plan. Companies that rely solely on their customers to guide their marketing efforts often find themselves lagging the competition. Customers rarely have the foresight to anticipate market trends and do not always have a clear view of how new products or services could satisfy their needs.

DEFINE SUPERIOR SERVICE. Based on what customers say, managers and employees must decide exactly what "superior service" means in the company. Such a statement should (1) be a strong statement of intent, (2) differentiate the company from others, and (3) have value to customers. Deluxe Corporation, a printer of personal checks, defines superior service quite simply: "Forty-eight hour turnaround; zero defects."[69]

SET STANDARDS AND MEASURE PERFORMANCE. To be able to deliver on its promise of superior service, a business must establish specific standards and measure overall performance against them. Satisfied customers should exhibit at least one of three behaviors: loyalty (increased customer retention rate), increased purchases (climbing sales and sales per customer), and resistance to rivals' attempts to lure them away with lower prices (market share and price tolerance).[70] Companies must track their performance on these and other service standards and reward employees accordingly.

EXAMINE YOUR COMPANY'S SERVICE CYCLE. What steps must a customer go through to get your product or service? Business owners often are surprised at the complexity that has seeped into their customer service systems as they have evolved over time. One of the most effective techniques is to work with employees to flowchart each component in the company's service cycle, including *everything* a customer has to do to get your product or service. The goal is to look for steps, policies, and procedures that are unnecessary, redundant, or unreasonable and then to eliminate them.

HIRE THE RIGHT EMPLOYEES. The key ingredient in the superior service equation is *people*. There is no substitute for friendly, courteous sales/service representatives. "You can't create world-class customer care if you hire run-of-the-mill employees," says customer service expert Ron Zemke.[71] Business owners must always be on the lookout for employees who are empathetic, flexible, articulate, creative, and able to think for themselves.

TRAIN EMPLOYEES TO DELIVER SUPERIOR SERVICE. Successful businesses train *every* employee who deals directly with customers; they don't leave customer service to chance. Superior service companies devote 1 to 5 percent of their employees' work hours to training, concentrating on how to meet, greet, and serve customers. Leading mail-order companies such as Lands' End and L.L. Bean spend *many* hours training the employees who handle telephone orders before they deal with their first customer.

EMPOWER EMPLOYEES TO OFFER SUPERIOR SERVICE. One of the single most important variables in determining whether or not employees deliver superior service is the degree to which they perceive they have permission to do so. The goal is to push decision making down the organization to the employees who have contact with customers. This includes giving them the latitude to circumvent "company policy" if it means improving customer satisfaction. If front-line workers don't have the power to solve disgruntled customers' problems, they fear being punished for overstepping their boundaries, become frustrated, and the superior service cycle breaks down. To be empowered, employees need knowledge and information, adequate resources, and managerial support.

USE TECHNOLOGY TO PROVIDE IMPROVED SERVICE. The role of technology is not to create a rigid bureaucracy but to free employees from routine clerical tasks, giving them more time and better tools to serve customers more effectively. Ideally, technology gives workers the information they need to help their customers and the time to serve them.

To use technology effectively, entrepreneurs must ask: "What is the best technology for our strategy?" This question then leads to four key service issues: (1) What is our primary service strategy? (i.e., what do we want customers to think of when they hear our name?) (2) What barriers are preventing our company from fully implementing this strategy now? (3) What, if anything, can technology do to overcome these barriers? (4) What is our strategy for encouraging our customers to adopt the new technology?[72]

A Company Example

StellarCon, a Raleigh, North Carolina–based construction firm that specializes in commercial projects, is distinguishing itself from its competitors with technology that solves many problems its customers have traditionally faced. Members of the family-run company say that the principal customer complaint is feeling "out of the loop" during the construction project, with no convenient way to get their questions answered. To eliminate that problem, StellarCon creates a password-protected Web site for every project that answers the typical questions clients have about their projects–from detailed budgets to updated schedules. Each site also gives customers access to live, remote-controlled Webcams so they can "tour" the site even if they are in another country. On-site superintendents use laptops to post daily updates to each site so customers get timely information. Creative use of technology enabled StellarCon to generate $30 million in revenues its first year, and repeat customers are already signing up![73]

REWARD SUPERIOR SERVICE. What gets rewarded gets done. Companies that want employees to provide stellar service must offer rewards for doing so. A recent National Science Foundation study concluded that when pay is linked to performance, employees' motivation and productivity climb by as much as 63 percent.[74]

GET TOP MANAGERS' SUPPORT. The drive toward superior customer service will fall far short of its target unless top managers support it fully. Success requires more than just a verbal commitment; it calls for managers' involvement and dedication to making service a core company value. Achieving customer satisfaction must become part of the strategic planning process and work its way into every nook and cranny of the organization. Once it does, employees will be able to provide stellar customer service with or without a checklist of "do's and don'ts."

VIEW CUSTOMER SERVICE AS AN INVESTMENT, NOT AN EXPENSE. The companies that lead the way when it comes to retaining their customers view the money they spend on customer service as an investment rather than an expense. One of the most effective ways for entrepreneurs to learn this lesson is to calculate the cost of poor customer service to their companies. Once they calculate it, the cost of lost customers due to poor service is so astonishing to most business owners that they quickly become customer service zealots. For instance, the owner of a small restaurant calculated that if every day he lost to poor service one customer who spent just $5 per week, his business was losing $94,900 in revenue per year! The restaurateur immediately changed his approach to customer service.

Emphasis on Speed

Technology, particularly the Internet, has changed the pace of business so dramatically that speed has become a major competitive weapon. Today's customers expect businesses to serve them at the speed of light! Providing a quality product at a reasonable price once was sufficient to keep customers happy, but that is not enough for modern customers who can find dozens of comparable products with a just few mouse clicks. Speed reigns. World-class companies recognize that reducing the time it takes to develop, design, manufacture, and deliver a product reduces costs, increases quality, improves customer satisfaction, and boosts market share. One study by McKinsey and Company found that high-tech products that come to market on budget but six months late earn 33 percent less profit over five years. Bringing the product out on time but 50 percent over budget cuts profits just 4 percent![75] Service companies also know that they must build speed into their business system if they are to satisfy their impatient, time-pressured customers.

Victory in this time-obsessed economy goes to the company that can deliver goods and services the fastest, not necessarily those that are the biggest and most powerful. Business is moving so rapidly today that companies "need to accomplish in 90 days what traditionally took a year," explains one entrepreneur.[76] Businesses that can satisfy their customers' insatiable appetites for speed have a distinct advantage.

A Company Example

England Inc., *which makes an average of 11,000 custom-built sofas and chairs each week, uses speed to set itself apart from other furniture makers. England has found ways to reduce the time required to build a custom-ordered sofa to less than three weeks. "In the furniture business, that's like greased lightning," says the owner of a furniture store who buys from England. The challenge is to offer customers enough variety so that they can get exactly the design and fabric they want but to standardize their offerings enough to keep prices reasonable ($500 to $1,500) and to get the finished product into the customer's hands long before any competitor can. Offering 85 different frames and 550 different fabrics, however, means that England faces 46,750 frame-and-fabric combinations! Every Monday night, England's computer system plots delivery schedules for all of the orders received for the week. Then the software plans the production schedule down to the minute for every sofa and chair and matches each order with a delivery truck. Bar-coded stickers ensure that every necessary part gets to the correct assembly station on time. Using the production schedule, the human resources department schedules the week's workforce. England requires the same level of discipline from its suppliers that it exercises in its manufacturing process. The company negotiates smaller, more frequent deliveries from its fabric suppliers, which England has culled from 40 to just four. Work crews can earn incentive pay by beating standard times posted. In all, the various components of the system combine in such a way that England is able to beat its competitors in getting furniture to its customers quickly.[77]*

YOU Be the Consultant . . .

The Power of the Little Blue and White Boxes

One day in 1930, Mabel Holmes noticed that a neighborhood boy, the child of a single father, was eating a homemade biscuit that resembled a hockey puck—hard and dry. Realizing that finding the time to make biscuits from scratch was a challenge for a single parent, Mabel decided to develop a ready-made biscuit mix that would be "so simple even a man can do it." She had no idea that the product she developed would become Jiffy, the nation's first prepared baking mix and now the market leader in the muffin-and-biscuit-mix category sold on practically every grocery store shelf in the country.

The Holmes family had been in the wholesale flour business since 1802, and at first, Jiffy was just a small sideline operation of the Chelsea Milling Company. Mabel's husband, Howard Samuel Holmes, ran Jiffy until his death in 1936, when their twin sons Dudley and Howard Sumner took it over and expanded the brand over the next several decades. They added a pie-crust mix in 1940 and a corn-muffin mix in 1950. By the 1960s the little blue and white boxes were selling so well that the Holmes family decided to close the flour wholesaling operation to focus on selling the Jiffy family of products. Today, the Jiffy product line includes 18 products, mixes for everyday products ranging from pizza crust and brownies to pancakes and cornbread.

The privately held family business is the market leader—not an easy task when the competition includes corporate giants General Mills and Pillsbury. Yet in the muffin-mix category, Jiffy commands 55.3 percent of the market when measured by unit sales. Just how does this small company in Chelsea, Michigan, do it? Current CEO Howdy Holmes, Mabel's grandson, credits the company's size and agility for much of its success. "In a larger company, the decision-making process is considerably more complicated," he says. "Here, it's done by three or four people, not three or four departments. We can make pricing decisions based solely on what makes sense, not on shareholder demands." Chelsea Milling focuses on efficient operations and handles every aspect of manufacturing, except printing its classic boxes, at its factory.

Chelsea's marketing strategy also has much to do with its success. Throughout its history, the company has *never* advertised or used one of the staples of grocery store marketing: coupons. Never using advertising sounds like a recipe for failure for a company making food products in this media-rich, advertising-laden world, but Holmes readily admits he thinks Chelsea Milling is an exception. He credits the company's long and rich history that has enabled it to build up generations of goodwill as one family member passes on the tradition of using Jiffy products to the next generation.

Despite its lack of advertising, Chelsea Milling *does* have a marketing strategy, and it is built on the principles of quality and value. "Our approach is to give people the best value, which is a combination of two things," says Holmes. "That's the highest-quality ingredients with the best price. The only way to do that is to take out the 30 percent to 52 percent of the end cost that's passed on to consumers by removing advertising, merchandising, and so forth."

Because Chelsea Milling does not incur any of these costs, Jiffy's prices are one-third to one-half less than its competitors. That significant price advantage gets customers' attention, which, in turn, gets the attention of supermarket retailers. "In our stores, Jiffy does three times the sales of the next closest item," says a spokesperson for Kroger, the nation's largest grocery chain. Even Kroger's private-label mixes can't compete with Jiffy because "we can't match them on cost."

Howdy Holmes, who says his former career as a professional race car driver was perfect training to take over a manufacturing company, saw the need for change when he took over the helm of the family business in 1987. The company had become too entrenched in outmoded business techniques in manufacturing, quality, accounting, and other key areas. Plus, there was no management succession plan in place. "Our business model worked against growth," he recalls. His goal was to transform Chelsea Milling "from a sole proprietorship into a professionally managed company." Today, thanks to a preventive maintenance program, enhanced manufacturing scheduling, upgraded quality management techniques, better accounting controls, and other improvements, Chelsea Milling's production capacity has shot up by 40 percent, to 1.6 million boxes of Jiffy mixes. If Holmes's other plans fall into place, the company will need all of it. Even in a slowing market, Jiffy's sales continue to climb. Plus, Holmes says, "Right now we're just in the retail market, but we are seriously looking at export. We are seriously looking at the institutional [market]. We are seriously looking at food service. All these are possibilities."

1. What is the basis for Chelsea Milling's marketing strategy? How effective is it?

2. How easily could a competitor duplicate Chelsea's marketing strategy for Jiffy? Explain.

3. How successful do you think a company launching a product such as Jiffy today would be if it never advertised? Explain.

4. How would you evaluate the opportunities Chelsea Milling faces for Jiffy products?

Sources: Paul Lukas, "Jiffy's Secret Recipe," *FSB*, December 2001/January 2002, pp. 56–60; "Company History," Chelsea Milling Company, www.jiffymix.com/history.html.

This philosophy of speed is called time compression management (TCM), and it involves three aspects: (1) speeding new products to market, (2) shortening customer response time in manufacturing and delivery, and (3) reducing the administrative time required to fill an order. Studies show plenty of room for improvement; most businesses waste 85 to 99 percent of the time it takes to produce products or services without ever realizing it!

A Company Example

*For example, when managers and employees at **United Electric Controls**, a family-owned maker of temperature and pressure controls and sensors, studied their production process, they were amazed at what they found. In their 50,000-square-foot factory, "We had one product that traveled 12 miles just in our plant," says one manager. Rearranging the plant's layout around products rather than processes solved the problem. "The product that once traveled 12 miles now travels 40 feet," he says. "The outcome was a reduction in lead time from 10 or 12 weeks to just a couple of days."* [78]

Although speeding up the manufacturing process is a common goal, companies using TCM have learned that manufacturing takes only 5 percent to 10 percent of the total time between an order and getting the product into the customer's hands. The rest is consumed by clerical and administrative tasks. "The primary opportunity for TCM lies in its application to the administrative process," says one manager.

Companies relying on TCM to help them turn speed into a competitive edge should:

- "Reengineer" the entire process rather than attempt to do the same things in the same way—only faster.
- Create cross-functional teams of workers and give them the power to attack and solve problems. In world-class companies, product teams include engineers, manufacturing workers, salespeople, quality experts—even customers.
- Set aggressive goals for reducing time and stick to the schedule. Some companies using TCM have been able to reduce cycle time from several weeks to just a few hours!
- Rethink the supply chain. Can you electronically link with your suppliers or your customers to speed up orders and deliveries?
- Instill speed in the culture. At Domino's Pizza, kitchen workers watch videos of the fastest pizza makers in the country.
- Use technology to find shortcuts wherever possible. Properly integrated into a company's strategy for speed, technology can restructure a company's operating timetable. Rather than build costly, time-consuming prototypes, many time-sensitive businesses use computer-aided design and computer-assisted manufacturing (CAD/CAM) to speed product design and testing.
- Put the Internet to work for you. Perhaps nothing symbolizes speed better than the Internet, and companies that harness its lightning-fast power can become leaders in TCM.

MARKETING ON THE WORLD WIDE WEB

Learning Objective

5. Discuss the marketing opportunities the World Wide Web (WWW) offers entrepreneurs and how to best take advantage of them.

Much like the telephone, the fax machine, and home shopping networks, the World Wide Web has become a revolutionary business tool. Although two-thirds of small business owners use the **World Wide Web (WWW)**, the vast network that links computers around the globe via the Internet and opens up endless oceans of information to its users, to research other companies, the majority of them are still struggling to understand how it can work for them and how they can establish a meaningful presence on it. Businesses get on the Web by using one of thousands of electronic gateways to set up an address (called a Universal Resource Locator, or URL) there. By establishing a creative, attractive Web site, the electronic storefront of a company on the Web, even the smallest companies can market their products and services to customers across the globe. The Web gives small businesses the power to broaden their marketing scope to unbelievable proportions. In fact, one of the greatest benefits to small business owners of launching a Web site is providing customers with another convenient shopping channel. According to a study by the Small Business Administration (SBA) Office of Advocacy, 67 percent of small businesses that established Web sites reported that their sites brought in new customers.[79] According to the Verizon Superpages.com Fourth Annual Small Business Internet Survey, 55 percent of small business owners with Web sites say their sites are either breaking even or are earning a profit.[80]

World Wide Web (WWW)—*the vast network that links computers around the globe via the Internet and opens up endless oceans of information to its users.*

With its ability to display colorful graphics, sound, animation, and video as well as text, the Web allows small companies to equal—even surpass—their larger rivals' Web presence. Although small companies cannot match the marketing efforts of their larger competitors dollar for dollar, a creative Web page can be "the great equalizer" in a small company's marketing program. "It's like advertising your product in the world's largest directory," says the president of the Internet Society. "The [World Wide Web] lets small companies expand far beyond their immediate region. [It is] a phenomenal commercial opportunity that offers businesses a worldwide marketing and distribution system."[81]

The number of Internet users worldwide has more than doubled from 352.2 million in 2000 to 709.1 million in 2004.[82] The rise in the number of potential customers is creating a huge increase in online revenues for businesses. In that same time period, e-commerce revenues climbed from $111 billion to $1.318 trillion.[83] Unfortunately, most small businesses are not yet taking advantage of the Web's tremendous marketing potential; only 33 percent of small companies have Web sites.[84] Of those small businesses that do have Web sites, only 24 percent actually generate revenues from online sales. The most common reasons small business owners cite for not creating a Web presence are concerns that their products and services are not suitable for online sales and the failure to see the benefit of selling online.[85] The result is a disproportionately small impact of small companies on the Web. According to Forrester Research, although small businesses make up 50 percent of all retail sales in the United States, they account for just 6 percent of all *online* sales![86]

Small companies that have established well-designed Web sites understand the Web's power as a marketing tool and are reaping the benefits of e-commerce. If a business has the proper marketing strategy in place, it can use the Web to magnify its ability to provide superior customer service at minimal cost. A customer-oriented Web site allows customers to gather information about a product or service, have their questions answered, download diagrams and photographs, place orders easily, and track the progress of their orders. As a marketing tool, the Web allows entrepreneurs to provide both existing and potential customers with meaningful information in an *interactive* rather than a passive setting. Well-designed Web sites often include interactive features that allow customers to access information about a company and its history, three-dimensional views or videos of its products and services in use, and other features such as question-and-answer sessions with experts or the ability to conduct e-mail conversations with company officials.

A Company Example

Rodney Moll is cofounder and CEO of **TrendSource***, a San Diego–based company that provides "mystery shopping" services to companies in a wide variety of industries ranging from hotels and restaurants to car dealers and video rental stores. More than 150,000 times a year, TrendSource employees masquerade as regular customers, visit clients' stores, and then file a complete report on their customer service experiences. Gathering, compiling, and presenting those data in a meaningful way used to take at least five days. TrendSource shoppers would either fax their handwritten forms to the company or leave messages with call centers. Recently, however, Moll established a secure Web site that uses its Rapid Knowledge Transfer system, which enables TrendSource employees to enter their shopping data instantly. Once the company summarizes the data, they become available to clients almost instantly on the Web with the help of security access codes. Not only has the new system enabled TrendSource to cut costs, but it also has reduced customer service times from five days to less than 30 hours! "It's improved our productivity and efficiency and made information available [to clients] virtually within a day," says Moll.[87]*

The Web gives small businesses the power to broaden their scope to unbelievable proportions. Web-based businesses are open around the clock seven days a week and can reach customers anywhere in the world. Plus, it gives entrepreneurs the flexibility to operate their companies from virtually anywhere in the world.

A Company Example

Jill-Anne Partain launched **Pilgrim Designs***, a company that makes unique handbags, with $500 she received as a college graduation gift. Although her handbags are the high-style designs one would expect to see in an upscale New York boutique, Partain opted to locate her business in Lexington, Virginia, and sell attractive handbags (which sell for up to $500) through her company's Web site. While she was attending college in the area and planning her* *business, Partain fell in love with the locale, where she would drive past abandoned textile factories and think that they would be the ideal location for her business. Her operating costs would be much lower in such a location, and there was plenty of room to expand as her company grew. The Web gave her that option. "Since I'm selling over the Web, it doesn't matter where my manufacturing is," Partain explains. Currently, Pilgrim Designs turns out about 5,000 handbags a year and generates more than $1.3 million in sales from one of those old converted Virginia textile mills. Partain is so pleased with her company's location that she has formed the Blue Ridge Mountain Business Initiative to encourage other entrepreneurs to launch businesses there. Pilgrim Designs' Web site, which Partain built herself, has received awards from* Harper's Bazaar *and* Inc. *magazines.*[88]

Small companies that have had the greatest success selling on the Web have marketing strategies that emphasize their existing strengths and core competencies. Their Web marketing strategies reflect their "brick-and-mortar" marketing strategies, often focusing on building relationships with their customers rather than merely scouting for a sale. These companies understand their target customers and know how to reach them using the Web. They create Web sites that provide meaningful information to their customers, that customize themselves based on each customer's interests, and that make it easy for customers to find what they want. In short, their Web sites create the same sense of trust and personal attention customers get when dealing with a local small business.

The World Wide Web also allows business owners to link their sites to other related Web sites, something advertisements in other media cannot offer. For instance, the home page of a company selling cookware might include hypertext links to Web pages containing recipes, cookbooks, foods, and other cooking resources. This allows small business owners to engage in cross-marketing with companies on the Web selling complementary products or services. Small businesses also have the ability to get quantifiable results from their Web-based marketing efforts. Many available software packages monitor the number of visitors to a company's Web site and track their movements in the site, telling entrepreneurs which features are most popular with customers.

The demographic profile of the typical Web user is very attractive to many entrepreneurs: young, educated, wealthy, and almost evenly split between males and females. Studies by Forrester Research show that the average household income of the typical Web shopper is $52,300, and 39 percent have college degrees.[89] Travel services, computer hardware and software, books, music, videos, and consumer electronics are among the best-selling items on the Web, but creative entrepreneurs say that they can use this powerful marketing tool to sell just about anything.

Mark Zeabin is the CEO of MHP Enterprises, a small family business in Nelson, British Columbia, that operates a most unusual Web-based business: **Casketfurniture.com***! As its name implies, the company, which is profitable, sells casket-shaped furniture, casket novelty products, "casket wear," and even furniture that is convertible into caskets ("simply remove the shelves"). Casketfurniture.com sells a full line of products over the Web, from the rustic CD coffin, which holds more than 100 CDs ($199.95), and the coffin coffee table ($2,495) to the casket phone booth ($2,236) and the casket entertainment center ($4,495). Zeabin's great-grandfather founded the casket-building business in British Columbia in 1927 to supply local communities, but Zeabin has taken the family business to another level. "With the evolution of the Internet," says Zeabin, "we are proud to offer our products globally."*[90]

Using the Web as a marketing tool requires more than establishing a Web site and waiting for customers to come calling. Just as in any marketing venture, the key to successful marketing on the World Wide Web is selling the right product or service at the right price to the right target audience. Entrepreneurs on the Web, however, also have two additional challenges: attracting Web users to their Web sites and converting them into paying customers. That requires setting up an electronic storefront that is inviting, easy to navigate, interactive, and offers more than a monotonous laundry list of standard items. It also requires promoting the Web site in all of a company's marketing material, from print ads and radio spots to business cards and company letterhead. With a solid marketing strategy

FIGURE 6.4 Cost to Set Up
a Small Business Web Site

Source: Joanne H. Pratt, *E-Biz:Strategies for Small Business Success*, U.S. Small Business Administration Office of Advocacy, www.sba.gov/advo/research/rs220tot.pdf, p. 35.

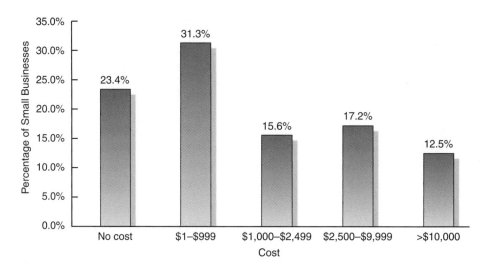

as a guide, small companies can—and are—selling everything from wine and vacations to jewelry and electronics successfully on the Web. Figure 6.4 provides a summary from an SBA study of the costs small companies incurred when setting up their Web sites.

THE MARKETING MIX

Learning Objective

6. Discuss the "four Ps" of marketing—product, place, price, and promotion—and their role in building a successful marketing strategy.

The major elements of a marketing strategy are the four Ps of marketing—**p**roduct, **p**lace, **p**rice, and **p**romotion. These four elements are self-reinforcing and, when coordinated, increase the sales appeal of a product or service. Small business managers must integrate these elements to maximize the impact of their product or service on the consumer. All four Ps must reinforce the image of the product or service the company presents to the potential customer. One long-time retailer claims, "None of the modern marvels of computerized inventory control and point-of-sale telecommunications have replaced the need for the entrepreneur who understands the customer and can translate that into the appropriate merchandise mix."[91]

Product

product life cycle—*describes the stages of development, growth, and decline in a products' life.*

introductory stage—*the stage in which a product or service must break into the market and overcome customer inertia.*

The product itself is an essential element in marketing. A product is any item or service that satisfies the need of a customer. Products can have form and shape, or they can be services with no physical form. Products travel through various stages of development. The **product life cycle** (see Figure 6.5) describes these stages of growth. Knowing which stage of the life cycle a product is in allows managers to make decisions about whether or not to continue selling the product and when to introduce new follow-up products.

In the **introductory stage**, marketers present their product to potential consumers. Initial high levels of acceptance are rare. Generally, new products must break into existing markets and compete with established products. Advertising and promotion help the new product be

FIGURE 6.5 The Product Life Cycle

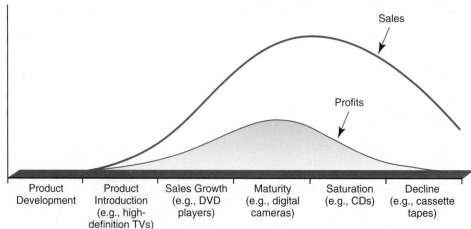

FIGURE 6.6 Time Between
Introduction of Products

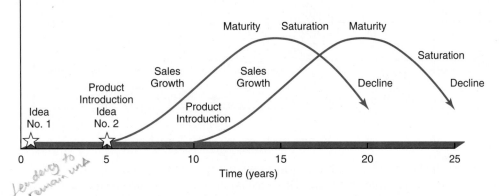

more quickly recognized. Potential customers must get information about the product, how to use it, and the needs it can satisfy. For instance, one Asian clothing maker has introduced a line of business suits with sachets of charcoal and jade powder sewn into the armpits and the crotch. The company says that the sachets not only absorb odors but they block electromagnetic radiation emitted by computer and television screens![92] The cost of marketing a product at this level of the life cycle is usually high because a company must overcome customer resistance and inertia. Thus, profits are generally low, or even negative, in the introductory stage.

After the introductory stage, the product enters the **growth and acceptance stage**. In the growth stage, consumers begin to compare the product in large enough numbers for sales to rise and profits to materialize. Products that reach this stage, however, do not necessarily become successful. If in the introductory or the growth stage the product fails to meet consumer needs, it does not sell and eventually disappears from the marketplace. According to Greg Stevens, president of a new-product research company, an average of just two new products are launched out of every 3,000 ideas generated; of the two actually launched, only one succeeds.[93] For successful products, sales and profit margins continue to rise through the growth stage.

In the **maturity and competition stage**, sales volume continues to rise, but profit margins peak and then begin to fall as competitors enter the market. Normally, this causes reduction in the product's selling price to meet competition and to hold its share of the market.

Sales peak in the **market saturation stage** of the product life cycle and give the marketer fair warning that it is time to introduce the next generation product.

The final stage of the product life cycle is the **product decline stage**. Sales continue to drop, and profit margins fall drastically. However, when a product reaches this stage of the cycle, it does not mean that it is doomed to failure. Products that have remained popular are always being revised. No firm can maintain its sales position without product innovation and change. Even Binney & Smith, the maker of Silly Putty, which was first introduced at the 1950 International Toy Fair (with lifetime sales of more than 300 million "eggs"), has introduced new gold, Day-Glo, and glow-in-the-dark colors. These innovations have caused the classic toy's sales to rebound, appealing to new generations of children.[94]

The time span of the stages in the product life cycle depends on the type of products involved. High-fashion and fad clothing have a short product life cycle, lasting for only four to six weeks. Products that are more stable may take years to complete a life cycle. Research conducted by MIT suggests that the typical product's life cycle lasts 10 to 14 years, but the length of that life cycle appears to be shrinking.[95]

Thomas Venable, owner of Spectrum Control, Inc., uses the concept of the product life cycle to plan the introduction of new products to his company's product line. Too often, companies wait too late into the life cycle of one product to introduce another. The result is that they are totally unprepared when a competitor produces "a better mousetrap" and their sales decline. "If you are not developing something new early in the current product's life cycle, you're living on borrowed time," says Venable. "If you wait until your line is mature, you're dead."[96]

In Venable's industry, a 12-year life cycle is common. His company's strategy is to begin turning out prototypes of sequel products two to three years before the maturity phase of the original product (see Figure 6.6). "The whole idea behind the process is to avoid crises," Venable says. "You want to be ready to go with the second product, just as the first one is about to die off."[97]

growth and acceptance stage—*the stage in which sales and profits materialize.*

maturity and competition stage—*the stage in which sales rise, but profits peak and then fall as competitors enter the market.*

market saturation stage—*stage in which sales peak, indicating the time to introduce the next generation product.*

product decline stage—*the stage in which sales continue to fall and profit margins decline drastically.*

FIGURE 6.7   Channels of
Distribution—Consumer Goods

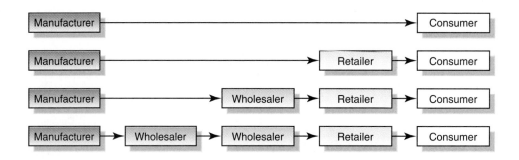

Place

Place (or method of distribution) has grown in importance as customers expect greater service and more convenience from businesses. This trend is one of the forces driving the rapid growth of the World Wide Web as a shopping tool. Entrepreneurs have come up with other clever ways to distribute their products and services and offer their customers more convenience. For instance, many traditionally stationary businesses have added wheels, becoming mobile animal clinics, computer shops, dentist offices, and windshield repair services.

Any activity involving movement of goods to the point of consumer purchase provides place utility. Place utility is directly affected by the marketing channels of distribution, the path that goods or services and their titles take in moving from producer to consumer. Channels typically involve a number of intermediaries who perform specialized functions that add valuable utility to the goods or service. These intermediaries provide time utility (making the product available *when* customers want to buy it) and place utility (making the product available *where* customers want to buy it).

A Company Example

In 1995, after observing the success of a classical music CD sold by lingerie retailer Victoria's Secret, New York producer and recording engineer Billy Straus launched **Rock River Communications**, *a company that produces branded music compilations. He finally convinced buyers at Pottery Barn to test market 15,000 copies of a jazz compilation titled* A Cool Christmas; *the retailer sold the entire order in just three weeks, opening the door to Rock River as the music supplier to other major retailers such as J. Crew, Eddie Bauer, Lane Bryant, Banana Republic, Old Navy, and, somewhat surprisingly, Jiffy Lube and Chef Boyardee. Rock River sells more than $8 million worth of music compilations annually, making it the equivalent of a midsize record label!*[98]

For consumer goods, there are four common channels of distribution (see Figure 6.7).

1. *Manufacturer to Consumer.* In some markets, producers sell their goods or services directly to consumers. Services, by nature, follow this channel of distribution. Dental care and haircuts, for example, go directly from creator to consumer.

2. *Manufacturer to Retailer to Consumer.* Another common channel involves a retailer as an intermediary. Many clothing items, books, shoes, and other consumer products are distributed in this manner.

3. *Manufacturer to Wholesaler to Retailer to Consumer.* This is the most common channel of distribution. Prepackaged food products, hardware, toys, and other items are commonly distributed through this channel.

4. *Manufacturer to Wholesaler to Wholesaler to Consumer.* A few consumer goods (e.g., agricultural goods and electrical components) follow this pattern of distribution.

Two channels of distribution are common for industrial goods (see Figure 6.8).

1. *Manufacturer to Industrial User.* The majority of industrial goods is distributed directly from manufacturers to users. In some cases, the goods or services are designed to meet the user's specifications.

2. *Manufacturer to Wholesaler to Industrial User.* Most expense items (paper clips, paper, rubber bands, cleaning fluids) that firms commonly use are distributed through wholesalers. For most small manufacturers, distributing goods through established wholesalers and agents is often the most effective route.

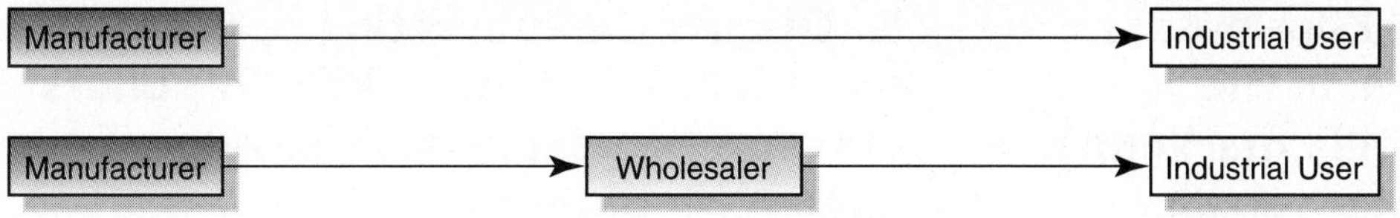

FIGURE 6.8 Channels of Distribution—Industrial Goods

Price

Almost everyone agrees that the price of the product or service is a key factor in the decision to buy. Price affects both sales volume and profits, and without the right price, both sales and profits will suffer. As we will see in the next chapter, the right price for a product or service depends on three factors: (1) a small company's cost structure, (2) an assessment of what the market will bear, and (3) the desired image the company wants to create in its customers' minds.

For many small businesses, nonprice competition—focusing on factors other than price—is a more effective strategy than trying to beat larger competitors in a price war. Nonprice competition, such as free trial offers, free delivery, lengthy warranties, and money-back guarantees, intends to play down the product's price and stress its durability, quality, reputation, or special features. We will discuss pricing in more detail in Chapter 8.

Promotion

Promotion involves both advertising and personal selling. Its goal is to inform and persuade consumers. Advertising communicates to potential customers through some mass medium the benefits of a good or service. Personal selling involves the art of persuasive sales on a one-to-one basis. A small company's promotional program can play a significant role in creating a specific image in its customers' minds—whether it is upscale, discount, or somewhere in between. "Marketing is not a battle of products; it's a battle of perceptions," says one marketing expert.[99] We will discuss promotion in more detail in Chapter 8.

CHAPTER SUMMARY

1. Describe the principles of building a guerrilla marketing plan and explain the benefits of preparing one.

A major part of the entrepreneur's business plan is the marketing plan, which focuses on a company's target customers and how best to satisfy their needs and wants. A solid marketing plan should:

■ determine customer needs and wants through market research.

■ pinpoint the specific target markets the company will serve.

■ analyze the firm's competitive advantages and build a marketing strategy around them.

■ create a marketing mix that meets customer needs and wants.

2. Explain how small businesses can pinpoint their target markets.

Sound market research helps the owner pinpoint his target market. The most successful businesses have well-defined portraits of the customers they are seeking to attract.

3. Discuss the role of market research in building a guerilla marketing plan and outline the market research process.

Market research is the vehicle for gathering the information that serves as the foundation of the marketing plan. Good research does *not* have to be complex and expensive to be useful. The steps in conducting market research include:

■ defining the objective—"What do you want to know?"

■ collecting the data from either primary or secondary sources.

■ analyzing and interpreting the data.

■ drawing conclusions and acting on them.

4. Describe how a small business can build a competitive edge in the marketplace using guerilla marketing strategies: customer focus, quality, convenience, innovation, service, and speed.

When plotting a marketing strategy, owners must strive to achieve a competitive advantage—some way to make their companies different from and better than the competition. Successful small businesses rely on the following to develop a competitive edge:

- find a niche and fill it
- don't just sell—entertain
- strive to be unique
- connect with the customer on an emotional level
- focus on the customer
- devotion to quality
- attention to convenience
- concentration on innovation
- dedication to service
- emphasis on speed

5. Discuss the marketing opportunities the World Wide Web (WWW) offers entrepreneurs and how to best take advantage of them.

The Web offers small business owners tremendous marketing potential on a par with their larger rivals. Entrepreneurs are just beginning to uncover the Web's profit potential, which is growing rapidly. Establishing a presence on the Web is important for companies targeting educated, wealthy, young customers. Successful Web sites are attractive, inviting, easy to navigate, interactive, and offer users something of value.

6. Discuss the "four Ps" of marketing—product, place, price, and promotion—and their role in building a successful marketing strategy.

The marketing mix consists of the "four Ps":

- *Product*. Entrepreneurs should understand where in the product life cycle their products are.
- *Place*. The focus here is on choosing the appropriate channel of distribution and using it most efficiently.
- *Price*. Setting the right price for a product or service is partly an art and partly a science.
- *Promotion*. Promotion involves both advertising and personal selling.

DISCUSSION QUESTIONS

1. Define the marketing plan. What lies at its center?
2. What objectives should a marketing plan accomplish?
3. How can market research benefit a small business owner? List some possible sources of market information.
4. Does market research have to be expensive and sophisticated to be valuable? Explain.
5. Describe several market trends that are driving markets into the new millennium and their impact on small businesses.
6. Why is it important for small business owners to define their target markets as part of their marketing strategies?
7. What is a competitive advantage? Why is it important for a small business owner to create a plan for establishing one?
8. Describe how a small business owner could use the following sources of competitive advantage:
   - focusing on a niche
   - entertailing
   - striving to be unique
   - creating an identity for the business
   - connecting with customers on an emotional level
   - focusing on the customer
   - devotion to quality
   - attention to convenience
   - concentration on innovation
   - dedication to service
   - emphasis on speed

9. One manager says, "When a company provides great service, its reputation benefits from a stronger emotional connection with its customers, as well as from increased confidence that it will stand behind its products." Do you agree? Explain. If so, describe a positive service experience you have had with a company and your impressions of that business. What are the implications of a company providing poor customer service? Once again, describe a negative service experience you have had with a company and your impressions of that business. How likely are you to do business with that company again?
10. What marketing potential does the World Wide Web offer small businesses? What does it take for a company to market successfully using the Web?
11. Explain the concept of the marketing mix. What are the four Ps?
12. List and explain the stages in the product life cycle. How can a small firm extend its product's life?
13. With a 70 percent customer retention rate (average for most U.S. firms, according to the American Management Association), every $1 million of business in 2000 will grow to more than $4 million by the year 2010. If you retain 80 percent of your customers, the $1 million will grow to a little over $6 million. If you can keep 90 percent of your customers, that $1 million will grow to more than $9.5 million. What can the typical small business do to increase its customer retention rate?

What steps can business owners take to become effective marketers even if they lack the resources of their larger competitors? After reviewing the material in Chapter 6, outline the steps of the guerrilla-marketing plan you intend to implement in your business.

If you are planning to buy a franchise, you should review the reference material on marketing a franchise on *The Business Disc*. From the menu across the top of your screen, select the "Reference" option and then click on "General Information." Click on "Marketing Your Franchise for Success" and review the concepts in this reference guide and in Chapter 6. Write a brief report summarizing your company's target market, the characteristics of the people or businesses in it, and the steps you plan to take to market your franchise successfully.

BUSINESS PLAN PRO

Business PlanPro

You will use the concepts in this chapter as well as those in Chapters 7 and 8 to create much of your business plan. Indeed, about one-fourth to one-third of your plan should be devoted to the marketing plan. In the following sections of the Business PlanPro you must "tell the story" of how you determined that a market exists for the products or services of your proposed business the marketing segments are targeting; the unique selling proposition you plan to use to differentiate your products and services; and how you will reach the market and motivate customers to purchase.

YOUR COMPANY

This series of steps in *Business Plan Pro* will allow you to create the basics of the executive summary. In part one of this section you can set forth the nature of the business. If the business is in actual operation, you should write a brief history of the business in this section. If the business is not in operation yet, this section should include your rationale for the venture.

PART TWO

In this section you should draw material from Chapter 4 of your textbook and the sections that deal with forms of ownership. Your response to this section of the business plan should reflect a detailed analysis of the various legal forms of ownership and why the form that you have selected is the best for your proposed business venture.

WHAT YOU ARE SELLING

Use the concepts contained in this chapter to help you describe what you are selling. Remember to consider the intangible needs your product or service meet.

SERVICE SUMMARY

Your plan should both discuss the unique nature of the services your business provides its customers and the factors that make these services superior to those offered by your competitors.

YOUR MARKET

Review the concepts in "Pinpointing the Target Market" on pages 176 and 177 and use them to help you develop a clear picture of your target customers. Be sure to include all the details you can about the specific market for your proposed product/services.

THE MARKET ANALYSIS SUMMARY

This one or two paragraph statement must demonstrate to your business plan reader that you have investigated your proposed market thoroughly. Like the financial aspect of your business plan, which focuses on cash flow, net income, and owner's equity, the market analysis projects numbers but analyzes them from a different perspective. Here your ultimate focus must remain on the customer.

MARKET ANALYSIS TABLE

Present the detailed target market analysis that you have conducted for your proposed new business venture. Be specific in developing a profile of the segments you are targeting and estimate the growth of each market segment over the five year time horizon. If you report exceptionally large percentage increases or decreases in any segment over the time period, be sure to explain both the causes of these changes as well as the impact on your business venture.

An explanation of each target market segment is included in the "Market Segmentation" section of the software. The more specifically you can describe each market segment, the better you will understand why each segment is important and how the marketing strategies you have developed will succeed.

TARGET MARKET SEGMENT STRATEGY

Chapters 6, 7, and 8 will contribute to defining the appropriate strategies for each segment which you have identified and defined. Locating a market segment is only part of the picture; now you must demonstrate the methods or techniques you will utilize to effectively reach your target customers.

"The Section Conclusion" should tie the marketing plan and its strategies together.

THE BUSINESS YOU'RE IN

In this section write a detailed explanation of the economic and competitive environment your business faces. If other external factors such as the political or legal/regulatory environment are important, include a detailed description of the interaction of all relevant factors and their potential impact on the economic viability of the venture.

SERVICE BUSINESS ANALYSIS

If your venture is a service business, or if services are an important part of the new venture, be sure to describe how your company will set apart its service offerings to gain a competitive advantage over competitors.

FACTORS OF COMPETITION

Always critical, this section must include a detailed and thorough discussion and analysis of each of the current *and* potential competitors. There is no substitute for this level of depth of analysis. The business plan must demonstrate that you have evaluated this critical factor and can identify, in realistic terms, how your business will successfully compete. Know why customers make purchasing decisions and how your proposed venture can gain their business. Be honest as you describe your competitors' strengths and weaknesses. Discuss the customer appeal, pricing, advertising, services of competitors' products and services.

YOUR SALES FORECAST/SALES STRATEGY

The focus of this section is on how you plan to sell your product/services. Again, it is very specific.
What are the key features that the sales presentation will form upon?
do you know how to qualify the buyer in the market?
how will you evaluate the buyer specific needs?
what are the signs that the buyer is interested?
And very important, how do you close the sale?
Every business is unique, and the sales strategy must be tailored to the relationship between the buyer's needs/wants and the key features of the products/services you are offering.

SALES FORECAST TABLE

Complete this table and be sure that your sales forecast and the cost of sales are as accurate as possible.

EXPLAIN SALES FORECAST

This is the narrative that explains the numbers in the Sales Forecast Table. Be sure that you include the assumptions on which you have developed your sales forecast. Explain why your sales are projected to increase or decrease over time. Include key events that may impact your sales and how and why they were included in your sales forecast. For example, if you know that the I believe Winter Olympics should be capitalized. Will be held in your area within the next four years /and you just happen to be selling hot chocolate near the slopes/ it is perfectly acceptable to include this in your sales forecast and accompanying narrative.

Finally, when you evaluate your numbers, and the assumptions that support them, are they realistic? Developing financial forecasts using published statistics from sources such as RMA Annual Statement Studies, market research, industry studies, and other sources lends credibility to your plan.

YOUR MARKETING PLAN

Competitive Edge

As with all components of the business plan—be detail oriented. Do not make a statement about your competitive edge that is simply a generalization and without an explanation of the strategies you will use to create this advantage. Incorporate material from your marketing and sales plan that will show how these strategic advantages will result in the number of customers you forecast.

MARKETING STRATEGY SUMMARY

A marketing strategy should present a clear link to generate sales revenue. Never assume that anything is obvious to the reader; spell it out with the use of detailed analysis and explanation of all assumptions on which the analysis rests. Your company's pricing, product, distribution, and promotion plans together should produce a unified marketing strategy.

1. Interview the owner of a local restaurant about its marketing strategy. From how large a geographic region does the restaurant draw its clientele? What is the firm's target market? What are its characteristics? Does the restaurant have a competitive edge?

2. Select a local small manufacturing operation and evaluate its primary product. What stage of the product life cycle is it in? What channels of distribution does the product follow after leaving the manufacturer?

3. Visit the Web site for the Small Business Administration's "Marketing Mall" at www.onlinewbc.gov/docs/market. Interview a local business owner, using the resources there as a guide. What sources for developing a competitive edge did you find? What weaknesses do you see? How do you recommend overcoming them? What recommendations can you make to help the owner make better use of its marketing techniques? Evaluate the business's approach to the four Ps of marketing. What guerrilla marketing strategies can you suggest to enhance current marketing efforts?

4. Contact three local small business owners and ask them about their marketing strategies. How have they achieved a competitive edge? Develop a series of questions to judge the sources of their competitive edge—a focus on the customer, devotion to quality, attention to convenience, concentration on innovation, dedication to service, and emphasis on speed. How do the businesses compare?

5. Select three local businesses (one large and two small) and play the role of "mystery shopper." How easy was it to do business with each company? How would you rate their service, quality, and convenience? Were salespeople helpful and friendly? Did they handle transactions professionally and courteously? How would you rate the business's appearance? How would you describe each company's competitive advantage? What future would you predict for each company? Prepare a brief report for your class on your findings and conclusions.

Chapter 7

E-Commerce and the Entrepreneur

The Internet remains a place where you can start with nothing and soon challenge the gods.

—Mark DiMassimo

The sure way to miss success is to miss the opportunity.

—Victor Charles

LEARNING OBJECTIVES

Upon completion of this chapter, you will be able to:

1. **DESCRIBE** the benefits of selling on the World Wide Web.

2. **UNDERSTAND** the factors an entrepreneur should consider before launching into e-commerce.

3. **EXPLAIN** the 12 myths of e-commerce and how to avoid falling victim to them.

4. **DISCUSS** the five basic approaches available to entrepreneurs wanting to launch an e-commerce effort.

5. **EXPLAIN** the basic strategies entrepreneurs should follow to achieve success in their e-commerce efforts.

6. **LEARN** the techniques of designing a killer Web site.

7. **EXPLAIN** how companies track the results from their Web sites.

8. **DESCRIBE** how e-businesses ensure the privacy and security of the information they collect and store from the Web.

9. **LEARN** how to evaluate the effectiveness of a company's Web site.

As a student of business, you are fortunate to witness the early stages of growth of a tool that is reshaping the way companies of all sizes do business: e-commerce. E-commerce is creating a new way of doing business, one that is connecting producers, sellers, and customers via technology in ways that have never been possible before. The result is a whole new set of companies built on business models that are turning traditional methods of commerce and industry on their heads. Companies that ignore the impact of the Internet on their markets run the risk of becoming as relevant to customers as a rotary-dial telephone. The most successful companies are embracing the Internet, not as merely another advertising medium or marketing tool but as a mechanism for transforming their companies and changing *everything* about the way they do business. As these companies discover new, innovative ways to use the Internet, computers, and communications technology to connect with their suppliers and to serve their customers better, they are creating a new industrial order. In short, e-commerce has launched a revolution. Just as in previous revolutions in the business world, some old established players are being ousted, and new leaders are emerging. The winners are discovering new business opportunities, new ways of designing work, and new ways of organizing and operating their businesses. Yet one lesson that the dot-com bubble burst in 2000 taught entrepreneurs is that business basics still apply, whether a company is on the Web or not. Companies engaging in e-commerce still have to take care of their customers and earn a profit to stay in business.

Perhaps the most visible changes are occurring in the world of retailing. Although e-commerce will not replace traditional retailing, no retailer, from the smallest corner store to industry giant Wal-Mart, can afford to ignore the impact of the World Wide Web on their business models. Companies can take orders at the speed of light from anywhere in the world and at any time of day. The Internet enables companies to collect more information on customers' shopping and buying habits than any other medium in history. This ability means that companies can focus their marketing efforts like never before—for instance, selling garden supplies to customers who are most likely to buy them and not wasting resources trying to sell to those who have no interest in gardening. The capacity to track customers' Web-based shopping habits allows companies to personalize their approaches to marketing and to realize the benefits of individualized (or one-to-one) marketing (refer to Chapter 6). Ironically, the same Web-based marketing approach that allows companies to get so personal with their customers also can make shopping extremely impersonal. Entrepreneurs who set up shop on the Web will likely never meet their customers face-to-face or even talk to them. Yet, those customers, who can live anywhere in the world, will visit the online store at all hours of the day or night and expect to receive individual attention. Making a Web-based marketing approach succeed requires a business to strike a balance, creating an e-commerce strategy that capitalizes on the strengths of the Web while meeting customers' expectations of convenience and service.

In the world of e-commerce, the new business models recognize the power the Internet gives customers. Pricing, for example, is no longer as simple as it once was for companies. Auction sites such as eBay and Priceline.com mean that entrepreneurs can no longer be content to take into account only local competitors when setting their own prices. With a few mouse clicks, customers can compare the prices of the same or similar products and services from companies across the globe. In the new wired and connected economy, the balance of power is shifting to customers, and new business models recognize this fact. Consider, for example, the challenges auto dealers face when selling to customers armed with dealer cost and pricing information gathered from any one of dozens of Web sites. Because they know the dealer's wholesale cost of a new car, these informed customers are taking price out of the buying equation, causing dealers to emphasize other factors such as service or convenience to build long-term relationships. Net profit margins on new cars average just 0.7 percent, compared to 1.7 percent on used cars, which are harder for online shoppers to pin a precise value on.[1] Auto dealerships are not the only companies facing this reality. One study by Ernst & Young found that 64 percent of Internet users research products online before buying them in stores or by telephone.[2]

In this fast-paced world of e-commerce, size no longer matters as much as speed and flexibility do. One of the Web's greatest strengths is its ability to provide companies with instantaneous customer feedback, giving them the opportunity to learn and to make necessary adjustments. Businesses, whatever their size, that are willing to experiment with different approaches to reaching customers and are quick to learn and adapt will grow and prosper; those that cannot will fall by the wayside. The Internet is creating a new industrial order, and companies that fail to adapt to it will soon become extinct. For instance, as profit margins on new cars have shrunk over the years due, in part, to the Web, smart auto dealers are finding ways to use the Web to make money.

Linda Cerrone, owner of a Nissan dealership in Tewksbury, Massachusetts, has created a Web site that allows customers to schedule service appointments or to order parts for their cars, both of which offer much higher profit margins than do car sales. An e-mail system automatically sends out reminders to customers for periodic maintenance or extended warranty offers. Shoppers also can peruse the dealership's inventory online, calculate monthly payments, and complete loan applications, reducing the time they must spend at the dealership when they purchase a car. Subscribing to four sales-referral Web sites generates an average of 10 sales a month. Cerrone also places ads for her used car inventory on specialty sites such as AutoTrader.com and Cars.com. Because of her Web-based marketing strategy, online sales comprise 10 percent of Cerrone's sales volume.[3]

By creating innovative, easy-to-use Web sites, auto dealerships such as Cerrone Nissan are changing the way traditional companies must compete.

High-volume, low-margin, commodity products are best suited for selling on the Web. Indeed, the items purchased most often online are books, music, videos, computer hardware and software, consumer electronics, and travel services. However, companies can—and do—sell practically anything over the Web, from antiques and pharmaceuticals to groceries and drug-free urine. The most commonly cited reasons among owners of small and mid-sized companies for taking their companies to the Web are (1) to reach new customers, (2) to sell goods and services, (3) to disseminate information more quickly, (4) to keep up with competitors, and (5) to reach global markets.[4]

Companies of all sizes are establishing a presence on the Web because that's where their customers are. The Department of Commerce reports that 54 percent of Americans are using the Internet, and the number of users continues to grow at a rapid pace of 2 million new users a month.[5] Consumers have adopted the Internet much more quickly than any other major innovation in the past. It reached 50 percent penetration in the United States in just seven years, compared to 30 years for the computer, 40 years for electricity, and more than 100 years for steam power.[6] Online shopping currently accounts for just 4.5 percent of total retail sales in the United States (nearly $100 billion), but online sales are growing by 30 to 40 percent a year, far faster than the 4 percent growth rate of off-line sales.[7] Although this torrid pace of growth will not last indefinitely, the Web represents a tremendous opportunity that businesses simply cannot afford to ignore.

BENEFITS OF SELLING ON THE WEB

As we saw in Chapter 6, only 33 percent of small companies have Web sites, and of those, only 24 percent actually generate revenues from online sales.[8] However, those small businesses that are doing business on the Web experience many benefits (see Figure 7.1). We now examine some of these benefits more closely.

- *The opportunity to increase revenues.* For many small businesses, launching a Web site is the equivalent of opening a new sales channel. Companies that launch e-commerce efforts soon discover that their sites are generating additional sales from new audiences of customers.

- *The ability to expand their reach into global markets.* The Web is the most efficient way for small businesses to sell their products to the millions of potential customers who live outside the borders of the United States. Tapping into these global markets through more traditional methods would be too complex and too costly for the typical small business. Yet, with the Web, a small company can sell its products efficiently to customers anywhere in the world at any time of day.

- *The ability to remain open 24 hours a day, seven days a week.* More than half of all retail sales occur after 6 P.M., when many traditional stores close. Extending the hours a brick-and-mortar store remains open can increase sales, but it also takes a toll on the business owner and the employees. With a Web site up and running, however, a small company can sell around the clock without having to incur additional staffing expenses. Customers never have to worry about whether or not an online store is "open."

- *The capacity to use the Web's interactive nature to enhance customer service.* Although selling on the Web can be highly impersonal because of the lack of human interaction, companies that design their sites properly can create an exciting, interactive experience for their online visitors. Customers

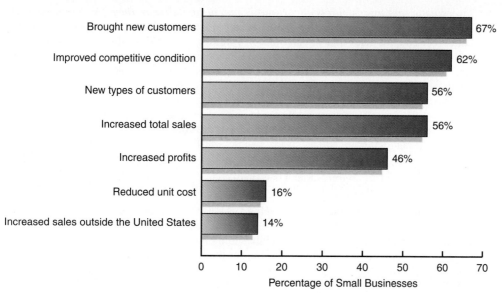

FIGURE 7.1 Benefits to Small Businesses of a Web Site

Source: Reprinted by permission of the National Federation of Independent Businesses, 2002.

can contact a company at any time of the day, can control the flow of information they get, and in some cases can interact with company representatives in real time. In addition, technology now allows companies to "personalize" their sites to suit the tastes and preferences of individual customers. Drawing on a database containing information customers have provided in the past, modern Web sites can customize themselves, displaying content that appeals to an individual visitor. For instance, a site selling clothing can greet a returning customer by name and ask if she is shopping for herself or for someone on her personal shopping list. Based on her response, the site can recall appropriate sizes and favorite styles and colors and can even make product recommendations.

■ ***The power to educate and to inform.*** Far more than most marketing media, the Web gives entrepreneurs the power to educate and to inform customers. Women and members of Generation Y, especially, crave product information before they make purchases. The Web allows business owners to provide more detailed information to visitors than practically any other medium. For instance, a travel company advertising an Alaskan tour in a newspaper or magazine might include a brief description of the tour, a list of the destinations, a telephone number, the price, and perhaps a photo or two. A Web-based promotion for the same tour could include all of this information as well as a detailed itinerary with dozens of breathtaking photographs; descriptions and photographs of all accommodations; advice on what to pack; airline schedules, seating configurations, and availability; information on optional side trips; comments from customers who have taken this tour before; and links to other Web sites about Alaska, the weather, and fun things to do in the region.[9]

■ ***The ability to lower the cost of doing business.*** The Web is one of the most efficient ways of reaching both new and existing customers. Properly promoted, a Web site can reduce a company's cost of generating sales leads, providing customer support, and distributing marketing materials. For instance, car dealers must spend $500 on average to get a potential customer into their showrooms; for a $40 listing fee, those same dealers can list a car on the popular auction site eBay, where they get an average of eight customers bidding to buy.[10] Online customer acquisition costs, the cost required for an online company to land a paying customer, have dropped from $29 in 2000 to less than $14 today.[11]

By integrating its Web site with its inventory control system, a company also can reduce its inventory costs by shortening the sales cycle. In addition, linking Web sales activity to suppliers enables a business to cut its purchasing costs.

A Company Example

Brady Corporation, an 87-year-old company that makes all types of signs—from identification tags to stop signs—faced a multitude of problems stemming from its outdated order-processing, accounts receivable, and quality control systems. Managers saw the opportunity the Web offered to correct errors, lower costs, and improve customer satisfaction. The company created Web-to-Workbench, a system that sends customer orders directly to the factory floor. Because the system allows customers to design and pay for their own signs online, Brady's accounts receivable problems have all but disappeared, and its order-processing costs fell 88 percent from $16 per order to just $2 per order! Because the system allows customers to preview the final design of their signs online, errors that used to result in millions of dollars of returned signs have been reduced dramatically. Customer satisfaction is higher because Brady now ships most orders within 24 hours of receiving them.[12]

- **The ability to spot new business opportunities and to capitalize on them.** E-commerce companies are poised to give customers just what they want when they want it. As the number of dual-career couples rises and the amount of available leisure time shrinks, consumers are looking for ways to increase the convenience of shopping, and the Web is fast becoming the solution they seek. Increasingly, customers view shopping as an unpleasant chore that cuts into already scarce leisure time, and they are embracing anything that reduces the amount of time they must spend shopping. Entrepreneurs who tap into customers' need to buy goods more conveniently and with less hassle are winning the battle for market share. New opportunities to serve customers' changing needs and wants are constantly arising, and the Web is the birthplace of many of them.

- **The ability to grow faster.** The Web has the power to accelerate a small company's growth. A study by *American City Journals* found that small companies that used the Internet grew 46 percent faster than those that did not.[13]

- **The power to track sales results.** The Web gives businesses the power to track virtually any kind of activity on their Web sites, from the number of visitors to the click-through rates on their banner ads. Because of the Web's ability to monitor traffic continuously, entrepreneurs can judge the value their sites are generating for their companies. When David Scifres, vice president of Internet Services at Camping World, a recreational vehicle dealer, redesigned the company's Web site for the first time, the software that tracked the site's performance indicated numerous problems. The performance measures told Scifres that the changes made the Web site worse! He quickly revamped the changes, and the site's **conversion rate**, the percentage of visitors to a Web site who actually make a purchase, climbed immediately from 39 percent to 52 percent![14]

In essence, the Web allows small businesses to match the efficiencies of big companies by increasing their reach and the scope of their operations, by connecting with suppliers and customers to lower costs, and by measuring the results of their e-commerce efforts.

A Company Example

Michael Bornstein, who had been running three successful skateboard stores in Southern California, wanted to expand his business and shift its focus to sell more profitable skateboard equipment and accessories. He decided that the Web was the key to success for his expansion strategy. First, he consolidated his three stores into two, and used the third as the Internet and mail-order center for **Skate America**. *After spending a year developing a business plan and a Web site, Bornstein launched the company. It took a few months before his site was picked up by search engines such as Yahoo; but then sales took off. Within two years, Bornstein closed his two retail stores to focus on Web sales. Bornstein has redesigned Skate America's Web site over the years, and today it is one of the most sophisticated in the industry, yet it remains one of the simplest for customers to use. Shoppers can create custom-designed skateboards or buy pre-built models and order parts or accessories with ease. Bornstein has linked his company's just-in-time inventory system to his Web site, which gives him an advantage over competitors because he avoids the problems of excess inventory. Because of Bornstein's successful e-commerce strategy, Skate America's sales have climbed from $1 million in its first year to more than $7 million today.[15]*

Learning Corporation

2. Understand the factors an entrepreneur should consider before launching into e-commerce.

FACTORS TO CONSIDER BEFORE LAUNCHING INTO E-COMMERCE

Despite the many benefits the Web offers, not every small business owner is ready to embrace e-commerce. Of those small business owners who have not taken their businesses online, 77 percent say their products and services are not suitable for sale on the Web. Another 37 percent say that they do not see any benefits to selling online.[16] Why are so many small companies hesitant to use the Web as a business tool? For many entrepreneurs, the key barrier is not knowing where or how to start an e-commerce effort, whereas for others cost and time concerns are major issues. Other roadblocks include the fear that customers will not use the Web site and the problems associated with ensuring online security.

Whatever their size, traditional companies must realize that selling their products and services on the Web is no longer a luxury. Business owners who are not at least considering creating a Web presence are putting their companies at risk. "Any company that wants to make it in the years ahead must make the technology and the processes of the Internet part of its core competence," says one experienced venture capitalist.[17] However, before launching an e-commerce effort, business owners should consider the following important issues:

- How a company exploits the Web's interconnectivity and the opportunities it creates to transform relationships with its suppliers and vendors, its customers, and other external stakeholders is crucial to its success.

- Web success requires a company to develop a plan for integrating the Web into its overall strategy. The plan should address issues such as site design and maintenance, creating and managing a brand name, marketing and promotional strategies, sales, and customer service.

- Developing deep, lasting relationships with customers takes on even greater importance on the Web. Attracting customers on the Web costs money, and companies must be able to retain their online customers to make their Web sites profitable.

- Creating a meaningful presence on the Web requires an ongoing investment of resources—time, money, energy, and talent. Establishing an attractive Web site brimming with catchy photographs of products is only the beginning.

- Measuring the success of its Web-based sales effort is essential to remaining relevant to customers whose tastes, needs, and preferences are always changing.

Doing business on the Web takes more time and energy than many entrepreneurs think. Answering the following questions will help entrepreneurs make sure they are ready to do business on the Web and avoid unpleasant surprises in their e-commerce efforts:

- What exactly do you expect a Web site to do for your company? Will it provide information only, reach new customers, increase sales to existing customers, improve communication with customers, enhance customer service, or reduce your company's cost of operation? Will customers be able to place orders from the site, or must they call your company to buy?

- How much can you afford to invest in an e-commerce effort?

- What rate of return do you expect to earn on that investment?

- How long can you afford to wait for that return?

- How well suited are your products and services for selling on the Web?

- How will the "back office" of your Web site work? Will your site be tied into your company's inventory control system?

- How will you handle order fulfillment? Can your fulfillment system handle the increase in volume you are expecting?

- What impact, if any, will your Web site have on your company's traditional channels of distribution?

- What mechanism will your site use to ensure secure customer transactions?

- How will your company handle customer service for the site? What provisions will you make for returned items?

- How do you plan to promote the site to draw traffic to it?

- What information will you collect from the visitors to your site? How will you use it? Will you tell visitors how you intend to use this information?

- Have you developed a privacy policy? Have you posted that policy on your company's Web site for customers?

- Have you tested your site with real, live customers to make sure that it is easy to navigate and easy to order from?

- How will you measure the success of your company's Web site? What objectives have you set for the site?

Table 7.1 provides a set of questions designed to help entrepreneurs assess their companies' potential to become an online success.

TABLE 7.1

Assessing Your Company's Online Potential

Considering launching an online company or transforming a brick-and-mortar business into a "dot-com" company? The following questions will help you assess your company's online potential.

1. Does your product have broad appeal to customers everywhere?

2. Do you want to sell your product to customers outside of your immediate geographical area?

3. Can the product you sell be delivered conveniently and economically?

4. Can your company realize significant cost advantages, such as lower rent, labor, inventory, and printing expenses, by going online?

5. Can you draw customers to your company's Web site with a reasonable investment?

Learning Objective

3. Explain the 12 myths of e-commerce and how to avoid falling victim to them.

12 MYTHS OF E-COMMERCE

Although many entrepreneurs have made their fortunes through e-commerce, setting up shop on the Web is no guarantee of success. Scores of entrepreneurs have plunged unprepared into the world of e-commerce only to discover that there is more to it than merely setting up a Web site and waiting for the orders to start pouring in. Make sure that you do not fall victim to one of the following e-commerce myths.

Myth 1. Setting Up a Business on the Web Is Easy and Inexpensive

A common misconception is that setting up an effective Web site for an online business is easy and inexpensive. Although practically anyone with the right software can post a static page in just a few minutes, creating an effective, professional, and polished Web site can be an expensive, time-consuming project. Most small businesses set up their Web pages as simple "electronic flyers," pages that post product information, a few photographs, prices, and telephone and fax numbers. Although these simple sites lack the capacity for true electronic commerce, they do provide a company with another way of reaching both new and existing customers.

Establishing a true transactional Web site will require several months and an investment ranging from $10,000 up to nearly $1 million, depending on the features and capacity it incorporates. According to a study by Jupiter Communications, setting up an e-commerce site takes most companies at least six months to complete (see Figure 7.2). The study also revealed that setting up the site was only the first investment required. Companies cited these follow-up investments: (1) redesign Web site, (2) buy more hardware to support Web site, (3) automate or expand warehouse to meet customer demand, (4) integrate Web site into inventory control system, and (5) increase customer call-center capacity.[18]

FIGURE 7.2 Time Required to Develop an E-Commerce Site

Source: Jupiter Communications.

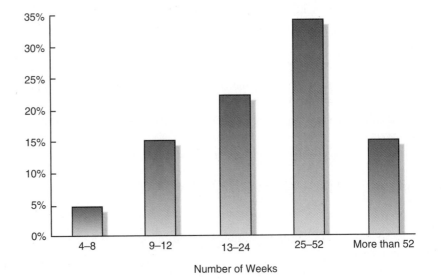

Number of Weeks

Myth 2. If I Launch a Site, Customers Will Flock to It

Some entrepreneurs think that once they set up their Web sites, their expenses end there. Not true! Without promotional support, no Web site will draw enough traffic to support a business. With more than 3 billion Web pages in existence and the number growing daily, getting a site noticed in the crowd has become increasingly difficult. Even listing a site with popular Web search engines cannot guarantee that customers surfing the Web will find your company's site. Just like traditional retail stores seeking to attract customers, virtual companies have discovered that drawing sufficient traffic to a Web site requires constant promotion—and lots of it! Setting up a Web site and then failing to drive customers to it with adequate promotional support is like setting up a physical store in a back alley; you may be in business, but nobody knows you're there!

Entrepreneurs with both physical and virtual stores must promote their Web sites at every opportunity by printing their URLs on everything related to their physical stores—on signs, in print and broadcast ads, on shopping bags, on merchandise labels, and anywhere else their customers will see it. Virtual shop owners should consider buying ads in traditional advertising media as well as using banner ads, banner exchange programs, and cross-marketing arrangements with companies selling complementary products on their own Web sites. Other techniques include creating a Web-based newsletter, writing articles that link to the company's site, or hosting a chat room that allows customers to interact with one another and with company personnel.

The key to promoting a Web site is networking, building relationships with other companies, customers, trade associations, online directories, and other Web sites your company's customers visit. "You need to create relationships with the businesses and people with whom you share common customers," says Barbara Ling, author of a book on e-commerce. "Then you need to create links between sites to help customers find what they are looking for." [19]

Myth 3. Making Money on the Web Is Easy

Promoters who hawk "get-rich-quick" schemes on the Web lure many entrepreneurs with the promise that making money on the Web is easy. It isn't. A study of e-commerce by the Small Business Administration reports that 35 percent of small businesses are losing money on their Web sites.[20] Making money on the Web is possible, but it takes time and a solid plan and requires an investment up front. As hundreds of new sites spring up every day, getting your company's site noticed requires more effort and marketing muscle than ever before. One study by management consulting firm Boston Consulting Group and shop.org, an Internet retailing trade association, found that Web retailers invested 65 percent of their revenues in marketing and advertising, compared to their off-line counterparts, who invested just 4 percent.[21]

Myth 4. Privacy Is Not an Important Issue on the Web

The Web allows companies to gain access to almost unbelievable amounts of information about their customers. Many sites offer visitors "freebies" in exchange for information about themselves. Companies then use this information to learn more about their target customers and how to market to them most effectively. A survey by Jupiter Media Metrix found that 70 percent of consumers expressed concern about online privacy.[22] Protecting online customers' privacy has become the topic of debate by many interested parties, including government agencies, consumer watchdog groups, customers, and industry trade associations. Jupiter Media Metrix estimates that if online companies adequately addressed privacy and security issues and alleviated customers' fear of breaches, online retail sales would be 24 percent higher![23]

Companies that collect information from their online customers have a responsibility to safeguard their customers' privacy, to protect that information from unauthorized use, and to use it responsibly. That means that businesses should post a privacy policy on their Web sites, explaining to customers how they intend to use the information they collect. Then they must be sure to follow it! One of the surest ways to alienate online customers is to abuse the information collected from them by selling it to third parties or by spamming customers with unwanted solicitations. BBBOnline offers a useful resource center designed to help small business owners wanting to establish or upgrade their Web site's privacy policies (www.bbbonline.org/understandingprivacy).

Businesses that publish privacy policies and then adhere to them build trust among their customers, an important facet of doing business on the Web. A study by Jupiter Communications found that 64 percent of Web customers distrust Web sites.[24] According to John Briggs, director of e-commerce for the Yahoo Network, customers "need to trust the brand they are buying and believe that their on-line purchases will be safe transactions. They need to feel comfortable that [their] personal data will not be sold and that they won't get spammed by giving their e-mail address. They need to know about shipping costs, product availability, and return policies up front."[25] Privacy *does* matter on the Web, and businesses that respect their customers' privacy will win their customers' trust. Trust is the foundation on which the long-term customer relationships that are so crucial to Web success are built.

Myth 5. The Most Important Part of Any E-Commerce Effort Is Technology

Although understanding the technology of e-commerce is an important part of the formula for success, it is *not* the most crucial ingredient. What matters most is the ability to understand the underlying business and to develop a workable business model that offers customers something of value at a reasonable price while producing a reasonable return for the company. The entrepreneurs who are proving to be most successful in e-commerce are those who know how their industries work inside and out and then build an e-business around their knowledge. They know that they can hire Webmasters, database experts, and fulfillment companies to design the technical aspects of their businesses but that nothing can substitute for a solid understanding of their industry, their target market, and the strategy needed to pull the various parts together. The key is seeing the Web for what it really is: another way to reach and serve customers with an effective business model.

A Company Example

*Founded in 1966 to publish printed guides for buyers of new and used cars, **Edmunds Publications** changed very little over the next two decades about the way it operated, selling its manuals to bookstores, libraries, financial institutions, and individuals. In 1988, however, Peter Steinlauf bought the small company and began making changes to realize the potential he saw in it. After moving the company to car-crazy California, Steinlauf began exploring other ways to publish the auto cost and pricing information customers found so valuable. A computer CD proved to be short-lived, but in 1994 when Steinlauf offered the information on a pre-Web text-only "gopher site" called the Electronic Newsstand, Edmunds became the first company to offer consumer automotive information (including dealer invoice prices) on the Internet. As word spread about the information Edmunds was posting, the volume of traffic on the Electronic Newsstand overwhelmed the site's capacity, and in 1995, Edmunds launched its own Web site, once again becoming the first automotive information site on the Web. Initially, Edmunds managers saw the Web site as a tool for marketing the company's print products, but they soon saw the power of the Web for transforming their entire business. Today, the Edmunds Web site contains more than 800,000 pages of information (which, unlike printed manuals, the company can update constantly) on a vast array of automotive topics, and more than 200,000 people a day visit it! The company still sells its information in print, but manuals account for less than 1 percent of its revenues. The immense volume of traffic the Edmunds site generates enables the company to provide automotive information free to users; Edmunds produces most of its $50 million in annual revenues by selling ads on its site to a wide variety of businesses targeting customers looking for automotive information.[26]*

The real key to Edmunds.com's success on the Web is the knowledge of collecting and publishing automotive information its managers and employees built over the years to which they then applied the technology of the Web. Unfortunately, too many entrepreneurs tackle e-commerce by focusing on technology first and then determine how that technology fits their business idea. "If you start with technology, you're likely to buy a solution in search of a problem," says Kip Martin, program director of META Group's Electronic Business Strategies. Instead, he suggests, "Start with the business and ask yourself what you want to happen and how you'll measure it. *Then* ask how the technology will help you achieve your goals. Remember: Business first, technology second."[27]

Myth 6. "Strategy? I Don't Need a Strategy to Sell on the Web! Just Give Me a Web Site, and the Rest Will Take Care of Itself."

Building a successful e-business is no different than building a successful brick-and-mortar business, and that requires a well-thought-out strategy. Building a strategy means that an entrepreneur must first develop a clear definition of the company's target audience and a thorough understanding of those customers' needs, wants, likes, and dislikes. To be successful, a Web site must be appealing to the customers it seeks to attract just as a traditional store's design and décor must draw foot traffic. If your Web site is to become the foundation for a successful e-business, you must create it with your target audience in mind.

A Company Example

In 1998, a group of real estate professionals launched **SafeRent**, *an online company aimed at helping landlords and apartment owners screen potential tenants. In addition to providing its customers access to standard credit reports and eviction histories, SafeRent uses a proprietary statistical model developed at Harvard University to give them a score for each potential tenant that predicts whether or not a particular rental agreement "will end happily for the landlord," says cofounder Linda Bush. Using information from rental applications that landlords enter on the company's Web site, SafeRent returns within 30 seconds a verdict on each potential tenant—accept, decline, or accept with conditions such as an additional deposit—for as little as $7.95 per search. Property managers nationwide use SafeRent services, generating more than $12 million in annual revenues for the company.*[28]

Myth 7. On the Web, Customer Service Is Not as Important as It Is in a Traditional Retail Store

Many Web sites treat customer service as an afterthought, and it shows. Sites that are difficult to navigate, slow to load, or confusing will turn customers away quickly, never to return. The fact is that customer service is just as important (if not more so) on the Web as it is in traditional brick-and-mortar stores.

There is plenty of room for improvement in customer service on the Web. Research by BizRate.com found that 75 percent of Web shoppers who fill their online shopping carts become frustrated and leave the site before checking out.[29] The most common reasons for leaving a site without purchasing include the following: (1) Customers could not find the items they were looking for, (2) the shopping cart was too hard to find, (3) checking out took too long, (4) the site did not look trustworthy, and (5) shipping charges were too high.[30]

In an attempt to improve the level of service they offer, many sites provide e-mail links to encourage customer interaction. Unfortunately, e-mail takes a very low priority at many e-businesses, a sign of poor customer service. One study by Jupiter Communications found that 42 percent of business Web sites took longer than five days to respond to e-mail inquiries, never replied at all, or simply were not accessible by e-mail![31] The lesson for e-commerce entrepreneurs is simple: Devote time, energy, and money to developing a functional mechanism for providing superior customer service. Those who do will build a sizable base of loyal customers who will keep coming back. Perhaps the most significant actions online companies can take to bolster their customer service efforts are creating a well-staffed and well-trained customer response team, offering a simple return process, and providing an easy order-tracking process so customers can check the status of their orders at any time. Establishing a policy of responding to all customer e-mails within 24 hours and sending customers order and shipping confirmations and "thank you for your order" e-mails can go a long way to enhancing online customer service. Amazon.com's 500-plus service representatives have access to a database that contains a customer's complete history with the company so they can serve customers faster and better. The database also keeps track of customers' purchase preferences and is the source of the site's ability to make customized product recommendations to shoppers.

Myth 8. Flash Makes a Web Site Better

Businesses that fall into this trap pour most of their e-commerce budgets into designing flashy Web sites with all of the "bells and whistles." The logic is that to stand out on the Web, a site really has to sparkle. That logic leads to a "more is better" mentality when designing a site. On the Web, however, "more" does *not* necessarily equate to "better."

*Rick Edler, owner of the **Edler Group**, a California real estate company, learned this lesson the hard way. Edler's first foray onto the Web was a simple site, one that followed the "electronic flyer" approach and cost just $285. A confessed gadget freak, Edler soon decided to revamp his company's site to incorporate lots of features and lots of flash. "We were going to dazzle everyone with all of the technology," he recalls. The site, which cost $7,000 to design, literally pulsed with color and motion as spinning graphics moved around the screen. It even included movie listings. But the site was a failure, never drawing much traffic at all. The busy design with all of its features meant that the site was very slow to download. "You just stared at it like you were watching a commercial," says Edler. "We were scaring people away." Edler quickly scrapped the site and for $2,000 built a much simpler one that allows buyers to get the details on a listing and take a video tour of a house. The site also includes links to other useful real estate pages. Customer response to the newly designed site (www.edlergroup.com) has been positive, and more importantly, the site is now helping realtors close sales.*[32]

Keep the design of your site simple. Although fancy graphics, bright colors, playful music, and spinning icons can attract attention, they also can be quite distracting, and, as Rick Edler learned, very slow to download.

Myth 9. It's What's Up Front That Counts

Designing an attractive Web site is important to building a successful e-business. However, designing the back office, the systems that take over once a customer places an order on a Web site, is just as important as designing the site itself. If the behind-the-scenes support is not in place or cannot handle the traffic from the Web site, a company's entire e-commerce effort will come crashing down. The potentially large number of orders that a Web site can generate can overwhelm a small company that has failed to establish the infrastructure needed to support the site. Although e-commerce can lower many costs of doing business, it still requires a basic infrastructure in the channel of distribution to process orders, maintain inventory, fill orders, and handle customer service. Many entrepreneurs hoping to launch virtual businesses are discovering the need for a "clicks-and-mortar" approach to provide the necessary infrastructure to serve their customers. "The companies with warehouses, supply-chain management, and solid customer service are going to be the ones that survive," says Daryl Plummer, head of the Gartner Group's Internet and new media division.[33]

To customers, a business is only as good as its last order, and many e-companies are not measuring up. One study suggests that only 30 percent of e-commerce Web sites feature real-time inventory lookup, which gives online shoppers the ability to see if an item they want to purchase is actually in stock.[34] In addition, only 7 percent of Web sites are linked to the back office.[35] These figures will increase as software to integrate Web sites with the back office becomes easier to use and more affordable, but in the meantime customers will have to endure late shipments, incorrect orders, and poor service.

Web-based entrepreneurs often discover that the greatest challenge their businesses face is not necessarily attracting customers on the Web but creating a workable order fulfillment strategy. Order fulfillment involves everything required to get goods from a warehouse into a customer's hands and includes order processing, warehousing, picking and packing, shipping, and billing. In a study of the connection between online companies' order fulfillment processes and their ultimate success or failure, researchers Sergui Netessine, Taylor Randall, and Nels Rudi found an important link. They concluded "that if an Internet company chooses its supply chain type logically—if it's aligned with its strategy, products, and operating environment—it's highly correlated with success."[36]

Some entrepreneurs choose to handle order fulfillment in-house with their own employees, whereas others find it more economical to hire specialized fulfillment houses to handle these functions. Virtual order fulfillment (or drop-shipping) suits many e-tailers perfectly. When a customer orders a product from its Web site, the company forwards the order to its wholesaler or distributor, who then ships the product to the customer with the online merchant's label on it.

***Spun.com**, an online CD retailer, has managed to generate a profit without incurring the expense of an estimated $8 million investment in inventory by using wholesale distributor Alliance Entertainment as its virtual order fulfillment source. Founded in 1998 by brothers Andrew and Steven Gundy, Spun.com also operates a music exchange, in which customers can trade used CDs, DVDs, and video games for online credit toward the purchase of new or used items.*[37]

Although e-tailers avoid the major problems that managing inventory presents, they lose control over delivery times and service quality. Also, finding a fulfillment house willing to handle a relatively small volume of orders at a reasonable price can be difficult for some small businesses, however. Major fulfillment providers include Federal Express, UPS, NewRoads, and NFI Interactive.

Myth 10. E-Commerce Will Cause Brick-and-Mortar Retail Stores to Disappear

The rapid growth of e-commerce does pose a serious threat to traditional retailers, especially those who fail to find ways to capitalize on the opportunities the Web offers them. However, it is unlikely that Web-based shopping will replace customers' need and desire to visit real stores selling real merchandise that they can see, touch, and try on. Some products simply lend themselves to selling in real stores more naturally than in online shops. For instance, furniture stores and supermarkets have struggled for success online. On the other hand, other items, particularly standard commodity products for which customers have little loyalty, are ideally suited for online sales. Virtual stores will continue to drive out of existence some traditional companies that resist creating new business models or are too slow to change. To remain competitive, traditional brick-and-mortar stores must find ways to blend their operations with an online presence to become click-and-mortar businesses that can make the convenience, the reach, and the low transaction costs of the Web work for them.

A Company Example

Jim McCann built a successful chain of 14 flower shops in New York and in 1986 bought the rights to the 1800-FLOWERS telephone number as part of his expansion plans. In 1992, McCann became one of the first retailers to go online, and in 1995, he launched the 1800flowers.com Web site. Today, his company, which has expanded into gourmet foods, candy, baskets, and unique gifts, has one of the most recognized brands in the gift retailing industry. Because physical locations give a brand more visibility and attract customers who do not shop online, McCann continues to add locations to the company's network of 120 stores and more than 40,000 affiliates across the United States. 1800flowers.com's network of physical stores and its ubiquitous Web presence make it a fierce competitor in the flower and gift industry.[38]

Myth 11. The Greatest Opportunities for E-Commerce Lie in the Retail Sector

As impressive as the growth rate and total volume for online retail sales are, they are dwarfed by those in the online business-to-business (B2B) sector, where businesses sell to one another rather than to retail customers. eMarketer estimates that global business-to-business e-commerce sales now total nearly $2 trillion.[39] That volume of sales is nearly seven times the amount of business-to-consumer e-commerce! Entrepreneurs who are looking to sell goods to other businesses on the Web will find plenty of opportunities available in a multitude of industries.

Business-to-business e-commerce is growing so rapidly because of its potential to boost productivity, slash costs, and increase profits. This brand of e-commerce is transforming the way companies purchase parts, supplies, and materials as well as the way they manage inventory and process transactions. The Web's power to increase the speed and the efficiency of the purchasing function represents a fundamental departure from the past. Experts estimate that transferring purchasing to the Web can cut total procurement costs by 10 percent and transaction costs by as much as 90 percent.[40] For instance, Chris Cogan, CEO of an Internet purchasing site for hotels, restaurants, and health care companies, explains, "We estimate [that] the average cost of executing a paper purchase order is $115." Businesses using his company's Web-based purchasing system "get that cost down to $10," he says.[41]

Business-to-business e-commerce is growing because of the natural link that exists with business-to-consumer e-commerce. As we have seen, one of the greatest challenges Web-based retailers face is obtaining and delivering the goods their customers order fast enough to satisfy customers' expectations. Increasingly, Web-based companies are connecting their front office sales systems and their back-office purchasing and order fulfillment systems with those of their suppliers. The result is a faster, more efficient method of filling customer orders. So far the most successful online business-to-business companies are those that have discovered ways of tying their front offices, their back offices, their suppliers, and their customers together into a single, smoothly functioning, Web-based network.

YOU Be the Consultant . . .

Changing the Rules of the Game

In 1997, Andrew Field had grown tired of the auto repair shop he owned, so he sold it and bought a print shop in tiny Livingston, Montana, that primarily served businesses in nearby Bozeman and Billings. His personal sales calls boosted revenues to about $80,000 a month, but no matter how hard he tried, he could not get past that sales plateau. The problem was that Express Color Printing was just breaking even at that point and generated no profit. Field was frustrated that he couldn't keep his high-cost presses in operation; every hour of downtime meant lost revenue for his business. "When a plane takes off with empty seats, that's revenue lost forever," Field explains. "Same thing if I have employees standing around and no jobs scheduled for three hours."

One day while fishing in the Yellowstone River, Field thought about the problem his printing business faced with idle press time. He realized that his was not the only printing company to have that problem. Then an idea struck him. Why not use the Web to pool the idle time on his presses with that of other printing companies and then sell it to customers who needed a last-minute print job? The Web would be the ideal way to provide a marketplace for these buyers and sellers of printing services.

In March 1999, Field launched a Web site, Printingforless.com, to handle all types of color printing jobs—from simple business cards to full-color brochures and posters. Field's Web site eliminates the complexity, inconvenience, and much of the time required in the typical design and printing process. The site allows customers to control the printing process from start to finish. Customers can read design tips and then submit electronic files containing their printing jobs through the Web site, whether they are for existing company stationery or for a new advertising brochure created in Microsoft Publisher. Capitalizing on the desktop publishing revolution, Printingforless.com accepts files in practically any format, including all Microsoft, Adobe, and Quark applications, among others. The site is surprisingly simple and intentionally does not overwhelm users with lots of sophisticated design techniques. "We're not trying to be fancy or entertaining," Field explains. "We want it to be a practical tool for business people." Everything a customer needs to place an order—designing process, pricing calculator, shipping information, project details, and payment information—appears on one page! "Printers don't like to publish prices," says Field. "We got hate mail [from competitors] when we started pricing online." Customers, however, love it. Within two days of submitting a printing job, production teams send customers an e-mail that includes a project number and a link to a proof of their projects so they can view it online. Once customers approve their proofs, the site takes them to a scheduling page that displays a calendar showing the shipping and delivery dates.

It is at this point that the genius of Field's idea takes hold. Like the airline industry, Printingforless.com actually books more jobs than its presses can handle. A Web-based service Field designed called PFL-Net attempts to schedule jobs on a Printingforless.com press first. If those presses are booked, the system makes the job available to other printers over the Web. Other affiliated printers handle their jobs in the same fashion so Field can accept one of their overflow orders if his presses are not busy. The process involves no bidding; printing partners simply log onto the site, accept a job, download the necessary files, and then handle the printing and shipping from their own plants. The entire process is invisible to customers.

With the help of PFL-Net, the Printingforless.com Web site now generates 95 percent of the company's revenues, far surpassing the amount the physical storefront produces. "Even our local customers decided they liked the Web better," says Field, whose Web-based strategy has proved to be a huge success. The site attracts more than 7,000 visitors on an average day and brings in 30 new customers a day. Company sales total $8 to $9 million a year and continue to grow. Typical of an entrepreneur's response to a challenge, Field's innovative idea of using the Web to save his business has transformed the way the printing industry operates.

1. Would Field's strategy for handling excess capacity be feasible without the Web? Explain.

2. In what ways does the Web enable Field's strategy to be successful?

3. Visit the Printingforless.com Web site. Does the site accomplish its goal of making the process simple for customers? Explain. Can you make any suggestions for improving the site's design?

Sources: Leigh Buchanan and Anne Stuart, "Printing Money," *Inc.*, December 2002, p. 74; Carole Matthews, "Printing for the Masses," *Inc.*, December 2, 2002, www.inc.com/articles/cust_serv/24898.html; Rich Karlgaard, "The Medium Is the Model," *Forbes*, September 30, 2002, p. 43; Printingforless.com, www.printingforless.com/press.html.

Myth 12. It's Too Late to Get on the Web

A common myth, especially among small companies, is that those businesses that have not yet moved onto the Web have missed a golden opportunity. E-commerce is still in its infancy. Companies are still figuring out how to succeed on the Web, learning which techniques work and which ones don't. For every e-commerce site that exists, a trio of others has failed. An abundance of business opportunities exists for those entrepreneurs insightful enough to spot them and clever enough to capitalize on them.

One fact of e-commerce that has emerged is the importance of speed. Companies doing business on the Web have discovered that those who reach customers first often have a significant advantage over their slower rivals. "The lesson of the Web is not how the big eat the small, but how the fast eat the slow," says a manager at a venture capital firm specializing in Web-based companies.[42]

Succumbing to this myth often leads entrepreneurs to make a fundamental mistake once they finally decide to go online: They believe they have to have a "perfect" site before they can launch it. Few businesses get their sites "right" the first time. In fact, the most successful e-commerce sites are constantly changing, removing what does not work and adding new features to see what does. Successful Web sites are much like a well-designed flower garden, constantly growing and improving, yet changing to reflect the climate of each season. Their creators worry less about creating the perfect site at the outset than about getting a site online and then fixing it, tweaking it, and updating it to meet changing customer demands. "The person trying to create the perfect (online) store will fail," says Gerry Goldsholle, founder of two Web sites aimed at small companies. "Part of the Internet process is 'try it, learn from it, and fix it.' Delay is your biggest enemy. If you delay, someone else will do it."[43]

APPROACHES TO E-COMMERCE

Learning Objective
4. Discuss the five basic approaches available to entrepreneurs wanting to launch an e-commerce effort.

A successful e-commerce effort requires much more than merely launching a Web site; entrepreneurs must develop a plan for integrating the Web into their overall business strategy. Many entrepreneurs choose to start their e-commerce efforts small and simply and then expand them as sales grow and their needs become more sophisticated. Others make major investments in creating full-blown, interconnected sites at the outset. The cost of setting up a Web site varies significantly, depending on which options an entrepreneur chooses. Generally, Web experts identify three basic pricing categories for creating a Web site: less than $10,000, between $10,000 and $30,000; and more than $30,000. When it comes to choosing an approach to e-commerce, there are no "right" or "wrong" answers; the key is creating a plan that fits into the small company's budget and meets its e-commerce needs as it grows and expands. Entrepreneurs looking to launch an e-commerce effort have five basic choices: (1) online shopping malls, (2) storefront-building services, (3) Internet service providers (ISPs), (4) hiring professionals to design a custom site, and (5) building a site in-house.

Online Shopping Malls

In the under $10,000 category, the simplest way for entrepreneurs to get their businesses online is to rent space for their products at an online shopping mall (also called a shopping portal). Online shopping malls are the equivalent of an electronic strip mall because they list on one site the product offerings from many different small companies. The primary advantages they offer are their simplicity and their low cost. To join an online mall, entrepreneurs simply provide descriptions and photographs of the products they sell. For a low monthly fee, the mall creates and maintains a virtual storefront for the company and funnels customer orders from it to the company.

The major disadvantages of using an online shopping mall are an individual store's lack of prominence and the lack of control entrepreneurs have over their sites. Most malls host dozens of businesses in a multitude of industries, and standing out in the crowd can be a challenge because all of the sites follow a similar (or the same) design. In addition, some malls are much more effective than others at promoting their resident businesses.

Storefront-Building Services

Also in the under $10,000 category are storefront-building services that help entrepreneurs create online shops that include features such as Web-hosting services, the ability to handle secure credit card transactions, databases for order fulfillment and customer tracking, advertising placement, and search engine registration—all for as little as $100 to $500 per month. Some storefront-building services offer to handle a limited number of transactions for free, although most businesses quickly outgrow the free service and end up paying the service the monthly fee for site hosting and operation. Most Internet portals such as Yahoo! (www.store.yahoo.com) and e-commerce service companies, such as FreeMerchant.com (www.freemerchant.com), Microsoft's bcentral.com (www.bcentral.com), Interland (www.interland.com), Bigstep.com (www.bigstep.com), or BizLand.com (www.bizland.com), offer these e-commerce services.

The major advantages of using these storefront-building services is their simplicity and their low cost. Setting up a store can take as little as a few hours, and the hosting company shoulders the burden of setting up and running the cyberstore, creating minimal headaches for the entrepreneur behind it. The downside of these services is that most of their sites look as though they came out of the same cookie-cutter approach because they rely on a limited number of templates to create store sites. It is extremely difficult to make a company's Web store stand out when every storefront is stamped from the same mold. Plus, most services limit the number of products they will handle at the base price on these sites to just 50 to 100.

Despite its drawbacks, using a storefront-building service offers a fast and easy way to create a virtual store that is open 24 hours a day, seven days a week.

A Company Example

After trying on his own for several months to set up an online store selling wines and spirits, George Randall turned to Yahoo! Store for help. He selected backgrounds and graphics from Yahoo! Store's templates, answered questions about the items he would sell and how he wanted them shipped, and soon had his virtual store, **Internet Wines & Spirits** *(www.internetwines.com) up and running. Each day, as many as 7,000 customers from all over the world visit the company's site, which now sells more than 3,000 items and generates one-third of the company's sales. "Overnight we became an international company," says Randall, noting that Internet Wines & Spirits routinely gets orders from Europe and the Far East.*[44]

Internet Service Providers and Application Service Providers

Another e-commerce option in the under $10,000 category is using an Internet service provider (ISP) or an application service provider (ASP) to create an online store. ISPs and ASPs provide many of the same features as storefront-design services except they offer their small business customers more design flexibility and the ability to customize their Web sites. ISP packages such as MindSpring Complete Commerce or VerioStore are not as easy to use as the templates from storefront-design services and typically require the entrepreneurs using them to know some basics of the hypertext markup language (HTML) used to design most Web sites. Although most ISPs provide basic design templates, experienced HTML users can modify them easily. ISP templates usually include shopping cart and catalog features as well as order and payment processing and report generation capabilities. ASPs' packages provide these same features. However, rather than requiring users to purchase e-commerce software, ASPs "rent" a variety of e-commerce applications, from site building and hosting to purchasing automation and accounting, to their customers on an as-needed basis.

In addition to hosting and running a company's virtual store, ISPs offer the ability to grow with a small company as its online store's sales volume climbs. Most base their fees on the number of visitors a site attracts and the amount of space it takes up on their server, so start-up stores offering a small product line can spend as little as $100 a month plus initial setup costs. Before choosing an ISP, entrepreneurs should investigate its operating history (specifically the amount of downtime the provider has experienced), the quality of its backup systems (in case of a crash), and its remaining capacity for hosting sites.

A Company Example

When Mike Dubelko launched his online store, **DVD.com,** *in 1996, ISPs were relatively expensive, so Dubelko and his staff created and managed their own small, simple Web site (www.dvd.com). Within six months, however, orders for the movies, games, and music the com-*

pany sold on the site shot up from just 50 per week to more than 2,000 per week, and the system Dubelko and his staff had built could not handle the volume. "We were totally overwhelmed," he recalls. "Our success was killing us." Dubelko located an ISP that could create a site capable of capturing and processing the thousands of orders the site generated. The redesigned site allowed customers to check the availability of any DVD and to track the status of their orders online. Today more than 100,000 online visitors browse through DVD Express's inventory of movies, music, and games each day.[45]

Hiring Professionals to Design a Custom Site

Businesses able to spend between $10,000 and $30,000 can afford to hire professionals to create their sites. The primary benefit this option offers is the unlimited ability to customize a site, making it anything an entrepreneur wants, including complete front-office and back-office integration. Just like building a custom-designed house, hiring professionals to design a site from the ground up gives entrepreneurs a high degree of control over the final result. Also, most Web development companies offer complete e-commerce solutions, including consulting and design services, Web hosting, site registration, and listings with search engines and directories.

A Company Example

*For most of its 32-year history, the **Lucas Group's** (an executive search firm) only technological investments were a telephone and a fax machine; the company did not get PCs until late in 1998! Recruiters kept their contact information in desktop Rolodex files and stored candidates' résumés in manila folders. When he arrived in 2000, managing partner Alex Baxter found that no one in the company was resisting the Web. "They just ignored it," he says. Recognizing that the company had fallen far behind its competition, Baxter hired a professional team to build a Web site and an easy-to-use in-house database. Now candidates can upload their résumés electronically to the company's Web site, which automatically routes them to the proper recruiter. Since going live in July 2000, the Web site has attracted more than 1,000 new corporate clients and has generated nearly $7 million in new revenues for the executive search firm!*[46]

Because custom-built sites require custom programming, they are much more expensive to create than sites based on preformatted templates. The Gartner Group estimates that building and launching an e-commerce site with complete front-office and back-office integration now costs more than $500,000![47] Expenses in that range are out of the question for most e-commerce entrepreneurs just starting out, and many small companies run their Web sites quite successfully without front-to-back integration.

Building a Web Site In-House

Building a Web site in-house gives an entrepreneur complete control over the site and its design, operation, and maintenance. However, hiring and supporting an in-house staff of Web designers can quickly run up the cost of creating and maintaining a custom Web site into the $250,000 to $500,000 range. Because of the high costs involved in hiring professional Web development companies or in maintaining a staff of Web designers, most entrepreneurs wanting to establish a Web presence do so by using either online shopping malls, storefront-building services, or Internet service providers.

STRATEGIES FOR E-SUCCESS

Learning Objective

5. Explain the basic strategies entrepreneurs should follow to achieve success in their e-commerce efforts.

The average Web user spends an average of 5 hours and 52 minutes online each week. Across a lifetime, the average baby boomer will spend 5 years and 6 months online; the average Generation Xer will spend 9 years and 11 months online; and the average Generation Y user will spend 23 years and 2 months online, almost one-third of a lifetime[48] However, converting these Web surfers into online customers requires a business to do more than merely set up a Web site and wait for the hits to start rolling up. You may be ready to sell, but no one knows you are there! Building sufficient volume for a site takes energy, time, money, creativity, and, perhaps most importantly, a well-defined marketing and promotional strategy. One business writer explains, "[Success in e-commerce] isn't glamorous at all. The difference between Web success and Web failure often hinges on how carefully people sift through details and fine-tune niggling plans. E businesses that actually get it . . . understand how to use the Web to push the envelope, to create new tools and business models."[49]

Although the Web is a unique medium for creating a company, launching an e-business is not much different from launching a traditional off-line company. The basic drivers of a successful business remain in place on the Web as well as on Main Street. To be successful, both off-line and online companies require solid planning and a well-formulated strategy that emphasizes customer service. The goals of e-commerce are no different from traditional off-line businesses—to increase sales, improve efficiency, and boost profits by serving customers better.

A Company Example

*When longtime friends Mike Morford, Blaine Donnelson, and Shannon Stowell launched **Altrec.com** (pronounced "all trek") in 1999, they saw an opportunity to create "an outdoor lifestyle destination Web site that brings together everything necessary for individuals to satisfy their passion for the outdoors." The online retailer sells outdoor gear from more than 300 of the world's top makers of clothing and accessories on a Web site built around "passion points" ranging from camping and fly fishing to snowboarding and mountain climbing. The site makes shopping extremely easy for customers with detailed product information, product comparison and sizing charts, 360-degree product views that offer a zoom option, customer product reviews, and many other features. Not only can customers buy equipment at Altrec.com, but they also can book trips to exotic locations, peruse photo galleries and diaries from traveling journalists, and even find locations for getting their outdoor equipment repaired. Customer service representatives provide around-the-clock assistance, answer questions, and can even guide customers (by taking long-distance control of their Web browsers) to the correct pages on the site! Altrec's unparalleled combination of product selection, superb customer service, and convenience has produced dramatic growth rates for the company; more than 600,000 guests visit its Web site each month.[50]*

How a company integrates the Web into its overall business strategy determines how successful it ultimately will become. Following are some guidelines for building a successful Web strategy for a small e-company.

Consider Focusing on a Niche in the Market

Rather than try to compete head-to-head with the dominant players on the Web who have the resources and the recognition to squash smaller competitors, entrepreneurs should consider focusing on serving a market niche. Smaller companies' limited resources usually are better spent serving niche markets than trying to be everything to everyone (recall the discussion of the focus strategy in Chapter 3). The idea is to concentrate on serving a small corner of the market the giants have overlooked. Niches exist in every industry and can be highly profitable, given the right strategy for serving them. A niche can be defined in many ways, including by geography, by customer profile, by product, by product usage, and many others.

The Web provides an ideal mechanism for reaching niche customers.

A Company Example

*For instance, **Dogbooties.com** reaches around the globe to find customers who own sled dogs, hunting dogs, dogs with tender feet, or who simply want their dogs to be on the cutting edge of fashion. In addition to dog booties, the company, founded in 1995 by copreneurs Louise and Greg Russell, sells other dog-related accessories. "The Internet allows us to reach all over the world inexpensively," says Greg.[51]*

A Company Example

*Chris Gwynn also focuses on a niche market with his company, **Fridgedoor.com**, which he bills as "the Web's magnet store." From Quincy, Massachusetts, Gwynn sells novelty and custom-designed refrigerator magnets. Customers looking for refrigerator magnets can find virtually any design from Betty Boop to the Virgin Mary.[52]*

As these two small companies prove, the Web, because of its broad reach, is the ideal mechanism for implementing a focus strategy because small companies can reach large numbers of customers with a common interest.

Develop a Community

On the Web, competitors are just a mouse click away. To attract customers and keep them coming back, e-companies have discovered the need to offer more than just quality products and excellent customer service. Many seek to develop a community of customers with similar interests, the nucleus of which is their Web site. The idea is to increase customer loyalty by giving customers the chance to interact with other like-minded visitors or with experts to discuss and learn more about topics they are passionate about. "It's not going to be a direct revenue source," says Howard Rheingold, author of The Virtual Community. "But it may offer you insight for creating new products. It may help you establish better relationships and more loyalty with your customers."[53]

E-mail lists, chat rooms, customer polls ("What is your favorite sports drink?"), Web logs (or blogs, regularly updated online journals), guest books, and message boards are powerful tools for building a community of visitors at a site because they give visitors the opportunity to have conversations about products, services, and topics that interest them.

Jim Coudal, founder of Coudal Partners Inc., a Chicago-based advertising agency, has relied on a Web log to attract customers from around the globe and to build a stellar reputation for creative ads since 1999. In addition to interesting text, Coudal's blog includes eye-catching photographs, links to articles on everything from advertising history to famous film directors, and information about the latest trends in advertising. Updated twice a day by one of the company's eight employees, the blog attracts 12,000 visitors to the site each week—and the company has never had to purchase an ad![54]

A Company Example

Like Coudal Partners, companies that successfully create a community around their Web sites turn mere customers into loyal fans who keep coming back and, better yet, invite others to join them.

Attract Visitors by Giving Away "Freebies"

One of the most important words on the Internet is *free*. Many successful e-merchants have discovered the ability to attract visitors to their site by giving away something free and then selling them something else. One e-commerce consultant calls this cycle of giving something away and then selling something "the rhythm of the Web."[55] The "freebie" must be something customers value, but it does *not* have to be expensive nor does it have to be a product. In fact, one of the most common giveaways on the Web is *information*. (After all, that's what most people on the Web are after!) Creating a free online or e-mail newsletter with links to your company's site, of course, and to others of interest is one of the most effective ways of driving potential customers to a site. Meaningful content presented in a clear, professional fashion is a must. Experts advise keeping online newsletters short—no more than about 600 words. Although HTML newsletters offer more eye-catching design options, 80 percent of all e-newsletters are in plain text to accommodate the large number of people whose e-mail software cannot display HTML.[56] *Poor Richard's E-Mail Publishing* by Chris Pirillo (Top Floor Publishing) offers much useful advice on creating online newsletters.

To attract customers to its travel planning Web site, Smarter Living offers customers travel tips and advice, articles filled with useful information, and a free newsletter that arrives at the end of each week and features a "deal alert," which details last-minute travel specials the company has discovered.

A Company Example

Make Creative Use of E-Mail, but Avoid Becoming a "Spammer"

Used properly and creatively, e-mail can be an effective, low-cost way to build traffic on a Web site. Just as with a newsletter, the e-mail's content should offer something of value to recipients. Supported by online newsletters or chat rooms, customers welcome well-constructed permission e-mail that directs them to a company's site for information or special deals, unlike unsolicited and universally despised e-mails known as "spam." More than 30 billion e-mails are sent worldwide each day, and more than 25 percent of them are spam![57]

To avoid having their marketing messages become part of that electronic clutter, companies should collect visitors' e-mail addresses when they register on a site to receive a "freebie." To be successful at collecting a sufficient number of e-mail addresses, a company must make clear to customers that they will receive messages that are meaningful to them and that the company will not sell e-mail addresses to others (which should be part of its posted privacy policy). Once a business has a customer's permission to send information in additional e-mail messages, it has a meaningful marketing opportunity to create a long-term customer relationship. For example, Ticketmaster, which sells 75 million tickets to concerts and performances each year, e-mails its customers the play lists from the most recent concert they attended along with an offer to purchase a concert T-shirt.[58]

Make Sure Your Web Site Says "Credibility"

As we learned earlier in this chapter, nearly two-thirds of customers do not trust Web sites. Unless a company can build trust in its Web site, selling is virtually impossible. A study by Princeton Survey Research Associates found that 80 percent of Web users say that being able to trust the information on a Web site is important.[59] Visitors begin to evaluate the credibility of a site as soon as they arrive. Does the site look professional? Are there misspelled words and typographical errors? If the site provides information, does it note the sources of that information? If so, are those sources legitimate? Are they trustworthy? Is the presentation of the information fair and objective, or is it biased? Does the company include a privacy policy posted in an obvious place?

One of the simplest ways to establish credibility with customers is to use brand names they know and trust. Whether a company sells nationally recognized brands or its own well-known private brand, using those names on its site creates a sense of legitimacy. People buy brand names they trust, and online companies can use that to their advantage. Businesses selling less well-known brands should use customer testimonials and endorsements (with their permission, of course) about a product or service.

Another effective way to build customer confidence is by joining an online seal program such as TRUSTe or BBBOnLine. The online equivalent of the Underwriter Laboratories stamp or the Good Housekeeping Seal of Approval, these seals mean that a company meets certain standards concerning the privacy of customers' information and the resolution of customer complaints. Providing a street address, an e-mail address, and a toll-free telephone number sends a subtle message to shoppers that a legitimate business is behind a Web site. Many small companies include photographs of their brick-and-mortar stores and of their employees to combat the Web's anonymity and to give shoppers the feeling that they are supporting a friendly small business. One small online retailer includes on his Web site short anecdotes about his dog, Cody, the official company mascot, and Cody's "views" on featured products. The response to the technique has been so strong that Cody has become a celebrity among the company's customers and has her own e-mail address.

Consider Forming Strategic Alliances

Most small companies engaged in e-commerce lack the brand and name recognition that larger, more established companies have. Creating that sort of recognition on the Web requires a significant investment of both time and money, two factors that most small companies find scarce. If building name recognition is one of the keys to success on the Web, how can small companies with their limited resources hope to compete? One option is to form strategic alliances with bigger companies that can help a small business achieve what it could not accomplish alone. Describing the need for small companies to consider forming strategic alliances, Philip Anderson of Dartmouth's Tuck School of Business says, "You need to build [market] share fast, and that means you have to have more resources than you can get your mitts on by yourself."[60]

Before plunging into a strategic alliance with a larger partner, however, entrepreneurs must understand their dark side. Research shows that 55 percent of strategic alliances unravel within three-and-a-half years.[61] The most common reasons for splitting up? One study found the following causes: incompatible corporate cultures (75 percent), incompatible management personalities (63 percent), and differences in strategic priorities (58 percent).[62]

TABLE 7.2

Questions to Ask *Before* Entering a Strategic Alliance

Reprinted by permission of Entrepreneur Media, Inc., February 2002, pg. 79, www.entrepreneur.com

Source: Robert McGarvey, "Made for Each Other?" *Entrepreneur,* February 2000, p. 79.

Unfortunately, most strategic alliances fail. In his book, *Partnering Intelligence: Creating Value for Your Business by Building Strong Alliances* (Davies-Black Publishing), Stephen M. Dent offers seven questions every entrepreneur should ask *before* forging an alliance.

1. What is your potential partner's business vision?

2. What are its strategies to achieve its vision?

3. Where does it want to go as a company?

4. What are its values and ethics?

5. What kind of corporate culture does it have?

6. What types of relationships and partnerships does it already have and how well are they working out?

7. Has it conducted an internal assessment of its strengths, weaknesses, and culture?

Based on the answers to these seven questions, entrepreneurs can assess how compatible potential partners are with their own business vision and goals.

Table 7.2 offers seven questions every entrepreneur should ask before entering into a strategic alliance with a partner.

Make the Most of the Web's Global Reach

Despite the Web's reputation as an international marketplace, many Web entrepreneurs fail to utilize fully its global reach. Approximately 665 million people around the world use the Internet, and almost 75 percent of them live outside the United States![63] Only 43 percent of Web users throughout the world speak English, and that percentage is declining. Limiting a global market to only a small portion of its potential by ignoring foreign customers makes little sense.

A Company Example

*When Lisa and Paul Beckham launched **BackWoods Grocery**, an online food and outdoor cookware site, they had no intentions of taking international orders because they thought dealing with tariffs, duties, and customs issues would be too complicated. An order from an English-speaking customer in Switzerland soon changed their minds, however. Lisa Beckham visited the U.S. Postal Service Web site to learn about shipping details and then let the customer (who paid the shipping charges) decide which method to use. To avoid the risks of currency fluctuations, Beckham accepted credit card payment in U.S. dollars only, and the customer's credit card issuer made the conversion. Today, BackWoods Grocery encourages foreign orders from Web customers; foreign sales account for just 2 percent of revenues but are growing fast.[64]*

E-companies wanting to draw significant sales from foreign markets must design their sites with these foreign customers in mind. A common mechanism is to include several "language buttons" on the opening page of a site that take customers to pages in the language of their choice. Experienced e-commerce companies have learned that offering a localized page for every country or region they target pays off in increased sales.

Virtual companies trying to establish a foothold in foreign markets by setting up Web sites dedicated to them run the same risk that actual companies do: offending international visitors by using the business conventions and standards they are accustomed to using in the United States. Business practices, even those used on the Web, that are acceptable, even expected, in the United States may be taboo in other countries. Color schemes can be important, too. Selecting the "wrong" colors and symbols on a site targeting people in a particular country can hurt sales and offend visitors. For example, in the United States and Asia, the "thumbs-up" gesture indicates a positive result, but in Europe and Latin America, it is an obscene gesture! A little research into the subtleties of a target country's culture and business practices can save a great deal of embarrassment and money! Creating secure, simple, and reliable payment methods for foreign customers also will boost sales.

When translating the content of their Web pages into other languages, e-companies must use extreme caution. This is *not* the time to pull out their notes from an introductory Spanish course

YOU Be the Consultant . . .

Two Companies That Get It Right

FROM THE TOP OF THE WORLD . . .

Earth Treks, a small company offering professional guide services and experiences for mountain and ice climbs, has found a way to keep customers returning frequently to its Web site (www.earthtreksclimbing.com): It takes them on climbs to exotic locations such as Ecuador's Cotopaxi volcano or to the most challenging summit in the world, the 29,035-foot peak of Mt. Everest. Company guides on these semiannual expeditions use laptop computers and satellite connections to post daily to the Web e-mail journals, digital photographs, and streaming video of their climbs, and climbing enthusiasts from all over the world log on to get the latest updates. Someone who has never been on a climb, especially one as difficult as ascending Mt. Everest, cannot really imagine what it is like, but Earth Treks does everything it can to make the experience real. On a recent excursion he led to Everest, company founder Chris Warner posted the following accounts:

May 23
I pulled myself up the last of this rock pitch and there, a rise or two above me, was the summit. 100 feet away, an undulating crest . . . I made it to the top just past 10 A.M., and searched for a place to sit down. Naoki handed me his camera and I snapped some photos of him. Clouds were hiding much of the view, but Lhotse looked incredible, with the Lhotse Coulior rising straight up the black face. Makalu was capped by clouds as was Cho Oyu . . .

May 26
Hey guys. Yes we did have a near disaster on our hands, and I did find myself in the unusual situation of spending two long days at 27,400 feet crying and weakening and hoping and working hard to find a way to keep hope and progress alive. I will write about it soon, but right now, my body and mind are not quite in the same place.

As many as 50,000 visitors logged onto the company's Web site the day Warner reached the summit of Mt. Everest. Earth Treks' Web-based marketing strategy has much to do with the fact that its revenues have doubled in just two years and continue to grow rapidly. Devoted climbers are fascinated by the online journals and pictures posted there and often book a climb with Earth Treks, but the site sends a clear message to visitors: If you are into climbing, whether as a hobby or as a serious obsession, this site is for you! The unique online experience creates a sense of community among Earth Treks' customers that many other companies find so elusive. The company is now receiving record numbers of requests from serious climbers who want to scale the world's most challenging summits.

An Earth Treks customer takes on one of the company's indoor climbing walls.

Courtesy of Earth Treks, Inc.

Earth Treks also is using its Web site to cultivate its next generation of customers. With the help of two local teachers, Warner started Shared Summits, a program in which students from ages 6 to 18 can follow climbers' adventures and learn about different countries, climates, geography, and cultures as well as about leadership and teamwork, and earn school credit. Due to the success of the program, the company now hosts kids' birthday parties and has record enrollment in its Youth Rox program, which trains youngsters the basics of climbing on its indoor climbing walls.

The Earth Treks' Web site has returned many times over the original $3,000 Warner spent to create it and the $7,200 a year he spends to maintain it.

. . . TO THE GOURMET'S KITCHEN.

Spencer Chesman, founder of one of the first gourmet food sites on the Web, has built a highly successful, multimillion-dollar business aimed at gourmands everywhere. Launched in 1997, from Yorktown Heights, New York, iGourmet is more than a one-stop shop for exotic foods; it has become a gourmet food *authority*. On its Web site (www.igourmet.com), customers can see large color pictures of every product and read complete descriptions as they shop. A recipe section and a "related items" button help customers find everything they need and boost sales of complementary products. Shoppers can browse the wine and cheese tastings iGourmet sponsors across the country, can sign up for a regularly published e-newsletter, get tips for hosting a party, and even read selections from the *Encyclopedia of Cheese*!

Those searching for just the right gift can use the iGourmet Gift Finder, which allows them to select a price range, and then the site pops up a few pages of gift suggestions in that range. Because many of the items it ships around the world are perishable, iGourmet developed a special foam-lined shipping chest that keeps items cool for up to 48 hours. Just in case, the company offers a 100 percent guaranteed return policy. If a customer is dissatisfied with any product from iGourmet, the company will refund the full purchase price within five business days. It's no

and begin their own translations. Hiring professional translation and localization services to convert a company's Web content into other languages minimizes the likelihood of a company unintentionally offending foreign customers.

Promote Your Web Site Online and Off-Line

E-commerce entrepreneurs have to use every means available—both online and off-line—to promote their Web sites and to drive traffic to them. In addition to using traditional online techniques such as registering with search engines, creating banner ads, and joining banner exchange programs, Web entrepreneurs must promote their sites off-line as well. Ads in other media such as direct mail or newspapers that mention a site's URL will bring customers to it. It is also a good idea to put the company's Web address on *everything* a company publishes, from its advertisements and letterhead to shopping bags, business cards—even employees' uniforms! The techniques for generating publicity for an off-line business covered in Chapter 8 can be just as effective for online businesses needing to make their domain names more well known without breaking their budgets. A passive approach to generating Web site traffic is a recipe for failure; entrepreneurs who are as innovative at promoting their e-businesses as they are at creating them can attract impressive numbers of visitors to their sites.

DESIGNING A KILLER WEB SITE

Learning Objective

6. Learn the techniques of designing a killer Web site.

World Wide Web users are not a patient lot. They sit before their computers, surfing the Internet, their fingers poised on their mouse buttons, daring any Web site to delay them with files that take a long time (to many, that's anything more than about 8 seconds) to load. Slow-loading sites or sites that don't deliver on their promises will cause a Web user to move on faster than a bolt of lightning can strike. Research shows that 59 percent of online customers buy from just a handful of sites that they consider safe and reliable and with which they are familiar.[65] With more than 3.6 million Web sites online, how can entrepreneurs design a Web site that will capture and hold potential customers' attention long enough to make a sale? What can they do to keep customers coming back on a regular basis? There is no sure-fire formula for stopping surfers in their tracks, but the following suggestions will help.

Understand Your Target Customer

Before launching into the design of their Web sites, entrepreneurs must develop a clear picture of their target customers. Only then are they ready to design a site that will appeal to their customers. The goal is to create a design in which customers see themselves when they visit. Creating a site in which customers find a comfortable fit requires a careful blend of market research, sales know-how, and aesthetics. The challenge for a business on the Web is to create the same image, style, and ambiance in its online presence as in its off-line stores.

Select a Domain Name That Is Consistent with the Image You Want to Create for Your Company and Register It

Entrepreneurs should never underestimate the power of the right domain name or universal resource locator (URL), which is a company's address on the Internet. It not only tells Web surfers where to find a company, but it also should suggest something about the company and what it does. Even the casual Web surfer could guess that the "toys.com" name belongs to a company selling children's toys. (It does; it belongs to eToys Inc., which also owns "etoys.com," "e-toys.com," and several other variations of its name.) Entrepreneurs must recognize that a domain name is part of the brand they are creating and should create the proper image for the company.

The ideal domain name should be:

- *Short.* Short names are easy for people to remember, so the shorter a company's URL is, the more likely potential customers are to recall it.
- *Memorable.* Not every short domain name is necessarily memorable. Some business owners use their companies' initials as their domain name (for example, www.sbfo.com for Stanley Brothers Furniture Outlet). The problem with using initials for a domain name is that customers rarely associate the two, which makes a company virtually invisible on the Web.
- *Indicative of a company's business or business name.* Perhaps the best domain name for a company is one that customers can guess easily if they know the company's name. For instance, mail-order catalog company J.Crew's URL is www.jcrew.com, and New Pig, a maker of absorbent materials for a variety of industrial applications, uses www.newpig.com as its domain name. (The company carries this concept over to its toll-free number, which is 1-800-HOT-HOGS.)
- *Easy to spell.* Even though a company's domain name may be easy to spell, it is usually wise to buy several variations of the correct spelling simply because some customers are not likely to be good spellers!

Just because an entrepreneur comes up with the perfect URL for his company's Web site does not necessarily mean that he can use it. Domain names are given on a first-come, first-served basis. Before business owners can use a domain name, they must ensure that someone else has not already taken it. The simplest way to do that is to go to a domain name registration service such as Network Solutions' Internic at www.networksolutions.com or Netnames at www.netnames.com to conduct a name search. Entrepreneurs who find the domain name they have selected already registered to someone else have two choices: They can select another name, or they can try to buy the name from the original registrant.

A Company Example

*After Becca Williams, founder of **Wallnutz**, a small company that sells paint-by-number wall murals for children's rooms, came up with the ideal name for her business, she discovered that someone else had already registered the domain name wallnutz.com. She contacted the original registrant and purchased the rights to the name.[66] Some businesses are able to buy the rights to their company names relatively cheaply, but not every online business is as fortunate. Business incubator eCompanies purchased the rights to the domain name "business.com" from an individual for $7.5 million![67]*

Finding unregistered domain names is becoming more difficult; 98 percent of the words in *Webster's English Dictionary* have been registered as Internet domain names![68] Once entrepreneurs find an unused name that is suitable, they should register it (plus any variations of it)—and the sooner, the better! Registering is quite easy: Simply use one of the registration services listed previously to fill out a form and pay $98, which registers the name for two years. The registration renewal fee is $49 per year, but discounts for multiple-year registrations apply. The next step is to register the domain name with the U.S. Patent and Trademark Office (USPTO) at a cost of $245. The USPTO's Web site (www.uspto.gov) not only allows users to register a trademark online, but it also offers useful information on trademarks and the protection they offer.

Be Easy to Find

With more than 3 billion pages already on the Web and more coming on every day, making your site easy for people to find is a real challenge. Because the Web is so expansive, many Web users rely on search engines to help them locate sites. Just 23 percent of Web users looking for a particular company will type the URL into a browser; the remaining 77 percent turn to search engines to locate the business or the site they are seeking.[69] Most of those surfers will type into the search engine keywords about what a company does ("industrial valves") rather than a particular company name ("Velan Valve Company"). That is why smart Web site designers embed codes called meta tags and title tags that contain keyword search phrases into their home pages that move their sites to the top of the most popular search engines such as Yahoo!, AltaVista, Dog Pile, Excite, Google, Go.com, Infospace, Lycos, Overture, WebCrawler, and others. (The key is figuring out which words and phrases your target customers are typing into search engines and then putting them into your site's meta tags and title tags; this is a never-ending process.) Unfortunately, business owners invest less than 1 percent of their marketing budgets on search engine marketing, which focuses on securing high-priority listings among search engines.[70] Search Engine Watch (www.searchenginewatch.com) offers many useful tips on search engine placement and registration as well as on using meta tags to increase the likelihood that a search engine will list a particular site.

Eventually, most search engines will find a newly posted site, but this may take weeks or even months. That's why many entrepreneurs choose to pay for search engine listings. Not only are their sites picked up more quickly, but they also move to the top of the search results list that searchers see. Rather than spend time themselves submitting their companies' URLs to search engine sites, entrepreneurs can use inexpensive software such as Traffic Builder or hire submission services such as bCentral's Submit It! to submit a site's address to hundreds of search engines. Registering with multiple search engines is critical because even the largest ones cover less than 20 percent of the Web![71]

Table 7.3 describes some techniques for getting the most out of search engine listings.

Give Customers What They Want

Although Web shoppers are price conscious, they rank fast delivery as the most important factor in their purchase decisions. Studies also show that surfers look for a large selection of merchandise available to them immediately. Remember that the essence of selling on the Web is

---

TABLE 7.3

Techniques for Optimizing Search Engine Use

Because of their widespread use among Web users, search engines are one of the most effective ways to drive traffic to your Web site. What can business owners do to optimize their use of search engines? The following tips will help:

- Submit your Web site to multiple search engines. To save time, consider using one of the automated search engine submission services such as Submit It!

- Consider paying for preferred placement in key search engines, but be sure the benefits outweigh the costs. Fees are usually set on a pay-per-click basis, which means you pay for search engine placement only when it works.

- Place as title tags, meta tags, and text on your Web pages keywords that Web users are likely to use in their searches.

- Find out which words users enter into search engines to find your products or services. Techniques include visiting competitors' Web sites and right-clicking to "View Source" to see which keywords they use, asking customers, using services such as Wordtracker that monitor popular search phrases, and relying on analytics software that tracks how users arrived at your site.

- Add links to other sites. Many "spider-based" search engines such as Google and AltaVista look for them.

- List your products or services separately. The more specific your Web site is, the more likely it will show up in keyword searches.

- Be patient, especially if you use free search engine placement. It often takes four to eight weeks before a site shows up in major search engines.

- Monitor search engine listing results using analytics software that tracks many important statistics such as the total number of visitors, which search engines they used, the keywords they typed in, and many others. These statistics can be valuable tools, helping business owners refine their search engine marketing techniques over time.

- Monitor search engine performance and productivity regularly. It changes constantly, and what worked three months ago may not be producing results today.

providing convenience to customers. Sites that allow them to shop whenever they want, to choose from a wide selection of products, to find what they are looking for quickly and easily, and to pay for it conveniently and securely will keep customers coming back.

Build Loyalty by Giving Online Customers a Reason to Return to Your Web Site

Typically, e-commerce sites experience 60 percent turnover rates among their customers every six weeks![72] Just as with brick-and-mortar retailers, e-tailers that constantly have to incur the expense of attracting new customers find it difficult to remain profitable because of the extra cost required to acquire customers. One of the most effective ways to encourage customers to return to a site is to establish an incentive program that rewards them for repeat purchases. "Frequent-buyer" programs that offer discounts or points toward future purchases, giveaways such as T-shirts emblazoned with a company's logo, or special services are common components of incentive programs. Incentive programs that are properly designed with a company's target customer in mind really work. A study by market research firm NFO Interactive found that 53 percent of online customers say they would return to a particular site to shop if it offered an incentive program.[73]

Establish Hyperlinks with Other Businesses, Preferably Those Selling Products or Services That Complement Yours

Listing the Web addresses of complementary businesses on a company's site and having them list its address on their sites offers customers more value and can bring traffic to your site that you otherwise would have missed. For instance, the owner of a site selling upscale kitchen gadgets should consider a cross-listing arrangement with sites that feature gourmet recipes, wines, and kitchen appliances.

Include an E-Mail Option and a Telephone Number in Your Site

Customers will appreciate the opportunity to communicate with your company. When you include e-mail access on your site, be sure to respond to it promptly. Nothing alienates cyber-customers faster than a company that is slow to respond or fails to respond to their e-mail messages. Also, be sure to include a toll-free telephone number for customers who prefer to call with their questions. Unfortunately, many companies either fail to include their telephone numbers on their sites or bury them so deeply within the sites' pages that customers never find them.

Give Shoppers the Ability to Track Their Orders Online

Many customers who order items online want to track the progress of their orders. One of the most effective ways to keep a customer happy is to send an e-mail confirmation that your company received the order and another e-mail notification when you ship the order. The shipment notice should include the shipper's tracking number and instructions on how to track the order from the shipper's site. Order and shipping confirmations instill confidence in even the most Web-wary shoppers.

Offer Web Shoppers a Special All Their Own

Give Web customers a special deal that you don't offer in any other advertising piece. Change your specials often (weekly, if possible) and use clever "teasers" to draw attention to the offer. Regular special offers available only on the Web give customers an incentive to keep visiting a company's site.

Follow a Simple Design

Catchy graphics and photographs are important to snaring customers, but designers must choose them carefully. Designs that are overly complex take a long time to download, and customers are likely to move on before they appear.

Specific design tips include:

- Avoid clutter. The best designs are simple and elegant with a balance of both text and graphics.

- Avoid huge graphic headers that must download first, prohibiting customers from seeing anything else on your site as they wait (or more likely, *don't* wait). Use graphics judiciously so that the site loads quickly. Zona Research reports that if a sight fails to load within 8 seconds, one-third of potential visitors will leave; a site failing to load within 12 seconds produces a 70 percent abandonment rate.[74]

- Include a menu bar at the top of the page that makes it easy for customers to find their way around your site.

- Make the site easy to navigate by including navigation buttons at the bottom of pages that enable customers to return to the top of the page or to the menu bar. This avoids what one expert calls "the pogo effect," where visitors bounce from page to page in a Web site looking for what they need. Without navigation buttons or a site map page, a company runs the risk of customers getting lost in its site and leaving.

- Regularly look for broken links on your site and purge them.

- Incorporate meaningful content in the site that is useful to visitors, well organized, easy to read, and current. The content should be consistent with the message a company sends in the other advertising media it uses. Although a Web site should be designed to sell, providing useful, current information attracts visitors, keeps them coming back, and establishes a company's reputation as an expert in the field.

- Include a "frequently asked questions (FAQ)" section. Adding this section to a page can reduce dramatically the number of telephone calls and e-mails that customer service representatives must handle. FAQ sections typically span a wide range of issues—from how to place an order to how to return merchandise—and cover whatever topics customers most often want to know about.

- Be sure to post prominently privacy and return policies as well as product guarantees the company offers.

- If your site is heavy on content, say, 100 or more pages, or has more than 100 products for sale, include a search tool that allows visitors to find the product or information they want. Smaller, simpler sites can get by without a search tool if they are organized properly. Setting up a search tool is easy with either a remote search service (available for a monthly fee) or off-the-shelf software.

- Avoid fancy typefaces and small fonts because they are too hard to read. Limit font and color choices to two or three to avoid a circus look.

- Be vigilant for misspelled words, typographical errors, and formatting mistakes; they destroy a site's credibility in no time.

- Avoid using small fonts on "busy" backgrounds; no one will read them!

- Use contrasting colors of text and graphics. For instance, blue text on a green background is nearly impossible to read.

- Be careful with frames. Using frames that are so thick that they crowd out text makes for a poor design.

- Test the site on different Web browsers and on different size monitors. A Web site may look exactly the way it was designed to look on one Web browser and be a garbled mess on another. Sites designed to display correctly on large monitors may not view well on small ones.

- Use your Web site to collect information from visitors, but don't tie up visitors immediately with a tedious registration process. Most will simply leave the site never to return. Offers for a free e-mail newsletter or a contest giveaway can give visitors enough incentive to register with a site.

Source: REPRINTED BY PERMISSION OF UNITED FEATURE SYNDICATE, INC.

- Avoid automated music that plays continuously and cannot be cut off.
- Make sure the overall look of the page is appealing. When a site is poorly designed, lacks information, or cannot support customer needs, that [company's] reputation is seriously jeopardized," says one expert.[75]
- Remember: Simpler usually is better.

Assure Customers That Their Online Transactions Are Secure

If you are serious about doing business on the Web, make sure that your site includes the proper security software and encryption devices. Computer-savvy customers are not willing to divulge their credit card numbers on sites are not secure.

Post Shipping and Handling Charges Up Front

A common gripe among online shoppers is that some e-tailers fail to reveal their shipping and handling charges early on in the checkout process. Jupiter Research reports that 63 percent of online buyers have abandoned an online shopping cart because they thought the shipping and handling charges were too high.[76] Responsible online merchants keep shipping and handling charges reasonable and display them early on in the buying process.

YOU Be the Consultant . . .

The Amazon.com of the Pool and Spa Industry

In the 10 years that he has sold pool and spa supplies through his online stores, Poolandspa.com, Dan Harrison has tried almost all of the most common ways of driving traffic to his site. However, none has been more successful than premier placement in key search engines, which has transformed Harrison into a search engine marketing aficionado. Harrison discovered early on in his business the importance of marketing and promotion, and over the years he has applied the lessons he learned in his brick-and-mortar business to his click-and-mortar company.

Poolandspa.com started life in 1980 as a small pool service company operated out of Harrison's basement in Smithtown, New York. By 1984, he had moved the company into a small store and became one of the first companies on Long Island to sell hot tub spas. In little more than a year, Harrison opened the first "all hot tub spa" store on Long Island. In the early 1990s, an economic recession hit the company's sales of luxury spas and spa rooms hard, and Harrison shifted his strategy to focus once again on pool and spa service and on selling aftermarket pool and spa accessories. He also undertook a more aggressive marketing campaign that included newspaper ads and direct mail. "We used to send out only two flyers a year for our pool service and product offers," he recalls, "but we boosted that up to two a month."

Using the mailing list of more than 2,000 spa owners the company had, Harrison decided to start publishing a newsletter, *The Long Island Hot Tub Newsletter*, which mixed both informative articles about spas with low-key sales pitches for products and services. Customers loved it, and sales increased as soon as the first newsletter went out. Harrison knew he had found a successful marketing technique.

In 1994, Harrison began to explore something he had heard about called the Internet. "It immediately interested us," he says, "because, at last, we could greatly expand our pool and spa chemical and accessory mail-order business nationwide for a very small investment." Going from "totally computer illiterate" to becoming one of the first small companies on the Internet was a challenge, but Harrison and his employees did it. In 1995, they launched a 150-page Web site called The Virtual Pool and Spa Store. In less than a year, the mailing list of 2,000 spa owners on Long Island who received *The Hot Tub Newsletter* had grown to more than 20,000 spa owners nationwide! Sales skyrocketed. In 1998, Harrison renamed the online store Poolandspa.com.

One of Poolandspa.com's most successful marketing campaigns, both online and off-line, came as a result of taking his dog, Moose, to work every day from the time he was a puppy. The German shepherd–husky mix had so much personality that he became the company's mascot, Moose the Hot Tub Dog. The press loved Moose, featuring him in numerous magazine and newspaper articles, and he appeared in every television commercial Poolandspa.com ran. When Moose died at age 11 in December 2002, the company was deluged with outpourings of sympathy. Customers from all across the country sent cards and flowers, and an industry publication, *Pool and Spa News Magazine*, ran his obituary.

The company still publishes *The Hot Tub Newsletter* and has added *The Swimming Pool Life* for pool owners. The Poolandspa.com Web site continues to serve as both a source of valuable information for customers as well as a sales channel. The site contains detailed product information, how-to articles, troubleshooting tips, "Ask the Spa Guy" and "Ask the Pool Guy" sections, chat rooms, message boards, and a fun and games section. The huge library of articles about pool and spa topics ("Everything you always wanted to know about pools and hot tub spas") on the Web site is a key part of the company's online marketing because most search engines pick them up, giving Poolandspa.com placement at or near the top of their listings. "Most of the traffic comes to the content, the articles, the pictures, the how-to's," says Harrison, "and we're skimming off the top of that the people who need to buy something." Because of the poolandspa.com site's longevity and Harrison's active search engine marketing strategy, most visitors arrive by way of free search engine listings. Still, Harrison spends considerably on paid search engine listings, where fees are on a pay-per-click basis. To track results of his listings, Harrison uses WebTrends, an analytics tool that gives him statistical feedback about his site's traffic—total visitor count, where visitors come from, and which keywords they use in their searches. Harrison says his goal is to make the company, which now generates more than $7 million in annual revenues, "THE place for pool and spa owners to shop for all their aftermarket needs—the Amazon.com of the pool and spa industry."

1. Why is search engine marketing so important to online businesses?

2. Conduct a Web search to develop a list of at least five techniques small companies can use to optimize their use of search engines.

3. What advice would you offer a business owner who has just launched an e-commerce company about driving traffic to the company's Web site?

Dan Harrison, founder of PoolandSpa.com, and Moose the Hot Tub Dog.
Courtesy of Long Island Hot Tubs

Sources: James Maguire, "Small Business Makes a Big Splash," *Small Business Computing*, May 16, 2003, www.smallbusinesscomputing.com/emarketing/print.php/22078; "The History of Poolsandspa.com," www.poolandspa.com/page810.htm; Rebecca Robledo, "A Dog's Life," *Pool and Spa News Magazine*, February 2003, p. 16; "Obituary: Moose the Hot Tub Dog Dies at Age 11," Poolandspa.com, www.poolandspa.com/page3016.htm.

Keep Your Site Updated

Customers want to see something new when they visit stores, and they expect the same when they visit virtual stores as well. Delete any hyperlinks that have disappeared and keep the information on your Web site current. One sure way to run off customers on the Web is to continue to advertise your company's "Christmas Special" in August! On the other hand, fresh information and new specials keep customers coming back.

Consider Hiring a Professional to Design Your Site

Pros can do it a lot faster and better than you can. However, don't give designers free rein to do whatever they want to with your site. Make sure it meets your criteria for an effective site that can sell.

Entrepreneurs must remember that on the World Wide Web every company, no matter how big or small it is, has the exact same screen size for its site. What matters most is not the size of your company but how you put that screen size to use.

TRACKING WEB RESULTS

Software Solutions

Learning Objective

7. Explain how companies track the results from their Web sites.

As they develop their Web sites, entrepreneurs seek to create sites that generate sales, improve customer relationships, or lower costs. How can entrepreneurs determine the effectiveness of their sites? **Web analytics**, tools that measure a Web site's ability to attract customers, generate sales, and keep customers coming back, help entrepreneurs know what works—and what doesn't—on the Web. In the early days of e-commerce, entrepreneurs strived to create sites that

Web analytics—*tools that measure a Web site's ability to attract customers, generate sales, and keep customers coming back.*

sticky site—*one that acts like electronic flypaper, capturing visitors' attention and offering them useful, meaningful information that makes them stay at the site.*

viral site—*one that visitors are willing to share with their friends.*

recency—*the length of time between a customer's visit to a Web site.*

conversion (or browse-to-buy) ratio—*measures the proportion of visitors to a site who actually make a purchase.*

counter—*the simplest mechanism for tracking activity on a Web site by counting the number of "hits" the site receives.*

log-analysis software—*programs that analyze server logs that record visitors' actions on a Web site and then generate meaningful reports for managers.*

click-stream analysis software—*software that allows entrepreneurs to determine the paths visitors take while on a site and to pinpoint the areas in which they spend the most—and the least—time.*

were both "sticky" and "viral." A **sticky site** is one that acts like electronic flypaper, capturing visitors' attention and offering them useful, interesting information that makes them stay at the site. The premise of stickiness is that the longer customers stay in a site, the more likely they are to actually purchase something and to come back to it. A **viral site** is one that visitors are willing to share with their friends. This "word-of-mouse" advertising is one of the most effective ways of generating traffic to a company's site. As the Web has matured as a marketing channel, however, the shortcomings of these simple measures have become apparent, and other e-metrics continue to emerge. E-businesses now focus on **recency**, the length of time between a customer's visits to a Web site. The more frequently customers visit a site, the more likely they are to become loyal customers. Another important measure of Web success is the **conversion (or browse-to-buy) ratio**, which measures the proportion of visitors to a site who actually make a purchase.

How can online entrepreneurs know if their sites are successful? Answering that question means that entrepreneurs must track visitors to their sites, the paths they follow within the site, and the activity they generate while there. A variety of methods for tracking Web results are available, but the most commonly used ones include counters and log-analysis software. The simplest technique is a **counter**, which records the number of "hits" a Web site receives. Although counters measure activity on a site, they do so only at the broadest level. If a counter records 10 hits, for instance, there is no way to know if those hits came as a result of 10 different visitors or as a result of just one person making 10 visits. Plus, counters cannot tell Web entrepreneurs where visitors to their sites come from or which pages they look at on the site.

A more meaningful way to track activity on a Web site is through **log-analysis software**. Server logs record every page, graphic, audio clip, or photograph that visitors to a site access, and log-analysis software analyzes these logs and generates reports describing how visitors behave when they get to a site. With this software, entrepreneurs can determine how many unique visitors come to their site and how many times repeat visitors come back. Owners of e-stores can discover which FAQ customers click on most often, which part of a site they stayed in the longest, which site they came from, and how the volume of traffic at the site affected the server's speed of operation. **Click-stream analysis** allows entrepreneurs to determine the paths visitors take while on a site and to pinpoint the areas in which they spend the most—and the least—time. These tools give the ability to infer what visitors think about a Web site, its products, its content, its design, and other features. Feedback from log-analysis software helps entrepreneurs redesign their sites to eliminate confusing navigation, unnecessary graphics, meaningless content, incomplete information, and other problems that can cause visitors to leave.

A Company Example

*Diana and Gregg Shapiro, co-owners of **All the Right Gifts** (www.alltherightgifts.com), an online shopping service that helps customers find gifts quickly and conveniently, use log-analysis software to manage their Web site and to keep it fresh and focused on what customers are most interested in. They can access their log reports any time of day and generate statistical analyses, tables, and graphs on practically any aspect of their site. "The data help us figure out which search engines are generating the best referrals and what keywords customers are keying in to find us," says Gregg. "Then we use this information to concentrate our marketing efforts in the best possible way."*[77]

Other tracking methods available to owners of e-businesses include:

■ *Clustering.* This software observes visitors to a Web site, analyzes their behavior, and then groups them into narrow categories. Companies then target each category of shoppers with products, specials, and offers designed to appeal to them.

■ *Collaborative filtering.* This software uses sophisticated algorithms to analyze visitors' interests by comparing them to other shoppers with similar tastes. Companies then use this information to suggest products an individual customer would most likely be interested in, given his or her profile.

■ *Profiling systems.* These programs tag individual customers on a site and note their responses to the various pages in the site. Based on the areas a customer visits most, the software develops a psychographic profile of the shopper. For instance, a visitor who reads an article on massage techniques might receive an offer for a book on acupuncture or a magazine focusing on alternative medicine.

- *Artificial intelligence (AI).* This software, sometimes called neural networking, is the most sophisticated of the group because it actually learns from users' behavior. The more these programs interact with customers, the "smarter" they become. Over time, they can help online marketers know which special offers work best with which customers, when customers are most likely to respond, and how to present the offer.

Return on Investment

Just like traditional businesses, e-businesses must earn a reasonable return on an entrepreneur's investment. The difficulty, however, is that much of the total investment required to build, launch, maintain, and market a Web site is not always obvious. Plus, the payoffs of a successful site are not easy to measure and do not always fit neatly into traditional financial models that calculate return on investment (ROI). For instance, how can a business with both a click- and brick presence determine exactly how many customers come into its retail store as a result of having visited its Web site? Can it quantify the increase in customer loyalty as a result of its e-commerce efforts? Many companies have discovered that the payoff from their online sales efforts are long term and hard to quantify accurately.

Owners of e-businesses are developing new measures unique to e-commerce to evaluate the performances of their companies. In addition to calculating ROI, many online businesses compute **cost per action (CPA)**, the amount it costs to produce a particular customer action such as registering for a newsletter, requesting information, downloading an article, and others. The actions a company uses should correlate to future sales. **Cost per order (CPO)** is a common measurement for online retailers. It measures the cost a company incurs to generate a customer order and can be calculated across all product lines or for a specific product. iGo, an online retailer of mobile computing and communication accessories (www.igo.com), has created an integrated set of performance measures that includes the lifetime value (LTV) of its customers and customer retention rates as well as several traditional financial measures.[78]

cost per action—*a measure of performance that calculates the amount it costs to produce a particular customer action.*

cost per order—*a measure of performance that calculates the amount it costs to generate a customer order.*

ENSURING WEB PRIVACY AND SECURITY

Privacy

The Web's ability to track customers' every move naturally raises concerns over the privacy of the information companies collect. E-commerce gives businesses access to tremendous volumes of information about their customers, creating a responsibility to protect that information and to use it wisely. According to the Pew Internet & American Life Project, 86 percent of Internet users say they worry about online privacy.[79] To make sure they are using the information they collect from visitors to their Web sites legally and ethically, companies should take the following steps:

TAKE AN INVENTORY OF THE CUSTOMER DATA COLLECTED. The first step to ensuring proper data handling is to assess exactly the type of data the company is collecting and storing. How are you collecting it? Why are you collecting it? How are you using it? Do visitors know how you are using the data? Do you need to get their permission to use it in this way? Do you use all of the data you are collecting?

DEVELOP A COMPANY PRIVACY POLICY FOR THE INFORMATION YOU COLLECT. A **privacy policy** is a statement explaining the nature of the information a company collects online, what it does with that information, and the recourse customers have if they believe the company is misusing the information. Several online privacy firms, such as TRUSTe (www.truste.org), BBBOnline (www.bbbonline.com), and BetterWeb (www.betterweb.com) offer Web "seal programs," the equivalent of a Good Housekeeping Seal of privacy approval. To earn a privacy seal of approval, a company must adopt a privacy policy, implement it, and monitor its effectiveness. Many of these privacy sites also provide online policy wizards, automated questionnaires that help e-business owners create comprehensive privacy statements.

privacy policy—*a statement explaining the nature of the information a company collects online, what it does with that information, and the recourse customers have if they believe the company is misusing the information.*

POST YOUR COMPANY'S PRIVACY POLICY PROMINENTLY ON YOUR WEB SITE AND FOLLOW IT. Creating a privacy policy is not sufficient; posting it in a prominent place on the Web site (which should be accessible from *every* page on the Web site), and then abiding by it make a policy meaningful. One of the worst mistakes a company can make is to publish its privacy policy online and then to fail to follow it. Not only is this unethical, but it also can lead to serious damage awards if customers take legal action against the company.

KBKids.com, an online retailer of children's toys, games, and videos, (www.kbkids.com), positions its privacy policy in a highly prominent position on its site using a large tab that links to a separate page. The page provides a comprehensive description of its policy, the way it collects information, how customers can view the information the company collects, and its affiliation with two privacy programs, TRUSTe and BBBOnLine. "We established a security and privacy policy to assure our customers that we respect the information they provide to us and that its only use is to help us serve them better," says KBKids.com's marketing vice president.[80]

Security

A company doing business on the Web faces two conflicting goals: to establish a presence on the Web so that customers from across the globe can have access to its site and to maintain a high level of security so that the business, its site, and the information it collects are safe from hackers and intruders intent on doing harm. Companies have a number of safeguards available to them, but hackers with enough time, talent, and determination usually can beat even the most sophisticated safety measures. If hackers manage to break into a system, they can do irreparable damage, stealing programs and data, modifying or deleting valuable information, changing the look and content of sites, or crashing sites altogether. For instance, hackers recently gained unauthorized access to a Web server at Capetown-Rio, a small marketing communications firm in Redmond, Washington, and deleted key files containing promotional campaigns for several of the company's most important customers.[81]

To minimize the likelihood of invasion by hackers, e-companies rely on several tools, including virus detection software, intrusion detection software, and firewalls. Perhaps the most basic level of protection, **virus detection software** scans computer drives for viruses, nasty programs written by devious hackers and designed to harm computers and the information they contain. The severity of viruses ranges widely, from relatively harmless programs that put humorous messages on a user's screen to those that erase a computer's hard drive or cause the entire system to crash. Because hackers are *always* writing new viruses to attack computer systems, entrepreneurs must keep their virus detection software up-to-date and must run it often. An attack by one virus can bring a company's entire e-commerce platform to a screeching halt in no time!

Intrusion detection software is essential for any company doing business on the Web. These packages constantly monitor the activity on a company's network server and sound an alert if they detect someone breaking into the company's computer system or if they detect unusual network activity. Intrusion detection software not only can detect attempts by unauthorized users to break into a computer system while they are happening, but it also can trace the hacker's location. Most packages also have the ability to preserve a record of the attempted break-in that will stand up in court so that companies can take legal action against cyber-intruders.

A **firewall** is a combination of hardware and software operating between the Internet and a company's computer network that allows employees to have access to the Internet but keeps unauthorized users from entering a company's network and the programs and data it contains. Establishing a firewall is essential to operating a company on the Web, but entrepreneurs must make sure that their firewalls are set up properly. Otherwise, they are useless! One recent study of more than 2,000 Web sites by ISCA.net, a security consulting firm, found even though every site had a firewall in place, more than 80 percent were vulnerable to attack with commonly available software because they were not properly designed.[82] Even with all of these security measures in place, it is best for a company to run its Web page on a separate server from the network that runs the business. If hackers break into the Web site, they still do not have access to the company's sensitive data and programs.

The Computer Security Institute (www.gocsi.com) offers articles, information, and seminars to help business owners maintain computer security. *The Business Security e-Journal* (www.lubrinco.com) is a free monthly newsletter on computer security, and *Information*

---

virus detection software—*programs that scan computer drives for viruses, nasty programs written by devious hackers and designed to harm computers and the information they contain.*

intrusion detection software—*programs that constantly monitor the activity on a company's network server and sound an alert if they detect someone breaking into the system or if they detect unusual network activity.*

firewall—*a combination of hardware and software that allows employees to have access to the Internet but keeps unauthorized users from entering a company's network and the programs and data it contains.*

Security Magazine (www.infosecuritymag.com), published by the International Computer Security Association (www.icsa.net), also offers helpful advice on maintaining computer security. For entrepreneurs who want to test their sites' security, the ICSA offers its Security Snapshot system (free of charge) that runs various security tests on a site and then e-mails a "Risk Index" score in six different categories, including the site's risk of hacker intrusion.

In e-commerce just as in traditional retail, sales do not matter unless a company gets paid! On the Web customers demand transactions they can complete with ease and convenience, and the simplest way to allow customers to pay for e-commerce transactions is with credit cards. From a Web customer's perspective, however, one of the most important security issues is the security of their credit card information.

Processing credit card transactions requires a company to obtain an Internet merchant account from a bank or financial intermediary. Setup fees for an Internet merchant account typically range from $500 to $1,000, but companies also pay monthly access and statement fees of between $40 and $80 plus a transaction fee of 10 to 60 cents per transaction. Once an online company has a merchant account, it can accept credit cards from online customers. To ensure the security of their customers' credit card numbers, online retailers typically use secure sockets layer (SSL) technology to encrypt customers' transaction information as it travels across the Internet. By using secure shopping cart features from storefront-building services or Internet service providers, even the smallest e-commerce stores can offer their customers secure online transactions.

Online credit card transactions also pose a risk for merchants; online companies lose an estimated $1 billion to online payment fraud each year.[83] The most common problem is **chargebacks**, online transactions that customers dispute. Unlike credit card transactions in a retail store, those made online involve no signatures, so Internet merchants incur the loss when a customer disputes an online credit card transaction. Experts estimate that payment fraud online is 12 times greater than in brick-and-mortar stores.[84] Research firm GartnerG2 says that one of every 20 Internet transactions is an attempted fraud.[85] A thief in Romania recently tried to use a stolen credit card to purchase eight handbags from Velma Handbags, a small company founded by Margaret Cobbs, but the company that handles her credit card transactions discovered the attempt and stopped the $380 transaction.[86]

One way to prevent fraud is to ask customers for their card verification value (CVV or CVV2), the three-digit number above the signature panel on the back of the credit card, as well as their card number and expiration date. Online merchants also can subscribe to a real-time credit card processing service that authorizes credit card transactions, but the fees can be high. Also, using a shipper that provides the ability to track shipments enables online merchants to prove that the customer actually received the merchandise and can help minimize the threat of payment fraud.

chargebacks—*online transactions that customers dispute.*

E-commerce is creating a new economy, one that is connecting producers, sellers, and customers via technology in ways that have never been possible before. In this fast-paced world of e-commerce, size no longer matters as much as speed and flexibility do. The Internet is creating a new industrial order, and companies that fail to adapt to it will soon become extinct.

1. Describe the benefits of selling on the World Wide Web.

Although a Web-based sales strategy does not guarantee success, the companies that have pioneered Web-based selling have realized many benefits, including the following:

- The opportunity to increase revenues.
- The ability to expand their reach into global markets.
- The ability to remain open 24 hours a day, seven days a week.
- The capacity to use the Web's interactive nature to enhance customer service.
- The power to educate and to inform.
- The ability to lower the cost of doing business.
- The ability to spot new business opportunities and to capitalize on them.
- The power to track sales results.

2. Understand the factors an entrepreneur should consider before launching into e-commerce.

Before launching an e-commerce effort, business owners should consider the following important issues:

- How a company exploits the Web's interconnectivity and the opportunities it creates to transform relationships with its suppliers and vendors, its customers, and other external stakeholders is crucial to its success.
- Web success requires a company to develop a plan for integrating the Web into its overall strategy. The plan should address issues such as site design and maintenance, creating and managing a brand name, marketing and promotional strategies, sales, and customer service.
- Developing deep, lasting relationships with customers takes on even greater importance on the Web. Attracting customers on the Web costs money, and companies must be able to retain their online customers to make their Web sites profitable.
- Creating a meaningful presence on the Web requires an ongoing investment of resources—time, money, energy, and talent. Establishing an attractive Web site brimming with catchy photographs of products is only the beginning.
- Measuring the success of its Web-based sales effort is essential to remaining relevant to customers whose tastes, needs, and preferences are always changing.

3. Explain the 12 myths of e-commerce and how to avoid falling victim to them.

The 12 myths of e-commerce are:

Myth 1. Setting up a business on the Web is easy and inexpensive.

Myth 2. If I launch a site, customers will flock to it.

Myth 3. Making money on the Web is easy.

Myth 4. Privacy is not an important issue on the Web.

Myth 5. The most important part of any e-commerce effort is technology.

Myth 6. "Strategy? I don't need a strategy to sell on the Web! Just give me a Web site, and the rest will take care of itself."

Myth 7. On the Web, customer service is not as important as it is in a traditional retail store.

Myth 8. Flash makes a Web site better.

Myth 9. It's what's up front that counts.

Myth 10. E-commerce will cause brick-and-mortar retail stores to disappear.

Myth 11. The greatest opportunities for e-commerce lie in the retail sector.

Myth 12. It's too late to get on the Web.

4. Discuss the five basic approaches available to entrepreneurs wanting to launch an e-commerce effort.

Entrepreneurs looking to launch an e-commerce effort have five basic choices: (1) online shopping malls, (2) storefront-building services, (3) Internet service providers (ISPs), (4) hiring professionals to design a custom site, and (5) building a site in-house.

5. Explain the basic strategies entrepreneurs should follow to achieve success in their e-commerce efforts.

Following are some guidelines for building a successful Web strategy for a small e-company:

- Consider focusing on a niche in the market.
- Develop a community of online customers.
- Attract visitors by giving away "freebies."
- Make creative use of e-mail, but avoid becoming a "spammer."
- Make sure your Web site says "credibility."

- Consider forming strategic alliances with larger, more established companies.
- Make the most of the Web's global reach.
- Promote your Web site online and off-line.

6. Learn the techniques of designing a killer Web site.

There is no sure-fire formula for stopping surfers in their tracks, but the following suggestions will help:

- Select a domain name that is consistent with the image you want to create for your company and register it.
- Be easy to find.
- Give customers what they want.
- Establish hyperlinks with other businesses, preferably those selling products or services that complement yours.
- Include an e-mail option and a telephone number in your site.
- Give shoppers the ability to track their orders online.
- Offer Web shoppers a special all their own.
- Follow a simple design for your Web page.
- Assure customers that their online transactions are secure.
- Keep your site updated.
- Consider hiring a professional to design your site.

7. Explain how companies track the results from their Web sites.

The simplest technique for tracking the results of a Web site is a counter, which records the number of "hits" a Web site receives. Another option for tracking Web activity is through log-analysis software. Server logs record every page, graphic, audio clip, or photograph that visitors to a site access, and log-analysis software analyzes these logs and generates reports describing how visitors behave when they get to a site.

8. Describe how e-businesses ensure the privacy and security of the information they collect and store from the Web.

To make sure they are using the information they collect from visitors to their Web sites legally and ethically, companies should take the following steps:

- Take an inventory of the customer data collected.
- Develop a company privacy policy for the information you collect.
- Post your company's privacy policy prominently on your Web site and follow it.

To ensure the security of the information they collect and store from Web transactions, companies should rely on virus and intrusion detection software and firewalls to ward off attacks from hackers.

9. Learn how to evaluate the effectiveness of a company's Web site.

Because the techniques used to evaluate traditional companies do not always fit e-commerce businesses, online entrepreneurs are developing new models to evaluate the performances of their companies that include measures of customer behavior and retention, financial returns, and site performance.

THE BUSINESS DISC

Launch *The Business Disc*, and continue from where you left off until you have completed Part I and are ready to begin Part II, "The First Year of Business."

BUSINESS PLAN PRO

Business PlanPro

Use the content of this chapter to update the components of your business plan. If necessary, modify your plan to incorporate your company's Web strategy.

Review the questions on page 217 to help you focus your company's Web strategy. How do you plan to create, support, and promote your site? Is the URL you plan to use available for registration?

DISCUSSION QUESTIONS

1. How have the Internet and e-commerce changed the ways companies do business?

2. Explain the benefits a company earns by selling on the Web.

3. Discuss the factors entrepreneurs should consider before launching an e-commerce site.

4. What are the 12 myths of e-commerce? What can an entrepreneur do to avoid them?

5. Explain the five basic approaches available to entrepreneurs for launching an e-commerce effort. What are the advantages, the disadvantages, and the costs associated with each one?

6. What strategic advice would you offer an entrepreneur about to start an e-company?

7. What design characteristics make for a successful Web page?

8. Explain the characteristics of an ideal domain name.

9. Describe the techniques that are available to e-companies for tracking results from their Web sites. What advantages does each offer?

10. What steps should e-businesses take to ensure the privacy of the information they collect and store from the Web?

11. What techniques can e-companies use to protect their banks of information and their customers' transaction data from hackers?

12. Why does evaluating the effectiveness of a Web site pose a problem for online entrepreneurs?

BEYOND THE CLASSROOM . . .

1. Work with a team of your classmates to come up with an Internet business you would be interested in launching. Come up with several suitable domain names for your hypothetical e-company. Once you have chosen a few names, go to a domain name registration service such as Network Solutions' Internic at www.networksolutions.com or Netnames at www.netnames.com to conduct a name search. How many of the names your team came up with were already registered to someone? If an entrepreneur's top choice for a domain name is already registered to someone else, what options does he or she have?

2. Select several online companies with which you are familiar and visit their Web sites. What percentage of them have privacy policies posted on their sites? How comprehensive are these policies? What percentage of the sites you visited belonged to a privacy watchdog agency such as TRUSTe or BBBOnLine? How important is a posted privacy policy for e-companies? Explain.

3. Visit five e-commerce sites on the Web and evaluate them on the basis of the Web site design principles described in this chapter. How well do they measure up? What suggestions can you offer for improving the design of each site? If you were a customer trying to make a purchase from each site, how would you respond to the design?

4. Visit the "Understanding Privacy" Web site at BBBOnLine (www.bbbonline.org/ understandingprivacy). Contact the owner of a Web-based business in your town and use the assessment tool "How's Your Privacy Quotient?" from the BBBOnLine Web site to evaluate the company's privacy policy. How does the company score on the PQ assessment tool? Use the resources on this site and others to develop a list of suggestions for improving the company's score.

Chapter

8

Integrated Marketing Communications and Pricing Strategies

There are two things that never live up to their advertising: sin and circuses.

—Anonymous

There is hardly anything in the world that someone cannot make a little worse and sell a little cheaper, and the people who consider price alone are this man's prey.

—John Ruskin

LEARNING OBJECTIVES

Upon completion of this chapter, you will be able to:

1. **DESCRIBE** the basis of a marketing communications plan.

2. **DESCRIBE** the operational elements of a marketing communications plan.

3. **DESCRIBE** the advantages and disadvantages of the various advertising media.

4. **DISCUSS** the four basic methods for preparing an advertising budget.

5. **EXPLAIN** practical methods for stretching a small business owner's advertising budget.

6. **DESCRIBE** effective pricing techniques for both introducing new products or services and for existing ones.

7. **EXPLAIN** the pricing methods and strategies for retailers, manufacturers, and service firms.

8. **DESCRIBE** the impact of credit on pricing.

Every business needs to construct, maintain, and continually evolve an integrated marketing communications system. Such a system is comprised of advertising, publicity or public relations, and personal selling with all parts focusing on the firm's targeted customers and delivering a consistent and reinforcing message that extols the benefits of the firm's product or services. Entrepreneurs who fail to communicate with their customers run a serious risk of declining sales. Their silence may be perceived by customers as a lack of interest on the part of the business.

In Chapter 6, the process of determining who the firm's customers or clients are was discussed in detail. The more precise and accurate this process is, the more highly focused and less expensive it becomes to communicate the messages of the business.

Developing an effective program to integrate marketing communications has become more of a challenge for business owners in recent years. Because of media overflow, overwhelming ad clutter, increasingly fragmented audiences, more advertising options, and more skeptical consumers, companies have had to become more innovative and creative in their promotional campaigns. Rather than merely turning up the volume on their campaigns, companies are learning to change their frequencies by trying new approaches in different forms of communication.

THE BASICS OF A MARKETING COMMUNICATIONS PLAN

Learning Objective

1. Describe the basis of a marketing communications plan.

Every small business needs a plan to assure that the money invested in its marketing communications is not wasted. A well-developed plan does not guarantee success, but it does increase the likelihood of achieving positive results.

Some entrepreneurs believe that because of limited budgets they cannot afford the luxury of marketing communications. This mind-set views the process as an expense they undertake only when their budgets permit—a leftover expense, something to spend money on if anything remains after paying the other bills. These owners discover, often after it's too late, that communicating with customers is not just an expense; it is an *investment* in a company's future. Advertising and promotion can be effective means of increasing sales by informing customers of the business and its goods or services, by improving the image of the firm and its products, or by persuading customers to purchase the firm's goods or services. A megabudget is *not* a prerequisite for building an effective communications campaign. With a little creativity and ingenuity, a small company can make its voice heard above the clamor of its larger competitors—and stay within a limited budget!

A Company Example

*For example, Scott Fiore, owner of **The Herbal Remedy**, a natural pharmacy in Littleton, Colorado, keeps his company's name in front of customers by using traditional advertising media, writing articles on herbal remedies for local magazines, and generating lots of publicity. Fiore, who spends about $1,400 a month on traditional advertising media, regularly buys radio ads that run during a popular talk show on health because he knows that the show reaches many of his target customers. On several occasions, the show's host has called Fiore to ask questions about a particular herb, giving The Herbal Remedy a promotional boost that normal advertising just cannot buy. Fiore also sponsors a series of free in-store seminars on a variety of health topics, and some have drawn standing-room-only crowds. One of the most effective forms of promotion for Fiore is word-of-mouth advertising from satisfied customers. Their positive experiences with The Herbal Remedy lead them to recommend the store to their friends, which has helped Fiore's customer base to grow rapidly. Fiore's promotional efforts are not only fun for both him and his customers, but they also create interest in his store's herbal products and keep his business thriving in the face of larger competitors—and for very little money.*[1]

The first step is to define the purpose of the company's marketing communications program by creating "...specific, realistic, and measurable objectives. In other words, the owner must decide, "What do I want to accomplish with my messages?" Some ads are designed to stimulate responses by encouraging customers to purchase a particular product in the immediate future. The object here is to trigger a purchase decision. Other ads seek to build the firm's image among its customers and the general public. These ads try to create goodwill by keeping the firm's name in the public's memory so that customers will recall the firm's name when they decide to purchase a product or service. Still other ads strive to draw new customers, build mailing lists, increase foot traffic in a store, or introduce a company or a product into a new territory. Good publicity promotes the firm or its products in a positive way. All personal selling is consistent with the market image created.

The next step in developing a communications plan is to analyze the firm and its target audience. A business owner who does not know who his target market is cannot effectively reach it! A marketing communications plan does not have to reach tens of thousands of people to be successful, but it must efficiently reach the people who are most likely to buy a company's product or services. An entrepreneur should address the following questions to focus a company's communications efforts.

- What business am I in?
- What image do I want to project?
- Who are my target customers and what are their characteristics?
- Through which media can they best be reached?
- What do my customers *really* purchase from me?
- What benefits can customers derive from my goods or services?
- How can I prove those benefits to my target customers?
- What sets my company, products, or services apart from the competition?
- How do I want to position my company in the market?
- What advertising approach do my competitors take?

Answering these questions will help entrepreneurs define their businesses and profile their customers, which will help focus the marketing message on a specific target market and get more for their advertising dollars. Defining these issues at the outset enables entrepreneurs to select the media that will reach their target audiences with the least amount of waste. For instance, the owner of a small photography studio specializing in portraits might know from experience that the target customers are "parents, ages 25 to 45, with children under 14" and that mothers are the ones who control the buying decision.

Once business owners have defined their target audience, they can design marketing messages and choose the media for transmitting them. At this stage, the owners decide what to say and how to say it. Creativity and originality count!

Unique Selling Proposition

Entrepreneurs should build their ads around a **unique selling proposition (USP)**, a key customer benefit of a product or service that sets it apart from its competition. To be effective, a USP must actually *be* unique—something the competition does not (or cannot) provide, as well as compelling enough to encourage customers to buy. One technique is to replace your company's name and logo with those of your top competitor. Does the ad still make sense? If so, the ad is not based on your company's unique selling proposition!

A successful USP answers the critical question every customer asks: "What's in it for me?" Can your product or service save customers time or money, make their lives easier or more convenient, improve their self-esteem, or make them feel better? If so, you have the foundation for building a USP. The USP becomes the heart of your advertising message. Unfortunately, many business owners never define their companies' USP, and the result is an uninspiring "me-too" message that cries out "buy from us" without offering customers any compelling reason to do so.

The best way to identify a meaningful USP is to describe the primary benefit your product or service offers customers and then to list other secondary benefits it provides. You are unlikely to have more than three top benefits. Be sure to look beyond just the physical characteristics of your product or service. Sometimes the most powerful USPs are the *intangible or psychological* benefits a product or service offers customers—for example, safety, security, acceptance, status, and others. You must be careful, however, to avoid stressing minuscule differences that are irrelevant to customers. Before developing an integrated marketing communications program, it is also important to develop a brief list of the facts that support your company's USP—for example, 24-hour service, a fully trained staff, awards won, and so on. By focusing the message on these top benefits and the facts supporting them, business owners can communicate their USPs to their target audiences in meaningful, attention-getting ways. Building a firm's marketing message around

unique selling proposition (USP)—*a key customer benefit of a product or service that sets it apart from its competition; it answers the customer's question: "What's in it for me?"*

a USP spells out for customers the specific benefit they get if they buy that product or service and why they should do business with your company rather than with the competition.

Table 8.1 describes a six-sentence advertising strategy designed to create powerful ads that focus on a USP.

Learning Objective

2. Describe the operational elements of a marketing communications plan.

THE OPERATIONAL ELEMENTS OF A MARKETING COMMUNICATIONS PLAN

The marketing communication plan is made operational by ensuring that all elements of the plan (advertising , publicity, and personal selling) achieve a consistent message that is based on the firm's unique selling proposition. Each element supports the others and is designed to continually reinforce a company's fundamental marketing message.

Advertising

advertising—*any sales presentation that is nonpersonal in nature and is paid for by an identified sponsor.*

Advertising is any sales presentation that is nonpersonal in nature and is paid for by an identified sponsor. The benefit accruing to a business from effective advertising is recognition that lasts for a long period of time. Effective advertising continually reinforces the positive perceptions customers have of the business. Successful entrepreneurs consciously strive to integrate advertising, publicity, and personal selling in ways that achieve the desired image in the mind of the customer and a clear message that is focused on the firm's unique selling proposition.

Effective advertising, in any form or format, is constructed on a strong, positive, and well-researched product/brand positioning statement that represents a precise understanding of whom your target audience is, how your product or services are capable of satisfying their needs and wants, and what message customers will respond most positively to.

Figure 8.1 illustrates the characteristics of a successful ad.

A company's target audience and the nature of its message determine the advertising media it will use. However, the process does not end with creating and broadcasting an ad. The final step involves evaluating the ad campaign's effectiveness. Did it accomplish the objectives it was designed to accomplish? Immediate-response ads can be evaluated in a number of ways. For instance, an owner can include coupons that customers redeem to get price reductions on products and services. Dated coupons identify customer responses over certain time periods. Some firms use hidden offers—statements hidden somewhere in an ad that offer customers special deals if they mention an ad or bring in a coupon from an ad. For example, Scott Fiore of The Herbal Remedy puts a "bring this ad in for 10 percent off" message in his print ads so he can track each ad's success rate and adjust his expenditures accordingly.

Business owners can also gauge an ad's effectiveness by measuring the volume of store traffic generated. Effective advertising should increase store traffic, which boosts sales of advertised

TABLE 8.1

A Six-Sentence Advertising Strategy

Source: Adapted from Jay Conrad Levinson, "The Six-Sentence Strategy," *Communication Briefings*, December 1994, p. 4.

Does your advertising deliver the message you want to the audience you are targeting? If not, try stating your strategy in six sentences:

Primary purpose. What is the primary purpose of this ad? "The purpose of Rainbow Tours' ads is to get people to call or write for a free video brochure."

Primary benefit. What USP can you offer customers? "We will stress the unique and exciting places our customers can visit."

Secondary benefits. What other key benefits support your USP? "We will also stress the convenience and value of our tours and the skill and experience of our tour guides."

Target audience. At whom are we aiming the ad? "We will aim our ads at adventurous male and female singles and couples, 21 to 34, who can afford our tours."

Audience reaction. What response do you want from your target audience? "We expect our audience to call or write to request our video brochure."

Company personality. What image do we want to convey in our ads? "Our ads will reflect our innovation, excitement, conscientiousness, and our warm, caring attitude toward our customers."

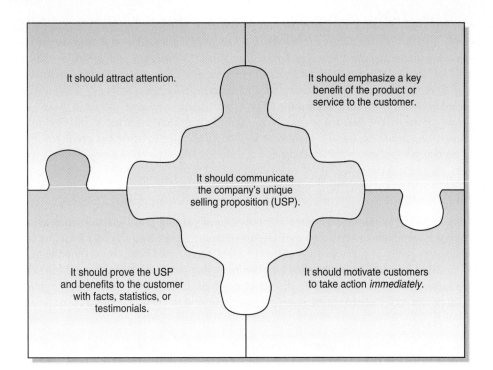

FIGURE 8.1 Five Fundamentals of a Successful Advertisement

Source: Adapted from Jerry Fisher, "Fine Print," *Entrepreneur,* November 1994, pp. 145–147.

It should attract attention.

It should emphasize a key benefit of the product or service to the customer.

It should communicate the company's unique selling proposition (USP).

It should prove the USP and benefits to the customer with facts, statistics, or testimonials.

It should motivate customers to take action *immediately*.

and nonadvertised items. Of course, if an advertisement promotes a particular bargain item, the owner can judge its effectiveness by comparing sales of the items to preadvertising sales levels. Remember: The ultimate test of an ad is whether or not it increases sales!

Ad tests can help determine the most effective methods of reaching potential customers. An owner can design two different ads (or use two different media or broadcast times) that are coded for identification and see which one produces more responses. For example, a business owner can use a split run of two different ads in a local newspaper. That is, he can place one ad in part of the paper's press run and another ad in the remainder of the run. Then he can measure the response level to each ad to compare its effectiveness. Figure 8.1 illustrates the characteristics of a successful ad, and Table 8.2 describes seven tests every advertisement should pass.

TABLE 8.2

Can Your Advertisement Pass These Seven Tests?

Source: Adapted from Galen Stilson, "Put Your Advertising Through These Quick Tests," Smart Business Supersite, www.smartbiz.com/sbs/columns/stll6.htm.

Test 1. The scan test. Scan the ad quickly, reading only the headline and any copy that is designed to stand out and looking at the photos or drawings that it includes. Can you tell what the ad is offering and, more importantly, does the benefit jump out at you?

Test 2. The comprehension test. Give the ad to someone who fits the profile of your target audience but who is unfamiliar with the product or service you are advertising. After reading the ad once, can that person tell you what the product or service is, what benefits it provides, what the offer is, and how to order?

Test 3. The differentiation test. Does the combination of ad copy and graphics differentiate your product or service from those of your competition? If a prospective customer read your ad and one of your chief competitor's ads, would she be able to tell how your product is different and better?

Test 4. The puffery test. Go through your copy and highlight every word or phrase that can be considered "sales puffery," such as "best," "greatest," "finest," and others. Can you eliminate these words and replace them with specific facts? If not, can you support the ad's claims with customer testimonials?

Test 5. The believability test. Give your ad to a potential customer and ask her to read through it. Ask her to highlight any claims in the ad that she finds hard to believe. Can you change them to make them more believable or offer facts to support them?

Test 6. The immediate clarity test. After the potential customer conducts the believability test, ask her to circle any words, phrases, or abbreviations that are not clear to her. Rewrite those parts of your ad.

Test 7. The USP test. Is the ad built around your company's USP? Does the USP come through in the message the ad sends to potential customers?

*Greg Schirf is the founder of **Schirf Brewing Company** in Park City, Utah. You might ask yourself why anyone would open a brewery in the state of Utah where 70 percent of the population are members of the Church of Latter Day Saints (Mormons), which forbids the consumption of alcohol. Greg Schirf's advertising creates great controversy in the conservative state of Utah, and the reaction of authorities to his ads generates a world of free publicity. Consider his irreverent ads, including "The Other Local Religion, Wasatch Beer" and "Polygamy Porter: Why Just Have One." Greg Schirf's ads have been successful in drawing attention to his products, but it's important to recognize that this style has great risk if the target market is offended by the message.[2]*

Publicity

publicity—*publicity - any commercial news covered by the media that boosts sales but for which a small company does not pay.*

Publicity or public relations is an intentional process of gaining positive recognition about a business or its products or services by writing interesting and newsworthy articles about what the business is doing or plans to do. **Publicity** is any commercial news covered by the media that is positive in nature, with the distinct possibility that it will increase recognition of the firm or its products. Publicity, unlike advertising, is free. In addition to being free, publicity has great power to influence an interested reader because it is viewed as more objective than advertising.

*After the launch of **Pumpkin Masters**, a company that makes pumpkin-carving kits complete with carving tools, elaborate templates, and instructions, John Bardeen was disappointed by the company's lackluster sales. Then, with the help of a loyal customer, the power of publicity changed Pumpkin Masters' fortune. With Bardeen's permission, the customer contacted ABC television and convinced the network to display pumpkins carved with the likenesses of the announcers on* Monday Night Football. *ABC showed the pumpkin carvings throughout the broadcast and opened the show with a scary pumpkin called "Skull" that Bardeen himself had carved. The national exposure jump-started Pumpkin Masters' sales immediately, and the company now sells more than 2 million pumpkin-carving kits each year.[3]*

The following tactics can help any small business owner stimulate publicity for her firm:

Write an article that will interest your customers or potential customers. Business owners often overlook the fact that newspapers and magazines are almost always in search of interesting and newsworthy material that fits their readerships. One investment advisor writes a monthly column for the local newspaper on timely topics such as retirement planning, minimizing your tax bill, and investing strategies for the new century. Not only do the articles help build her credibility as an expert, but they also have attracted new customers to her business. When writing articles, remember to keep them short, with 200 to 300 words for a new product release, 500 to 1,000 words on how your products or services solved a unique problem or helped a customer, and at the most a 3,000-word feature article if addressing a very relevant issue on which you or your firm is considered an authority or expert. Whenever possible, support your article with photos, charts, or diagrams that further illustrate your message and improve reader understanding.

Sponsor an offbeat event designed to attract attention. Karen Neuburger, owner of Karen Neuburger's Sleepwear, throws pajama parties in stores across the country to promote her line of sleepwear. Local news media almost always cover the party, giving Neuburger's company lots of free exposure.[4]

Involve celebrities "on the cheap." Few small businesses can afford to hire celebrities as spokespersons for their companies. Some companies have discovered other ways to get celebrities to promote their products, however. For instance, when Karen Neuburger learned that Oprah Winfrey is a "pajama connoisseur," she sent the talk show host a pair of her pajamas. The move paid off; Neuburger has appeared on Oprah's popular television show on three separate occasions.[5]

Contact local TV and radio stations and offer to be interviewed. Many local news or talk shows are looking for guests to talk about topics of interest to their audiences (especially in January and February). Even local shows can reach new customers.

Publish a newsletter. With a personal computer and desktop publishing software, any entrepreneur can publish a professional-looking newsletter. Freelancers can offer design and editing advice. Use the newsletter to reach present and potential customers.

Contact local business and civic organizations and offer to speak to them. A powerful, informative presentation can win new business. (Be sure your public speaking skills are up to par first! If not, consider joining Toastmasters.)

Offer or sponsor a seminar. Teaching people about a subject you know a great deal about builds confidence and goodwill among potential customers. The owner of a landscaping service and nursery offers a short course in landscape architecture and always sees sales climb afterward!

Write news releases and fax or e-mail them to the media. The key to having a news release picked up and printed is finding a unique angle on your business or industry that would interest an editor. Keep it short, simple, and interesting. E-mail press releases should be shorter than printed ones—typically four or five paragraphs rather than one or two pages—and they should include a company's Web site address.

*Steve Hoffman, cofounder of **LavaMind**, a CD-ROM game and Web site development company, uses e-mail press releases to generate publicity for his company. Hoffman's e-mail press releases have led to articles in the* New York Times, Wall Street Journal, *and* Business Week, *and others as well as to television coverage on ABC, PBS, and CNBC. Hoffman says that half of LavaMind's sales have come as a result of the publicity generated by his e-mail releases.*[6]

Volunteer to serve on community and industry boards and committees. You can make your town a better place to live and work and raise your company's visibility at the same time.

Sponsor a community project or support a nonprofit organization or charity. Not only will you be giving something back to the community, but you will also gain recognition, goodwill, and, perhaps, customers for your business.

The owner of a dry cleaning business received the equivalent of thousands of dollars' worth of advertising from the publicity generated by a program called "Give the gift of warmth." Customers donated winter coats, which the company cleaned for free and then distributed to the needy.

Promote a cause. Business owners who have a passion for a cause should act on its behalf. Socially responsible acts often turn into highly successful public relations efforts that attract valuable publicity.

Sponsorships and Special Events

Although sponsorships of special events are a relatively new advertising medium for small companies, a growing number of small businesses are finding that sponsoring special events attracts a great deal of interest and provides a lasting impression of the company in customers' minds. As customers become increasingly harder to reach through any single advertising medium, companies of all sizes are finding that sponsoring special events—from wine tastings and beach volleyball tournaments to fitness walks and car races—is an excellent way to reach their target audiences. According to the *IEG Sponsorship Report*, companies in North America spend more than $7 billion each year on sponsorships.[7]

Sports events, such as basketball tournaments, soccer matches, and NASCAR races, draw the greatest interest from sponsors. In fact, NASCAR events boast the largest increase in attendance since 1990 of any professional sport, a fact that has not escaped sponsors.[8] Companies also have discovered that NASCAR sponsorships work. Research suggests that NASCAR fans have the highest degree of loyalty to a sponsor's product than any other sport (72 percent versus 52 percent for tennis, 47 percent for golf, and 36 percent for football).[9] Getting your company's name on a race car is not cheap, however. The least expensive part of the car on which to put a company logo is the lower quarter panel, with the cost ranging from $25,000 to $75,000. The most expensive part of the car to sponsor? No surprise: the hood, at a cost of $4 to $6 million![10]

Although most small companies cannot afford the cost of sponsoring a NASCAR race car, there are plenty of more affordable events that generate impressive opportunities for increasing name recognition and customer awareness. For instance, according to the International Festival and Events Association, the number of festivals and events in the United States has doubled to more than 50,000 in the past 15 years.[11] Because of their local character, many of these festival, fairs, and events are ideally suited for small business sponsors. For instance, the owner of one small art gallery generates thousands of dollars' worth of publicity and

NASCAR fans exhibit high levels of loyalty to sponsors' products. NASCAR sponsors also benefit from reams of publicity for their companies and the products they sell.

Courtesy of Nigel Kinrade Photography.

recognition for her company with her sponsorship of a local art show. The gala event features a sidewalk art exhibit, a "meet the artists" luncheon, and a competition among local artists. Hundreds of potential customers flock to her gallery on the night the winners are announced. The sponsorship costs the gallery owner a few thousand dollars, but the "buzz" it generates for her company is worth many times the cost!

Small companies do not have to rely on other organizations' events to generate advertising opportunities; they can create their own special events. Creativity and uniqueness are essential ingredients in any special event promotion, and most entrepreneurs excel at those.

A Company Example

*For example, the owner of **For Paws**, a California pet boutique, sponsors free "doggy brunches" each week, complete with "kibble quiche" and "wheat-germ woofies." The shop also caters birthday parties, beach parties (picture a dog with a whistle around his neck, a muscle T-shirt, and a dab of Noxzema on his nose), and other gala events for its four-legged customers and their owners.[12]*

The following tips will ensure that a small company gets the most promotional impact from its sponsorship of an event:

■ Do not count on sponsorships for your entire advertising campaign. Sponsorships are most effective when they are part of a coordinated advertising effort. Most sponsors spend no more than 10 percent of their advertising budgets on sponsorships.

■ Look for an event that is appropriate for your company and its products and services. The owner of a small music store in an upscale mountain resort sponsors a local jazz festival every summer during the busy tourist season and generates lots of business among both residents and tourists. Ideally, an event's audience should match the sponsoring company's target audience. Otherwise, the sponsorship will be a waste of money.

■ Research the event and the organization hosting it *before* agreeing to become a sponsor. How well attended is the event? What is the demographic profile of the event's visitors? Is it well organized?

■ Try to become a dominant (or, ideally, the only) sponsor of the event. A small company can be easily lost in a crowd of much larger companies sponsoring the same event. If sole sponsorship is too expensive, make sure that your company is the only one from its industry sponsoring the event.

■ Clarify the costs and level of participation required for sponsorship up front.

■ Get involved. Do not simply write a check for the sponsorship fee and then walk away. Find an event that is meaningful to you, your company, and its employees and take an active role in it. Your sponsorship dollars will produce a higher return if you do.

Hybrid Forms of Promotion and Advertising

In some cases the line between what is advertising and what is promotion has become blurry. In recent years, entrepreneurs have begun to explore new methods of placing their products or services before the targeted market in a more subtle fashion. *Sponsorship* of participants in sporting events or entertainment comes first to mind, such as laundry detergent manufacturers that sponsor NASCAR race teams or musical group tours. The key is to have your product or service identified with an individual, group, or sport that your target customers admire.

The next step up the hierarchy is *product placement*, a term that broadly describes the strategy of having your product seen in successful movies or television programs. It is highly sophisticated yet subtle brand exposure. For example, Roxy, the California clothing company that targets younger consumers with its trendy clothing styles, coproduces a television show for MTV. Throughout the show, the cast wears Roxy clothing exclusively.[13]

Branded content is the ultimate integration of advertising and entertainment. Branded content creates an entertainment product (documentary, music video, book, or even Broadway play) to reflect the brand's image or spirit. As an example, Nike's documentary, "The Road to Paris," profiles champion cyclist and Nike endorser, Lance Armstrong.[14]

Personal Selling

Advertising often marks the beginning of a sale, but personal selling usually is required to close the sale. **Personal selling** is the personal contact between salespeople and potential customers resulting from sales efforts. Effective personal selling can give the small company a definite advantage over its larger competitors by creating a feeling of personal attention. Personal selling deals with the salesperson's ability to match customer needs to the firm's goods and services. Top salespeople have the following profile:

personal selling—*the personal contact between salespeople and potential customers resulting from sales efforts.*

- They are enthusiastic and alert to opportunities. They realize that the next great account they may find through a chance social meeting rather than a scheduled sales call. Star sales representatives also demonstrate deep concentration, high energy, and drive.
- They are experts in the products or services they sell. They understand how their product lines or services can help their customers and, they are able to articulate this to customers.
- Top salespeople concentrate on select accounts. They focus on customers with the greatest sales potential.
- They plan thoroughly. On every sales call, the best representatives act with a purpose to close the sale.
- Top salespeople use a direct approach. They get right to the point with customers.
- They work from the customer's perspective. They have empathy for their customers and know their customers' businesses and their needs.
- They use "past success stories." They encourage customers to express their problems and then present solutions using examples of past successes.
- They leave sales material with clients. The material gives the customer the opportunity to study company and product literature in more detail.[15]
- Top salespeople see themselves as problem solvers, not just vendors. Their perspective is "How can I be a valuable resource for my customers?"
- They measure their success not just by sales volume but also by customer satisfaction.[16]

Effective selling is never an accident, and it is wrong to assume that anyone can be successful at personal selling. Selling requires training about the product or service. You cannot effectively sell what you do not understand. And what may be worse, an uninformed salesperson may misrepresent the firm's products or services. Hire capable individuals who display empathy for customers, are personally motivated to succeed, are patient, and possess the ability to focus on the satisfaction of the customer's buying needs.

Sales training needs to be a blend of product or service knowledge as well as the most important basic selling skills of listening to customers and closing the sale.

The Selling Process

Small business owners can improve their sales representatives' "batting averages" by following some basic guidelines:

ESTABLISH A SELLING SYSTEM.   A successful sales call usually is the result of a systematic sales approach.

1. *Create a feeling of mutual trust and respect.* Establish a rapport with the prospect at the outset. Customers seldom buy from salespeople they dislike or distrust.

2. *Ask the prospect questions that will reveal the key criteria that must be met to obtain the sale.* Customers tend to have a few "must" criteria that will influence their willingness to buy; identify these and then base your selling approach on meeting or exceeding these key criteria. The goal is to identify the prospect's needs, preferences, concerns, and problems.

3. *Demonstrate, explain, and show.* Make clear the features and benefits of your product or service and point out how they meet the prospect's needs or solve his problems.

4. *Validate.* Prove the claims about your product or service. If possible, offer the prospect names and numbers of other satisfied customers (with their permission, of course). Testimonials really work.

5. *Overcome objections.* Listen for objections from the prospect. Try to determine the *real* objection and confront it. Work to overcome it. Objections can be the salesperson's best friend; they tell you what must be "fixed" before the prospect will commit to an order. Remember to focus on the customer's buying criteria.

6. *Close.* Ask for a decision. Good sales representatives know when the prospect flashes the green light on a sale. They stop talking and ask for the order.

BE EMPATHETIC AND STRESS VALUE.   The best salespeople look at the sale from the customer's viewpoint, not their own! Doing so encourages the sales representative to stress *value* to the customer.

SET MULTIPLE OBJECTIVES.   Before making a sales call, salespeople should set three objectives:

1. *The primary objective*—the most reasonable outcome expected from the meeting. It may be to get an order or to learn more about a prospect's needs.

2. *The minimum objective*—the very least the salesperson will leave with. It may be to set another meeting or to identify the prospect's primary objections.

3. *The visionary objective*—the most optimistic outcome of the meeting. This objective forces the salesperson to be open-minded and to shoot for the top.

MONITOR SALES EFFORTS AND RESULTS.   Selling is just like any other business activity and must be controlled. At a minimum, the business owner should know:

1. Actual sales versus projected sales
2. Sales generated per call made
3. Total sales costs
4. Sales by product, salesperson, territory, customer, and so on
5. Profit contribution by product, salesperson, territory, customer, and so on

Learning Objective

3. Describe the advantages and disadvantages of the various advertising media.

A Company Example

SELECTING ADVERTISING MEDIA

One of the most important decisions an entrepreneur must make is which media to use in disseminating the advertising message. The medium used to transmit the message influences the consumer's perception—and reception—of it. By choosing the proper advertising media, a business owner can reach his target audience effectively at minimum cost. Similarly, the right message communicated in the wrong medium will not increase sales.

*For instance, when they launched **Micro Express**, a computer services firm, the founders allocated an annual advertising budget of $50,000, most of it for ads in large newspapers. For seven years, major newspapers remained the company's primary advertising medium. Then managers began to examine their customer base more closely and discovered that their customers were large companies rather than the small companies and home users at whom its ads* *were targeted. Realizing that Micro Express's advertising had been missing its mark, the company switched to direct mailings to* Fortune 1000 *companies. Not only do the direct-mail ads cost the company less, but its sales are also climbing again. "We see a much higher return now that we spend $10,000 a year on the right promotional efforts compared to the $50,000 we spent per year targeting the wrong customers," says President Jim Mickel.*[17]

Key Advertising Concepts

Although no single formula exists for determining the ideal medium to use, there are several important characteristics that make some media better suited than others. Understanding the qualities of the various media available can simplify an owner's decision. Before selecting the vehicle for the message, the owner should consider several questions:

How large is my firm's trading area? How big is the geographical region from which the firm will draw its customers? The size of this area influences the choice of media.

Who are my target customers and what are their characteristics? Determining a customer profile often points to the appropriate medium to use to get the message across most effectively.

Which media are my target customers most likely to watch, listen to, or read? Until he knows who his target audience is, a business owner cannot select the proper advertising media to reach it.

What budget limitations do I face? Every business owner must direct the firm's advertising program within the restrictions of its operating budget. Certain advertising media cost more than others.

What media do my competitors use? It is helpful for the small business manager to know the media his competitors use, although he should *not* automatically assume that they are the best. An approach that differs from the traditional one may produce better results.

How important is repetition and continuity of my advertising message? Generally, an ad becomes effective only after it is repeated several times, and many ads must be continued for some time before they produce results. Some experts suggest that an ad must be run at least six times in most mass media before it becomes effective.

How does each medium compare with others in its audience, its reach, and its frequency? **Audience** measures the number of paid subscribers a particular medium attracts and is called *circulation* in most print media such as newspapers and magazines. **Reach** is the total number of people exposed to an ad at least once in a period of time, usually four weeks. **Frequency** is the average number of times a person is exposed to an ad in that same time period.

What does the advertising medium cost? There are two types of advertising costs the small business manager must consider: the absolute cost and the relative cost. **Absolute cost** is the actual dollar outlay a business owner must make to place an ad in a particular medium for a specific time period. An even more important measure is an ad's **relative cost,** the ad's cost per potential customer reached. Relative cost is most often expressed as **cost per thousand (CPM)**, the cost of the ad per 1,000 customers reached. Suppose a manager decides to advertise his product in one of two newspapers in town. The *Sentinel* has a circulation of 21,000 and charges $1,200 for a quarter-page ad. The *Democrat* has a circulation of 18,000 and charges $1,300 for the same space. Reader profiles of the two papers suggest that 25 percent of *Sentinel* readers and 37 percent of the *Democrat* readers are potential customers. Using this information, the manager computes the following relative costs:

audience—*a measure of the number of paid subscribers a particular medium attracts.*

reach—*the total number of people exposed to an ad at least once in a period of time, usually four weeks.*

frequency—*the average number of times a person is exposed to an ad in a period of time.*

absolute cost—*the actual dollar outlay a business owner must make to place an ad in a particular medium for a specific period of time.*

relative cost—*the cost of an ad per potential customer reached.*

cost per thousand (CPM)—*the cost of an ad per 1,000 customers reached.*

	Sentinel	Democrat
Circulation	21,000	18,000
Percentage of readers that are potential customers (p.c.)	×25%	×37%
Potential customers reached	5,250	6,660
Absolute cost of ad	$1,200	$1,300

Relative cost of ad (CPM) $\dfrac{\$1,200}{5.250} = .22857$ or $228.57 1,000 per p.c. $\dfrac{\$1,300}{6,600} = .19520$ or $195.20 1,000 per p.c.

Although the *Sentinel* has a larger circulation and a lower absolute cost for running the ad, the *Democrat* will serve the small business owner better because it offers a lower cost per thousand potential customers (CPM) reached. It is important to note that this technique does not give a reliable comparison across media; it is a meaningful comparison only within a single medium. Differences among the format, presentation, and coverage of ads in different media are so vast that such comparisons are not meaningful.

Traditional Media Options

Figure 8.2 gives a breakdown of U.S. business advertising expenditures by medium. Choosing advertising media is no easy task because each has distinctive advantages, disadvantages, and cost. The "right" message in the "wrong" medium will miss its mark.

word-of-mouth advertising—*advertising in which satisfied customers recommend a business to friends, family members, and acquaintances.*

WORD-OF-MOUTH ADVERTISING AND ENDORSEMENTS. Perhaps the most effective and certainly the least expensive form of advertising is **word-of-mouth advertising** in which satisfied customers recommend a business to friends, family members, and acquaintances. Unsolicited testimonials are powerful because they carry so much weight among potential customers. The best way to generate positive word-of-mouth advertising is to provide the superior quality and service discussed in chapter 6. Providing that level of service and quality leads to loyal customers who become walking advertisements for the companies they believe in. Word-of-mouth advertising can make or break a business because *dissatisfied* customers also speak out against businesses that treat them poorly. To ensure that the word-of-mouth advertising a company generates is positive, business owners must actually do what they want their customers to say they do!

A Company Example

*For instance, Fred Anderson, owner of **Anderson's Landscape Construction**, a landscape planning and design service that targets upscale homes, relies totally on word-of-mouth advertising for his company's sales. Anderson counts on referrals from professional architects and from satisfied customers to generate new business. If a customer is unhappy about any aspect of a project his company has done, Anderson fixes it to the customer's satisfaction at no extra charge, which surprises some people.*[18]

A customer endorsement is an effective way of converting the power of word of mouth to an advertising message. The more recognized the person making the endorsement, the more potential customers will be influenced to buy. For example, Brad Johnson, quarterback for the Tampa Bay Buccaneers, has appeared on local Tampa Bay stations endorsing Fantastic Sams for haircuts. After their stunning win in Super Bowl XXXVII, the endorsement became even more meaningful to Tampa fans. Of course, unpaid and unsolicited endorsements are the most valuable. In a cynical world, many potential customers are turned off by what they believe is simply a paid statement from a person who may or may not have used the product.

The ultimate in word-of-mouth advertising is the holy grail of advertising, something experts call "buzz." Buzz occurs when a product is hot and everyone is talking about it.

FIGURE 8.2 Advertising Expenditures by Medium

Source: McCann-Erickson, Inc. *Statistical Abstract of the United States, 2002,* p. 772.

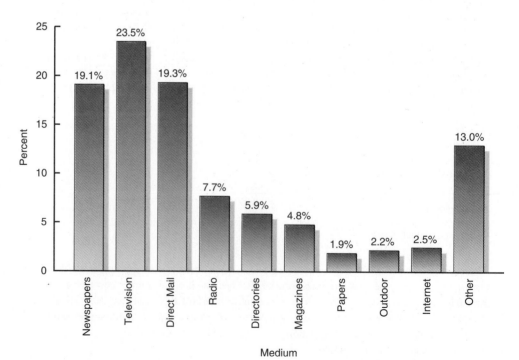

From the mood rings of the 1970s to the redesigned Volkswagen Beetle of the 1990s, buzz drives the sales of many products. The Internet has only magnified the power of buzz to influence a product's sales. Buzz on the Web has become a powerful force in influencing the popularity of a firm's products or services. What can business owners do to start a buzz about their companies or their products or services? Sometimes buzz starts on its own, leaving a business owner struggling to keep up with the fury it creates. More often than not, however, business owners can give it a nudge by creating interest, mystique, and curiosity in a product or service or by ensuring its scarcity. Ty Inc. has managed to keep collectors interested for years by "retiring" some of its Beanie Baby patterns every year to ensure that demand for them outstrips supply.

NEWSPAPERS. Traditionally, the local newspaper has been the medium that most advertisers rely on to get their messages across to customers. Although the number of newspapers in the United States has declined in recent years, this medium attracts nearly one-fifth of all advertising dollars nationwide.

Newspapers provide several *advantages* to the small business advertiser:

Selected geographical coverage. Newspapers are geared to a specific geographic region, and they reach potential customers across all demographic classes.

Flexibility. Newspaper advertisements can be changed readily on very short notice. The owner can select the size of the ad and its location in the paper.

Timeliness. Papers almost always have very short closing times, the publication deadline prior to which the advertising copy must be submitted.

Communication potential. Newspaper ads can convey a great deal of information by employing attractive graphics and copy.

Low costs. Newspapers normally offer advertising space at low absolute cost and, because of their blanket coverage of a geographic area, at low relative cost as well.

Prompt responses. Newspaper ads typically produce relatively quick customer responses. A newspaper ad is likely to generate sales the very next day, and advertisers who use coupons can track the response to an ad.

Of course, newspaper advertisements also have *disadvantages*:

Wasted readership. Because newspapers reach such a variety of people, at least a portion of an ad's coverage will be wasted on those who are not potential customers.

Reproduction limitations. The quality of reproduction in newspapers is limited, especially when it is compared to that of magazines and direct mail.

Source: REPRINTED BY PERMISSION OF NEWSPAPER ENTERPRISE ASSOCIATION, INC.

Lack of prominence. One frequently cited drawback of newspapers is that they carry so many ads that a small company's message might be lost in the crowd. The typical newspaper is 62 percent advertising.

Declining readership. Newspaper circulation as a percentage of U.S. households has dropped from 98 percent in 1970 to 70 percent today. Newspaper ads would be least effective for small businesses targeting young people, who are least likely to read newspapers.

Short ad life. The typical newspaper is soon discarded and, as a result, an ad's life is extremely short. Business owners can increase the effectiveness of their ads by giving them greater continuity. Spot ads can produce results, but maintaining a steady flow of business requires some degree of continuity in advertising.

BUYING NEWSPAPER SPACE. Newspapers typically sell ad space by lines and columns or inches and columns. For instance, a 4-column × 100-line ad occupies four columns and 100 lines of space (14 lines are equal to 1 column inch). For this ad, the small business owner would pay the rate for 400 lines. Most papers offer discounts for bulk, long-term, and frequency contracts and for full-page ads. Advertising rates vary from one paper to another, depending on such factors as circulation and focus. A small business owner would do well to investigate the circulation statements, advertising rates, and reader profiles of the various newspapers available before selecting one.

RADIO. Newspapers offer blanket advertising coverage of a region, but radio permits advertisers to appeal to specific audiences over large geographic areas. By choosing the appropriate station, program, and time for an ad, a small company can reach virtually *any* target market.

Radio advertising offers several *advantages*:

Universal infiltration. Radio's nearly universal presence gives advertisements in this medium a major advantage. Virtually every home and car in the United States is equipped with a radio, which means that these advertising messages receive a tremendous amount of exposure in the target market. Radio reaches 94 percent of all consumers each week![19]

Market segmentation. Radio advertising is flexible and efficient because advertisers can choose stations directed toward a specific market within a broad geographic region. Radio stations design their formats to appeal to specific types of audiences, which makes an advertiser's job much easier.

Flexibility and timeliness. Radio commercials have short closing times and can be changed quickly.

Friendliness. Radio ads are more "active" than ads in printed media because they use the spoken word to influence customers. Vocal subtleties used in radio ads are impossible to convey through printed media. Table 8.3 offers a guide to producing effective radio copy.

Radio advertisements also have a number of *disadvantages*:

Poor listening. Radio's intrusiveness into the public life almost guarantees that customers will hear ads, but they may not listen to them.

Need for repetition. Radio ads must be broadcast repeatedly to be effective.

Limited message. Because radio ads are limited to one minute or less, the message must be brief and not overly complex.

BUYING RADIO TIME. The small business owner can zero in on a specific advertising target by using the appropriate radio station. Stations follow various formats—from rap to rhapsodies—to appeal to specific audiences. Radio advertising time usually sells in 15-second, 30-second, and 60-second increments, with the latter being the most common. Fixed spots are guaranteed to be broadcast at the times specified in the owner's contract with the station. Preemptible spots are cheaper than fixed spots, but the advertiser risks being preempted by an advertiser willing to pay the fixed rate for a time slot. Floating spots are the least expensive, but the advertiser has no control over broadcast times. Many stations offer package plans, using flexible combinations of fixed, preemptible, and floating spots.

Radio rates vary depending on the time of day they are broadcast and, like television, there are prime time slots known as drive-time spots. Although exact hours may differ from station to station, the following classifications are common (listed in descending order of cost):

- *Mention the business often.* This is the single most important and inflexible rule in radio advertising. Also make sure listeners know how to find your business. If the address is complicated, use landmarks.
- *Stress the benefit to the listener.* Don't say "Bryson's has new fall fashions." Say "Bryson's fall fashions make you look fabulous."
- *Use attention-getters.* Radio has a whole battery—music, sound effects, unusual voices. Crack the barrier with sound.
- *Zero in on your audience.* Know to whom you're selling. Radio's selectivity attracts the right audience. It's up to you to communicate in the right language.
- *Keep the copy simple and to the point.* Don't try to impress listeners with vocabulary. "To be or not to be" may be the best-known phrase in the language . . . and the longest word has just three letters.
- *Sell early and often.* Don't back into the selling message. At most, you've got 60 seconds. Make the most of them. Don't be subtle.
- *Write for the ear.* Write conversationally.
- *Prepare your copy.* Underline words you want to emphasize.
- *Triple space.* Type clean, legible copy. Make the announcer rehearse.
- *Use positive action words.* Use words such as *now* and *today*, particularly when you're writing copy for a sale. Radio has qualities of urgency and immediacy. Take advantage of them by including a time limit or the date the sale ends.
- *Put the listener in the picture.* Radio's theater of the mind means you don't have to talk about a new car. With sounds and music, you can put the listener behind the wheel.
- *Focus the spot on getting a response.* Make it clear what you want the listener to do. Don't try to get a mail response. Use phone numbers only, and repeat the number three times. End the spot with the phone number.
- *Don't stay with a loser.* Direct-response ads produce results right way—or not at all. Don't stick with a radio spot that is not generating sales. Change it.

Class AA: Morning drive time—6 A.M. to 10 A.M.

Class A: Evening drive time—4 P.M. to 7 P.M.

Class B: Home worker time—10 A.M. to 4 P.M.

Class C: Evening time—7 P.M. to Midnight

Class D: Nighttime—Midnight to 6 A.M.

Some stations may also have different rates for weekend time slots.

TELEVISION. In advertising dollars spent, television now ranks first in popularity of all media. Although the cost of national TV ads precludes their use by most small businesses, local spots can be an extremely effective means of broadcasting a small company's message. A 30-second commercial on network television may cost more than $500,000, but a 30-second spot on local cable television, which now is in 67 percent of all U.S. homes, may go for $200 or less.

Television offers a number of distinct *advantages*:

Broad coverage. Television ads provide extensive coverage of a sizable region, and they reach a significant portion of the population. About 98 percent of the homes in the United States have a television, and the average household spends 7 hours and 12 minutes each day tuned in to television.[20]

Visual advantage. The primary benefit of television is its capacity to present an advertiser's product or service in a graphic, vivid manner with sight, sound, and action.

Flexibility. Television ads can be modified quickly to meet the rapidly changing conditions in the marketplace. Advertising on TV is the closest substitute for personal selling.

Design and production assistance. Few small business owners have the skills to prepare an effective television commercial. Although professional production firms might easily charge $50,000 for a commercial production, the television station from which a business owner purchases air time may be willing to offer design and production assistance very inexpensively.

Television advertising also has several *disadvantages*:

Brief exposure. Most television ads are on the screen for only a short time and require substantial repetition to achieve the desired effect.

zappers—television viewers who flash from one channel to another, especially during commercials.

Clutter. The typical person sees 1,500 advertising messages a day, and more ads are on the way. With so many ads beaming across the airwaves, a small business's advertising message could easily become lost in the shuffle.

"Zapping." **Zappers**, television viewers who flash from one channel to another, especially during commercials, pose a real threat to TV advertisers. Zapping means TV advertisers are not reaching the audiences they hope to reach. The remote control has transformed television viewers into channel surfers during commercial breaks.

Fragmented audience. As the number of channels available proliferates, the question of where to advertise becomes more difficult to answer. Network television has lost audience steadily over the past 20 years to cable television. About 96 percent of cable television households receive more than 30 channels.[21]

Costs. TV commercials can be expensive to create. A 30-second ad can cost several thousand dollars to develop, even before the owner purchases airtime. Table 8.4 offers some suggestions for developing creative television commercials.

USING TELEVISION CREATIVELY. Although television ads are not affordable for every small business, many entrepreneurs have found creative ways to use the power of television advertising without spending a fortune. Two popular methods include creating infomercials and using home shopping networks. **Infomercials** (also called direct-response television), full-length television commercials packed with information, testimonials, and a sales pitch, are popular tools for selling everything from mops to computers. Producing and airing a half-hour infomercial can be expensive, often costing $50,000 or more, but entrepreneurs can save money by doing some of the work themselves and hiring freelance professionals for a share of the profits.

infomercials—full-length television commercials packed with information, testimonials, and a sales pitch.

A Company Example

*After he launched **Smart Inventions**, Jon Nokes set out across the country to promote his latest product, the SmartMop, a unique mop from Finland with a self-wringing feature. In its first year, SmartMop generated $1.8 million in sales, but Nokes knew he could do much better if only he could let customers see the benefits of the SmartMop. Nokes worked with a production company to create a 28-minute infomercial for $60,000 to demonstrate the user-friendly mop. Consumer response to the infomercial amazed even Nokes. Whenever the infomercial aired, orders poured in—so fast, in fact, that Nokes had to invest in a larger manufacturing facility to keep up with demand. After a year of airing the infomercial, sales of the SuperMop had climbed to $44 million![22]*

To become an infomercial star, a product should meet the following criteria:[23]

- Be unique and of good quality.
- Solve a common problem.
- Be easy to use and easy to demonstrate.
- Appeal to a mass audience.
- Have an aha! factor that makes customers think "What a great idea!"

TABLE 8.4

Guidelines for Creative TV Ads

Source: Adapted from How to Make a Creative Television Commercial, Television Bureau of Advertising, Inc.

- *Keep it simple.* Avoid confusing the viewer by sticking to a simple concept.
- *Have one basic idea.* The message should focus on a single, important benefit to the customer. Why should people buy from your business?
- *Make your point clear.* The customer benefit should be obvious and easy to understand.
- *Make it unique . . . different.* To be effective, a television ad must reach out and grab the viewer's attention. Take advantage of television's visual experience.
- *Get viewer attention.* Unless viewers watch the ad, its effect is lost.
- *Involve the viewer.* To be most effective, an ad should portray a situation to which the viewer can relate. Common, everyday experiences are easiest for people to identify with.
- *Use emotion.* The most effective ads evoke an emotion from the viewer—a laugh, a tear, or a pleasant memory.
- *Consider production values.* Television offers vivid sights, colors, motions, and sounds. Use them!
- *Prove the benefit.* Television allows an advertiser to prove a product's or service's customer benefit by actually demonstrating it.
- *Identify your company well and often.* Make sure your store's name, location, and product line stand out. The ad should portray your company's image.

Shopping networks such as QVC and the Home Shopping Network offer entrepreneurs another route to television. Time on these networks is free, but getting a product accepted is tough. One buyer for QVC says that the network subjects about 500 products to an extensive review every week, but that only 5 percent are selected to appear on television.[24] Shopping networks look for products that offer quality, have "demonstration appeal," and are typically priced between $15 and $40 (although there are exceptions). Landing a product on one of these networks may be a challenge, but entrepreneurs who do often sell thousands of units in a matter of minutes!

MAGAZINES. Another advertising medium available to the small business owner is magazines. Today, customers have more than 18,600 magazine titles from which to choose.[25] Magazines have a wide reach; nearly 9 out of 10 adults read an average of 7 different magazines per month. The average magazine attracts 6 hours and 3 minutes of total adult reading time, and studies show that the reader is exposed to 89 percent of the ads in the average copy.[26]

Magazines offer several *advantages* for advertisers:

Long life spans. Magazines have a long reading life because readers tend to keep them longer than other printed media. The result is that each magazine ad has a good chance of being seen several times.

Multiple readership. The average magazine has a readership of 3.9 adult readers, and each reader spends about 1 hour and 33 minutes with each copy. Many magazines have a high "passalong" rate—they are handed down from reader to reader.

Target marketing. By selecting the appropriate special interest periodical, small business owners can reach customers with a high degree of interest in their goods or services. Specialty magazines have proliferated in recent years, giving businesses the opportunity to advertise in magazines such as *Surfer Girl* or *Ferrets* that target specific audiences.

Ad quality. Magazine ads usually are of high quality, resulting in strong visual appeal. Photographs and drawings can be reproduced very effectively, and color ads are readily available.

Magazines also have several *disadvantages*:

Costs. Magazine advertising rates vary according to their circulation rates; the higher the circulation, the higher the rate. Thus, local magazines, whose rates are often comparable to newspaper rates, may be the best bargain for small businesses.

Long closing times. Another disadvantage of magazines is the relatively long closing times they require. For a weekly periodical, the closing date for an ad may be several weeks before the actual publication date, making it difficult for advertisers to respond quickly to changing market conditions.

Lack of prominence. Another disadvantage of magazine ads arises from their popularity as an advertising vehicle. The effectiveness of a single ad may be reduced because of a lack of prominence; 48.3 percent of the typical magazine content is devoted to advertising.[27] Proper ad positioning, therefore, is critical to an ad's success. Research shows that readers "tune out" right-hand pages and look mainly at left-hand pages.

DIRECT MAIL. Direct mail has long been a popular method of small business advertising and includes such tools as letters, postcards, catalogs, discount coupons, brochures, computer disks, and videotapes mailed to homes or businesses. The earliest known catalogs were printed by fifteenth-century printers. Today, direct-mail marketers sell virtually every kind of product imaginable from Christmas trees and lobsters to furniture and clothing (the most popular mail-order purchase). Responding to the convenience of "shopping at home," customers purchase more than $500 billion worth of goods and services through mail order each year!

Direct mail offers a number of distinct *advantages* to the small business owner:

Selectivity. The greatest strength of direct-mail advertising is its ability to target a specific audience to receive the message. Depending on mailing list quality, an owner can select an audience with virtually any set of characteristics. Small business owners can develop, rent, or purchase a mailing list of prospective residential, commercial, or industrial customers.

Flexibility. Another advantage of direct mail is its capacity to tailor the message to the target. The advertiser's presentation to the customer can be as simple or as elaborate as necessary. In addition, the advertiser controls the timing of the campaign; she can send the ad when it is most appropriate.

Reader attention. With direct mail, the advertiser's message does not have to compete with other ads for the reader's attention. People enjoy getting mail.

Rapid feedback. Direct-mail advertisements produce quick results. In most cases the ad will generate sales within three to four days after customers receive it.

Measurable results and testable strategies. Because they control their mailing lists, direct marketers can readily measure the results their ads produce. Also, direct mail allows advertisers to test different ad layouts, designs, and strategies (often within the same "run") to see which one "pulls" the greatest response. Table 8.5 offers guidelines for creating direct-mail ads that really work.

Effectiveness. The right message targeted at the right mailing list can make direct mail one of the most efficient forms of advertising. Direct mail to the right people produces results.

Direct-mail ads also suffer from several *disadvantages*:

Inaccurate mailing lists. The key to the success of the entire mailing is the accuracy of the customer list. A poor list is a waste of money.

Clutter. The average person in the United States receives over 600 pieces of direct mail each year. With that volume of direct mail, it can be difficult for an advertisement to get customers' attention.

High relative costs. Relative to the size of the audience reached, the cost of designing, producing, and mailing an advertisement via direct mail is high. But if the mailing is well planned and properly executed, it can produce a high percentage of returns, making direct mail one of the least expensive advertising methods in terms of results.

High throwaway rate. Often called junk mail, direct-mail ads become "junk" when an advertiser selects the wrong audience or broadcasts the wrong message. In fact, the typical direct-mail advertising campaign produces only a 2 percent response rate. To boost returns small business owners can supplement their traditional direct-mail pieces with toll-free (800) numbers and carefully timed follow-up phone calls.

"HIGH-TECH" DIRECT MAIL AND THE WORLD WIDE WEB. Sending out ads on computer diskettes and CDs is an excellent way to reach upscale households and businesses. Not only do computer-based ads give advertisers the power to create flashy, attention-grabbing designs, but they also hold the audience's attention.

Compact discs (CDs) offer advertisers the same benefits as computer disks with one extra— more space to do it in. Companies are using CDs with interactive ads to sell everything from cars to computers. The ads usually contain videos, computer games, quizzes, animation, music, graphics, and other features to engage more of their audiences' senses. In a world where U.S. households receive *4.5 million tons* of paper each year in the form of direct-mail ads, multimedia ads can offer a distinct advantage: They get noticed.

HOW TO USE DIRECT MAIL. The key to a direct mailing's success is the right mailing list. Even the best direct-mail ad will fail if sent to the "wrong" customers. Owners can develop lists themselves, using customer accounts, telephone books, city and trade directories, and other sources. Other sources for mailing lists include companies selling complementary but not competing products; professional organizations' membership lists; business or professional magazine's subscription lists; and mailing list brokers who sell lists for practically any need. Advertisers can locate list brokers through *The Direct Marketing List Source* from the Standard Rate and Data Service found in most public libraries.

THE WORLD WIDE WEB The past decade has witnessed the World Wide Web reshape the way companies conduct business and transform e-commerce into a major economic force. Just as the Web has become a common tool for conducting business, it also has become a popular medium for advertisers. Increasingly, small businesses are turning to the World Wide Web as a valuable way to reach their customers and to build an awareness of their products and services. For instance, when lingerie seller Victoria's Secret ran an ad during the Super Bowl to promote its first live lingerie fashion show broadcast over the Web, the response was phenomenal! More than 1.5 million people tuned in to Victoria's Secret Web site to watch the fashion show, proving the power of combining the Web with traditional advertising media. The Internet has proved to be the fastest-growing advertising medium in history. Using the time required for radio, television, and the Internet to reach 50 million users as a basis for comparing the three media, the Internet is the clear winner. Radio required 38 years to reach that milestone, and television took 13 years; the Internet, however, hit 50 million users in just five years!

The Web's multimedia capabilities makes it an ideal medium for companies to demonstrate their products and services with full motion, color, and sound and to get customers involved in

TABLE 8.5

Guidelines for Creating Direct-Mail Ads That Really Work

Sources: Adapted from Kim T. Gorcon, "Copy Right," *Business Start-Ups,* June 1998, pp. 18–19; Paul Hughes, "Profits Due," *Entrepreneur,* February 1994, pp. 74–78; "Why They Open Direct Mail," *Communication Briefings,* December 1993, p. 5; Ten Lammers, "The Elements of Perfect Pitch," *Inc.,* March 1992, pp. 53–55; "Special Delivery." *Small Business Reports,* February 1993, p. 6; Gloria Green and James W. Peltier. "How to Develop a Direct Mail Program," *Small Business Forum,* Winter 1993/1994. pp. 30–45; Susan Headden, "The Junk Mail Deluge," *U.S. News & World Report,* December 8, 1997, pp. 40–48.

"Mail order means trend watching, meticulous planning, and devouring news and information on the industry, your niche, technology, politics, and the world—and that's just for starters," says one observer. "You'll have to deal with the laws of a vast federal bureaucracy and 50 states (plus a couple hundred countries if you go international), the intricacies of designing and mailing a catalog, and the fickle nature of a demanding public."

You'll also have to write copy that will get results. Try these proven techniques:

Promise readers your most important benefit in the headline or first paragraph.

Use short "action" words and paragraphs.

Make the copy look easy to read—lots of "white space."

Use eye-catching words such as *free, you, save, guarantee, new, profit, benefit, improve,* and others.

Consider using computerized "handwriting" somewhere on the page or envelope; it attracts attention.

Forget grammatical rules; write as if you were speaking to the reader.

Repeat the offer three or more times in various ways.

Back up claims and statements with proof and endorsements whenever possible.

Ask for the order or a response.

Ask questions such as "Would you like to lower your home's energy costs?" in the copy.

Use high-quality paper and envelopes (those with windows are best) because they stand a better chance of being opened and read. Brown envelopes that resemble government correspondence work well.

Envelopes that resemble bills almost always get opened.

Address the envelope to an individual, not "Occupant."

Use stamps if possible. They get more letters opened than metered postage.

Use a postscript (P.S.) always—they are the most often read part of a printed page. Make sure the P.S. contains a "hook" that will encourage the recipient to read on.

Make sure the order form is clear and easy to fill out; include a fax number for ordering, too.

the demonstrations. Businesses that normally use direct mail can bring the two-dimensional photos and product descriptions in their print catalogs to life, avoid the expense of mailing them, and attract new customers that traditional mailings might miss.

A Company Example

*Charlie Hoeveler, CEO of **US Sports Camps, Inc.**, a company that stages summer camps in a variety of sports on college campuses across the nation, has found the Web to be the ideal vehicle for promoting and managing the administrative details of the hundreds of camps the company runs. For years, US Sports Camps used direct-mail campaigns and ads in sports-oriented magazines to enroll youngsters in its camps. Today, the company touts its Web site (www.ecamps.com) with banner ads on Yahoo! and in all of its other promotional literature. The site, with its online registration form, has attracted hundreds of new customers and has boosted the company's international clientele 200 percent! The sports-specific bulletin boards on the Web site attract potential customers even in the off-season. Hoeveler, who says that he has "a perfect product for the Web," hopes eventually to "see 40 percent or 50 percent of sales come through the site." [28]*

Advertisements on the Web take five basic forms: banner ads, cookies, full-page ads, "push" technology ads, and e-mail ads. **Banner ads** are small, rectangular ads that reside on Web sites, much like roadside billboards, touting a company's product or service. When visitors to a site click on the banner ad, they go straight to the advertiser's home page. One measure of a banner ad's effectiveness is the number of impressions it produces. An **impression** occurs every time an ad appears on a Web page, whether or not the user clicks on the ad to explore it. Another common way of judging banner ads is the **click-through rate**, which is calculated by dividing the number of times customers actually click on the banner ad by the number of impressions for that ad. The cost of a banner ad to an advertiser depends on the number of users who actually click on it. The cost of creating a banner ad ranges from practically nothing for do-it-yourselfers to as much as $3,000 if the ad is designed by a professional and includes animation and high levels of interactivity.

banner ads—*small, rectangular ads that reside on Web sites much like roadside billboards, touting a company's product or service.*

impression—*occurs every time an ad appears on a Web page, whether or not the user clicks on it.*

click-through rate—*a value calculated by dividing the number of times customers actually click on a banner ad by the number of impressions for that ad.*

Deborah Edlhuber, founder of Prairie Frontier, a small company selling wildflower and prairiegrass seed, drives traffic to her company's Web site with the help of a banner exchange program.

Courtesy of Praire Frontier, LLC.

A Company Example

Banner ads do not have to be expensive, however. Many small business owners increase the exposure their banner ads receive by joining a banner exchange program, which are similar to advertising cooperatives. In a banner exchange program, member companies can post their banners on each other's sites. These programs work best for companies selling complementary products or services. For instance, a small company selling gourmet food products over the Web might exchange banner ads with a company using the Web to sell fine wines or one selling upscale kitchen tools and appliances. Two of the largest banner exchange Web sites are Microsoft bCentral (formerly LinkExchange) and SmartClicks.

*Deborah Edlhuber, owner of **Prairie Frontier**, a small company selling wildflower and prairie-grass seed, uses a banner exchange program to drive traffic to her company's Web site. Through the exchange, Edlhuber places her banner ads she creates herself on several dozen gardening and photographic sites. Prairie Frontier's Web site now draws more than 1,700 hits a day, many of them from her banner exchange partners. "They definitely bring people to my site," says Edlhuber, "and I can track the click-throughs."* [29]

The primary disadvantage of banner ads is that Web users can easily ignore them. These ads have become such a part of the Web page landscape that frequent users may tend to ignore them. As this phenomena expands, Web designers search for the "best" page placement for banner ads, as well as any "bells and whistles" that will attract the browser and encourage them to click through. One newer form of Web advertising is more difficult to ignore. Known as an **interstitial or pop-up**, this is a separate window of advertising that pops open spontaneously, blocking the site behind it. It is designed to grab consumers' attention for the few nanoseconds it takes them to close the window. The danger, of course, is that the attention received is not necessarily positive. These ads are often perceived as an annoying intrusion. A slight variation on this is the "pop-under" ad that immediately goes behind the active screen but stays open until the browser window is closed.

Cookies are small programs that attach to users' computers when they visit certain Web sites. These programs track the locations users visit while in the site and use this electronic footprint to send pop-up ads that would be of interest to the user. For instance, a Web user who frequently visits garden sites might find ads for garden tools and seed companies popping up on her screen. Many sites that require users to register before they can enter are collecting information to create cookie files. Cookies cannot access a user's computer, read sensitive information such as credit card numbers or passwords, or send such data back to the company that created the cookie. Nor can they alter the files on a computer's hard drive. Cookies can, however, track users' Web browsing patterns, revealing which pages they view and how often they view them. Because cookies record users' Web use and habits transparently (and usually without users' express permission), their use has become somewhat controversial. Some companies use the information they glean from cookies to make inferences about customers' interests and then target ads at them based on those inferences.

Full-page ads are those that download to Web users' screens before they can access certain Web sites. They are common on popular game sites that attract a high volume of Web traffic. **Push technology ads** appear on users' screens when they download information such as news, sports, or entertainment from another site. For instance, a Web user downloading sports information might receive an ad for athletic shoes or T-shirts with the information. One advantage of Web advertising is its ability to track the results that an ad produces. Web technology allows advertisers to count the number of visitors to a site and to track the number of people who actually click on the ads placed there.

With more than 150 million users, e-mail is the most common application on the Internet, and e-mail advertising capitalizes on that popularity. **E-mail advertising**, in which companies

interstitial or pop-up—*a separate window of advertising that pops open spontaneously, blocking the site behind it.*

cookies—*small programs that attach to users' computers when they visit certain Web sites and that track users' Web browsing patterns.*

full-page ads—*ads that download to users' Web screens before they can access certain Web sites.*

push technology ads—*ads that appear on users' screens when they download information such as news, sports, or entertainment from another site.*

e-mail advertising—*advertising in which companies broadcast their advertising messages via e-mail.*

broadcast their advertising messages via e-mail, grew from just 3 percent of total Web advertising expenditures to 15 percent in 2003.[30] E-mail advertising takes two forms: permission e-mail and spam. As its name suggests, **permission e-mail** involves sending e-mail ads to customers with their permission; **spam** is unsolicited commercial e-mail. Approximately 20 percent of all e-mail in the United States is commercial, and it is split evenly between permission e-mail and spam.[31] Because most e-mail users see spam as a nuisance, they often view companies that use it ("spammers") in a negative light. Entrepreneurs would be wise to exclude spam from their Web advertising plans. However, permission e-mail can be an effective—and money-saving—advertising tool. Although a banner ad's response rate is just 1 to 5 percent, permission e-mail messages often produce response rates of 25 percent![32] The cost for traditional direct-mail campaigns ranges from $1 to $2 per piece compared to only $0.01 to $0.25 per piece for e-mail.[33]

permission e-mail— *commercial e-mail sent to customers with their consent.*

spam—*unsolicited commercial e-mail.*

For an online advertisement to be really effective consumers must want to receive the message. When customers request information, it is referred to as opt-in e-mail. The return communications should be personal and relevant and respect the reader.

Building an e-mail list simply requires attention to the basics of marketing. The goal is to have qualified potential buyers identify themselves to you by sharing their e-mail addresses. Successful marketers offer rewards to those willing to share their e-mail addresses. The reward may be a one-time discount, special offer, special report, entry in a sweepstakes, or drawing for a prize. Once a small company obtains potential customers' e-mail addresses, the next step is to send a message that is useful and of interest to them. The message must be geared to their interests and should show how your product or service will satisfy their needs or wants.[34]

Many companies have success with creative e-mail newsletters sent to customers.

A Company Example

*For example, **Paul Frederick**, a maker of fine men's shirts, sends a weekly e-mail newsletter to customers (with their permission) that covers everything from fashion do's and don'ts to the hottest new styles. The electronic newsletter contains links to the company's Web site, where customers can browse through the catalog, use the "Create Your Shirt" feature to design their own shirts, and take advantage of special deals for online customers. The combination of its e-mail advertising campaign and its user-friendly Web site gives Paul Frederick an edge over its rivals.*

Entrepreneurs can test e-mail promotions and online advertising messages to ensure maximum impact, just as is done with print material, only faster and at little cost. Too often, business owners simply assume that they know how to promote their products or services and never test various messages for effectiveness in producing new sales. Entrepreneurs can test a variety of messages using different product discounts to test the price sensitivity of the market, free gift offers, e-mail formats, or even a "hard" sell versus a "soft" sell. If you don't experiment, you will never gain additional knowledge of customers that allows for the implementation of successful e-mail marketing.[35]

OUTDOOR ADVERTISING. National advertisers have long used outdoor ads. This medium is proving to be popular among small firms (especially retailers) as well. Spending on outdoor ads is growing at a rate faster than that of most other media at nearly 10 percent a year. Very few small businesses rely solely on outdoor advertising; instead, they supplement other advertising media with billboards. With a creative outdoor campaign, a small company can make a big impact—even on a small budget.

Outdoor advertising offers certain *advantages* to the small business:

High exposure. Outdoor advertising offers a high-frequency exposure; studies suggest that the typical billboard reaches an adult 29 to 31 times each month. Most people tend to follow the same routes in their daily traveling, and billboards are there waiting for them when they pass by.

Broad reach. The nature of outdoor ads makes them effective devices for reaching a large number of potential customers within a specific area. Not only has the number of cars on the road increased, but the number of daily vehicle trips people take has also climbed. In addition, the people outdoor ads reach tend to be younger, wealthier, and better educated than the average person.

Flexibility. Advertisers can buy outdoor advertising units separately or in a number of packages. Through its variety of graphics, design, and unique features, outdoor advertising enables the small advertiser to match his message to the particular audience.

Cost efficiency. Outdoor advertising offers one of the lowest costs per thousand customers reached of all advertising media. Experts estimate the cost per thousand viewers (CPM) for outdoor ads is about $2, compared to $5 for drive-time radio spots, $9 for magazine ads, and $10 to $20 for newspaper ads and prime-time television spots.[36]

Outdoor ads also have several *disadvantages*:

Brief exposure. Because billboards are immobile, the reader is exposed to the advertiser's message for only a short time—typically no more than five seconds. As a result, the message must be short and to the point.

Limited ad recall. Because customers often are zooming past outdoor ads at high speed, they are exposed to an advertising message very briefly, which limits their ability to retain the message.

Legal restrictions. Outdoor billboards are subject to strict regulations and to a high degree of standardization. Many cities place limitations on the number and type of signs and billboards allowed along the roadside.

Lack of prominence. A clutter of billboards and signs along a heavily traveled route tends to reduce the effectiveness of a single ad that loses its prominence among the crowd of billboards.

USING OUTDOOR ADS. Until the 1990s, billboards were mostly hand-painted. Today, however, technology has changed the face of outdoor advertising dramatically. Computerized painting techniques render truer, crisper, and brighter colors and have improved the quality of outdoor ads significantly. Vinyl surfaces accept print-quality images and are extremely durable. Digital technology, three-dimensional effects, computerized lighting, and other advances allow companies to create animated, continuous motion ads that really capture viewers' attention at reasonable costs. Because the outdoor ad is stationary and the viewer is in motion, a small business owner must pay special attention to its design. An outdoor ad should:

- Identify the product and the company clearly and quickly.
- Use a simple background. The background should not compete with the message.
- Rely on large illustrations that jump out at the viewer.
- Include clear, legible type. All lowercase or a combination of uppercase and lowercase letters work best. Very bold or very thin typefaces become illegible at a distance.
- Use black-and-white designs. Research shows that black-and-white outdoor ads are more effective than color ads. If color is important to the message, pick color combinations that contrast both hue and brightness—for example, black on yellow.
- Emphasize simplicity; short copy and short words are best. Don't try to cram too much onto a billboard. One study found that ads with fewer than eight words were most effective, and those containing more than 10 words were least effective.
- Be located on the right-hand side of the highway.

One of the latest trends in outdoor advertising is "talking billboards." The text directs viewers to tune into a specific radio frequency, where they hear a short commercial. Those who tune in hear jokes, skits, and, of course, a commercial for the company and its products. Underwear maker Joe Boxer uses talking billboards with a great deal of success.[37]

Entrepreneurs are finding other creative ways to use outdoor advertising to get their messages across to customers. Tom Scott and Tom First, cofounders of Nantucket Nectars, send "mobile marketing squads" out in purple Winnebagos emblazoned with the company's logo to concerts, races, football games, and other events, where they hand out free samples of Nantucket Nectars' products.[38] Beach 'N Billboard, a small company in New Jersey, will imprint company logos and advertisements into the sand at the beach. Some companies now even advertise their products and services using stickers on pieces of fruit sold in grocery stores![39]

TRANSIT ADVERTISING. Transit advertising includes advertising signs inside and outside some 70,000 public transportation vehicles throughout the country's urban areas. The medium is likely to grow as more cities look to public transit systems to relieve transportation problems. Transit ads offer a number of *advantages*:

Wide coverage. Transit advertising offers advertisers mass exposure to a variety of customers. The message literally goes to where the people are. This medium also reaches people with a wide variety of demographic characteristics.

Repeat exposure. Transit ads provide repeated exposure to a message. The typical transit rider averages 24 rides per month and spends 61 minutes per day riding.

Low cost. Even small business owners with limited budgets can afford transit advertising. One study shows that transit advertising costs average only $0.30 per thousand.[40]

Flexibility. Transit ads come in a wide range of sizes, numbers, and duration. With transit ads, an owner can select an individual market or any combination of markets across the country.

Transit ads also have several *disadvantages*:

Generality. Even though a small business can choose the specific transit routes on which to advertise, it cannot target a particular segment of the market through transit advertising. The effectiveness of transit ads depends on the routes that public vehicles travel and on the people they reach, which, unfortunately, the advertiser cannot control.

Limited appeal. Unlike many media, transit ads are not beamed into the potential customer's residence or business. The result is that customers cannot keep them for future reference. Also, these ads do not reach with great frequency the upper-income, highly educated portion of the market.

Brief message. Transit ads do not permit the small advertiser to present a detailed description or a demonstration of the product or service for sale. Although inside ads have a relatively long exposure (the average ride lasts 22.5 minutes), outside ads must be brief and to the point.

DIRECTORIES. Directories are an important advertising medium for reaching those customers who have already made purchase decisions. The directory simply helps these customers locate the specific product or service they have decided to buy. Directories include telephone books, industrial or trade guides, buyer guides, annuals, catalog files, and yearbooks that list various businesses and the products they sell.

Directories offer several *advantages* to advertisers:

Prime prospects. Directory listings reach customers who are prime prospects, because they have already decided to purchase an item. The directory just helps them find what they are looking for.

Long life. Directory listings usually have long lives. A typical directory may be published annually.

However, there are certain *disadvantages* to using directories:

Lack of flexibility. Listings and ads in many directories offer only a limited variety of design features. Business owners may not be as free to create unique ads as in other printed media.

Ad clutter. In many directories, ads from many companies are clustered together so closely that no single ad stands out from the rest.

Obsolescence. Because directories are commonly updated only annually, some of their listings become obsolete. This is a problem for a small firm that changes its name, location, or phone number.

When choosing a directory, the small business owner should evaluate several criteria:

- *Completeness.* Does the directory include enough listings that customers will use it?
- *Convenience.* Are the listings well organized and convenient? Are they cross-referenced?
- *Evidence of use.* To what extent do customers actually use the directory? What evidence of use does the publisher offer?
- *Age.* Is the directory well established and does it have a good reputation?
- *Circulation.* Do users pay for the directory or do they receive complimentary copies? Is there an audited circulation statement?

TRADE SHOWS. Trade shows provide manufacturers and distributors with a unique opportunity to advertise to a preselected audience of potential customers who are inclined to buy. Literally thousands of trade shows are sponsored each year, and carefully evaluating and selecting a few shows can produce profitable results for a business owner. A study by the Center for Exhibition Industry Research found that trade show success does *not* depend on how much an exhibitor spends; instead, success is a function of planning, preparation, and follow-up.[41]

Trade shows offer the following *advantages*:

A natural market. Trade shows bring together buyers and sellers in a setting where products can be explained, demonstrated, and handled. Comparative shopping is easy, and the buying process is more efficient.

Preselected audience. Trade exhibits attract potential customers with a specific interest in the goods or services being displayed. There is a high probability that these prospects will make a purchase.

New customer market. Trade shows offer exhibitors a prime opportunity to reach new customers and to contact people who are not accessible to sales representatives.

Cost advantage. As the cost of making a field sales call continues to escalate, more companies are realizing that trade shows are an economical method for making sales contacts and presentations.

There are, however, certain *disadvantages* associated with trade shows:

Increasing costs. The cost of exhibiting at trade shows is rising quickly. Registration fees, travel and setup costs, sales salaries, and other expenditures may be a barrier to some small firms.

Wasted effort. A poorly planned exhibit ultimately costs the small business more than its benefits are worth. Too many firms enter exhibits in trade shows without proper preparation, and they end up wasting their time, energy, and money on unproductive activities.

To avoid these disadvantages, business owners should:

- Establish objectives for the show. Do you want to generate 100 new sales leads, make new product presentations to 500 potential customers, or make $5,000 in sales?
- Communicate with key potential customers *before* the show; send them invitations or invite them to stop by your booth for a special gift.
- Make your display memorable. Be sure your exhibit shows your company and its products or services in the best light.
- Have knowledgeable salespeople staffing the booth. Research shows that the most important factor to trade show attendees is knowledgeable, friendly, professional people tending the exhibit.[42]
- Demonstrate your product or service; let customers see it in action.
- Learn to distinguish between serious customers and "tire-kickers."
- Distribute literature that clearly communicates the product or service sold.
- Project a professional image at all times.
- Follow up promptly on sales leads. The most common mistake trade show participants make is failing to follow up on the sales leads the show generated. If you are not going to follow up leads, why bother to attend the show in the first place?

SPECIALTY ADVERTISING. As advertisers have shifted their focus to "narrowcasting" their messages to target audiences and away from "broadcasting," specialty advertising has grown in popularity. Advertisers now spend more than $3 billion annually on specialty items. This category includes all customer gift items imprinted with the company's name, address, telephone number, and slogan. Specialty items are best used as reminder ads to supplement other forms of advertising and help to create goodwill among existing and potential customers.

Specialty advertising offers several *advantages*:

Reaching select audiences. Advertisers have the ability to reach specific audiences with well-planned specialty items.

A Company Example

*For instance, **Corhart Refractories Corporation** wanted to increase the number of steel executives reached at a trade show. The company mailed the executives invitations in a box containing a set of radio earphones. To get the radio (without which the earphones were useless), the executives had to stop by Corhart's booth. An overflow crowd stopped to get their radios, imprinted with Corhart's logo.[43]*

Personalized nature. By carefully choosing a specialty item, a business owner can "personalize" his advertisement. When choosing advertising specialties, a small business owner should use items that are unusual, related to the nature of the business, and meaningful to customers.

Versatility. The rich versatility of specialty advertising is limited only by the business owner's imagination. Advertisers print their logos on everything from pens and scarves to wallets and caps.

There are *disadvantages* to specialty advertising:

Potential for waste. Unless the owner chooses the appropriate specialty item, he will be wasting his time and money. The options are virtually infinite.

Costs. Some specialty items can be quite expensive. Plus, some owners have a tendency to give advertising materials to anyone—even to those who are not potential customers.

POINT-OF-PURCHASE ADS. In the last several years, in-store advertising has become more popular as a way of reaching the customer at a crucial moment—the point of purchase. Research suggests that consumers make 66 percent of all buying decisions at the point of sale.[44] Self-service stores are especially well suited for in-store ads because they remind people of the products as they walk the aisles. These in-store ads are not just blasé signs or glossy photographs of the product in use. Some businesses use in-store music interspersed with household hints and, of course, ads. Another ploy involves tiny devices that sense when a customer passes by and triggers a prerecorded sales message. Other machines emit scents—chocolate chip cookies or piña coladas—to appeal to passing customers' sense of smell.[45] Joe Boxer now sells its boxer shorts in pop-top aluminum cans from vending machines that use motion sensors to detect passing shoppers. When triggered, the machine talks to customers, with comments including, "Hey you! Hey you! Have you changed your underwear lately?"[46]

In sum, small business owners have an endless array of advertising tools, techniques, and media available to them. Even postage stamps, bathroom walls, sides of cows, and parking meters offer advertising space! Table 8.6 summarizes the different advertising media and their suitability for reaching particular customer groups.

PREPARING AN ADVERTISING BUDGET

One of the most challenging decisions confronting a small business owner is how much to invest in advertising. The amount the owner wants to spend and the amount the firm can afford to spend on advertising usually differ significantly. There are four methods of determining an advertising budget: what is affordable; matching competitors; percentage of sales; and objective and task.

Learning Objective

4. Discuss the four basic methods for preparing an advertising budget.

YOU Be the Consultant . . .

Fat Free But Not Famous—Yet

When she was in college, Candace Vanice was a french fry fanatic, but she worried about the fat content of fries cooked the traditional way. "I waited and waited for someone to create fat-free french fries, but no one did," recalls Vanice. "So, I got busy in my own kitchen. I explored a great number of approaches that did not work, but one recipe showed great promise." That recipe was based on her mother's recipe for crispy french toast, a dish Vanice had enjoyed while growing up. After much experimenting with seasonings, Vanice created french fries that tasted as good as the ones at fast-food restaurants but with one major advantage: They contained no fat!

In 1994, Vanice applied for and received a patent for her fat-free fries, and she launched a company, Marvel LLC, to market them. She quickly learned that breaking into the food business and getting a new product on grocers' shelves is no easy task. To gain widespread acceptance in supermarkets, a new product needs a food broker to push it. The problem 27-year-old Vanice faced was that both food brokers and supermarkets are reluctant to carry products that are not supported by big-time marketing and advertising campaigns. Vanice's company, like most fledgling start-ups, did not have the financial resources to launch an extensive advertising program.

Vanice had faith in her product, however, and believed that customers would flock to buy her fat-free fries once they tasted them. She contacted several supermarkets in her hometown of Kansas City and started handing out free samples. She also hired a sampling agency to give away free product samples in stores in the surrounding area. As Vanice and the sampling agency handed out fries, they collected customer feedback, asking people to fill out surveys about the fries. According to customers, her fries were an overwhelming hit! The only remaining question was how to raise the visibility of 8th Wonder Fat Free Fries enough to convince food brokers and supermarkets to carry them. That would be a challenge because Marvel LLC had practically no money for advertising.

1. Work with a team of your classmates to develop a creative advertising and promotional plan for Marvel LLC. What unique selling proposition should Vanice use?

2. How should Vanice use publicity to draw attention to her 8th Wonder Fat Free Fries?

3. According to one marketing expert, "A product can be copied or imitated, but a brand cannot." What can entrepreneurs such as Candace Vanice do to build brand name recognition when they do not have the advertising budgets large companies have?

Sources: Adapted from Don Debalak, "French Twist," *Business Start-Ups*, November 1999, pp. 78–81; Marvel LLC, www.fatfreefries.com; Sheryl Nance-Nash, "Making a Name for Your Brand," *Fortune*, July 20, 1998, pp. 156[L]–156[M].

TABLE 8.6
Advertising Media Comparison
Chart

Media	Coverage	Special Characteristics
Newspapers	Selected geographic coverage. Entire city or metropolitan area with major newspapers. Single town with smaller, weekly papers.	Top advertising media; attracts about 23% of advertising expenditures.
Radio	Market area radio station serves. Stations' formats range from country and easy listening to rap and golden oldies.	Ability to reach almost any market by choosing proper station. The average household has 5.6 radios, and 95 percent of the cars in the United States have radios.
Television	Market area TV station serves; could be local (cable) or national (major network).	Powerful medium; especially effective at reaching younger, less educated audiences.
Magazines	Local magazines typically cover a particular city or region.	Magazines usually target specific audiences, from wealthy owners of country estates to low-income apartment dwellers.
Direct mail	Advertiser chooses the audience.	An effective advertising medium for small companies in virtually *any* business.
World Wide Web (WWW)	Anyone in the world who is wired to the WWW.	Reaches upscale, well-educated consumers anywhere in the world.
Outdoor advertising	Ranges from a neighborhood to an entire metropolitan area.	An excellent medium to supplement other forms of advertising.
Transit advertising	Urban areas.	Typically does not reach upper-income, well-educated audience.
Directories	Customers who have already made a purchase decision.	Many directories available; the key is picking the right ones.
Trade shows	Preselected audience.	Potential customers are inclined to buy.
Specialty advertising	Advertiser chooses the audience.	Allows advertiser to "narrowcast" message rather than broadcast it.
Special events and promotions	Advertiser chooses the audience.	Allow advertiser maximum flexibility and creativity in ads.
Point-of-purchase ads	Existing customers.	Two-thirds of buying decisions are made at the point of sale.

Under the what-is-affordable method, the owner sees advertising as a luxury. She views advertising completely as an expense, not as an investment that produces sales and profits in the future. Therefore, as the name implies, management spends whatever it can afford on advertising. Too often, the advertising budget is allocated funds after all other budget items have been financed. The result is an inadequate advertising budget. This method also fails to relate the advertising budget to the advertising objective.

Another approach is to match the advertising expenditures of the firm's competitors, either in a flat dollar amount or as a percentage of sales. This method assumes that a firm's advertising needs and strategies are the same as those of its competitors. Although competitors' actions can be helpful in establishing a floor for advertising expenditures, relying on this technique can lead to blind imitation instead of a budget suited to the small firm's circumstances.

Advantages	Disadvantages	Tips
Extensive coverage; low absolute and relative costs; timeliness.	Blanket coverage means some ads are wasted on those who are not potential customers; limited reproduction quality; significant ad clutter.	Research newspaper's reader profile; focus on placing ads in proper sections.
Universal infiltration; radio ads are more "active" than print ads, giving advertisers the ability to be more creative with ads.	Need to repeat ads for effectiveness; no visual possibilities; brief ads mean limited message potential.	Make sure station's listener profile matches company's target audience. Keep ad copy simple.
Visual advantage—advertiser can *show* customers product or service benefits; cable stations bring TV ads into price ranges that small businesses can afford.	Brief exposure to ads, often because of zapping; creating TV commercials can be expensive.	Consider infomercials. They may be obnoxious to many, but they work, if properly done. Try to evoke emotion in ads.
Long life spans for ads; most magazines have multiple readers; high ad quality.	Long closing times for ads require advance planning; ad clutter can reduce ads' effectiveness.	As in newspaper advertising, proper placement is the key. Left-hand pages are better.
Ability to select a specific audience and tailor a message to it; captures reader's attention, at least for a moment.	Will become junk mail if improperly targeted; high relative cost because of low response rates.	Plan direct-mail ads so that you can measure results; use catchy words—*free, save, new*.
Attractive audience profile; rapid growth of the WWW as a marketing tool; ability to use full-color, sound, animation, etc.	Audience may bypass ads without ever seeing them; advertising clutter is a problem and will grow as WWW use grows.	Make site interactive, if possible; games, puzzles, and contests can be effective draws.
Multiple exposures; a bargain because of its low relative cost.	Brief exposure requires limited messages; lack of prominence.	Keep ads short and simple; use clear, legible type.
Wide coverage and repeat exposure to ads; low relative cost.	Difficulty in reaching specific target audiences; brief exposure requires limited message.	Use contrasting colors and designs that give ads a two-dimensional appearance.
Target prime prospects; long ad life.	Danger of listing or directory becoming obsolete; ad clutter.	Design ad so that it stands out from the crowd.
Ample time for personal selling; ability to demonstrate products.	High cost of traveling to show, setting up, and staffing booth.	Make the most of sales time and follow up leads.
Ability to reach specific audience and to personalize the message.	Potential for waste and high costs.	Specialty items should prompt customer recall.
Reach some customers when all other attempts fail.	Require time to plan and coordinate; can be expensive.	Creativity is a must if a specialty promotion is to be successful.
Reach customer at a crucial moment: the point of purchase.	Require customers to come into the business first.	Capture the customer's attention first; then sell.

The most commonly used method of establishing an advertising budget is the simple percentage-of-sales approach. This method relates advertising expenditures to actual sales results. Tying advertising expenditures to sales is generally preferred to relating them to profits because sales tend to fluctuate less than profits. One expert suggests a useful rule of thumb when establishing an advertising budget: 10 percent of projected sales the first year in business; 7 percent the second year; and at least 5 percent each year after that. Relying totally on such broad rules can be dangerous, however. They may not be representative of a small company's advertising needs.

The objective-and-task method is the most difficult and least used technique for establishing an advertising budget. It also is the method most often recommended by advertising experts. With this method, an owner links advertising expenditures to specific objectives. Although the previous methods break down the total amount of funds allocated to advertising, the task

FIGURE 8.3 Advertising
Planning Calendar

October

Sunday	Monday	Tuesday	Wednesday	Thursday	Friday	Saturday
Advertising Budget for October: 9% of Sales = $2,275 Co-op Ads = $550 Total $2,825	October Advertising Expenditures: $2,845 Under/(Over) Budget: ($20) Remaining Balance: $6,400			**1** WPCC Radio 5 Spots $125 Billboard $350	**2** The Chronicle 140 lines $100	**3**
4	**5**	**6**	**7**	**8**	**9** The Chronicle 140 lines $100	**10**
11	**12**	**13** Meet w/ Leslie Re: November Ad Campaigns 2pm	**14**	**15** Envelope "Stuffer" in Invoices Halloween Sale $175	**16** The Chronicle 140 lines $100	**17** WPCC Radio 5 Spots $100
18	**19**	**20** WPCC Radio 5 Spots $125	**21**	**22** Direct Mail Halloween Sale Promo "Preferred Customers" $120	**23** The Chronicle 140 lines $100	**24** WPCC Radio 5 Spots $100
25	**26** WPCC Radio 5 Spots $125	**27** WPCC Radio 5 Spots $125	**28** WPCC Radio 5 Spots $125	**29** WPCC Radio 5 Spots $125	**30** The Chronicle Half-Page Spread Sale $300	**31** Halloween WPCC Radio Live Remote Broadcast $425

method builds up the advertising funds by analyzing what it will cost to accomplish these objectives. For example, suppose that a manager wants to boost sales of a particular product 10 percent by attracting local college students. He may determine that a nearby rock radio station would be the best medium to use. Then he must decide on the number and frequency of the ads and estimate their costs.

A manager follows this same process for each advertising objective. A common problem with the method is the tendency for the manager to be overly ambitious in setting advertising objectives, which leads to unrealistically high advertising expenditures. The manager may be forced to alter objectives, or the plans to reach them, to bring the advertising budget back to a reasonable level. However, the plan can still be effective.

Most small companies find it useful to plan in advance their advertising expenditures on a weekly basis. This short-term planning ensures a more consistent advertising effort throughout the year. A calendar like the one pictured in Figure 8.3 can be one of the most valuable tools in planning a small company's advertising program. The calendar enables the owner to prepare for holidays and special events, to monitor actual and budgeted expenditures, and to ensure that ads are scheduled on the appropriate media at the proper times.

ADVERTISE BIG ON A SMALL BUDGET

5. Explain practical methods for stretching a small business owner's advertising budget.

The typical small business does not have the luxury of an unlimited advertising budget. Most cannot afford to hire a professional ad agency. This does not mean, however, that a small company should assume a second-class advertising posture. Most advertising experts say that, unless a small company spends more than $10,000 a year on advertising, it probably doesn't need an ad agency. For most, hiring freelance copywriters and artists on a per-project basis is a much better bargain. With a little creativity and a dose of ingenuity, small business owners can stretch their advertising dollars and make the most of what they spend. Three useful techniques to do this are cooperative advertising, shared advertising, and publicity.

Cooperative Advertising

cooperative advertising—
an arrangement in which a manufacturing company shares the cost of advertising with a small retailer if the retailer features its products in those ads.

In **cooperative advertising**, a manufacturing company shares the cost of advertising with a small retailer if the retailer features its products in those ads. Both the manufacturer and the retailer get more advertising per dollar by sharing expenses.

David Lang, owner of a small lawn equipment store, purchases his inventory from 10 different manufacturers, nine of whom offer cooperative advertising programs. "Without [the manufacturers' help], we could only spend $20,000 a year [on advertising]," says Lang. "But now we can spend $40,000 because we're getting $20,000 back." [47]

Unlike Lang, who uses every dollar of cooperative advertising available to him, most small business owners fail to take advantage of manufacturers' cooperative advertising programs. Manufacturers, whose products cover the entire retail spectrum, make available an estimated $15 billion of co-op ad dollars each year; yet, more than two-thirds of it goes unused! [48]

*Barbara Malki, co-owner of **Cahaba Cycles**, is now a believer in the power of cooperative advertising, although she admits that she has not always been. "Two years ago," she says, "I was leaving co-op money on the table. I'm more aggressive about it now. [Now] I . . . use every co-op dollar." Cahaba Cycles recoups about 10 percent of its annual advertising budget through cooperative advertising.* [49]

Shared Advertising

In **shared advertising**, a group of similar businesses forms a syndicate to produce generic ads that allow the individual businesses to dub in local information. The technique is especially useful for small businesses that sell relatively standardized products or services such as legal assistance, autos, and furniture. Because the small firms in the syndicate pool their funds, the result usually is higher-quality ads and significantly lower production costs.

shared advertising—*an arrangement in which a group of similar businesses forms a syndicate to produce generic ads that allow the individual businesses to dub in local information.*

Other cost-saving suggestions for advertising expenditures include the following:

Repeat ads that have been successful. In addition to reducing the cost of ad preparation, this may create a consistent image in a small firm's advertising program.

Use identical ads in different media. If a billboard has been an effective advertising tool, an owner should consider converting it to a newspaper or magazine ad or a direct-mail flyer.

Hire independent copywriters, graphic designers, photographers, and other media specialists. Many small businesses that cannot afford a full-time advertising staff buy their advertising services a la carte. They work directly with independent specialists and usually receive high-quality work that compares favorably to that of advertising agencies without paying a fee for overhead.

Concentrate advertising during times when customers are most likely to buy. Some small business owners make the mistake of spreading an already small advertising budget evenly—and thinly—over a 12-month period.

PUBLIC RELATIONS As we discussed earlier in this chapter, the press can be either a valuable friend or a fearsome foe to a any business, depending on how well the owner handles her firm's public relations. Too often, entrepreneurs take the attitude, "My business is too small to be concerned about public relations." However, wise small business managers recognize that investing time and money in public relations benefits both the community and the company. The community gains the support of a good business citizen, and the company earns a positive image in the marketplace.

Many small businesses rely on media attention to get noticed, and getting that attention takes a coordinated effort. Public relations doesn't just happen; an owner must work at getting her company noticed by the media. Although publicity may not be free, it definitely can lower the company's advertising expenditures and still keep its name before the public. Because small companies' advertising budgets are limited, public relations takes on significant importance.

Bob Mayberry, a car dealer in Monroe, North Carolina, recently bought a 1961 Ford squad car like the one used on the 1960s hit TV series The Andy Griffith Show. *Not only does the car lure potential customers onto his lot, but it also has gotten the dealership into several newspaper articles. "We have sold a lot of cars from it," says Mayberry.* [50]

One successful public relations technique is **cause marketing**, in which a small business sponsors and promotes fund-raising activities of nonprofit groups and charities while raising its own visibility in the community.

*For example, during the Muscular Dystrophy Association's annual telethon, a local shop, Cookies Cook'n, donated over 100 pounds of cookies and brownies to feed telephone volunteers. Several giant cookies were auctioned off during the telethon, and the small cookie shop's name was mentioned frequently. **Cookies Cook'n** got more television exposure for donating these cookies than it could have gotten spending its entire advertising budget on TV commercials.[51]*

cause marketing—*an arrangement in which a small business sponsors and promotes fund-raising activities of nonprofit groups and charities while raising its own visibility in the community.*

PRICING: A CREATIVE BLEND OF ART AND SCIENCE

Deciding how and where to advertise is not the only key to marketing success; small business owners also must determine prices for their goods and services that will draw customers and produce a profit. Unfortunately, too many small business owners set prices according to vague, poorly defined techniques or even hunches. Price is an important factor in the relationship with customers, and haphazard-pricing techniques can confuse and alienate customers and endanger a firm's profitability. Setting prices is not only one of the toughest decisions small business owners' face, but it also is one of the most important. Improper pricing has destroyed countless businesses when owners mistakenly thought their prices were sufficient to generate a profit.

Price is the monetary value of a product or service in the marketplace; it is a measure of what the customer must exchange in order to obtain various goods and services. As the media continuously reinforces, this is an era where shoppers seek value for their money. Price also is a signal of a product's or service's value to an individual, and different customers assign different values to the same goods and services. From an owner's viewpoint, price must be compatible with the customer's perception of value. "Pricing is not just a math problem," says one business writer. "It's a psychology test."[52] The psychology of pricing is an art much more than it is a science. Value often becomes what the customer perceives it to be. For example, price reflects this notion of perceived value nowhere better than that of the products of the Swiss watch industry. Rolex, Cartier, Patek Philippe, Chopard, Toric, Blanepain, and Corum are legendary brands of ultrapremium handmade watches selling from $10,000 to $50,000. Owning one of these watches is a mark of financial success, yet each is less accurate at keeping time than a $10 quartz-driven Timex.[53] A similar example of price insensitivity can be found in fountain pens. In recent years, Renaissance Pen Company has marketed pens made from gold and platinum and encrusted with diamonds selling for as much as $230,000. Or how about one that contains the crystallized DNA of Abraham Lincoln for only $1,650?[54] Value for these examples is not found in superior technical performance but rather in their scarcity and uniqueness. Although entrepreneurs must recognize the shallow depth of the market for such ultraluxury items, the ego-satisfying ownership of limited-edition watches, pens, cars, jewelry, and so on is the psychological force supporting this pricing strategy.

Two Potent Forces: Image and Competition

PRICE CONVEYS IMAGE. A company's pricing policies communicate important information about its overall image to customers. For example, the prices charged by a posh men's clothing store reflect a completely different image from those charged by a factory outlet. Customers look at prices to determine what type of store they are dealing with. High prices frequently convey the idea of quality, prestige, and uniqueness to the customer. Accordingly, when developing a marketing approach to pricing, a small business manager must establish prices that are compatible with what its customers expect and are willing to pay. Too often, small business owners *underprice* their goods and services, believing that low prices are the only way they can achieve a competitive advantage. One study by the Copernicus consulting firm found that only 15 percent to 35 percent of customers consider price to be the chief criterion when selecting a product or service.[55]

A common mistake small business owners make is failing to recognize the extra value, convenience, service, and quality they give their customers—all things many customers are willing to pay for. These companies fall into the trap of trying to compete solely on the basis of price when they lack the sales volume—and, hence, the lower costs—of their larger rivals. It is a recipe for failure. "People want quality," says one merchant selling upscale goods at upscale prices. "They want value. But if you lower prices, they think that you are lowering the value and lowering the quality."[56]

*Discounting the prices on its once popular Izod polo shirts nearly cost **Lacoste** its entire business. Demand for the shirts, which sported a unique crocodile logo, slumped as prices fell. Discounting had eroded the company's distinctive image. Today, the company is trying to rebuild its upscale image and the cachet of its shirts by charging premium prices. Sales have been climbing.[57]*

A Company Example

The secret to setting prices properly is based on understanding the firm's target market, the customer groups at which the small company is aiming its goods or services. Target market, business image, and price are closely related.

*For instance, **Crème de la Crème** child care centers charge a staggering $14,000 a year in tuition, compared to a national average tuition of $5,400, and parents are clamoring to enroll their children. (Some applicants have not even been conceived yet!) Despite its premium prices, Crème de la Crème had a six-month waiting list in only its first year. How did the company manage this spectacular record? The key is differentiating itself from other child care centers and marketing those differences to well-to-do parents who want only the best for their preschool children. A Crème de la Crème center features a 3,600-volume library, a math lab, television and dance studios, and a state-of-the-art computer lab. The company pays 40 percent above the norm for teachers, 90 percent of whom have college degrees, compared to just 31 percent nationwide. Specialized teachers handle important subjects such as music and foreign languages and keep the student–teacher ratio low. Twenty security monitors ensure students' safety as they play tennis, stage plays in an open-air theater, or frolic in well-equipped playgrounds.[58]*

A Company Example

COMPETITION AND PRICES.   When setting prices, business owners should take into account their competitors' prices, but they should *not* automatically match or beat them. Two factors are vital to studying the effects of competition on the small firm's pricing policies: the location of the competitors and the nature of the competing goods. In most cases, unless a company can differentiate the quality and the quantity of extras it provides, it must match the prices charged by nearby competitors for identical items. For example, if a self-service station charges a nickel more per gallon for gasoline than does another self-service station across the street, customers will simply go across the street to buy. Without the advantage of a unique business image— quality of goods sold, value of services provided, convenient location, favorable credit terms— a small company must match local competitors' prices or lose sales. Although the prices that distant competitors charge are not nearly as critical to the small business as are those of local competitors, it can be helpful to know them and to use them as reference points. Before matching any competitor's prices, however, small business owners should consider the rival's motives. The competition may be establishing its price structure based on a unique set of criteria and a totally different strategy.

The nature of the competitors' goods also influences the small firm's pricing policies. The manager must recognize which products are substitutes for those he sells and then strive to keep his prices in line with them. For example, the local sandwich shop should consider the hamburger restaurant, the taco shop, and the roast beef shop as competitors because they all serve fast foods. Although none of them offers the identical menu of the sandwich shop, they're all competing for the same quick meal dollar. Of course, if a small business can differentiate its products or services by creating a distinctive image in the consumer's mind, it can charge prices higher than those of its competitors. Because competitors' prices can have a dramatic impact on a small company's own prices, entrepreneurs should make it a habit to monitor their rivals' prices, especially on identical items.

Generally, small business managers should avoid head-to-head price competition with other firms that can more easily achieve lower prices through lower cost structures. Most locally owned drugstores cannot compete with the prices of large national drug chains. However, many local drugstores operate successfully by using nonprice competition; these stores offer more personal service, free delivery, credit sales, and other extras that the chains have eliminated. Nonprice competition can be an effective strategy for a small business in the face of larger, more powerful enterprises, especially because there are many dangers in experimenting with price changes. For instance, price shifts cause fluctuations in sales volume that the small firm may not be able to tolerate. Also, frequent price changes may damage the company's image and its customer relations.

One of the most deadly games a small business can get into with competitors is a price war. Price wars can eradicate companies' profit margins and scar an entire industry for years. "Many entrepreneurs cut prices to the point of unprofitability just to compete," says one business writer. "In doing so, they open the door to catastrophe. Less revenue often translates into lower quality, poorer service, sloppier salesmanship, weaker customer loyalty, and financial disaster."[59] Price wars usually begin when one competitor thinks he can achieve higher volume instantaneously by lowering prices. Rather than sticking to their strategic guns, competitors believe they must follow suit.

Entrepreneurs usually overestimate the power of price cuts, however. Sales volume rarely rises enough to offset the lower profit margins of a lower price. If you have a 25 percent gross profit margin, and you cut your price by 10 percent, you have to roughly triple your sales volume just to break even. In a price war, a company may cut its prices so severely that it is impossible to achieve the volume necessary to offset the lower profit margins. Even when price cuts work, their effects often are temporary. Customers lured by the lowest price usually have almost no loyalty to a business. The lesson: The best way to survive a price war is to stay out of it by emphasizing the unique features, benefits, and value your company offers its customers!

Setting prices with a customer orientation is more important than trying to choose the ideal price for a product. In fact, for most products there is an acceptable price range, not a single ideal price. This price range is the area between the price ceiling defined by customers in the market and the price floor established by the firm's cost structure. A manager's goal should be to position the firm's prices within this acceptable price range. The final price that business owners set depends on the desired image they want to create for the business in the customer's mind—discount, middle of the road, or prestige (see Figure 8.4).

Setting appropriate prices requires more than just choosing a number based solely on intuition. Rather, proper pricing policies require information, facts, and analysis. The factors that small business owners must consider when determining the final price for goods and services include the following:

- Product/service costs
- Market factors—supply and demand
- Sales volume
- Competitors' prices

FIGURE 8.4 What Determines Price?

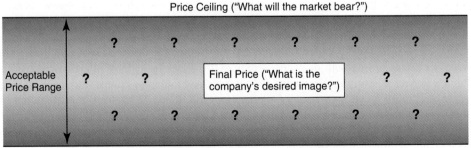

- The company's competitive advantage
- Economic conditions
- Business location
- Seasonal fluctuations
- Psychological factors
- Credit terms and purchase discounts
- Customers' price sensitivity
- Desired image

Although business owners may not be able to charge the ideal price for a product or service, they should set the price high enough to cover costs and earn a reasonable profit but low enough to attract customers and generate an adequate sales volume. Furthermore, the right price today may be completely inappropriate tomorrow because of changing market and competitive conditions. For many businesses, the pricing decision has become more difficult because the World Wide Web gives customers access to incredible amounts of information about the prices of items ranging from cars to computers. Increasingly, customers are using the Web to find the lowest prices available.

PRICING STRATEGIES AND TACTICS

There is no limit to the number of variations in pricing strategies and tactics. This wide variety of options is exactly what allows the small business manager to be so creative. This section will examine some of the more commonly used tactics under a variety of conditions. Pricing always plays a critical role in a firm's overall strategy; pricing policies must be compatible with a company's total marketing plan.

Learning Objective

6. Describe effective pricing techniques for introducing new products or services and for existing ones.

Introducing a New Product

Most small business managers approach setting the price of a new product with a great deal of apprehension because they have no precedent on which to base their decision. If the new product's price is excessively high, it is in danger of failing because of low sales volume. However, if its price is too low, the product's sales revenue might not cover costs. When pricing any new product, the owner should try to satisfy three objectives:

1. *Getting the product accepted.* No matter how unusual a product is, its price must be acceptable to the firm's potential customers.
2. *Maintaining market share as competition grows.* If a new product is successful, competitors will enter the market, and the small company must work to expand or at least maintain its market share. Continuously reappraising the product's price in conjunction with special advertising and promotion techniques helps to retain a satisfactory market share.
3. *Earning a profit.* Obviously, a small firm must establish a price for the new product higher than its cost. Entrepreneurs should not introduce a new product at a price below cost because it is much easier to lower a price than to increase it once the product is on the market.

*Linda Calder, owner of **Calder & Calder Promotions**, a company that produces trade shows, knows how difficult it can be to raise prices. When she launched her company, Calder decided to set her price below the average price of competing trade show production companies because she thought that would give her a competitive edge. "My fee was so low ... I sold out but did not make a profit," she says. Realizing her mistake, Calder raised prices in her second year, but her customers balked. Her sales fell by 50 percent.*[60]

A Company Example

Small business managers have three basic strategies to choose from when establishing a new product's price: a penetration pricing strategy, a skimming pricing strategy, and a sliding-down-the-demand-curve strategy.

MARKET PENETRATION. If a small business introduces a product into a highly competitive market in which a large number of similar products are competing for acceptance, the product must penetrate the market to be successful. To gain quick acceptance and extensive distribution in the mass market, the firm should introduce the product with a low price. In other words, it should set the price just above total unit cost to develop a wedge in the market and quickly achieve a high volume of sales. The resulting low profit margins may discourage other competitors from entering the market with similar products.

In most cases, a penetration pricing strategy is used to introduce relatively low-priced goods into a market with no elite segment and little opportunity for differentiation exists. The introduction is usually accompanied by heavy advertising and promotional techniques, special sales, and discounts. Entrepreneurs must recognize that penetration pricing is a long-range strategy; until customers accept the product, profits are likely to be small. If the strategy works and the product achieves mass market penetration, sales volume will increase, and the company will earn adequate profits. The objectives of the penetration strategy are to break into the market quickly, to generate a high sales volume as soon as possible, and to build market share. Many consumer products, such as soap, shampoo, and lightbulbs, are introduced through penetration pricing strategies.

SKIMMING.   A skimming pricing strategy often is used when a company introduces a new product into a market with little or no competition. Sometimes the firm employs this tactic when introducing a product into a competitive market that contains an elite group that is able to pay a higher price. Here a firm uses a higher-than-normal price in an effort to quickly recover the initial developmental and promotional costs of the product. Start-up costs usually are substantial due to intensive promotional expenses and high initial production costs. The idea is to set a price well above the total unit cost and to promote the product heavily in order to appeal to the segment of the market that is not sensitive to price. Such a pricing tactic often reinforces the unique, prestigious image of a store and projects a quality picture of the product. Another advantage of this technique is that the owner can correct pricing mistakes quickly and easily. If the firm sets a price that is too low under a penetration strategy, raising the price can be very difficult. If a firm using a skimming strategy sets a price too high to generate sufficient volume, it can always lower the price. Successful skimming strategies require a company to differentiate its products or services from those of the competition, justifying the above-average price.

SLIDING DOWN THE DEMAND CURVE.   One variation of the skimming price strategy is called sliding down the demand curve. Using this tactic, the small company introduces a product at a high price. Then technological advancements enable the firm to lower its costs quickly and to reduce the product's price before its competition can. By beating other businesses in a price decline, the small company discourages competitors and gradually, over time, becomes a high-volume producer. Computers are a prime example of a product introduced at a high price that quickly cascaded downward as companies forged important technological advances.

Sliding is a short-term pricing strategy that assumes that competition will eventually emerge. But even if no competition arises, the small business almost always lowers the product's price to attract a larger segment of the market. Yet, the initial high price contributes to a rapid return of start-up costs and generates a pool of funds to finance expansion and technological advances.

Pricing Established Goods and Services

Each of the following pricing tactics or techniques can become part of the toolbox of pricing tactics entrepreneurs can use to set prices of established goods and services.

ODD PRICING.   Although studies of consumer reactions to prices are mixed and generally inconclusive, many small business managers use the technique known as **odd pricing**. These managers prefer to establish prices that end in odd numbers (5, 7, 9) because they believe that merchandise selling for $12.95 appears to be much cheaper than the same item priced at $13.00. Psychological techniques such as odd pricing are designed to appeal to certain customer interests, but their effectiveness remains to be proven.

PRICE LINING.   **Price lining** is a technique that greatly simplifies the pricing function. Under this system, the manager stocks merchandise in several different price ranges, or price lines. Each category of merchandise contains items that are similar in appearance, quality, cost,

odd pricing—*a pricing technique that sets prices that end in odd numbers to create the psychological impression of low prices.*

price lining—*a technique that sets the same price for products that have similar features and appear within the same line.*

performance, or other features. For example, most music stores use price lines for their DVDs and CDs to make it easier for customers to select items and to simplify stock planning. Most lined products appear in sets of three—good, better, and best—at prices designed to satisfy different market segment needs and incomes.

LEADER PRICING. Leader pricing is a technique in which the small retailer marks down the customary price (i.e., the price consumers are accustomed to paying) of a popular item in an attempt to attract more customers. The company earns a much smaller profit on each unit because the markup is lower, but purchases of other merchandise by customers seeking the leader item often boost sales and profits. In other words, the incidental purchases that consumers make when shopping for the leader item boost sales revenue enough to offset a lower profit margin on the leader. Grocery stores frequently use leader pricing.

leader pricing—a technique that involves marking down the normal price of a popular item in an attempt to attract more customers who make incidental purchases of other items at regular prices.

GEOGRAPHICAL PRICING. Small businesses whose pricing decisions are greatly affected by the costs of shipping merchandise to customers across a wide range of geographical regions frequently employ one of the geographical pricing techniques. For these companies, freight expenses comprise a substantial portion of the cost of doing business and may cut deeply into already narrow profit margins. One type of geographical pricing is **zone pricing**, in which a small company sells its merchandise at different prices to customers located in different territories. For example, a manufacturer might sell at one price to customers east of the Mississippi and at another to those west of the Mississippi. The United States Postal Service's varying parcel post charges offer a good example of zone pricing. A small business must be able to show a legitimate basis (e.g., differences in selling or transporting costs) for the price discrimination or risk violating Section 2 of the Clayton Act.

zone pricing—a technique that involves setting different prices for customers located in different territories because of different transportation costs.

Another variation of geographic pricing is uniform **delivered pricing**, a technique in which a firm charges all of its customers the same price regardless of their location, even though the cost of selling or transporting merchandise varies. The firm calculates the proper freight charges for each region and combines them into a uniform fee. The result is that local customers subsidize the firm's charges for shipping merchandise to distant customers.

delivered pricing—a technique in which a company charges all customers the same price regardless of their locations

A final variation of geographical pricing is **FOB-Factory**, in which the small company sells its merchandise to customers on the condition that they pay all shipping costs. In this way, the company can set a uniform price for its product and let each customer cover the freight costs.

FOB-Factory—a pricing method in which a company sells merchandise to customers on the condition that they pay all shipping costs.

OPPORTUNISTIC PRICING. When products or services are in short supply, customers are willing to pay more for products they need. Some businesses use such circumstances to maximize short-term profits by engaging in price gouging. Many customers have little choice but to pay the higher prices. **Opportunistic pricing** may backfire, however, because customers know that unreasonably high prices mean that a company is exploiting them. For example, after the devastating Los Angeles earthquake, one convenience store jacked up prices on virtually every item, selling small bottles of water for $8 each. Neighborhood residents had no choice but to pay the higher prices. After the incident, many customers remembered the store's unfair prices and began to shop elsewhere. The convenience store's sales slipped and never recovered.

opportunistic pricing—a pricing method that involves charging customers unreasonably high prices when goods or services are in short supply.

DISCOUNTS. Many small business managers use **discounts or markdowns**—reductions from normal list prices—to move stale, outdated, damaged, or slow-moving merchandise. A seasonal discount is a price reduction designed to encourage shoppers to purchase merchandise before an upcoming season. For instance, many retail clothiers offer special sales on winter coats in midsummer. Some firms grant purchase discounts to special groups of customers, such as senior citizens or students, to establish a faithful clientele and to generate repeat business. For example, one small drugstore located near a state university offered a 10 percent student discount on all purchases and was quite successful in developing a large volume of student business.

discounts (markdowns)—reductions from normal list prices.

Multiple unit pricing is a promotional technique that offers customers discounts if they purchase in quantity. Many products, especially those with relatively low unit value, are sold using multiple unit pricing. For example, instead of selling an item for 50 cents, a small company might offer five for $2.

multiple unit pricing—a technique offering customers discounts if they purchase in quantity.

SUGGESTED RETAIL PRICES.   Many manufacturers print suggested retail prices on their products or include them on invoices or in wholesale catalogs. Small business owners frequently follow these suggested retail prices because this eliminates the need to make a pricing decision. Nonetheless, following prices established by a distant manufacturer may create problems for the small firm. For example, a haberdasher may try to create a high-quality, exclusive image through a prestige pricing policy, but manufacturers may suggest discount outlet prices that are incompatible with the small firm's image. Another danger of accepting the manufacturer's suggested price is that it does not take into consideration the small firm's cost structure or competitive situation. A manufacturer cannot force a business to accept a suggested retail price or require a business to agree not to resell merchandise below a stated price because such practices violate the Sherman Antitrust Act and other legislation.

Learning Objective

7-A. Explain the pricing methods and strategies for retailers.

PRICING STRATEGIES AND METHODS FOR RETAILERS

As customers have become more price conscious, retailers have changed their pricing strategies to emphasize value. This value/price relationship allows for a wide variety of highly creative pricing and marketing practices. As discussed previously, delivering high levels of recognized value in products and services is one key to retail customer loyalty.

Markup

markup (or markon)—*the difference between the cost of a product or service and its selling price.*

The basic premise of a successful business operation is selling a good or service for more than it costs. The difference between the cost of a product or service and its selling price is called **markup** (or **markon**). Markup can be expressed in dollars or as a percentage of either cost or selling price:

$$\text{Dollar markup} = \text{Retail price} - \text{Cost of merchandise}$$

$$\text{Percentage (of retail price) markup} = \frac{\text{dollar markup}}{\text{retail price}}$$

$$\text{Percentage (of cost) markup} = \frac{\text{dollar markup}}{\text{cost of unit}}$$

For example, if a man's shirt costs \$15, and the manager plans to sell it for \$25, markup would be as follows:

$$\text{Dollar markup} = \$25 - \$15 = \$10$$

$$\text{Percentage (of retail price) markup} = \frac{\$10}{\$25} = \$40\%$$

$$\text{Percentage (of cost) markup} = \frac{\$10}{\$15} = 66.67\%$$

Notice that the cost of merchandise used in computing markup includes not only the wholesale price of the merchandise but also any incidental costs (e.g., selling or transportation charges) that the retailer incurs and a profit minus any discounts (quantity, cash) that the wholesaler offers.

Once a business owner has a financial plan, including sales estimates and anticipated expenses, she can compute the firm's initial markup. The initial markup is the *average* markup required on all merchandise to cover the cost of the items, all incidental expenses, and a reasonable profit:

$$\frac{\text{Initial}}{\text{dollar}} = \frac{\text{operating expenses} + \text{reductions} + \text{profits}}{\text{net sales} + \text{reductions}}$$
$$\text{markup}$$

where operating expenses are the cost of doing business, such as rent, utilities, and depreciation; and reductions include employee and customer discounts, markdowns, special sales, and the cost of stockouts.

For example, if a small retailer forecasts sales of $380,000, expenses of $140,000, and $24,000 in reductions, and she expects a profit of $38,000, the initial markup percentage will be:

$$\text{Initial markup percentage} = \frac{140{,}000 + 24{,}000 + 38{,}000}{380{,}000 + 24{,}000} = 50\%$$

This retailer, thus, knows that an average markup of 50 percent is required to cover costs and generate an adequate profit.

Some businesses employ a standard markup on all of their merchandise. This technique, which is usually used in retail stores carrying related products, applies a standard percentage markup to all merchandise. Most stores find it much more practical to use a flexible markup, which assigns various markup percentages to different types of products. Because of the wide range of prices and types of merchandise they sell, department stores frequently rely on a flexible markup. It would be impractical for them to use a standard markup on all items because they have such a divergent cost and volume range. For instance, the markup percentage for socks is not likely to be suitable as a markup for washing machines.

Once an owner determines the desired markup percentage, she can compute the appropriate retail price. Knowing that the markup of a particular item represents 40 percent of the retail price

$$\begin{aligned}\text{Cost} &= \text{retail price} - \text{markup} \\ &= 100\% - 40\% \\ &= 60\% \text{ of retail price}\end{aligned}$$

And assuming that the cost of the item is $18.00, the retailer can rearrange the percentage (of retail price) markup formula:

$$\text{Retail price} = \frac{\text{dollar cost}}{\text{percentage cost}}$$

Solving for retail price, the retailer computes a price of the following:

$$\text{Retail price} = \frac{\$18.00}{0.60} = \$30.00$$

Thus, the owner establishes a retail price of $30.00 for the item using a 40 percent markup.

Finally, retailers must verify that the retail price they have calculated is consistent with their planned initial markup percentage. Will it cover costs and generate the desired profit? Is it congruent with the firm's overall price image? Is the final price in line with the company's strategy? Is it within an acceptable price range? How does it compare to the prices charged by competitors? And, perhaps most important, are the customers willing and able to pay this price?

Follow-the-Leader Pricing

Some small companies make no effort to be price leaders in their immediate geographic areas and simply follow the prices that their competitors establish. Entrepreneurs wisely monitor their competitors' pricing policies and individual prices by reviewing their advertisements or by hiring part-time or full-time comparison shoppers. But then these retailers use this information to establish a "me too" pricing policy, which eradicates any opportunity to create a special price image for their businesses. Although many retailers must match competitors' prices on identical items, maintaining a follow-the-leader pricing policy may not be healthy for a small business because it robs the company of the opportunity to create a distinctive image in its customers' eyes.

Below-Market Pricing

Some small businesses choose to create a discount image in the market by offering goods at below-market prices. By setting prices below those of their competitors, these firms hope to attract a sufficient level of volume to offset the lower profit margins. Many retailers using a below-market pricing strategy eliminate most of the extra services that their above-market-pricing competitors offer. For instance, these businesses trim operating costs by cutting out services like delivery, installation, credit granting, and sales assistance. Below-market pricing strategies can be risky for small companies because they require them to constantly achieve high sales volume to remain competitive.

Adjustable or Dynamic Pricing

For most of the history of business, price was set through face-to-face bargaining. A merchant knew his customers and their price sensitivity and bargaining skills. The result was that the final price for identical merchandise or services could vary significantly. In the mass marketing era of the latter half of the twentieth century when individual identity became blurred, the trend became to have an established "fixed" price for the goods or service.

With the Internet, the marketplace is beginning to see the reemergence of adjustable or **dynamic pricing**. Computer software is blending the disciplines of microeconomics, mathematics, and psychology into programs capable of analyzing a customer's price sensitivity based on that potential customer's previous purchasing behaviors. The airline and hospitality industries have been employing adjustable pricing for some time. For this reason, people on the same flight may have paid different prices for their tickets. Software firms such as ProfitLogic, Optivo, Enduse.com., Zillant, and KhL Metrics all employ a blending of consumer data with sophisticated mathematical models to help retailers set prices in ways they believe will maximize profits.[61]

dynamic pricing—*price is set by the interaction of buyer and seller at the point of purchase.*

Learning Objective

7-B. Explain the pricing methods and strategies for manufacturers.

PRICING CONCEPTS FOR MANUFACTURERS

For manufacturers, the pricing decision requires the support of accurate, timely accounting records. The most commonly used pricing technique for manufacturers is cost-plus pricing. Using this method, the manufacturer establishes a price composed of direct materials, direct labor, factory overhead, selling and administrative costs, plus the desired profit margin. Figure 8.5 illustrates the cost-plus pricing components.

The main advantage of the cost-plus pricing method is its simplicity. Given the proper cost accounting data, computing a product's final selling price is relatively easy. Also, because he adds a profit onto the top of the firm's costs, the manufacturer is guaranteed the desired profit margin. This process, however, does not encourage the manufacturer to use his resources efficiently. Even if the company fails to employ its resources in the most effective manner, it will

FIGURE 8.5 Cost-Plus Pricing Components

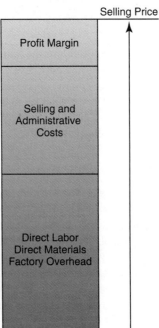

still earn a reasonable profit, and thus, there is no motivation to conserve resources in the manufacturing process. Finally, because manufacturers' cost structures vary so greatly, cost-plus pricing fails to consider the competition sufficiently. Despite its drawbacks, the cost-plus method of establishing prices remains prominent in many industries such as construction and printing.

Direct Costing and Price Formulation

One requisite for a successful pricing policy in manufacturing is a reliable cost accounting system that can generate timely reports to determine the costs of processing raw materials into finished goods. The traditional method of product costing is called **absorption costing**, because all manufacturing and overhead costs are absorbed into the finished product's total cost. Absorption costing includes direct materials, direct labor, plus a portion of fixed and variable factory overhead in each unit manufactured. Full absorption financial statements are used in published annual reports and in tax reports and are very useful in performing financial analysis. However full-absorption statements are of little help to the manufacturer when determining prices or the impact of price changes.

A more useful technique for managerial decision making is **variable (or direct) costing**, in which the cost of the products manufactured includes only those costs that vary directly with the quantity produced. In other words, variable costing encompasses direct materials, direct labor, and factory overhead costs that vary with the level of the firm's output of finished goods. Those factory overhead costs that are fixed (rent, depreciation, insurance) are *not* included in the costs of finished items. Instead, they are considered to be expenses of the period.

> **absorption costing**—the traditional method of product costing in which all manufacturing and overhead costs are absorbed into the product's total cost.
>
> **variable (direct) costing**—a method of product costing that includes in the product's cost only those costs that vary directly with the quantity produced.

The manufacturer's goal when establishing prices is to discover the cost combination of selling price and sales volume that covers the variable costs of producing a product and contributes toward covering fixed costs and earning a profit. The problem with using full-absorption costing for this is that it clouds the true relationships among price, volume, and costs by including fixed expenses in unit cost. Using a direct-costing basis yields a constant unit cost for the product no matter what volume of production. The result is a clearer picture of the price–volume–costs relationship.

The starting point for establishing product prices is the direct-cost income statement. As Table 8.7 indicates, the direct-cost statement yields the same net income as does the full-absorption income statement. The only difference between the two statements is the format. The full-absorption statement allocates costs such as advertising, rent, and utilities according to the activity that caused them, but the direct-cost income statement separates expenses into fixed and variable. Fixed expenses remain constant regardless of the production level, but variable expenses fluctuate according to production volume.

When variable costs are subtracted from total revenues, the result is the manufacturer's contribution margin—the amount remaining that contributes to covering fixed expenses and earning a profit. Expressing this contribution margin as a percentage of total revenue yields the firm's contribution percentage. Computing the contribution percentage is a critical step in establishing prices through the direct-costing method. This manufacturer's contribution percentage is 36.5 percent ($288,000 ÷ 790,000).

Computing the Break-Even Selling Price

The manufacturer's contribution percentage tells what portion of total revenues remains after covering variable costs to contribute toward meeting fixed expenses and earning a profit. This manufacturer's contribution percentage is 36.5 percent, which means that variable costs absorb 63.5 percent of total revenues. In other words, variable costs should be 63.5 percent ($1.00 - 0.365 = 0.635$) of the product's selling price. Suppose that this manufacturer's variable costs include the following:

Material	$2.08/unit
Direct labor	$4.12/unit
Variable factory overhead	$0.78/unit
Total variable cost	$6.98/unit

The minimum price at which the manufacturer would sell the item for is $6.98. Any price below this would not cover variable costs. To compute the break-even selling price for this product, use the following equation:

$$\text{Break-even selling price} = \frac{\text{profit (variable cost per unit} \times \text{quantity produced)} + \text{total fixed cost}}{\text{quantity produced}}$$

TABLE 8.7

Full-Absorption Versus Direct-Cost Income Statement

Full-Absorption Income Statement

Sales Revenue		$790,000
Cost of Goods Sold		
Materials	250,500	
Direct Labor	190,200	
Factory Overhead	120,200	560,900
Gross Profit		$229,100
Operating Expenses		
General and Administrative	66,100	
Selling	112,000	
Other	11,000	
Total Operating Expenses		189,100
Net Income (before taxes)		$ 40,000

Direct-Cost Income Statement

Sales Revenue (100%)		$790,000
Variable Costs		
Materials	250,500	
Direct Labor	190,200	
Variable Factory Overhead	13,200	
Variable Selling Expenses	48,100	
Total Variable Costs (63.54%)		502,000
Contribution Margin (36.46%)		288,000
Fixed Costs		
Fixed Factory Overhead	107,000	
Fixed Selling Expenses	63,900	
General and Administrative	66,100	
Other Fixed Expenses	11,000	
Total Fixed Expenses (31.39%)		248,000
Net Income (before taxes) (5.06%)		$ 40,000

To break even, the manufacturer assumes $0 profit. Suppose that his plans are to produce 50,000 units of the product and that fixed costs will be $110,000. The break-even selling price is as follows:

$$\text{Break-even selling price} = \frac{\$0 + (\$6.98 \times 50,000 \text{ units}) + \$110,000}{50,000 \text{ units}}$$

$$= \frac{\$459,000}{50,000 \text{ units}}$$

$$= \$9.18/\text{unit}$$

Thus, $2.20 ($9.18/unit − $6.98/unit) of the $9.18 break-even price contributes to meeting fixed production costs. But suppose the manufacturer wants to earn a $50,000 profit. Then the selling price is:

$$\text{Selling price} = \frac{\$50,000 + (\$6.98/\text{units} \times 50,000 \text{ units}) + \$110,000}{50,000 \text{ units}}$$

$$= \frac{\$509,000}{50,000 \text{ units}}$$

$$= \$10.18/\text{unit}$$

Now the manufacturer must decide whether customers will purchase 50,000 units at $10.18. If not, he must decide either to produce a different, more profitable product or to lower the selling price. Any price above $9.18 will generate some profit, although less than that desired. In the short run, the manufacturer could sell the product for less than $9.18 if competitive factors so dictated, but not below $6.98 because this would not cover the variable cost of production.

Because the manufacturer's capacity in the short run is fixed, pricing decisions should be aimed at employing these resources most efficiently. The fixed costs of operating the plant cannot be avoided, and the variable costs can be eliminated only if the firm ceases offering the product. Therefore, the selling price must be at least equal to the variable costs (per unit) of making the product. Any price above this amount contributes to covering fixed costs and providing a reasonable profit.

Of course, over the long run, the manufacturer cannot sell below total costs and continue to survive. So, selling price must cover total product cost—both fixed and variable—and generate a reasonable profit.

PRICING STRATEGIES AND METHODS FOR SERVICE FIRMS

Learning Objective

7-C. Explain the pricing methods and strategies for service firms.

A service firm must establish a price based on the materials used to provide the service, the labor employed, an allowance for overhead, and a profit. As in the manufacturing operation, a service firm must have a reliable, accurate accounting system to keep a tally of the total costs of providing the service. Most service firms base their prices on an hourly rate, usually the actual number of hours required to perform the service. Some companies, however, base their fees on a standard number of hours, determined by the average number of hours needed to perform the service. For most firms, labor and materials comprise the largest portion of the cost of the service. To establish a reasonable, profitable price for service, a small business owner must know the cost of materials, direct labor, and overhead for each unit of service. Using these basic cost data and a desired profit margin, an owner of a small service firm can determine the appropriate price for the service.

Consider a simple example for pricing a common service—television repair. Ned's T.V. Repair Shop uses the direct-costing method to prepare an income statement for exercising managerial control (see Table 8.8). Ned estimates that he and his employees spent about 12,800 hours in the actual production of television service. So total cost per productive hour for Ned's T.V. Repair Shop comes to the following:

$$\frac{\$172,000}{12,800 \text{ hours}} = \$13.44/\text{hour}$$

Now Ned must add in an amount for his desired profit. He expects a net operating profit of 18 percent on sales. To compute the final price he uses this equation:

$$\begin{aligned} \text{Price} \\ \text{per hour} \end{aligned} = \begin{aligned} \text{total cost per} \\ \text{productive hour} \end{aligned} \times \frac{1.00}{(1.00 - \text{Net profit target as \% of sales})}$$

$$= \$13.44 \times 1.219$$
$$= \$16.38/\text{hour}$$

A price of $16.38 per hour will cover Ned's costs and generate the desired profit. The wise service shop owner computes his cost per production hour at regular intervals throughout the year. Rapidly

TABLE 8.8

Direct-Cost Income Statement, Ned's T.V. Repair Shop

Sales Revenue	_____	$199,000
Variable Expenses		
Labor	$52,000	
Materials	40,500	
Variable Factory Overhead	11,500	
Total Variable Expenses	_____	104,000
Fixed Expenses		
Rent	$ 2,500	
Salaries	38,500	
Fixed Overhead	27,000	
Total Fixed Expenses		68,000
Net Income		$27,000

rising labor costs and material prices dictate that the service firm's price per hour be computed even more frequently. As in the case of the retailer and the manufacturer, Ned must evaluate the pricing policies of competitors and decide whether his price is consistent with his firm's image.

Of course, the price of $16.38 per hour assumes that each job requires the same amount of materials. If this is not a valid assumption, Ned must recalculate the price per hour *without* including the cost of materials:

$$\text{Cost per productive hour} = \frac{\$172,000 - 40,500}{12,800 \text{ hours}}$$
$$= \$10.27/\text{hour}$$

Adding in the desired 18 percent net operating profit on sales:

$$\text{Price per hour} = \$10.27/\text{hour} \times \frac{1.00}{(1.00 - 0.18)}$$
$$= \$10.27/\text{hour} \times 1.219$$
$$= \$12.52/\text{hour}$$

Under these conditions Ned would charge $12.52 per hour plus the actual cost of materials used and any markup on the cost of material. A repair job that takes four hours to complete would have the following price:

Cost of service (4 hours × $12.52/hour)	$50.08
Cost of materials	$21.00
Markup on material (10%)	$2.10
Total price	$73.18

Learning Objective

8. Describe the impact of credit on pricing.

THE IMPACT OF CREDIT ON PRICING

Consumers crave convenience when they shop, and one of the most common conveniences they demand is the ability to purchase goods and services on credit. Small businesses that fail to offer customers credit lose sales to competitors that do. Yet, companies that do sell on credit incur additional expenses for offering this convenience. Small companies have three options for selling to customers on credit: credit cards, installment credit, and trade credit.

Credit Cards

Credit cards have become a popular method of payment among customers. Approximately 70 percent of the adult U.S. population uses credit cards to make purchases, and the typical U.S. household has 10 credit cards.[62] The number of credit cards in circulation in the United States exceeds 1 billion, an average of about four cards per person! The average customer uses a credit card 5.5 times per month to charge an average of $547.[63] Customers use credit cards to pay for $28 out of every $100 spent on consumable goods and services.[64] One study found that accepting credit cards increases the probability, speed, and magnitude of customer spending. In addition, surveys show that customers rate businesses offering credit options higher on key performance measures such as reputation, reliability, and service.[65] In short, accepting credit cards broadens a small company's customer base and closes sales it would normally lose if customers had to pay in cash.

The convenience of credit cards is not free to business owners, however. Companies must pay to use the system, typically 1 to 6 percent of the total credit card charges, which they must factor into the prices of their products or services. They also pay a transaction fee of 5 to 25 cents per charge. Given customer expectations, small businesses cannot drop major cards, even when the big card companies raise the fees that merchants must pay. Fees operate on a multi-step process. On a $100 Visa or MasterCard purchase, a processing bank buys the credit card slip from the retailer for $97.44. Then that bank sells the slip to the bank that issued the card for about $98.80. The remaining $1.20 discount is called the interchange fee, which is what the processing bank passes along to the issuing bank. Before it can accept credit cards, a business must obtain merchant status from either a bank or an independent sales organization (ISO).

More small businesses also are equipping their stores to handle debit card transactions, which act as electronic checks, automatically deducting the purchase amount from a customer's checking account. The equipment is easy to install and to set up, and the cost to the company is negligible. The payoff can be big, however, in the form of increased sales. "How can you possibly lose when you're offering customers another avenue for purchasing merchandise?" says Mark Knauff, who recently installed a debit card terminal in his guitar shop.[66]

Installment Credit

Small companies that sell big-ticket consumer durables—such as major appliances, cars, and boats—frequently rely on installment credit. Because very few customers can purchase such items in a single lump-sum payment, small businesses finance them over an extended time. The time horizon may range from just a few months up to 30 or more years. Most companies require customers to make an initial down payment for the merchandise and then finance the balance for the life of the loan. The customer repays the loan principal plus interest on the loan. One advantage of installment loans for a small business is that the owner retains a security interest as collateral on the loan. If a customer defaults on the loan, the owner still holds the title to the merchandise. Because installment credit absorbs a small company's cash, many rely on financial institutions such as banks and credit unions to provide installment credit. When a firm has the financial strength to "carry its own paper," the interest income from the installment loan contract often yields more than the initial profit on the sale of the product. For some businesses, such as furniture stores, this has traditionally been a major source of income.

Trade Credit

Companies that sell small-ticket items frequently offer their customers trade credit—that is, they create customer charge accounts. The typical small business bills its credit customers each month. To speed collections, some offer cash discounts if customers pay their balances early; others impose penalties on late payers. Before deciding to use trade credit as a competitive weapon, the small business owner must make sure that the firm's cash position is strong enough to support the additional pressure.

CHAPTER SUMMARY

1. Describe the basis of a marketing communications plan.

- What is to be achieved with the message?
- Knowledge of the firm's targeted market to ensure that the message is properly focused.
- Build the message on the firm's unique selling proposition.

2. Describe the advantages and disadvantages of the various advertising media.

- Advertising.
- Publicity and public relations.
- Hybrid forms of promotion and advertising.
- Personal selling.

3. Describe the advantages and disadvantages of the various advertising media.

- The medium used to transmit an advertising message influences the consumer's perception—and reception—of it.
- Media options include newspapers, radio, television, magazines, direct mail, the World Wide Web, outdoor advertising, transit advertising, directories, trade shows, special events and promotions, and point-of-purchase ads.

4. Discuss four basic methods for preparing an advertising budget.

- Establishing an advertising budget presents a real challenge to the small business owner.
- Here are four basic methods: what is affordable; matching competitors; percentage of sales; objective and task.

5. Explain practical methods for stretching the small business owner's advertising budget.

- Despite their limited advertising budgets, small businesses do not have to take a second-class approach to advertising. Three techniques that can stretch a small company's advertising dollars are cooperative advertising, shared advertising, and publicity.

6. Describe effective pricing techniques for introducing new goods or services and for existing ones.

- Pricing a new product is often difficult for the small business manager, but it should accomplish three objectives: getting the product accepted; maintaining market share as the competition grows; and earning a profit. Generally, there are three major pricing strategies used to introduce new products into the market: penetration, skimming, and sliding down the demand curve.
- Pricing techniques for existing products and services include odd pricing, price lining, leader pricing, geographical pricing, opportunistic pricing, discounts, and suggested retail pricing.

7. Explain the pricing methods and strategies for retailers, manufacturers, and service firms.

- Pricing for the retailer means pricing to move merchandise. Markup is the difference between the cost of a product or service and its selling price. Most retailers compute their markup as a percentage of retail price, but some retailers put a standard markup on all their merchandise; more frequently, they use a flexible markup.

- A manufacturer's pricing decision depends on the support of accurate cost accounting records. The most common technique is cost-plus pricing, in which the manufacturer charges a price that covers the cost of producing a product plus a reasonable profit. Every manufacturer should calculate a product's break-even price, the price that produces neither a profit nor a loss.

- Service firms often suffer from the effects of vague, unfounded pricing procedures and frequently charge the going rate without any idea of their costs. A service firm must set a price based on the cost of materials used, labor involved, overhead, and a profit. The proper price reflects the total cost of providing a unit of service.

8. Describe the impact of credit on pricing.

- Offering consumer credit enhances a small company's reputation and increases the probability, speed, and magnitude of customers' purchases. Small firms offer three types of consumer credit: credit cards, installment credit, and trade credit (charge accounts).

DISCUSSION QUESTIONS

1. What are the four elements of promotion? How do they support one another?
2. Briefly outline the steps in creating an advertising plan. What principles should the small business owner follow when creating an effective advertisement?
3. What factors should a small business manager consider when selecting advertising media?
4. Create a table to summarize the advantages and disadvantages of the following advertising media:

Newspapers	Direct mail
Radio	Outdoor advertising
Television	Transit advertising
Magazines	Directories
Specialty advertising	Trade shows
World Wide Web	Sponsorships and promotions

5. What are fixed spots, preemptible spots, and floating spots in radio advertising?
6. Describe the characteristics of an effective outdoor advertisement.
7. Describe the common methods of establishing an advertising budget. Which method is most often used? Which technique is most often recommended? Why?

8. How does pricing affect a small firm's image?
9. What competitive factors must the small firm consider when establishing prices?
10. Describe the strategies a small business could use in setting the price of a new product. What objectives should the strategy seek to achieve?
11. Define the following pricing techniques: odd pricing, price lining, leader pricing, geographical pricing, and discounts.
12. Why do many small businesses use the manufacturer's suggested retail price? What are the disadvantages of this technique?
13. What is a markup? How is it used to determine individual price?
14. What is a standard markup? A flexible markup?
15. What is cost-plus pricing? Why do so many manufacturers use it? What are the disadvantages of using it?
16. Explain the difference between full-absorption costing and direct costing. How does absorption costing help a manufacturer determine a reasonable price?
17. Explain the technique for a small service firm setting an hourly price.
18. What benefits does a small business get by offering customers credit? What costs does it incur?

THE BUSINESS DISC

Launch *The Business Disc* and return to the section where Harry describes the basics of pricing. If you have passed that point in the program, you can easily return to it. From the "Go To" menu, select "Events from PART 1 - B," and click on "Harry on Pricing." If you haven't reached that point, continue from where you left off. **Note: If you skip ahead you will not be able to set your price**. Explain Harry's

"formula" for setting the price for a product or service. What is a company's break-even point? Explain the factors that influence the price your company can charge for its products or services. If you have not done so already, complete the "Set Your Price Form" on *The Business Disc*. Now that you have read Chapter 8, do you want to change the prices you established? Explain.

Business PlanPro

Upon completion of this chapter you will likely need to modify some of the marketing sections in your business plan to provide the reader additional details regarding the advertising, promotion and pricing of your products or services.

BEYOND THE CLASSROOM . . .

1. Contact a small retailer, manufacturer, and a service firm and interview each one about his or her advertising program.

    a. Are there specific advertising objectives?

    b. What media does the owner employ? Why?

    c. How does the manager evaluate an ad's effectiveness?

    d. What assistance does the manager receive in designing ads?

2. Contact several small business owners and determine how they establish their advertising budgets. Why do they use the method they do?

3. Collect two or three advertisements for local small businesses and evaluate them on a scale of 1 (low) to 10 (high) using the following criteria: attention-getting, distinctive, interesting, brevity, personal appeal, credibility, USP focused, convincing, motivating, and effectiveness. How would you change the ads to make them more effective?

4. Browse through a magazine and find two ads that use sex to sell a good or service—one that you consider effective and one that you consider offensive. Compare your ads and reasoning with those of your classmates. What implications does your discussion have for advertisers?

5. Interview a successful small retailer and ask the following questions: Does the retailer seek a specific image through its prices? What type of outlet would you consider the retailer to be? What role do its competitors play in the business owner's pricing? Does the owner use specific pricing techniques such as odd pricing, price lining, leader pricing or geographical pricing? How are discounts calculated? What markup percentage does the firm use? How are prices derived? What are the firm's cost structures?

6. Select an industry that has several competing small firms in your area. Contact these firms and compare their approaches to determining prices. Do prices on identical or similar items differ? Why?

7. Use the Web to research the use of cookies in online advertising. What benefits do cookies offer Web users? Web advertisers? What ethical concerns do you have concerning cookies? Explain. Should marketers be able to use cookies?

CHAPTER

9

Managing Cash Flow

Whatever you have, spend less.
—Samuel Johnson

A deficit is what you have when you haven't got as much as when you had nothing.
—Gerald F. Lieberman

LEARNING OBJECTIVES

Upon completion of this chapter, you will be able to:

1. **EXPLAIN** the importance of cash management to a small business's success.

2. **DIFFERENTIATE** between cash and profits.

3. **UNDERSTAND** the five steps in creating a cash budget and use them to create a cash budget.

4. **DESCRIBE** fundamental principles involved in managing the "big three" of cash management: accounts receivable, accounts payable, and inventory.

5. **EXPLAIN** the techniques for avoiding a cash crunch in a small company.

Cash—a four-letter word that has become a curse for many small businesses. Lack of this valuable asset has driven countless small companies into bankruptcy. Unfortunately, many more firms will become failure statistics because their owners have neglected the principles of cash management that can spell the difference between success and failure. "Everything is about cash," says entrepreneur-turned-venture-capitalist Guy Kawasaki, "raising it, conserving it, collecting it."[1] Indeed, developing a cash forecast is essential for new businesses because early profit levels usually do not generate sufficient cash to keep the company afloat. A common cause of business failures is that owners neglect to forecast how much cash their companies will need until they reach the point of generating positive cash flow. Another problem, especially in start-up and fast-growth companies, is overemphasis on increasing sales with little concern for collecting the receivables those sales create. The result is always the same: a cash crisis.

Controlling the financial aspects of a business using the traditional analysis of basic financial statements with ratios (the topic of Chapter 10) is immensely important; however, by themselves, these techniques are insufficient to achieve business success. Entrepreneurs are prone to focus on their companies' income statements—particularly sales and profits. The income statement, of course, shows only part of a company's financial picture. It is entirely possible for a business to earn a profit and still go out of business *by running out of cash*. In other words, managing a company's total financial performance effectively requires an entrepreneur to look beyond the "bottom line" and focus on what it takes to keep a company going—cash.

"This [monitoring your cash flow statement] is more important than watching your income statement or balance sheet," says Scott Trenner, owner of **S.T. Lube**, *a company that operates six Jiffy Lube franchises. Trenner knows firsthand the importance of positive cash flow. His company ran into serious cash flow problems as he focused on rapid growth. "I was building a multi-million-dollar empire," he recalls, "but my revenues never caught up with my expenses." Cash was so tight that Trenner had trouble meeting the payroll for his company's 65 employees. "I once had to get a two-week, $30,000 loan from my father when we were struggling," he recalls. The turning point came when Trenner created a statement to track and analyze his company's cash flow. "We stopped focusing only on expansion and started paying attention to day-to-day management," he says. "By keeping a close eye on our cash flow statement, we went from a negative cash flow to a positive cash flow of $1,000 a week and turned around a $140,000 deficit in three years."[2]*

CASH MANAGEMENT

Learning Objective

1. Explain the importance of cash management to a small business's success.

cash management—*the process of forecasting, collecting, disbursing, investing, and planning for the cash a company needs to operate smoothly*

A survey by the National Federation of Independent Businesses found that 67 percent of small business owners say they have at least occasional problems managing cash flow; 19 percent of business owners report cash flow as a continuing problem.[3] The only way to avoid this potentially business-crushing predicament is by using the principles of cash management. **Cash management** involves forecasting, collecting, disbursing, investing, and planning for the cash a company needs to operate smoothly. Cash management is a vital task because cash is the most important yet least productive asset that a small business owns. A business must have enough cash to meet its obligations or it will be declared bankrupt. Creditors, employees, and lenders expect to be paid on time, and cash is the required medium of exchange. But some firms retain an excessive amount of cash to meet any unexpected circumstances that might arise. These dormant dollars have an income-earning potential that owners are ignoring, and this restricts a firm's growth and lowers its profitability. Investing these dollars, even for a short time, can add to a company's earnings. Proper cash management permits the owner to adequately meet the cash demands of the business, to avoid retaining unnecessarily large cash balances, and to stretch the profit-generating power of each dollar the business owns.

Although cash flow difficulties afflict companies of all sizes and ages, young companies, especially, are cash sponges, soaking up every available dollar and always hungry for more. The reason usually is that their cash-generating "engines" are not operating at full speed yet and cannot provide enough power to generate the cash necessary to cover rapidly climbing operating expenses. Entrepreneurs must manage cash flow from the day they launch their businesses.

Henry Ford displays the first car built by the Ford Motor Company. Within a month of its launch, Ford's company nearly failed because of a cash crisis before growing into one of the largest companies in the world.

Courtesy of Getty Images Inc. - Hulton Archive Photos.

FIRST · CAR

A Company Example

Shortly after he launched his new company on June 16, 1903, entrepreneur Henry Ford ran headlong into a cash crisis that nearly wiped out the **Ford Motor Company**. *Start-up expenses (including $10,000 to the Dodge brothers for engines and other parts and $640 to the Hartford Rubber Works for 64 tires) quickly soaked up Ford's $28,000 in start-up capital that he and 11 associates had invested. By July 10, the company's cash balance had fallen to a mere $223.65. Another payroll and more parts orders were just around the corner, and the 25-day-old company was already on the brink of a financial collapse. On July 11, an investor saved the day with a $5,000 contribution. Four days later the Ford Motor Company sold its first car to Dr. E. Pfennig of Chicago, pushing the company's cash balance to $6,486.44. From this shaky financial beginning grew one of the largest automakers in the world![4]*

Managing cash flow is also an acute problem for rapidly growing businesses. In fact, fast-track companies are most likely to suffer cash shortages. Many successful, growing, and profitable businesses fail because they become insolvent; they do not have adequate cash to meet the needs of a growing business with a booming sales volume. If a company's sales are up, its owner also must hire more employees, expand plant capacity, increase the sales force, build inventory, and incur other drains on the firm's cash supply. During rapid growth, cash collections typically fall behind, compounding the problem. Cash flows out of these high-growth companies much faster than it comes in. The head of the National Federation of Independent Businesses says that many small business owners "wake up one day to find that the price of success is no cash on hand. They don't understand that if they're successful, inventory and receivables will increase faster than profits can fund them."[5] The resulting cash crisis may force the owner to lose equity control of the business or, ultimately, declare bankruptcy and close. Table 9.1 shows how to calculate the additional cash required to support an increase in sales.

The first step in managing cash more effectively is to understand the company's **cash flow cycle**—the time lag between paying suppliers for merchandise or materials and receiving payment from customers for the product or service (see Figure 9.1). The longer this cash flow cycle, the more likely the business owner is to encounter a cash crisis. Preparing a cash forecast that recognizes this cycle, however, will help avoid a crisis. Understanding the cash flow patterns of a business over the course of a year is essential to creating a successful cash management strategy. Business owners should calculate their cash flow cycles whenever they prepare their financial statements (or at least quarterly). On a *daily* basis, business owners should generate reports showing the following items:

cash flow cycle—*the time lag between paying suppliers for merchandise or materials and receiving payment from customers.*

TABLE 9.1

How Much Cash Is Required to Support an Increase in Sales?

Source: Adapted from Norm Brodsky, "Paying for Growth: How Much Cash You Need to Carry New Sales" *Inc.* Online Tools & Apps: Worksheet, www.inc.com/tools/details/0,6152, CNT61_HOM1_LOC0_NAVhome_ TOL11648,00.html.

Too often, entrepreneurs believe that increasing sales is the ideal solution to a cash crunch only to discover (often after it is too late) that it takes extra cash to support extra sales. The following worksheet demonstrates how to calculate the amount of additional cash required to support an increase in sales.

To make the calculation, a business owner needs the following information:

- the increase in sales planned ($)
- the time frame for adding new sales (days)
- the company's gross profit margin, gross profit ÷ net sales (%)
- the estimated additional expenses required to generate additional sales ($)
- the company's average collection period (days)

To calculate the amount of additional cash needed, use the following formula:

Extra cash required = ((New sales − Gross profit + Extra overhead) × (Average collection period × 1.20*)) ÷ (Time frame in days for adding new sales)

Consider the following example:

The owner of Ardent Company wants to increase sales by $75,000 over the next year. The company's gross profit margin is 30 percent of sales (so its gross profit on these additional sales would be $75,000 × 30% = $22,500), its average collection period is 47 days, and managers estimate that generating the additional sales will require an increase in expenses of $21,300. The additional cash that Ardent will need to support this higher level of sales is:

Extra cash required = (($75,000 − $22,500 + 21,300) × (47 × 1.2)) ÷ 365 = $11,404

Advent will need $11,404 in extra cash to support the additional sales of $75,000 it plans to bring in over the next year.

*The extra 20 percent is added as a cushion.

total cash on hand, bank balance, summary of the day's sales, summary of the day's cash receipts and cash disbursements, and a summary of accounts receivable collections. Compiling these reports into monthly summaries provides the basis for making reliable cash forecasts.

The next step in effective cash management is to analyze the cash flow cycle, looking for ways to reduce its length. Reducing the cycle from 240 days to, say, 150 days would free up incredible amounts of cash that this company could use to finance growth and dramatically reduce its borrowing costs. What steps would you suggest the owner of the business whose cash flow cycle is illustrated in Figure 9.1 take to reduce its length?

Table 9.2 describes the five key cash management roles every entrepreneur must fill.

FIGURE 9.1

The Cash Flow Cycle

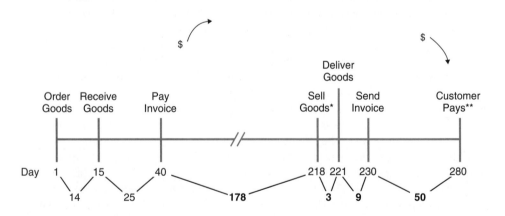

* Based on Average Inventory Turnover:

$$\frac{365 \text{ days}}{2.05 \text{ times/year}} = 178 \text{ days}$$

** Based on Average Collection Period:

$$\frac{365 \text{ days}}{7.31 \text{ times/year}} = 50 \text{ days}$$

TABLE 9.2

Five Cash Management Roles of the Entrepreneur

Source: Adapted from Bruce J. Blechman, "Quick Change Artist," *Entrepreneur,* January 1994, pp. 18–21.

Role 1: Cash Finder. This is the entrepreneur's first and foremost responsibility. You must make sure there is enough capital to pay all present (and future) bills. This is not a one-time task; it is an ongoing job.

Role 2: Cash Planner. As cash planner, an entrepreneur makes sure the company's cash is used properly and efficiently. You must keep track of its cash, make sure it is available to pay bills, and plan for its future use. Planning requires you to forecast the company's cash inflows and outflows for the months ahead with the help of a cash budget (discussed later in this chapter).

Role 3: Cash Distributor. This role requires you to control the cash needed to pay the company's bills and the priority and the timing of those payments. Forecasting cash disbursements accurately and making sure the cash is available when payments come due are essential to keeping the business solvent.

Role 4: Cash Collector. As cash collector, your job is to make sure your customers pay *their* bills on time. Too often, entrepreneurs focus on pumping up sales, while neglecting to collect the cash from those sales. Having someone in your company responsible for collecting accounts receivable is essential. Uncollected accounts drain a small company's pool of cash very quickly.

Role 5: Cash Conserver. This role requires you to make sure your company gets maximum value for the dollars it spends. Whether you are buying inventory to resell or computers to keep track of what you sell, it is important to get the most for your money. Avoiding unnecessary expenditures is an important part of this task. The goal is to spend cash so it will produce a return for the company.

CASH AND PROFITS ARE NOT THE SAME

Learning Objective

2. Differentiate between cash and profits.

When analyzing cash flow, entrepreneurs must understand that cash and profits are not the same. Attempting to discern the status of a small company's cash position by analyzing its profitability is futile; profitability is not necessarily highly correlated with cash flow. Profit (or net income) is the difference between a company's total revenue and its total expenses. It measures how efficiently a business is operating. Cash is the money that is free and readily available to use in a business. **Cash flow** measures a company's liquidity and its ability to pay its bills and other financial obligations on time by tracking the flow of cash into and out of the business over a period of time. Many small business owners soon discover that profitability does not guarantee liquidity. As important as earning a profit is, no business owner can pay suppliers, creditors, employees, the government, and lenders in profits; that requires *cash*! Although profits are tied up in many forms, such as inventory, computers, or machinery, cash is the money that flows through a business in a continuous cycle without being tied up in any other asset. "Businesses fail not because they are making or losing money," warns one financial expert, "but because they simply run out of cash."[6]

cash flow—*a method of tracking a company's liquidity and its ability to pay its bills and other financial obligations on time by tracking the flow of cash into and out of the business over a period of time.*

Figure 9.2 shows the flow of cash through a typical small business. Cash flow is the volume of actual cash that comes into and goes out of the business during an accounting period.

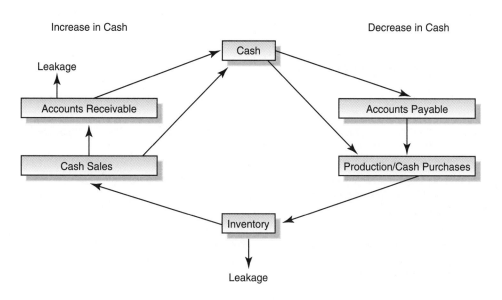

FIGURE 9.2

Cash Flow

Decreases in cash occur when the business purchases, on credit or for cash, goods for inventory or materials for use in production. A business sells the resulting inventory either for cash or on credit. When a company takes in cash or collects payments on accounts receivable, its cash balance increases. Notice that purchases for inventory and production *lead* sales; that is, these bills typically must be paid *before* sales are generated. But collection of accounts receivable *lags* behind sales; that is, customers who purchase goods on credit may not pay until next month.

THE CASH BUDGET

The need for a cash budget arises because in every business the cash flowing in is rarely "in sync" with the cash flowing out of the business. This uneven flow of cash creates periodic cash surpluses and shortages, making it necessary for entrepreneurs to track the flow of cash through their businesses so they can project realistically the cash available throughout the year. Many managers operate their businesses without knowing the pattern of their cash flows, believing that the process is too complex or time consuming. In reality, entrepreneurs simply cannot afford to disregard the process of cash management. They must ensure that their businesses have on hand an adequate, but not excessive, supply of cash to meet their operating needs. The goal of cash management is to have enough cash available to meet the company's cash needs at a given time.

How much cash is enough? What is suitable for one business may be totally inadequate for another, depending on each firm's size, nature, seasonal pattern of sales, and particular situation. The small business manager should prepare a **cash budget**, which is nothing more than a "cash map," showing the amount and the timing of the cash receipts and the cash disbursements day by day, week by week, or month by month. It is used to predict the amount of cash the firm will need to operate smoothly over a specific period of time, and it is a valuable tool in managing a company successfully. A cash budget can illuminate a host of approaching problems, giving entrepreneurs adequate time to handle, or better yet, avoid them. A cash budget reveals important clues about how well a company balances its accounts payable and accounts receivable, controls inventory, finances its growth, and makes use of the cash it has.

One consultant recalls how a cash budget helped salvage a once successful service firm that had fallen on hard times. The five-year-old firm with $20 million in annual billings began to lose money and was having trouble paying its bills. After working with the consultant, the company began sending customer invoices much faster and implemented a much stricter collection policy. The new collection system involved employees in collecting overdue payments and took immediate action when an account became overdue. Managers set up a receivables report and reviewed it at weekly staff meetings. They also beefed up the company's financial reports, added a cash budget, and used it to make managerial decisions. Within six months, the company's cash balance had improved dramatically (a turnaround of $1.5 million), managers were able to pay down a line of credit at the bank, and the business was back on track again!

PREPARING A CASH BUDGET

Typically, small business owners should prepare a projected monthly cash budget for at least one year into the future and quarterly estimates for another. The forecast must cover all seasonal sales fluctuations. The more variable a firm's sales pattern, the shorter its planning horizon should be. For example, a firm whose sales fluctuate widely over a relatively short time frame might require a weekly cash budget. The key is to track cash flows over time. The timing of a company's cash flow is as important as the amounts. "An alert cash flow manager keeps an eye not on cash receipts or on cash demands as average quantities but on cash as a function of the *calendar*," says one business owner.[7]

Regardless of the time frame selected, a cash budget must be in writing for an entrepreneur to properly visualize a company's cash position. Creating a written cash plan is not an excessively time-consuming task and can help the owner avoid unexpected cash shortages, a situation that can cause a business to fail. One financial consultant describes "a client who won't be able to make the payroll this month. His bank agreed to meet the payroll for him—but banks don't like to be surprised like that," he adds.[8] Preparing a cash budget will help business owners avoid such adverse surprises and will also let an owner know if he is keeping excessively large amounts of cash on hand. Computer spreadsheets such as Microsoft Excel and Lotus 1-2-3 make the job fast and easy to complete.

The cash budget is based on the cash method of accounting, which means that cash receipts and cash disbursements are recorded in the forecast *only when the cash transaction is expected to take place*. For example, credit sales to customers are not reported until the company expects to receive the cash from them. Similarly, purchases made on credit are not recorded until the owner expects to pay them. Because depreciation, bad debt expense, and other noncash items involve no cash transfers, they are omitted entirely from the cash budget.

The cash budget is nothing more than a forecast of the firm's cash inflows and outflows for a specific time period, and it will never be completely accurate. But it does give an entrepreneur a clear picture of the firm's estimated cash balance for the period, pointing out where external cash infusions may be required or where surplus cash balances may be available to invest. Also, by comparing actual cash flows with projections, an owner can revise his forecast so that future cash budgets will be more accurate.

Joseph Popper, CEO of **Computer Gallery**, *knows how deadly running out of cash can be for a small company and does everything he can to make sure his business avoids that trap. Popper uses a computer spreadsheet to extract key sales, collection, and disbursement totals and to generate the resulting cash balance each day. Even when he is traveling, Popper keeps up with his company's daily cash balance. He has the spreadsheet results sent to an Internet service, which e-mails them to his alphanumeric pager every day he is out of the office. "We've been paranoid about cash from day one," Popper says. But his system keeps accounts receivable in control, ensures that the company's available cash is working hard, and improves his relationship with the company's banker.[9]*

Formats for preparing a cash budget vary depending on the pattern of a company's cash flow. Table 9.3 shows a monthly cash budget for a small department store over a four-month period. Each monthly column should be divided into two sections—estimated and actual (not shown)—so that each succeeding cash forecast can be updated according to actual cash transactions. Comparing forecasted amounts to actual cash flows and learning the causes of any significant discrepancies allow entrepreneurs to improve the accuracy of future cash budgets. There are five basic steps in completing a cash budget:

1. Determining an adequate minimum cash balance.
2. Forecasting sales.
3. Forecasting cash receipts.
4. Forecasting cash disbursements.
5. Determining the end-of-month cash balance.

Step 1: Determining an Adequate Minimum Cash Balance

What is considered an excessive cash balance for one small business may be inadequate for another, even though the two firms are in the same business. Some suggest that a firm's cash balance should equal at least one-fourth of its current debts, but this general rule clearly will not work for all small businesses. The most reliable method of deciding cash balance is based on past experience. Past operating records should indicate the proper cash cushion needed to cover any unexpected expenses after all normal cash outlays are deducted from the month's cash receipts. For example, past records may indicate that it is desirable to maintain a cash balance equal to five days' sales. Seasonal fluctuations may cause a firm's minimum cash balance to change. For example, the desired cash balance for a retailer in December may be greater than in June.

TABLE 9.3 Cash Budget for Small Department Store

Assumptions:

Cash balance on December 31 = $12,000

Minimum cash balance desired = $10,000

Sales are 75% credit and 25% cash.

Credit sales are collected in the following manner:

- 60% collected in the first month after the sale
- 30% collected in the second month after the sale
- 5% collected in the third month after the sale
- 5% are never collected

Sales forecasts are as follows:	Pessimistic	Most Likely	Optimistic
October (actual)		$300,000	
November (actual)		350,000	
December (actual)		400,000	
January	$120,000	150,000	$175,000
February	160,000	200,000	250,000
March	160,000	200,000	250,000
April	250,000	300,000	340,000

The store pays 70% of sales price for merchandise purchased and pays for each month's anticipated sales in the preceding month.

Rent is $2,000 per month.

An interest payment of $7,500 is due in March.

A tax prepayment of $50,000 must be made in March.

A capital addition payment of $130,000 is due in February.

Utilities expenses amount to $850 per month.

Miscellaneous expenses are $70 per month.

Interest income of $200 will be received in February.

Wages and salaries are estimated to be

January—$30,000

February—$40,000

March—$45,000

April—$50,000

Step 2: Forecasting Sales

The heart of the cash budget is the sales forecast. It is the central factor in creating an accurate picture of the firm's cash position because sales ultimately are transformed into cash receipts and cash disbursements. For most businesses, sales constitute the major source of the cash flowing into the business. Similarly, sales of merchandise require that cash be used to replenish inventory. As a result, the cash budget is only as accurate as the sales forecast from which it is derived.

For an established business, a sales forecast is based on past sales, but owners must be careful not to be excessively optimistic in projecting sales. Economic swings, increased competition, fluctuations in demand, normal seasonal variations, and other factors can drastically affect sales patterns and, therefore, a company's cash flow. Most businesses, from retailers and hotels to accounting firms and builders, have sales patterns that are "lumpy" and not evenly distributed throughout the year. For instance, 40 percent of all toy sales take place in the last six weeks of the year, and companies that make fruitcakes typically generate 50 percent to 90 percent of their sales during the holiday season, making proper cash management an essential activity.[10] Several quantitative techniques, which are beyond the scope of this text (linear regression, multiple regression, time series analysis, exponential smoothing), are available to

	Oct.	Nov.	Dec.	Jan.	Feb.	Mar.	Apr.
Cash Receipts:							
Sales	$300,000	$350,000	$400,000	$120,000	$160,000	$160,000	$250,000
Credit Sales	225,000	262,500	300,000	90,000	120,000	120,000	187,500
Collections:							
60%—1st month after sale				$180,000	$54,000	$72,000	$72,000
30%—2nd month after sale				78,750	90,000	27,000	36,000
5%—3rd month after sale				11,250	13,125	15,000	4,500
Cash Sales				30,000	40,000	40,000	62,500
Interest				0	200	0	0
Total Cash Receipts				$300,000	$197,325	$154,000	$175,000
Cash Disbursements:							
Purchases				$112,000	$112,000	$175,000	$133,000
Rent				2,000	2,000	2,000	2,000
Utilities				850	850	850	850
Interest				0	0	7,500	0
Tax Prepayment				0	0	50,000	0
Capital Addition				0	130,000	0	0
Miscellaneous				70	70	70	70
Wages/Salaries				30,000	40,000	45,000	50,000
Total Cash Disbursements				$144,920	$284,920	$280,420	$185,920
End-of-Month Balance:							
Cash (beginning of month)				$12,000	$167,080	$79,485	$10,000
+ Cash Receipts				300,000	197,325	154,000	175,000
− Cash Disbursements				144,920	284,920	280,420	185,920
Cash (end of month)				167,080	79,485	(46,935)	(920)
Borrowing/Repayment				0	0	56,935	10,920
Cash (end of month [after borrowing])				$167,080	$ 79,485	$ 10,000	$ 10,000

(continues)

owners of existing businesses with an established sales pattern for forecasting sales. These methods enable the small business owner to extrapolate past and present sales trends to arrive at a fairly accurate sales forecast.

The task of forecasting sales for the new firm is more difficult but not impossible. For example, the new owner might conduct research on similar firms and their sales patterns in the first year of operation to come up with a forecast. The local Chamber of Commerce and trade associations in the various industries also collect such information. Publications such as *Robert Morris Associates' Annual Statement Studies*, which profiles financial statements for companies of all sizes in hundreds of industries, are also a useful tool. Market research is another source of information that may be used to estimate annual sales for the fledgling firm. Other potential sources that may help predict sales include census reports, newspapers, radio and television customer profiles, polls and surveys, and local government statistics. Talking with owners of similar businesses (outside the local trading area, of course) can provide entrepreneurs with realistic estimates of start-up sales. Table 9.4 provides an example of how one entrepreneur used such marketing information to derive a sales forecast for his first year of operation.

No matter what techniques entrepreneurs employ, they must recognize that even the best sales estimates will be wrong. Many financial analysts suggest that the owner create *three*

TABLE 9.3   Cash Budget for Small Department Store *(continued)*

Cash Budget—Most Likely Sales Forecast							
	Oct.	Nov.	Dec.	Jan.	Feb.	Mar.	Apr.
Cash Receipts:							
Sales	$300,000	$350,000	$400,000	$150,000	$200,000	$200,000	$300,000
Credit Sales	225,000	262,500	300,000	112,000	150,000	150,000	225,000
Collections:							
60%—1st month after sale				$180,000	$67,500	$90,000	$90,000
30%—2nd month after sale				78,750	90,000	33,750	45,000
5%—3rd month after sale				11,250	13,125	15,000	5,625
Cash Sales				37,500	50,000	50,000	75,000
Interest				0	200	0	0
Total Cash Receipts				$307,500	$220,825	$188,750	$215,625
Cash Disbursements:							
Purchases				$140,000	$140,000	$210,000	$175,000
Rent				2,000	2,000	2,000	2,000
Utilities				850	850	850	850
Interest				0	0	7,500	0
Tax Prepayment				0	0	50,000	0
Capital Addition				0	130,000	0	0
Miscellaneous				70	70	70	70
Wages/Salaries				30,000	40,000	45,000	50,000
Total Cash Disbursements				$172,920	$312,920	$315,420	$227,920
End-of-Month Balance:							
Cash (beginning of month)				$12,000	$146,580	$54,485	$10,000
+ Cash Receipts				307,500	220,825	188,750	215,625
− Cash Disbursements				172,920	312,920	315,420	227,920
Cash (end of month)				146,580	54,485	(72,185)	(2,295)
Borrowing/Repayment				0	0	82,185	12,295
Cash (end of month [after borrowing])				$146,580	$ 54,485	$ 10,000	$ 10,000

estimates—an optimistic, a pessimistic, and a most likely sales estimate—and then make a separate cash budget for each forecast (a very simple task with a computer spreadsheet). This dynamic forecast enables the owner to determine the range within which his sales will likely be as the year progresses.

Step 3: Forecasting Cash Receipts

As noted earlier, sales constitute the primary source of cash receipts. When a firm sells goods and services on credit, the cash budget must account for the delay between the sale and the actual collection of the proceeds. Remember: You cannot spend cash you haven't collected yet! For instance, an appliance store might not collect the cash from a refrigerator sold in February until April or May, and the cash budget must reflect this delay. To project accurately the firm's cash receipts, the owner must analyze the accounts receivable to determine the collection pattern. For example, past records may indicate that 20 percent of sales are for cash, 50 percent are paid in the month following the sale, 20 percent are paid two months after the sale, 5 percent

	Oct.	Nov.	Dec.	Jan.	Feb.	Mar.	Apr.
Cash Receipts:							
Sales	$300,000	$350,000	$400,000	$175,000	$250,000	$250,000	$340,000
Credit Sales	225,000	262,500	300,000	131,250	187,500	187,500	255,000
Collections:							
60%—1st month after sale				$180,000	$78,750	$112,500	$112,500
30%—2nd month after sale				78,750	90,000	39,375	56,250
5%—3rd month after sale				11,250	13,125	15,000	6,563
Cash Sales				43,750	62,500	62,500	85,000
Interest				0	200	0	0
Total Cash Receipts				$313,750	$244,575	$229,375	$260,313
Cash Disbursements:							
Purchases				$175,000	$175,000	$238,000	$217,000
Rent				2,000	2,000	2,000	2,000
Utilities				850	850	850	850
Interest				0	0	7,500	0
Tax Prepayment				0	0	50,000	0
Capital Addition				0	130,000	0	0
Miscellaneous				70	70	70	70
Wages/Salaries				30,000	40,000	45,000	50,000
Total Cash Disbursements				$207,920	$347,920	$343,420	$269,920
End-of-Month Balance:							
Cash [beginning of month]				$ 12,000	$117,830	$ 14,485	$ 10,000
+ Cash Receipts				313,750	244,575	229,375	296,125
– Cash Disbursements				207,920	317,920	343,120	269,920
Cash (end of month)				117,830	14,485	(99,560)	36,205
Borrowing/Repayment				0	0	109,560	0
Cash (end of month [after borrowing])				$117,830	$ 14,485	$ 10,000	$ 36,205

after three months, and 5 percent are never collected. In addition to cash and credit sales, the small business may receive cash in a number of forms—interest income, rental income, dividends, and others.

Collecting accounts receivable promptly poses problems for many small companies; in fact, difficulty in collecting accounts receivable is the primary cause of cash flow problems cited by small business owners (see Figure 9.3).[11] Figure 9.4 demonstrates how vital it is to act promptly once an account becomes past due. Notice how the probability of collecting an outstanding account diminishes the longer the account is delinquent. Table 9.5 illustrates the high cost of failing to collect accounts receivable on time.

Step 4: Forecasting Cash Disbursements

Most owners of established businesses have a clear picture of the firm's pattern of cash disbursements. In fact, many cash payments, such as rent, loan repayments, and interest, are fixed amounts due on specified dates. The key factor in forecasting disbursements for a cash budget

TABLE 9.4

Forecasting Sales for a Business
Start-Up

Robert Adler wants to open a repair shop for imported cars. The trade association for automotive garages estimates that the owner of an imported car spends an average of $485 per year on repairs and maintenance. The typical garage attracts its clientele from a trading zone (the area from which a business draws its customers) with a 20-mile radius. Census reports show that the families within a 20-mile radius of Robert's proposed location own 84,000 cars, of which 24 percent are imports. Based on a local consultant's market research, Robert believes he can capture 9.9 percent of the market this year. Robert's estimate of his company's first year's sales are as follows:

Number of cars in trading zone	84,000	autos
× Percent of imports	× 24	%
= Number of imported cars in trading zone	20,160	imports
Number of imports in trading zone	20,160	imports
× Average expenditure on repairs and maintenance	× $485	
= Total import repair sales potential	$9,777,600	
Total import repair sales potential	$9,777,600	
× Estimated share of the market	× 9.9	%
= Sales estimate	$967,982	

Now Robert Adler can convert this annual sales estimate of $967,982 into monthly sales estimates for use in his company's cash budget.

is to record them in *the month in which they will be paid, not when the obligation is incurred*. Of course, the number of cash disbursements varies with each particular business, but the following disbursement categories are standard: purchase of inventory or raw materials; wages and salaries; rent, taxes, loans and interest; selling expenses; fixed asset purchases; overhead expenses; and miscellaneous expenses.

Usually, an owner's tendency is to underestimate cash disbursements, which can result in a cash crisis. To prevent this, wise entrepreneurs cushion their cash disbursement accounts, assuming they will be higher than expected. This is particularly important for

FIGURE 9.3

Collecting Delinquent Accounts

Source: Commercial Collection Agency
Section of the Commercial Law League
of America.

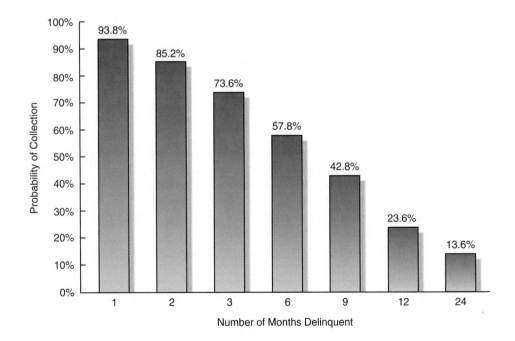

ing the potential customer's credit references. The savings from lower bad debt expenses can more than offset the cost of using a credit reporting service such as TRW or Dun & Bradstreet. The National Association of Credit Management (www.nacm.org) is another important source of credit information because it collects information on many small businesses that other reporting services ignore. The cost to check a potential customer's credit at reporting services such as these ranges from $15 to $85, a small price to pay when considering selling thousands of dollars' worth of goods or services to a new customer. The Internet has made the job of credit checking much easier. Sites such as Dun & Bradstreet (www.dnb.com), Experian (www.experian.com), Equifax (www.equifax.com), Veritas Credit Corporation (www.veritas-usa.com), and KnowX (www.knowx.com) help entrepreneurs gather credit information on potential customers. Unfortunately, few small businesses take the time to conduct a credit check; in one study, just one-third of the businesses protected themselves by checking potential customers' credit.[21]

The next step involves establishing a firm written credit policy and letting every customer know in advance the company's credit terms. Industry practices often dictate credit terms (30 days is common), but a business does not have to abide by industry standards. A credit agreement must state clearly all the terms the business will enforce if the account goes bad—including interest, late charges, attorney's fees, and others. Failure to specify these terms in the contract means they *cannot* be added later after problems arise. When will you invoice? How soon is payment due: immediately, 30 days, 60 days? Will you add a late charge? If so, how much? The credit policies should be as tight as possible and within federal and state credit laws. According to the American Collectors Association, if a business is writing off more than 5 percent of sales as bad debts, the owner should tighten its credit and collection policy.[22]

The third step in an effective credit policy is to send invoices promptly because customers rarely pay *before* they receive their bills. The cornerstone of collecting accounts receivable on time is making sure you invoice your customers or send them their periodic billing statements promptly. "The sooner you mail your invoice, the sooner the check will be in the mail," says one entrepreneur. "In the manufacturing environment, get the invoice en route to the customer as soon as the shipment goes out the door," he advises. "Likewise, service industries with billable hours should keep track of hours daily or weekly and bill as often as the contract or agreement with the client permits."[23] Some businesses use **cycle billing**, in which a company bills a portion of its credit customers each day of the month to smooth out uneven cash receipts.

Small business owners can take several steps to encourage prompt payment of invoices:

- Ensure that all invoices are clear, accurate, and timely.
- State clearly a description of the goods or services purchased and an account number.
- Make sure that the prices and the language on invoices agree with the price quotations on purchase orders or contracts.
- Highlight the balance due and the terms of sale (e.g., "net 30") on all invoices. A study by Xerox Corporation found that highlighting with color the balance due section of invoices increased the speed of collection by 30 percent.[24]
- Include a telephone number and a contact person in your organization in case the customer has a question or a dispute.

When an account becomes overdue, a small business owner must take *immediate* action. The longer an account is past due, the lower is the probability of collecting it. As soon as an account becomes overdue, many business owners send a "second notice" letter requesting immediate payment. If that fails to produce results, the next step is a telephone call. When contacting a delinquent customer by phone, the goal is to get a commitment to pay the full amount of the bill by a specific date (*not* "soon" or "next week"). Following up with an e-mail to the customer summarizing the telephone commitment also helps. If the customer still refuses to pay the bill, collection experts recommend the following:

- Sending a letter from the company's attorney.
- Turning the account over to a collection attorney.
- As a last resort, hiring a collection agency. (The Commercial Law League of America (www.clla.org) can provide a list of reputable agencies.)

cycle billing—*a method in which a company bills a portion of its credit customers each day of the month in order to smooth out uneven cash receipts.*

Although collection agencies and attorneys will take 25 to 50 percent of any accounts they collect, they are often worth the price. According to the American Collectors Association, only 5 percent of accounts more than 90 days delinquent will be paid voluntarily. When dealing with delinquent customers, business owners must be sure to abide by the provisions of the federal Fair Debt Collection Practices Act, which prohibits any kind of harassment when collecting debts (e.g., telephoning repeatedly, issuing threats of violence, telling third parties about the debt, or using abusive language). The primary rule when collecting past-due accounts is "*Never lose your cool.*" Establishing a friendly but firm attitude that treats customers with respect is more likely to produce payment than hostile threats.

Table 9.6 outlines 10 collection blunders small business owners typically make and how to avoid them.

OTHER TECHNIQUES FOR ACCELERATING ACCOUNTS RECEIVABLE. Small business owners can rely on a variety of other techniques to speed cash inflow from accounts receivable:

- Speed up orders by having customers e-mail or fax them to you.
- Send invoices when goods are shipped—not a day or a week later; consider faxing or e-mailing invoices to reduce "in transit" time to a minimum. Most small business accounting software has features that allow users to e-mail the invoices they generate.
- Indicate in conspicuous print the invoice due date and any late payment penalties. (Check with an attorney to be sure all finance charges comply with state laws.)
- Restrict a customer's credit until past-due bills are paid.
- Deposit customer checks and credit card receipts *daily*.
- Identify the top 20 percent of your customers (by sales volume), create a separate file system for them, and monitor them closely. Twenty percent of the typical company's customers generate 80 percent of all accounts receivable.

TABLE 9.6

10 Collection Blunders and How to Avoid Them

Sources: Adapted from "Tips for Collecting Cash," *FSB*, May 2002, p. 72; Janine Latus Musick, "Collecting Payments Due," *Nation's Business*, January 1999, pp. 44–46; Bob Weinstein, "Collect Calls," *Entrepreneur*, August 1995, pp. 66–69; Elaine Pofeldt, "Collect Calls," *Success*, March 1998, pp. 22–24.

Business owners often make mistakes when trying to collect the money their customers owe. Checking potential credit customers' credit records and creating a thorough sales contract that spells out exactly what happens if the account becomes past due can help minimize collection problems. Sooner or later, however, even the best system will encounter late payers. What happens then? Business owners should avoid these collection blunders.

Blunder 1: Delaying collection phone calls. Many entrepreneurs waste valuable time and resources sending four or five "past-due" letters to delinquent customers, usually with limited effectiveness.

Instead: Once a bill becomes past due, call the customer within a week to verify that he received the bill and that it is accurate. Ask for payment.

Blunder 2: Failing to ask for payment in clear terms. To avoid angering a customer, some entrepreneurs ask meekly, "Do you think you could take care of this bill soon?"

Instead: Firmly, but professionally, ask for payment of the full amount by a specific date.

Blunder 3: Sounding desperate. Some entrepreneurs show weakness by saying that they must have payment or they "can't meet payroll" or "can't pay bills." That gives the customer more leverage to negotiate additional discounts or time.

Instead: Ask for payment simply because the invoice is past due—without any other explanation. Don't apologize for your request; it's *your* money.

Blunder 4: Talking tough. Getting nasty with delinquent customers does not make them pay any faster and may be a violation of the Fair Debt Collections Practices Act.

Instead: Remain polite and professional when dealing with past-due customers, even if you think they don't deserve it. *Never* lose your temper. Don't ruin your reputation by being rude.

Blunder 5: Trying to find out the customer's problem. Some entrepreneurs think it is necessary to find out why a delinquent customer has not paid a bill.

Instead: Don't waste time playing private investigator. Focus on the "business at hand," collecting your money.

Blunder 6: Asking customers how much they can pay. When customers claim that they cannot pay the bill in full, inexperienced entrepreneurs ask, "Well, how much can you pay?" They don't realize that they have just turned control of the situation over to the delinquent customer.

Instead: Take charge of negotiations from the outset. Let the customer know that you expect full payment. If you cannot get full payment immediately, suggest a new deadline. Only as a last resort should you offer an extended payment plan.

Blunder 7: Continuing to talk after you get a promise to pay. Some entrepreneurs "blow the deal" by not knowing when to stop talking. They keep interrogating a customer after they have a promise to pay.

Instead: Wrap up the conversation as soon as you have a commitment. Summarize the agreement, thank the customer, and end the conversation on a positive note.

Blunder 8: Calling without being prepared. Some entrepreneurs call customers without knowing exactly which invoices are past due and what amounts are involved. The effort is usually fruitless.

Instead: Have all account details in front of you when you call and be specific in your requests.

Blunder 9: Trusting your memory. Some entrepreneurs think they can remember previous collection calls, conversations, and agreements.

Instead: Keep accurate records of all calls and conversations. Take notes about each customer contact and resulting agreements.

Blunder 10: Letting your computer control your collection efforts. Inexperienced entrepreneurs tend to think that their computers can manage debt collection for them.

Instead: Recognize that a computer is a valuable tool in collecting accounts but that you are in control. "Past-due" notices from a computer may collect some accounts, but your efforts will produce more results. Getting to know the people who handle the invoices at your customers' businesses can be a major advantage when collecting accounts.

- Ask customers to pay at least a portion of the purchase price up front. To preserve her company's cash flow, Jane Conner, owner of the Whitefish Gymnastics Club, requires her customers to pay for their 10-week exercise classes after the first session.[25]

- Watch for signs that a customer may be about to declare bankruptcy. If that happens, creditors typically collect only a small fraction, if any, of the debt owed.

■ Consider using a bank's lockbox collection service (located near customers) to reduce mail time on collections. In a **lockbox** arrangement, customers send payments to a post office box the company's bank maintains. Several times each day, the bank collects payments and deposits them immediately in the company's account. The procedure sharply reduces processing and clearing times, especially if the lockboxes are located close to the firm's biggest customers' business addresses. The system can be expensive to operate and is most economical for companies with a high volume of large checks.

■ Track the results of the company's collection efforts. Managers and key employees should receive a weekly report on the status of the company's outstanding accounts receivable.

A Company Example

*Although project managers at **Ransom Environmental**, an environmental consulting company in Newburyport, Massachusetts, viewed collecting accounts receivable as a necessary evil, CEO Steve Ransom decided his company had to make collections a priority to improve cash flow. Ransom began distributing a receivables status report at the company's weekly operations meetings. Given to every manager, the report features a receivables-aging chart showing whose customers were behind on their payments and by how many days. Ransom Environmental quickly began to see an improvement in its collection patterns and in its cash flow. The company's average collection period has fallen from 75 days to 60 days, and faster collections have boosted cash flow, enabling Ransom to save between $1,000 and $2,000 a month in interest on its line of credit.*[26]

Another strategy small companies can use to protect the cash they have tied up in receivables is coupling a security agreement with a financing statement. This strategy falls under Article 9 of the Uniform Commercial Code (UCC), which governs a wide variety of business transactions, from the sale of goods to security interests. A **security agreement** is a contract in which a business selling an asset on credit gets a security interest in that asset (the collateral), protecting its legal rights in case the buyer fails to pay. To get the protection it seeks in the security agreement, the seller must file a financing statement, the UCC-1 form, with the proper state or county office (a process the UCC calls "perfection"). The UCC-1 form gives notice to other creditors and to the general public that the seller holds a secured interest in the collateral named in the security agreement. The UCC-1 form must include the name, address, and signature of the buyer; a description of the collateral; and the name and address of the seller.

Suppose that Lanford Mechanical sells a piece of manufacturing machinery to Abbott Chemical Company for $64,000, accepting $12,000 in cash and retaining the $52,000 balance on account, payable over 24 months. As part of the sales contract (which also is governed by the UCC, Article 2), Lanford gets Abbott to sign a security agreement, giving Lanford a security interest in the machine. If Lanford files the financing statement (UCC-1 form) with the secretary of state for a small fee, it has perfected its security interest in the machine. If Abbott fails to pay the account balance in full, Lanford can repossess the machine and sell it to satisfy the remaining balance. If Abbott were to declare bankruptcy, Lanford is not guaranteed payment, but its filing puts its claim to the machinery ahead of those of unsecured creditors. Lanford's degree of safety on this large credit sale is much higher with a security agreement and a properly filed financing statement.

Accounts Payable

The second element of the "big three" of cash management is accounts payable. The timing of payables is just as crucial to proper cash management as the timing of receivables, but the objective is exactly the opposite. Entrepreneurs should strive to stretch out payables as long as possible *without damaging their companies' credit rating*. Otherwise, suppliers may begin demanding prepayment or C.O.D. terms, which severely impairs a company's cash flow, or they simply stop doing business with it. When one computer manufacturer ran into cash flow problems, it deferred payments to its suppliers for as long as 100 days (compared to an industry average of about 40 days). Because of the company's slow payments, many suppliers simply stopped selling to the computer maker.[27] One cash management consultant says, "Some companies pay too early and wind up forgoing the interest they could have earned on their cash.

Others pay too late and either wind up with late penalties or being forced to buy on a C.O.D. basis, which really kills them."[28] It is perfectly acceptable for small business owners to regulate payments to their companies' advantage. Efficient cash managers set up a payment calendar each month that allows them to pay their bills on time and to take advantage of cash discounts for early payment.

*Nancy Dunis, CEO of **Dunis & Associates**, a Portland, Oregon, marketing firm, recognizes the importance of controlling accounts payable. "Our payables must be functioning just right to keep our cash flow running smoothly," says Dunis. She has set up a simple five-point accounts payable system:*[29]

1. ***Set scheduling goals.*** *Dunis strives to pay her company's bills 45 days after receiving them and to collect all her receivables within 30 days. Even though "it doesn't always work that way," her goal is to make the most of her cash flow.*

2. ***Keep paperwork organized.*** *Dunis dates every invoice she receives and carefully files it according to her payment plan. "This helps us remember when to cut the check," she says, and "it helps us stagger our payments, over days or weeks"—significantly improving the company's cash flow.*

3. ***Prioritize.*** *Dunis cannot stretch out all of her company's creditors for 45 days; some demand payment sooner. Those suppliers are at the top of the accounts payable list.*

4. ***Be consistent.*** *"Companies want consistent customers," says Dunis. "With a few exceptions," she explains, "most businesses will be happy to accept 45-day payments, so long as they know you'll always pay your full obligation at that point."*

5. ***Look for warning signs.*** *Dunis sees her accounts payable as an early warning system for cash flow problems. "The first indication I get that cash flow is in trouble is when I see I'm getting low on cash and could have trouble paying my bills according to my staggered filing system," she says. Other signs that a business is heading for cash flow problems include difficulty making principal and interest payments on loans and incurring penalties for late payment of routine bills.*

Business owners should verify all invoices before paying them. Some unscrupulous vendors will send out invoices for goods they never shipped or services they never rendered, knowing that many business owners will simply pay the bill without checking its authenticity. A common invoice scam aimed at small business owners involves bogus operators sending bills for ads in nonexistent printed or online "yellow pages" directories. In some cases, the directories actually do exist, but their distribution is so limited that ads in them are useless. A survey by the real Yellow Pages Publishers Association found that one-third of businesses had received bogus bills for Yellow Pages advertising.[30] To avoid falling victim to such scams, someone in the company—for instance, the accounts payable clerk—should have the responsibility of verifying *every* invoice received.

Generally, it is a good idea for owners to take advantage of cash discounts vendors offer. A cash discount (e.g., "2/10, net 30"—take a 2 percent discount if you pay the invoice within 10 days; otherwise, total payment is due in 30 days) offers a price reduction if the owner pays an invoice early. Failing to take advantage of this particular cash discount is the equivalent of borrowing at an interest rate of 36.7 percent! A clever cash manager also will negotiate the best possible credit terms with his suppliers. Almost all vendors grant their customers trade credit, and small business owners should take advantage of it. However, because trade credit is so easy to get, entrepreneurs must be careful not to overuse and abuse it, putting their businesses in a precarious financial position.

Favorable credit terms can make a tremendous difference in a company's cash flow. Table 9.7 shows the same most likely cash budget from Table 9.2 with one exception: Instead of purchasing on C.O.D. terms (Table 9.2), the owner has negotiated net 30 payment terms (Table 9.7). Notice the drastic improvement in the company's cash flow resulting from improved credit terms.

If owners do find themselves financially strapped when payment to a vendor is due, they should avoid making empty promises that "the check is in the mail" or sending unsigned checks. Instead, they should openly discuss the situation with the vendor. Most vendors will

TABLE 9.7

Cash Budget,[a] Most Likely Sales Forecast

	Jan.	Feb.	Mar.	Apr.
Cash Receipts:				
Sales	$150,000	$200,000	$200,000	$300,000
Credit Sales	112,500	150,000	150,000	225,000
Collections:				
60%—1st month after sale	$180,000	$67,500	$90,000	$90,000
30%—2nd month after sale	78,750	90,000	33,750	45,000
5%—3rd month after sale	11,250	13,125	15,000	5,625
Cash Sales	37,500	50,000	50,000	75,000
Interest	0	200	0	9
Total Cash Receipts	$307,500	$220,825	$188,750	$215,625
Cash Disbursements:				
Purchases[a]	$105,000	$140,000	$140,000	$210,000
Rent	2,000	2,000	2,000	2,000
Utilities	850	850	850	850
Interest	0	0	7,500	0
Tax Prepayment	0	0	50,000	0
Capital Addition	0	130,000	3	0
Miscellaneous	70	70	70	70
Wage/Salaries	30,000	40,000	45,000	50,000
Total Cash Disbursements[a]	$137,920	$312,920	$245,420	$262,920
End-of-Month Balance:				
Cash (beginning of month)[a]	$12,000	$181,580	$89,485	$32,815
+ Cash Receipts	307,500	220,825	188,750	215,625
− Cash Disbursements[a]	137,920	312,920	245,420	262,920
Cash (end of month)[a]	181,580	89,485	32,815	(14,480)
Borrowing	0	0	0	24,480
Cash (end of month [after borrowing])[a]	$181,580	$89,485	$32,815	$10,000

[a] After negotiating "net 30" trade credit terms.

work out payment terms for extended credit. One small business owner who was experiencing a cash crisis claims:

> One day things got so bad I just called up a supplier and said, "I need your stuff, but I'm going through a tough period and simply can't pay you right now." They said they wanted to keep me as a customer, and they asked if it was okay to bill me in three months. I was dumbfounded: *They didn't even charge me interest.*[31]

Small business owners also can improve their firms' cash flow by scheduling controllable cash disbursements so that they do not come due at the same time. For example, paying employees every two weeks (or every month) rather than every week reduces administrative costs and gives the business more time to use its cash. Owners of fledgling businesses may be able to conserve cash by hiring part-time employees or by using freelance workers rather than full-time, permanent workers. Scheduling insurance premiums monthly or quarterly rather than annually also improves cash flows.

Wise use of business credit cards is another way to stretch the firm's cash balance. However, entrepreneurs should avoid cards that charge transaction fees. Credit cards differ in their interest-charging policies; many begin charging interest from the date of purchase, but some charge interest only from the invoice date.

Inventory

Inventory is a significant investment for many small businesses and can create a severe strain on cash flow. The typical grocery store now stocks more than 49,000 items, three times as many as it did 20 years ago, and many other types of businesses are following this pattern.[32] Offering customers a wider variety of products is one way a business can outshine its competitors, but product proliferation increases the need for tight inventory control to avoid a cash crisis. Although inventory represents the largest capital investment for most businesses, few owners use any formal methods for managing it. As a result, the typical small business not only has too much inventory but also too much of the *wrong* kind of inventory! Because inventory is illiquid, it can quickly siphon off a company's pool of available cash. "Small companies need cash to grow," says one consultant. "They've got to be able to turn [cash] over quickly. That's difficult to do if a lot of money is tied up in excess inventory."[33]

Surplus inventory yields a zero rate of return and unnecessarily ties up the firm's cash. "The cost of carrying inventory is expensive," says one small business consultant. "A typical manufacturing company pays 25 percent to 30 percent of the value of the inventory for the cost of borrowed money, warehouse space, materials handling, staff, lift-truck expenses, and fixed costs. This shocks a lot of people. Once they realize it, they look at inventory differently."[34] Marking down items that don't sell will keep inventory lean and allow it to turn over frequently. Even though volume discounts lower inventory costs, large purchases may tie up the company's valuable cash. Wise business owners avoid overbuying inventory, recognizing that excess inventory ties up valuable cash unproductively. In fact, only 20 percent of a typical business's inventory turns over quickly, so owners must watch constantly for stale items. If a small business must pay suppliers within 30 days of receiving an inventory shipment and then the merchandise sits on the shelf for another 30 to 60 days, the pressure on its cash flow intensifies.

Carrying too little inventory is not desirable because companies with excessive "stockouts" lose sales (and eventually customers if the problem persists). However, carrying too much inventory usually results in slow-moving inventory and a low inventory turnover ratio. Experienced business owners understand the importance of shedding slow-moving inventory, even if the price they get is below their normal markup.

A Company Example

Recognizing the high cost of holding inventory, Cindy Revenaugh, vice president of sales at **Channeled Resources***, a company that sells recycled paper products, gives her sales force the power to sell slow-moving items at any price that is not below the company's cost. "We just want to move the stuff and get cash for it," says Revenaugh. "Even if they sell it at cost, it's better than letting it sit here."[35]*

Carrying too much inventory increases the chances that a business will run out of cash. "The cash that pays for goods is channeled into inventory," says one business writer, "where its flow is dead-ended until the inventory is sold and the cash is set free again. The cash flow trick is to commit just enough cash to inventory to meet demand."[36] Scheduling inventory deliveries at the latest possible date will prevent premature payment of invoices. Finally, given goods of comparable quality and price, an entrepreneur should purchase goods from the fastest supplier to keep inventory levels low.

Monitoring the "big three" of cash management can help every business owner avoid a cash crisis while making the best use of available cash. According to one expert, maximizing cash flow involves "getting money from customers sooner; paying bills at the last moment possible; consolidating money in a single bank account; managing accounts payable, accounts receivable, and inventory more effectively; and squeezing every penny out of your daily business."[37]

AVOIDING THE CASH CRUNCH

Learning Objective

5. Explain the techniques for avoiding a cash crunch in a small company.

Nearly every small business has the potential to improve its cash position with little or no investment. The key is to make an objective evaluation of the company's financial policies, searching for inefficiency in its cash flow. Young firms cannot afford to waste resources, especially one as vital as cash. By utilizing the following techniques, entrepreneurs can get maximum benefit from their companies' pool of available cash.

Barter

Bartering, the exchange of goods and services for other goods and services rather than for cash, is an effective way to conserve cash. An ancient concept, bartering regained popularity during recent recessions. Over the last decade, more than 700 barter exchanges have cropped up, catering primarily to small- and medium-sized businesses looking to conserve cash. More than 500,000 companies—most of them small—engage in more than $16.1 billion worth of barter each year.[38] Every day, entrepreneurs across the nation use bartering to buy much needed materials, services, equipment, and supplies—*without* using cash.

A Company Example

When Jerry Trombo relocated his printing business, **Litho Graphics***, he traded printing services for moving services, painting, carpeting, furnishings, a computer, and a newly paved driveway. For the year, Litho Graphics conducted more than $50,000 worth of bartering, an amount representing 8 percent of the company's sales—and involving no cash! "I don't buy anything unless I pick up the barter catalogue," says Trombo, who has been bartering through an exchange for more than 11 years. "I'll do anything to avoid spending cash."* [39]

In addition to conserving cash, companies that use barter also have the opportunity to transform slow-moving inventory into much-needed products and services. Barter companies pay, on average, trade credits equal to three times the amount inventory liquidators would pay for the same merchandise.[40] Buying goods and services with barter also offers the benefit of a built-in discount. Although a company gets credit for the retail value of the goods or services it offers, the real cost to the company is less and depends on its gross profit margin. For instance, the owner of an Italian restaurant bartered $1,000 worth of meals for some new furniture, but his actual cost of the meals was only $680, given his gross profit margin of 32 percent. Business owners who barter also say that joining a barter exchange brings in customers who normally would not buy from them.

In a typical barter exchange, businesses accumulate trade credits when they offer goods or services through the exchange. Then they can use their trade credits to purchase other goods and services from other members of the exchange. The typical exchange charges a $500 membership fee and a 10 percent transaction fee (5 percent from the buyer and 5 percent from the seller) on every deal. The exchange tracks the balance in each member's account and typically sends a monthly statement summarizing account activity.

Online barter exchanges such as Intagio.com, International Trade Exchange, and Ubarter.com have become extremely popular because of their convenience and the wide variety of items they list on their exchanges. A business owner can barter for advertising time and space, hotel stays, catering services, car rentals, airline tickets, office supplies, printing services, photography, carpet, cell phones, and many other products and services. Online barter exchanges usually charge lower membership and transaction fees than their off-line counterparts. Before joining a barter exchange, business owners should investigate the fee structure, the selection and the prices of its goods and services, and its geographical coverage.

Trim Overhead Costs

High overhead expenses can strain a small firm's cash supply to the breaking point; simple cost-cutting measures can save big money. Frugal small business owners can trim their overhead in a number of ways.

PERIODICALLY EVALUATE EXPENSES.   Business owners not only should attempt to keep their operating costs low, but they also should evaluate them periodically to make sure they have not gotten out of line. Comparing current expenses with past levels is helpful and so is comparing a company's expenses against industry standards. Useful resources for determining typical expenses in an industry include *Robert Morris Associates' Annual Statement Studies, Dun & Bradstreet's Industry Norms and Key Business Ratios*, and *Prentice Hall's Almanac of Business and Industrial Financial Ratios*. We will describe these resources in more detail in the next chapter.

Linda Nespole, a manager at **Hi-Shear Technology***, an aerospace subcontractor, used this technique to cut thousands of dollars from her company's operating expenses each year. When Hi-Shear's cash flow was squeezed recently, Nespole began tracking some of the company's largest operating expenses, mostly utility bills, and discovered some unusually large increases. Basic repairs, preventive maintenance, and more efficient fixtures cut costs and generated enough savings to pay for themselves within just a few months. Nespole expanded her list and began charting company expenses and acting on trends she saw. The result was major cost savings in everything from telephone charges to retirement plan costs. Tracking and controlling expenses has become a priority for Hi-Shear's 125 employees, and the company's cash flow has never been better![41]*

A Company Example

WHEN PRACTICAL, LEASE INSTEAD OF BUY.   By leasing automobiles, computers, office equipment, machinery, and other assets rather than buying them, an entrepreneur can conserve valuable cash. The value of such assets is not in *owning* them but in *using* them. Businesses can lease practically any kind of equipment—from office furniture and computers to construction equipment and manufacturing machinery. According to a recent survey, 73 percent of small companies use leasing as a cash management strategy.[42] "These companies are long on ideas, short on capital, and in need of flexibility as they grow and change," says Suzanne Jackson of the Equipment Leasing Association of America. "They lease for efficiency and convenience."[43]

Although total lease payments typically are greater than those for a conventional loan, most leases offer 100 percent financing, which means the owner avoids the large capital outlays required as down payments on most loans. Also, leasing is an "off-the-balance-sheet" method of financing and requires no collateral. A lease is considered an operating expense on the income statement, not a liability on the balance sheet. Thus, leasing conserves a company's borrowing capacity. Lease agreements also are flexible. Leasing companies typically offer a variety of terms and allow businesses to stretch payments over a longer time period than those of a conventional loan. "There are so many ways to tailor a lease agreement to a company's individual equipment and financial needs that you might call it a personalized rental agreement," says the owner of a small construction firm.[44]

Leasing also protects a business against obsolescence, especially when it comes to equipment such as computer hardware and software, whose technological life is limited to perhaps three years.

When Kai Adams, Brad Monarch, and Tim Haines opened the **Sebago Brewing Company***, a restaurant-pub in South Portland, Maine, they borrowed $175,000 through a Small Business Administration loan and invested an equal amount of their own money. Installing beer brewing equipment, outfitting the kitchen, and furnishing the dining room (plus holding some cash in reserve for working capital) took most of their start-up funds. Still, the partners knew that they needed one more crucial ingredient to make their restaurant a success: a sophisticated computer system that would track every aspect of its operation minute by minute and give them the control they needed. The only catch was the system cost $30,000 that they did not have! So Adams, Monarch, and Haines decided to lease the computer setup. "It took a lot of money to open this restaurant," says Adams, "and we really had to be selective about what we spent our capital on. Leasing the computer system freed up cash flow for our opening." Having since opened two more outlets, the entrepreneurs continue to lease everything from computers to dishwashers. The benefits include lower initial capital outlays, flexibility in updating equipment, and, in many cases, transferring the cost of maintenance to the lessor.[45]*

A Company Example

AVOID NONESSENTIAL OUTLAYS.   By forgoing costly ego indulgences like ostentatious office equipment, first-class travel, and flashy company cars, entrepreneurs can make the most efficient use of a company's cash. Before putting scarce cash into an asset, every business owner should put the decision to the acid test: "What will this purchase add to my company's ability to compete and to become more successful?" Making across-the-board spending cuts to conserve cash is dangerous, however, because the owner runs the risk of cutting expenditures that literally drive the business. One common mistake during business slowdowns is cutting marketing and advertising expenditures. Economic slowdowns present a prime opportunity for smart business owners to bring increased attention to their products and services and to gain market share if they hold the line on their marketing and advertising budgets as their competitors cut back. The secret to successful cost saving is cutting *nonessential* expenditures. "If the lifeblood of your company is marketing, cut it less," advises one advertising executive. "If it is customer service, that is the last thing you want to cut back on. Cut from areas that are not essential to business growth."[46]

NEGOTIATE FIXED LOAN PAYMENTS TO COINCIDE WITH YOUR COMPANY'S CASH FLOW CYCLE. Many banks allow businesses to structure loans so that they can skip specific payments when their cash flow ebbs to its lowest point. Negotiating such terms gives businesses the opportunity to customize their loan repayments to their cash flow cycles.

*For example, Ted Zoli, president of **Torrington Industries**, a construction-materials supplier and contracting business, consistently uses "skipped payment loans" in his highly seasonal business. "Every time we buy a piece of construction machinery," he says, "we set it up so that we're making payments for eight or nine months, and then skipping three or four months during the winter."* [47]

BUY USED OR RECONDITIONED EQUIPMENT, ESPECIALLY IF IT IS "BEHIND-THE-SCENES" MACHINERY. One restaurateur saved thousands of dollars in the start-up phase of his business by buying used equipment from a restaurant equipment broker.

HIRE PART-TIME EMPLOYEES AND FREELANCE SPECIALISTS WHENEVER POSSIBLE. Hiring part-time workers and freelancers rather than full-time employees saves on the cost of both salaries and benefits.

CONTROL EMPLOYEE ADVANCES AND LOANS. An entrepreneur should grant only those advances and loans that are necessary and should keep accurate records on payments and balances.

DEVELOP A SYSTEM TO BATTLE CHECK FRAUD. Consumers and businesses in the United States write more than 42 billion checks a year for retail payments, totaling some $39.5 trillion! Of those checks, about 251 million are returned because of insufficient funds, a closed account, or some other problem.[48] About 70 percent of all "bounced" checks occur because nine out of ten customers fail to keep their checkbooks balanced; the remaining 30 percent of bad checks are the result of fraud.[49] Simple techniques for minimizing losses from bad checks include requesting proper identification (preferably with a photograph) from customers, recording customers' telephone numbers, and training cashiers to watch for forged or counterfeit checks. Perhaps the most effective way to battle bad checks is to subscribe to an electronic check approval service. The service works at the cash register, and approval takes only a minute or less. The fee a small business pays to use the service depends on the volume of checks. For most small companies, charges amount to 1 to 2 percent of the cleared checks' value.

CHANGE YOUR SHIPPING TERMS. Changing the firm's shipping terms from "F.O.B (free on board) buyer," in which the *seller* pays the cost of freight, to "F.O.B seller," in which the *buyer* absorbs all shipping costs, can improve cash flow.

SWITCH TO ZERO-BASED BUDGETING. Zero-based budgeting (ZBB) primarily is a shift in the philosophy of budgeting. Rather than build the current year budget on *increases* from the previous year's budget, ZBB starts from a budget of zero and evaluates the necessity of every item. "Start with zero and review all expenses, asking yourself whether each one is necessary," says one business consultant.[50]

Be on the Lookout for Employee Theft

Companies lose billions of dollars each year to employee theft. Because they often rely on informal procedures for managing cash (or no procedures at all), small business owners are most likely to become victims of embezzlement and fraud by their employees. One source of the problem is the entrepreneur's attitude that "we're all family here; no one would steal from family." Although establishing a "police state" environment and trusting no one is not conducive to a positive work environment, putting in place adequate financial control systems is essential. Separating among at least two employees key cash management duties such as writing checks and handling bank statements and conducting regular financial audits can be effective deterrents to employee theft.

Keep Your Business Plan Current

Before approaching any potential lender or investor, a business owner must prepare a solid business plan. Smart owners keep their plans up-to-date in case an unexpected cash crisis forces them to seek emergency financing. Revising the plan annually also forces the owner to focus on managing the business more effectively.

YOU Be the Consultant . . .

The Trusted Employee

Lloyd and Jim Graff, co-owners of Graff-Pinkert, a company in Oak Forest, Illinois, that buys and sells machines that make metal components, ran the family-owned business the way their father, who founded the company, had: on trust and a handshake. After all, they were still doing business with many of the same companies their father had done business with over the years. The Graffs extended that same level of trust to their family of 18 employees. If an employee needed money for a deposit on a home or for a family medical emergency, the Graffs would extend a loan—interest free. Many employees and their families were friends outside of work and spent recreational time together.

That's why the Graffs were shocked and dismayed when they discovered that one of their workers, Patty Preston (not her real name), had been embezzling money from the business for more than four years. An 11-year employee and a mother of three children, Preston was a bookkeeper for Graff-Pinkert. Her illicit activities came to light while Preston was on vacation. Preston had neglected to deposit Jim Graff's last few payroll checks into his personal bank account. When he mentioned it in front of several workers, one of them grew concerned and revealed that she believed Preston had charged several Rugrats videotapes for her kids on the company's account at Home Depot. Another employee said that Preston also had purchased a storage shed for her home on a company account.

Jim immediately began to investigate the employees' allegations and discovered that they were true; Preston had been using company funds to purchase personal items. He contacted his brother, who was on vacation at the time. "I fired her for being a petty crook," Lloyd says. It didn't take long for the Graffs to discover that Preston's crime was anything but petty. To finance a gambling habit and a luxurious lifestyle, she had embezzled more than $200,000 from Graff-Pinkert, a huge amount for a company whose annual sales were between $8 and $10 million. "Jim and I walked around punch-drunk as the enormity of the crime mounted up," recalls Lloyd. "It was a real blow to our confidence. The people who worked with her were horrified, even angrier than Jim and me. This was a co-worker they trusted. They felt violated."

Preston's duties included, among other things, writing checks and reconciling the company bank statement. Her embezzlement scheme was simple. She would write a check to a legitimate vendor or supplier and have one of the Graffs sign it. Then she would go to her typewriter and, using correction tape, change the name on the check, making it payable to her own credit card company. Because she also handled the bank statement, she could cover her tracks, and no one else saw what she was doing. Because they were focused on managing the company's rapid growth and because they saw their employees as part of an extended family, the Graffs never noticed the crime that was taking place right before their eyes. The small accounting firm, the same one their father had hired decades before, somehow never caught the embezzlement in their annual audits.

Graff-Pinkert had no fidelity insurance protecting them against employee theft, and they wanted to recover at least some of the money Preston had stolen. Because Preston had mailed fraudulent checks across state lines, she had committed a federal crime. The Graffs contacted the FBI and filed a lawsuit against Preston in federal court. In a settlement, Preston relinquished to Graff-Pinkert $72,000 she had accumulated in her profit-sharing plan. Because she had blown most of the money gambling in nearby casinos, Preston had few assets from which to make restitution to the company. At her sentencing, Preston said nothing, not even uttering an apology to the Graffs or to the handful of employees who showed up. The judge sentenced her to 24 months in a federal penitentiary and ordered her to continue to pay restitution to the company upon her release. The Graffs receive checks for small amounts, sometimes just $25, irregularly from Preston, who now works as a hotel maid. Although they scrutinize their bank statements more carefully now, the Graffs' business philosophy hasn't changed. "We're more skeptical but not cynical," says Lloyd. "We still approach it as a family business. If we couldn't run it that way, I'd hang it up."

1. Identify some of the factors that led Graff-Pinkert to become a victim of embezzlement. What impact does this crime have on a company's cash flow?

2. What recommendations would you make to the Graffs about protecting their business from embezzlement in the future?

3. Working with several of your classmates, use the resources of the Web to develop a list of steps entrepreneurs should take to prevent their businesses from becoming victims of employee theft and embezzlement.

Source: Adapted from John Grossmann, "A Thief Within," *Inc.*, May 2003, pp. 42–44.

Invest Surplus Cash

Because of the uneven flow of receipts and disbursements, a company will often temporarily have more cash than it needs—for a week, month, quarter, or even longer. When this happens, most small business owners simply ignore the surplus because they are not sure how soon they will need it. They believe that relatively small amounts of cash sitting around for just a few days or weeks are not worth investing. However, this is not the case. Small business owners who put surplus cash to work *immediately* rather than allowing it to sit idle soon discover that the yield adds up to a significant amount over time. This money can help ease the daily cash crunch during business troughs. "Your

Check fraud costs businesses billions of dollars a year.

Courtesy of Corbis/Stock Market, © Chuck Savage/Corbis.

money market account— *an interest bearing account that allows depositors to write checks without tying up their money for a specific period of time.*

zero balance account (ZBA)— *a checking account that never has any funds in it. A company keeps its money in an interest-bearing master account tied to the ZBA; when a check is drawn on the ZBA, the bank withdraws enough money from the master account to cover it.*

sweep account— *a checking account that automatically sweeps all funds in a company's checking account above a predetermined minimum into an interest-bearing account.*

goal . . . should be to identify every dollar you don't need to pay today's bills and to keep that money invested to improve your cash flow," explains a consultant.[51]

However, when investing surplus cash, an entrepreneur's primary objective should *not* be to earn the maximum yield (which usually carries with it maximum risk); instead, the focus should be on the safety and the liquidity of the investments. Making high-risk investments with a company's cash cushion makes no sense and could jeopardize its future. The need to minimize risk and to have ready access to the cash restricts an entrepreneur's investment options to just a few such as money market accounts, zero balance accounts, and sweep accounts. A **money market account** is an interest-bearing account offered by a variety of financial institutions ranging from banks to mutual funds. Money market accounts pay interest while allowing depositors to write checks (most have minimum check amounts) without tying their money up for a specific period of time. A **zero balance account** is a checking account that technically never has any funds in it but is tied to a master account. The company keeps its money in the master account where it earns interest, but it writes checks on the ZBA. At the end of the day, the bank pays all of the checks drawn on the ZBA; then it withdraws enough money from the master account to cover them. ZBAs allow a company to keep more cash working during the float period, the time between a check being issued and its being cashed. A **sweep account** automatically "sweeps" all funds in a company's checking account above a predetermined minimum into an interest-bearing account, enabling it to keep otherwise idle cash invested until it is needed to cover checks.

CONCLUSION

Successful owners run their businesses "lean and mean." Trimming wasteful expenditures, investing surplus funds, and carefully planning and managing the company's cash flow enable them to compete effectively. The simple but effective techniques covered in this chapter can improve every small company's cash position. One business writer says, "In the day-to-day course of running a company, other people's capital flows past an imaginative CEO as opportunity. By looking forward and keeping an analytical eye on your cash account as events unfold (remembering that if there's no real cash there when you need it, you're history), you can generate leverage as surely as if that capital were yours to keep."[52]

CHAPTER SUMMARY

1. Explain the importance of cash management to a small business's success.

■ Cash is the most important but least productive asset the small business has. The manager must maintain enough cash to meet the firm's normal requirements (plus a reserve for emergencies) without retaining excessively large, unproductive cash balances.

■ Without adequate cash, a small business will fail.

2. Differentiate between cash and profits.

■ Cash and profits are *not* the same. More businesses fail for lack of cash than for lack of profits.

■ Profits, the difference between total revenue and total expenses, are an accounting concept. Cash flow represents the flow of actual cash (the only thing businesses can use to pay bills) through a business in a continuous cycle. A business can be earning a profit and be forced out of business because it runs out of cash.

3. Understand the five steps in creating a cash budget and use them to create a cash budget.

■ The cash budgeting procedure outlined in this chapter tracks the flow of cash through the business and enables the owner to project cash surpluses and cash deficits at specific intervals.

■ The five steps in creating a cash budget are as follows: determining an adequate minimum cash balance, forecasting sales, forecasting cash receipts, forecasting cash disbursements, and determining the end-of-month cash balance.

4. Describe fundamental principles involved in managing the "big three" of cash management: accounts receivable, accounts payable, and inventory.

■ Controlling accounts receivable requires business owners to establish clear, firm credit and collection policies and to screen customers *before* granting them credit. Sending invoices promptly and acting on past-due accounts quickly also improve cash flow. The goal is to collect cash from receivables as quickly as possible.

■ When managing accounts payable, a manager's goal is to stretch out payables as long as possible without damaging the company's credit rating. Other techniques include verifying invoices before paying them, taking advantage of cash discounts, and negotiating the best possible credit terms.

■ Inventory frequently causes cash headaches for small business managers. Excess inventory earns a zero rate of return and ties up a company's cash unnecessarily. Owners must watch for stale merchandise.

5. Explain the techniques for avoiding a cash crunch in a small company.

■ Trimming overhead costs by bartering, leasing assets, avoiding nonessential outlays, using zero-based budgeting, and implementing an internal control system boost a firm's cash flow position.

■ Investing surplus cash also maximizes the firm's earning power. The primary criteria for investing surplus cash are security and liquidity.

DISCUSSION QUESTIONS

1. Why must entrepreneurs concentrate on effective cash flow management?
2. Explain the difference between cash and profit.
3. Outline the steps involved in developing a cash budget.
4. How can an entrepreneur launching a new business forecast sales?
5. What are the "big three" of cash management? What effect do they have on a company's cash flow?
6. Outline the basic principles of managing a small firm's receivables, payables, and inventory.
7. How can bartering improve a company's cash position?
8. What steps can entrepreneurs take to conserve the cash within their companies?
9. What should be a small business owner's primary concern when investing surplus cash?

THE BUSINESS DISC

Launch *The Business Disc* and return to the section where Harry describes the cash flow statement. If you have passed that point in the program, you can easily return to it. From the "Go To" menu, select "Events from PART 1 - B," and click on "Harry Introduces: Cash-Flow Statement." If you haven't reached that point, continue from where you left off. What does a cash-flow statement track? Why does Harry suggest that you add 10 percent of the total to your estimated disbursements? How does the sales forecast affect your company's cash-flow statement?

Develop a list of all of the costs you expect to incur as you operate your business. If you have not done so already, complete the disbursement section of the cash flow statement using this information. Now that you have read Chapter 9, do you see any cost estimates you want to change? Explain. How accurate did your initial estimates prove to be?

Business PlanPro

Section 7.1 of the Business PlanPro, "Important Assumptions," includes financial assumptions you must make to as part of your business plan.

Section 7.4 "Project Cash Flow" will allow you to conduct a proforma cash flow analysis or, if this is an acquisition of an existing business, assess the capability of the business to generate "free cash".

BEYOND THE CLASSROOM . . .

1. Interview several local small business owners about their cash management policies. Do they know how much cash their businesses have during the month? How do they track their cash flows? Do they use some type of cash budget? If not, ask if you can help the owner develop one. Does the owner invest surplus cash? If so, where?

2. Volunteer to help a small business owner develop a cash budget for his or her company. What patterns do you detect? What recommendations can you make for improving the company's cash management system?

3. Contact the International Reciprocal Trade Association (www.irta.net) and get a list of the barter exchanges in your state. Interview the manager of one of the exchanges and prepare a report on how barter exchanges work and how they benefit small businesses. Ask the manager to refer you to a small business owner who benefits from the barter exchange and interview him or her. How does the owner use the exchange? How much cash has bartering saved? What other benefits has the owner discovered?

4. Use the resources of the World Wide Web to research leasing options for small companies. The Equipment Leasing Association of America (www.elaonline.com) and its Lease Assistant site (www.leaseassistant.org) are good places to start. What advantages does leasing offer? Disadvantages? Identify and explain the various types of leases.

5. Contact a local small business owner who sells on credit. Is collecting accounts receivable on time a problem? What steps does the owner take to manage the company's accounts receivable? Do late payers strain the company's cash flow? How does the owner deal with customers who pay late?

*Ignorance is not bliss—it is
oblivion.*

—Philip Wylie

*It is better to solve problems
than crises.*

—John Guinther

LEARNING OBJECTIVES

Upon completion of this chapter, you will be able to:

1. **UNDERSTAND** the importance of preparing a financial plan.

2. **DESCRIBE** how to prepare the basic financial statements and use them to manage a small business.

3. **CREATE** projected (pro forma) financial statements.

4. **UNDERSTAND** the basic financial statements through ratio analysis.

5. **EXPLAIN** how to interpret financial ratios.

6. **CONDUCT** a break-even analysis for a small company.

financial management—a process that provides entrepreneurs with relevant financial information in an easy-to-read format on a timely basis; it allows entrepreneurs to know not only how their businesses are doing financially but also why they are performing that way.

Fashioning a well-designed, logical financial plan as part of a comprehensive business plan is one of the most important steps to launching a new business venture. Entrepreneurs who fail to develop workable strategies for earning a profit within a reasonable time eventually will suffer the ultimate business penalty: failure. Potential lenders and investors demand a realistic financial plan before putting their money into a start-up company. More importantly, a financial plan is a vital tool that helps entrepreneurs manage their businesses more effectively, steering their way around the pitfalls that cause failures. Proper **financial management** requires putting in place a system that provides entrepreneurs with relevant financial information in an easy-to-read format on a timely basis; it allows entrepreneurs to know not only *how* their businesses are doing financially but also *why* their companies are performing that way. Smart entrepreneurs put their companies' numbers to work for them so they can make their businesses more successful.

Unfortunately, failure to collect and analyze basic financial data is a common mistake among entrepreneurs. According to one survey, one-third of all entrepreneurs run their companies *without any kind of financial plan.*[1] Another study found that only 11 percent of small business owners analyzed their financial statements as part of the managerial planning and decision-making process.[2] To reach profit objectives, entrepreneurs must be aware of their firms' overall financial position and the changes in financial status that occur over time.

This chapter focuses on some very practical tools that will help entrepreneurs develop a workable financial plan, keep them aware of their company's financial plan, and enable them to plan for profit. They can use these tools to help them anticipate changes and plot an appropriate profit strategy to meet them head on. These profit planning techniques are not difficult to master, nor are they overly time consuming. We will discuss the techniques involved in preparing projected (pro forma) financial statements, conducting ratio analysis, and performing break-even analysis.

BASIC FINANCIAL STATEMENTS

Learning Objective

2. Describe how to prepare the basic financial statements and use them to manage a small business.

Before we begin building projected financial statements, it would be helpful to review the basic financial reports that measure a company's financial position: the balance sheet, the income statement, and the statement of cash flows. The level of financial sophistication among small business owners may not be high, but the extent of financial reporting among small businesses is. Most small businesses regularly produce summary financial information, almost all of it in the form of these traditional financial statements.

The Balance Sheet

balance sheet—a financial statement that provides a snapshot of a business's financial position, estimating its worth on a given date; it is built on the fundamental accounting equation: Assets = Liabilities + Owner's equity.

current assets—assets such as cash and other items to be converted into cash within one year or within the company's normal oberating cycle.

fixed assets—assets acquired for long-term use in a business.

liabilities—creditors' claims against a company's assets.

current liabilities—those debts that must be paid within one year or within the normal operating cycle of a company.

The **balance sheet** takes a "snapshot" of a business's financial position, providing owners with an estimate of its worth on a given date. Its two major sections show what assets the business owns and what claims creditors and owners have against those assets. The balance sheet is usually prepared on the last day of the month. Figure 10.1 shows the balance sheet for Sam's Appliance Shop for the year ended December 31, 200X.

The balance sheet is built on the fundamental accounting equation: Assets = Liabilities + Owner's equity. Any increase or decrease on one side of the equation must be offset by an increase or decrease on the other side; hence, the name *balance sheet*. It provides a baseline from which to measure future changes in assets, liabilities, and equity. The first section of the balance sheet lists the firm's assets (valued at cost, not actual market value) and shows the total value of everything the business owns. **Current assets** consist of cash and items to be converted into cash within one year or within the normal operating cycle of the company, whichever is longer, such as accounts receivable and inventory, and **fixed assets** are those acquired for long-term use in the business. Intangible assets include items that, although valuable, do not have tangible value, such as goodwill, copyrights, and patents.

The second section shows the business's **liabilities**—the creditors' claims against the company's assets. **Current liabilities** are those debts that must be paid within one year or within the normal operating cycle of the company, whichever is longer, and **long-term liabilities** are those that come due after one year. This section of the balance sheet also shows the **owner's equity**, the value of the owner's investment in the business. It is the balancing factor on the balance sheet, representing all of the owner's capital contributions to the business plus all accumulated (or retained) earnings not distributed to the owner(s).

FIGURE 10.1   Balance
Sheet, Sam's Appliance Shop

Assets

Current Assets

Cash		$ 49,855
Accounts Receivable	$179,225	
Less Allowance for Doubtful Accounts	6,000	$173,225
Inventory		$455,455
Prepaid Expenses		$ 8,450
Total Current Assets		$686,985

Fixed Assets

Land		$ 59,150
Buildings	$ 74,650	
Less Accumulated Depreciation	7,050	$ 67,600
Equipment	$ 22,375	
Less Accumulated Depreciation	1,250	$ 21,125
Funiture and Fixtures	$ 10,295	
Less Accumulated Depreciation	1,000	$ 9,295
Total Fixed Assets		$157,170
Intangibles (Goodwill)		$ 3,500
Total Assets		$847,655

Liabilities

Current Liabilities

Accounts Payable	$152,580
Notes Payable	83,920
Accrued Wages/Salaries Payable	38,150
Accrued Interest Payable	42,380
Accrued Taxes Payable	50,820
Total Current Liabilities	$367,850

Long-Term Liabilities

Mortgage	$127,150
Note Payable	85,000
Total Long-Term Liabilities	$212,150

Owner's Equity

Sam Lloyd, Capital	$267,655
Total Liabilities and Owner's Equity	$847,655

The Income Statement

The **income statement** (or profit and loss statement or "P&L") compares expenses against revenue over a certain period of time to show the firm's net profit (or loss). The income statement is a "moving picture" of a firm's profitability over time. The annual P&L statement reports the bottom line of the business over the fiscal/calendar year. Figure 10.2 shows the income statement for Sam's Appliance Shop for the year ended December 31, 200X.

To calculate net profit or loss, an entrepreneur records sales revenues for the year, which include all income that flows into the business from sales of goods and services. Income from other sources (rent, investments, interest) also must be included in the revenue section of the income statement. To determine net sales revenue, owners subtract the value of returned items and refunds from gross revenue. **Cost of goods sold** represents the total cost, including shipping, of the merchandise sold during the accounting period. Manufacturers, wholesalers, and retailers calculate cost of goods sold by adding purchases to beginning inventory and subtracting ending inventory. Service companies typically have no cost of goods sold.

long-term liabilities—liabilities that come due after one year.

owner's equity—the value of the owner's investment in the business.

income statement—a financial statement that represents a moving picture of a business, comparing its expenses against its revenue over a period of time to show its net profit (or loss).

cost of goods sold—the total cost, including shipping, of the merchandise sold during the accounting period.

FIGURE 10.2 Income
Statement, Sam's Appliance Shop

Net Sales Revenue		$1,870,841
Credit Sales	$1,309,589	
Cash Sales	561,252	
Cost of Goods Sold		
Beginning Inventory, 1/1/xx	$ 805,745	
+ Purchases	939,827	
Goods Available for Sale	$1,745,572	
– Ending Inventory, 12/31/xx	455,455	
Cost of Goods Sold		$1,290,117
Gross Profit		$ 580,724
Operating Expenses		
Advertising	$ 139,670	
Insurance	46,125	
Depreciation		
Building	18,700	
Equipment	9,000	
Salaries	224,500	
Travel	4,000	
Entertainment	2,500	
Total Operating Expenses		$ 444,495
General Expenses		
Utilities	$ 5,300	
Telephone	2,500	
Postage	1,200	
Payroll Taxes	25,000	
Total General Expenses		$ 34,000
Other Expenses		
Interest Expense	$ 39,850	
Bad Check Expense	1,750	
Total Other Expenses		$ 41,600
Total Expenses		$ 520,095
Net Income		$ 60,629

Net sales revenue minus cost of goods sold results in a company's gross profit. Dividing gross profit by net sales revenue produces the **gross profit margin**, a percentage that every small business owner should watch closely. If a company's gross profit margin slips too low, it is likely that it will operate at a loss (negative net income). Many business owners whose companies are losing money mistakenly believe that the problem is inadequate sales volume; therefore, they focus on pumping up sales at any cost. In many cases, however, the losses their companies are incurring are the result of an inadequate gross profit margin, and pumping up sales only deepens their losses! Repairing a poor gross profit margin requires a company to raise prices, cut manufacturing or purchasing costs, refuse orders with low profit margins, or add new products with more attractive profit margins. Monitoring the gross profit margin over time and comparing it to those of other companies in the same industry are important steps to maintaining a company's long-term profitability.

gross profit margin—*gross profit divided by net sales revenue.*

Operating expenses include those costs that contribute directly to the manufacture and distribution of goods. General expenses are indirect costs incurred in operating the business. "Other expenses" is a catch-all category covering all other expenses that don't fit into the other two categories. Total revenue minus total expenses gives the net income (or loss) for the accounting period. Comparing a company's current income statement to those of prior accounting periods often reveals valuable information about key trends and a company's progress toward its financial goals. Figure 10.3 shows how long it typically takes small companies to become profitable.

operating expenses—*those costs that contribute directly to the manufacture and distribution of goods.*

Percentage of small companies
that became profitable after . . .

- No answer 3%
- Not yet profitable 18%
- 0–12 months 49%
- More than 36 months 10%
- 25–36 months 8%
- 13–24 months 12%

The Statement of Cash Flows

The **statement of cash flows** shows the changes in the firm's working capital from the beginning of the year by listing both the sources of funds and the uses of these funds. Many small businesses never need to prepare such a statement, but in some cases creditors, investors, new owners, or the IRS may require this information.

To prepare the statement, the owner must assemble the balance sheets and the income statements summarizing the present year's operations. She begins with the company's net income for the period (from the income statement). Then she adds the sources of the company's funds—borrowed funds, owner contributions, decreases in accounts receivable, increases in accounts payable, decreases in inventory, depreciation, and any others. Depreciation is listed as a source of funds because it is a noncash expense that has already been deducted as a cost of doing business. But because the owner has already paid for the item being depreciated, its depreciation is a source of funds. Next the owner subtracts the uses of these funds—plant and equipment purchases, dividends to owners, repayment of debt, increases in accounts receivable, decreases in accounts payable, increases in inventory, and so on. The difference between the total sources and the total uses is the increase or decrease in working capital. By investigating the changes in the firm's working capital and the reasons for them, owners can create a more practical financial action plan for the future of the enterprise.

These financial statements are more than just complex documents used only by accountants and financial officers. When used in conjunction with the analytical tools described in the following sections, they can help entrepreneurs map a firm's financial future and actively plan for profit. Mere preparation of these statement is not enough, however; owners and employees must *understand and use* the information contained in them to make the business more effective and efficient.

statement of cash flows—*a financial statement showing the changes in a company's working capital from the beginning of the year by listing both the sources and the uses of those funds.*

CREATING PROJECTED FINANCIAL STATEMENTS

Creating projected financial statements helps the small business owner transform business goals into reality. Budgets answer such questions as: What profit can the business expect to obtain? If the owner's profit objective is *x* dollars, what sales level must she achieve? What fixed and variable expenses can she expect at that level of sales? The answers to these and other questions are critical in formulating a functional financial plan for the small business.

This section will focus on creating projected income statements and balance sheets for a small start-up. These projected (or pro forma) statements are a crucial component of every

Learning Objective

3. Create projected (pro forma) financial statements.

business plan because they estimate the profitability and the overall financial condition of a company in the future. They are an integral part of convincing potential lenders and investors to provide the financing needed to get the company off the ground (the topic of Chapter 12). Also, because these statements project a firm's financial position through the end of the forecasted period, they help entrepreneurs plan the route to improved financial strength and healthy business growth. To be useful, however, these forecasts must be *realistic*! "A business plan is not complete until it contains a set of financial projections that are not only inspiring but also logical and defensible," says one business writer.[3]

Because an established business has a history of operating data from which to construct pro forma financial statements, the task is not nearly as difficult as it is for the beginning business. When creating pro forma financial statements for a brand new business, an entrepreneur typically relies on published statistics summarizing the operation of similar-size companies in the same industry. These statistics are available from a number of sources (described later), but this section draws on information found in *Robert Morris Associates' Annual Statement Studies*, a compilation of financial data on thousands of companies across hundreds of industries [organized by Standard Industrial Classification (SIC) Code].

Pro Forma Statements for the Small Business

One of the most important tasks confronting the entrepreneur launching a new enterprise is to determine the funds needed to begin operation as well as those required to keep going through the initial growth period. The amount of money needed to begin a business depends on the type of operation, its location, inventory requirements, sales volume, and other factors. But every new firm must have enough capital to cover all start-up costs, including funds to rent or buy plant, equipment, and tools, as well as pay for advertising, wages, licenses, utilities, and other expenses. In addition, entrepreneurs must maintain a reserve of capital to carry the company until it begins to make a profit. Too often entrepreneurs are overly optimistic in their financial plans and fail to recognize that expenses initially exceed income for most small firms. This period of net losses is normal and may last from just a few months to several years. Owners must be able to meet payrolls, maintain adequate inventory, take advantage of cash discounts, grant customer credit, and meet personal obligations during this time.

THE PRO FORMA INCOME STATEMENT. Although they are projections, financial forecasts must be based in reality; otherwise, the resulting financial plan is nothing more than a hopeless dream. When creating a projected income statement, an entrepreneur has two options: to develop a sales forecast and work down or set a profit target and work up. Developing a realistic sales forecast for a business start-up is not always easy, but with creativity and research it is possible. Talking with owners of existing businesses in the industry (outside of the local trading area, of course) can provide meaningful insight into the sales levels a company can expect to generate in its early years. For a reasonable fee, entrepreneurs can access published aggregated financial statistics that industry trade associations collect on the companies in their industries. Other organizations, such as Robert Morris Associates and Dun & Bradstreet, publish useful financial information for a wide range of industries. Web searches and trips to the local library will produce the desired information. Interviews with potential customers and test marketing an actual product or service also can reveal the number of customers a company can expect to attract. Multiplying the number of customers by projected prices yields a revenue estimate. One method for checking the accuracy of a sales revenue estimate is to calculate the revenue other companies in the same industry generate per employee and compare it to your own projected revenue per employee. A value that is out of line with industry standards is not likely to be realistic.

Many entrepreneurs prefer the other method of creating a projected income statement, targeting a profit figure and then determining the sales level they must achieve to reach it. Of course, it is important to compare this sales target against the results of the marketing plan to determine whether or not it is realistic. The next step is to estimate the expenses the business will incur in securing those sales. In any small business, the annual profit must be large enough to produce a return for the time the owners spend operating the business, plus a return on their investment in the business.

An entrepreneur who earns less in his own business than he could earn working for someone else must weigh carefully the advantages and disadvantages of choosing the path of entrepreneurship. Why be exposed to all of the risks, sacrifices, and hard work of beginning and operating a small business if the rewards are less than those of remaining in the secure employment of another? Although there are many nonfinancial benefits of owning a business, the net profit after taxes a company generates should be at least as much as an entrepreneur could earn by working for someone else.

An adequate profit must also include a reasonable return on the owner's total investment in the business. The owner's total investment is the amount contributed to the company at its inception plus any retained earnings (profits from previous years funneled back into the operation). If a would-be owner has $70,000 to invest and can invest it in securities and earn 10 percent, she should not consider investing it in a small business that would yield only 3 percent.

An entrepreneur's target income is the sum of a reasonable salary for the time spent running the business and a normal return on the amount invested in the firm. Determining how much this should be is the first step in creating the pro forma income statement.

An entrepreneur then must translate this target profit into a net sales figure for the forecasted period. To calculate net sales from a target profit, the owner needs published statistics for this type of business. Suppose an entrepreneur wants to launch a small retail bookstore and has determined that his target income is $29,000 annually. Statistics gathered from *Robert Morris Associates' Annual Statement Studies* show that the typical bookstore's net profit margin (net profit ÷ by net sales) is 9.3 percent. Using this information, he can compute the sales level required to produce a net profit of $29,000:

$$\text{Net profit margin} = \frac{\text{Net profit}}{\text{Net sales (annual)}}$$

$$9.3\% = \frac{\$29,000}{\text{Net sales (annual)}}$$

$$\text{Net sales} = \frac{\$29,000}{0.093}$$

$$= \$311,828$$

Now this entrepreneur knows that to make a net profit of $29,000 (before taxes), he must achieve annual sales of $311,828. To complete the projected income statement, the owner simply applies the appropriate statistics from *Annual Statement Studies* to the annual sales figure. Because the statistics for each income statement item are expressed as percentages of net sales, he merely multiplies the proper percentage by the annual sales figure to obtain the desired value. For example, cost of goods sold usually comprises 61.4 percent of net sales for the typical small bookstore. So the owner of this new bookstore expects his cost of goods sold to be the following:

$$\text{Cost of goods sold} = \$311,828 \times 0.614 = \$191,462$$

The bookstore's complete projected income statement is shown as follows:

Net sales	(100%)	$311,828
– Cost of goods sold	(61.4%)	191,462
Gross profit margin	(38.6%)	$120,366
– Operating expenses	(29.3%)	$91,366
Net profit (before taxes)	(9.3%)	$29,000

At this point, the business appears to be a lucrative venture. But remember: This income statement represents a sales goal that the owner may not be able to reach. The next step is to determine whether this required sales volume is reasonable. One useful technique is to break down the required annual sales volume into *daily* sales figures. Assuming the store will be open six days per week for 50 weeks (300 days), the owner must average $1,039 per day in sales:

$$\text{Average daily sales} = \frac{\$311,828}{300 \text{ days}}$$

$$= \$1,039 / \text{day}$$

This calculation gives the owner a better perspective of the sales required to yield an annual profit of $29,000.

To determine whether the profit expected from the business will meet or exceed the target income, the entrepreneur should also create an income statement based on a realistic sales estimate. The previous analysis shows an entrepreneur the sales level needed to reach a desired profit. But what happens if sales are lower? Higher? The entrepreneur requires a reliable sales forecast using the market research techniques described in Chapter 6.

Suppose, for example, that after conducting a marketing survey of local customers and talking with nearby business owners, the prospective bookstore operator projects annual sales for the proposed business to be only $285,000. The entrepreneur must take this expected sales figure and develop a pro forma income statement.

Net sales	(100%)	$285,000
– Cost of goods sold	(61.4%)	174,990
Gross profit margin	(38.6%)	110,010
– Operating Expenses	(29.3%)	83,505
Net profit (before taxes)	(9.3%)	$26,505

Based on sales of $285,000, this entrepreneur should expect a net profit (before taxes) of $26,505. If this amount is acceptable as a return on the investment of time and money in the business, he should proceed with his planning.

At this stage in developing the financial plan, the owner should create a more detailed picture of the venture's expected operating expenses. One common method is to use the operating statistics data found in *Dun & Bradstreet's Cost of Doing Business* reports. These booklets document typical selected operating expenses (expressed as a percentage of net sales) for 190 different lines of businesses. Contacting potential vendors, suppliers, and providers to get estimates of expenses increases the accuracy of the expected expenses on a projected income statement. One entrepreneur who was preparing a business plan for the launch of an upscale women's clothing store contacted local utility companies, insurance agencies, radio and television stations, and other vendors to get estimates of her utility, insurance, advertising, and other general expenses.

To ensure that no business expenses have been overlooked in the preparation of the business plan, entrepreneurs should list all of the expenses they will incur and have an accountant review the list. Sometimes in their estimates of expenses entrepreneurs neglect to include salaries for themselves, which immediately raises a red flag among lenders and investors. Without drawing a salary, how will an entrepreneur pay her own personal bills? At the other extreme, lenders and investors frown on exorbitantly high salaries for owners of business start-ups. Typically, salaries are not the best use of cash in a start-up; one guideline is to draw a salary that is about 25 to 30 percent below the market rate for a similar position (and to make adjustments from there if conditions warrant). Also, as the company grows, executive salaries should be among the *last* expenses to be increased. Reinvesting the extra money back into the company for essentials will accelerate its growth rate even more. Figures 10.4 and 10.5 show two useful forms designed to help entrepreneurs estimate both monthly and start-up expenses. Totals derived from this list of expenses should approximate the total expense figures calculated from published statistics. Naturally, an entrepreneur should be more confident in his own list of expenses because it reflects his particular set of circumstances.

THE PRO FORMA BALANCE SHEET.   In addition to projecting a small company's net profit or loss, an entrepreneur must develop a pro forma balance sheet outlining the fledgling firm's assets and liabilities. Most entrepreneurs' primary concern is profitability because, on the surface, the importance of a business's assets is less obvious. In many cases, small companies begin their lives on weak financial footing because entrepreneurs fail to determine their firms' total asset requirements. To prevent this major oversight, entrepreneurs should prepare a projected balance sheet listing every asset their businesses will need and all the claims against these assets.

ASSETS.   Cash is one of the most useful assets the business owns; it is highly liquid and can quickly be converted into other tangible assets. But how much cash should a small business

FIGURE 10.4 Anticipated Expenses

Source: U.S. Small Business Administration. *Checklist for Going into Business.* Small Marketers Aid no. 71, Washington, DC, 1982, pp. 6–7.

Worksheet No. 2
Estimated Monthly Expenses

Your estimate of monthly expenses based on sales of $_____ per year

Your estimate of how much cash you need to start your business (see column 3)

What to put in column 2 (These figures are typical for one kind of business. You will have to decide how many months to allow for in your business.)

Item	Column 1	Column 2	Column 3
Salary of owner-manager	$	$	2 times column 1
All other salaries and wages			3 times column 1
Rent			3 times column 1
Advertising			3 times column 1
Delivery expense			3 times column 1
Supplies			3 times column 1
Telephone and telegraph			3 times column 1
Other utilities			3 times column 1
Insurance			Payment required by insurance company
Taxes, including Social Security			4 times column 1
Interest			3 times column 1
Maintenance			3 times column 1
Legal and other professional fees			3 times column 1
Miscellaneous			3 times column 1
Starting Costs You Have To Pay Only Once			Leave column 2 blank
Fixtures and equipment			Fill in worksheet 3 and put the total here
Decorating and remodeling			Talk it over with a contractor
Installation of fixtures and equipment			Talk to suppliers from whom you buy these
Starting inventory			Suppliers will probably help you estimate this
Deposits with public utilities			Find out from utilities companies
Legal and other professional fees			Lawyer, accountant, and so on
Licenses and permits			Find out from city offices what you have to have
Advertising and promotion of opening			Estimate what you'll use
Accounts receivable			What you need to buy more stock until credit customers pay
Cash			For unexpected expenses or losses, special purchases, etc.
Other			Make a separate list and enter total
Total Estimated Cash You Need To Start		$	Add up all the numbers in column 2

have at its inception? Obviously, there is no single dollar figure that fits the needs of every small firm. One practical rule of thumb, however, suggests that the company's cash balance should cover its operating expenses (less depreciation, a noncash expense) for one inventory

FIGURE 10.5 Anticipated

Expenditures for Fixtures and

Equipment

Source: U.S. Small Business
Administration, *Checklist for Going into
Business*, Small Marketers Aid no. 71,
Washington, DC, 1982, p. 12.

Worksheet No. 3
List of Furniture, Fixtures, and Equipment

Leave out or add items to suit your business. Use separate sheets to list exactly what you need for each of the items below.	If you plan to pay cash in full, enter the full amount below and in the last column.	If you are going to pay by installments, fill out the columns below. Enter in the last column your down payment plus at least one installment.			Estimate of the cash you need for furniture, fixtures, and equipment
		Price	Down payment	Amount of each installment	
Counters	$	$	$	$	$
Storage shelves, cabinets					
Display stands, shelves, tables					
Cash register					
Safe					
Window display fixtures					
Special lighting					
Outside sign					
Delivery equipment if needed					
Total Furniture, Fixtures, and Equipment (Enter this figure also in worksheet 2 under "Starting Costs You Have to Pay Only Once.") $					

turnover period. Using this guideline, the cash balance for the small bookstore is calculated as follows:

Operating expenses = $83,505 (from projected income statement)

Less: depreciation (0.9% of annual sales) of $2,565

Equals: cash expenses (annual) = $80,940

$$\text{Cash requirement} = \frac{\text{Cash expenses}}{\text{Average inventory turnover}}$$

$$= \frac{\$80,940}{3.5 \text{ times a year}}$$

$$= \$23,126$$

*From *RMA Annual Statement Studies*.

Notice the inverse relationship between the small firm's average turnover ratio and its cash requirement. The smaller the number of inventory turns a company generates, the higher is its cash requirement.

Another decision facing the entrepreneur is how much inventory the business should carry. A rough estimate of the inventory requirement can be calculated from the information found on the projected income statement and from published statistics:

$$\text{Cost of goods sold} = \$174,990 \text{ (from projected income statement)}$$

$$\text{Average inventory turnover} = \frac{\text{Cost of goods sold}}{\text{Inventory level}} = 3.5 \text{ times / year}$$

Substituting,

$$3.5 \text{ times / year} = \frac{\$174,990}{\text{Inventory level}}$$

Solving algebraically,

$$\text{Inventory level} = \$49,997$$

Entrepreneurs can use the planning forms shown in Figures 10.3 and 10.4 to estimate fixed assets (land, building, equipment, and fixtures). Suppose the estimate of fixed assets is as follows:

Fixtures	$17,500
Office equipment	2,850
Computers/Cash register	3,125
Signs	3,200
Miscellaneous	1,500
Total	$28,175

LIABILITIES.   To complete the projected balance sheet, the owner must record all of the small firm's liabilities, the claims against its assets. The bookstore owner was able to finance 50 percent of the inventory and fixtures through suppliers and has a short-term note payable in the amount of $3,750. The only other major claim against the firm's assets is a note payable to the entrepreneur's father-in-law for $30,000.

The final step is to compile all of these items into a projected balance sheet, as shown in Figure 10.6.

RATIO ANALYSIS

Learning Objective

4. Understand the basic financial statements through ratio analysis.

Once an entrepreneur has the business "up and running" with the help of a solid financial plan, the next step is to keep the company moving in the right direction with the help of proper financial controls. Establishing these controls—and using them consistently—is one of the keys to keeping a business vibrant and healthy. "If you don't keep a finger on the pulse of your company's finances, you risk making bad decisions," explains one business writer. "You could be in serious financial trouble and not even realize it."[4]

A smoothly functioning system of financial controls is essential to achieving business success. Such a system can serve as an early warning device for underlying problems that could destroy a young business. According to one writer:

A company's financial accounting and reporting systems will provide signals, through comparative analysis, of impending trouble, such as:

■ Decreasing sales and falling profit margins.

■ Increasing corporate overheads.

Assets		Liabilities	
Current Assets		**Current Liabilities**	
Cash	$ 23,126	Accounts Payable	$ 24,998
Inventory	49,997	Note Payable	3,750
Miscellaneous	1,800		
Total Current Assets	$ 74,923	Total Current Liabilities	$ 28,748
Fixed Assets		**Long-Term Liabilities**	
Fixtures	$ 17,500	Note Payable	$ 30,000
Office equipment	2,850		
Computers/Cash register	3,125	Total Liabilities	58,748
Signs	3,200		
Miscellaneous	1,500		
Total Fixed Assets	$ 28,175	**Owner's Equity**	44,350
Total Assets	$103,098	**Total Liabilities and Owner's Equity**	$103,098

FIGURE 10.6   Projected Balance Sheet for a Small Bookstore

■ Growing inventories and accounts receivable.

These are all signals of declining cash flows from operations, the lifeblood of every business. As cash flows decrease, the squeeze begins:

■ Payments to vendors become slower.

■ Maintenance on production equipment lags.

■ Raw material shortages appear.

■ Equipment breakdowns occur.

All of these begin to have a negative impact on productivity. Now the downward spiral has begun in earnest. The key is hearing and focusing on the signals.[5]

ratio analysis—*a method of expressing the relationship between any two accounting elements that allows business owners to analyze their companies' financial performances.*

What are these signals, and how does an entrepreneur go about hearing and focusing on them? One extremely helpful tool is ratio analysis. **Ratio analysis**, a method of expressing the relationships between any two elements on financial statements, provides a convenient technique for performing financial analysis. When analyzed properly, ratios serve as barometers of a company's financial health. "You owe it to yourself to understand each ratio and what it means to your business," says one accountant. "Ratios point out potential trouble areas so you can correct them before they multiply."[6] Ratio analysis allows entrepreneurs to determine if their companies are carrying excessive inventory, experiencing heavy operating expenses, overextending credit, taking on too much debt, managing to pay their bills on time, and to answer other questions relating to the efficient and effective operation of the overall business. Unfortunately, few business owners actually use ratio analysis; one study discovered that only 27 percent of small business owners compute financial ratios and use them to manage their businesses![7]

Clever business owners use financial ratio analysis to identify problems in their businesses while they are still problems, not business-threatening crises. Tracking these ratios over time permits an owner to spot a variety of "red flags" that are indications of these problem areas. This is critical to business success because business owners cannot solve problems they do not know exist!

A Company Example

*At **Atkinson-Baker & Associates**, a Los Angeles court-reporting service, every one of the firm's 50 employees is responsible for tracking every day a key financial statistic relating to his or her job. CEO Alan Atkinson-Baker believes that waiting until the month's end to compile financial ratios takes away a company's ability to respond to events as they happen. "Employees have statistics for their jobs, and it helps them see how well they are producing," he says. Because the statistics are linked directly to their jobs, employees quickly learn which numbers to track and how to compile or to calculate them. "Each day everybody reports their statistics," explains Atkinson-Baker. "It all goes into a computer . . . and we keep track of it all." A spreadsheet summarizes the calculations and generates 27 graphs so managers can analyze trends in a meeting the following morning. One rule the company developed from its financial analysis is "Don't spend more today than you brought in yesterday." Atkinson-Baker explains, "You can never run into trouble as long as you stick to that rule." He also notes that effective financial planning would be impossible without timely data. "When we have had problem areas, the statistics have helped us catch them before they become a bigger problem," he says.[8]*

Business owners also can use ratio analysis to increase the likelihood of obtaining a bank loan. By analyzing his financial statements with ratios, an owner can anticipate potential problems and identify important strengths in advance. And loan officers *do* use ratios to analyze the financial statements of companies applying for loans, comparing them against industry averages and looking for trends over time.

But how many ratios should the small business manager monitor to maintain adequate financial control over the firm? The number of ratios that an owner could calculate is limited only by the number of accounts on a firm's financial statements. However, tracking too many ratios only creates confusion and saps the meaning from an entrepreneur's financial analysis. The secret to successful ratio analysis is *simplicity*, focusing on just enough ratios to provide a clear picture of a company's financial standing.

12 Key Ratios

In keeping with the idea of simplicity, we will describe 12 key ratios that will enable most business owners to monitor their companies' financial positions without becoming bogged down in financial details. This chapter presents explanations of these ratios and examples based on the balance sheet and the income statement for Sam's Appliance Shop shown in Figures 10.1 and 10.2. We will group them into four categories: liquidity ratios, leverage ratios, operating ratios, and profitability ratios.

LIQUIDITY RATIOS. Liquidity ratios tell whether or not the small business will be able to meet its short-term financial obligations as they come due. These ratios can forewarn a business owner of impending cash flow problems. A small company with solid liquidity not only is able to pay its bills on time, but it also has enough cash to take advantage of attractive business opportunities as they arise. The primary measures of liquidity are the current ratio and the quick ratio.

> **liquidity ratios**—*tell whether a small business will be able to meet its short-term obligations as they come due.*

1. CURRENT RATIO. The **current ratio** measures a small firm's solvency by indicating its ability to pay current liabilities (debts) from current assets. It is calculated in the following manner:

> **current ratio**—*measures a small firm's solvency by indicating its ability to pay current liabilities out of current assets.*

$$\text{Current ratio} = \frac{\text{Current assets}}{\text{Current liabilities}}$$

$$= \frac{\$686,985}{\$367,850}$$

$$= 1.87:1$$

Sam's Appliance Shop has $1.87 in current assets for every $1 it has in current liabilities.

Current assets are those that an owner expects to convert into cash in the ordinary business cycle and normally include cash, notes/accounts receivable, inventory, and any other short-term marketable securities. Current liabilities are those short-term obligations that come due within one year and include notes/accounts payable, taxes payable, and accruals.

The current ratio is sometimes called the *working capital ratio* and is the most commonly used measure of short-term solvency. Typically, financial analysts suggest that a small business maintain a current ratio of at least 2:1 (i.e., two dollars of current assets for every one dollar of current liabilities) to maintain a comfortable cushion of working capital. Generally, the higher a company's current ratio, the stronger its financial position; but a high current ratio does not guarantee that a company is using its assets in the most profitable manner. For example, a business may have an abundance of accounts receivable (many of which may not even be collectible) or may be overinvesting in inventory.

With its current ratio of 1.87, Sam's Appliance Shop could liquidate its current assets at 53.5 percent (1 ÷ 1.87 = .535) of its book value and still manage to pay its current creditors in full.

2. QUICK RATIO. The current ratio sometimes can be misleading because it does not show the quality of a company's current assets. As we have already seen, a company with a large number of past-due receivables and stale inventory could boast an impressive current ratio and still be on the verge of financial collapse. The **quick ratio** (or the **acid test ratio**) is a more conservative measure of a company's liquidity because it shows the extent to which its most liquid assets cover its current liabilities. This ratio includes only a company's "quick assets," excluding the most illiquid asset of all—inventory. It is calculated as follows:

> **quick ratio**—*a conservative measure of a firm's liquidity, measuring the extent to which its most liquid assets cover its current liabilities.*

$$\text{Quick ratio} = \frac{\text{Quick assets}}{\text{Current liabilities}}$$

$$= \frac{\$686,985 - \$455,455}{\$367,850}$$

$$= 0.63:1$$

Sam's Appliance Shop has 63 cents in quick assets for every $1 of current liabilities.

Quick assets include cash, readily marketable securities, and notes/accounts receivables, assets that can be converted into cash immediately if needed. Most small firms determine quick assets by subtracting inventory from current assets because they cannot convert inventory into cash quickly. Also, inventory is the asset on which losses are most likely to occur in case of liquidation.

The quick ratio is a more specific measure of a firm's ability to meet its short-term obligations and is a more rigorous test of its liquidity. It expresses capacity to pay current debts if all sales income ceased immediately. Generally, a quick ratio of 1:1 is considered satisfactory. A ratio of less than 1:1 indicates that the small firm is overly dependent on inventory and on future sales to satisfy short-term debt. A quick ratio of more than 1:1 indicates a greater degree of financial security.

leverage ratios—*measure the financing supplied by a firm's owners against that supplied by its creditors; they are a gauge of the depth of a company's debt.*

LEVERAGE RATIOS. **Leverage ratios** measure the financing supplied by a firm's owners against that supplied by its creditors; they are a gauge of the depth of a company's debt. These ratios show the extent to which an entrepreneur relies on debt capital (rather than equity capital) to finance operating expenses, capital expenditures, and expansion costs. As such, it is a measure of the degree of financial risk in a company. Generally, small businesses with low leverage ratios are less affected by economic downturns, but the returns for these firms are lower during economic booms. Conversely, small firms with high leverage ratios are more vulnerable to economic slides because their debt loads demolish cash flow; however, they have greater potential for large profits.

Over the past decade, American businesses have relied increasingly on debt financing to fuel their growth and expansion. Nonfinancial businesses in the United States have $4.9 trillion in outstanding debt, which is double the amount in 1995.[9]

A Company Example

*Typical of these debt-laden companies is **LodgeNet Entertainment Corporation**, which offers pay-per-view movies, video games, cable television, and express checkout to hotel customers. To finance attempts to reach new markets and to take on new partners in strategic alliances, LodgeNet has relied on debt financing so heavily that its debt load has risen twice as fast as its sales over the past six years. (The company's sales are less than $200 million per year, and its total debt is $262 million.) LodgeNet's interest expense eats up $23 million per year, limiting its ability to invest in a new direct Web access service it offers its customers.[10]*

debt ratio—*measures the percentage of total assets financed by a company's creditors compared to its owners.*

DEBT RATIO. A small company's **debt ratio** measures the percentage of total assets financed by its creditors compared to its owners. The debt ratio is calculated as follows:

$$\text{Debt ratio} = \frac{\text{Total debt (or liabilities)}}{\text{Total assets}}$$

$$= \frac{\$367,850 + \$212,150}{\$847,655}$$

$$= 0.68:1$$

Creditors have claims of 68 cents against every $1 of assets that Sam's Appliance Shop owns.

Total debt includes all current liabilities and any outstanding long-term notes and bonds. Total assets represent the sum of the firm's current assets, fixed assets, and intangible assets. A high debt ratio means that creditors provide a large percentage of a company's total financing and, therefore, bear most of its financial risk. Owners generally prefer higher leverage ratios; otherwise, business funds must come either from the owners' personal assets or from taking on new owners, which means giving up more control over the business. Also, with a greater portion of a firm's assets financed by creditors, the owner is able to generate profits with a smaller personal investment. Creditors, however, typically prefer moderate debt ratios because a lower debt ratio indicates a smaller chance of creditor losses in case of liquidation. To lenders and creditors, high debt ratios mean a higher risk of default.

According to a senior analyst at Dun & Bradstreet's Analytical Services, "If managed properly, debt can be beneficial because it's a great way to have money working for you. You're leveraging your assets, so you're making more money than you're paying out in interest." However, excessive debt can be the downfall of a business. "As we pile up debt on our personal credit cards our lifestyles are squeezed," he says. "The same thing happens to a business. Overpowering debt sinks thousands of businesses each year."[11]

4. DEBT TO NET WORTH RATIO. A small firm's **debt to net worth** (or **debt to equity) ratio** also expresses the relationship between the capital contributions from creditors and those from owners and measures how highly leveraged a company is. This ratio shows a company's capital structure by comparing what the business "owes" to "what it is worth." It is a measure of the small firm's ability to meet both its creditor and owner obligations in case of liquidation. The debt to net worth ratio is calculated as follows:

debt to net worth (debt to equity) ratio—*expresses the relationship between the capital contributions from creditors and those from owners and measures how highly leveraged a company is.*

$$\text{Debt to net worth ratio} = \frac{\text{Total debt (or liabilities)}}{\text{Tangible net worth}}$$

$$= \frac{\$367,850 + \$212,150}{\$267,655 - \$3,500}$$

$$= 2.20:1$$

Sam's Appliance Shop owes creditors \$2.20 for every \$1 of equity that Sam owns.

Total debt is the sum of current liabilities and long-term liabilities, and tangible net worth represents the owners' investment in the business (capital + capital stock + earned surplus + retained earnings) less any intangible assets (e.g., goodwill) the firm owns.

The higher this ratio, the more leverage a business is using, and the lower the degree of protection afforded creditors if the business should fail. Also, a higher debt to net worth ratio means that the firm has less capacity to borrow; lenders and creditors see the firm as being "borrowed up." Conversely, a low ratio typically is associated with a higher level of financial security, giving the business greater borrowing potential.

As a company's debt to net worth ratio approaches 1:1, the creditors' interest in the business approaches that of the owners'. If the ratio is greater than 1:1, creditors' claims exceed those of the owners', and the business may be undercapitalized. In other words, the owner has not supplied an adequate amount of capital, forcing the business to be overextended in terms of debt.

5. TIMES INTEREST EARNED RATIO. The **times interest earned ratio** is a measure of a small firm's ability to make the interest payments on its debt. It tells how many times a company's earnings cover the interest payments on the debt it is carrying. This ratio measures the size of the cushion a company has in covering the interest cost of its debt load. The times interest earned ratio is calculated as follows:

times interest earned ratio—*measures a small firm's ability to make the interest payments on its debt.*

$$\text{Times interest earned} = \frac{\text{Earnings before interest and taxes (or EBIT)}}{\text{Total interest expense}}$$

$$= \frac{\$60,629 + \$39,850}{\$39,850}$$

$$= 2.52:1$$

Sam's Appliance Shop's earnings are 2.5 times greater than its interest expense.

EBIT is the firm's profit *before* deducting interest expense and taxes; the denominator measures the amount the business paid in interest over the accounting period.

A high ratio suggests that the company would have little difficulty meeting the interest payments on its loans; creditors see this as a sign of safety for future loans. Conversely, a low ratio is an indication that the company is overextended in its debts; earnings will not be able to cover its debt service if this ratio is less than 1. "I look for a [times interest earned] ratio of higher than three-to-one," says one financial analyst, "which indicates that management has considerable breathing room to make its debt payments. When the ratio drops below one-to-one, it clearly indicates management is under tremendous pressure to raise cash. The risk of default or bankruptcy is very high."[12] Many creditors look for a times interest earned ratio of at least 4:1 to 6:1 before pronouncing a company a good credit risk.

Although low to moderate levels of debt can boost a company's financial performance, trouble looms on the horizon for businesses whose debt loads are so heavy that they must starve critical operations, research and development, customer service, and others just to pay interest on the debt. Because their interest payments are so large, highly leveraged companies find that they are restricted when it comes to spending cash, whether on an acquisition, normal operations, or capital spending.

Like dynamite, debt financing can be a powerful tool, but companies must handle it carefully, or it can be deadly.

Courtesy of Getty Images Inc. - Hulton Archive Photos.

Debt is a powerful financial tool, but companies must handle it carefully—just as a demolitionist handles dynamite. And, like dynamite, too much debt can be deadly. Unfortunately, some companies that have pushed their debt loads beyond the safety barrier (see Figure 10.7) are struggling to survive. Managed carefully, however, debt can boost a company's performance and improve its productivity. Its treatment in the tax code also makes debt a much cheaper means of financing growth than equity. When companies with AA financial ratings borrow at, say, 8 percent, the after-tax cost is about 5.75 percent (because interest payments to lenders are tax deductible); equity financing often costs twice as much.

Table 10.1 describes how lenders view liquidity and leverage.

operating ratios—*help an entrepreneur evaluate a small company's overall performance and indicate how effectively the business employs its resources.*

OPERATING RATIOS. **Operating ratios** help an entrepreneur evaluate a small company's overall performance and indicate how effectively the business employs its resources. The more effectively its resources are used, the less capital a small business will require. These five operating ratios are designed to help an entrepreneur spot those areas she must improve if her business is to remain competitive.

average inventory turnover ratio—*measures the number of times its average inventory is sold out, or turned over, during an accounting period.*

6. AVERAGE INVENTORY TURNOVER RATIO. A small firm's **average inventory turnover ratio** measures the number of times its average inventory is sold out, or turned over, during the accounting period. This ratio tells the owner whether or not an entrepreneur is managing inventory properly. It apprises the owner of whether the business inventory is understocked, overstocked, or obsolete. The average inventory turnover ratio is calculated as follows:

$$\text{Average inventory turnover ratio} = \frac{\text{Cost of goods sold}}{\text{Average inventory}}$$

$$= \frac{\$1,290,117}{(\$805,745 + \$455,455) \div 2}$$

$$= 2.05 \text{ times / year}$$

FIGURE 10.7 The Right Amount of Debt Is a Balancing Act

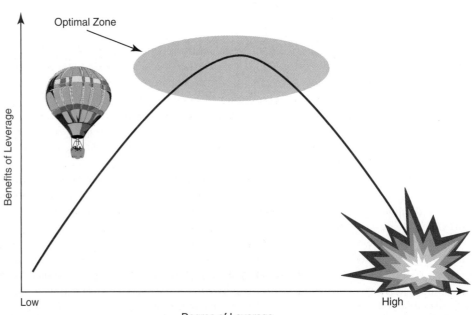

Benefits of Leverage

Optimal Zone

Low — Degree of Leverage — High

TABLE 10.1

How Lenders View Liquidity and
Leverage

Source: Adapted from David H. Bangs,
Jr., *Financial Troubleshooting,* (Dover, NH:
Upstart Publishing, 1992), p. 124.

	Liquidity	**Leverage**
Low	If chronic, this is often evidence of mismanagement. It is a sign that the owner has not planned for the company's working capital needs. In most businesses characterized by low liquidity, there is usually no financial plan. This situation is often associated with last-minute or "Friday night" financing.	This is a very conservative position. With this kind of leverage, lenders are likely to lend money to satisfy a company's capital needs. Owners in this position should have no trouble borrowing money.
Average	This is an indication of good management. The company is using its current assets wisely and productively. Although they may not be impressed, lenders feel comfortable making loans to companies with adequate liquidity.	If a company's leverage is comparable to that of other businesses of similar size in the same industry, lenders are comfortable making loans. The company is not overburdened with debt and is demonstrating its ability to use its resources to grow.
High	Some lenders look for this because it indicates a most conservative company. However, companies that constantly operate this way usually are forgoing growth opportunities because they are not making the most of their assets.	Businesses that carry excessive levels of debt scare most lenders off. Companies in this position normally will have a difficult time borrowing money unless they can show lenders good reasons for making loans. Owners of these companies must be prepared to sell lenders on their ability to repay.

Sam's Appliance Shop turns its inventory about two times a year, or once every 178 days.

Average inventory is the sum of the value of the firm's inventory at the beginning of the accounting period and its value at the end of the accounting period, divided by 2.

This ratio tells the owner how fast the merchandise is moving through the business and helps her balance the company's inventory on the fine line between oversupply and undersupply. To

A healthy average inventory turnover
ratio means that inventory is moving
through a business at a brisk pace.

Courtesy of Corbis Bettman, © Keith
Wood/Corbis.

determine the average number of days units remain in inventory, the owner can divide the average inventory turnover ratio into the number of days in the accounting period (e.g., 365 days ÷ average inventory turnover ratio). The result is called *days' inventory* (or *average age of inventory*). Auto dealerships often use the average age of inventory as a measure of their performance.

An above-average inventory turnover indicates that the small business has a healthy, salable, and liquid inventory and a supply of quality merchandise supported by sound pricing policies. A below-average inventory turnover suggests an illiquid inventory characterized by obsolescence, overstocking, stale merchandise, and poor purchasing or pricing procedures.

Businesses that turn their inventories more rapidly require a smaller inventory investment to produce a particular sales volume. That means that these companies tie up less cash in inventory that idly sits on shelves. For instance, if Sam's could turn its inventory *four* times each year instead of just *two*, the company would require an average inventory of just $322,529 instead of the current level of $630,600 to generate sales of $1,870,841. Increasing the number of inventory turns would free up more than $308,000 in cash currently tied up in excess inventory! Sam's would benefit from improved cash flow and higher profits.

The inventory turnover ratio can be misleading, however. For example, an excessively high ratio could mean the firm has a shortage of inventory and is experiencing stockouts. Similarly, a low ratio could be the result of planned inventory stockpiling to meet seasonal peak demand. Another problem is that the ratio is based on an inventory balance calculated from two days out of the entire accounting period. Thus, inventory fluctuations due to seasonal demand patterns are ignored, which may bias the resulting ratio. There is no universal, ideal inventory turnover ratio. Financial analysts suggest that a favorable turnover ratio depends on the type of business, its size, its profitability, its method of inventory valuation, and other relevant factors.

average collection period ratio—*measures the number of days it takes to collect accounts receivable.*

7. AVERAGE COLLECTION PERIOD RATIO. A small firm's **average collection period ratio** (or days sales outstanding, DSO) tells the average number of days it takes to collect accounts receivable. To compute the average collection period ratio, you must first calculate the firm's receivables turnover. Given that Sam's *credit* sales for the year were $1,309,589, then the company's receivables turnover ratio would be as follows:

$$\text{Receivables turnover ratio} = \frac{\text{Credit sales}}{\text{Accounts receivable}}$$

$$= \frac{\$1,309,589}{\$179,225}$$

$$= 7.31 \text{ times / year}$$

Sam's Appliance Shop turns over its receivables 7.31 times per year. This ratio measures the number of times the firm's accounts receivable turn over during the accounting period. The higher the firm's receivables turnover ratio, the shorter the time lag between the sale and the cash collection.

Use the following to calculate the firm's average collection period ratio:

$$\text{Average collection period ratio} = \frac{\text{Days in accounting period}}{\text{Receivables turnover ratio}}$$

$$= \frac{365 \text{ days}}{7.31 \text{ times / year}}$$

$$= 50.0 \text{ days}$$

The lower a company's average collection period is, the faster it is collecting its receivables. Sam's Appliance Shop's accounts receivable are outstanding for an average of 50 days. Typically, the higher a firm's average collection period ratio, the greater its chance of incurring bad debt losses.

One of the most useful applications of the collection period ratio is to compare it to the industry average and to the firm's credit terms. Such a comparison will indicate the degree of the small company's control over its credit sales and collection techniques. A healthy collection period ratio depends on the industry in which a company operates. For instance, a study by REL Consultancy Group found that the average collection period for companies selling technology hardware is 69 days; for retailers of food, it is just 10 days.[13] Perhaps the most meaningful analysis is comparing the collection period ratio to a company's credit terms. One rule of thumb suggests that a company's collection period ratio should be no more than one-third greater than its credit terms. For example, if a small company's credit terms are net 30, its average collection period ratio should be no more than 40 days. A ratio greater than 40 days would indicate poor collection procedures.

Slow payers represent a great risk to many small businesses. Many entrepreneurs proudly point to rapidly rising sales only to find that they must borrow money to keep their companies going because their credit customers are paying their bills in 45, 60, or even 90 days instead of the desired 30. Slow receivables are a real danger because they usually lead to a cash crisis that threatens a company's survival. Table 10.2 shows how to calculate the savings associated with lowering a company's average collection period ratio.

8. AVERAGE PAYABLE PERIOD RATIO. The converse of the average collection period, the **average payable period ratio,** tells the average number of days it takes a company to pay its accounts payable. Like the average collection period, it is measured in days. To compute this ratio, first calculate the payables turnover ratio. Sam's payables turnover ratio is as follows:

average payable period ratio—*measures the number of days it takes a company to pay its accounts payable.*

$$\text{Payables turnover} = \frac{\text{Purchases}}{\text{Accounts payable}}$$

$$= \frac{\$939,827}{\$152,580}$$

$$= 6.16 \text{ times / year}$$

To find the average payable period, use the following computation:

$$\text{Average payable period} = \frac{\text{Days in accounting period}}{\text{Payables turnover ratio}}$$

$$= \frac{365 \text{ days}}{6.16 \text{ times per year}}$$

$$= 59.3 \text{ days}$$

Sam's Appliance Shop takes an average of 59 days to pay its accounts with suppliers.

An excessively high average payables period ratio indicates the presence of a significant amount of past-due accounts payable. Although sound cash management calls for a business owner to keep her cash as long as possible, slowing payables too drastically can severely damage the company's credit rating. Ideally, the average payable period would match (or exceed) the time it takes to convert inventory into sales and ultimately into cash. In this case, the company's vendors would be financing its inventory and its credit sales. Amazon.com reaps the benefits of this situation; it does not pay its vendors until after it collects from its customers.[14]

One of the most meaningful comparisons for this ratio is against the credit terms suppliers offer (or an average of the credit terms offered). If the average payable ratio slips beyond vendors' credit terms, it is an indication that the company is suffering from a sloppy accounts payable procedure or from cash shortages, and its credit rating is in danger. If this ratio is significantly lower than vendors' credit terms, it may be a sign that the firm is not using its cash most effectively.

9. NET SALES TO TOTAL ASSETS RATIO. A small company's **net sales to total assets ratio** (also called the **total asset turnover ratio**) is a general measure of its ability to generate sales in relation to its assets. It describes how productively the firm employs its assets to produce sales revenue. The total assets turnover ratio is calculated as follows:

net sales to total assets (total asset turnover) ratio—*measures a company's ability to generate sales in relation to its asset base.*

$$\text{Total assets turnover ratio} = \frac{\text{Net sales}}{\text{Net total assets}}$$

$$= \frac{\$1,870,841}{\$847,655}$$

$$= 2.21:1$$

TABLE 10.2

How Lowering Your Average Collection Period Can Save You Money

Source: Adapted from "Days Saved, Thousands Earned," *Inc.*, November 1995, p. 98.

Too often, entrepreneurs fail to recognize the importance of collecting their accounts receivable on time. After all, collecting accounts is not as glamorous or as much fun as generating sales. Lowering a company's average collection period ratio, however, *can* produce tangible—and often significant—savings. The following formula shows how to convert an improvement in a company's average collection period ratio into dollar savings:

$$\text{Annual Savings} = \frac{(\text{Credit sales} \times \text{Annual interest rate} \times \text{Number of days average collection period is lowered})}{365}$$

where

credit sales = company's annual credit sales in $

annual interest rate = the interest rate at which the company borrows money

number of days average collection period is lowered = the difference between the previous year's average collection period ratio and the current one

Example:

Sam's Appliance Shop's average collection period ratio is 50 days. Suppose that the previous year's average collection period ratio was 58 days, an eight-day improvement. The company's credit sales for the most recent year were $1,309,589. If Sam borrows money at 8.75 percent, this six-day improvement has generated savings for Sam's Appliance Shop of

$$\text{Savings} = \frac{\$1,309,589 \times 8.75\% \times 8 \text{ days}}{365 \text{ days}} = \$2,512$$

By collecting his accounts receivable just six days faster on the average, Sam has saved his business more than $2,512! Of course, if a company's average collection period ratio rises, the same calculation will tell the owner how much that costs.

Sam's Appliance Shop is generating $2.21 in sales for every dollar of assets.

The denominator of this ratio, net total assets, is the sum of all of a company's assets (cash, inventory, land, buildings, equipment, tools, everything owned) less depreciation. This ratio is meaningful only when compared to that of similar firms in the same industry category. A total assets turnover ratio below the industry average indicates that a small firm is not generating an adequate sales volume for its asset size.

net sales to working capital ratio—*measures how many dollars in sales a business generates for every dollar of working capital.*

10. NET SALES TO WORKING CAPITAL RATIO. The **net sales to working capital ratio** measures how many dollars in sales the business generates for every dollar of working capital (Working capital = Current assets − Current liabilities). Also called the *turnover of working capital ratio*, this proportion tells the owner how efficiently working capital is being used to generate sales. It is calculated as follows:

$$\text{Net sales to working capital ratio} = \frac{\text{Net sales}}{\text{Current assets} - \text{Current liabilities}}$$

$$= \frac{\$1,870,841}{\$686,985 - \$367,850}$$

$$= 5.86:1$$

Sam's Appliance Shop is generating $5.86 in sales for every dollar of working capital.

An excessively low net sales to working capital ratio indicates that a small firm is not employing its working capital efficiently or profitably. On the other hand, an extremely high ratio may indicate an inadequate level of working capital to maintain a suitable level of sales, which puts creditors in a more vulnerable position. Monitoring this ratio over time is very helpful in maintaining sufficient working capital as the small business grows. It is critical for the small firm to keep a satisfactory level of working capital to nourish its expansion, and the net sales to working capital ratio helps define the level of working capital required to support higher sales volumes.

PROFITABILITY RATIOS. **Profitability ratios** indicate how efficiently a small company is being managed. They provide the owner with information about a company's bottom line; in other words, they describe how successfully the firm is using its available resources to generate a profit.

profitability ratios—*indicate how efficiently a small company is being managed.*

11. NET PROFIT ON SALES RATIO. The **net profit on sales ratio** (also called the *profit margin on sales* or *net profit margin*) measures a company's profit per dollar of sales. The computed percentage shows the portion of each sales dollar remaining after deducting all expenses. The profit margin on sales is calculated as follows:

net profit on sales ratio—*measures a company's profit per dollar of sales.*

$$\text{Net profit on sales ratio} = \frac{\text{Net profit}}{\text{Net sales}}$$

$$= \frac{\$60,629}{\$1,870,841}$$

$$= 3.24\%$$

For every dollar in sales Sam's Appliance Shop generates, Sam keeps 3.24 cents in profit.

Many small business owners believe that a high profit margin on sales is necessary for a successful business operation, but this is a myth. To evaluate this ratio properly, the owner must consider a firm's asset value, its inventory and receivables turnover ratios, and its total capitalization. For example, the typical small supermarket earns an average net profit of only one or two cents on each dollar of sales, but its inventory may turn over as many as 25 times a year. If a firm's profit margin on sales is below the industry average, it may be a sign that its prices are too low, that its costs are excessively high, or both.

If a company's net profit on sales ratio is excessively low, the owner first should check the gross profit margin (net sales minus cost of goods sold expressed as a percentage of net sales). Of course, a reasonable gross profit margin varies from industry to industry. For instance, a service company may have a gross profit margin of 75 percent, whereas a manufacturer's may be 35 percent. The key is to know what a reasonable gross profit margin is for your particular business. If this margin slips too low, it puts a company's future in immediate jeopardy. An inadequate gross profit margin cannot cover all of a company's business expenses and still be able to generate a profit.

Monitoring the net profit margin is especially important for fast-growing companies where sales are climbing rapidly. Unbridled growth can cause expenses to rise faster than sales, eroding a company's net profit margin. Success can be deceptive: Sales are rising, but profits are shrinking. Ideally, a company reaches a point at which it achieves **operating leverage**, a situation in which increases in operating efficiency mean that expenses as a percentage of sales revenues flatten or even decline. As a result, the company's net profit margin will climb as it grows.

operating leverage—*a situation in which increases in operating efficiency mean that expenses as a percentage of sales revenue flatten or even decline.*

A Company Example

In 1994, when Rick Sapio launched **Mutuals.com***, a mutual fund advisory and account management service, he was able to raise $14 million in equity capital from private and institutional investors. That largess and the ease with which he raised it gave Sapio an excuse for ignoring the importance of operating leverage. "We were not accountable to being a profitable company at the beginning," he says, "and our energies weren't focused on [analyzing] expenses. We were looking only at revenue." Even though Mutuals.com's sales were growing at an average of 113 percent a year, the company lost money consistently. Sapio decided to get serious about controlling costs. Every day at 4:37 P.M., just after the markets close, Sapio and his top managers gather to assess the company's financial results for that day, and each person is responsible for reporting one revenue item and one expense item. "Every line item on our financial statement has a name attached to it," says Sapio. Since 1999, the company's revenues have increased 190 percent and expenses are actually dropping about 4 percent a year, producing a solid net profit margin of 15 percent.*[15]

12. NET PROFIT TO EQUITY RATIO. The **net profit to equity ratio** (or *return on net worth ratio*) measures the owners' rate of return on investment. Because it reports the percentage of the owners' investment in the business that is being returned through profits annually, it

net profit to equity ratio—*measures the owners' rate of return on investment.*

is one of the most important indicators of a firm's profitability or a management's efficiency. The net profit to equity ratio is computed as follows:

$$\text{Net profit to equity} = \frac{\text{Net profit}}{\text{Owners' equity (or net worth)}}$$

$$= \frac{\$60,629}{\$267,655}$$

$$= 22.65\%$$

Sam is earning 22.65 percent on the money he has invested in this business.

This ratio compares profits earned during the accounting period with the amount the owner has invested in the business at that time. If this interest rate on the owners' investment is excessively low, some of this capital might be better employed elsewhere.

INTERPRETING BUSINESS RATIOS

Ratios are useful yardsticks when measuring a small firm's performance and can point out potential problems before they develop into serious crises. But calculating these ratios is not enough to ensure proper financial control. In addition to knowing how to calculate these ratios, entrepreneurs must understand how to interpret them and apply them to managing their businesses more effectively and efficiently.

A Company Example

*For instance, with the help of financial ratios, Linda Nespole, a top manager at **Hi-Shear Technology**, an aerospace subcontracting company in Torrance, California, noticed the company's performance beginning to slip. Given the signals her analysis revealed, she immediately devised a strategy to restore Hi-Shear's financial position, focusing first on cost-cutting measures. Simply charting the company's major costs led Nespole to discover leaking water pipes and inefficient lighting that were driving up costs unnecessarily. Some basic repairs lowered utility costs significantly, and a new, more efficient lighting system paid for itself in just six months. Nespole's cost-saving attitude took hold throughout the entire company, and soon all 125 employees were finding ways to keep costs down—from switching long-distance carriers to cutting the cost of its 401(k) retirement plan by 30 percent.[16]*

Not every business measures its success with the same ratios. In fact, key performance ratios vary dramatically across industries and even within different segments of the same

YOU Be the Consultant . . .

Yes, But Are Those Profits Real?

It was so easy to do . . . and so easy to justify. Then things began to get out of control.

After years at the helm of the high-flying Comptronix Corporation, an Alabama electronics company, William Hebding admitted that he and two other top officers had improperly inflated the company's profits by engaging in fraudulent accounting practices. The managers disclosed that they had recorded as capital assets some expenses such as salaries and start-up costs and had overstated Comptronix's inventory holdings to decrease its cost of goods sold. The reason was to shore up a weakening balance sheet and to give the illusion that profits were holding at the levels to which investors had grown accustomed. After the scandal broke, Mr. Hebding and his two accomplices were quickly fired.

As headlines tell tales of illegal activities at major companies such as Enron and WorldCom, small companies get caught up in the fray. Comptronix's story has become all too common as fierce competitive conditions exert increasing pressure on companies' profits. "When companies are desperate to stay afloat, inventory fraud is the easiest way to produce profits and dress up the balance sheet," says one accounting expert. The tactic is so simple, yet so effective, primarily because detecting fraudulent adjustments to inventory is so difficult, even for auditors at top accounting firms. In a typical audit, accountants take a small sample of the goods and raw materials in stock and compare an actual count with the company's inventory records. One auditor claims that it is extremely difficult, if not impossible, for an outside auditor to spot inventory fraud "if top management is directing it." One accounting expert reports that inventory fraud has increased fourfold within the past five years.

Measurement Specialties, a maker of electronic sensors, scales, and tire gauges, saw its shares pummeled when the once-profitable company surprised investors with a sudden loss of $3.8 million that put the company in technical default on $29 million worth of loans. Shortly afterward, First Union, Measurement Specialties' lead lender, expressed doubts about the company's management. After the Securities and Exchange Commission launched an investigation into the company's accounting practices, the board of directors ousted CEO Joseph Mallon but allowed him to stay on as chairman of the board. Measurement Specialties brought in a new chief financial officer, who determined that the company had been overvaluing its inventory to make its cost of goods sold appear lower than it was. In just two years, the value of the company's reported inventory had climbed 578 percent! Further investigation also revealed that the company had misclassified a $5.8 million short-term loan as accounts payable.

Some companies, feeling the same pressure to perform, are engaging in a common practice known as "earnings management," in which managers modify allowances for warranty costs or returned items or reclassify expenses into other categories. Aware that one quarter of unexpected financial results can ruin a company's prospects for future growth, some managers are tweaking their companies' financial reports. Their goal? To make their companies' financial statements look as good as possible for investors. "We're painting a picture for investors," says one Silicon Valley accountant. "They want to know that it's business as usual."

Another questionable practice among some companies involves recognizing barter revenue. For instance, a Web-based company might barter $10,000 worth of banner ads to another company for $10,000 worth of computer equipment. It would report the $10,000 as revenue and then amortize the cost of the equipment over a span of several years. Recorded this way, the transaction artificially inflates the company's sales revenue and makes its income statement look stronger than it really is.

Another frequent technique used by Web-based businesses is categorizing the costs of storing, packaging, and shipping inventory (known as "fulfillment costs") under "sales and marketing expenses" rather than recording them as part of "cost of goods sold" on the income statement. Shifting these fulfillment costs to a company's cost of goods sold would lower *significantly* its gross profit margin, a number that investors watch very closely. Even though recording these expenses as part of its cost of goods sold would produce a more accurate picture of a company's financial position, a lower gross profit margin would most likely dampen investors' enthusiasm for its stock. "Companies are under a lot of pressure to keep current [financial statements] looking good," rationalizes one accountant. "The business may be trending in one direction or the other, but we have to always make it look good. Companies work hard to protect [their] margins. It's all about painting the picture."

1. Refer to the balance sheet and income statement for Sam's Appliance Shop (Figures 10.1 and 10.2) and do some "creative accounting" of your own. Inflate the inventory values by a significant amount and see what happens to net worth and profits.

2. Recalculate the 12 key ratios for Sam's Appliance Shop. Compare the results. Which version would look better to a banker? Why?

3. Who loses when the managers of a company commit inventory fraud? What are the ethical implications of such practices?

4. What dangers does the practice of "earnings management" hold for companies and their investors?

Source: Adapted from Nathan Vardi, "Mismeasurement," *Forbes,* September 2, 2002, pp. 202–203; David Raymond, "The Number Runners," *Forbes ASAP,* April 3, 2000, pp. 128–129; Tim Kendall, "Show Me the Money," *Forbes ASAP,* November 29, 1999, p. 36; Lee Berton, "Tech Concerns Fudge Figures to Buoy Stocks," *Wall Street Journal,* May 19, 1994, pp. B1, B2; Lee Berton, "Convenient Fiction," *Wall Street Journal,* December 14, 1992, pp. A1, A4; Eileen Buckley, "No Accounting for Internet Accounting," *The Industry Standard,* April 10, 2000, p. 58; Elizabeth MacDonald, "Are Those Revenue for Real?" *Forbes,* May 29, 2000, pp. 108–110; Daniel Roth, "Under the Microscope," *FSB,* July/August 2002, pp. 52–55.

industry. Entrepreneurs must know and understand which ratios are most crucial to their companies' success and focus on monitoring and controlling those. Sometimes business owners develop ratios and measures that are unique to their own operations to help them achieve success. Known as **critical numbers**, these indicators measure key financial and operational aspects of a company's performance. When these critical numbers are headed in the right direction, a business is on track to achieve its objectives. The owner of a delivery company breaks his business into four categories and tracks critical numbers for each one. Every Monday morning, he gets a report comparing the previous week's critical numbers to the previous 28 weeks and the same week for the previous three years. "In 30 seconds, I can see what's going on in every part of my delivery business," he says. "I get another sheet for my storage business because I need to track a different set of numbers there, but the idea is the same." [17] Examples of critical numbers at other companies include:

critical numbers—*indicators that measure key financial and operational aspects of a company's performance; when these numbers are moving in the right direction, a business is on track to achieve its objectives.*

- The gross profit margin of a manufacturer of pallets.
- Sales per labor hour at a supermarket.
- The utilization ratio, billable hours as a percentage of total hours worked at an Internet service provider.
- The load factor, the percentage of seats filled with passengers, at an airline. [18]

Critical numbers may be different for two companies that compete in the same industry. The key is knowing what *your* company's critical numbers are, monitoring them, and then driving them in the right direction. That requires communicating the importance of these critical numbers to employees and giving them feedback on how well the business is achieving them.

A Company Example

For instance, one California retail chain established the daily customer count and the average sale per customer as its critical numbers. The company organized a monthly contest with prizes and posted charts tracking each store's performance. Soon employees were working hard to improve their stores' performances over the previous year and to outdo other stores in the chain. The healthy rivalry among stores boosted the company's performance significantly. [19]

Another valuable way to utilize ratios is to compare them with those of similar businesses in the same industry. By comparing the company's financial statistics to industry averages, an entrepreneur is able to locate problem areas and maintain adequate financial controls. "By themselves, these numbers are not that meaningful," says one financial expert on ratios, "but when you compare them to [those of] other businesses in your industry, they suddenly come alive because they put your operation in perspective." [20]

The principle behind calculating these ratios and comparing them to industry norms is the same as that of most medical tests in the health care profession. Just as a healthy person's blood pressure and cholesterol levels should fall within a range of normal values, so should a financially healthy company's ratios. A company cannot deviate too far from these normal values and remain successful for long. When deviations from "normal" do occur (and they will), a business owner should focus on determining the cause of the deviations (see Table 10.3). In some cases, such deviations are the result of sound business decisions, such as taking on inventory in preparation for the busy season, investing heavily in new technology, and others. In other instances, however, ratios that are out of the normal range for a particular type of business are indicators of what could become serious problems for a company. Properly used, ratio analysis can help owners identify potential problem areas in their businesses early on—*before* they become crises that threaten their very survival.

Several organizations regularly compile and publish operating statistics, including key ratios, that summarize the financial performance of many businesses across a wide range of industries. The local library should subscribe to most of these publications:

Robert Morris Associates. Established in 1914, Robert Morris Associates publishes its *Annual Statement Studies*, showing ratios and other financial data for more than 350 different industrial, wholesale, retail, and service categories.

Dun & Bradstreet, Inc. Since 1932, Dun & Bradstreet has published *Key Business Ratios*, which covers 22 retail, 32 wholesale, and 71 industrial business categories. Dun & Bradstreet also publishes *Cost of Doing Business*, a series of operating ratios compiled from the IRS's *Statistics of Income.*

TABLE 10.3
Putting Your Ratios to the Test

Source: Adapted from George M. Dawson, "Divided We Stand," *Business Start-Ups*, May 2000, p. 34.

When comparing your company's ratios to your industry's standards, ask the following questions:

1. Is there a significant difference in my company's ratio and the industry average?

2. If so, is this a *meaningful* difference?

3. Is the difference good or bad?

4. What are the possible causes of this difference? What is the most likely cause?

5. Does this cause require that I take action?

6. What action should I take to correct the problem?

Vest Pocket Guide to Financial Ratios. This handy guide, published by Prentice Hall, gives key ratios and financial data for a wide variety of industries.

Industry Spotlight. Published by Schonfeld & Associates, this publication, which can be customized for any one of more than 150 industries, contains financial statement data and key ratios from more than 95,000 tax returns. *Industry Spotlight* also provides detailed financial information for both profitable companies and those with losses.

Bank of America. Periodically, the Bank of America publishes many documents relating to small business management, including the *Small Business Reporter*, which details costs of doing business ratios.

Trade Associations. Virtually every type of business is represented by a national trade association, which publishes detailed financial data compiled from its membership. For example, owners of small supermarkets could contact the National Association of Retail Grocers or check the *Progressive Grocer*, its trade publication, for financial statistics relevant to their operations.

Government Agencies. Several government agencies (the Federal Trade Commission, Interstate Commerce Commission, Department of Commerce, Department of Agriculture, and Securities and Exchange Commission) offer a great deal of financial operating data on a variety of industries, although the categories are more general. In addition, the IRS annually publishes *Statistics of Income*, which includes income statement and balance sheet statistics compiled from income tax returns. The IRS also publishes the *Census of Business*, which gives a limited amount of ratio information.

What Do All of These Numbers Mean?

Learning to interpret financial ratios just takes a little practice! This section will show you how it's done by comparing the ratios already computed from the operating data for Sam's to those taken from *Robert Morris Associate's Annual Statement Studies*. (The industry median is the ratio falling exactly in the middle when sample elements are arranged in ascending or descending order.)

You Be the Consultant . . .

All Is Not Paradise in Eden's Garden: Part I

Joe and Kaitlin Eden, co-owners of Eden's Garden, a small nursery, lawn, and garden supply business, have just received their year-end financial statements from their accountant. At their last meeting with their accountant, Shelley Edison, three months ago, the Edens had mentioned that they seemed to be having trouble paying their bills on time. "Some of our suppliers have threatened to put us on 'credit hold,'" said Joe.

"I think you need to sit down with me very soon and let me show you how to analyze your financial statements so you can see what's happening in your business," Shelley told them at that meeting. Unfortunately, that was the beginning of Eden's Garden's busy season, and the Edens were so busy running the company that they never got around to setting a time to meet with Shelley.

"Now that business has slowed down a little, perhaps we should call Shelley and see what she can do to help us understand what our financial statements are trying to tell us," said Kaitlin.

"Right. Before it's too late to do anything about it . . ." said Joe, pulling out the following financial statements.

(continued on page 348)

Balance Sheet, Eden's Garden

Assets

Current Assets

Cash		$6,457
Accounts Receivable	$29,152	
Less Allowance for Doubtful Accounts	$3,200	$25,952
Inventory		$88,157
Supplies		$7,514
Prepaid Expenses		$1,856
Total Current Assets		$129,936

Fixed Assets

Land		$59,150
Buildings	$51,027	
Less Accumulated Depreciation	$2,061	$48,966
Autos	$24,671	
Less Accumulated Depreciation	$12,300	$12,371
Equipment	$22,375	
Less Accumulated Depreciation	$1,250	$21,125
Furniture and Fixtures	$10,295	
Less Accumulated Depreciation	$1,000	$9,295
Total Fixed Assets		$150,907
Intangibles (Goodwill)		$0
Total Assets		$280,843

Liabilities

Current Liabilities

Accounts Payable	$54,258
Notes Payable	$20,150
Credit Line Payable	$8,118
Accrued Wages/Salaries Payable	$1,344
Accrued Interest Payable	$1,785
Accrued Taxes Payable	$1,967
Total Current Liabilities	$87,622

Long-Term Liabilities

Mortgage	$72,846
Note Payable	$47,000
Total Long-Term Liabilities	$119,846

Owner's Equity

Joe and Kaitlin Edens, Capital	$73,375
Total Liabilities and Owner's Equity	$280,843

Income Statement, Eden's Garden

Net Sales Revenue*		$689,247

Cost of Goods Sold

Beginning Inventory, 1/1/xx	$78,271	
+ Purchases	$403,569	
Goods Available for Sale	$481,840	
– Ending Inventory, 12/31/xx	$86,157	
Cost of Goods Sold		$395,683
Gross Profit		$293,564

Operating Expenses

Advertising	$22,150	
Insurance	$9,187	
Depreciation		
Building	$26,705	
Autos	$7,895	
Equipment	$11,200	
Salaries	$116,541	
Uniforms	$4,018	
Repairs and Maintenance	$9,097	
Travel	$2,658	
Entertainment	$2,798	
Total Operating Expenses		$212,249

General Expenses

Utilities	$7,987	
Telephone	$2,753	
Professional Fees	$3,000	
Postage	$1,892	
Payroll Taxes	$11,589	
Total General Expenses		$27,221

Other Expenses

Interest Expense	$21,978	
Bad Check Expense	$679	
Miscellaneous Expense	$1,248	
Total Other Expenses		$23,905
Total Expenses		$263,375
Net Income		$30,189

*Credit sales represented $289,484 of this total.

1. Assume the role of Shelley Edison. Using the financial statements for Eden's Garden, calculate the 12 ratios covered in this chapter.

2. Do you see any ratios that, on the surface, look suspicious? Explain.

	Sam's Appliance Shop	**Industry Median**

Liquidity Ratios—tell whether or not a small business will be able to meet its maturing obligations as they come due.

1. Current ratio = 1.87:1 1.50:1

Sam's Appliance Shop falls short of the rule of thumb of 2:1, but its current ratio is above the industry median by a significant amount. Sam's should have no problem meeting its short-term debts as they come due. By this measure, the company's liquidity is solid.

2. Quick ratio =   0.63:1   0.50:1

Again, Sam's is below the rule of thumb of 1:1, but the company passes this test of liquidity when measured against industry standards. Sam's relies on selling inventory to satisfy short-term debt (as do most appliance shops). If sales slump, the result could be liquidity problems for Sam's. Sam should consider building a cash reserve as a precautionary measure.

Leverage Ratios—measure the financing supplied by a firm's owners against that supplied by its creditors and serve as a gauge of the depth of a company's debt.

3. Debt ratio =   0.68:1   0.64:1

Creditors provide 68 percent of Sam's total assets, very close to the industry median of 64 percent. Although Sam's does not appear to be overburdened with debt, the company might have difficulty borrowing additional money, especially from conservative lenders.

4. Debt to net worth ratio = 2.20:1   1.90:1

Sam's Appliance Shop owes creditors $2.20 for every $1.00 the owners have invested in the business (compared to $1.90 in debt to every $1.00 in equity for the typical business). Although this is not an exorbitant amount of debt, many lenders and creditors will see Sam's as "borrowed up." The company's borrowing capacity is limited because creditors' claims against the business are more than twice those of the owners. Sam should consider increasing his owner's equity in the business through retained earnings or by paying down some of the company's debt.

5. Times interest earned =   2.52:1   2.0:1

Sam's earnings are high enough to cover the interest payments on its debt by a factor of 2.52, slightly better than the typical firm in the industry, whose earnings cover its interest payments just two times. Sam's Appliance Shop has a cushion (although a small one) in meeting its interest payments.

Operating Ratios—evaluate the firm's overall performance and show how effectively it is putting its resources to work.

6. Average inventory turnover ratio = 2.05 times/year   4.0 times/year

Inventory is moving through Sam's at a very slow pace, *half* that of the industry median. The company has a problem with slow-moving items in its inventory and, perhaps, too much inventory. Which items are they, and why are they slow moving? Does Sam's need to drop some product lines? Sam must analyze his company's inventory and reevaluate his inventory control procedures.

7. Average collection period ratio = 50.0 days   19.3 days

Sam's Appliance Shop collects the average account receivable after 50 days (compared with the industry median of 19 days), more than two-and-a-half times longer. A more meaningful comparison is against Sam's credit terms; if credit terms are net 30 (or anywhere close to that), Sam's has a dangerous collection problem, one that drains cash and profits and demands *immediate* attention! The owner must implement the cash management procedures pertaining to accounts receivable mentioned in Chapter 8.

8. Average payable period ratio = 59.3 days   43 days

Sam's payables are nearly 40 percent slower than those of the typical firm in the industry. Stretching payables too far could seriously damage the company's credit rating, causing suppliers to cut off future trade credit. This could be a sign of cash flow problems or a sloppy accounts payable procedure. This problem also demands *immediate* attention. Once again, Sam must implement proper cash management procedures to resolve this problem.

9. Net sales to total assets ratio = 2.21:1   2.7:1

Sam's Appliance Shop is not generating enough sales, given the size of its asset base. This could be the result of a number of factors—improper inventory, inappropriate pricing, poor location, poorly trained sales personnel, and many others. The key is to find the cause . . . *fast!*

10. Net sales to working capital ratio = 5.86:1   10.8:1

Sam's generates just $5.86 in sales for every $1 in working capital, just over half of what the typical firm in the industry does. Given the previous ratio, the message is clear: Sam's simply is not producing an adequate level of sales. Improving the number of inventory turns will boost this ratio; otherwise, Sam's is likely to experience a working capital shortage soon.

Profitability Ratios—measure how efficiently a firm is operating and offer information about its bottom line.

11. Net profit on sales ratio = 3.24%   7.6%

   After deducting all expenses, 3.24 cents of each sales dollar remains as profit for Sam's—less than half the industry median. Sam's should check the company's gross profit margin and investigate its operating expenses, checking them against industry standards and looking for those that are out of balance.

12. Net profit to equity ratio = 22.65%   12.6%

   Sam's Appliance Shop's owners are earning 22.65 percent on the money they have invested in the business. This yield is nearly twice that of the industry median and, given the previous ratio, is more a result of the owners' relatively low investment in the business than an indication of its superior profitability. Sam is using O.P.M. (other people's money) to generate a profit in the business.

   When comparing ratios for their individual businesses to published statistics, small business owners must remember that the comparison is made against averages. The owner must strive to achieve ratios that are at least as good as these average figures. The goal should be to manage the business so that its financial performance is above average. As they compare their company's financial performance to those covered in the published statistics, they inevitably will discern differences between them. They should note those items that are substantially out of line from the industry average. However, a ratio that varies from the average does not *necessarily* mean that the small business is in financial jeopardy. Instead of making drastic changes in financial policy, entrepreneurs must explore *why* the figures are out of line.

<table>
<tr><td>**A Company Example**</td><td>*Greg Smith, CEO of **Petra Group**, a systems integrator with $1.5 million in annual sales, once gave little thought to comparing his company's financial performance against industry standards. Then Petra Group's sales flattened and Smith's company faced the prospect of losing money for the first time. Smith worked with an accounting firm, using information from Robert Morris Associates and a nonprofit organization that provides similar studies, to analyze his company's financial position. Comparing his numbers to industry statistics, Smith quickly saw that his payroll expenses for his 15-person company were too high to allow the company to generate a profit. He also discovered that Petra Group's debt ratio was too high. To restore his company's financial strength, Smith reduced his staff by two and began relying more on temporary employees and independent contractors. He realigned Petra Group's financing, reducing the company's line of credit from $100,000 to just $35,000. The analysis also revealed several strengths for the company. For instance, the company's average collection period was 36.5 days compared to an industry average of 73 days! Smith continues to use ratio comparisons to make key decisions for his company, and he credits the initial financial analysis with getting his company back on the track to profitability.*[21]</td></tr>
</table>

   In addition to comparing ratios to industry averages, owners should analyze their firms' financial ratios over time. By themselves, these ratios are "snapshots" of a company's financial postion at a single instant; but by examining these trends over time, an entrepreneur can detect gradual shifts that otherwise might go unnoticed until a financial crisis is looming (see Figure 10.8).

Learning Objective

6. Conduct a break-even analysis for a small company.

BREAK-EVEN ANALYSIS

Another key component of every sound financial plan is break-even analysis. A small company's **break-even point** is the level of operation (sales dollars or production quantity) at which it neither earns a profit nor incurs a loss. At this level of activity, sales revenue equals expenses—that is, the firm "breaks even." By analyzing costs and expenses, an entrepreneur can calculate the minimum level of activity required to keep the firm in operation. These techniques can then be refined to project the sales needed to generate the desired profit. Most potential lenders and investors will require entrepreneurs to prepare a break-even analysis to assist them in evaluating the earning potential of the new business. In addition to its being a simple, useful screening device for financial institutions, break-even analysis can also serve as a planning device for the small business owner. It occasionally will show a poorly prepared entrepreneur just how unprofitable a proposed business venture is likely to be.

break-even point—*the level of operation (sales dollars or production quantity) at which a company neither earns a profit nor incurs a loss.*

$$\text{Sales (\$)} = \frac{\text{Total fixed expenses} + \text{Desired net income}}{\text{Contribution margin expressed as a percentage of sales}}$$

$$= \frac{\$177,375 + \$80,000}{0.26}$$

$$= \$989,904$$

To achieve a net profit of $80,000 (before taxes), the Magic Shop must generate net sales of $989,904.

Break-Even Point in Units

Some small businesses may prefer to express the break-even point in units produced or sold instead of in dollars. Manufacturers often find this approach particularly useful. The following formula computes the break-even point in units:

$$\text{Break-even volume} = \frac{\text{Total fixed costs}}{\text{Sales price per unit} - \text{Variable cost per unit}}$$

For example, suppose that Trilex Manufacturing Company estimates its fixed costs for producing its line of small appliances at $390,000. The variable costs (including materials, direct labor, and factory overhead) amount to $12.10 per unit, and the selling price per unit is $17.50. So, Trilex computes its contribution margin this way:

$$\text{Contribution margin} = \text{Price per unit} - \text{Variable cost per unit}$$
$$= \$17.50 \text{ per unit} - \$12.10 \text{ per unit}$$
$$= \$5.40 \text{ per unit}$$

So, Trilex's break-even volume is as follows:

$$\text{Break-even volume (units)} = \frac{\text{Total fixed costs}}{\text{Per unit contribution margin}}$$

$$= \frac{\$390,000}{\$5.40 \text{ per unit}}$$

$$= 72,222 \text{ units}$$

To convert this number of units to break-even sales dollars, Trilex simply multiplies it by the selling price per unit:

YOU Be the Consultant . . .

Where Do We Break Even?

Anita Dawson is doing some financial planning for her music store. Based on her budget for the upcoming year, Anita is expecting net sales of $495,000. She estimates that cost of goods sold will be $337,000 and that other variable expenses will total $42,750. Using the past year as a guide, Anita anticipates fixed expenses of $78,100.

Anita recalls an earlier meeting with her accountant, who mentioned that her store had already passed the break-even point eight-and-one-half months into the year. She was pleased but really didn't know how the accountant came up with that calculation. Now Anita is considering expanding her store into a vacant building next to her existing location and taking on three new product lines. The company's cost structure would change, adding another $66,000 to fixed costs and $22,400 to variable expenses. Anita believes the expansion could generate additional sales of $102,000.

She wonders what she should do.

1. Calculate Anita's break-even point without the expansion plans. Draw a break-even chart.

2. Compute the break-even point assuming that Anita decides to expand.

3. Would you recommend that Anita expand her business? Explain.

$$\text{Break-even sales} = 72{,}222 \text{ units} \times \$17.50 \text{ per unit} = \$1{,}263{,}889$$

Trilex could compute the sales required to produce a desired profit by treating the profit as if it were a fixed cost:

$$\text{Sales (units)} = \frac{\text{Total fixed costs} + \text{Desired net income}}{\text{Per unit contribution margin}}$$

For example, if Trilex wanted to earn a $60,000 profit, its required sales would be:

$$\text{Sales (units)} = \frac{390{,}000 + 60{,}000}{5.40} = 83{,}333 \text{ units}$$

which would require 83,333 units × $17.50 per unit = $ 1,458,328 in sales.

Constructing a Break-Even Chart

The following outlines the procedure for constructing a graph that visually portrays the firm's break-even point (that point where revenues equal expenses):

Step 1. On the horizontal axis, mark a scale measuring sales volume in dollars (or in units sold or some other measure of volume). The break-even chart for the Magic Shop shown in Figure 10.9 uses sales volume in dollars because it applies to all types of businesses, departments, and products.

Step 2. On the vertical axis, mark a scale measuring income and expenses in dollars.

Step 3. Draw a fixed expense line intersecting the vertical axis at the proper dollar level parallel to the horizontal axis. The area between this line and the horizontal axis represents the firm's fixed expenses. On the break-even chart for the Magic Shop shown in Figure 10.9, the fixed expense line is drawn horizontally beginning at $177,375 (point *A*). Because this line is parallel to the horizontal axis, it indicates that fixed expenses remain constant at all levels of activity.

Step 4. Draw a total expense line that slopes upward beginning at the point where the fixed cost line intersects the vertical axis. The precise location of the total expense line is determined by plotting the total cost incurred at a particular sales volume. The total cost for a given sales level is found by the following formula:

Total expenses = Fixed expenses + Variable expenses expressed as a % of sales × Sales level

Arbitrarily choosing a sales level of $950,000, the Magic Shop's total costs would be as follows:

$$\text{Total expenses} = \$177{,}375 + (0.74 \times \$950{,}000)$$
$$= \$880{,}375$$

Thus, the Magic Shop's total cost is $880,375 at a net sales level of $950,000 (point *B*). The variable cost line is drawn by connecting points *A* and *B*. The area between the total cost line and the horizontal axis measures the total costs the Magic Shop incurs at various levels of sales. For example, if the Magic Shop's sales are $850,000, its total costs will be $806,375.

Step 5. Beginning at the graph's origin, draw a 45-degree revenue line showing where total sales volume equals total income. For the Magic Shop, point *C* shows that sales = income = $950,000.

Step 6. Locate the break-even point by finding the intersection of the total expense line and the revenue line. If the Magic Shop operates at a sales volume to the left of the break-even point, it will incur a loss because the expense line is higher than the revenue line over this range. This is shown by the triangular section labeled "Loss Area." On the other hand, if the firm operates at a sales volume to the right of the break-even point, it will earn a profit because the revenue line lies above the expense line over this range. This is shown by the triangular section labeled "Profit Area."

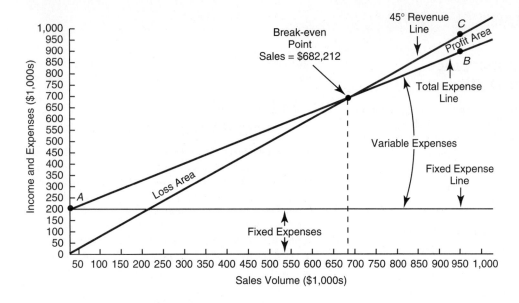

FIGURE 10.9 Break-Even Chart, The Magic Shop

Using Break-Even Analysis

Break-even analysis is a useful planning tool for the potential small business owner, especially when approaching potential lenders and investors for funds. It provides an opportunity for integrated analysis of sales volume, expenses, income, and other relevant factors. Break-even analysis is a simple, preliminary screening device for the entrepreneur faced with the business start-up decision. It is easy to understand and use. With just a few calculations, the small business owner can determine the effects of various financial strategies on the business operation. It is a helpful tool for evaluating the impact of changes in investments and expenditures.

A Company Example

For instance, before Steve Wynn opened the $630 million dollar **Mirage***, an opulent casino–hotel complex in Las Vegas, a cost–revenue analysis showed that the complex needed revenues of $365 million a year—$1 million a day—just to break even! Although many people doubted the casino-hotel's ability to generate that level of revenue, the Mirage has done so consistently. In its first year of operation, the Mirage brought in an average of $1.97 million each day![22]*

Although few small companies have break-even points as high as the Mirage's (much to the relief of entrepreneurs!), the break-even point can be just as useful. Greg Smith, for instance, knows that Petra Group's break-even point is $23,000 per week, and he compares sales to that figure every week.[23]

Break-even analysis does have certain limitations. It is too simple to use as a final screening device because it ignores the importance of cash flows. Also, the accuracy of the analysis depends on the accuracy of the revenue and expense estimates. Finally, the assumptions pertaining to break-even analysis may not be realistic for some businesses. Break-even calculations assume the following: Fixed expenses remain constant for all levels of sales volume; variable expenses change in direct proportion to changes in sales volume; and changes in sales volume have no effect on unit sales price. Relaxing these assumptions does not render this tool useless, however. For example, the owner could employ nonlinear break-even analysis using a graphical approach.

1. Understand the importance of preparing a financial plan.

■ Launching a successful business requires an entrepreneur to create a solid financial plan. Not only is such a plan an important tool in raising the capital needed to get a company off the ground, but it also is an essential ingredient in managing a growing business.

■ Earning a profit does not occur by accident; it takes planning.

2. Describe how to prepare the basic financial statements and use them to manage the small business.

■ Entrepreneurs rely on three basic financial statements to understand the financial conditions of their companies:

1. *The balance sheet.* Built on the accounting equation: Assets = Liabilities + Owner's equity (capital), it provides an estimate of the company's value on a particular date.

2. *The income statement.* This statement compares the firm's revenues against its expenses to determine its net profit (or loss). It provides information about the company's bottom line.

3. *The statement of cash flows.* This statement shows the change in the company's working capital over the accounting period by listing the sources and the uses of funds.

3. Create projected (pro forma) financial statements.

■ Projected financial statements are a basic component of a sound financial plan. They help the manager plot the company's financial future by setting operating objectives and by analyzing the reasons for variations from targeted results. Also, the small business in search of start-up funds will need these pro forma statements to present to prospective lenders and investors. They

also assist in determining the amount of cash, inventory, fixtures, and other assets the business will need to begin operation.

4. Understand the basic financial statements through ratio analysis.

■ The 12 key ratios described in this chapter are divided into four major categories: *liquidity ratios*, which show the small firm's ability to meet its current obligations; *leverage ratios*, which tell how much of the company's financing is provided by owners and how much by creditors; *operating ratios*, which show how effectively the firm uses its resources; and *profitability ratios*, which disclose the company's profitability.

■ Many agencies and organizations regularly publish such statistics. If there is a discrepancy between the small firm's ratios and those of the typical business, the owner should investigate the reason for the difference. A below average ratio does not necessarily mean that the business is in trouble.

5. Explain how to interpret financial ratios.

■ To benefit from ratio analysis, the small company should compare its ratios to those of other companies in the same line of business and look for trends over time.

■ When business owners detect deviations in their companies' ratios from industry standards, they should determine the cause of the deviations. In some cases, such deviations are the result of sound business decisions; in other instances, however, ratios that are out of the normal range for a particular type of business are indicators of what could become serious problems for a company.

6. Conduct a break-even analysis for a small company.

■ Business owners should know their firm's break-even point, the level of operations at which total revenues equal total costs; it is the point at which companies neither earn a profit nor incur a loss. Although just a simple screening device, break-even analysis is a useful planning and decision-making tool.

DISCUSSION QUESTIONS

1. Why is developing a financial plan so important to an entrepreneur about to launch a business?

2. How should a small business manager use the 12 ratios discussed in this chapter?

3. Outline the key points of the 12 ratios discussed in this chapter. What signals does each give the manager?

4. Describe the method for building a projected income statement and a projected balance sheet for a beginning business.

5. Why are pro forma financial statements important to the financial planning process?

6. How can break-even analysis help an entrepreneur planning to launch a business?

Launch *The Business Disc* and return to the section where Harry describes business record keeping and monthly sales projections. From the "Go To" menu, select "Events from PART 1 - B," and click on "Harry Talks About: Record Keeping." Summarize the various types of financial records you must keep for your business. Why is it important to keep these records? How long should you retain these records? Do you plan to maintain these records by hand or will you use a computer?

From the "Go To" menu, select "Events from PART 1 - B," and click on "Harry Discusses Monthly Sales Projections." Describe the factors that will influence the pattern of monthly sales for your business. How will the monthly sales for your business fluctuate? If you have not done so already, complete the sales projection form using this information. How accurate did your sales forecast prove to be? What gross profit margin are you earning in your type of business? How does it compare to other companies in this same business? (Review the information in Chapter 10 to determine how you can estimate this percentage and get comparison figures.)

Develop a list of your company's start-up costs. If you have not done so already, complete the "Start-up Cost Form" on *The Business Disc* using this information. Including Harry's suggestions for the first few months' expenses, how much money will you need to launch your business? How much of this amount can you provide?

What is depreciation? Complete the "Depreciation Form" on *The Business Disc*. Should you include depreciation on your cash flow statement? Explain.

BUSINESS PLAN PRO

Business PlanPro

The material from this chapter will enable you to complete sections 7.1, 7.2, 7.3, 7.5, and 7.6 in the "Financial Plan" section of *Business Plan Pro*.

These sections will allow you to conduct a break-even analysis for the business; produce a projected balance sheet; and lastly, conduct key ratio analysis that investors expect to see.

BEYOND THE CLASSROOM . . .

1. Ask the owner of a small business to provide your class with copies of the firm's financial statements (current or past).

   - Using these statements, compute the 12 key ratios described in this chapter.
   - Compare the firm's ratios with those of the typical firm in this line of business.
   - Interpret the ratios and make suggestions for operating improvements.
   - Prepare a break-even analysis for the owner.

2. Find a publicly held company of interest to you that provides its financial statements on the Web. You can conduct a Web search using the company's name or you can find lists of companies at the Securities and Exchange Commission's EDGAR database at www.sec.gov/cgi-bin/srch-edgar. Analyze the company's financial statements by calculating the 12 ratios covered in this chapter and compare these ratios to industry averages found in *Robert Morris Associates' Annual Statement Studies* or *Dun and Bradstreet's Cost of Doing Business* reports.

3. Download the annual report for a company that interests you. Calculate the 12 ratios discussed in this chapter and then compare them to the industry median using *Robert Morris Associates' Annual Statement Studies* or a similar resource. Do you spot any problem areas? Strengths? What recommendations can you make to improve the company's financial position? What do you project the company's future to be?

Chapter
11

Crafting a Winning Business Plan

The more concrete and complete the plan, the more likely it is to earn the respect of outsiders and their support in necessary financial matters.

—Jesse Werner

Good judgment comes from experience, and often experience comes from bad judgment.

—Rita Mae Brown

LEARNING OBJECTIVES

Upon completion of this chapter, you will be able to:

1. **EXPLAIN** why every entrepreneur should create a business plan and list the benefits of such a plan.

2. **DESCRIBE** the elements of a solid business plan.

3. **UNDERSTAND** the keys to making an effective business plan presentation.

4. **EXPLAIN** the "five Cs of credit" and why they are important to potential lenders and investors reading business plans.

Any entrepreneur who is in business or is about to launch a business needs a well-conceived and factually based business plan to increase the likelihood of success. For decades, research has proven that companies that engage in business planning outperform those that do not. Unfortunately, studies also show that small companies are especially lackadaisical in their approach to developing business plans. A recent survey by the market research company Willard & Shullman Group Ltd. found that only 14 percent of the small companies surveyed had created an annual written business plan. The study also reported that 60 percent of small companies had no written plans of any type! [1]

WHY DEVELOP A BUSINESS PLAN?

A **business plan** is a written summary of an entrepreneur's proposed business venture, its operational and financial details, its marketing opportunities and strategy, and its managers' skills and abilities. There is no substitute for a well-prepared business plan, and there are no shortcuts to creating one. The plan serves as an entrepreneur's road map on the journey toward building a successful business. It describes the direction the company is taking, what its goals are, where it wants to be, and how it's going to get there. The plan is written proof that the entrepreneur has performed the necessary research and has studied the business opportunity adequately. In short, the business plan is the entrepreneur's best insurance against launching a business destined to fail or mismanaging a potentially successful company.

A business plan serves three essential functions. First and most important, it guides the company's operations by charting its future course and devising a strategy for success. The plan provides a battery of tools—a mission statement, goals, objectives, market analysis, budgets, financial forecasts, target markets, strategies—to help entrepreneurs lead a company successfully. It gives managers and employees a sense of direction, but only if everyone is involved in creating, updating, or altering it. As more team members become committed to making the plan work, the plan takes on special meaning. It gives everyone targets to shoot for, and it provides a yardstick for measuring actual performance against those targets, especially in the crucial and chaotic start-up phase. Creating a plan also forces entrepreneurs to subject their ideas to the test of reality. Can this business idea actually produce a profit?

The second function of the business plan is to attract lenders and investors. Too often small business owners approach potential lenders and investors without having prepared to sell themselves and their business concept. Simply scribbling a few rough figures on a note pad to support a loan application is not enough. Applying for loans or attempting to interest investors without a solid business plan rarely attracts needed capital. Rather, the best way to secure the necessary capital is to prepare a sound business plan. Entrepreneurs must pay attention to detail because it is germane to their sales presentation to potential lenders and investors. In most cases, the quality of the firm's business plan weighs heavily in the decision to lend or invest funds. It is also potential lenders' and investors' first impression of the company and its managers. Therefore, the finished product should be highly polished and professional in both form and content.

A business plan must prove to potential lenders and investors that a venture will be able to repay loans and produce an attractive rate of return. Entrepreneur and author Neal Stephenson, who started several high-tech companies before focusing on a writing career, explains his experience writing a business plan:

> As I was trying to write my plan, something came into focus for me that should have been obvious from the very beginning. I was proposing to borrow a lot of money from strangers and gamble it on doing something. If it didn't work, these people would lose their money, which is a very sobering prospect. It really shakes you up and makes you think very hard about what it is you are doing. . . . We're using other people's real money, and those people could get hurt. [2]

Third, building a business the plan forces potential entrepreneurs to look at their business ideas in the harsh light of reality. It also requires owners to assess their ventures' chances of success more objectively. A well-assembled plan helps prove to outsiders that a business idea

Learning Objective

1. Explain why every entrepreneur should create a business plan and list the benefits of such a plan.

business plan—*a written summary of an entrepreneur's proposed business venture, its operational and financial details, its marketing opportunities and strategy, and its managers' skills and abilities.*

can be successful. To get external financing, an entrepreneur's plan must pass three tests with potential lenders and investors: (1) the reality test, (2) the competitive test, and (3) the value test.[3] The first two tests have both external and internal components as described next.

Reality Test

The external component of the reality test revolves around proving that a market for the product or service really does exist. It focuses on industry attractiveness, market niches, potential customers, market size, degree of competition, and similar factors. Entrepreneurs who pass this part of the reality test prove in the marketing portion of their business plans that there is strong demand for their business idea.

The internal component of the reality test focuses on the product or service itself. Can the company *really* build or provide it for the cost estimates in the business plan? Is it truly different from what competitors are already selling? Does it offer customers something of value?

Competitive Test

The external part of the competitive test evaluates the company's relative position to its key competitors. How do the company's strengths and weaknesses match up with those of the competition? Do these comparisons threaten the new company's success and survival?

The internal competitive test focuses on management's ability to create a company that will gain an edge over existing rivals. To pass this part of the competitive test, a plan must prove the quality, skill, and experience of the venture's management team. What other resources does the company have that can give it a competitive edge in the market?

Value Test

To convince lenders and investors to put their money into the venture, a business plan must prove to them that it offers a high probability of repayment or an attractive rate of return. Entrepreneurs usually see their businesses as good investments because they consider the intangibles of owning a business—gaining control over their own destinies, freedom to do what they enjoy, and others; lenders and investors, however, look at a venture in colder terms: dollar-for-dollar returns. A plan must convince lenders and investors that they will earn an attractive return on their money.

The same business basics that investors have employed for decades to evaluate the financial potential of a new venture are still valid today. Gone are the valuations of new ventures that were based on market assumptions that were, at best, flawed and overly optimistic. The collapse of the dot-coms at the end of the twentieth century proved that "smoke and mirrors" do not replace financial basics.

Today earning projections based on real numbers are important. The business model must hold water, so to speak. The venture must have a long-term strategic vision and a practical focus on operations. Entrepreneurs must be able to clearly demonstrate their knowledge of:

1. Supplies and all related cost of goods
2. Unit labor cost
3. Market-determined selling price and gross profit margins
4. Break-even point[4]

Sometimes the greatest service a business plan provides an entreprenur is the realization that "it just won't work." The time to find out a potential business idea won't succeed is in the planning stages *before* an entrepreneur commits significant resources to a venture. In other cases it reveals important problems to overcome before launching a company.

The real value in preparing a business plan is not so much in the plan itself as it is in the process an entrepreneur goes through to create the plan. Although the finished product is useful, the process of building a plan requires an entrepreneur to subject his idea to an objective, critical evaluation. What the entrepreneur learns about his company, its target market, its financial requirements, and other factors can be essential to making the venture a success. This process allows the entrepreneur to replace "I think" with "I know" and to make mistakes on paper, which is much cheaper than making them in reality. Simply put, building a business plan reduces the risk and uncertainty in launching a company by teaching the entrepreneur to do it the right way!

Because a business plan is a reflection of its creator, it should demonstrate that the entrepreneur has thought seriously about the venture and what will make it succeed. Preparing a solid plan demonstrates that the entrepreneur has taken the time to commit the idea to paper. Building a plan also forces the entrepreneur to consider both the positive and the negative aspects of the business. A detailed and thoughtfully developed business plan makes a positive first impression on those who read it. In most cases, potential lenders and investors read a business plan before they ever meet with the entrepreneur behind it. Sophisticated investors will not take the time to meet with an entrepreneur whose business plan fails to reflect a serious investment of time and energy. They know that an entrepreneur who lacks this discipline to develop a good business plan likely lacks the discipline to run a business.

The business plan should reflect the fire and passion an entrepreneur has for the venture. For this reason an entrepreneur cannot allow others to prepare the business plan for him because outsiders cannot understand the business nor envision the proposed company as well as he can. The entrepreneur is the driving force behind the business idea and is the one who can best convey the vision and the enthusiasm he has for transforming that idea into a successful business. Also, because the entrepreneur will make the presentation to potential lenders and investors, he must understand every detail of the business plan. Otherwise, an entrepreneur cannot present it convincingly and in most cases the financial institution or investor will reject it. Investors want to feel confident that an entrepreneur has realistically evaluated the risk involved in the new venture and has a strategy for addressing it. And, as you can expect, they also want to see proof that a business will be profitable and produce a reasonable rturn on their investment.

Perhaps the best way to understand the need for a business plan is to recognize the validity of the "two-thirds rule," which says that only two-thirds of the entrepreneurs with a sound and viable new business venture will find financial backing. Those that do find financial backing will only get two-thirds of what they initially requested, and it will take them two-thirds longer to get the financing than they anticipated.[5] The most effective strategy for avoiding the two-thirds rule is to build a business plan!

THE ELEMENTS OF A BUSINESS PLAN

Smart entrepreneurs recognize that every business plan is unique and must be tailor-made. They avoid the off-the-shelf, "cookie-cutter" approach that produces look-alike plans. The elements of a business plan may be standard, but the way an entrepreneur tells her story should be unique and reflect her personal excitement about the new venture. If this is a first attempt at writing a business plan, it may be very helpful to seek the advice of individuals with experience in this process. Accountants, business professors, attorneys, and consultants with Small Business Development Centers can be excellent sources of advice in creating and refining a plan (for a list of Small Business Development Center locations, see the Small Business Administration's SBDC Web page at www.sba.gov/SBDC). Entrepreneurs also can use business planning software available from several companies to create their plans. Some of the most popular programs include Business Plan Pro* (Palo Alto Software), BizPlan Builder (Jian Tools), PlanMaker (Power Solutions for Business), and Plan Write (Business Resources Software). These planning packages help entrepreneurs organize the material they have researched and gathered, and they provide helpful tips on plan writing and templates for creating financial statements. These planning packages produce professional-looking business plans, but entrepreneurs who use them face one drawback: The plans they produce often look the same, as if they came from the same mold. That can be a turn-off for professional investors, who see hundreds of business plans each year.

Initially, the prospect of writing a business plan may appear to be overwhelming. Many entrepreneurs would rather launch their companies and "see what happens" than invest the

---

*Business Plan Pro is available at a nominal cost with this textbook.

necessary time and energy defining and researching their target markets, defining their strategies, and mapping out their finances. After all, building a plan is hard work! However, it is hard work that pays many dividends—not all of them immediately apparent. Entrepreneurs who invest their time and energy building plans are better prepared to face the hostile environment in which their companies will compete than those who do not. Earlier, we said that a business plan is like a road map that guides an entrepreneur on the journey to building a successful business. If you were making a journey to a particular destination through unfamiliar, harsh, and dangerous territory, would you rather ride with someone equipped with a road map and a trip itinerary or with someone who didn't believe in road maps or in planning trips, destinations, and layovers? Although building a business plan does not *guarantee* success, it *does* raise an entrepreneur's chances of succeeding in business.

A business plan typically ranges from 25 to 50 pages in length. Shorter plans usually are too sketchy to be of any value, and those much longer than this run the risk of never getting used or read! This section explains the most common elements of a business plan. However, entrepreneurs must recognize that, like every business venture, every business plan is unique. An entrepreneur should view the following elements as a starting point for building a plan and should modify them as needed to better tell the story of his new venture.

The Executive Summary

To summarize the presentation to each potential financial institution or investor, the entrepreneur should write an executive summary. It should be concise—a maximum of two pages—and should summarize all of the relevant points of the business venture. The executive summary is a synopsis of the entire plan, capturing its essence in a capsulized form. It should explain the basic business model and briefly describe the owners and key employees, target market(s), and financial highlights (e.g., sales projections, dollar amount requested, how the funds will be used, and how and when any loans will be repaid).

The executive summary is a written version of what is known as "the elevator pitch." Imagine yourself on an elevator with a potential lender or investor. Only the two of you are on the elevator, and you have that person's undivided attention for the duration of the ride, but the building is not very tall! To convince the investor that your business is a great investment, you must boil your message down to its essence—key points that you can communicate in just a matter of one or two minutes.

The executive summary *must* capture the reader's attention. If it misses the mark, the chances of the remainder of the plan being read are minimal. A well-developed, coherent summary introducing the financial proposal establishes a favorable first impression of the entrepreneur and the business and can go a long way toward obtaining financing. Although the executive summary is the first part of the business plan, it should be the last section written.

Mission Statement

As you learned in Chapter 3, a mission statement expresses in words an entrepreneur's vision for what her company is and what it is to become. It is the broadest expression of a company's purpose and defines the direction in which it will move. It anchors a company in reality and serves as the thesis statement for the entire business plan.

Company History

The owner of an existing small business should prepare a brief history of the operation, highlighting the significant financial and operational events in the company's life. This section should describe when and why the company was formed, how it has evolved over time, and what the owner envisions for the future. It should highlight the successful accomplishment of past objectives such as developing prototypes, earning patents, achieving market-share targets, or securing long-term customer contracts. This section also should convey the firm's image in the marketplace.

FIGURE 11.1 The Relationship Among Mission, Goals, and Objectives

Mission → Goals → Objectives

Business and Industry Profile

To acquaint lenders and investors with the industry in which a company competes, an entrepreneur should describe it in the business plan. This section should begin with a statement of the company's general business goals and a narrower definition of its immediate objectives. Together they should spell out what the business plans to accomplish, how, when, and who will do it. **Goals** are broad, long-range statements of what a company plans to achieve in the future that guide its overall direction and express its *raison d'être*. In other words, they address the question: "Why am I in business?" Answering such a basic question appears to be obvious, but, in fact, many entrepreneurs cannot define the basis of their businesses.

Objectives, on the other hand, are short-term, specific performance targets that are attainable, measurable, and controllable. Every objective should reflect some general business goal and include a technique for measuring progress toward its accomplishment. To be meaningful, an objective must have a time frame for achievement. Both goals and objectives should relate to the company's basic mission (see Figure 11.1).

When summarizing a small company's background, an entrepreneur should describe the present state of the art in the industry and what she will need to succeed in the market segment in which her business will compete. She should then identify the current applications of the product or service in the market and include projections for future applications.

This section should provide the reader with an overview of the industry or market segment in which the new venture will operate. Industry data such as market size, growth trends, and the relative economic and competitive strength of the major firms in the industry all set the stage for a better understanding of the viability of the new product or service. Strategic issues such as ease of market entry and exit, the ability to achieve economies of scale or scope, and the existence of cyclical or seasonal economic trends further help readers evaluate the new venture. This part of the plan also should describe significant industry trends and an overall outlook for its future. Information about the evolution of the industry helps the reader comprehend its competitive dynamics. The *U.S. Industrial Outlook Handbook* is an excellent

goals—*broad, long-range statements of what a company plans to achieve in the future that guide its overall direction and express its raison d'être.*

objectives—*short-term, specific performance targets that are attainable, measurable, and controllable.*

"Our old mission statement was more eloquent, and dignified, but not nearly as effective."

reference that profiles a variety of industries and offers projections for future trends in them. Another useful resource of industry and economic information is the *Summary of Commentary on Current Economic Conditions*, more commonly known as the *Beige Book*. Published eight times a year by the Federal Reserve, the *Beige Book* provides detailed statistics and trends in key business sectors and in the overall economy. It offers valuable information on topics ranging from tourism and housing starts to consumer spending and wage rates. Entrepreneurs can find this wealth of information at their fingertips on the Web at the Federal Reserve's Web site.

This section of the plan also should describe the existing and anticipated profitability of the industry. Any significant entry or exit of firms or consolidations and mergers should be discussed in terms of their impact on the competitive behavior of the market. The entrepreneur also should mention any events that have significantly affected the industry in the past 10 years.

Business Strategy

An even more important part of the business plan is the owner's view of the strategy needed to meet—and beat—the competition. In the previous section, the entrepreneur defined *where* he wants to take his business by establishing goals and objectives. This section addresses the question of *how* to get there—business strategy. Here an entrepreneur must explain how he plans to gain a competitive edge in the market and what sets the business apart from the competition. He should comment on how he plans to achieve business goals and objectives in the face of competition and government regulation and should identify the image that the business will try to project. An important theme in this section is what makes the company unique in the eyes of its customers. One of the quickest routes to business failure is trying to sell "me-too" products or services that offer customers nothing new, better, bigger, faster, or different. The foundation for this part of the business plan comes from the material in Chapter 3, "Strategic Management and the Entrepreneur."

This segment of the business plan should outline the methods the company can use to meet the key success factors cited earlier. If, for example, a strong, well-trained sales force is considered critical to success, the owner must devise a plan of action for assembling one.

Description of Firm's Product/Service

An entrepreneur should describe the company's overall product line, giving an overview of how customers use its goods or services. Drawings, diagrams, and illustrations may be required if the product is highly technical. It is best to write product and service descriptions so that laypeople can understand them. A statement of a product's position in the product life cycle might also be helpful. An entrepreneur should include a summary of any patents, trademarks, or copyrights protecting the product or service from infringement by competitors. Finally, it is helpful provide an honest of comparison of the company's products or services with those of competitors, citing specific advantages or improvements that make the company's goods or services unique and indicating plans for creating the next generation of goods and services that will evolve from the present product line.

The emphasis of this section should be on defining the *benefits* customers get by purchasing the company's products or services, rather than on just a "nuts and bolts" description of the *features* of those products or services. A **feature** is a descriptive fact about a product or service ("an ergonomically designed, more comfortable handle"). A **benefit** is what a customer gains from the product or service feature ("fewer problems with carpal tunnel syndrome and increased productivity"). Advertising legend Leo Burnett once said, "Don't tell the people how good you make the goods; tell them how good your goods make them."[6] This part of the plan must describe how a business will transform tangible product or service *features* into important, but often intangible, customer *benefits*—for example, lower energy bills, faster access to the Internet, less time writing checks to pay monthly bills, greater flexibility in building floating structures, shorter time required to learn a foreign language, or others. Remember: Customers buy benefits, *not* product or service features.

Manufacturers should describe their production process, strategic raw materials required, sources of supply they will use, and their costs. They should also summarize the production

feature—*a descriptive fact about a product or service.*

benefit—*what a customer gains from the product or service.*

method and illustrate the plant layout. If the product is based on a patented or proprietary process, a description (including diagrams, if necessary) of its unique market advantages is helpful. It is also helpful to explain the company's environmental impact and how the entrepreneur plans to mitigate any negative environmental consequences the process may produce.

*For example, as the value of the automobiles Americans drive increases, so does their desire to have their cars look "showroom" clean. There are 75,000 car washes in the United States varying in service and quality. Matthew Lieb and Chris Jones created **SWASH** as a state-of-the-art, no-muss, no-fuss, stand-alone entity where customers can select the services the equipment will provide and remain in their vehicles. All services are delivered by software-controlled equipment that never lays a brush on the car and the process is environmentally friendly from start to finish.*

Stressing these types of facts to investors can help differentiate a company's product or process from competitors.

Marketing Strategy

One crucial concern of entrepreneurs and the potential lenders and investors who finance their companies is whether or not there is a real market for the proposed good or service. Every entrepreneur must, therefore, describe the company's target market and its characteristics. Defining the target market and its potential is one of the most important—and most challenging—parts of building a business plan. Creating a successful business depends on an entrepreneur's ability to attract real customers who are willing and able to spend real money to buy its products or services. Perhaps the worst marketing error an entrepreneur can commit is failing to define his target market and trying to make his business "everything to everybody." Small companies usually are much more successful by focusing on a specific market niche where they can excel at meeting customers' special needs or wants.

One new and evolving target market for small businesses is teenagers. By 2010, the number of teens will grow to 35 million, which will make them a larger target market than the much-touted baby boomers. According to the U.S. Department of Labor, the average teenager gets a staggering $50 a week in disposable income from parents, and market research shows that teens are willing to spend what they have. This group is often characterized as being the product of dual-income parents who provide their offspring with more cash than attention. Adolescence has always been a period of exploration and rebellion that results in unique attire, haircuts, and other visible signs of differences from those of their parents' generation. Today, fueled with cash and credit cards, this target market has attracted attention as their appetite for the external trappings that help them achieve peer approval results in a dizzying cycle of new "hot trend" purchases. Psychologists, manufacturers, and retailers alike analyze this market segment in hopes of gaining an edge in the accurate prediction of what the market will want.

Successful entrepreneurs know that a solid understanding of their target markets is the first step in building an effective marketing strategy. Indeed, every other aspect of marketing depends on having a clear picture of their customers and their unique needs and wants.

Questions this part of the business plan should address include: Who are the most promising customers or prospects? What are their characteristics? Where do they live? What do they buy? Why do they buy? When do they buy? What expectations do they have about the product or service? Will the business focus on a niche? How does the company seek to position itself in its market(s)?

Proving that a profitable market exists involves two steps: showing customer interest and documenting market claims.

Although many teens get either no allowance or an allowance in the $10 to $20 range, the amount of money that many parents actually give over the course of the week is substantially higher. Spending by this demographic group is quickly closing in on $200 billion a year.

Courtesy of Getty Images, Inc.-Taxi

YOU Be the consultant . . .

Are All Dot-Com Ventures Dead?

The market shakeout among the dot-coms in recent years has produced a negative perception about the financial viability of all new dot-com ventures. Is this negativity warranted, or should any new business venture be judged on its business model and forecasted financial outcomes? Today's sophisticated investors recognize that e-commerece still is in its infancy and that entrepreneurs are still trying to work out business models that will produce success in such a fast-paced, dynamic environment. A plan sporting elaborate descriptions of target customers and spreadsheets with detailed financial projections five years into the future simply is not that credible. Investors know that most e-commerce companies will fail, a situation that is not likely to change in the near future.

The financial section of an e-business plan also is much shorter than in a traditional business plan. Rather than producing reams of spreadsheets showing the outcomes of multiple scenarios many years into the future, successful Internet entrepreneurs are sticking with perhaps one or two scenarios projected just two years out. Investors recognize that few e-businesses generate sufficient revenue to make a profit, especially in the early years when development costs are so high. As e-commerce matures and becomes more stable, investors will expect more traditional types of financial forecasts.

Investors also demand less detail in the section of the plan that describes a company's target market. Normally, an entrepreneur includes in a traditional plan a thorough analysis of the market and the characteristics of the customers that comprise it. A plan for an e-business, however, recognizes that markets and the techniques for reaching customers effectively change rapidly in e-commerce. Investors want entrepreneurs behind Internet companies to summarize the market opportunity and its potential for growth.

Two areas in an e-business plan require more attention than in a traditional plan: the explanation of the business concept and the description of the management team. Before investors put any money into an e-business, they must have a crystal-clear understanding of it and how it is superior to any current business model. "You had better have a very simple way to powerfully differentiate your company," advises venture capitalist Guy Kawasaki. E-commerce plans include definitions of industry-specific terms, diagrams of technology, hyperlinks to Web sites, and charts showing how a company works.

Just as in a traditional business, investors evaluating an e-commerce plan are looking for a skilled, experienced management team that can prove it has the wherewithal to launch a company and manage it through the tremulous start-up phase. "Launching an e-business is not for the weak-minded nor the weak-hearted," says one expert. Investors are especially interested in how the company will draw customers to its Web site and how it will handle and fulfill orders from them once they arrive. An e-business plan, therefore, should contain a Web site map that shows how all of the pages on the site will look and be linked to one another. Presentations can also include a DVD version of the Web site's characteristics or a live hook-up that shows the investor exactly what the customer will experience when using the site. This can be a bit risky—the worst that can happen sometimes will happen when "going live" in front of a group of potential investors! A plan should also describe how the company's back office, the systems that take over once a customer places an order on the site, will work and the volume of traffic it can handle.

Just as with a traditional business plan, the executive summary in an e-business plan is extremely important because it is the first section investors read. If it fails to capture investors' attention and interest, the probability that they will read the rest of the plan is miniscule.

1. In what ways are a plan for a traditional business and one for an e-business similar? Different?

2. Suppose that a good friend comes to you and announces that he is going to launch an Internet business but needs financing to do it. You ask about his business plan. "I don't have the time to write a business plan," he says. What do you tell him?

3. Assume that you convince your friend that he should write a business plan. He asks your advice on how to write the plan. What advice would you offer?

Sources: Adapted from Mark Henricks, "Short and Sweet," *Business Start-Ups,* May 2000, p. 20; Joel Kirtzman, "The New Age of Business Plans," *Fortune,* September 27, 2000, p. 262 (N); Robert Calem, Sherly Nance-Nash, Michael Scully, and Carlye Adler, "Napkin Plans . . . The Main Street Mayor . . . Silicon Goes Celluloid," *Fortune,* May 24, 1999, p. 296 (I); Guy Kawaski, "Needbucks.com" *Forbes,* January 10, 2000, p. 1998.

SHOWING CUSTOMER INTEREST.   An entrepreneur must be able to prove that her target customers need or want her good or service and are willing to pay for it. This phase is relatively straightforward for a company with an existing product or service but can be quite difficult for one with only an idea or a prototype. In this case the entrepreneur might offer the prototype to several potential customers in order to get written testimonials and evaluations to show to investors. Or the owner could sell the product to several customers at a discount. This would prove that there are potential customers for the product and would allow demonstrations of the product in operation. Getting a product into customers' hands is also an excellent way to get valuable feedback that can lead to significant design improvements and increased sales down the road.

DOCUMENTING MARKET CLAIMS.   Too many business plans rely on vague generalizations such as, "This market is so huge that if we get just 1 percent of it, we will break even in eight months." Such statements are not backed by facts and usually reflect an entrepreneur's unbridled optimism. In most cases, they are also unrealistic! Market share determination is not obtained by a "shoot from the hip" generalization; to the contrary, sophisticated investors expect to be shown the detailed research that supports the claims made about the potential of the market.

Entrepreneurs must support claims of market size and growth rates with *facts*, and that requires market research. Results of market surveys, customer questionnaires, and demographic studies lend credibility to an entrepreneur's frequently optimistic sales projections. (Refer to the market research techniques and resources in Chapter 6.) Many entrepreneurs build financial models for their potential businesses by applying facts and formulas based on data available from the relevent trade or professional associations, local market data, and, with the assistance of the Small Business Development Center, data that are available in independent federal databases or from sources such as Dun & Bradstreet or Robert Morris Associates.

Quantitative market data are important because they form the basis for all of the company's financial projections in the business plan. One technique involves **business prototyping**, in which entrepreneurs test their business models on a small scale before committing serious resources to a business that might not work. Business prototyping recognizes that every business idea is a hypothesis that needs to be tested before an entrepreneur takes it to full scale. If the test supports the hypothesis and its accompanying assumptions, it is time to launch a company. If the prototype flops, the entrepreneur scraps the business idea with only minimal losses and turns to the next idea.

The World Wide Web makes business prototyping practical, fast and easy.

> **business prototyping**—*a process in which entrepreneurs test their business models on a small scale before committing serious resources to a business that may or may not work.*

> **A Company Example**
>
> *For instance, after successfully selling antiques on the online auction site EBay, Nona Cunane decided to test the market for products she was more interested in: upscale designer clothing for women. When her business prototype proved to be successful on EBay, Cunane launched an online company of her own, **Stylebug.com**. The Bear, Delaware-based business sells more than $800,000 of women's clothing a year, about half of it still on EBay.[7]*

An effective market analysis also should identify the following:

Advertising: Once an entrepreneur defines her company's target market, she can design a promotion and advertising campaign to reach those customers most effectively and efficiently. Which media are most effective in reaching the target market? How will they be used? How much will the promotional campaign cost? How can the company benefit from publicity?

Market size and trends: How large is the potential market? Is it growing or shrinking? Why? Are the customer's needs changing? Are sales seasonal? Is demand tied to another product or service?

Location: For many businesses, choosing the right location is a key success factor. For retailers, wholesalers, and service companies, the best location usually is one that is most convenient to their target customers. By combining census data and other market research with digital mapping software, entrepreneurs can locate sites with the greatest concentrations of their customers and the least interference from competitors. Which specific sites put the company in the path of its target customers? Do zoning regulations restrict the use of the site? For manufacturers, the location issue often centers on finding a site near key raw materials or near major customers. Using demographic reports and market research to screen potential sites takes the guesswork out of choosing the "right" location for a business.

Pricing: What does the product or service cost to produce or deliver? What is the company's overall pricing strategy? What image is the company trying to create in the market? Will the planned price support the company's strategy and desired image? (See Figure 11.2.) Can it produce a profit? How does the planned price compare to those of similar products or services? Are customers willing to pay it? What price tiers exist in the market? How sensitive are customers to price changes? Will the business sell to customers on credit? Will it accept credit cards?

Distribution: How will the product or service be distributed? What is the average sale? How many sales calls does it take to close a sale? What are the incentives for salespeople? What can the company do to make it as easy as possible for customers to buy?

This portion of the plan also should describe the channels of distribution that the business will use (mail, in-house sales force, sales agent, retailers). The entrepreneur should summarize the firm's overall pricing and promotion strategies, including the advertising budget, media used, and publicity efforts. The company's warranties and guarantees for its products and services should be addressed as well.

Competitor Analysis

An entrepreneur should discuss the new venture's competition. Failing to assess competitors realistically makes entrepreneurs appear to be poorly prepared, naive, or dishonest, especially to potential lenders and investors. This section of the plan should include an analysis of each significant competitor. Entrepreneurs who believe they have no competitors are only fooling themselves. Gathering information on competitors' market shares, products, and strategies is usually not difficult. Trade associations, customers, industry journals, marketing representatives, and sales literature are valuable sources of data. This section of the plan should focus on demonstrating that the entrepreneur's company has an advantage over its competitors. Who are the company's key competitors? What are their strengths and weaknesses? What are their strategies? What images do they have in the marketplace? How successful are they? What distinguishes the entrepreneur's product or service from others already on the market, and how will these differences produce a competitive edge?

Description of the Management Team

The most important factor in the success of a business venture is the quality of its management, and financial officers and investors weigh heavily the ability and experience of the firm's managers in their financing decisions. Thus, a plan should describe the qualifications of business officers, key directors, and any person with at least 20 percent ownership in the company. *Remember: Lenders and investors prefer experienced managers.* A management team with industry experience and a proven record of success goes a long way in adding credibility to the new venture.

Résumés in a plan should summarize an individual's education, work history (emphasizing managerial responsibilities and duties), and relevant business experience. When compiling a personal profile, an entrepreneur should review the primary reasons for small business failure (refer to Chapter 1) and show how her team will use its skills and experience to avoid them. Entrepreneurs should not cover up previous business failure, however. Failing in business no

FIGURE 11.2 The Link Between Pricing Perceived Quality and Company Image

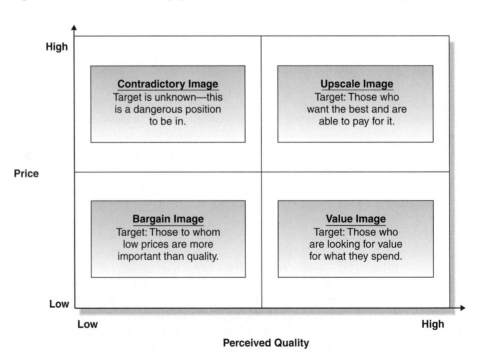

longer has a terrible stigma attached to it. In fact, many investors are suspicious of entrepreneurs who have never experienced a business failure.

When considering investing in a business, lenders and investors look for the experience, talent, and integrity of the people who will breathe life into the plan. This portion of the plan should show that the company has the right people organized in the right fashion for success. One experienced private investor advises entrepreneurs to remember the following:

- Ideas and products don't succeed; people do. Show the strength of your management team. A top-notch management team with a variety of proven skills is crucial.

- Show the strength of key employees and how you will retain them. Most small companies cannot pay salaries that match those at large businesses, but stock options and other incentives can improve employee retention.

- A board of directors or advisors consisting of industry experts lends credibility and can enhance the value of the management team.[8]

Plan of Operation

To complete the description of the business, the owner should construct an organizational chart identifying the business's key positions and the personnel occupying them. Assembling a management team with the right stuff is difficult, but keeping it together until the company is established may be harder. Thus, the entrepreneur should describe briefly the steps taken to encourage important officers to remain with the company. Employment contracts, shares of ownership, and perks are commonly used to keep and motivate such employees.

Finally, a description of the form of ownership (partnership, joint venture, S corporation, or LLC) and of any leases, contracts, and other relevant agreements pertaining to the business is helpful.

Forecasted or Pro Forma Financial Statements

One of the most important sections of the business plan is an outline of the proposed company's financial statements—the "dollars and cents" of the proposed venture. For an existing business, lenders and investors use past financial statements to judge the health of the company and its ability to repay loans or generate adequate returns; therefore, an owner should supply copies of the firm's financial statements from the past three years. Ideally, these statements should be audited by a certified public accountant because most financial institutions prefer that extra reliability, although a financial review of the statements by an accountant sometimes may be acceptable.

Whether assembling a plan for an existing business or for a start-up, an entrepreneur should carefully prepare monthly projected (or pro forma) financial statements for the operation for the next year (and for two or three more years by quarter) using past operating data, published statistics, and judgment to derive three sets of forecasts of the income statement, balance sheet, cash budget (always!), and schedule of planned capital expenditures. (Refer to Chapter 10, "Creating a Successful Financial Plan," for a discussion on creating projected financial statements.) The forecasts should cover pessimistic, most likely, and optimistic conditions to reflect the uncertainty of the future. When in doubt, be up front and include some contingencies for any costs that you are unsure about.

It is essential that all three sets of forecasts be realistic. Entrepreneurs must avoid the tendency to "fudge the numbers" just to make their businesses look good. Lenders and investors compare these projections against published industry standards and can detect unrealistic forecasts. In fact, some venture capitalists automatically discount an entrepreneur's financial projections by as much as 50 percent. Upon completing the forecasts, an entrepreneur should perform a break-even analysis and a ratio analysis on the projected figures.

It is also important to include a statement of the *assumptions* on which these financial projections are based. Potential lenders and investors want to know how an entrepreneur derived forecasts for sales, cost of goods sold, operating expenses, accounts receivable, collections, accounts payable, inventory, taxes, and other items. Spelling out such assumptions gives a plan more credibility and reduces the tendency to include overly optimistic estimates of sales growth and profit margins. In addition to providing valuable information to potential lenders and investors, projected financial statements help an entrepreneur run her business more effectively and more efficiently. They establish important targets for financial performance and make it easier for an entrepreneur to maintain control over routine expenses and capital expenditures.

The Loan or Investment Proposal

The loan or investment proposal section of the business plan should state the purpose of the financing, the amount requested, and the plans for repayment or, in the case of investors, an attractive exit strategy. When describing the purpose of the loan or investment, an entrepreneur must specify the planned use of the funds. General requests for funds using terms such as "for modernization," "working capital," or "expansion" are unlikely to win approval. Instead, entrepreneurs should use more detailed descriptions such as "to modernize production facilities by purchasing five new, more efficient looms that will boost productivity by 12 percent" or "to rebuild merchandise inventory for fall sales peak, beginning in early summer." Entrepreneurs should state the precise amount requested and include relevant backup data, such as vendor estimates of costs or past production levels. An entrepreneur should not hesitate to request the amount of money needed but should not inflate the amount anticipating the financial officer to "talk her down." Remember: Lenders and investors are normally very familiar with industry cost structures.

Another important element of the loan or investment proposal is the repayment schedule or exit strategy. A lender's main consideration in granting a loan is the assurance that the applicant will repay, whereas an investor's major concern is earning a satisfactory rate of return. Financial projections must reflect a firm's ability to repay loans and produce adequate yields. Without this proof, a request for additional funds stands little chance of being accepted. It is necessary for the entrepreneur to produce tangible evidence showing the ability to repay loans or to generate attractive returns. "Plan an exit for the investor," advises the owner of a financial consulting company. "Generally, the equity investor's objective with early stage funding is to earn a 30 percent to 50 percent annual return over the life of the investment. To enhance the investor's interest in your enterprise, show how they can 'cash out' perhaps through a public offering or acquisition."[9]

Finally, the owner should have a timetable for implementing the proposed plan. He should present a schedule showing the estimated start-up date for the project and noting any significant milestones along the way. Entrepreneurs tend to be optimistic, so document how and why the timetable of events is realistic.

It is beneficial to include an evaluation of the risks of a new venture. Evaluating risk in a business plan requires an entrepreneur to walk a fine line, however. Dwelling too much on everything that can go wrong will discourage potential lenders and investors from financing the venture. Ignoring the project's risks makes those who evaluate the plan tend to believe an entrepreneur to be either naive, dishonest, or unprepared. The best strategy is to identify the most significant risks the venture faces and then to describe the plans the entrepreneur has developed to avoid them altogether or to overcome the negative outcome if the event does occur.

There is a difference between a *working* business plan—the one the entrepreneur is using to guide her business—and the *presentation* business plan—the one she is using to attract capital. Although coffee rings and penciled-in changes in a working plan don't matter (in fact, they're a good sign that the entrepreneur is actually using the plan), they have no place on a plan going to someone outside the company. A plan is usually the tool that an entrepreneur uses to make a first impression on potential lenders and investors. To make sure that impression is a favorable one, an entrepreneur should follow these tips:

- First impressions are crucial. Make sure the plan has an attractive (not necessarily expensive) cover.
- Make sure the plan is free of spelling and grammatical errors and "typos." It is a professional document and should look like one.
- Make it visually appealing. Use color charts, figures, and diagrams to illustrate key points. Don't get carried away, however, and end up with a "comic book" plan.
- Include a table of contents to allow readers to navigate the plan easily. Reviewers should be able to look through a plan and quickly locate the sections they want to see.
- Make it interesting. Boring plans seldom get read.

- A plan must prove that the business will make money. In one survey of lenders, investors, and financial advisors, 81 percent said that, first and foremost, a plan should prove that a venture will earn a profit.[10] Start-ups do not necessarily have to be profitable immediately, but sooner or later (preferably sooner), they must make money.

- Use computer spreadsheets to generate financial forecasts. They allow entrepreneurs to perform valuable "what if" (sensitivity) analysis in just seconds.

- *Always* include cash flow projections. Entrepreneurs sometimes focus excessively on their proposed venture's profit forecasts and ignore cash flow projections. Although profitability is important, lenders and investors are much more interested in cash flow because they know that's where the money to pay them back or to cash them out comes from.

- The ideal plan is "crisp," long enough to say what it should but not so long that it is a chore to read.

- Tell the truth. Absolute honesty is always critical when preparing a business plan.

When a visitor to New York City once asked a native New Yorker the question, "How do I get to Carnegie Hall?" the answer was, "practice, practice, practice."

*The same is true for the fortunate candidates selected to participate in the Springboard Venture Capital Forums, a nonprofit organization that aggressively recruits the best and brightest female entrepreneurs. The success rate of its graduates in raising venture capital is astounding, with nearly 40 percent raising in excess of $700 million from venture capitalists and "angels." A recent venture capital forum presented 23 entrepreneurs selected by Springboard from a pool of 150 applicants. Ultimately, the 23 entrepreneurs have 10 minutes to present their business plans to an audience of 200 to 300 potential investors. **Springboard Enterprise** requires that each of the finalists rehearse, present, be critiqued, rework her presentation, and begin the cycle again. In the most recent round, the 23 finalists had the consultants of the prestigious global consulting firm McKinsey and Company provide each of them with a one-hour critique of their presentation. The consultants focused on the presentation's content, quality of the visuals, use of time, and the presenter's style of delivery. A week later came the dress rehearsals with a round of suggestions from a panel of venture capitalists, executive coaches, consultants, and lawyers. Twenty-four hours before the forum, the 23 entrepreneurs participate in a technical dress rehearsal. This is the last opportunity to put the final touches on the 10-minute presentation.*

For most of this group of entrepreneurs, the final presentation reflected all the days, weeks, and months of preparation and rehearsal. Most of the presentations were extremely professional and well received. Springboard Enterprise again delivered the "goods," and the venture capitalists and private investors had an opportunity on one day to preview 23 high-potential business plans.[11]

MAKING THE BUSINESS PLAN PRESENTATION

Lenders and investors are favorably impressed by entrepreneurs who are informed and prepared when requesting a loan or investment. When attempting to secure funds from professional venture capitalists or private investors, the written business plan almost always precedes the opportunity to meet "face-to-face." Typically, an entrepreneur's time for presenting her business opportunity will be quite limited. (When presenting a plan to a venture capital forum, the allotted time is usually no more than 15 to 20 minutes, and at some forums, the time limit is a mere five or six minutes.) When the opportunity arises, an entrepreneur must be well prepared. It is important to rehearse, rehearse, and then rehearse some more. It is a mistake to begin by leading the audience into a long-winded explanation about the technology on which the product or service is based. Within minutes most of the audience will be lost, and so is any chance the entrepreneur has of obtaining the necessary financing for her new venture.

Some helpful tips for making a business plan presentation to potential lenders and investors include:

- Demonstrate enthusiasm about the venture but don't be overly emotional.
- Know your audience thoroughly and work to establish a rapport with them.
- "Hook" investors quickly with an up-front explanation of the new venture, its opportunities, and the anticipated benefits to them.

Entrepreneurs typically have a limited amount of time to present their ideas to potential lenders and investors. Planning, preparation, and enthusiasm are key elements to a successful presentation.

Courtesy of Getty Images - EyeWire, Inc.

■ Hit the highlights; specific questions will bring out the details later. Don't get caught up in too much detail in early meetings with lenders and investors.

■ Keep your presentation simple by limiting it to the two or three (no more) major points you must get across to your audience.

■ Avoid the use of technological terms that will likely be above most of the audience. Do at least one rehearsal before someone who has no special technical training. Tell him to stop you anytime he does not understand what you are talking about. When this occurs (and it likely will), rewrite that portion of your presentation.

■ Use visual aids. Although they make it easier for people to follow your presentation, do not make the visual aids the "star" of the presentation. They should merely support and enhance your message.

■ Close by reinforcing the nature of the opportunity. Be sure you have sold the benefits the investors will realize when the business is a success.

■ Be prepared for questions. In many cases, there is seldom time for a long "Q&A" session, but interested investors may want to get you aside to discuss the details of the plan.

■ Follow up with every investor to whom you make a presentation. Don't sit back and wait; be proactive. They have what you need—investment capital. Demonstrate that you have confidence in your plan and have the initiative necessary to run a business successfully.

Learning Objective

4. Explain the "five Cs of credit" and why they are important to potential lenders and investors reading business plans.

five Cs of credit—*criteria lenders and investors use to evaluate the creditworthiness of entrepreneurs seeking financing: capital, capacity, collateral, character, and conditions.*

WHAT LENDERS AND INVESTORS LOOK FOR IN A BUSINESS PLAN

Banks will rarely be a new venture's sole source of capital because a bank's return is limited by the interest rate it negotiates, but its risk could be the entire amount of the loan if the new business fails. Once a business is operational and has established a financial track record, however, banks become a regular source of financing. For this reason the small business owner needs to be aware of the criteria lenders and investors use when evaluating the creditworthiness of entrepreneurs seeking financing. Lenders and investors refer to these criteria as the **five Cs of credit:** capital, capacity, collateral, character, and conditions.

Capital

A small business must have a stable capital base before any lender is willing to grant a loan. Otherwise the lender would be making, in effect, a capital investment in the business. Most banks refuse to make loans that are capital investments because the potential for return on the investment is limited strictly to the interest on the loan, and the potential loss would probably exceed the reward. In fact, the most common reasons that banks give for rejecting small business loan applications are undercapitalization and too much debt. Banks expect a small company to have an equity base of investment by the owner(s) that will help support the venture during times of financial strain, which are common during the start-up and growth phases of a business. Lenders and investors see capital as a risk-sharing strategy with entrepreneurs.

Capacity

A synonym for capacity is cash flow. Lenders and investors must be convinced of the firm's ability to meet its regular financial obligations and to repay loans, and that takes cash. In Chapter 9, we saw that more small businesses fail from lack of cash than from lack of profit.

It is possible for a company to be showing a profit and still have no cash—that is, to be technically bankrupt. Lenders expect small businesses to pass the test of liquidity, especially for short-term loans. Potential lenders and investors examine closely a small company's cash flow position to decide whether it has the capacity necessary to survive until it can sustain itself.

Collateral

Collateral includes any assets an entrepreneur pledges to a lender as security for repayment of a loan. If the company defaults on the loan, the lender has the right to sell the collateral and use the proceeds to satisfy the loan. Typically, banks make very few unsecured loans (those not backed by collateral) to business start-ups. Bankers view the entrepreneurs' willingness to pledge collateral (personal or business assets) as an indication of their dedication to making the venture a success. A sound business plan can improve a banker's attitude toward the venture.

Character

Before extending a loan to or making an investment in a small business, lenders and investors must be satisfied with an entrepreneur's character. The evaluation of character frequently is based on intangible factors such as honesty, integrity, competence, polish, determination, intelligence, and ability. Although the qualities judged are abstract, this evaluation plays a critical role in the decision to put money into a business or not.

YOU Be the Consultant . . .

Battle of the Plans

Unlike most summer campers, the girls attending Camp Startup in Wellesley, Massachusetts, do not take lessons in handling canoes, tying knots, or ornithology. Instead, these entrepreneurs-to-be are learning how to put together a business plan for a fictitious company they plan to launch. Like the participants in Camp Startup, students in colleges and universities across the United States are also creating business plans for companies they hope to start or, in some cases, have already launched. For some, what is at stake involves much more than just a good grade. They are competing for real start-up money and valuable feedback from judges in business plan competitions. In the typical business plan competition, students submit plans and make presentations to panels of judges that include venture capitalists, successful entrepreneurs, private investors, and potential lenders.

More than 50 colleges and universities across the United States sponsor business plan competitions, and it is not uncommon for the winners to attract impressive amounts of venture capital from judges. "I have been amazed at the quality of the plans and the companies coming out of these competitions," says Steve Kaplan of the University of Chicago. One student team at Harvard's business plan competition went on to launch the company for which they created the plan, Chemdex, an e-commerce site that buys and sells life science products. The young entrepreneurs raised $13 million from one of the nation's most well-known venture capital firms and has since made a public stock offering . . . and it was only a *runner-up* in the competition! The winning company was an Internet consulting company named Zefer that attracted $100 million in start-up capital, the largest private funding ever for an Internet start-up.

Although most of the leading schools in the field of entrepreneurship sponsor business plan competitions, perhaps the most famous contest is MIT's $50K Entrepreneurship Competition, which has stimulated the creation of more than 50 companies that have gone on to attract $175 million in venture financing and have created more than 600 jobs! When Mike Cassidy and his two partners won the $50K

competition with their plan for Stylus Innovation, a computer software company, Cassidy and his team parlayed the status of their victory into $125,000 in additional venture capital. Cassidy managed the fast-growing company for several years before selling it for $13 million. Unwilling to retire at age 33, he began looking for an Internet company to manage. Cassidy returned to MIT's Web site, where he found descriptions of the businesses the student teams were proposing for the $50K competition. One business in particular, Direct Hit Technologies, an Internet search engine company, caught Cassidy's attention. He approached Gary Culliss, who came up with the idea for Direct Hit, and within days signed on as the company's CEO. Culliss's team did not win a warm-up round of the $50K competition it entered, but with Cassidy's help, the entrepreneurs began reworking the business plan. The retooling worked, and Direct Hit scored a direct hit, winning $30,000 in the competition. Culliss and Cassidy went on to raise $1.4 million in venture capital and to launch Direct Hit successfully, at which time they graciously returned the $30,000 prize money that got them started.

1. If your school does not already have a business plan competition, work with a team of your classmates in a brainstorming session to develop ideas for creating one. What would you offer as a prize? How would you finance the competition? Whom would you invite to judge it? How would you structure the competition?

2. Use the World Wide Web to research business plan competitions at other colleges and universities across the nation. Using the competitions at these schools as benchmarks and the ideas you generated in Question 1, develop a format for a business plan competition at your school.

3. Assume that you are a member of a team of entrepreneurial students entered in a prestigious business plan competition. Outline your team's strategy for winning the competition.

Sources: Adapted from Jane Hodges, "Eat S'Mores? No. Draft a Business Plan," *Fortune*, September 27, 1999, p. 294; Marc Ballon, "MIT Springboard Sends Internet Company Aloft," *Inc.*, December 1998, pp. 23–25; MIT $50K Entrepreneurship Competition, http://50k.mit.edu; Alex Frankel, "Battle of the Business Plans," *Forbes ASAP*, August 23, 1999, pp. 22–24; Michael Warshaw, "The Best Business Plan on the Planet," *Inc.*, August 1999, pp. 80–90.

Lenders and investors know that most small businesses fail because of incompetent management, and they try to avoid extending loans to high-risk entrepreneurs. A solid business plan and a polished presentation by the entrepreneur can go far in convincing the banker of the owner's capability.

Conditions

The conditions surrounding a funding request also affect an entrepreneur's chances of receiving financing. Lenders and investors consider factors relating to a business's operation such as potential growth in the market, competition, location, strengths, weaknesses, opportunities, and threats. Again, the best way to provide this relevant information is in a business plan. Another important condition influencing the banker's decision is the shape of the overall economy, including interest rate levels, inflation rate, and demand for money. Although these factors are beyond an entrepreneur's control, they still are an important component in a banker's decision.

The higher a small business scores on these five Cs, the greater its chance will be of receiving a loan. The wise entrepreneur keeps this in mind when preparing a business plan and presentation.

CONCLUSION

Although there is no guarantee of success when launching a business, the best way to ensure against failure is to create a business plan. A good plan serves as an entrepreneurial strategic compass that keeps a business on course as it travels into an uncertain future. Also, a solid plan is essential to raising the capital needed to start a business; lenders and investors demand it. It is absolutely essential for the business plan to be built on facts and realistic assumptions. Nothing destroys an entrepreneur's credibility faster than a document or presentation that lacks substance and is viewed by potential investors as a complete fabrication or an exercise in wishful thinking. Of course, building a business plan is just one step along the path to launching a business. Building a successful business requires entrepreneurs to put the plan into action. The remaining chapters in this book focus on putting your business plan to work.

BUSINESS PLAN FORMAT

Although every company's business plan will be unique, reflecting its individual circumstances, certain elements are universal. The following outline summarizes these components:

I   Executive Summary (not to exceed two pages)
    A. Company name, address, and phone number
    B. Name(s), addresses, and phone number(s) of all key people
    C. Brief description of the business, its products and services, and the customer problems they solve
    D. Brief overview of the market for your products and services
    E. Brief overview of the strategies that will make your firm a success
    F. Brief description of the managerial and technical experience of key people
    G. Brief statement of the financial request and how the money will be used
    H. Charts or tables showing highlights of financial forecasts

II   Vision and Mission statement
    A. Entrepreneur's vision for the company
    B. "What business are we in?"
    C. Values and principles on which the business stands
    D. What makes the business unique? What is the source of its competitive advantage?

III   Company History (for existing businesses only)
    A. Company founding
    B. Financial and operational highlights
    C. Significant achievements

IV   Business and Industry Profile
    A. Stage of growth (start-up, growth, maturity)
    B. Company goals and objectives
        1. Operational
        2. Financial
        3. Other
    C. Industry analysis
        1. Industry background and overview
        2. Significant trends

3. Growth rate

4. Key success factors in the industry

5. Outlook for the future

V   Business strategy

A. Desired image and position in market

B. SWOT analysis

1. Strengths

2. Weaknesses

3. Opportunities

4. Threats

C. Competitive strategy

1. Cost-leadership

2. Differentiation

3. Focus

VI   Company Products and Services

A. Description

1. Product or service features

2. Customer benefits

3. Warranties and guarantees

4. Uniqueness

B. Patent or trademark protection

C. Description of production process (if applicable)

1. Raw materials

2. Costs

3. Key suppliers

D. Future product or service offerings

VII Marketing Strategy

A. Target market

1. Complete demographic profile

2. Other significant customer characteristics

B. Customers' motivation to buy

C. Market size and trends

1. How large is the market?

2. Is it growing or shrinking? How fast?

D. Advertising and promotion

1. Media used—reader, viewer, listener profiles

2. Media costs

3. Frequency of usage

4. Plans for generating publicity

E. Pricing

1. Cost structure

a. Fixed

b. Variable

2. Desired image in market

3. Comparison against competitors' prices

F. Distribution strategy

1. Channels of distribution used

2. Sales techniques and incentives

VIII Location and Layout
    A. Location
        1. Demographic analysis of location vs. target customer profile
        2. Traffic count
        3. Lease/Rental rates
        4. Labor needs and supply
        5. Wage rates
    B. Layout
        1. Size requirements
        2. Americans with Disabilities compliance
        3. Ergonomic issues
        4. Layout plan (suitable for an appendix)

IX   Competitor Analysis
    A. Existing competitors
        1. Who are they? Create a competitive profile matrix.
        2. Strengths
        3. Weaknesses
    B. Potential competitors: Companies that might enter the market
        1. Who are they?
        2. Impact on your business if they enter

X   Description of management team
    A. Key managers and employees
        1. Their backgrounds
        2. Experience, skills, and know-how they bring to the company
    B. Resumes of key managers and employees (suitable for an appendix)

XI   Plan of Operation
    A. Form of ownership chosen and reasoning
    B. Company structure (organization chart)
    C. Decision making authority
    D. Compensation and benefits packages

XII   Financial Forecasts (suitable for an appendix)
    A. Financial statements
        1. Income statement
        2. Balance sheet
        3. Cash flow statement
    B. Break-even analysis
    C. Ratio analysis with comparison to industry standards (most applicable to existing businesses)

XIII Loan or Investment Proposal
    A. Amount requested
    B. Purpose and uses of funds
    C. Repayment or "cash out" schedule (exit strategy)
    D. Timetable for implementing plan and launching the business

XIV Appendices—Supporting documentation, including market research, financial statements, organization charts, resumes, and other items.

1. Explain why every entrepreneur should create a business plan.

■ A business plan serves two essential functions. First and most important, it guides the company's operations by charting its future course and devising a strategy for following it. The second function of the business plan is to attract lenders and investors. Applying for loans or attempting to interest investors without a solid business plan rarely attracts needed capital.

2. Explain the benefits of preparing a plan.

■ Preparing a sound business plan clearly requires time and effort, but the benefits greatly exceed the costs. Building the plan forces a potential entrepreneur to look at her business idea in the harsh light of reality. It also requires the owner to assess the venture's chances of success more objectively. A well-assembled plan helps prove to outsiders that a business idea can be successful.

■ The *real* value in preparing a business plan is not so much in the plan itself as it is in the process the entrepreneur goes through to create the plan. Although the finished product is useful, the process of building a plan requires an entrepreneur to subject his idea to an objective, critical evaluation. What the entrepreneur learns about his company, its target market, its financial requirements, and other factors can be essential to making the venture a success.

3. Describe the elements of a solid business plan.

■ Although a business plan should be unique and tailor-made to suit the particular needs of a small company, it should cover these basic elements: an executive summary, a mission statement, a company history, a business and industry profile, a description of the company's business strategy, a profile of its products or services, a statement explaining its marketing strategy, a competitor analysis, owners' and officers' résumés, a plan of operation, financial data, and the loan or investment proposal.

4. Understand the keys to making an effective business plan presentation.

■ Lenders and investors are favorably impressed by entrepreneurs who are informed and prepared when requesting a loan or investment.

■ Tips include: Demonstrate enthusiasm about the venture, but don't be overly emotional; "hook" investors quickly with an up-front explanation of the new venture, its opportunities, and the anticipated benefits to them; use visual aids; hit the highlights of your venture; don't get caught up in too much detail in early meetings with lenders and investors; avoid the use of technological terms that will likely be above most of the audience; rehearse your presentation before giving it; close by reinforcing the nature of the opportunity; and be prepared for questions.

5. Explain the "five Cs of credit" and why they are important to potential lenders and investors reading business plans.

■ Small business owners need to be aware of the criteria bankers use in evaluating the creditworthiness of loan applicants—the five Cs of credit: capital, capacity, collateral, character, and conditions.

■ Capital—Lenders expect small businesses to have an equity base of investment by the owner(s) that will help support the venture during times of financial strain.

■ Capacity—A synonym for capacity is cash flow. The bank must be convinced of the firm's ability to meet its regular financial obligations and to repay the bank loan, and that takes cash.

■ Collateral—Collateral includes any assets the owner pledges to the bank as security for repayment of the loan.

■ Character—Before approving a loan to a small business, the banker must be satisfied with the owner's character.

■ Conditions—The conditions (interest rates, the health of the nation's economy, industry growth rates, etc.) surrounding a loan request also affect the owner's chance of receiving funds.

DISCUSSION QUESTIONS

1. Why should an entrepreneur develop a business plan?
2. Describe the major components of a business plan.
3. How can an entrepreneur seeking funds to launch a business convince potential lenders and investors that a market for the product or service really does exist?

4. How would you prepare to make a formal presentation of your business plan to a venture capital forum?
5. What are the five Cs of credit? How does a banker use them when evaluating a loan request?

THE BUSINESS DISC

Before you begin this section, you should review the reference material on writing a business plan on *The Business Disc*. From the menu across the top of your screen, select the "Reference" option and then click on the following document: "Business Plans and Planning." Click on "The Business Plan: Roadmap to Success," "How to Write a Business Plan," and "Business Plan for a . . . (choose the type of business you are launching). Review the concepts in these reference guides and in Chapter 11.

Why is it necessary to prepare a business plan before launching a business? Develop an outline of the business plan you will create for your company. By now, you should have created most of these components. Assemble them according to your outline.

BUSINESS PLAN PRO

Business PlanPro

This chapter on the creation of a successful business plan will complete the missing element in the *Business Plan Pro* software. Section 6, "Personnel Plan," will allow you to identify the key persons for the business. When you calculate the relevant payroll data, you will need to incorporate this information into the "Financial Plan" section.

The next step is to integrate the details of the plan with the help of section 5.4, which allows you to set the key milestones for all work to be performed.

This will be the vehicle through which all of the components of your business plan will be linked together to determine the required steps to implement the plan.

Who is responsible for each step in the plan? When is each step to begin and when does it need to be completed? ? Set deadlines for key activities, and establish budgets for each task in the plan.

Explain Milestones
Explain in detail how each of the activities are interrelated with other activities, as well as how personnel must work together to ensure the smooth integration of every element of the plan. You will often discover that each element of the plan has many more detailed subelements that become obvious as the process of building the plan takes place.

Finally, it is time to write the executive summary (remember the elevator pitch!) and finish and polish each section.

When you have completed these final steps, ask another person—preferably someone with a good business background—to read over your plan. Ask that person(s) to tell you what they were unable to understand about the plan. Their questions allow you to rewrite the plan for increased clarity.

Congratulations—YOU HAVE A BUSINESS PLAN!

1. Contact a local entrepreneur who recently launched a business. Did he or she prepare a business plan before starting the company? Why or why not? If the entrepreneur did not create a plan, is he or she considering doing so now? If the entrepreneur did create a plan, what benefits did he or she gain from the process? How long did it take to complete the plan? How did he or she put the plan to use during the start-up phase? Does he or she intend to keep the business plan updated? What advice does he or she have to offer another entrepreneur about to begin writing a business plan?

2. Interview a local banker who has experience in making loans to small businesses. Ask him or her the following questions.

   a. How important is a well-prepared business plan?

   b. How important is a smooth presentation?

   c. How does the banker evaluate the owner's character?

   d. How heavily does the bank weigh the five Cs of credit?

   e. What percentage of small business owners are well prepared to request a bank loan?

   f. What are the major reasons for the bank's rejection of small business loan applications?

3. Interview a small business owner who has requested a bank loan or an equity investment from external sources. Ask him or her these questions:

   a. Did you prepare a written business plan before approaching the financial officer?

   b. If the answer is "yes" to part a, did you have outside or professional help in preparing it?

   c. How many times have your requests for additional funds been rejected? What reasons were given for the rejection?

Chapter

12

Sources of Financing: Debt and Equity

If you don't know who the fool is in a deal, it's you.

—Michael Wolff

There's many a pessimist who got that way by financing an optimist.

—Anonymous

LEARNING OBJECTIVES

Upon completion of this chapter, you will be able to:

1. **EXPLAIN** the differences in the three types of capital small businesses require: fixed, working, and growth.

2. **DESCRIBE** the differences in equity capital and debt capital and the advantages and disadvantages of each.

3. **DISCUSS** the various sources of equity capital available to entrepreneurs, including personal savings, friends and relatives, angels, partners, corporations, venture capital, and public stock offerings.

4. **DESCRIBE** the process of "going public," as well as its advantages and disadvantages and the various simplified registrations and exemptions from registration available to small businesses wanting to sell securities to investors.

5. **DESCRIBE** the various sources of debt capital and the advantages and disadvantages of each: banks, asset-based lenders, vendors (trade credit), equipment suppliers, commercial finance companies, savings and loan associations, stockbrokers, insurance companies, credit unions, bonds, private placements, Small Business Investment Companies (SBICs), and Small Business Lending Companies (SBLCs).

6. **IDENTIFY** the various federal loan programs aimed at small businesses.

7. **DESCRIBE** the various loan programs available from the Small Business Administration.

8. **DISCUSS** valuable methods of financing growth and expansion internally.

Raising the money to launch a new business venture has always been a challenge for entrepreneurs. Capital markets rise and fall with the stock market, overall economic conditions, and investors' fortunes. These swells and troughs in the availability of capital make the search for financing look like a wild rollercoaster ride. For instance, during the late 1990s, founders of dot-com companies were able to attract mountains of cash from private and professional investors, even if their businesses existed only on paper! Investors flocked to initial public offerings from practically any dot-com company. The market for capital became bipolar: easy-money times for dot-coms and tight-money times for "not-coms." Even established, profitable companies in "old economy" industries such as manufacturing, distribution, real estate, and brick-and-mortar retail could not raise the capital they needed to grow. Then, early in 2000, the dot-com bubble burst, and financing an Internet business also became extremely challenging.

Today, the challenge of attracting capital to start or to expand a business remains. Most entrepreneurs, especially those in less glamorous industries or those just starting out, face difficulty finding outside sources of financing. Many banks shy away from making loans to start-ups, venture capitalists have become more risk averse, private investors have grown cautious, and making a public stock offering remains a viable option for only a handful of promising companies with good track records and fast-growth futures. The result has been a credit crunch for entrepreneurs looking for small to moderate amounts of start-up capital. Entrepreneurs and business owners needing between $100,000 and $3 million are especially hard hit because of the vacuum that exists at that level of financing.

In the face of this capital crunch, business's need for capital has never been greater. Experts estimate the small business financing market to be $170 billion a year; yet, that still is not enough to satisfy the capital appetites of entrepreneurs and their cash-hungry businesses.[1] When searching for the capital to launch their companies, entrepreneurs must remember the following "secrets" to successful financing:

- *Choosing the right sources of capital for a business can be just as important as choosing the right form of ownership or the right location.* It is a decision that will influence a company for a lifetime, so entrepreneurs must weigh their options carefully before committing to a particular funding source. "It is important that companies in need of capital align themselves with sources that best fit their needs," says one financial consultant. "The success of a company often depends on the success of that relationship."[2]

- *The money is out there; the key is knowing where to look.* Entrepreneurs must do their homework *before* they set out to raise money for their ventures. Understanding which sources of funding are best suited for the various stages of a company's growth and then taking the time to learn how those sources work are essential to success.

- *Raising money takes time and effort.* Sometimes entrepreneurs are surprised at the energy and the time required to raise the capital needed to feed their cash-hungry, growing businesses. The process usually includes lots of promising leads, most of which turn out to be dead ends. Meetings with and presentations to lots of potential investors and lenders can crowd out the time needed to manage a growing company. Entrepreneurs also discover that raising capital is an ongoing job. "The fund-raising game is a marathon, not a sprint," says Jerusha Stewart, founder of iSpiritus Soul Spa, a store selling personal growth and well-being products.[3]

- *Creativity counts.* Although some traditional sources of funds now play a lesser role in small business finance than in the past, other sources—from large corporations and customers to international venture capitalists and state or local programs—are taking up the slack. To find the financing their businesses demand, entrepreneurs must use as much creativity in attracting financing as they did in generating the ideas for their products and services. For instance, after striking out with traditional sources of funding, EZConserve, a company that makes software that provides energy management tools for large PC networks, turned to the nonprofit group Northwest Energy Efficiency Alliance and received a sizable grant as well as marketing assistance that fueled its growth.[4]

- *The World Wide Web puts at entrepreneurs' fingertips vast resources of information that can lead to financing; use it.* The Web often offers entrepreneurs, especially those looking for relatively small amounts of money, the opportunity to discover sources of funds that they otherwise might miss. The Web site created for this book (www.prenhall.com/zimmerer) provides links to many useful sites related to raising both start-up and growth capital. The Web also provides a low-cost, convenient way for entrepreneurs to get their business plans into potential investors' hands anywhere in the world. When searching for sources of capital, entrepreneurs must not overlook this valuable tool!

- *Be thoroughly prepared before approaching potential lenders and investors.* In the hunt for capital, tracking down leads is tough enough; don't blow a potential deal by failing to be ready to present your business idea to potential lenders and investors in a clear, concise, convincing way. That, of course, requires a solid business plan.
- *Entrepreneurs cannot overestimate the importance of making sure that the "chemistry" among themselves, their companies, and their funding sources is a good one.* Too many entrepreneurs get into financial deals because they needed the money to keep their businesses growing only to discover that their plans do not match those of their financial partners.

Rather than rely primarily on a single source of funds as they have in the past, entrepreneurs must piece together capital from multiple sources, a method known as **layered financing**. They have discovered that raising capital successfully requires them to cast a wide net to capture the financing they need to launch their businesses.

> **layered financing**—the technique of raising capital from multiple sources.

*The founders of **Med-Channel**, an Internet-based company that focuses on the medical supply industry, demonstrate the "patchwork" of start-up financing that has become so common. In addition to the initial capital the founders provided, the company raised $42 million in its early stages from 11 private investors. Then Med-Channel received a cash infusion from two venture capital firms. As the company grew, it turned to two investment banks and large corporations, including Johnson & Johnson and an Italian pharmaceutical company, to satisfy its capital requirements.*[5]

> **A Company Example**

This chapter will guide you through the myriad of financing options available to entrepreneurs, focusing on both sources of equity (ownership) and debt (borrowed) financing.

PLANNING FOR CAPITAL NEEDS

Learning Objective

1. Explain the differences among the three types of capital small businesses require: fixed, working, and growth.

Becoming a successful entrepreneur requires one to become a skilled fund-raiser, a job that usually requires more time and energy than most business founders think. In start-up companies, raising capital can easily consume as much as one-half of the entrepreneur's time and can take many months to complete. Most entrepreneurs are seeking less than $1 million (indeed, most need less than $100,000), which may be the toughest money to secure. Where to find this seed money depends, in part, on the nature of the proposed business and on the amount of money required. For example, the originator of a computer software firm would have different capital requirements than the founder of a coal mining operation. Although both entrepreneurs might approach some of the same types of lenders or investors, each would be more successful targeting specific sources of funds best suited to their particular financial needs.

Capital is any form of wealth employed to produce more wealth. It exists in many forms in a typical business, including cash, inventory, plant, and equipment. Entrepreneurs need three different types of capital:

> **capital**—any form of wealth employed to produce more wealth.

Fixed Capital

Fixed capital is needed to purchase a company's permanent or fixed assets such as buildings, land, computers, and equipment. Money invested in these fixed assets tends to be frozen because it cannot be used for any other purpose. Typically, large sums of money are involved in purchasing fixed assets, and credit terms usually are lengthy. Lenders of fixed capital expect the assets purchased to improve the efficiency and, thus, the profitability of the business and to create improved cash flows that ensure repayment.

> **fixed capital**—capital needed to purchase a company's permanent or fixed assets such as land, buildings, computers, and equipment.

Working Capital

Working capital represents a business's temporary funds; it is the capital used to support a company's normal short-term operations. Accountants define working capital as current assets minus current liabilities. The need for working capital arises because of the uneven flow of cash into and out of the business due to normal seasonal fluctuations. Credit sales, seasonal sales swings, or unforeseeable changes in demand will create fluctuations in *any* small company's cash flow. Working capital normally is used to buy inventory, pay bills, finance credit

> **working capital**—capital needed to support a business's short-term operations; it represents a company's temporary funds.

sales, pay wages and salaries, and take care of any unexpected emergencies. Lenders of working capital expect it to produce higher cash flows to ensure repayment at the end of the production/sales cycle.

Growth Capital

growth capital—*capital needed to finance a company's growth or its expansion in a new direction.*

Growth capital, unlike working capital, is not related to the seasonal fluctuations of a small business. Instead, growth capital requirements surface when an existing business is expanding or changing its primary direction. For example, a small manufacturer of silicon microchips for computers saw his business skyrocket in a short time period. With orders for chips rushing in, the growing business needed a sizable cash infusion to increase plant size, expand its sales and production workforce, and buy more equipment. During times of such rapid expansion, a growing company's capital requirements are similar to those of a business start-up. Like lenders of fixed capital, growth capital lenders expect the funds to improve a company's profitability and cash flow position, thus ensuring repayment.

Although these three types of capital are interdependent, each has certain sources, characteristics, and effects on the business and its long-term growth that entrepreneurs must recognize.

Learning Objective

2. Describe the differences between equity capital and debt capital and the advantages and disadvantages of each.

EQUITY CAPITAL VERSUS DEBT CAPITAL

Equity capital represents the personal investment of the owner (or owners) in a business and is sometimes called *risk capital* because these investors assume the primary risk of losing their funds if the business fails.

A Company Example

*For instance, private investor Victor Lombardi lost the $3.5 million he invested in a start-up called **NetFax**, a company that was developing the technology to send faxes over the Internet. When NetFax's patent application stalled, the company foundered. Just three years after its launch, NetFax ceased operations, leaving Lombardi's investment worthless.*[6]

equity capital—*represents the personal investment of the owner(s) in a business and is sometimes called risk capital.*

If a venture succeeds, however, founders and investors share in the benefits, which can be quite substantial. The founders of and early investors in Yahoo, Sun Microsystems, Federal Express, Intel, and Microsoft became multimillionaires when the companies went public and their equity investments finally paid off. To entrepreneurs, the primary advantage of equity capital is that it does not have to be repaid like a loan does. Equity investors are entitled to share in the company's earnings (if there are any) and usually to have a voice in the company's future direction.

The primary disadvantage of equity capital is that the entrepreneur must give up some—perhaps *most*—of the ownership in the business to outsiders. Although 50 percent of something is better than 100 percent of nothing, giving up control of your company can be disconcerting and dangerous.

A Company Example

*For instance, when Gary Hoover launched **Bookstop Inc.**, a book superstore, he relied on equity financing so much that he was left with just 6 percent of his company's stock. Seven years after start-up, the venture capitalists who owned most of the stock fired Hoover from the company he founded!*[7]

Entrepreneurs are more likely to give up significant amounts of equity in their businesses in the start-up phase than in any other.

debt capital—*the financing that a small business owner has borrowed and must repay with interest.*

Debt capital is the financing that a small business owner has borrowed and must repay with interest. Very few entrepreneurs have adequate personal savings to finance the complete start-up costs of a small business; many of them must rely on some form of debt capital to launch their companies. Lenders of capital are more numerous than investors, although small business loans can be just as difficult (if not more difficult) to obtain. Although borrowed capital allows entrepreneurs to maintain complete ownership of their businesses, it must be carried as a liability on the balance sheet as well as be repaid with interest at some point in the future. In addition, because lenders consider small businesses to be greater risks than bigger corporate customers, they require higher interest rates on loans to small companies because of the risk-return trade-off—the higher the risk, the greater the return demanded. Most small firms pay the prime rate—the interest rate banks charge their most creditworthy customers—*plus* a few percentage points. Still, the cost of debt financing often is lower than that of equity financing. Because of the higher risks associated with providing equity capital to small companies, investors demand greater returns than lenders. Also, unlike equity financing, debt financing does not require an entrepreneur to dilute her ownership interest in the company. We now turn our attention to nine common sources of equity capital.

SOURCES OF EQUITY FINANCING

Learning Objective

3. Discuss the various sources of equity capital available to entrepreneurs.

Personal Savings

The *first* place entrepreneurs should look for start-up money is in their own pockets. It's the least expensive source of funds available! "The sooner you take outside money, the more ownership in your company you'll have to surrender," warns one small business expert.[8] Entrepreneurs apparently see the benefits of self-sufficiency; the most common source of equity funds used to start a small business is the entrepreneur's pool of personal savings.

A Company Example

*In 1979, when Robert MacLeod and Stephen Byckiewicz launched **Kiss My Face**, a company that sells a line of soaps and shampoos, they could not persuade a bank to lend them any money, so they pooled all they had—just $10,000—and invested it in the business. Sales were thin in the early years, but they climbed steadily with the help of creative marketing and the strategic partnerships with larger companies that MacLeod and Byckiewicz forged. The entrepreneurs financed their company's growth with retained earnings and some debt but retained 100 percent ownership. Today, Kiss My Face is debt free and tallies sales of more than $18 million. "We're very happy to have maintained complete control of our business," says MacLeod.[9]*

Lenders and investors *expect* entrepreneurs to put their own money into a business start-up. If an entrepreneur is not willing to risk his own money, potential investors are not likely to risk their money in the business either. Furthermore, failing to put up sufficient capital of their own means that entrepreneurs must either borrow an excessive amount of capital or give up a significant portion of ownership to outsiders to fund the business properly. Excessive borrowing in the early days of a business puts intense pressure on its cash flow, and becoming a minority shareholder may dampen a founder's enthusiasm for making a business successful. Neither outcome presents a bright future for the company involved.

Friends and Family Members

Although most entrepreneurs look to their own bank accounts first to finance a business, few have sufficient resources to launch their businesses alone. In fact, three out of four people who start businesses do so with capital from outside sources.[10] After emptying their own pockets, where should entrepreneurs turn for capital? The second place most entrepreneurs look is to friends and family members who might be willing to invest in a business venture. Because of their relationships with the founder, these people are most likely to invest. Often they are more patient than other outside investors and are less meddlesome in a business's affairs than many other types of investors. "Most of our relatives just told us to pay them back when we could," says an entrepreneur who used $30,000 from family members to launch a gourmet coffee business.[11]

Investments from family and friends are an excellent source of seed capital and can get a start-up far enough along to attract money from private investors or venture capital companies. Inherent dangers lurk in family business investments, however. Unrealistic expectations or misunderstood risks have destroyed many friendships and have ruined many family reunions. To avoid such problems, an entrepreneur must honestly present the investment opportunity and the nature of the risks involved to avoid alienating friends and family members if the business fails. On the other hand, some investments return more than friends and family members ever could have imagined. In 1995, Mike and Jackie Bezos invested $300,000 in their son Jeff's start-up business, Amazon.com. Today, Mike and Jackie own 6 percent of Amazon.com's stock, and their shares are worth billions of dollars![12]

Angels

After dipping into their own pockets and convincing friends and relatives to invest in their business ventures, many entrepreneurs still find themselves short of the seed capital they need. Frequently, the next stop on the road to business financing is private investors. These private investors or **"angels"** are wealthy individuals, often entrepreneurs themselves, who invest in business start-ups in exchange for equity stakes in the companies. Angel investors have provided much-needed capital to entrepreneurs for many years. In 1938, when World War I flying ace Eddie Rickenbacker needed money to launch Eastern Airlines, millionaire Laurance Rockefeller provided it.[13] Alexander Graham Bell, inventor of the telephone, used angel capital to start Bell Telephone in 1877.

In many cases, angels invest in businesses for more than purely economic reasons (for instance, because they have a personal interest in the industry), and they are willing to put money into companies in the earliest stages, long before venture capital firms and institutional investors jump in. Angel financing, the fastest-growing segment of the small business capital market, is ideal for companies that have outgrown the capacity of investments from friends and family but are still too small to attract the interest of venture capital companies. For instance, after raising the money to launch Amazon.com from family and friends, Jeff Bezos turned to angels because venture capital firms were not interested in a business start-up. Bezos attracted $1.2 million from a dozen angels before landing $8 million from venture capital firms a year later.[14]

Angels are a primary source of start-up capital for companies in the embryonic stage through the growth stage, and their role in financing small businesses is significant. Experts estimate that 400,000 angels invest $50 billion a year in 30,000 to 60,000 small companies, most of them in the start-up phase.[15] Because the angel market is so fragmented and disorganized, we may never get a completely accurate estimate of its investment in business start-ups. Although they may disagree on the exact amount of angel investments, experts concur on one fact: Angels are the largest single source of external equity capital for small businesses. Their investments in young companies dwarf those of professional venture capitalists, providing at least two to five times more capital to 20 to 30 times as many companies.

Angels fill a significant gap in the seed capital market. They are most likely to finance start-ups with capital requirements in the $10,000 to $2 million range, well below the $3 million to $10 million minimum investments most professional venture capitalists prefer. Because a $500,000 deal requires about as much of a venture capitalist's time to research and evaluate as a $5 million deal does, venture capitalists tend to focus on big deals, where their returns are bigger. Angels also tolerate risk levels that would make venture capitalists shudder; as much as 80 percent of angel-backed companies fail.[16] One angel investor, a former executive at Oracle Corporation, says that of the 10 companies he has invested in, seven have flopped. Three of the start-ups, however, have produced fifty-fold returns![17] Because of the inherent risks in start-up companies, many venture capitalists have shifted their investment portfolios away from start-ups toward more established firms. That's why angel financing is so important: Angels often finance deals that no venture capitalist will consider.

The typical angel invests in companies at the start-up or infant growth stage and accepts 24 percent of the investment opportunities presented, makes an average of two investments every three years, and has invested an average of $80,000 of equity in 3.5 firms. Ninety percent say they're satisfied with their investment decisions.[18] When evaluating a proposal, angels look for qualified managers, a business with a clearly defined niche, market potential, and a competitive advantage. They also want to see market research that proves the existence of a sizable customer base.

Entrepreneurs in search of capital quickly learn that the real challenge lies in *finding* angels. Most angels have substantial business and financial experience, and many of them are entrepreneurs or former entrepreneurs. Because most angels frown on "cold calls" from entrepreneurs they don't know, locating them boils down to making the right contacts. Networking is the key. Asking friends, attorneys, bankers, stockbrokers, accountants, other business owners, and consultants for suggestions and introductions is a good way to start. Angels almost always invest their money locally, so entrepreneurs should look close to home for them—typically within a 50- to 100-mile radius. Angels also look for businesses they know something about, and most expect to invest their knowledge, experience, and energy as well as their money in a company. In fact, the advice and the network of contacts that angels bring to a deal can sometimes be as valuable as their money!

A Company Example

*John McCallum, founder of **VetExchange**, an Internet-based service provider for veterinarians, found that the contacts and the advice angel investors brought to his company were invaluable. "Our angels are networked across the country," says McCallum. "They have relationships you can't imagine." One angel, a former entrepreneur, gave McCallum valuable advice on a key strategic issue recently. "He's dealt with the same issue five times before," he says.[19]*

Angels tend to invest in clusters as well, many of them through one of the nation's 170 angel capital networks. With the right approach, an entrepreneur can attract an angel who might share the deal with some of his cronies.

A Company Example

*In 1995, Hans Severiens, a professional investor, created the **Band of Angels**, a group of about 150 angels (mostly Silicon Valley millionaires, many of whom are retired entrepreneurs) who meet monthly in Portola Valley, California, to listen to entrepreneurs pitch their business plans. The Band of Angels reviews about 30 proposals each month before inviting three entrepreneurs to make 20-minute presentations at their monthly meeting. Interested members often team up with one another to invest in the businesses they consider most promising. Over the years, the Band of Angels has invested a total of more than $90 million in promising young companies. The average investment is $600,000, which usually nets the angels between 15 percent and 20 percent of a company's stock. At one meeting, Craig McMullen, CEO of Cardiac Focus, a company that is developing a disposable vest to help doctors map patients' cardiac arrythmias without surgery, made a pitch for $2 million. Cardiac Focus needed the money to complete its management team, perform clinical trials, and file for approval from the FDA. Within weeks of the presentation, 14 members of the Band of Angels decided to invest, giving Cardiac Focus the capital it needed to reach the next phase of growth.[20]*

The Internet has expanded greatly the ability of entrepreneurs in search of capital and angels in search of businesses to find one another. Dozens of angel networks have opened on the World Wide Web, including AngelMoney.com, Business Angels International, Garage.com, the Capital Network, JumpStart Investments, the Capital Connection, WomenAngels.net, and many others. The Small Business Administration's Access to Capital Electronic Network, ACE-Net, is a Web-based listing service that provides a marketplace for entrepreneurs seeking between $250,000 and $5 million in capital and angels looking to invest in promising businesses. Entrepreneurs pay $450 a year to list information about their companies on the site, which potential angels can access at any time.

Angels are an excellent source of "patient money," often willing to wait seven years or longer to cash out their investments. They earn their returns through the increased value of the business, not through dividends and interest. For example, more than 1,000 early investors in Microsoft Inc. are now multimillionaires. Members of the Tech Coast Angels, a network of angel investors in California, purchased stock in a fledgling computer networking company called Sandpiper Networks at 70 cents a share, which they later sold for $97 a share![21] Angels' return-on-investment targets tend to be lower than those of professional venture capitalists. Although venture capitalists shoot for 60 percent to 75 percent returns annually, private investors usually settle for 20 percent to 50 percent (depending on the level of risk involved in the venture). Private investors typically take less than 50 percent ownership leaving the majority ownership to the company founder(s). The lesson: If an entrepreneur needs relatively small amounts of money to launch a company, angels are a primary source.

Partners

As we saw in Chapter 4, entrepreneurs can take on partners to expand the capital foundation of a business.

A Company Example

*When Lou Bucelli and Tim Crouse were searching for the money to launch **CME Conference Video**, a company that produces and distributes videotapes of educational conferences for physicians, they found an angel willing to put up $250,000 for 40 percent of the business. Unfortunately, their investor backed out when some of his real estate investments went bad, leaving the partners with commitments for several conferences but no cash to produce and distribute the videos. With little time to spare, Bucelli and Crouse decided to form a series of limited partnerships with people they knew, one for each videotape they would produce. Six limited partnerships produced $400,000 in financing, and the tapes generated $9.1 million in sales for the year. As the general partners, Bucelli and Crouse retained 80 percent of each partnership. The limited partners earned returns of up to 80 percent in just six months. Within two years, their company was so successful that venture capitalists started calling. To finance their next round of growth, Bucelli and Crouse sold 35 percent of their company to a venture capital firm for $1.3 million.[22]*

Before entering into any partnership arrangement, however, entrepreneurs must consider the impact of giving up some personal control over operations and of sharing profits with others. Whenever entrepreneurs give up equity in their businesses (through whatever mechanism), they run the risk of losing control over it. As the founder's ownership in a company becomes increasingly diluted, the probability of losing control of its future direction and the entire decision-making process increases.

A Company Example

*At age 19, Scott Olson started a company that manufactured in-line skates—a company that he had big dreams for. **Rollerblades Inc.** grew quickly but soon ran into the problem that plagues so many fast-growing companies—insufficient cash flow. Through a series of unfortunate incidents, Olsen began selling shares of ownership in the company for the money he desperately needed to bring his innovative skate designs to market. Ultimately, investors ended up with 95 percent of the company, leaving Olson with the remaining scant 5 percent. Frustrated at not being able to determine the company's direction, Olson soon left to start another company. "It's tough to keep control," he says. "For every penny you get in the door, you have to give something up."[23]*

Corporate Venture Capital

Large corporations have gotten into the business of financing small companies. Today, about 300 large corporations across the globe, including Intel, Motorola, Cisco Systems, UPS, and Johnson & Johnson, invest in fledgling companies, most often those in the product development and sales growth stages. Today, 20 percent of all venture capital invested comes from corporations.[24] Young companies not only get a boost from the capital injections large companies give them, but they also stand to gain many other benefits from the relationship. The right corporate partner may share technical expertise, distribution channels, marketing know-how, and provide introductions to important customers and suppliers. Another intangible yet highly important advantage an investment from a large corporate partner gives a small company is credibility. Doors that otherwise would be closed to a small company magically open when the right corporation becomes a strategic partner.

A Company Example

*When Keith Brown launched **BuildSoft Inc.**, a company that links residential builders, suppliers, and subcontractors over the Internet, he began looking for corporate investors who would also serve as partners, giving BuildSoft the tools it needed to gain a competitive advantage. Within seven months, Brown had negotiated a $104 million dollar deal with 12 giants in the construction industry, including Lennar and Owens Corning. Not only did the corporations supply valuable capital to the growing company, but they also attracted customers and provided access to products and marketing and distribution expertise.[25]*

Foreign corporations such as Nestle S.A., the Swiss food giant, Hitachi, a Japanese maker of electronics, and Orange S.A., one of France's largest companies, are also interested in investing in small U.S. businesses. Often these corporations are seeking strategic partnerships to gain access to new technology, new products, or access to lucrative U.S. markets. In return, the small companies they invest in benefit from the capital infusion as well as from their partners' international experience and connections. In other cases, small companies are turning to their customers for the resources they need to fuel their rapid growth. Recognizing how interwoven their success is with that of their suppliers, corporate giants such as AT&T, ChevronTexaco, and Ford now offer financial support to many of the small businesses they buy from.

Jeff Brown, CEO of **RadioFrame Networks**, *found not only a customer in France's wireless technology giant Orange S.A. but also an investor. RadioFrame's technology improves the performance of wireless networks inside buildings, making it a perfect fit with Orange's primary business. Through its venture capital division, Orange invested $1.5 million in the 55-person company, giving it enough fuel to feed its growth.*[26]

Venture Capital Companies

Venture capital companies are private, for-profit organizations that assemble pools of capital and then use them to purchase equity positions in young businesses they believe have high-growth and high-profit potential, producing annual returns of 300 to 500 percent within five to seven years. More than 1,300 venture capital firms operate across the United States today, investing billions of dollars (see Figure 12.1) in promising small companies in a wide variety of industries. *Pratt's Guide to Venture Capital Sources*, published by Venture Economics, is a valuable resource for entrepreneurs looking for venture capital. The guide, available in most libraries, includes contact information as well as investment preferences for hundreds of venture capital firms.

venture capital companies—*private, for-profit organizations that purchase equity positions in young businesses they believe have high-growth and high-profit potential.*

Colleges and universities have entered the venture capital business; more than 100 colleges across the nation now have venture funds designed to invest in promising businesses started by their students, alumni, and faculty.[27] Even the Central Intelligence Agency (CIA) has launched a venture capital firm called In-Q-Tel that invests in companies that are developing new technologies that could benefit the CIA. One of In-Q-Tel's investments is in a company that is developing a three-dimensional Web browser that allows users to see "live" versions of the Web sites they visit.[28]

Venture capital firms, which provide about 7 percent of all funding for private companies, have invested billions of dollars in high-potential small companies over the years, including such notable businesses as Apple Computer, FedEx, Microsoft Inc., Intel, and Genentech.[29] In many of these deals, several venture capital companies invested money, experience, and advice across several stages of growth. Table 12.1 offers a humorous look at how venture capitalists decipher the language of sometimes overly optimistic entrepreneurs.

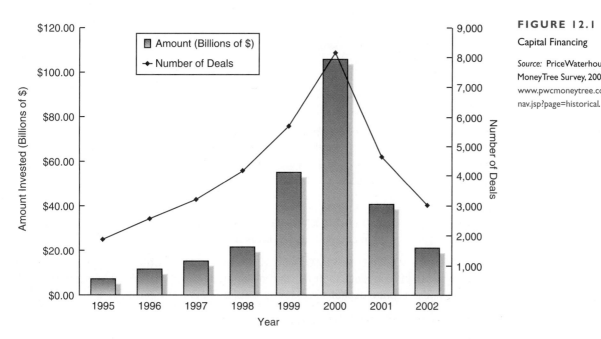

FIGURE 12.1 Venture Capital Financing

Source: PriceWaterhouseCoopers MoneyTree Survey, 2003, www.pwcmoneytree.com/moneytree/nav.jsp?page=historical.

TABLE 12.1

Deciphering the Language of the Venture Capital Industry

Sources: Adapted from Suzanne McGee, "A Devil's Dictionary of Financing," *Wall Street Journal,* June 12, 2000, p. C13; John F. Budd Jr., "Cracking the CEO's Code," *Wall Street Journal,* March 27, 1995, p. A20; "Venture-Speak Defined," *Teleconnect,* October 1990, p. 42; Cynthia E. Griffin, "Figuratively Speaking," *Entrepreneur,* August 1999, p. 26.

By nature, entrepreneurs tend to be optimistic. When screening business plans, venture capitalists must make an allowance for entrepreneurial enthusiasm. Here's a dictionary of phrases commonly found in business plans and their accompanying venture capital translations.

Exploring an acquisition strategy—Our current products have no market.

We're on a clear P2P (pathway to profitability)—We're still years away from earning a profit.

Basically on plan—We're expecting a revenue shortfall of 25 percent.

Internet business model—Potentially-bigger fools have been identified.

A challenging year—Competitors are eating our lunch.

Considerably ahead of plan—Hit our plan in one of the last three months.

Company's underlying strength and resilience—We still lost money, but look how we cut our losses.

Core business—Our product line is obsolete.

Currently revising budget—The financial plan is in total chaos.

Cyclical industry—We posted a huge loss last year.

Entrepreneurial CEO—He is totally uncontrollable, bordering on maniacal.

Facing unprecedented economic, political, and structural shifts—It's a tough world out there, but we're coping the best we can.

Highly leverageable network—No longer works but has friends who do.

Ingredients are there—Given two years, we might find a workable strategy.

Investing heavily in R&D—We're trying desperately to catch the competition.

Limited downside—Things can't get much worse.

Long sales cycle—Yet to find a customer who likes the product enough to buy it.

Major opportunity—It's our last chance.

Niche strategy—A small-time player.

On a manufacturing learning curve—We can't make the product with positive margins.

Passive investor—She phones once a year to see if we're still in business.

Positive results—Our losses were less than last year.

Repositioning the business—We've recently written off a multimillion-dollar investment.

Selective investment strategy—The board is spending more time on yachts than on planes.

Solid operating performance in a difficult year—Yes, we lost money and market share, but look how hard we tried.

Somewhat below plan—We expect a revenue shortfall of 75 percent.

Expenses were unexpectedly high—We grossly overestimated our profit margins.

Strategic investor—One who will pay a preposterous price for an equity share in the business.

Strongest fourth quarter ever—Don't quibble over the losses in the first three quarters.

Sufficient opportunity to market this product no longer exists—Nobody will buy the thing.

Too early to tell—Results to date have been grim.

A team of skilled, motivated, and dedicated people—We've laid off most of our staff, and those who are left should be glad they still have jobs.

Turnaround opportunity—It's a lost cause.

Unique—We have no more than six strong competitors.

Volume sensitive—Our company has massive fixed costs.

Window of opportunity—Without more money fast, this company is dead.

Work closely with the management—We talk to them on the phone once a month.

A year in which we confronted challenges—At least we know the questions even if we haven't got the answers.

POLICIES AND INVESTMENT STRATEGIES. Venture capital firms usually establish stringent policies to implement their overall investment strategies.

INVESTMENT SIZE AND SCREENING. Most venture capital firms seek investments in the $3 million to $10 million range to justify the cost of investigating the large number of proposals they receive. The venture capital screening process is *extremely* rigorous. The typical venture capital company invests in less than 1 percent of the applications it receives! For example, the average venture capital firm screens about 1,200 proposals a year, but more than 90 percent are rejected immediately because they do not match the firm's investment criteria. The remaining 10 percent are investigated more thoroughly at a cost ranging from $2,000 to $3,000 per proposal. At this time, approximately 10 to 15 proposals will have passed the screening process, and these are subjected to comprehensive review. The venture capital firm will invest in three to six of these remaining proposals.

OWNERSHIP AND CONTROL. Most venture capitalists prefer to purchase ownership in a small business through common stock or convertible preferred stock. Typically, a venture capital company seeks to purchase 20 percent to 40 percent of a business, but in some cases, a venture capitalist may buy 70 percent or more of a company's stock, leaving its founders with a minority share of ownership.

Most venture capitalists prefer to let the founding team of managers employ its skills to operate a business *if* they are capable of managing its growth. However, it is quite common for venture capitalists to join the boards of directors of the companies they invest in or to send in new managers or a new management team to protect their investments. "We change management in the companies we fund about 40 percent of the time," says Janet Effland, a partner in the venture capital firm Apax Partners.[30] In other words, venture capitalists are *not* passive investors! Some serve only as financial and managerial advisors, whereas others take an active role in managing the company—recruiting employees, providing sales leads, choosing attorneys and advertising agencies, and making daily decisions. The majority of these active venture capitalists say they are forced to step in because the existing management team lacked the talent and experience to achieve growth targets.

STAGE OF INVESTMENT. Most venture capital firms invest in companies that are either in the early stages of development (called early stage investing) or in the rapid-growth phase (called expansion stage investing). Others specialize in acquisitions, providing the financing for managers and employees of a business to buy it out. On average, 91 percent of all venture capital goes to businesses in these stages, although some venture capital firms are showing more interest in companies in the start-up phase because of the tremendous returns that are possible by investing then.[31] Most venture capital firms do not make just a single investment in a company. Instead, they invest in a company over time across several stages, where their investments often total $10 to $15 million.

INVESTMENT PREFERENCES. The venture capital industry has undergone important changes over the past decade. Venture capital funds now are larger and more specialized. As the industry matures, venture capital funds increasingly are focusing their investments in niches—everything from low-calorie custards to the Internet. Some will invest in almost any industry but prefer companies in particular stages, from start-up to expansion. Traditionally, however, only 9 percent of venture capital financing goes to companies in the start-up (seed) stage, when entrepreneurs are forming a company or developing a product or service. Most of the start-up businesses that attract venture capital are technology companies—software, biotechnology, telecommunications, and networking.[32]

WHAT VENTURE CAPITALISTS LOOK FOR. Small business owners must realize that it is very difficult for any small business, especially fledgling or struggling firms, to pass the intense screening process of a venture capital company and qualify for an investment. Venture capital firms finance only about 3,600 deals in a typical year. Two factors make a deal attractive to venture capitalists: high returns and a convenient (and profitable) exit strategy. When evaluating potential investments, venture capitalists look for the following features:

COMPETENT MANAGEMENT. The most important ingredient in the success of any business is the ability of the management team, and venture capitalists recognize this. To venture capitalists, the ideal management team has experience, managerial skills, commitment, and the ability to build teams. One financing expert explains, "Venture capitalists are really buying into the management of your company. If the light isn't on at the top, it's dim all the way down."[33]

FIGURE 12.2 Average
Returns on Venture Capital
Investments

Source: Paul Keaton, "The Reality of
Venture Capital," Small Business Forum,
Arkansas Small Business Development
Center, http://asbdc.ualr.edu/bizfacts/-
501.asp?print=Y, p. 8.

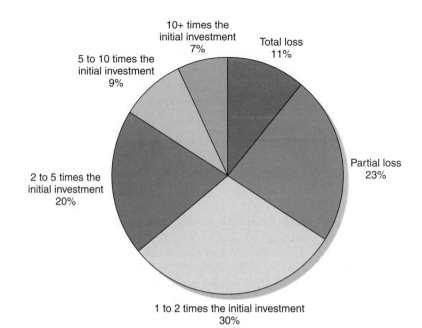

A Company Example

FurnitureFind.com, an online furniture retailer that not only survived but also thrived in the dot-com fallout, recently attracted a multimillion-dollar investment from HQ Venture Capital in Austin, Texas. Because its founders had been in the bricks-and-mortar retail furniture business for many years and understood the industry, FurnitureFind.com emerged as one of the online market leaders. "We were impressed by the strength of the management team," says HQ Venture Capital's CEO. The founder's experience and the company's proven business model convinced venture capitalists that FurnitureFind.com will become "the dominant online franchise in the category." [34]

COMPETITIVE EDGE. Investors are searching for some factor that will enable a small business to set itself apart from its competitors. This distinctive competence may range from an innovative product or service that satisfies unmet customer needs to a unique marketing or R&D approach. It must be something with the potential to create a sustainable competitive edge, making the company a leader in its industry.

GROWTH INDUSTRY. Hot industries attract profits—and venture capital. Most venture capital firms focus their searches on prospects in rapidly expanding fields because they believe the profit potential is greater in these areas. Venture capital firms are most interested in young companies that have enough growth potential to become at least $100 million businesses within three to five years. Venture capitalists know that most of the businesses they invest in will flop, so their winners have to be *big* winners (see Figure 12.2). One venture capital investor says, "If you want to get really good returns, your hits generally have to earn 10 times your investment in three to five years." [35]

VIABLE EXIT STRATEGY. Venture capitalists not only look for promising companies with the ability to dominate a market, but they also want to see a plan for a feasible exit strategy, typically to be executed within three to five years. Venture capital firms realize the return on their investments when the companies they invest in either make an initial public offering or are acquired by or merged into another business.

INTANGIBLE FACTORS. Some other important factors considered in the screening process are not easily measured; they are the intuitive, intangible factors the venture capitalist detects by gut feeling. This feeling might be the result of the small firm's solid sense of direction, its strategic planning process, the chemistry of its management team, or a number of other factors.

Entrepreneurs in search of financing must understand the implications of accepting venture capital.

A Company Example

When his daughter developed a seizure disorder that required taking bitter medicine four times a day, Kenny Kramm began experimenting with different flavorings that could be mixed with regular medicines to make them taste better without affecting their efficacy. He finally found success with a banana flavoring that proved to be a huge hit not only with his *daughter but also with the customers at the pharmacy his parents owned. Kramm went on to develop 42 more flavors ranging from orange Creamsicle to chocolate silk pie, which became the basis for his company, **FlavorX**, launched in 1995 with $1 million he invested and raised from family members, friends, and private investors. Building brand awareness required significant expenditures on advertising and a sales force to call on pharmacies and veterinarians. (Pets appreciate the flavors, too!) The large amounts of capital needed to stoke the company's growth required Kramm to turn to venture capitalists. In return for company stock, several venture capital firms invested $2 million in FlavorX, leaving Kramm with 34 percent of the company, whose sales now exceed $5 million a year.[36]*

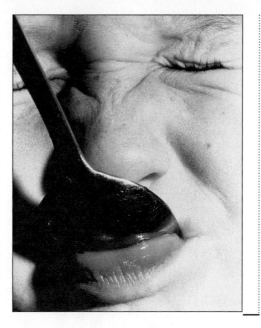

Thanks to Kenny Kramm, founder of FlavorX, and the venture capital firms that invested in his business, taking medicine no longer has to be a bitter experience.

Courtesy of FlavorX, Inc.

Despite its many benefits, venture capital is not suited for every entrepreneur. "VC money comes at a price," warns one entrepreneur. "Before boarding a one-way money train, ask yourself if this is the best route for your business and personal desires, because investors are like department stores the day after Christmas—they expect a lot of returns in a short period of time."[37]

Public Stock Sale ("Going Public")

In some cases, entrepreneurs can "go public" by selling shares of stock in their corporations to outside investors. In an **initial public offering**, a company raises capital by selling shares of its stock to the general public for the first time. A public offering is an effective method of raising large amounts of capital, but it can be an expensive and time-consuming process filled with regulatory nightmares. Once a company makes an initial public offering (IPO), *nothing* will ever be the same again. Managers must consider the impact of their decisions not only on the company and its employees but also on its shareholders and the value of their stock.

Going public isn't for every business. In fact, most small companies do not meet the criteria for making a successful public stock offering. Over the past 20 years, an average of 440 companies per year have made initial public offerings of their stock, although the number of IPOs has fallen off significantly since 2000 (see Figure 12.3). Only about 20,000 companies in the United States—less than 1 percent of the total—are publicly held. Few companies with less than $20 million in annual sales manage to go public successfully. It is extremely difficult for a start-up company with no track record of success to raise money with a public offering. Instead, the investment bankers who underwrite public stock offerings typically look for established companies with the following characteristics:

initial public offering—*a method of raising equity capital in which a company sells shares of its stock to the general public for the first time.*

- consistently high growth rates.

- a strong record of earnings.

- three to five years of audited financial statements that meet or exceed SEC standards. After the Enron and WorldCom scandals, investors are demanding impeccable financial statements.

- a solid position in a rapidly growing industry. In 2000, the median age of companies making IPOs was three years; today it is 15 years.[38]

- a sound management team with experience and a strong board of directors.

Entrepreneurs who are considering taking their companies public should first consider carefully the advantages and the disadvantages of an IPO. The *advantages* include the following:

FIGURE 12.3   Initial Public
Offerings (IPOs)

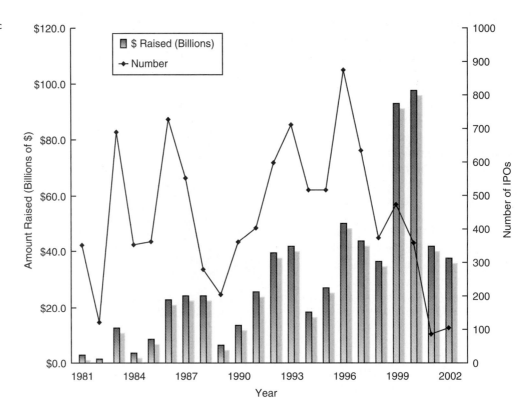

ABILITY TO RAISE LARGE AMOUNTS OF CAPITAL. The biggest benefit of a public offering is the capital infusion the company receives. After going public, the corporation has the cash to fund R&D projects, expand plant and facilities, repay debt, or boost working capital balances without incurring the interest expense and the obligation to repay associated with debt financing.

A Company Example

*For instance, **JetBlue**, the low-cost airline founded by David Neeleman, raised $158 million when the company made an initial public offering, selling 5.87 million shares of stock for $27 each, more than the $22 to $24 anticipated price range in its S-1 filing with the SEC. JetBlue used the offering proceeds for working capital and to purchase new aircraft.*[39]

IMPROVED CORPORATE IMAGE. All of the media attention a company receives during the registration process makes it more visible. Plus, becoming a public company in some industries improves its prestige and enhances its competitive position, one of the most widely recognized, intangible benefits of going public.

IMPROVED ACCESS TO FUTURE FINANCING. Going public boosts a company's net worth and broadens its equity base. Its improved stature and financial strength make it easier for the firm to attract more capital—both debt and equity—and to grow.

ATTRACTING AND RETAINING KEY EMPLOYEES. Public companies often use stock-based compensation plans to attract and retain quality employees. Stock options and bonuses are excellent methods for winning employees' loyalty and for instilling a healthy ownership attitude among them *if* the company's stock performs well in the market. Employee stock ownership plans (ESOPs) and stock purchase plans are popular recruiting and motivational tools in many small corporations, enabling them to hire top-flight talent they otherwise would not be able to afford.

USING STOCK FOR ACQUISITIONS. A company whose stock is publicly traded can acquire other businesses by offering its own shares rather than cash. Acquiring other companies with shares of stock eliminates the need to incur additional debt.

LISTING ON A STOCK EXCHANGE. Being listed on an organized stock exchange, even a small regional one, improves the marketability of a company's shares and enhances its image. Most publicly held companies' stocks do not qualify for listing on the nation's largest exchanges—the New York Stock Exchange (NYSE) and the American Stock Exchange (AMEX). However, the AMEX recently created a new market for small-company stocks, The Emerging Company Marketplace. Most small companies' stocks are traded on either the National Association of Securities Dealers Automated Quotation (NASDAQ) system's National Market System (NMS) and its emerging small-capitalization exchange or one of the nation's regional stock exchanges.

Despite these advantages, many factors can spoil a company's attempted IPO. In fact, only 5 percent of the companies that attempt to go public ever complete the process.[40] The *disadvantages* of going public include the following:

DILUTION OF FOUNDER'S OWNERSHIP. Whenever entrepreneurs sell stock to the public, they automatically dilute their ownership in their businesses. Most owners retain a majority interest in the business, but they may still run the risk of unfriendly takeovers years later after selling more stock.

LOSS OF CONTROL. If enough shares are sold in a public offering, a founder risks losing control of the company. If a large block of shares falls into the hands of dissident stockholders, they could vote the existing management team (including the founder) out.

*George Stathakis, owner of the highly successful chain of **Stax's** restaurants in Greenville, South Carolina, recalls investment bankers approaching him about taking his company public to fund its growth, but he refused them all. "The one thing you don't have when you go public is control," he says, " and that's something my partners and I just couldn't handle."*[41]

A Company Example

LOSS OF PRIVACY. Taking their companies public can be a big ego boost for owners, but they must realize that their companies are no longer solely theirs. Information that was once private must be available for public scrutiny. The initial prospectus and the continuous reports filed with the Securities and Exchange Commission (SEC) disclose a variety of information about the company and its operations—from financial data and raw material sources to legal matters and patents to *anyone*—including competitors. Loss of privacy and loss of control are the most commonly cited reasons that CEOs choose not to attempt IPOs.[42]

REPORTING TO THE SEC. Operating as a publicly held company is expensive. Publicly held companies must file periodic reports with the SEC, which often requires a more powerful accounting system, a larger accounting staff, and greater use of attorneys and other professionals. The cost of complying with the SEC's accounting and filing requirements alone can cost $150,000 or more a year.

*Chief operating officer John Henderson and the top managers at **High Falls Brewing Company**, a brewery in Rochester, New York, recently transformed the once publicly held company into a privately owned business. Henderson says that the reporting requirements of running a publicly held company "took a lot more time than I expected" and that operating the brewery as a private business is "a huge relief."*[43]

A Company Example

FILING EXPENSES. A public stock offering usually is an expensive way to generate funds for start-up or expansion. For the typical small company, the cost of a public offering is around 12 percent of the capital raised. On small offerings, costs can eat up as much as 40 percent of the capital raised; however, on offerings above $20 million, just 5 percent typically goes to cover expenses.[44] Once an offering exceeds $10 million, its relative issuing costs drop. The largest cost is the underwriter's commission, which is typically 7 percent of the proceeds on offerings less than $10 million and 13 percent on those over that amount.

ACCOUNTABILITY TO SHAREHOLDERS. The capital that entrepreneurs manage is no longer just their own. The manager of a publicly held firm is accountable to the company's shareholders. Indeed, the law requires that managers recognize and abide by a relationship built on trust. Profit and return on investment become the primary concerns for investors. If the stock price of a newly public company falls, shareholder lawsuits are inevitable.

"We threw an IPO and nobody came."

Investors whose shares decline in value often sue the company's managers for fraud and the failure to disclose the potential risks to which their investments expose them.

PRESSURE FOR SHORT-TERM PERFORMANCE. In privately held companies, entrepreneurs are free to follow their strategies for success, even if those strategies take years to produce results. When a company goes public, however, entrepreneurs quickly learn that shareholders are impatient and expect results immediately. Founders are under constant pressure to produce growth in profits and in market share, which requires them to maintain a delicate balance between short-term results and long-term strategy.

TIMING. As impatient as they can be, entrepreneurs often find the time demands of an initial public offering frustrating and distracting. Managing the IPO takes time away from managing the company. Working on an IPO can consume as much as 75 percent of top managers' time. "You want to make sure you're not becoming a chief 'going public' officer as opposed to a chief executive officer," advises an investment banker.[45]

A Company Example

When one company that produced sports entertainment software decided to go public, managers spent so much time focusing on the demands of the IPO that the company failed to get a new product to market in time for the Christmas season. Because it missed this crucial deadline, the company never recovered and went out of business.[46]

During this time, a company also runs the risk that the overall market for IPOs or for a particular industry may go sour. Factors beyond managers' control, such as declines in the stock market and potential investors' jitters, can quickly slam shut a company's "window of opportunity" for an IPO. For instance, when the NASDAQ began sinking in 2000, many companies planning IPOs, including InternetConnect (broadband networking services) and Plumtree Software (Web-portal software for large companies), withdrew their proposed stock offerings. Plumtree finally did pull off its IPO, but it was forced to cut its offering price to $8.50 from the $13 to $15 estimate listed in its SEC filings.[47]

THE REGISTRATION PROCESS. Taking a company public is a complicated, bureaucratic process that usually takes several months to complete. Many experts compare the IPO process to running a corporate marathon, and both the company and its management team must be in shape and up to the grueling task. The typical entrepreneur *cannot* take his company public alone. It requires a coordinated effort from a team of professionals, including

TABLE 12.2

Timetable for an Initial Public Offering

Sources: Adapted from "Initial Public Offering," *Entrepreneur,* June 14, 2002, www.entrepreneur.com/article/0,46-21,300892,00.html; PriceWaterhouseCoopers "Going Public Timetable," www.pwcglobal.com/Extweb/industry.nsf/docid/2C9CA8A7F060404A85256AC5007A86B8#.

Time	Action
Week 1	Conduct organizational meeting with IPO team, including underwriter, attorneys, accountants, and others. Begin drafting registration statement.
Week 5	Distribute first draft of registration statement to IPO team and make revisions.
Week 6	Distribute second draft of registration statement and make revisions.
Week 7	Distribute third draft of registration statement and make revisions.
Week 8	File registration statement with the SEC. Begin preparing presentations for road show to attract other investment bankers to the syndicate. Comply with blue-sky laws in states where offering will be sold.
Week 12	Receive comment letter on registration statement from SEC. Amend registration statement to satisfy SEC comments.
Week 13	File amended registration statement with SEC. Prepare and distribute preliminary offering prospectus (called a "red herring") to members of underwriting syndicate. Begin road show meetings.
Week 15	Receive approval for offering from SEC (unless further amendments are required). Issuing company and lead underwriter agree on final offering price. Prepare, file, and distribute final offering prospectus.
Week 16	Company and underwriter sign the final agreement. Underwriter issues stock, collects the proceeds from the sale, and delivers proceeds (less commission) to company.

company executives, an accountant, a securities attorney, a financial printer, and at least one underwriter. Table 12.2 shows a typical timetable for an IPO. The key steps in taking a company public include:

CHOOSE THE UNDERWRITER. The single most important ingredient in making a successful IPO is selecting a capable **underwriter (or investment banker)**. The underwriter serves two primary roles: helping to prepare the registration statement for the issue and promoting the company's stock to potential investors. The underwriter works with company managers as an advisor to prepare the registration statement that must be filed with the SEC, promoting the issue, pricing the stock, and providing after-market support. Once the registration statement is finished, the underwriter's primary job is selling the company's stock through an underwriting syndicate of other investment bankers it develops.

underwriter (or investment banker)—*a financial company that serves two important roles: helping to prepare the registration statement for an issue and promoting the company's stock to potential investors.*

NEGOTIATE A LETTER OF INTENT. To begin an offering, the entrepreneur and the underwriter must negotiate a **letter of intent**, which outlines the details of the deal. The letter of intent covers a variety of important issues, including the type of underwriting, its size and price range, the underwriter's commission, and any warrants and options included. It almost always states that the underwriter is not bound to the offering until it is executed—usually the day before or the day of the offering. However, the letter usually creates a binding obligation for the company to pay any direct expenses the underwriter incurs relating to the offer.

letter of intent—*an agreement between the underwriter and the company about to go public that outlines the details of the deal.*

PREPARE THE REGISTRATION STATEMENT. After a company signs the letter of intent, the next task is to prepare the **registration statement** to be filed with the Securities and Exchange Commission (SEC). This document describes both the company and the stock offering and discloses information about the risks of investing. It includes information on the use of the proceeds, the company's history, its financial position, its capital structure, the risks it faces, its managers' experience, and *many* other details. The statement is extremely comprehensive and may take months to develop. To prepare the statement, entrepreneurs must rely on their team of professionals.

registration statement—*the document a company must file with the SEC that describes both the company and its stock offering and discloses information about the risk of investing.*

FILE WITH THE SEC. When the statement is finished (with the exception of pricing the shares, proceeds, and commissions, which cannot be determined until just before the issue goes to market), the company officially files the statement with the SEC and awaits the review of the Division of Corporate Finance, a process that takes 30 to 45 days (or more). The division sends notice of any deficiencies in the registration statement to the company's attorney in a comment letter. The company and its team of professionals must cure all of the deficiencies in the statement noted by the comment letter. Finally, the company files the revised registration statement, along with a pricing amendment (giving the price of the shares, the proceeds, and the commissions).

WAIT TO GO EFFECTIVE. While waiting for the SEC's approval, the managers and the underwriters are busy. The underwriters are building a syndicate of other underwriters who will market the company's stock. (No stock sales can be made prior to the effective date of the offering, however.) The SEC also limits the publicity and information a company may release during this quiet period (which officially starts when the company reaches a preliminary agreement with the managing underwriter and ends 90 days after the effective date).

Securities laws do permit a **road show**, a gathering of potential syndicate members sponsored by the managing underwriter. Its purpose is to promote interest among potential underwriters in the IPO by featuring the company, its management, and the proposed deal. The managing underwriter and key company officials barnstorm major financial centers at a grueling pace.

A Company Example

*During the road show for **Plumtree Software**, a provider of expensive Web-portal software that raised $40 million in its IPO, CEO John Kunzie logged 45,000 miles to court potential investors in 80 different meetings in just 21 days.*[48]

On the last day before the registration statement becomes effective, the company signs the formal underwriting agreement. The final settlement, or closing, takes place a few days after the effective date for the issue. At this meeting the underwriters receive their shares to sell and the company receives the proceeds of the offering.

Typically, the entire process of going public takes from 60 to 180 days, but it can take much longer if the issuing company is not properly prepared for the process.

MEET STATE REQUIREMENTS. In addition to satisfying the SEC's requirements, a company also must meet the securities laws in all states in which the issue is sold. These state laws (or "blue-sky" laws) vary drastically from one state to another, and the company must comply with them.

Simplified Registrations and Exemptions

The IPO process just described (called an S-1 filing) requires maximum disclosure in the initial filing and discourages most small businesses from using it. Fortunately, the SEC allows several exemptions from this full-disclosure process for small businesses. Many small businesses that go public choose one of the simplified options the SEC has designed for small companies. The SEC has established the following simplified registration statements and exemptions from the registration process:

REGULATION S-B. Regulation S-B is a simplified registration process for small companies seeking to make initial or subsequent public offerings. Not only does this regulation simplify the initial filing requirements with the SEC, but it also reduces the ongoing disclosure and filings required of companies. Its primary goals are to open the doors to capital markets to smaller companies by cutting the paperwork and the costs of raising capital. Companies using the simplified registration process have two options: Form SB-1, a "transitional" registration statement for companies issuing less than $10 million worth of securities over a 12-month period, and Form SB-2, reserved for small companies seeking more than $10 million in a 12-month period.

To be eligible for the simplified registration process under process under Regulation S-B, a company:

■ must be based in the United States or Canada
■ must have revenues of less than $25 million

- must have outstanding publicly held stock worth no more than $25 million
- must not be an investment company
- must provide audited financial statements for two fiscal years

The goal of Regulation S-B's simplified registration requirements is to enable smaller companies to go public without incurring the expense of a full-blown registration. Total costs for a Regulation S-B registration are approximately $35,000.

REGULATION D (RULE 504): SMALL COMPANY OFFERING REGISTRATION (SCOR). Created in the late 1980s, the Small Company Offering Registration (also known as the Uniform Limited Offering Registration, ULOR) now is available in 47 states. A little-known tool, SCOR is designed to make it easier and less expensive for small companies to sell their stock to the public by eliminating the requirement for registering the offering with the SEC. The whole process typically costs less than half of what a traditional public offering costs. Entrepreneurs using SCOR will need an attorney and an accountant to help them with the issue, but many can get by without a securities lawyer, which can save tens of thousands of dollars. Some entrepreneurs even choose to market their companies' securities themselves (for example, to customers), saving the expense of hiring a broker. However, selling an issue is both time and energy consuming, and most SCOR experts recommend hiring a professional securities or brokerage firm to sell the company's shares. The SEC's objective in creating SCOR was to give small companies the same access to equity financing that large companies have via the stock market while bypassing many of the same costs and filing requirements. The capital ceiling on a SCOR issue is $1 million (except in Texas, where there is no limit), and the price of each share must be at least $5. That means that a company can sell no more than 200,000 shares (making the stock less attractive to stock manipulators). A SCOR offering requires only minimal notification to the SEC. The company must file a standardized disclosure statement, the U-7, which consists of 50 fill-in-the-blank questions. The form, which asks for information such as how much money the company needs, what the money will be used for, what investors receive, how investors can sell their investments, and other pertinent questions, closely resembles a business plan but also serves as a state securities offering registration, a disclosure document, and a prospectus. Entrepreneurs using SCOR may advertise their companies' offerings and can sell them directly to any investor with no restrictions and no minimums. An entrepreneur can sell practically any kind of security through a SCOR offering, including common stock, preferred stock, convertible preferred stock, stock options, stock warrants, and others.

A Company Example

Steve Crane and Art Aviles, Jr., cofounders of **CorpHQ**, *a Web portal that links small and home-based business owners in an online community, decided to bypass venture capital and relied on a SCOR offering to attract their first round of outside capital. The entrepreneurs believed that taking their company public not only would save them money but also would create greater opportunities for future financing efforts, both of which have proved to be true. Early on, Crane and Aviles recognized the need to promote their newly public company, whose shares trade on the OTC Bulletin Board, in the investment community. "Our success as a public company depends not only on how well we do financially but also how well we market our company and our story to the financial markets," says Crane.*[49]

A SCOR offering offers entrepreneurs needing equity financing several *advantages*:

- Access to a sizable pool of equity funds without the expense of full registration with the SEC. Companies often can complete a SCOR offering for less than $25,000.
- Few restrictions on the securities to be sold and on the investors to whom they can be sold.
- The ability to market the offering through advertisements to the public.
- New or start-up companies can qualify.
- No requirement of audited financial statements for offerings less than $500,000.
- Faster approval of the issue from regulatory agencies.
- The ability to make the offering in several states at once.

There are, of course, some *disadvantages* to using SCOR to raise needed funds:

- Not every state yet recognizes SCOR offerings.
- Partnerships cannot make SCOR offerings.
- A company can raise no more than $1 million in a 12-month period.
- An entrepreneur must register the offering in every state in which shares of stock will be sold to comply with their blue-sky laws, although current regulations allow simultaneous registration in multiple states.
- The process can be time consuming, distracting an entrepreneur from the daily routine of running the company. A limited secondary market for the securities may limit investors' interest. Currently, SCOR shares must be traded through brokerage firms that make small markets in specific stocks. However, the Pacific Stock Exchange and the NASDAQ's electronic bulletin board recently began listing SCOR stocks, so the secondary market for them has broadened.

REGULATION D (RULES 505 AND 506): PRIVATE PLACEMENTS. Rules 505 and 506 of Regulation D, also known as the Private Placement Memorandum, are exemptions from federal registration requirements that give emerging companies the opportunity to sell stock through private placements without actually going public. In a private placement, the company sells its shares directly to private investors without having to register them with the SEC or incur the expenses of an IPO. Instead, a knowledgeable attorney simply draws up an investment agreement that meets state and federal requirements between the company and its private investors.

A Company Example

*For example, **PatchLink.com**, a company that provides software solutions for businesses over the Internet, raised $5.6 million in a private equity placement made through online broker-dealer OffRoad Capital. PatchLink used the money to expand its engineering, sales, and marketing staff and to launch new products. "We ended up raising more money than we expected to without giving up any more of the company," says CEO Sean Moshir.*[50]

A *Rule 505* offering has a higher capital ceiling than a SCOR offering ($5 million) in a 12-month period but imposes more restrictions (no more than 35 nonaccredited investors, no advertising of the offer, and more stringent disclosure requirements).

Rule 506 imposes no ceiling on the amount that can be raised, but, like a Rule 505 offering, it limits the issue to 35 nonaccredited investors and prohibits advertising the offer to the public. There is no limit on the number of accredited investors, however. Rule 506 also requires detailed disclosure of relative information, but the extent depends on the dollar size of the offering.

These Regulation D rules minimize the expense and the time required to raise equity capital for small businesses. Fees for private placements typically range from 1 to 5 percent rather than the 7 to 13 percent underwriters normally charge for managing a public offering. Offerings made under Regulation D do impose limitations and demand certain disclosures, but they only require a company to file a simple form (Form D) with the SEC within 15 days of the first sale of stock.

SECTION 4(6). Section 4(6) covers private placements and is similar to Regulation D, Rules 505 and 506. It does not require registration on offers up to $5 million if they are made only to accredited investors.

INTRASTATE OFFERINGS (RULE 147). Rule 147 governs intrastate offerings, those sold only to investors in a single state by a company doing business in that state. To qualify, a company must be incorporated in the state, maintain its executive offices there, have 80 percent of its assets there, derive 80 percent of its revenues from the state, and use 80 percent of the offering proceeds for business in the state. There is no ceiling on the amount of the offering, but only residents of the state in which the issuing company operates can invest.

A Company Example

*Years ago, Ben Cohen and Jerry Greenfield founded a small ice cream manufacturing business named after themselves that struck a chord with customers. **Ben & Jerry's Homemade** grew rapidly, and the founders needed $600,000 to build a new manufacturing plant in*

Vermont where the company was based. They decided to "give the opportunity to our neighbors to grow with our company" by making an intrastate offering under Rule 147. Cohen and Greenfield registered their offering of 73,500 shares of stock with Vermont's Division of Banking and Insurance. Ben & Jerry's Homemade sold the entire offering (mostly to loyal customers) by placing ads in newspapers and stickers on ice cream containers that touted "Get a Scoop of the Action!" [51]

REGULATION A. Regulation A, although currently not used often, allows an exemption for offerings up to $5 million over a 12-month period. Regulation A imposes few restrictions, but it is more costly than the other types of exempted offerings, usually running between $80,000 and $120,000. The primary difference between a SCOR offering and a Regulation A offering is that a company must register its SCOR offering only in the states where it will sell its stock; in a Regulation A offering, the company also must file an offering statement with the SEC. Like a SCOR offering, a Regulation A offering requires only a simplified question-and-answer SEC filing and allows a company to sell its shares directly to investors.

*For instance, when **Blue Fish Clothing Inc.**, an all-natural women's clothing company, needed money to fuel its rapid growth, founder Jennifer Barclay decided to make a direct public offering under Regulation A, selling 800,000 shares at $5 each. "Banks wouldn't provide the funds, and venture capital firms wanted a huge percentage of the company," says Barclay. Blue Fish publicized its $4 million offering through mailings, advertisements, fish-shaped hanging tags on its garments, and word of mouth among its base of 30,000 loyal customers and supporters. Blue Fish, whose shares are traded on the Chicago Stock Exchange, used the offering's proceeds to build new retail stores, to install a computerized information system, and to expand its management team.* [52]

`A Company Example`

DIRECT STOCK OFFERINGS. Many of the simplified registrations and exemptions discussed here give entrepreneurs the power to sidestep investment bankers and sell their companies' stock offerings directly to investors and, in the process, save themselves thousands of dollars in underwriting fees. By cutting out the underwriter's commission and many legal and most registration fees, entrepreneurs willing to handle the paperwork requirements and to market their own shares typically can make direct public offerings (DPOs) for 6 to 10 percent of the total amount of the issue, compared with 13 percent for a traditional stock offering.

__Real Goods Trading Company__, a retailer of environmentally friendly products, was a pioneer of direct public offerings over the Web. In 1991, the company engineered a successful DPO that raised $1 million and followed with two more DPOs in later years that generated $3.6 million each! More than 5,000 of the company's loyal customers became investors. In fact, managers discovered that once customers became shareholders, they purchased nearly twice as much merchandise as customers who were not shareholders! Managers at Real Goods found that using the Web to reach potential investors was not only one of the best bargains but also one of the most effective methods for selling its stock to the public. [53]

`A Company Example`

The World Wide Web (WWW) opens an easy-to-use avenue for direct public offerings and is one the fastest-growing sources of capital for small businesses. Much of the Web's appeal as a fund-raising tool stems from its ability to reach large numbers of prospective investors very quickly and at a low cost. "This is the only form of instantaneous international contact with an enormous population," says one Web expert. "You can put your prospectus out to the world." [54] Companies making direct stock offerings on the Web most often make them under either Regulation A or Regulation D. Direct public offerings work best for companies that have a single product or related product lines and a base of customers who are loyal to the company. In fact, the first company to make a successful DPO over the Internet was Spring Street Brewing, a microbrewery founded by Andy Klein. Klein raised $1.6 million in a Regulation A offering in 1996. Companies that make successful direct public offerings of their stock over the Web must meet the same standards as companies making stock offerings using more traditional methods. Experts caution Web-based fund seekers to make sure their electronic prospectuses meet SEC and state requirements.

Table 12.3 provides a summary of the major types of exemptions and simplified offerings. Of these, the limited offerings and private placements are most commonly used.

TABLE 12.3

Simplified Registration and Exemptions: Comparative Table

Source: Deciding to Go Public, New York: Ernst & Young, 1993, pp. 70–71.

Private and Limited Offerings Regulation D

	Rule 504	Rule 505	Rule 506
Dollar Limit	$1 million in any 12-month period	$5 million in any 12-month period	None
Limit on Number of Purchasers	No	35 nonaccredited, unlimited accredited	35 nonaccredited, unlimited accredited
Qualification for Purchasers	No	No	Nonaccredited must be sophisticated
Qualifications of Issuers	Not available for investment companies, blank check companies, or reporting companies	Not available for investment companies or those disqualified by "bad boy" provisions	No
Disclosure Requirements	Not specified	Only if one or more nonaccredited purchasers	Only if one or more nonaccredited purchasers
Financial Statement Requirements	Not specified	Period varies for audited statements	Period varies for audited statements
General Solicitation and Advertising Prohibited	No	Yes	Yes
Resale Restrictions	No	Yes	Yes

	Private Placements Section 4(6)	Intrastate Offerings Rule 147	Unregistered Public Offerings Regulation A	Small Business Issuers Registration Form SB-1	Small Business Issuers Registration Form SB-2
Dollar Limit	$5 million	None	$5 million in any 12-month period	$10 million in any 12-month period	None
Limit on Number of Purchasers	No	No	No	No	No
Qualification for Purchasers	All must be accredited	All must be registrants of a single state	No	No	No
Qualifications of Issuers	No	Must be resident and do business in same state as purchasers	Available for U.S. and Canadian companies only; not available for reporting companies, blank check companies, investment companies, sale of oil and gas or mineral rights, or those disqualified by "bad boy" provisions	Available for U.S. and Canadian companies with revenue and public float of less than $25 million; not available for investment companies or susidiaries whose parent is not qualified to use the form	Available for U.S. and Canadian companies with revenue and public float of less than $25 million; not available for investment companies or subsidiaries whose parent is not qualified to use the form
Disclosure Requirements	Not specified	Not specified	Yes	Yes	Yes
Financial Statement Requirements	Not specified	Not specified	2 years of unaudited statements	2 years of unaudited statements	2 years of unaudited statements
General Solicitation and Advertising Prohibited	Yes	No	No	No	No
Resale Restrictions	Yes	Yes	Yes	No	No

YOU Be the Consultant . . .

Filled with Promise, but Low on Capital

After graduation, Astro Teller and three college buddies from Carnegie Mellon University worked as consultants to technology companies such as Motorola and Compaq Computers on projects involving wearable computers. Before long, they had launched a company of their own, BodyMedia, built around a product they had developed called the SenseWear armband. The 3-ounce device, which straps onto a person's arm, includes metallic sensors that monitor the wearer's perspiration levels, skin temperature, and internal temperature and then combines them into a constant measure of his or her calorie burn rate. The clever product has a wireless device that sends all captured information to a PC, where it can be displayed for easy analysis. It can run for four consecutive days before its batteries need to be recharged. Users can program the SenseWear armband to signal when they have reached a calorie goal or when it is time to take medicine. The device may be just the tool a dieter is looking for, a lifesaving device for those with medical conditions such as diabetes, and the solution to medical researchers' problems of collecting reliable data on their patients.

BodyMedia CEO Teller, who has a Ph.D. in artificial intelligence and is the grandson of Edward Teller, the inventor of the atomic bomb, saw the SenseWear armband as the centerpiece of a Web-based health portal that would track a person's daily statistics on exercise, sleep, and calorie expenditures. Unfortunately, potential lenders and investors didn't see things quite as clearly as Teller and his cofounders. "We had no credibility," says CFO Jeff Swoveland. "We kissed every frog. Nobody wanted to hear the pitch."

Teller and his friends managed to launch their company, but they knew they would need the endorsement of physicians to be able to raise the capital they needed to realize the company's potential. For five months, they worked the halls at the University of Pittsburgh Medical Center before David Kupfer, an expert in behavioral health, helped them convince the hospital to invest $2.5 million to turn the prototype into a real product. Teller soon abandoned the Web portal idea and decided to focus on selling SenseWear, which would be priced around $900, to large corporations for their employees with the idea that it would help lower their rapidly escalating health insurance costs. By 2001, however, a sluggish economy had reduced corporate America's spending on employee wellness, and Teller was in need of a device to monitor BodyMedia's cash burn rate as accurately as the SenseWear device monitored users' calorie burn rates. A falling stock market had diminished the number of IPOs to a trickle, and venture capital firms were watching the

Astro Teller, CEO of BodyMedia Inc., needs second-round financing to bring to market SenseWear armband, a device that monitors the wearer's vital signs and calorie burn rate. What recommendations can you offer Teller?

Courtesy of BodyMedia, Inc.

value of their investments and their pools of capital evaporate. BodyMedia, projected to generate sales of $700,000 in the upcoming year, was in danger of running out of money, having gone through most of the original $2.5 million from the hospital. Teller shifted the company's strategy to focus on selling the product to makers and distributors of medical testing equipment such as Roche Diagnostics, a $5 billion global giant. Teller is convinced that his company and its product will succeed, and he is setting out to attract its much-needed second round of financing.

1. What role do factors that are beyond entrepreneurs' control—such as a faltering economy or a falling stock market—have on their ability to attract the capital they need?

2. Explain why the following funding sources would or would not be appropriate for BodyMedia: family and friends, angel investors, an initial public offering, a traditional bank loan, asset-based borrowing, or one of the many federal or SBA loans.

3. Work with a team of your classmates to devise a workable strategy for raising the capital BodyMedia needs to market the SenseWear device.

Sources: Adapted from Bob Parks, "Armed for Success," *Business 2.0,* April 2003, pp. 46–48; Brad Lemley, "TEDMED," *Discover,* April 2003, www.discover.com/apr_03/gthere.html?article=featted.html; BodyMedia, www.bodymedia.com.

prime rate—*the interest rate banks charge their most creditworthy customers.*

THE NATURE OF DEBT FINANCING

Debt financing involves the funds that the small business owner borrows and must repay with interest. Lenders of capital are more numerous than investors, although small business loans can be just as difficult (if not more difficult) to obtain. Although borrowed capital allows entrepreneurs to maintain complete ownership of their businesses, it must be carried as a liability on the balance sheet as well as be repaid with interest at some point in the future. In addition, because small businesses are considered to be greater risks than bigger corporate customers, they must pay higher interest rates because of the risk-return trade-off—the higher the risk, the greater the return demanded. Most small firms pay the **prime rate**, the interest rate banks charge their most creditworthy customers, *plus* two to three percentage points. Still, the cost of debt financing often is lower than that of equity financing. Because of the higher risks associated with providing equity capital to small companies, investors demand greater returns than lenders. Also, unlike equity financing, debt financing does not require an entrepreneur to dilute her ownership interest in the company.

Entrepreneurs seeking debt capital are quickly confronted with an astounding range of credit options varying greatly in complexity, availability, and flexibility. Not all of these sources of debt capital are equally favorable, however. By understanding the various sources of capital—both commercial and government lenders—and their characteristics, entrepreneurs can greatly increase the chances of obtaining a loan.

We now turn to the various sources of debt capital.

Sources of Debt Capital

COMMERCIAL BANKS Commercial banks are the very heart of the financial market for small businesses, providing the greatest number and variety of loans to small companies. One study by the Small Business Administration found that commercial banks provide 64 percent of the credit available to small businesses, compared to 12.3 percent supplied by commercial finance companies, the next most prominent source of small business lending. The study also revealed that 67 percent of all small businesses that borrow from traditional sources get financing from banks![55] For small business owners, banks are lenders of *first* resort.

Banks tend to be conservative in their lending practices and prefer to make loans to established small businesses rather than to high-risk start-ups. One expert estimates that only 5 to 8 percent of business start-ups get bank financing.[56] Bankers want to see evidence of a company's successful track record before committing to a loan. They are concerned with a firm's operating past and will scrutinize its financial reports to project its position in the future. They also want proof of the stability of the company's sales and the ability of the product or service to generate adequate cash flows to ensure repayment of the loan. If they do make loans to a start-up venture, banks like to see sufficient cash flows to repay the loan, ample collateral to secure it, or a Small Business Administration (SBA) guarantee to insure it. Studies suggest that small banks (those with less than $300 million in assets) are most likely to lend money to small businesses.[57]

A Company Example

Some banks are willing to extend loans to start-up companies, however. Rasheed Refaey turned to bank financing to cover unexpected cost overruns in the construction and start-up of his restaurant, **Tasca-Kitchen & Wine Bar***. Refaey already had raised $500,000 from private investors and did not want to give up any more equity in his business, so he turned to a small community bank for a $250,000 loan. His solid business plan coupled with an introduction by consultants at a nearby Small Business Development Center convinced bank officers to make the loan. Business at the restaurant is booming, giving Refaey plenty of cash to repay the loan.*[58]

When evaluating a loan application, banks focus on a company's capacity to create positive cash flow because they know that's where the money to repay their loans will come from. The first question in most bankers' minds when reviewing an entrepreneur's business plan is "Can this business generate sufficient cash to repay the loan?" Even though they rely on collateral to secure their loans, the last thing banks want is for a borrower to default, forcing them to sell the collateral (often at "fire sale" prices) and use the proceeds to pay off the loan. *That's* why bankers stress cash flow when analyzing a loan request, especially for a business start-up. "Cash is more important than your mother," jokes one experienced borrower.[59]

Short-Term Loans

Short-term loans, extended for less than one year, are the most common type of commercial loan banks make to small companies. These funds typically are used to replenish the working capital account to finance the purchase of more inventory, boost output, finance credit sales to customers, or take advantage of cash discounts. As a result, an owner repays the loan after converting inventory and receivables into cash. There are several types of short-term loans.

COMMERCIAL LOANS (OR TRADITIONAL BANK LOANS). A basic short-term loan is the commercial bank's specialty. Business owners use commercial loans for a specific expenditure—to buy a particular piece of equipment or to make a specific purchase, and terms usually require repayment as a lump sum within three to six months. Two types of commercial loans exist: secured and unsecured. A secured loan is one in which the borrower's promise to repay is secured by giving the bank an interest in some asset (collateral). Although secured loans give banks a safety cushion in case the borrower defaults on the loan, they are much more expensive to administer and maintain. With an unsecured loan, the bank grants a loan to a business owner without requiring him to pledge any specific collateral to support the loan in case of default. Until a small business is able to prove its financial strength to the bank's satisfaction, it will probably not qualify for an unsecured commercial loan. For both secured and unsecured commercial loans, an owner is expected to repay the total amount of the loan at maturity. Sometimes the interest due on the loan is prepaid—deducted from the total amount borrowed.

LINES OF CREDIT. One of the most common requests entrepreneurs make of banks is to establish a **line of credit**, a short-term loan with a preset limit that provides much-needed cash flow for day-to-day operations. With an approved line of credit, a business owner can borrow up to the predetermined ceiling at any time during the year quickly and conveniently by writing himself a loan. Banks set up lines of credit that are renewable for anywhere from 90 days to several years, and they usually limit the open line of credit to 40 to 50 percent of a firm's present working capital, although they will lend more for highly seasonal businesses. Bankers may require a company to rest its line of credit during the year, maintaining a zero balance, as proof that the line of credit is not a perpetual crutch. Like commercial loans, lines of credit can be secured or unsecured. A business typically pays a small handling fee (1 to 2 percent of the maximum amount of credit) plus interest on the amount borrowed—usually prime plus three points or more.

line of credit—*a short-term bank loan with a preset limit that provides working capital for day-to-day operations.*

Table 12.4 describes the five most common reasons bankers reject small business loan applications and how to avoid them.

FLOOR PLANNING. Floor planning is a form of financing frequently employed by retailers of big-ticket items that are easily distinguishable from one another (usually by serial number), such as automobiles, boats, and major appliances. For example, a commercial bank finances Auto City's purchase of its inventory of automobiles and maintains a security interest in each car in the order by holding its title as collateral. Auto City pays interest on the loan monthly and repays the principal as it sells the cars. The longer a floor-planned item sits in inventory, the more it costs the business owner in interest expense. Banks and other floor planners often discourage retailers from using their money without authorization by performing spot checks to verify prompt repayment of the principal as items are sold.

Intermediate and Long-Term Loans

Banks primarily are lenders of short-term capital to small businesses, although they will make certain intermediate and long-term loans. Intermediate and long-term loans, which are normally secured by collateral, are extended for one year or longer and are normally used to increase fixed- and growth-capital balances. Small companies often face a greater challenge qualifying for intermediate and long-term loans because of the increased risk to which they expose the bank. Commercial banks grant these loans for constructing a plant, purchasing real estate and equipment, expanding a business, and other long-term investments. Loan repayments are normally made monthly or quarterly. One of the most common types of intermediate loans is an installment loan, which banks make to small firms for purchasing equipment, facilities, real estate, and other fixed assets. When financing equipment, a bank usually lends the small business from 60 to 80 percent of the equipment's value in return for a security interest in

TABLE 12.4

The Six Most Common Reasons
Bankers Reject Small Business
Loan Applications (and How You
Can Avoid Them)

Sources: Adapted from Anne Field,
"Getting the Bank to Yes," *Success,* May
1999, pp. 67–71; J. Tol Broome, Jr., "How
to Get a 'Yes' from Your Banker,"
Nation's Business, April 1996, p. 37.

Reason 1. "Our bank doesn't make small business loans." Cure: Before applying for a bank loan, research banks to find out which ones actively seek the type of loan you need. Some banks don't emphasize loans under $500,000, whereas others focus almost exclusively on small company loans. The Small Business Administration's reports, *Micro-Business-Friendly Banks in the United States* and *Small Business Lending in the United States,* are valuable resources for locating the banks in your area that are most likely to make small business loans.

Reason 2. "I don't know enough about you or your business." Cure: Develop a detailed business plan that explains what your company does (or will do) and describes how you will gain a competitive edge over your rivals. Also be prepared to supply business credit references and a personal credit history.

Reason 3. "You haven't told me why you need the money." Cure: A solid business plan will explain how much money you need and how you plan to use it. Make sure your request is specific; avoid requests for loans "for working capital." Don't make the mistake of answering the question, "How much money do you need?" with "How much will you lend me?"

Reason 4. "Your numbers don't support your loan request." Cure: Include a cash flow forecast in your business plan. Bankers analyze a company's balance sheet and income statement to judge the quality of its assets and its profitability, but bankers lend primarily on the basis of cash flow. They know that's how you'll repay the loan. If adequate cash flow isn't available, don't expect a loan. Prove to the banker that you know what your company's cash flow is and how to manage it.

Reason 5. "You don't have enough collateral." Cure: Be prepared to pledge your company's assets—and perhaps your personal assets—as collateral for the loan. Bankers like to have the security of collateral before they make a loan. They also expect more than $1 in collateral for every $1 of money they lend. Banks typically lend 80 to 90 percent of the value of real estate, 70 to 80 percent of the value of accounts receivable, and just 10 to 50 percent of the value of inventory pledged as collateral.

Reason 6. "Your business does not support the loan on its own." Cure: Be prepared to provide a personal guarantee on the loan. By doing so, you're telling the banker that if your business cannot repay the loan, you will. Many bankers see their small business clients and their companies as one and the same. Even if you choose a form of ownership that provides you with limited personal liability, most bankers will ask you to override that protection by personally guaranteeing the loan.

There's no magic to getting a bank to approve your loan request. The secret is proper preparation and building a solid business plan that enhances your credibility as a business owner with your banker. Use your plan to prove that you have what it takes to survive and thrive.

the equipment. The loan's amortization schedule, which is based on a set number of monthly payments, typically coincides with the length of the equipment's usable life. In financing real estate (commercial mortgages), banks typically will lend up to 75 to 80 percent of the property's value and will allow a lengthier repayment schedule of 10 to 30 years.

Another common type of loan banks make to small businesses is a **term loan**. Typically unsecured, banks grant these loans to businesses whose past operating history suggests a high probability of repayment. Some banks make only secured term loans, however. Term loans impose restrictions (called covenants) on the business decisions an entrepreneur makes concerning the company's operations. For instance, a term loan may set limits on owners' salaries, prohibit further borrowing without the bank's approval, or maintain certain financial ratios (recall the discussion of ratio analysis in Chapter 10). Entrepreneurs must understand all of the terms attached to term loans before accepting them.

term loan—*a bank loan that imposes restrictions (covenants) on the business decisions an entrepreneur makes concerning the company's operations.*

Nonbank Sources of Debt Capital

Although they are usually the first stop for entrepreneurs in search of debt capital, banks are not the only lending game in town. We now turn our attention to other sources of debt capital that entrepreneurs can tap to feed their cash-hungry companies.

ASSET-BASED LENDERS Asset-based lenders, which are usually smaller commercial banks, commercial finance companies, or specialty lenders, allow small businesses to borrow money by pledging otherwise idle assets such as accounts receivable, inventory, or purchase orders as collateral. This form of financing works especially well for manufacturers, wholesalers, distributors, and other companies with significant stocks of inventory or accounts receivable. Even unprofitable companies whose financial statements could not convince loan officers to make traditional loans can get asset-based loans. These cash-poor but asset-rich companies can use normally unproductive assets—accounts receivable, inventory, fixtures, and purchase orders—to finance rapid growth and the cash crises that often accompany it.

Like banks, asset-based lenders consider a company's cash flow, but they are more interested in the quality of the assets pledged as collateral. The amount a small business can borrow through asset-based lending depends on the **advance rate**, the percentage of an asset's value that a lender will lend. For example, a company pledging $100,000 of accounts receivable might negotiate a 70 percent advance rate and qualify for a $70,000 asset-based loan. Advance rates can vary dramatically depending on the quality of the assets pledged and the lender. Because inventory is an illiquid asset (i.e., hard to sell), the advance rate on inventory-based loans is quite low, usually 10 percent to 50 percent. A business pledging high-quality accounts receivable as collateral, however, may be able to negotiate up to an 85 percent advance rate. The most common types of asset-based financing are discounting accounts receivable and inventory financing.

advance rate—the percentage of an asset's value that a lender will lend.

DISCOUNTING ACCOUNTS RECEIVABLE.   The most common form of secured credit is accounts receivable financing. Under this arrangement, a small business pledges its accounts receivable as collateral; in return, the lender advances a loan against the value of approved accounts receivable. The amount of the loan tendered is not equal to the face value of the accounts receivable, however. Even though the bank screens the firm's accounts and accepts only qualified receivables, it makes an allowance for the risk involved because some will be written off as uncollectible. A small business usually can borrow an amount equal to 55 to 80 percent of its receivables, depending on their quality. Generally, lenders will not accept receivables that are past due.

Many commercial finance companies engage in accounts receivable financing.

A Company Example

Kyle Jodice, founder of **Milnucorp**, *a small distributor of products ranging from Hula-Hoops to tank parts, uses accounts receivable financing from Action Capital, a commercial finance company in Atlanta, to get the cash he needs to purchase inventory. Action Capital advances money based on Milnucorp's accounts receivable. After Action Capital collects payment from Milnucorp's customers, typically within 40 to 60 days, the commercial finance company remits the payments to Jodice after subtracting the amount of the loan and the interest it charges.*[60]

INVENTORY FINANCING.   Here, a small business loan is secured by the company's inventory of raw materials, work in process, and finished goods. If an owner defaults on the loan, the lender can claim the pledged inventory, sell it, and use the proceeds to satisfy the loan (assuming the bank's claim is superior to the claims of other creditors). Because inventory usually is not a highly liquid asset and its value can be difficult to determine, lenders are willing to lend only a portion of its worth, usually no more than 50 percent of the inventory's value. Most asset-based lenders avoid inventory-only deals; they prefer to make loans backed by inventory *and* more secure accounts receivable.

A Company Example

David LaTorre, CFO of **Design Resource Group International**, *used inventory financing to enable his company to land a contract with a large multinational corporation to install a complete office furnishing system. Design Resource Group's rapid growth was stretching its capital base, and traditional financing sources such as banks were hesitant to lend to a small company without an established record of success. LaTorre turned to Westgate Financial Corporation, a company specializing in asset-based financing, for help. Pledging the purchase order from the multinational corporation as collateral, LaTorre negotiated a loan from Westgate that enabled it to purchase the necessary inventory and complete the job. When the multinational corporation paid the invoice, LaTorre repaid the loan out of the proceeds.*[61]

Asset-based financing is a powerful tool. A small business that could obtain a $1 million line of credit with a bank would be able to borrow as much as $3 million by using accounts receivable as collateral. It is also an efficient method of borrowing because a small business owner has the money he needs when he needs it. In other words, the business pays only for the capital it actually needs and uses.

To ensure the quality of the assets supporting the loans they make, lenders must monitor borrowers' assets, perhaps as often as once a month, making paperwork requirements on these loans intimidating, especially to first-time borrowers. Also, asset-based loans are more expensive than traditional bank loans because of the cost of originating and maintaining them and the higher risk involved. Rates usually run from two to seven percentage points above the prime rate. Because of this rate differential, small business owners should not use asset-based loans over the long term; their goal should be to establish their credit through asset-based financing and then to move up to a line of credit.

Trade Credit

Because of its ready availability, trade credit is an extremely important source of financing to most entrepreneurs. When banks refuse to lend money to a start-up business because they see it as a bad credit risk, an entrepreneur may be able to turn to trade credit for capital. Getting vendors to extend credit in the form of delayed payments (for example, "net 30" credit terms) usually is much easier for small businesses to obtain than bank financing. Essentially, a company receiving trade credit from a supplier is getting a short-term, interest-free loan for the amount of the goods purchased.

It is no surprise that businesses receive three dollars of credit from suppliers for every two dollars they receive from banks as loans.[62] Vendors and suppliers often are willing to finance a small business's purchases of goods from 30 to 60 days, interest free.

A Company Example

*For instance, Gus Walboldt, owner of **AMCAL**, a fine-art publishing company, uses supplier financing as an integral part of his company's 20-year growth plan. Because calendars represent a large portion of AMCAL's sales, its business is highly seasonal, which creates significant cash flow problems. "We would spend half the year flush with cash [and the other half] cash poor," says Walboldt. Walboldt worked out a financing arrangement with the companies that print the calendars. AMCAL pays the printers' labor and material costs when the calendars are printed during the summer months and then covers their profit margins when its cash flow swells in the fall.[63]*

The key to maintaining trade credit as a source of funds is establishing a consistent and reliable payment history with every vendor.

Equipment Suppliers

Most equipment vendors encourage business owners to purchase their equipment by offering to finance the purchase. This method of financing is similar to trade credit but with slightly different terms. Usually, equipment vendors offer reasonable credit terms with only a modest down payment with the balance financed over the life of the equipment (often several years). In some cases, the vendor will repurchase equipment for salvage value at the end of its useful life and offer the business owner another credit agreement on new equipment. Some companies get equipment loans to lease rather than to purchase fixed assets. Start-up companies often use trade credit from equipment suppliers to purchase equipment and fixtures such as counters, display cases, refrigeration units, machinery, and the like. It pays to scrutinize vendors' credit terms, however; they may be less attractive than those of other lenders.

Commercial Finan ce Companies

When denied bank loans, small business owners often look to commercial finance companies for the same types of loans. Commercial finance companies are second only to banks in making loans to small businesses and, unlike their conservative counterparts, are willing to tolerate more risk in their loan portfolios. Of course, their primary consideration is collecting their loans, but finance companies tend to rely more on obtaining a security interest in some type of collateral, given the higher-risk loans that make up their portfolios. Because commercial finance companies depend on collateral to recover most of their losses, they do not require the complete financial projections of future operations that most banks do. However, this does *not* mean that they do not carefully evaluate a company's financial position before making a loan.

Approximately 150 large commercial finance companies such as AT&T Small Business Lending, GE Capital Small Business Finance, and others make a variety of loans to small companies, ranging from asset-based loans and business leases to construction and Small Business Administration loans. Dubbed "the Wal-Marts of finance," commercial finance companies usually offer many of the same credit options as commercial banks do. However, because their loans are subject to more risks, finance companies charge a higher interest rate than commercial banks (usually at least prime plus 4 percent). Their most common methods of providing credit to small businesses are asset-based—accounts receivable financing and inventory loans. Specific rates on these loans vary but can be as high as 20 to 30 percent (including fees), depending on the risk a particular business presents and the quality of the assets involved.

In addition to short-term financing for small businesses, commercial finance companies also extend intermediate and long-term loans for real estate and fixed assets.

When Anna Kinney wanted to build a new building to house her metal fabrication business, **AMK Manufacturing***, 20 banks rejected her loan application, even though she owned all of the equipment in her company and had a track record of success. Kinney then turned to Allied Capital, a Washington, DC–based commercial finance company, that quickly approved a 25-year loan for $300,000 backed by a guarantee from the Small Business Administration.*[64]

A Company Example

Savings and Loan Associations

Savings and loan associations (S&Ls) specialize in loans for real property. In addition to their traditional role of providing mortgages for personal residences, savings and loan associations offer financing on commercial and industrial property. In the typical commercial or industrial loan, the S&L will lend up to 80 percent of the property's value with a repayment schedule of up to 30 years. Minimum loan amounts are typically $50,000, but most S&Ls hesitate to lend money for buildings specially designed for a particular customer's needs. S&Ls expect the mortgage to be repaid from the firm's future profits.

Stock Brokerage Houses

Stockbrokers are getting into the lending business, too, and many of them offer loans to their customers at lower interest rates than banks. These **margin loans** carry lower rates because the collateral supporting them—the stocks and bonds in the customer's portfolio—is of high quality and is highly liquid. Moreover, brokerage firms make it easy to borrow. Usually, brokers set up a line of credit for their customers when they open a brokerage account. To tap that line of credit, the customer simply writes a check or uses a debit card. Typically, there is no fixed repayment schedule for a margin loan; the debt can remain outstanding indefinitely, as long as the market value of the borrower's portfolio of collateral meets minimum requirements. Aspiring entrepreneurs can borrow up to 50 percent of the value of their stock portfolios, up to 70 percent of their bond portfolios, and up to 90 percent of the value of their government securities. For example, one woman borrowed $60,000 to buy equipment for her New York health club, and a St. Louis doctor borrowed $1 million against his brokerage account to help finance a medical clinic.[65]

There is risk involved in using stocks and bonds as collateral on a loan. Brokers typically require a 30 percent cushion on margin loans. If the value of the borrower's portfolio drops, the broker can make a **margin call**—that is, the broker can call the loan in and require the borrower to provide more cash and securities as collateral. Recent swings in the stock market have translated into margin calls for many entrepreneurs, requiring them to repay a significant portion of their loan balances within a matter of days—or hours. If an account lacks adequate collateral, the broker can sell off the customer's portfolio to pay off the loan.

Over the past two decades, stock brokers have been adding traditional loans to their line of small business financial services, but start-up companies rarely meet their stringent standards. For established companies, however, these loans can be an important source of funds.

margin loans—*loans from stockbrokers that use the stocks and bonds in the borrower's portfolio as collateral.*

margin call—*occurs when the value of a borrower's portfolio drops and the broker calls the loan in, requiring the borrower to put up more cash and securities as collateral.*

*Kevin Nikkhoo, founder of **Vertex Systems Inc.**, a $10 million-a-year technology consulting firm, negotiated a small business loan from Morgan Stanley to finance the company's rapid growth. After negotiating with banks and other potential sources of funds, Nikkhoo decided to go with Morgan Stanley because it offered better terms and the potential to provide more funding as Vertex grew.[66]*

Insurance Companies

policy loan—*a loan insurance companies make on the basis of the amount of money a customer has paid into a policy in the form of premiums.*

For many small businesses, life insurance companies can be an important source of business capital. Insurance companies offer two basic types of loans: policy loans and mortgage loans. **Policy loans** are extended on the basis of the amount of money paid through premiums into the insurance policy. It usually takes about two years for an insurance policy to accumulate enough cash surrender value to justify a loan against it. Once he accumulates cash value in a policy, an entrepreneur may borrow up to 95 percent of that value for any length of time. Interest is levied annually, but borrowers can defer repayment indefinitely. However, the amount of insurance coverage is reduced by the amount of the loan. Policy loans typically offer very favorable interest rates, often at or below prevailing loan rates at banks and other lending institutions. Only insurance policies that build cash value—that is, combine a savings plan with insurance coverage—offer the option of borrowing. These include whole life (permanent insurance), variable life, universal life, and many corporate-owned life insurance policies. Term life insurance, which offers only pure insurance coverage, has no borrowing capacity.

mortgage loan—*a loan insurance companies make on a long-term basis for real property worth at least $500,000.*

Insurance companies make **mortgage loans** on a long-term basis on real property worth a minimum of $500,000. They are based primarily on the value of the real property being purchased. The insurance company will extend a loan of up to 75 or 80 percent of the real estate's value and will allow a lengthy repayment schedule over 25 or 30 years so that payments do not strain the firm's cash flows excessively.

Credit Unions

credit union—*a nonprofit financial cooperative that promotes saving and provides loans to its members.*

Credit unions, nonprofit financial cooperatives that promote saving and provide loans to their members, are best known for making consumer and car loans. However, many are also willing to lend money to their members to launch businesses. More than 10,000 federally and state-chartered credit unions operate in the United States, and they make loans to their members totaling more than $172 billion a year, many of them for the purpose of starting a business.[67]

Credit unions don't make loans to just anyone; to qualify for a loan, an entrepreneur must be a member. Lending practices at credit unions are very much like those at banks, but they usually are willing to make smaller loans. Entrepreneurs around the globe are turning to credit unions to finance their businesses, sometimes borrowing tiny amounts of money.

*When **Joseph Ogwal**, a refugee of war-torn Sudan, arrived in South Africa, he had nothing—literally. Ogwal, who has a degree in electronics engineering, wanted to start his own business to earn enough money to bring his family to South Africa, so he turned to the Cape Metropole South African Credit Co-Operative (SACCO) for a small loan. With his $115 loan, Ogwal launched a consumer electronics repair business that already is earning a profit. With another loan from the credit union, he plans to expand his business, launching a training center for repair technicians.[68]*

Bonds

Bonds, which are corporate IOUs, have always been a popular source of debt financing for large companies. Few small business owners realize that they can also tap this valuable source of capital. Although the smallest businesses are not viable candidates for issuing bonds, a growing number of small companies are finding the funding they need through bonds when banks and other lenders say no. Because of the costs involved, issuing bonds usually is best suited for companies generating sales between $5 million and $30 million and have capital requirements between $1.5 million and $10 million. Although they can help small companies raise much-needed capital, bonds have certain disadvantages. The issuing company must follow the same regulations that govern businesses selling stock to public investors. Even if the bond issue is private, the company must register the offering and file periodic reports with the SEC.

Small manufacturers needing money for fixed assets have access to an attractive, relatively inexpensive source of funds in industrial development bonds (IDBs), which were created to give manufacturers access to capital at rates lower than they could get from traditional lenders. In 1999, Congress created the mini-bond program, which allows small companies to issue bonds through a streamlined application process and lower fees. Typically, the amount of money small companies issuing IDBs seek to raise is at least $1 million, but some small manufacturers have raised as little as $500,000 using IDBs. Even though the paperwork and legal costs associated with making an IDB issue can run up to 2 to 3 percent of the financing amount, that is a relative bargain for borrowing long-term money at a fixed interest rate.

*After using bank loans for many years to finance his company's capital needs, Ned Golterman, co-owner of **Golterman & Sabo**, a small building materials company, decided to issue mini-bonds. Not only was Golterman able to avoid much of the complicated paperwork associated with a typical bond issue, but he also managed to get long-term financing for his company at a rate two percentage points below the best bank loan rate he could find and favorable repayment terms.[69]*

Private Placements

Earlier in this chapter, we saw how companies can raise capital by making private placements of their stock (equity). Private placements are also available for debt instruments. A private placement involves selling debt to one or a small number of investors, usually insurance companies or pension funds. Private placement debt is a hybrid between a conventional loan and a bond. At its heart, it is a bond, but its terms are tailored to the borrower's individual needs, as a loan would be.

Privately placed securities offer several advantages over standard bank loans. First, they usually carry fixed interest rates rather than the variable rates banks often charge. Second, the maturity of private placements is longer than most bank loans: 15 years rather than five. Private placements do not require hiring expensive investment bankers. Finally, because private investors can afford to take greater risks than banks, they are willing to finance deals for fledgling small companies.

Small Business Investment Companies (SBICs)

Small Business Investment Companies (SBICs), created in 1958 when Congress passed the Small Business Investment Act, are privately owned financial institutions that are licensed and regulated by the SBA. Their function is to use a combination of private capital and federally guaranteed debt to provide long-term capital to small businesses. There are two types of SBICs: regular SBICs and specialized SBICs (SSBICs). More than 100 SSBICs provide credit and capital to small businesses that are at least 51 percent owned by minorities and socially or economically disadvantaged people. Since their inception in 1969, SSBICs have helped finance nearly 25,000 minority-owned companies with investments totaling $2.34 billion.[70] Most SBICs prefer later-round financing over funding raw start-ups. Because of changes in their financial structure made a few years ago, however, SBICs now are better equipped to invest in start-up companies. In fact, about 55 percent of SBIC investments go to companies that are no more than three years old.[71] Funding from SBICs helped launch companies such as Apple Computer, Federal Express, Staples, Sun Microsystems, and Callaway Golf.

Since 1960, SBICs have provided more than $34 billion in long-term debt and equity financing to some 105,000 small businesses, adding many thousands of jobs to the American economy.[72] Both SBICs and SSBICs must be capitalized privately with a minimum of $5 million to $10 million, at which point they qualify for up to three dollars in long-term SBA loans for every dollar of private capital invested in small businesses. As a general rule, both SBICs and SSBICs may provide financial assistance only to small businesses with a net worth of less than $18 million and average after-tax earnings of $6 million during their past two years. However, employment and total annual sales standards vary from industry to industry. SBICs are limited to a maximum investment or loan amount of 20 percent of their private capital to a single client, whereas SSBICs may lend or invest up to 30 percent of their private capital in a single small business.

SBICs provide both debt and equity financing to small businesses. Because of SBA regulations affecting the financing arrangements an SBIC can offer, most SBICs extend their investments as loans with an option to convert the debt instrument into an equity interest later. Most SBIC loans are in the much-needed range of $100,000 and $5 million, and the

Small Business Investment Companies (SBICs)— *privately owned financial institutions that are licensed and regulated by the SBA; they use a combination of private and public funds to provide long-term capital to small businesses.*

loan term is longer than most banks allow. The average SBIC loan is $664,200.[73] When they make equity investments, SBICs are prohibited from obtaining a controlling interest in the companies in which they invest (no more than 49 percent ownership). The average SBIC equity investment is $1.13 million, far below the average equity investment by venture capital firms of $12 million.[74] The most common forms of SBIC financing (in order of their frequency) are a loan with an option to buy stock, a convertible debenture, a straight loan, and preferred stock.

Outback Steakhouse, a highly successful restaurant chain based on an Australian theme, received early financing from an SBIC, Kitty Hawk Capital I, that allowed it to grow. In 1990, Outback had been in business less than three years when the SBIC decided to invest $151,000 to boost the company's working capital balance. That capital infusion gave Outback the financing it needed to get to the next level. The company made an initial public offering in 1991 and today generates sales of more than $2.5 billion a year![75]

Outback Steakhouse, which now has locations around the globe, truly is a success story for the SBIC industry.

Small Business Lending Companies (SBLCs)

Small Business Lending Companies (SBLCs) make only intermediate and long-term SBA-guaranteed loans. They specialize in loans that many banks would not consider and operate on a nationwide basis. For instance, most SBLC loans have terms extending for at least 10 years. The maximum interest rate for loans of seven years or longer is 2.75 percent above the prime rate; for shorter-term loans, the ceiling is 2.25 percent above prime. Another feature of SBLC loans is the expertise the SBLC offers borrowing companies in critical areas.

SBLCs also screen potential investors carefully, and most of them specialize in particular industries. The result is a low loan default rate of roughly 4 percent. Corporations own most of the nation's SBLCs, giving them a solid capital base.

FEDERALLY SPONSORED PROGRAMS

Federally sponsored lending programs have suffered from budget reductions in the past several years. Current trends suggest that the federal government is reducing its involvement in the lending business, but many programs are still quite active and some are actually growing.

Economic Development Administration (EDA)

The Economic Development Administration, a branch of the Commerce Department, offers loan guarantees to create new business and to expand existing businesses in areas with below-average income and high unemployment. Focusing on economically distressed communities, the EDA finances long-term investment projects needed to stimulate economic growth and to create jobs by making loan guarantees. The EDA guarantees loans up to 80 percent of business loans between $750,000 and $10 million. Entrepreneurs apply for loans through private lenders, for whom an EDA loan guarantee significantly reduces the risk of lending. Start-up companies must supply 15 percent of the guaranteed amount in the form of equity, and established businesses must make equity investments of at least 15 percent of the guaranteed amount. Small businesses can use the loan proceeds in a variety of ways, including supplementing working capital and purchasing equipment to buying land and renovating buildings.

EDA business loans are designed to help replenish economically distressed areas by creating or expanding small businesses that provide employment opportunities in local communities. To qualify for a loan the business must be located in the disadvantaged area, and its presence must directly benefit local residents. Some communities experiencing high unemployment or suffering from the effects of devastating natural disasters have received EDA Revolving Loan Fund Grants to create loan pools for local small businesses.

Department of Housing and Urban Development (HUD)

HUD sponsors several loan programs to assist qualified entrepreneurs in raising needed capital. The Community Development Block Grants (CDBGs) are extended to cities and counties that, in turn, lend or grant money to entrepreneurs to start small businesses that will strengthen the local economy. Grants are aimed at cities and towns in need of revitalization and economic stimulation. Some grants are used to construct buildings and plants to be leased to entrepreneurs, sometimes with an option to buy. Others are earmarked for revitalizing a crime-ridden area or making start-up loans to entrepreneurs or expansion loans to existing business owners. No ceilings or geographic limitations are placed on CDBG loans and grants, but projects must benefit low- and moderate-income families.

The city of **Wichita, Kansas,** *and* **Cessna Aircraft Company** *used the loan guarantee provision of the CDBG program to purchase a large tract in a troubled neighborhood and to renovate it. They built the Cessna Learning Work Complex, which included a light assembly factory and a training/day care center for Cessna trainees from the local area. The renovation stimulated investments in the community, including a new bank, a library, a senior citizens center, and a housing complex.*[76]

A Company Example

HUD also makes loans to small businesses through its Enterprise Community Loan Program, including microloans (up to $15,000), façade loans (up to $50,000 for exterior improvements to buildings), and commercial revitalization loans (up to $50,000 for purchasing fixed assets or for working capital).

U.S. Department of Agriculture's Rural Business-Cooperative Service

The U.S. Department of Agriculture (USDA) provides financial assistance to certain small businesses through its Rural Business-Cooperative Service (RBS). The RBS program is open to all types of businesses (not just farms) and is designed to create nonfarm employment opportunities in rural areas—those with populations below 50,000 and not adjacent to a city where densities exceed 100 people per square mile. Entrepreneurs in many small towns, especially those with populations below 25,000, are eligible to apply for loans through the RBS program, which makes almost $900 million in loan guarantees each year.

The RBS does make a limited number of direct loans to small businesses, but the majority of its activity is in loan guarantees. Through its Business and Industry Guaranteed Loan Program, the RBS will guarantee as much as 90 percent of a bank's loan up to $25 million (although actual guarantee amounts are almost always far less) for qualified applicants. Entrepreneurs apply for loans through private lenders, who view applicants with loan guarantees much more favorably than those without such guarantees. The RBS guarantee reduces a lender's risk dramatically because the guarantee means that the government agency would pay off the loan balance (up to the ceiling) if the entrepreneur defaults on the loan.

To make a loan guarantee, the RBS requires much of the same documentation as most banks and most other loan guarantee programs. Because of its emphasis on developing employment in rural areas, the RBS requires an environmental-impact statement describing the jobs created and the effect the business has on the area. The Rural Business-Cooperative Service also makes grants available to businesses and communities for the purpose of encouraging small business development and growth.

Small Business Innovation Research (SBIR) Program

Started as a pilot program by the National Science Foundation in the 1970s, the SBIR program has expanded to 11 federal agencies, ranging from NASA to the Department of Defense. These agencies award cash grants or long-term contracts to small companies wanting to initiate or to expand their research and development (R&D) efforts. SBIR grants give innovative small companies the opportunity to attract early-stage capital investments *without* having to give up significant equity stakes or taking on burdensome levels of debt. The SBIR process involves three phases. Phase I grants, which determine the feasibility and commercial potential of a technology or product, last for up to six months and have a ceiling of $100,000. Phase II grants,

YOU Be the Consultant . . .

Two Financing Puzzles

CREATIVE CAPITAL

Lissa D'Aquanni's candy-making business, The Chocolate Gecko, had humble beginnings but a great deal of promise. After working as an executive for several nonprofit organizations, D'Aquanni decided to go into business for herself and launched her company from the basement of her Albany, New York, home. When her home-based company's sales climbed to $44,000, D'Aquanni decided it was time to leave the neighborhood behind and move into a location that could support her plans for growth. Just three blocks away from her home, she found an older building for sale that was in need of renovation and repair. She approached traditional lenders for help financing the $300,000 project, but without a proven track record and no collateral to speak of, they refused. They urged D'Aquanni to consider renting the building rather than buying it. D'Aquanni's plans called for her to purchase the building, and she wasn't backing down just because of a setback in financing.

D'Aquanni had faced challenges attracting capital before, but she had gotten the funding she needed by being creative. For instance, shortly after she had launched her business, D'Aquanni needed $5,000 to purchase molds and a temperer so she could meet demand for the upcoming Christmas season. Recalling a strategy she had read about in a small business magazine, she sold discounted gift certificates to her customers. For every $100 in gift certificates her customers bought, D'Aquanni offered $25 worth of free chocolates. Within two weeks, she had raised the $5,000 she needed to purchase the supplies. An unanticipated benefit of her capital-raising strategy was a broader customer base. "A lot of folks mailed them as gift certificates to friends, family, and co-workers, and most of those people ordered chocolates," she says. To conserve cash in her business, D'Aquanni also barters for goods and services when she can. Both her accountant and her Web site designer take chocolates rather than cash as payment for their services.

D'Aquanni knows that most likely she will have to resort to another creative financing strategy to come up with the money she needs to purchase and renovate the building to house her growing business.

STALLED OUT

John Acosta is frustrated because his business, Jolly Technologies, has stalled for a lack of capital. Acosta invented a garage door opener that installs on motorcycles in just minutes and has invested more than $30,000 of his own money in the company since founding it in 1998. To date, he has managed to sell more than $50,000 worth of the openers at $40 each through magazine ads, from the company's Web site, and at motorcycle shows. Acosta estimates that he needs $100,000 to fine-tune the product and market it effectively.

Like Lissa D'Aquanni, Acosta has run into dead ends seeking financing through traditional financing sources. Financial advisors have suggested that Acosta sell the company to someone with the financial resources to develop and market the product or to give majority control to distributors in return for using their established marketing channels. Acosta refuses to consider those options. "I don't want to relinquish power," he says. "I want to make this company work."

1. Describe the advantages and the disadvantages of both equity capital and debt capital for Lissa D'Aquanni and John Acosta.

2. Explain why the following funding sources would or would not be appropriate for these entrepreneurs: family and friends, angel investors, an initial public offering, a traditional bank loan, asset-based borrowing, or one of the many federal or SBA loans.

3. Work with a team of your classmates to brainstorm ways that Lissa D'Aquanni and John Acosta could attract the capital they need for their businesses. What steps would you recommend they take before they approach the potential sources of funding you have identified?

Sources: Adapted from Crystal Detamore-Rodman, "Out on a Limb," *Entrepreneur B.Y.O.B.*, March 2003, pp. 78–83; The Chocolate Gecko, www.chocolategecko.com; Jolly Technologies, www.jollytec.com.

---

designed to develop the concept into a specific technology or product, run for up to 24 months with a ceiling of $750,000. Approximately 40 percent of all Phase II applicants receive funding. Phase III is the commercialization phase, in which the company pursues commercial applications of the research and development conducted in Phases I and II and must use private or non-SBIR federal funding to bring a product to market.

Competition for SBIR funding is intense; only 12 percent of the small companies that apply receive funding. So far, more than 36,000 SBIR awards totaling in excess of $10 billion have gone to small companies that traditionally have had difficulty competing with big corporations for federal R&D dollars. The government's dollars have been well invested. Nearly 40 percent of small businesses receiving second-phase SBIR awards have achieved commercial success with their products.[77]

Integrated Systems Inc. of Sunnyvale, California, used SBIR funding to develop technology for writing embedded software that allowed robots to load munitions safely. The company, whose stock now trades on the NASDAQ, went on to transfer the technology to commercial applications, including software that controls robots in the auto manufacturing process and "intelligent" gas pumps that allow customers to pay at the pump with a credit card.[78]

The Small Business Technology Transfer (STTR) Program

The Small Business Technology Transfer (STTR) Program complements the Small Business Innovation Research Program. Whereas the SBIR focuses on commercially promising ideas that originate in small businesses, the STTR uses companies to exploit the vast reservoir of commercially promising ideas that originate in universities, federally funded R&D centers, and nonprofit research institutions. Researchers at these institutions can join forces with small businesses and can spin off commercially promising ideas while remaining employed at their research institutions. Five federal agencies award grants of up to $500,000 in three phases to these research partnerships.

SMALL BUSINESS ADMINISTRATION (SBA)

Learning Objective

7. Describe the various loan programs available from the Small Business Administration.

The Small Business Administration (SBA) has several programs designed to help finance both start-up and existing small companies that cannot qualify for traditional loans because of their thin asset base and their high risk of failure. In its 50-plus years of operation, the SBA has helped nearly 20 million small businesses through a multitude of programs, enabling many of them to get the financing they need for start-up or for growth. The SBA's $45 billion loan portfolio makes it the largest single financial backer of small businesses in the nation.[79] To be eligible for SBA funds, a business must meet the SBA's criteria that define a small business. Also, some types of businesses, such as those engaged in gambling, pyramid sales schemes, or real estate investment, among others, are ineligible for SBA loans.

The loan application process can take from between three days to several months, depending on how well prepared the entrepreneur is and which bank is involved. To speed up processing times, the SBA has established a Certified Lender Program (CLP) and a Preferred Lender Program (PLP). Both are designed to encourage banks to become frequent SBA lenders. When a bank makes enough good loans to qualify as a certified lender, the SBA promises a fast turnaround time for the loan decision—typically three to ten business days. About 850 lenders across the country are SBA certified lenders. When a bank becomes a preferred lender, it makes the final lending decision itself, subject to SBA review. In essence, the SBA delegates the application process, the lending decision, and other details to the preferred lender. The SBA guarantees up to 75 percent of PLP loans in case the borrower fails and defaults on the loan. The minimum PLP loan guarantee is $100,000, whereas the maximum is $500,000. About 500 lenders across the United States meet the SBA's preferred lender standards. Using certified or preferred lenders can reduce the processing time for an SBA loan considerably.

To further reduce the paperwork requirements involved in its loans, the SBA created the **Low Doc** (for "low documentation") **Loan Program**, which allows small businesses to use a simple one-page application for all loan applications. Before the Low Doc Loan Program, a typical SBA loan application required an entrepreneur to complete at least 10 forms, and the SBA often took 45 to 90 days to make a decision about an application. Under the Low Doc Loan Program, response time is just three days.

To qualify for a Low Doc loan, a company must have average sales below $5 million during the previous three years and employ fewer than 100 people. Businesses can use Low Doc loans for working capital, machinery, equipment, and real estate. The SBA guarantees 80 percent of loans up to $100,000 and 75 percent of loans over that amount up to the loan ceiling of $150,000. Borrowers must be willing to provide a personal guarantee for repayment of the loan principal. Interest rates are prime plus 2.75 percent on loans of seven years or longer and prime plus 2.25 percent on loans of less than seven years. The average Low Doc loan is $79,500.

Low Doc Loan Program—*a program initiated by the SBA in an attempt to simplify and streamline the application process for small business loans.*

Richard Smith, owner of a whitewater rafting business, needed money to expand his 20-year-old company and to buy new equipment. Smith, however, was hesitant to approach the SBA because he wanted to avoid "myriads of paperwork." At his banker's urging, Smith decided to try the Low Doc Loan Program, and within days of submitting his application, he received a $100,000 loan.[80]

SBA Express Program—*an SBA program that allows participating lenders to use their own loan procedures to make SBA-guaranteed loans.*

Another program designed to streamline the application process for SBA loan guarantees is the **SBA Express Program**, in which participating lenders use their own loan procedures and applications to make loans of up to $250,000 to small businesses. Because the SBA guarantees up to 50 percent of the loan, banks are often more willing to make smaller loans to entrepreneurs who might otherwise have difficulty meeting lenders' standards. Loan maturities on SBA*Express* loans typically are between five and ten years, but loan maturities for fixed assets can be up to 25 years.

SBA Loan Programs

7(A) Loan Guaranty Program—*an SBA loan program in which loans made by private lenders to small businesses are guaranteed up to a ceiling by the SBA.*

7(A) LOAN GUARANTY PROGRAM. The SBA works with local lenders (both bank and nonbank) to offer a variety of loan programs all designed to help entrepreneurs who cannot get capital from traditional sources gain access to the financing they need to launch and grow their businesses. By far, the most popular SBA loan program is the **7(A) Loan Guaranty Program** (see Figure 12.4). Private lenders extend these loans to small businesses, but the SBA guarantees them (80 percent of loans up to $100,000; 75 percent of loans above $100,000 up to the loan guarantee ceiling of $750,000). In other words, the SBA does not actually lend any money; it merely acts as an insurer, guaranteeing the lender this much repayment in case the borrower defaults on the loan. Because the SBA assumes most of the credit risk, lenders are more willing to consider riskier deals that they normally would refuse.

*For instance, when their sports-equipment-bag company, **Buck's Bags**, began to experience explosive growth that outstripped cash flow, Larry Lee and Dara Lee Howerton applied for an SBA guaranteed loan at their banker's suggestion. The Howertons have received four SBA-guaranteed loans totaling more than $600,000, using the loans to move into a larger plant, buy new equipment, and hire new workers. With the SBA loan guarantees, Buck's Bags' sales have soared. "The SBA was very helpful in getting us through our rapid-growth years," says Larry Lee. "I don't know what we would have done without them."[81]*

Qualifying for an SBA loan guarantee requires cooperation among the entrepreneur, the participating bank, and the SBA. The participating bank determines the loan's terms and sets the interest rate within SBA limits. Contrary to popular belief, SBA-guaranteed loans do *not* carry special deals on interest rates. Typically, rates are negotiated with the participating bank, with a

FIGURE 12.4 SBA 7(A) Guaranteed Loans

Source: U.S. Small Business Administration.

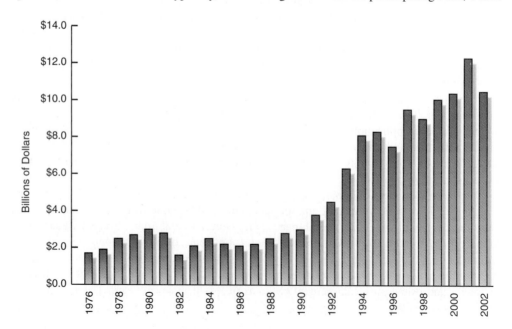

ceiling of prime plus 2.25 percent on loans of less than seven years and prime plus 2.75 percent on loans of seven to 25 years. Interest rates on loans of less than $25,000 can run up to prime plus 4.75 percent. The average interest rate on SBA-guaranteed loans is prime plus 2 percent (compared to prime plus 1 percent on conventional bank loans). The SBA also assesses a one-time guaranty fee of up to 3.875 percent for all loan guarantees.

The mean loan through the 7(A) guaranty program is $232,500, and the average duration of an SBA loan is 12 years—longer than the average commercial small business loan. In fact, longer loan terms are a distinct advantage of SBA loans. At least half of all bank business loans are for less than one year. By contrast, SBA real estate loans can extend for up to 25 years (compared to just 10 to 15 years for a conventional loan), and working capital loans have maturities of seven years (compared with two to five years at most banks). These longer terms translate into lower payments, which are better suited for young, fast-growing, cash-strapped companies.

THE CAPLINE PROGRAM. In addition to its basic 7(a) Loan Guaranty Program (through which the SBA makes about 84 percent of its loans), the SBA provides guarantees on small business loans for start-up, real estate, machinery and equipment, fixtures, working capital, exporting, and restructuring debt through several other methods. About two-thirds of all SBA's loan guarantees are for machinery and equipment or working capital. The **CAPLine Program** offers short-term capital to growing companies needing to finance seasonal buildups in inventory or accounts receivable under five separate programs, each with maturities up to five years: seasonal line of credit (provides advances against inventory and accounts receivable to help businesses weather seasonal sales fluctuations), contract line of credit (finances the cost of direct labor and materials costs associated with performing contracts), builder's line of credit (helps small contractors and builders finance labor and materials costs), standard asset-based line of credit (an asset-based revolving line of credit for financing short-term needs), and small asset-based line of credit (an asset-based revolving line of credit up to $200,000). CAPLine is aimed at helping cash-hungry small businesses by giving them a credit line to draw on when they need it. These loans built around lines of credit are what small companies need most because they are so flexible, efficient, and, unfortunately, so hard for small businesses to get from traditional lenders.

> **CAPLine Program**—an SBA program that makes short-term capital loans to growing companies needing to finance seasonal buildups in inventory or accounts receivable.

LOANS INVOLVING INTERNATIONAL TRADE. For small businesses going global, the SBA has the **Export Working Capital (EWC) Program**, which is designed to provide working capital to small exporters. The SBA works in conjunction with the Export-Import Bank to administer this loan guarantee program. Applicants file a one-page loan application, and the response time normally is 10 days or less. The maximum loan is $1,111,111 and proceeds must be used to finance small business exports.

> **Export Working Capital (EWC) Program**—an SBA loan program that is designed to provide working capital to small exporters.

Crown Products Inc., a small company generating more than $16 million in annual sales by exporting grocery products to more than 70 countries, typifies the small companies that benefit most from the EWC program. In its early years, Crown's retained earnings and its owners financed the company's growth. But as its growth accelerated, the company's cash needs began to outstrip its internal funding sources. With the help of the Hibernia National Bank, owners Kee Lee, Sun Kim, and Jeffrey Teague were able to land a $750,000 line of credit that fueled its international growth.[82]

> **A Company Example**

The **International Trade Program** is for small businesses that are engaging in international trade or are adversely affected by competition from imports. The SBA allows global entrepreneurs to combine loans from the Export Working Capital Program with those from the International Trade Program for a maximum guarantee of $1,250,000. Loan maturities range from one to 25 years.

> **International Trade Program**—an SBA loan program for small businesses that are engaging in international trade or are adversely affected by competition from imports.

SECTION 504 CERTIFIED DEVELOPMENT COMPANY PROGRAM. The SBA's Section 504 program is designed to encourage small businesses to expand their facilities and to create jobs. Section 504 loans provide long-term, fixed-asset financing to small companies to purchase land, buildings, or equipment. Three lenders play a role in every 504 loan: a bank, the SBA, and a **certified development company (CDC)**. A CDC is a nonprofit organization licensed by the SBA and designed to promote economic growth in local communities. Some 270 CDCs operate across the United States. An entrepreneur generally is required to make a down payment of just 10 percent of the total project cost. The CDC puts

> **certified development company (CDC)**—a nonprofit organization licensed by the SBA and designed to promote growth in local communities by working with commercial banks and the SBA to make long-term loans to small businesses.

up 40 percent at a long-term fixed rate, supported by an SBA loan guarantee in case the entrepreneur defaults. The bank provides long-term financing for the remaining 50 percent, also supported by an SBA guarantee. The major advantages of Section 504 loans are their fixed rates and terms, their 10- and 20-year maturities, and the low down payment required. The maximum loan amount is $1.3 million.

A Company Example

*When Chris Lamm decided to relocate his wholesale seafood business from Oakland's Jack London Square, his two-year search led him to an ideal site in nearby Hayward, California. His company, **Joe Pucci & Sons Seafood**, had grown to 60 employees and needed more space. With the help of the Capital Access Group, a local development company, Lamm was able to buy a 44,000-square-foot building located on two acres that once housed a Mervyn's department store. The building was a perfect fit for the seafood company's needs with loading docks, a large parking lot, and plenty of room to handle the company's expansion. Lamm, who went to work for the company in 1993 and purchased it in 2001, put down 10 percent of the cost and borrowed the maximum $1.3 million from the CDC. A loan from a local bank rounded out the financing package.*[83]

As attractive as they are, 504 loans are not for every business owner. The SBA imposes several restrictions on 504 loans:

- For every $35,000 the CDC loans, the project must create at least one new job or achieve a public policy goal such as rural development, expansion of exports, minority business development, and others.
- Machinery and equipment financed must have a useful life of at least 10 years.
- The borrower must occupy at least two-thirds of a building constructed with the loan, or the borrower must occupy at least half of a building purchased or remodeled with the loan.
- The borrower must qualify as a small business under the SBA's definition and must not have a tangible net worth in excess of $7 million and does not have an average net income in excess of $2.5 million after taxes for the preceding two years.

Because of strict equity requirements, existing small businesses usually find it easier to qualify for 504 loans than do start-ups.

MICROLOAN PROGRAM. About three-fourths of all entrepreneurs need less than $100,000 to launch their businesses. Indeed, most entrepreneurs require less than $50,000 to start their companies. Unfortunately, loans of that amount can be the most difficult to get. Lending these relatively small amounts to entrepreneurs starting businesses is the purpose of the SBA's **Microloan Program**. Called microloans because they range from just a hundred dollars to as much as $35,000, these loans have helped thousands of people take their first steps toward entrepreneurship. Banks typically have shunned loans in such small amounts because they considered them to be unprofitable. In an attempt to "fill the void" in small loans to start-up companies, the SBA launched the Microloan Program in 1992; today, more than 150 authorized lenders make SBA-backed microloans. The size of the average microloan is $10,500 with a maturity of three years (the maximum term is six years), and lenders' standards are less demanding than those on conventional loans. All microloans are made through nonprofit intermediaries approved by the SBA.

Microloan Program—an SBA program that makes small loans, some as small as $100, to entrepreneurs.

A Company Example

*Jonathan Reese and Jason Salfi needed capital to fund the growth of **Comet Skateboard**, the skateboard manufacturing company they cofounded, but, given their lack of collateral, sparse credit history, and small loan need, no bank was interested. However, two $20,000 SBA-guaranteed microloans from the Oakland Business Development Corporation gave the fledgling company the solid financial footing it needed to grow. Reese and Salfi's business plan calls for steady growth that will enable them to qualify for a bank line of credit and to ultimately attract venture capital.*[84]

Prequalification Loan Program—an SBA program designed to help disadvantaged entrepreneurs "prequalify" for SBA loan guarantees before approaching commercial lenders.

PREQUALIFICATION LOAN PROGRAM. The **Prequalification Loan Program** is designed to help disadvantaged entrepreneurs such as those in rural areas, minorities, women, the disabled, those with low incomes, veterans, and others prepare loan applications and "prequalify" for SBA loan guarantees before approaching banks and lending institutions for business loans. Because lenders are much more likely to approve loans that the SBA has prequalified, these entrepreneurs have greater access to the capital they need. The maximum loan under this program is $250,000, and loan maturities range from seven to 25 years. A local Small Business Development Center usually helps entrepreneurs prepare their loan applications at no charge.

DISASTER LOANS. As their name implies, **disaster loans** are made to small businesses devastated by some kind of financial or physical loss. The maximum disaster loan usually is $1.5 million, but Congress often raises that ceiling when circumstances warrant. Disaster loans carry below-market interest rates. Loans for physical damage above $10,000 and financial damage of more than $5,000 require an entrepreneur to pledge some kind of collateral, usually a lien on the business property. The SBA has helped entrepreneurs whose businesses have been disrupted by a variety of disasters, ranging from hurricanes on the Southeast Coast and earthquakes on the West Coast to floods and tornadoes in the Midwest to the terrorist attacks of September 11, 2001.

> **disaster loans**—an SBA loan program that makes loans to small businesses devastated by some kind of financial or physical loss.

STATE AND LOCAL LOAN DEVELOPMENT PROGRAMS

Many states have created their own loan and economic development programs to provide funds for business start-ups and expansions. They have decided that their funds are better spent encouraging small business growth rather than "chasing smokestacks"—trying to entice large businesses to locate in their boundaries. These programs come in a wide variety of forms, but they all tend to focus on developing small businesses that create the greatest number of jobs and economic benefits. Although each state's approach to economic development is somewhat unique, one common element is some kind of small business financing program: loans, loan guarantees, development grants, venture capital pools, and others. One approach many states have had success with is **Capital Access Programs (CAPs)**. First introduced in Michigan in 1986, many states now offer CAPs that are designed to encourage lending institutions to make loans to businesses that do not qualify for traditional financing because of their higher risk. Under a CAP, a bank and a borrower each pay an up-front fee (a portion of the loan amount) into a loan-loss reserve fund at the participating bank, and the state matches this amount. The reserve fund, which normally ranges from 6 to 14 percent of the loan amount, acts as an insurance policy against the potential loss a bank might experience on a loan and frees the bank to make loans that it otherwise might refuse. One study of CAPs found that 55 percent of the entrepreneurs who received loans under a CAP would not have been granted loans without the backing of the program.[85]

> **Capital Access Programs (CAPs)**—a state lending program that encourages lending institutions to make loans to businesses that do not qualify for traditional financing because of their higher risk.

Even cities and small towns have joined in the effort to develop small businesses and help them grow. More than 7,500 communities across the United States operate **revolving loan funds** (RLFs) that combine private and public funds to make loans to small businesses, often at below-market interest rates. As money is repaid into the funds, it is loaned back out to other entrepreneurs. A study by the Corporation for Enterprise Development of RLFs in seven states found that the median RLF loan was $40,000 with a maturity of five years.[86]

> **revolving loan fund**—a program offered by communities that combine private and public funds to make loans to small businesses, often at below-market interest rates.

Brian Hale transformed his passion for snowmobiles, dirt bikes, and ATVs into a thriving business with the help of a loan from the Central Vermont Revolving Loan Fund. Hale's company, **J.B. Motorsports and Salvage**, *repairs as well as refurbishes and sells these vehicles to customers looking for bargains. He used his loan to purchase an inventory of parts and to purchase a computer system to help him run the business more efficiently.[87]*

> **A Company Example**

INTERNAL METHODS OF FINANCING

Small business owners do not have to rely solely on financial institutions and government agencies for capital; their businesses have the capacity to generate capital. This type of financing, called **bootstrap financing**, is available to virtually every small business and encompasses factoring, leasing rather than purchasing equipment, using credit cards, and managing the business frugally.

> **Learning Objective**
>
> **8.** Discuss valuable methods of financing growth and expansion internally.

FIGURE 12.5 Where Do
Small Businesses Get Their
Financing?

Source: *Trends for 2000*, a survey by
Arthur Andersen and National Small
Business United.

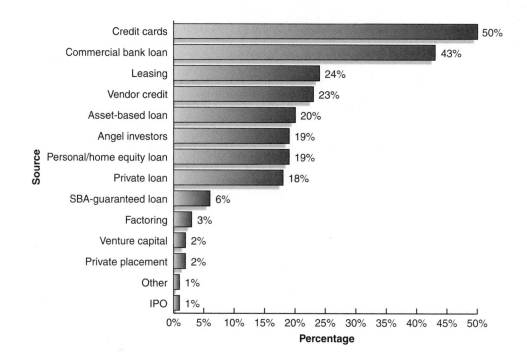

bootstrap financing—
*internal methods of financing a
company's need for capital.*

factor—*a financial institution
that buys a business's accounts
receivable at a discount.*

FACTORING ACCOUNTS RECEIVABLE. Instead of carrying credit sales on its own books (some of which may never be collected), a small business can sell outright its accounts receivable to a factor. A **factor** buys a company's accounts receivable and pays for them in two parts. The first payment, which the factor makes immediately, is for 50 to 80 percent of the accounts' agreed-upon (and usually discounted) value. The factor makes the second payment, which makes up the balance less the factor's service fees, when the original customer pays the invoice. Factoring is a more expensive type of financing than loans from either banks or commercial finance companies, but for businesses that cannot qualify for those loans, factoring may be the only choice!

Factoring deals are either with recourse or without recourse. Under deals arranged with recourse, a small business owner retains the responsibility for customers who fail to pay their accounts. The business owner must take back these uncollectible invoices. Under deals arranged without recourse, however, the owner is relieved of the responsibility for collecting them. If customers fail to pay their accounts, the factor bears the loss. Because the factoring company assumes the risk of collecting the accounts, it normally screens the firm's credit customers, accepts those judged to be creditworthy, and advances the small business owner a portion of the value of the accounts receivable. Factors will discount anywhere from 5 to 40 percent of the face value of a company's accounts receivable, depending on a small company's:

■ customers' financial strength and credit ratings.
■ industry and its customers' industries because some industries have a reputation for slow payments.
■ history and financial strength, especially in deals arranged with recourse.
■ credit policies.[88]

LEASING. Leasing is another common bootstrap financing technique. Today, small businesses can lease virtually any kind of asset—from office space and telephones to computers and heavy equipment. By leasing expensive assets, the small business owner is able to use them without locking in valuable capital for an extended period of time. In other words, the manager can reduce the long-term capital requirements of the business by leasing equipment and facilities, and she is not investing her capital in depreciating assets. Also, because no down payment is required and because the cost of the asset is spread over a longer time (lowering monthly payments), a company's cash flow improves.

LOCATION OPTIONS FOR RETAIL AND SERVICE BUSINESSES

Learning Objective

3. Outline the location options for retail and service businesses.

There are six basic areas where retail and service business owners can locate: the central business district (CBD), neighborhoods, shopping centers and malls, near competitors, outlying areas, and at home. According to the International Council of Shopping Centers, the average cost to lease space in a shopping center is about $15 per square foot. At a regional mall, rental rates run from $20 to $40 per square foot, and in central business locations, the average cost is $43 per square foot (although rental rates can vary significantly in either direction of that average, depending on the city).[15] Of course, cost is just one factor a business owner must consider when choosing a location.

Central Business District

The central business district (CBD) is the traditional center of town—the downtown concentration of businesses established early in the development of most towns and cities. Entrepreneurs derive several advantages from a downtown location. Because the firm is centrally located, it attracts customers from the entire trading area of the city. Also, a small business usually benefits from the customer traffic generated by the other stores in the district. However, locating in a CBD does have certain disadvantages. Many CBDs are characterized by intense competition, high rental rates, traffic congestion, and inadequate parking facilities.

Beginning in the 1950s, many cities saw their older downtown business districts begin to decay as residents moved to the suburbs and began shopping at newer, more convenient malls. Today, however, many of these CBDs are experiencing rebirth as cities restore them to their former splendor and shoppers return. Many customers find irresistible the charming atmosphere that traditional downtown districts offer with their rich mix of stores, their unique architecture and streetscapes, and their historic character. Cities have begun to reverse the urban decay of their downtown business districts through proactive revitalization programs designed to attract visitors and residents alike to cultural events by locating major theaters and museums in the downtown area. In addition, many cities are providing economic incentives to real estate developers to build apartment and condominium complexes in the heart of the downtown area. Vitality is returning as residents live and shop in the once nearly abandoned downtown areas. The "ghost-town" image is being replaced by both younger and older residents who love the convenience and excitement of life at the center of the city. One real estate developer experienced in Main Street locations says that his research shows that the best downtown streets for retailers are located in densely populated, affluent areas, are one-way, offer on-street parking, and are shaded by mature trees.[16]

Shopping malls and centers in the United States account for $1.23 billion in sales a year. The typical customer spends an average of 76.4 minutes and $68.20 per mall visit.

Courtesy of Corbis Bettmann, © Owen Franken/Corbis.

*Working through the **National Main Street Program**, residents in Burlington, Iowa, have revitalized their downtown district. When three historic buildings, including an old stone mill, that had fallen into disrepair were about to be demolished, residents sprang into action and began a cooperative program to refurbish the old buildings and to recruit businesses to them. The effort was successful, and Burlington has since seen 80 new businesses open downtown, representing a total investment of $4.5 million!*[17]

Neighborhood Locations

Small businesses that locate near residential areas rely heavily on the local trading areas for business. Businesses that provide convenience as a major attraction for customers find that locating on a street or road just outside major residential areas provides the needed traffic counts essential for success. Gas stations and convenience stores seem to thrive in these high-traffic areas. One study of food stores found that the majority of the typical grocer's customers live within a five-mile radius. The primary advantages of a neighborhood location include relatively low operating costs and rents and close contact with customers.

Shopping Centers and Malls

The first regional shopping mall, Northgate Shopping Center in Seattle, Washington, was built in 1950 and featured a full-service department store as its anchor and a central pedestrian walkway. Since then, shopping centers and malls have become a mainstay of the American landscape. Since 1970 the number of shopping malls and centers in the United States has climbed from 11,000 to more than 46,300, and they occupy 5.77 billion square feet of retail space.[18] Because many different types of stores exist under one roof, shopping malls give meaning to the term *one-stop shopping*. In a typical month, some 201 million adults visit a mall or shopping center.[19] There are four distinct types of shopping centers:

- *Neighborhood Shopping Centers.* The typical neighborhood shopping center is relatively small, containing from three to 12 stores and serving a population of up to 40,000 people who live within a 10-minute drive. The anchor store in these centers is usually a supermarket or a drugstore.
- *Community Shopping Centers.* The community shopping center contains from 12 to 50 stores and serves a population ranging from 40,000 to 150,000 people. The leading tenant is a department or variety store.
- *Regional Shopping Malls.* The regional shopping mall serves a much larger trading area, usually from 10 to 15 miles or more in all directions. It contains from 50 to 100 stores and serves a population in excess of 150,000 people living within a 20- to 40-minute drive. The anchor is typically one or more major department stores.
- *Power Centers.* A power center combines the drawing strength of a large regional mall with the convenience of a neighborhood shopping center. Anchored by large specialty retailers, these centers target older, wealthier baby boomers, who want selection and convenience. Anchor stores usually account for 80 percent of power center space, compared with 50 percent in the typical strip shopping center. Just as in a shopping mall, small businesses can benefit from the traffic generated by anchor stores, but they must choose their locations carefully so that they are not overshadowed by their larger neighbors.

When evaluating a mall or shopping center location, an entrepreneur should consider the following questions:

- Is there a good fit with other products and brands sold in the mall or center?
- Who are the other tenants? Which stores are the "anchors" that will bring people into the mall or center?
- Demographically, is the center a good fit for your products or services? What are its customer demographics?
- How much foot traffic does the mall or center generate? How much traffic passes the specific site you are considering?
- How much vehicle traffic does the mall or center generate? Check its proximity to major population centers, the volume of tourists it draws, and the volume of drive-by freeway traffic. A mall or center that scores well on all three is probably a winner.
- What is the vacancy rate? The turnover rate?

- How much is the rent and how is it calculated? Most mall tenants pay a base amount of rent plus a percentage of their sales.
- Is the mall or center successful? How many dollars in sales does it generate per square foot? Compare its record against industry averages. The International Council of Shopping Centers in New York (www.icsc.org) is a good source of industry information.

A mall location is no longer a guarantee of success. Malls have been under pressure lately, and many weaker ones have closed. Additionally, the demographic makeup of the shopper often changes over time, creating a new socioeconomic customer base that may or may not be compatible with the customer profile attracted to your business. Others have undergone extensive renovations, adding entertainment features to their existing retail space in an attempt to generate more traffic. The basic problem is an oversupply of malls; the United States has 20 feet of mall retail space for every person in the United States!

Near Competitors

One of the most important factors in choosing a retail or service location is the compatibility of nearby stores with the retail or service customer. For example, stores selling high-priced goods find it advantageous to locate near competitors to facilitate comparison shopping. Locating near competitors might be a key factor for success in those businesses selling goods that customers shop for and compare on the basis of price, quality, color, and other factors.

Although some business owners avoid locations near direct competitors, others see locating near rivals as an advantage. For instance, restaurateurs know that successful restaurants attract other restaurants, which, in turn, attract more customers. Many cities have at least one "restaurant row," where restaurants cluster together; each restaurant feeds customers to the others.

Locating near competitors has its limits, however. Clustering too many businesses of a single type into a small area ultimately will erode their sales once the market reaches the saturation point. When an area becomes saturated with competitors, the shops cannibalize sales from one another, making it difficult for any of them to be successful.

Outlying Areas

Generally, it is not advisable for a small business to locate in a remote area because accessibility and traffic flow are vital to retail and service success, but there are exceptions. Some small firms have turned their remote locations into trademarks. One small gun shop was able to use its extremely remote location to its advantage by incorporating this into its advertising to distinguish itself from its competitors. This location strategy is usually only effective if there are few comparable competitors. There must be an overwhelmingly compelling reason for a potential customer to travel to an outlying area to shop.

An entrepreneur should consider the cost of a location (rental or lease expense) in light of its visibility to potential customers. If a less expensive location is difficult to find and has a low traffic count, the owner will need to spend a disproportionately large amount of money to advertise both where the business is located as well as how to find it. A superior and highly visible location may have a total lower cost when less advertising is needed. Many customers do not want to "go exploring" to find a business and, consequently, never bother to try.

Home-Based Businesses

For more than 24 million people, home is where the business is, and their numbers are swelling. According to the Department of Commerce, home-based businesses represent the fastest-growing segment of the U.S. economy.[20] One recent study found that 52 percent of all small companies are home-based.[21] Although a home-based retail business is usually not feasible, locating a service business at home is quite popular. Many service companies do not have customers come to their places of business, so an expensive office location is unnecessary. For instance, customers typically contact plumbers or exterminators by telephone, and the work is performed in customers' homes.

Entrepreneurs locating their businesses at home reap several benefits. Perhaps the biggest benefit is the low cost of setting up the business. Most often, home-based entrepreneurs set up shop in a spare bedroom or basement, avoiding the cost of renting, leasing, or buying a building. With a few basic pieces of office equipment—a computer, printer, fax machine, copier, telephone answering system, and scanner—a lone entrepreneur can perform just like a major corporation.

A Company Example

*For instance, David Gans runs **Truth and Fun Inc.**, a state-of-the-art production studio, from a spare bedroom in his Oakland, California, home. From his high-tech, in-home studio, Gans produces a weekly radio show, the "Grateful Dead Hour," that he beams by satellite to 90 radio stations across the country. "The equipment has gotten so powerful and inexpensive that one human being working from home can produce the exact same quality program as National Public Radio," says Gans.*[22]

Choosing a home location has certain disadvantages, however. Interruptions are more frequent, the refrigerator is all too handy, work is always just a few steps away, and isolation can be a problem. Another difficulty facing some home-based entrepreneurs involves zoning laws. As their businesses grow and become more successful, entrepreneurs' neighbors often begin to complain about the increased traffic, noise, and disruptions from deliveries, employees, and customers who drive through their residential neighborhoods to conduct business. Many communities now face the challenge of passing updated zoning laws that reflect the reality of today's home-based businesses while protecting the interests of residential homeowners.

THE LOCATION DECISION FOR MANUFACTURERS

Learning Objective

4. Explain the site selection process for manufacturers.

The criteria for the location decision for manufacturers are very different from those of retailers and service businesses; however, the decision can have just as much impact on the company's success. In some cases, a manufacturer has special needs that influence the choice of a location. For instance, when one manufacturer of photographic plates and film was searching for a location for a new plant, it had to limit its search only to those sites with a large supply of available fresh water, a necessary part of its process. In other cases, the location decision is controlled by zoning ordinances. If a manufacturer's process creates offensive odors or excessive noise, it may be even further restricted in its choices.

TABLE 13.1

Rating the Suitability of Sites for a Business

Common Factors	Factor Importance (10 high—1 low)	
Located to serve the customer (demographic trends)		
Cost of the location (rent or purchase price)		
Quantity and quality of the labor supply		
Zoning restrictions		
General business climate		
Transportation		
—For customers (highways, public transportation)		
—For raw material or inventories (rail, barge, air freight)		
Proximity to raw material or inventory		
Quality of public services (fire and police protection)		
Taxes (if owning)		
Adequacy for future expansion		
Value of the site in future years		
Labor cost and anticipated productivity		

Zoning maps show potential manufacturers the areas of the city or county set aside for industrial development. Most cities have developed industrial parks in cooperation with private industry. These industrial parks typically are equipped with sewage and electrical power sufficient for manufacturing. Many locations are not so equipped, and it can be extremely expensive for a small manufacturer to have such utilities brought to an existing site.

The type of transportation facilities required dictates location of a plant in some cases. Some manufacturers may need to locate on a railroad siding, whereas others may only need reliable trucking service. If raw materials are purchased by the carload, for economies of scale, the location must be convenient to a railroad siding. Bulk materials are sometimes shipped by barge and, consequently, require a facility convenient to a navigable river or lake. The added cost of using multiple shipping methods (e.g., rail to truck or barge to truck) can significantly increase shipping costs and make a location unfeasible for a manufacturer.

In some cases the perishibility of the product dictates location. Vegetables and fruits must be canned in close proximity to the fields in which they are harvested. Fish must be processed and canned at the water's edge. Location is determined by quick and easy access to the perishable products.

Table 13.1 provides a rating system to determine the suitability of various locations.

Foreign Trade Zones

Foreign trade zones can be an attractive location for small manufacturers that engage in global trade and are looking to minimize the tariffs they pay on the materials and parts they import and the goods they export. A **foreign trade zone** is a specially designated area in or near a U.S. customs port of entry that allows resident companies to import materials and components from foreign countries; assemble, process, manufacture, or package them; and then ship the finished

foreign trade zone—*a specially designated area in or near a U.S. customs port of entry that allows resident companies to import materials and components from foreign countries; assemble, process, manufacture, or package them; and then ship the finished product while either reducing or eliminating tariffs and duties.*

	Actual Scores for Alternative Sites (10 high—1 low)				Total Scores for Alternative Sites (Factor Importance × Actual Score)			
	Site A	Site B	Site C	Site D	Site A	Site B	Site C	Site D
Total					_____	_____	_____	_____
					_____	_____	_____	_____

Highest-scoring site is: _____

product while either reducing or eliminating tariffs and duties. As far as tariffs and duties are concerned, a company located in a foreign trade zone is treated as if it is located outside the United States. For instance, a maker of speakers might import components from around the world and assemble them at its plant located in a foreign trade zone. The company would pay no duties on the components it imports or on the speakers it exports to other foreign markets. The only duties the manufacturer would pay is on the speakers it sells in the United States.

Empowerment Zones

empowerment zone—an area designated as economically disadvantaged in which businesses are offered tax breaks on the investments they make within zone boundaries.

Originally created to encourage companies to locate in economically blighted areas, **empowerment zones** offer businesses tax breaks on the investments they make within zone boundaries. Companies can get federal tax credits, grants, and loans for hiring workers living in empowerment zones and for investments they make in plant and equipment in the zones. Empowerment zones operate in both urban and rural areas, ranging from Los Angeles, California, to Sumter, South Carolina. Boston, Massachusetts, has a technology-oriented business incubator located within a federal empowerment zone called TechSpace, which provides high-potential start-up businesses with a full-service facility featuring completely integrated information technology and business services.

Business Incubators

business incubator—an organization that combines low-cost, flexible rental space with a multitude of support services for its small business residents.

For many start-up companies, a business incubator may make the ideal initial location. A **business incubator** is an organization that combines low-cost, flexible rental space with a multitude of support services for its small business residents. The overwhelming reason for establishing an incubator is to enhance economic development by attracting new business ventures to an area, as well as to diversify the local economy. An incubator's goal is to nurture young companies during the volatile start-up period and to help them survive until they are strong enough to go out on their own. Common sponsors of incubators include colleges or universities (25 percent), government agencies (16 percent), economic development agencies (16 percent), with the remainder split among partnerships among government, nonprofit agencies and/or private developers and private investment groups. Technology incubators account for 37 percent of all incubators, and 47 percent are mixed-use operations, attracting a wide variety of businesses. The remaining 16 percent focus on service companies and those engaged in light manufacturing or specific niches.[23]

The shared resources incubators typically provide their tenants include secretarial services, a telephone system, computers and software, fax machines, and meeting facilities and, sometimes, management consulting services and financing. Not only do these services save young companies money, but they also save them valuable time. Entrepreneurs can focus on getting their products and services to market faster than competitors rather than searching for the resources they need to build their companies. The typical incubator has entry requirements that prospective residents must meet. Incubators also have criteria that establish the conditions a business must maintain to remain in the facility as well as the expectations for "graduation" into the business community.

More than 950 incubators operate across the United States. Perhaps the greatest advantage of choosing to locate a start-up company in an incubator is a greater chance for success; according to the National Business Incubation Association, graduates from incubators have a success rate of 87 percent. The average incubator houses 20 ongoing businesses employing 55 people.[24]

A Company Example

*When the biotech company that he ran from a spare bedroom in his home acquired the exclusive license to a breakthrough system that delivers medicine straight to the heart, James Grabek knew it was time to take his company, **Comedicus, Inc.**, to the next level. Fearful of losing control of his business, Grabek ultimately turned to Genesis Business Centers, a business incubator in Minneapolis, Minnesota. Harlon T. Jacobs, president of Genesis, offered Grabek access to $50,000 in financing, free office space, and management assistance in exchange for just 5 percent of the company's stock. Grabek decided to nurture his business in the incubator and quickly accepted the offer. Within 15 months, Genesis had helped Comedicus raise $1 million in a private placement and land $4 million in licensing agreements with major pharmaceutical companies. "It was a turning point that catapulted us into the corporate world," Grabek says of his decision to move into the incubator.[25]*

YOU Be the Consultant . . .

The "Cheers" of Bel Air

Downtown Bel Air, Maryland, faces many of the same challenges that thousands of other small towns and large cities across the United States are facing. Located about 40 minutes northeast of Baltimore, Bel Air is in a fast-growing area, but little of that growth is occurring in the town's central business district. The five-and-dime store, the shoe shop, the hardware store, and Richardson's Pharmacy (which boasted an old-fashioned soda fountain) either closed or moved to suburban malls years ago. Most of the buildings in the downtown area are filled with municipal government offices, law firms, accounting firms, and insurance agencies.

Although few merchants remain in downtown locations, Dave Wolff and his wife Jane chose a storefront in the middle of Main Street as the location for their coffee shop, Fine Grind. "We definitely wanted a Main Street location," says Wolff, who rejected the higher-priced sites in several malls near town. He points to the high concentration of white-collar workers in the downtown area who would serve as potential customers for Fine Grind.

Wolff has higher aspirations than mere business success. He wants to be the cornerstone in Bel Air's revitalization effort and to bring "a sense of community" to the town that seems to have lost that. "I'm hoping there's going to be a renaissance on Main Street," he says. "I think I'm the beginning." Wolff was able to supplement the money he invested in the business with a low-interest loan from a state program aimed at revitalizing downtown areas.

Before launching his business, Wolff spent many hours studying the layout, the techniques, and the unique personalities that the proprietors of old-fashioned candy stores, drugstores, and other retail operations used in the early days of the last century. He read books and pored over old photographs and then began applying what he learned to the design of his own shop. He brought in glass canisters of Tootsie Rolls, licorice, jelly beans, and other colorful candies. He bought a large brass espresso machine and put it behind a beautiful long bar hand-crafted from polished wood from an old gymnasium floor. The tables in Fine Grind are made from the same wood.

Not long after opening, people began coming to Bel Air's downtown district just to visit Fine Grind, which is exactly what Wolff wanted to happen. To lure customers in, Wolff allows local artists to display their work on the walls of his shop. One Saturday each month, he stays open later than normal to host an art exhibit with entertainment by a local musician. Although only three people (the artist, the musician, and Wolff) came to the first opening, the events now draw standing-room-only crowds. Wolff also dedicates one evening each month to a local book club (a large bookstore chain in a nearby mall refused to let the book club meet in its store), and another evening the members of a poetry club come in for a poetry reading. During the summer months, Wolff offers live music every Saturday night. Every Saturday morning, Wolf and his family get up early and head to the local farmer's market where they sell coffee and snacks from a booth. Customers also can buy Fine Grind's products from the company's Web site (www.finegrind.net).

Customers have turned Fine Grind into a local hangout, and, like a good bartender, Wolff knows all of his regular customers' favorite drinks. "We call this the 'Cheers' of Bel Air," says Bonnie Maivelett, a regular who comes in with her husband Bob practically every morning, referring to the popular TV show from the 1980s about a Boston pub "where everybody knows your name." Since Fine Grind opened, several other entrepreneurs have opened businesses in the downtown area, including several restaurants, an Irish pub, a T-shirt shop, and others. That's exactly what David Wolff hoped would happen when he launched Fine Grind.

1. What advantages and disadvantages does choosing a downtown location offer an entrepreneur like David Wolff?

2. Assume the role of consultant. Suppose that officials in a town with which you are familiar approached you about revitalizing the central business district. What advice would you offer them?

3. What factors should entrepreneurs evaluate when comparing a downtown location against a location in a shopping center or mall?

Source: Adapted from Hilary Stout, "When Building Up a Business Means Turning Around a Town," *Wall Street Journal*, June 11, 2000, p. B1.

LAYOUT AND DESIGN CONSIDERATIONS

Learning Objective

5. Describe the criteria used to analyze the layout and design considerations of a building, including the Americans with Disabilities Act.

Once an entrepreneur chooses the best location for her business, the next question deals with designing the proper layout for the building to maximize sales (retail) or productivity (manufacturing or service). **Layout** is the logical arrangement of the physical facilities in a business that contributes to efficient operations, increased productivity, and higher sales. Planning for the most effective and efficient layout in a business environment can produce dramatic improvements in a company's operating effectiveness and efficiency. An attractive, effective layout can help a company's recruiting efforts. One study conducted by the American

Association of Interior Designers found that employees rated the look and feel of their workspaces as the third most important consideration (after salary and benefits) when deciding whether or not to accept or to quit a job.[26]

*In most U.S. businesses you can find the chairperson and CEO by simply searching for the office that is larger than the others with better furniture and the most picturesque view of the outdoors. That process would not help you very much at **SEI Investments** in Oaks, Pennsylvania, a suburb of Philadelphia. Alfred P. West, Jr. doesn't have an office, nor does anyone else. As he puts it, "We don't use personal space to distinguish ourselves." This open work atmosphere encourages employees to be flexible and creative. Actually, that is not an exaggeration because everything is on wheels, which allows employees to move their desks whenever they want. This work climate has earned SEI Investments a place for three years running on Fortune's list of "100 Best Companies to Work For."* [27]

The following factors have a significant impact on a building's layout and design.

Size

layout—*the logical arrangement of the physical facilities in a business that contributes to efficient operations, increased productivity, and higher sales.*

A building must be large enough to accommodate a business's daily operations comfortably. If it is too small at the outset of operations, efficiency will suffer. There must be enough room for customers' movement, inventory, displays, storage, work areas, offices, and restrooms. Haphazard layouts undermine employee productivity and create organizational chaos. Too many small business owners start their operations in locations that are already overcrowded and lack the ability to be expanded. The result is that an owner is forced to make a costly move to a new location within the first few years of operation.

If an entrepreneur plans to expand, will the building accommodate it? Will hiring new employees, purchasing new equipment, expanding production areas, increasing service areas, and other growth require a new location? How fast is the company expected to grow over the next three to five years? Lack of adequate room in the building may become a limitation on a company's growth. Most small businesses wait too long before moving into larger quarters, and they fail to plan their new space arrangements properly. To avoid such problems, some experts recommend that new businesses plan their space requirements one to two years ahead and update the estimates every six months. When preparing the plan, managers should include the expected growth in the number of employees, manufacturing, selling, or storage space requirements and the number and location of branches to be opened.

Construction and External Appearance

Is the construction of the building sound? It pays to have an expert look it over before buying and leasing the property. Beyond the soundness of construction, does the building have an attractive external and internal appearance? The physical appearance of the building provides customers with their first impression of a business. This is especially true in retail businesses. Many retailers provide the customer with a consistent building appearance as they expand (e.g., fast-food restaurants and motels). Is the building's appearance consistent with the entrepreneur's desired image for the business?

Small retailers must recognize the importance of creating the proper image for their stores and how their shops' layouts and physical facilities influence this image. The store's external appearance contributes significantly to establishing its identity in the customer's mind. In many ways the building's appearance sets the tone for what the customer can expect in the way of quality and service. The appearance should, therefore, reflect the business's "personality." Should the building project an exclusive image or an economical one? Is the atmosphere informal and relaxed or formal and businesslike? Physical facilities send important messages to customers. Communicating the right signals through layout and physical facilities is an important step in attracting a steady stream of customers. Retail consultant Paco Underhill advises merchants to "seduce" passersby with their storefronts. "The seduction process should start a minimum of 10 paces away," he says.[28] Mr. Underhill says, "A store's interior architecture is fundamental to the customers experience—the stage upon which a retail company functions."[29]

The following tips will help entrepreneurs create window displays that will sell:

- *Keep displays simple.* Simple, uncluttered, and creative arrangements of merchandise draw the most attention and have the greatest impact on potential customers.
- *Keep displays clean and current.* Dusty, dingy displays or designs that are outdated send a negative message to passersby.
- *Change displays frequently.* Customers do not want to see the same merchandise on display every time they enter a store. Experts recommend changing displays at least quarterly, but stores selling trendy items should change their displays twice a month.
- *Get expert help if necessary.* Not all business owners have a knack for designing window displays. Their best bet is to hire a professional or to work with the design department at a local college or university.

Entrances

All entrances to a business should invite customers in. Wide entry ways and attractive merchandise displays that are set back from the doorway can draw customers into a business. A store's entrance must catch customers' attention and draw them inside. "That's where you want somebody to slam on the brakes and realize they're going someplace new," says retail consultant Paco Underhill.[30] Retailers with heavy traffic flows such as supermarkets or drugstores often install automatic doors to ensure a smooth traffic flow into and out of their stores. Retailers should remove any barriers that interfere with customers' easy access to the storefront. Broken sidewalks, sagging steps, mud puddles, and sticking or heavy doors not only create obstacles that might discourage potential customers, but they also create legal hazards for a business if they cause customers to be injured.

The Americans with Disabilities Act

The **Americans with Disabilities Act (ADA)**, passed in July 1990, requires practically all businesses to make their facilities available to physically challenged customers and employees. In addition, the law requires businesses with 15 or more employees to accommodate physically challenged candidates in their hiring practices. Most states have similar laws, many of them more stringent than the ADA, that apply to smaller companies as well. The rules of these state laws and the ADA's Title III are designed to ensure that mentally and physically challenged customers have equal access to a firm's goods or services. For instance, the act requires business owners to remove architectural and communication barriers when "readily achievable." The ADA allows flexibility in how a business achieves this equal access, however. For example, a restaurant could either provide menus in braille or could offer to have a staff member read the menu to blind customers. A small dry cleaner might not be able to add a wheelchair ramp to its storefront without incurring significant expense, but the owner could comply with the ADA by offering curbside pickup and delivery services for disabled customers at no extra charge.

Americans with Disabilities Act (ADA)— *a law that requires businesses with 15 or more employees to make their facilities available to physically challenged customers and employees.*

Although the law allows a good deal of flexibility in retrofitting existing structures, buildings that were occupied after January 25, 1993, must be designed to comply with all aspects of the law. For example, buildings with three stories or more must have elevators; anywhere the floor level changes by more than one-half inch, an access ramp must be in place. In retail stores, checkouts aisles must be wide enough—at least 36 inches—to accommodate wheelchairs. Restaurants must have 5 percent of their tables accessible to wheelchair-bound patrons.

Complying with the ADA does not necessarily require businesses to spend large amounts of money. The Justice Department estimates that more than 20 percent of the cases customers have filed under Title III involved changes the business owners could have made at no cost, and another 60 percent would have cost less than $1,000![31] In addition, companies with $1 million or less in annual sales or with 30 or fewer full-time employees that invest in making their locations more accessible to all qualify for a tax credit. The credit is 50 percent of their expenses between $250 and $10,500. Businesses that remove physical, structural, and transportation barriers for disabled employees and customers also qualify for a tax deduction of up to $15,000.

The Americans with Disabilities Act also prohibits any kind of employment discrimination against anyone with a physical or mental disability. A physically challenged person is considered to be "qualified" if he can perform the essential functions of the job. The employer must make "reasonable accommodation" for a physically challenged candidate or employee without causing "undue hardship" to the business.

The Americans with Disabilities Act has affected, in a positive way, how businesses deal with this segment of its customers and employees. The Department of Justice offers a program that provides business owners with free information and technical assistance concerning the ADA. The Department of Justice also has an ADA hot line that owners can call for information and publications on the ADA (800-514-0301).

Signs

One of the lowest-cost and most effective methods of communicating with customers is a business sign. Signs tell potential customers what a business does, where it is, and what it is selling. America is a very mobile society, and a well-designed, well-placed sign can be a powerful tool for reaching potential customers.

A sign should be large enough for passersby to read from a distance, taking into consideration the location and speed of surrounding traffic arteries. To be most effective, the message should be short, simple, and clear. A sign should be legible in both daylight and at night; proper illumination is a must. Contrasting colors and simple typefaces are best. The most common problems with business signs are that they are illegible, poorly designed, improperly located, poorly maintained, and have color schemes that are unattractive or are hard to read.

Before investing in a sign, an entrepreneur should investigate the local community's sign ordinance. In some cities and towns, local regulations impose restrictions on the size, location, height, and construction materials used in business signs.

Building Interiors

Like exterior considerations, the functional aspects of building interiors are very important and require careful attention to detail. Designing a functional, efficient interior is not easy. Technology has changed drastically the way employees, customers, and the environment interact with one another.

A Company Example

*Layout of a store contributes to its ability to achieve its mission. Consider **Blockbuster**, the world's leading provider of videos, that recently announced the complete redesign of 4,412 company-operated U.S. stores. Its layout goal was to create clearly delineated retail and rental boutique-style sections. The use of new color-blocked signage designed for identification of key sections, as well as other customer-friendly layout changes, were all designed to help Blockbuster "be the complete source to our customers for movies and games, in a format of their choice, rental or retail, new and used."* [32]

ergonomics—*the science of adapting work and the work environment to complement employees' strengths and to suit customers' needs.*

Piecing together an effective layout is not a haphazard process. **Ergonomics**, the science of adapting work and the work environment to complement employees' strengths and to suit customers' needs, is an integral part of a successful design. For example, chairs, desks, and table heights that allow people to work comfortably can help employees perform their jobs faster and more easily. Design experts claim that improved lighting, better acoustics, and proper climate control benefit the company as well as employees. An ergonomically designed workplace can improve workers' productivity significantly and lower days lost due to injuries and accidents. Unfortunately, many businesses fail to incorporate ergonomic design principles into their layouts, and the result is costly. The most frequent and most expensive workplace injuries are musculoskeletal disorders (MSDs), which cost U.S. businesses $20 billion in workers' compensation claims each year. According to the Occupational Safety and Health Administration (OSHA), MSDs account for 34 percent of all lost-work day injuries and illnesses and one-third of all workers' compensation claims. [33] Workers who spend their days staring at computer monitors (a significant and growing proportion of the workforce) often are victims of MSDs.

The most common MSD is carpal tunnel syndrome (CTS), which occurs when repetitive motion causes swelling in the wrist that pinches the nerves in the arm and hand. Studies by the Bureau of Labor Statistics show that more than 42 percent of carpal tunnel syndrome cases require more than 30 days away from work. [34] The good news for employers, however, is that preventing injuries, accidents, and lost days does *not* require spending thousands of dollars on ergonomically correct solutions. Most of the solutions to MSDs are actually quite simple and inexpensive.

Source: REPRINTED BY PERMISSION OF RANDY GLASBERGEN.

SIT UP STRAIGHT OR I'LL ERASE YOUR HARD DRIVE.

"It's called Ergonomics."

Sequins International, *a maker of sequined fabrics and trimmings in Woodside, New York, uses adjustable chairs and machinery as well as automatic spooling devices to reduce workers' repetitive motions and taxing physical demands. These simple changes eliminated carpal tunnel syndrome and cut workers' compensation costs to just $800, down from $98,000 in just one year.*[35]

> **A Company Example**

Other solutions are decidedly low tech.

*For instance, when **Designer Checks**, a maker of custom checks based in Anniston, Alabama, consulted with an occupational therapist, owner Grady Burrow learned that one of the best ways to fight MSDs among its computer-dependent workforce is simply to take frequent breaks and to move around. Department heads began scheduling regular exercise breaks designed to stretch employees' necks, shoulders, and hands. Before long, many managers began livening up their exercise breaks with music and dancing! Visitors to Designer Check's plant are likely to see managers and employees take to the production floor for a rousing rendition of the macarena or the hokey pokey.*[36]

> **A Company Example**

When planning store, office, or plant layouts, business owners usually focus on minimizing costs. Although staying within a budget is important, minimizing injuries and enhancing employees' productivity with an effective layout should be the overriding issues. Many exhaustive studies have concluded that changes in office design have a direct impact on workers' performance, job satisfaction, and ease of communication. In a reversal of the trend toward open offices separated by nothing more than cubicles, businesses are once again creating private offices in their workspaces. Many businesses embraced open designs, hoping that they would lead to greater interaction among workers. Many companies, however, have discovered that most office workers need privacy and quiet surroundings to be productive. Michael Brill, an office space consultant, studied 11,000 workers to determine the factors that most affect their productivity and found that the ability to do distraction-free work topped the list.[37] Rather than encourage teamwork, open offices leave workers distracted, frustrated, and less productive—just like the characters in the Dilbert cartoon strip.

*ment***Flyswat Inc.**, *a company that develops customized tools and services for Internet browsing, designed the interior of its building to appeal to its twenty-something, high-tech workforce. Cofounders John Rodkin, Leo Chang, and Raymond Crouse created a 150-square-foot indoor beach, complete with 3,000 pounds of sand, in their third-floor San Francisco office! Employees can scrunch the sand between their toes while gazing at banana trees, bird of paradise plants, tiki torches, and walls, floors, and ceilings painted to resemble grass and sky. "Why bother?" visitors*

> **A Company Example**

ask. Because Flyswat employees often spend 60-plus hours a week there, the company founders want to give them a fun, enjoyable place to work. The company buys dinner for its workers four nights a week, maintains a fully stocked kitchen, and offers showers and a laundry room.[38]

On a more technical level, when evaluating an existing building's interior, an entrepreneur must be sure to determine the integrity of its structural components. Are the building's floors sufficiently strong to hold the business's equipment, inventories, and personnel? Strength is an especially critical factor for manufacturing firms that use heavy equipment. When multiple floors exist, are the upper floors anchored as solidly as the primary floor? Can inventory be moved safely and easily from one area of the plant to another? Is the floor space adequate for safe and efficient movement of goods and people? Consider the cost of maintaining the floors. Hardwood floors may be extremely attractive but require expensive and time-consuming maintenance. Carpeted floors may be extremely attractive in a retail business but may be totally impractical for a quality manufacturing firm. Entrepreneurs must consider both the utility and durability and maintenance requirements, attractiveness, and, if important, effectiveness in reducing noise.

Like floors, walls and ceilings must be both functional and attractive. On the functional side, walls and ceilings should be fireproof and soundproof. Are the colors of walls and ceilings compatible, and do they create an attractive atmosphere here for customers and employees? For instance, many Web-related companies use bright, bold colors in their designs because they appeal to their young employees. On the other hand, more conservative firms such as accounting firms and law offices decorate with more subtle, subdued tones because they convey an image of trustworthiness and honesty. Upscale restaurants that want their patrons to linger over dinner use deep, luxurious tones and soft lighting to create the proper ambiance. Fast-food restaurants, on the other hand, use strong, vibrant colors and bright lighting to encourage customers to get in and out quickly, ensuring the fast table turnover they require to be successful. In most cases, ceilings should be done in light colors to reflect the store's lighting.

For many businesses, a drive-through window adds another dimension to the concept of customer convenience and is a relatively inexpensive way to increase sales. Although drive-through windows are staples at fast-food restaurants and banks, they can add value for customers in a surprising number of businesses.

*For instance, when Marshall Hoffman relocated his business, **Steel Supply Company**, to a building that had been used as a bank, the idea of using the drive-through window intrigued him. Looking for a way to improve customer service, Hoffman transformed the former bank lobby into his showroom floor and began advertising the convenience of buying steel at the drive-through window. Customers place their steel orders by telephone, pull up to the window and pay, and receive a ticket. The order goes by computer to a warehouse Hoffman built on the site. By the time the customer pulls up to the warehouse, the order is waiting! The window has been a hit with customers. Since moving into its new location, Steel Supply's sales have grown from $3.5 million to more than $6 million.*[39]

Lights and Fixtures

Good lighting allows employees to work at maximum efficiency. Proper lighting is measured by what is ideal for the job being done. Proper lighting in a factory may be quite different from that required in an office or retail shop. Retailers often use creative lighting to attract customers to a specific display. Jewelry stores provide excellent examples of how lighting can be used to display merchandise.

Lighting is often an inexpensive investment when considering its impact on the overall appearance of the business. Few people seek out businesses that are dimly lit because they convey an image of untrustworthiness. The use of natural and artificial light in combination can give a business an open and cheerful look. Many restaurant chains have added greenhouse glass additions to accomplish this.

LAYOUT: MAXIMIZING REVENUES, INCREASING EFFICIENCY, AND REDUCING COST

The ideal layout for a building depends on the type of business it houses and on the entrepreneur's strategy for gaining a competitive edge. Retailers design their layouts with the goal of maximizing sales revenue; manufacturers see layout as an opportunity to increase efficiency and productivity and to lower costs.

YOU Be the Consultant . . .

Not Your Typical CPA Firm

Lipschulz, Levin and Gray (LLG) is not the typical public accounting firm, a fact that is obvious to even the most casual observer who enters the company's offices in Northbrook, Illinois. Rather than the traditional conservative decor found in most CPA offices, LLG's is quite contemporary and very different. First, there are no offices. No employees (officially called "team members") have enclosed offices; nor do they reside in honeycombs of Dilbert-like cubicles. The same holds true of LLG's partners (called "members"). *Everyone* in the company works in an open expanse with no private offices. The flexible workspace the owners created *really* is flexible. Even the office furniture, including desks, is on wheels so that team members can move it around as needed to collaborate with colleagues.

The transformation from a staid, traditional accounting firm began in 1988, when the partners did some soul-searching in an attempt to find out why the company was earning so little money, employee turnover was high, morale was low, and attracting quality workers was virtually impossible. "We ended up with everybody else's dregs," says managing partner Steve Siegel. A survey of the company's clients revealed that most of them stereotyped LLG as just another boring accounting firm filled with "bean counters." It was then that the partners began taking bold steps toward shaking off every remnant of the boring CPA firm. They started with their name. Although they retained the founding partners names as the firm's official moniker, the partners adopted a nickname that most of their clients continue to use: the Bean Counters. The name conveyed an image of fun and confronted head-on the stereotype of accountants who were as exciting as airline food.

Then managers made some important decisions about the layout of the office space, which, at the time, assigned workers to cubicles and partners to plush private offices. As a result of several planning retreats, managers decided to reduce the size of the workforce, some of the reductions coming through normal attrition but others the result of firings. Morale slipped, and the office space the company leased to house nearly 60 workers looked rather vacant with just 32. Then the partners made a key decision. "We were wasting [a lot of] space," says Siegel, so the partners decided to put the extra space to better use. They installed a miniature golf course right in the middle of the office!

One goal managers hoped to achieve was to get employees out of their offices and cubicles so they could communicate more effectively and be more creative. A "closed door mentality" continued to prevail at LLG, however. Siegel decided that if people were intimidated by doors, the doors would come down. Before long, walls and cubicles began to disappear as well. One day, at a brainstorming session around the miniature golf course, a partner half-jokingly suggested that one way to increase the level of communication in the office was to put the office furniture on wheels. Almost as soon as he suggested it, the manager looked up and said, "Oh gosh. We're going to do this, aren't we?" They did.

Given the drastic changes in office design the partners were making, it became obvious that the company needed a more suitable space to make them all work. Fortunately, the lease was about to end, so LLG hired an architect to help them find and then create a suitable space. Within two years, the architect presented the partners with a set of plans for an office that was 60 percent smaller, was minimalist in nature, but was extremely functional and comfortable. The partners of LLG were sold on the design, and today that office is home to the Bean Counters. It is an open community without cubicles or offices, yet its creative use of space encourages interaction among team members while allowing them to concentrate on their work when necessary. The space is wired for every type of technology, including a "Welcome Wall" dominated by a big-screen television that constantly flashes quotations about various topics such as business, life, and creativity. Architects also incorporated the company's sense of humor into the design. A four-by-nine-foot abacus made of steel conduit and brightly colored plastic balls graces one wall. The entire work space is designed to encourage the continued development of LLG's most valuable resource: the intellectual capital of its team members.

The new layout is working. In addition to its traditional accounting work, LLG has launched four new business consulting divisions, called Sharp Circles. Client referrals have doubled and income has tripled over the past decade. Communication among team members has never been better, and a distinct sense of innovation pervades the office. In addition, employee turnover has plummeted, and clients are more satisfied with the Bean Counters' work. Siegel and the other partners say that the new office and its layout are an important part of LLG's success. "We could not have gotten those Sharp Circle businesses up and running in the old building," he says. "The old building was such a huge impediment to sitting and meeting and just talking about things. Just being next to each other and hearing what's going on has allowed us to get things going."

1. What impact does the space in which people work have on their ability to do their jobs effectively?

2. Use the resources in your library and on the World Wide Web to learn more about ergonomics and layout. Then select a work space (perhaps on your campus or in a local business) and spend some time watching how people work in it. Finally, develop a list of recommendations for improving the design of the space to enhance workers' ability to do their jobs.

Source: Adapted from Nancy K. Austin, "Tear Down the Walls," *Inc.,* April 1999, pp. 66–76.

Layout for Retailers

Retail layout is the arrangement of merchandise in a store and its method of display. A retailer's success depends, in part, on a well-designed floor display. A retail layout should pull customers into the store and make it easy for them to locate merchandise, compare prices, quality, and features, and ultimately make a purchase. In addition, the floor plan should take customers past displays of other items that they may buy on impulse. Between 65 and 70 percent of all buying decisions are made once a customer enters a store, which means that the right layout can boost sales significantly. One study found that 68 percent of the items bought on major shopping trips (and 54 percent on smaller trips) were impulse purchases. Shoppers in this study were heavily influenced by in-store displays, especially those at the ends of aisles (called end-cap displays).[40]

Retailers have always recognized that some locations within a store are superior to others. Customer traffic patterns give the owner a clue to the best location for the highest gross margin items. Merchandise purchased on impulse and convenience goods should be located near the front of the store. Items people shop around for before buying and specialty goods will attract their own customers and should not be placed in prime space. Prime selling space should be restricted to products that carry the highest markups.

Layout in a retail store evolves from a clear understanding of customers' buying habits. If customers come into the store for specific products and have a tendency to walk directly to those items, placing complementary products in their path will boost sales. Observing customer behavior can help the owner identify the "hot spots" where merchandise sells briskly and "cold spots" where it may sit indefinitely. By experimenting with factors such as traffic flow, lighting, aisle size, music type and audio levels, signs, and colors, an owner can discover the most productive store layout.

Retailers have three basic layout patterns to choose from: the grid, the free-form, and the boutique. The **grid layout** arranges displays in rectangular fashion so that aisles are parallel. It is a formal layout that controls the traffic flow through the store. Supermarkets and discount stores use the grid layout because it is well suited to self-service stores. This layout uses the available selling space most efficiently, creates a neat, organized environment, and facilitates shopping by standardizing the location of items. Figure 13.2 shows a typical grid layout.

Unlike the grid layout, the **free-form layout** is informal, using displays of various shapes and sizes. Its primary advantage is the relaxed, friendly shopping atmosphere it creates, which encourages customers to shop longer and increases the number of impulse purchases they make. Still, the free-form layout is not as efficient as the grid layout in using selling space, and it can create security problems if not properly planned. Figure 13.3 illustrates a free-form layout.

The **boutique layout** divides the store into a series of individual shopping areas, each with its own theme. It is like building a series of specialty shops into a single store. The boutique layout is more informal and can create a unique shopping environment for customers; small department stores sometimes use this layout (see Figure 13.4).

Business owners should display merchandise as attractively as their budgets allow. Customers' eyes focus on displays, which tell them the type of merchandise the business sells. It is easier for customers to relate to one display than to a rack or shelf of merchandise. Open displays of merchandise can surround the focus display, creating an attractive selling area. Spacious aisles provide shoppers an open view of merchandise and reduce the likelihood of shoplifting. One study found that shoppers, especially women, are reluctant to enter narrow aisles in a store. Narrow aisles force customers to jostle past one another (called the "butt-brush factor"), which makes them extremely nervous. The same study also found that placing shopping baskets in several areas around a store can increase sales. Seventy-five percent of shoppers who pick up a basket buy something, compared to just 34 percent of customers who do not pick up a basket.[41]

Retailers can also boost sales by displaying together items that complement each other. For example, displaying ties near dress shirts or handbags next to shoes often leads to multiple sales. Placement of items on store shelves is important, too, and storeowners must keep their target customers in mind when stocking shelves. For example, putting hearing aid batteries on bottom shelves where the elderly have trouble getting to them or placing popular children's toys on top shelves where little ones cannot reach them can hurt sales. Even

grid layout—*a formal arrangement of displays arranged in a rectangular fashion so that aisles are parallel.*

free-form layout—*an informal arrangement of displays of various shapes and sizes.*

boutique layout—*an arrangement that divides a store into a series of individual shopping areas, each with its own theme.*

FIGURE 13.2   The Grid Layout

Meats   Deli   Dairy Products

Bread and Baked Goods

Frozen Foods

Frozen Foods

Drinks and Juices

Housewares

Paper Products

Packaged Goods

Canned Goods

Canned Goods

Fresh Fruits and Vegetables

Checkout Stands and Impulse Displays

Snack Items

Health and Beauty Items

Exit   Entrance

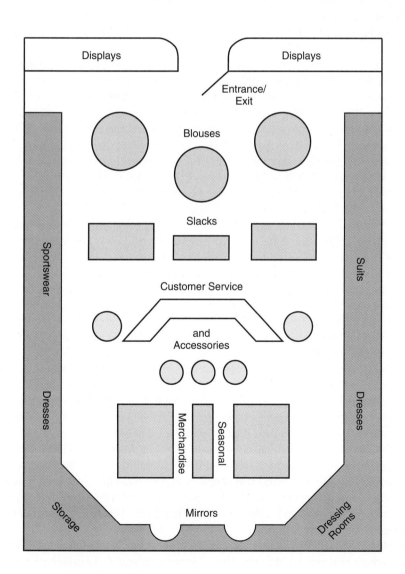

FIGURE 13.3   The Free-Form Layout

Displays   Displays

Entrance/Exit

Blouses

Slacks

Sportswear

Suits

Customer Service

and Accessories

Dresses

Dresses

Merchandise

Seasonal

Storage

Mirrors

Dressing Rooms

FIGURE 13.4 The Boutique
Layout

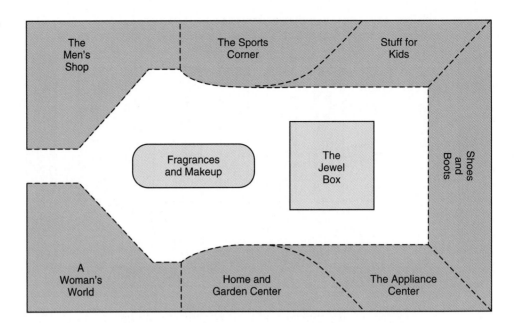

background music can be a merchandising tool if the type of music playing in a store matches the demographics of its target customers. Music can be a stimulant to sales because it has been proven to reduce resistance, warps the sense of time allowing shoppers to stay longer in the store, and helps to produce a positive mental association between the music and the intended image of the store.[42]

One good example of this can be found in the collection of antique stores clustered in Ozark, Missouri. Each of the stores tunes into either local "oldies" stations or more "down-home" bluegrass tunes on their stereo systems. It is not uncommon in these stores for people to browse for hours while humming along to their favorite tunes.

Retailers must remember to separate the selling and nonselling areas of a store. Never waste prime selling space with nonselling functions (storage, office, dressing area, etc.). Although nonselling activities are necessary for a successful retail operation, they should not take precedence and occupy valuable selling space. Many retailers place their nonselling departments in the rear of the building, recognizing the value of each foot of space in a retail store and locating their most profitable items in the best selling areas.

Not every portion of a small store's interior space is of equal value in generating sales revenue. Certain areas contribute more to revenue than others. The value of store space depends on floor location in a multistory building, location with respect to aisles and walkways, and proximity to entrances. Space values decrease as distance from the main entry-level floor increases. Selling areas on the main level contribute a greater portion to sales than those on other floors in the building because they offer greater exposure to customers than either basement or higher-level locations. Therefore, main-level locations carry a greater share of rent than other levels. Figure 13.5 offers one example of how rent and sales could be allocated by floors.

The layout of aisles in the store has a major impact on the customer exposure merchandise receives. Items located on primary walkways should be assigned a higher share of rental costs and should contribute a greater portion to sales revenue than those displayed along secondary aisles. Figure 13.6 shows that high-value areas are exposed to two secondary aisles.

Space values also depend on their relative position to the store entrance. Typically, the farther away an area is from the entrance, the lower its value. Another consideration is that most shoppers turn to the right entering a store and move around it counterclockwise. (This apparently is culturally determined. Studies of shoppers in Australia and Great Britain find that they turn *left* upon entering a store.) Finally, only about one-fourth of a store's customers will go more than halfway into the store. Using these characteristics, Figure 13.7 illustrates space values for a typical small store layout.

Understanding the value of store space ensures proper placement of merchandise. The items placed in the high-rent areas of the store should generate adequate sales and contribute enough to profit to justify their high-value locations.

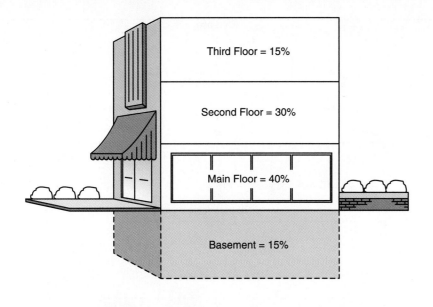

FIGURE 13.5 Rent
Allocation by Floors

Source: Retailing. 6th ed. 1997 Prentice
Hall. © Dale M. Lewison.

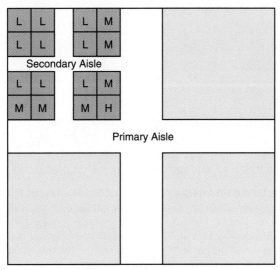

FIGURE 13.6 Rent
Allocation Based on Traffic Aisles

Source: Retailing. 6th ed. 1997 Prentice
Hall. © Dale M. Lewison.

The decline in value of store space from front to back of the shop is expressed in the 40-30-20-10 rule. This rule assigns 40 percent of a store's rental cost to the front quarter of the shop, 30 percent to the second quarter, 20 percent to the third quarter, and 10 percent to the final quarter. Similarly, each quarter of the store should contribute the same percentage of sales revenue.

For example, suppose that a small department store anticipates $720,000 in sales this year. Each quarter of the store should generate the following sales volume:

Front quarter	$720,000 × 0.40 =	$288,000
Second quarter	$720,000 × 0.30 =	$216,000
Third quarter	$720,000 × 0.20 =	$144,000
Fourth quarter	$720,000 × 0.10 =	$72,000
Total		$720,000

Layout for Manufacturers

Manufacturing layout decisions take into consideration the arrangement of departments, workstations, machines, and stock-holding points within a production facility. The general objective is to arrange these elements to ensure a smooth workflow (in a production facility) or a particular traffic pattern (in a service facility or organization).

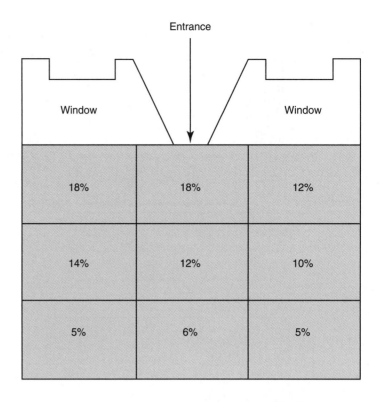

Manufacturing facilities have come under increasing scrutiny as firms attempt to improve quality, decrease inventories, and increase productivity through facilities that are integrated, flexible, and controlled. Facility layout has a dramatic effect on product mix, product processing, and material handling, storage, and control, as well as production volume and quality.

FACTORS IN MANUFACTURING LAYOUT.   The ideal layout for a manufacturing operation depends on a number of factors, including the following:

■ *Type of product.* Product design and quality standards; whether the product is produced for inventory or for order; and the physical properties such as the size of materials and products, special handling requirements, susceptibility to damage, and perishability.

■ *Type of production process.* Technology used; types of materials handled; means of providing a service; and processing requirements in terms of number of operations involved and amount of interaction between departments and work centers.

■ *Ergonomic considerations.* To ensure worker safety; to avoid unnecessary injuries and accidents; and to increase productivity.

■ *Economic considerations.* Volume of production; costs of materials, machines, workstations, and labor; pattern and variability of demand; and length of permissible delays.

■ *Space availability within the facility itself.*

TYPES OF MANUFACTURING LAYOUTS.   Manufacturing layouts are categorized by either the work flow in a plant or by the production system's function. There are three basic types of layouts that manufacturers can use separately or in combination—product, process, and fixed position—and they are differentiated by their applicability to different conditions of manufacturing volume.

product (line) layout *—an arrangement of workers and equipment according to the sequence of operations performed on a product.*

PRODUCT LAYOUTS. In a **product (or line) layout**, a manufacturer arranges workers and equipment according to the sequence of operations performed on the product (see Figure 13.8). Conceptually, the flow is an unbroken line from raw material input or customer arrival to finished goods to customer's departure. This type of layout is applicable to rigid-flow, high-volume, continuous process or a mass-production operation, or when the service or product is highly standardized. Automobile assembly plants, paper mills, and oil refineries are examples of product layouts.

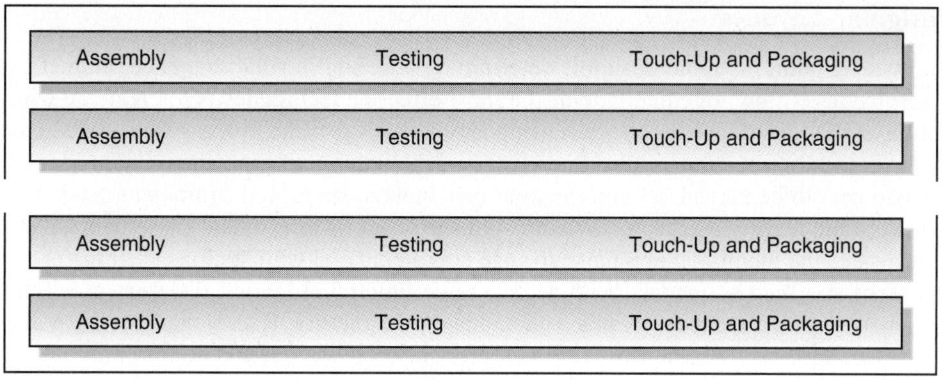

FIGURE 13.8 Product
Layout

Assembly	Testing	Touch-Up and Packaging
Assembly	Testing	Touch-Up and Packaging

Assembly	Testing	Touch-Up and Packaging
Assembly	Testing	Touch-Up and Packaging

Product layouts offer the advantages of lower material handling costs; simplified tasks that can be done with low-cost, lower-skilled labor; reduced amounts of work-in-process inventory; and relatively simplified production control activities. All units are routed along the same fixed path, and scheduling consists primarily of setting a production rate.

Disadvantages of product layouts are their inflexibility, monotony of job tasks, high fixed investment in specialized equipment, and heavy interdependence of all operations. A break-down in one machine or at one workstation can idle the entire line. This layout also requires business owners to duplicate many pieces of equipment in the manufacturing facility, which for a small firm can be cost prohibitive.

PROCESS LAYOUTS. In a **process layout**, a manufacturer groups workers and equipment according to the general function they perform, without regard to any particular product or customer (see Figure 13.9). Process layouts are appropriate when production runs are short, when demand shows considerable variation and the costs of holding finished goods inventory are high, or when the service or product is customized.

Process layouts have the advantages of being flexible for doing custom work and promoting job satisfaction by offering employees diverse and challenging tasks. Its disadvantages are the higher costs of materials handling, more skilled labor, lower productivity, and more complex production control. Because the work flow is intermittent, each job must be individually routed through the system, scheduled at the various work centers, and have its status monitored.

FIXED POSITION LAYOUTS. In **fixed position layouts**, materials do not move down a line as in a production layout but rather, due to the weight, size, or bulk of the final product, are assembled in one spot. In other words, workers and equipment go to the material rather than having the material flow down a line to them. Aircraft assembly plants and shipyards typify this kind of layout.

FUNCTIONAL LAYOUTS. Many layouts are designed with more than one objective or function in mind and, therefore, combinations of the various layouts are common. For example, a super-market, though primarily arranged on the basis of marketing, is partly a storage layout; a cafe-teria represents not only a layout by marketing function but also by work flow (a food assembly line); and a factory may arrange its machinery in a process layout but perform assembly opera-tions in a fixed sequence, as in a product layout.

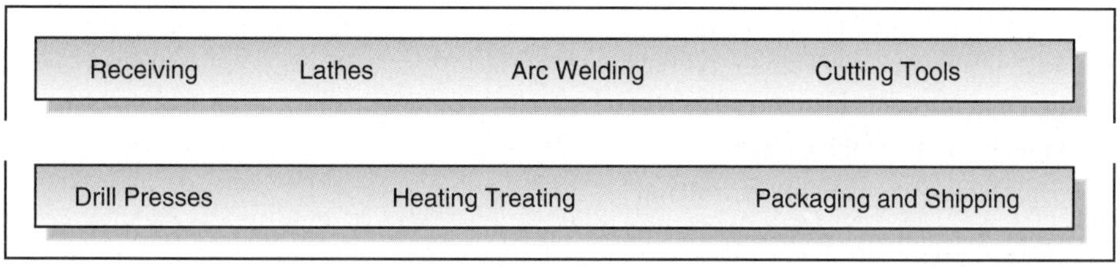

process layout —an arrangement of workers and equipment according to the general function they perform, without regard to any particular product or customer.

fixed position layout —an arrangement in which materials do not move down a production line but rather, because of their weight, size, or bulk, are assembled in one spot.

FIGURE 13.9 Process
Layout

Receiving	Lathes	Arc Welding	Cutting Tools

Drill Presses	Heating Treating	Packaging and Shipping

Designing Layouts

The starting point in layout design is determining how and in what sequence product parts or service tasks flow together. One of the most effective techniques is to create an overall picture of the manufacturing process using assembly charts and process flowcharts. Given the tasks and their sequence, plus knowledge of the volume of products to be produced or of customers to be served, an entrepreneur can analyze space and equipment needs to get an idea of the facility's capacity. When using a product or line layout, these demands take precedence, and manufacturers must arrange equipment and workstations to fit the production tasks and their sequence. With a process or functional layout, different products or customers with different needs place demands on the facility. Rather than having a single best flow, there may be one flow for each product or customer, and compromises in efficiency may be necessary. As a result, the layout for any one product or customer may not result in the achievement of optimal capacity but is flexible to serve the specific situation.

ANALYZING PRODUCTION LAYOUTS. Although there is no general procedure for analyzing the numerous interdependent factors that enter into layout design, specific layout problems lend themselves to detailed analysis. Two important criteria for selecting and designing a layout are worker effectiveness and material handling costs. A layout should be designed to improve job satisfaction and to use workers at the highest skill level for which they are being paid. This applies just as much to an office layout, where engineers may spend half a workday delivering blueprints, which a clerk could do, as it does to a plant layout, where machinists leave their stations to travel a long distance to secure needed tools.

A Company Example

*When a team of manufacturing specialists purchased the **Alexander Doll Company**, a maker of collectible dolls that was founded in 1923, the company's six-story manufacturing operation in New York's Harlem needed a major overhaul. The new owners were experts in designing lean, efficient production systems, and they immediately set about creating one for this classic and well-known maker of dolls. An analysis of the existing layout revealed the use of many archaic principles, which resulted in a work-in-process inventory of more than 90,000 partly finished dolls and a cycle time (the time between receiving a customer's order and delivering a finished doll) of 16 weeks. As they redesigned the factory layout, the new owners involved the 470 employees, who now work in teams of seven or eight. With the new design, work-in-process inventory has fallen by 96 percent, and the company now fills orders within one or two weeks. The new layout played a major role in the company's revitalization.*[43]

Manufacturers can lower materials handling costs by using layouts designed so that product flow is automated whenever possible and flow distances and times are minimized. The extent of automation depends on the level of technology and amount of capital available, as well as behavioral considerations of employees. Flow distances and times are usually minimized by locating sequential processing activities or interrelated departments in adjacent areas. The following features are important to a good manufacturing layout:

1. planned materials flow pattern
2. straight-line layout where possible
3. straight, clearly marked aisles
4. backtracking kept to a minimum
5. related operations close together
6. minimum of in-process inventory
7. easy adjustment to changing conditions
8. minimum materials handling distances
9. minimum of manual handling
10. no unnecessary rehandling of material
11. minimum handling between operations
12. materials delivered to production employees

13. material efficiently removed from the work area

14. materials handling being done by indirect labor

15. orderly materials handling and storage

16. good housekeeping

BUILD, BUY, OR LEASE?

Learning Objective

7. Evaluate the advantages and disadvantages of building, buying, or leasing a building.

Once an entrepreneur has a good idea of the specific criteria to be met for a building to serve the needs of her business, the issue turns to what she can afford to spend. The ability to obtain the best possible physical facilities in relation to available cash may depend largely on whether an entrepreneur decides to build, buy, or lease a building.

The Decision to Build

If a business had unlimited funds, the owner could design and build a perfect facility. However, few new business owners have this luxury. Constructing a new facility can project a positive image to potential customers. The business looks new and, consequently, creates an image of being modern, efficient, and top quality. A new building can incorporate the most modern features during construction, and these might significantly lower operating costs. When such costs are critical to remaining competitive, it may be reasonable to build.

In some rapidly growing areas, there are few existing buildings to buy or lease that meet an entrepreneur's requirements. In these situations, a business owner must consider the cost of constructing a building as a significant factor in her initial estimates of capital needs and break-even point. Constructing a building has high initial fixed expenses that an owner must weigh against the facility's ability to attract additional sales revenue and to reduce operating costs.

The Decision to Buy

In many cases, there may be an ideal building in the area where an entrepreneur wants to locate. Buying the facility allows her to remodel it without seeking permission from anyone else. As with building, buying can put a drain on the business's financial resources, but the owner knows exactly what her monthly payments will be. Under a lease, rental rates can (and usually do) increase over time. If an owner believes that the property will actually appreciate in value, then purchasing it can be a wise investment. In addition, an owner can depreciate the building each year, and both depreciation and interest are tax-deductible expenses.

When considering purchasing a building, the owner should use the same outline of facilities requirements developed for the building option to ensure that this property will not be excessively expensive to modify for her use. Remodeling can add a significant initial expense. The layout of the building may be suitable in many ways, but it may not be ideal for a particular business. Even if a building housed the same kind of business, its existing layout may be completely unsuitable for the way the new owner plans to operate.

Building or buying a building greatly limits an entrepreneur's mobility, however. Some business owners prefer to stay out of the real estate business to retain maximum flexibility and mobility. Plus, not all real estate appreciates in value. Surrounding property can become run down and, consequently, lower a property's value despite the owner's efforts to keep it in excellent condition.

The Decision to Lease

The major advantage of leasing is that it requires no large initial cash outlay, so the business's funds are available for purchasing inventory or for current operations. Firms that are short on cash will inevitably be forced to lease facilities. All lease expenses are tax deductible.

One major disadvantage of leasing is that the property owner might choose not to renew the lease. A successful business might be forced to move to a new location, and such relocation can be extremely costly and could result in a significant loss of established customers. In many cases it is almost like starting the business again. Also, if a business is successful, the property owner may ask for a significant increase in rent when the lease renewal is negotiated. The owner of the building is well aware of the costs associated with moving and has the upper hand in the negotiations. In some lease arrangements the owner is compensated, in addition to a monthly rental fee, by a percentage of the tenant's gross sales. This is common in malls and shopping centers.

Still another disadvantage to leasing is the limitation on remodeling. If the building owner believes that modifications will reduce the future rental value of the property, he will likely require a long-term lease at increased rent. In addition, all permanent modifications of the structure become the property of the building owner.

CHAPTER SUMMARY

1. Explain the stages in the location decision: choosing the region, the state, the city, and the final site.

- The location decision is one of the most important decisions an entrepreneur will make, given its long-term effects on the company. An entrepreneur should look at the choice as a series of increasingly narrow decisions: Which region of the country? Which state? Which city? Which site? Choosing the right location requires an entrepreneur to evaluate potential sites with her target customers in mind. Demographic statistics are available from a wide variety of sources, but government agencies such as the Census Bureau have a wealth of detailed data that can guide an entrepreneur in her location decision.

2. Describe the location criteria for retail and service businesses.

- For retailers, the location decision is especially crucial. Retailers must consider the size of the trade area, the volume of customer traffic, number of parking spots, availability of room for expansion, and the visibility of a site.

3. Outline the basic location options for retail and service businesses.

- Retail and service businesses have six basic location options: central business districts (CBDs), neighborhoods, shopping centers and malls, near competitors, outlying areas, and at home.

4. Explain the site selection process for manufacturers.

- A manufacturer's location decision is strongly influenced by local zoning ordinances. Some areas offer industrial parks designed specifically to attract manufacturers. Two crucial factors for most manufacturers are the reliability (and the cost of transporting) raw materials and the quality and quantity of available labor.

- A foreign trade zone is a specially designated area in or near a U.S. customs port of entry that allows resident companies to import materials and components from foreign countries; assemble, process, manufacture, or package them; and then ship the finished product while either reducing or eliminating tariffs and duties.

- Empowerment zones offer businesses tax breaks on the investments they make within zone boundaries.

- Business incubators are locations that offer flexible, low-cost rental space to their tenants as well as business and consulting services. Their goal is to nurture small companies until they are ready to "graduate" into the business community. Many government agencies and universities offer incubator locations.

5. Describe the criteria used to analyze the layout and design considerations of a building, including the Americans with Disabilities Act.

- When evaluating the suitability of a particular building, an entrepreneur should consider several factors: size (is it large enough to accommodate the business with some room for growth?); construction and external appearance (is the building structurally sound and does it create the right impression for the business?); entrances (are they inviting?); legal issues (does the building comply with the Americans with Disabilities Act? If not how much will it cost to bring it up to standard?); signs (are they legible, well located, and easy to see?); interior (does the interior design contribute to our ability to make sales, and is it ergonomically designed?); lights and fixtures (is the lighting adequate for the tasks workers will be performing, and what is the estimated cost of lighting?).

6. Explain the principles of effective layouts for retailers, service businesses, and manufacturers.

- Layout for retail stores and service businesses depends on the owner's understanding of her customers' buying habits. Retailers have three basic layout options from which to choose: grid, free-form, and boutique. Some areas of a retail store generate more sales per square foot and are, therefore, more valuable.

- The goal of a manufacturer's layout is to create a smooth, efficient work flow. Three basic options exist: product layout, process layout, and fixed position layout. Two key considerations are worker productivity and materials handling costs.

7. Evaluate the advantages and disadvantages of building, buying, and leasing a building.

- Building a new building gives an entrepreneur the opportunity to design exactly what he wants in a brand-new facility; however, not every small business owner can afford to tie up significant amounts of cash in fixed assets. Buying an existing building gives a business owner the freedom to renovate as needed, but this can be an expensive alternative. Leasing a location is a common choice because it is economical, but the business owner faces the uncertainty of lease renewals, rising rents, and renovation problems.

DISCUSSION QUESTIONS

1. How do most small business owners choose a location? Is this wise?

2. What factors should a manager consider when evaluating a region in which to locate a business? Where are such data available?

3. Outline the factors important when selecting a state in which to locate a business.

4. What factors should a seafood processing plant, a beauty shop, and an exclusive jewelry store consider in choosing a location? List factors for each type of business.

5. What intangible factors might enter into the entrepreneur's location decision?

6. What are zoning laws? How do they affect the location decision?

7. What is the trade area? What determines a small retailer's trade area?

8. Why is it important to discover more than just the number of passersby in a traffic count?

9. What types of information can the entrepreneur collect from census data?

10. Why may a "cheap location" not be the "best location"?

11. What is a foreign trade zone? An empowerment zone? A business incubator? What advantages and disadvantages does each one of these offer a small business locating there?

12. Why is it costly for a small firm to choose a location that is too small?

13. What function does a small firm's sign serve? What are the characteristics of an effective business sign?

14. Explain the Americans with Disabilities Act. Which businesses does it affect? What is its purpose?

15. What is ergonomics? Why should entrepreneurs utilize the principles of ergonomics in the design of their facilities?

16. Explain the statement: "Not every portion of a small store's interior space is of equal value in generating sales revenue." What areas are most valuable?

17. What are some of the key features that determine a good manufacturing layout?

18. Summarize the advantages and disadvantages of building, buying, and leasing a building.

THE BUSINESS DISC

Launch *The Business Disc* and return to the section where Harry describes various options for a location for your business: urban residential, downtown, shopping center, highway, or at home. From the "Go To" menu, select "Events from PART 1 - A," and click on "Harry explains various location options." Develop a list of the factors that would characterize the ideal location for your business. How would the factors on your list influence the location choices presented on *The Business Disc*? What are the advantages and the disadvantages of the location you chose?

1. Select a specific type of business you would like to go into one day and use census data and Commerce Department reports from the World Wide Web or the local library to choose a specific site for the business in the local region. What location factors are critical to the success of this business? Would it be likely to succeed in your hometown?

2. Interview a sample of local small business owners. How did they decide on their particular locations? What are the positive and negative features of their existing locations?

3. Locate the most recent issue of either *Entrepreneur* or *Fortune* describing the "best cities for (small) business." (For *Entrepreneur*, it is usually the October issue, and for *Fortune*, it is normally an issue in November.) Which cities are in the top 10? What factors did the magazine use to select these cities? Pick a city and explain what makes it an attractive destination for locating a business there.

4. Select a manufacturing operation, a wholesale business, or a retail store, and evaluate their layouts using the guidelines presented in this chapter. What changes would you recommend? Why? Does the layout contribute to a more effective operation?

5. Choose one of the businesses you studied in Exercise 4 and design an improved layout for the operation. How expensive would these alterations be?

6. Visit the Web site for the Census Bureau at www.census.gov. Go to the census data for your town and use this information to discuss its suitability as a location for the following types of businesses:

   - a new motel with 25 units
   - a bookstore
   - an exclusive women's clothing shop
   - a Mexican restaurant
   - a residential plumber
   - a day care center
   - a high-quality stereo shop
   - a family hair care center

7. Use the resources on the World Wide Web or the local library to prepare a demographic profile of your hometown or city or of the town or city in which you attend college. Using the demographic profile as an analytical tool, what kinds of businesses do you think would be successful there? Unsuccessful? Explain. Use these same resources to prepare an analysis of the competition in the area.

Chapter

14

Global Aspects of Entrepreneurship

National borders are no longer defensible against the invasion of knowledge, ideas, and financial data.

—Walter Wriston

"Pepsi brings your ancestors back from the grave."

—Chinese translation of "Pepsi comes alive."

LEARNING OBJECTIVES

Upon completion of this chapter, you will be able to:

1. **EXPLAIN** why "going global" has become an integral part of many small companies' marketing strategies.

2. **DESCRIBE** the principal strategies small businesses have for going global.

3. **EXPLAIN** how to build a thriving export program.

4. **DISCUSS** the major barriers to international trade and their impact on the global community.

5. **DESCRIBE** the trade agreements that will have the greatest influence on foreign trade in the twenty-first century.

Until recently, the world of international business was much like the field of astronomy before Copernicus revolutionized the study of the planets and the stars with his theory of planetary motion. In the sixteenth century, the Copernican system replaced the Ptolemaic system, which held that the earth was the center of the universe with the sun and all the other planets revolving around it. The Copernican system, however, placed the sun at the center of the solar system with all of the planets revolving around it. Astronomy would never be the same.

In the same sense, business owners across the globe have been guilty of having Ptolemaic tunnel vision when it came to viewing international business opportunities. Like their pre-Copernican counterparts, owners saw an economy that revolved around the nations that served as their home bases. Market opportunities stopped at their homeland's borders. Global trade was only for giant corporations that had the money and the management to tap foreign markets and enough resources to survive if the venture flopped. This scenario no longer holds true in the twenty-first century.

Today, the global marketplace is as much the territory of small, upstart companies as it is that of giant multinational corporations. Powerful, affordable technology, increased access to information on conducting global business, and the growing interdependence of the world's economies have made it easier for companies of all sizes to engage in international trade.

It is no longer a surprise to entrepreneurs that they face global competition in the marketplace. The new economic world order is the result of the interaction of many dynamic forces. Culture, politics, and the basic social fabric of nations are evolving an unprecedented pace as change is facilitated by technology and challenged by global economic and competitive forces. Early twenty-first-century entrepreneurs recognize that the markets of today are small in comparison to the market potential of tomorrow. The world market for goods and services continues to expand, fueled by a global economy that welcomes consumers with new wealth. Technology, which continues to become increasingly affordable and powerful, links trading partners whether they are giant corporations or individual owners with small companies.

The interdependence of nations is highlighted daily as billions of dollars in trade takes place with little or no interference. Global business is accepted as a natural phenomenon, and new entries join daily. The tools of global business are not beyond the reach of any entrepreneur. This chapter is designed to demonstrate the nature and scope of the opportunities available to entrepreneurs who accept the challenge to "go global." In fact, two-thirds of the world's purchasing power lies outside of the borders of the United States!

Successful global ventures are built on a match between the needs of the market and the products and services of the seller.

<A Company Example>

*This is reflected in an opportunity discovered by **AMD Telemedicine** on a visit to Scandinavia. Denmark, Norway, and Sweden are all increasingly employing telemedicine in health care. As an example, Denmark currently imports $850 million of medical equipment and technology each year. U.S. products are viewed as "world class" and in high demand. The match between the health care needs of the Scandinavian countries and the products of the small U.S.-based company AMD Telemedicine demonstrates the basics upon which all global business can be conducted.[1]*

<A Company Example>

*The United States Chamber of Commerce established **Trade Roots**, an international trade leadership program that networks over 3,000 local U.S. Chambers of Commerce. The program also facilitates the transfer of current information on the benefits and methods for its members' involvement in international trade. Blending this program with a multiagency publication by the U.S. government called* Export Programs Guide *provides entrepreneurs with a substantial amount of resources at their fingertips.[2]*

<Learning Objective>

1. Explain why "going global" has become an integral part of many small companies' marketing strategies.

WHY GO GLOBAL?

The main reason to go global is not unlike the reason given by the legendary bank robber, Willie Sutton, who, when asked why he robbed banks, replied, "That's where the money is." The same is true for global business today. Failure to cultivate global markets can be a lethal mistake for modern businesses, whatever their size. Increasingly, small businesses will be under pressure to expand into international markets and to consider themselves businesses without borders.

Going global can put tremendous strain on a small company, but entrepreneurs who take the plunge into global business can reap the following benefits:

- *Offset sales declines in the domestic market.* Markets in foreign countries may be booming when those in the United States are sagging. In this way, global business acts as a countercyclical balance.

- *Increase sales and profits.* Two forces are working in tandem to make global business increasingly attractive: income rising to levels where potential sales are now possible and the realization that 96 percent of the planet's population is outside of the United States.

- *Extend their products' life cycle.* Some companies have been able to take products that had reached the maturity stage of the product life cycle in the United States and sell them successfully in foreign markets.

- *Lower manufacturing costs.* In industries characterized by high levels of fixed costs, businesses that expand into global markets can lower their manufacturing costs by spreading those fixed costs over a larger number of units.

- *Improve competitive position and enhance reputation.* Going up against some of the toughest competition in the world forces a company to hone its competitive skills.

- *Raise quality levels.* Customers in many global markets are much tougher to satisfy than those in the United States. One reason Japanese products have done so well worldwide is that Japanese companies must build products to satisfy their customers at home who demand extremely high quality and are sticklers for detail. Businesses that compete in global markets learn very quickly how to boost their quality levels to world-class standards.

- *Become more customer oriented.* Delving into global markets teaches business owners about the unique tastes, customs, preferences, and habits of customers in many different cultures. Responding to these differences imbues businesses with a degree of sensitivity toward their customers, both domestic and foreign.

Becoming a global entrepreneur does require a modification in a company's mind-set. Success in a global economy also requires constant innovation; staying nimble enough to use speed as a competitive weapon; maintaining a high level of quality and constantly improving it; being sensitive to foreign customers' unique requirements; adopting a more respectful attitude toward foreign habits and customs; hiring motivated, multilingual employees; and retaining a desire to learn constantly about global markets. In short, the path to success requires businesses to become "insiders" rather than just "exporters." Entrepreneurs must remain the "hunters" in the global market or they will find themselves the "hunted."

As with any new venture, entrepreneurs need to prepare. In this case, it is critical to ask, and answer, the following questions about their business.

1. Is there a profitable market in which the firm has the potential to be successful for an extended period of time?

2. Does the firm have the specific resources, skills, and commitment to succeed in this venture?

3. Are there pressures domestically that are forcing the firm to seek global opportunities?

4. Do entrepreneurs know the culture, history, economics, value system, and so on of the countries they are considering? Will you be comfortable doing business there?

5. Is there a viable exit strategy if the conditions change or the new venture is not successful?

6. Can the company afford *not* to go global?

Entrepreneurs must see their companies from a global perspective. An absence of global thinking is one of the barriers that most often limits their ability to move beyond known markets. Indeed, learning to *think globally* may be the first—and most threatening—obstacle an entrepreneur must overcome on the way to creating a truly global business. Global thinking is the ability to appreciate, understand, and respect the different beliefs, values, behavior, and business practices of companies and people in different cultures and countries. This means entrepreneurs must "do their homework" about every aspect of a potential host country when they believe they can successfully sell their product in that market. The U.S. government, through the Department of Commerce, has a vast amount of current information about all nations, including economic data that can be useful in the evaluation of a potential opportunity. Doing business globally presents extraordinary opportunities only to those who are prepared. Never assume that business "there" is conducted like business "here."

Construction is a major segment of the United States economy (8 percent of GDP or $800+ billion a year). Yet the global construction market is estimated to be in excess of $3.5 trillion. This vast and lucrative market will require U.S-based construction companies that are known for their skills in engineering, construction and project management, and specialized technology to form joint ventures with firms in the host country. Many foreign governments mandate these conditions to ensure that local construction firms benefit as well as learn the specialized skills of U.S. construction companies.[3] An example of how parties to a trade agreement benefit is International Chem-Crete.

*With the assistance of the United States Department of Commerce, Texas-based **International Chem-Crete** was able to establish relationships with the Egyptian company Technomechanic. This relationship allows the distribution of Chem-Crete chemical-based products for use in the repair of Egypt's infrastructure. On the same trade mission, International Chem-Crete established another agreement with the Moroccan firm YNNA Holdings. This arrangement is expected to generate 500 to 1,000 new jobs in Morocco. Examples such as this are truly "win-win" situations that have the potential to benefit to all parties involved.*[4]

Learning Objectives

2. Describe the principal strategies for going global.

STRATEGIES FOR GOING GLOBAL

Entrepreneurs have eight strategic options to choose from when going global. The principal strategies include launching a World Wide Web site, relying on trade intermediaries, creating joint ventures, foreign licensing, franchising, engaging in countertrading and bartering, exporting, and establishing international locations (see Figure 14.1). Whatever strategic options the entrepreneur selects, the mind-set of the organization's leadership must become broader. Becoming a global business depends on instilling a global culture throughout the organization that permeates *everything* the company does. Entrepreneurs who routinely conduct international business have developed a global mind-set for themselves and their companies.

An entrepreneur also must understand the needs of the customers in the new marketplace. Consider the case of Pentaura Ltd., a Greenville, South Carolina, manufacturer of high-quality, handmade furniture, that sought assistance from the Japan External Trade Organization (JETRO). In addition to helping Pentaura navigate the intricacies of the Japanese economy, JETRO recommended that the firm modify the height of its tables to accommodate the smaller stature and compact living space of Japanese customers.[5] In this case, product acceptance was improved through product modification to the physical needs of the customer.

Creating a World Wide Web

Perhaps in our technology-rich global environment the fastest, least expensive, and lowest-cost strategic option to establishing a global business presence is creating a Web site. Because the Web is global, with a well-designed Web site, entrepreneurs can extend their reach to customers

FIGURE 14.1 Eight Strategies for Going Global

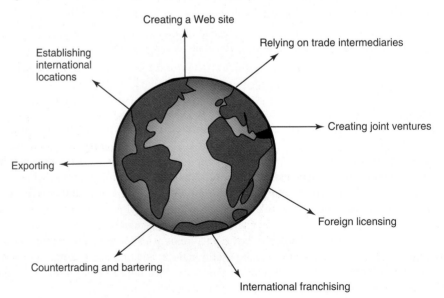

Creating a Web site

Relying on trade intermediaries

Establishing international locations

Creating joint ventures

Exporting

Foreign licensing

Countertrading and bartering

International franchising

anywhere in the world—and without breaking the budget! A company's Web site is available to anyone anywhere in the world and provides exposure 24 hours a day to a firm's products or services seven days a week. For some small companies, the Web has become as essential a tool to doing business as the telephone and the fax machine.

Establishing a presence on the Web has become an important part of a company's strategy for reaching customers outside the United States. A study by the International Development Conference estimates the number of World Wide Web users to be 500 million worldwide. Approximately 143 million of them live in the United States, leaving 357 million potential Web customers outside this country's borders.[6] Figure 14.2 provides a comparison of the Web-using population by world region.

Most small companies follow a three-step evolutionary approach to conducting global business on the Web.

Step 1. *Connecting to e-mail.* Even though it lacks the ability to provide the engaging images, sounds, and animation available on the Web, e-mail gives entrepreneurs the ability to communicate with customers anywhere in the world quickly and easily. E-mail correspondence often is the first step to establishing lasting relationships with international customers. Not only is e-mail communication less expensive than international telephone calls, but it also overcomes many of the problems associated with different time zones.

Step 2. *Using the Web to conduct international market research.* Once they discover the power of the Internet through e-mail, entrepreneurs soon begin to explore the Web's capacity to generate sales leads by researching customers and market characteristics in other countries. With the help of the Web, they begin to see the world as their market.

Step 3. *Building a globally accessible Web site.* This step allows a business to both educate potential customers about the products and services the company offers as well as generate inquiries and, hopefully, orders. With the introduction in recent years of highly secure transactions software, orders a company can accept quickly and safely. The Internet provides the entrepreneur with the quickest and easiest way to go global. Unfortunately, small companies miss out on millions of dollars in potential Web sales every year because their Web sites are not set up to handle international transactions!

Anthropologists tell us that all civilizations made and drank wine, but could a small northern California winery successfully market its products globally? **Next Wine** *turned to the Internet as the vehicle to reach the market. Dain Duston, president of the firm, struggles to make the "little things" work while meeting the regulations on the sale of wine in various countries. It was necessary to have the Web information translated accurately into multiple languages. For this task, Next Wine turned to SDL International, a firm that offers translation services for the Internet. This is an example of two small businesses working together to achieve a presence in a global market.*[7]

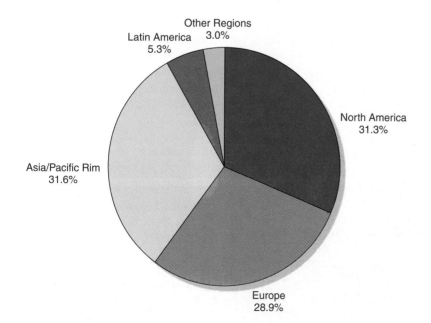

FIGURE 14.2 Internet Users Worldwide by Region

Source: United Nations Conference on Trade Development, E-Commerce and Development Report 2002, p. 8.

Trade Intermediaries

Another alternative for low-cost and low-risk entry into international markets is to use a trade intermediary. **Trade intermediaries** are domestic agencies that serve as distributors in foreign countries for domestic companies of all sizes. They rely on their networks of contacts, their extensive knowledge of local customs and markets, and their experience in international trade to market products effectively and efficiently all across the globe. Although a broad array of trade intermediaries is available, the following are ideally suited for small businesses.

EXPORT MANAGEMENT COMPANIES. **Export management companies (EMCs)** are an important channel of foreign distribution for small companies just getting started in international trade or for those lacking the resources to assign their own people to foreign markets. Most EMCs are merchant intermediaries, working on a buy-and-sell arrangement with domestic small companies. They provide small businesses with a low-cost, efficient, independent, international marketing department, offering services ranging from market research and advice on patent protection to arranging financing and handling shipping. More than 1,000 EMCs operate across the United States, and many of them specialize in particular products or product lines.

The greatest benefits EMCs offer small companies are ready access to global markets and an extensive knowledge base on foreign trade, both of which are vital for entrepreneurs who are inexperienced in conducting global business. In return for their services, EMCs usually earn an extra discount on the goods they buy from their clients or, if they operate on a commission rate, a higher commission than domestic distributors earn on what they sell. Finding an EMC is not difficult. The Federation of International Trade Associations (FITA) provides useful information for small companies about global business and trade intermediaries on its Web site (http.fita.org). Industry trade associations and publications and the U.S. Department of Commerce's Export Assistance Centers* also can help entrepreneurs locate EMCs and other trade intermediaries.

EXPORT TRADING COMPANIES. Another tactic for getting into international markets with a minimum of cost and effort is through export trading companies (ETCs). **Export trading companies** are businesses that buy and sell products in a number of countries, and they typically offer a wide range of services such as exporting, importing, shipping, storing, distributing, and others to their clients. Unlike EMCs, which tend to focus on exporting, ETCs usually perform both import and export trades across many countries' borders. However, like EMCs, ETCs lower the risk of exporting for small businesses. Some of the largest ETCs in the world are based in the United States and Japan. In fact, many businesses that have navigated successfully Japan's complex system of distribution have done so with the help of ETCs.

In 1982, Congress passed the Export Trading Company Act to allow producers of similar products to form ETC cooperatives without the fear of violating antitrust laws. The goal was to encourage U.S. companies to export more goods by allowing businesses in the same industry to band together to form ETCs.

MANUFACTURER'S EXPORT AGENTS. Manufacturer's export agents (MEAs) act as international sales representatives in a limited number of markets for various noncompeting domestic companies. Unlike the close, long-term partnering relationship formed with most EMCs, the relationship between the MEA and a small company is a short-term one, and the MEA typically operates on a commission basis.

EXPORT MERCHANTS. Export merchants are domestic wholesalers that do business in foreign markets. They buy goods from many domestic manufacturers and then market them in foreign

*A searchable list of the Export Assistance Centers is available at the Export. gov Web site
http://www.export.gov/comm_svc/eac.html.

---

trade intermediaries— *domestic agencies that serve as distributors in foreign countries for domestic companies of all sizes.*

export management companies—*merchant intermediaries that provide small businesses with a low-cost, efficient, off-site international marketing department.*

export trading companies—*businesses that buy and sell products in a number of countries and offer a wide variety of services to their clients.*

With a global mindset and a solid international business strategy, entrepreneurs can capture a share of the $6.4 trillion in global trade each year.

Courtesy of Corbis - NY.

markets. Unlike MEAs, export merchants often carry competing lines, which means they have little loyalty to suppliers. Most export merchants specialize in particular industries: office equipment, computers, industrial supplies, and others.

RESIDENT BUYING OFFICES.   Another approach to exporting is to sell to a resident buying office, a government-owned or privately owned operation of one country established in another country for the purpose of buying goods made there. Many foreign governments and businesses have set up buying offices in the United States. Selling to them is just like selling to domestic customers because the buying office handles all the details of exporting.

FOREIGN DISTRIBUTORS.   Some small businesses work through foreign distributors to reach international markets. Domestic small companies export their products to distributors that handle all of the marketing, distribution, and service functions in the foreign country. They also offer exporting small businesses the benefits of knowledge of their local markets, the ability to cover a given territory thoroughly, and prompt sales and service support.

> *Ed Anderson, founder of **Lil' Orbits**, a Minnesota-based company that makes doughnut machines, sold his machinery only in the United States for nearly 15 years with great success. Then he began to wonder why his doughnut-making hardware wouldn't sell in international markets as well. In 1987, he placed a $40 ad in a U.S. Department of Commerce publication and was flooded with inquiries from foreign distributors. Today, Lil' Orbits has 42 long-time foreign distributors that sell the company's line of seven machines around the world. The company collects more than 60 percent of its $10 million annual revenue from abroad.*[8]

A Company Example

THE VALUE OF USING TRADE INTERMEDIARIES.   Trade intermediaries such as these are becoming increasingly popular among businesses attempting to branch out into world markets because they make that transition much faster and easier. Most small businesses simply do not have the knowledge, resources, or confidence to go global alone. Intermediaries' global networks of buyers and sellers allow their small business customers to build their international sales much faster and with fewer hassles and mistakes.

The key to establishing a successful relationship with a trade intermediary is conducting a thorough screening to determine what type of intermediary—and which one in particular—will best serve a small company's needs. A company looking for an intermediary should develop a list of criteria by which to measure candidates' suitability and then compile a list of potential candidates using some of the sources listed in Table 14.1. After compiling a list of potential intermediaries, entrepreneurs should evaluate each one using the criteria to narrow the field to the most promising ones. Interviewing a principal from each intermediary on the final list should tell entrepreneurs which ones are best able to meet their companies' needs. Finally, before signing any agreement with a trade intermediary, it is wise to conduct thorough background and credit checks. Entrepreneurs with experience in global trade also suggest entering short-term agreements of about a year with new trade intermediaries to allow time to test their ability and willingness to live up to their promises.

Joint Ventures

Joint ventures, both domestic and foreign, lower the risk of entering global markets for small businesses. They also give small companies more clout in foreign lands. In a **domestic joint venture,** two or more U.S. small businesses form an alliance for the purpose of exporting their goods and services. For export ventures, participating companies get antitrust immunity, allowing them to cooperate freely. The businesses share the responsibility and the cost of getting export licenses and permits, and they split the venture's profits. Establishing a joint venture with the right partner has become an essential part of maintaining a competitive position in global markets for a growing number of industries.

domestic joint venture—*an alliance of two or more U.S. small companies for the purpose of exporting their goods and services abroad.*

In a **foreign joint venture,** a domestic small business forms an alliance with a company in the target nation. The host partner brings to the joint venture valuable knowledge of the local market and its method of operation as well as of the customs and the tastes of local customers, making it much easier to conduct business in the foreign country. Sometimes foreign countries place certain limitations on joint ventures. Some nations, for example, require host companies to own at least 51 percent of the venture.

foreign joint venture—*an alliance between a U.S. small business and a company in the target nation.*

The most important ingredient in the recipe for a successful joint venture is choosing the right partner. A productive joint venture is much like a marriage, requiring commitment and understanding. In addition to picking the right partners, a second key to creating a successful

TABLE 14.1

Resources for Locating a Trade
Intermediary

Trade intermediaries make doing business around the world much easier for small companies, but finding the right one can be a challenge. Fortunately, several government agencies offer a wealth of information to businesses interested in reaching into global markets with the help of trade intermediaries. Entrepreneurs looking for help in breaking into global markets should contact the International Trade Administration, the U.S. Commerce Department, and the Small Business Administration first to take advantage of the following services:

- *Agent/Distributor Service (ADS)*. Provides customized searches to locate interested and qualified foreign distributors for a product or service. (Search cost $250 per country)
- *Commercial Service International Contacts (CSIC) List*. Provides contact and product information for more than 82,000 foreign agents, distributors, and importers interested in doing business with U.S. companies.
- *Country Directories of International Contacts (CDIC) List*. Provides the same kind of information as the CSIC list but is organized by country.
- *Industry Sector Analyses (ISAs)*. Offer in-depth reports on industries in foreign countries, including information on distribution practices, end users, and top sales prospects.
- *International Market Insights (IMIs)*. Include reports on specific foreign market conditions, upcoming opportunities for U.S. companies, trade contacts, trade show schedules, and other information.
- *Trade Opportunity Program (TOP)*. Provides up-to-the-minute, prescreened sales leads around the world for U.S. businesses, including joint venture and licensing partners, direct sales leads, and representation offers.
- *International Company Profiles (ICPs)*. Commercial specialists will investigate potential partners, agents, distributors, or customers for U.S. companies and will issue profiles on them.
- *Commercial News USA*. A government-published magazine that promotes U.S. companies' products and services to 259,000 business readers in 152 countries at a fraction of the cost of commercial advertising. Small companies can use *Commercial News USA* to reach new customers around the world for as little as $395.
- *Gold Key Service*. For a small fee, business owners wanting to target a specific country can use the Department of Commerce's Gold Key Service in which experienced trade professionals arrange meetings with prescreened contacts whose interests match their own.
- *Matchmaker Trade Delegations Program*. Helps small U.S. companies establish business relationships in major markets abroad by introducing them to the right contacts.
- *Multi-State/Catalog Exhibition Program*. Working with state economic development offices, the Department of Commerce presents companies' product and sales literature to hundreds of interested business prospects in foreign countries.
- *International Fair Certification Program*. Promotes U.S. companies' participation in foreign trade shows that represent the best marketing opportunities for them.
- *National Trade Data Bank (NTDB)*. Most of the information listed previously is available on the NTDB, the U.S. government's most comprehensive database of world trade data. With the NTDB, small companies have access to information that only *Fortune 500* companies could afford.
- *Economic Bulletin Board (EBB)*. Provides online trade leads and valuable market research on foreign countries compiled from a variety of federal agencies.
- *U.S. Export Assistance Centers*. The Department of Commerce has established 19 export centers (SEACs) around the country to serve as one-stop shops for entrepreneurs needing export help. Call (800) 872-8723.
- *Trade Information Center*. Helps locate federal export assistance, provides export assistance, and offers a 24-hour automated fax retrieval system that gives entrepreneurs free information on export promotion programs, regional market information, and international trade agreements. Call USA-TRADE.
- *Office of International Trade*. The Small Business Administration provides a variety of export development assistance, how-to publications, and information on foreign markets.
- *Export Hotline*. Provides no-cost trade information on more than 50 industries in 80 countries. Call (800) 872-9767.
- *Export Opportunity Hotline*. Trade specialists have access to online databases and reports from government and private agencies concerning foreign markets. Call (202) 628-8389.

alliance is to establish common objectives. Defining *exactly* what each party in the joint venture hopes to accomplish at the outset will minimize the opportunity for misunderstandings and disagreements later on. One important objective should always be to use the joint venture as a learning experience, which requires a long-term view of the business relationship.

Often joint ventures fail because entrepreneurs didn't do the following:

- Define at the outset important issues such as each party's contributions and responsibilities, the distribution of earnings, the expected life of the relationship, and the circumstances under which the parties can terminate the relationship.

- Understand in depth their partner's reasons and objectives for joining the venture.
- Select a partner who shares their company's values and standards of conduct.
- Spell out in writing exactly how the venture will work and where decision-making authority lies.
- Select a partner whose skills are different from but compatible with those of their own companies.
- Prepare a "prenuptial agreement" that spells out what will happen in case of a business "divorce."

Foreign Licensing

Rather than sell their products or services directly to customers overseas, some small companies enter foreign markets by licensing businesses in other nations to use their patents, trademarks, copyrights, technology, processes, or products. In return for licensing these assets, the small company collects royalties from the sales of its foreign licenses. Licensing is a relatively simple way for even the most inexperienced business owners to extend their reach into global markets.

Licensing is ideal for companies whose value lies in unique products or services, a recognized name, or proprietary technology. Although many businesses consider licensing only their products to foreign companies, the licensing potential for intangibles such as processes technology, copyrights, and trademarks often is greater. Some entrepreneurs discover that they can make more money from licensing their know-how for production or product control than they can from actually selling a finished product in a highly competitive foreign market. Foreign licensing enables a small business to enter foreign markets quickly, easily, and with virtually no capital investment. Risks to the company include the potential of losing control over its manufacturing and marketing and creating a competitor if the licensee gains too much knowledge and control. Securing proper patent, trademark, and copyright protection beforehand can minimize those risks, however.

International Franchising

Over the past decade, a growing number of franchises have been attracted to international markets to boost sales and profits as the domestic market has become increasingly saturated with outlets and much tougher to wring growth from. International franchisors sell virtually every kind of product or service imaginable—from fast food to child day care—in international markets. In some cases, the products and services sold in international markets are identical to those sold in the United States. However, most franchisors have learned that they must modify their products and services to suit local tastes and customs. As you travel the world, you will discover that American fast-food giants like McDonald's and Domino's make significant modifications in their menu to remain attractive to the demands of local customers.

*For instance, **Domino's Pizza** operates restaurants in more than 50 countries, where local franchises offer pizza toppings that are quite different from traditional ones used in the United States, including squid (Japan), pickled ginger (India), green peas (Brazil), and reindeer sausage (Iceland) to cater to customers' palates. The dough, the sauce, and the cheese are standard in every location, however. At **McDonald's** locations around the world, Big Macs share the menu with Vegetable McNuggets in India, teriyaki burgers in Japan, and McHuevos (a burger topped with a poached egg and mayonnaise) in Uruguay.*

Although franchise outlets span the globe, Canada is the primary market for U.S. franchisors, with Japan and Europe following. These markets are most attractive to franchisors because they are similar to the U.S. market: rising personal incomes, strong demand for consumer goods, growing service economies, and spreading urbanization. There is little doubt that franchising is becoming a two-way street and that globalization will continue to be a powerful force in the growth of the strategic marketing option. Early entry into emerging markets with cultural sensitivity to national tastes is a key to long-term success.

Countertrading and Bartering

countertrade—*a transaction in which a company selling goods in a foreign country agrees to promote investment and trade in that country.*

A **countertrade** involves a transaction in which a company selling goods in a foreign country agrees to promote investment and trade in that country. The goal of the transaction is to help offset the capital drain from the foreign country's purchases. As entrepreneurs enter more and more developing countries, they will need to develop skills at implementing this strategy. In some cases, small and medium-sized businesses find it advantageous to work together with large corporations that have experience in implementing this strategy.

Countertrading does suffer numerous drawbacks. Countertrade transactions can be complicated, cumbersome, and time consuming. They also increase the chances that a company will get stuck with merchandise that it cannot move. They can lead to unpleasant surprises concerning the quantity and quality of products required in the countertrade. Still, countertrading offers one major advantage: Sometimes it's the only way to make a sale!

Entrepreneurs must weigh the advantages against the disadvantages for their company before committing to a countertrade deal. Because of its complexity and the risks involved, countertrading is not the best choice for a novice entrepreneur looking to break into the global marketplace.

bartering—*the exchange of goods and services for other goods and services.*

Bartering, the exchange of goods and services for other goods and services, is another way of trading with countries lacking convertible currency. In a barter exchange, a company that manufactures electronics components might trade its products for the coffee that a business in a foreign country processes, which it then sells to a third company for cash. Barter transactions require finding a business with complementary needs, but they are much simpler than countertrade transactions.

Learning Objective

3. Explain how to build a thriving export program.

EXPORTING

Until recently, small businesses were reluctant to undertake exporting because of the perception that the process was overly complex and required sophisticated skills. More than 200,000 U.S. companies currently export; however, experts estimate that at least twice as many are capable of exporting but are not doing so. The biggest barrier facing companies that have never exported is not knowing where or how to start. The following steps provide guidance to an entrepreneur on how to establish an exporting program:

1. *Recognize that even the tiniest companies and least experienced entrepreneurs have the potential to export.* A company's size has nothing to do with the demand for its products abroad. If the products meet the needs of global customers, there is the potential to export. U.S. businesses export nearly $700 billion worth of merchandise a year, and with the right approach, small companies can snare their share of that business.

2. *Analyze your product or service.* Is it special? New? Unique? High quality? Priced favorably because of lower costs or exchange rates? In which countries would there be sufficient demand for it? In many foreign countries, products from America are in demand because they have an air of mystery about them! Exporters quickly learn the value foreign customers place on quality.

3. *Analyze your commitment.* Are you willing to devote the time and energy to develop export markets? Does your company have the necessary resources? Export start-ups can take from six to eight months (or longer) to develop, but entering foreign markets isn't as tough as most entrepreneurs think. Table 14.2 summarizes key issues managers must address in the export decision.

4. *Research markets and pick your target.* Nearly two-thirds of small businesses export to just one country. Before investing in a costly sales trip abroad, however, entrepreneurs should make a trip to the local library or the nearest branch of the Department of Commerce. Exporters can choose from a multitude of guides, manuals, books, newsletters, videos, and other resources to help them research potential markets. Some of the most helpful tools for researching foreign markets are the Country and Industry Market Reports available at the U.S. government's export Web portal (http://www.export.gov/marketresearch.html), which provide detailed information on the economic, political, regulatory, and investment environment for countries ranging from Afghanistan to Zimbabwe. Armed with research, small business owners can avoid wasting a lot of time and money on markets with limited potential for their products and can concentrate on those with the greatest promise. Research shows export entrepreneurs whether they need to modify their existing products and services to suit the tastes and preferences of their foreign target customers. Sometimes foreign customers' lifestyles, housing needs, body size, and cultures require exporters to make alterations in their product lines. Such modifications can sometimes spell the difference between success and failure in the global market. Table 14.3 offers questions to guide entrepreneurs conducting export research.

TABLE 14.2

Management Issues in the Export

Decision

Source: Adapted from *A Basic Guide to Exporting* (Washington, DC: U.S. Department of Commerce, 1986), p. 3.

I. Experience

    1. With what countries has your company already conducted business (or from what countries have you received inquiries about your product or service)?

    2. What product lines do foreign customers ask about most often?

    3. Prepare a list of sale inquiries for each buyer by product and by country.

    4. Is the trend of inquiries or sales increasing or decreasing?

    5. Who are your primary domestic and foreign competitors?

    6. What lessons has your company learned from past export experience?

II. Management and Personnel

    1. Who will be responsible for the export entity's organization and staff? (Do you have an export "champion"?)

    2. How much top management time

    a. *Should* you allocate to exporting?

    b. *Can* you afford to allocate to exporting?

    3. What does management expect from its exporting efforts? What are your company's export goals and objectives?

    4. What organizational or structure will your company require to ensure that it can service export sales properly? (Note the political implications, if any.)

    5. Who will implement the plan?

III. Production Capacity

    1. To what extent is your company using its existing production capacity? Is there any excess? If so, how much?

    2. Will filling export orders hurt your company's ability to make and service domestic sales?

    3. What will additional production for export markets cost your company?

    4. Are there seasonal or cyclical fluctuations in your company's workload? When? Why?

    5. Is there a minimum quantity foreign customers must order for a sale to be profitable?

    6. To what extent would your company need to modify its products, packaging, and design specifically for its export targets? Is your product quality adequate for foreign customers?

    7. What pricing structure will your company use? Will prices be competitive?

    8. How will your company collect payment of its export sales?

IV. Financial Capacity

    1. How much capital will your company need to begin exporting? Where will it come from?

    2. How will you allocate the initial costs of your company's export effort?

    3. Does your company have other expansion plans that would compete with an exporting effort?

    4. By what date do you expect your company's export program to pay for itself?

    5. How important is establishing a global presence to your company's future success?

5. *Develop a distribution strategy.* Should you use an trade intermediary or sell directly to foreign customers? Small companies just entering international markets may prefer to rely on trade intermediaries to break new ground.

6. *Find your customer.* Small businesses can rely on a host of export specialists to help them track down foreign customers. (Refer to Table 14.1 for a list of some of the resources available from the government.) The U.S. Department of Commerce and the International Trade Administration should be the first stops on an entrepreneur's agenda for going global. These agencies have the market research available for locating the best target markets for a particular company and specific customers in those markets. Industry Sector Analyses (ISAs), International Market Insights (IMIs), and Customized Market Analyses (CMAs) are just some of the reports and services global entrepreneurs find most useful. They also have knowledgeable staff specialists experienced in the details of global trade and in the intricacies of foreign cultures.

A Company Example

Jimmy Kaplanges, head of **GP66 Chemical Corporation**, *a small producer of industrial degreasers, has led his company into exporting its products to Brazil, Spain, France, and Greece. He also saw plenty of opportunity for the company's products in China, but Kaplanges knew that cracking that*

TABLE 14.3

Questions to Guide International Market Research

Source: Adapted from *A Basic Guide to Exporting* (Washington, DC: Department of Commerce, 1986), p. 11.

- Is there an overseas market for your company's products or services?
- Are there specific target markets that look most promising?
- Which new markets abroad are most likely to open up or expand?
- How big is the market your company is targeting, and how fast is it growing?
- What are the major economic, political, legal, social, technological, and other environmental factors affecting this market?
- What are the demographic and cultural factors affecting this market (e.g., disposable income, occupation, age, gender, opinions, activities, interests, tastes, and values)?
- Who are your company's present and potential customers abroad?
- What are their needs and desires? What factors influence their buying decisions: price, credit terms, delivery terms, quality, brand name, and the like?
- How would they use your company's product or service? What modifications, if any, would be necessary to sell to your target customers?
- Who are your primary competitors in the foreign market?
- How do competitors distribute, sell, and promote their products? What are their prices?
- What are the best channels of distribution for your product?
- What is the best way for your company to gain exposure in this market?
- Are there any barriers such as tariffs, quotas, duties, or regulations to selling your product in this market? Are there any incentives?
- Are there any potential licensing or joint venture partners already in this market?

market was more than GP66 Chemical could accomplish on its own. That's when Kaplanges turned to the Export Assistance Center in the company's hometown of Baltimore, Maryland. Kaplanges credits the trade specialist there, Nasir Abbasi, with helping his company enter the Chinese market successfully. Sales to Chinese customers have climbed from $3 million to more than $12 million.[9]

7. *Find financing.* One of the biggest barriers to small business exports is lack of financing. Access to adequate financing is a crucial ingredient in a successful export program because the cost of generating foreign sales often is higher and collection cycles are longer than in domestic markets. The trouble is that bankers and other sources of capital don't always understand the intricacies of international sales and view financing them as excessively risky. Also, among major industrialized nations, the U.S. government spends the least per capita to promote exports.

Several federal, state, and private programs are operating to fill this export financing void, however. Programs such as the Small Business Administration's Export Working Capital Program (90 percent loan guarantees up to $750,00), the Export-Import Bank (www.exim.gov), the Overseas Private Investment Corporation, and a variety of state-sponsored programs offer export-minded entrepreneurs both direct loans and loan guarantees. (A list of all state foreign trade assistance offices is available in the Commerce Department's *National Export Directory*.) In recent years, the Export-Import Bank has emphasized loans and loan guarantees for small exporters; 81 percent of its lending volume has gone to small companies.[10] The Bankers Association for Foreign Trade (www.baft.org) is an association of 450 banks that matches exporters needing foreign trade financing with interested banks.

A Company Example

When Robert Cavallarin was traveling in Europe in 1989, he realized that he and partner Steve Macri, co-owners of S&S Seafood, could export Maine lobsters to Europe. Unfortunately, Cavallarin and Macri could not get the $100,000 in financing necessary to start their export venture, despite the fact that they had orders from seafood importers in hand. Macri turned to a trade consultant for help, and soon S&S Seafood had a business plan for its proposed export business and a contact at the Export-Import Bank. With a 90 percent loan guarantee from the Export-Import Bank, S&S Seafood was able to secure a $100,000 bank loan and begin exporting. Today, the company has eight employees and generates annual sales of $12 million, 95 percent of which comes from exports to Europe and Asia.[11]

8. *Ship your goods.* Export novices usually rely on international freight forwarders and custom-house agents—experienced specialists in overseas shipping—for help in navigating the bureaucratic morass of packaging requirements and paperwork demanded by customs. These specialists, also known as transport architects, are to exporters what travel agents are to passengers and normally charge relatively small fees for a valuable service. They move shipments of all sizes to destinations all over the world efficiently, saving entrepreneurs many headaches.

TABLE 14.4

Common International Shipping Terms and Their Meanings

Source: Adapted from *Guide to the Finance of International Trade*, edited by Gordon Platt (HSBC Trade Services, Marine Midland Bank, and the *Journal of Commerce*), /infoserv2.ita.doc.gov/efm/efm.nsf/503d177e3c6f0b48525675900112e24/6218a8703573b329852567590004c41f3/$FILE/Finance_.pdf/pp. 6-10.

Shipping Term Used	Seller's Responsibility	Buyer's Responsibility	Shipping Method
FOB ("Free on Board") (Seller)	Deliver goods to carrier and provide export license and clean on-board receipt. Bear risk of loss until goods are delivered to carrier.	Pay shipping, freight, and insurance charges. Bear risk of loss while goods are in transit.	All
FOB ("Free on Board") (Buyer)	Deliver goods to the buyer's place of business and provide export license and clean on-board receipt. Pay shipping, freight, and insurance charges.	Accept delivery of goods after documents are tendered.	All
FAS ("Free Along Side")	Deliver goods alongside ship. Provide an "alongside" receipt.	Provide export license and proof of delivery of the goods to the carrier. Bear risk of loss once goods are delivered to the carrier.	Ship
CFR ("Cost and Freight")	Deliver goods to carrier, obtain export licenses, and pay export taxes. Provide buyer with clean bill of lading. Pay freight and shipping charges. Bear risk of loss until goods are delivered to buyer.	Pay insurance charges. Accept delivery of goods after documents are tendered.	Ship
CIF ("Cost, Insurance, and Freight")	Same as CFR plus pay insurance charges and provide buyer with insurance policy.	Accept delivery of goods after documents are tendered.	Ship
CPT ("Carriage Paid to . . .")	Deliver goods to carrier, obtain export licenses, and pay export taxes. Provide buyer with clean transportation documents. Pay shipping and freight charges.	Pay insurance charges. Accept delivery of goods after documents are tendered.	All
CIP ("Carriage and Insurance Paid to . . .")	Same as CPT plus pay insurance charges and provide buyer with insurance policy.	Accept delivery of goods after documents are tendered.	All
DDU ("Delivered Duty Unpaid")	Obtain export license and pay import duty, pay insurance charges, and provide buyer documents for taking delivery.	Take delivery of goods and pay import duties.	All
DDP ("Delivered Duty Paid")	Obtain export license, pay insurance charges, and provide buyer documents for taking delivery.	Take delivery of goods.	All

Shipping terms, always important for determining which party in a transaction pays the cost of shipping and bears the risk of loss or damage to the goods, take on heightened importance in international transactions. Table 14.4 explains the implications of some of the most common shipping terms used in international transactions.

9. *Collect your money.* Collecting foreign accounts can be more complex than collecting domestic ones, but by picking their customers carefully and checking their credit references closely, entrepreneurs can minimize bad-debt losses. Financing foreign sales often involves special credit arrangements such as letters of credit and bank (or documentary) drafts. A **letter of credit** is an

letter of credit—*an agreement between an exporter's bank and a foreign buyer's bank that guarantees payment to the exporter for a specific shipment of goods.*

FIGURE 14.3 How a Letter of Credit Works

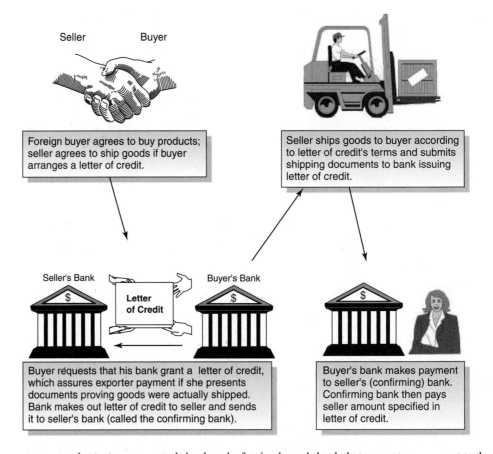

Seller   Buyer

Foreign buyer agrees to buy products; seller agrees to ship goods if buyer arranges a letter of credit.

Seller ships goods to buyer according to letter of credit's terms and submits shipping documents to bank issuing letter of credit.

Seller's Bank   **Letter of Credit**   Buyer's Bank

Buyer requests that his bank grant a letter of credit, which assures exporter payment if she presents documents proving goods were actually shipped. Bank makes out letter of credit to seller and sends it to seller's bank (called the confirming bank).

Buyer's bank makes payment to seller's (confirming) bank. Confirming bank then pays seller amount specified in letter of credit.

bank draft—*a document the seller draws on the buyer, requiring the buyer to pay the face amount either on sight or on a specified date.*

foreign sales corporations—*a shell company created in an approved U.S. territory or a foreign country that allows a business to reduce its income tax liability.*

agreement between an exporter's bank and a foreign buyer's bank that guarantees payment to the exporter for a specific shipment of goods once the exporter delivers specific documents about the shipment. In essence, a letter of credit reduces the financial risk for the exporter by substituting a bank's creditworthiness for that of the purchaser (see Figure 14.3). A **bank draft** is a document the seller draws on the buyer, requiring the buyer to pay the face amount (the purchase price of the goods) either on sight (a sight draft) or on a specified date (a time draft) once the goods have been shipped. Rather than use letters of credit or drafts, some exporters simply require cash on delivery (COD). Insisting on cash payments up front, however, may cause some foreign buyers to reject a deal. The parties to an international deal should always come to an agreement in advance on an acceptable method of payment.

Planned carefully and taken one step at a time, exporting can be a highly profitable route for small businesses. Many small companies are forming **foreign sales corporations** (FSCs, pronounced "fisks") to take advantage of a tax benefit that is designed to stimulate exports. Although large companies have used the tax advantages of FSCs for many years, a rapidly growing number of small exporters are beginning to catch on. More than 5,000 U.S. corporations have created FSCs in the past decade, and the number is growing by 25 percent a year. By forming a FSC, a company can shelter about 15 percent of its profits on foreign sales from federal—and, in some cases, state—income taxes. Setting up a FSC requires a company to establish a shell corporation in the Virgin Islands, Barbados, or one of another 40 tax-friendly offshore locations that have tax treaties with the United States. The company also must have fewer than 25 shareholders and one non-U.S. resident board member.

Small companies with $5 million or less in export sales can create small FSCs, which offer the same benefits as regular FSCs but are subject to less stringent procedural requirements. Most companies that establish FSCs use a FSC management company in the designated territory or country to do so. Once it establishes a FSC, a small company can allocate up to 23 percent of its export profits to the FSC, where these profits are taxed at lower rates than normal. Because it costs about $2,000 to set up a small FSC and about $3,000 per year to maintain one, a business should earn at least $50,000 in export profits a year to make the tax savings from a FSC worthwhile. Because of complaints from the World Trade Organization that FSCs give U.S. companies an exclusive and unfair trade advantage, Congress changed the law in 2003, allowing foreign companies that pay taxes in the United States to take advantage of FSCs as well. Further changes to the law may be pending.

Establishing International Locations

Once established in international markets, some small businesses set up permanent locations there. Establishing an office or a factory in a foreign land can require a substantial investment reaching beyond the budgets of many small companies. Plus, setting up an international office can be an incredibly frustrating experience in some countries. Business infrastructures are in disrepair or nonexistent. Getting a telephone line installed can take months in some places, and finding reliable equipment to move goods to customers is nearly impossible. Securing necessary licenses and permits from bureaucrats often takes more than filing the necessary paperwork; in some nations, bureaucrats expect payments to "grease the wheels of justice." Such payments are often viewed as bribery and result in many businesses avoiding some countries. Finding the right person to manage an international office is crucial to success; it also is a major challenge, especially for small businesses. Small companies usually have lean management staffs and cannot afford to send key people abroad without running the risk of losing their focus.

The major advantages to establishing an international location can be the combination of lower production and marketing costs, as well as developing an intimate knowledge of customer preferences.

The U.S. tool and die industry never saw a need to look for business outside its local markets because business was always there. Then came the 1990s with low-price foreign competitors, a serious shortage of skilled workers, and the deleterious effects of tariffs on the price of raw materials. Metz Tool and Die of Rockforth, Illinois, had built a reputation for exceptional quality and, until this time, had never needed to "think globally." With orders drastically down and

A Company Example

production capacity skyrocketing, Don Metz began to work with the U.S. Export Assistance Center in the identification of foreign markets for the firm's services. Within a year, Metz Tool and Die landed $250,000 in orders from Mexican firms with additional potential orders for $500,000 to $600,000 in future sales.[12]

Learning Objective

4. Discuss the major barriers to international trade and their impact on the global economy.

BARRIERS TO INTERNATIONAL TRADE

Governments have always used a variety of barriers to block free trade among nations in an attempt to protect businesses within their own borders. The benefit of protecting their own companies, however, comes at the expense of foreign businesses, which face limited access to global markets. Numerous trade barriers—domestic and international—restrict the freedom of businesses in global trading. Even with these barriers, international trade has grown 26-fold to more than $6.4 *trillion* over the past 30 years.[13]

Domestic Barriers

Sometimes the biggest barriers potential exporters face are right here at home. Three major domestic roadblocks are common: attitude, information, and financing. Perhaps the biggest barrier to small businesses exporting is the attitude "I'm too small to export. That's just for big corporations." The first lesson of exporting is "Take nothing for granted about who can export and what you can and cannot export." The first step to building an export program is recognizing that the opportunity to export exists.

Another reason entrepreneurs neglect international markets is a lack of information about how to get started. The key to success in international markets is choosing the correct target market and designing the appropriate strategy to reach it. That requires access to information and research. Although a variety of government and private organizations make volumes of exporting and international marketing information available, many small business owners never use it. A successful global marketing strategy also recognizes that not all international markets are the same. Companies must be flexible, willing to make adjustments to their products and services, promotional campaigns, packaging, and sales techniques.

An additional obstacle is the inability of small firms to obtain adequate export financing. Financial institutions that serve smaller firms are often not experienced with this type of financing and are unwilling to accept the perceived higher risk.

International Barriers

Domestic barriers aren't the only ones export-minded entrepreneurs must overcome. Trading nations also erect obstacles to free trade. Two types of international barriers are common: tariff and nontariff.

tariff—*a tax, or duty, that a government imposes on goods and services imported into that country.*

TARIFF BARRIERS. A **tariff** is a tax, or duty, that a government imposes on goods and services imported into that country. Imposing tariffs raises the price of the imported goods—making them less attractive to consumers—and protects the makers of comparable domestic products and services. Established in the United States in 1790 by Alexander Hamilton, the tariff system generated the majority of federal revenues for about 100 years. The U.S. tariff code lists duties on more than 8,000 items ranging from ice cream to watches.

NONTARIFF BARRIERS. Many nations have lowered the tariffs they impose on products and services brought into their borders, but they rely on other nontariff structures as protectionist trade barriers.

quota—*a limit on the amount of product imported into a country.*

QUOTAS. Rather than impose a direct tariff on certain imported products, nations often use quotas to protect their industries. A **quota** is a limit on the amount of a product imported into a country. Worried about the Japanese economic juggernaut, the European Union has limited Japanese automakers' share of the European market to just 16 percent. In the U.S. auto market, the Japanese have agreed to "voluntary quotas," limiting the number of autos shipped here. The United States imposes more than 3,000 quotas on clothing and textile imports.

Japan, often criticized for its protectionist attitude toward imports, traditionally used tariffs and quotas to keep foreign competitors out. Japan's tariffs are now among the world's lowest—averaging just 2 percent—but quotas still exist on many products.

EMBARGOES. An **embargo** is a total ban on imports of certain products. The motivation for embargoes is not always economic. For instance, because of South Africa's history of apartheid policies, many nations have embargoed imports of Krugerrands (gold coins). Traditionally, Taiwan, South Korea, and Israel have banned imports of Japanese autos.

embargo—a total ban on imports of certain products.

DUMPING. In an effort to grab market share quickly, some companies have been guilty of **dumping** products: selling large quantities of them in foreign countries below cost. The United States has been a dumping target for steel, televisions, shoes, and computer chips in the past. Under the U.S. Antidumping Act, a company must prove that the foreign company's prices are lower here than in the home country and that U.S. companies are directly harmed.

dumping—the practice of selling large quantities of products in foreign countries below cost in an attempt to gain market share.

Political Barriers

Entrepreneurs who go global quickly discover a labyrinth of political tangles. Although many U.S. business owners complain of excessive government regulation in the United States, they are often astounded by the complex web of governmental and legal regulations and barriers they encounter in foreign countries.

Companies doing business in politically risky lands face the very real dangers of government takeovers of private property; attempts at coups to overthrow ruling parties; kidnapping, bombings, and other violent acts against businesses and their employees; and other threatening events. Their investments of millions of dollars may evaporate overnight in the wake of a government coup or the passage of a law nationalizing an industry (giving control of an entire industry to the government).

Business Barriers

American companies doing business internationally quickly learn that business practices and regulations in foreign lands can be quite different from those in the United States. Simply duplicating the practices they have adopted (and have used successfully) in the domestic market and using them in foreign markets is not always a good idea. Perhaps the biggest shock comes in the area of human resources management, where international managers discover that practices common in the United States, such as overtime, women workers, and employee benefits, are restricted, disfavored, or forbidden in other cultures. Business owners new to international business sometimes are shocked at the wide range of labor costs they encounter and the accompanying wide range of skilled labor available. In some countries, what appear to be "bargain" labor rates turn out to be excessively high after accounting for the quality of the labor force and the benefits their governments mandate: from company-sponsored housing, meals, and clothing to profit sharing and extended vacations. In many nations, labor union are present in almost every company, yet they play a very different role from the unions in the United States. Although management–union relations are not as hostile as in the United States and strikes are not as common, unions can greatly complicate a company's ability to compete effectively.

Cultural Barriers

The **culture** of a nation includes the beliefs, values, view, and mores that its inhabitants share. Differences in cultures among nations create another barrier to international trade. The diversity of languages, business philosophies, practices, and traditions makes international trade more complex than selling to the business down the street. Consider the following examples:

culture—the beliefs, values, and mores that the inhabitants of a nation share.

- A U.S. entrepreneur, eager to expand into the European Union, arrives at his company's potential business partner's headquarters in France. Confidently, he strides into the meeting room, enthusiastically pumps his host's hand, slaps him on the back, and says, "Tony, I've heard a great deal about you; please, call me Bill." Eager to explain the benefits of his product, he opens his briefcase and gets right down to business. The French executive politely excuses himself and leaves the room before negotiations ever begin, shocked by the American's rudeness and ill manners. Rudeness and ill manners? Yes—from the French executive's perspective.

■ Another American business owner flies to Tokyo to close a deal with a Japanese executive. He is pleased when his host invites him to play a round of golf shortly after he arrives. He plays well and manages to win by a few strokes. The Japanese executive invites him to play again the next day, and again he wins by a few strokes. Invited to play another round the following day, the American asks, "But when are we going to start doing business?" His host, surprised by the question, says, "But we have been doing business."

■ An American businesswoman in London is invited to a party hosted by an advertising agency. Unsure of her ability to navigate the streets and subways of London alone, she approaches a British colleague who was driving to the party and asks him, "Could I get a ride with you?" After he turns bright red from embarrassment, he regains his composure and politely says, "Lucky for you I know what you meant." Unknowingly, the young woman had requested a sexual encounter with her colleague, not a lift to the party![14]

■ An American businessman grows tired of trying to speak over the persistent chanting of a nearby group of Islamic men. Exasperated, he looks harshly at the group and said to his Muslim host, "Can't somebody shut those guys up?" Only then did he discover that "those guys" were Islamic priests chanting a call to prayer—and that he had just blown the deal he was trying to land.[15]

■ An American goes to Malaysia to close a sizable contract. In an elaborate ceremony, he is introduced to a man he thinks is named "Roger." Throughout the negotiations, he calls the man "Rog" not realizing that his potential client was a "rajah," a title of nobility, not a name.[16]

■ One company selling a razor aimed at women in Holland creates a television commercial showing a woman's leg and the product's name. Unfortunately, the ad proves to be completely ineffective because the product's name is slang for "homosexual," and Dutch viewers think the leg belongs to a transvestite.[17]

When American businesspeople enter international markets for the first time, they often are amazed at the differences in foreign cultures' habits and customs. In the first scenario just described, for instance, had the entrepreneur done his homework, he would have known that the French are very formal (backslapping is *definitely* taboo!) and do not typically use first names in business relationships (even among long-time colleagues). In the second scenario, a global manager would have known that the Japanese place a tremendous importance on developing personal relationships before committing to any business deals. Thus, he would have seen the golf games for what they really were: an integral part of building a business relationship.

Understanding and heeding these often subtle cultural differences is one of the most important keys to international business success. Conducting a business meeting with a foreign executive in the same manner as one with an American businessperson could doom the deal from the outset. Business customs and behaviors that are acceptable, even expected, in this country may be taboo in others.

Entrepreneurs who fail to learn the differences in the habits and customs of the cultures in which they hope to do business are at a distinct disadvantage. The stories of business executives who unknowingly insulted their foreign counterparts are both lengthy, legendary, and a continuing reminder of the cost associated with a failure to prepare for dealing in a culture different from one's own.

Culture, customs, and the norms of behavior differ greatly among nations and making the correct impression is extremely critical to building a long-term business relationship. Consider the following few examples:

■ Japanese executives conduct business much like the British: with an emphasis on formality, thoughtfulness, and respect. Don't expect to hear Japanese executives say no, even during a negotiation; they don't want to offend or to appear confrontational. Instead of "no," the Japanese negotiator will say, "It is very difficult," "Let us think about that," or "Let us get back to you on that." Similarly, "yes" from a Japanese executive doesn't necessarily mean that. It could mean, "I understand," "I hear you," or "I don't understand what you mean, but I don't want to embarrass you."

■ In Japan and South Korea, exchanging business cards, known in Japan as *meishi,* is an important business function (unlike Great Britain, where exchanging business cards is less popular). A Western executive who accepts a Japanese companion's card and then slips it into his pocket or scribbles notes on it has committed a major blunder. Tradition there says a business card must be treated just as its owner would be—with respect. Travelers should present their own cards using both hands with the card positioned so the recipient can read it. (The flip side should be printed in Japanese, an expected courtesy.)

- Greeting a Japanese executive properly includes a bow and a handshake—showing respect for both cultures. In many traditional Japanese businesses, exchanging gifts at the first meeting is appropriate. Also, a love of golf (the Japanese are fanatical about the game) is a real plus for winning business in Japan.

- In Great Britain, businesspeople consider it extremely important to conduct business "properly"—with formality and reserve. Boisterous behavior such as backslapping or overindulging in alcohol and ostentatious displays of wealth are considered ill-mannered. The British do not respond to hard-sell tactics but do appreciate well-mannered executives. Politeness and impeccable manners are useful tools for conducting business successfully here.

- Appearance and style are important to Italian businesspeople; they judge the polish and the expertise of the company's executives as well as the quality of its products and services. Italians expect presentations to be organized, clear, and exact. A stylish business wardrobe also is an asset in Italy. Physical contact is an accepted part of Italian society. Don't be surprised if an Italian businessperson uses a lingering handshake or touches you occasionally when doing business.

- In Mexico, making business appointments through a well-connected Mexican national will go a long way to assuring successful business deals. "People in Mexico do business with somebody they know, they like, or they're related to," says one expert. Because family and tradition are top priorities for Mexicans, entrepreneurs who discuss their family heritages and can talk knowledgeably about Mexican history are a step ahead. In business meetings, making extended eye contact is considered impolite.

- In China, entrepreneurs will need an ample dose of the "three Ps": patience, patience, patience. Nothing in China—especially business—happens fast! In conversation and negotiations, periods of silence are common; they are a sign of politeness and contemplation. The Chinese view personal space much differently than Americans; in normal conversation, they will stand much closer to their partners.

- In the Pacific Rim, entrepreneurs must remember that each country has its own unique culture and business etiquette. Starting business relationships with customers in the Pacific Rim usually requires a third-party contact because Asian executives prefer to do business with people they know. Also, building personal relationships is important. Many business deals take place over informal activities in this part of the world.

- American entrepreneurs doing business in the Pacific Rim should avoid hard-sell techniques, which are an immediate turnoff to Asian businesspeople. Harmony, patience, and consensus make good business companions in this region. It is also a good idea to minimize the importance of legal documents in negotiations. Although getting deals and trade agreements down in writing always is advisable, attempting to negotiate detailed contracts (as most American businesses tend to do) would insult most Asians, who base their deals on mutual trust and benefits.

INTERNATIONAL TRADE AGREEMENTS

Learning Objective

5. Discuss the trade agreements that will have the greatest influence on foreign trade in the twenty-first century.

With the fundamental assumption that free trade among nations results in enhanced economic well-being for all who participate, the last five decades have witnessed a gradual opening of trade among nations. Hundreds of agreements have been negotiated among nations in this time frame, with each contributing to free trade across the globe.

WTO

The World Trade Organization (WTO) was established in January 1995 and replaced the General Agreement on Tariffs and Trade (GATT), the first global tariff agreement, which was designed to reduce tariffs among member nations. In 2003, the WTO had 146 member countries, including the newest member, China. These member countries represent over 97 percent of all world trade. An additional 30 nations are actively seeking membership. The rules and agreements of the WTO are the result of negotiations among its members. The WTO actively implements the rules established by GATT and continues to negotiate additional trade agreements. Through the agreements of the WTO, members commit themselves to nondiscriminatory trade practices. These agreements spell out the rights and obligations of each member country. Each member country receives guarantees that its exports will be treated fairly and consistently in other member countries' markets. Specifically addressed have been banking, insurance, telecommunications, and tourism under the WTO's General Agreement on Trade in Services (GATS). In addition, the WTO's intellectual property agreement, which covers patents, copyrights, and trademarks, amounts to the rules for trade and investment in ideas and creativity.

In addition to the development of agreements among members, the WTO is involved in the resolution of trade disputes among members. The WTO system is designed to encourage dispute resolutions through consultation. If this approach fails, the WTO has a stage-by-stage procedure that can culminate in a ruling by a panel of experts.

NAFTA

The North American Free Trade Agreement (NAFTA) created a free trade area among Canada, Mexico, and the United States. A free trade area is an association of countries that have agreed to eliminate trade barriers, both tariff and nontariff, among partner nations. Under the provision of NAFTA, these barriers were eliminated for trade among the three countries, but each remained free to set its own tariffs on imports from nonmember nations.

NAFTA forged a unified United States–Canada–Mexico market of an estimated 400 million people with a total annual output of more than $6.5 trillion of goods and services. This important trade agreement binds together the three nations on the North American continent into a single trading unit stretching from the Yukon to the Yucatan. Because Canada and the United States already had a free trade agreement in effect, the businesses that will benefit most from NAFTA are those already doing business, or those wanting to do business, with Mexico. Before NAFTA took effect on January 1, 1994, the average tariff on U.S. goods entering Mexico was 10 percent. Under NAFTA, these tariffs will be reduced to zero on most goods over the next 10 to 15 years. NAFTA's provisions encourage trade among the three nations, make that trade more profitable and less cumbersome, and open up new opportunities for a wide assortment of companies.

YOU Be the Consultant . . .

Safe Water Systems

Since 1996, Safe Water Systems has exported 1,400 solar water pasteurizers to nearly 50 countries in Asia, Central America, and Africa. Will Hartzell, president of the firm, knows that his product has the potential to save lives. Eighty percent of all illnesses in the developing world are directly related to the consumption of waterborne pathogens in unsafe drinking water.

The concept behind Safe Water Systems' technology is really very simple. The solar water pasteurizers use the sun's rays to heat the water to the point where all harmful bacteria and viruses are disinfected. It achieves the same result as boiling but at a lower temperature over a longer period of time. The solar units are designed to last about 25 years, don't need electricity, and require virtually no maintenance, making them ideal for undeveloped rural locations and an efficient alternative to purifying water by boiling. Where firewood cannot be gathered, wood or other fuels must be purchased, with the cost often consuming up to 25 percent of a family's income. Millions of people cannot afford to buy fuel, have no

way to disinfect their drinking water, and, consequently, suffer illnesses or die. Each year 5 million people die as a result of contaminated drinking water. Placed at the water source of a local village or clinic, the water enters the solar water pasteurization system, where it is heated for two and one-half hours or so, and there you have it—drinkable water!

According to the World Health Organization, 1.2 billion people do not have access to drinking that is from disease-causing microbes. The World Health Organization predicts that by 2025, this number will increase to more than 2 billion.

Safe Water Systems has used the guidance provided by the U.S. Export Assistance Centers in Honolulu, where the firm is located, to cope with the often confusing regulations of developing countries.

1. What additional steps can a small company such as Safe Water Systems take to distribute its products in developing countries more effectively?

2. Should the U.S. government intercede with governments of other countries to ask them to eliminate any barriers to the distribution of lifesaving products?

Source: Curt Cultice, "The Heat Is On: Solar Technology Creates Potable Water," *Export America: Success Stories*, [www.export.gov/exportAmerica/SuccessStories/ss_SafeWater_0103.html].

Among NAFTA's provisions are:

- *Tariff reductions.* Immediate reduction, then gradual phasing out, of most tariffs on goods traded among the three countries.
- *Elimination of nontariff barriers.* Most nontariff barriers to free trade are to be eliminated by 2008.
- *Simplified border processing.* Mexico, in particular, opens its border and interior to U.S. truckers and simplifies border processing.
- *Tougher health and safety standards.* Industrial standards involving worker health and safety are to become more stringent and more uniform.

The aim of NAFTA is to create increased economic opportunities for the citizens of all three countries through the promotion of trade. South and Central American countries generally favor the geographic expansion of this agreement to include them based on the economic gains achieved by Mexico.

CONCLUSION

To remain competitive, businesses must assume a global posture. Global effectiveness requires managers to be able to leverage workers' skills, company resources, and an understanding of customers across borders and throughout cultures across the world. Managers also must concentrate on maintaining competitive cost structures and a focus on the core of every business—the *customer!* Although there are no surefire rules for going global, small businesses wanting to become successful international competitors should observe these guidelines.

- Make yourself at home in all three of the world's key markets: North America, Europe, and Asia. This triad of regions is forging a new world order in trade that will dominate global markets for years to come.
- Appeal to the similarities within the various regions in which you operate but recognize the differences in their specific cultures. Although the European Union is a single trading bloc composed of 15 countries, smart entrepreneurs know that each country has its own cultural uniqueness and do not treat them as a unified market.
- Develop new products for the world market. Make sure your products and services measure up to world-class quality standards.
- Familiarize yourself with foreign customs and languages; constantly scan, clip, and build a file on other cultures: their lifestyles, values, customs, and business practices.
- Learn to understand your customers from the perspective of *their* culture, not your own. Bridge cultural gaps by being willing to adapt your business practices to suit their preferences and customs.
- "Glocalize": Make global decisions about products, markets, and management but allow local employees to make tactical decisions about packaging, advertising, and service.
- Train employees to think globally, send them on international trips, and equip them with state-of-the-art communications technology.
- Hire local managers to staff foreign offices and branches.
- Do whatever seems best wherever it seems best, even if people at home lose jobs or responsibilities.
- Consider using partners and joint ventures to break into foreign markets you cannot penetrate on your own.

By its very nature, going global can be a frightening experience. Most entrepreneurs who have already made the jump, however, have found that the benefits outweigh the risks and that their companies are much stronger because of it.

CHAPTER SUMMARY

1. Explain why "going global" has become an integral part of many small companies' marketing strategies.

- Companies that move into international business can reap many benefits, including offsetting sales declines in the domestic market; increasing sales and profits; extending their products' life cycles; lowering manufacturing costs; improving competitive position; raising quality levels; and becoming more customer oriented.

2. Describe the principal strategies small businesses have for going global.

- Perhaps the simplest and least expensive way for a small business to begin conducting business globally is to establish a site on the World Wide Web. Companies wanting to sell goods on the Web should establish a secure ordering and payment system for online customers.

- Trade intermediaries such as export management companies, export trading companies, manufacturer's export agents, export merchants, resident buying offices, and foreign distributors can serve as a small company's "export department."

- In a domestic joint venture, two or more U.S. small companies form an alliance for the purpose of exporting their goods and services abroad. In a foreign joint venture, a domestic small business forms an alliance with a company in the target area.

- Some small businesses enter foreign markets by licensing businesses in other nations to use their patents, trademarks, copyrights, technology, processes, or products.

- Franchising has become a major industry for the United States. The International Franchise Association estimates that more than 20 percent of the nation's 4,000 franchisors have outlets in foreign countries.

- Some countries lack a hard currency that is convertible into other currencies, so companies doing business there must rely on countertrading or bartering. A countertrade is a transaction in which a business selling goods in a foreign country agrees to promote investment and trade in that country. Bartering involves trading goods and services for other goods and services.

- Although small companies account for 97 percent of the companies involved in exporting, they generate only 33 percent of the dollar value of the nation's exports. However, small companies, realizing the incredible profit potential it offers, are making exporting an ever-expanding part of their marketing plans. Nearly half of the U.S. companies with annual revenues under $100 million export goods.

- Once established in international markets, some small businesses set up permanent locations there. Although they can be very expensive to establish and maintain, international locations give businesses the opportunity to stay in close contact with their international customers.

3. Explain how to build a thriving export program.

- Building a successful export program takes patience and research. Steps include realizing that even the tiniest firms have the potential to export; analyzing your product or service; analyzing your commitment to exporting; researching markets and picking your target; developing a distribution strategy; finding your customer; finding financing; shipping your goods; and collecting your money.

4. Discuss the major barriers to international trade and their impact on the global economy.

- Three domestic barriers to international trade are common: the attitude that "we're too small to export," lack of information on how to get started in global trade, and a lack of available financing.

- International barriers include tariffs, quotas, embargoes, dumping, and political and cultural barriers.

5. Describe the trade agreements that will have the greatest influence on foreign trade in the twenty-first century.

- Created in 1947, the General Agreement on Tariffs and Trade (GATT), the first global tariff agreement, was designed to reduce tariffs among member nations and to facilitate trade across the globe.

- The World Trade Organization (WTO) was established in 1995 to implement the GATT tariff agreements. The WTO has over 140 member nations and represents over 97 percent of all global trade. The WTO is the governing body that resolves trade disputes among members.

- The North American Free Trade Agreement (NAFTA) created a free trade area among Canada, Mexico, and the United States. The agreement created an association that knocked down trade barriers, both tariff and nontariff, among these partner nations.

DISCUSSION QUESTIONS

1. Why must entrepreneurs learn to think globally?
2. What forces are driving small businesses into international markets?
3. What advantages does going global offer a small business owner? What are the risks?
4. Outline the eight strategies that small businesses can use to go global.
5. Describe the various types of trade intermediaries small business owners can use. What functions do they perform?
6. What is a domestic joint venture? A foreign joint venture? What advantages does taking on an international partner through a joint venture offer? What are the disadvantages?
7. What mistake are first-time exporters most likely to make? Outline the steps a small company should take to establish a successful export program.
8. What are the benefits of establishing international locations? What are the disadvantages?
9. Describe the barriers businesses face when trying to conduct business internationally. How can a small business owner overcome these obstacles?
10. What is a tariff? A quota? What impact do they have on international trade?
11. What impact have the GATT, WTO, and NAFTA trade agreements had on small companies wanting to go global? What provisions are included in these trade agreements?
12. What advice would you offer an entrepreneur interested in launching a global business effort?

THE BUSINESS DISC

Launch *The Business Disc*. From the menu across the top of your screen, select the "Reference" option and then click on "International Trade." Here you will find several reference guides that offer useful information to entrepreneurs. Click on "Breaking Into the Trade Game: A Small Business Guide," "SBA Automated Trade Locator Assistance System," and "Question and Answer Guide to Trade Finance." Review the concepts in these reference guides and in Chapter 14.

What prevents most small business owners from exporting? Describe the resources available to entrepreneurs who are interested in finding foreign markets for their products. What steps should an entrepreneur take to become an exporter? What steps can entrepreneurs take to ensure that foreign customers pay for the merchandise they order? What should entrepreneurs do to minimize the cultural barriers they face when doing business internationally?

BEYOND THE CLASSROOM . . .

1. Go to lunch with a student from a foreign country. Discuss what products and services are most needed. How does the business system there differ from ours? How much government regulation affects business? What cultural differences exist? What trade barriers has the government erected?

2. Review several current business publications and prepare a brief report on which nations seem to be the most promising for U.S. entrepreneurs. What steps should a small business owner take to break into those markets? Which nations are the least promising? Why?

3. Select a nation that interests you and prepare a report on its business customs and practices. How are they different from those in the United States? How are they similar?

15 Leading the Growing Company and Planning for Management Succession

Anybody who accepts mediocrity—in school, on the job, in life—is a person who compromises, and when a leader compromises, the whole organization compromises.

—Charles Knight

The buck stops here.

—Harry S. Truman

LEARNING OBJECTIVES

Upon completion of this chapter, you will be able to:

1. **EXPLAIN** the challenges involved in the entrepreneur's role as leader and what it takes to be a successful leader.

2. **DESCRIBE** the importance of hiring the right employees and how to avoid making hiring mistakes.

3. **EXPLAIN** how to build the kind of company culture and structure to support the entrepreneur's mission and goals and to motivate employees to achieve them.

4. **DISCUSS** the ways in which entrepreneurs can motivate their workers to higher levels of performance.

5. **DESCRIBE** the steps in developing a management succession plan for a growing business that will allow a smooth transition of leadership to the next generation.

LEADERSHIP IN THE NEW ECONOMY

Learning Objective

1. Explain the challenges involved in the entrepreneur's role as leader and what it takes to be a successful leader.

To be successful, an entrepreneur must assume a wide range of roles, tasks, and responsibilities, but none is more important than the role of leader. Some entrepreneurs initially are uncomfortable in this role, but they must learn to be effective leaders if their companies are to grow and reach their potential. **Leadership** is the process of influencing and inspiring others to work to achieve a common goal and then giving them the power and the freedom to achieve it. Without leadership ability, entrepreneurs—and their companies—never rise above mediocrity. Leadership skills are not easy to learn. In the past, many small business managers relied on fear and intimidation as leadership tools. Today, however, the workforce is more knowledgeable, has more options, is more skilled, and consequently demands a more sophisticated style of leadership.

leadership—*the process of influencing and inspiring others to work to achieve a common goal and then giving them the power and the freedom to achieve it.*

The rapid pace of change in the new economy also is placing new demands on leaders. Technology is changing the ways in which people work, the ways in which the various parts of an organization operate and interconnect, and the ways in which competitors strive for market dominance. To remain in the game, companies must operate at this new speed of business, and that requires a new style of leadership. Leaders of small companies must gather information and make decisions with lightning speed, and they must give workers the resources and the freedom to solve problems and exploit opportunities as they arise. Effective leaders now empower employees to act in the best interest of the business. They demonstrate trust in their employees and respect for their ability to make decisions. Many entrepreneurs have discovered that the old style of leadership has lost its effectiveness and that they must develop a new, more fluid and flexible style of leadership that better fits the needs of modern workers and competitive conditions.

Until recently, experts compared the leader's job to that of a symphony orchestra conductor. Like the symphony conductor, an entrepreneur made sure that everyone in the company was playing the same score, coordinated individual efforts to produce a harmonious sound, and directed the orchestra members as they played. The conductor (entrepreneur) retained virtually all of the power and made all of the decisions about how the orchestra would play the music without any input from the musicians themselves. Today's successful entrepreneur, however, is more like the leader of a jazz band, which is known for its improvisation, innovation, creativity, and freewheeling style. Max DePree, former head of Herman Miller, Inc., a highly successful office furniture manufacturer, explains the connection this way:

> Jazz band leaders must choose the music, find the right musicians, and perform—in public. But the effect of the performance depends on so many things—the environment, the volunteers playing in the band, the need for everybody to perform as individuals and as a group, the absolute dependence of the leader on the members of the band, the need for the followers to play well. . . . The leader of the jazz band has the beautiful opportunity to draw the best out of the other musicians. We have much to learn from jazz band leaders, for jazz, like leadership, combines the unpredictability of the future with the gifts of individuals.[1]

Management and leadership are not the same; yet both are essential to a company's success. Leadership without management is unbridled; management without leadership is uninspired. Leadership gets a small business going; management keeps it going. In other words, leaders are the architects of small businesses; managers are the builders. Some entrepreneurs are good managers yet are poor leaders; others are powerful leaders but are weak managers. The best bet for the latter is to hire people with solid management skills to help them execute the vision they have for their companies. Stephen Covey, author of *Principle-Centered Leadership*, explains the difference between management and leadership this way:

> Leadership deals with people; management deals with things. You manage things; you lead people. Leadership deals with vision; management deals with logistics toward that vision. Leadership deals with doing the right things; management focuses on doing things right. Leadership deals with examining the paradigms on which you are operating; management operates within those paradigms. Leadership comes first, then management, but both are necessary.[2]

Leadership and management are intertwined; one without the other means that a small business is going nowhere. Leadership is especially important for companies in the growth phase, when entrepreneurs are hiring employees (often for the first time) and must keep the company and everyone in it focused on its mission as growth tests every seam in the organizational structure. At this stage, selling everyone in the company on the mission, goals, and objectives for which the leader is aiming is crucial to a business's survival and success.

Effective leaders exhibit certain behaviors. They:

- *Create a set of values and beliefs for employees and passionately pursue them.* Values are the foundation on which vision is built. Leaders should be like beacons in the night, constantly shining light on the principles, values, and beliefs on which they founded their companies. Values are set forth from the top—employees look to their leaders for guidance in making decisions.

- *Define and then constantly reinforce the vision they have for the company.* Effective leaders have a clear vision of where they want their companies to go, and they concentrate on communicating that vision to those around them. Leaders articulate the firm's vision to every employee often.

- *Respect and support their employees.* To gain the respect of their employees, leaders must first respect those who work for them. Successful leaders put their employees first dedicated workforce is a company's most valuable resource, and they treat their employees that way.

- *Set the example for their employees.* A leader's words ring hollow if he fails to "practice what he preaches." Few signals are transmitted to workers faster than a leader who sells employees on one set of values and principles and then acts according to a different set. Employees expect leaders to "walk the talk." That is why integrity is perhaps the most important determinant of a leader's effectiveness.

- *Create a climate of trust in the organization.* Leaders who demonstrate integrity soon win the trust of their employees, an essential ingredient in the success of any organization. Honest, open communication and a consistent pattern of leaders doing what they say they will do serve to build trust in a business. An environment of trust becomes especially important when a company encounters a crisis. Workers are willing to band together to tackle the problem facing the company without sensing the need to protect their turf.

- *Focus employees' efforts on challenging goals and keep them driving toward those goals.* When asked by a student intern to define leadership, one entrepreneur said, "Leadership is the ability to convince people to follow a path they have never taken before to a place they have never been—and upon finding it to be successful, to do it over and over again."[3]

- *Provide the resources employees need to achieve their goals.* Effective leaders know that workers cannot do their jobs well unless they have the tools they need. They not only provide workers with the physical resources they need to excel but also the necessary intangible resources such as training, coaching, and mentoring.

- *Communicate with their employees.* Leaders recognize that helping workers see the company's overarching goal is just one part of effective communication; encouraging employee feedback and then listening are just as vital. In other words, they know that communication is a two-way street. Open communication takes on even greater importance when a company faces a difficult or uncertain future.

- *Value the diversity of their workers.* Smart business leaders recognize the value of their workers' varied skills, abilities, backgrounds, and interests. When channeled in the right direction, diversity can be a powerful weapon in achieving innovation and maintaining a competitive edge. Good leaders get to know their workers and to understand the diversity of their strengths. Especially important to young workers in the new economy is a leader's capacity for empathy, the ability to see things from another person's viewpoint (see Figure 15.1).

- *Celebrate their workers' successes.* Effective leaders recognize that workers want to be winners and do everything they can to encourage top performance among their people. The rewards they give are not always financial; in many cases, it may be as simple as a handwritten congratulatory note.

- *Encourage creativity among their workers.* Rather than punish workers who take risks and fail, effective leaders are willing to accept failure as a natural part of innovation and creativity. They know that innovative behavior is the key to future success and do everything they can to encourage it among workers.

- *Maintain a sense of humor.* One of the most important tools a leader can have is a sense of humor. Without it, work can become dull and unexciting for everyone.

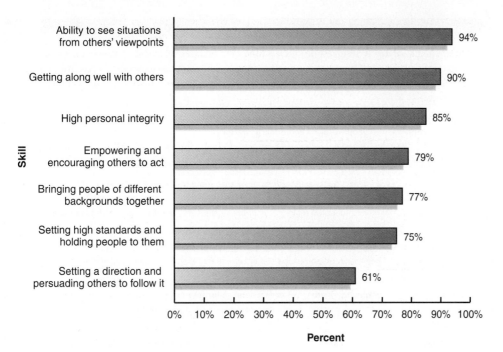

FIGURE 15.1 Generation X on Leadership: Skills That Gen-Xers Value Most in Leaders

Source: Peter D. Hart Research Associates, Inc., 1999.

*Former **Southwest Airlines'** CEO Herb Kelleher is famous for creating a work environment where fun is the watchword. Kelleher, who appeared at one employee function on a Harley-Davidson motorcycle and at another dressed as Elvis Presley, encouraged employees to have fun at work. Flight attendants sometimes pop out of overhead bins as passengers board, or they tell jokes over the plane's public address system. Crews have been known to liven up the preflight safety demonstrations with song and dance routines. On Halloween, employees dress up in costumes and hand out cake to passengers. The culture of fun at Southwest Airlines has built an esprit de corps that gives Southwest a unique advantage that competitors cannot match, and clown prince Herb Kelleher was its architect.[4]*

A Company Example

■ *Create an environment in which people have the motivation, the training, and the freedom to achieve the goals they have set.* Great leaders know that *their* success is determined by the success of their followers. They create a work climate that enables others to achieve maximum performance.

■ *Become a catalyst for change when change is needed.* With market and competitive climates changing so rapidly, small company leaders must make sure that their companies change along with them. Although leaders must cling to the values and principles that form the bedrock of their companies, they must be willing to change, sometimes radically, the policies, procedures, and processes within their businesses. If a company is headed in the wrong direction, the leader's job is to recognize that and to get the company moving in the right direction. Effective leaders understand that to preserve their businesses, they must change them constantly.

■ *Keep their eyes on the horizon.* Effective leaders are never satisfied with what they and their employees accomplished yesterday. They know that yesterday's successes are not enough to sustain their companies indefinitely. They see the importance of building and maintaining sufficient momentum to carry their companies to the next level. A proactive stance is essential and strategic thinking a must.

Leading an organization, whatever its size, is one of the biggest challenges any manager faces. Yet, for an entrepreneur, leadership success is one of the key determinants of the company's success. In addition to the uncertainties of dealing with people, the job of the organizational leader is constantly changing. In these challenging times, leaders must clearly envision the future, share repeatedly and forcefully their vision for the firm, provide each employee with the tools needed to perform the job, the training to remain current, and the freedom that enables co-workers to manage and improve the process.

Table 15.1 offers useful tips on how to become a successful leader.

To be effective, a small business leader must perform four vital tasks:

■ Hire the right employees and constantly improve their skills.

■ Build an organizational culture and structure that allow both workers and the company to reach their potential.

■ Motivate workers to higher levels of performance.

■ Plan for "passing the torch" to the next generation of leadership.

TABLE 15.1

Tips for Becoming a Successful Leader in the New Economy

Source: Adapted from "Make Yourself a Leader," *Fast Company,* June 1999, tear-out booklet.

Leadership in the old days often meant that leaders had all of the answers and that employees were to follow them to the "promised land." Today, however, workers require a different style of leadership, one that involves more listening, empowering, delegating, and team building. The following tips can help you become a more effective leader.

1. *Leaders are both confident and modest.* Being a leader is not about making yourself more powerful; it's about making the people around you more powerful.

2. *Leaders are authentic.* No one believes in a leader who fails to "walk the talk." Leadership requires integrity and sincerity. These characteristics are the building blocks of trust.

3. *Leaders are good listeners.* Successful leaders know that some of the best ideas come from the people who actually do a job every day, and these leaders are willing to listen to employees. The chief enemy of involving workers in decision making is grandiosity, the belief that the leader has all of the answers.

4. *Leaders are good at giving encouragement, and they are never satisfied.* Leaders constantly test their own stamina and courage and those of the people in their organizations by raising the standards of performance. They are an organization's top cheerleaders when people succeed and are supportive when people fail.

5. *Leaders make unexpected connections.* Leaders arrange for interaction among people who otherwise might not get together. Then they listen for innovative ideas that result from those interactions and act on them.

6. *Leaders provide direction.* However, that does not mean that they have all of the answers, as the Wizard of Oz seemed to have. Modern leaders know how to ask probing, revealing questions of others that provide insight into the best course of action. Steve Miller, a manager at Royal Dutch Shell, says. "No leader can have all the answers. . . . The actual solutions about how best to meet the challenges of the moment have to be made by the people closest to the action. . . . The leader has to empower these frontline people, to challenge them, to provide them with the resources they need, and then hold them accountable."

7. *Leaders protect their people from danger and expose them to reality.* The surest way leaders can protect their organizations from danger is to keep everyone focused on the vision. Exposing people to reality means forcing the organization to face up to the need for change. Although many people are uncomfortable with and resistant to change, leaders know that their organizations must change or risk being left behind.

8. *Leaders create change and stand for values that don't change.* Although change is essential to an organization's survival, a leader must protect those values and principles that are central to the company's core. Losing these would cause the company to lose its identity. However, leaders must always watch for habits and assumptions that the company must change if it is to continue to prosper.

9. *Leaders lead by example.* Leaders recognize that they are always under the microscope and that workers are always interpreting leaders' actions. That is why leaders must live by the principles they espouse. Leaders use small gestures to send big messages.

10. *Leaders don't blame; they learn.* Leaders know that creativity and innovation carry with them the risk of failure. They also understand that creativity and innovation are essential to the organization's survival and do not punish people just because they tried and failed. Their attitude is: Try, fail, learn, and try again.

11. *Leaders look for and network with other leaders.* Successful leaders are *not* Lone Rangers. They look for allies and the opportunity to network with others so they can learn to become more effective leaders. Leaders build relationships.

12. *The job of the leader is to make more leaders.* In the past, the assumption was that an organization needed just one strong leader. Today, the organization with the most leaders usually wins! Your ultimate challenge is not just to become an effective leader but also to create more leaders in your company.

HIRING THE RIGHT EMPLOYEES

Learning Objective

2. Describe the importance of hiring the right employees and how to avoid making hiring mistakes.

The decision to hire a new employee is an important one for every business, but its impact is magnified many times in a small company. Every new hire a business owner makes determines the heights to which the company can climb—or the depths to which it will plunge. "Bad hires" can poison a small company's culture. Hiring mistakes are also incredibly expensive, and no organization, especially a small one, can afford too many of them. One study concluded that an employee hired into a typical entry-level position who quits after six months costs a company about $17,000 in salary, benefits, and training. In addition, the intangible costs—time invested in the new employee, lost opportunities, reduced morale among co-workers, and business setbacks—are seven times the direct costs of a "bad hire." In other words, the total price tag for this "bad hire" is about $136,000![5]

Avoiding Hiring Mistakes

As crucial as finding good employees is to a small company's future, it is no easy task. Today, increased demand for skilled knowledge workers and relatively low levels of unemployment have combined to create a hiring crisis for business owners. The severity of this labor shortage will worsen, too, thanks to demographic trends. Currently, the ratio of workers to retirees is 4:1. By 2011, when baby boomers begin retiring, this ratio will begin dropping, reaching 3:1 in 2020 before bottoming out at 2:1 in 2030.[6] Competition among businesses for quality workers is intense, and the battle for talent has taken on higher stakes. Rapidly advancing technology and increasing globalization give companies of all sizes access to most of the same resources so that the balance of competitive power shifts to those companies with superior human resources. Small businesses must mentally equate the search for quality new employees with their survival. There is no way to successfully compete without high-quality employees. Consequently, small firms must approach the hiring process with a commitment to fill the open positions with high-quality employees, even if this process takes longer than expected.

Managerial talent is both expensive and a good investment when entrepreneurs want to grow their business and recognize that they cannot do it alone.

*That was exactly the case for Doug Harrison, founder and CEO of the **Scooter Store**. The company is now a $200 million provider of power wheelchairs and scooters for the physically challenged. It took Doug seven and a half years to develop his business model to a point where he felt it was time to grow the business to a higher level of sales. He needed experienced and expensive management talent. In fact, he paid the new managers more than he was making in salary. Doug sold them on his plan, turned them loose, and they delivered the goods—you might say he got what he paid for![7]*

Even though the importance of hiring decisions is magnified in small companies, small businesses are most likely to make hiring mistakes because they lack the human resources experts and the disciplined hiring procedures large companies have. The hiring process is informal and its results often unpredictable. In the early days of a company, entrepreneurs rarely take the time to create job descriptions and specifications; instead, they usually hire people because they know or trust them rather than for their job skills. Then, as the company grows, business owners hire people to fit in around these existing employees, often creating a very unusual, inefficient organizational structure built around jobs that are poorly planned and designed.

The following guidelines can help small business managers avoid making costly hiring mistakes:

ELEVATE RECRUITING TO A STRATEGIC POSITION IN THE COMPANY. Assembling a quality workforce begins with a sound recruiting effort. By investing time and money at this crucial phase of the staffing process, entrepreneurs can generate spectacular savings down the road by avoiding costly hiring mistakes. The recruiting process also is the starting point for building quality into a company. Recruiting is so important that smart entrepreneurs no longer leave the task to human resource managers, choosing instead to become actively involved in the process themselves. Truly aggressive entrepreneurs *never* stop recruiting because top quality talent is hard to find and extremely valuable.

Attracting a pool of qualified job candidates requires not only constant attention but also creativity, especially among smaller companies that often find it difficult to match the more generous offers large companies make. With a sound recruiting strategy and a willingness to look in new places, however, smaller companies *can* hire and retain high caliber employees. The following techniques will help.

Look inside the company first. One of the best sources for top prospects is right inside the company itself. A promotion from within policy serves as an incentive for existing workers to upgrade their skills. Additonally, an entrepreneur already knows the employee's work habits, and the employee already understands the company's culture.

Encourage employee referrals. To cope with the shortage of available talent, many companies are offering their employees (and others) bonuses for referring candidates who come to work and prove to be valuable employees. Employees serve as reliable screens because they do not want to jeopardize their reputations with their employer. Rewards companies offer to employees for successful referrals range from weekend getaways to cash. At Redback Network, a high-tech networking company, referral bonuses range from $2,500 to $10,000 (for especially hard-to-fill positions)![8]

Perficient, an Internet services company, was growing so fast that CEO Jack McDonnell needed to increase the company's workforce from nine employees to 180 employees in just 10 months. Using outside recruiters proved to be too time-consuming and costly, so McDonnell offered employees $5,000 referral bonuses. The incentive worked so well that one team leader posted an ad on an Internet job bulletin board and began interviewing candidates who responded on weekends. His efforts led to three new hires for Perficient and $15,000 in bonuses for himself![9]

Make employment advertisements stand out. Getting employment ads noticed in traditional media is becoming more difficult because they get lost in the swarm of ads from other companies.

*Roger Mody, founder of **Signal Corporation**, an information technology provider, uses humor to make his employment ads stand out and to communicate the sense of fun in the company's culture. One recent ad ran a photo of Mody after a company pie-eating contest with the tag line "And you should see us on casual day." Although newspaper ads still top employers' list of ad placement, some businesses are attracting candidates through other media such as billboards and online ads.*

Use the Internet as a recruiting tool. The Internet is one of the fastest-growing media for employment ads because it offers tremendous reach at a relatively low cost and is effective, especially for companies recruiting high-tech workers. Many companies post jobs on several of the many job bulletin boards on the Web, including Monster, HotJobs, Career Builder, Employment Guide, and others.

*Darlene Chapin, recruiting manager at **Cheetah Technologies**, a computer network-management company, says the Internet has proved to be the most effective recruiting tool she uses. Chapin emphasizes that the Internet is just one part of a comprehensive recruiting effort. Cheetah also uses ads in newspapers and technical publications, employee referrals, career fairs, college visits, and other methods to find employees.[10]*

The wording of Internet ads is extremely important. In their ads, entrepreneurs should be specific about the qualifications a candidate must have and should describe the benefits their companies offer in an honest but appealing manner.

Recruit on campus. For many employers college and university campuses remain an excellent source of workers, especially for entry-level positions. After screening résumés, a recruiter can interview a dozen or more high-potential students in just one day. On some campuses, competition for the best students is so intense that companies are going to extreme measures. For example, large signing bonuses for graduates in "hot" career fields are becoming more common.

Forge relationships with schools and other sources of workers. Some employers have found forging long-term relationships with schools and other institutions to be a valuable source of workers. As colleges and universities begin to offer students greater internship opportunities, a small business can gain greatly by hosting one or more students for a semester or for the summer. The company has an opportunity to observe the student's work habits and to sell the student on a permanent position after graduation.

C.P. Shipping of Tampa, Florida, has found that hiring international students as interns is particularly valuable because of the students' knowledge of the language and culture of locations where the company does business.

Recruit "retired" workers. Many businesses are drawing on a pool of workers with much to offer: senior citizens. With a lifetime of work experience and time on their hands, "retired" workers can be the ideal solution to many entrepreneurs' labor problems. Currently, only 13 percent of Americans over the age of 65 work, but changes in Social Security laws now allowing them to earn more may encourage more retirees to return to take on part-time jobs.

Bonne Bell, a small cosmetics firm in Lakewood, Ohio, has 87 senior citizens on its payroll. (The oldest is 89, and 30 percent of them are over 70.) The company's owner, Jess Bell, who is 75, says the program has been a huge success for the seniors and her company. "We realized that many seniors are simply not ready to retire when they reach 65," she says.[11]

A Company Example

Wal-Mart and McDonald's are other examples of companies that have used this strategy effectively. Older employees can also be a valuable asset to smaller firms.

Consider using offbeat recruiting techniques. To attract the workers they need to support their growing businesses, some entrepreneurs have resorted to rather unconventional recruiting techniques such as the following:[12]

- Sending young recruiters to where college students gather on spring break.
- Having an airplane tow a banner over competitors' offices that reads "Don't make a career mistake."
- Launching a monthly industry networking meeting for local workers at Internet companies.
- Keeping a file of all of the workers mentioned in the "People on the Move" column in the business section of the local newspaper and then contacting them a year later to see if they are happy in their jobs.

Offer what workers want. Of course, adequate compensation is an important consideration for job candidates, but other less tangible factors also weigh in a prospect's decision to accept a job. For young knowledge workers especially, a fun, yet professionally challenging, work environment can be as important as salary. In fact, a survey by O'Conner Kenny Partners Inc., found that the factor topping college students' list when evaluating a job offer is "a fun working environment."[13]

*That's why Bill Ziercher, CEO of **Sterling Direct**, a direct marketing company, emphasizes having fun in his business. Employees have a contest for the sloppiest desk of the week, in which the winner has the privilege of displaying "Pat the Pig" (a Beanie Baby) on his or her desk. Ziercher also holds regular events such as the recent on-site beach party, complete with karaoke machine and Super Soaker water guns and often gives away tickets to sporting events as part of other contests.[14]*

A Company Example

CREATE PRACTICAL JOB DESCRIPTIONS AND JOB SPECIFICATIONS. Small business owners must recognize that what they do *before* they ever start interviewing candidates for a position determines to a great extent how successful they will be at hiring winners. The first step is to perform a **job analysis**, the process by which a firm determines the duties and nature of the jobs to be filled and the skills and experience required of the people who are to fill them. Without a proper job analysis, a hiring decision is, at best, a coin toss. The first objective of a job analysis is to develop a **job description**, a written statement of the duties, responsibilities, reporting relationships, working conditions, methods and techniques used, and materials and equipment used in a job. A results-oriented job description explains what a job entails and the duties the person filling it is expected to perform. A detailed job description should include a job title, job summary, duties to be performed, nature of supervision, the job's relationship to other jobs in the company, working conditions, definitions of job-specific terms, and general comments needed to clarify any of the preceding categories.

Preparing job descriptions is a task most small business owners overlook; however, this may be one of the most important parts of the hiring process because it creates a "blueprint" for the job. It is important for a business owner to define the tasks that need to be accomplished. Without this blueprint, a manager tends to hire the person with experience whom they like the best. Useful sources of information for writing job descriptions include the manager's knowledge of the job, the worker(s) currently holding the job, and O*Net, a Web site that replaced the *Dictionary of Occupational Titles (D.O.T)*, and lists more than 20,000 job titles and descriptions. O*Net serves as a useful tool for getting a small business owner started when writing job descriptions. Table 15.2 provides an example of the description drawn from O*Net for an unusual job.

The second objective of a job analysis is to create a **job specification**, a written statement of the qualifications and characteristics needed for a job in terms of education, skills, and experience. A job specification shows a small business manager what kind of person to recruit and establishes the standards an applicant must meet to be hired. When writing job specifications,

job analysis—*the process by which a firm determines the duties and nature of the jobs to be filled and the skills and experience required of the people who are to fill them.*

job description—*a written statement of the duties, responsibilities, working conditions, and materials and equipment used in a job.*

job specification—*a written statement of the qualifications and characteristics needed for a job in terms of education, skills, and experience.*

TABLE 15.2

A Sample Job Description from O*Net

Worm Picker—gathers worms to be used as fish bait: walks about grassy areas, such as gardens, parks, and golf courses, and picks up earthworms (commonly called dew worms and nightcrawlers). Sprinkles chlorinated water on lawn to cause worms to come to the surface and locates worms by use of lantern or flashlight. Counts worms, sorts them, and packs them into containers for shipment.

some managers define the traits a candidate needs to do a job well. Does the person have to be a good listener, empathetic, well organized, decisive, a "self-starter?" Should she have experience in Java or C++ programming? One of the best ways to develop a list of these traits is to study the top performers currently working for the company and focus on the characteristics that make them successful. Table 15.3 provides an example that links the tasks for a sales representative's job (drawn from a job description) to the traits or characteristics a small business owner identified as necessary to succeed in that job.

PLAN AN EFFECTIVE INTERVIEW. Once an entrepreneur knows what she must look for in a job candidate, she can develop a plan for conducting an informative job interview. Too often, small business owners go into an interview unprepared, and as a result, they fail to get the information they need to judge the candidate's qualifications, qualities, and suitability for the job. Conducting an effective interview requires an entrepreneur to know what she wants to get out of the interview in the first place and to develop a series of questions to extract that information. The following guidelines will help an owner develop interview questions that will give her meaningful insight into an applicant's qualifications, personality, and character:

Develop a series of core questions and ask them of every candidate. To give the screening process more consistency, smart business owners rely on a set of relevant questions they ask in every interview. Of course, they also customize each interview using impromptu questions based on an individual's responses.

Ask open-ended questions (including on-the-job "scenarios") rather than questions calling for "yes or no" answers. These types of questions are most effective because they encourage candidates to talk about their work experience in a way that will disclose the presence or the absence of the traits and characteristics the business owner is seeking.

Create hypothetical situations candidates would be likely to encounter on the job and ask how they would handle them. Building the interview around such questions gives the owner a preview of the candidate's work habits and attitudes.

Probe for specific examples in the candidate's past work experience that demonstrate the necessary traits and characteristics. A common mistake interviewers make is failing to get candidates to provide the detail they need to make an informed decision.

Job Task	Trait or Characteristic
Generate and close new sales	"outgoing"; persuasive; friendly
Make 15 "cold calls" per week	"self-starter"; determined; optimistic; independent; confident
Analyze customers' needs and recommend proper equipment	good listener; patient; empathetic
Counsel customers about options and features needed	organized; polished speaker; "other oriented"
Prepare and explain financing methods	honest; "numbers oriented"; comfortable with computers and spreadsheets
Retain existing customers	customer oriented; relationship builder

Ask candidates to describe a recent success and a recent failure and how they dealt with them. Smart entrepreneurs look for candidates who describe them both with equal enthusiasm because they know that peak performers put as much into their failures as they do their successes and usually learn something valuable from their failures.

Table 15.4 lists some interview questions one manager uses to uncover the traits and characteristics he seeks in a top-performing sales representative.

CONDUCT THE INTERVIEW. An effective interview contains three phases: breaking the ice, asking questions, and selling the candidate on the company.

Breaking the ice. In the opening phase of the interview the manager's primary job is to diffuse the tension that exists because of the nervousness of both parties. Many skilled interviewers use the job description to explain the nature of the job and the company's culture to the applicant. Then they use "icebreakers," questions about a hobby or special interest, to get the candidate to relax.

Asking questions. During the second phase of the interview, the employer asks the questions from her question bank to determine the applicant's suitability for the job. Her primary job at this point is to listen. Effective interviewers spend about 25 percent of the interview talking and about 75 percent listening. They also take notes during the interview to help them ask follow-up questions based on a candidate's comments and to evaluate a candidate after the interview is over. Experienced interviewers also pay close attention to a candidate's nonverbal clues, or body language, during the interview. They know that candidates may be able to say exactly what they want with their words, but that their body language does not lie!

Small business owners must be careful to make sure they avoid asking candidates illegal questions. At one time, interviewers could ask wide-ranging questions covering just about every area of an applicant's background. Today, interviewing is a veritable minefield of legal liabilities, waiting to explode in the unsuspecting interviewer's face. Although the Equal Employment Opportunity Commission (EEOC) as the government agency responsible for enforcing employment laws does not outlaw specific questions, it does recognize that some questions can result in employment discrimination. If a candidate files charges of employment discrimination against a company, the burden of proof shifts to the employer to prove that all preemployment questions are job related and are nondiscriminatory. In addition, many states have passed laws that forbid the use of certain questions or screening tools in interviews. To avoid trouble, business owners should keep in mind why they are asking a particular question. The goal is to identify individuals who are qualified to do the job well. By steering clear of questions about subjects that are peripheral to the job itself, employers are less likely to ask questions that will land them in court. Wise business owners ask their attorneys to review their bank of questions

Trait or Characteristic	Question
"outgoing"; persuasive; friendly; "self-starter"; determined; optimistic; independent; confident	How do you persuade reluctant prospects to buy?
good listener; patient; empathetic; organized; polished speaker; "other oriented"	What would you say to a fellow salesperson who was getting more than his share of rejections and was having difficulty getting appointments?
honest; customer oriented, relationship builder	How do you feel when someone questions the truth of what you say? What do you do in such situations?
Other questions:	If you owned a company, why would you hire yourself? If you were head of your department, what would you do differently? How do you recognize the contributions of others in your department? If you weren't in sales, in what other job would you be?

TABLE 15.4

Interview Questions for Candidates for a Sales Representative Position

before using them in an interview. Table 15.5 offers a quiz entitled "Is It Legal?" to help you understand the kinds of questions that are most likely to create charges of discrimination.

Selling the candidate on the company. In the final phase of the interview, the employer tries to sell her company to desirable candidates. This phase begins by allowing the candidate to ask questions about the company, the job, or other issues. Again, experienced interviewers note the nature of these questions and the insights they give into the candidate's personality. This part of the interview offers the employer a prime opportunity to explain to the candidate why her company is an attractive place to work. Remember: The best candidates will have other offers, and it's up to you to make sure they leave the interview wanting to work for your company. Finally, before closing the interview, the employer should thank the candidate and tell him what happens next (for example, "We'll be contacting you about our decision within two weeks").

Table 15.6 outlines a 10-step process for hiring and retention and Table 15.7 describes 10 interviewing mistakes small business owners must avoid.

CHECK REFERENCES. Small business owners should take the time to check every applicant's references. Although many business owners see checking references as a formality and pay little attention to it, others realize the need to protect themselves (and their customers) from hiring unscrupulous workers. Is it really necessary? Yes! According to the Society for Human Resource Management, more than half of candidates either exaggerated or falsified information about their previous employment on their résumés.[15] Checking references thoroughly can help employers uncover false or exaggerated information. Rather than contacting only the references listed, experienced employers call applicants' previous employers and talk to their immediate supervisors to get a clear picture of the applicant's job performance, character, and work habits. After talking with the references a candidate for a top financial position his company had listed, one entrepreneur took the time to contact the applicant's previous employers. He soon discovered that the candidate had stolen money and misused company credit cards in a previous job. *None of the references listed mentioned the incident.*

Experienced small business owners understand that the hiring process provides them with one of the most valuable raw materials their companies count on for success—capable, hardworking people. They know that hiring an employee is not a single event but the beginning of a long-term relationship. Table 15.8 features some strange but true incidents that employers have encountered during the selection process.

Learning Objective

3. Explain how to build the kind of company culture and structure to support an entrepreneur's mission and goals and motivate employees to achieve them.

BUILDING THE RIGHT ORGANIZATIONAL CULTURE AND STRUCTURE

Culture

culture—*the distinctive, unwritten, informal code of conduct that governs an organization's behavior, attitudes, relationships, and style.*

A company's **culture** is the distinctive, unwritten, informal code of conduct that governs its behavior, attitudes, relationships, and style. It is the essence of "the way we do things around here" and often originates with the founder. In many small companies, culture plays as important a part in gaining a competitive edge as strategy does. It has a powerful impact on the way people work together in a business, how they do their jobs, and how they treat their customers. Company culture manifests itself in many ways—from how workers dress and act to the language they use. For instance, at some companies, the unspoken dress code requires workers to wear suits and ties, but at many companies employees routinely come to work in jeans and T-shirts and enjoy perks such as Friday afternoon parties! The culture at some small companies is more an extension of college life than a transition to corporate life, which suits these companies' young, college-educated workers just fine!

In many companies, the culture creates its own language. At Disney, for instance, workers are not "employees"; they are "cast members." They don't merely go to work; their jobs are "parts in a performance." Disney's customers are "guests." When a cast member treats someone to lunch, it's "on the mouse." Anything negative—such as a cigarette butt on a walkway—is "a bad Mickey," and anything positive is "a good Mickey."

Creating a culture that supports a company's strategy is no easy task, but the entrepreneurs who have been most successful at it believe in having a set of overarching beliefs to serve as powerful guides for everyday action. Culture arises from an entrepreneur's consistent and relent-

TABLE 15.5

Is It Legal?

Some interview questions can land an employer in legal hot water. Review the following interview questions and then decide whether you think each one is "legal" or "illegal."

Legal Illegal

❏	❏	1.	Are you currently using illegal drugs?
❏	❏	2.	Have you ever been arrested?
❏	❏	3.	Do you have any children or are you planning to have children?
❏	❏	4.	When and where were you born?
❏	❏	5.	Is there any limit on your ability to work overtime or to travel?
❏	❏	6.	How tall are you? How much do you weigh?
❏	❏	7.	Do you drink alcohol?
❏	❏	8.	How much alcohol do you drink per week?
❏	❏	9.	Would your religious beliefs interfere with your ability to do this job?
❏	❏	10.	What contraceptive practices do you employ?
❏	❏	11.	Are you HIV-positive?
❏	❏	12.	Have you ever filed a lawsuit or a workers' compensation claim against a former employer?
❏	❏	13.	Do you have any physical or mental disabilities that would interfere with your doing this job?
❏	❏	14.	Are you a U.S. citizen?
❏	❏	15.	What is your race?

Small business owners can use the "OUCH" test as a guide for determining whether an interview question might be considered discriminatory:

■ Does the question *Omit* references to race, religion, color, sex, or national origin?

■ Does the question *Unfairly* screen out a particular class of people?

■ Can you *Consistently* apply the question to every applicant?

■ Does the question *Have* job-relatedness and business necessity?

Answers: 1. Legal. 2. Illegal. Employers cannot ask about an applicant's arrest record, but they can ask if a candidate has ever been convicted of a crime. 3. Illegal. Employers cannot ask questions that would lead to discrimination against a particular group (e.g., women). 4. Illegal. The Civil Rights Act of 1964 bans discrimination on the basis of race, color, sex, religion, or national origin. 5. Legal. 6. Illegal. Unless a person's physical characteristics are important for high job performance (e.g., lifting 100-pound sacks of flour), employers cannot ask candidates such questions. 7. Legal. 8. Illegal. Notice the fine line between question 7 and question 8; this is what makes interviewing a challenge! 9. Illegal. This question would violate the Civil Rights Act of 1964. 10. Illegal. What relevance would this have to an employee's job performance? 11. Illegal. Under the Americans with Disabilities Act, which prohibits discrimination against people with disabilities, people with HIV or AIDS are considered "disabled." 12. Illegal. Workers who file such suits are protected from retribution by a variety of federal and state laws. 13. Illegal. This question would also violate the Americans with Disabilities Act. 14. Illegal. This question violates the Civil Rights Act of 1964. 15. Illegal. Employers cannot ask questions about a job applicant's race. The Civil Rights Act of 1964 bans discrimination on the basis of race, color, sex, religion, or national origin.

less pursuit of a set of core values that everyone in the company can believe in. In some cases, the original organizational culture set forth by the founder may prove to be ineffective and successors face the challenge of introducing a new culture; consider the People Soft example.

A Company Example

*Few firms have experienced a greater corporate culture change in the past decade than the employees of **PeopleSoft**. The firm's founder, David A. Duffield, turned the reins of his firm over to Craig Conway, a product of the Larry Ellison school of "take-no-prisoners" management at Oracle. Before long PeopleSoft was in serious financial difficulty. Duffield's leadership style created a corporate culture described, even in the software development industry, as peculiar. Duffield had provided free breakfasts for all employees, allowed employees to bring their pets to the office, and practiced a participative management style.*

TABLE 15.6	10-Step Hiring and Retention Process
The 10-Step Hiring and Retention Process	

10-Step Hiring and Retention Process

Step 1. Ask yourself the following questions: Do I really need to replace the person who left? What happens if I don't? Can others assume the responsibility and tasks?

Step 2. Look inside. Whenver, possible promote from within.

Step 3. Before you interview potential candidates, develop a set of standards against which you will judge each candidate. Don't compromise.

Step 4. When interviewing, ask pertinent questions that will help you identify individuals with a track record of producing tangible results.

Step 5. Ask others in your organization to spend time with a candidate to get a second opinion.

Step 6. Focus on determining the candidate's skills at problem solving, teamwork (if relevant), and other specifically relevant job performances.

Step 7. After your selection and the candidate's acceptance, be sure that the transition into the new position is smooth. Examples of this include having the new employee's workstation well equipped, co-workers aware of the new employee's arrival, and a welcome function where all parties can be introduced.

Step 8. Assign each new employee a mentor to ensure that he or she learns the job from an employee who will start them on the right track.

Step 9. Whenever possible, plan a dinner with the new employee's family and yours. You sold the job to the new hire; now do the same for the spouse.

Step 10. For the first four to six months meet briefly with the new hire on a regular basis. New employees view your business through "fresh eyes" and can often help the firm recognize new opportunities.

Craig Conway wore power suits, expected others to do so as well, and did not greet employees with a big hug, as Duffield often would. Gone were the free breakfasts and pets and in came strategic planning and "corporate discipline." Many key executives left to form other firms or work with competitors. However, Conway held firm and in September 2000 released PeopleSoft's Internet-based product PeopleSoft 8, which has proved to be a market success. The firm is now financially sound.[16]

TABLE 15.7	
10 Interviewing Mistakes	

1. Succumbing to pressure to hire fast, which often arises as a result of failing to begin the search process far enough in advance. Plan ahead!

2. Falling victim to the halo effect, the tendency to attribute a host of positive attributes (e.g., intelligence, sense of humor, honesty, etc.) to a candidate based on one positive attribute (e.g., well spoken). This tendency is called the horn effect when it works in a negative fashion.

3. Asking leading or "canned" questions, those in which it is obvious to everyone involved, including the job applicant, what the "right" answer should be.

4. Talking too much. A common mistake inexperienced interviewers make is doing most of the talking while the candidate has to work hard just to become part of the conversation. Remember the 25/75 rule!

5. Failing to take notes during the interview. Jotting down key points, questions, and impressions as they occur will be of tremendous value when it's time to make a final decision about a particular candidate.

6. Accepting generalizations from a candidate. Effective interviewers probe for specific results and examples from candidates so they can verify applicants' qualifications and characteristics more objectively.

7. Asking questions that could lead to charges of discrimination and land the company in a nasty lawsuit. Keep questions job focused and consistent.

8. Failing to check a candidate's references. This routine procedure may uncover inconsistencies and falsehoods in the candidate's background. It can help small business owners avoid making a "bad hire" and lawsuits charging them with "negligent hiring." Ask former employers, "Would you hire him or her again?"

9. Making snap judgments. A common tendency among novice interviewers is to make a decision about a candidate in the first few minutes of an interview and then to spend the rest of the interview justifying that decision.

10. Committing candidate-order error. Experienced interviewers know that the order in which they interview candidates can affect their evaluations of them. Most recent candidates tend to have the advantage. Be aware of this tendency.

TABLE 15.8
Strange but True!

Source: "Hiring Horrors," *Your Company,*
April 1999, p. 14: Mike B. Hall, "From Job
Applicants," Joke-of-the-Day,
www.jokeoftheday.com, December 8,
2000; Karen Axelton. "L-L-L-Losers!"
Business Start-Ups, April 2000, p. 13.

If you read enough résumés, conduct enough interviews, and check enough references, sooner or later you will encounter something bizarre. Consider the following examples (all true).

- After having lunch with a job candidate, a business owner took the applicant to her office for more discussion. The discussion ended, however, when the applicant dozed off and began snoring.
- On his résumé, one candidate wrote, "It's best for employers if I not work with people." Another included the following note; "Please don't misconstrue my 14 jobs as job hopping. I have never quit a job."
- An interviewer told a man applying for a clerical job to relax before taking a typing test. He flexed his fingers and then took off his shirt!
- An applicant at a warehouse proudly reviewed his prison record for the interviewer, adding that he had gotten much better: Rather than steal from his grandmother, he stole only from her friends and beat her up only if she refused to give him money.
- When asked about his personal interests, one candidate proudly replied, "Donating blood. Fourteen gallons so far!"
- At the end of an interview, the interviewer asked the candidate if he had any questions. His only question: "Is the office close enough so I can run home three times a day to Water Pik my teeth?"
- One candidate asked if he could bring his rabbit to work with him, adding that the rabbit was focused and reliable but that he himself had been fired before.
- When asked about why he had been fired from several jobs, one candidate said that his previous employers had conspired to place an evil curse on him.
- When asked what his ideal job would be, another candidate showed his lack of motivation, saying, "To lie in bed all day, eat chocolate, and get paid."

Recommendations from previous employers can sometimes be quite entertaining, too. The following are statements from managers about workers.

- "Works well when under constant supervision and cornered like a rat in a trap."
- "This young lady has delusions of adequacy."
- "A photographic memory but with the lens cover glued on."
- "If you were to give him a penny for his thoughts, you'd get change."
- "If you stand close enough to him, you can hear the ocean."

Nurturing the right culture in a company can enhance a company's competitive position by improving its ability to attract and retain quality workers and by creating an environment in which workers can grow and develop. Which organizational culture will be most effective is never easy to determine. However, one thing is certain: The culture must support exceptional performance and be compatible with the firm's stated values and benefits. Companies that have been successful in creating supportive cultures rely on the following principles.

RESPECT FOR WORK AND LIFE BALANCE. Successful companies recognize that their employees have lives away from work. One recent study of Generation X workers found that those companies that people most wanted to work for erased the traditional barriers between home life and work life by making it easier for employees to deal with the pressures they face away from their jobs. These businesses offer flexible work schedules, part-time jobs, job sharing, telecommuting, sabbaticals, on-site day care, and dry cleaning.

Roger Greene, founder of **Ipswitch Inc.***, a software company in Lexington, Massachusetts, has built his company on the concept of work–life balance. Company policy discourages employees from working late into the night and on weekends, and Greene recently raised the minimum vacation period for employees to five weeks a year. "Live life as it goes along and do neat things while you're working and enjoy every year of your life," he advises his employees. Ipswitch's rate of employee turnover is half that of the industry average.*[17]

A Company Example

It is logical to believe that grief equates to lower productivity, but it is rare to see how expensive grief is to our economy. The Grief Recovery Institute reports that workplace grief results in the loss of $75 billion in productivity. The Grief Index on page 500 illustrates its findings.

Although these data are subjective and not exact, they represent an attempt to quantify the effects of the loss of 2.4 million loved ones each year. Employee assistance programs can be very valuable in helping individuals cope with the emotional loss and the corresponding period

Source: The Gerief Recovery Institute

The Grief Index

Death of a Loved One Cost: $37.6 billion	**Death of an Acquaintance** Cost: $7 billion
Divorce/Marital Woes Cost: $11 billion	**Money Trouble at Home** Cost: $4.6 billion
Family Crisis Cost: $9 billion	**Pet Loss** Cost: $2.4 billion

of depression that can produce declining productivity. Entrepreneurs need to recognize that proactive intervention in these cases both demonstrates a genuine interest in the employee's loss, as well as helping the individual overcome the loss and return sooner to full productivity.[18]

A SENSE OF PURPOSE. As you learned in Chapter 3, "Strategic Management and the Entrepreneur," one of the most important jobs an entrepreneur faces is defining the company's vision and then communicating it effectively to everyone the company touches. Effective companies use a strong sense of purpose to make employees feel connected to the company's mission. At motorcycle legend Harley-Davidson, employees are so in tune with the company's mission that some of them have tatooed the company's name on their bodies!

A SENSE OF FUN. For some companies, the barriers between work and play are blurred. The founders of these businesses see no reason for work and fun to be mutually exclusive. In fact, they believe that workplaces that create a sense of fun make it easier to recruit quality workers and encourage them to be more productive and more customer oriented. Employees are encouraged to participate in activities designed to build their skills in teamwork and human relations. These "fun" events improve employees' ability to work in teams in a creative and productive manner.

DIVERSITY. Effective companies not only accept cultural diversity in their workforces, but they also embrace it, actively seeking out workers with different backgrounds. Today businesses must recognize that a workforce that has a rich mix of cultural diversity gives the company more talent, skills, and abilities from which to draw. The result is a stronger company.

A Company Example

*That was the approach taken by the shareholder-owned, publicly-chartered mortgage funding organization **Fannie Mae**. The organization's goal was to have a workforce that "mirrors" American demographics. The results are impressive and include an increase in minority-held management positions from 9 percent in 1994 to 24 percent in 2001. In addition, managerial positions held by females increased from 40 percent to more than 45 percent.[19]*

A study of the demographics of the United States quickly reveals the steady march toward an increasingly diverse population. The workforce is beginning to reflect the diversity of our culture and its composition. In the 100 largest cities in America, non-Hispanic white males now are a minority. Surrounding the issue of a diverse American culture lies the continually intensifying problem of the shortage of skilled workers.

Entrepreneurs must articulate the positive value of a diverse workforce and then compete in the labor market to attract and retain the best-qualified workers. In the case of diversity, both society and the organization are the beneficiaries of an effective diversity program. Fred Kleisner, chairman and CEO of Wyndham International (Wyndham Hotels), explains, "I want diversity to be more than a corporate initiative. . . . I want it to be a living part of our culture, a belief system and service philosophy that permeate from each of our employees."[20]

INTEGRITY. Employees want to work for companies that stand for honesty and integrity. They do not want to check their own personal values systems at the door when they report to work. Indeed, many workers take pride in the fact that they work for companies that are ethical

YOU Be the Consultant . . .

Last Resort Workers

Tim Rock, owner of Rock Communications, a small printing company in Newton, Iowa, was concerned about the growth prospects of his business, not because of a lack of customers but because of a lack of employees. Rock was constantly short of workers. "Every day we'd be one or two or five people short," says Rock. Then one day, while driving down Interstate 80, Rock thought of the prison just outside of town and the number of men there with plenty of time on their hands. Why not hire some of the inmates to work at his company? Rock wrote a letter to the warden and soon a dozen inmates arrived at Rock Communications for work. It was an extreme solution to Rock's labor problems, but it is one that has worked out well. In the five years that Rock has been hiring workers from the prison, he has seen dozens of men cycle through his business. Most stayed only a few months, but 13 former prisoners are now full-time employees. Rock also has a team of 60 part-time senior adults who assemble advertising inserts the company prints every week.

Like Tim Rock, Jerry Strahan is always in desperate need of employees. Strahan, general manager of Lucky Dogs, Inc., a 52-year-old hot dog vending company in New Orleans, is constantly looking for vendors to take the company's 22 pushcarts out into the streets of the French Quarter. Although the work requires no special skills other than the ability to make change, finding workers in New Orleans willing to push 650-pound carts shaped like a giant hot dog is tougher than it sounds. "We've tried ads and employment agencies," says Strahan, "but most people can't take the streets." Lucky Dogs now recruits at mission centers for the homeless and at the Salvation Army. "We've tried to get better people," Strahan says, "but with no success." Many show up on Lucky Dogs' doorstep after hearing about the opportunity for work from current employees.

The result is a rather motley workforce made up of drifters, alcoholics, petty thieves, and brawlers that is, at best, a challenge to manage and to motivate. "I tell the vendors, 'You need to be neat, you need to be clean, you need to be on time, you need to be polite, and you need to be conscientious,'" says Strahan. "But the vendors say to me, 'Jerry, if I could be all those things, I'd be working in an office on Poydras Street. Can we go for three out of five?'" One off-and-on employee has stayed with the company for 14 years, despite his occasional tendency to show up for work dressed like Doris Day or John Wayne.

Strahan is willing to go for three out of five and, frankly, is happy when he gets it. Erratic behavior and actions that would get workers fired on the spot in most companies are acceptable at Lucky Dogs. "We make a set of rules, and they're good for about 10 minutes," says Strahan, only half joking. "You have to be very forgiving when they're not followed; otherwise, you don't have the carts out. You can't eliminate the madness. Sometimes you can control it." At Lucky Dogs, for instance, it's not unusual for employees to scream at their supervisors, to show up drunk, or to fail to show up for work altogether. "Most companies will say, 'If you show up for work drunk, you're fired,'" says Strahan. "Here, if you show up for work drunk, I've got to give you a C-minus because you showed up."

With the pool of potential workers so small, Lucky Dogs does not turn away many applicants. Those who are clean, able to make change, and have an ID get a chance to work. Strahan does not bother to check references on applicants, either. In an attempt to keep employee theft to a minimum, Lucky Dogs requires vendors to turn in their receipts often during a shift. Strahan does have one rule that, if broken, results in immediate dismissal: Any vendor caught stealing from another vendor will be fired.

To manage (if you can call it that) this rather unruly crew of workers, a Strahan admits that he breaks almost every conventional rule in the field of human resources management. Yet, he somehow manages to pull it off. He's been involved in shouting matches with employees and then a few minutes later ends up lending them money. When one worker showed up for his shift so intoxicated that he could barely stand, Strahan asked him to explain. "I thought I was pregnant," said the man. Without missing a beat, Strahan deadpanned, "In your condition, you probably shouldn't be working. Why don't you go home and we'll talk about it tomorrow?" Perhaps Strahan's style is best described as management by looking the other way. Although he has worked in his current job at Lucky Dogs for more than 28 years, he doubts that he could succeed at another company. "I don't think my skills would translate to a normal company," he says.

1. Why must employers such as Tim Rock and Jerry Strahan resort to such extreme measures to find workers?

2. What techniques would you recommend for motivating workers such as those described in this feature?

3. Are there other options for recruiting employees that you might suggest Rock and Strahan explore?

Source: Adapted from Ann Harrington, "Does Anybody Here Want a Job?" *Fortune,* May 15, 2000, pp. 489–498. Leigh Buchanan, "The Taming of the Crew," *Inc.,* August 1999, pp. 27–40.

and socially responsible. They expect their companies to communicate with them openly and honestly about issues that matter to them.

PARTICIPATIVE MANAGEMENT. Company owners and managers must trust and empower employees at all levels of the organization to make decisions and to take the actions they need to do their jobs well. As a firm grows, management must empower employees to act

"We need to focus on diversity. Your goal is to hire
people who all look different, but think just like me."

without direct supervision. For instance, at Nantucket Nectars, a small juice company, the management style is so participative that there is no established organizational hierarchy and no secretaries.

LEARNING ENVIRONMENT.   Today companies encourage and support lifelong learning among their employees. Every day is an opportunity to learn and improve the ability to contribute to the firm and to grow as a person. That attitude is a strong magnet for the best and the brightest young workers, who know that to stay at the top of their fields, they must always be learning.

Managing Growth and a Changing Culture

As companies grow from start-up businesses, going through the growth phase and beyond, they often experience dramatic changes in their cultures. Procedures become more formal, operations grow more widespread, jobs take on more structure, communication becomes more difficult, and the company's personality begins to change. As more workers come on board, employees find it more difficult to know everyone in the company and what their jobs are. Unless an entrepreneur works hard to maintain her company's unique culture, she may wake up one day to find that she has sacrificed that culture—and the competitive edge that goes with it—in the name of growth.

Ironically, growth can sometimes be a small company's biggest enemy, causing a once successful business to spiral out of control into oblivion. The problem stems from the fact that the organizational structure (or lack of it!) and the style of management that make an entrepreneurial start-up so successful often cannot support the business as it grows into adolescence and maturity. As a company grows, not only does its culture tend to change but so does its need for a management infrastructure capable of supporting that growth. Compounding the problem is the entrepreneur's tendency to see all growth as good. After all, who wouldn't want to be the founder of a small company whose rapid growth makes it destined to become the next rising star in the industry? Yet, achieving rapid growth and managing it are two distinct challenges. Entrepreneurs must be aware of the challenges rapid growth brings with it; otherwise they may find their companies crumbling around them as they reach warp speed.

In many cases, small companies achieve impressive growth because they bypass the traditional organizational structures, forgo rigid policies and procedures, and maintain maximum flexibility. One study of business growth found that small companies have the edge over their larger rivals:[21]

- Large companies' inability to react quickly is a major barrier to their growth. Small companies are naturally quick to respond.
- Rigid internal structures keep big companies from growing rapidly. Small companies typically bypass traditional structures.
- Large companies focus on expanding existing product and service lines, whereas small businesses concentrate more on creating new ones.
- Large companies are concerned with minimizing risks and defending their market share. Small companies are more willing to takes the risks necessary to conquer new markets.
- Large companies are reluctant to eradicate market research and technology that have worked in the past. Entrepreneurial companies have more of a "clean slate" approach to research and technology.

But growth brings with it change: changes in management style, organizational strategy, and methods of operations. Growth produces organizational complexity. In this period of transition, the entrepreneur's challenge is to walk a fine line between retaining the small-company traits that are the seeds of the business's success and incorporating the elements of the infrastructure essential to supporting and sustaining the company's growth.

Structure

Entrepreneurs rely on six different management styles to guide their companies as they grow. The first three (craftsman, classic, and coordinator) involve running a company without any management assistance and are best suited for small companies in the early stages of growth; the last three (entrepreneur-plus-employee team, small partnership, big-team venture) rely on a team approach to run the company as its growth rate heats up.[22]

THE CRAFTSMAN.   One of the earliest management styles to emerge was the craftsman. These entrepreneurs literally run a one-man (or one-woman) show; they do everything themselves because their primary concern is with the quality of the products or services they produce. Woodworkers, cabinetmakers, glassblowers, and other craftsmen rely on this style of management. The benefits of this style include minimal operating expenses (no employees to pay), very simple operations (no workers' compensation, incentive plans, or organizational charts), no supervision problems, and the entrepreneur's total control over both the business and its quality.

Of course, one disadvantage of the craftsman management style is that the entrepreneur must do everything in the business, including those tasks that she does not enjoy. The biggest disadvantage of this style, however, is the limitations it puts on a company's ability to grow. A business can grow only so big without the craftsman taking on other workers and delegating authority to them. Before choosing this management style, a craftsman must decide: "How large do I want my business to become?"

THE CLASSIC.   As business opportunities arise, a craftsman quickly realizes that she could magnify the company's capacity to grow by hiring other people to work. The classic entrepreneur brings in other people but does not delegate any significant authority to them, choosing instead to "watch over everything" herself. She insists on tight supervision, constantly monitors employees' work, and performs all of the critical tasks herself. Classic entrepreneurs do not feel comfortable delegating the power and the authority for making decisions to anyone else; they prefer to keep a tight rein on the business and on everyone who works there.

Even though this management style gives a business more growth potential than the craftsman style, there is a limit to how much an entrepreneur can accomplish. Therefore, entrepreneurs who choose to operate this way must limit the complexity of their businesses if they are to grow at all. An inherent danger of this style is the entrepreneur's tendency to "micromanage" every aspect of the business rather than spend her time focusing on those tasks that are most important and most productive for the company.

THE COORDINATOR. The coordinator style of management gives an entrepreneur the ability to create a fairly large company with very few employees. In this type of business (often called a virtual corporation because the company is actually quite "hollow"), the entrepreneur farms out a large portion of the work to other companies and then coordinates all of the activities from "headquarters." By hiring out at least some of the work (in some cases, most of the work), the entrepreneur is free to focus on pumping up sales and pushing the business to higher levels. Some coordinators hire someone to manufacture their products, pay brokers to sell them, and arrange for someone to collect their accounts receivable! With the help of just a few workers, a coordinator can build a multimillion-dollar business!

Although the coordinator style sounds like an easy way to build a business, it can be very challenging to implement. The business's success is highly dependent on its suppliers and their ability to produce quality products and services in a timely fashion. Getting suppliers to perform on time is one of the hardest tasks. Plus, if the entrepreneur hires someone else to manufacture the product, she loses control over its quality.

THE ENTREPRENEUR-PLUS-EMPLOYEE TEAM. As their companies grow, many entrepreneurs see the need to shift to a team-based management style. The entrepreneur-plus-employee team gives an entrepreneur the power to grow the business beyond the scope of the manager-only styles. In this style, the entrepreneur delegates authority to key employees, but she retains the final decision-making authority in the company. Of course, the transition from a management style in which the entrepreneur retains almost total authority to one based on delegation requires some adjustments for employees and especially for the entrepreneur! Employees have to learn to make decisions on their own, and the manager must learn to give workers the authority, the responsibility, and the information to make them. Delegating requires a manager to realize that there are several ways to accomplish a task and that sometimes employees will make mistakes. Still, delegation allows a manager to get the maximum benefit from each employee while freeing herself up to focus on the most important tasks in the business.

A Company Example

*Many executives believe that their leadership style is the product of a major life experience. Jack Kahl, founder of **Manco**, says that his mother's leadership when he was seven and his father was diagnosed with tuberculosis, formed the model he follows in business. His mother pulled the children together into a team to cope with the family's financial difficulties. All the children worked to support the needs of the family. Jack Kahl learned consensual leadership from his mother and built a successful business based on its application.*[23]

THE SMALL PARTNERSHIP. As the business world grows more complex and interrelated, many entrepreneurs find that there is strength in numbers. Rather than manage a company alone, they choose to share the managerial responsibilities with one or more partners (or shareholders). As we saw in Chapter 3 concerning forms of ownership, the benefits are many. Perhaps the biggest advantage is the ability to share responsibility for the company with others who have a real stake in the company and are willing to work hard to make it a success. Some of the most effective partnerships are those in which the owners' skills complement one another, creating natural "fault lines" for dividing responsibilities. Of course, the downside to this management style includes the necessity of giving up total control over the business and the potential for personality conflicts and disputes over the company's direction.

THE BIG-TEAM VENTURE. The broadest-based management style is the big-team venture, which typically emerges over time as a company grows. The workload demands on a small number of partners can quickly outstrip the time and energy they can devote to them, even if they are effective delegators. Once a company reaches this point, managers must expand the breadth of the management team's experience to handle the increasing level of responsibility that results from the sheer size of the company. If the company's operations have become global in scope as it has grown, the need for such a management team is even more pronounced. For entrepreneurial ventures that have grown to this size, the big-team venture is almost a necessity.

Any of these management styles can be successful for an entrepreneur if it matches her personality and the company's goals. The key is to plan for the company's growth and to lay out a strategy for managing the changes the company will experience as it grows. Entrepreneurs should annually evaluate their companies and themselves and ask if change is needed.

Making Teams Work

Large companies have been using self-directed work teams for years to improve quality, increase productivity, raise morale, lower costs, and boost motivation; yet, team-based management only recently began to catch on in small firms. In fact, a team approach may be best suited to small companies. Even though converting a traditional company to teams requires a major change in management style, it is usually easier to implement with a small number of workers. A **self-directed work team** is a group of workers from different functional areas of a company who work together as a unit largely without supervision, making decisions and performing tasks that once belonged only to managers. Some teams may be temporary, attacking and solving a specific problem, but many are permanent components of an organization's structure. As their name implies, these teams manage themselves, performing such functions as setting work schedules, ordering raw materials, evaluating and purchasing equipment, developing budgets, hiring and firing team members, solving problems, and a host of other activities. The goal is to get people working together to serve customers better.

self-directed work team—*a group of workers from different functional areas of a company who work together as a unit largely without supervision, making decisions and performing tasks that once belonged only to managers.*

Managers in companies using teams don't just sit around drinking coffee, however. In fact, they work just as hard as before, but the nature of their work changes dramatically. Before teams, managers were "bosses" who made most of the decisions affecting their subordinates alone and hoarded information and power for themselves. In a team environment, managers take on the role of "coaches" who empower those around them to make decisions affecting their work and share information with workers. As facilitators, their job is to support and to serve the teams functioning in the organization and to make sure they produce results. Not every entrepreneur feels comfortable in the roles of facilitator and coach, but for a team-based approach to succeed, an entrepreneur must learn to adapt.

Companies have strong competitive reasons for using team-based management. Companies that use teams effectively report significant gains in quality, reductions in cycle time, lower costs, increased customer satisfaction, and improved employee motivation and morale. A team-based approach is not for every organization, however. Teams are not easy to start, and switching from a traditional organizational structure to a team-based one is filled with potential pitfalls. Teams work best in environments where the work is interdependent and people must interact with one another to accomplish their goals. Although a team approach might succeed in a small plant making gas grills, it would most likely fail miserably in a real estate office, where salespeople work independently of one another with little interaction required to make a sale.

In some cases, teams have been a company's salvation from failure and extinction; in others, the team approach has flopped. What's the difference? What causes teams to fail? The following errors are common:[24]

- *Assigning teams inappropriate tasks.* One of the biggest mistakes managers make with teams is assigning them to tasks that individuals ought to be performing.

- *Creating "make-nice" teams.* For a team to perform effectively it must have a clear purpose, and every team member must understand it. Unfortunately, managers sometimes create a team but fail to give it any meaningful work assignments other than to "make nice with one another."

- *Failing to provide adequate training for team members and team leaders.* Some organizations form teams and then expect employees, long accustomed to individual responsibilities, to magically become team players and contributors. Teams are very complex social systems influenced by pressures from within and buffeted by forces from without, and workers need training to become effective team players.

- *Sabotaging teams with underperformers.* Rather than fire poor performers (always an unpleasant task), some managers put them on teams, hoping that the members will either discipline them or get rid of them. It never works. Underperfomers undermine team performance.

- *Switching to team responsibilities but keeping pay individually oriented.* One of the quickest ways to destroy a team system is to pay team members based on their individual performances.

Teams work best in creative environments, and entrepreneurs who use them must establish an organizational structure that supports them. Teams do not fit naturally into a company's layers of hierarchy, and managers must adjust appraisal, compensation, and motivation systems to suit a team-based approach. Employees serving on teams also need support in the form of training in the team process. Successful teams do not just happen; they require planning, adequate resources, and managerial support. In essence, building a successful team-based structure requires some effort on an entrepreneur's part. To ensure teams' success, managers must:

- *Make sure that teams are appropriate for the company and the nature of its work.* A good starting point is to create a "map" of the company's work flow that shows how workers build a product or deliver a service. Is the work interdependent, complex, and interactive? Would teamwork improve the company's performance?

- *Make sure that teams are appropriate for the task to be accomplished.* Nothing ensures the failure of a team faster than assigning it a task that individuals should be performing.

- *Form teams around the natural work flow and give them specific tasks to accomplish.* Teams can be effective only if managers challenge them to accomplish specific, measurable objectives.

- *Provide adequate support and training for team members and leaders.* Team success requires a new set of skills. Workers must learn how to communicate, resolve conflict, support one another, and solve problems as a team. Smart managers see that workers get the training they need.

- *Involve team members in determining how their performances will be measured, what will be measured, and when it will be measured.* Doing so gives team members a sense of ownership and pride about what they are accomplishing.

- *Make at least part of team members' pay dependent on team performance.* Companies that have used teams successfully still pay members individually, but they make successful team work a major part of an individual's performance review. For teams to succeed, at least part of team members' compensation must be based on the team's performance.

Whole Foods, a natural foods supermarket founded in 1978, relies on employees' participation in self-directed work teams to run its more than 200 stores. Company founders John Mackey, Craig Weller, and Mark Skiles decided to use a highly decentralized management structure built around self-directed teams early in the life of the business, creating the team structure when they opened their second store. Their goal was to allow decisions to be made at the level closest to customers and to help workers feel connected to the company. Whole Food's growth has been phenomenal over the years, but the company still uses the team concept; in fact, its workers are known as "team members," not "employees." Stores have an average of 10 teams, and every employee, including part-time workers, is a member of a team. Teams handle their own hiring, firing, training, purchasing, and scheduling. Management shares extensive financial information with teams, and a part of every team member's compensation is based on the team's performance. Managers at Whole Foods credit the team structure with maintaining an innovative atmosphere, with keeping team members highly motivated, and with sustaining the company's growth and above-average profitability.[25]

motivation—*the degree of effort an employee exerts to accomplish a task; it shows up as excitement about work.*

Table 15.9 shows the four stages that teams go through on their way to performing effectively and accomplishing results.

THE CHALLENGE OF MOTIVATING WORKERS

Motivation is the degree of effort an employee exerts to accomplish a task; it shows up as excitement about work. Motivating workers to higher levels of performance is one of the most difficult and challenging tasks facing a small business manager. Few things are more frustrating to a business owner than an employee with a tremendous amount of talent who lacks the desire to use it. Employees who consistently display a lack of excitement about work and never seem to "live up" to their potential stand out in small firms. Nonmotivated workers create friction because entrepreneurs are themselves almost always highly motivated overachievers. This section discusses four aspects of motivation: empowerment, job design, rewards and compensation, and feedback.

TABLE 15.9
The Stages of Team Development

Source: Mark Frohman, "Do Teams . . . But Do Them Right," *Industry Week,* April 3, 1995, p. 22.

Stage	Description	Leader Focus
1. Start-up	High expectations Unclear goals and roles	Task focus Provide goals and structure Supervise start-up and define accountability
2. Reality strikes	Recognition of time and effort required Roadblocks Frustration	Task and process emphasis Clarify expectations and roles Encourage open discussions and address concerns Ensure proper skills and resource
3. Realigning expectations	Goals and roles reset Cooperation and trust begin to produce progress	Process focus Promote participation and team decision making Encourage peer support Provide feedback
4. Performance	Involvement, openness, and teamwork Commitment to process and task achievement	Monitoring and feedback focus Let team take responsibility for solving problems and making decisions Monitor progress and supply feedback

Empowerment

One of the principles underlying the team-based management style discussed in the previous section is empowerment. **Empowerment** involves giving workers at every level of the organization the power, the freedom, and the responsibility to control their own work, to make decisions, and to take action to meet the company's objectives. Competitive forces and a more demanding workforce challenge business owners and managers to share power with everyone in the organization, whether they use a team-based approach or not.

Empowering employees requires a different style of management and leadership from that of the traditional manager. Many old-style managers are unwilling to share power with anyone because they fear doing so weakens their authority and reduces their influence. In fact, exactly the opposite is true! Business owners who share information, responsibility, authority, and power soon discover that their success (and their companies' success, too) is magnified many times over. Empowered workers become more successful on the job, which means the entrepreneur also becomes more successful.

Empowerment builds on what real business leaders already know: that the people in their organizations bring with them to work an amazing array of talents, skills, knowledge, and abilities. Workers are willing—even anxious—to put these to use; unfortunately, in too many small businesses, suffocating management styles and poorly designed jobs quash workers' enthusiasm and motivation. Enlightened business owners recognize their workers' abilities, develop them, and then give workers the freedom and the power to use those abilities. Motivated and trained employees work best when given the opportunity to use their own creativity and imagination.

When implemented properly, empowerment can produce impressive results, not only for the small business but also for newly empowered employees. For the business, benefits typically include significant productivity gains, quality improvements, more satisfied customers, improved morale, and increased employee motivation. When one manufacturing plant switched to empowered process improvement teams, workers used their newfound freedom to unleash a torrent of new ideas aimed at improving the company's performance. The teams were able to reduce cycle time for several key products by as much as 33 percent to 60 percent, producing huge savings and improving customer satisfaction. Other suggestions by the teams enabled the materials storage department to triple its productivity![26]

empowerment—*the process of giving workers at every level of the organization the power, the freedom, and the responsibility to control their own work, to make decisions, and to take action to meet the company's objectives.*

For workers, empowerment offers the chance to do a greater variety of work that is more interesting and challenging. Empowerment challenges workers to make the most of their creativity, imagination, knowledge, and skills. This method of management encourages them to take the initiative to identify and solve problems on their own and as part of a team. As empowered workers see how the various parts of a company's manufacturing or service systems fit together, they realize their need to acquire more skills and knowledge to do their jobs well. Entrepreneurs must realize that empowerment and training go hand in hand.

Not every worker wants to be empowered, however. Some will resist, wanting only to "put in their eight hours and go home." One expert estimates that companies moving to empowerment can expect to lose about 5 percent of their workforce. "Out of every 100 employees, five are diehards who will be impossible to change," he says. Another 75 percent will accept empowerment and thrive under it, if it is done properly. The remaining 20 percent will pounce eagerly on empowerment because it is something they "have been waiting to do . . . their whole [work] lives," he says.[27] Empowerment works best when a business owner:

- *Is confident enough to give workers all of the authority and responsibility they can handle.* Early on, this may mean giving workers the power to tackle relatively simple assignments. But, as their confidence and ability grow, most workers are eager to take on more responsibility.

- *Plays the role of coach and facilitator, not the role of meddlesome boss.* One surefire way to make empowerment fail is to give associates the power to attack a problem and then to hover over them, criticizing every move they make. Smart owners empower their workers and then get out of the way so they can do their jobs!

- *Recognizes that empowered employees will make mistakes.* The worst thing an owner can do when empowered employees make mistakes is to hunt them down and punish them. That teaches everyone in the company to avoid taking risks and to always play it safe—something no innovative small business can afford.

- *Hires people who can blossom in an empowered environment.* Empowerment is not for everyone. Owners quickly learn that as costly as hiring mistakes are, such errors are even more costly in an empowered environment. Ideal candidates are high-energy self-starters who enjoy the opportunity to grow and to enhance their skills.

- *Trains workers continuously to upgrade their skills.* Empowerment demands more of workers than traditional work methods. Managers are asking workers to solve problems and make decisions they have never made before. To handle these problems well, workers need training, especially in effective problem-solving techniques, communication, teamwork, and technical skills. Investing in employee training also improves employee retention.

- *Trusts workers to do their jobs.* Once workers are trained to do their jobs, owners must learn to trust them to assume responsibility for their jobs. After all, they are the *real* experts; they face the problems and challenges every day. One Japanese study found that workers "in the trenches" knew 100 percent of the problems in a company; supervisors knew 74 percent; and top managers knew just 4 percent![28]

- *Listens to workers when they have ideas, solutions, or suggestions.* Because they are the experts on the job, employees often come up with incredibly insightful, innovative ideas for improving them—if business owners give them the chance. Failing to acknowledge or to act on employees' ideas sends them a clear message: Their ideas really don't count.

- *Shares information with workers.* For empowerment to succeed, business owners must make sure workers get adequate information, the raw material for good decision making. Some companies have gone beyond sharing information to embrace **open-book management**, in which employees have access to all of a company's records, including its financial statements. The goal of open-book management is to enable employees to understand why they need to raise productivity, improve quality, cut costs, and improve customer service. Open-book management becomes the ultimate form of employee involvement. Under open-book management, employees (1) see and learn to understand the company's financial statements and other critical numbers in measuring its performance; (2) learn that a significant part of their jobs is making sure those critical numbers move in the right direction; and (3) have a direct stake in the company's success through profit sharing, ESOPs, or performance-based bonuses. To work, open-book management must not only make sure that workers understand how their company makes a profit but also how they can influence its financial results. One expert writes, "Instead of telling employees how to cut defects, [open-book management] asks them to boosts profits—and lets them figure out how. Instead of giving them a reengineered job, it turns them into businesspeople. They experience the

open-book management—
the process of giving employees access to all of a company's records, including its financial statements, so they can understand why they need to raise productivity, improve quality, cut costs, and improve customer service.

challenge—and the sheer fun and excitement—of matching wits with the marketplace, toting up the score, and sharing in the proceeds. . . . There's no better motivation."[29]

- *Recognizes workers' contributions.* One of the most important tasks a business owner has is to recognize jobs well done. Some businesses reward workers with monetary awards; others rely on recognition and praise; still others use a combination of money and praise. Whatever system an owner chooses, the key to keeping a steady flow of ideas, improvements, suggestions, and solutions is to recognize the people who supply them.

*The **Great Harvest Bread Company** was founded in 1976 by Pete and Laura Wakeman in Dillon, Montana and has grown through franchising to 137 stores. The business does $60 million a year in sales systemwide and has become an example of a firm that learns from listening to its franchisees. One new franchisee came up with an idea for how she could implement the Great Harvest Bread Company's corporate value of "giving back generously to the local community." Her idea for a "Baker for the Day" program allowed each store to work in its community with local community groups to make and sell bread on Sunday (a day when the store is normally closed), with all of the profits on that day contributed to the community project. The program was a success and has been implemented by many other franchisees.*[30]

Job Design

Over the years, managers have learned that the job itself and the way it is designed can be a source of motivation (or demotivation!) for workers. In some companies, work is organized on the principle of **job simplification**, breaking the work down into its simplest form and standardizing each task, as in some assembly-line operations. The scope of jobs organized in such a way is extremely narrow, resulting in impersonal, monotonous, and boring work that creates little challenge or motivation for workers. Job simplification invites workers to "check their brains at the door" and offers them little opportunity for excitement, enthusiasm, or pride in their work. The result can be apathetic, unmotivated workers who don't care about quality, customers, or costs.

job simplification—*the type of job design that breaks work down into its simplest form and standardizes each task.*

To break this destructive cycle, some companies have redesigned jobs so that they offer workers intrinsic rewards and motivation. Three strategies are common: job enlargement, job rotation, and job enrichment.

Job enlargement (or horizontal job loading) adds more tasks to a job to broaden its scope. For instance, rather than an employee simply mounting four screws in computers coming down an assembly line, a worker might assemble, install, and test the entire motherboard (perhaps as part of a team). The idea is to make the job more varied and to allow employees to perform a more complete unit of work.

job enlargement—*the type of job design that adds more tasks to a job to broaden its scope.*

Job rotation involves cross-training employees so they can move from one job in the company to others, giving them a greater number and variety of tasks to perform. As employees learn other jobs within an organization, both their skills and their understanding of the company's purpose and processes improve. Cross-trained workers are more valuable because they give a company the flexibility to shift workers from low-demand jobs to those where they are most needed. As an incentive for workers to learn to perform other jobs within an operation, some companies offer skill-based pay, a system under which the more skills workers acquire, the more they earn.

job rotation—*the type of job design that involves cross-training employees so they can move from one job in the company to others, giving them a greater number and variety of tasks to perform.*

Job enrichment (or vertical job loading) involves building motivators into a job by increasing the planning, decision-making, organizing, and controlling functions—traditional managerial tasks—workers perform. The idea is to make every employee a manager—at least a manager of his own job. Notice that empowerment, the management technique discussed in the previous section, is based on the principle of job enrichment.

job enrichment—*the type of job design that involves building motivators into a job by increasing the planning, decision-making, organizing, and controlling functions workers perform.*

To enrich employees' jobs, a business owner must build five core characteristics into them:

- *Skill variety* is the degree to which a job requires a variety of different skills, talents, and activities from the worker. Does the job require the worker to perform a variety of tasks that demand a variety of skills and abilities or does it force him to perform the same task repeatedly?
- *Task identity* is the degree to which a job allows the worker to complete a whole or identifiable piece of work. Does the employee build an entire piece of furniture (perhaps as part of a team) or does he merely attach four screws?

- *Task significance* is the degree to which a job substantially influences the lives or work of others—employees or final customers. Does the employee get to deal with customers, either internal or external? One effective way to establish task significance is to put employees in touch with customers so they can see how customers use the product or service they make.

- *Autonomy* is the degree to which a job gives a worker the freedom, independence, and discretion in planning and performing tasks. Does the employee make decisions affecting his work or must he rely on someone else (e.g., the owner, a manager, or a supervisor) to "call the shots?"

- *Feedback* is the degree to which a job gives the worker direct, timely information about the quality of his performance. Does the job give employees feedback about the quality of their work or does the product (and all information about it) simply disappear after it leaves the worker's station?

Some organizational design questions do not have simple-to-apply textbook answers.

A Company Example

Consider the struggles of Douglas Green, founder of **Green Design Furniture Company** *of Portland, Maine. Green struggled to design an operating system that minimizes labor and material cost while ensuring exceptionally high-quality products. In search of this outcome, he invested in sophisticated furniture-making equipment he hoped would reduce his cost of production. Labor cost with the new equipment was approximately $50 per hour. Then, after an attempt to involve employees in the design of the production, scheduling, and workplace environment, Green discovered that labor cost rose from $50 to $70. The new employee-designed system was creating a bottleneck in production. The result was that production declined and orders were shipping late. In response, Green began to build furniture "to stock" in hopes that he would have the necessary inventory to meet demand. Inventory increased by more than 2000 percent and cost of goods sold increased dramatically. Green and his employees redesigned the production system once again, and costs fell. The average time between receiving an order and shipping is also improving. Job design and production layout are not "cookie-cutter" problems. Even experienced entrepreneurs like Douglas Green must constantly struggle to fine-tune a model that can result in a fair return on their invested capital.*[31]

As the nation's workers and the companies employing them continue to change, business is changing the way people work, moving away from a legion of full-time employees in traditional 8-to-5, full-time, on-site jobs. Significant changes in the demographic profile of the nation's workforce are requiring employers to change the way they organize jobs. By 2010, workers will be older, more racially and culturally diverse, and less loyal to any individual employer. In addition, the shortage of workers will worsen. The effect of these changes on business owners will be significant. Companies will be required to offer an ever broader array of work schedules and structures, including flextime, job sharing, flexplace, and telecommuting.

flextime—*an arrangement under which employees work a normal number of hours but have flexibility about when they start and stop work.*

Flextime is an arrangement under which employees work a normal number of hours but have flexibility about when they start and stop work. Most flextime arrangements require employees to build their work schedules around a set of "core hours," such as 11 A.M. to 2 P.M., but give them the freedom to set their schedules outside of those core hours. For instance, one worker might choose to come in at 7 A.M. and leave at 3 P.M. to attend her son's soccer game, whereas another may work from 11 A.M. to 7 P.M. Flextime not only raises worker morale, but it also makes it easier for companies to attract high-quality young workers who want rewarding careers without sacrificing their lifestyles. In addition, companies using flextime schedules often experience lower levels of tardiness, turnover, and absenteeism. Linda Field, founder of Field & Associates, a marketing and public relations firm in Houston, Texas, says that offering flextime helps her employees keep their work and their lives in balance and brings her company a larger pool of more qualified applicants.[32]

Flextime is becoming a popular job design strategy. A recent survey by the Society for Human Resource Management found that 55 percent of the nation's workers have flexible schedules, up from just 15 percent in 1991.[33] That percentage will grow because flextime is an important job design strategy for some companies that find it difficult to recruit capable, qualified full-time workers. Research shows that when considering job offers candidates weigh heavily the flexibility of the work schedule companies offer.

Job sharing is a work arrangement in which two or more people share a single full-time job. For instance, two college students might share the same 40-hour-a-week job, one working mornings and the other working afternoons. Salary and benefits are prorated between the workers sharing a job. Because job sharing is a simple solution to the growing challenge of life-and-work balance, it will become more popular in the future. A recent study by the Society of Human Resource Management found that 22 percent of companies in the United States currently offer job sharing.[34] Companies already using it are finding it easier to recruit and retain qualified workers. "Employers get the combined strengths of two people, but they only have to pay for one," says one hotel sales manager, herself a job sharer.[35]

Flexplace is a work arrangement in which employees work at a place other than the traditional office, such as a satellite branch closer to their homes or, in many cases, at home. Flexplace is an easy job design strategy for companies to use because of **telecommuting**. Using modern communication technology such as e-mail, voice mail, fax machines, and portable computers, employees have more flexibility in choosing where they work. Today, it is quite simple for workers to hook up electronically to their workplaces (and to all of the people and the information there) from practically anywhere on the planet. Telecommuting employees get the flexibility they seek, and they also benefit from reduced commuting times and expenses, not to mention a less expensive wardrobe (bathrobes and bunny slippers compared to business suits and wingtips). Companies reap many benefits as well, including improved employee morale, less absenteeism, lower turnover, and higher productivity. One study of companies using telecommuting found that employee turnover fell by 20 percent and that productivity climbed between 15 percent and 20 percent.[36]

Despite the many benefits that telecommuting offers both employers and employees, small companies are less likely to use it as a job design strategy than large businesses. Although 90 percent of companies with more than 5,000 employees use telecommuting; only 40 percent of small businesses do.[37]

*Iris Feinberg, president of **Trillium Group** of Decatur, Georgia, has 45 of her 65 employees telecommuting, but this work option is only available once employees have proven themselves in the office setting. No employee is guaranteed the opportunity to telecommute. Trillium Group requires employees to work in-house full time for the first 90 days before they become eligible, and employees who do work from home are required to report to the office one day a week. Their experience has been that success in telecommuting results when all work expectations have been spelled out and both parties agree to them and to keeping the lines of communication open. Supervisors visit employees who are telecommuting to ensure that the agreement is being met. Trillium Group has found that the opportunity to telecommute has helped to reduce employee turnover by retaining good employees. Feinberg believes that, "With the right people in place, the right system to accommodate work-at-home employees, and the right policies to manage them, telecommuting can strengthen staff members' ties to the company, even while they work from a distance."[38]*

A Company Example

Before implementing telecommuting, entrepreneurs must address the following important issues:

- Does the nature of the work fit telecommuting? Obviously, some jobs are better suited to telecommuting than others.
- Have you selected the right employees for telecommuting? Telecommuting is not suitable for every job or for every worker. Experienced managers say that employees who handle it best are experienced workers who know their jobs well, are self-disciplined, and are good communicators.
- Can you monitor compliance with federal wage and hour laws for telecommuters? Generally, employers must keep the same employment records for telecommuters that they do for traditional office workers.
- Are you adequately insured? Employers should be sure that the telecommuting equipment employees use in their homes is covered under their insurance policies.
- Can you keep in touch? Telecommuting works well as long as long-distance employees stay in touch with headquarters.
- Have you created an equitable telecommuting policy? One danger of telecommuting is that it can create resentment among employees who remain office-bound.

job sharing—*a work arrangement in which two or more people share a single full-time job.*

flexplace—*a work arrangement in which employees work at a place other than the traditional office, such as a satellite branch closer to their homes or at home.*

telecommuting—*an arrangement under which employees working from their homes use modern communications equipment to hook up electronically to their workplaces.*

hoteling—an arrangement in
which employees who spend
most of their time away from the
office use the same office space
at different times.

A variation of telecommuting that is growing in popularity is **hoteling**, in which employees who spend most of their time away from the office use the same office space at different times, just as travelers use the same hotel room on different days. Hoteling requires advance planning and coordination, but businesses that use it have been able to reduce the cost of leasing office space, sometimes by as much as 50 percent. Flexible office designs and furnishings allow workers to configure these "hot offices" (so called because they usually turn over so quickly that the seats are still hot from the previous user) to suit their particular needs.

A Company Example

When Lou Hoffman, founder of a professional services firm in San Jose, California, realized that employees were using only 45 percent of the company's existing office space regularly, he implemented hoteling. One-third of the company's 65 employees began sharing office space on a rotating basis, and Hoffman added temporary workstations to handle the occasional overflows and schedule conflicts. Hoffman estimates that hoteling saved his company $130,000 in less than one year![39]

Rewards and Compensation

The rewards an employee gets from the job itself are intrinsic rewards, but managers have at their disposal a wide variety of extrinsic rewards (those outside the job itself) to motivate workers. The key to using rewards to motivate involves tailoring them to the needs and characteristics of the workers. Rewards and compensation must be based on offering incentives that are really important to people. Consequently, it is critical to take the time to find out what those are and structure recognition around those in the context of the job. For instance, to a technician making $25,000 a chance to earn a $3,000 performance bonus would most likely be a powerful motivator. To an executive earning $175,000 a year, it may not be.

One of the most popular rewards is money. Cash is an effective motivator—up to a point. Over the last 20 years, many companies have moved to **pay-for-performance compensation systems**, in which employees' pay depends on how well they perform their jobs. In other words, extra productivity equals extra pay. By linking employees' compensation directly to the company's financial performance, a business owner increases the likelihood that workers will achieve performance targets that are in their best interest and in the company's best interest. These systems work only when employees see a clear connection between their performances and their pay, however. That's where small businesses have an advantage over large businesses. Because they work for small companies, employees can see more clearly the impact their performances have on the company's profitability and ultimate success than their counterparts at large corporations.

pay-for-performance
compensation system—a
compensation system in which
employees' pay depends on how
well they perform their jobs.

To make sure that the salaries they pay are competitive, entrepreneurs can consult a variety of sources. The Bureau of Labor Statistics publishes the *Occupational Outlook Handbook*, which provides pay rates and job forecasts for hundreds of occupations. The Bureau of Labor Statistics Web site (www.bls.gov) contains wage and salary data by region. Other useful sources are the *American Wages and Salary Survey* published by Gale Research, the *American Almanac of Jobs and Salaries*, JobStar (www.jobsmart.org), and Wageweb (www.wageweb.com).

Money isn't the only motivator business owners have at their disposal, of course. In fact, money tends to be only a short-term motivator. In addition to the financial compensation they provide, most companies offer their employees a wide array of benefits, ranging from stock options and medical insurance to retirement plans and tuition reimbursement. **Stock options**, a plan under which the employees can purchase shares of a company's stock at a fixed price, have become a popular benefit for employees, especially in the new economy. Stock options take on real value once the fair market price of a company's stock exceeds the exercise price, the price at which employees can purchase stock. (Note that if the fair market price of a stock never exceeds the exercise price, the stock option is useless.) When trying to attract and retain quality employees, many small companies rely on stock options to gain an edge over larger companies offering bigger salaries.

stock options—a plan under
which employees can purchase
shares of a company's stock at a
fixed price.

A Company Example

*For example, Dick Plodzien, CEO of **Spencer Reed Group, Inc.**, a privately owned executive search and staffing company in Overland Park, Kansas, uses stock options to attract and retain quality employees. Not only has the stock option plan slowed the number of employees defecting to larger companies offering bigger salaries, but it also has enabled Plodzien to entice several executives to leave billion-dollar companies to join Spencer Reed.*[40]

Sometimes stock options produce a huge payoff for employees. Workers at highly successful companies such as Microsoft and Dell have retired early as multimillionaires thanks to stock options.

In an economy where they must compete aggressively for employees, entrepreneurs must recognize that compensation and benefits are no longer "one-size-fits-all" issues. The diversity of today's workforce requires employers to be highly flexible and innovative in the compensation and benefits they provide. To attract and retain quality workers, creative entrepreneurs offer employees a set of benefits designed to appeal to their individual needs and preferences. This diversity has led to the popularity of cafeteria benefit plans, in which employers provide certain base benefits and then allocate a specific dollar amount for employees to select the benefits that suit their needs best. Beyond flexible benefits plans, many small companies are setting themselves apart from others by offering unique benefits such as the following:[41]

- Clothing retailer Eddie Bauer offers employees on-site massages to ease tension and to enhance creativity.
- Starbucks, a chain of coffee shops, provides its employees with a personal concierge service that handles employees' errands. Need to make reservations at a restaurant and to order flowers for your friend's birthday celebration? The concierge will take care of it for you!
- Numerous Silicon Valley companies provide catered meals, on-site kitchens filled with fruit and snacks, and gymnasiums and athletic fields for employees. At Clif Bar, a 65-employee company that makes energy bars, employees on breaks can scale the 22-foot-high climbing wall located in the company gym. Clif Bar also hires trainers to conduct classes in aerobics, weight lifting, and other workouts on company time.
- At its San Jose, California headquarters, Cisco Systems Inc. operates a child care center for its employees' children, complete with Internet cameras so parents can connect to the Internet and check on their kids.
- One company that writes software for the insurance industry has an ultramodern exercise facility open 24 hours a day for its employees. Not only does the facility help recruit and retain workers, but the company's health insurance costs also have declined since it opened.
- Employees at Adobe Systems Inc. get a three-week paid sabbatical leave every five years to pursue some topic of interest to them.
- When workers at Gould Evans Goodman Associates, a Kansas City architectural firm, need a break, they can retreat to one of the company's "spent tents," camping tents set up in a corner complete with pillows, sleeping bags, soothing music, and alarm clocks (of course!).

Besides the wages, salaries, and attractive benefits they use as motivators, creative entrepreneurs have discovered that intangible incentives can be more important sources of employee motivation. After its initial impact, money does not have a lasting motivational effect (which for small businesses, with their limited resources, is a plus). Often for workers the most meaningful motivational factors are the simplest ones—praise, recognition, feedback, job security, promotions, and others—things that any small business, no matter how limited its budget, can do. When the economy is in a downturn, a business that can display its commitment to employees through a record of job security has a powerful tool to recruit good employees.

Entrepreneurs find that younger workers, especially "Generation Xers," respond best to intangible rewards and not to monetary rewards. Wanting more balance in their work and personal lives than their baby boomer parents, Generation X workers are looking for workplaces that offer challenging assignments coupled with a sense of fun. They respond best to constant feedback that is specific and accurate and to managers who take the time to celebrate their successes. The following suggestions will help entrepreneurs motivate and reward their Generation X employees:

- Give them challenging assignments that allow them to learn more skills. Generation X workers value education and want to upgrade their knowledge continuously.
- Give them jobs that require diverse skills and have an observable impact on the company's mission.
- Treat them as individuals and allow them to express their individuality at work.
- Avoid an authoritarian approach. They thrive in a participative work environment.

The New Company Town

The company office complex in the new economy looks very different from the nondescript, open offices so popular in the 1980s and 1990s with their walls painted institutional tan and lined with the cubicles that cartoon character Dilbert toils in every day. With a war raging among companies to attract the most qualified workers, many businesses are using their offices and a host of unique perks as recruiting and retention tools. Some companies provide their employees with in-house or take-home meals to free them from the drudgery of cooking for themselves. Others offer concierge services to help employees take care of the thousands of details that make up everyday life such as buying gifts, picking up laundry, or making reservations. Some offer on-site child care facilities and classes on gardening, sculpting, public speaking, karate, or scuba diving. The goal of these benefits is not only to attract and retain quality workers but also to free them up to focus on doing their jobs. Companies know that many workers will be on site from dawn to dusk and are doing everything they can to make employees' lives easier and more manageable. "Companies are taking the best aspects of home and incorporating them into work," says one expert.

What's behind these companies' efforts? Workers in the United States seem to be busier than ever, leaving little time for fun activities. Taking up that precious time with mundane tasks makes no sense, and that is the appeal of on-site services at work. "Time is a commodity I don't have a lot of," says Sheila Childs, a product manager in BMC software's research and development department and the mother of four children. "The amenities definitely make it comfortable for you to be [at work]." Childs's story is echoed in millions of homes across the United States. A study by the International Labor Organization found that the typical worker in the United States works 1,966 hours per year, even more than the 1,889 hours the legendary workaholic Japanese employee does!

BMC Software in Houston, Texas, has created a unique company campus designed to appeal to every aspect of its high-tech workers' busy lives. BMC has built what comes close to being a self-contained community so complete that one worker says. "You never have to leave the place." When employees are not in their offices, they can lounge on hammocks strung between trees on the company's grounds, lift weights in the gym, play a pickup game on the basketball court, practice their putting on the green, play horseshoes, or get in a friendly game of beach volleyball. Walking past the herb garden, employees might see cooks busily gathering fresh oregano to use in a company-provided lunch. On each floor of BMC's two glass towers is a large kitchen well stocked with fruit, popcorn, soft drinks, and coffee. Employees can dine in spacious booths and watch television on the big-screen TV. A sign in a hallway says "Massage Therapy This Way." In the lobby, a Steinway player piano plays a repertoire of both snappy tunes and relaxing minuets as employees and guests move about. A company valet picks up employees' cars scheduled for washes and oil changes. Also within the office complex are a bank, a store, a dry cleaner, a hairdresser, and a nail salon.

1. What are the benefits to companies and to workers of the services and facilities such as the one at BMC Software? What potential disadvantages do you see with companies offering these services and facilities?

2. Would *you* want to work at a company such as BMC Software? Explain.

Source: Jerry Useem, "Welcome to the New Company Store," *Fortune*, January 10, 2000, pp. 62–70.

■ Trust them. One of the biggest turnoffs for Generation X employees is a manager who constantly checks up on them, indicating a lack of trust.

■ Offer them varied assignments and frequent rewards (not necessarily money). Generation X workers want to be challenged by a variety of tasks, and they expect frequent feedback on their performance.

Praise is another simple yet powerful motivational tool. People enjoy getting praise, especially from a manager or business owner; it's just human nature. As Mark Twain once said, "I can live for two months on a good compliment." Praise is an easy and inexpensive reward for employees producing extraordinary work. A short note to an employee for a job well done costs practically nothing; yet it can be a potent source of motivation. How often have you had an employer say "thank-you" when you performed well?

A Company Example

*At **Mary Kay Cosmetics'** annual meeting, praise and saying "thank-you" are the watchwords. Indeed, they are the main reasons more than 36,000 beauty consultants from around the world gather in Dallas every year. At the meeting, superstar saleswomen receive praise and recognition from their peers and from top managers in sessions that resemble a cross between an awards banquet and a tent revival. Women come away with crowns, sashes, pins, bracelets, and, of course, those coveted pink Cadillacs—and a zealous fervor to go out and sell lots of makeup! "This is a company that understands that positive emotions can be good for the soul," says Gloria Mayfield Hayes, senior sales director.[42]*

One of the surest ways to kill high performance is simply to fail to recognize it and the employees responsible for it. Failing to praise good work eventually conveys the message that an entrepreneur either doesn't care about exceptional performance or cannot distinguish between good work and poor work. In either case, through inaction, the business owner destroys employees' motivation to excel.

Because they lack the financial resources of bigger companies, small business owners must be more creative when it comes to giving rewards that motivate workers. In many cases, however, using rewards other than money gives small businesses an advantage because they usually have more impact on employee performance over time. Rewards do not have to be expensive to be effective.

The late Mary Kay Ash, founder of Mary Kay Cosmetics, believed that praise is a powerful motivator. Every year, more than 36,000 beauty consultants gather in Dallas to receive rewards for a job well done, a tradition that Mary Kay herself started.

Courtesy of Corbis Bettmann, © Douglas Kirkland/Corbis.

A Company Example

At **Mackay Envelope Corporation**, managers "go around and try to catch people in the act of doing something right," says owner Harvey Mackay. "Managers have a fistful of tickets to Vikings and Timberwolves games, to the opera and to Broadway shows, and we reward them right on the spot. We praise them in front of mother, God, and country!" he says.[43]

In the future, managers will rely more on nonmonetary rewards such as praise, recognition, game tickets, dinners, letters of commendation, and others to create a work environment where employees take pride in their work, enjoy it, are challenged by it, and get excited about it: in other words, act like owners of the business themselves. The goal is to let employees know that "every person is important" (see Table 15.10).

Table 15.11 offers the "20 Top Ways to Motivate Employees," which is based on the results of a survey of some of the nation's leading motivational experts.

Feedback

Business owners not only must motivate employees to excel in their jobs, but they must also focus their efforts on the right targets. Providing feedback on progress toward those targets can be a powerful motivating force in a company. To ensure that the link between her vision for the company and its operations is strong, an entrepreneur must build a series of specific performance measures that serve as periodic monitoring points. For each critical element of the organization's performance (e.g., product or service quality, financial performance, market position, productivity, employee development, etc.), the owner should develop specific measures that connect daily operational responsibilities with the company's overall strategic direction. These measures become the benchmarks for measuring employees' performances and the company's progress. The adage "what gets measured and monitored gets done" is true for most organizations. By connecting the company's long-term strategy to its daily operations and measuring performance, an entrepreneur makes it clear to everyone in the company what is most important. Jack Stack,

---

TABLE 15.10

Xvxry Pxrson Is Important

Source: "You Arx a Kxy Pxrson," *Pasadena Weekly Journal of Business,* 155 S. El Molino Avenue, Suite 101, Pasadena, California 91101.

One business owner let employees know how valuable they are with the following memo:

You Arx a Kxy Pxrson

Xvxn though my typxwritxr is an old modxl, it works vxry wxll—xxcxpt for onx kxy. You would not think that with all thx othxr kxys functioning propxrly, onx kxy not working would hardly bx noticxd; but just onx kxy out of whack sxxms to ruin thx wholx xffort.

You may say to yoursxlf—"Wxll, I'm only onx pxrson. No onx will noticx if I don't do my bxst." But it doxs makx a diffxrxnce bxcausx to bx xffxctivx, an organization nxxds activx participation by xvxry onx to thx bxst of his or hxr ability.

So thx nxxt timx you think you arx not important, rxmxbxr my old typxwritxr. You arx a kxy pxrson.

TABLE 15.11

The Top 20 Ways to Motivate Employees

Source: Shari Caudron, "The Top 20 Ways to Motivate Employees," *Industry Week*, April 3, 1995, pp. 12–18.

1. Give employees the information they need to do a good job. Employees need timely information to do their jobs, starting with the company's mission and goals and moving on to information on their specific job responsibilities.

2. Provide regular feedback. Communication should be an ongoing event, giving employees the opportunity to measure and improve their performances.

3. Ask employees for their input and involve them in the decisions that affect their jobs. The people who are performing a job are the real experts, so why not involve them in the decision-making process? At one manufacturing plant, workers, not managers, made all of the decisions relating to the purchase of a $3 million piece of equipment. After all, they were the ones who would be using it.

4. Establish easy-to-use channels of communication. Managers should give employees the opportunity to express their ideas and suggestions on workplace issues. Effective managers learn to become good listeners.

5. Learn from employees themselves what motivates them. Because what motivates each employee is different, managers must customize the rewards they offer. The best way to find out what employees want is to get to know them and then ask them.

6. Learn what on-the-job activities employees choose to do when they have free time and then create opportunities for them to perform those activities on a more regular basis. Employees do well at those tasks they enjoy most.

7. Personally congratulate employees for jobs well done. A survey of 1,500 employees from a variety of work settings found that the most powerful motivator was recognition. Not only is it powerful, but it also doesn't cost anything.

8. Recognize the power of a manager's presence. Employees like frequent contact with their managers, however brief, because it indicates that the manager recognizes the importance of their work.

9. Write personal notes to employees about their performances. Such tangible recognition is a powerful motivator. These notes often make it to the home hall of fame—the refrigerator door.

10. Publicly recognize employees for good work. Given that one-on-one recognition is such an important motivator, consider the power of public recognition to accelerate an employee's performance.

11. Include morale-building meetings that celebrate team success. Although they don't have to be elaborate, team success celebrations help employees build camaraderie and a sense of togetherness.

12. Give employees good jobs to do. Boring, routine, unchallenging work saps employee motivation faster than anything. Proper job design is an important part of effective motivation.

13. Make sure employees have the tools available to do their best work. Like good mechanics, smart managers know that doing a job well requires the right tools. Plus, when managers provide good equipment, employees see it as an investment in their abilities.

14. Recognize employees' personal needs. With so many dual-career families in our society, workers appreciate companies that acknowledge and care for their personal needs by offering flextime, on-site day care, personal time allowances, and other conveniences.

15. Use performance as the basis for promotions. Although it makes sense to promote those employees who are the best and the most productive, too many companies continue to use seniority or politics to determine who gets promoted.

16. Establish a comprehensive promote-from-within policy. One of the best ways to spur employees to higher levels of performance is to show them that doing so leads to promotions within the company.

17. Emphasize the company's commitment to long-term employment. Although no company can offer a blanket "no-layoff" guarantee in this age, managers can communicate a "lifetime employment without guarantees" attitude. Job security for top performers is an important source of motivation.

18. Foster a sense of community. Forming a company around teams is a great way to start, but encouraging employees to recognize fellow workers for top performances can do wonders.

19. Pay people competitively based on what they are worth. If employees believe they are compensated fairly, they won't be preoccupied with their paychecks, and a company can get the most from its nonfinancial awards.

20. Give employees a financial reason to excel by offering them a share of the profits or a share of the company. Employees begin to act like owners when they are owners. Sharing ownership—or at least profits—gives them a major incentive to do everything they can to see that the company prospers.

the father of "open-book" management and CEO of Springfield Remanufacturing Corporation, explains the importance of focusing every employee's attention on key performance targets:

> To be successful in business, you have to be going somewhere, and everyone involved in getting you there has to know where it is. That's a basic rule, a higher law, but most companies miss . . . the fact that you have a much better chance of winning if everyone knows what it takes to win.[44]

Getting or giving feedback implies that a business owner has established meaningful targets that serve as standards of performance for her, her employees, and the company as a whole. One characteristic successful people have in common is that they set goals and objectives—usually challenging ones—for themselves. Business owners are no different. Successful entrepreneurs usually set targets for performance that make them stretch to achieve, and then they encourage their employees to do the same. The result is that they keep their companies constantly moving forward.

For feedback to have impact as a motivating force in a business requires business owners to follow the procedure illustrated in Figure 15.2.

DECIDING WHAT TO MEASURE. The first step in the feedback loop is deciding what to measure. Every business is characterized by a set of numbers that are critical to its success, and these critical numbers are what the entrepreneur should focus on. Obvious critical numbers include sales, profits, profit margins, cash flow, and other standard financial measures. However, running beneath these standard and somewhat universal measures of performance is an undercurrent of critical numbers that are unique to a company's operations. In most cases, these are the numbers that actually drive profits, cash flow, and other financial measures and are the company's real critical numbers.

For instance, in a conversation with another business owner, a hotel franchisee said that his company's critical number was profit and that the way to earn a profit was to control costs. His managerial efforts focused on making sure that his employees knew exactly what to do, how to do it, and how much they could spend doing it. The only problem was that the hotel was losing money.

"Tell me," said his friend, "how do you make money in this business?"

"We fill rooms," said the hotelier.

"How many rooms do you have to fill to break even?"

"Seventy-one percent," came the reply, "but we're only running at 67 percent."

"How many people know that?" asked his friend?

"Two," he said.

"Maybe that's your problem," observed his friend.

The hotel owner quickly realized that one of his company's most critical numbers was occupancy rate; that's what drove profits! His managerial focus had been misguided, and he had failed to get his employees involved in solving the problem. The hotel owner put together an incentive plan for

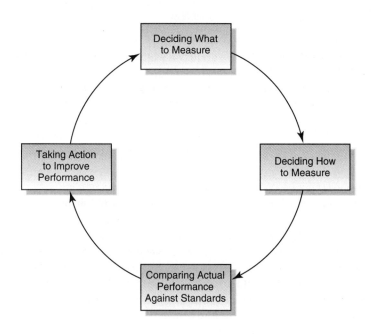

FIGURE 15.2 The Feedback Loop

employees based on occupancy rate. Once the rate surpassed 71 percent, employees qualified for bonuses; the higher the occupancy rate, the bigger the bonuses. He also involved employees in identifying other critical numbers, such as customer retention rates and customer satisfaction levels, and began tracking results and posting them for everyone to see. Before long, every employee in the hotel was involved in and excited about exceeding their targets. The occupancy rate, customer retention rate, and customer satisfaction scores all shot up. The hotel owner had learned not only what his company's critical number was but also how to use it to motivate employees![45]

DECIDING HOW TO MEASURE. Once a business owner identifies his company's critical numbers, the issue of how to best measure them arises. In some cases, identifying the critical numbers defines the measurements the owner must make (e.g., the occupancy rate at the hotel just mentioned) and measuring them simply becomes a matter of collecting and analyzing data. In other cases, the method of measurement is not as obvious or as tangible. For instance, in some businesses, social responsibility is a key factor, but how should a manager measure his company's performance on such an intangible concept? One of the best ways to develop methods for measuring such factors is to use brainstorming sessions involving employees, customers, and even outsiders. For example, one company used this technique to develop a "fun index," which used the results of an employee survey to measure how much fun employees had at work (and, by extension, how satisfied they were with their work, the company, and their managers).

Whatever method a business owner designs to measure a company's critical numbers, it must meet two criteria: validity and reliability. **Validity** is the extent to which a measuring device or technique actually measures what it is intended to measure and how well it measures that factor. **Reliability** is the extent to which a measurement device or technique produces consistent measurements of a factor over time. To be reliable, a measurement technique must be stable. Without measurements that are both valid and reliable, a company could be chasing after solutions to performance gaps that do not really exist! The performance gap appears only because the measurements are faulty or misleading. To avoid this problem, managers and employees should carefully define the measurements they will use to track performance and determine the procedure used to collect and to analyze the data.

COMPARING ACTUAL RESULTS WITH STANDARDS. In this stage of the feedback loop, the idea is to look for deviations in either direction from the performance standards the company has set for itself. In other words, opportunities to improve performance arise when there is a gap between "what should be" and "what is." The most serious deviations usually are those where actual performance falls far below the standard. Managers and employees must focus their efforts on figuring out why actual performance is substandard. The goal is not to hunt down the guilty party (or parties) for punishment but to discover the cause of the subpar performance and fix it. Managers should not ignore deviations in the other direction, however. When actual performance consistently exceeds the company's standards, it is an indication that the standards are set too low. The company should look closely at "raising the bar another notch" to spur motivation.

TAKING ACTION TO IMPROVE PERFORMANCE. When managers or employees detect a performance gap, their next challenge is to decide on which course of action will eliminate it most effectively. Typically, several suitable alternatives to solving a performance problem exist; the key is finding an acceptable solution that solves the problem quickly, efficiently, and effectively.

Performance Appraisal

One of the most common methods of providing feedback on employee performance is through **performance appraisal**, the process of evaluating an employee's actual performance against desired performance standards. Most performance appraisal programs strive to accomplish three goals: (1) to give employees feedback about how they are doing their jobs, which can be an important source of motivation; (2) to provide a business owner and an employee the opportunity to develop a plan for developing the employee's skills and abilities and for improving his performance; and (3) to establish a basis for determining promotions and salary increases. Although the primary purpose of performance appraisals is to encourage and to help employees improve their performances, too often they turn into uncomfortable confrontations that do nothing more than upset the employee, aggravate the business owner, and destroy trust and morale. Why? Because most business owners don't understand how to conduct an effective performance appraisal.

validity—the extent to which a measuring device or technique actually measures what it is intended to measure and how well it measures that factor.

reliability—the extent to which a measurement device or technique produces consistent measurements of a factor over time.

performance appraisal—the process of evaluating an employee's performance against desired performance standards.

Although American business owners have been conducting performance appraisals for more than 90 years, most companies, their managers, and their employees are dissatisfied with the entire process. Common complaints include unclear standards and objectives; managers who lack information about employees' performances; managers who are unprepared or who lack honesty and sincerity; and managers who use general, ambiguous terms to describe employees' performances. Perhaps the biggest complaint concerning appraisals is that they happen only periodically—most often just once a year. Employees do not have the opportunity to receive any ongoing feedback on a regular basis. All too often, a manager saves up all of the negative feedback to give an employee and then dumps it on him in the annual performance review. Not only does it destroy the employee's motivation, but it also does nothing to improve the employee's performance. What good does it do to tell an employee that six months before he botched an assignment that caused the company to lose a customer? The lack of ongoing feedback is like asking employees to bowl in the dark. They can hear some pins falling, but they have no idea which ones are left standing for the next frame. Without detailed feedback, how motivated would you be to keep bowling? Managers should address problems when they occur rather than wait until the performance appraisal session. Continuous feedback, both positive and negative, is a much more effective way to improve employees' performances and to increase their motivation to produce.

MAKING PERFORMANCE APPRAISALS WORK. If done properly, performance appraisals can be effective ways to provide employee feedback and to improve workers' performances. However, it takes planning and preparation on the business owner's part. The following guidelines can help a business owner create a performance appraisal system that actually works:

- *Link the employee's performance criteria to the job description discussed earlier in this chapter.* To evaluate an employee's performance effectively, a manager must understand very well the job the employee performs.

- *Establish meaningful, job-related, observable, measurable, and fair performance criteria.* The criteria should describe behaviors and actions, not traits and characteristics. What kind of behavior constitutes a solid performance in this job?

- *Prepare for the appraisal session by outlining the key points you want to cover with the employee.* Important points to include are the employee's strengths and weaknesses and developing a plan for improving his performance.

- *Invite the employee to provide an evaluation of his own job performance based on the performance criteria.* In one small company, workers rate themselves on a one-to-five scale in categories of job-related behavior and skills as part of the performance appraisal system. Then they meet with their supervisors to compare their evaluations with those of their supervisors and discuss them. Workers also evaluate their bosses as part of the review process.

- *Be specific.* One of the most common complaints employees have about the appraisal process is that managers' comments are too general to be of any value. Offer the employee specific examples of his desirable or undesirable behavior.

- *Keep a record of employees' critical incidents—both positive and negative.* The most productive evaluations are those based on a manager's direct observation of their employees' on-the-job performances. Such records also can be vital in case legal problems arise.

- *Discuss an employee's strengths and weaknesses.* An appraisal session is not the time to "unload" about everything an employee has done wrong over the past year. Use it as an opportunity to design a plan for improvement and to recognize employees' strengths, efforts, and achievements.

- *Incorporate employees' goals into the appraisal.* Ideally, the standard against which to measure an employee's performance is against the goals he has played a role in setting. Workers are more likely to be motivated to achieve goals that they have helped establish.

- *Keep the evaluation constructive.* Avoid the tendency to belittle employees. Do not dwell on past failures. Instead, point out specific things they should do better and help them develop meaningful goals for the future and a strategy for getting there.

- *Focus on behaviors, actions, and results.* Problems arise when managers move away from tangible results and actions and begin to critique employees' abilities and attitudes. Such criticism creates a negative tone for the appraisal session and undercuts its primary purpose.

- *No surprises.* If a business owner is doing her job well, performance appraisals should contain no surprises for employees or the business owner. The ideal time to correct improper behavior or slumping performance is when it happens, not months later. Managers should provide employees with continuous feedback on their performances and use the appraisal session to keep employees on the right track.

■ *Plan for the future.* Smart business owners use appraisal sessions as gateways to workers' future success. They spend only about 20 percent of the time discussing past performance; they use the remaining 80 percent of the time to develop goals, objectives and a plan for the future.

Many companies are encouraging employees to evaluate each other in **peer reviews** or to evaluate their bosses in **upward feedback**, both part of a technique called 360-degree feedback in which employees get feedback from above, from below, and from all around. An increasing number of U.S. companies now use 360-degree evaluations as part of their performance appraisal systems. For instance, at W.L. Gore and Associates, the maker of Gore-Tex fabric, employees' pay increases depend on biannual peer reviews.[46] Peer appraisals such as those at W.L. Gore can be especially useful because an employee's co-workers see his on-the-job performance every day. As a result, peer evaluations tend to be more accurate and more valid than those of some managers. Plus, they may capture behavior that managers might miss. Disadvantages of peer appraisals include potential retaliation against co-workers who criticize, the possibility that appraisals will be reduced to "popularity contests," and workers who refuse to offer any criticism because they feel uncomfortable evaluating others. Some bosses using upward feedback report similar problems, including personal attacks and extreme evaluations by vengeful subordinates.

MANAGEMENT SUCCESSION: PASSING THE TORCH OF LEADERSHIP

More than 90 percent of all companies in the United States are family owned. Not all family-owned businesses are small, however; one-third of the *Fortune* 500 companies are family businesses. Unfortunately, 70 percent of first-generation businesses fail to survive into the second generation; of those that do survive, only 12 percent make it to the third generation, and just 3 percent make it to the fourth generation and beyond.[47] Sibling rivalries, fights over control of the business, and personality conflicts often lead to nasty battles that can tear families apart and destroy once-thriving businesses.

The best way to avoid deadly turf battles and conflicts is to develop a succession plan for the company. Although business founders inevitably want their businesses to survive them and almost 81 percent intend to pass them on to their children, they seldom support their intentions with a plan to accomplish that goal. About 25 percent of all family business owners do *not* have a formal management succession plan![48] These owners dream of their businesses continuing in the family but take no significant steps to make their dreams a reality. In many situations the reason for failing to develop a succession plan is that the entrepreneur is unwilling to make tough, and potentially, disruptive decisions that require selecting a succcessor. It is not uncommon for family feuds to erupt over who is (and is not) selected as successor in the family business.

Most of the family businesses in existence today were started after World War II, and their founders are ready to pass the torch of leadership on to the next generation. Experts estimate that between 1993 and 2013, $4.8 trillion in wealth will be transferred from one generation to the next, much of it through family businesses.[49] For a smooth transition from one generation to the next, these companies need a succession plan. Without a succession plan, family businesses face an increased risk of faltering or failing in the next generation. Those businesses with the greatest probability of surviving are the ones whose owners prepare a succession plan well before it is time to "pass the torch of leadership" to the next generation. Succession planning also allows business owners to minimize the impact of taxes on their businesses, their estates, and their successors' wealth as well.

Succession planning reduces the tension and stress created by these conflicts by gradually "changing the guard." A well-developed succession plan is like the smooth, graceful exchange of a baton between runners in a relay race. The new runner still has maximum energy; the concluding runner has already spent her energy by running at maximum speed. The athletes never come to a stop to exchange the baton; instead, the handoff takes place on the move. The race is a skillful blend of the talents of all team members—an exchange of leadership is so smooth and powerful that the business never falters, but accelerates, fueled by a new source of energy at each leg of the race.

How to Develop a Management Succession Plan

Creating a succession plan involves the following steps:

Step 1.   *Select the successor.* Entrepreneurs should never assume that their children want to take control of the family business. Above all, they should not be afraid to ask the question: "Do you really want to take over the family business?" Too often, children in this situation tell Mom and Dad what they want to hear out of loyalty, pressure, or guilt. It is critical to remember at this juncture in the life of a business that children do not necessarily inherit their parents' entrepreneurial skills and desires. By leveling with the children about the business and their options regarding a family succession, the owner will know which heirs, if any, are willing to assume leadership of the business. When naming a successor, merit is a better standard to use than birth order. When considering a successor, an entrepreneur should take the following actions:

- Make it clear to all involved that they are not required to join the business on a full-time basis. Family members' goals, ambitions, and talents should be foremost in their career decisions.

- Do not assume that a successor must always come from within the family. Simply being born into a family does *not* guarantee that a person will make a good business leader.

- Give family members the opportunity to work outside the business first to learn for themselves how others conduct business. Working for others will allow them to develop knowledge, confidence, and credibility before stepping back into the family business.

     One of the worst mistakes entrepreneurs can make is to postpone naming a successor until just before they are ready to step down. The problem is especially acute when more than one family member works for the company and is interested in assuming leadership of it. Sometimes founders avoid naming successors because they don't want to hurt the family members who are not chosen to succeed them. However, both the business and the family will be better off if, after observing the family members as they work in the business, the founder picks a successor based on that person's skills and abilities.

Step 2.   *Create a survival kit for the successor.* Once he identifies a successor, an entrepreneur should prepare a survival kit and then brief the future leader on its contents, which should include all of the company's critical documents (wills, trusts, insurance policies, financial statements, bank accounts, key contracts, corporate bylaws, and so forth). The founder should be sure that the successor reads and understands all the relevant documents in the kit. Other important steps the owner should take to prepare the successor to take over leadership of the business include:

- Create a strategic analysis for the future. Working with the successor, entrepreneurs should identify the primary opportunities and the challenges facing the company and the requirements for meeting them.

- On a regular basis, share with the successor their vision of the business's future direction, describing key factors that have led to its success and those that will bring future success.

- Be open and listen to the successor's views and concerns.

- Teach and learn at the same time.

- Relate specifically how the firm's key success factors have produced tangible results.

- Tie the key success factors to performance and profitability.

- Explain the strategies of the business and the operational key success factors.

- Discuss the values and philosophy of the business and how they have inspired and influenced past actions.

- Discuss the people in the business and their strengths and weaknesses.

- Discuss the philosophy underlying the firm's compensation policy and explain why employees are paid what they are.

- Make a list of the firm's most important customers and its key suppliers or vendors and review the history of all dealings with the parties on both lists.

- Discuss how to treat these key players to ensure the company's continued success and its smooth and error-free ownership transition.

- Develop a job analysis by taking an inventory of the activities involved in leading the company. This analysis can show successors those activities on which they should be spending most of their time.

- Document as much process knowledge—"how we do things"—as possible. After many years in their jobs, business owners are not even aware of their vast reservoirs of knowledge. For them, making decisions is a natural part of their business lives. They do it effortlessly because they have so much knowledge and experience. It is easy to forget that a successor will not have the benefit of those years of experience unless the founder communicates it.

A Company Example *Morry Stein, the head of* **Camp Echo Lake**, *a family-run youth camp, took the time to develop a successor's survival kit in case something happened to him. When he was killed tragically in an airplane crash, Stein's sons, Tony and George, and his wife were able to use the written instructions to help make the difficult transition. In the kit he left behind, Stein included the names of his most trusted advisors, advice for handling different employees, where to find important company documents, and a touching pep talk for his family. The transition went smoothly not only because of the survival kit Stein had prepared but also because he had taken the time to sit down regularly with both of his sons to discuss "the state of the camp" as he called it. "About ten years ago, we started having business meetings around the dining room table at my parents' house," explains Tony. "We talked about new program ideas, the future of camping, how we could raise tuition, when we would enter the business, what our strengths were, and what we liked to do."* [50]

Step 3. *Groom the successor.* The discussions that set the stage for the transition of leadership are time-consuming and require openness by both parties. This is the process by which business founders transfer their knowledge to the next generation. In fact, grooming the successor is the founder's greatest teaching and development responsibility, and it takes time. To implement the succession plan, the founder must be:

- Patient, realizing that the transfer of power is gradual and evolutionary and that the successor should earn responsibility and authority one step at a time until the final transfer of power takes place.
- Willing to accept that the successor will make mistakes.
- Skillful at using the successor's mistakes as a teaching tool.
- An effective communicator and an especially tolerant listener.
- Capable of establishing reasonable expectations for the successor's performance.
- Able to articulate the keys to the successor's performance.

Grooming a successor can begin at an early age simply by involving children in the family business and observing which ones have the greatest ability and interest in the company.

A Company Example *At age 9, Jay Alexander started going to work with his father at the family business,* **Alexander Machinery**, *a maker of textile and road construction equipment. At 11, Jay approached his father and asked for a job in the company, beginning a long succession of jobs over the next 12 years. "I've worked practically every job in the company," says Jay. "I've never worked anywhere else." When Jay's father, Bill, decided to step away from the business he founded, Jay was the natural choice as his successor, although Jay's sister also works for the company. "This business has come naturally to him," says Bill.* [51]

Step 4. *Promote an environment of trust and respect.* Another priceless gift a founder can leave a successor is an environment of trust and respect. Trust and respect on the part of the founder and others fuel the successor's desire to learn and excel and build the successor's confidence in making decisions. Developing a competent successor over a five- to ten-year period is realistic. Empowering the successor by gradually delegating responsibilities creates an environment in which all parties can objectively view the growth and development of the successor. Customers, creditors, suppliers, and staff members can gradually develop confidence in the successor. The final transfer of power is not a dramatic, wrenching change but a smooth, coordinated passage.

Step 5. *Cope with the financial realities of estate and gift taxes.* The final step in developing a workable management succession plan involves structuring the transition so as to minimize the impact of estate, gift, and inheritance taxes on family members and the business. Entrepreneurs who fail to consider the impact of these taxes may force their heirs to sell a successful business just to pay the estate's tax bill. Recent tax legislation reduces the impact of taxes on transferring family businesses from one generation to the next. However, without proper estate planning, an entrepreneur's family members will incur a painful tax bite when they inherit the business. According to the Arthur Andersen/MassMutual Survey of American Family Businesses, only 25 percent of all small business owners have completed an estate plan, even though they have 70 to 80 percent of their net worth tied up in their businesses![52] Entrepreneurs should be actively engaged in estate planning no later than age 45; those who start businesses early in their lives or whose businesses grow rapidly may need to begin as early as age 30. A variety of options exist that may prove to be helpful in reducing the estate tax liability. Each operates in a different fashion, but their objective remains the same: to remove a portion of business owners' assets out of their estates so that when they die, those assets will not be subject to estate taxes. Many of these estate planning tools need time to work their magic, so the key is to put them in place early on in the life of the business.

BUY/SELL AGREEMENT. One of the most popular estate planning techniques is the buy/sell agreement. A survey by the Chartered Life Underwriters and the Chartered Life Financial Consultants found that 76 percent of small business owners who have estate plans have created buy/sell agreements.[53] A **buy/sell agreement** is a contract that co-owners often rely on to ensure the continuity of a business. In a typical arrangement, the co-owners create a contract stating that each agrees to buy the others out in case of the death or disability of one. That way, the heirs of the deceased or disabled owner can "cash out" of the business while leaving control of the business in the hands of the remaining owners. The buy/sell agreement specifies a formula for determining the value of the business at the time the agreement is to be executed. One problem with buy/sell agreements is that the remaining co-owners may not have the cash available to buy out the disabled or deceased owner. To resolve this issue, many businesses buy life and disability insurance for each of the owners in amounts large enough to cover the purchase price of their respective shares of the business.

> **buy/sell agreement**—*a contract among co-owners of a business stating that each agrees to buy out the others in case of the death or disability of one.*

LIFETIME GIFTING. The owners of a successful business may transfer money to their children (or other recipients) from their estate throughout the parents' lives. Current federal tax regulations allow individuals to make gifts of $10,000 per year, per parent, per recipient, that are exempt from federal gift taxes. Each child would be required to pay income taxes on the $10,000 gift they receive, but the children are usually in lower tax brackets than those of the giver. For instance, husband-and-wife business owners could give $1.2 million worth of stock to their three children and their spouses over a period of 10 years without incurring any estate or gift taxes at all.

SETTING UP A TRUST. A **trust** is a contract between a grantor (the company founder) and a trustee (generally a bank officer or an attorney) in which the grantor gives to the trustee legal title to assets (e.g., stock in the company), which the trustee agrees to hold for the beneficiaries (children). The beneficiaries can receive income from the trust, or they can receive the property in the trust, or both, at some specified time. Trusts can take a wide variety of forms, but two broad categories of trusts are available: revocable trusts and irrevocable trusts. A **revocable trust** is one which a grantor can change or revoke during his lifetime. Under present tax laws, however, the only trust that provides a tax benefit is an **irrevocable trust**, in which the grantor cannot require the trustee to return the assets held in trust. The value of the grantor's estate is lowered because the assets in an irrevocable trust are excluded from the value of the estate. However, an irrevocable trust places severe restrictions on the grantor's control of the property placed in the trust. Business owners use several types of irrevocable trusts to lower their estate tax liabilities:

> **trust**—*a contract between a grantor (the company founder) and a trustee in which the grantor gives the trustee assets (e.g., company stock), which the trustee holds for the trust's beneficiaries (e.g., the grantor's heirs).*
>
> **revocable trust**—*a trust which a grantor can change or revoke during his lifetime.*
>
> **irrevocable trust**—*a trust in which a grantor cannot require the trustee to return the assets held in trust.*

- *Bypass trust.* The most basic type of trust is the bypass trust, which allows a business owner to put $1.3 million into trust naming his spouse as the beneficiary upon his death. The spouse receives the income from the trust throughout her life, but the principal in the trust goes to the couple's heirs free of estate taxes upon the spouse's death.

- *Irrevocable life insurance trust.* This type of trust allows a business owner to keep the proceeds of a life insurance policy out of his estate and away from estate taxes, freeing up that money to pay the taxes on the remainder of the estate. To get the tax benefit, business owners must be sure that the business or the trust (rather than themselves) own the insurance policy. The disadvantage of an irrevocable life insurance trust is that if the owner dies within three years of establishing it, the insurance proceeds do become part of his estate and are subject to estate taxes.

- *Irrevocable asset trust.* An irrevocable asset trust is similar to a life insurance trust except that it is designed to pass the assets in the parents' estate on to their children. The children do not have control of the assets while the parents are still living, but they do receive the income from those assets. Upon the parents' death, the assets in the trust go to the children without being subjected to the estate tax.

- *Grantor retained annuity trust (GRAT).* A grantor retained annuity trust (GRAT) is a special type of irrevocable trust and has become one of the most popular tools for entrepreneurs to transfer

Who's Next?

Dick Strossner wants the family business to continue into the next generation, but so far, none of the younger members in the family have shown much interest in taking over the bakery started by his father in 1947. Strossner, 57, owns 80 percent of the bakery's stock. His sister, who manages the business's financial affairs, owns 10 percent, and Strossner's son, Richard, owns the remaining 10 percent. Both Dick and his sister have worked in Strossner's Bakery since they were teenagers.

When Strossner's parents decided to gradually get out of the business in 1976. Dick was the natural choice to take over management of the bakery because he had been working in the family business for nearly two decades. "Dad taught me almost everything I know about baking," he says. "He did a lot of things I didn't respect and understand until I took over." Although Dick took control of the company, his father continued to work in the family business until he died at the age of 82. The transition from one generation of leadership to the next was not always smooth. Strossner began to experiment with the business, trying new products and different approaches, some of which his father said would never work. He introduced computers to the bakery (an idea Dad was against) and shifted its product mix from bread and Danish pastries to cakes and Danish pastries. Although his father disagreed with some of the experiments a Strossner says, he never interfered, allowing Dick to try whatever he wanted. In most cases, Strossner recalls, his father was right about which ideas would work and which ones would not. "Dad was a major asset for the business," says Strossner, "I really needed him." Under Dick's leadership, the bakery has grown and now includes both a catering business and a florist operation.

With his own retirement not too far away, Strossner is now considering the best way to deal with the issue of management succession. He hopes his son, who currently is not working in the bakery, will take over the leadership reins for the next generation. "I'm thinking he will be back." Strossner says. "He's worked in every single facet of the business." If his son chooses not to return to the bakery. Strossner says his employees are skilled enough and experienced enough to run the business without him. He also wants to start relinquishing control of the family business in time to avoid the bite of heavy estate taxes. Currently. Strossner's estate planning is based on insurance policies. "If I were to go away today. I have enough insurance to cover the taxes," he says.

1. What advice would you offer Dick Strossner concerning a management succession plan?

2. What steps should Strossner take to develop a management succession plan?

3. What tools would you suggest Strossner use for minimizing estate taxes?

Source: Adapted from Jenny Munre, "Bridging the Generation Gap," *Upstate Business*, October 8, 2000, pp. 8–9.

ownership of a business while maintaining control over it and minimizing estate taxes. Under a GRAT, an owner can put property in an irrevocable trust for a maximum of 10 years. While the trust is in effect, the grantor retains the voting power and receives the interest income from the property in the trust. At the end of the trust (not to exceed 10 years), the property passes to the beneficiaries (heirs). The beneficiaries are required to pay a gift tax on the value of the assets placed in the GRAT. However, the IRS taxes GRAT gifts only according to their discounted present value because the heirs did not receive use of the property while it was in trust. The primary disadvantage of using a GRAT in estate planning is that if the grantor dies during the life of the GRAT, its assets pass back into the grantor's estate. These assets then become subject to the full estate tax.

Establishing a trust requires meeting many specific legal requirements and is not something business owners should do on their own. It is much better to hire experienced attorneys, accountants, and financial advisors to assist. Although the cost of establishing a trust can be high, the tax savings they generate are well worth the expense.

estate freeze—*a strategy that minimizes estate taxes by creating two classes of stock for a business: preferred voting stock for the parents and nonvoting common stock for the children.*

ESTATE FREEZE. An **estate freeze** minimizes estate taxes by having family members create two classes of stock for the business: (1) preferred voting stock for the parents and (2) nonvoting common stock for the children. The value of the preferred stock is frozen whereas the common stock reflects the anticipated increased market value of the business. Any appreciation in the value of the business after the transfer is not subject to estate taxes. However, the parent must pay gift taxes on the value of the common stock given to the children. The value of the common stock is the total value of the business less the value of the voting preferred stock retained by the parents. The parents also must accept taxable dividends at the market rate on the preferred stock they own.

FAMILY LIMITED PARTNERSHIP.   Creating a **family limited partnership (FLP)** allows business-owning parents to transfer their company to their children (thus lowering their estate taxes) while still retaining control over it for themselves. To create a family limited partnership, the parents (or parent) set up a partnership among themselves and their children. The parents retain the general partnership interest, which can be as low as 1 percent, and the children become the limited partners. As general partners, the parents control both the limited partnership and the family business. In other words, nothing in the way the company operates has to change. Over time, the parents can transfer company stock into the limited partnership, ultimately passing ownership of the company to their children. One of the principal tax benefits of an FLP is that it allows discounts on the value of the shares of company stock the parents transfer into the limited partnership. Because a family business is closely held, shares of ownership in it, especially minority shares, are not as marketable as those of a publicly held company. As a result, company shares transferred into the limited partnership are discounted at 20 to 50 percent of their full market value, producing a large tax savings for everyone involved. The average discount is 40 percent, but that amount varies based on the industry and the individual company involved. An FLP is an ideal part of a succession plan when there has been a buildup of substantial value in a business and the older generation has a substantial amount of liquidity. Because of their ability to reduce estate and gift taxes, family limited partnerships have become one of the most popular estate planning tools in recent years.

Developing a succession plan and preparing a successor requires a wide variety of skills, some of which the business founder will not have. That's what it is important to bring experts into the process when necessary. Entrepreneurs often call on their attorneys, accountants, insurance agents, and financial planners to help them build a succession plan that works best for their particular situations. Because the issues involved can be highly complex and charged with emotion, bringing in trusted advisors to help improves the quality of the process and provides an objective perspective.

family limited partnership—*a strategy that allows business-owning parents to transfer their company to their children (lowering their estate taxes) while still retaining control over it for themselves.*

CHAPTER SUMMARY

1. Explain the challenges involved in the entrepreneur's role as leader and what it takes to be a successful leader.

■ Leadership is the process of influencing and inspiring others to work to achieve a common goal and then giving them the power and the freedom to achieve it.

■ Management and leadership are not the same, yet both are essential to a small company's success. Leadership without management is unbridled; management without leadership is uninspired. Leadership gets a small business going; management keeps it going.

2. Describe the importance of hiring the right employees and how to avoid making hiring mistakes.

■ The decision to hire a new employee is an important one for every business, but its impact is magnified many times in a small company. Every "new hire" a business owner makes determines the heights to which the company can climb—or the depths to which it will plunge.

■ To avoid making hiring mistakes, entrepreneurs should develop meaningful job descriptions and job specifications, plan and conduct an effective interview, and check references before hiring any employee.

3. Explain how to build the kind of company culture and structure to support the entrepreneur's mission and goals and to motivate employees to achieve them.

■ Company culture is the distinctive, unwritten code of conduct that governs the behavior, attitudes, relationships, and style of an organization. Culture arises from an entrepreneur's consistent and relentless pursuit of a set of core values that everyone in the company can believe in. Small companies' flexible structures can be a major competitive weapon.

■ Entrepreneurs rely on six different management styles to guide their companies as they grow. The first three (craftsman, classic, and coordinator) involve running a company without any management assistance and are best suited for small companies in the early stages of growth; the last three (entrepreneur-plus-employee team, small partnership, big-team venture) rely on a team approach to run the company as its growth rate heats up.

■ Team-based management is growing in popularity among small firms. Companies that use teams effectively report significant gains in quality, reductions in cycle time, lower costs, increased customer satisfaction, and improved employee motivation and morale.

4. Discuss the ways in which entrepreneurs can motivate their workers to higher levels of performance.

■ Motivation is the degree of effort an employee exerts to accomplish a task; it shows up as excitement about work. Four important tools of motivation include empowerment, job design, rewards and compensation, and feedback.

■ Empowerment involves giving workers at every level of the organization the power, the freedom, and the responsibility to control their own work, to make decisions, and to take action to meet the company's objectives.

■ Job design techniques for enhancing employee motivation include job enlargement, job rotation, job enrichment, flextime, job sharing, and flexplace (which includes telecommuting).

■ Money is an important motivator for many workers, but it is not the only one. The key to using rewards such as recognition and praise and to motivate involves tailoring them to the needs and characteristics of the workers.

■ Giving employees timely, relevant feedback about their job performances through a performance appraisal system can also be a powerful motivator.

5. Describe the steps in developing a management succession plan for a growing business that will allow a smooth transition of leadership to the next generation.

■ As their companies grow, entrepreneurs must begin to plan for passing the leadership baton to the next generation well in advance. A succession plan is a crucial element in successfully transferring a company to the next generation. Preparing a succession plan involves five steps: (1) select the successor; (2) create a survival kit for the successor; (3) groom the successor; (4) promote an environment of trust and respect; and (5) cope with the financial realities of estate taxes.

DISCUSSION QUESTIONS

1. What is leadership? What is the difference between leadership and management?

2. What behaviors do effective leaders exhibit?

3. Why is it so important for small companies to hire the right employees? What can small business owners do to avoid making hiring mistakes?

4. What is a job description? A job specification? What functions do they serve in the hiring process?

5. Outline the procedure for conducting an effective interview.

6. What is company culture? What role does it play in a small company's success? What threats does rapid growth pose for a company's culture?

7. Explain the six different management styles entrepreneurs rely on to guide their companies as they grow (craftsman, classic, coordinator, entrepreneur-plus-employee team, small partnership, and big-team venture).

8. What mistakes do companies make when switching to team-based management? What can they do to avoid these mistakes? Explain the four phases teams typically go through.

9. What is empowerment? What benefits does it offer workers? The company? What must a small business manager do to make empowerment work in a company?

10. Explain the differences among job simplification, job enlargement, job rotation, and job enrichment. What impact do these different job designs have on workers?

11. Is money the "best" motivator? How do pay-for-performance compensation systems work? What other rewards are available to small business managers to use as motivators? How effective are they?

12. Suppose that a mail-order catalog company selling environmentally friendly products identifies its performance as a socially responsible company as a "critical number" in its success. Suggest some ways for the owner to measure this company's "social responsibility index."

13. What is performance appraisal? What are the most common mistakes managers make in performance appraisals? What should small business managers do to avoid making these mistakes?

14. Why is it so important for a small business owner to develop a management succession plan? Why is it so difficult for most business owners to develop such a plan? What are the steps that are involved in creating a succession plan?

15. Briefly describe the options a small business owner wanting to pass the family business on to the next generation can take to minimize the impact of estate taxes.

Launch *The Business Disc* and return to the section where Harry talks about hiring employees. From the Go To menu, select "Events from PART 1-A," and click on "Meet with Harry about Hiring Employees." How many employees, if any, did you need to run your business successfully? Develop a list of the employee benefits (both required and optional) your company will offer employees. You may want to review the reference guide "Human Resource Management" (under the "General Information" heading of the "Reference" option in the menu) and the information in Chapter 15. Develop a job description and a job specification for each position you will need to fill in your company.

How much did you pay your employees? What factors influence the wages you decide to pay?

BEYOND THE CLASSROOM . . .

1. Visit a local business that has experienced rapid growth in the past three years and ask the owner about the specific problems he or she had to face due to the organization's growth. How did the owner handle these problems? Looking back, what would he or she do differently?

2. Contact a local small business with at least 20 employees. Does the company have job descriptions and job specifications? What process does the owner use to hire a new employee? What questions does the owner typically ask candidates in an interview?

3. Ask the owner of a small manufacturing operation to give you a tour of his or her operation. During your tour, observe the way jobs are organized. To what extent does the company use the following job design concepts: job simplification? job enlargement? job rotation? job enrichment? flextime? job sharing? Based on your observations, what recommendations would you make to the owner about the company's job design?

4. Contact five small business owners about their plans for passing their businesses on to the next generation. Do they intend to pass the business along to a family member? Do they have a management succession plan? When do they plan to name a successor? Have they developed a plan for minimizing the effects of estate taxes? How many more years do they plan to work before retiring?

5. Entrepreneurs say that they have learned much about leadership from the movies! "Films beg to be interpreted and discussed," says one leadership consultant, "and from those discussions businesspeople come up with principles for their own jobs." A recent survey of small company CEOs by *Inc.* magazine* resulted in the following list of the best movies for leadership lessons: *Apollo 13* (1995), *The Bridge on the River Kwai* (1957), *Dead Poets Society* (1989), *Elizabeth* (1998), *Glengarry Glen Ross* (1992), *It's a Wonderful Life* (1946), *Norma Rae* (1979), *One Flew Over the Cuckoo's Nest* (1975), *Twelve Angry Men* (1957), and *Twelve O'Clock High* (1949). Rent one of these films and watch it with a group of your classmates. After viewing the movie, discuss the leadership lessons you learned from it and report the results to the other members of your class.

*Leigh Buchanan and Mike Hofman, "Everything I Know About Leadership, I Learned from the Movies," *Inc.*, March 2000, pp. 58–70.

A

3. *Knowle*
   ence in
   provide
   throw a
   who wi

COMPA

Sluggers Ba
a chance to
location for
fortable an
Sluggers a

COMPA

Sluggers Ba
Steele and
investors w
continuity c

START-U

Our start-u
land, buildi

Sluggers Batting Cage, LLC
A Business Plan

Sluggers B

Item
Start-Up
Land
Building
Pitching
Batting E
Dimple E
Helmets
Radar Gu
Paper Ma
Decor
Legal Fee
Cleaning
Furniture
Compute
Vending
Token Ca
Miscellar

Linzie M. Steele, Owner
342 Birchwood Drive
Hartsville, SC 29550

Chapter 1

1. *NFIB Small Business Policy Guide*, National Federation of Independent Businesses (Washington, DC), 2000, p. 2.

2. William J. Dennis, *Business Starts and Stops*, Wells Fargo and National Federation of Independent Businesses Education Foundation, 1999, p. 3.

3. Geoff Williams, "2001: An Entrepreneurial Odyssey," *Entrepreneur*, April 1999, p. 106; "What's In, What's Out," *Success*, February 1999, p. 12.

4. Howard H. Stevens, "We Create Entrepreneurs," *Success*, September 1995, p. 51.

5. *Global Entrepreneurship Monitor 2002 Executive Report*, Babson College, Ewing Marion Kauffman Foundation, and London Business School, 2002, p. 8.

6. Chantelle Ludski, "A Day in the Life: Entrepreneurship," mba.com, www.mba.comlNR/exeres/4ECE6033-C16C-4DC4-816E-B04DEAA021A3,frameless.htm; "Gogetter Goes Back to School," *The Daily Mail*, April 25, 2002, www.thisismoney.com/ 20020422/sb47233.html; Tricia Bisoux, "Brave New Ventures," *BizEd*, May/June 2002, pp. 27–34.

7. Charles Burck, "The Real World of the Entrepreneur," *Fortune*, April 5, 1993, p. 62.

8. David McClelland, *The Achieving Society*, (Princeton, NJ: Van Nostrand, 1961), p. 16.

9. Evan T. Robbins, "E Is for Entrepreneurship," *Syllabus*, November 2002, p. 24.

10. *National Small Business Poll: Success, Satisfaction, and Growth*, National Federation of Independent Businesses (Washington, DC), 2002, p. 2.

11. Gayle Sato Stodder, "Goodbye Mom & Pop," *Entrepreneur*, May 1999, p. 112.

12. Lea Goldman, "Machine Dreams," *Forbes*, May 27, 2002, pp. 149–150; Walter S. Mossberg, "A Vacuum That Even a Couch-Potato Could Love," *Wall Street Journal*, September 18, 2002, pp. D1, D12; iRobot Corporation, www.irobot.com/corp/default.asp.

13. Gayle Sato Stodder, "Are You Satisfied?" *Entrepreneur*, October 1999, p. 88.

14. Jeff Bailey, "Desire—More Than Need—Builds a Business," *Wall Street Journal*, May 21, 2002, p. B4.

15. Geoff Williams, "Keep It Coming," *Entrepreneur B.Y.O.B.*, April 2002, pp. 100–102; Skywire Software LLC, www.skywiresoftware.com/default.aspx.

16. Gayle Sato Stodder, "Never Say Die," *Entrepreneur*, December 1990, p. 95.

17. George Gendron, "The Origin of the Entrepreneurial Species," *Inc.*, February 2000, p. 107.

18. "The History of Soaps and Detergents," *Inventors*, www.inventors.about.com/library/inventors/blsoap.htm.

19. Julie Rose, "The New Risk Takers," *FSB*, March 2002, p. 30.

20. Bob Weinstein, "Success Secrets," *Business Start-Ups*, August 1995, p. 47.

21. John Case, "The Origins of Entrepreneurship," *Inc.*, June 1989, p. 52.

22. Cynthia Hodnett, "Young People Parlay Interests into Job," *Greenville News*, January 13, 2003, pp. 1E, 2E.

23. Leigh Buchanan, "After-School Special," *Inc.*, May 1, 2001, www.inc.com/articles/leadership_strat/leading_company/social_resnonsibility.

24. Gayle Sato Stodder, "Are You Satisfied?" *Entrepreneur*, October 1999, p. 86.

25. David Armstrong and Brendan Coffey, "The Forbes 400," *Forbes*, September 30, 2002, pp. 99–124.

26. Tony Cook, "Secrets of the Millionaire Next Door," *Reader's Digest*, November 1997, p. 135.

27. Aliza Pilar Sherman, "The Idol Life," *Entrepreneur*, January 2002, pp. 55–57; Julia Boorstin, Jonah Freedman, and Christopher Tkaczyk, "America's 40 Richest Under 40," *Fortune*, September 16, 2002, pp. 169–175; David Armstrong and Brendan Coffey, "The Forbes 400," *Forbes*, September 30, 2002, pp. 99–124.

28. Amanda C. Kooser, Gisela M. Pedroza, April Y. Pennington, Devlin Smith, and Nichole L. Torres, "Got ID?" *Entrepreneur*, November 2002, pp. 67–77; Funko Inc., www.wackywobblers.com.

29. *NFIB Small Business Policy Guide*, National Federation of Independent Businesses (Washington, DC), 2003, p. 16.

30. Robert Johnson, "Owners Pressured to Work Through Vacation Season," *Wall Street Journal*, July 27, 1999, p. B2.

31. Chantelle Ludski, "A Day in the Life: Entrepreneurship," mba.com, www.mba.com/NR/exeres/4ECE6033-C16C-4DC4-816E-B04DEAA021A3, frameless.htm.

32. Anne Fisher, "Is Your Business Taking Over Your Life?" *Inc.*, *FSB*, November 2001, pp. 32–40.

33. Donna Fenn, "Time-Out," *Inc.*, July 2001, pp. 34–40.

34. William J. Dennis, "National Small Business Poll," Volume 2, Issue 5, NFIB Foundation Series, 2002, p. 1.

35. Michelle Prather, "Pedal Pushers," *Business Start-Ups*, August 2000, p. 12; L.A. Bike Tours, LLC, www.labiketours.com.

36. David Lidsky, "Tech Skeptic", *FSB*, January 24, 2003, www.fortune.com/fortune/smallbusiness/skeptic/0,15704,411307,00.html; Donna M McGuire, "Is Your Web Site Profitable?" *Small Business Information*, January 26, 2003, sbinformation.miningco.com/library/weekly/uc012603a.htm.

37. Patricia Fusco, "Internet Future Bright for Business," *Small Business Computing*, January 14, 2003, www.smallbusinesscomputing.com/biztools/article.php/1569091.

38. Susan Greco, "The Messenger Is the Medium," *Inc.*, September 2001, pp. 162–163.

39. "Opportunities in Exporting," Office of International Trade, U.S. Small Business Administration, www.sba.gov/OIT/txt/export/whyexport.html.

40. Kenneth Klee, "Going Global? Our Ten Tests Can Help You Get Started," *FSB*, March 2001, pp. 98–103.

41. "The Meaning of Generation X," JobCircle: Entrepreneurship, 2002, www.jobcircle.com/career/articles/3020.html.

42. Julie Sloane, "Most Likely to Succeed," *FSB*, November 2002, p. 22.

43. "One in 18 U.S. Women Is a Business Owner," Center for Women's Business Research, July 16, 2002, www.nfwbo.org/Research/7-16-2002/7-16-2002.htm.

44. "Women-Owned Businesses in the United States, 2002: A Fact Sheet," Center for Women's Business Research, 2002, www.nfwbo.org/USStateFacts/US.pdf; Debra Phillips, Cynthia E. Griffin, Heather Page, and Melissa Campanelli, "Quick Guide for Women Entrepreneurs," *Entrepreneur*, January 1999, www.entrepreneur.com/mag/article/0,15-39,266807,00.html.

45. "Women-Owned Businesses in the United States, 2002: A Fact Sheet," Center for Women's Business Research, 2002, www.nfwbo.org/USStateFacts/US.pdf.

46. "Women-Owned Businesses in the United States, 2002: A Fact Sheet," Center for Women's Business Research, 2002, www.nfwbo.org/USStateFacts/US.pdf.

47. Aliza Pilar Sherman, "Big Plans," *Entrepreneur*, February 2002, www.entepreneur.com/article/0,4621,296515,00.html.

48. Ibid; Julie Blackledge, "PharmaFab(ulous)", *Fort Worth Business Press*, July 2002, www.fwbusinesspress.com.

49. Ellen McGirt, "Small Business," *Money*, December 2002, p. 37; Anne Robertson, "Minorities Say Climate Improving," *Business Journal of Phoenix*, February 23, 2001, phoenix.bizjournals.com/phoenix/stories/2001/02/26/story4.html.

50. "Minority Share of U. S. Business Ownership Nears 15 Percent," SBA Number 02-02 ADVO, February 4, 2002, www.sba.gov/advo/press/02-02.html.

51. Minorities in Business, 2001, U.S. Small Business Administration, Office of Advocacy (Washington, DC), www.sba.gov/advo/stats/min01.pdf.

52. Jim Hopkins, "Asian Business Owners Gaining Clout," *USA Today*, February 27, 2002, www.usatoday.com/money/covers/2002-02-27-asian-biz.htm.

53. Nichole Torres, "From Part Time to Full Time," *Entrepreneur*, April 2002, www.entrepreneur.com/Your_Business/YB_SegArticle/0,4621,298297—,00.html.

54. *NFIB Small Business Policy Guide* (Washington, DC: NFIB Education Foundation, 2003), p. 20.

55. Joanne H. Pratt, "Small Business Research Summary, Home-Based Business: The Hidden Economy," U.S. Small Business Administration Office of Advocacy, No. 194, March 2000, pp. 1–2.

56. "Practical Car Accessories for Canines Brings Profits," *Home Business Magazine Online*, www.homebusinessmag.com/tarticle1.html?aID=214&mID=1&c1D=17&sID=0.

57. "Facts and Figures: Family Business in the U.S," *Family Business Magazine*, www.business.com/bdcframe.asp?ticker=&src=http%3A//rd.business.com/index.asp%3Fbdcz%3Di.1.1.ml.e%26bdcr%3D1%26bdcu%3Dhttp%253 A//www.familybusinessmagazine.com/%26bdcs%3D0CD38920-C1E8-4F F8-B724-77BBCF2BA89F%26bdcf%3D0D92C0F3-4149-444B-938 BEFABD06FCD31%26bdcp%3D%26partner%3Dbdc%26title%3DFamil y%2520Business%2520magazine&back=http%3A//www.business.com/directory/media_and_entertainment/publishing/magazines/family_business_publishing/family_business_magazine/index.asp%3Fpartner%3Dinc &path=/directory/media_and_entertainment/publishing/magazines/family_business_publishing/family_business_magazine.

58. Ibid.

59. Kathy Spencer-Mention, "All in the Family," *Greenville News*, November 3, 2002, pp. 1D, 12D.

60. Udayan Gupta, "And Business Makes Three: Couples Working Together," *Wall Street Journal*, February 26, 1990, p. B2.

61. Bob Weinstein, "For Better or Worse," *Your Company*, Spring 1992, pp. 28–31.

62. Echo M. Garrett "And Business Makes Three," *Small Business Reports*, September 1993, pp. 27–31.

63. Mares Green, "Couples Find Challenge, Pleasure Working Together," *Greenville News*, January 5, 2003, p. 1E.

64. "Going Places," *Entrepreneur*, June 1994, p. 14.

65. David Whitford, "Hard Times in the Heartland," *FSB*, November 2001, pp. 54–64.

66. Jeff Bailey, "Anger Can Power the Creation of New Companies," *Wall Street Journal*, June 4, 2002, p. B5.

67. *NFIB Small Business Policy Guide* (Washington, DC: NFIB Education Foundation, 2003), p. 21.

68. *Small Business by the Numbers*, U.S. Small Business Administration (Washington, DC, 2003), www.sba.gov/advo/stats/sbfaq.pdf.

69. "Cognetics Corporate Quiz," Cognetics, Inc., www.cogonline.com/Inde.xL.htm; Garry Powers, "Wanted: More Small, Fast-Growing Firms," *Business & Economic Review*, April–June 1999, pp. 19–22.

70. Erskine Bowles, "Training Ground," *Entrepreneur*, March 1994, p. 168.

71. *Small Business by the Numbers*, U.S. Small Business Administration (Washington, DC, 2003), www.sba.gov/advo/stats/sbfaq.pdf.

72. *NFIB Small Business Policy Guide* (Washington, DC: NFIB Education Foundation, 2003), p. 33.

73. John LaFalce, "The Driving Force," *Entrepreneur*, February 1990, pp. 161–166.

74. Bruce G. Posner, "Why Companies Fail," *Inc.*, June 1993, p. 102.

75. Rob Walker, "Starting Over After *Startup.com*," *Fortune*, March 4, 2002, pp. 43–44.

76. Eugene Carlson, "Spreading Your Wings," *Wall Street Journal*, October 16, 1992, p. R2.

77. Sharon Nelton, "Coming to Grips with Growth," *Nation's Business*, February 1998, pp. 26–32.

78. Geoff Williams, "Pick Your Spot," *Entrepreneur B.Y.O.B.*, June 2002, pp. 102–109.

79. Michael Warsaw, "Great Comebacks," *Success*, July/August, 1995, p. 43.

80. Marc Gunther, "They All Want a Piece of Bill Gross," *Fortune*, November 11, 2002, p. 140.

81. Robert Huber, "Failure: The Seven Mistakes Entrepreneurs Make and How to Avoid Them," *Success*, March 1998, p. 60; "The Triangle," Integrity Publishing Company, www.integritypublishing.com/ex%20triangle%20web%20pages/xtri.execstaff.htm.

82. Tahl Raz, "60-Second Business Plan: Talking Trash," *Inc.*, November 1, 2002, www.inc.com/magazine/20021101/24819.html; Marjorie Censer, "From the Ground Up: Student Entrepreneurs Create New Compost," *Daily Princetonian*, December 13, 2002, www.dailyprincetonian.com/archives/2002/12/13/news/6667.shtml.

83. G. David Doran, Michelle Prather, Elaine Teague, and Laura Tiffany, "Young Guns," *Business StartUps*, April 1999, pp. 28–35.

84. Barbara Carton, "Help Wanted," *Wall Street Journal*, May 22, 1995, p. R10.

Chapter 2

1. Cynthia E. Griffin, "It's a Bra!" *Entrepreneur*, April 2001, p. 44; T&J Designs LLC, www.bellybra.com.

2. "Small Serial Innovators: The Small Firm Contribution to Technical Change," CHI Research, U.S. Small Business Administration Office of Advocacy, No. 225, February 2003, www.sba.gov/advo/research/rs225.pdf.

3. "The Power of Innovation," *Inc.*, State of Small Business 2001, p. 103; Leigh Buchanan, "Built to Invent," *Inc.*, August 2002, p. 53.

4. Warren Bennis, "Cultivating Creative Collaboration," *Industry Week*, August 18, 1997, p. 86.

5. "Polaroid, R.I.P.," *Fortune*, November 12, 2001, p. 44; Robert Epstein, "How to Get a Great Idea," *Reader's Digest*, December 1992, p. 103.

6. Roger von Oech, *A Whack on the Side of the Head* (New York: Warner Books, 1990), p. 108.

7. Gisela M. Pedroza, "Road Dogs," *Entrepreneur B.Y.O.B.*, May 2002, p. 112; Ruff Rider LLC, www.ruffrider.com.

8. Michael Maiello, "They Almost Changed the World," *Forbes*, December 23, 2002, p. 217.

9. Peter Carbonara, "30 Great Small Business Ideas," *Your Company*, August/September 1998, pp. 32–58.

10. Robert Fulghum, "Time to Sacrifice the Queen," *Reader's Digest*, August 1993, pp. 136–138.

11. Carla Goodman, "Sparking Your Imagination," *Entrepreneur*, September 1997, p. 32.

12. Ibid.

13. Ibid.

14. Joseph Rosenbloom, "The Lifetime Achiever," *Inc.*, September 2002, pp. 80–82.

15. Betty Edwards, *Drawing on the Right Side of the Brain* (Los Angeles: J.P. Tarcher, Inc., 1979), p. 32.

16. Roger von Oech, *A Whack on the Side of the Head* (New York: Warner Books, 1990), pp. 21–167; "Obstacles to Creativity," Creativity Web, www.ozemail.com.au/~caveman/Creative/Basics/obstacles.htm.

17. Sara J. Welch, "Walking on Water," *Successful Meetings*, October 2002, pp. 75–76.

18. Joel Millman, "Trendy Sprout Thrives on Water from Sea," *Wall Street Journal*, February 26, 2003, pp. B1–B2.

19. Karen Axelton, "Imagine That," *Entrepreneur*, April 1998, p. 96; "Thomas Edison Biography," http://edison-ford-estate.com/ed_bio.htm.

20. Sally Fegley, "Painting the Town," *Entrepreneur*, July 1997, p. 14.

21. Joseph Schumpeter, "The Creative Response in Economic History," *Journal of Economic History*, November 1947, pp. 149–159.

22. *Bits & Pieces*, January 1994, p. 6.

23. "Make Your Company an Idea Factory," *FSB*, May/June 2000, p. 124.

24. Robert Epstein, "How to Get a Great Idea," *Reader's Digest*, December 1992, p. 102.

25. Thea Singer and Leigh Buchanan, "A Field Guide to Innovation," *Inc.*, August 2002, pp. 63–70.

26. Ibid.

27. Ibid.

28. Stephanie Barlow, "Turn It On," *Entrepreneur*, May 1993, p. 52.

29. Mark Henricks, "Good Thinking," *Entrepreneur*, May 1996, p. 70.

30. Kip Crosby, "Stumbling into the Future," *Forbes ASAP*, November 20, 2000, pp. 105–112; John Steele Gordon with Michael Maiello, "Pioneers Die Broke," *Forbes*, December 23, 2002, pp. 258–264.

31. Don Debelak, "Ideas Unlimited," *Business Start-Ups*, May 1999, pp. 57–58.

32. Leslie Miller, "Write Your True Love into a Romance Novel," *USA Today*, February 6, 2002, www.usatoday.com/tech/news/2001-02-01-ebrief.htm; Gisela M. Pedroza, "Novel Idea," *Entrepreneur, B.Y.O.B.*, July 2002, p. 104.

33. Geoff Williams, "Innovative Model," *Entrepreneur*, September 2002, p. 66.

34. Roy Rowan, "Those Hunches Are More Than Blind Faith," *Fortune*, April 23, 1979, p. 112.

35. Michael Waldholz, "A Hallucination Inspires a Vision for AIDS Drug," *Wall Street Journal*, September 29, 1993, pp. B1, B5.

36. Kate O'Sullivan, "Insect Inside," *Inc.*, November 15, 2001, p. 52.

37. Carla Goodman, "Sparking Your Imagination," *Entrepreneur*, September 1997, pp. 32–36.

38. Janean Chun, "Theory of Creativity," *Entrepreneur*, October 1997, p. 130.

39. Emily Barker, "The Green Giant," *Inc.*, September 2002, pp. 84–85.

40. Chun, "Theory of Creativity," p. 10.

41. Thea Singer, "Your Brain on Innovation," *Inc.*, September 2002, pp. 86–88.

42. Paul Bagne, "When to Follow a Hunch," *Reader's Digest*, May 1994, p. 77.

43. Susan Hansen, "The Action Hero," *Inc.*, September 2002, pp. 82–84.

44. "Ceiling Fan Leads to Physics Theory," *Laurens County Advertiser*, December 19, 1993, p. 4.

45. Thea Singer and Lea Buchanan, "Who? What? Where? Why? When? How?" *Inc.*, August 2002, p. 66.

46. Waldholz, "A Hallucination Inspires a Vision for AIDS Drug," p. B5.

47. Thea Singer and Leah Buchanan, "Seeing It Fresh," *Inc.*, August 2002, p. 68.

48. Epstein, "How to Get a Great Idea," p. 104.

49. Waldholz, "A Hallucination Inspires a Vision for AIDS Drug," p. B5.

50. Chun, "Theory of Creativity," pp. 130–131.

51. Ed Brown, "A Day at Innovation U," *Fortune*, April 12, 1999, pp. 163–165.

52. The Hall of Science and Exploration, "Academy of Achievement: Linus Pauling, PhD," www.achievement.org/autodoc/page/pau0pro-1.

53. Brown, "A Day at Innovation U," p. 165.

54. Ibid.

55. *General Information Concerning Patents* (Washington, DC: U.S. Patent and Trademark Office, 1997), p. 15; Tomima Edmark, "Bright Idea," *Entrepreneur*, April 1997, p. 98; Tomima Edmark, "What Price Protection?" *Entrepreneur*, September 1998, pp. 109–110; U.S. Patent and Trademark Office, "Attorneys and Agents," www.uspto.gov/web/offices/pac/doc/general/attorney.htm.

56. "Snapshot," *Entrepreneur*, January 2003, p. 22.

57. "U.S. Patent Statistics," U.S. Patent and Trademark Office, www.uspto.gov/web/offices/ac/ido/oeip/taf/us_stat.pdf.

58. Michael S. Malone, "The Smother of Invention," *Forbes ASAP*, June 24, 2002, pp. 32–40.

59. Kris Frieswick, "License to Steal?" *CFO*, September 2001, pp. 89–91; Megan Barnett, "Patents Pending," *U.S. News & World Report*, June 10, 2002, pp. 33–34; Tomima Edmark, "On Guard," *Entrepreneur*, August 1997, pp. 92–94; Tomima Edmark, "On Guard," *Entrepreneur*, February 1997, pp. 109–111.

60. Michael J. McCarthy, "Fake King Cobras Tee Off Maker of High End Clubs," *Wall Street Journal*, February 11, 1997, pp. A1, A8.

61. Rebecca Quick and Ken Bensinger, "Sleaze E-Commerce," *Wall Street Journal Weekend Journal*, May 14, 1999, pp. W1, W10.

62. Michael B. Sapherstein, "The Registrability of the Harley-Davidson Roar: A Multimedia Analysis," www.bc.edu/bc_org/avp/law/st_org/iptf/articles/content/1998101101.html; Tomima Edmark, "How Much Is Too Much?" *Entrepreneur*, February 1998, pp. 93–95.

63. Todd Spangler, "Zippo Snuffs Out Imitations," *The State*, February 25, 2003, pp. B1, B11.

64. Nancy Ganz, "Protecting Your Good Name," *Nation's Business*, September 1995, p. 6.

65. *Global Software Piracy Study*, Business Software Alliance (Washington, DC, May 2001), p. 1, www.bsa.org/resources/2001-05-21.55.pdf.

Chapter 3

1. Alvin Toffler, "Shocking Truths About the Future," *Journal of Business Strategy*, July/August 1996, p. 6.

2. Thomas A. Stewart, "You Think Your Company's So Smart? Prove It," *Fortune*, April 30, 2001, p. 188.

3. Verne Harnish, "The X Factor," *FSB*, December 2002/January 2003, pp. 81–84; "Learn About Us," The Container Store, www.containerstore.com/learn/index.jhtml#stores.

4. Thomas A. Stewart, "Intellectual Capital: Ten Years Later, How Far We've Come," *Fortune*, May 28, 2001, p. 188.

5. Gary Hamel, "Innovation's New Math," *Fortune*, July 9, 2001, p. 130.

6. Harnish, "The X Factor," pp. 81–84.

7. Alan Cohen, "The Great Race," *FSB*, December 2002/January 2003, pp. 42–48.

8. Melanie Wells, "Out of the Tube," *Forbes*, November 26, 2001, p. 200; "Tom's of Maine Common Good Report," www.tomsofmaine.com/downloads/pdf/common_good_report_2001.pdf.

9. Ken Blanchard, "The New Bottom Line," *Entrepreneur*, February 1998, p. 127.

10. Mike Hoffman, "Archive," *Inc.*, April 2002, p. 132; "HP History and Facts," Hewlett-Packard, www.hp.com/hpinfo/abouthp/histnfacts.

11. Thomas A. Stewart, "Why Values Statements Don't Work," *Fortune*, June 10, 1996, p. 137.

12. Michael Barrier, "Back from the Brink," *Nation's Business*, September 1995, p. 21.

13. Richard Schneider, "Chain Reaction," *Guideposts*, April 2003, pp. 18–19; Chick-fil-A, www.chickfila.com/Company.asp.

14. Ellyn Spragins, "Unmasking Your Motivations," *FSB*, November 2002, p. 86; "Workplace 2000 Employee Insight Survey: A Report of Key Findings," MeaningfulWorkplace.com, www.meaningfulworkplace.com/survey.

15. Spragins, "Unmasking Your Motivations," p. 86.

16. Chris Penttila, "Missed Mission," *Entrepreneur*, May 2002, pp. 73–74.

17. "Our Mission Statement," Ben and Jerry's Homemade, Inc., www.benjerry.com/our-company/our_mission.

18. John R. McPherson, Adrian V. Mitchell, and Mark R. Mitten, "Fast-Food Fight," *The McKinsey Quarterly*, Number 2, 2003, www.mckinseyquarterly.com/article_abstract.asp?ar=1295&L2=16&L3=17&srid=17&gp=0.

19. Cora Daniels, "Businesses of War," *FSB*, December 2001/January 2002, p. 24.

20. Paul Glader, "One Industry Is Booming in the Aftermath of Attacks," *Wall Street Journal*, November 7, 2001, pp. B1, B4.

21. Jim Hopkins, "Big Businesses Can't Swallow These Little Fish," *USA Today*, March 27, 2002, p. 28-B.

22. Jenny Munro, "Changing Times," *Greenville News Business*, March 9, 2003, pp. 1, 8–9.

23. Mark Henricks, "Analyze This," *Entrepreneur*, June 1999, pp. 72–75.

24. "Survey Shows Competition Is Most Significant Business Worry," *South Carolina Business Journal*, October 1998, p. 8; Stephanie Gruner, "What Worries CEOs," *Inc.*, February 1997, p. 98.

25. "To the Point," *Beyond Computing*, July/August 1998, p. 21.

26. Carolyn Z. Lawrence, "Know Your Competition," *Business Start-Ups*, April 1997, p. 51.

27. Beth Kwon, "Toolbox: Staying Competitive," *FSB*, December 2002/January 2003, p. 89.

28. Shari Caudron, "I Spy, You Spy," *Industry Week*, October 3, 1994, p. 36.

29. Stephen D. Solomon, "Spies Like You," *FSB*, June 2001, pp. 76–82.

30. Lawrence, "Know Your Competition," pp. 51–56.

31. Stephanie Gruner, "Spies Like Us," *Inc.*, August 1998, p. 45.

32. John DeVore, "Keeping Up with the Jones Co." *Small Business Computing*, October 1999, p. 26.

33. Erika Brown, "Analyze This," *Forbes*, April 1, 2002, pp. 96–98.

34. Laton McCartney, "Getting Smart About Knowledge Management," *Industry Week*, May 4, 1998, p. 30.

35. George Pór, "The Knowledge Ecology," *BizEd*, November/December 2001, p. 33.

36. Tim McCollum, "All the News That's Fit to Net," *Nation's Business*, June 1998, pp. 59–62.

37. Christopher Caggiano, "Low-Tech Smarts," *Inc.*, January 1999, pp. 79–80.

38. Lewis Carroll, *Alice in Wonderland* (Mount Vernon, NY: Peter Pauper Press, 1937), pp. 78–79.

39. Mark Henricks, "In the BHAG," *Entrepreneur*, August 1999, pp. 65–67.

40. Joseph C. Picken and Gregory Dess, "The Seven Traps of Strategic Planning," *Inc.*, November 1996, p. 99.

41. April Y. Pennington, "Snapshot," *Entrepreneur*, June 2002, p. 21; "Our Story," True Confections, www.trueconfections.com//ourstory.php.

42. Michael E. Porter, *Competitive Strategy* (New York: Free Press, 1980), Chapter 2.

43. Melanie Wells, "Lord of the Skies," *Forbes*, October 14, 2002, pp. 130–138.

44. Mark Tatge, "Propped Up," *Forbes*, November 11, 2002, p. 158.

45. Brendan Coffey, "Every Penny Counts," *Forbes*, September 30, 2002, pp. 68–70; Amber McDowell, "Discount Retailers Prosper Amid Economic Instability," *Greenville News Business*, December 23, 2002, pp. 6, 13.

46. "History of It's A Wrap," www.itsawrappws.com/history.html; "Store Information," www.itsawrappws.com/shop.html; "Client Information," www.itsawrappws.com/industry1.html.

47. Celia Farber, "Anice Hotel," *Inc.*, June 2002, pp. 88–90; Shelly Branch, "Havin' an Ice Team," *Fortune*, March 1, 1999, pp. 277–278; Eleena De Lisser, "The Hot New Travel Spot Is Freezing Cold," *Wall Street Journal*, October 16, 2002, pp. D1, D4; Ice Hotel, www.icehotel.com.

48. Debra Phillips, "Leaders of the Pack," *Entrepreneur*, September 1996, p. 127.

49. Victoria Reynolds, "Breaking Big," *FSB*, June 2002, p. 24.

50. Alex Taylor III, "Road Kill," *Fortune*, November 12, 2001, pp. F182[C]–F182[F].

51. Joel Kurtzman, "Is Your Company Off Course? Now You Can Find Out Why," *Fortune*, February 17, 1997, p. 128.

52. Michelle Bitoun, "Show Them the Data," *Trustee*, September 2002, p. 35.

53. Mark Henricks, "Who's Counting?" *Entrepreneur*, July 1998, pp. 70–73.

54. Robert S. Kaplan and David P. Norton, "The Balanced Scorecard— Measures That Drive Performance," *Harvard Business Review*, January–February 1992, pp. 71–79.

Chapter 4

1. Michael Parisi and Brian Balkovic, "Sole Proprietorship Returns 2000," Internal Revenue Service, September 2002.

2. Jacquelyn Lynn, "Partnership Procedures," *Business Start-Ups*, June 1996, p. 73.

3. Frances Huffman, "Irreconcilable Differences," *Entrepreneur*, February 1992, p. 108.

4. "Partnerships," Dogwood Stable, www.dogwoodstable.com.

5. Chief Justice John Marshall, cited by Roger L. Miller and Gaylord A. Jentz, *Business Law Today* (St. Paul, MN: West Publishing Co., 1994), p. 632.

6. Joan Szabo, "Join the Corps," *Entrepreneur*, October 1999, p. 71.

7. Kylo-Patrick Hart, "Step 4: Decide Your Legal Structure," *Business Start-Ups*, August 1996, pp. 62–64.

8. Dale D. Buss, "New Dynamics for a New Era," *Nation's Business*, June 1999, pp. 45–48; "History of Franchising," FranInfo, www.franinfo.com/history.html.

9. Laura Tiffany, "Breaking the Mold," *Business Start-Ups*, April 1999, pp. 42–47; "Why Buy a Franchise?" *The Franchise Doctor*, www.franchisedoc.com/whybuy.html; Buss, "New Dynamics for a New Era," pp. 45–48.

10. Chieh Chieng, "Do You Want to Know a Secret?" *Entrepreneur*, January 1999, p. 176.

11. Anne Field, "Piping-Hot Performance," *Success*, March 1999, pp. 76–80.

12. Andrew A. Caffey, "Franchises That Offer Creative Financing," *Business Start-Ups*, September 1996, pp. 62–68.

13. www.primroseschools.com, 2003.

14. Chana R. Schoenberger, "A Burger with a Side of Losses," *Forbes*, December 9, 2002, p. 168.

15. Gregory Matusky, "The Franchise Hall of Fame," *Inc.*, April 1994, pp. 86–89.

16. North American Securities Administrators Association, "State Regulators Identify 'Top Ten Frauds,'" www.nasaa.org/whoweare/media/topten.html.

17. Anne Field, "Piping-Hot Performance," p. 79.

18. Steven J. Stark, "Have It Your Way," *Success*, April 1999, pp. 57–59.

19. Chieh Chieng, "No Holes Barred," *Business Start-Ups*, March 1999, p. 64; and Carlye Adler, "Would You Pay $2 million for This Franchise?" *Fortune Small Business*, May 2002.

20. Asia Pacific Economic Cooperation, "Consultative Survey on Franchising in APEC Member Economies," http://strategis.ic.gc.ca/SSG/ae00275e.html.

21. Jeffrey Tannenbaum, "Franchisers see a Future in East Bloc," *Wall Street Journal*, June 5, 1990, p. B1.

22. Jay Solomon, "How Mr. Bambang Markets Big Macs in Muslim Indonesia," *Wall Street Journal*, October 26, 2001, p. A-1.

23. Dale D. Buss, "New Dynamics for a New Era," pp. 45–48; "History of Franchising," FranInfo, www.franinfo.com/history.html.

24. Dan Morse, "Franchisees Test the Water Before Taking the Plunge," *Wall Street Journal*, May 11, 1999, p. B2.

25. Roberta Maynard, "Why Franchisers Look Abroad," *Nation's Business*, October 1995, pp. 65–72.

26. Gabrielle Solomon, "Co-Branding Alliances: Arranged Marriages Made by Marketers," *Fortune*, October 12, 1998, p. 188[N]; Gordon Williams, "Roadside Attraction," *Financial World*, October 21, 1996, pp. 96–98; Lynn Beresford, "Seeing Double," *Entrepreneur*, October 1995, pp. 164–167; Roberta Maynard, "The Hit Parade for 2000," *Nation's Business*, April 1997, pp. 68–74.

27. Gabrielle Solomon, "Co-Branding Alliances: Arranged Marriages Made by Marketers," p. 188[N].

Chapter 5

1. Nicole L. Torres, "Fixer-Upper," *Entrepreneur/BYOB*, November 2001, pp. 120–128.

2. Elaine W. Teague, "Playing for Keeps," *Entrepreneur*, August 1998, pp. 104–107.

3. Jill Andresky Fraser, "When It's a Seller's Market," *Inc.*, July 1999, pp. 60–70.

4. Gianna Jacobson, "Mission: Acquisition," *Success*, October 1997, pp. 62–66; Thomas Owens, "Growth Through Acquisition, " *Small Business Reports*, August 1990, p. 63.

5. John Case, "Buy Now—Avoid the Rush," *Inc.*, February 1991, p. 38.

6. Andrea Hock, "When a Business Is Family-Owned; Determining Value Is Art Not Science," *New York Law Journal*, May 29, 2001, p. 3.

7. Kris Frieswick, "Power to the People," *CFO*, April 2002, p. 34; Julie Rose, "Selling (His Soul) to Dannon?" *FSB*, January 2003, pp. 39–42.

8. Peter Nulty, "Smart Ways to Sell Your Business," *Fortune*, March 17, 1996, pp. 97–98.

9. Arthur Lubow, "Mom & Me," *Inc.*, April 1999, pp. 55–63; Michael Liedtke, "Young Inventor Sells Toy Firm," *Upstate Business*, February 7, 1999, p. 3.

10. Jill Andresky Fraser, "Putting Your Company on the Block," *Inc.*, April 2001, pp. 106–107.

11. Laura M. Litvan, "Selling Off, Staying On," *Nation's Business*, August 1995, pp. 29–30.

12. Peter Collins, "Cashing Out and Maintaining Control," *Small Business Reports*, December 1989, p. 28.

13. Charles Stein, "Want to Make a Deal? Find a Rich European Suitor," *FSB*, January 2000, p. 34.

Chapter 6

1. Mark Henricks, "Soft Sell," *Entrepreneur*, September 1998, pp. 139–144; Neil DiBernado, "D&B Survey Finds the Smaller the Business, the Less Marketing Savvy," http://dnb.com/newsview/0898news1.htm.

2. Dale D. Buss, "The Little Guys Strike Back," *Nation's Business*, July 1996, p. 19.

3. Geoff Williams, "Impact!" *Entrepreneur*, October 2002, pp. 64–69.

4. Howard Dana Shaw, "Customer Care Checklist," *In Business*, September/October, 1987, p. 28.

5. Katherine Hobson, "Chic—and Comfortable," *U.S. News & World Report*, May 13, 2002, p. 40; Chico's FAS, www.chicos.com.

6. Jamie Mejia and Gabriel Sama, "Media Players Say 'Si' to Latino Magazines," *Wall Street Journal*, May 15, 2002, p. B4.

7. E. Richard Walton, "Latino Publisher Plans Expansion," *Greenville News*, November 2, 2002, p. 1B.

8. Mejía and Gabriel Sama, "Media Players Say 'Sí' to Latino Magazines," p. B4.

9. NPR's "Morning Edition," January 5, 2000.

10. James M. Pethokoukis, "Bye-Bye Burgers," *U.S. News & World Report*, December 2, 2002, pp. 36–37.

11. Gisela M. Pedroza, "A Case of Amnasia," *Entrepreneur*, June 2002, pp. 22–24.

12. Roberta Maynard, "New Directions in Marketing" *Nation's Business*, July 1995, p. 26.

13. Jim Ammeen, "Making a Niche a Perfect Fit," *Nation's Business*, February 1999, p. 8.

14. Maureen Tkacik, "Hey Dude, This Sure Isn't the Gap," *Wall Street Journal*, February 12, 2002, pp. B1, B4.

15. Nancy L. Croft, "Smart Selling," *Nation's Business*, March 1988, pp. 51–52.

16. Al Cole, "Cinematic Chic," *Modern Maturity*, March–April 1998, p. 24.

17. Larry Selden and Geoffrey Colvin, "A Measure of Success," *Business 2.0*, November 2001, p. 59.

18. Stephen M. Silverman, "Retail Retold," *Inc. Technology*, Summer 1995, pp. 23–26.

19. Jason Fry, "Know Your Customer," *Wall Street Journal*, October 15, 2001, pp. R18–R19.

20. Angela Garber Wolf, "Million-Dollar Questionnaire," *Small Business Computing*, January 2002, pp. 47–48.

21. Meg Whittemore, "Retailing Looks to a New Century," *Nation's Business*, December 1994, p. 20.

22. Nick Wreden, "From Customer Satisfaction to Customer Loyalty," *Beyond Computing*, January/February 1999, pp. 12–14.

23. Paul Hughes, "Service Savvy," *Business Start-Ups*, January 1996, p. 48.

24. G. Lieberman and Sons, www.glieberman.com/activskin; Nichole L. Torres, "Bunch of Hosiers," *Entrepreneur*, August 2002, pp. 26–28; Kevin Helliker, "Kingsize, Not Queen: Some Men Have Taken to Wearing Pantyhose," *Wall Street Journal*, February 19, 2002, pp. A1, A10.

25. Roberta Maynard, "Rich Niches," *Nation's Business*, November 1993, pp. 39–42.

26. Dale D. Buss, "Entertailing," *Nation's Business*, December 1997, p. 18.

27. Buss, "Entertailing," pp. 12–18.

28. Kevin Helliker, "Rare Retailer Scores by Targeting Men Who Hate to Shop," *Wall Street Journal*, December 17, 2002, pp. A1–A11.

29. Shirley Leung, "Novel Delivery Puts Business on the Right Track," *Wall Street Journal*, April 23, 2002, p. B5.

30. Heidi Ernst, "Space Men," *Your Company*, October 1999, p. 20; Space Adventures, www.spaceadventures.com.

31. Mike Hofman, "Emotional Branding," *Inc.*, May 2002, pp. 70–79.

32. *Entrepreneur*, October 2001, p. 24.

33. Ranjay Gulati, Sarah Huffman, and Gary Neilson, "The Barista Principle: Starbucks and the Rise of Relational Capital," *Strategy + Business*, Issue 28, Third Quarter 2002, pp. 58–69.

34. Aimee L. Stern, "How to Build Customer Loyalty," *Your Company*, Spring 1995, p. 37.

35. "Deadly Game of Losing Customers," *In Business*, May 1988, p. 189.

36. Jerry Fisher, "The Secret's Out," *Entrepreneur*, May 1998, pp. 112–119; Jim Campbell, "Good Customer Service Pays Off," *UP*, November 1988, pp. 12–13.

37. "Keeping Customers for Life," *Communication Briefings*, September 1990, p. 3.

38. Rahul Jacob, "Why Some Customers Are More Equal Than Others," *Fortune*, September 19, 1994, pp. 215–224.

39. Patricia Sellers, "Companies That Serve You Best," *Fortune*, May 31, 1993, p. 75.

40. Susan Hauser, "Out of Print? Not Walter Powell," *Wall Street Journal*, January 24, 2002, p. A16.

41. William A. Sherden, "The Tools of Retention," *Small Business Reports*, November 1994, pp. 43–47.

42. Hobson, "Chic—and Comfortable," p. 40.

43. "Ways & Means," *Reader's Digest*, January 1993, p. 56.

44. Kate O'Sullivan, "Major Concessions," *Inc.*, May 2002, p. 34.

45. Thomas Mucha, "The Payoff for Trying Harder," *Business 2.0*, July 2002, pp. 84–87.

46. Erika Brown, "What Women Want," *Forbes*, November 12, 2001, p. 124.

47. Emily Barker, "You Just Don't Get It," *Inc.*, November 2001, p. 120.

48. Faye Rice, "How to Deal with Tougher Customers," *Fortune*, December 3, 1990, pp. 39–40.

49. Philip Siekman, "A Big Maker of Tiny Batches," *Fortune*, May 27, 2002, pp. 152[c]–152[F].

50. Rahul Jacob, "TQM: More Than a Dying Fad," *Fortune*, October 18, 1993, p. 67.

51. Jacob, "TQM: More Than a Dying Fad," p. 67.

52. Janie Magruder, "Tidy Up Your Cleaning Regimen," *Greenville News*, May 3, 2003, pp. 1H, 5H.

53. Dave Zielinski, "Improving Service Doesn't Require a Big Investment," *Small Business Reports*, February 1991, p. 20.

54. Zielinski, "Improving Service Doesn't Require a Big Investment," p. 20.

55. A Little White Wedding Chapel, www.alittlewhitechapel.com/html/tunnel_of_love.html.

56. Emily Nelson, "Marketers Push Individual Portions and Families Bite," *Wall Street Journal*, July 23, 2002, pp. A1, A6.

57. Lucy McCauley, "Measure What Matters," *Fast Company*, May 1999, p. 100.

58. Ben Szobody, "Chefs Get Personal," *Greenville News*, May 19, 2002, p. 1F.

59. Michael Dell, "Thrive in a Sick Economy," *Business 2.0*, December 2002/January 2003, p. 88.

60. Bob Weinstein, "Bright Ideas," *Business Start-Ups*, August 1995, p. 57.

61. Alan Deutschman, "America's Fastest Risers," *Fortune*, October 7, 1991, p. 58.

62. Erika Rasmussion, "A New Kind of Bar Exam," *FSB*, September 2002, p. 18.

63. Jeffrey Pfeffer, "The Face of Your Business," *Business 2.0*, December 2002/January 2003, p. 58.

64. "Hold That Price!" *Success*, May 1995, p. 25.

65. Brian L. Clark, "Interview: Pat Croce," *FSB*, November 2001, p. 44.

66. "Keeping Customers for Life," *Communication Briefings*, September 1990, p. 3.

67. Mark Henricks, "Satisfaction Guaranteed," *Entrepreneur*, May 1991, p. 122.

68. Scott McCormack, "Making Waves," *Forbes*, April 5, 1999, pp. 76–78.

69. Ron Zemke and Dick Schaaf, "The Service Edge," *Small Business Reports*, July 1990, pp. 57–60.

70. Thomas A. Stewart, "After All You've Done for Your Customers, Why Are They Still NOT HAPPY?" *Fortune*, December 11, 1995, pp. 178–182.

71. Mark Henricks, "5 Best Customer Service Ideas," *Entrepreneur*, March 1999, p. 122.

72. Leonard L. Berry, "Customer Service Solutions," *Success*, July/August 1995, pp. 90–95.

73. Julie Sloane, "Digital Makeover," *FSB*, June 2002, p. 78.

74. Zemke and Schaaf, "The Service Edge," p. 60.

75. Desiree De Meyer, "Get to Market Faster," *Smart Business*, October 2001, pp. 62–65; Brian Dumaine, "How Managers Can Succeed Through Speed," *Fortune*, February 13, 1989, pp. 54–59.

76. Geoff Williams, "Speed Freaks," *Entrepreneur*, September 1999, p. 120.

77. Dan Morse, "Tennessee Producer Tries New Tactic in Sofas: Speed," *Wall Street Journal*, November 19, 2002, pp. A1, A20.

78. Mark Henricks, "Time Is Money," *Entrepreneur*, February 1993, p. 44.

79. Joanne H. Pratt, *E-Biz:Strategies for Small Business Success*, U.S. Small Business Administration Office of Advocacy, www.sba.gov/advo/research/rs220tot.pdf, p. 10.

80. "David Lidsky," Tech Skeptic," *FSB*, January 24, 2003, www.fortune.com/fortune/smallbusiness/skeptic/0,15704,411307,00.html; Donna M. McGuire, "Is Your Web Site Profitable?" *Small Business Information*, January 26, 2003, http://sbinformation.miningco.com/library/weekly/uc012603a.htm.

81. Veronica Byrd and Brian L. Clark, "Increasing Your Net Profits," *Your Company*, June/July 1996, p. 24.

82. Noah Elkin, "Web's Face Resembles World," *eMarketer*, December 12, 2001, www.emarketer.com/analysis/world_regions/20011212_wr.html.

83. "Business-to-Business E-Commerce Revenues," Deery Design, www.deerydesign.com/didUknow/chart/b2b.htm; "Business-to-Consumer E-Commerce Revenues," Deery Design, www.deerydesign.com/didUknow/chart/b2c.htm.

84. "David Lidsky," Tech Skeptic," *FSB*, January 24, 2003, www.fortune.com/fortune/smallbusiness/skeptic/0,15704,411307,00.html.

85. Pratt, *E-Biz:Strategies for Small Business Success*, U.S. Small Business Administration Office of Advocacy, www.sba.gov/advo/research/rs220tot.pdf, p. 13.

86. David G. Propson, "Small Biz Gets Small Piece of the Pie," *Small Business Computing*, November 1999, p. 24.

87. Tom Dinome, "Shop Talk," *Small Business Computing*," December 2001, p. 32.

88. Leigh Buchanan, "Virginia Is for Manufacturers," *Inc.*, December 2002, p. 84.; Pilgrim Designs, www.pilgrimdesigns.com.

89. Susan Solomon, "Make Your Web Content Gender Aware," *Small Business Computing*, February 5, 2003, www.smallbusinesscomputing.com/webmaster/print.php/1579571.

90. Pratt, *E-Biz:Strategies for Small Business Success*, U.S. Small Business Administration Office of Advocacy, www.sba.gov/advo/research/rs220tot.pdf, p. 50; Casketfurniture.com, www.casketfurniture.com.

91. Stanley J. Winkelman, "Why Big-Name Stores Are Losing Out," *Fortune*, May 8, 1989, pp. 14–15.

92. Chris Prystay and Meeyoung Song, "Fragrant Fabrics: Peppermint 3-Piece Is Hot in Korea," *Wall Street Journal*, October 21, 2002, pp. A1, A8.

93. Jeannie Mandelker, "Crush Rivals by Launching Great Products," *Your Company*, October/November 1997, pp. 54–60.

94. "Silly Putty Stretches into Cyberspace for Its 50th Anniversary," Sillyputty.com, www.sillyputty.com/campus_news/campus_news_web.htm.

95. Mandelker, "Crush Rivals by Launching Great Products," pp. 54–60; "Fast Break," *Success*, September 1998, p. 14.

96. Paul B. Brown, "The Eternal Second Act," *Inc.*, June 1988, pp. 119–120.

97. Brown, "The Eternal Second Act," p. 120.

98. Andy Raskin, "Why Retail Rocks," *Business 2.0*, June 2002, pp. 55–57.

99. Bob Weinstein, "Set in Stone," *Business Start-Ups*, October 1995, p. 27.

Chapter 7

1. Jonathan Fahey, "Dealers 1, Internet 0," *Forbes*, April 29, 2002, pp. 56–57.

2. Gary Hamel and Jeff Sampler, "The E-Corporation," *Fortune*, December 7, 1998, pp. 81–92.

3. Fahey, "Dealers 1, Internet 0," pp. 56–57.

4. Andrew Raskin, "Setting Your Sites," *Inc. Technology*, No. 2, 1999, p. 20.

5. *A Nation Online: How Americans Are Expanding Their Use of the Internet*, U.S. Department of Commerce (Washington, DC: February 2002), p. 1; Yochi J. Dreazen, "U.S. Says Web Use Has Risen to 54% of the Population," *Wall Street Journal*, February 4, 2002, p. B4.

6. Jerry Useem, "Our 10 Principles of the New Economy, Slightly Revised," *Business 2.0*, August/September 2001, p. 85.

7. "Online Sales Soar According to Latest Shop.org/Forrester Study," May 15, 2003, www.shop.org/press/03/051503.html; Fred Vogelstein, "What Went Right: E-Commerce," *Fortune*, December 30, 2002, p. 166.

8. David Lidsky, "Tech Skeptic," *FSB*, January 24, 2003, www.fortune.com/fortune/smallbusiness/skeptic/0,15704,411307,00.html.

9. "Marketing on the World Wide Web," Alaska Internet Marketing, www.alaskaoutdoors.com/Misc/info.html.

10. Jonathan Fahey, "Wheels of Fortune," *Forbes*, January 6, 2003, pp. 48–49.

11. *The State of Retailing Online 6.0*, Shop.org/Forrester Research, www.shop.org/research/SRO6ExecSumm.html.

12. Maria Atanasov, "A Good Sign," *Smart Business*, February 2002, pp. 66–67.

13. "Part One," *FSB*, October 2001, pp. 16–17.

14. Lane Anderson, "Oops! Learn from Your Mistakes," *Smart Business*, March 2002, p. 63.

15. Lynn Morrissey, "Helping Small Business Grow," *Forbes* insert, September 2, 2002.

16. Joanne H. Pratt, *E-Biz: Strategies for Small Business Success*, U.S. Small Business Administration Office of Advocacy (Washington, DC), October 2002, p. 13.

17. "e or Be Eaten," *Fortune*, November 8, 1999, p. 87.

18. "Reality Bites" *Wall Street Journal*, May 1, 2000, p. B18.

19. Claire Tristram, "Many Happy Returns," *Small Business Computing*, May 1999, p. 73.

20. Pratt, *E-Biz: Strategies for Small Business Success*, p. ii.

21. Melissa Campanelli, "E-Business Busters," *Entrepreneur*, January 2000, pp. 46–50.

22. "Privacy Worries Plague E-Biz," *Small Business Computing*, June 13, 2002, www.smallbusinesscomputing.com/emarketing/print.php/1365361.

23. Ibid.

24. Jodi Mardesich, "The Web Is No Shopper's Paradise," *Fortune*, November 8, 1999, pp. 188–198.

25. "Survival of the Fastest," *Inc. Technology*, No. 4, 1999, p. 57.

26. Anne Stuart, "This Year's Model," *Inc.*, December 2002, p. 94; "Company Profile and History," www.edmunds.com/help/about/profile.html.

27. Steve Bennett and Stacey Miller, "The E-Commerce Plunge," *Small Business Computing*, February 2000, p. 50.

28. Leigh Buchanan and Anne Stuart, "Rental Health," *Inc.*, December 2002, pp. 74, 76; "SafeRent History," www1.saferent.com/about/history.php.

29. Robert McGarvey, "Dot Dot Dot," *Entrepreneur*, April 2000, pp. 96–101; Bronwyn Fryer and Lee Smith, ".Com or Bust," *Forbes Small Business*, December 1999/January 2000, pp. 38–49; Alice Hill, "5 Reasons Customers Abandon Their Shopping Carts (and What You Can Do About It)," *Smart Business*, March 2001, pp. 80–84.

30. Hill, "5 Reasons Customers Abandon Their Shopping Carts (and What You Can Do About It)," pp. 80–84.

31. Bronwyn Fryer, "When Something Clicks," *Inc. Technology*, No. 1, 2000, pp. 62–72; Tristram, "Many Happy Returns," pp. 70–75; Mardesich, "The Web Is No Shopper's Paradise," pp. 188–198.

32. Emily Barker, Anne Marie Borrego, and Mike Hoffman, "I Was Seduced by the Web Economy," *Inc.*, February 2000, pp. 48–70.

33. Fred Vogelstein, "A Cold Bath for Dot-Com Fever," *U.S. News & World Report*, September 13, 1999, p. 37.

34. Mardesich, "The Web Is No Shopper's Paradise," pp. 188–198.

35. Bethany McLean, "More Than Just Dot-Coms," *Fortune*, December 6, 1999, pp. 130–138.

36. "Can E-Tailers Find Fulfillment with Drop Shipping?" *Inc.*, July 18, 2002, www.inc.com/articles/biz_online/do_biz_online/sell_online/24433.html.

37. "Can E-Tailers Find Fulfillment with Drop Shipping?" *Inc.*, July 18, 2002, www.inc.com/articles/biz_online/do_biz_online/sell_online/24433.html; "About Us," Spun.com, www.spun.com/help/aboutus.jsp.

38. David Pecaut, "Myths and Realities of Online Retailing," Boston Consulting Group, www.bcg.com/publications/publication_view.jsp?pubID=416&language=English; "Company Overview," 1800flowers.com, www.1800flowers.com/about/index.asp.

39. Joanne H. Pratt, *E-Biz: Strategies for Small Business Success*, U.S. Small Business Administration Office of Advocacy (Washington, DC), October 2002, p. 24.

40. Robert McGarvey, "From: Business to Business," *Entrepreneur*, June 2000, pp. 96–103; William J. Holstein, "Rewiring the 'Old Economy,'" *U.S. News & World Report*, April 10, 2000, pp. 38–40.

41. McGarvey, "From: Business to: Business," p. 98.

42. Bronwyn Fryer and Lee Smith, ".Com or Bust," *FSB*, December 1999/January 2000, p. 41.

43. Dana Dratch, "These E-Gardening Tips Will Help Your Web Site Grow from Sprout to Giant," *Bankrate.com*, February 29, 2000, www.bankrate.com/brm/news/biz/Ecommerce/20000117.asp.

44. Brad Grimes, "E-Commerce Made Easy," *Your Company*, April 1999, pp. 71–78; Internet Wines & Spirits, www.internetwines.com.

45. Anne Ashby Gilbert, "Going Small Time," *Fortune*, September 27, 1999, pp. 262[A]–262[F].

46. Anne Stuart, "The Search Engine," *Inc.*, December 2002, p. 96.

47. Ibid.

48. Michelle Prather, "Life Online," *Business Start-Ups*, May 2000, p. 17.

49. Eryn Brown, "9 Ways to Win on the Web," *Fortune*, May 24, 1999, p. 112.

50. Melissa Campanelli, "Dot.common Sense," *Entrepreneur*, May 2002, pp. 34–36; "Company Overview," Altrec.com, www.altrec.com/company/press/company.html.

51. Joanne H. Pratt, *E-Biz: Strategies for Small Business Success*, U.S. Small Business Administration Office of Advocacy (Washington, DC), October 2002, pp. 14, 28; dogbooties.com, www.dogbooties.com.

52. Melissa Campanelli, "Caught in the Web of Lies," *Entrepreneur*, January 2003, p. 37; fridgedoor.com, www.fridgedoor.com.

53. Geoff Williams, "Among Friends," *Entrepreneur*, June 2002, p. 30.

54. Matthew Fogel, "Blogging for Dollars," *Inc.*, May 2003, p. 36.

55. Ralph F. Wilson, "The Five Mutable Laws of Web Marketing," *Web Marketing Today* (www.wilsonweb.com/wmta/basic-principles.htm), April 1, 1999, pp. 1–7.

56. Kim T. Gordon, "Weigh Your Opt-Ins," *Entrepreneur*, October 2002, www.entrepreneur.com/Your_Business/YB_SegArticle/0,4621,303101,00.html.

57. Paul Soltoff, "The Future of E-Mail," *Small Business Computing*, March 26, 2003, www.smallbusinesscomputing.com/emarketing/print.php/2170261.

58. Melanie Warner and Daniel Roth, "10 Companies That Get It," *Fortune*, November 8, 1999, pp. 115–117.

59. Melissa Campanelli, "Straight Talking," *Entrepreneur*, October 2002, pp. 47–48.

60. Robert McGarvey, "Find Your Partner," *Entrepreneur*, February 2000, p. 74.

61. Robert McGarvey, "Irreconcilable Differences," *Entrepreneur*, February 2000, p. 75.

62. Ibid.

63. Steve Cooper, "Global Village," *Entrepreneur*, April 2002, p. 30.

64. Melissa Campanelli, "Spanning the Globe," *Entrepreneur*, August 2000, www.entrepreneur.com/Your_Business/YB_PrintArticle/0,2361,277783,00.html.

65. "How to Get Customers to Come Back to Your Site," *Entrepreneur*, October 28, 2002, www.entrepreneur.com/article/o,4621,304098,00.html.

66. "Finding and Securing a Domain Name," *Entrepreneur*, April 14, 2003, www.entrepreneur.com/Your_Business/YB_PrintArticle/0,2361,307741,00.html; Linda Formichelli, "The Domain Game," *Home Office Magazine*, January 2001, www.entrepreneur.com/Your_Business/YB_SegArticle/0,4621,285164,00.html.

67. Robert A. Mamis, "The Name Game," *Inc.'s The State of Small Business 2000*, pp. 141–144.

68. Alfred Gingold, "Click Here," *My Generation*, July–August 2001, p. 51.

69. Joanna L. Krotz, "Rise to the Top of Search Results," *Microsoft bCentral*, May 18, 2003, http://bcentral.com/articles/krotz/110.asp?format=print.

70. Ibid.

71. Amy Austin, "Making Your Site Stand Out," *Small Business Computing*, October 1999, Advertising Insert.

72. Melissa Campanelli, "Good Incentive," *Entrepreneur*, August 2001, pp. 82–84.

73. Ibid.

74. Melissa Campanelli, "Spring Cleaning," *Entrepreneur*, April 2003, p. 44; Dan Blacharski, "Now Loading . . . .", *Entrepreneur*, April 16, 2000, www.entrepreneur.com/Your_Business/YB_SegArticle/0,4621,271233,00.html.

75. Stavraka, "There's No Stopping E-Business. Are You Ready?" *Forbes*, December 13, 1999, Special Advertising Section.

76. Michele Marrinan, "The Shipping News," *Small Business Computing*, December 2001, pp. 47–48.

77. Melissa Campanelli, "Hot on the Trail," *Entrepreneur*, August 1999, pp. 40–43.

78. Nick Wreden, "Computing Your Web Site Payoff," *Beyond Computing*, April 2000, pp. 50–53.

79. *Pew Internet & American Life Project*, 2002, www.pewinternet.org/reports/reports.asp?Report=19&Section=ReportLevel1&Field=Level1ID&ID=43; Bob Tedeschi, "Privacy vs. Profits," *Smart Business*, October 2001, pp. 56–60.

80. J. D. Tuccille, "Don't Be Big Brother," *Small Business Computing*, July 1999, pp. 42–43.

81. Melissa Campanelli, "A Wall of Fire," *Entrepreneur*, February 2000, pp. 48–49.

82. Ibid.

83. "Insane Stat," *Business 2.0*, March 6, 2001, p. 30.

84. David Lidsky, "Hello, Sucker," *FSB*, May 2002, p. 82.

85. Ibid.

86. Susan Greco, "The Fraud Bogeyman," *Inc.*, February 2001, pp. 103–104.

Chapter 8

1. Michelle Prather, "Selling Points," *Business Start-Ups*, July 1999, p. 96.

2. Donna Fenn, "Honey, Hand Me a Polygamy Porter," *Inc.*, May, 2002, pp. 94–97.

3. Thomas Love, "Creating Demand for a New Product," *Nation's Business*, August 1998, p. 11.

4. Debra Phillips, "Fast Track," *Entrepreneur*, April 1999, p. 42.

5. Ibid.

6. Monique Harris, "Fast Pitch," *Business Start-Ups*, December 1999, pp. 71–75.

7. Harvey Meyer, "And Now, Some Words About Sponsors," *Nation's Business*, March 1999, pp. 38–41.

8. Roy S. Johnson, "Speed Sells," *Fortune*, April 12, 1999, pp. 56–62.

9. Erick Schonfeld, "Coming to a Speedway Near You," *Fortune*, March 31, 1997, p. 38.

10. Cora Daniels, "Not Your Showroom Model," *Fortune*, April 12, 1999, pp. 62–72.

11. Meyer, "And Now, Some Words About Sponsors," pp. 38–41.

12. Carrie Dolan, "Putting on the Dog Just Comes Naturally in Fey Marin County," *Wall Street Journal*, September 19, 1985, p. 1.

13. Maureen Tkacik, "Roxy Builds TV, Book Series Around Its Own Surf Wear," *Wall Street Journal*, February 19, 2003, p. B1.

14. Warren Berger, "Just Do It, Again," *Business 2.0*, September 2002, pp. 77–84.

15. Dale D. Buss, "Sell Your Way to Success," *Nation's Business*, February 1999, pp. 14–19; "Traits of Top Salespeople," *Small Business Reports*, December 1990, pp. 7–8; Roberta Maynard, "Finding the Essence of Good Salespeople," February 1998, p. 10; Landy Chase, "2000 and Beyond: The Golden Age of Professional Selling," *The Small Business Journal*, www.tsbj.com/editorial/02050501.htm.

16. Jaclyn Fierman, "The Death and Rebirth of the Salesman," *Fortune*, July 25, 1994, pp. 80–91.

17. Nancy J. Wagner, "Picking a Medium for Your Message," *Nation's Business*, February 1999, pp. 56–57.

18. Mark Henricks, "Spread the Word," *Entrepreneur*, February 1998, pp. 120–125.

19. "Radio Facts," Radio Advertising Bureau, www.rab.com/station/mgfb99/fac2.html.

20. "Trends in Television," Television Bureau of Advertising, www.tvb.org/tvfacts/trends/tv/executive.html.

21. "Media Facts," Radio Advertising Bureau, www.rab.com/station/mediafact/medfcts98/tv.html.

22. G. David Doran, "Station Breaks," *Entrepreneur*, September 1998, pp. 147–151.

23. Ibid.

24. Don Debelak, "Broadcast News," *Business Start-Ups*, September 1998, pp. 90–91; Doran, "Station Breaks," pp. 147–151.

25. "Fact Sheets," Magazine Publishers of America, www.magazine.org/resources/fact_sheets/ed1_8_99.html.

26. *The Dynamics of Change in Markets and Media*, from a Magazine Publishers Association seminar, New York.

27. "Fact Sheets," Magazine Publishers of America, www.magazine.org/resources/fact_sheets/ed3_8_99.html.

28. Leigh Buchanan, "The Best of the Small Business Web: Pitching Camp," *Inc. Technology 1999*, No. 4, pp. 74–75.

29. Bronwyn Fryer, "(Your Message Here)," *Inc. Technology 1999*, No. 1, pp. 76–79; Leigh Buchanan, "The Best of the Small Business Web: Seed Money," *Inc. Technology 1999*, No. 4, pp. 72–74, 108.

30. "E-Mail Marketing Worth $4.6 Billion in 2003," *eMarketer*, February 4, 2000, www.emarketer.com/estats/020400_email.html.

31. "E-Mail Marketing Report," *eMarketer*, January 2000, www.emarketer.com/estats/sell_email.html.

32. Jane Weaver, "Marketing Secrets for the New Economy," *PC Computing*, January 2000, pp. 90–100.

33. "E-Mail Marketing Worth $4.6 Billion in 2003," *eMarketer*, February 4, 2000, www.emarketer.com/estats/020400_email.html.

34. Jeanne Jennings, "How to Optimize E-Mail List Growth," *Small Business Computing.Com*, February 3, 2003.

35. Jared Blank, "The Four Basic E-Mail Campaign Test," *Small Business Computing.Com*, February 3, 2003.

36. Outdoor Advertising Association of America, www.oaaa.org; MARC Gunther, *Fortune*, March 1, 1999, "The Great Outdoors," pp. 150–157.

37. Debra Phillips, "Now Hear This," *Entrepreneur*, July 1999, p. 32.

38. Joel Kurtzman, "Advertising for All the Little Guys," *Fortune*, April 12, 1999, p. 162[L].

39. Debra Phillips, "To Infinity and Beyond," *Entrepreneur*, May 1999, p. 46.

40. *TAA Rate Directory of Transit Advertising* (New York: Transit Advertising Association), p. 2.

41. Tad Simons, "Trick of the Trade," *Presentations*, December 1998, pp. 131–135.

42. Leann Anderson, "On with the Show," *Entrepreneur*, August 1998, p. 94.

43. Bernie Ward, "Everything's the Medium," *Sky*, May 1989, pp. 96–110.

44. "Point of Purchase (POP) Advertising," Smart Business Supersite, www.smartbiz.com/sbs/arts/hph8.htm.

45. Ronald Alsop, "To Share Shoppers, Companies Test Talking, Scented Displays," *Wall Street Journal*, June 12, 1986, p. 31.

46. Rodney Ho, "Vending Machines Make Change," *Wall Street Journal*, July 7, 1999, pp. B1, B4.

47. Denise Osburn and Dawn Kopecki, "A Way to Stretch Ad Dollars," *Nation's Business*, May 1994, p. 68.

48. Osburn and Kopecki, "A Way to Stretch Ad Dollars," p. 68.

49. Jane Easter Bahls, "Ad It Up," *Entrepreneur*, December 1994, pp. 47–49.

50. "Advertising Vehicles: Businesses Discover New Use for Old Cars," *The Greenville News*, June 19, 1993, p. 1D.

51. Sara Delano, "Give and You Shall Receive," *Inc.*, February 1983, p. 128.

52. Howard Scott, "The Tricky Art of Raising Prices," *Nation's Business*, February 1999, p. 32.

53. Joshua Levine, "Time Is Money," *Forbes*, September 18, 2000, pp. 178–185.

54. Joann S. Lublin, "Fountain Pen Fashion: Try 5,072 Diamonds or Abe Lincoln's DNA," *Wall Street Journal*, August, 14, 2001, p. A.1.

55. Robert Shulman and Richard Miniter, "Discounting Is No Bargain," *Wall Street Journal*, December 7, 1998, p. A30.

56. William Echilkson, "The Return of Luxury," *Fortune*, October 17, 1994, p. 18.

57. Shulman and Richard Miniter, "Discounting Is No Bargain," p. A30.

58. Brenda Biondo, "Think *Your* Day Care Is Expensive?" *USA Weekend*, February 4–6, 2000, p. 10.

59. Gayle Sato Stodder, "Paying the Price," *Entrepreneur*, October 1994, p. 54.

60. Carolyn Z. Lawrence, "The Price Is Right," *Business Start-Ups*, February 1996, p. 67.

61. Michael Menduno, "Priced to Perfection," *Business 2. Com*, March 6, 2001, pp. 40–41, Amy Cortese, "The Power of Optimal Pricing," *Business 2.0*, September 2002, pp. 68–70, and John Edwards, "Cyber Pricing," *CFO*, June 2001, p. 16.

62. American Consumer Credit Counseling, www.consumercredit.com/cardstats.htm; Bob Weinstein, "Getting Carded," *Entrepreneur*, September 1995, pp. 76–80.

63. "ICMA Quick Card Facts and Glossary," International Card Manufacturers Association, www.icma.com/info/cardfacts.htm; Lucy Lazarony, "What Your Address Says About How You Use Credit Cards," Bankrate.com, www.bankrate.com/brm/news/cc/19990816.asp.

64. "Business Bulletin," *Wall Street Journal*, July 26, 1990, p. A1.

65. Richard J. Maturi, "Charging Ahead," *Entrepreneur*, July 1990, p. 56.

66. Bob Weinstein, "Getting Carded," p. 76.

Chapter 9

1. Wendy Taylor and Marty Jerome, "Dead Men Talking," *Smart Business*, December 2001/January 2002, p. 19.

2. "Help! My Firm Is Hemorrhaging Cash," *Your Company*, April/May 1996, pp. 10–11.

3. *National Small Business Poll: The Cash Flow Problem*, National Federation of Independent Businesses (Washington, DC: 2002), p. 2.

4. Jerry Useem, "The Icon That Almost Wasn't," *Inc: The State of Small Business 1998*, p. 142; "History," Ford Motor Company, www.ford.com/en/heritage/history/default.htm.

5. Daniel Kehrer, "Big Ideas for Your Small Business," *Changing Times*, November 1989, p. 58.

6. Douglas Bartholomew, "4 Common Financial Management Mistakes . . . And How to Avoid Them," *Your Company*, Fall 1991, p. 9.

7. Robert A. Mamis, "Money In, Money Out," *Inc.*, March 1993, p. 98.

8. Bartholomew, "4 Common Financial Management Mistakes . . . And How to Avoid Them," p. 9.

9. Phaedra Hise, "Paging for Cash Flow," *Inc.*, December 1995, p. 131.

10. Kortney Stringer, "Neither Anthrax Nor the Economy Stops the Fruitcake," *Wall Street Journal*, December 19, 2001, pp, B1, B4; Dirk Smillie, "Signs of Life," *Forbes*, November 11, 2002, p. 160.

11. *National Small Business Poll: The Cash Flow Problem*, National Federation of Independent Businesses (Washington, DC: 2002), p. 1.

12. Jill Andresky Fraser, "Monitoring Daily Cash Trends," *Inc.*, October 1992, p. 49.

13. William G. Shepherd, Jr., "Internal Financial Strategies," *Venture*, September 1985, p. 66.

14. David H. Bangs, *Financial Troubleshooting: An Action Plan for Money Management in the Small Business* (Dover, NH: Upstart Publishing Company, 1992), p. 61.

15. Ilan Mochari, "A Simple Little System," *Inc.*, October 1999, p. 87.

16. "Cash Flow/Cash Flow Management," *Small Business Reporter*, No. 9, p. 5.

17. William Bak, "Make 'Em Pay," *Entrepreneur*, November 1992, p. 64.

18. Sean P. Melvin, "It's Payback Time," *Entrepreneur*, April 2002, pp. 67–68.

19. Richard G. P. McMahon and Scott Holmes, "Small Business Financial Management Practices in North America: A Literature Review," *Journal of Small Business Management*, April 1991, p. 21.

20. Ilan Mochari, "Collect from the Worst," *Inc.*, September 1999, p. 101.

21. "The Check Isn't in the Mail," *Small Business Reports*, October 1991, p. 6.

22. American Collectors Association, www.collector.com; Howard Muson, "Collecting Overdue Accounts," *Your Company*, Spring 1993, p. 4.

23. Richard J. Maturi, "Collection Dues and Don'ts," *Entrepreneur*, January 1992, p. 326.

24. Elaine Pofeldt, "Collect Calls," *Success*, March 1998, pp. 22–24.

25. Janine Latis Musick, "Collecting Payments Due," *Nation's Business*, January 1999, pp. 44–46.

26. Ilan Mochari, "Top Billing," *Inc.*, October 1999, p. 89.

27. Jim Carlton, "Tight Squeeze," *Wall Street Journal*, March 26, 1996, pp. A1, A6.

28. Jill Andresky Fraser, "A Confidence Game," *Inc.*, December 1989, p. 178.

29. Jill Andresky Fraser, "How to Get Paid," *Inc.*, March 1992, p. 105.

30. Eleena deLisser, "Yellow-Pages Con Artists Are Pushing Online Editions," *Wall Street Journal*, November 16, 1999, p. B2.

31. Shepherd, "Internal Financial Strategies," p. 68.

32. Mark Henricks, "No Long-Term Parking," *Entrepreneur*, January 2002, www.entrepreneur.com/article/0,4621,295660.html.

33. Stephanie Barlow, "Frozen Assets," *Entrepreneur*, September 1993, p. 53.

34. Roberta Maynard, "Can You Benefit from Barter?" *Nation's Business*, July 1994, p. 6.

35. "301 Great Ideas for Selling Smarter," *Inc.*, January 1, 1998, p. 47.

36. Mamis, "Money In, Money Out," p. 102.

37. Jeffrey Lant, "Cash Is King," *Small Business Reports*, May 1991, p. 49.

38. "Barter Statistics," International Reciprocal Trade Association, www.irta.com; Melissa Campanelli, "Fair Trade," *Entrepreneur*, August 2001, pp. 33–35.

39. Ronaleen Roha, "How Bartering Saves Cash," *Kiplinger's Personal Finance Magazine*, February 1996, p. 103.

40. Campanelli, "Fair Trade," pp. 33–35.

41. Ilan Mochari, "A Simple Little System," *Inc.*, October 1, 1999, p. 142.

42. "Leasing Basics," Equipment Lease Association's Lease Assistant, 2002, www.leaseassistant.org.

43. Jill Amadio, "To Lease or Not to Lease?" *Entrepreneur*, February 1998, p. 133.

44. Jack Wynn, "To Use But Not to Own," *Nation's Business*, January 1991, p. 38.

45. Mark Henricks, "To Say the Leased," *Entrepreneur*, February 2002, pp. 61–62; Michelle Marinan, "Love It, or Lease It," *Small Business Computing*, March 2000, pp. 39–40; Juan Hovey, "Equip Your Future Through a Lease," *Nation's Business*, May 1999, pp. 47–48.

46. Roger Thompson, "Business Copes with the Recession," *Nation's Business*, January 1991, p. 20.

47. Bruce G. Posner, "Skipped-Payment Loans," *Inc.*, September 1992, p. 40.

48. "Check and ACH Statistics," ACA International, www.acainternational.org/images/Press/Checks.doc.pdf; "The Use of Checks and Other Noncash Payment Instruments in the United States, Federal Reserve Board, www.federalreserve.gov/pubs/bulletin/2002/0802_2nd.pdf, 2002, pp. 360–361.

49. "How to Win the Battle of Bad Checks," *Collection*, Fall 1990, p. 3.

50. Thompson, "Business Copes with the Recession," p. 21.

51. Jill Andresky Fraser, "Better Cash Management," *Inc.*, May 1993, p. 42.

52. Mamis, "Money In, Money Out," p. 103.

Chapter 10

1. "Odds and Ends," *Wall Street Journal*, July 25, 1990, p. B1.

2. Richard G. P. MaMahon and Scott Holmes, "Small Business Financial Management Practices in North America: A Literature Review," *Journal of Small Business Management*, April 1991, p. 21.

3. Paul A. Broni, "Make Your Financials Add Up," *Inc.*, March 21, 2002, www.inc.com/articles/write_bz_plan/24019.html.

4. William Bak, "The Numbers Game," *Entrepreneur*, April 1993, p. 54.

5. Diedrich Von Soosten, "The Roots of Financial Destruction," *Industry Week*, April 5, 1993, pp. 33–34.

6. Richard Maturi, "Take Your Pulse," *Business Start-Ups*, January 1996, p. 72.

7. G. Dean Palmer, "Marketing and Management Strategies of Small Rural Retailers in South-Side Virginia," Small Business Advancement National Center, University of Central Arkansas (Conway, Arkansas, 1995), www.sbaer.uca.edu/Research/1995/SSBIA/95swi052.txt.

8. Jill Andresky Fraser, "When Staffers Track Results," *Inc.*, October 1993, p. 42; Dan Callahan, "Everybody's an Accountant," *Business Ethics*, January/February 1994, p. 37.

9. Gregory Zuckerman, "Climb of Corporate Debt Trips Analysts' Alarm," *Wall Street Journal*, December 31, 2001, pp. C1–C2.

10. Rishawn Biddle, "Gloom Service," *Forbes*, January 24, 2000, p. 140.

11. Bak, "The Numbers Game," p. 57.

12. "Analyzing Creditworthiness," *Inc.*, November 1991, p. 196.

13. Scott Herhold, "Warning Sign," *Business 2.0*, August/September 2001, pp. 198–199.

14. Kayte Vanscoy, "Dead or Alive?" *Smart Business*, August 2001, p. 32.

15. Emily Barker, "Finance: Cheap Executive Officer," *Inc.*, April 1, 2002, pp. 114–116.

16. Ilan Mochari, "A Simple Little System," *Inc.*, October 1999, p. 87.

17. Bo Burlingham, "*Inc.* Query: Number Crunching," *Inc.*, February 1, 2002, www.inc.com/articles/finance/fin_manage/basic_fin_manage/23857.html.

18. John Case, "Critical Numbers in Action," *Inc.*, January 21, 2000, www.inc.com/articles/finance/fin_manage/forecast/15981.html.

19. Ibid.

20. William F. Doescher, "Taking Stock," *Entrepreneur*, November 1994, p. 64.

21. Ilan Mochari, "Significant Figures," *Inc.*, July 2000, p. 128.

22. Robert Macy, "Mirage Megaresort Changed Face and Fortunes of Las Vegas," *Greenville News*, November 25, 1999, p. 22A.

23. Mochari, "Significant Figures," p. 128.

Chapter 11

1. Dan Morse, "Many Small Businesses Don't Devote Time to Planning," *Wall Street Journal*, September 7, 1999, p. B2.

2. Michael Warshaw, "A Novel Plan," *Inc.*, October 1999, p. 21.

3. Steve Marshall Cohen, "Reality Check," *Business Start-Ups*, October 1995, pp. 74–75.

4. David Newton, "Model Behavior," *Entrepreneur*, March, 2002, pp. 68–71.

5. Steve Marshall Cohen, "Money Rules," *Business Start-Ups*, July 1995, p. 79.

6. "Advice from the Great Ones," *Communication Briefings*, January 1992, p. 5.

7. Jacquelyn Lynn, "Let the Bidding Begin," *Entrepreneur*, September 2003 www.entrepreneur.com/article/0,4621,310583,00.html.

8. Conversation with Charles Burke, CEO, Burke Financial Associates.

9. Conversation with Charles Burke, CEO, Burke Financial Associates.

10. Karen Axelton, "Good Plan, Stan," *Business Start-Ups*, March 2000, p. 17.

11. Susan Greco, "Finding The Perfect Pitch," *Inc.*, June, 2002, pp. 87–98.

Chapter 12

1. Paul DeCeglie, "What About Me?" *Business Start-Ups*, June 2000, p. 45.

2. Udayan Gupta, "The Right Fit," *Wall Street Journal*, May 22, 1995, p. R8.

3. Aliza Pilar Sherman, "The Opposite Sex," *Entrepreneur*, September 2002, p. 36.

4. U.N. Umesh and Patrick Criteser, "Venture Capital's Foul Weather Friends," *Wall Street Journal*, January 14, 2003, p. B13; "Press Releases," Northwest Energy Efficiency Alliance, www.nwalliance.org/news/pressreleases.asp.

5. Luisa Kroll, "P2P or Bust," *Forbes: Best of the Web*, July 17, 2000, pp. 94–96.

6. Silvia Sansoni, "Burned Angels," *Forbes*, April 19, 1999, pp. 182–185.

7. Toni Mack, "They Stole My Baby," *Forbes*, February 12, 1996, pp. 90–91.

8. Elizabeth Fenner, "How to Raise the Cash You Need," *Money Guide*, Summer 1991, p. 45.

9. Carrie Coolidge, "The Bootstrap Brigade," *Forbes*, December 28, 1998, pp. 90–91.

10. Ibid.

11. Fenner, "How to Raise the Cash You Need," p. 45.

12. Paul Kvinta, "Frogskins, Shekels, Bucks, Moolah, Cash, Simoleans, Dough, Dinero: Everybody Wants It. Your Business Needs It. Here's How to Get It," *Smart Business*, August 2000, pp. 74–89.

13. Joseph R. Bell, Kenneth M. Huggins, and Christine McClatchey, "Profiling the Angel Investor," presented at Small Business Insitute Director's Association Conference, February 7, 2002, San Diego California, p. 1; "Biography: Laurance Spelman Rockefeller," InfoPlease.com, www.infoplease.com/ipa/A0771997.html.

14. Pamela Sherrid, "Angels of Capitalism," *U.S. News & World Report*, October 13, 1997, pp. 43–45.

15. Wendy Taylor and Marty Jerome, "Pray," *Smart Business*, July 2000, p. 45; Sherrid, "Angels of Capitalism," pp. 43–45; Paul Kvinta, "Frogskins, Shekels, Bucks, Moolah, Cash, Simoleans, Dough, Dinero: Everybody Wants It. Your Business Needs It. Here's How to Get It," *Smart Business*, August 2000, pp. 74–89; Thea Singer, "Where the Money Is," *Inc.*, September 2000, pp. 52–57; Bonnie Azab Powell, "Angel Investors Fill Void Left by Risk Capital," *New York Times*, July 6, 2001, p. 28.

16. Taylor and Jerome, "Pray," p.45.

17. Silvia Sansoni, "Burned Angels," *Forbes*, April 19, 1999, pp. 182–185.

18. Roger Barnes, "Touched by an Angel," *Black Enterprise*, June 2001, pp. 242–247; Susan Greco, "Get$$$Now.com," *Inc.*, September 1999, pp. 35–38; "Digging for Dollars," *Wall Street Journal*, February 24, 1989, p. R25; Quentin Hardy, "Where Angels Dare to Tread," *Forbes*, October 28, 2002, pp. 303–304.

19. Kvinta, "Frogskins, Shekels, Bucks, Moolah, Cash, Simoleans, Dough, Dinero: Everybody Wants It. Your Business Needs It. Here's How to Get It," p. 78.

20. Powell, "Angel Investors Fill Void Left by Risk Capital," p. 28; Paul Kvinta, "Frogskins, Shekels, Bucks, Moolah, Cash, Simoleans, Dough, Dinero: Everybody Wants It. Your Business Needs It. Here's How to Get It."

21. Hardy, "Where Angels Dare to Tread."

22. Nancy Scarlato, "Money," *Business Start-Ups*, December 1995, pp. 50–51; Gianna Jacobsen, "Raise Money Now," *Success*, November 1995, pp. 39–50.

23. Mark Henricks, "Stand Your Ground," *Entrepreneur*, January 1993, p. 264.

24. *Corporate Venture Capital Report* (New York: Ernst & Young, 2002), p. 3; Alistair Christopher, "Corporate Venture Capital: Moving to the Head of the Class," *Venture Capital Journal*, November 1, 2000, www.findarticles.com/cf_dls/m0ZAL/2000_Nov_1/66502342/print.jhtml.

25. Ian Springsteel, "Need More Money? Find a Big White Knight," *FSB*, September 2000, pp. 33–36.

26. Mark Henricks, "Answering the Call," *Entrepreneur*, July 2002, pp. 19–21.

27. Arlyn Tobias Gajilan, "Big Money on Campus," *Your Company*, October 1999, p. 34.

28. Warren P. Strobel, "The Spy Who Funded Me (and My Start-Up)," *U.S. News & World Report*, July 17, 2000, pp. 38–39; Rick E. Yannuzzi, "In-Q-Tel: A New Partnership Between the CIA and the Private Sector," *Defense Intelligence Journal*, Volume 9, Number 1, Winter 2000, pp. 25–38.

29. "What Is Venture Capital?" *Venture Capital Journal*, 2001, pp. 32–36; Paul DeCeglie, "What About Me?" *Business Start-Ups*, June 2000, pp. 45–51.

30. Janet Effland, "How to Bet on the Next Big Thing," *Business 2.0*, December 2002/January 2003, p. 90.

31. Singer, "Where the Money Is," pp. 52–55; National Venture Capital Association, www.nvca.org; PriceWaterhouseCoopers MoneyTree Survey, www.pwcmoneytree.com/moneytree/index.jsp.

32. PriceWaterhouseCoopers Money Tree Survey, www.pwcmoneytree.com/moneytree/index.jsp.

33. Anne B. Fisher, "Raising Capital for a New Venture," *Fortune*, June 13, 1994, p. 101.

34. Brian Carroll, "FurnitureFind.com Gets Capital Infusion," *Furniture Today*, July 16, 2002, www.furnituretoday.com/news/news07-16-02d.shtml; "About Us," FurnitureFind.com, www.furniturefind.com/findanswers/info.asp?strInfo=ffhis; Joseph McCafferty, "Adventure Capital," *CFO*, September 2002, p. 19.

35. Stewart Alsop, "The Rules of Venture Capital," *Fortune*, April 15, 2002, p. 76.

36. Chandrani Ghosh, "Problem Licked," *Forbes*, July 8, 2002, p. 158; Anne Stuart, "Where Do Great Ideas Come From?" *Inc.*, October 15, 2002, pp. 40–42; "About FlavorX," www.flavorx.com/about.asp?T=I.

37. Dave Pell, "What's Old Is New Again," *FSB*, July/August 2000, p. 122.

38. Jennifer Pellet, "Public Opinion," *Entrepreneur*, October 2002, pp. 76–81.

39. "JetBlue IPO Soars," *CNNMoney*, money.cnn.com/2002/04/12/markets/ipo/jetblue/index.htm; Julia Boorstin, "JetBlue's IPO Takes Off," *Fortune*, April 29, 2002, p. 150; JetBlue Airways, S-1/A SEC Filing, p. 3, http://hoovers.10kwizard.com/filing.php?repo=tenk&ipage=1708589&doc=1&back=3&eRid=&type=.

40. David R. Evanson, "Tales of Caution in Going Public," *Nation's Business*, June 1996, p. 58.

41. Francis B. Allgood, "Stathakis Keeps Stax's on Track," *GSA Business*, March 11, 2002, p. 3.

42. Roberta Maynard, "Are You Ready to Go Public?" *Nation's Business*, January 1995, pp. 30–32.

43. Tim Reason, "Off the Street," *CFO*, May 2003, pp. 54–58.

44. Jill Andresky Fraser, "The Price of Going Public," *Inc.*, June 2002, p. 86; Philip W. Taggart, Roy Alexander, and Robert M. Arnold, "Deciding Whether to Go Public," *Nation's Business*, May 1991, p. 52.

45. Pellet, "Public Opinion," p. 79.

46. David R. Evanson and Art Beroff, "Synchronize Your Watches," *Entrepreneur*, November 1999, pp. 74–77.

47. Luisa Kroll, "R-E-S-P-E-C-T," *Forbes*, July 22, 2002, pp. 184–185; "Internet Connect Withdraws $100M IPO, Cites Market Conditions," *IPO Monitor*, September 29, 2000, www.ipomonitor.com/nt/56966.html.

48. Kroll, "R-E-S-P-E-C-T," pp. 184–185.

49. David R. Evanson and Art Beroff, "It Ain't Over . . ." *Entrepreneur*, December 1999, pp. 66–69; CorpHQ, www.corphq.com.

50. Andresky Fraser, "Entrepreneurs in Search of a Deal," *Inc.*, April 2000, pp. 116–120; "PatchLink.com Closes $5.6 Million Funding Round Led by OffRoad Capital," corporate.patchlink.com/news/ Release.asp?ReleaseID=44.

51. Telephone interview with David Barash, Ben & Jerry's Homemade.

52. Paul DeCeglie, "Public Enemy?" *Business Start-Ups*, November 1999, pp. 38–48; "Small Green Firms Use Direct Public Offerings," *In Business*, May/June 1996, p. 10; "A Fishy Success," *Business Ethics*, July/August 1996, p. 6; Drew Field Direct Public Offerings: Client Summaries, Blue Fish Clothing, www.dfdpo.com/clientsum9.htm.

53. "About Us," Real Goods Trading Company, www.realgoods.com/about/history.cfm; "Real Goods Trading Company," Drew Field Direct Public Offering, www.dfdpo.com/clientsum5.htm.

54. Gianna Jacobson, "Find Your Fortune on the Internet," *Success*, November 1995, p. 50.

55. *Micro-Business-Friendly Banks in the United States, 2001 Edition*, U.S. Small Business Administration, Office of Advocacy (Washington, DC: 2002), p. 2.

56. Karen Axelton, "Don't Bank on It," *Business Start-Ups*, May 1998, p. 116.

57. Cynthia E. Griffin, "Money in the Bank," *Entrepreneur*, July 2000, pp. 84–89; *Micro-Business-Friendly Banks in the United States, 2001 Edition*, U.S. Small Business Administration, Office of Advocacy, (Washington, DC: 2002), p. 2.

58. Anne Field, "Getting the Bank to Yes," *Success*, May 1999, pp. 67–71.

59. Daniel M. Clark, "Banks and Bankability," *Venture*, September 1989, p. 29.

60. Anne Ashby Gilbert, "Where to Go When the Bank Says No," *Fortune*, October 12, 1998, pp. 188[C]–188[F].

61. Crystal Detamore-Rodman, "Can I Take Your Orders?" *Entrepreneur*, August 2002, pp. 49–51.

62. "What Is Business Credit?" National Association of Credit Management, www.nacm.org/aboutnacm/what.html; "Financing Small Business," *Small Business Reporter*, c3, p. 9.

63. Jill Andresky Fraser, "When Supplier Credit Helps Fuel Growth," *Inc.*, March 1995, p. 117.

64. Gilbert, "Where to Go When the Bank Says No," pp. 188[C]–188[F].

65. Scott McMurray, "Personal Loans from Brokers Offer Low Rates," *Wall Street Journal*, January 7, 1986, p. 31.

66. Crystal Detamore-Rodman, "Going for Broker," *Entrepreneur*, September 2002, pp. 52–54.

67. "Credit Union Statistics," Credit Union National Association, www.cuna.org/download/us_totals.pdf.

68. "Joseph Ogwal: Building a Stable Future for His Family," World Council of Credit Unions, www.woccu.org/cudev/microfinance/afr_splt.htm.

69. Sean P. Melvin, "Itsy-Bitsey Bonds," *Entrepreneur*, January 2002, pp. 78–82.

70. *SBIC Program Statistical Package*, U.S. Small Business Administration (Washington, DC), 2003, www.sba.gov/INV/stat/table1.pdf.

71. *SBIC Program Statistical Package*, U.S. Small Business Administration (Washington, DC), 2003, www.sba.gov/INV/stat/table3.pdf.

72. *SBIC Program Statistical Package*, U.S. Small Business Administration (Washington, DC), 2003, www.sba.gov/INV/stat/table1.pdf.

73. *SBIC Program Statistical Package*, U.S. Small Business Administration (Washington, DC), 2003, www.sba.gov/INV/tables/2001/stats/allsbic1.pdf.

74. *SBIC Program Statistical Package*, U.S. Small Business Administration (Washington, DC), 2003, www.sba.gov/INV/tables/2001/stats/allsbic4.pdf.

75. "Success Stories: Outback Steakhouse," National Association of Small Business Investment Companies, www.nasbic.com/success/stories/outback.cfm;

"Company Statistics," Outback Steakhouse, www.corporate-ir.net/ireye/ir_site.zhtml?ticker=osi&script=950&layout=11&item_id='ps=1*pg=2.

76. "Section 108 Case Studies," U.S. Department of Housing and Urban Development, www.hud.gov/offices/cpd/communitydevelopment/programs/108/casestudies.cfm.

77. "Technology: SBIR/STTR," U.S. Small Business Administration, www.sba.gov/sbir/indexwhatwedo.html.

78. "SBIR/STTR Program Successes: Integrated Systems, Inc., "U.S. Department of Defense, www.acq.osd.mil/sadbu/sbir/success/index.htm.

79. "Overview and History of the SBA," U.S. Small Business Administration, www.sba.gov/aboutsba/history.html.

80. Laura M. Litvan, "Some Rest for the Paperwork Weary," *Nation's Business*, June 1994, pp. 38–40; Robert W. Casey, "Getting Down to Business," *Your Company*, Summer 1994, pp. 30–33.

81. Anna Barron Billingsley, "Dream Weavers," *Region Focus*, Fall 1999, pp. 20–23.

82. Roberta Reynes, "Borrowing Tailored for Exporters," *Nation's Business*, March 1999, pp. 29–30.

83. Katherine Conrad, "Fish Wholesaler Flees from Oakland," *East Bay Business Times*, August 30, 2002, www.capitalaccess.com/suc_FishWholesaler.pdf.

84. Nichole Torres, "Lilliputian Loans," *Entrepreneur*, October 2001, www.entrepreneur.com/Your_Business/YB_SegArticle/0,4621,292934,00.html.

85. Ziona Austrian and Zhongcai Zhang, "An Inventory and Assessment of Pollution Control and Prevention Financing Programs," Great Lakes Environmental Finance Center, Levin College of Urban Affairs, Cleveland State University, www.csuohio.edu/glefc/inventor.htm#sba.

86. Sharon Nelton, "Loans That Come Full Circle," *Nation's Business*, June 1999, pp. 35–36.

87. "Central Vermont Revolving Loan Fund," cvcac.org/Services/revolvingloan.htm.

88. Roberta Reynes, "A Big Factor in Expansion," *Nation's Business*, January 1999, pp. 31–32; Bruce J. Blechman, "The High Cost of Credit," *Entrepreneur*, January 1993, pp. 22–25.

89. Chris Sandlund, "The Golden Egg," *Entrepreneur*, May 2002, pp. 44–46; Phaedra Hise, "Don't Start a Business Without One," *Inc.*, February 1998, pp. 50–53.

90. Hise, "Don't Start a Business Without One."

Chapter 13

1. Roberta Maynard, "A Growing Outlet for Small Firms," *Nation's Business*, August 1996, pp. 45–48.

2. Jeffrey A. Tannenbaum, "Phoenix Tops List of Fertile Areas for Small Companies," *Wall Street Journal*, December 7, 1999, p. B2.

3. Michelle Prather, "Hit the Spot," *Business Start-Ups*, April 1999, p. 104.

4. "Employment Cost Trends," Bureau of Labor Statistics, http://stats.bls.gov/news.release/ecec.t07.htm.

5. Tim W. Ferguson, "Sun, Fun, and Ph.D.s, Too," *Forbes*, May 31, 1999, pp. 220–233.

6. Mark Henricks, "A Tale of 25 Cities," *Entrepreneur*, October 2000, pp. 86–94.

7. Elaine Appleton, "E-Town, USA," *Inc. Technology*, 2000, Number 3, pp. 56–61.

8. Henricks, "A Tale of 25 Cities."

9. Leslie Wines, "Escape to Spokane," *Journal of Business Strategy*, May/June 1996, p. 35.

10. Joel Kotkin, "Here Comes the Neighborhood," *Inc.*, July 2000, pp. 113–123.

11. Kevin Helliker, "Monster Movie Theaters Invade the Cinema Landscape," *Wall Street Journal*, May 13, 1997, pp. B1, B13; "It All Started on the Silver Screen," AMC Theaters, www.amctheaters.com/about/history.html.

12. Prather, "Hit the Spot."

13. "C-Store Saturation Analysis," www.c-store.com/saturation.htm.

14. Bernard J. LaLonde, "New Frontiers in Store Location," *Supermarket Merchandising*, February 1963, p. 110.

15. Maynard, "A Growing Outlet for Small Firms."

16. Mitchell Pacelle, "More Stores Spurn Malls for Village Square," *Wall Street Journal*, February 16, 1996, p. B1.

17. "Some Great Things Happening in Main Street Communities," Main Street National Trust for Historic Preservation, www.mainst.org/AboutMainStreet/communities.htm.

18. *Scope 2000*, International Council of Shopping Centers, www.icsc.org/srch/rsrch/scope/current/index.html.

19. Ibid.

20. Nichole L. Torres, "No Place Like Home," *Start-Ups*, September 2000, pp. 38–45. "Executive Overview," National Association of Home-Based Business's U.S.A. Home-Based Business Information Superhighway, www.usahomebusiness.com/homesite2.htm.

21. Joanne H. Pratt, "Home-based Business: The Hidden Economy," *Small Business Research Summary*, No. 194, March 2000, U.S. Small Business Administration Office of Advocacy, www.sba.gov/ADVO/research/rs194.pdf.

22. Susan Gregory Thomas, "Home Offices That Really Do the Job," *U.S. News and World Report*, October 28, 1996, pp. 84–87.

23. "Business Incubation Facts," National Business Incubation Association, www.nbia.org/info/fact_sheet.html.

24. Ibid.

25. Lori Ioannou, "Start-Ups with a Catch," *Fortune*, July 20, 1998, pp. 156[C]–156[D].

26. Marci McDonald, "The Latte Connections," *U.S. News & World Report*, March 20, 1999, pp. 63–66.

27. Nancy D. Holt, "Alfred P. West, Jr., SEI Investments", *Wall Street Journal*, February 19, 2003.

28. Laura Tiffany, "The Rules of . . . Retail," *Business Start-Ups*, December 1999, p. 106.

29. Paul Keegan, "The Architect of Happy Customers," *Business 2.0.* August 2002, pp. 85–87.

30. Tiffany, "The Rules of . . . Retail."

31. "Educational Kit," President's Committee on Employment of People with Disabilities, www50.pcepd.gov/pcepd/archives/pubs/ek99/wholedoc.htm#decisions.

32. "Blockbuster, Inc., Transforms More Than 4,400 Stores Nationwide", *P.R. Newswire*, November 1, 2002, p. 3.

33. "Proposal for an Ergonomics Program Standard," The Occupational Health and Safety Administration, www.osha-slc.gov/ergonomics-standard/ergo-faq.html.

34. Melissa J. Perenson, "Straighten Up," *Small Business Computing*, October 1999, pp. 77–80.

35. "Work Week," *Wall Street Journal*, November 16, 1999, p. A1.

36. Shane McLaughlin, "You Put Your Left Foot In," *Inc. Technology*, 1998, No. 2, p. 18.

37. Leigh Gallagher, "Get Out of My Face," *Forbes*, October 18, 1999, pp. 105–106.

38. Laura Tiffany, "Personal Space," *Entrepreneur*, May 2000, p. 22; Brenda Moore, "We Don't Want to Know What People Wear to Work," *Wall Street Journal*, California Edition, September 29, 1999, p. CA2.

39. Heather Page, "Pedal to the Metal," *Entrepreneur*, August 1996, p. 15.

40. "Business Bulletin," *Wall Street Journal*, April 15, 1999, p. A1.

41. Kenneth Labich, "This Man Is Watching You," *Fortune*, July 19, 1999, pp. 131–134.

42. Colleen Bazdarich, "In The Buying Mood? Maybe It's the Muzak," *Business 2.0*, March 2002, p. 100.

43. Alex Taylor III, "It Worked for Toyota. Can It Work for Toys?" *Fortune*, January 11, 1999, p. 36.

Chapter 14

1. www.export.gov/comm_svc/press_room/news/success/adm.html.

2. Leslie M. Schweitzer, "Trade Roots," *Export America*, February 2003, pp. 10–11,; William Corley, "Export Programs Guide," *Export America*, March 2003, pp. 12–13.

3. www.trade.gov/exportamerica/new opportunities/no_construction.html.

4. www.export.gov/comm_svc/press_room/news/articles/chem-crete_success.html.

5. Rudolph Bell, "Japanese Connection," *Upstate Business*, September 5, 1999, pp. 1, 8–9.

6. Larry Pearl and Sandeep Thakar, "Taking Your Business Worldwide," *FSB*, March 23, 2000, www.esb.com/fortunesb/articles/o, 2227, 634.00, html.

7. Michael Grebb, "Business Without Borders," *Destination Sobo.com*, September 2001, pp. 36–41.

8. John R. Engen, "Rolling in Dough," *Success*, June 1997, p. 29.

9. Roberta Maynard, "A Simplified Route to Markets Abroad," *Nation's Business*, November 1997, pp. 46–48.

10. J. Russell Boner, "Tap American's Top Export Leaders to Expand Abroad," *Your Company*, October/November 1997, p. 28.

11. Ibid.

12. John Ward, "A Mold Maker Finds a Mexican Match," *Export America*, May 2003, pp. 8–9.

13. Charlotte Mulhern, "Fast Forward," *Entrepreneur,* October 1997, p. 34.

14. Lawrence Van Gelder, "It Pays to Watch Words, Gestures While Abroad," *Greenville News*, April 7, 1996, p. 8E.

15. Sandy Asirvatham, "Old World Order," *Success*, October 1998, pp. 73–75.

16. Edward T. Hall, "The Silent Language of Overseas Business," *Harvard Business Review*, May–June 1960, pp. 5–14.

17. Christopher D. Lancette, "Hitting the Spot," *Entrepreneur*, September 1999, p. 40.

Chapter 15

1. Max DePree, *Leadership Jazz* (New York: Currency Doubleday, 1992), pp. 8–9.

2. Francis Huffman, "Taking the Lead," *Entrepreneur*, November 1993, p. 101.

3. John Mariotti, "The Role of a Leader," *Industry Week*, February 1, 1999, p. 75.

4. Katrina Brooker, "Southwest Airlines: Can Anyone Replace Herb?" *Fortune*, April 17, 2000, www.fortune.com/fortune/fortune500/sou.html; "The Best of Herb Kelleher," pp. 60–70; Herb Kelleher, "A Culture of Commitment," *Leader to Leader*, No. 4, Spring 1997, www.drucker.org/leaderbooks/121/spring97/kelleher.html; Kathleen Melymuka, "Down-to-Earth Technology Helps Make Herb Kelleher's Southwest Airlines a Soaring Success," *Computerworld*, www.idg.net/crd_kelleher_10166.html.

5. Kayte Vanscoy, "The Hiring Crisis," *Smart Business*, July 2000, pp. 85–97; Michael Barrier, "Hire Without Fear," *Nation's Business*, May 1999, pp. 16–23; "Hiring Mistakes," *Practical Supervision*, October 1994, pp. 4–5.

6. Christopher Caggiano, "Recruiting Secrets," *Inc.*, October 1998, pp. 30–42.

7. Verne Harnish, "Ready, Set, Grow," *FSB*, September 2001, pp. 55–58.

8. Karen Southwick, "To Survive: Hire Up," *Forbes ASAP*, April 3, 2000, pp. 117–118.

9. Jill Hecht Maxwell, "An Inside Job," *Inc.*, July 2000, p. 126.

10. Christopher Caggiano, "The Truth About Internet Recruiting," *Inc.*, December 1999, p. 156.

11. Jane Shealy, "Recruiting and Retaining Top Talent," *Success*, September 2000, p. 86.

12. Caggiano, "Recruiting Secrets," pp. 30–42; Vanscoy, "The Hiring Crisis," pp. 85–97.

13. Laurie Francisco, "Extreme Measures," *Business Start-Ups*, June 2000, p. 13.

14. Caggiano, "Recruiting Secrets," pp. 30–42; Jane Shealy, "Playing for Keeps," *Success*, December 2000/January 2001, pp. 62–64.

15. Jill Hecht Maxwell, "Of Résumés and Rap Sheets," *Inc. Technology 2000*, No. 2, p. 27.

16. Ian Mount, "Attention Underlings: That's Conway to You and I Am a People Person," *Business 2.0*, February 2002, pp. 52–58.

17. Eleena De Lisser, "Start-Up Attracts Staff with a Ban on Midnight Oil," *Wall Street Journal*, August 23, 2000, pp. B1, B6.

18. Jeffery Zaslow, "Putting a Price Tag on Grief," *Wall Street Journal*, November 20, 2002, p. D12.

19. Roy Harris, "The Illusion of Inclusion: Why Most Corporate Diversity Efforts Fail," *CFO*, May 2001, pp. 42–50.

20. "Keeping Your Edge': Managing a Diverse Corporate Culture," *Fortune.com*, p. 58, Judith Turnock, "The 21st Century Workforce," *Forbes*, July 22, 2002; Jeremy Kahn, "Diversity," *Fortune*, July 9, 2001, pp. 114–116, Mike Hofman, "It Takes All Kinds," *Inc.*, July 2001, pp. 70–75.

21. Anna Brady, "Small Is as Small Does," *Journal of Business Strategy*, January/February 1996, pp. 44–52.

22. Ronald E. Merrill and Henry D. Sedgwick, "To Thine Own Self Be True," *Inc.*, August 1994, pp. 50–56.

23. Carol Hymowitz, "Effective Leaders Say One Pivotal Experience Sealed Their Careers," *Wall Street Journal*, August 27, 2002, p. B1.

24. Mark Fischetti, "Team Doctors, Report to ER," *Fast Company*, February–March 1998, pp. 170–177; Robert McGarvey, "Joining Forces," *Entrepreneur*, September 1996, pp. 80–83; "Whoa, Team," *Journal of Business Strategy*, January/February 1996, p. 8.

25. Ed Carberry, "Hypergrowth Strategy: Create an Ownership Culture," *Inc.*, December 12, 1999, www.inc.com/casestudies/details/1.345.CAS15825_CNT_GDE65.00.html.

26. Theodore B. Kinni, "America's Best," *Industry Week*, October 21, 1996, p. 84.

27. Theodore B. Kinni, "The Empowered Workforce," *Industry Week*, September 19, 1994, p. 37.

28. David Maize, "Where It Pays to Have a Good Idea," *Reader's Digest*, June 1995, pp. 100–104.

29. John Case, "The Open-Book Revolution," *Inc.*, June 1995, pp. 26–43.

30. Michael Hopkins, "Zen and the Art of the Self-Managing Company," *Inc.*, November 2000, pp. 54–63.

31. Christopher Helman, "Green Wood," *Forbes*, September 15, 2003, pp. 106–107.

32. Linda Field, "A Little Leeway Goes a Long Way," *Nation's Business*, November 1998, p. 6.

33. Robert McGarvey, "Time on Their Side," *Entrepreneur*, July 1999, pp. 79–81.

34. Carol Kleiman, "Job Sharing Working Its Way into Mainstream," *Greenville News*, August 6, 2000, p. 3G.

35. Kleiman, "Job Sharing Working Its Way Into Mainstream."

36. Peg Verone, "House Rules," *Success*, July 1998, pp. 22–24.

37. Eleena De Lisser, "Firms with Virtual Environments Appeal to Workers," *Wall Street Journal*, October 5, 1999, p. B2.

38. Gwen Moran, "It's 3:00 P.M. . . . Do You Know Where Your Telecommuters Are?" *destinationsoho.com*, June 2001, pp. 39–43.

39. Mark Henricks, "Musical Chairs," *Entrepreneur*, April 1999, pp. 77–79.

40. Jill Andresky Fraser, "Know Your Options," *Inc.*, February 1998, pp. 112–113.

41. Jacquelyn Lynn, "Rub It In," *Entrepreneur*, September 1999, p. 46; Anne Fisher, "The 100 Best Companies to Work For in America," *Fortune*, January 12, 1998, pp. 69–70; Joann S. Lublin, "Climbing the Walls on Company Time," *Wall Street Journal*, December 1, 1998, pp. B1, B16; Pui-Wing Tam, "Silicon Valley Belatedly Boots Up Programs to Ease Employees' Lives," *Wall Street Journal*, August 29, 2000, pp. B1, B14; Quentin Hardy, "Aloft in a Career Without Fetters," *Wall Street Journal*, September 29, 1998, pp. B1, B14; Jerry Useem, "Welcome to the New Company Town," *Fortune*, January 10, 2000, pp. 62–70.

42. Ronald Lieber, "Why Employees Love These Companies," *Fortune*, January 12, 1998, pp. 72–74; Alan Farnham, "Mary Kay's Lessons in Leadership," *Fortune*, September 20, 1993, pp. 68–77.

43. Scott Smith, "Mackay's Way," *Success*, September 2000, p. 16.

44. Jack Stack, "That Championship Season," *Inc.*, July 1996, p. 27.

45. Jack Stack, "The Logic of Profit," *Inc.*, March 1996, p. 17.

46. Justin Martin, "So, You Want to Work for the Best . . ." *Fortune*, January 12, 1998, pp. 77–78.

47. Janet Moore, "Like Father, Like Daughter," *Upstate Business*, October 8, 2000, p. 9; "Facts on Family Business in the U.S.," Family Firm Institute, www.ffi.org.

48. Ibid.

49. The Arthur Andersen/MassMutual American Family Business Survey, 1997, www.massmutual.com/fbn/index.htm; Sharon Nelton, "Major Shifts in Leadership Lie Ahead," *Nation's Business*, June 1997, pp. 56–58.

50. Patricia Schiff Estess, "Overnight Succession," *Entrepreneur*, February 1996, pp. 80–83.

51. Woody White, "Planning Eases Transfer of Control of Family Business," *Upstate Business*, October 8, 2000, p. 1.

52. The Arthur Andersen/MassMutual American Family Business Survey, 1997.

53. Amanda Walmac, "Get an Estate Plan to Protect Your Family," *Your Company*, Forecast 1997, pp. 48–54.

INDEX

U.S. Department of Commerce, 472–473
  Export Assistance Centers, 466
U.S. Export Assistance Centers, 470
US Franchise Systems, 120
US Funding Corporation, 120
U.S. Global Outlook, 181
U.S. Industrial Outlook Handbook, 363
U.S. Patent and Trademark Office
  (USPTO), 58, 234
US Sports Camps, Inc., 265
U.S. Statistical Abstract, 427
Used or reconditioned equipment, purchasing, 318
Useem, Jerry, 514
USP test, advertising, 251
uspto.gov, 234

V

Vaidyanathan, Ravi, 50
Validity, 518
Value, market vs. book, 149
Value of store space, 454–456
Value test for the business plan, 360–361
Vanderbilt, Cornelius, 7
Vanice, Candace, 271
Vardi, Nathan, 345
Variable costing, 284
Variable expenses, 352
Variance, 434
Vassallo, Steve, 56
Velma Handbags, 243
Venable, Thomas, 205
Venture capital companies, 389–393
  competitive edge, 392
  growth industry, 392
  industry language, 390
  intangible factors, 392
  investment preferences, 391
  investment size and screening, 390–391
  management, 391
  ownership and control, 391
  policies and investment strategies, 390
  stage of investment, 391
  viable exit strategy, 392
  what venture capitalists look for, 391
Venzke, Ben, 76
VerioStore, 226
Veritas Credit Corporation, 309
Vertex Pharmaceuticals, 50, 53–54
Vertex Systems Inc., 410
Vertical job loading, 509–510
Vest Pocket Guide to Financial Ratios, 347
VetExchange, 387
Victoria's Secret, 89, 206, 264
ViewPoint International, 190–191
Viral site, 240
Virtual Community, The (Rheingold), 229
Virtual order fulfillment, 222
Virus detection software, 242
Vision, 71–72
  format, 375
Visionary objective, 256

Vital Resources Inc., 421
Volte, Lee, 57
von Oech, Roger, 42
Vulcanization, 48

W

Wageweb, 512
Waite, Ted, 430
Wakeman, Pete and Laura, 509
Walboldt, Gus, 408
Wallnutz, 234
Wal-Mart, 76, 86, 174, 213
  and recruitment of older workers, 493
Warner, Kurt, 11
Warshaw, Michael, 374
Washington, George, 58
Watson, Thomas J., 28
Weaknesses, 75
Web analytics, 239–240
Web Consultants, 289
Web services, pricing, 289
WebCrawler, 235
Web-to-Workbench, 215
Weller, Craig, 506
Wellsprings of Knowledge (Leonard-
  Barton), 81
Wendy's, 177
  franchisees and national advertising program, 120
Werner, Jesse, 358
West, Alfred P., Jr., 446
Western Auto, 118
Weyerhauser, Frederick, 7
Whack on the Side of the Head, A (Occh), 42
Whiteboards, 82
Whitefish Gymnastics Club, 311
Whole Foods, 506
Wiese, Andy, 17
Wiggins, Dave, 50, 52
Wilcox, Ella Wheeler, 67
Wilder, Billy, 8
Williams, Becca, 234
Wilson, Ron, 54
Window displays, 446–447
Witchita, Kansas, and CDBG program, 413
Witt, Katarina, 42
Witty, Adam, 15
W.L. Gore and Associates, 520
Wolff, Dave, 445
Wolff, Jane, 445
Wolff, Michael, 381
Women entrepreneurs, 16
Women, and product information, 215
Women for Hire, 175
WomenAngels.net, 387
Woodplay, 142
Woods, Tiger, 12
Word-of-mouth advertising, 258–259
Working capital, 383–384
Working capital ratio, 335
Workplace grief, 499–500

World Trade Organization (WTO), 476,
  481–482
  General Agreement on Trade in Services
    (GATS), 482
World Wide Web (WWW), 13, 35, 80, 382
  and angel networks, 387
  and business prototyping, 367
  and counterfeit market, 59
  defined, 201
  direct mail, 264–267
    banner ads, 265–266
    click-through rate, 265
    cookies, 266
    e-mail advertising, 266
    e-mail list, building, 267
    full-page ads, 266
    impression, 265
    interstitial, 266
    permission e-mail, 266
    pop-up, 266
    push technology ads, 266
    spam, 266
  and direct public offerings, 401–402
  and "high-tech" direct mail, 264–265
  and market research, 178, 181
  marketing on, 201–204
  See also Internet
WorldCom, 345
Wriston, Walter, 463
Wycoff, Joyce, 38–39
Wylie, Philip, 323
Wyndham International (Wyndham Hotels), 501
Wynn, Steve, 355

Y

Yahoo!, 235, 384
Yahoo Network, 220
Yahoo! Store, 226
Yamaguchi, Kristi, 42
Yellow Pages advertising, 313
Young entrepreneurs, 14
YourNovel.com, 48

Z

Zappers, 262
Zeabin, Mark, 203
Zefer, 374
Zefer Corporation, 434
Zemke, Ron, 198
Zero balance account (ZBA), 320
Zero-based budgeting (ZBB), 318
Zien, Karen Anne, 36
Ziercher, Bill, 493
Zillant, 284
Zip Code Atlas and Market Planner, 428
Zip Code Business Patterns, 433
Zippo Manufacturing Company, 60
Zoli, Ted, 318
Zone pricing, 281
Zoning, 434
  maps, 443